The Hargadines of Maryland & Delaware

The Hargadines of Maryland and Delaware

The Descendants of William Hargadine and Katherine Lamsin

Samuel Emmett Hargadine V

Fifth Great Grandson of William Hargadine

Compass
Flower
Press
Compass Flower Press
Columbia, Missouri

Library of Congress Control Number: 2024912807

ISBN: 978-1-951960-62-9

This book is dedicated to VII.

When Samuel Emmett Hargadine (1821-1895) was alive he could not have known that a legacy was about to happen with his descendants.

Samuel Emmett Hargadine	(1821-1895)
Samuel Emmett Hargadine II	(1864-1921)
Samuel Emmett Hargadine III	(1897-1979)
Samuel Emmett Hargadine IV	(1930-2020)
Samuel Emmett Hargadine V	(1958-)
Samuel Emmett Hargadine VI	(1987-)
Samuel Emmett Hargadine VII	(2023-)

I had the privilege of knowing SEH III, IV and VI, all honorable men, and cannot wait to see what kind of man SEH VII turns out to be.

Foreword

My interest in family genealogy started in the early days of the internet. Websites like ancestry.com and findagrave.com were in their infancy and not particularly good. Prior to these sites becoming what they are today, researchers used Family Group Sheets that were photocopied over and over, so the quality of the print was faint, and you were lucky if you received one that was typed. My original mentors were family members that researched our history decades before I got interested in it and they called people on the phone, wrote to people the old-fashioned way, which is now referred to as "snail mail." This was before cell phones were even thought of and long distance was relatively expensive.

My research has focused on two main families. The Hargadines, my father's side, and the Straubes, my mother's side. Then there are the thousands of surnames that married into both families. Both sides had family Bibles that archived births and deaths as they occurred. If you are lucky, you have someone in your ancestry that has applied for membership in either the Daughters or Sons of the American Revolution. Membership and lineage in these societies were investigated and genealogical research had to be accurate to become a member. There are at least two known applications that I found and was able to use either as a source for current information or as confirmation of information that I already had.

While my research spans a couple of decades, it was not continuous, non-stop work. It is a hobby that lends itself to winter when you are stuck inside, and in between the demands of family and career. As I type this, I am semi-retired, the family is grown and gone, and I have picked up where I left off. The information on the internet is much more complete and easier to find. It still requires due diligence because there are hundreds of people with the same name.

In the early days I had research partners. Two of the best researchers I know are Norma Pugmire and Tim Chambers. The three of us were in separate parts of the U.S. and connected via the internet emailing dozens of times a day with whatever tidbit we had discovered on our own. We were machines, and I remember often sending something late at night when everyone should be in bed only to get a response back because they were up doing the same thing. Norma's birth name was Clifton, and our common ancestors were Joseph Henry Clifton (b. 1834) and Sarah A. Hargadine (b. 1842). Tim Chambers' common ancestors are William Henry Chambers (b. 1849) and Mary Ann Hargadine (b. 1850) who married in 1870. Both Norma and Tim are first class genealogists and were much better than I at logging their sources, which leaves a trail that often was necessary to determine how a conclusion was made.

The Hargadine ancestry line survived primarily because of the size of the families. There were several with ten or more children. Not all but many had large families, sometimes with multiple spouses, if a partner died at an early age, which was not rare.

One interesting note regarding the Hargadine women that married, is that there are at least twenty families where Hargadine was listed as a middle name which was a custom in the 1800s and 1900s. Examples are Samuel Hargadine Snow (b.1868) and Robert Hargadine Hurd (b.1910). I have had phone calls from individuals whose middle name was Hargadine, and they did not know why. Luckily, I was able to go back a few generations for them and find the two ancestors that married.

The Hargadine tale starts in Delaware and Maryland just prior to the Revolutionary War. The earliest known records found were of the military Muster Rolls. The Hargadine heritage prior to arriving in America is most likely either England or Ireland. My thinking had always leaned towards Ireland however a recent DNA test came back as descending from England. To follow the migration west you simply look at where they are buried. There are descendants in almost every state, but the largest burial settlements are in Kent County Delaware, the Peoria County Illinois area, and Edwards and Kiowa Counties in Kansas. Brookfield, Missouri, and St. Louis have many buried there as well.

This work is published as a means of furthering the work of any person engaged in genealogical research on the family lines listed. It does not represent complete research into all available sources. It has been said that genealogy work is never done. As you are reading this there is no doubt that there are recent discoveries, and you may even have facts of which I am not aware. I certainly hope so, and you are welcome to communicate discrepancies or additions to the compiler.

Many thanks to the following people who have contributed, collaborated, and traded family history over the years. Without these cousins, some more distant than others, this effort would never have ended up being what it is at this moment.

The information in this genealogical effort came from many sources in addition to those shown in footnotes. Since contributions came from many individuals, some of the original source materials were not noted, but are believed to be true, thus are included with documented material. These may include:

- Oral interviews of family members.
- Federal, state county, city, and township census records.
- Public court records, military records.
- Church records, funeral and crematory service records, cemetery records.
- Family records including family Bibles, birth certificates, marriage certificates, death certificates, estate documents.

Norma Jean Clifton Pugmire

Timothy (**Tim**) John Chambers

Patricia Millard Passwater

Clyde Deloss Hargadine *

Sharon (**Shari**) Lee Hargadine Dolan

Viola (**Mom Vi**) Belle Cox Hargadine *

* Genealogy researchers long before the internet was invented.

Contents

Introduction

The following pages list data for all known family members as of February 19, 2024.

Each immediate family is presented in their own section that contains a graphical family tree as well as a description with information about each referenced person and their children. The child section provides information about the children of the preceding couple. When a child has offspring of their own, this is presented in a separate family section for that child. In this case a '+' is used to denote that an individual will appear later in the book as a parent with his/her own children. For children with partners but no offspring, the partner data is given with the reference family. Roman numerals followed by a period are used to indicate the birth order.

In the chapter titled "Family of the Starting Person" the ancestors of William Hargadine and Katherine Lamsin are presented in an enhanced Pedigree Chart which displays the graphic representation of their direct-line ancestors and the children of the couple. This chapter contains information about the couple whose offspring are listed in the later chapters.

The chapter titled "Families of his Descendants" provides details (as known as of the publication date) for the offspring of William Hargadine and Katherine Lamsin. There is a chapter for each generation. Relatives are listed in the order of the nearness of their relationship.

If a burial date or cause of death is included then I've actually seen or have a copy of the death certificate. If there is no burial place listed then it can be assumed there is no online reference to where an individual is buried. There are instances where the death certificate will say someone is buried in a specific cemetery but the decedent ends up buried somewhere else. There are also individuals that have two findagrave.com numbers or locations. This is usually because one is a cenotaph and the other is the actual burial location. A common example is a war memorial where someone is listed but not buried there.

Sources for the information provided are given in the footnotes.

This document reports the details of 2,013 individuals, of whom 1,033 are male and 978 are female. The sex of two individuals is unknown because they are infant burials. Of the 1,106 individuals with recorded birth and death dates, the average lifespan was 67.3 years. Of these, 568 males averaged 65.1 years, and 537 females averaged 69.7 years. The longest living male was Levi Taylor Clifton (1878–1979), who died aged 100. The longest living female was Hazel Doris Helm (1908–2012), who died aged 103.

Momentous events during our ancestors' lives:

Revolutionary War	1775 – 1783
California Gold Rush	1848 - 1855
Civil War	1861 – 1865
Lincoln Assassination	April 15,1865
First flight	December 17, 1903
Kitty Hawk, North Carolina	
WWI	1914 – 1918
Prohibition Era	1919 – 1933
19th Amendment	August 18, 1920
Ratified Women's Right to Vote	
Great Depression	1929 - 1939
WWII	1939 – 1945
Attack on Pearl Harbor	December 7, 1941
Korean Conflict	1950 – 1953
Kennedy Assassination	1963
Vietnam War	1954 – 1975
First Man on the Moon	1969
Watergate Scandal	1970
Elvis Presley Dies	1977
World Trade Center Attacked	September 11, 2001
Covid-19 Pandemic	March 11, 2020

Family of the Starting Person

Family of William Hargadine and Katherine Lamsin

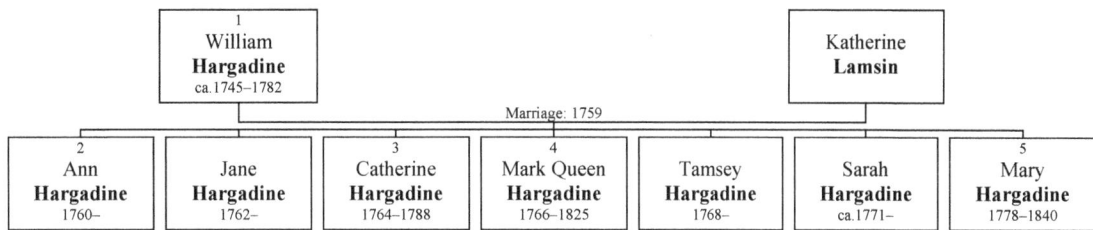

1.   **William Hargadine** was born about 1745 in Maryland, USA. He died in Queen Anne's County, Maryland, on October 20, 1782, at the age of 37.

More facts and events for William Hargadine:

Individual Note: 1776   Executor for the estate of the widow, Ann Bush. Tammie (Tamsey), William's wife, received a bequest.

Individual Note: 1778   Queen Anne's County, Maryland
Took the Oath of Fidelity and Allegiance in Queen Anne's County

William married **Katherine Lamsin** in 1759 in Maryland, USA. They had seven children.

Children of William Hargadine and Katherine Lamsin:

+   2   f   I. **Ann Hargadine** was born in Saint John's Parish, Hillsboro, Caroline County, Maryland, on September 07, 1760.

        f   II. **Jane Hargadine** was born in Saint John's Parish, Hillsboro, Caroline County, Maryland, on May 09, 1762.

+   3   f   III. **Catherine Hargadine** was born in Saint John's Parish, Hillsboro, Caroline County, Maryland, on November 17, 1764. She died in 1788 at the age of 23.

+   4   m   IV. **Mark Queen Hargadine** was born in Saint John's Parish, Hillsboro, Caroline County, Maryland, on September 16, 1766. He died in Kent County, Delaware, in 1825 at the age of 58.

        f   V. **Tamsey Hargadine** was born on September 13, 1768.

        f   VI. **Sarah Hargadine** was born about 1771.

+   5   f   VII. **Mary Hargadine** was born in Saint John's Parish, Hillsboro, Caroline County, Maryland, on March 09, 1778. She died in Caroline County, Maryland, in 1840 at the age of 61.

Family of the Starting Person

Families of his Descendants

1st Generation

Family of Ann Hargadine and John Dodd

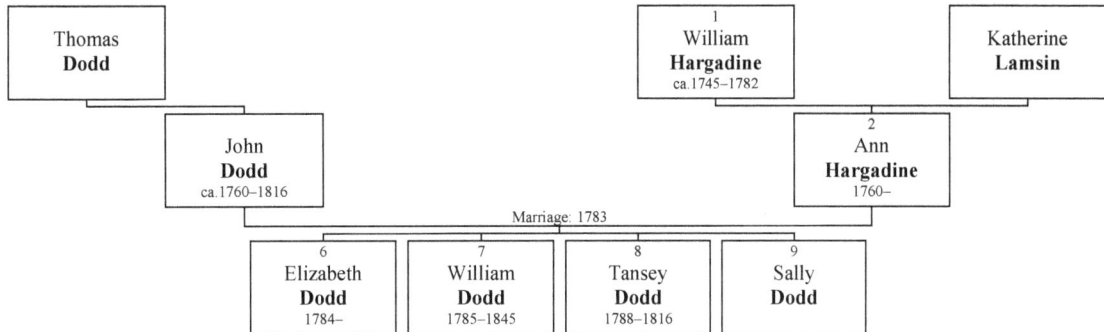

```
┌─────────────┐                    ┌─────────────┐    ┌─────────────┐
│   Thomas    │                    │      1      │    │  Katherine  │
│    Dodd     │                    │   William   │    │   Lamsin    │
│             │                    │  Hargadine  │    │             │
└─────────────┘                    │  ca.1745-1782│   └─────────────┘
        ┌──────────────┐           └─────────────┘  ┌─────────────┐
        │    John      │                            │     2       │
        │    Dodd      │                            │    Ann      │
        │  ca.1760-1816│                            │  Hargadine  │
        └──────────────┘        Marriage: 1783      │   1760-     │
                                                    └─────────────┘
        ┌─────────┐  ┌─────────┐  ┌─────────┐  ┌─────────┐
        │    6    │  │    7    │  │    8    │  │    9    │
        │Elizabeth│  │ William │  │ Tansey  │  │  Sally  │
        │  Dodd   │  │  Dodd   │  │  Dodd   │  │  Dodd   │
        │  1784-  │  │1785-1845│  │1788-1816│  │         │
        └─────────┘  └─────────┘  └─────────┘  └─────────┘
```

2.   **Ann Hargadine** was born on Sunday, September 07, 1760, in Saint John's Parish, Hillsboro, Caroline County, Maryland. She was the daughter of William Hargadine (1) and Katherine Lamsin.

Ann married **John Dodd** on Thursday, July 17, 1783, in Saint John's Parish, Hillsboro, Caroline County, Maryland. They had four children.

John was born in Caroline County, Maryland, about 1760. He was the son of Thomas Dodd.

John reached 56 years of age and died in Iberville Parish, Louisiana, on January 04, 1816.

Children of Ann Hargadine and John Dodd:

+   6   f   I. **Elizabeth Dodd** was born in Hillsboro, Caroline County, Maryland, on March 01, 1784.

+   7   m   II. **William Dodd** was born in Maryland, USA, in 1785. He died in Plaquemine, Iberville Parish, Louisiana, on June 06, 1845, at the age of 60.

+   8   f   III. **Tansey Dodd** was born in South Carolina, USA, in 1788.[1] She died in Iberville Parish, Louisiana, in February 1816 at the age of 28.[1]

+   9   f   IV. **Sally Dodd**.

Family of Catherine Hargadine and Thomas Purnell

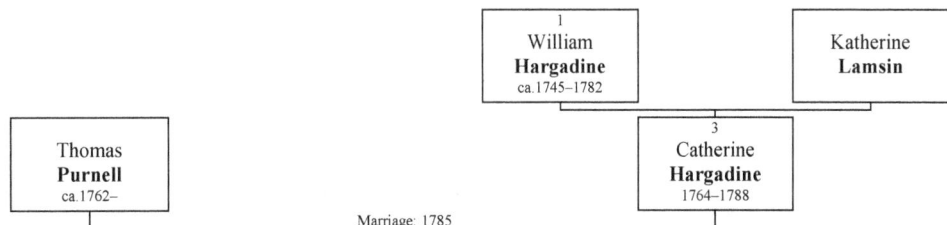

```
                                   ┌─────────────┐    ┌─────────────┐
                                   │      1      │    │  Katherine  │
                                   │   William   │    │   Lamsin    │
                                   │  Hargadine  │    │             │
                                   │  ca.1745-1782│   └─────────────┘
        ┌─────────────┐            └─────────────┘  ┌─────────────┐
        │   Thomas    │                             │     3       │
        │   Purnell   │                             │  Catherine  │
        │  ca.1762-   │                             │  Hargadine  │
        └─────────────┘        Marriage: 1785       │  1764-1788  │
                                                    └─────────────┘
```

---

1   Ancestry.com, Public Member Trees (Provo, UT, USA, Ancestry.com Operations, Inc., 2006), Ancestry.com, Record for Tansy Dodd. https://search.ancestry.co.uk/cgi-bin/sse.dll?db=1030&h=202073588575&indiv=try.

3.   **Catherine Hargadine** was born on Saturday, November 17, 1764, in Saint John's Parish, Hillsboro, Caroline County, Maryland. She was the daughter of William Hargadine (1) and Katherine Lamsin.

Catherine died in 1788 at the age of 23.

Catherine married **Thomas Purnell** on Tuesday, June 07, 1785, in Caroline, Caroline County, Maryland.[2] Thomas was born about 1762.

Family of Mark Hargadine and Rachel Broadway

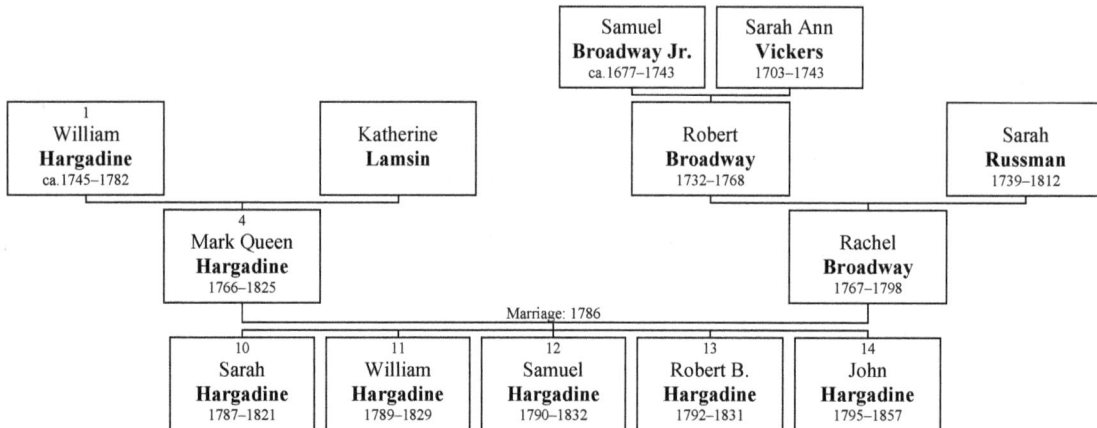

4.   **Mark Queen Hargadine** was born on Tuesday, September 16, 1766, in Saint John's Parish, Hillsboro, Caroline County, Maryland. He was the son of William Hargadine (1) and Katherine Lamsin.

Mark Queen died in Kent County, Delaware, in 1825 at the age of 58.

Mark Queen married **Rachel Broadway** on Thursday, August 24, 1786, in Kent County, Delaware. They had five children.

Rachel was born in Kent County, Delaware, in 1767. She was the daughter of Robert Broadway and Sarah Russman.

Rachel reached 31 years of age and died in Kent County, Delaware, on July 28, 1798.

Children of Mark Queen Hargadine and Rachel Broadway:

+   10   f   I. **Sarah Hargadine** was born in Queen Anne's County, Maryland, on June 24, 1787. She was also known as **Sally**.

Sarah died in 1821 at the age of 33.

+   11   m   II. **William Hargadine** was born in Queen Anne's County, Maryland, on March 03, 1789. He died in Clark County, Ohio, on October 07, 1829, at the age of 40.

---

2   Marriage Records for Caroline County, Maryland 1774-1815.

+ 12 m III. **Samuel Hargadine** was born in Kent County, Delaware, on November 05, 1790. He died in Kent County, Delaware, on July 06, 1832, at the age of 41. Samuel was buried in Lockwood Family Cemetery, Kent County, Delaware (Find a Grave ID 11036358).

+ 13 m IV. **Robert B. Hargadine** was born in Kent County, Delaware, on August 23, 1792. He died in 1831 at the age of 38.

+ 14 m V. **John Hargadine** was born in Kent County, Delaware, on March 08, 1795. He died in Kent County, Delaware, on November 06, 1857, at the age of 62. John was buried in Hargadine Family Cemetery; Dover, Kent County, Delaware (Find a Grave ID 13265786).

Family of Mary Hargadine and Sylvester Purnell

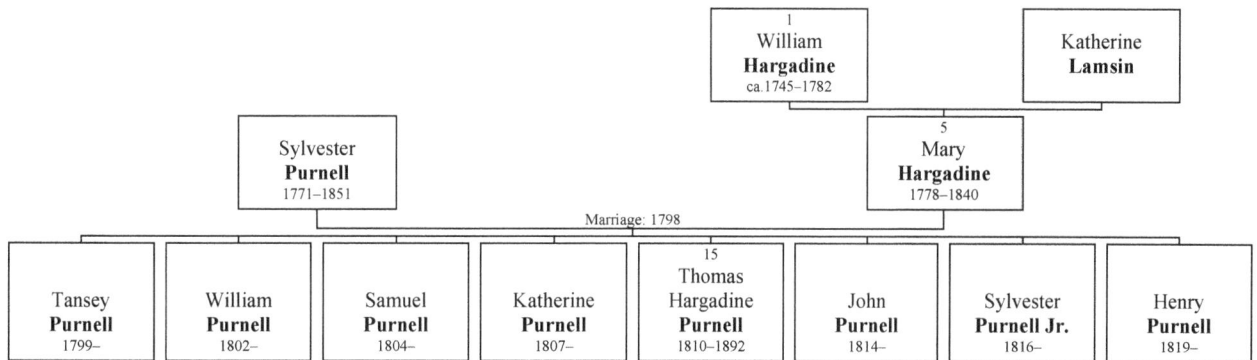

5. **Mary Hargadine** was born on Monday, March 09, 1778, in Saint John's Parish, Hillsboro, Caroline County, Maryland. She was the daughter of William Hargadine (1) and Katherine Lamsin.

Mary died in Caroline County, Maryland, in 1840 at the age of 61.

At the age of 19, Mary married **Sylvester Purnell** on Thursday, February 08, 1798, in Caroline County, Maryland, when he was 26 years old. They had eight children.

Sylvester was born in Caroline County, Maryland, on Friday, May 10, 1771. He reached 79 years of age and died in Caroline County, Maryland, on January 04, 1851.

Children of Mary Hargadine and Sylvester Purnell:

f I. **Tansey Purnell** was born in Caroline County, Maryland, on September 06, 1799.

m II. **William Purnell** was born in Caroline County, Maryland, on October 21, 1802.

m III. **Samuel Purnell** was born in Caroline County, Maryland, on July 04, 1804.

f IV. **Katherine Purnell** was born in Caroline County, Maryland, on July 07, 1807.

+   15   m   V. **Thomas Hargadine Purnell** was born in Caroline County, Maryland, on May 16, 1810. He died in Kent County, Delaware, on July 16, 1892, at the age of 82.

              m   VI. **John Purnell** was born in Caroline County, Maryland, on October 10, 1814.

              m   VII. **Sylvester Purnell Jr.** was born in Caroline County, Maryland, on December 21, 1816.

              m   VIII. **Henry Purnell** was born in Caroline County, Maryland, on November 18, 1819.

2nd Generation

Family of Elizabeth Dodd and John Godwin

	Thomas **Dodd**			[1] William **Hargadine** ca.1745–1782	Katherine **Lamsin**
		John **Dodd** ca.1760–1816		[2] Ann **Hargadine** 1760–	
John **Godwin**			[6] Elizabeth **Dodd** 1784–		

Marriage: 1804

6.   **Elizabeth Dodd** was born on Monday, March 01, 1784, at Saint John's Parish in Hillsboro, Caroline County, Maryland. She was the daughter of John Dodd and Ann Hargadine (2).

Elizabeth married **John Godwin** on Thursday, February 09, 1804, in Talbot County, Maryland.

Family of William Dodd and Mary Pritchett

Thomas **Dodd**		[1] William **Hargadine** ca.1745–1782	Katherine **Lamsin**	
	John **Dodd** ca.1760–1816		[2] Ann **Hargadine** 1760–	
	[7] William **Dodd** 1785–1845			Mary Elizabeth **Pritchett** 1794–1863

Marriage: 1816

7.   **William Dodd** was born in 1785 in Maryland, USA. He was the son of John Dodd and Ann Hargadine (2).

William died in Plaquemine, Iberville Parish, Louisiana, on June 06, 1845, at the age of 60.

William married **Mary Elizabeth Pritchett** on Saturday, January 27, 1816, in Davidson County, Tennessee. Mary Elizabeth was born in North Carolina, USA, in 1794. She was also known as **Betsy**.

Mary Elizabeth reached 69 years of age and died in Plaquemine, Iberville Parish, Louisiana, in 1863.

Tansey Dodd

8.　　**Tansey Dodd** was born in 1788 in South Carolina, USA.[3] She was the daughter of John Dodd and Ann Hargadine (2).

Tansey died in Iberville Parish, Louisiana, in February 1816 at the age of 28.[3]

Marriages with William Saulsbury and Edwin Smith (Page 39) are known.

Family of Tansey Dodd and William Saulsbury

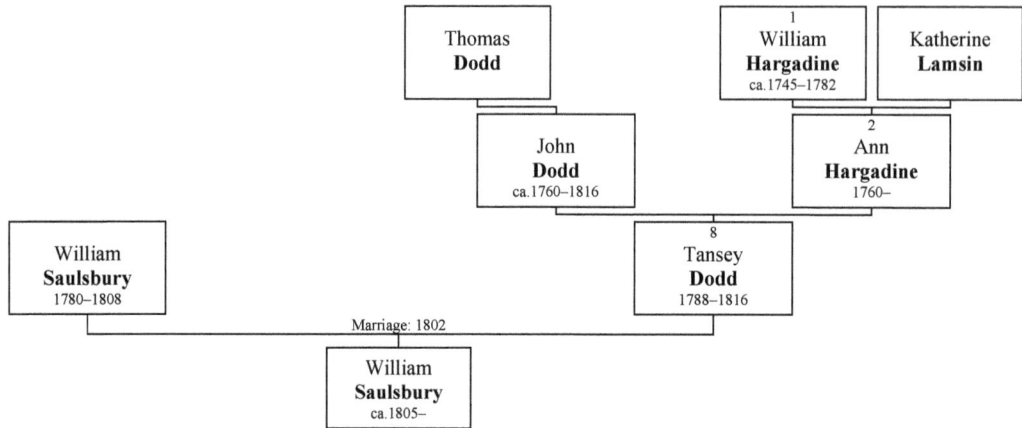

Here are the details about **Tansey Dodd's** first marriage, with William Saulsbury. You can read more about Tansey on page 38.

Tansey Dodd married **William Saulsbury** on Friday, August 27, 1802, in Caroline County, Maryland. They had one son.

William was born in Maryland, USA, in 1780.[4] He reached 28 years of age and died in Davidson County, Tennessee, in 1808.

Son of Tansey Dodd and William Saulsbury:

　　　m　　　I. **William Saulsbury** was born about 1805.

3　　Ancestry.com, Public Member Trees (Provo, UT, USA, Ancestry.com Operations, Inc., 2006), Ancestry.com, Record for Tansy Dodd. https://search.ancestry.co.uk/cgi-bin/sse.dll?db=1030&h=202073588575&indiv=try.

4　　Ancestry.com, Public Member Trees (Provo, UT, USA, Ancestry.com Operations, Inc., 2006), Ancestry.com, Record for William Sr. Saulsbury. https://search.ancestry.co.uk/cgi-bin/sse.dll?db=1030&h=280083293374&indiv=try.

Family of Tansey Dodd and Edwin Smith

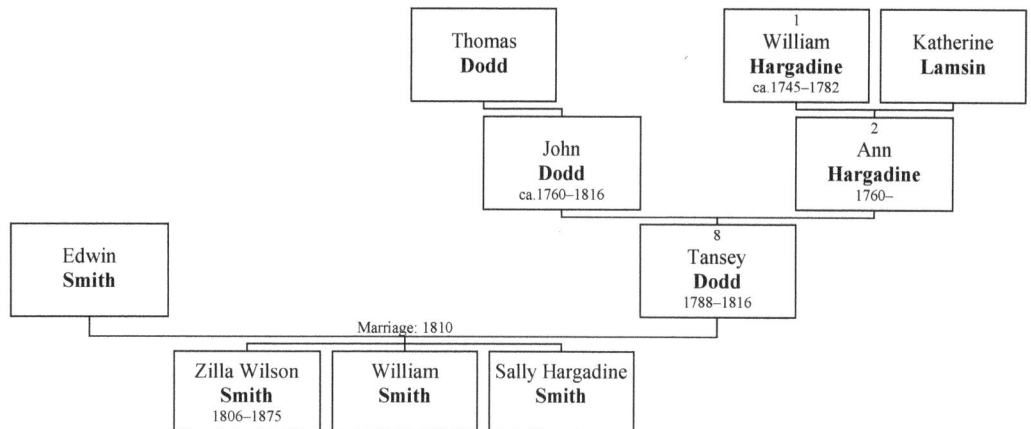

Here are the details about **Tansey Dodd's** second marriage, with Edwin Smith. You can read more about Tansey on page 38.

Tansey Dodd married **Edwin Smith** on Sunday, March 25, 1810, in Davidson County, Tennessee. They had three children.

Children of Tansey Dodd and Edwin Smith:

f I. **Zilla Wilson Smith** was born in Tennessee in 1806.[5] She died in Florida in 1875 at the age of 69.[5]

m II. **William Smith**.

f III. **Sally Hargadine Smith**.

Family of Sally Dodd and John Lewis

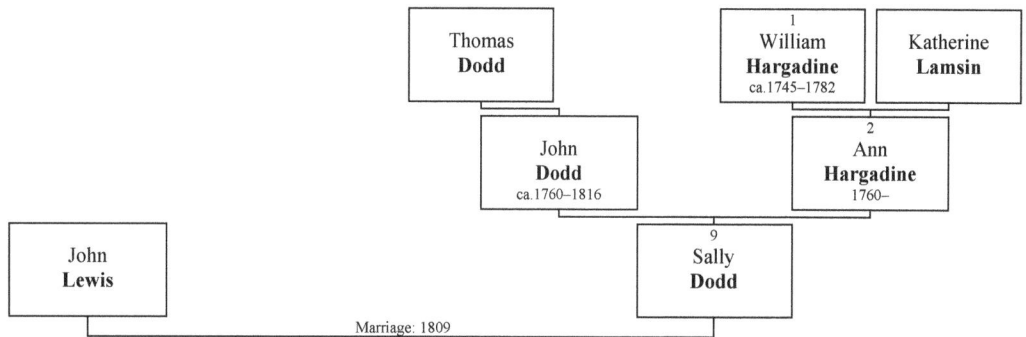

9. **Sally Dodd**. She was the daughter of John Dodd and Ann Hargadine (2).

Sally married **John Lewis** on Tuesday, July 04, 1809, in Davidson County, Tennessee.[6]

5 Ancestry.com, Public Member Trees (Provo, UT, USA, Ancestry.com Operations, Inc., 2006), Ancestry.com, Record for Zillia Willson Smith. https://search.ancestry.co.uk/cgi-bin/sse.dll?db=1030&h=18196735310&indiv=try.

6 Lucas, Marriage Record Book 1, Davidson County, TN.

Family of Sarah Hargadine and Jacob Chambers

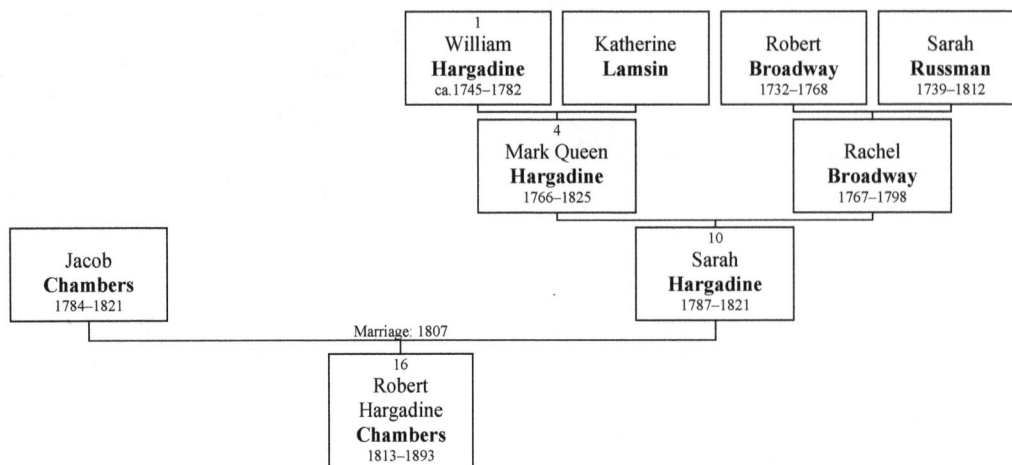

10.   **Sarah Hargadine** was born on Sunday, June 24, 1787, in Queen Anne's County, Maryland. She was the daughter of Mark Queen Hargadine (4) and Rachel Broadway. She was also known as **Sally**.

Sarah died in 1821 at the age of 33.

Sarah married **Jacob Chambers** on Friday, June 26, 1807, in Kent County, Delaware. They had one son.

Jacob was born in Delaware, USA, in 1784. He reached 37 years of age and died in Maryland, USA, in 1821.

Son of Sarah Hargadine and Jacob Chambers:

+   16   m   I.   **Robert Hargadine Chambers** was born in Maryland, USA, on September 26, 1813.[7] He died in Marion County, Iowa, on June 06, 1893, at the age of 79.[8] Robert Hargadine was buried in Olive Chapel Cemetery, Attica, Marion County, Iowa (Find a Grave ID 104711078).

---

7   Newspaper Obituary and Lawrence N. Chambers.

8   Marion County, Iowa Death Records + Tombstone.

Family of William Hargadine and Elizabeth Griffin

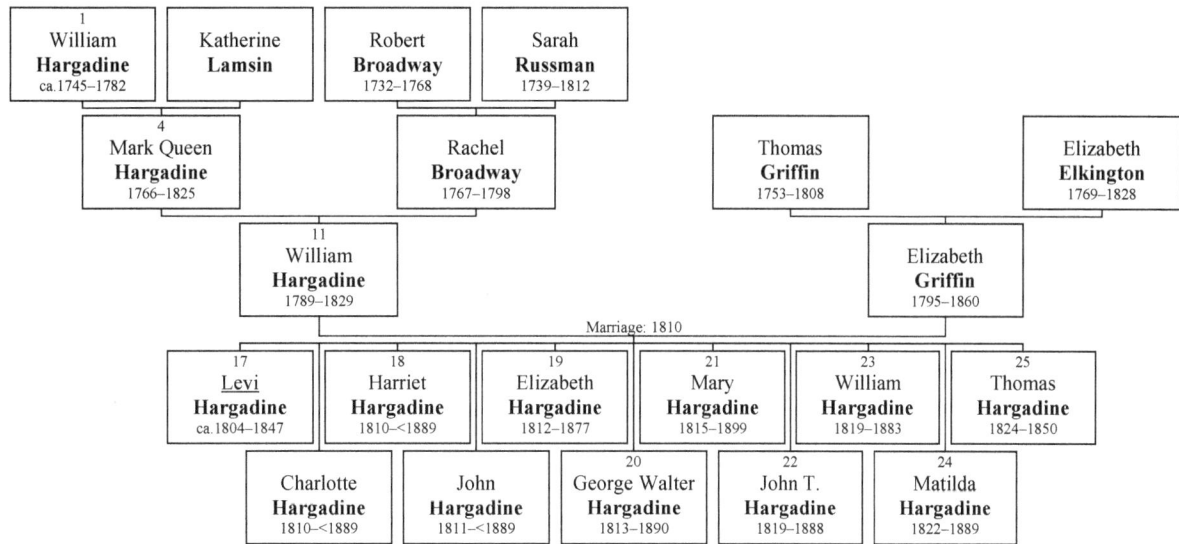

1 William **Hargadine** ca.1745–1782	Katherine **Lamsin**	Robert **Broadway** 1732–1768	Sarah **Russman** 1739–1812

4 Mark Queen **Hargadine** 1766–1825	Rachel **Broadway** 1767–1798

Thomas **Griffin** 1753–1808	Elizabeth **Elkington** 1769–1828

11
William
Hargadine
1789–1829

Elizabeth
Griffin
1795–1860

Marriage: 1810

17 Levi **Hargadine** ca.1804–1847	**18** Harriet **Hargadine** 1810–<1889	**19** Elizabeth **Hargadine** 1812–1877	**21** Mary **Hargadine** 1815–1899	**23** William **Hargadine** 1819–1883	**25** Thomas **Hargadine** 1824–1850

Charlotte **Hargadine** 1810–<1889	John **Hargadine** 1811–<1889	**20** George Walter **Hargadine** 1813–1890	**22** John T. **Hargadine** 1819–1888	**24** Matilda **Hargadine** 1822–1889

11.   **William Hargadine** was born on Tuesday, March 03, 1789, in Queen Anne's County, Maryland. He was the son of Mark Queen Hargadine (4) and Rachel Broadway.

William served in the military in 1812. War of 1812. He died in Clark County, Ohio, on October 07, 1829, at the age of 40.

William married **Elizabeth Griffin** on Saturday, April 14, 1810, in Queen Anne's County, Maryland. They had eleven children.

Elizabeth was born in Queen Anne's County, Maryland, in 1795.[9, 10] She was the daughter of Thomas Griffin and Elizabeth Elkington.

Elizabeth reached 65 years of age and died in Clark County, Ohio, on October 31, 1860.[11] She was buried in Pleasant Hill Cemetery, New Moorefield, Clark County, Ohio (Find a Grave ID 6097772).[11]

More facts and events for Elizabeth Griffin:

Individual Note: March 26, 1855   Applied for bounty land due to husband's military service

Children of William Hargadine and Elizabeth Griffin:

+   17   m   I. **Levi Hargadine** was born in Ohio, USA, about 1804. He died in Peoria, Peoria County, Illinois, on May 09, 1847, at the age of 43. Levi was buried in La Salle Cemetery, Rome, Peoria County, Illinois (Find a Grave ID 44542916).

9   FamilySearch.org, United States Census, 1850, FamilySearch, "United States Census, 1850," database with images, <i>FamilySearch</i> (https://www.familysearch.org/ark:/61903/1:1:MX32-4P3 : 21 December 2020), Elizabeth Hargadine in household of Jacob Arbogast, Moorefield Township, Clark, Ohio, United States; citing family , NARA microfilm publication (Washington, D.C.: National Archives and Records Administration, n.d.).

10   FamilySearch.org, United States Census, 1860, FamilySearch, "United States Census, 1860," database with images, <i>FamilySearch</i> (https://familysearch.org/ark:/61903/1:1:MCGF-JBS : 18 February 2021), Elizabeth Hargadine in entry for Daniel Brindel, 1860.

11   FamilySearch.org, Find A Grave Index, FamilySearch, "Find A Grave Index," database, <i>FamilySearch</i> (https://www.familysearch.org/ark:/61903/1:1:QVVW-VK4Q : 6 February 2023), Elizabeth Griffin Hargadine, Burial, New Moorefield, Clark, Ohio, United States of America, Pleasant Hill Cemetery; citing record ID 6097772, <i>Find a Grave</i>, http://www.findagrave.com.

	f	II.	**Charlotte Hargadine** was born in Clark County, Ohio, in 1810. She died before September 18, 1889.

+ 18 f III. **Harriet Hargadine** was born in Clark County, Ohio, in 1810. She died before September 18, 1889.

    m IV. **John Hargadine** was born in Clark County, Ohio, in 1811. He died before September 18, 1889.

+ 19 f V. **Elizabeth Hargadine** was born in Ohio, USA, on May 20, 1812. She died on April 30, 1877, at the age of 64. Elizabeth was buried in Pleasant Hill Cemetery, New Moorefield, Clark County, Ohio (Find a Grave ID 6095528).

+ 20 m VI. **George Walter Hargadine** was born in Queen Anne's County, Maryland, on June 13, 1813. He died in Chenoa, McLean County, Illinois, on April 06, 1890, at the age of 76. George Walter was buried in Chenoa Cemetery, McLean County, Illinois (Find a Grave ID 55010445).

+ 21 f VII. **Mary Hargadine** was born in Ohio, USA, on December 28, 1815. She died in Moorefield Twp., Clark, Ohio, on May 31, 1899, at the age of 83. Mary was buried in Pleasant Hill Cemetery, New Moorefield, Clark County, Ohio (Find a Grave ID 6095933).

+ 22 m VIII. **John T. Hargadine** was born in Clark County, Ohio, in 1819. He was also known as **Jack**.

        John T. died in Lost Creek Township, Miami County, Ohio, on November 10, 1888, at the age of 69. He was buried in Casstown Cemetery, Casstown, Miami County, Ohio (Find a Grave ID 11670301).

+ 23 m IX. **William Hargadine** was born in Bellefontaine, Logan County, Ohio, on August 01, 1819. He died in Aurora, Kane County, Illinois, on February 15, 1883, at the age of 63. His cause of death was cancer. He was buried in Lucas Chapel Cemetery, Lincoln, Logan County, Illinois (Find a Grave ID 232012520).

+ 24 f X. **Matilda Hargadine** was born in Ohio, USA, in 1822. She died on September 18, 1889, at the age of 67.

+ 25 m XI. **Thomas Hargadine** was born in Ohio, USA, on May 20, 1824.[12] He died in Clark County, Ohio, on November 13, 1850, at the age of 26.[13] Thomas

---

12   FamilySearch.org, United States Census, 1850, FamilySearch, "United States Census, 1850," database with images, <i>FamilySearch</i> (https://www.familysearch.org/ark:/61903/1:1:MX3K-LDN : 21 December 2020), Thos Argedine in household of Daniel Brindle, Moorefield Township, Clark, Ohio, United States; citing family , NARA microfilm publication (Washington, D.C.: National Archives and Records Administration, n.d.).

13   FamilySearch.org, Find A Grave Index, FamilySearch, "Find A Grave Index," database, <i>FamilySearch</i> (https://www.familysearch.org/ark:/61903/1:1:QVVW-VK47 : 6 February 2023), Thomas Hargadine, ; Burial, New Moorefield, Clark, Ohio, United States of America, Pleasant Hill Cemetery; citing record ID 6097770, <i>Find a Grave</i>, http://www.findagrave.com.

was buried in Pleasant Hill Cemetery, New Moorefield, Clark County, Ohio (Find a Grave ID 6097770).[13]

Family of Samuel Hargadine and Mary Lockwood

12. **Samuel Hargadine** was born on Friday, November 05, 1790, in Kent County, Delaware. He was the son of Mark Queen Hargadine (4) and Rachel Broadway.

Samuel served in the military on May 07, 1813. Delaware Militia. He died in Kent County, Delaware, on July 06, 1832, at the age of 41. Samuel was buried in Lockwood Family Cemetery, Kent County, Delaware (Find a Grave ID 11036358).

More facts and events for Samuel Hargadine:

Individual Note: 1831   Kent County Constable

At the age of 25, Samuel married **Mary Lockwood** on Tuesday, September 03, 1816, in Kent County, Delaware, when she was 22 years old.[14] They had three children.

Mary was born on Thursday, October 03, 1793. She was the daughter of Thomas Lockwood and Eunity Virdin. She was also known as **Lockwood**.

Mary reached 67 years of age and died on November 18, 1860. She was buried in Lockwood Family Cemetery, Kent County, Delaware (Find a Grave ID 111022847).

Children of Samuel Hargadine and Mary Lockwood:

| | f | I. | **Eliza Hargadine** was born on March 10, 1825. She died on October 26, 1826, at the age of 1. |

+   26   f   II. **Emiline Hargadine** was born in Delaware, USA, on April 16, 1827. She was also known as **Emily**.

Emiline died in Delaware, USA, on June 29, 1899, at the age of 72. She was buried in Hillside Cemetery and Memorial Gardens, Roslyn, Montgomery County, Pennsylvania (Find a Grave ID 139171923).

---

14   Kent County Records, Vol. 22, page 323.

+ 27   m   III. **Robert B. Hargadine** was born in Kent County, Delaware, on January 31, 1829. He died in Oakland, Alameda County, California, on January 13, 1877, at the age of 47. Robert B. was buried in Hargadine Cemetery, Ashland, Jackson County, Oregon (Find a Grave ID 11178298).

Robert Hargadine

13.   **Robert B. Hargadine** was born on Thursday, August 23, 1792, in Kent County, Delaware. He was the son of Mark Queen Hargadine (4) and Rachel Broadway.

Robert B. worked as a Farmer. He died in 1831 at the age of 38.

Marriages with Ann Kenton and Nancy Anderson (Page 45) are known.

Family of Robert Hargadine and Ann Kenton

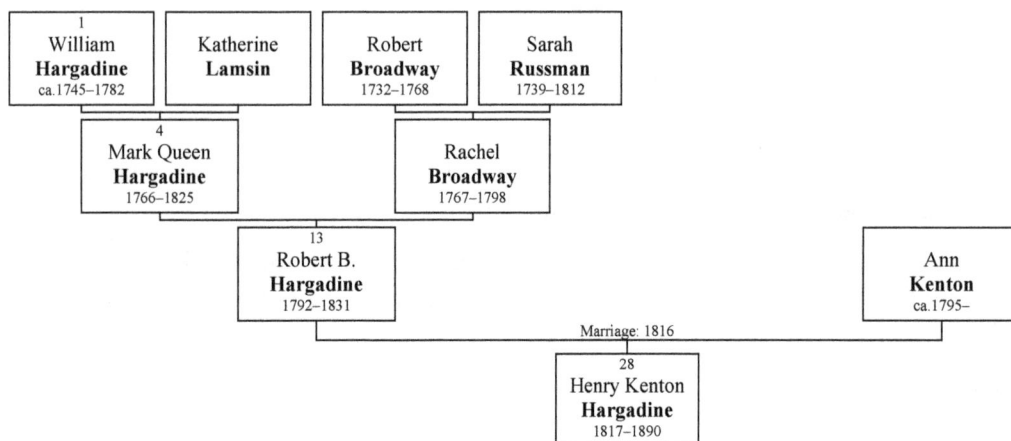

```
┌──────────────┐  ┌──────────────┐  ┌──────────────┐  ┌──────────────┐
│      1        │  │              │  │              │  │              │
│  William      │  │  Katherine   │  │  Robert      │  │  Sarah       │
│  Hargadine    │  │  Lamsin      │  │  Broadway    │  │  Russman     │
│  ca.1745–1782 │  │              │  │  1732–1768   │  │  1739–1812   │
└──────────────┘  └──────────────┘  └──────────────┘  └──────────────┘
        ┌──────────────┐              ┌──────────────┐
        │      4        │             │              │
        │  Mark Queen   │             │  Rachel      │
        │  Hargadine    │             │  Broadway    │
        │  1766–1825    │             │  1767–1798   │
        └──────────────┘              └──────────────┘
              ┌──────────────┐                        ┌──────────────┐
              │     13        │                       │              │
              │  Robert B.    │                       │  Ann         │
              │  Hargadine    │                       │  Kenton      │
              │  1792–1831    │                       │  ca.1795–    │
              └──────────────┘                        └──────────────┘
                              Marriage: 1816
                       ┌──────────────┐
                       │     28        │
                       │  Henry Kenton │
                       │  Hargadine    │
                       │  1817–1890    │
                       └──────────────┘
```

Here are the details about **Robert B. Hargadine's** first marriage, with Ann Kenton. You can read more about Robert B. on page 44.

Robert B. Hargadine married **Ann Kenton** on Saturday, September 21, 1816, in Kent County, Delaware. They had one son.

Ann was born in Kent County, Delaware, about 1795.

Son of Robert B. Hargadine and Ann Kenton:

+ 28   m   I. **Henry Kenton Hargadine** was born in Kent County, Delaware, on May 25, 1817. He died in Kent County, Delaware, on January 10, 1890, at the age of 72. Henry Kenton was buried in Odd Fellows Cemetery, Camden, Kent County, Delaware (Find a Grave ID 7795556).

Family of Robert Hargadine and Nancy Anderson

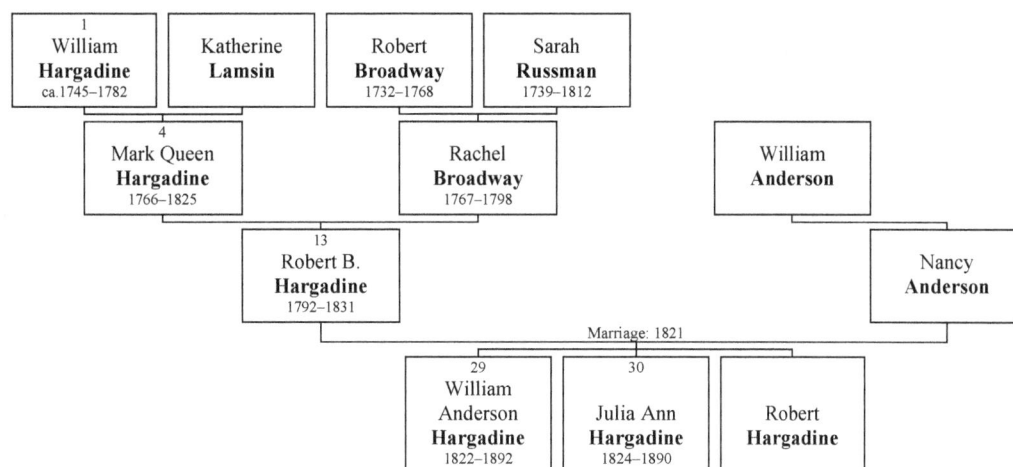

Here are the details about **Robert B. Hargadine's** second marriage, with Nancy Anderson. You can read more about Robert B. on page 44.

Robert B. Hargadine married **Nancy Anderson** on Thursday, February 08, 1821, in Kent County, Delaware. They had three children. She was the daughter of William Anderson.

Children of Robert B. Hargadine and Nancy Anderson:

+ 29 m I. **William Anderson Hargadine** was born in Frederica, Kent County, Delaware, on January 06, 1822. He died in Saint Louis, Saint Louis County, Missouri, on January 04, 1892, at the age of 69. William Anderson was buried in Bellefontaine Cemetery, Saint Louis, St. Louis City, Missouri, on January 06, 1892 (Find a Grave ID 21038).

+ 30 f II. **Julia Ann Hargadine** was born in Kent County, Delaware, on March 15, 1824. She died on July 21, 1890, at the age of 66. Julia Ann was buried in Wesley Methodist Church Cemetery, Dover, Kent County, Delaware (Find a Grave ID 7566639).

   m III. **Robert Hargadine**.

John Hargadine

14. **John Hargadine** was born on Sunday, March 08, 1795, in Kent County, Delaware. He was the son of Mark Queen Hargadine (4) and Rachel Broadway.

John died in Kent County, Delaware, on November 06, 1857, at the age of 62. He was buried in Hargadine Family Cemetery; Dover, Kent County, Delaware (Find a Grave ID 13265786).

Marriages with Sarah Cubbage and Ann McCoy (Page 47) are known.

Family of John Hargadine and Sarah Cubbage

Here are the details about **John Hargadine's** first marriage, with Sarah Cubbage. You can read more about John on page 45.

At the age of 23, John Hargadine married **Sarah Cubbage** on Wednesday, January 13, 1819, in Kent County, Delaware, when she was 21 years old. They had four children.

Sarah was born in Kent County, Delaware, on Saturday, January 28, 1797. She was the daughter of John Cubbage. She was also known as **Sallie**.

Sarah reached 46 years of age and died in Kent County, Delaware, on January 30, 1843. She was buried in Hargadine Family Cemetery; Dover, Kent County, Delaware (Find a Grave ID 13265866).

Children of John Hargadine and Sarah Cubbage:

+ 31   f   I. **Mary Hargadine** was born in Kent County, Delaware, on November 12, 1819. She died in Kent County, Delaware, on June 15, 1879, at the age of 59. Mary was buried in Bethesda Church Cemetery, Pearsons Corner, Kent County, Delaware (Find a Grave ID 11262695).

+ 32   m   II. **Samuel Emmett Hargadine I** was born in Kent County, Delaware, on July 05, 1821.[15–18] He died in Brookfield, Linn County, Missouri, on May 12, 1895, at the age of 73.[15] Samuel Emmett was buried in Rose Hill Cemetery, Brookfield, Linn County, Missouri, on May 15, 1895 (Find a Grave ID 131197208).[15]

---

15   FamilySearch.org, Find A Grave Index, FamilySearch, "Find A Grave Index," database, <i>FamilySearch</i> (https://www.familysearch.org/ark:/61903/1:1:QVGB-4WQH : 11 January 2023), Samuel Emmett Hargadine, ; Burial, Brookfield, Linn, Missouri, United States of America, Rose Hill Cemetery; citing record ID 131197208, <i>Find a Grave</i>, http://www.findagrave.com.

16   FamilySearch.org, United States Census, 1870, FamilySearch, "United States Census, 1870," <i>FamilySearch</i> (https://www.familysearch.org/ark:/61903/1:1:M4BP-DVK : Fri Oct 06 14:54:24 UTC 2023), Entry for Samuel Hargadine and Marian Hargadine, 1870.

17   FamilySearch.org, United States Census, 1850, FamilySearch, "United States Census, 1850," <i>FamilySearch</i> (https://www.familysearch.org/ark:/61903/1:1:MD4D-J9S : Wed Oct 04 05:43:55 UTC 2023), Entry for Samuel Harganton and Marium Harganton, 1850.

18   FamilySearch.org, United States Census, 1880, FamilySearch, "United States Census, 1880," <i>FamilySearch</i> (https://www.familysearch.org/ark:/61903/1:1:M6XK-68P : Fri Oct 06 10:11:48 UTC 2023), Entry for Samuel Hargadine and Marians Hargadine, 1880.

+ 33 f III. **Sarah Ann Hargadine** was born in Kent County, Delaware, on June 17, 1825. She was also known as **Sallie**.

Sarah Ann died in Kent County, Delaware, on November 16, 1896, at the age of 71. She was buried in Lakeside Cemetery, Dover, Kent County, Delaware (Find a Grave ID 7588812).

+ 34 m IV. **John C. Hargadine Jr.** was born in Kent County, Delaware, on November 02, 1829. He died in Kent County, Delaware, on March 09, 1868, at the age of 38. John C. was buried in Hargadine Family Cemetery; Dover, Kent County, Delaware (Find a Grave ID 13265800).

Family of John Hargadine and Ann McCoy

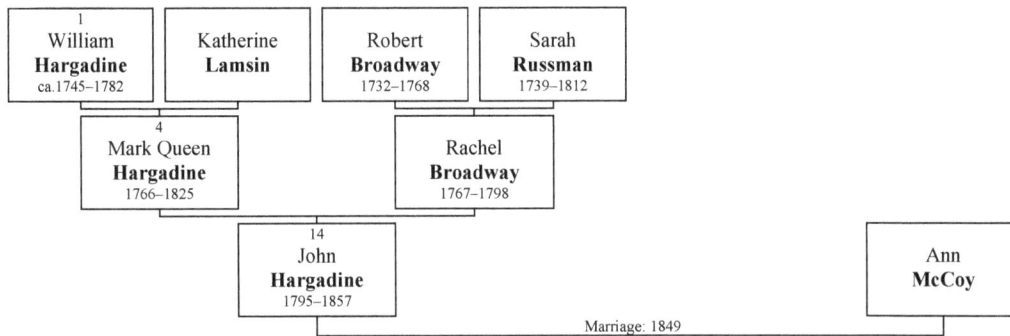

Here are the details about **John Hargadine's** second marriage, with Ann McCoy. You can read more about John on page 45.

John Hargadine married **Ann McCoy** on Thursday, January 18, 1849, in Kent County, Delaware.

Thomas Purnell

15. **Thomas Hargadine Purnell** was born on Wednesday, May 16, 1810, in Caroline County, Maryland. He was the son of Sylvester Purnell and Mary Hargadine (5).

Thomas Hargadine died in Kent County, Delaware, on July 16, 1892, at the age of 82.

Marriages with Mary Elizabeth Downs and Susannah Dill (Page 49) are known.

Family of Thomas Purnell and Mary Downs

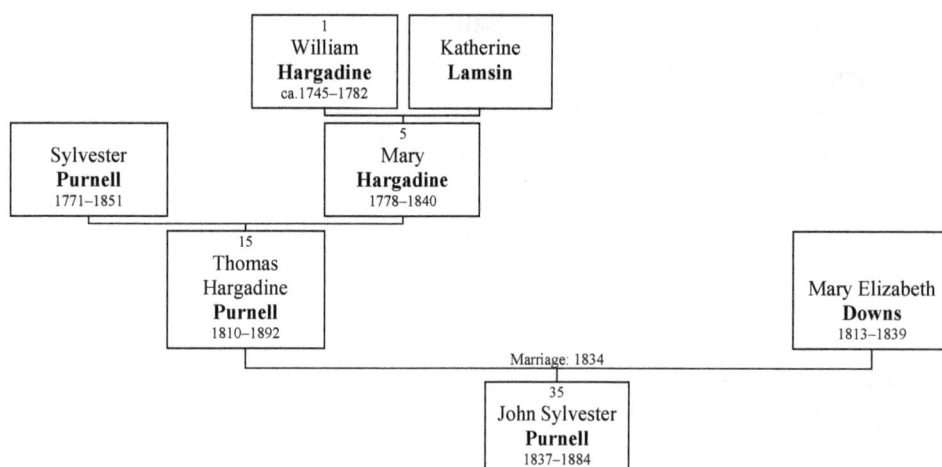

Here are the details about **Thomas Hargadine Purnell's** first marriage, with Mary Elizabeth Downs. You can read more about Thomas Hargadine on page 47.

At the age of 23, Thomas Hargadine Purnell married **Mary Elizabeth Downs** on Sunday, April 20, 1834, in Worcester County, Maryland, when she was 20 years old. They had one son.

Mary Elizabeth was born in Kent County, Maryland, on Sunday, May 09, 1813.[19, 20] She reached 25 years of age and died in Kent County, Delaware, on April 14, 1839.[19]

More facts and events for Mary Elizabeth Downs:

Individual Note: DAR ID Number 161055

Son of Thomas Hargadine Purnell and Mary Elizabeth Downs:

+   35   m   I. **John Sylvester Purnell** was born in Delaware, USA, on September 27, 1837. He died in Delaware, USA, on October 20, 1884, at the age of 47.

Family of Thomas Purnell and Susannah Dill

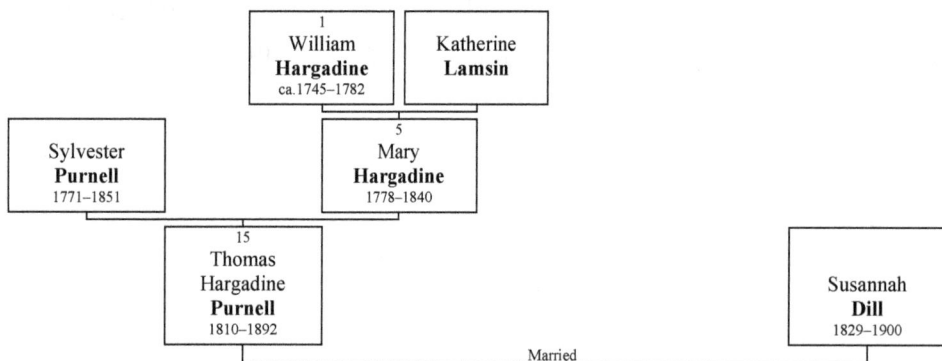

---

19   Ancestry.com, Public Member Trees (Provo, UT, USA, Ancestry.com Operations, Inc., 2006), Ancestry.com, Record for Mary Elizabeth Downs. https://search.ancestry.co.uk/cgi-bin/sse.dll?db=1030&h=122243013704&indiv=try.

20   The National Society of the Daughters of the American Revolution.

Here are the details about **Thomas Hargadine Purnell's** second marriage, with Susannah Dill. You can read more about Thomas Hargadine on page 47.

Thomas Hargadine Purnell married **Susannah Dill**. Susannah was born in Delaware, USA, in 1829.

She reached 71 years of age and died in New Castle, New Castle County, Delaware, on April 30, 1900. Susannah was buried in Harrington, Kent County, Delaware.

3rd Generation

Family of Robert Chambers and Eleanor Dixon

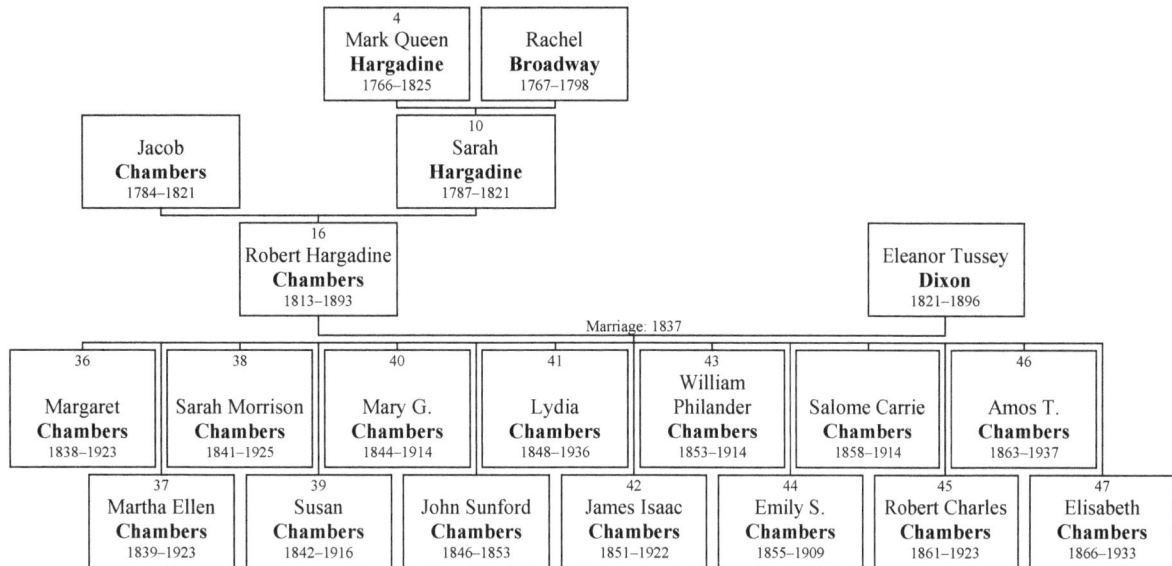

16. **Robert Hargadine Chambers** was born on Sunday, September 26, 1813, in Maryland, USA.[21] He was the son of Jacob Chambers and Sarah Hargadine (10).

Robert Hargadine died in Marion County, Iowa, on June 06, 1893, at the age of 79.[22] He was buried in Olive Chapel Cemetery, Attica, Marion County, Iowa (Find a Grave ID 104711078).

At the age of 23, Robert Hargadine married **Eleanor Tussey Dixon** on Thursday, August 24, 1837, in Butler County, Ohio, when she was 15 years old.[23] They had fourteen children.

Eleanor Tussey was born in Delaware, USA, on Tuesday, October 16, 1821. She was also known as **Ellen**.

Eleanor Tussey reached 74 years of age and died in Marion County, Iowa, on April 10, 1896. She was buried in Olive Chapel Cemetery, Attica, Marion County, Iowa (Find a Grave ID 104711259).

Children of Robert Hargadine Chambers and Eleanor Tussey Dixon:

+ 36   f   I. **Margaret Chambers** was born in Montgomery County, Indiana, on September 15, 1838.[21] She died in Attica, Marion County, Iowa, on March 31, 1923, at the age of 84.[21] Her cause of death was: burned to death. She was buried in Olive Chapel Cemetery, Attica, Marion County, Iowa (Find a Grave ID 51963791).

+ 37   f   II. **Martha Ellen Chambers** was born in Montgomery County, Indiana, on November 11, 1839.[21] She died in Osceola, Clarke County, Iowa, on July

---

21   Newspaper Obituary and Lawrence N. Chambers.

22   Marion County, Iowa Death Records + Tombstone.

23   Butler County, Ohio Marriage Records.

08, 1923, at the age of 83.[24] Martha Ellen was buried in Ottawa Cemetery, Ottawa, Clarke County, Iowa (Find a Grave ID 63567498).

+ 38   f   III. **Sarah Morrison Chambers** was born in Montgomery County, Indiana, on February 18, 1841.[21] She died in Springfield, Greene County, Missouri, on November 01, 1925, at the age of 84.[21] Sarah Morrison was buried in Hillcrest Cemetery, Mountain Grove, Wright County, Missouri (Find a Grave ID 33939755).

+ 39   f   IV. **Susan Chambers** was born in Montgomery County, Indiana, on July 19, 1842.[21] She died in Murray, Clarke County, Iowa, on April 14, 1916, at the age of 73.[25]

+ 40   f   V. **Mary G. Chambers** was born in Montgomery County, Indiana, on July 31, 1844.[26] She died in Knoxville, Marion County, Iowa, on January 07, 1914, at the age of 69.[21] Mary G. was buried in Graceland Cemetery, Knoxville, Marion County, Iowa (Find a Grave ID 180264777).

   m   VI. **John Sunford Chambers** was born in Montgomery County, Indiana, on May 17, 1846.[21] He died on December 15, 1853, at the age of 7.[27]

+ 41   f   VII. **Lydia Chambers** was born in Montgomery County, Indiana, on November 19, 1848.[21] She died in Colfax, Jasper County, Iowa, on July 01, 1936, at the age of 87.[21]

+ 42   m   VIII. **James Isaac Chambers** was born in Montgomery County, Indiana, on June 24, 1851.[21] He died in Knoxville, Marion County, Iowa, on October 22, 1922, at the age of 71.[21] James Isaac was buried in Zion Cemetery, Pershing, Marion County, Iowa (Find a Grave ID 16350132).

+ 43   m   IX. **William Philander Chambers** was born in Montgomery County, Indiana, on May 20, 1853.[28] He died in Knoxville, Marion County, Iowa, on September 14, 1914, at the age of 61.[28] William Philander was buried in Graceland Cemetery, Knoxville, Marion County, Iowa (Find a Grave ID 15554223).

+ 44   f   X. **Emily S. Chambers** was born in Montgomery County, Indiana, on May 14, 1855.[21] She died in Oregon, USA, on February 17, 1909, at the age of 53.[21]

   f   XI. **Salome Carrie Chambers** was born in Marion County, Iowa, on April 29, 1858.[29] She died in Knoxville, Marion County, Iowa, on September 08, 1914, at the age of 56.[29] Salome Carrie was buried in Olive Chapel Cemetery, Attica, Marion County, Iowa (Find a Grave ID 104711165).

---

24   Newspaper Obituary.

25   Tombstone in Murray Cemetery.

26   Newspaper Obituary and Lawrence N. Chambers and Tombstone.

27   Notes from when Lawrence Chambers interviewed his father, Robert Chambers.

28   Lawrence N. Chambers and Ruth Hawks Wright.

29   Newspaper Obituary and Lawrence N. Chambers + Tombstone.

+ 45   m   XII. **Robert Charles Chambers** was born in Attica, Marion County, Iowa, on August 23, 1861.[21] He died in Grand Junction, Greene County, Iowa, on November 06, 1923, at the age of 62.[21] Robert Charles was buried in Junction Township Cemetery, Grand Junction, Greene County, Iowa (Find a Grave ID 40455269).

+ 46   m   XIII. **Amos T. Chambers** was born in Marion County, Iowa, on September 24, 1863.[21] He died in California, USA, in 1937 at the age of 73.[21] Amos T. was buried in Bellevue Memorial Park, Ontario, San Bernardino County, California (Find a Grave ID 149799175).

+ 47   f   XIV. **Elisabeth Chambers** was born in Marion County, Iowa, on February 21, 1866.[21] She was also known as **Lizzie**.

       Elisabeth died in Portland, Multnomah County, Oregon, on January 16, 1933, at the age of 66.[21] She was buried in River View Cemetery, Portland, Multnomah County, Oregon (Find a Grave ID 136096395).

Family of Levi Hargadine and Anna Hurd

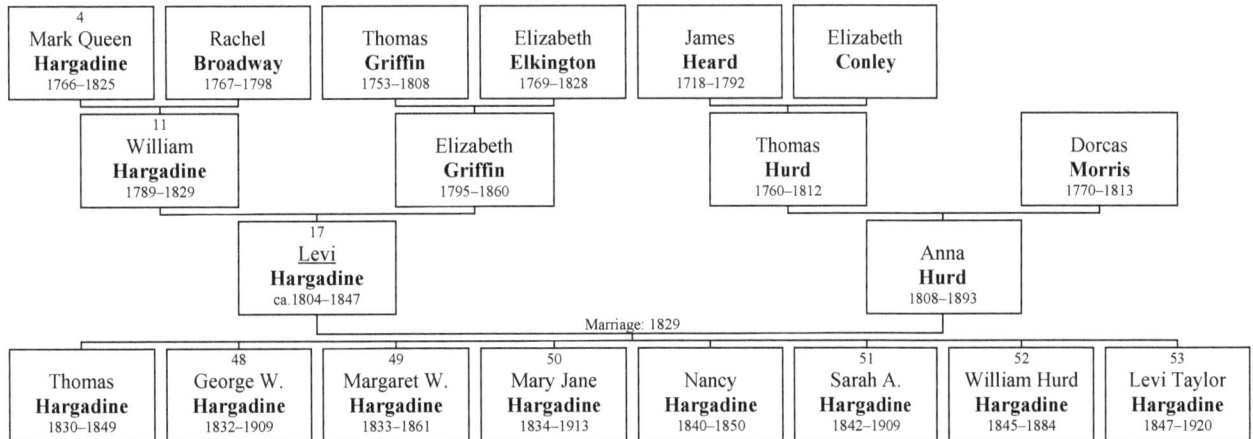

17.   ***Levi Hargadine** was born about 1804 in Ohio, USA. He was the son of William Hargadine (11) and Elizabeth Griffin.

     Levi died in Peoria, Peoria County, Illinois, on May 09, 1847, at the age of 43. He was buried in La Salle Cemetery, Rome, Peoria County, Illinois (Find a Grave ID 44542916).

     More facts and events for Levi Hargadine:

Individual Note:	*Levi Hargadine has been added as a child of William and Elizabeth Griffin with an asterisk. Many on the internet have already stated it as a fact, however when queried can't provide a source. Most researchers suspect that Levi is William and Elizabeth's son, as do I. A preponderance of the evidence suggests this and when trying to prove a negative, what else is feasible, all indicators point to William being the father. For this work to be credible it isn't proven 100% and must be stated that way.

At the age of 25, Levi married **Anna Hurd** on Thursday, November 19, 1829, in Champaign County, Ohio, when she was 21 years old. They had eight children.

Anna was born in Pennsylvania, USA, on Sunday, April 24, 1808. She was the daughter of Thomas Hurd and Dorcas Morris.

Anna reached 84 years of age and died in Iowa, USA, on April 15, 1893. She was buried in Calhoun Cemetery, Harrison County, Iowa (Find a Grave ID 47669691).

Children of <u>Levi</u> Hargadine and Anna Hurd:

	m	I.	**Thomas Hargadine** was born in Ohio, USA, on October 03, 1830. He died in Peoria County, Illinois, on February 08, 1849, at the age of 18. Thomas was buried in La Salle Cemetery, Rome, Peoria County, Illinois (Find a Grave ID 44542917).
+ 48	m	II.	**George W. Hargadine** was born in Moorefield, Clark County, Ohio, on November 07, 1832.[30] He died in Omaha, Douglas County, Nebraska, on August 14, 1909, at the age of 76. George W. was buried in Chillicothe City Cemetery, Chillicothe, Peoria County, Illinois.
+ 49	f	III.	**Margaret W. Hargadine** was born in Medina, Peoria County, Illinois, in 1833. She died on June 08, 1861, at the age of 28. Margaret W. was buried in La Salle Cemetery, Rome, Peoria County, Illinois (Find a Grave ID 44542836).
+ 50	f	IV.	**Mary Jane Hargadine** was born in Ohio, USA, on September 13, 1834.[31] She died in Guss, Taylor County, Iowa, on July 30, 1913, at the age of 78.[32] Mary Jane was buried in Guss Cemetery, Guss, Taylor County, Iowa (Find a Grave ID 95382556).
	f	V.	**Nancy Hargadine** was born in Illinois, USA, on May 09, 1840. She died in Peoria County, Illinois, on April 10, 1850, at the age of 9. Her cause of death was whooping cough. She was buried in La Salle Cemetery, Rome, Peoria County, Illinois.
+ 51	f	VI.	**Sarah A. Hargadine** was born in Peoria, Peoria County, Illinois, on September 05, 1842.[33] She died in Modale, Harrison County, Iowa, on February 10, 1909, at the age of 66.[33] Sarah A. was buried in Calhoun Cemetery, Harrison County, Iowa, on February 13, 1909 (Find a Grave ID 47669695).[33]
+ 52	m	VII.	**William Hurd Hargadine** was born in Illinois, USA, on January 02, 1845. He died on February 27, 1884, at the age of 39. William Hurd was buried in La Salle Cemetery, Rome, Peoria County, Illinois (Find a Grave ID 44542919).

---

[30] 1900 Census Douglas County, Nebraska Omaha City (Vol 14, ED 58, Sheet 2) June 2, 1900.

[31] Tim Chambers, Vanalstines.GED, Date of Import: Mar 11, 2001.

[32] http://www.geocities.com/Heartland/Ridge/7026/main/d200.htm#P383.

[33] Norma Pugmire Gedcom file, Date of Import: Feb 2, 2000.

+ 53 m VIII. **Levi Taylor Hargadine** was born in Medina, Peoria County, Illinois, on April 08, 1847. He died in Dunlap, Radnor Twp., Peoria County, Illinois, on September 22, 1920, at the age of 73. Levi Taylor was buried in La Salle Cemetery, Rome, Peoria County, Illinois (Find a Grave ID 24825520).

Family of Harriet Hargadine and Simon Gibson

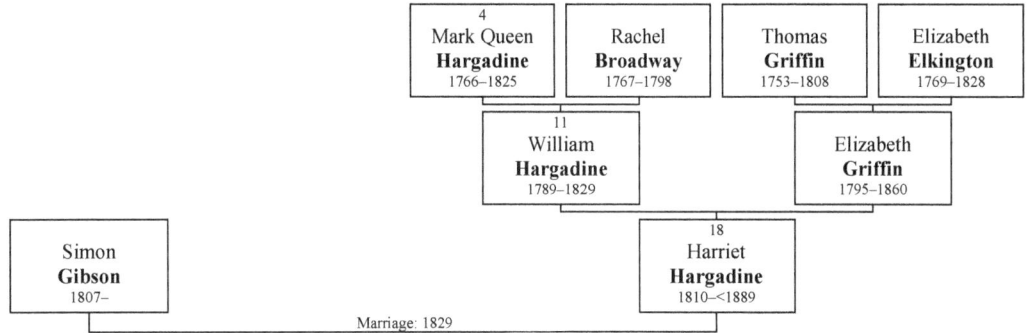

4 Mark Queen **Hargadine** 1766–1825	Rachel **Broadway** 1767–1798	Thomas **Griffin** 1753–1808	Elizabeth **Elkington** 1769–1828

11 William **Hargadine** 1789–1829	Elizabeth **Griffin** 1795–1860

Simon **Gibson** 1807–	18 Harriet **Hargadine** 1810–<1889

Marriage: 1829

18. **Harriet Hargadine** was born in 1810 in Clark County, Ohio. She was the daughter of William Hargadine (11) and Elizabeth Griffin.

Harriet died before September 18, 1889.

Harriet married **Simon Gibson** in 1829 in Clark County, Ohio. Simon was born in Ohio, USA, in 1807.

Family of Elizabeth Hargadine and Jacob Arbogast

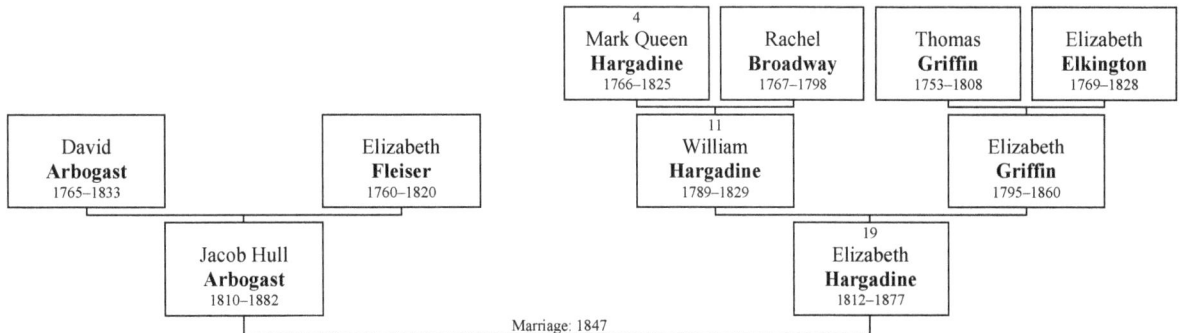

4 Mark Queen **Hargadine** 1766–1825	Rachel **Broadway** 1767–1798	Thomas **Griffin** 1753–1808	Elizabeth **Elkington** 1769–1828

David **Arbogast** 1765–1833	Elizabeth **Fleiser** 1760–1820	11 William **Hargadine** 1789–1829	Elizabeth **Griffin** 1795–1860

Jacob Hull **Arbogast** 1810–1882	19 Elizabeth **Hargadine** 1812–1877

Marriage: 1847

19. **Elizabeth Hargadine** was born on Wednesday, May 20, 1812, in Ohio, USA. She was the daughter of William Hargadine (11) and Elizabeth Griffin.

Elizabeth died on April 30, 1877, at the age of 64. She was buried in Pleasant Hill Cemetery, New Moorefield, Clark County, Ohio (Find a Grave ID 6095528).

At the age of 34, Elizabeth married **Jacob Hull Arbogast** on Saturday, May 08, 1847, in Clark County, Ohio, when he was 36 years old. Jacob Hull was born in Virginia, USA, on Wednesday, May 09, 1810. He was the son of David Arbogast and Elizabeth Fleiser.

Jacob Hull reached 72 years of age and died in Madison County, Indiana, on December 14, 1882. He was buried in Moss Cemetery, Anderson, Madison County, Indiana (Find a Grave ID 15889336).

Family of George Hargadine and Anna Jones

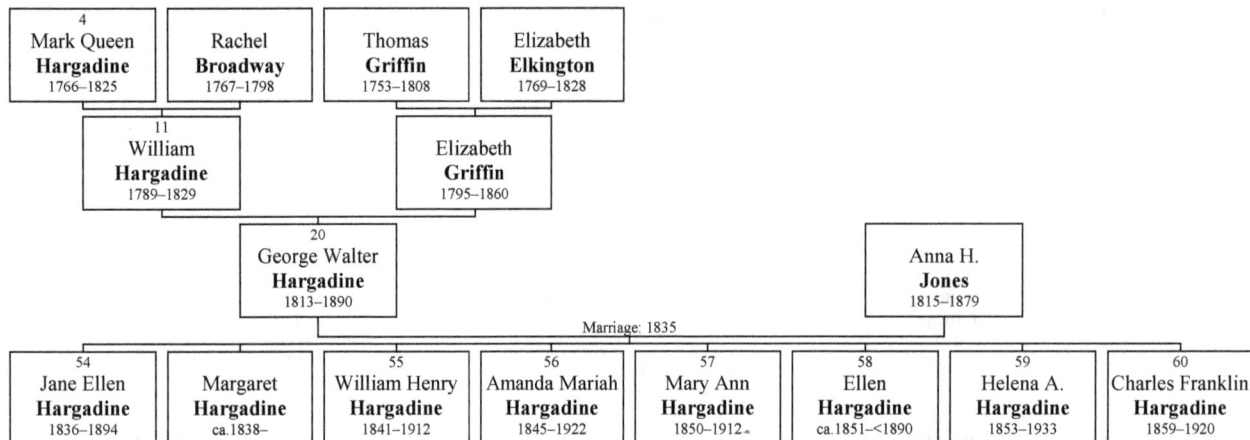

20. **George Walter Hargadine** was born on Sunday, June 13, 1813, in Queen Anne's County, Maryland. He was the son of William Hargadine (11) and Elizabeth Griffin.

George Walter worked as a Farmer. He died in Chenoa, McLean County, Illinois, on April 06, 1890, at the age of 76. George Walter was buried in Chenoa Cemetery, McLean County, Illinois (Find a Grave ID 55010445).

At the age of 22, George Walter married **Anna H. Jones** on Wednesday, October 21, 1835, in Clark County, Ohio, when she was 20 years old. They had eight children.

Anna H. was born in Ohio, USA, on Saturday, February 25, 1815. She reached 63 years of age and died in Chenoa, McLean County, Illinois, on January 15, 1879. Anna H. was buried in Chenoa Cemetery, McLean County, Illinois (Find a Grave ID 55010504).

Children of George Walter Hargadine and Anna H. Jones:

+ 54 f I. **Jane Ellen Hargadine** was born in Clark County, Ohio, on December 26, 1836. She died in Chenoa, McLean County, Illinois, on June 02, 1894, at the age of 57. Jane Ellen was buried in Springdale Cemetery and Mausoleum, Peoria, Peoria County, Illinois, on June 04, 1894 (Find a Grave ID 119219149).

   f II. **Margaret Hargadine** was born about 1838.[34]

+ 55 m III. **William Henry Hargadine** was born in Moorefield Twp., Clark County, Ohio, on January 12, 1841. He died in Kinsley County, Kansas, on July 01, 1912, at the age of 71. His cause of death was cerebral hemorrhage. He was buried in Bethel Cemetery, Hodges, Edwards County, Kansas (Find a Grave ID 67563434).

---

34 FamilySearch.org, United States Census, 1860, FamilySearch, "United States Census, 1860," database with images, <i>FamilySearch</i> (https://familysearch.org/ark:/61903/1:1:MXCW-7J5 : 18 February 2021), Margaret Hargadine in entry for George W Hargadine, 1860.

+   56   f   **IV. Amanda Mariah Hargadine** was born in Moorefield Twp., Clark County, Ohio, on November 16, 1845. She died in Wray, Yuma County, Colorado, on December 23, 1922, at the age of 77. Her cause of death was carcinoma of liver. She was buried in Grandview Cemetery, Wray, Yuma County, Colorado, on December 26, 1966 (Find a Grave ID 50355873).

+   57   f   **V. Mary Ann Hargadine** was born in Medina, Peoria County, Illinois, on January 05, 1850. She died in Chenoa, McLean County, Illinois, on December 20, 1912, at the age of 62. Her cause of death was "dropsy." She was buried in Chenoa Cemetery, McLean County, Illinois, on December 21, 1912 (Find a Grave ID 80966705).

+   58   f   **VI. Ellen Hargadine** was born in Peoria County, Illinois, about 1851. She died before April 06, 1890.

+   59   f   **VII. Helena A. Hargadine** was born in Medina, Peoria County, Illinois, on August 16, 1853. She died in Bloomington, McLean County, Illinois, on December 26, 1933, at the age of 80. Her cause of death was pyloric stenosis. She was buried in Hudson Cemetery, Hudson, McLean County, Illinois (Find a Grave ID 11880055).

+   60   m   **VIII. Charles Franklin Hargadine** was born in Medina, Peoria County, Illinois, on December 09, 1859. He died in Arcadia, Iron County, Missouri, on February 21, 1920, at the age of 60. Charles Franklin was buried in Knights of Pythias Cemetery, Ironton, Iron County, Missouri, on February 22, 1920 (Find a Grave ID 158189091).

Family of Mary Hargadine and Daniel Brandle

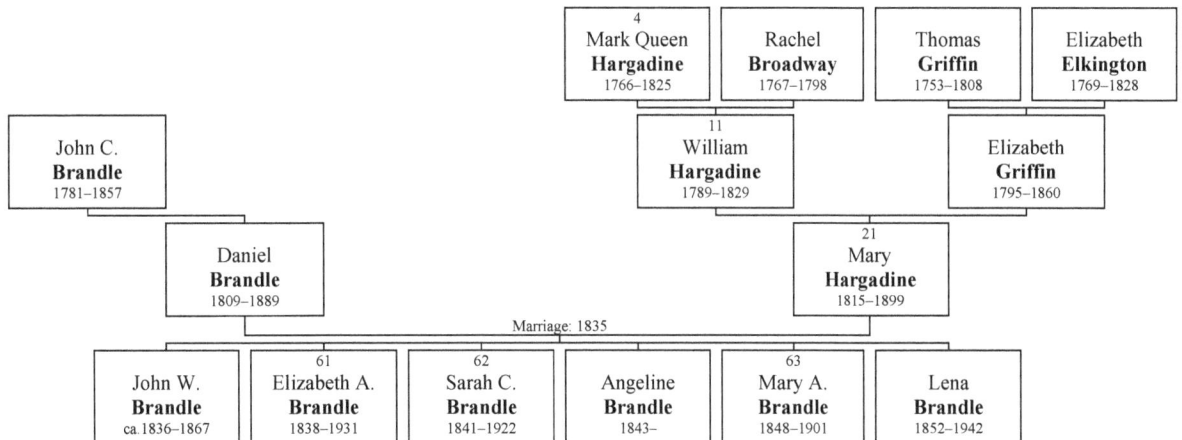

21. **Mary Hargadine** was born on Thursday, December 28, 1815, in Ohio, USA. She was the daughter of William Hargadine (11) and Elizabeth Griffin.

Her religious affiliation was Methodist Protestant Church. She died in Moorefield Twp., Clark, Ohio, on May 31, 1899, at the age of 83. Mary was buried in Pleasant Hill Cemetery, New Moorefield, Clark County, Ohio (Find a Grave ID 6095933).

At the age of 19, Mary married **Daniel Brandle** on Thursday, October 29, 1835, when he was 26 years old. They had six children.

Daniel was born in Dauphin County, Pennsylvania, on Wednesday, January 11, 1809. He was the son of John C. Brandle.

Daniel reached 80 years of age and died in Dauphin County, Pennsylvania, on September 18, 1889. He was buried in Pleasant Hill Cemetery, New Moorefield, Clark County, Ohio (Find a Grave ID 6095935).

Children of Mary Hargadine and Daniel Brandle:

m   I. **John W. Brandle** was born about August 08, 1836. He died on November 03, 1867, at the age of 31. John W. was buried in Pleasant Hill Cemetery, New Moorefield, Clark County, Ohio (Find a Grave ID 6095927).

+ 61   f   II. **Elizabeth A. Brandle** was born in Clark County, Ohio, on March 09, 1838. She died in Dayton, Montgomery County, Ohio, on May 14, 1931, at the age of 93. Elizabeth A. was buried in Ferncliff Cemetery, Springfield, Clark County, Ohio (Find a Grave ID 45844575).

+ 62   f   III. **Sarah C. Brandle** was born in Ohio, USA, in 1841.[35] She was also known as **Sallie**.

Sarah C. died in Springfield, Clark County, Ohio, on November 20, 1922, at the age of 81.[35] She was buried in Ferncliff Cemetery, Springfield, Clark County, Ohio, on November 22, 1922 (Find a Grave ID 58292798).[35]

f   IV. **Angeline Brandle** was born in 1843.

+ 63   f   V. **Mary A. Brandle** was born in 1848. She died in 1901 at the age of 53. Mary A. was buried in Pleasant Hill Cemetery, New Moorefield, Clark County, Ohio (Find a Grave ID 6095633).

f   VI. **Lena Brandle** was born in Clark County, Ohio, on December 18, 1852. She died in Springfield, Clark County, Ohio, on December 19, 1942, at the age of 90. Lena was buried in Pleasant Hill Cemetery, New Moorefield, Clark County, Ohio, on December 22, 1942 (Find a Grave ID 6095937).

---

35   Ancestry.com, Public Member Trees (Provo, UT, USA, Ancestry.com Operations, Inc., 2006), Ancestry.com, Record for Sarah C. Brandle. https://search.ancestry.co.uk/cgi-bin/sse.dll?db=1030&h=232061998133&indiv=try.

Family of John Hargadine and Elenor Mater

22.   **John T. Hargadine** was born in 1819 in Clark County, Ohio. He was the son of William Hargadine (11) and Elizabeth Griffin. He was also known as **Jack**.

John T. served in the military on October 27, 1861. Enlisted, G County 66th Inf Reg. IL. He died in Lost Creek Township, Miami County, Ohio, on November 10, 1888, at the age of 69. John T. was buried in Casstown Cemetery, Casstown, Miami County, Ohio (Find a Grave ID 11670301).

John T. married **Elenor Mater** on Thursday, February 02, 1843, in Troy, Miami County, Ohio. They had two daughters.

Elenor was born in England in 1817. She reached 73 years of age and died on January 04, 1890. Elenor was buried in Casstown Cemetery, Casstown, Miami County, Ohio (Find a Grave ID 11670304). 1850 Census - http://www.tdn-net.com/genealogy/census/lstcrekc.htm Hargadine, John 1850 037b Lostcreek Twp

1860 Census - Post Office - Fletcher, Miami Co., Ohio enumerated on 11 Jul 1860 Page 239 B
John Hargadine age 44 m farm laborer value of personal estate -$100 born in Virginia
Ellen Hargadine age 43 f born in England
Mary Hargadine age 14 f born in Ohio School
Elizabeth A. Hargadine age 9 f born Ohio School

1870 Census - page 354
John Hardadine age 49 m w day laborer $500 $200 born Ohio
Ellen Hardadine age 53 f w keeping house born England
Elisabeth Hardadine age 19 f w at home born Ohio

1880 Census - page 127 D
John Hargadine w m age 61 m day laborer born Ohio, father born Kentucky, mother born Kentucky
Ellen Hargadine w f age 63 m keeping house born England, Father born Scotland, Mother born England
Katie E. Martin w f age 19 s housekeeping born Ohio, father born Ohio, mother born Ohio

1880 http://www.tdn-net.com/genealogy/census/lstcrekc.htm
Luker, Caleb 1880 126A Lostcreek Twp

Daughters of John T. Hargadine and Elenor Mater:

+   64   f   I. **Elizabeth A. Hargadine** was born in Ohio, USA, in July 1848. She died in California, USA, on August 24, 1937, at the age of 89.

+   65   f   II. **Mollie Hargadine**. She was also known as **Mary**.

Family of William Hargadine and Eliza Wigginton

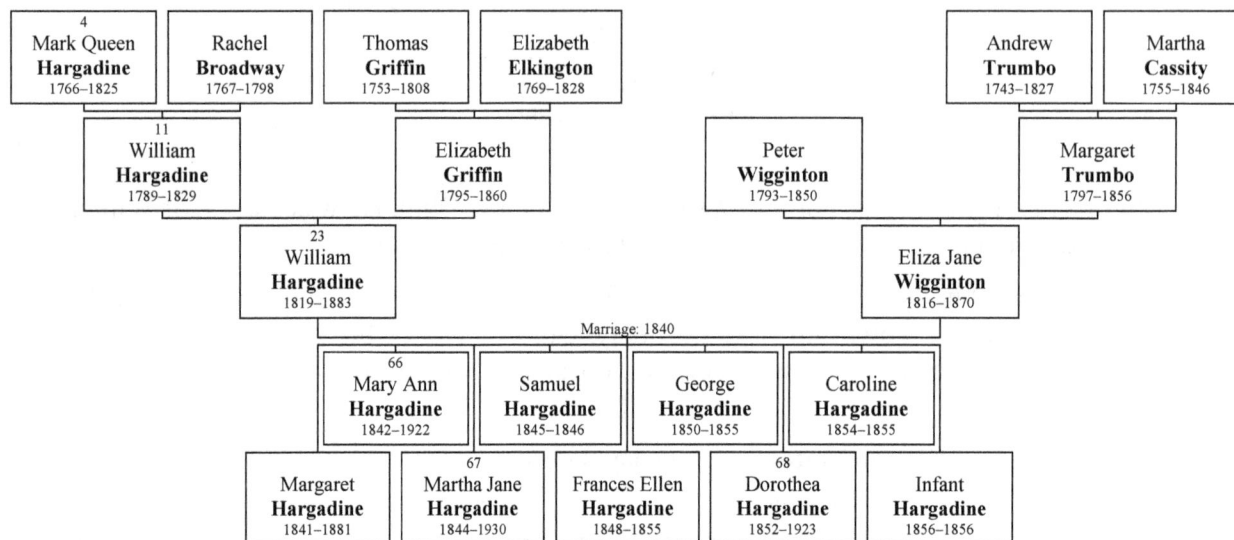

| 4 Mark Queen **Hargadine** 1766–1825 | Rachel **Broadway** 1767–1798 | Thomas **Griffin** 1753–1808 | Elizabeth **Elkington** 1769–1828 | | Andrew **Trumbo** 1743–1827 | Martha **Cassity** 1755–1846 |

| 11 William **Hargadine** 1789–1829 | Elizabeth **Griffin** 1795–1860 | Peter **Wigginton** 1793–1850 | Margaret **Trumbo** 1797–1856 |

| 23 William **Hargadine** 1819–1883 | Eliza Jane **Wigginton** 1816–1870 |

Marriage: 1840

| 66 Mary Ann **Hargadine** 1842–1922 | Samuel **Hargadine** 1845–1846 | George **Hargadine** 1850–1855 | Caroline **Hargadine** 1854–1855 |

| Margaret **Hargadine** 1841–1881 | 67 Martha Jane **Hargadine** 1844–1930 | Frances Ellen **Hargadine** 1848–1855 | 68 Dorothea **Hargadine** 1852–1923 | Infant **Hargadine** 1856–1856 |

23.   **William Hargadine** was born on Sunday, August 01, 1819, in Bellefontaine, Logan County, Ohio. He was the son of William Hargadine (11) and Elizabeth Griffin.

William worked as a Farmer, trader, landowner, city planner and dealer in cattle. He died in Aurora, Kane County, Illinois, on February 15, 1883, at the age of 63. His cause of death was cancer. He was buried in Lucas Chapel Cemetery, Lincoln, Logan County, Illinois (Find a Grave ID 232012520).

At the age of 21, William married **Eliza Jane Wigginton** on Tuesday, September 29, 1840, in Sangamon County, Illinois, when she was 24 years old. They had nine children.

Eliza Jane was born in Bourbon County, Kentucky, on Tuesday, August 13, 1816. Eliza Jane reached 53 years of age and died in Logan County, Illinois, on January 07, 1870. She was buried in Lucas Chapel Cemetery, Lincoln, Logan County, Illinois (Find a Grave ID 232012542). (Lincoln Courier - August 26, 1953)

William Hargadine Came to Illinois From Ohio in 1830. William Hargadine was born August 1, 1819 in Logan County Ohio and came to Logan County, Illinois in the early 1830s. Taking up farming, he located in the present Lucas Chapel community.

Eliza Jane Wigginton, a daughter of Peter and Margaret Trumbo Wigginton, was born August 13, 1816 in Loudoun County, Virginia. She was of English descent.

The Wigginton family came to Illinois from Virginia by way of Kentucky in 1828. Mr. Hargadine and Eliza Wigginton were married about 1840 and moved into the present Pool Hill neighborhood. Several children were born to this union.

One daughter, Martha, became the wife of Lewis Ogle. Frank Ogle of this city is a son.

John Merrilees was born in Edinburgh, Scotland, October 20, 1846, the son of John and Jane Marr Merrilees. The family came to this country in 1851 and lived in New York state for a few years before settling in Delavan.

John, Jr., followed the carpenter trade, and while working in the new town of Lincoln, met and married Dora Hargadine on August 1, 1874.

Miss Hargadine, the youngest daughter of William and Eliza Hargadine, was born July 4, 1852. Mrs. C. C. Applegate and Mrs. G. S. Houston of Lincoln are surviving daughters of this family.

Mr. and Mrs. Hargadine moved to Lincoln in the middle 1850s. In 1861 he served on the town board and was a member of the tree planting committee for Kickapoo, McLean, Logan, Broadway, and Fourth Streets. These streets became beauty spots of the city. He also was alderman of the Third Ward in 1873.

Owned Bowling Alley

At one time he was owner and operator of a bowling alley where the Arcade building is now. At the death of Mrs. Hargadine in January of 1870, Mrs. Merrilees moved her family in her father's home on Fourth Street, the present home of the McGough sisters.

Prior to his death in 1883, Mr. Hargadine had become the owner of several hundred acres of farming land and numerous pieces of town property. This was bought primarily through mortgages and redemptions of forfeited homesteads. In the late 70s he became interested in cattle, often riding horse-back into the northern states and driving back large herds for local feeders.

Mr. and Mrs. Hargadine were buried in the Lucas Chapel cemetery.

In the early 1890s Mr. Merrilees was the carpenter specializing in hand work especially balustrades and railings. He did such work in the John A. Lutz home in Lincoln and the Wright Funeral home, both landmarks today.

So with the passing of time, the descendants of William and Eliza Hargadine have increased until in 1953 there are 75 living in Central Illinois. She was the daughter of Peter Wigginton and Margaret Trumbo.

Children of William Hargadine and Eliza Jane Wigginton:

f I. **Margaret Hargadine** was born in Logan County, Illinois, on August 04, 1841. She was also known as **Maggie**.

Margaret died in Logan County, Illinois, on February 15, 1881, at the age of 39. She was buried in Lucas Chapel Cemetery, Lincoln, Logan County, Illinois (Find a Grave ID 232012597).

+ 66 f II. **Mary Ann Hargadine** was born in Logan County, Illinois, on October 29, 1842. She died in Holdrege, Phelps County, Nebraska, on July 24, 1922, at the age of 79. Mary Ann was buried in Prairie Home Cemetery, Holdrege, Phelps County, Nebraska (Find a Grave ID 35771032).

+ 67 f III. **Martha Jane Hargadine** was born in Logan County, Illinois, on February 20, 1844. She was also known as **Mattie**.

Martha Jane died in Lincoln, Logan County, Illinois, on November 09, 1930, at the age of 86. She was buried in Old Union Cemetery, Lincoln, Logan County, Illinois (Find a Grave ID 166820433).

m IV. **Samuel Hargadine** was born in Sangamon County, Illinois, on October 26, 1845. He died on February 03, 1846. Samuel was buried in Kern Cemetery, Sangamon County, Illinois (Find a Grave ID 37549864).

f   V. **Frances Ellen Hargadine** was born in Logan County, Illinois, on August 16, 1848. She died in Logan County, Illinois, on January 25, 1855, at the age of 6. Frances Ellen was buried in Lucas Chapel Cemetery, Lincoln, Logan County, Illinois (Find a Grave ID 232012646).

m   VI. **George Hargadine** was born in Logan County, Illinois, on March 20, 1850. He died in Logan County, Illinois, on February 08, 1855, at the age of 4. George was buried in Lucas Chapel Cemetery, Lincoln, Logan County, Illinois (Find a Grave ID 232012717).

+ 68   f   VII. **Dorothea Hargadine** was born in Logan County, Illinois, on July 04, 1852. She died on February 20, 1923, at the age of 70.

f   VIII. **Caroline Hargadine** was born on July 22, 1854. She died on May 10, 1855. Caroline was buried in Lucas Chapel Cemetery, Lincoln, Logan County, Illinois (Find a Grave ID 232012780).

m   IX. **Infant Hargadine** was born on May 15, 1856. He died on May 18, 1856. Infant was buried in Lucas Chapel Cemetery, Lincoln, Logan County, Illinois (Find a Grave ID 232012938).

Family of Matilda Hargadine and Levi Hoak

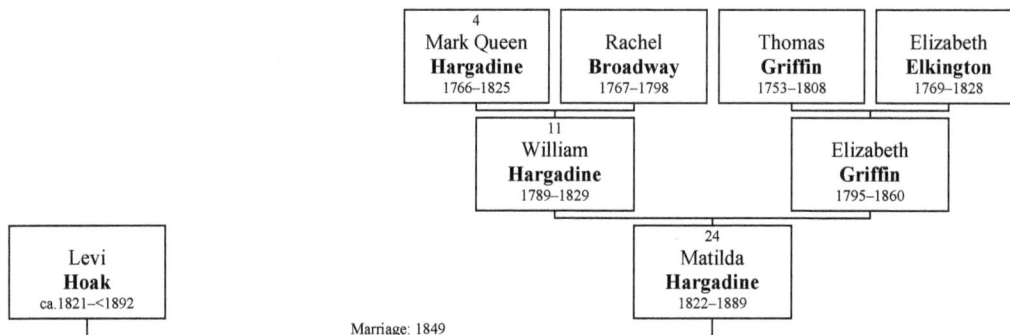

24.   **Matilda Hargadine** was born in 1822 in Ohio, USA. She was the daughter of William Hargadine (11) and Elizabeth Griffin.

Matilda died on September 18, 1889, at the age of 67.

Matilda married **Levi Hoak** on Tuesday, August 14, 1849, in Clark County, Ohio. Levi was born in Ohio, USA, about 1821.

He died in Springfield, Clark County, Ohio, before 1892.

Family of Thomas Hargadine and Margaret

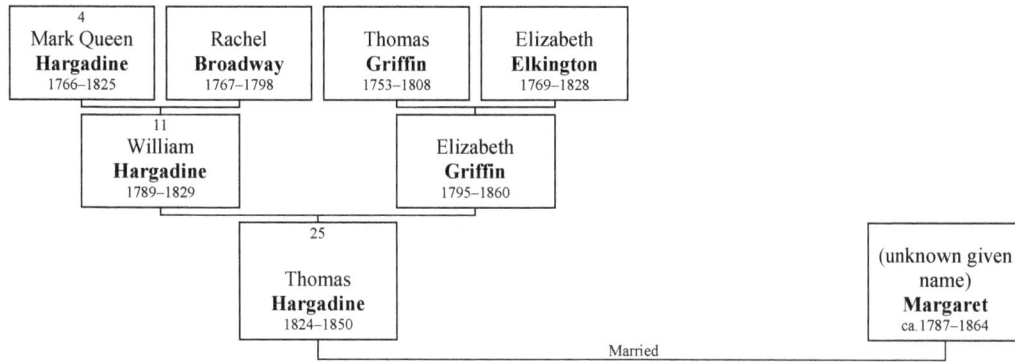

25.   **Thomas Hargadine** was born on Thursday, May 20, 1824, in Ohio, USA.[36] He was the son of William Hargadine (11) and Elizabeth Griffin.

Thomas served in the military in 1812. 35th Regiment; Brown's Maryland Militia; Rank of Private. He died in Clark County, Ohio, on November 13, 1850, at the age of 26.[37] Thomas was buried in Pleasant Hill Cemetery, New Moorefield, Clark County, Ohio (Find a Grave ID 6097770).[37]

He married **(unknown given name) Margaret**. (unknown given name) was born about 1787. She was also known as **Peggy**.

She reached 77 years of age and died on February 24, 1864. She was buried in La Salle Cemetery, Rome, Peoria County, Illinois.

Family of Emiline Hargadine and Thomas McClary

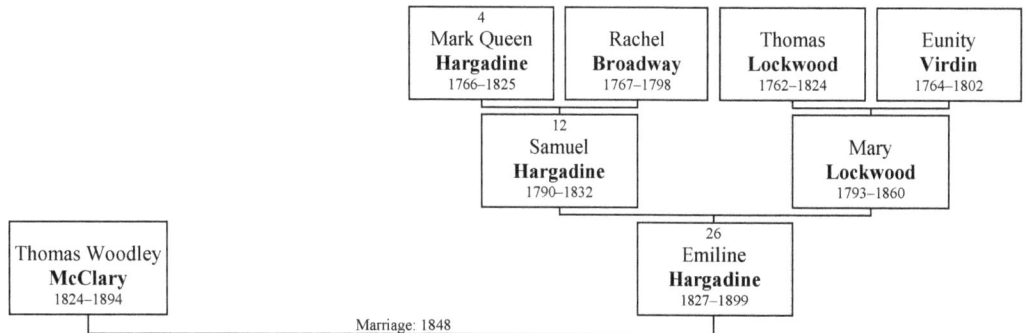

26.   **Emiline Hargadine** was born on Monday, April 16, 1827, in Delaware, USA. She was the daughter of Samuel Hargadine (12) and Mary Lockwood. She was also known as **Emily**.

---

36   FamilySearch.org, United States Census, 1850, FamilySearch, "United States Census, 1850," database with images, <i>FamilySearch</i> (https://www.familysearch.org/ark:/61903/1:1:MX3K-LDN : 21 December 2020), Thos Argedine in household of Daniel Brindle, Moorefield Township, Clark, Ohio, United States; citing family , NARA microfilm publication (Washington, D.C.: National Archives and Records Administration, n.d.).

37   FamilySearch.org, Find A Grave Index, FamilySearch, "Find A Grave Index," database, <i>FamilySearch</i> (https://www.familysearch.org/ark:/61903/1:1:QVVW-VK47 : 6 February 2023), Thomas Hargadine; Burial, New Moorefield, Clark, Ohio, United States of America, Pleasant Hill Cemetery; citing record ID 6097770, <i>Find a Grave</i>, http://www.findagrave.com.

Emiline died in Delaware, USA, on June 29, 1899, at the age of 72. She was buried in Hillside Cemetery and Memorial Gardens, Roslyn, Montgomery County, Pennsylvania (Find a Grave ID 139171923).

Emiline married **Rev. Thomas Woodley McClary** on Thursday, April 13, 1848.[38] Thomas Woodley was born in Willow Grove, Kent County, Delaware, in 1824.

He served in the military: Civil War Union Army Chaplain, 3rd Delaware Volunteer Infantry. Thomas Woodley reached 70 years of age and died in Philadelphia, Philadelphia County, Pennsylvania, on November 05, 1894. He was buried in Hillside Cemetery and Memorial Gardens, Roslyn, Montgomery County, Pennsylvania (Find a Grave ID 139171926).

Family of Robert Hargadine and Martha Kilgore

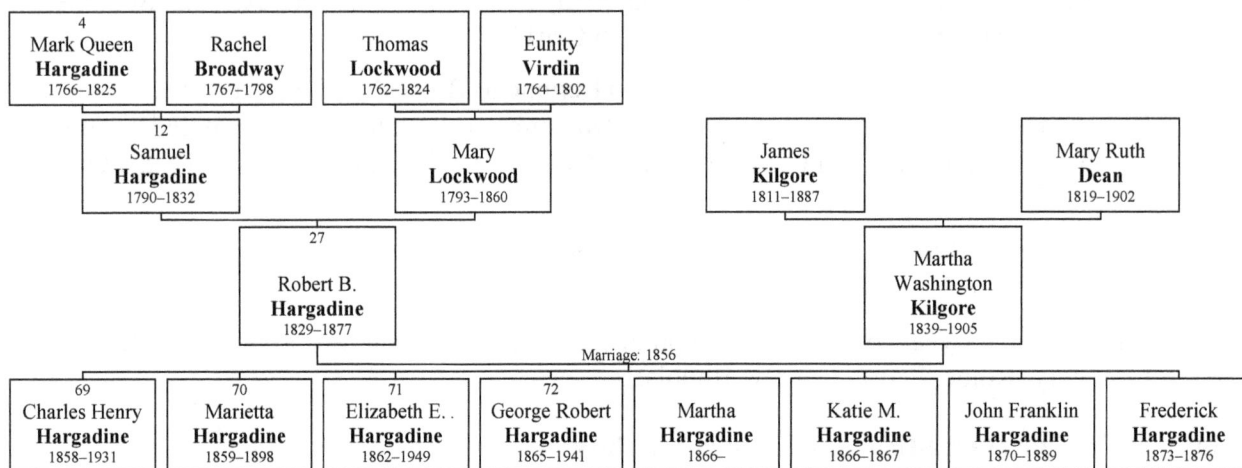

4 Mark Queen **Hargadine** 1766–1825	Rachel **Broadway** 1767–1798	Thomas **Lockwood** 1762–1824	Eunity **Virdin** 1764–1802		James **Kilgore** 1811–1887		Mary Ruth **Dean** 1819–1902

12 Samuel **Hargadine** 1790–1832	Mary **Lockwood** 1793–1860

27
Robert B.
Hargadine
1829–1877

Martha
Washington
Kilgore
1839–1905

Marriage: 1856

69 Charles Henry **Hargadine** 1858–1931	70 Marietta **Hargadine** 1859–1898	71 Elizabeth E. . **Hargadine** 1862–1949	72 George Robert **Hargadine** 1865–1941	Martha **Hargadine** 1866–	Katie M. **Hargadine** 1866–1867	John Franklin **Hargadine** 1870–1889	Frederick **Hargadine** 1873–1876

27. **Robert B. Hargadine** was born on Saturday, January 31, 1829, in Kent County, Delaware. He was the son of Samuel Hargadine (12) and Mary Lockwood.

Robert B. served in the military on October 20, 1855. Sergeant during Oregon Indian wars, Company J. He died in Oakland, Alameda County, California, on January 13, 1877, at the age of 47. Robert B. was buried in Hargadine Cemetery, Ashland, Jackson County, Oregon (Find a Grave ID 11178298).

Robert B. married **Martha Washington Kilgore** on Wednesday, February 06, 1856. They had eight children.

Martha Washington was born in Ohio, USA, in February 1839. She was the daughter of James Kilgore and Mary Ruth Dean.

Martha Washington reached 66 years of age and died in Ashland, Jackson County, Oregon, on September 05, 1905. Her cause of death was Chronic Myocardial Degeneration. Martha Washington was buried in Hargadine Cemetery, Ashland, Jackson County, Oregon (Find a Grave ID 11178304).

---

38   Donald O. Virdin, THE HARGADINES AND OTHER DELAWARE AND MARYLAND FAMILIES (Published by Raymond B. Clark, Jr. P.O. Box 352, St. Michaels, Maryland 21663), Family History Library, 35 N.W. Temple, Salt Lake City, Utah 84150, Quoting Kent County Marriage Records, Volume 90, page 2.

Children of Robert B. Hargadine and Martha Washington Kilgore:

+ 69   m   I. **Charles Henry Hargadine** was born on February 11, 1858. He died in Santa Monica, Los Angeles County, California, in 1931 at the age of 72. Charles Henry was buried in Hargadine Cemetery, Ashland, Jackson County, Oregon (Find a Grave ID 11178322).

+ 70   f   II. **Marietta Hargadine** was born in Oregon, USA, on July 02, 1859. She was also known as **Etta**.

Marietta died in Ashland, Jackson County, Oregon, on June 21, 1898, at the age of 38. She was buried in Hargadine Cemetery, Ashland, Jackson County, Oregon (Find a Grave ID 11178341).

+ 71   f   III. **Elizabeth E. Hargadine** was born in Ashland, Jackson County, Oregon, on August 02, 1862. She was also known as **Lizzie**.

Elizabeth E. died in Ashland, Jackson County, Oregon, on August 06, 1949, at the age of 87. She was cremated in Grants Pass, Oregon, on August 09, 1949 (Find a Grave ID 11178327).

+ 72   m   IV. **George Robert Hargadine** was born in Ashland, Jackson County, Oregon, on September 09, 1865. He died in Ashland, Jackson County, Oregon, on April 02, 1941, at the age of 75. George Robert was buried in Hargadine Cemetery, Ashland, Jackson County, Oregon, on April 04, 1941 (Find a Grave ID 23304338).

         f   V. **Martha Hargadine** was born on January 28, 1866.

         f   VI. **Katie M. Hargadine** was born in Ashland, Jackson County, Oregon, on May 28, 1866. She died in Ashland, Jackson County, Oregon, on December 08, 1867, at the age of 1. Katie M. was buried in Hargadine Cemetery, Ashland, Jackson County, Oregon, on December 08, 1867 (Find a Grave ID 11178337).

         m   VII. **John Franklin Hargadine** was born in 1870. He died in Ashland, Jackson County, Oregon, on March 03, 1889, at the age of 19. John Franklin was buried in Hargadine Cemetery, Ashland, Jackson County, Oregon, on March 04, 1889 (Find a Grave ID 150292572).

         m   VIII. **Frederick Hargadine** was born in Ashland, Jackson County, Oregon, on February 23, 1873. He died in Ashland, Jackson County, Oregon, on April 26, 1876, at the age of 3. Frederick was buried in Hargadine Cemetery, Ashland, Jackson County, Oregon (Find a Grave ID 11178315).

Family of Henry Hargadine and Ruth Whittaker

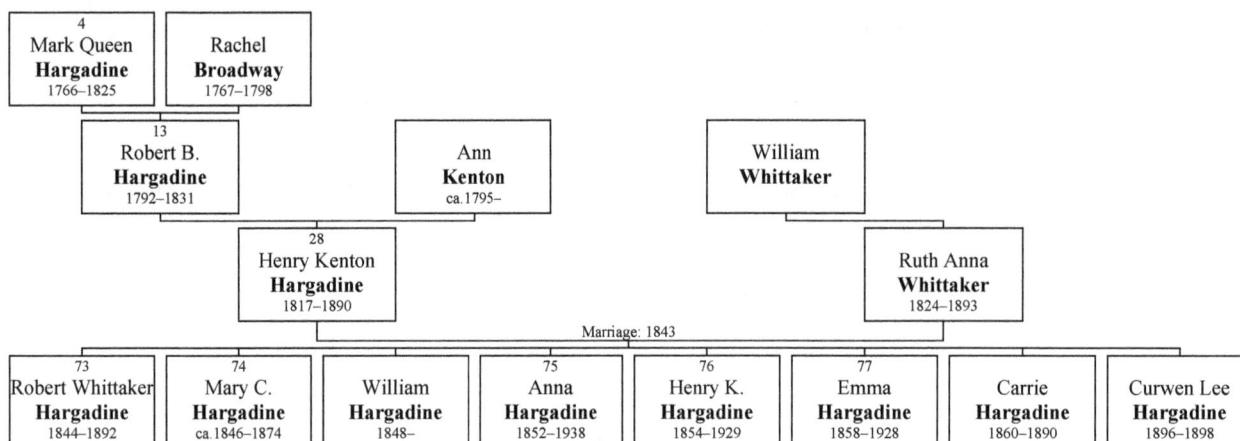

```
┌─────────────┐ ┌─────────────┐
│      4      │ │   Rachel    │
│ Mark Queen  │ │  Broadway   │
│ Hargadine   │ │ 1767–1798   │
│ 1766–1825   │ │             │
└─────────────┘ └─────────────┘
```

```
┌─────────────┐        ┌─────────────┐              ┌─────────────┐
│     13      │        │     Ann     │              │   William   │
│  Robert B.  │        │   Kenton    │              │  Whittaker  │
│  Hargadine  │        │  ca.1795–   │              │             │
│  1792–1831  │        │             │              │             │
└─────────────┘        └─────────────┘              └─────────────┘
```

```
        ┌─────────────┐                          ┌─────────────┐
        │     28      │                          │  Ruth Anna  │
        │ Henry Kenton│                          │  Whittaker  │
        │  Hargadine  │                          │  1824–1893  │
        │  1817–1890  │                          │             │
        └─────────────┘                          └─────────────┘
                      Marriage: 1843
```

73	74		75	76	77		
Robert Whittaker **Hargadine** 1844–1892	Mary C. **Hargadine** ca.1846–1874	William **Hargadine** 1848–	Anna **Hargadine** 1852–1938	Henry K. **Hargadine** 1854–1929	Emma **Hargadine** 1858–1928	Carrie **Hargadine** 1860–1890	Curwen Lee **Hargadine** 1896–1898

28. **Henry Kenton Hargadine** was born on Sunday, May 25, 1817, in Kent County, Delaware. He was the son of Robert B. Hargadine (13) and Ann Kenton.

Henry Kenton died in Kent County, Delaware, on January 10, 1890, at the age of 72. He was buried in Odd Fellows Cemetery, Camden, Kent County, Delaware (Find a Grave ID 7795556).

At the age of 26, Henry Kenton married **Ruth Anna Whittaker** on Wednesday, June 21, 1843, in Kent County, Delaware, when she was 19 years old. They had eight children.

Ruth Anna was born in Kent County, Delaware, on Friday, June 04, 1824. Ruth Anna reached 68 years of age and died in Kent County, Delaware, on January 09, 1893. She was buried in Odd Fellows Cemetery, Camden, Kent County, Delaware (Find a Grave ID 7795554). Burial info:
http://searches.rootsweb.com/cgi-bin/ifetch2?/u1/data/de+index+1028529+F

More About HENRY KENTON HARGADINE:
Burial: Odd Fellows Cemetery -Camden, Kent, Delaware
Census 1: 16 August 1850, Murderkill Hundred, Kent County, Delaware (Pg. 231, Sht 462)
Census 2: 14 July 1860, Murderkill Hundred, Kent County, Delaware (Pg. 260)
Census 3: 20 June 1870, North Murderkill Hundred, Kent County, Delaware (Pg. 168, Sht. 38)
Census 4: 22 June 1880, Canterbury, North Murderkill Hundred, Kent County, Delaware (ED 40, Pg. 271D, Sht. 72)

More About RUTH ANA WHITTAKER:
Burial: Odd Fellows Cemetery -Camden, Kent, Delaware
Census 1: 16 August 1850, Murderkill Hundred, Kent County, Delaware (Pg. 231, Sht 462)
Census 2: 14 July 1860, Murderkill Hundred, Kent County, Delaware (Pg. 260)
Census 3: 20 June 1870, North Murderkill Hundred, Kent County, Delaware (Pg. 168, Sht. 38)
Census 4: 22 June 1880, Canterbury, North Murderkill Hundred, Kent County, Delaware (ED 40, Pg. 271D, Sht. 72) She was the daughter of William Whittaker.

Children of Henry Kenton Hargadine and Ruth Anna Whittaker:

+ 73   m   I. **Robert Whittaker Hargadine** was born in Canterbury, Kent County, Delaware, on April 28, 1844. He died in Felton, Kent County, Delaware, on August 31, 1892, at the age of 48. Robert Whittaker was buried in Holy Cross Catholic Cemetery, Dover, Kent County, Delaware (Find a Grave ID 6345526).

+ 74   f   II. **Mary C. Hargadine** was born in Delaware, USA, about 1846. She died on August 07, 1874, at the age of 28. Mary C. was buried in Saint Peter's Episcopal Churchyard, Lewes, Sussex County, Delaware (Find a Grave ID 7713162).

     m   III. **William Hargadine** was born in Delaware, USA, in 1848.

+ 75   f   IV. **Anna Hargadine** was born in Kent County, Delaware, on August 25, 1852. She was also known as **Annie**.

          Anna died in Viola, Kent County, Delaware, on July 05, 1938, at the age of 85. She was buried in Odd Fellows Cemetery, Camden, Kent County, Delaware (Find a Grave ID 45752463).

+ 76   m   V. **Henry K. Hargadine** was born in Viola, Kent County, Delaware, on December 16, 1854. He died in Woodside, Kent County, Delaware, on October 17, 1929, at the age of 74. His cause of death was Chronic Myocarditis. He was buried in Barratts Chapel Cemetery, Frederica, Kent County, Delaware, on October 19, 1929 (Find a Grave ID 29366382).

+ 77   f   VI. **Emma Hargadine** was born in Delaware, USA, on October 27, 1858. She died in Kent County, Delaware, on February 08, 1928, at the age of 69. Emma was buried in Canterbury Cemetery, Canterbury, Kent County, Delaware, on February 10, 1928 (Find a Grave ID 5091580).

     f   VII. **Carrie Hargadine** was born on June 20, 1860. She died on December 02, 1890, at the age of 30. Carrie was buried in Odd Fellows Cemetery, Camden, Kent County, Delaware (Find a Grave ID 111022517).

     m   VIII. **Curwen Lee Hargadine** was born in 1896. He died in 1898 at the age of 2. Curwen Lee was buried in Barratts Chapel Cemetery, Frederica, Kent County, Delaware (Find a Grave ID 29366372).

Family of William Hargadine and Acrata McCreery

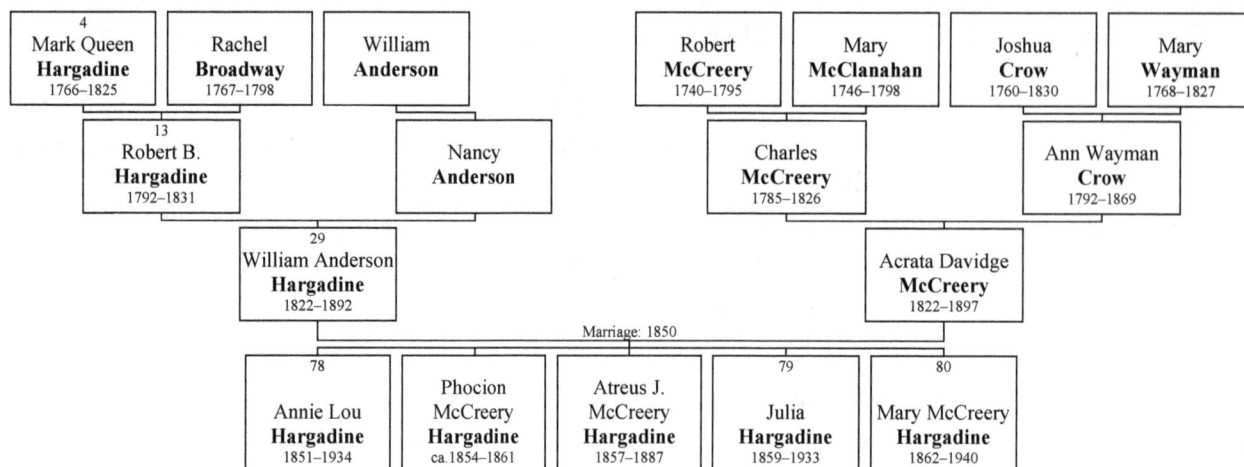

29.   **William Anderson Hargadine** was born on Sunday, January 06, 1822, in Frederica, Kent County, Delaware. He was the son of Robert B. Hargadine (13) and Nancy Anderson.

William Anderson worked as a merchant; Hargadine & McKittrick Dry Goods, St. Louis. He died in Saint Louis, Saint Louis County, Missouri, on January 04, 1892, at the age of 69. William Anderson was buried in Bellefontaine Cemetery, Saint Louis, St. Louis City, Missouri, on January 06, 1892 (Find a Grave ID 21038).

William Anderson married **Acrata Davidge McCreery** in 1850. They had five children.

Acrata Davidge was born on Saturday, November 02, 1822. Acrata Davidge reached 74 years of age and died in Saint Louis, Saint Louis County, Missouri, on January 09, 1897. She was buried on January 10, 1897, in Bellefontaine Cemetery, Saint Louis, St. Louis City, Missouri (Find a Grave ID 36903476). Burial: 6 January 1892, Bellefontaine Cemetery -St. Louis, St. Louis, Missouri
Census 1: 29 June 1860, St. Louis, St. Louis County, Missouri (Pg. 345, Sht 79, Ward 6)
Census 2: 4 June 1870, St. Louis City, St. Louis County, Missouri (Pg. 642, Sht 17, Subd. 13)
Census 3: 2 June 1880, St. Louis City, St. Louis County, Missouri (ED 69, Pg. 19, Sht 6)
Occupation: Merchant; Hargadine & McKittrick Dry Goods, St. Louis

—
1880 Census Place: St. Louis, St. Louis, Missouri
Source: FHL Film 1254720 National Archives Film T9-0720   Page 19B   First Enumeration
Relation Sex Marr Race Age Birthplace
William A. HARGADINE Self M M W 56 DE Occ: Wholesale Merchant Fa: DE Mo: DE
Acrata HARGADINE Wife F M W 56 KY Occ: Keeping House Fa: KY Mo: MD
Althens Mc Crary HARGARDINE Son M S W 23 MO   Fa: DE Mo: KY
Mary Mc Crary HARGADINE Dau F S W 18 MO   Fa: DE Mo: KY
Margaret MC FADDEN Other F S W 35 IRE Occ: Servant Fa: IRE Mo: IRE
Kate MORAN Other F S W 22 IRE Occ: Servant Fa: IRE Mo: IRE
Norah BERGEN Other F S W 22 IRE Occ: Servant Fa: IRE Mo: IRE
Joanna O BRIEN Other F S W 25 IRE Occ: Servant Fa: IRE Mo: IRE
Thomas SHANNON Other M S W 40 IRE Occ: Servant Fa: IRE Mo: IRE
William JONES Other M S B 35 VA Occ: Servant Fa: VA Mo: VA She was the daughter of Charles McCreery and Ann Wayman Crow.

Children of William Anderson Hargadine and Acrata Davidge McCreery:

+ 78   f   I. **Annie Lou Hargadine** was born in Saint Louis, Saint Louis County, Missouri, on September 07, 1851. She died in Saint Louis, Saint Louis County, Missouri, on July 25, 1934, at the age of 82. Annie Lou was buried in Bellefontaine Cemetery, Saint Louis, St. Louis City, Missouri (Find a Grave ID 99158870).

        m   II. **Phocion McCreery Hargadine** was born in Saint Louis, Saint Louis County, Missouri, about 1854. He died in Saint Louis, Saint Louis County, Missouri, in May 1861 at the age of 7. His cause of death was Encephalitis. He was buried in Bellefontaine Cemetery, Saint Louis, St. Louis City, Missouri, on May 22, 1861.

        m   III. **Atreus J. McCreery Hargadine** was born in Saint Louis, Saint Louis County, Missouri, on January 22, 1857. He died in Saint Louis, Saint Louis County, Missouri, on January 29, 1887, at the age of 30. Atreus J. McCreery was buried in Bellefontaine Cemetery, Saint Louis, St. Louis City, Missouri (Find a Grave ID 99057624).

+ 79   f   IV. **Julia Hargadine** was born in Missouri, USA, on August 12, 1859. She died on June 14, 1933, at the age of 73. Julia was buried in Bellefontaine Cemetery, Saint Louis, St. Louis City, Missouri (Find a Grave ID 99080321).

+ 80   f   V. **Mary McCreery Hargadine** was born in Saint Louis, Saint Louis County, Missouri, on April 04, 1862. She died in Washington D.C. on March 28, 1940, at the age of 77. Mary McCreery was buried in Bellefontaine Cemetery, Saint Louis, St. Louis City, Missouri, on April 03, 1940 (Find a Grave ID 99058156).

Family of Julia Hargadine and Robert Wright

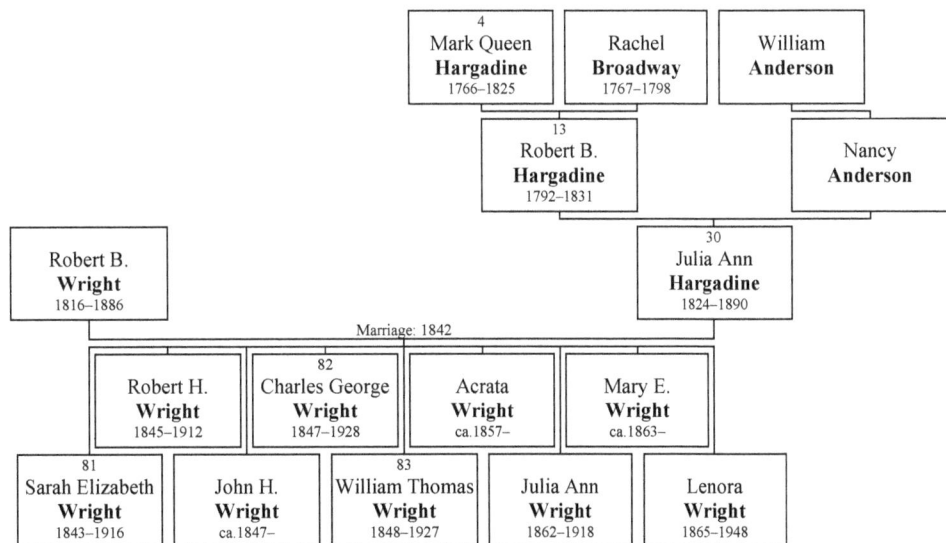

30.   **Julia Ann Hargadine** was born on Monday, March 15, 1824, in Kent County, Delaware. She was the daughter of Robert B. Hargadine (13) and Nancy Anderson.

Julia Ann died on July 21, 1890, at the age of 66. She was buried in Wesley Methodist Church Cemetery, Dover, Kent County, Delaware (Find a Grave ID 7566639).

At the age of 17, Julia Ann married **Robert B. Wright** on Thursday, February 03, 1842, in Kent County, Delaware, when he was 25 years old. They had nine children.

Robert B. was born in Kent County, Delaware, on Monday, September 16, 1816. He reached 69 years of age and died on June 01, 1886. Robert B. was buried in Wesley Methodist Church Cemetery, Dover, Kent County, Delaware (Find a Grave ID 7566641).

Children of Julia Ann Hargadine and Robert B. Wright:

+ 81   f   I. **Sarah Elizabeth Wright** was born on March 17, 1843. She died in New Castle, New Castle County, Delaware, on April 05, 1916, at the age of 73. Sarah Elizabeth was buried in Dover, Kent County, Delaware, on May 08, 1916.

        m   II. **Robert H. Wright** was born in Delaware, USA, on March 17, 1845. He died in Baltimore, Baltimore County, Maryland, on April 26, 1912, at the age of 67. Robert H. was buried in Chester Cemetery, Chestertown, Kent County, Maryland (Find a Grave ID 151429492).

        m   III. **John H. Wright** was born in Delaware, USA, about 1847.

+ 82   m   IV. **Charles George Wright** was born in Delaware, USA, on January 09, 1847. He died in Dover, Kent County, Delaware, on June 17, 1928, at the age of 81. Charles George was buried in Lakeside Cemetery, Dover, Kent County, Delaware (Find a Grave ID 7803777).

+ 83   m   V. **William Thomas Wright** was born in Kent County, Delaware, on February 10, 1848.[39] He died in Delaware, USA, on June 13, 1927, at the age of 79.[39] William Thomas was buried in Spring Hill Cemetery, Easton, Talbot County, Maryland (Find a Grave ID 67441058).

        f   VI. **Acrata Wright** was born in Delaware, USA, about 1857.

        f   VII. **Julia Ann Wright** was born in Delaware, USA, in 1862. She died in Dover, Kent County, Delaware, on April 24, 1918, at the age of 56. Julia Ann was buried in Lakeside Cemetery, Dover, Kent County, Delaware (Find a Grave ID 207441369).

        f   VIII. **Mary E. Wright** was born in Delaware, USA, about 1863.

        f   IX. **Lenora Wright** was born in Delaware, USA, in 1865. She died in 1948 at the age of 83. Lenora was buried in Lakeside Cemetery, Dover, Kent County, Delaware (Find a Grave ID 7800388).

---

[39]   Ancestry.com, Public Member Trees (Provo, UT, USA, Ancestry.com Operations, Inc., 2006), Ancestry.com, Record for William Thomas Wright. https://search.ancestry.co.uk/cgi-bin/sse.dll?db=1030&h=7501965283&indiv=try.

Family of Mary Hargadine and William Virdin

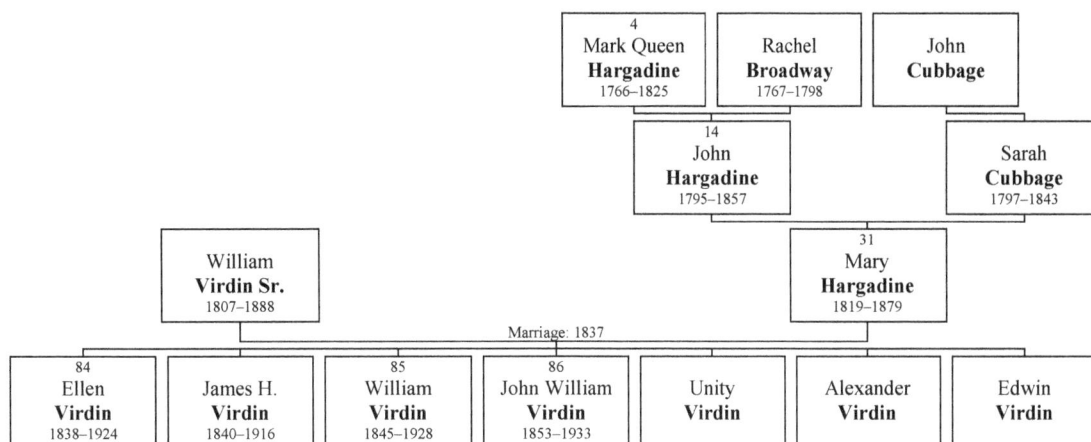

31. **Mary Hargadine** was born on Friday, November 12, 1819, in Kent County, Delaware. She was the daughter of John Hargadine (14) and Sarah Cubbage.

Mary died in Kent County, Delaware, on June 15, 1879, at the age of 59. She was buried in Bethesda Church Cemetery, Pearsons Corner, Kent County, Delaware (Find a Grave ID 11262695).

At the age of 17, Mary married **William Virdin Sr.** on Tuesday, June 06, 1837, in Kent County, Delaware, when he was 30 years old. They had seven children.

William was born on Monday, March 16, 1807. He reached 81 years of age and died on December 12, 1888. William was buried in Bethesda Church Cemetery, Pearsons Corner, Kent County, Delaware (Find a Grave ID 11262699).

Children of Mary Hargadine and William Virdin Sr.:

+ 84 f I. **Ellen Virdin** was born on November 09, 1838. She died on December 30, 1924, at the age of 86. Ellen was buried in Lakeside Cemetery, Dover, Kent County, Delaware (Find a Grave ID 7779889).

 m II. **James H. Virdin** was born on April 12, 1840. He died in Wyoming, Kent County, Delaware, on December 21, 1916, at the age of 76. James H. was buried in Odd Fellows Cemetery, Camden, Kent County, Delaware (Find a Grave ID 7795586).

+ 85 m III. **William Virdin** was born in 1845. He died in Dover, Kent County, Delaware, on March 18, 1928, at the age of 83. William was buried in Lakeside Cemetery, Dover, Kent County, Delaware (Find a Grave ID 7777123).

+ 86 m IV. **John William Virdin** was born in Delaware, USA, in March 1853. He died in Delaware, USA, on November 12, 1933, at the age of 80. John William was buried in Odd Fellows Cemetery, Camden, Kent County, Delaware (Find a Grave ID 191161853).

 f V. **Unity Virdin.**

 m VI. **Alexander Virdin.**

 m VII. **Edwin Virdin.**

Family of Samuel Hargadine and Mariam Irons

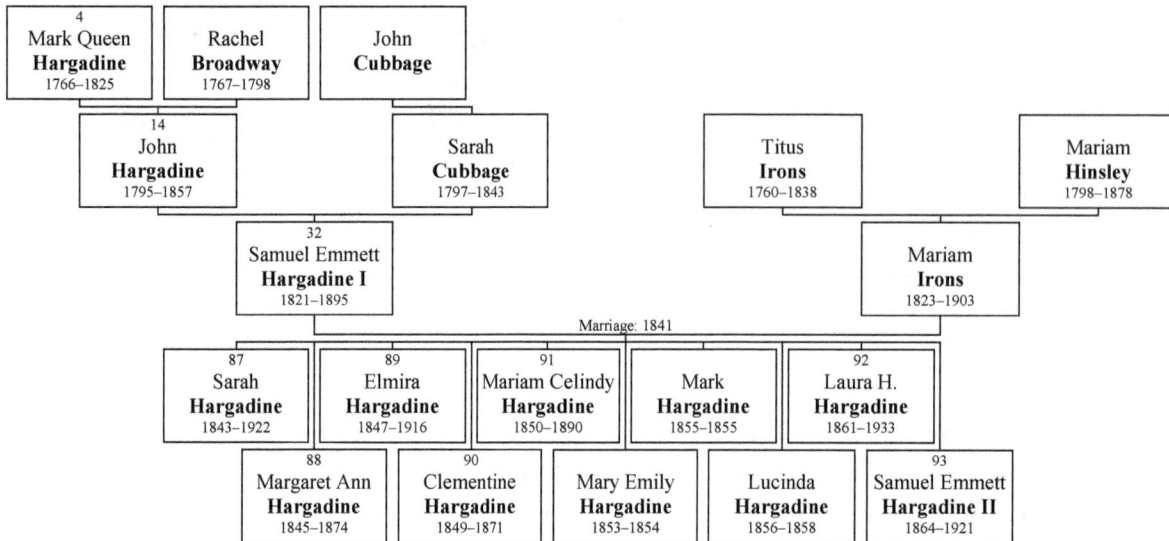

32. **Samuel Emmett Hargadine I** was born on Thursday, July 05, 1821, in Kent County, Delaware.[40–43] He was the son of John Hargadine (14) and Sarah Cubbage.

Samuel Emmett worked as a Sheriff of Kent County, Delaware between 1871 and 1875. He died in Brookfield, Linn County, Missouri, on May 12, 1895, at the age of 73.[40] Samuel Emmett was buried in Rose Hill Cemetery, Brookfield, Linn County, Missouri, on May 15, 1895 (Find a Grave ID 131197208).[40]

At the age of 20, Samuel Emmett married **Mariam Irons** on Thursday, November 18, 1841, in Kent County, Delaware, when she was 18 years old. They had ten children.

Mariam was born in Templeville, Queen Annes County, Maryland, on Friday, August 01, 1823.[41–46] She was the daughter of Titus Irons and Mariam Hinsley.

40   FamilySearch.org, Find A Grave Index, FamilySearch, "Find A Grave Index," database, <i>FamilySearch</i> (https://www.familysearch.org/ark:/61903/1:1:QVGB-4WQH : 11 January 2023), Samuel Emmett Hargadine, ; Burial, Brookfield, Linn, Missouri, United States of America, Rose Hill Cemetery; citing record ID 131197208, <i>Find a Grave</i>, http://www.findagrave.com.

41   FamilySearch.org, United States Census, 1870, FamilySearch, "United States Census, 1870," <i>FamilySearch</i> (https://www.familysearch.org/ark:/61903/1:1:M4BP-DVK : Fri Oct 06 14:54:24 UTC 2023), Entry for Samuel Hargadine and Marian Hargadine, 1870.

42   FamilySearch.org, United States Census, 1850, FamilySearch, "United States Census, 1850," <i>FamilySearch</i> (https://www.familysearch.org/ark:/61903/1:1:MD4D-J9S : Wed Oct 04 05:43:55 UTC 2023), Entry for Samuel Harganton and Marium Harganton, 1850.

43   FamilySearch.org, United States Census, 1880, FamilySearch, "United States Census, 1880," <i>FamilySearch</i> (https://www.familysearch.org/ark:/61903/1:1:M6XK-68P : Fri Oct 06 10:11:48 UTC 2023), Entry for Samuel Hargadine and Marians Hargadine, 1880.

44   FamilySearch.org, United States Census, 1900, FamilySearch, "United States Census, 1900," <i>FamilySearch</i> (https://www.familysearch.org/ark:/61903/1:1:M3ZJ-1YV : Thu Oct 05 15:46:48 UTC 2023), Entry for Sam Schenck and Laura Schenck, 1900.

45   FamilySearch.org, Find A Grave Index, FamilySearch, "Find A Grave Index," database, <i>FamilySearch</i> (https://www.familysearch.org/ark:/61903/1:1:QVGB-4WQ4 : 11 January 2023), Mariam Irons Hargadine; Burial, Brookfield, Linn, Missouri, United States of America, Rose Hill Cemetery; citing record ID 131197174, <i>Find a Grave</i>, http://www.findagrave.com.

46   FamilySearch.org, FamilySearch FamilyTree, FamilySearch.

Mariam reached 79 years of age and died in Wilmington, New Castle County, Delaware, on March 16, 1903.[45] She was buried on March 19, 1903, in Rose Hill Cemetery, Brookfield, Linn County, Missouri (Find a Grave ID 131197174).[45]

Children of Samuel Emmett Hargadine I and Mariam Irons:

+ 87 f   I. **Sarah Hargadine** was born in Delaware, USA, on February 10, 1843. She was also known as **Sallie**.

    Sarah died in Wilmington, New Castle County, Delaware, on August 14, 1922, at the age of 79. She was buried in Glenwood Cemetery, Smyrna, Kent County, Delaware, on August 16, 1922 (Find a Grave ID 11160895).

+ 88 f   II. **Margaret Ann Hargadine** was born on January 17, 1845. She died on June 09, 1874, at the age of 29. Margaret Ann was buried in Glenwood Cemetery, Smyrna, Kent County, Delaware (Find a Grave ID 11169052).

+ 89 f   III. **Elmira Hargadine** was born in Templeville, Caroline County, Maryland, on March 04, 1847. She was also known as **Ella**.

    Elmira died in Brookfield, Linn County, Missouri, on April 23, 1916, at the age of 69. She was buried in Rose Hill Cemetery, Brookfield, Linn County, Missouri (Find a Grave ID 83950092).

+ 90 f   IV. **Clementine Hargadine** was born on September 13, 1849. She died on February 07, 1871, at the age of 21. Clementine was buried in Glenwood Cemetery, Smyrna, Kent County, Delaware (Find a Grave ID 11236609).

+ 91 f   V. **Mariam Celindy Hargadine** was born in Maryland, USA, on November 12, 1850. She was also known as **Mellie**. Mariam Celindy died on November 11, 1890, at the age of 39.

    f   VI. **Mary Emily Hargadine** was born in Kent County, Delaware, on June 23, 1853. She died in Kent County, Delaware, on May 31, 1854. Mary Emily was buried in Hargadine Family Cemetery; Dover, Kent County, Delaware (Find a Grave ID 13265843).

    m   VII. **Mark Hargadine** was born on April 26, 1855. He died on April 26, 1855. Mark was buried in Hargadine Family Cemetery; Dover, Kent County, Delaware (Find a Grave ID 13265830).

    f   VIII. **Lucinda Hargadine** was born on November 23, 1856. She died on September 29, 1858, at the age of 1. Lucinda was buried in Hargadine Family Cemetery; Dover, Kent County, Delaware (Find a Grave ID 13265814).

+ 92 f   IX. **Laura H. Hargadine** was born in Delaware, USA, on February 04, 1861.[47] She died in Brookfield, Linn County, Missouri, on June 26, 1933, at the age of 72. Laura H. was buried in Rose Hill Cemetery, Brookfield, Linn County, Missouri (Find a Grave ID 83488117).

---

47   Neil Becker. FTW, Date of Import: May 19, 2004.

+ 93   m   X. **Samuel Emmett Hargadine II** was born in Leipsic, Kent County, Delaware, on July 26, 1864. He died in Brookfield, Linn County, Missouri, on September 21, 1921, at the age of 57. His cause of death was cancer of stomach. He was buried in Rose Hill Cemetery, Brookfield, Linn County, Missouri, on September 23, 1921 (Find a Grave ID 131195781).

Family of Sarah Hargadine and John Carson

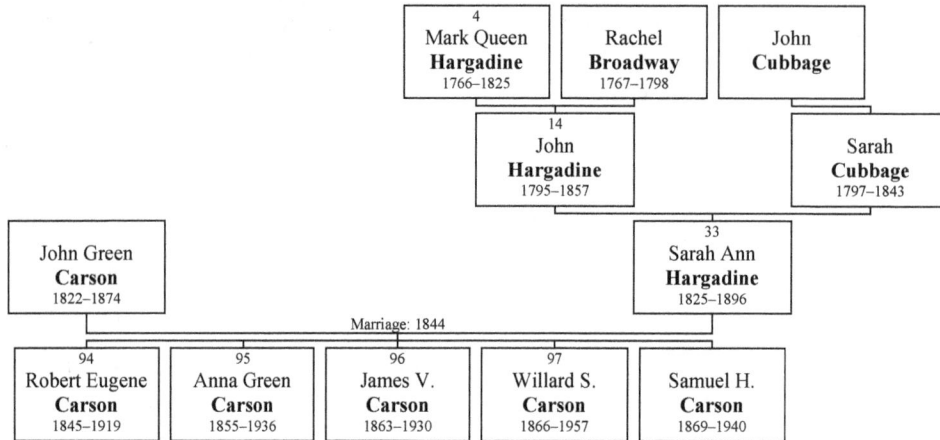

33.   **Sarah Ann Hargadine** was born on Friday, June 17, 1825, in Kent County, Delaware. She was the daughter of John Hargadine (14) and Sarah Cubbage. She was also known as **Sallie**.

Sarah Ann died in Kent County, Delaware, on November 16, 1896, at the age of 71. She was buried in Lakeside Cemetery, Dover, Kent County, Delaware (Find a Grave ID 7588812).

At the age of 18, Sarah Ann married **John Green Carson** on Thursday, April 25, 1844, in Kent County, Delaware, when he was 22 years old. They had five children.

John Green was born in Delaware, USA, on Saturday, February 23, 1822. He reached 52 years of age and died on September 29, 1874. John Green was buried in Lakeside Cemetery, Dover, Kent County, Delaware (Find a Grave ID 7588811).

Children of Sarah Ann Hargadine and John Green Carson:

+ 94   m   I. **Robert Eugene Carson** was born in Dover, Kent County, Delaware, on February 05, 1845. He died in Dover, Kent County, Delaware, on April 22, 1919, at the age of 74. Robert Eugene was buried in Lakeside Cemetery, Dover, Kent County, Delaware (Find a Grave ID 7588806).

+ 95   f   II. **Anna Green Carson** was born in Dover, Kent County, Delaware, on May 25, 1855. She died in Harrington, Kent County, Delaware, on December 10, 1936, at the age of 81. Anna Green was buried in Greensboro Cemetery, Greensboro, Caroline County, Maryland (Find a Grave ID 45482606).

+ 96   m   III. **James V. Carson** was born in Delaware, USA, on April 17, 1863. He died in Kent County, Delaware, on March 29, 1930, at the age of 66. James V. was buried in Lakeside Cemetery, Dover, Kent County, Delaware (Find a Grave ID 7588798).

+ 97   m   IV. **Willard S. Carson** was born on April 22, 1866. He died on February 07, 1957, at the age of 90. Willard S. was buried in Lakeside Cemetery, Dover, Kent County, Delaware (Find a Grave ID 7588810).

     m   V. **Samuel H. Carson** was born in near Dover, Kent County, Delaware, on November 21, 1869. He died on November 16, 1940, at the age of 70. Samuel H. was buried in Lakeside Cemetery, Dover, Kent County, Delaware (Find a Grave ID 7588809).

Family of John Hargadine and Elizabeth Craig

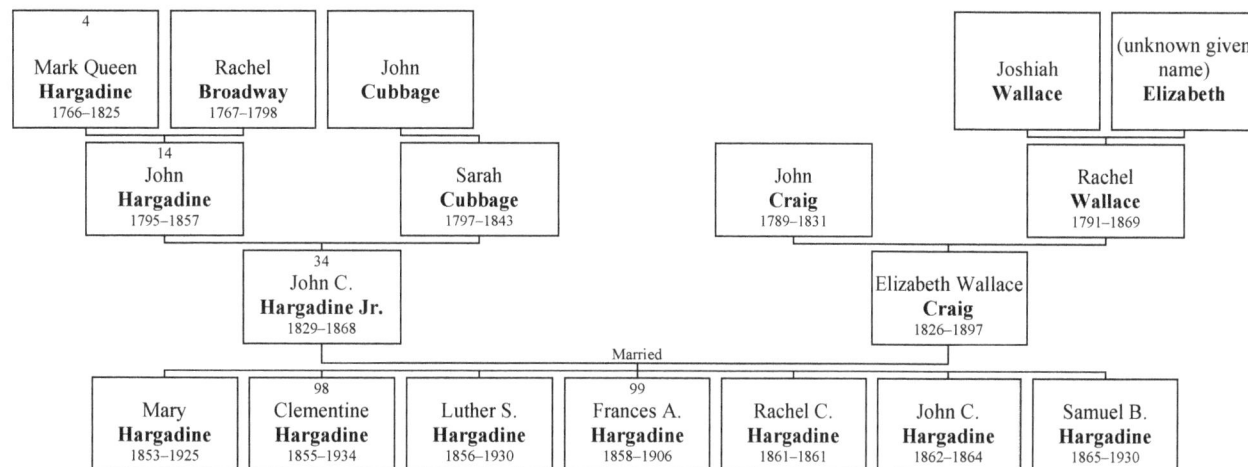

4 Mark Queen **Hargadine** 1766–1825	Rachel **Broadway** 1767–1798	John **Cubbage**			Joshiah **Wallace**	(unknown given name) **Elizabeth**
14 John **Hargadine** 1795–1857		Sarah **Cubbage** 1797–1843	John **Craig** 1789–1831		Rachel **Wallace** 1791–1869	
34 John C. **Hargadine Jr.** 1829–1868			Elizabeth Wallace **Craig** 1826–1897			
Married						

Mary **Hargadine** 1853–1925	98 Clementine **Hargadine** 1855–1934	Luther S. **Hargadine** 1856–1930	99 Frances A. **Hargadine** 1858–1906	Rachel C. **Hargadine** 1861–1861	John C. **Hargadine** 1862–1864	Samuel B. **Hargadine** 1865–1930

34.   **John C. Hargadine Jr.** was born on Monday, November 02, 1829, in Kent County, Delaware. He was the son of John Hargadine (14) and Sarah Cubbage.

John C. died in Kent County, Delaware, on March 09, 1868, at the age of 38. He was buried in Hargadine Family Cemetery; Dover, Kent County, Delaware (Find a Grave ID 13265800).

He married **Elizabeth Wallace Craig**. They had seven children.

Elizabeth Wallace was born in Kent County, Delaware, on Saturday, December 30, 1826. She was the daughter of John Craig and Rachel Wallace. She was also known as **Eliza Wallace Craig**.

Elizabeth Wallace reached 70 years of age and died in Kent County, Delaware, on April 26, 1897. She was buried in Hargadine Family Cemetery; Dover, Kent County, Delaware (Find a Grave ID 13265778).

Children of John C. Hargadine Jr. and Elizabeth Wallace Craig:

     f   I. **Mary Hargadine** was born on December 14, 1853. She died in Kent County, Delaware, on February 15, 1925, at the age of 71. Mary was buried in Hargadine Family Cemetery; Dover, Kent County, Delaware, on February 18, 1925 (Find a Grave ID 13265837).

+ 98   f   II. **Clementine Hargadine** was born on June 15, 1855. She died on April 03, 1934, at the age of 78. Clementine was buried in Hargadine Family Cemetery; Dover, Kent County, Delaware (Find a Grave ID 13265875).

m III. **Luther S. Hargadine** was born on September 02, 1856. He died in Kent County, Delaware, on June 30, 1930, at the age of 73. Luther S. was buried in Hargadine Family Cemetery; Dover, Kent County, Delaware, on July 03, 1930 (Find a Grave ID 13265820).

+ 99 f IV. **Frances A. Hargadine** was born on August 25, 1858. She died in Kent County, Delaware, on February 28, 1906, at the age of 47. Frances A. was buried in Hargadine Family Cemetery; Dover, Kent County, Delaware (Find a Grave ID 13265767).

f V. **Rachel C. Hargadine** was born on March 15, 1861. She died on April 22, 1861. Rachel C. was buried in Hargadine Family Cemetery; Dover, Kent County, Delaware (Find a Grave ID 13265852).

m VI. **John C. Hargadine** was born in June 1862. He died on April 05, 1864, at the age of 1. John C. was buried in Hargadine Family Cemetery; Dover, Kent County, Delaware (Find a Grave ID 13265809).

m VII. **Samuel B. Hargadine** was born on June 30, 1865. He died on December 29, 1930, at the age of 65. Samuel B. was buried in Hargadine Family Cemetery; Dover, Kent County, Delaware, on January 02, 1931 (Find a Grave ID 13265860).

John Purnell

35. **John Sylvester Purnell** was born on Wednesday, September 27, 1837, in Delaware, USA. He was the son of Thomas Hargadine Purnell (15) and Mary Elizabeth Downs.

John Sylvester died in Delaware, USA, on October 20, 1884, at the age of 47.

Marriages with Margaret Carter and Marian Williams (Page 77) are known.

Family of John Purnell and Margaret Carter

Here are the details about **John Sylvester Purnell's** first marriage, with Margaret Carter. You can read more about John Sylvester on page 76.

John Sylvester Purnell married **Margaret Carter** on Friday, October 14, 1859, in Delaware, USA. Margaret was born in 1839.

She reached 22 years of age and died on October 15, 1861.

Family of John Purnell and Marian Williams

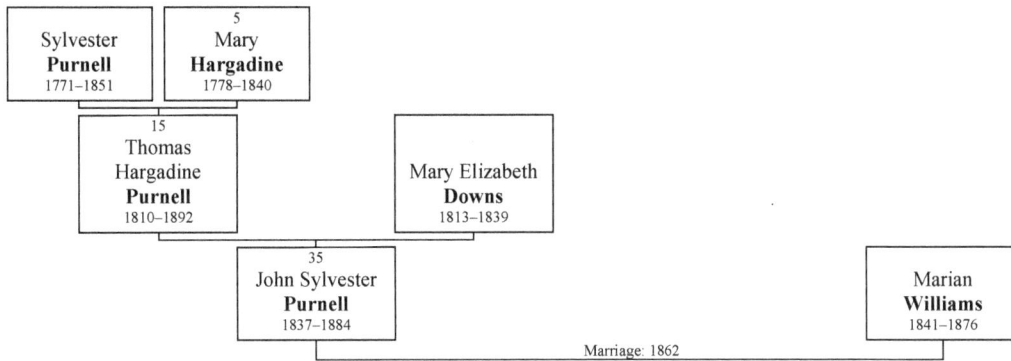

Here are the details about **John Sylvester Purnell's** second marriage, with Marian Williams. You can read more about John Sylvester on page 76.

At the age of 25, John Sylvester Purnell married **Marian Williams** on Wednesday, December 17, 1862, when she was 21 years old. Marian was born on Saturday, May 08, 1841.

She reached 35 years of age and died on December 28, 1876.

4th Generation

Family of Margaret Chambers and Edmon Wayman

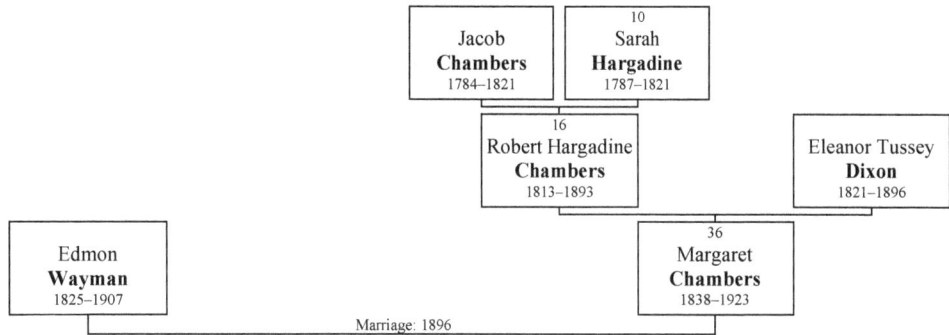

```
                              ┌──────────┐ ┌──────────┐
                              │  Jacob   │ │    10    │
                              │ Chambers │ │  Sarah   │
                              │1784–1821 │ │Hargadine │
                              │          │ │1787–1821 │
                              └──────────┘ └──────────┘
                              ┌──────────────┐      ┌──────────────┐
                              │      16      │      │Eleanor Tussey│
                              │Robert Hargadine│    │    Dixon     │
                              │  Chambers    │      │  1821–1896   │
                              │  1813–1893   │      └──────────────┘
                              └──────────────┘
┌──────────┐                        ┌──────────┐
│  Edmon   │                        │    36    │
│ Wayman   │                        │ Margaret │
│1825–1907 │                        │ Chambers │
│          │                        │1838–1923 │
└──────────┘                        └──────────┘
              Marriage: 1896
```

36. **Margaret Chambers** was born on Saturday, September 15, 1838, in Montgomery County, Indiana.[48] She was the daughter of Robert Hargadine Chambers (16) and Eleanor Tussey Dixon.

Margaret died in Attica, Marion County, Iowa, on March 31, 1923, at the age of 84.[48] Her cause of death was Burned to death. Margaret was buried in Olive Chapel Cemetery, Attica, Marion County, Iowa (Find a Grave ID 51963791).

At the age of 57, Margaret married **Edmon Wayman** on Thursday, September 10, 1896, in Marion County, Iowa, when he was 71 years old.[49] Edmon was born in Tennessee, USA, on Tuesday, August 02, 1825.[50]

He reached 82 years of age and died in Attica, Marion County, Iowa, on August 10, 1907. Edmon was buried in Olive Chapel Cemetery, Attica, Marion County, Iowa (Find a Grave ID 51963924).

Family of Martha Chambers and James Carson

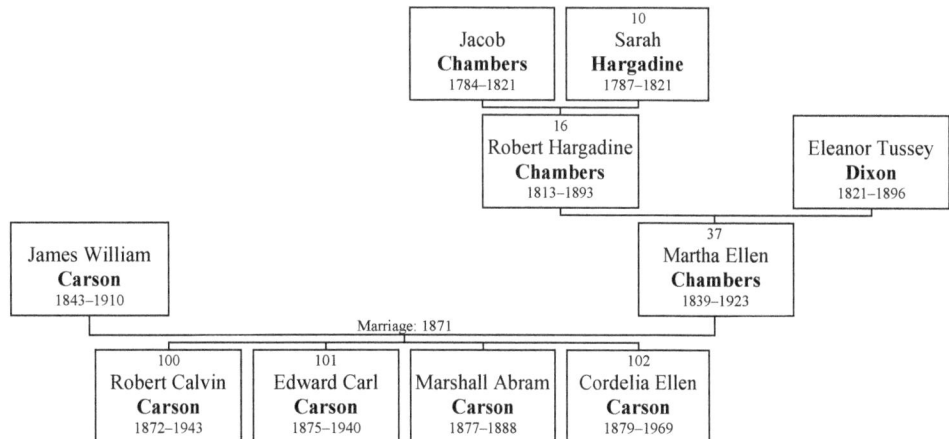

```
                              ┌──────────┐ ┌──────────┐
                              │  Jacob   │ │    10    │
                              │ Chambers │ │  Sarah   │
                              │1784–1821 │ │Hargadine │
                              │          │ │1787–1821 │
                              └──────────┘ └──────────┘
                              ┌──────────────┐      ┌──────────────┐
                              │      16      │      │Eleanor Tussey│
                              │Robert Hargadine│    │    Dixon     │
                              │  Chambers    │      │  1821–1896   │
                              │  1813–1893   │      └──────────────┘
                              └──────────────┘
┌──────────────┐                    ┌──────────────┐
│James William │                    │      37      │
│   Carson     │                    │ Martha Ellen │
│  1843–1910   │                    │  Chambers    │
│              │                    │  1839–1923   │
└──────────────┘                    └──────────────┘
              Marriage: 1871
┌──────────┐ ┌──────────┐ ┌──────────────┐ ┌──────────────┐
│   100    │ │   101    │ │              │ │     102      │
│ Robert   │ │  Edward  │ │Marshall Abram│ │Cordelia Ellen│
│ Calvin   │ │   Carl   │ │   Carson     │ │   Carson     │
│ Carson   │ │  Carson  │ │  1877–1888   │ │  1879–1969   │
│1872–1943 │ │1875–1940 │ └──────────────┘ └──────────────┘
└──────────┘ └──────────┘
```

---

48   Newspaper Obituary and Lawrence N. Chambers.

49   Marion County Iowa Marriage Records.

50   Tombstone.

37. **Martha Ellen Chambers** was born on Monday, November 11, 1839, in Montgomery County, Indiana.[51] She was the daughter of Robert Hargadine Chambers (16) and Eleanor Tussey Dixon.

Martha Ellen died at Harken Hospital in Osceola, Clarke County, Iowa, on July 08, 1923, at the age of 83.[52] She was buried in Ottawa Cemetery, Ottawa, Clarke County, Iowa (Find a Grave ID 63567498).

At the age of 31, Martha Ellen married **James William Carson** on Thursday, September 28, 1871, in Marion County, Iowa, when he was 28 years old.[53] They had four children.

James William was born in Fayette County, Pennsylvania, on Monday, July 10, 1843.[54] He reached 66 years of age and died in Ottawa, Clarke County, Iowa, on May 10, 1910.[55] James William was buried in Ottawa Cemetery, Ottawa, Clarke County, Iowa (Find a Grave ID 63567491).

Children of Martha Ellen Chambers and James William Carson:

+ 100 m I. **Robert Calvin Carson** was born in Clarke County, Iowa, on September 27, 1872.[56] He died in Creston, Union County, Iowa, on August 06, 1943, at the age of 70.[57] Robert Calvin was buried in Ottawa Cemetery, Ottawa, Clarke County, Iowa (Find a Grave ID 63567476).

+ 101 m II. **Edward Carl Carson** was born in Ottawa, Clarke County, Iowa, on December 23, 1875.[56] He died in Clarke County, Iowa, on January 03, 1940, at the age of 64. Edward Carl was buried in Woodburn Cemetery, Woodburn, Clarke County, Iowa (Find a Grave ID 63791573).

  m III. **Marshall Abram Carson** was born in Iowa, USA, in 1877.[58] He died in Clarke County, Iowa, in 1888 at the age of 11.[59]

+ 102 f IV. **Cordelia Ellen Carson** was born in Clarke County, Iowa, on February 28, 1879.[60] She was also known as **Nellie**.

  Cordelia Ellen died in 1969 at the age of 89. She was buried in Snow Hill Cemetery, Lincoln Township, Page County, Iowa.

---

51 Newspaper Obituary and Lawrence N. Chambers.

52 Newspaper Obituary.

53 Marion County Iowa Marriage Records.

54 Age listed as 67 years when he died on tombstone.

55 Tombstone in Ottawa Cemetery in Jackson Township.

56 Birth month and year given in 1900 Census.

57 Tombstone in Ottawa Cemetery.

58 Tombstone.

59 Mother's Newspaper Obituary.

60 Age given as 1 year in 1880 Iowa Soundex.

Family of Sarah Chambers and William Bruffey

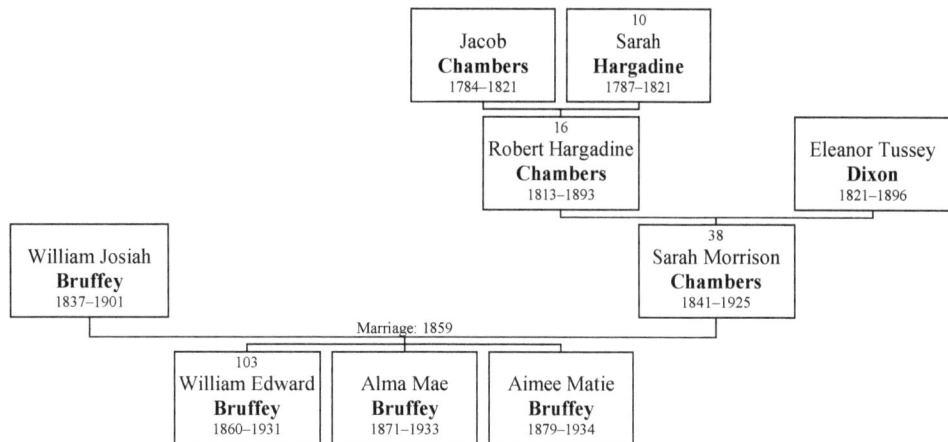

38.   **Sarah Morrison Chambers** was born on Thursday, February 18, 1841, in Montgomery County, Indiana.[61] She was the daughter of Robert Hargadine Chambers (16) and Eleanor Tussey Dixon.

Sarah Morrison died in Springfield, Greene County, Missouri, on November 01, 1925, at the age of 84.[61] She was buried in Hillcrest Cemetery, Mountain Grove, Wright County, Missouri (Find a Grave ID 33939755).

At the age of 18, Sarah Morrison married **William Josiah Bruffey** on Thursday, February 24, 1859, in Marion County, Iowa, when he was 21 years old.[62] They had three children.

William Josiah was born in Huntersville, Pocahontas County, West Virginia, on Sunday, April 02, 1837.[63] He was also known as **Joe**.

William Josiah reached 64 years of age and died in Mountain Grove, Wright County, Missouri, on April 28, 1901.[64] He was buried in Hillcrest Cemetery, Mountain Grove, Wright County, Missouri (Find a Grave ID 33939673).

Children of Sarah Morrison Chambers and William Josiah Bruffey:

+   103   m   I.   **William Edward Bruffey** was born in Attica, Marion County, Iowa, on October 01, 1860.[65] He died in Springdale, Washington County, Arkansas, on January 05, 1931, at the age of 70. William Edward was buried in Hillcrest Cemetery, Mountain Grove, Wright County, Missouri (Find a Grave ID 33939805).

           f   II.   **Alma Mae Bruffey** was born in Iowa, USA, on December 09, 1871.[66] She died on November 13, 1933, at the age of 61. Alma Mae was buried in

---

61   Newspaper Obituary and Lawrence N. Chambers.

62   Marion County, Iowa Marriage Records 1845-1915.

63   Birth month and year given in 1900 Census.

64   Present in 1900 Census; wife was head of household in 1920 Census.

65   Age given as 20 years in 1880 Iowa Soundex.

66   Age given as 9 years in 1880 Iowa Soundex.

Peninsula Memorial Park, Newport News, Newport News City, Virginia (Find a Grave ID 93076770).

f III. **Aimee Matie Bruffey** was born in Iowa, USA, on April 24, 1879.[63] She died in Springfield, Greene County, Missouri, on August 13, 1934, at the age of 55. Aimee Matie was buried in Hillcrest Cemetery, Mountain Grove, Wright County, Missouri (Find a Grave ID 33939790).

Family of Susan Chambers and Jamison Clark

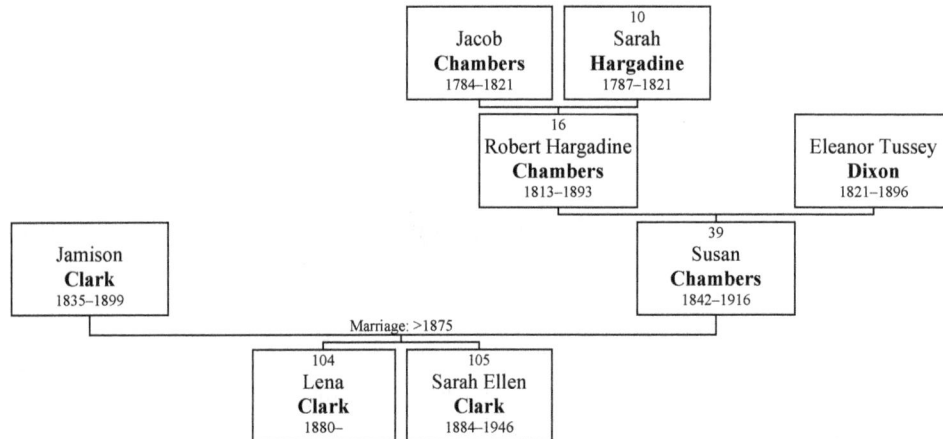

39. **Susan Chambers** was born on Tuesday, July 19, 1842, in Montgomery County, Indiana.[67] She was the daughter of Robert Hargadine Chambers (16) and Eleanor Tussey Dixon.

Susan died in Murray, Clarke County, Iowa, on April 14, 1916, at the age of 73.[68]

Susan married **Jamison Clark** after 1875. They had two daughters.

Jamison was born in Virginia, USA, on Wednesday, June 17, 1835.[69] He reached 64 years of age and died on November 22, 1899.[68]

Daughters of Susan Chambers and Jamison Clark:

+ 104 f I. **Lena Clark** was born in Iowa, USA, in July 1880.[70]

+ 105 f II. **Sarah Ellen Clark** was born in Murray, Clarke County, Iowa, on June 19, 1884.[70, 71] She died in Santa Cruz County, California, on May 10, 1946, at the age of 61.[71] Sarah Ellen was buried in Golden Gate National Cemetery, San Bruno, San Mateo County, California (Find a Grave ID 3553344).[71]

---

67   Newspaper Obituary and Lawrence N. Chambers.

68   Tombstone in Murray Cemetery.

69   Age at death written on tombstone as 64 years 5 months and 5 days.

70   Birth month and year given in 1900 Census.

71   Ancestry.com, Public Member Trees (Provo, UT, USA, Ancestry.com Operations, Inc., 2006), Ancestry.com, Record for Sarah Ellen Clark. https://search.ancestry.co.uk/cgi-bin/sse.dll?db=1030&h=162182227685&indiv=try.

Family of Mary Chambers and Isiah Ball

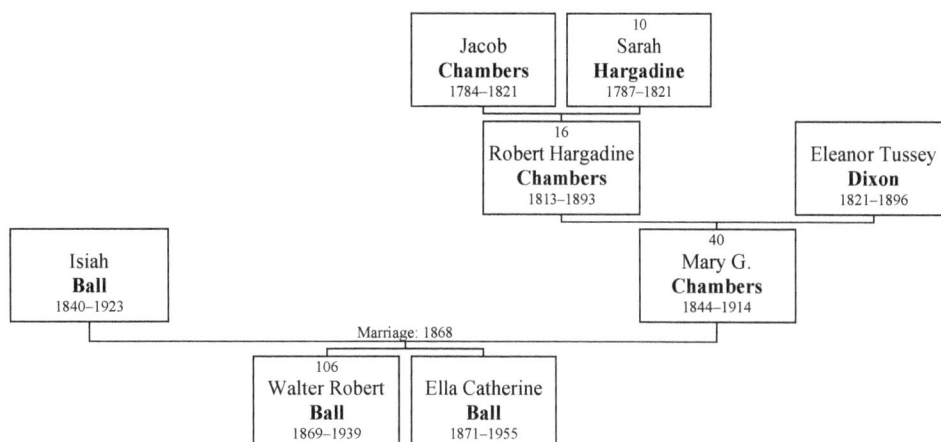

```
                              ┌─────────────┬────10────────┐
                              │   Jacob     │    Sarah     │
                              │  Chambers   │  Hargadine   │
                              │  1784–1821  │  1787–1821   │
                              └──────┬──────┴──────────────┘
                       ┌────16──────────────┐        ┌──────────────┐
                       │ Robert Hargadine   │        │Eleanor Tussey│
                       │    Chambers        │        │    Dixon     │
                       │    1813–1893       │        │  1821–1896   │
                       └──────────┬─────────┘        └──────┬───────┘
                                  └──────────40──────────────┘
   ┌──────────────┐                      │   Mary G.    │
   │    Isiah     │                      │  Chambers    │
   │     Ball     │                      │  1844–1914   │
   │  1840–1923   │                      └──────────────┘
   └──────┬───────┘     Marriage: 1868
          └──────────────────┬──────────────────┘
                    ┌───106───────┬──────────────┐
                    │Walter Robert│Ella Catherine│
                    │    Ball     │    Ball       │
                    │  1869–1939  │  1871–1955    │
                    └─────────────┴──────────────┘
```

40.   **Mary G. Chambers** was born on Wednesday, July 31, 1844, in Montgomery County, Indiana.[72] She was the daughter of Robert Hargadine Chambers (16) and Eleanor Tussey Dixon.

Mary G. died in Knoxville, Marion County, Iowa, on January 07, 1914, at the age of 69.[73] She was buried in Graceland Cemetery, Knoxville, Marion County, Iowa (Find a Grave ID 180264777).

At the age of 24, Mary G. married **Isiah Ball** on Monday, September 07, 1868, in Montgomery County, Indiana, when he was 27 years old.[74] They had two children.

Isiah was born on Tuesday, November 17, 1840.[75] He reached 82 years of age and died in Knoxville, Marion County, Iowa, on February 11, 1923.[75] Isiah was buried in Graceland Cemetery, Knoxville, Marion County, Iowa (Find a Grave ID 48175560).

Children of Mary G. Chambers and Isiah Ball:

+ 106   m   I. **Walter Robert Ball** was born in Wayne County, Indiana, on June 16, 1869.[75] He died in Des Moines, Polk County, Iowa, on April 19, 1939, at the age of 69.[75] Walter Robert was buried in Graceland Cemetery, Knoxville, Marion County, Iowa (Find a Grave ID 135716729).

           f   II. **Ella Catherine Ball** was born in 1871.[75] She died in Oregon City, Clackamas County, Oregon, on March 28, 1955, at the age of 84.[75] Ella Catherine was buried in Graceland Cemetery, Knoxville, Marion County, Iowa (Find a Grave ID 135716638).

---

72   Newspaper Obituary and Lawrence N. Chambers and Tombstone.

73   Newspaper Obituary and Lawrence N. Chambers.

74   Montgomery County, Indiana Marriage Records.

75   Tombstone in Graceland Cemetery.

Family of Lydia Chambers and John Ghrist

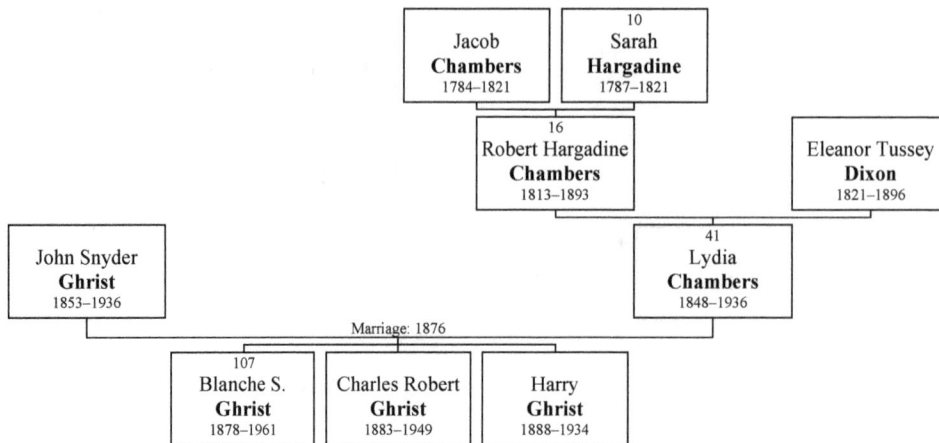

41.   **Lydia Chambers** was born on Sunday, November 19, 1848, in Montgomery County, Indiana.[76] She was the daughter of Robert Hargadine Chambers (16) and Eleanor Tussey Dixon.

Lydia died in Colfax, Jasper County, Iowa, on July 01, 1936, at the age of 87.[76]

At the age of 27, Lydia married **John Snyder Ghrist** on Thursday, April 06, 1876, in Marion, Linn County, Iowa, when he was 23 years old. They had three children.

John Snyder was born in Pennsylvania, USA, on Thursday, January 20, 1853.[77] He reached 83 years of age and died in Colfax, Jasper County, Iowa, on March 08, 1936. John Snyder was buried on March 10, 1936, in Colfax Cemetery, Colfax, Jasper County, Iowa (Find a Grave ID 20431658).

Children of Lydia Chambers and John Snyder Ghrist:

+   107   f   I. **Blanche S. Ghrist** was born in Marion, Linn County, Iowa, on May 19, 1878.[78, 79] She died in Los Angeles, California, on April 05, 1961, at the age of 82.[78] Blanche S. was buried in Oakview Cemetery, Albia, Monroe County, Iowa (Find a Grave ID 23193005).

        m   II. **Charles Robert Ghrist** was born in Marion, Linn County, Iowa, on April 04, 1883.[80] He died at Bell Nursing Home in Chariton, Lucas County, Iowa, on October 01, 1949, at the age of 66. Charles Robert was buried in Colfax Cemetery, Colfax, Jasper County, Iowa, on October 04, 1949.

        m   III. **Harry Ghrist** was born in Iowa, USA, on September 21, 1888.[80] He served in the military: WWII Veteran; Disabled.
            Harry died on May 27, 1934, at the age of 45. He was buried in Colfax Cemetery, Colfax, Jasper County, Iowa (Find a Grave ID 20431627).

---

76   Newspaper Obituary and Lawrence N. Chambers.

77   1900 Iowa Soundex.

78   Ancestry.com, Public Member Trees (Provo, UT, USA, Ancestry.com Operations, Inc., 2006), Ancestry.com, Record for Blanche S. Ghrist. https://search.ancestry.co.uk/cgi-bin/sse.dll?db=1030&h=42262304840&indiv=try.

79   Age given as 2 years in 1880 Iowa Census.

80   Birth month and year given in 1900 Iowa Census.

Family of James Chambers and Mary Rankin

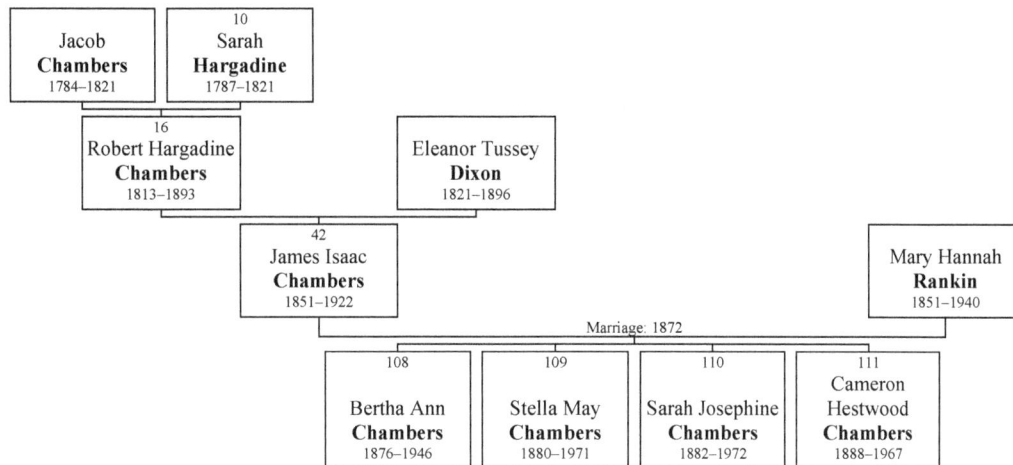

42. **James Isaac Chambers** was born on Tuesday, June 24, 1851, in Montgomery County, Indiana.[81] He was the son of Robert Hargadine Chambers (16) and Eleanor Tussey Dixon.

    James Isaac died in Knoxville, Marion County, Iowa, on October 22, 1922, at the age of 71.[81] He was buried in Zion Cemetery, Pershing, Marion County, Iowa (Find a Grave ID 16350132).

    At the age of 21, James Isaac married **Mary Hannah Rankin** on Wednesday, December 25, 1872, in Marion County, Iowa, when she was 21 years old.[82] They had four children.

    Mary Hannah was born in Marion County, Iowa, on Friday, May 09, 1851.[83] She reached 88 years of age and died in Knoxville, Marion County, Iowa, on February 29, 1940.[83] Mary Hannah was buried in Zion Cemetery, Pershing, Marion County, Iowa (Find a Grave ID 16350160).

Children of James Isaac Chambers and Mary Hannah Rankin:

+ 108   f   I. **Bertha Ann Chambers** was born in Farm southeast of Knoxville, Marion County, Iowa, on February 07, 1876.[84] She died in Knoxville, Marion County, Iowa, on August 13, 1946, at the age of 70.[84] Bertha Ann was buried in Zion Cemetery, Pershing, Marion County, Iowa (Find a Grave ID 66718662).

+ 109   f   II. **Stella May Chambers** was born in Attica, Marion County, Iowa, on June 28, 1880.[85] She died in Knoxville, Marion County, Iowa, on June 23, 1971, at the age of 90.[85] Stella May was buried in Zion Cemetery, Pershing, Marion County, Iowa (Find a Grave ID 66774914).

---

81   Newspaper Obituary and Lawrence N. Chambers.

82   History of Marion County (Volume II pages 80-81) by John W. Wright.

83   Tombstone in Zion Chapel Cemetery.

84   Newspaper Clipping.

85   Tombstone.

+ 110 f III. **Sarah Josephine Chambers** was born in Indiana Township, Marion County, Iowa, on November 18, 1882.[86] She was also known as **Josie**.

Sarah Josephine died in Albia, Monroe County, Iowa, on October 27, 1972, at the age of 89. She was buried in Oakview Cemetery, Albia, Monroe County, Iowa (Find a Grave ID 16350096).

+ 111 m IV. **Cameron Hestwood Chambers** was born in Marion County, Iowa, on October 16, 1888.[87] He died in Knoxville, Marion County, Iowa, on September 12, 1967, at the age of 78.[87] Cameron Hestwood was buried in Breckenridge Cemetery, Harvey, Marion County, Iowa (Find a Grave ID 16456705).

William Chambers

43. **William Philander Chambers** was born on Friday, May 20, 1853, in Montgomery County, Indiana.[88] He was the son of Robert Hargadine Chambers (16) and Eleanor Tussey Dixon.

William Philander died in Knoxville, Marion County, Iowa, on September 14, 1914, at the age of 61.[88] He was buried in Graceland Cemetery, Knoxville, Marion County, Iowa (Find a Grave ID 15554223).

Marriages with Hannah Ellen Nelson and Minnie Robuck (Page 88) are known.

Family of William Chambers and Hannah Nelson

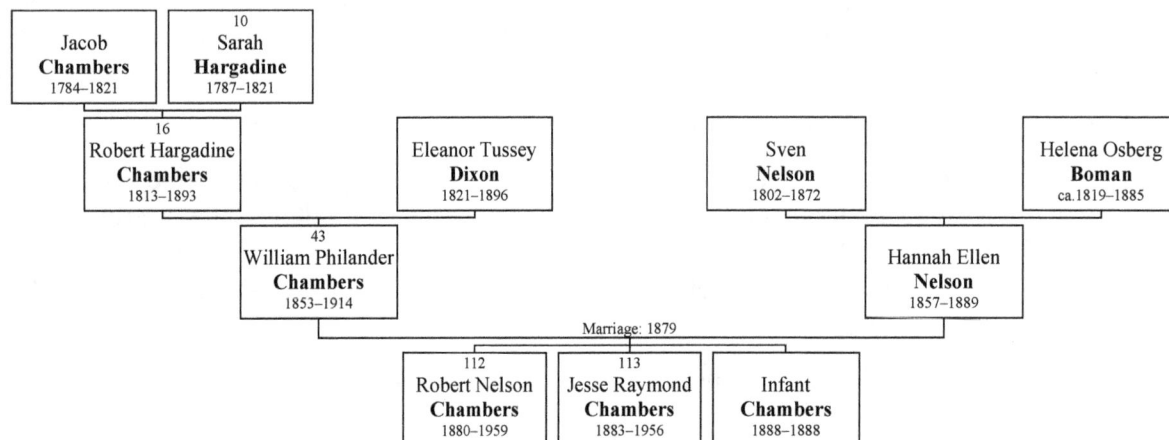

Here are the details about **William Philander Chambers's** first marriage, with Hannah Ellen Nelson. You can read more about William Philander on page 86.

---

86 Marion County, Iowa Birth Records.

87 Tombstone in Breckenridge Cemetery.

88 Lawrence N. Chambers and Ruth Hawks Wright.

At the age of 26, William Philander Chambers married **Hannah Ellen Nelson** on Friday, September 12, 1879, in Marion County, Iowa, when she was 22 years old.[89] They had three sons.

Hannah Ellen was born in Henry County, Illinois, on Tuesday, January 13, 1857.[90] She was the daughter of Sven Nelson and Helena Osberg Boman.

Hannah Ellen reached 32 years of age and died in Clarke County, Iowa, on May 21, 1889. She was buried in Ottawa Cemetery, Ottawa, Clarke County, Iowa (Find a Grave ID 155265089).

Sons of William Philander Chambers and Hannah Ellen Nelson:

+ 112   m   I. **Robert Nelson Chambers** was born in Columbia, Marion County, Iowa, on August 18, 1880.[88] He died in Davenport, Scott County, Iowa, on December 12, 1959, at the age of 79.[91] Robert Nelson was buried in Graceland Cemetery, Knoxville, Marion County, Iowa (Find a Grave ID 135668230).

+ 113   m   II. **Jesse Raymond Chambers** was born in Columbia, Marion County, Iowa, on March 31, 1883.[88] He died in Loveland, Larimer County, Colorado, on September 14, 1956, at the age of 73.[88] Jesse Raymond was buried in Loveland Burial Park, Loveland, Larimer County, Colorado (Find a Grave ID 150047205).

       m   III. **Infant Chambers** was born in 1888.[92] He died in 1888.[92]

Family of William Chambers and Minnie Robuck

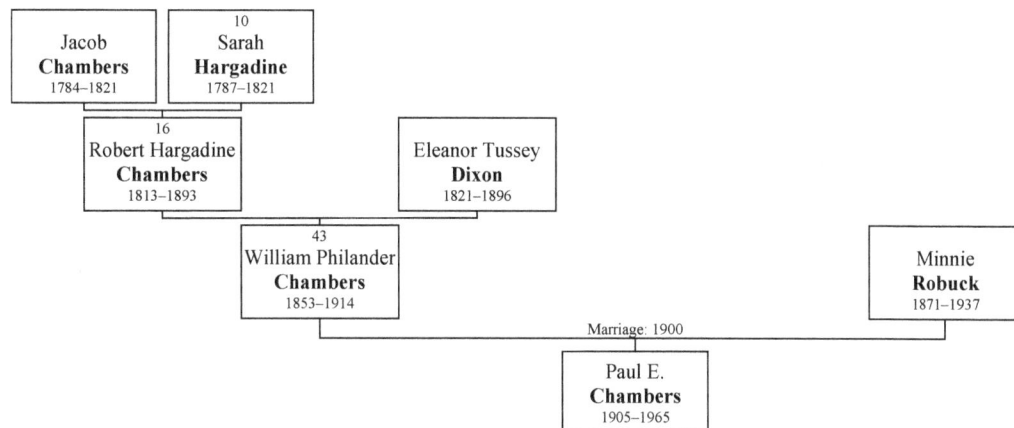

Here are the details about **William Philander Chambers's** second marriage, with Minnie Robuck. You can read more about William Philander on page 86.

---

89   Copy of Marriage License.

90   Lawrence Chambers from his father Robert Nelson Chambers.

91   Lawrence Nelson Chambers.

92   Lawrence Chambers notes from interview with his father.

At the age of 46, William Philander Chambers married **Minnie Robuck** on Saturday, March 03, 1900, in Marion County, Iowa, when she was 28 years old.[93] They had one son.

Minnie was born in Attica, Marion County, Iowa, on Monday, November 06, 1871.[94] She reached 65 years of age and died in Marion County, Iowa, on September 04, 1937.[95] Minnie was buried in Graceland Cemetery, Knoxville, Marion County, Iowa (Find a Grave ID 15554227).

Son of William Philander Chambers and Minnie Robuck:

m   I. **Paul E. Chambers** was born in Marion County, Iowa, on April 24, 1905.[96] He died in Flats, McPherson County, Nebraska, on April 23, 1965, at the age of 59.[97]

Family of Emily Chambers and Henry Peterson

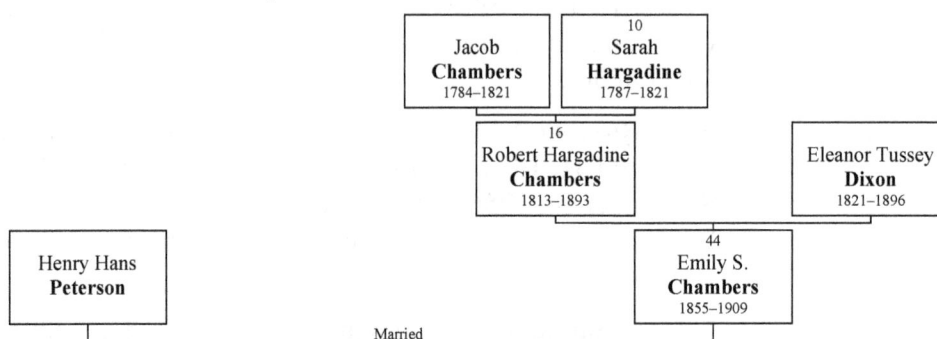

44.   **Emily S. Chambers** was born on Monday, May 14, 1855, in Montgomery County, Indiana.[98] She was the daughter of Robert Hargadine Chambers (16) and Eleanor Tussey Dixon.

Emily S. died in Oregon, USA, on February 17, 1909, at the age of 53.[98]

She married **Mr. Henry Hans Peterson**.

---

93   Marion County, Iowa Marriage Records 1900 - 1915.

94   Birth month and year given in 1900 Census.

95   Tombstone in Graceland Cemetery.

96   Obituary.

97   Funeral Notice.

98   Newspaper Obituary and Lawrence N. Chambers.

Family of Robert Chambers and Cora Zink

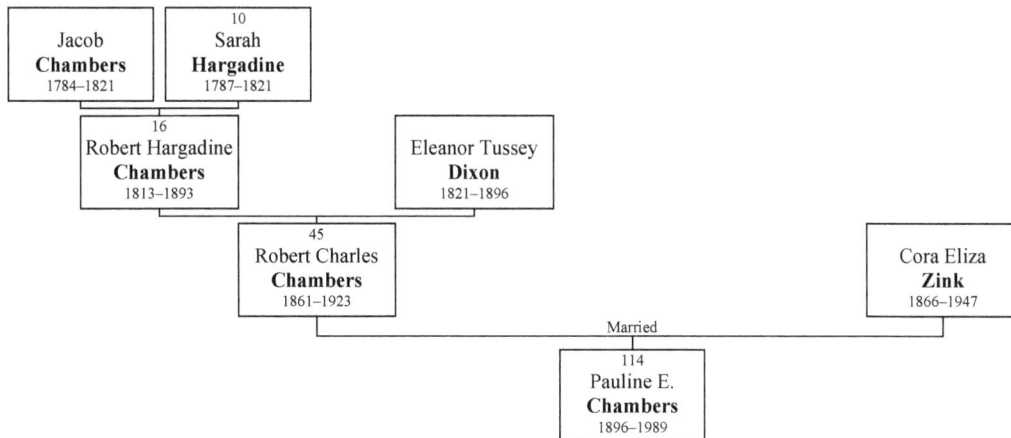

45. **Robert Charles Chambers** was born on Friday, August 23, 1861, in Attica, Marion County, Iowa.[99] He was the son of Robert Hargadine Chambers (16) and Eleanor Tussey Dixon.

Robert Charles died in Grand Junction, Greene County, Iowa, on November 06, 1923, at the age of 62.[99] He was buried in Junction Township Cemetery, Grand Junction, Greene County, Iowa (Find a Grave ID 40455269).

He married **Cora Eliza Zink**. They had one daughter.

Cora Eliza was born in Newton, Jasper County, Iowa, on Saturday, September 08, 1866.[100, 101] She reached 80 years of age and died in Grand Junction, Greene County, Iowa, on January 03, 1947.[100] Cora Eliza was buried in Junction Township Cemetery, Grand Junction, Greene County, Iowa (Find a Grave ID 40455264).[100]

Daughter of Robert Charles Chambers and Cora Eliza Zink:

+ 114 f I. **Pauline E. Chambers** was born in Osceola, Clarke County, Iowa, on March 29, 1896.[101] She died in 1989 at the age of 92. Pauline E. was buried in Junction Township Cemetery, Grand Junction, Greene County, Iowa (Find a Grave ID 40455492).

---

99 Newspaper Obituary and Lawrence N. Chambers.

100 Ancestry.com, Public Member Trees (Provo, UT, USA, Ancestry.com Operations, Inc., 2006), Ancestry.com, Record for Cora Eliza Zink. https://search.ancestry.co.uk/cgi-bin/sse.dll?db=1030&h=292268163481&indiv=try.

101 Birth month and year given in 1900 Census.

Family of Amos Chambers and Annette Eastlack

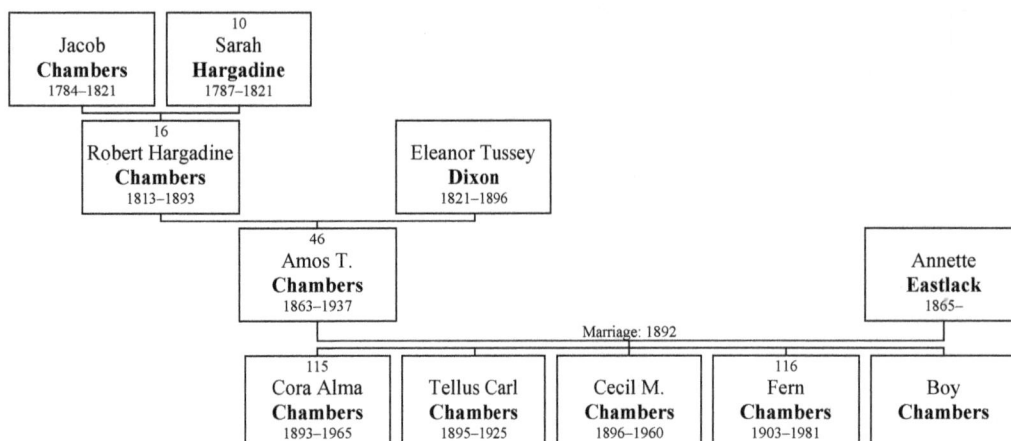

46.   **Amos T. Chambers** was born on Thursday, September 24, 1863, in Marion County, Iowa.[102] He was the son of Robert Hargadine Chambers (16) and Eleanor Tussey Dixon.

Amos T. died in California, USA, in 1937 at the age of 73.[102] He was buried in Bellevue Memorial Park, Ontario, San Bernardino County, California (Find a Grave ID 149799175).

Amos T. married **Annette Eastlack** on Thursday, January 21, 1892, in Monroe County, Iowa. They had five children.

Annette was born in Indiana, USA, in July 1865.[103]

Children of Amos T. Chambers and Annette Eastlack:

+   115   f   I. **Cora Alma Chambers** was born in Murray, Clarke County, Iowa, on March 08, 1893.[103] She died in Phoenix, Maricopa County, Arizona, on September 04, 1965, at the age of 72. Her cause of death was acute coronary thrombosis with myocardial infarction, arteriosclerosis. She was cremated on September 08, 1965 (Find a Grave ID 228140275).

        m   II. **Tellus Carl Chambers** was born in Iowa, USA, on May 05, 1895.[103] He was also known as **Tully**.

                Tellus Carl died on December 20, 1925, at the age of 30. He was buried in Bellevue Memorial Park, Ontario, San Bernardino County, California (Find a Grave ID 20879236).

        m   III. **Cecil M. Chambers** was born in Iowa, USA, in September 1896.[103] He died in 1960 at the age of 63. Cecil M. was buried in Bellevue Memorial Park, Ontario, San Bernardino County, California (Find a Grave ID 133571195).

+   116   f   IV. **Fern Chambers** was born in 1903. She died in 1981 at the age of 78. Fern was buried in Bellevue Memorial Park, Ontario, San Bernardino County, California (Find a Grave ID 151101256).

        m   V. **Boy Chambers**.

---

102   Newspaper Obituary and Lawrence N. Chambers.

103   From the 1900 Census Information.

Family of Elisabeth Chambers and Ely Ellrod

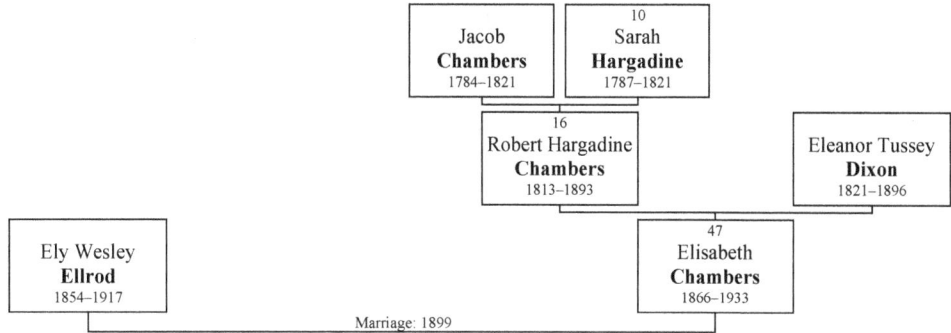

```
                          ┌─────────────┬──────────────10──┐
                          │   Jacob     │     Sarah        │
                          │  Chambers   │   Hargadine      │
                          │  1784–1821  │   1787–1821      │
                          └──────┬──────┴──────────────────┘
                          ┌──────────────16───┐          ┌──────────────┐
                          │ Robert Hargadine  │          │ Eleanor Tussey│
                          │    Chambers       │          │    Dixon      │
                          │   1813–1893       │          │  1821–1896    │
                          └─────────┬─────────┘          └───────┬───────┘
                                    └──────────┬──────────────47─┘
  ┌─────────────┐                        │   Elisabeth    │
  │ Ely Wesley  │                        │   Chambers     │
  │   Ellrod    │                        │   1866–1933    │
  │  1854–1917  │                        └────────────────┘
  └──────┬──────┘
         └────────────── Marriage: 1899 ──────────────┘
```

47. **Elisabeth Chambers** was born on Wednesday, February 21, 1866, in Marion County, Iowa.[104] She was the daughter of Robert Hargadine Chambers (16) and Eleanor Tussey Dixon. She was also known as **Lizzie**.

Elisabeth died in Portland, Multnomah County, Oregon, on January 16, 1933, at the age of 66.[104] She was buried in River View Cemetery, Portland, Multnomah County, Oregon (Find a Grave ID 136096395).

Elisabeth married **Mr. Ely Wesley Ellrod** on Tuesday, January 24, 1899, in Clarke, Iowa, USA. Ely Wesley was born in Iowa, USA, in 1854.

He reached 63 years of age and died in Portland, Multnomah County, Oregon, on April 04, 1917. Ely Wesley was buried in River View Cemetery, Portland, Multnomah County, Oregon (Find a Grave ID 136096403).

Family of George Hargadine and Hannah Carter

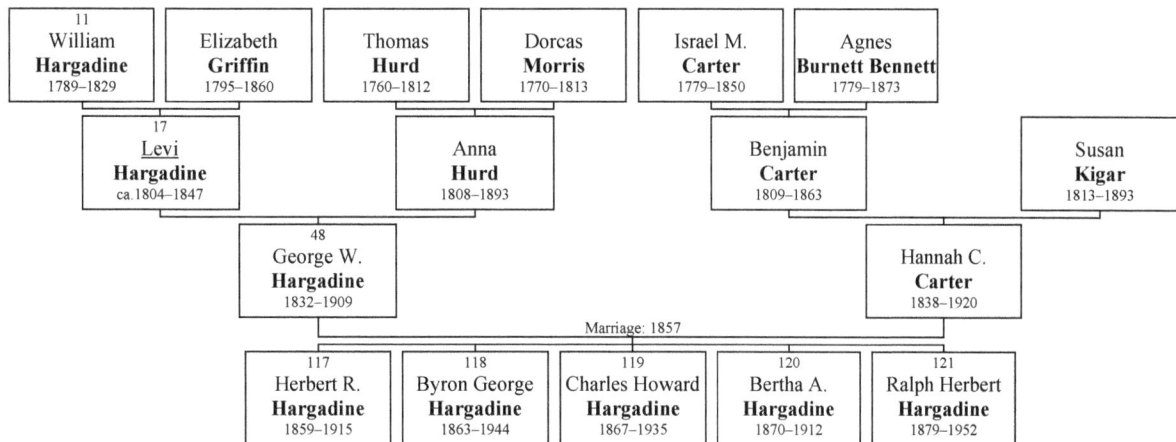

```
┌────────11──┬──────────┬──────────┬──────────┐ ┌──────────┬──────────┐
│  William   │Elizabeth │  Thomas  │  Dorcas  │ │ Israel M.│  Agnes   │
│ Hargadine  │ Griffin  │   Hurd   │  Morris  │ │  Carter  │Burnett Bennett│
│ 1789–1829  │1795–1860 │1760–1812 │1770–1813 │ │1779–1850 │1779–1873 │
└─────┬──────┴──────────┴────┬─────┴──────────┘ └────┬─────┴──────────┘
 ┌────────17──┐          ┌──────────┐          ┌──────────────┐     ┌──────────┐
 │   Levi     │          │   Anna   │          │  Benjamin    │     │  Susan   │
 │ Hargadine  │          │   Hurd   │          │   Carter     │     │  Kigar   │
 │ ca.1804–1847│         │1808–1893 │          │  1809–1863   │     │1813–1893 │
 └─────┬──────┘          └────┬─────┘          └──────┬───────┘     └────┬─────┘
       └─────────48──┐            └──────┬────────────┘   ┌──────────────┐
             │George W.   │              │     Hannah C.  │
             │ Hargadine  │              │       Carter   │
             │ 1832–1909  │              │     1838–1920  │
             └─────┬──────┘              └───────┬────────┘
                   └────── Marriage: 1857 ───────┘
   ┌──────117─┬──────118─┬──────119─┬──────120─┬──────121─┐
   │Herbert R.│Byron George│Charles Howard│Bertha A.│Ralph Herbert│
   │Hargadine │ Hargadine│ Hargadine│Hargadine │ Hargadine│
   │1859–1915 │1863–1944 │1867–1935 │1870–1912 │1879–1952 │
   └──────────┴──────────┴──────────┴──────────┴──────────┘
```

48. **George W. Hargadine** was born on Wednesday, November 07, 1832, in Moorefield, Clark County, Ohio.[105] He was the son of Levi Hargadine (17) and Anna Hurd.

---

[104] Newspaper Obituary and Lawrence N. Chambers.

[105] 1900 Census Douglas County, Nebraska Omaha City (Vol 14, ED 58, Sheet 2) June 2, 1900.

George W. died in Omaha, Douglas County, Nebraska, on August 14, 1909, at the age of 76. He was buried in Chillicothe City Cemetery, Chillicothe, Peoria County, Illinois.

George W. married **Hannah C. Carter** on Thursday, December 17, 1857, in Peoria County, Illinois. They had five children.

Hannah C. was born in Union County, Ohio, in June 1838.[105] She was the daughter of Benjamin Carter and Susan Kigar.

Hannah C. reached 81 years of age and died in Omaha, Douglas County, Nebraska, on January 03, 1920.

Children of George W. Hargadine and Hannah C. Carter:

+ 117 m I. **Herbert R. Hargadine** was born in Illinois, USA, on June 23, 1859. He died on April 12, 1915, at the age of 55. Herbert R. was buried in Ashland Cemetery, Saunders County, Nebraska (Find a Grave ID 41928399).

+ 118 m II. **Byron George Hargadine** was born in Lasalle County, Illinois, in September 1863.[105] He died in Omaha, Douglas County, Nebraska, on September 10, 1944, at the age of 81.

+ 119 m III. **Charles Howard Hargadine** was born in Illinois, USA, in October 1867. He died in Omaha, Douglas County, Nebraska, in April 1935 at the age of 67. Charles Howard was buried in Forest Lawn Memorial Park, Omaha, Douglas County, Nebraska, on April 10, 1935 (Find a Grave ID 136311888).

+ 120 f IV. **Bertha A. Hargadine** was born in Chillicothe, Peoria County, Illinois, on December 02, 1870. She died in Spooner, Washburn County, Wisconsin, on October 28, 1912, at the age of 41. Her cause of death was carcinoma of the liver and carcinoma of the lung. She was buried in Chillicothe, Peoria County, Illinois.

+ 121 m V. **Ralph Herbert Hargadine** was born in Groveland Twp., LaSalle County, Illinois, on September 06, 1879. He was also known as **Jackson R. Davis**.

Ralph Herbert died in Long Beach, Los Angeles County, California, on March 03, 1952, at the age of 72. He was buried in Forest Lawn Memorial Park, Long Beach, Los Angeles County, California (Find a Grave ID 200477703).

Family of Margaret Hargadine and William Clyne

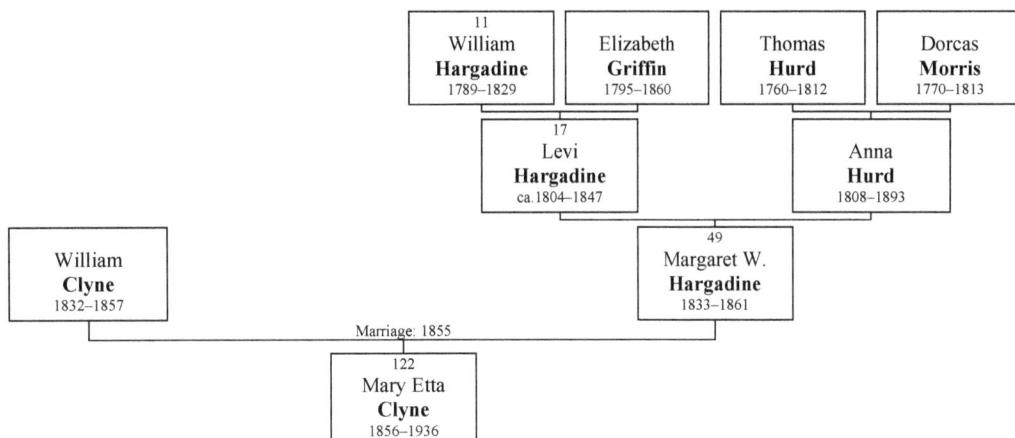

```
                                    ┌──────────┐  ┌──────────┐   ┌──────────┐  ┌──────────┐
                                    │    11    │  │          │   │          │  │          │
                                    │ William  │  │Elizabeth │   │  Thomas  │  │  Dorcas  │
                                    │Hargadine │  │ Griffin  │   │   Hurd   │  │  Morris  │
                                    │1789–1829 │  │1795–1860 │   │1760–1812 │  │1770–1813 │
                                    └──────────┘  └──────────┘   └──────────┘  └──────────┘
                                          ┌──────────┐              ┌──────────┐
                                          │    17    │              │          │
                                          │   Levi   │              │   Anna   │
                                          │Hargadine │              │   Hurd   │
                                          │ca.1804–1847│            │1808–1893 │
                                          └──────────┘              └──────────┘
  ┌──────────┐                                   ┌──────────┐
  │          │                                   │    49    │
  │ William  │                                   │Margaret W.│
  │  Clyne   │                                   │Hargadine │
  │1832–1857 │                                   │1833–1861 │
  └──────────┘          Marriage: 1855           └──────────┘
                        ┌──────────┐
                        │   122    │
                        │Mary Etta │
                        │  Clyne   │
                        │1856–1936 │
                        └──────────┘
```

49.   **Margaret W. Hargadine** was born in 1833 in Medina, Peoria County, Illinois. She was the daughter of Levi Hargadine (17) and Anna Hurd.

Margaret W. died on June 08, 1861, at the age of 28. She was buried in La Salle Cemetery, Rome, Peoria County, Illinois (Find a Grave ID 44542836).

At the age of 22, Margaret W. married **William Clyne** on Sunday, December 16, 1855, in Peoria County, Illinois, when he was 23 years old. They had one daughter.

William was born in Scotland on Sunday, April 22, 1832.

William reached 24 years of age and died on January 24, 1857. He was buried in La Salle Cemetery, Rome, Peoria County, Illinois (Find a Grave ID 139620289).

Daughter of Margaret W. Hargadine and William Clyne:

+   122   f   I. **Mary Etta Clyne** was born in Illinois, USA, on June 17, 1856. She died in Medina, Peoria County, Illinois, on February 10, 1936, at the age of 79. Her cause of death was carcinoma of the intestines, cirrhosis of liver. She was buried in La Salle Cemetery, Rome, Peoria County, Illinois, on February 13, 1936 (Find a Grave ID 23286807).

Family of Mary Hargadine and Charles Van Alstine

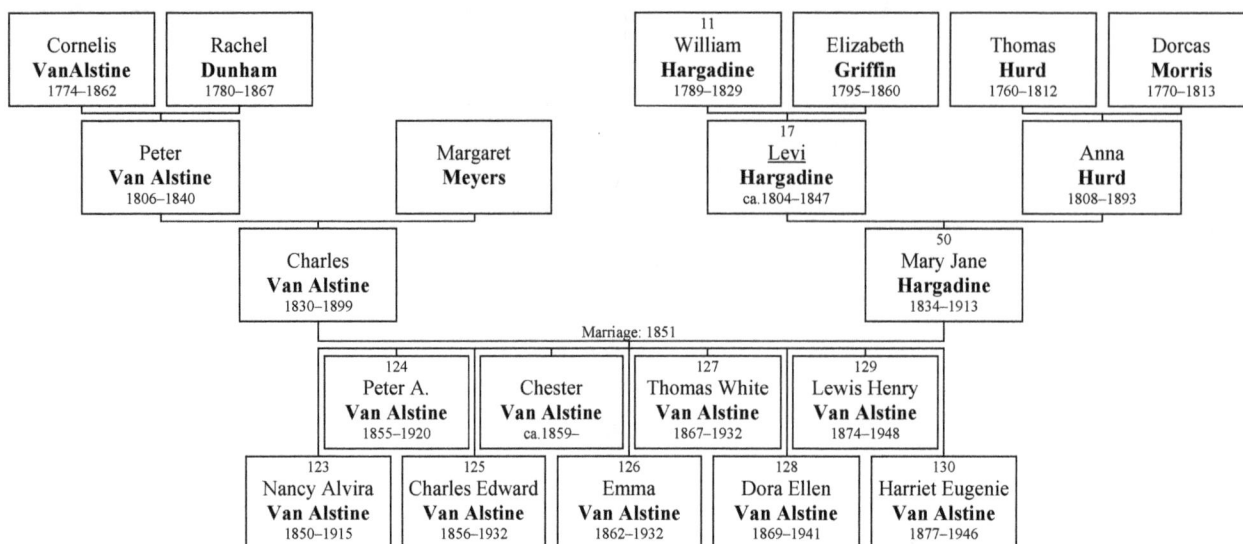

| Cornelis **VanAlstine** 1774–1862 | Rachel **Dunham** 1780–1867 | | 11 William **Hargadine** 1789–1829 | Elizabeth **Griffin** 1795–1860 | Thomas **Hurd** 1760–1812 | Dorcas **Morris** 1770–1813 |

| Peter **Van Alstine** 1806–1840 | Margaret **Meyers** | 17 Levi **Hargadine** ca.1804–1847 | Anna **Hurd** 1808–1893 |

| Charles **Van Alstine** 1830–1899 | 50 Mary Jane **Hargadine** 1834–1913 |

Marriage: 1851

| 124 Peter A. **Van Alstine** 1855–1920 | Chester **Van Alstine** ca.1859– | 127 Thomas White **Van Alstine** 1867–1932 | 129 Lewis Henry **Van Alstine** 1874–1948 |

| 123 Nancy Alvira **Van Alstine** 1850–1915 | 125 Charles Edward **Van Alstine** 1856–1932 | 126 Emma **Van Alstine** 1862–1932 | 128 Dora Ellen **Van Alstine** 1869–1941 | 130 Harriet Eugenie **Van Alstine** 1877–1946 |

50. **Mary Jane Hargadine** was born on Saturday, September 13, 1834, in Ohio, USA.[106] She was the daughter of Levi Hargadine (17) and Anna Hurd.

Mary Jane died in Guss, Taylor County, Iowa, on July 30, 1913, at the age of 78.[107] She was buried in Guss Cemetery, Guss, Taylor County, Iowa (Find a Grave ID 95382556).

At the age of 16, Mary Jane married **Charles Van Alstine** on Sunday, April 06, 1851, in Peoria County, Illinois, when he was 20 years old. They had nine children.

Charles was born in Chautauqua County, New York, on Friday, July 16, 1830.[106] He was the son of Peter Van Alstine and Margaret Meyers.

Charles reached 68 years of age and died in Guss, Taylor County, Iowa, on June 18, 1899.[106] He was buried in Guss Cemetery, Guss, Taylor County, Iowa (Find a Grave ID 57720960).[106]

Children of Mary Jane Hargadine and Charles Van Alstine:

+ 123 f I. **Nancy Alvira Van Alstine** was born in Olena, Henderson County, Illinois, on December 27, 1850.[106] She died in Omaha, Douglas County, Nebraska, on June 29, 1915, at the age of 64. Nancy Alvira was buried in Evergreen Cemetery, Red Oak, Montgomery County, Iowa (Find a Grave ID 26152434).

+ 124 m II. **Peter A. Van Alstine** was born in Henderson County, Illinois, on February 26, 1855.[106] He died in McDonough County, Illinois, on February 19, 1920, at the age of 64. Peter A. was buried in Mount Auburn Cemetery, Colchester, McDonough County, Illinois (Find a Grave ID 82893699).

+ 125 m III. **Charles Edward Van Alstine** was born in Pottawattamie County, Iowa, in July 1856.[106] He was also known as **Ed**.

---

106   Tim Chambers, Vanalstines.GED, Date of Import: Mar 11, 2001.

107   http://www.geocities.com/Heartland/Ridge/7026/main/d200.htm#P383.

Charles Edward died in Nodaway, Taylor County, Iowa, on September 15, 1932, at the age of 76.

m IV. **Chester Van Alstine** was born in Illinois, USA, about 1859.[106]

+ 126 f V. **Emma Van Alstine** was born in Illinois, USA, in October 1862.[106] She died in Wasco County, Oregon, on September 15, 1932, at the age of 69. Emma was buried in Kelly Cemetery, Maupin, Wasco County, Oregon (Find a Grave ID 155713925).

+ 127 m VI. **Thomas White Van Alstine** was born in Peoria, Peoria County, Illinois, on June 17, 1867.[106] He died in Taylor County, Iowa, on September 15, 1932, at the age of 65.[106] Thomas White was buried in Prairie Rose Cemetery, Corning, Adams County, Iowa (Find a Grave ID 80093109).[106]

+ 128 f VII. **Dora Ellen Van Alstine** was born in Peoria, Peoria County, Illinois, on August 16, 1869.[108] She died in Atkinson, Holt County, Nebraska, on April 12, 1941, at the age of 71. Dora Ellen was buried in Stuart Cemetery, Stuart, Holt County, Nebraska (Find a Grave ID 115024401).

+ 129 m VIII. **Lewis Henry Van Alstine** was born in Illinois, USA, in June 1874.[106] He died on October 14, 1948, at the age of 74. Lewis Henry was buried in Graceland Cemetery, Mitchell, Davison County, South Dakota (Find a Grave ID 105095310).

+ 130 f IX. **Harriet Eugenie Van Alstine** was born in Villisca, Montgomery County, Iowa, on May 20, 1877.[106] She died in Oregon, USA, on May 24, 1946, at the age of 69. Harriet Eugenie was buried in Pine Grove Cemetery, Hood River, Hood River County, Oregon (Find a Grave ID 29269441).

Family of Sarah Hargadine and Joseph Clifton

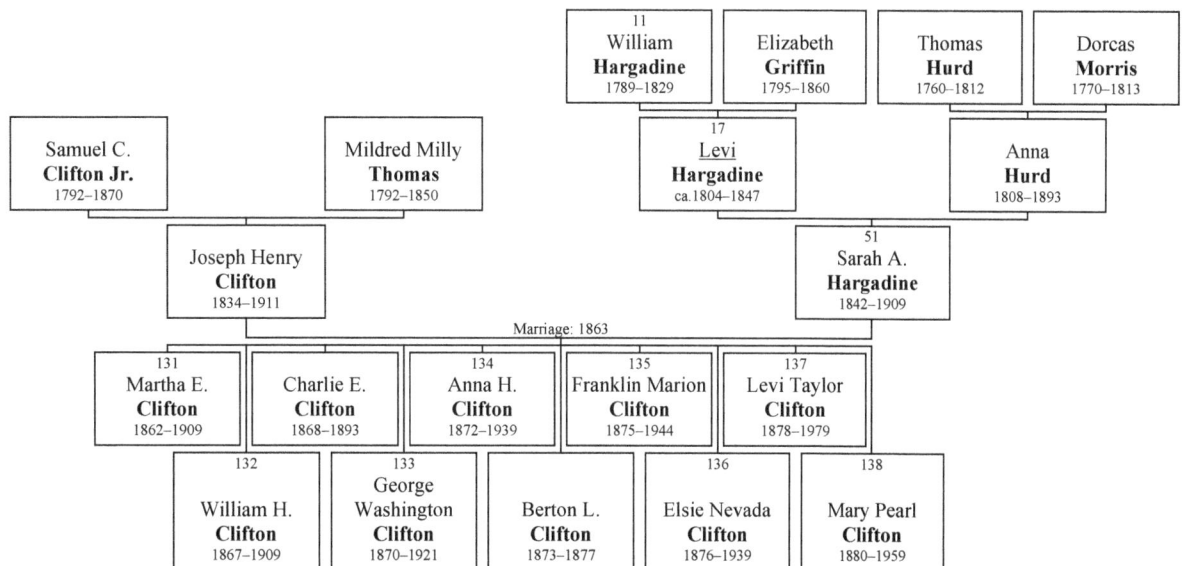

---

108 Tim Chambers, Date of Import: Mar 11, 2001.

51.   **Sarah A. Hargadine** was born on Monday, September 05, 1842, in Peoria, Peoria County, Illinois.[109] She was the daughter of <u>Levi</u> Hargadine (17) and Anna Hurd.

Sarah A. died in Modale, Harrison County, Iowa, on February 10, 1909, at the age of 66.[109] She was buried in Calhoun Cemetery, Harrison County, Iowa, on February 13, 1909 (Find a Grave ID 47669695).[109]

Sarah A. married **Joseph Henry Clifton** in 1863 in Peoria, Peoria County, Illinois.[109] They had ten children.

Joseph Henry was born in Peoria, Peoria County, Illinois, on Monday, June 23, 1834.[109] He was the son of Samuel C. Clifton Jr. and Mildred Milly Thomas.

Joseph Henry reached 77 years of age and died in Blair, Washington County, Nebraska, on December 30, 1911.[109] He was buried on January 02, 1912, in Calhoun Cemetery, Harrison County, Iowa (Find a Grave ID 47669693).[109]

Children of Sarah A. Hargadine and Joseph Henry Clifton:

+   131   f   I. **Martha E. Clifton** was born in Peoria, Peoria County, Illinois, on November 28, 1862.[109] She was also known as **Katie**.

Martha E. died in Decatur, Burt County, Nebraska, on March 18, 1909, at the age of 46.[109] She was buried in Calhoun Cemetery, Harrison County, Iowa (Find a Grave ID 232989891).

+   132   m   II. **William H. Clifton** was born in Peoria, Peoria County, Illinois, on April 25, 1867.[109] He died on March 24, 1909, at the age of 41.[109]

        m   III. **Charlie E. Clifton** was born in Peoria, Peoria County, Illinois, on October 03, 1868.[109] He died in Calhoun, Harrison County, Iowa, on May 21, 1893, at the age of 24.[109] Charlie E. was buried in Calhoun Cemetery, Harrison County, Iowa (Find a Grave ID 47669696).[109]

+   133   m   IV. **George Washington Clifton** was born in Peoria, Peoria County, Illinois, on March 21, 1870.[109] He died in Wessington Springs Township, Jerauld County, South Dakota, on September 22, 1921, at the age of 51.[109] George Washington was buried in Rose Hill Memorial Gardens, Missouri Valley, Harrison County, Iowa (Find a Grave ID 155535120).[109]

+   134   f   V. **Anna H. Clifton** was born in LaSalle, LaSalle County, Illinois, on January 14, 1872.[109] She died in Omaha, Douglas County, Nebraska, on December 08, 1939, at the age of 67.[109] Anna H. was buried in Blair Cemetery, Blair, Washington County, Nebraska, on December 10, 1939 (Find a Grave ID 77018111).[109]

        m   VI. **Berton L. Clifton** was born in Peoria, Peoria County, Illinois, on October 18, 1873.[109] He died on December 18, 1877, at the age of 4.[109]

+   135   m   VII. **Franklin Marion Clifton** was born in Peoria, Peoria County, Illinois, on April 26, 1875.[109] He died in Okmulgee, Okmulgee County, Oklahoma, on June 24, 1944, at the age of 69.[109] Franklin Marion was buried in

---

109   Norma Pugmire Gedcom file, Date of Import: Feb 2, 2000.

Okmulgee Cemetery, Okmulgee, Okmulgee County, Oklahoma, on June 29, 1944 (Find a Grave ID 122913383).

+ 136 f VIII. **Elsie Nevada Clifton** was born in Adams County, Iowa, on December 23, 1876.[109] She died in Long Beach, Los Angeles County, California, on August 18, 1939, at the age of 62.[109] Elsie Nevada was buried in Rose Hills Memorial Park, Whittier, Los Angeles County, California (Find a Grave ID 127285911).

+ 137 m IX. **Levi Taylor Clifton** was born in Clarks, Merrick County, Nebraska, on December 09, 1878.[109] He died in Seattle, King County, Washington, on May 10, 1979, at the age of 100.[109] Levi Taylor was buried in Calvary Mausoleum, Seattle, King County, Washington, on May 12, 1979 (Find a Grave ID 76264110).[109]

+ 138 f X. **Mary Pearl Clifton** was born in Clarks, Merrick County, Nebraska, on August 27, 1880.[109] She died in Los Angeles, Los Angeles County, California, on October 05, 1959, at the age of 79.[109]

Family of William Hargadine and Anne Evans

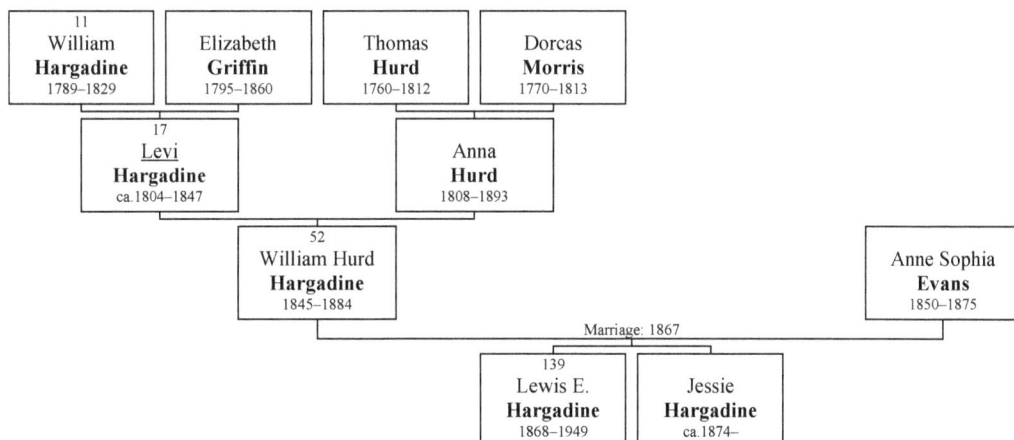

52. **William Hurd Hargadine** was born on Thursday, January 02, 1845, in Illinois, USA. He was the son of Levi Hargadine (17) and Anna Hurd.

William Hurd died on February 27, 1884, at the age of 39. He was buried in La Salle Cemetery, Rome, Peoria County, Illinois (Find a Grave ID 44542919).

William Hurd married **Anne Sophia Evans** on Sunday, January 27, 1867, in Peoria County, Illinois. They had two sons.

Anne Sophia was born in Illinois, USA, in 1850. She reached 25 years of age and died at During childbirth with Jessie in Groveland, La Salle County, Illinois, in 1875. Anne Sophia was buried in Minonk Township Cemetery, Woodford County, Illinois.

Sons of William Hurd Hargadine and Anne Sophia Evans:

+ 139 m I. **Lewis E. Hargadine** was born in Dunlap, Peoria County, Illinois, on April 16, 1868. He was also known as **Lewis**.

Lewis E. died in Speer, Stark County, Illinois, on July 05, 1949, at the age of 81. He was buried in Saint Mary of the Woods Cemetery, Princeville, Peoria County, Illinois, on July 07, 1949 (Find a Grave ID 31412732).

m   II. **Jessie Hargadine** was born about 1874. He was buried in Minonk Township Cemetery, Woodford County, Illinois.

Family of Levi Hargadine and Louisa Hurd

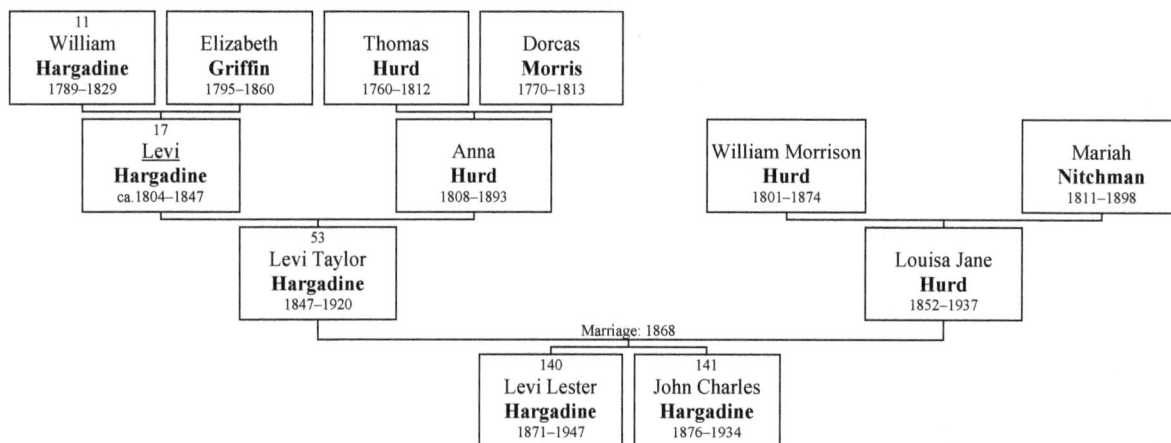

53.   **Levi Taylor Hargadine** was born on Thursday, April 08, 1847, in Medina, Peoria County, Illinois. He was the son of Levi Hargadine (17) and Anna Hurd.

Levi Taylor died in Dunlap, Radnor Twp., Peoria County, Illinois, on September 22, 1920, at the age of 73. He was buried in La Salle Cemetery, Rome, Peoria County, Illinois (Find a Grave ID 24825520).

At the age of 21, Levi Taylor married **Louisa Jane Hurd** on Monday, June 01, 1868, in Illinois, USA, when she was 16 years old. They had two sons.

Louisa Jane was born in Urbana, Champaign County, Ohio, on Monday, February 16, 1852. Louisa Jane reached 85 years of age and died in Radnor Township, Peoria County, Illinois, on November 26, 1937. Her cause of death was heart disease. Louisa Jane was buried on November 28, 1937, in La Salle Cemetery, Rome, Peoria County, Illinois (Find a Grave ID 24825522).

Married Fifty Years

    Mr. and Mrs. Taylor Hargadine were married fifty years ago June 1st. They spent the day with their nephew, Lewie Hargadine, and family of Jubilee.

    Returning home in the evening, they were surprised to find seventy five of their friends and relatives gathered to help them celebrate their golden wedding anniversary. Gold and white crepe paper and flowers were used in the decorations.

    After supper was served the guests, departed at a late hour, leaving many beautiful and appropriate gifts to remind Mr. and Mrs. Hargadine of this pleasant occasion.

    Five dollar gold piece, Mrs. And Mrs. John Shaw; Gold bowl cream ladle, Mr. and Mrs. George Shaw; Gold bowl berry spoon, Mr. and Mrs. Wm. Myers; Gold plated salt and pepper shakers and box of cigars, Mr. and Mrs. Fred Mayer; Gold tie pin and hat pin, Mr. and Mrs. Truitt Rice. Watch chain and brooch, Mr. and Mrs. Wallace Hurd and the families of Lester and John Hargadine. One dollar Mr. and Mrs. Wiley Reynolds; Casserole, Mr. and Mrs. John Sturms; Glass stemmed jelly dish, Mr. and Mrs. Henry Meyers and Mrs. John Meyers; Cake plate, Mr. and Mrs. Jno. Ernst; Eight pie plates, Mr. and Mrs. Roy Ruse and Miss Hazel Kimbal; Four pie plates, Mr. and Mrs. Graham; Bed spread, Mr. and Mrs. Ernest Aby and daughter. She was the daughter of William Morrison Hurd and Mariah Nitchman.

Sons of Levi Taylor Hargadine and Louisa Jane Hurd:

+ 140   m   I. **Levi Lester Hargadine** was born in Medina, Peoria County, Illinois, on December 20, 1871. He died in North Chillicothe, Peoria County, Illinois, on July 31, 1947, at the age of 75. His cause of death was carcinoma of prostate with metastasis. He was buried in La Salle Cemetery, Rome, Peoria County, Illinois, on August 02, 1947 (Find a Grave ID 24825518).

+ 141   m   II. **John Charles Hargadine** was born in Medina, Peoria County, Illinois, on August 22, 1876. He died in Peoria, Peoria County, Illinois, on January 27, 1934, at the age of 57. His cause of death was fractured skull and hemorrhage of brain due to injuries accidentally received. He was buried in Prospect Cemetery, Dunlap, Peoria County, Illinois, on January 31, 1934 (Find a Grave ID 22160967).

Family of Jane Hargadine and John Yates

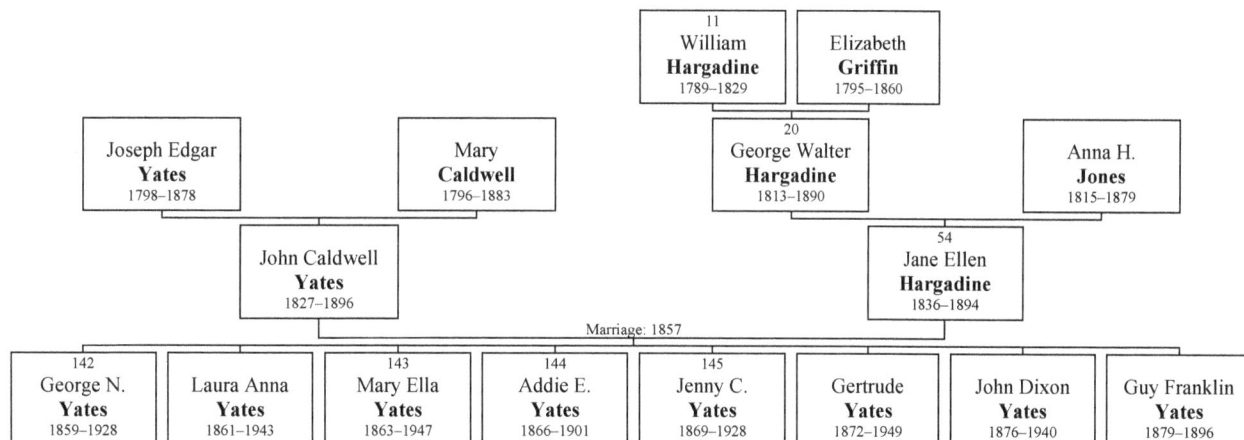

54.   **Jane Ellen Hargadine** was born on Monday, December 26, 1836, in Clark County, Ohio. She was the daughter of George Walter Hargadine (20) and Anna H. Jones.

Jane Ellen died in Chenoa, McLean County, Illinois, on June 02, 1894, at the age of 57. She was buried in Springdale Cemetery and Mausoleum, Peoria, Peoria County, Illinois, on June 04, 1894 (Find a Grave ID 119219149).

At the age of 20, Jane Ellen married **John Caldwell Yates** on Tuesday, June 16, 1857, in Peoria County, Illinois, when he was 29 years old. They had eight children.

John Caldwell was born in Ohio County, West Virginia, on Friday, August 17, 1827. He was the son of Joseph Edgar Yates and Mary Caldwell.

He worked as a Judge. John Caldwell reached 68 years of age and died in Peoria County, Illinois, on March 14, 1896. He was buried in Springdale Cemetery and Mausoleum, Peoria, Peoria County, Illinois (Find a Grave ID 25338289).

Children of Jane Ellen Hargadine and John Caldwell Yates:

+ 142 m I. **George N. Yates** was born in Peoria County, Illinois, on December 06, 1859. He died in Peoria, Peoria County, Illinois, on November 28, 1928, at the age of 68. George N. was buried in Mount Hawley Cemetery, Peoria, Peoria County, Illinois, on November 30, 1928 (Find a Grave ID 22160515).

      f II. **Laura Anna Yates** was born in Illinois, USA, on August 17, 1861. She died in Plummer, Benewah County, Idaho, on April 26, 1943, at the age of 81. Laura Anna was buried in Springdale Cemetery and Mausoleum, Peoria, Peoria County, Illinois (Find a Grave ID 173369333).

+ 143 f III. **Mary Ella Yates** was born on August 12, 1863. She died in Filley, Gage County, Nebraska, on May 28, 1947, at the age of 83. Mary Ella was buried in Filley Cemetery, Filley, Gage County, Nebraska (Find a Grave ID 59312714).

+ 144 f IV. **Addie E. Yates** was born on June 05, 1866. She died on August 19, 1901, at the age of 35. Addie E. was buried in Springdale Cemetery and Mausoleum, Peoria, Peoria County, Illinois (Find a Grave ID 136695218).

+ 145 f V. **Jenny C. Yates** was born on November 18, 1869. She died on August 19, 1928, at the age of 58. Jenny C. was buried in Smithville Cemetery, Hanna City, Peoria County, Illinois (Find a Grave ID 133133752).

      f VI. **Gertrude Yates** was born in Peoria County, Illinois, on May 22, 1872. She died in Los Angeles County, California, on September 17, 1949, at the age of 77. Gertrude was buried in Springdale Cemetery and Mausoleum, Peoria, Peoria County, Illinois (Find a Grave ID 173325688).

      m VII. **John Dixon Yates** was born in Peoria County, Illinois, on May 26, 1876.[110] He died in Hermosa Beach, Los Angeles County, California, on July 05, 1940, at the age of 64.[110] John Dixon was buried in Inglewood Park Cemetery, Inglewood, Los Angeles County, California (Find a Grave ID 110771470).

      m VIII. **Guy Franklin Yates** was born in Peoria, Peoria County, Illinois, on November 10, 1879. He died in Peoria, Peoria County, Illinois, on March 21, 1896, at the age of 16. Guy Franklin was buried in Springdale Cemetery and Mausoleum, Peoria, Peoria County, Illinois (Find a Grave ID 119216349).

---

[110] California Death Index.

Family of William Hargadine and Sarah Sprague

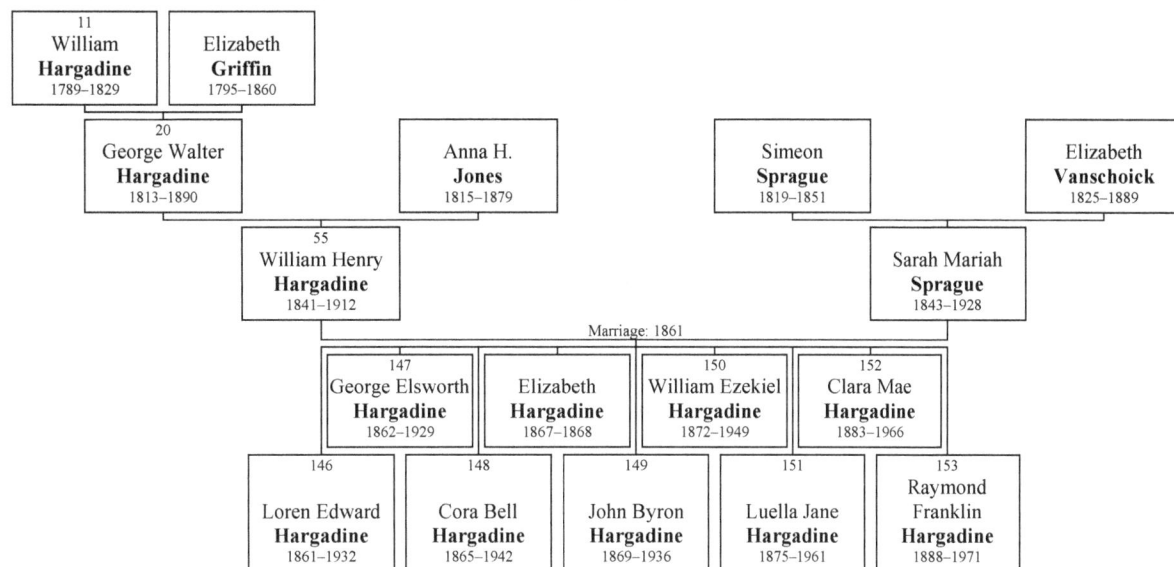

55.   **William Henry Hargadine** was born on Tuesday, January 12, 1841, in Moorefield Twp., Clark County, Ohio. He was the son of George Walter Hargadine (20) and Anna H. Jones.

William Henry died in Kinsley County, Kansas, on July 01, 1912, at the age of 71. His cause of death was cerebral hemorrhage. William Henry was buried in Bethel Cemetery, Hodges, Edwards County, Kansas (Find a Grave ID 67563434).

At the age of 20, William Henry married **Sarah Mariah Sprague** on Wednesday, September 11, 1861, in Peoria County, Illinois, when she was 17 years old. They had nine children.

Sarah Mariah was born in Peoria, Peoria County, Illinois, on Saturday, November 25, 1843. She was the daughter of Simeon Sprague and Elizabeth Vanschoick.

Sarah Mariah reached 84 years of age and died in Kinsley, Edwards County, Kansas, on May 13, 1928. She was buried in Bethel Cemetery, Hodges, Edwards County, Kansas (Find a Grave ID 67563105).

Children of William Henry Hargadine and Sarah Mariah Sprague:

+   146   m   I. **Loren Edward Hargadine** was born in Chenoa, McLean County, Illinois, on October 10, 1861. He was also known as **Ed**.

Loren Edward died in Kinsley, Edwards County, Kansas, on March 15, 1932, at the age of 70. He was buried in Bethel Cemetery, Hodges, Edwards County, Kansas (Find a Grave ID 67562844).

+   147   m   II. **George Elsworth Hargadine** was born in Chenoa, McLean County, Illinois, on January 01, 1862. He died on July 22, 1929, at the age of 67. George Elsworth was buried in Prairie Lawn Cemetery, Wellington, Sumner County, Kansas (Find a Grave ID 63279785).

+   148   f   III. **Cora Bell Hargadine** was born in Chenoa, McLean County, Illinois, on December 08, 1865. She died in Edwards County, Kansas, on August 17, 1942, at the age of 76. Cora Bell was buried in Bethel Cemetery, Hodges, Edwards County, Kansas (Find a Grave ID 67570823).

		f	IV.	**Elizabeth Hargadine** was born in Illinois, USA, in 1867. She was also known as **Lizzie**.

Elizabeth died in Illinois, USA, on August 29, 1868, at the age of 1. She was buried in Chenoa Cemetery, McLean County, Illinois (Find a Grave ID 198490269).

+ 149 m   V. **John Byron Hargadine** was born in Chenoa, McLean County, Illinois, on July 04, 1869. He was also known as **Jack**.

John Byron died in Haviland, Kiowa County, Kansas, on May 27, 1936, at the age of 66. He was buried in Bethel Cemetery, Hodges, Edwards County, Kansas (Find a Grave ID 67562830).

+ 150 m   VI. **William Ezekiel Hargadine** was born in Chenoa, McLean County, Illinois, on April 17, 1872. He was also known as **Will**.

William Ezekiel died in Edwards County, Kansas, on November 12, 1949, at the age of 77. He was buried in Bethel Cemetery, Hodges, Edwards County, Kansas (Find a Grave ID 67563044).

+ 151 f   VII. **Luella Jane Hargadine** was born in Chenoa, McLean County, Illinois, on March 01, 1875. She died in Kinsley, Edwards County, Kansas, on January 08, 1961, at the age of 85. Luella Jane was buried in Hillside Cemetery, Kinsley, Edwards County, Kansas (Find a Grave ID 11471653).

+ 152 f   VIII. **Clara Mae Hargadine** was born in Chenoa, McLean County, Illinois, on September 26, 1883. She died in Protection, Comanche County, Kansas, on October 04, 1966, at the age of 83. Clara Mae was buried in Protection Cemetery, Protection, Comanche County, Kansas (Find a Grave ID 21542845).

+ 153 m   IX. **Raymond Franklin Hargadine** was born in Mullinville, Kiowa County, Kansas, on January 26, 1888. He died in Seattle, King County, Washington, on March 28, 1971, at the age of 83. Raymond Franklin was buried in Old Carson Cemetery, Skamania County, Washington, on April 01, 1971 (Find a Grave ID 43234197).

Family of Amanda Hargadine and James Drommond

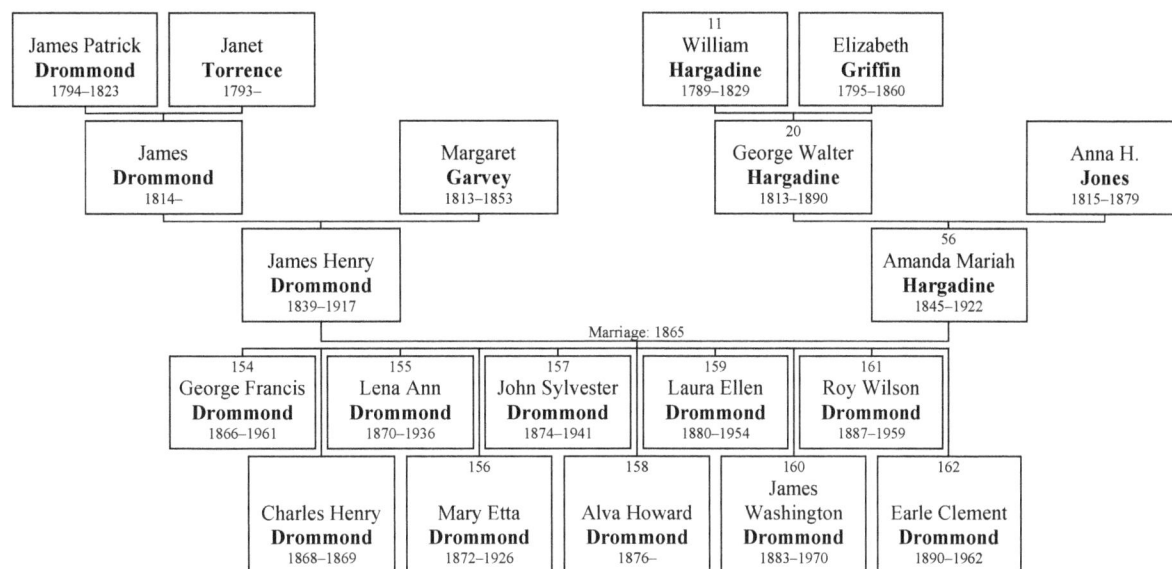

56. **Amanda Mariah Hargadine** was born on Sunday, November 16, 1845, in Moorefield Twp., Clark County, Ohio. She was the daughter of George Walter Hargadine (20) and Anna H. Jones.

Amanda Mariah died in Wray, Yuma County, Colorado, on December 23, 1922, at the age of 77. Her cause of death was carcinoma of liver. Amanda Mariah was buried in Grandview Cemetery, Wray, Yuma County, Colorado, on December 26, 1966 (Find a Grave ID 50355873).

At the age of 19, Amanda Mariah married **James Henry Drommond** on Thursday, April 13, 1865, in Lawn Ridge, Marshall County, Illinois, when he was 25 years old. They had ten children.

James Henry was born in Milwaukee, Milwaukee County, Wisconsin, on Thursday, September 19, 1839. He was the son of James Drommond and Margaret Garvey.

He served in the military: Co H, 47th Illinois Infantry; enlisted at the age of 22. James Henry reached 77 years of age and died in Wray, Yuma County, Colorado, on August 15, 1917. He was buried on August 17, 1917, in Grandview Cemetery, Wray, Yuma County, Colorado (Find a Grave ID 50356047).

Children of Amanda Mariah Hargadine and James Henry Drommond:

+ 154 m I. **George Francis Drommond** was born in Peoria, Peoria County, Illinois, on November 17, 1866. He died in Loveland, Larimer County, Colorado, on July 16, 1961, at the age of 94. George Francis was buried in Grandview Cemetery, Wray, Yuma County, Colorado (Find a Grave ID 56943092).

           m II. **Charles Henry Drommond** was born in Ford County, Illinois, on April 14, 1868. He died on August 11, 1869, at the age of 1. Charles Henry was buried in Lyman Township Cemetery, Roberts, Ford County, Illinois (Find a Grave ID 53755646).[111]

+	155	f	III. **Lena Ann Drommond** was born in Lyman Twp., Ford County, Illinois, on January 30, 1870. She died in 1936 at the age of 65. Lena Ann was buried in Crown Hill Cemetery, Wheat Ridge, Jefferson County, Colorado (Find a Grave ID 34249816).
+	156	f	IV. **Mary Etta Drommond** was born in Lyman Twp., Ford County, Illinois, on April 26, 1872. She died in Englewood, Arapahoe County, Colorado, on April 03, 1926, at the age of 53. Her cause of death: accidentally killed by a truck. She was buried in Grandview Cemetery, Wray, Yuma County, Colorado (Find a Grave ID 17059444).
+	157	m	V. **John Sylvester Drommond** was born in Lyman Twp., Ford County, Illinois, on March 23, 1874. He died in Colorado Springs, El Paso County, Colorado, on November 22, 1941, at the age of 67. John Sylvester was buried in Evergreen Cemetery, Colorado Springs, El Paso County, Colorado (Find a Grave ID 34611285).
+	158	m	VI. **Alva Howard Drommond** was born in Chenoa, McLean County, Illinois, on December 06, 1876.
+	159	f	VII. **Laura Ellen Drommond** was born in Weston, McLean County, Illinois, on January 18, 1880. She died in Wray, Yuma County, Colorado, on September 26, 1954, at the age of 74. Laura Ellen was buried in Grandview Cemetery, Wray, Yuma County, Colorado (Find a Grave ID 9393640).
+	160	m	VIII. **James Washington Drommond** was born in Eppards Point Township, Livingston County, Illinois, on February 02, 1883. He died in Wray, Yuma County, Colorado, on December 21, 1970, at the age of 87. James Washington was buried in Grandview Cemetery, Wray, Yuma County, Colorado, on December 23, 1970 (Find a Grave ID 50358395).
+	161	m	IX. **Roy Wilson Drommond** was born in Haigler, Dundy County, Nebraska, on May 05, 1887. He died on September 30, 1959, at the age of 72. Roy Wilson was buried in Grandview Cemetery, Wray, Yuma County, Colorado (Find a Grave ID 50359537).
+	162	m	X. **Earle Clement Drommond** was born in Haigler, Dundy County, Nebraska, on July 10, 1890. He died in Wray, Yuma County, Colorado, on January 08, 1962, at the age of 71. Earle Clement was buried in Grandview Cemetery, Wray, Yuma County, Colorado (Find a Grave ID 50538843).

---

[111] Obituary for George F. Drommond, At the age of 11 he moved with his family to Weston, Illinois, where they lived for two years. A brother, Charles, died during that time and was buried at Chatsworth, Illinois.

Family of Mary Hargadine and William Chambers

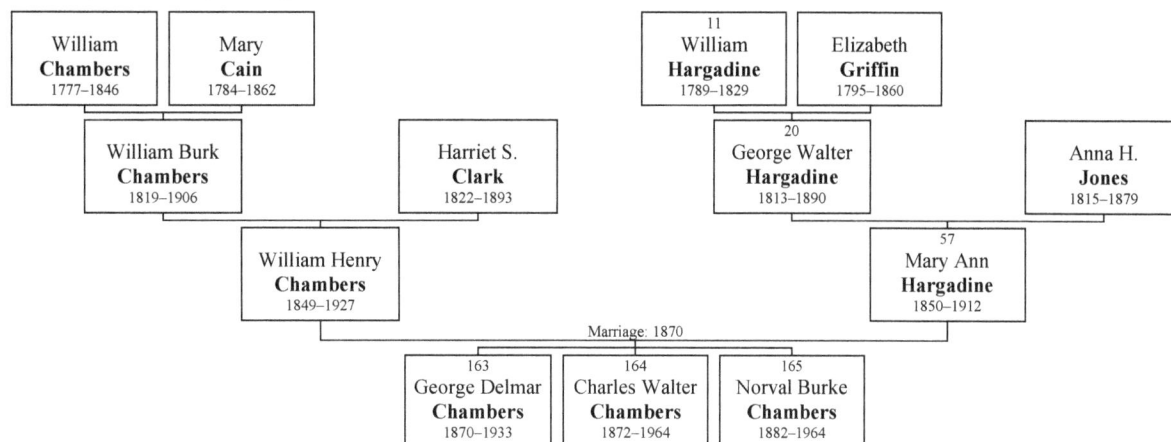

57.   **Mary Ann Hargadine** was born on Saturday, January 05, 1850, in Medina, Peoria County, Illinois. She was the daughter of George Walter Hargadine (20) and Anna H. Jones.

Mary Ann died in Chenoa, McLean County, Illinois, on December 20, 1912, at the age of 62. Her cause of death was dropsy. Mary Ann was buried in Chenoa Cemetery, McLean County, Illinois, on December 21, 1912 (Find a Grave ID 80966705).

At the age of 20, Mary Ann married **William Henry Chambers** on Tuesday, March 08, 1870, in Pontiac, Livingston County, Illinois, when he was 20 years old. They had three sons.

William Henry was born in Newton, Camden County, New Jersey, on Tuesday, December 25, 1849. He was the son of William Burk Chambers and Harriet S. Clark.

William Henry reached 77 years of age and died in Bloomington, McLean County, Illinois, on May 09, 1927. His cause of death was myocarditis. William Henry was buried in Chenoa Cemetery, McLean County, Illinois (Find a Grave ID 88603883).

Sons of Mary Ann Hargadine and William Henry Chambers:

+   163   m   I. **George Delmar Chambers** was born in Chenoa, McLean County, Illinois, on June 16, 1870. He died in Bloomington, McLean County, Illinois, on December 09, 1933, at the age of 63. George Delmar was buried in Park Hill Cemetery and Mausoleum, Bloomington, McLean County, Illinois, on December 11, 1933 (Find a Grave ID 58544177).

+   164   m   II. **Charles Walter Chambers** was born in Chenoa, McLean County, Illinois, on November 01, 1872. He died in Saint Louis, Saint Louis County, Missouri, on April 13, 1964, at the age of 91. Charles Walter was buried in Park Hill Cemetery and Mausoleum, Bloomington, McLean County, Illinois, on April 15, 1964 (Find a Grave ID 58543841).

+   165   m   III. **Norval Burke Chambers** was born in Chenoa, McLean County, Illinois, on September 21, 1882. He died in Bloomington, McLean County, Illinois, on July 09, 1964, at the age of 81. Norval Burke was buried in Chenoa Cemetery, McLean County, Illinois, on July 12, 1964 (Find a Grave ID 80966677).

Family of Ellen Hargadine and William Nelson

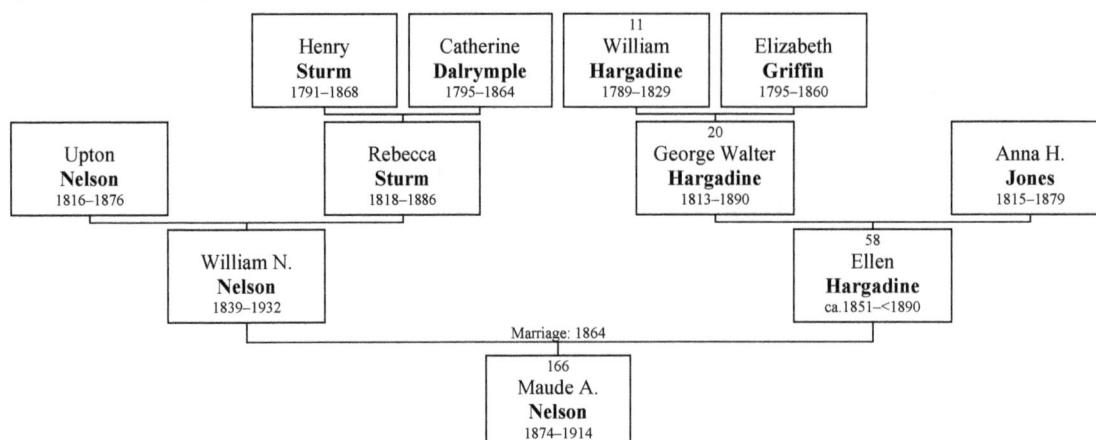

```
┌──────────────┐ ┌──────────────┐ ┌──────11──────┐ ┌──────────────┐
│    Henry     │ │  Catherine   │ │   William    │ │  Elizabeth   │
│    Sturm     │ │  Dalrymple   │ │  Hargadine   │ │   Griffin    │
│  1791–1868   │ │  1795–1864   │ │  1789–1829   │ │  1795–1860   │
└──────────────┘ └──────────────┘ └──────────────┘ └──────────────┘
┌──────────────┐ ┌──────────────┐ ┌──────20──────┐ ┌──────────────┐
│    Upton     │ │   Rebecca    │ │George Walter │ │   Anna H.    │
│    Nelson    │ │    Sturm     │ │  Hargadine   │ │    Jones     │
│  1816–1876   │ │  1818–1886   │ │  1813–1890   │ │  1815–1879   │
└──────────────┘ └──────────────┘ └──────────────┘ └──────────────┘
      ┌──────────────┐              ┌──────58──────┐
      │  William N.  │              │    Ellen     │
      │    Nelson    │              │  Hargadine   │
      │  1839–1932   │              │ ca.1851–<1890│
      └──────────────┘              └──────────────┘
                Marriage: 1864
              ┌──────166─────┐
              │   Maude A.   │
              │    Nelson    │
              │  1874–1914   │
              └──────────────┘
```

58. **Ellen Hargadine** was born about 1851 in Peoria County, Illinois. She was the daughter of George Walter Hargadine (20) and Anna H. Jones.

Ellen died before April 06, 1890.

At the age of 13, Ellen married **William N. Nelson** on Monday, October 10, 1864, in Peoria County, Illinois, when he was 25 years old. They had one daughter.

William N. was born in Stark County, Illinois, on Sunday, February 10, 1839. He was the son of Upton Nelson and Rebecca Sturm.

William N. reached 93 years of age and died in Latour, Johnson County, Missouri, on March 27, 1932. He was buried in Pleasanton Cemetery, Pleasanton, Linn County, Kansas (Find a Grave ID 62270034).

Daughter of Ellen Hargadine and William N. Nelson:

+ 166   f   I. **Maude A. Nelson** was born in Peoria, Peoria County, Illinois, in 1874.[112] She died in Pleasanton, Linn County, Kansas, in 1914 at the age of 40. Maude A. was buried in Pleasanton Cemetery, Pleasanton, Linn County, Kansas (Find a Grave ID 62208874).

112   FamilySearch.org, United States Census, 1910, FamilySearch, "United States Census, 1910," database with images, <i>FamilySearch</i> (https://familysearch.org/ark:/61903/1:1:M2CK-SS5 : accessed 23 January 2023), Maude Murphy in household of Edward Murphy, Potosi, Linn, Kansas, United States; citing enumeration district (ED) ED 122, sheet 8B, family 115, NARA microfilm publication T624 (Washington D.C.: National Archives and Records Administration, 1982), roll 445; FHL microfilm 1,374,458.

Family of Helena Hargadine and George Jewell

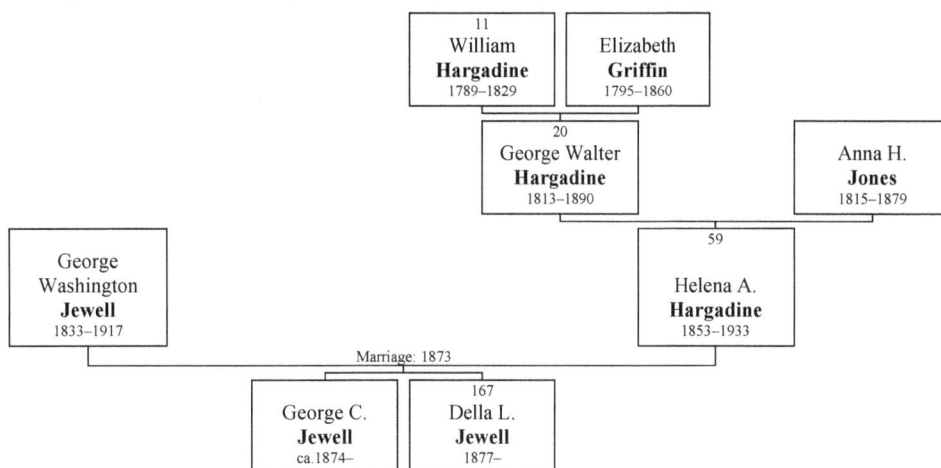

59. **Helena A. Hargadine** was born on Tuesday, August 16, 1853, in Medina, Peoria County, Illinois. She was the daughter of George Walter Hargadine (20) and Anna H. Jones.

Helena A. died in Bloomington, McLean County, Illinois, on December 26, 1933, at the age of 80. Her cause of death was pyloric stenosis. Helena A. was buried in Hudson Cemetery, Hudson, McLean County, Illinois (Find a Grave ID 11880055).

At the age of 20, Helena A. married **George Washington Jewell** on Thursday, October 23, 1873, in Mc Lean County, Illinois, when he was 40 years old. They had two children.

George Washington was born in Martonsburg, Lincoln County, Ohio, on Monday, July 15, 1833. He reached 84 years of age and died in Bloomington, McLean County, Illinois, on August 03, 1917. George Washington was buried in Hudson Cemetery, Hudson, McLean County, Illinois (Find a Grave ID 11880044).

Children of Helena A. Hargadine and George Washington Jewell:

	m	I.	**George C. Jewell** was born about 1874.
+ 167	f	II.	**Della L. Jewell** was born in Pennsylvania, USA, in November 1877.

Family of Charles Hargadine and Jennie Bay

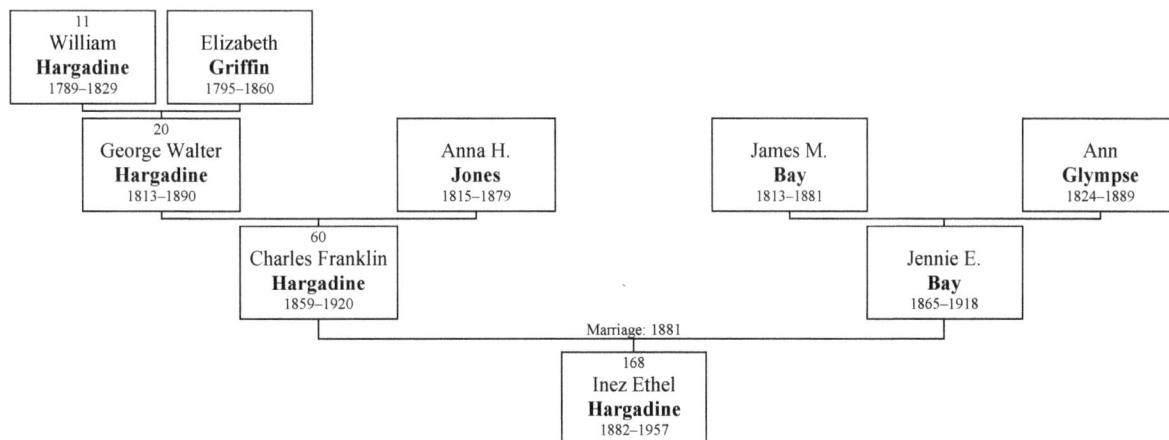

60. **Charles Franklin Hargadine** was born on Friday, December 09, 1859, in Medina, Peoria County, Illinois. He was the son of George Walter Hargadine (20) and Anna H. Jones.

Charles Franklin died in Arcadia, Iron County, Missouri, on February 21, 1920, at the age of 60. He was buried in Knights of Pythias Cemetery, Ironton, Iron County, Missouri, on February 22, 1920 (Find a Grave ID 158189091).

At the age of 21, Charles Franklin married **Jennie E. Bay** on Wednesday, April 06, 1881, in McLean County, Illinois, when he was 15 years old. They had one daughter.

Jennie E. was born in Illinois, USA, on Saturday, August 12, 1865. He was the son of James M. Bay and Ann Glympse.

Jennie E. reached 53 years of age and died in Chicago, Cook County, Illinois, on October 22, 1918. He was buried on October 24, 1918, in Rosehill Cemetery and Mausoleum, Chicago, Cook County, Illinois (Find a Grave ID 158189144).

Daughter of Charles Franklin Hargadine and Jennie E. Bay:

+   168   f   I. **Inez Ethel Hargadine** was born in Illinois, USA, on January 16, 1882. She died in Chicago, Cook County, Illinois, on February 12, 1957, at the age of 75. Inez Ethel was buried in Rosehill Cemetery and Mausoleum, Chicago, Cook County, Illinois, on February 15, 1957.

Family of Elizabeth Brandle and Samuel Hunter

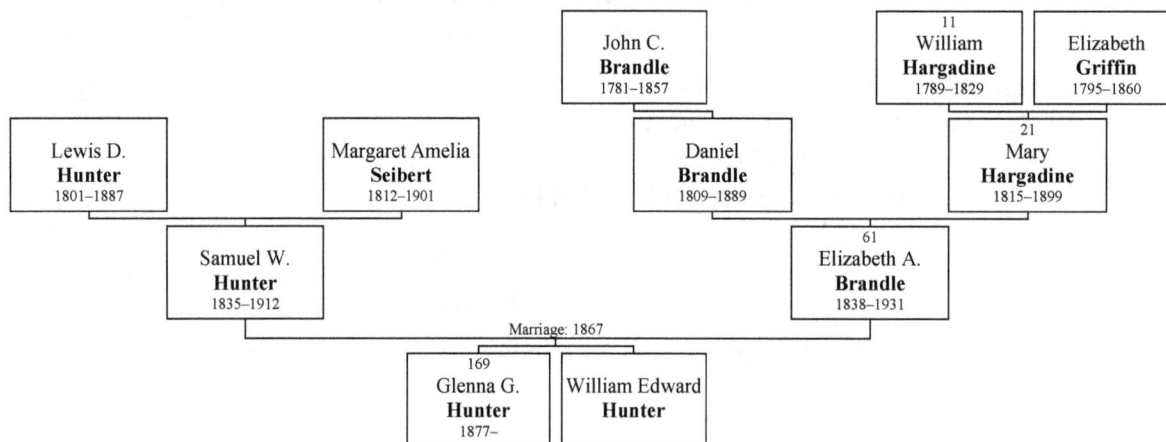

61. **Elizabeth A. Brandle** was born on Friday, March 09, 1838, in Clark County, Ohio. She was the daughter of Daniel Brandle and Mary Hargadine (21).

Elizabeth A. died at Miami Valley Hospital in Dayton, Montgomery County, Ohio, on May 14, 1931, at the age of 93. She was buried in Ferncliff Cemetery, Springfield, Clark County, Ohio (Find a Grave ID 45844575).

At the age of 29, Elizabeth A. married **Samuel W. Hunter** on Thursday, November 07, 1867, when he was 32 years old. They had two children.

Samuel W. was born in Clark County, Ohio, on Saturday, October 17, 1835. He was the son of Lewis D. Hunter and Margaret Amelia Seibert.

Samuel W. reached 76 years of age and died in Clark County, Ohio, on February 23, 1912. He was buried in Ferncliff Cemetery, Springfield, Clark County, Ohio (Find a Grave ID 45844508).

Children of Elizabeth A. Brandle and Samuel W. Hunter:

+ 169   f   I. **Glenna G. Hunter** was born in Clark County, Ohio, on February 03, 1877.

         m   II. **William Edward Hunter**.

Family of Sarah Brandle and Joseph Normand

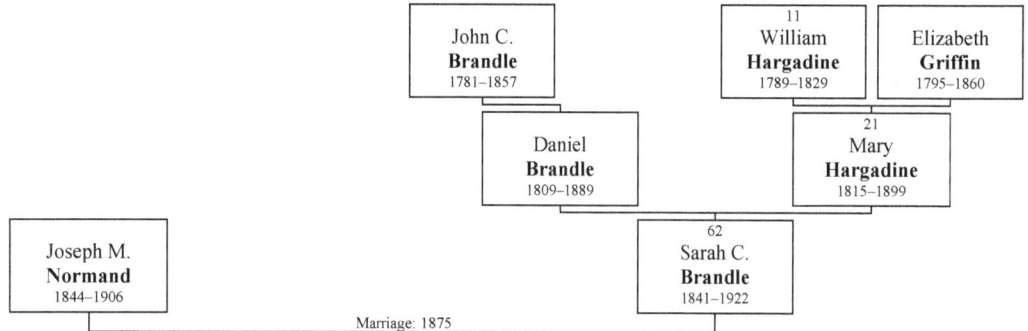

62.   **Sarah C. Brandle** was born in 1841 in Ohio, USA.[113] She was the daughter of Daniel Brandle and Mary Hargadine (21). She was also known as **Sallie**.

Sarah C. died in Springfield, Clark County, Ohio, on November 20, 1922, at the age of 81.[113] She was buried in Ferncliff Cemetery, Springfield, Clark County, Ohio, on November 22, 1922 (Find a Grave ID 58292798).[113]

At the age of 34, Sarah C. married **Joseph M. Normand** on Wednesday, February 10, 1875, when he was 30 years old.[113] Joseph M. was born in Brooklyn, Kings County, New York, on Sunday, September 08, 1844.[113]

He reached 62 years of age and died on December 24, 1906.[113] Joseph M. was buried on December 24, 1906, in Ferncliff Cemetery, Springfield, Clark County, Ohio.[113]

Family of Mary Brandle and Henry Beard

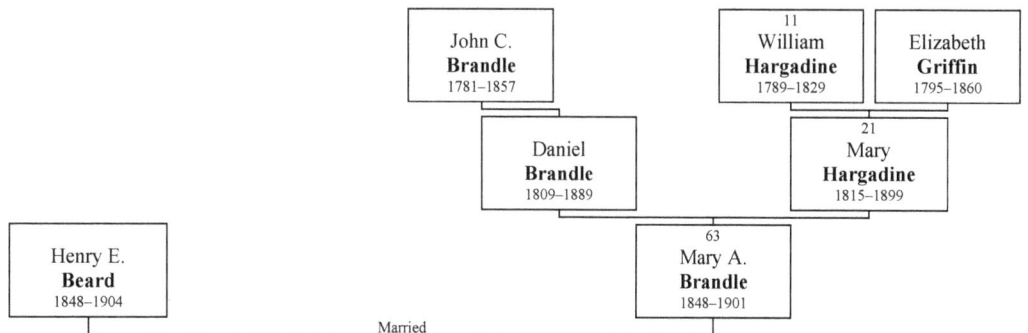

---

[113]   Ancestry.com, Public Member Trees (Provo, UT, USA, Ancestry.com Operations, Inc., 2006), Ancestry.com, Record for Sarah C. Brandle. https://search.ancestry.co.uk/cgi-bin/sse.dll?db=1030&h=232061998133&indiv=try.

63.   **Mary A. Brandle** was born in 1848. She was the daughter of Daniel Brandle and Mary Hargadine (21).

Mary A. died in 1901 at the age of 53. She was buried in Pleasant Hill Cemetery, New Moorefield, Clark County, Ohio (Find a Grave ID 6095633).

She married **Henry E. Beard**. Henry E. was born in Ohio, USA, in 1848.

He reached 56 years of age and died in 1904. Henry E. was buried in Pleasant Hill Cemetery, New Moorefield, Clark County, Ohio (Find a Grave ID 6095632).

Family of Elizabeth Hargadine and Caleb Luker

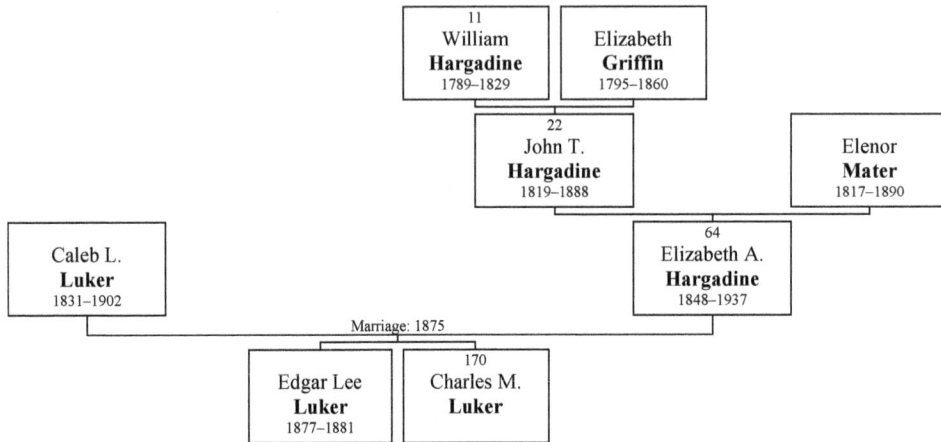

64.   **Elizabeth A. Hargadine** was born in July 1848 in Ohio, USA. She was the daughter of John T. Hargadine (22) and Elenor Mater.

Elizabeth A. died in California, USA, on August 24, 1937, at the age of 89.

Elizabeth A. married **Caleb L. Luker** on Saturday, March 13, 1875, in Miami County, Ohio. They had two sons.

Caleb L. was born in New Jersey, USA, in June 1831. He worked as an Auctioneer.

Caleb L. reached 71 years of age and died in Troy, Ashland County, Ohio, on December 15, 1902. He was buried in Casstown Cemetery, Casstown, Miami County, Ohio.

Sons of Elizabeth A. Hargadine and Caleb L. Luker:

         m   I. **Edgar Lee Luker** was born in Ohio, USA, on July 02, 1877. He died on February 21, 1881, at the age of 3. Edgar Lee was buried in Casstown Cemetery, Casstown, Miami County, Ohio.

+   170   m   II. **Charles M. Luker** was born in Ohio, USA.

Family of Mollie Hargadine and Samuel Martin

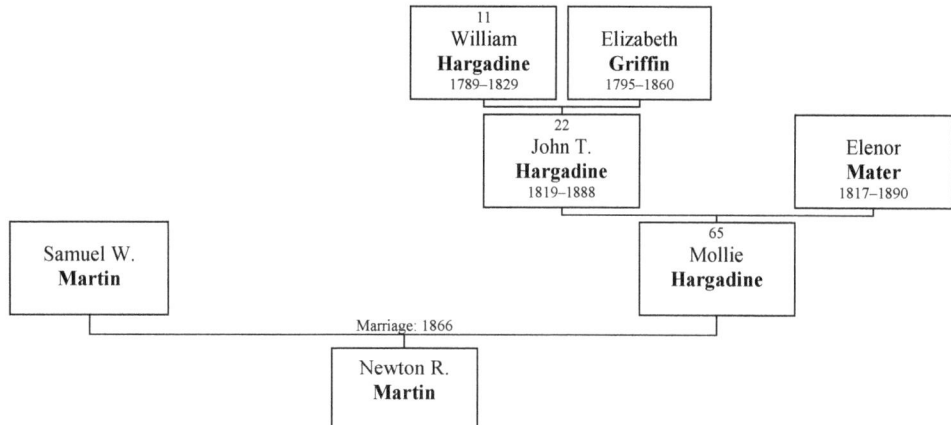

65.   **Mollie Hargadine.** She was the daughter of John T. Hargadine (22) and Elenor Mater. She was also known as **Mary**.

Mollie married **Samuel W. Martin** on Thursday, March 22, 1866, in Miami County, Ohio. They had one son.

Son of Mollie Hargadine and Samuel W. Martin:

      m   I. **Newton R. Martin**.

Family of Mary Hargadine and Joseph Coffman

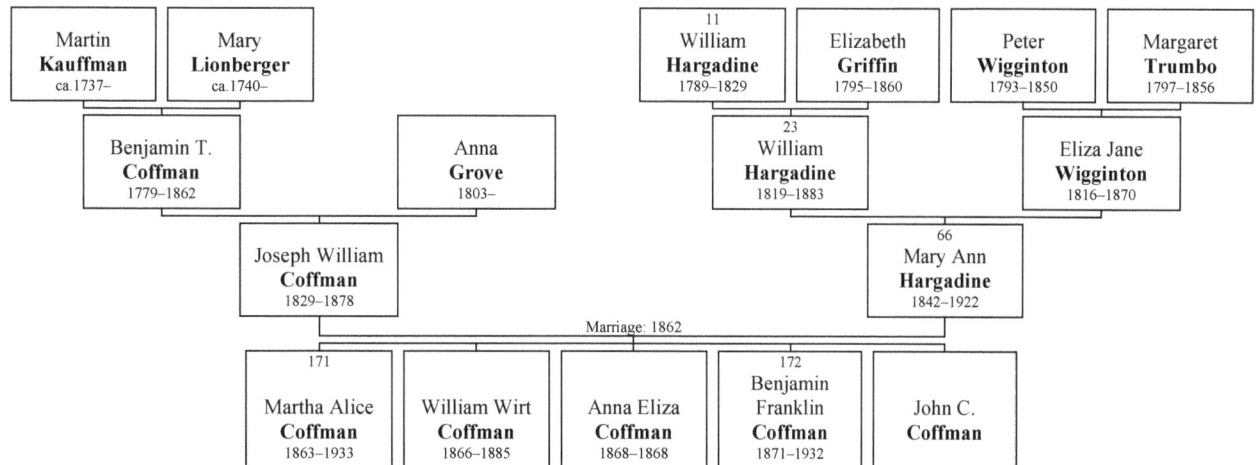

66.   **Mary Ann Hargadine** was born on Saturday, October 29, 1842, in Logan County, Illinois. She was the daughter of William Hargadine (23) and Eliza Jane Wigginton.

Mary Ann died in Holdrege, Phelps County, Nebraska, on July 24, 1922, at the age of 79. She was buried in Prairie Home Cemetery, Holdrege, Phelps County, Nebraska (Find a Grave ID 35771032).

At the age of 19, Mary Ann married **Joseph William Coffman** on Tuesday, March 18, 1862, in Lincoln, Logan County, Illinois, when he was 32 years old. They had five children.

Joseph William was born in Page County, Virginia, on Tuesday, March 31, 1829. He was the son of Benjamin T. Coffman and Anna Grove.

Joseph William reached 48 years of age and died in Lincoln, Logan County, Illinois, on January 13, 1878. His cause of death was cancerous tumor. Joseph William was buried in Lucas Chapel Cemetery, Lincoln, Logan County, Illinois (Find a Grave ID 74926142).

Children of Mary Ann Hargadine and Joseph William Coffman:

+ 171   f   I. **Martha Alice Coffman** was born in Lincoln, Logan County, Illinois, on February 28, 1863.[114, 115] She died in Holdrege, Phelps County, Nebraska, on April 14, 1933, at the age of 70.[114, 115] Martha Alice was buried in Prairie Home Cemetery, Holdrege, Phelps County, Nebraska (Find a Grave ID 35323785).[114, 115]

        m   II. **William Wirt Coffman** was born on March 24, 1866. He died in Logan County, Illinois, on February 24, 1885, at the age of 18. William Wirt was buried in Lucas Chapel Cemetery, Lincoln, Logan County, Illinois (Find a Grave ID 28899554).

        f   III. **Anna Eliza Coffman** was born on February 04, 1868. She died on February 15, 1868. Anna Eliza was buried in Lucas Chapel Cemetery, Lincoln, Logan County, Illinois (Find a Grave ID 80135473).

+ 172   m   IV. **Benjamin Franklin Coffman** was born on August 06, 1871. He died on June 26, 1932, at the age of 60. Benjamin Franklin was buried in Fairlawn Cemetery, Decatur, Macon County, Illinois (Find a Grave ID 64982460).

        m   V. **John C. Coffman**.

Family of Martha Hargadine and Lewis Ogle

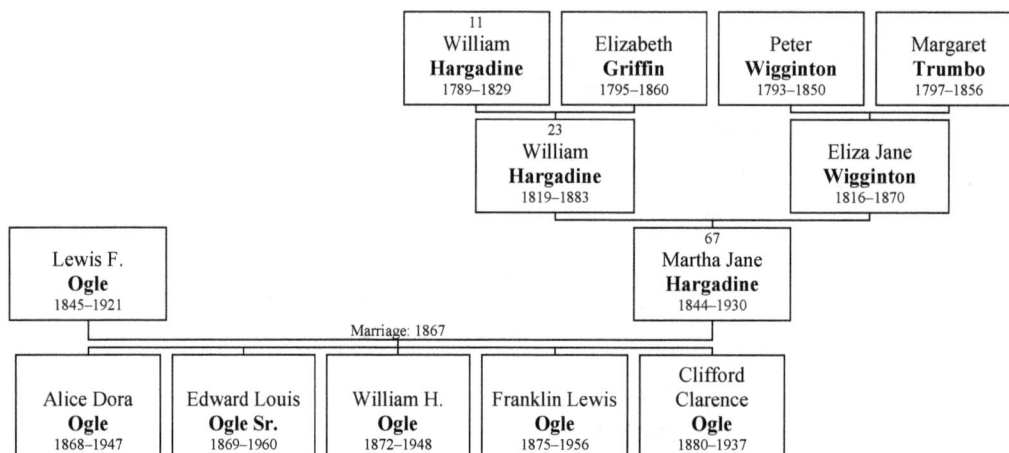

11 William **Hargadine** 1789–1829	Elizabeth **Griffin** 1795–1860	Peter **Wigginton** 1793–1850	Margaret **Trumbo** 1797–1856

23 William **Hargadine** 1819–1883	Eliza Jane **Wigginton** 1816–1870

Lewis F. **Ogle** 1845–1921	67 Martha Jane **Hargadine** 1844–1930

Marriage: 1867

Alice Dora **Ogle** 1868–1947	Edward Louis **Ogle Sr.** 1869–1960	William H. **Ogle** 1872–1948	Franklin Lewis **Ogle** 1875–1956	Clifford Clarence **Ogle** 1880–1937

67.   **Martha Jane Hargadine** was born on Tuesday, February 20, 1844, in Logan County, Illinois. She was the daughter of William Hargadine (23) and Eliza Jane Wigginton. She was also known as **Mattie**.

---

114   LDS Ancestral File.

115   Leffler.FTW, Date of Import: Jan 3, 2002.

Martha Jane died in Lincoln, Logan County, Illinois, on November 09, 1930, at the age of 86. She was buried in Old Union Cemetery, Lincoln, Logan County, Illinois (Find a Grave ID 166820433).

At the age of 23, Martha Jane married **Lewis F. Ogle** on Sunday, October 20, 1867, in Logan County, Illinois, when he was 22 years old. They had five children.

Lewis F. was born in Maryland, USA, on Sunday, March 30, 1845. He reached 75 years of age and died in Lincoln, Logan County, Illinois, on March 10, 1921. Lewis F. was buried in Old Union Cemetery, Lincoln, Logan County, Illinois (Find a Grave ID 166820450).

Children of Martha Jane Hargadine and Lewis F. Ogle:

f	I.	**Alice Dora Ogle** was born in Lincoln, Logan County, Illinois, on July 23, 1868. She died in Lincoln, Logan County, Illinois, on February 17, 1947, at the age of 78. Alice Dora was buried in Old Union Cemetery, Lincoln, Logan County, Illinois (Find a Grave ID 166820417).
m	II.	**Edward Louis Ogle Sr.** was born in Illinois, USA, on December 26, 1869. He died on September 24, 1960, at the age of 90. Edward Louis was buried in East Lawn Cemetery, Urbana, Champaign County, Illinois (Find a Grave ID 97656455).
m	III.	**William H. Ogle** was born in Illinois, USA, in May 1872. He died in Danville, Vermilion County, Illinois, in 1948 at the age of 75. William H. was buried in Old Union Cemetery, Lincoln, Logan County, Illinois (Find a Grave ID 166820404).
m	IV.	**Franklin Lewis Ogle** was born in Illinois, USA, on March 17, 1875. He died in Lincoln, Logan County, Illinois, on October 08, 1956, at the age of 81. Franklin Lewis was buried in Holy Cross Cemetery, Lincoln, Logan County, Illinois (Find a Grave ID 218079103).
m	V.	**Clifford Clarence Ogle** was born in Illinois, USA, on October 24, 1880. He died in Lincoln, Logan County, Illinois, on May 20, 1937, at the age of 56. Clifford Clarence was buried in Old Union Cemetery, Lincoln, Logan County, Illinois (Find a Grave ID 58291309).

Family of Dorothea Hargadine and John Merrilees

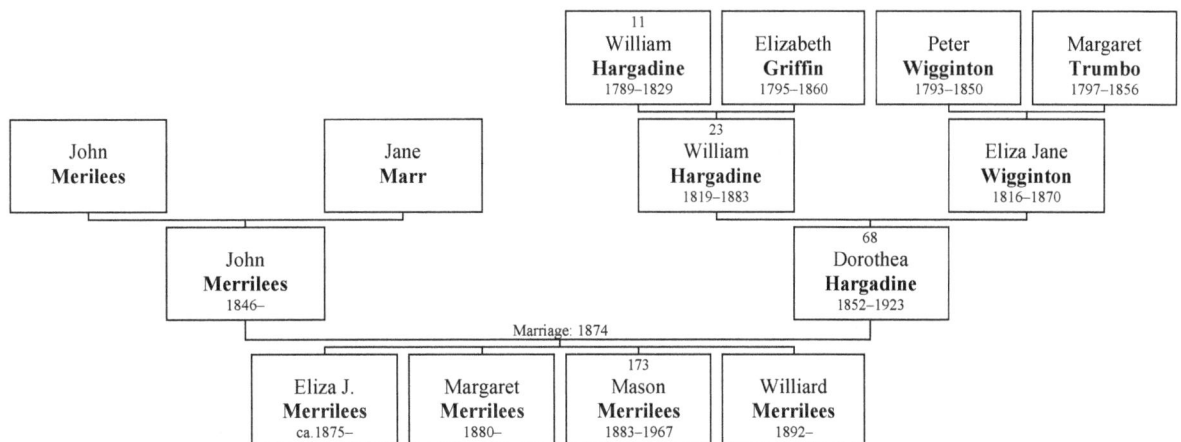

68. **Dorothea Hargadine** was born on Sunday, July 04, 1852, in Logan County, Illinois. She was the daughter of William Hargadine (23) and Eliza Jane Wigginton.

Dorothea died on February 20, 1923, at the age of 70.

At the age of 22, Dorothea married **John Merrilees** on Saturday, August 01, 1874, in Logan County, Illinois, when he was 27 years old. They had four children.

John was born in Edinburgh, Scotland, on Tuesday, October 20, 1846. He was the son of John Merilees and Jane Marr.

He worked as a Carpenter.

Children of Dorothea Hargadine and John Merrilees:

	f	I.	**Eliza J. Merrilees** was born about 1875.
	f	II.	**Margaret Merrilees** was born in June 1880.
+ 173	f	III.	**Mason Merrilees** was born on February 17, 1883. She died in Lincoln, Logan County, Illinois, in June 1967 at the age of 84.
	m	IV.	**Williard Merrilees** was born in Illinois, USA, in March 1892.

Family of Charles Hargadine and Carrie Casey

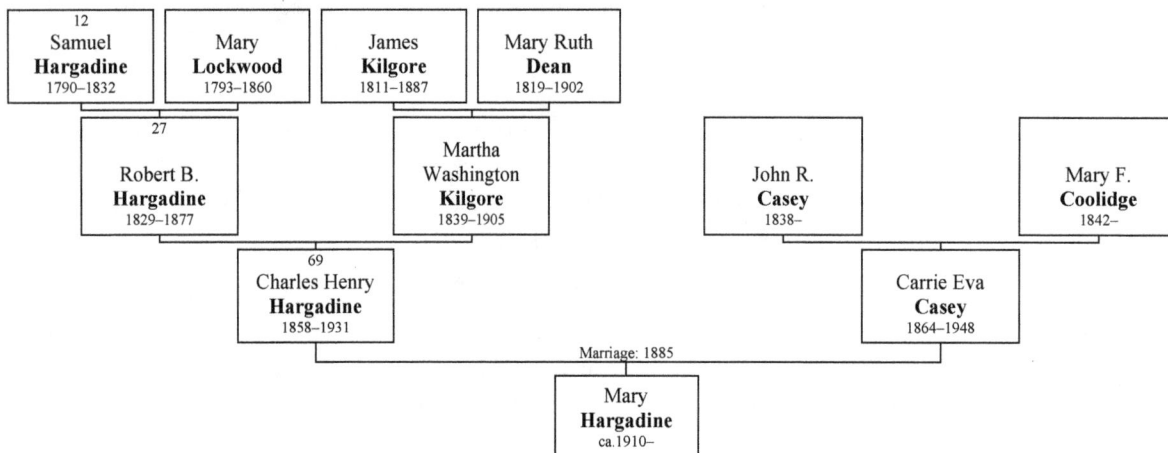

```
┌──────────┬──────────┬──────────┬──────────┐
│    12    │          │          │          │
│  Samuel  │   Mary   │  James   │ Mary Ruth│
│Hargadine │ Lockwood │  Kilgore │   Dean   │
│1790–1832 │1793–1860 │1811–1887 │1819–1902 │
└────┬─────┴─────┬────┴────┬─────┴────┬─────┘
  ┌──┴───┐    ┌──┴────┐                   
  │  27  │    │Martha │   ┌────────┐  ┌────────┐
  │Robert B. │ │Washington││John R. │  │Mary F. │
  │Hargadine │ │ Kilgore ││ Casey  │  │Coolidge│
  │1829–1877 │ │1839–1905││ 1838–  │  │ 1842–  │
  └────┬─────┘ └───┬─────┘└───┬────┘  └───┬────┘
     ┌──┴──┐           ┌──────┴──────┐
     │  69 │           │ Carrie Eva  │
     │Charles Henry│   │   Casey     │
     │Hargadine │      │  1864–1948  │
     │1858–1931 │      └──────┬──────┘
     └────┬─────┘             
       Marriage: 1885
          ┌──────────┐
          │   Mary   │
          │Hargadine │
          │ ca.1910– │
          └──────────┘
```

69. **Charles Henry Hargadine** was born on Thursday, February 11, 1858. He was the son of Robert B. Hargadine (27) and Martha Washington Kilgore.

Charles Henry died in Santa Monica, Los Angeles County, California, in 1931 at the age of 72. He was buried in Hargadine Cemetery, Ashland, Jackson County, Oregon (Find a Grave ID 11178322).

At the age of 27, Charles Henry married **Carrie Eva Casey** on Wednesday, May 20, 1885, in Ashland, Jackson County, Oregon, when she was 20 years old. They had one daughter.

Carrie Eva was born in Iowa, USA, on Friday, November 11, 1864. She was the daughter of John R. Casey and Mary F. Coolidge.

Carrie Eva reached 83 years of age and died in Los Angeles County, California, on September 03, 1948.

Daughter of Charles Henry Hargadine and Carrie Eva Casey:

    f   I. **Mary Hargadine** was born about 1910.

Family of Marietta Hargadine and Andrew Kyle

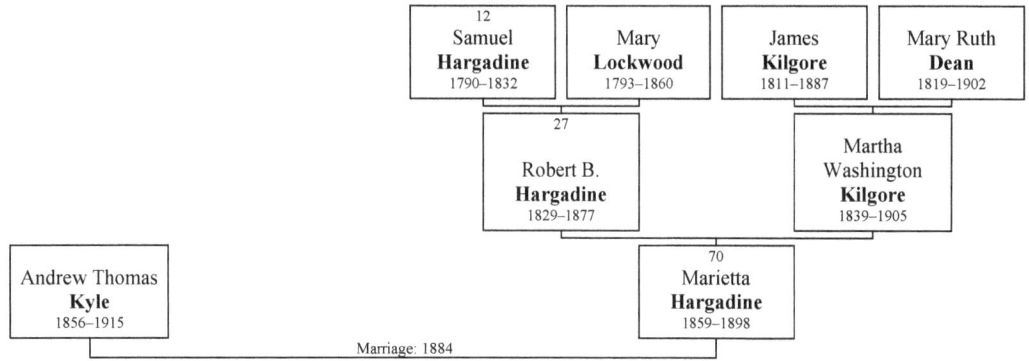

70.   **Marietta Hargadine** was born on Saturday, July 02, 1859, in Oregon, USA. She was the daughter of Robert B. Hargadine (27) and Martha Washington Kilgore. She was also known as **Etta**.

Marietta died in Ashland, Jackson County, Oregon, on June 21, 1898, at the age of 38. She was buried in Hargadine Cemetery, Ashland, Jackson County, Oregon (Find a Grave ID 11178341).

At the age of 25, Marietta married **Andrew Thomas Kyle** on Wednesday, September 17, 1884, in Ashland, Jackson County, Oregon, when he was 27 years old. Andrew Thomas was born in Kansas, USA, on Thursday, September 25, 1856.

He reached 58 years of age and died in Great Falls, Cascade County, Montana, on January 18, 1915. Andrew Thomas was buried in Old Highland Cemetery, Great Falls, Cascade County, Montana (Find a Grave ID 37180987).

Family of Elizabeth Hargadine and Alexander Ogilvie

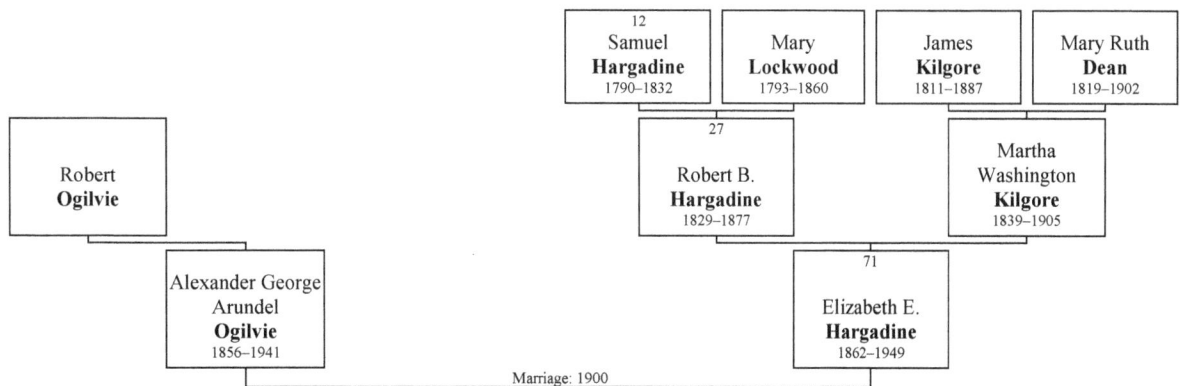

71.   **Elizabeth E. Hargadine** was born on Saturday, August 02, 1862, in Ashland, Jackson County, Oregon. She was the daughter of Robert B. Hargadine (27) and Martha Washington Kilgore. She was also known as **Lizzie**.

Elizabeth E. died in Ashland, Jackson County, Oregon, on August 06, 1949, at the age of 87. She was cremated—Grants Pass, Oregon, on August 09, 1949 (Find a Grave ID 11178327).

Elizabeth E. married **Alexander George Arundel Ogilvie** in 1900 in Ashland, Jackson County, Oregon. Alexander George Arundel was born in Devonshire, England, on Monday, September 01, 1856. He was the son of Robert Ogilvie.

Alexander George Arundel reached 85 years of age and died in Ashland, Jackson County, Oregon, on October 01, 1941. He was cremated—Grants Pass, Oregon (Find a Grave ID 160243684).

George Hargadine

72.   **George Robert Hargadine** was born on Saturday, September 09, 1865, in Ashland, Jackson County, Oregon. He was the son of Robert B. Hargadine (27) and Martha Washington Kilgore.

George Robert died in Ashland, Jackson County, Oregon, on April 02, 1941, at the age of 75. He was buried in Hargadine Cemetery, Ashland, Jackson County, Oregon, on April 04, 1941 (Find a Grave ID 23304338).

Marriages with Allie Averil and Beatrice Baker (Page 117) are known.

Family of George Hargadine and Allie Averil

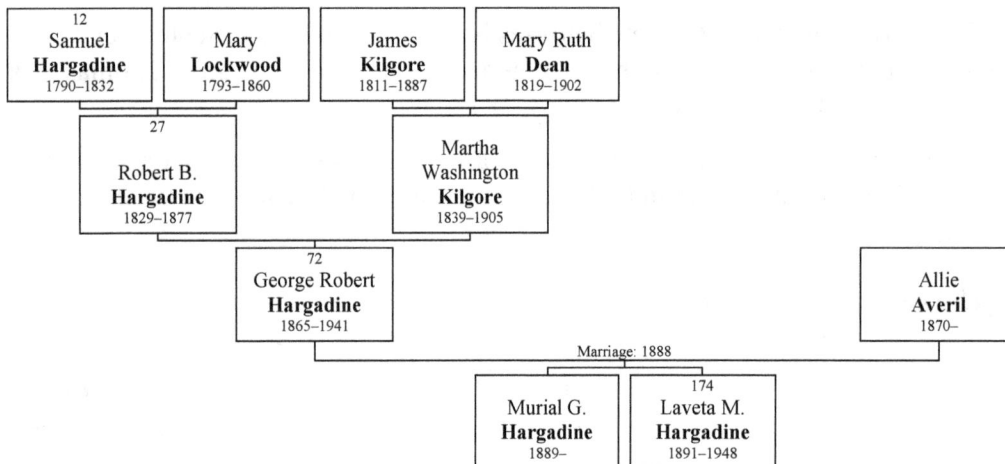

	12					
Samuel **Hargadine** 1790–1832	Mary **Lockwood** 1793–1860	James **Kilgore** 1811–1887	Mary Ruth **Dean** 1819–1902			

27
Robert B. **Hargadine** 1829–1877

Martha Washington **Kilgore** 1839–1905

72
George Robert **Hargadine** 1865–1941

Allie **Averil** 1870–

Marriage: 1888

174
Murial G. **Hargadine** 1889–

Laveta M. **Hargadine** 1891–1948

Here are the details about **George Robert Hargadine's** first marriage, with Allie Averil. You can read more about George Robert on page 116.

George Robert Hargadine married **Allie Averil** on Friday, November 16, 1888. They had two daughters.

Allie was born in Minnesota, USA, in 1870.[116]

---

[116]   1900 Oregon, Jackson County, East Ashland Precinct - June 4, ED# 93 Sheet #4B.

Daughters of George Robert Hargadine and Allie Averil:

| | f | | I. | **Murial G. Hargadine** was born on December 08, 1889. |

+   174   f   II. **Laveta M. Hargadine** was born in Oregon, USA, on March 24, 1891. She died in San Bernardino, San Bernardino County, California, on December 17, 1948, at the age of 57.

Family of George Hargadine and Beatrice Baker

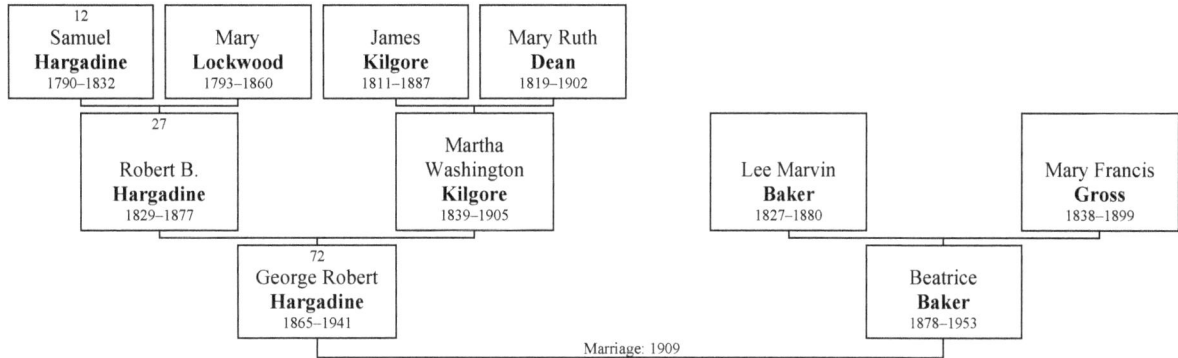

Here are the details about **George Robert Hargadine's** second marriage, with Beatrice Baker. You can read more about George Robert on page 116.

George Robert Hargadine married **Beatrice Baker** in September 1909. Beatrice was born in Oregon, USA, in 1878. She was the daughter of Lee Marvin Baker and Mary Francis Gross.

Beatrice reached 75 years of age and died in Jackson County, Oregon, on October 19, 1953. She was buried in Hargadine Cemetery, Ashland, Jackson County, Oregon (Find a Grave ID 23304290).

Family of Robert Hargadine and Mary Carter

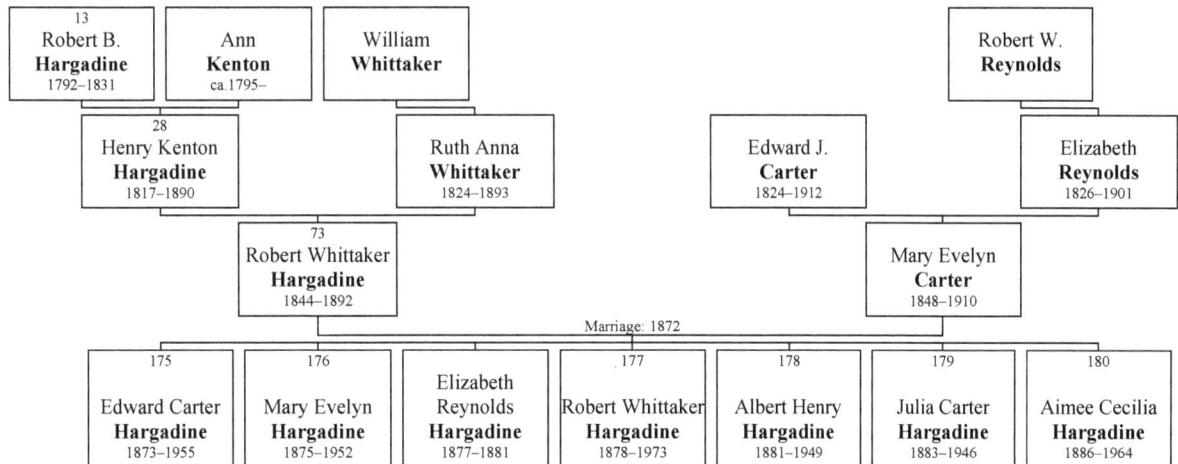

73.   **Dr. Robert Whittaker Hargadine** was born on Sunday, April 28, 1844, in Canterbury, Kent County, Delaware. He was the son of Henry Kenton Hargadine (28) and Ruth Anna Whittaker.

Robert Whittaker worked as a medical doctor. He died in Felton, Kent County, Delaware, on August 31, 1892, at the age of 48. Robert Whittaker was buried in Holy Cross Catholic Cemetery, Dover, Kent County, Delaware (Find a Grave ID 6345526).

More facts and events for Robert Whittaker Hargadine:

Individual Note: Medical Doctor

At the age of 28, Robert Whittaker married **Mary Evelyn Carter** on Thursday, October 31, 1872, when she was 24 years old. They had seven children.

Mary Evelyn was born in Henderson, Caroline County, Maryland, on Thursday, May 18, 1848. She was the daughter of Edward J. Carter and Elizabeth Reynolds.

After the death of Dr. Hargadine, Mary Carter was appointed postmaster of Felton by President Grover Cleveland. Mary Evelyn reached 62 years of age and died at St. Agnes Hospital in Philadelphia, Pennsylvania, on July 29, 1910. Her cause of death was cerebral hemorrhage. Mary Evelyn was buried on July 31, 1910, in Holy Cross Catholic Cemetery, Dover, Kent County, Delaware (Find a Grave ID 6345535).

Children of Robert Whittaker Hargadine and Mary Evelyn Carter:

+ 175   m   I. **Edward Carter Hargadine** was born in Felton, Kent County, Delaware, on November 22, 1873.[117] He died in Ramsey County, Minnesota, on April 29, 1955, at the age of 81.

+ 176   f   II. **Mary Evelyn Hargadine** was born in Felton, Kent County, Delaware, on September 12, 1875. She died in Great Falls, Cascade County, Montana, on May 09, 1952, at the age of 76.[118] Mary Evelyn was buried in Highland Cemetery, Great Falls, Cascade County, Montana (Find a Grave ID 9510564).

         f   III. **Elizabeth Reynolds Hargadine** was born on January 31, 1877. The nature of the relationship to the parents is marked as related.

                  She died on April 23, 1881, at the age of 4. Elizabeth Reynolds was buried in Holy Cross Catholic Cemetery, Dover, Kent County, Delaware (Find a Grave ID 6345517).

+ 177   m   IV. **Robert Whittaker Hargadine** was born in Felton, Kent County, Delaware, on December 17, 1878. He died in St. Paul, Ramsey County, Minnesota, in January 1973 at the age of 94.

+ 178   m   V. **Albert Henry Hargadine** was born in Felton, Kent County, Delaware, on October 05, 1881. He died in Great Falls, Cascade County, Montana, on November 23, 1949, at the age of 68. Albert Henry was buried in Holy Cross Catholic Cemetery, Dover, Kent County, Delaware, on November 26, 1949 (Find a Grave ID 6345492).

---

[117]   Death Certificate, CertID# 1955-MN-026578.
[118]   Montana Death Index, 1907-1953.

+   179   f   VI. **Julia Carter Hargadine** was born in Felton, Kent County, Delaware, on August 12, 1883. She died in Pheonix, Maricopa County, Arizona, on November 17, 1946, at the age of 63. Julia Carter was buried in Saint Francis Catholic Cemetery, Phoenix, Maricopa County, Arizona, on November 21, 1946 (Find a Grave ID 70526028).

+   180   f   VII. **Aimee Cecilia Hargadine** was born in Delaware, USA, on March 14, 1886. She died in Glasgow, Valley County, Montana, on January 02, 1964, at the age of 77. Aimee Cecilia was buried in Highland Cemetery, Glasgow, Valley County, Montana (Find a Grave ID 210159324).

Family of Mary Hargadine and Walter Burton

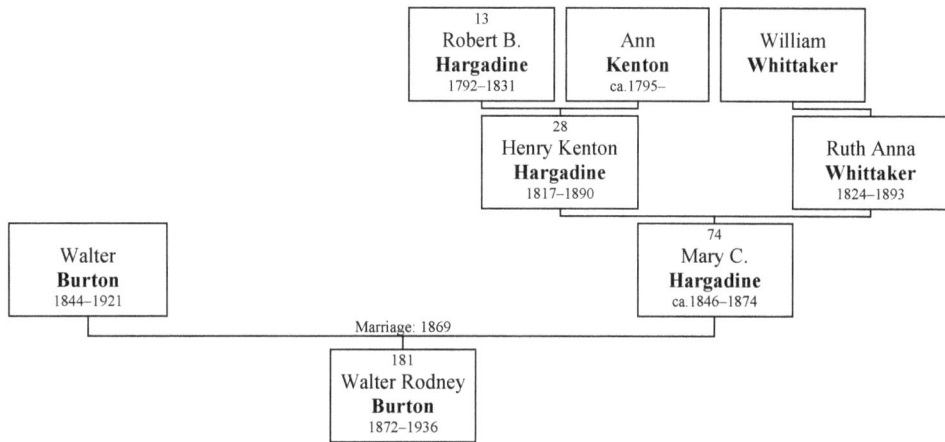

74.   **Mary C. Hargadine** was born about 1846 in Delaware, USA. She was the daughter of Henry Kenton Hargadine (28) and Ruth Anna Whittaker.

Mary C. died on August 07, 1874, at the age of 28. She was buried in Saint Peter's Episcopal Churchyard, Lewes, Sussex County, Delaware (Find a Grave ID 7713162).

At the age of 23, Mary C. married **Walter Burton** on Friday, November 05, 1869, when he was 24 years old. They had one son.

Walter was born in Lewes, Sussex County, Delaware, on Monday, November 18, 1844. He worked as a Was the owner of the Hotel Henlopen and Willard Hotel in Washington.

Walter reached 76 years of age and died in Rehoboth Beach, Sussex County, Delaware, on September 12, 1921. He was buried in Saint Peter's Episcopal Churchyard, Lewes, Sussex County, Delaware (Find a Grave ID 7716668).

Son of Mary C. Hargadine and Walter Burton:

+   181   m   I. **Walter Rodney Burton** was born in 1872. He died in 1936 at the age of 64. Walter Rodney was buried in Saint Peter's Episcopal Churchyard, Lewes, Sussex County, Delaware (Find a Grave ID 7716670).

Family of Anna Hargadine and William Dill

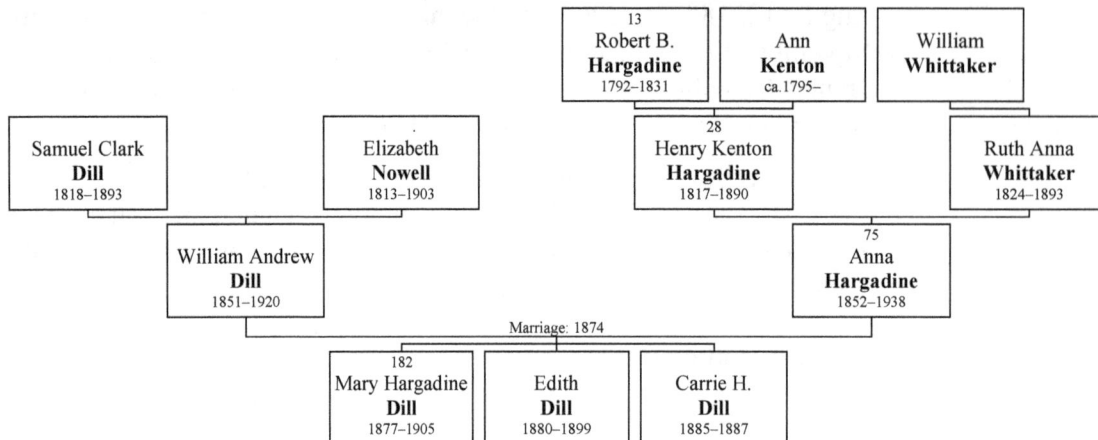

| | 13
Robert B.
Hargadine
1792–1831 | Ann
Kenton
ca.1795– | William
Whittaker |

Samuel Clark **Dill** 1818–1893
Elizabeth **Nowell** 1813–1903
28 Henry Kenton **Hargadine** 1817–1890
Ruth Anna **Whittaker** 1824–1893

William Andrew **Dill** 1851–1920
75 Anna **Hargadine** 1852–1938

Marriage: 1874

182 Mary Hargadine **Dill** 1877–1905
Edith **Dill** 1880–1899
Carrie H. **Dill** 1885–1887

75. **Anna Hargadine** was born on Wednesday, August 25, 1852, in Kent County, Delaware. She was the daughter of Henry Kenton Hargadine (28) and Ruth Anna Whittaker. She was also known as **Annie**.

Anna died in Viola, Kent County, Delaware, on July 05, 1938, at the age of 85. She was buried in Odd Fellows Cemetery, Camden, Kent County, Delaware (Find a Grave ID 45752463).

Anna married **William Andrew Dill** in 1874. They had three daughters.

William Andrew was born in Kent County, Delaware, on Tuesday, February 18, 1851. He was the son of Samuel Clark Dill and Elizabeth Nowell.

William Andrew reached 68 years of age and died in Viola, Kent County, Delaware, on February 11, 1920. He was buried in Odd Fellows Cemetery, Camden, Kent County, Delaware (Find a Grave ID 45752431).

Daughters of Anna Hargadine and William Andrew Dill:

+ 182   f   I. **Mary Hargadine Dill** was born in Kent County, Delaware, on April 24, 1877. She died in Greenwood, Sussex County, Delaware, on January 20, 1905, at the age of 27. Mary Hargadine was buried in Odd Fellows Cemetery, Camden, Kent County, Delaware (Find a Grave ID 45752389).

          f   II. **Edith Dill** was born in Kent County, Delaware, on February 14, 1880. She died in Viola, Kent County, Delaware, on March 05, 1899, at the age of 19. Edith was buried in Odd Fellows Cemetery, Camden, Kent County, Delaware (Find a Grave ID 45752552).

          f   III. **Carrie H. Dill** was born in Kent County, Delaware, on October 01, 1885. She died in Kent County, Delaware, on March 11, 1887, at the age of 1. Carrie H. was buried in Odd Fellows Cemetery, Camden, Kent County, Delaware (Find a Grave ID 45752577).

Family of Henry Hargadine and Laura Jones

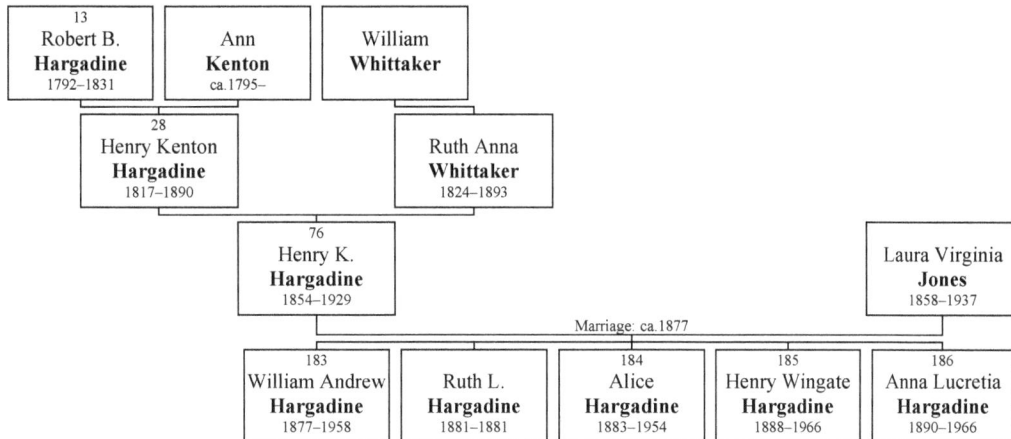

76. **Henry K. Hargadine** was born on Saturday, December 16, 1854, in Viola, Kent County, Delaware. He was the son of Henry Kenton Hargadine (28) and Ruth Anna Whittaker.

Henry K. worked as a Farmer near Canterbury. He died in Woodside, Kent County, Delaware, on October 17, 1929, at the age of 74. His cause of death was chronic myocarditis. He was buried in Barratts Chapel Cemetery, Frederica, Kent County, Delaware, on October 19, 1929 (Find a Grave ID 29366382).

Henry K. married **Laura Virginia Jones** about 1877 in Bridgeville, Sussex County, Delaware. They had five children.

Laura Virginia was born in Viola, Kent County, Delaware, in May 1858. She reached 78 years of age and died in 1937. Laura Virginia was buried in Barratts Chapel Cemetery, Frederica, Kent County, Delaware (Find a Grave ID 29366391).

Children of Henry K. Hargadine and Laura Virginia Jones:

+ 183   m   I. **William Andrew Hargadine** was born in Delaware, USA, on November 08, 1877. He died in 1958 at the age of 80. William Andrew was buried in Barratts Chapel Cemetery, Frederica, Kent County, Delaware (Find a Grave ID 29366398).

            f   II. **Ruth L. Hargadine** was born on July 12, 1881. She died on July 21, 1881. Ruth L. was buried in Barratts Chapel Cemetery, Frederica, Kent County, Delaware (Find a Grave ID 29366395).

+ 184   f   III. **Alice Hargadine** was born in Viola, Kent County, Delaware, on October 24, 1883. She died on September 22, 1954, at the age of 70. Alice was buried in Lakeside Cemetery, Dover, Kent County, Delaware (Find a Grave ID 7802648).

+ 185   m   IV. **Henry Wingate Hargadine** was born in Woodside, Kent County, Delaware, on October 08, 1888. He died on October 01, 1966, at the age of 77. Henry Wingate was buried in Barratts Chapel Cemetery, Frederica, Kent County, Delaware (Find a Grave ID 29366385).

+ 186   f   V. **Anna Lucretia Hargadine** was born in Delaware, USA, on June 04, 1890. She died in Seaford, Sussex County, Delaware, on July 04, 1966, at the age of 76. Anna Lucretia was buried in Odd Fellows Cemetery, Seaford, Sussex County, Delaware, on July 06, 1966 (Find a Grave ID 86288948).

Family of Emma Hargadine and Charles Barger

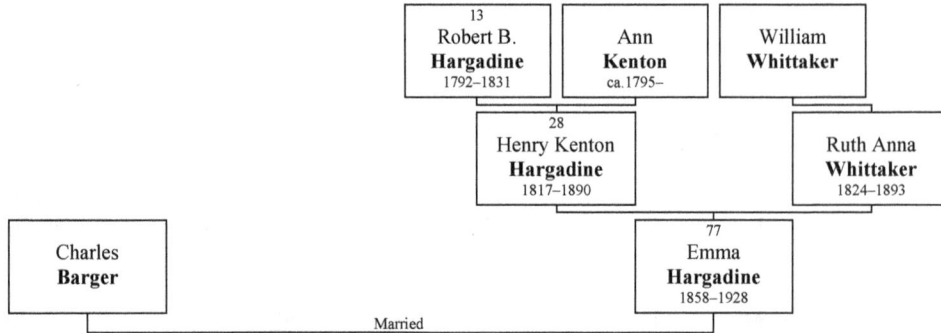

77.   **Emma Hargadine** was born on Wednesday, October 27, 1858, in Delaware, USA. She was the daughter of Henry Kenton Hargadine (28) and Ruth Anna Whittaker.

Emma died in Kent County, Delaware, on February 08, 1928, at the age of 69. She was buried in Canterbury Cemetery, Canterbury, Kent County, Delaware, on February 10, 1928 (Find a Grave ID 5091580).

She married **Charles Barger**.

Family of Annie Hargadine and William Thomson

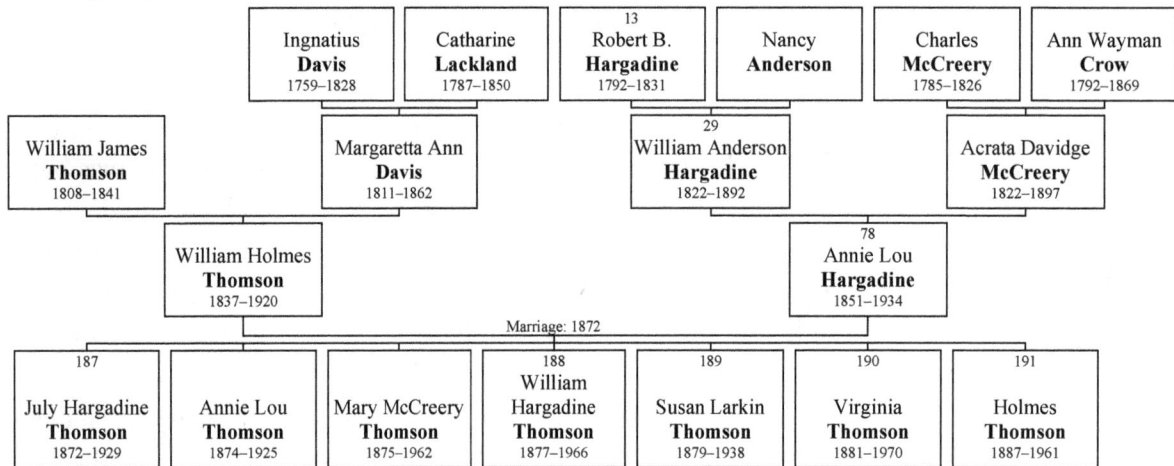

78.   **Annie Lou Hargadine** was born on Sunday, September 07, 1851, in Saint Louis, Saint Louis County, Missouri. She was the daughter of William Anderson Hargadine (29) and Acrata Davidge McCreery.

Annie Lou died in Saint Louis, Saint Louis County, Missouri, on July 25, 1934, at the age of 82. She was buried in Bellefontaine Cemetery, Saint Louis, St. Louis City, Missouri (Find a Grave ID 99158870).

At the age of 20, Annie Lou married **William Holmes Thomson** on Tuesday, January 23, 1872, when he was 34 years old. They had seven children.

William Holmes was born in Frederick, Frederick County, Maryland, on Sunday, April 16, 1837. He was the son of William James Thomson and Margaretta Ann Davis.

William Holmes reached 83 years of age and died in Saint Louis, Saint Louis County, Missouri, on June 23, 1920. He was buried in Bellefontaine Cemetery, Saint Louis, St. Louis City, Missouri (Find a Grave ID 136699259).

Children of Annie Lou Hargadine and William Holmes Thomson:

+ 187 f I. **July Hargadine Thomson** was born in Saint Louis, Saint Louis County, Missouri, on December 09, 1872. She died in Saint Louis, Saint Louis County, Missouri, on October 16, 1929, at the age of 56. July Hargadine was buried in Bellefontaine Cemetery, Saint Louis, St. Louis City, Missouri (Find a Grave ID 99059481).

f II. **Annie Lou Thomson** was born in Saint Louis, Saint Louis County, Missouri, on July 03, 1874. She was also known as **Nannie**.

Annie Lou died in Saint Louis, Saint Louis County, Missouri, on February 06, 1925, at the age of 50. She was buried in Bellefontaine Cemetery, Saint Louis, St. Louis City, Missouri (Find a Grave ID 99157183).

f III. **Mary McCreery Thomson** was born in Saint Louis, Saint Louis County, Missouri, on December 24, 1875. She died in Saint Louis, Saint Louis County, Missouri, on January 02, 1962, at the age of 86. Mary McCreery was buried in Bellefontaine Cemetery, Saint Louis, St. Louis City, Missouri (Find a Grave ID 99156556).

More facts and events for Mary McCreery Thomson:

Individual Note: DAR ID # 25762

+ 188 m IV. **William Hargadine Thomson** was born in Saint Louis, Saint Louis County, Missouri, on July 05, 1877. He died in Dallas, Dallas County, Texas, on October 18, 1966, at the age of 89. William Hargadine was buried in Sparkman Hillcrest Memorial Park, Dallas, Dallas County, Texas (Find a Grave ID 170461505).

+ 189 f V. **Susan Larkin Thomson** was born in Saint Louis, Saint Louis County, Missouri, on June 20, 1879. She died in El Paso, El Paso County, Texas, on August 10, 1938, at the age of 59. Susan Larkin was buried in Arlington National Cemetery, Arlington, Arlington County, Virginia (Find a Grave ID 49171749).

+ 190 f VI. **Virginia Thomson** was born in Saint Louis, Saint Louis County, Missouri, on January 11, 1881. She died in Saint Louis, Saint Louis County, Missouri, in February 1970 at the age of 89. Virginia was buried in Bellefontaine Cemetery, Saint Louis, St. Louis City, Missouri (Find a Grave ID 99078737).

+   191   f   VII. **Holmes Thomson** was born on November 06, 1887. She died on May 13, 1961, at the age of 73. Holmes was buried in Bellefontaine Cemetery, Saint Louis, St. Louis City, Missouri (Find a Grave ID 99077730).

Family of Julia Hargadine and Edward Glasgow

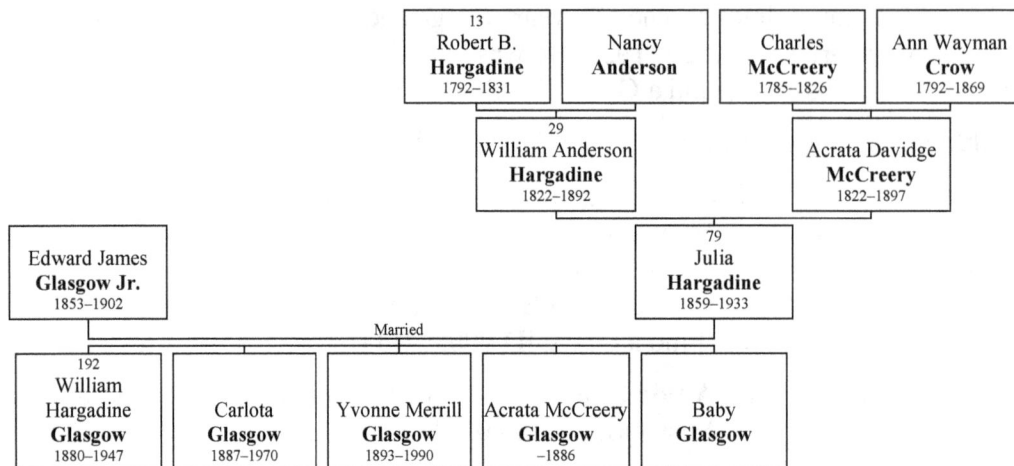

79.   **Julia Hargadine** was born on Friday, August 12, 1859, in Missouri, USA. She was the daughter of William Anderson Hargadine (29) and Acrata Davidge McCreery.

Julia died on June 14, 1933, at the age of 73. She was buried in Bellefontaine Cemetery, Saint Louis, St. Louis City, Missouri (Find a Grave ID 99080321).

She married **Edward James Glasgow Jr.** They had five children.

Edward James was born in Missouri, USA, on Sunday, March 27, 1853. He reached 49 years of age and died on May 10, 1902. Edward James was buried in Bellefontaine Cemetery, Saint Louis, St. Louis City, Missouri (Find a Grave ID 99080214).

Children of Julia Hargadine and Edward James Glasgow Jr.:

+   192   m   I. **William Hargadine Glasgow** was born in Saint Louis, Saint Louis County, Missouri, on November 09, 1880. He died on June 21, 1947, at the age of 66. William Hargadine was buried in Bellefontaine Cemetery, Saint Louis, St. Louis City, Missouri (Find a Grave ID 99080462).

        f   II. **Carlota Glasgow** was born on June 21, 1887. She died on April 11, 1970, at the age of 82. Carlota was buried in Bellefontaine Cemetery, Saint Louis, St. Louis City, Missouri (Find a Grave ID 99078812).

        f   III. **Yvonne Merrill Glasgow** was born on August 17, 1893. She died on September 10, 1990, at the age of 97. Yvonne Merrill was buried in Bellefontaine Cemetery, Saint Louis, St. Louis City, Missouri (Find a Grave ID 147356896).

        f   IV. **Acrata McCreery Glasgow**. Acrata McCreery died on December 15, 1886. She was buried in Bellefontaine Cemetery, Saint Louis, St. Louis City, Missouri (Find a Grave ID 147356497).

V. **Baby Glasgow**. Baby was buried in Bellefontaine Cemetery, Saint Louis, St. Louis City, Missouri, on December 02, 1890.

Family of Mary Hargadine and Otto Von Schrader

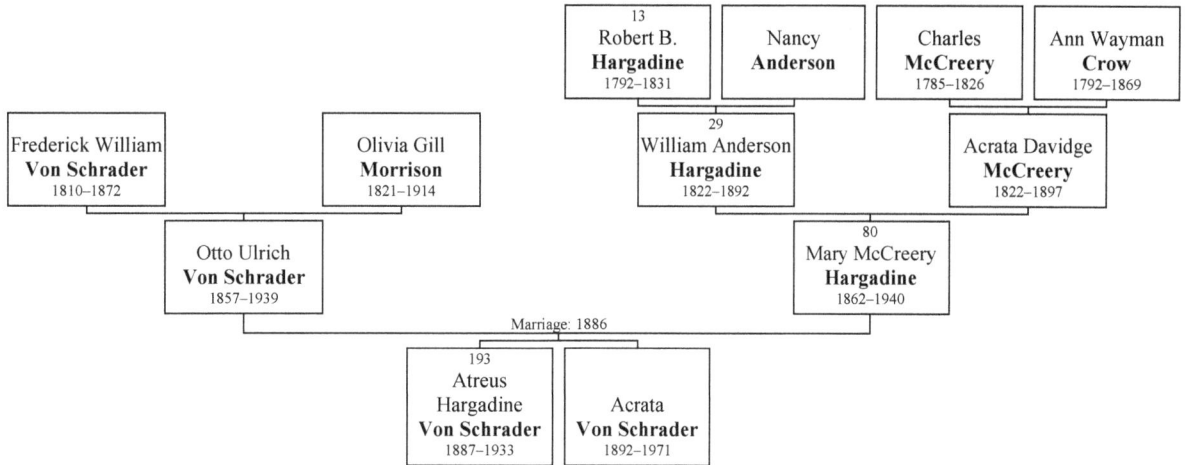

80. **Mary McCreery Hargadine** was born on Friday, April 04, 1862, in Saint Louis, Saint Louis County, Missouri. She was the daughter of William Anderson Hargadine (29) and Acrata Davidge McCreery.

Mary McCreery died in Washington D.C. on March 28, 1940, at the age of 77. She was buried in Bellefontaine Cemetery, Saint Louis, St. Louis City, Missouri, on April 03, 1940 (Find a Grave ID 99058156).

At the age of 24, Mary McCreery married **Otto Ulrich Von Schrader** on Wednesday, June 02, 1886, when he was 29 years old. They had two children.

Otto Ulrich was born in Belleville, St. Clair County, Illinois, on Friday, May 08, 1857. He was the son of Frederick William Von Schrader and Olivia Gill Morrison.

Otto Ulrich reached 82 years of age and died in Washington, District of Columbia, USA, on December 06, 1939. He was buried in Bellefontaine Cemetery, Saint Louis, St. Louis City, Missouri (Find a Grave ID 99058514).

Children of Mary McCreery Hargadine and Otto Ulrich Von Schrader:

+ 193   m   I. **Atreus Hargadine Von Schrader** was born on November 06, 1887. He died on October 06, 1933, at the age of 45. Atreus Hargadine was buried in Bellefontaine Cemetery, Saint Louis, St. Louis City, Missouri (Find a Grave ID 99079007).

     f   II. **Acrata Von Schrader** was born in Missouri, USA, in May 1892. She died in October 1971 at the age of 79. Acrata was buried in Bellefontaine Cemetery, Saint Louis, St. Louis City, Missouri (Find a Grave ID 172163789).

Sarah Wright

81. **Sarah Elizabeth Wright** was born on Friday, March 17, 1843. She was the daughter of Robert B. Wright and Julia Ann Hargadine (30).

Sarah Elizabeth died in New Castle, New Castle County, Delaware, on April 05, 1916, at the age of 73. She was buried in Dover, Kent County, Delaware, on May 08, 1916.

Marriages with John H. Boggs and William Nobel Hall (Page 127) are known.

Family of Sarah Wright and John Boggs

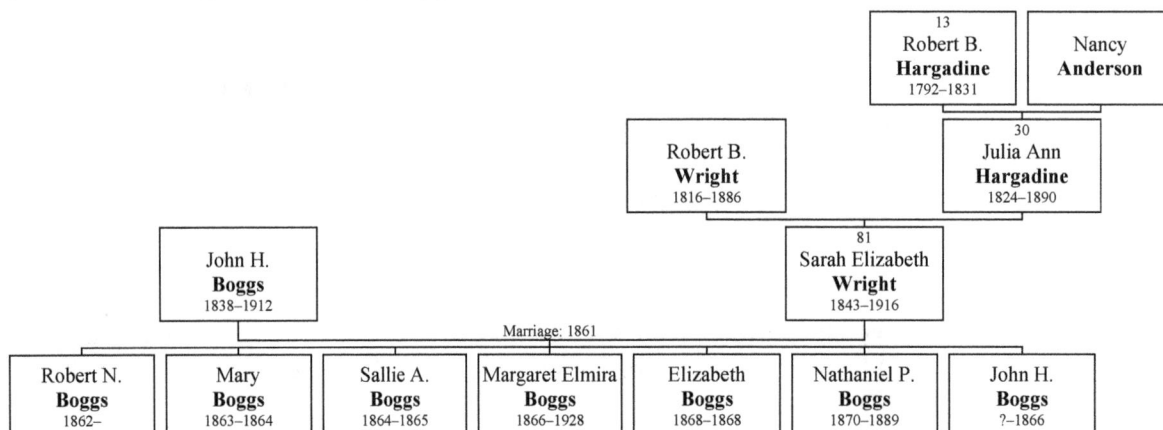

Here are the details about **Sarah Elizabeth Wright's** first marriage, with John H. Boggs. You can read more about Sarah Elizabeth on page 126.

Sarah Elizabeth Wright married **John H. Boggs** on Tuesday, June 25, 1861, in Delaware, USA. They had seven children.

John H. was born in 1838. He reached 74 years of age and died in 1912. John H. was buried in Ewells Methodist Church Cemetery, Clayton, Kent County, Delaware (Find a Grave ID 7567546).

Children of Sarah Elizabeth Wright and John H. Boggs:

m   I. **Robert N. Boggs** was born on May 27, 1862.

f   II. **Mary Boggs** was born on May 02, 1863. She died on March 11, 1864.

f   III. **Sallie A. Boggs** was born on July 23, 1864. She died on August 13, 1865, at the age of 1.

f   IV. **Margaret Elmira Boggs** was born on November 15, 1866. She died in Wilmington, New Castle County, Delaware, on May 21, 1928, at the age of 61. Her cause of death was diabetes mellitis. She was buried in Silverbrook Cemetery and Memorial Park, Wilmington, New Castle County, Delaware.

f   V. **Elizabeth Boggs** was born on July 16, 1868. She died on July 26, 1868.

m   VI. **Nathaniel P. Boggs** was born on September 17, 1870. He died on September 13, 1889, at the age of 18.

m   VII. **John H. Boggs** was born on September 30. He died on September 27, 1866.

Family of Sarah Wright and William Hall

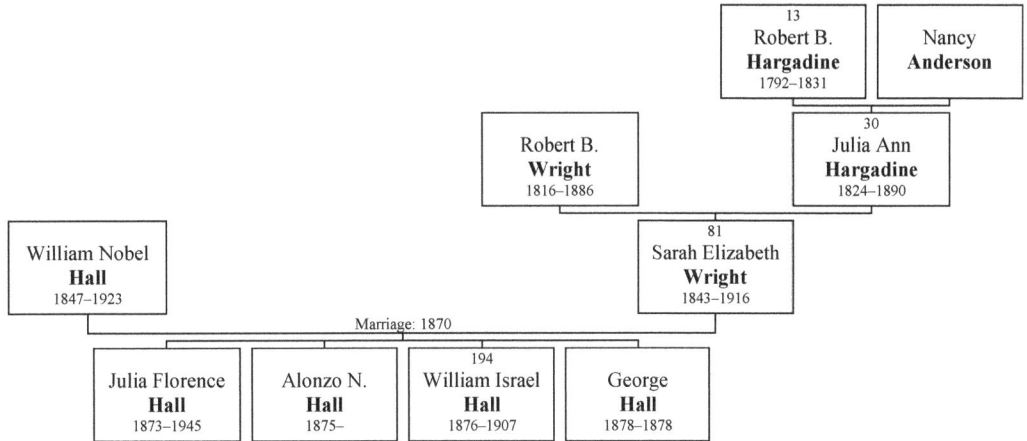

Here are the details about **Sarah Elizabeth Wright's** second marriage, with William Nobel Hall. You can read more about Sarah Elizabeth on page 126.

At the age of 27, Sarah Elizabeth Wright married **William Nobel Hall** on Thursday, August 11, 1870, when he was 23 years old. They had four children.

William Nobel was born on Saturday, March 27, 1847. He reached 75 years of age and died on January 23, 1923.

Children of Sarah Elizabeth Wright and William Nobel Hall:

f   I. **Julia Florence Hall** was born on September 08, 1873. She died in Greenbrier County, West Virginia, on March 14, 1945, at the age of 71.

m   II. **Alonzo N. Hall** was born on March 14, 1875.

+ 194   m   III. **William Israel Hall** was born on June 12, 1876. He died in New Castle County, Delaware, on September 15, 1907, at the age of 31. His cause of death was a railroad accident. He was buried in Lakeside Cemetery, Dover, Kent County, Delaware (Find a Grave ID 198356405).

m   IV. **George Hall** was born on April 22, 1878. He died on April 22, 1878.

Family of Charles Wright and Sallie Sipple

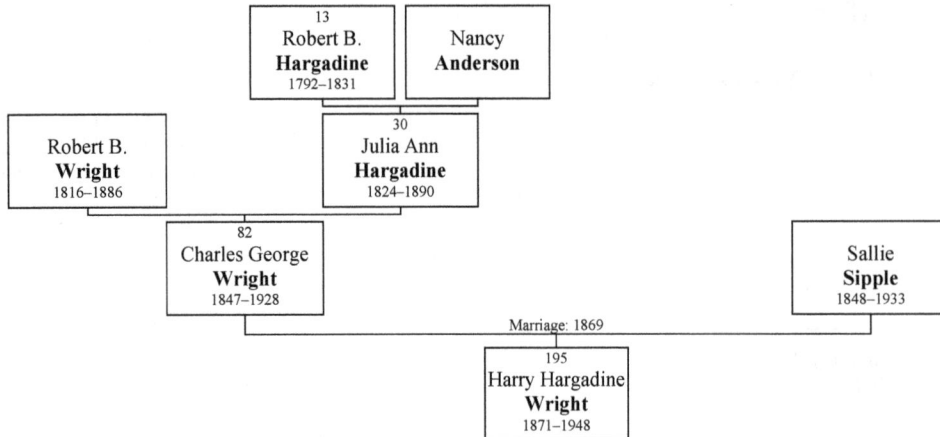

```
                        ┌─────────────┐ ┌─────────────┐
                        │     13      │ │   Nancy     │
                        │  Robert B.  │ │  Anderson   │
                        │  Hargadine  │ │             │
                        │  1792–1831  │ │             │
                        └─────────────┘ └─────────────┘
        ┌─────────────┐        ┌─────────────┐
        │  Robert B.  │        │     30      │
        │   Wright    │        │  Julia Ann  │
        │  1816–1886  │        │  Hargadine  │
        │             │        │  1824–1890  │
        └─────────────┘        └─────────────┘
                ┌─────────────┐                        ┌─────────────┐
                │     82      │                        │   Sallie    │
                │Charles George│                       │   Sipple    │
                │   Wright    │                        │  1848–1933  │
                │  1847–1928  │                        │             │
                └─────────────┘                        └─────────────┘
                           Marriage: 1869
                        ┌─────────────┐
                        │    195      │
                        │Harry Hargadine│
                        │   Wright    │
                        │  1871–1948  │
                        └─────────────┘
```

82. **Charles George Wright** was born on Saturday, January 09, 1847, in Delaware, USA. He was the son of Robert B. Wright and Julia Ann Hargadine (30).

Charles George died in Dover, Kent County, Delaware, on June 17, 1928, at the age of 81. He was buried in Lakeside Cemetery, Dover, Kent County, Delaware (Find a Grave ID 7803777).

Charles George married **Sallie Sipple** in 1869. They had one son.

Sallie was born in Delaware, USA, on Wednesday, October 18, 1848. She reached 84 years of age and died in Dover, Kent County, Delaware, on March 09, 1933. Sallie was buried in Lakeside Cemetery, Dover, Kent County, Delaware (Find a Grave ID 7803797).

Son of Charles George Wright and Sallie Sipple:

+   195   m   I. **Harry Hargadine Wright** was born in Delaware, USA, in 1871. He died in Wilmington, New Castle County, Delaware, in 1948 at the age of 77. Harry Hargadine was buried in Silverbrook Cemetery and Memorial Park, Wilmington, New Castle County, Delaware (Find a Grave ID 116979676).

Family of William Wright and Emily Robinson

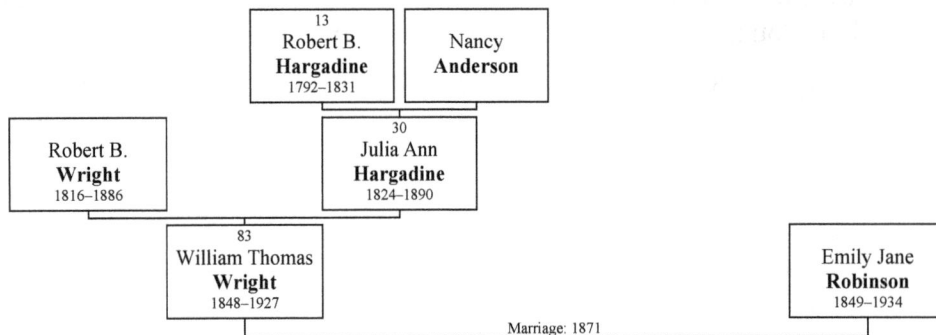

```
                        ┌─────────────┐ ┌─────────────┐
                        │     13      │ │   Nancy     │
                        │  Robert B.  │ │  Anderson   │
                        │  Hargadine  │ │             │
                        │  1792–1831  │ │             │
                        └─────────────┘ └─────────────┘
        ┌─────────────┐        ┌─────────────┐
        │  Robert B.  │        │     30      │
        │   Wright    │        │  Julia Ann  │
        │  1816–1886  │        │  Hargadine  │
        │             │        │  1824–1890  │
        └─────────────┘        └─────────────┘
                ┌─────────────┐                        ┌─────────────┐
                │     83      │                        │ Emily Jane  │
                │William Thomas│                       │  Robinson   │
                │   Wright    │                        │  1849–1934  │
                │  1848–1927  │                        │             │
                └─────────────┘                        └─────────────┘
                           Marriage: 1871
```

83.   **William Thomas Wright** was born on Thursday, February 10, 1848, in Kent County, Delaware.[119] He was the son of Robert B. Wright and Julia Ann Hargadine (30).

William Thomas died in Delaware, USA, on June 13, 1927, at the age of 79.[119] He was buried in Spring Hill Cemetery, Easton, Talbot County, Maryland (Find a Grave ID 67441058).

William Thomas married **Emily Jane Robinson** on Tuesday, December 12, 1871, in Talbot County, Maryland.[119] Emily Jane was born in Delaware, USA, in 1849.[119]

She reached 85 years of age and died in 1934.[119] Emily Jane was buried in Spring Hill Cemetery, Easton, Talbot County, Maryland (Find a Grave ID 67441109).

Family of Ellen Virdin and Samuel Wallace

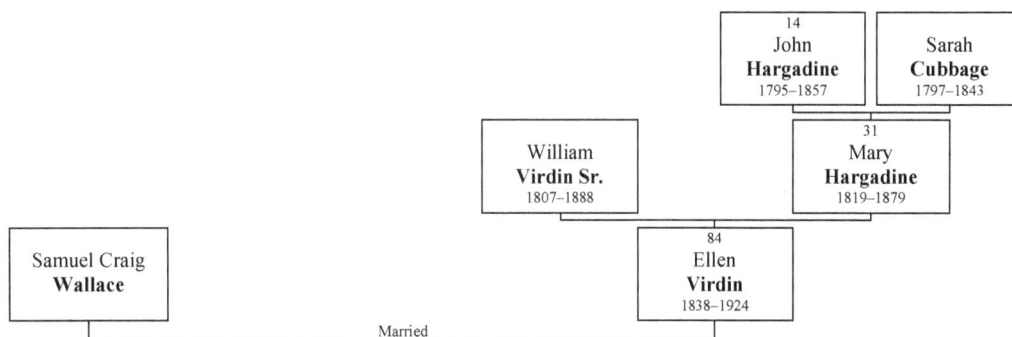

84.   **Ellen Virdin** was born on Friday, November 09, 1838. She was the daughter of William Virdin Sr. and Mary Hargadine (31).

Ellen died on December 30, 1924, at the age of 86. She was buried in Lakeside Cemetery, Dover, Kent County, Delaware (Find a Grave ID 7779889).

She married **Samuel Craig Wallace**.

Family of William Virdin and Emily Craig

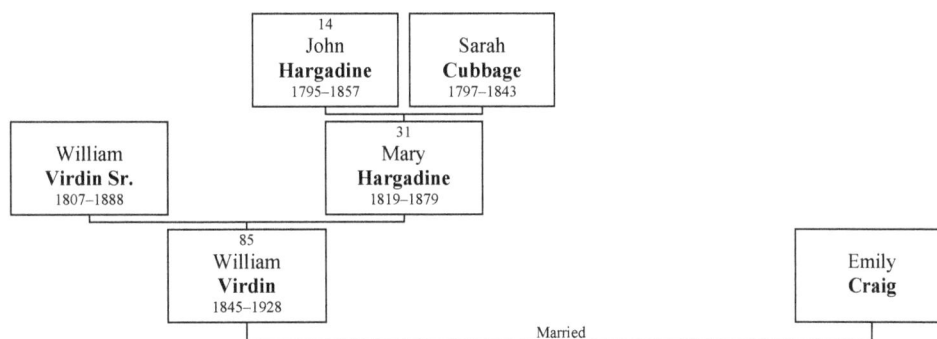

85.   **William Virdin** was born in 1845. He was the son of William Virdin Sr. and Mary Hargadine (31).

---

119   Ancestry.com, Public Member Trees (Provo, UT, USA, Ancestry.com Operations, Inc., 2006), Ancestry.com, Record for William Thomas Wright. https://search.ancestry.co.uk/cgi-bin/sse.dll?db=1030&h=75019652835&indiv=try.

William died in Dover, Kent County, Delaware, on March 18, 1928, at the age of 83. He was buried in Lakeside Cemetery, Dover, Kent County, Delaware (Find a Grave ID 7777123).

He married **Emily Craig**.

Family of John Virdin and Anna Ford

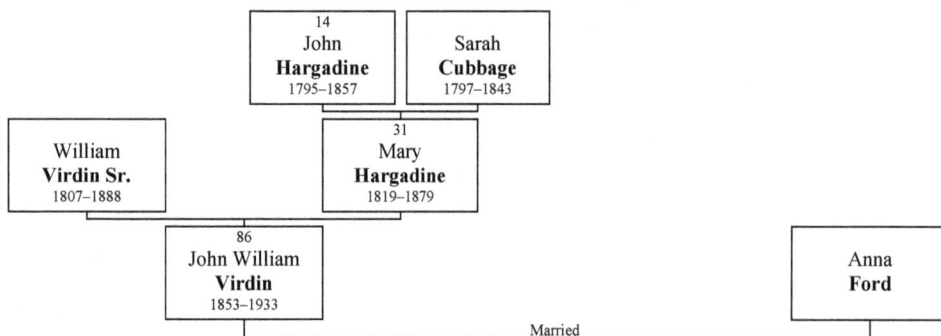

86.   **John William Virdin** was born in March 1853 in Delaware, USA. He was the son of William Virdin Sr. and Mary Hargadine (31).

John William died in Delaware, USA, on November 12, 1933, at the age of 80. He was buried in Odd Fellows Cemetery, Camden, Kent County, Delaware (Find a Grave ID 191161853).

He married **Anna Ford**.

Sarah Hargadine

87.   **Sarah Hargadine** was born on Friday, February 10, 1843, in Delaware, USA. She was the daughter of Samuel Emmett Hargadine I (32) and Mariam Irons. She was also known as **Sallie**.

Sarah died in Wilmington, New Castle County, Delaware, on August 14, 1922, at the age of 79. She was buried in Glenwood Cemetery, Smyrna, Kent County, Delaware, on August 16, 1922 (Find a Grave ID 11160895).

Marriages with John Severson Truax and Joseph Van Gasken Hoffecker (Page 132) are known.

Family of Sarah Hargadine and John Truax

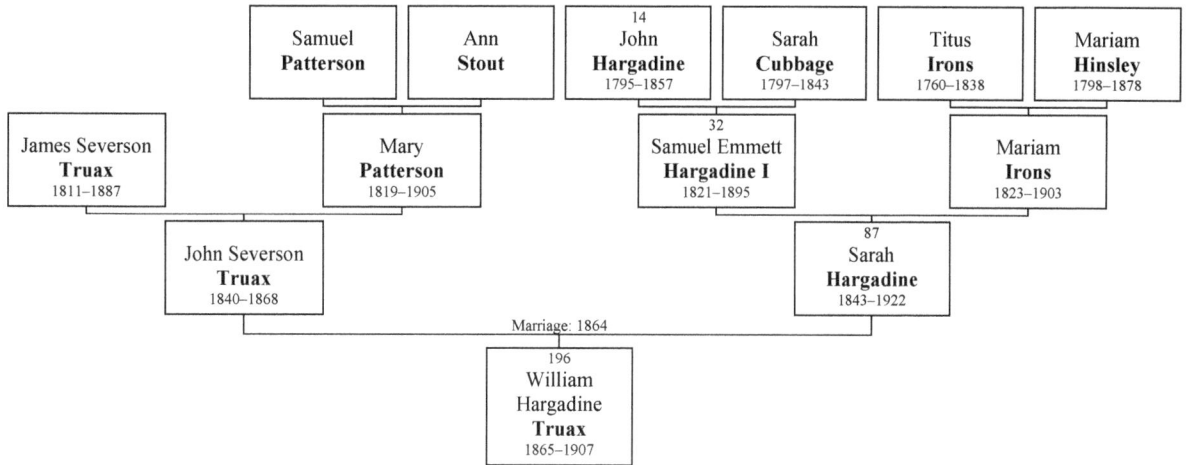

Samuel **Patterson**	Ann **Stout**	14 John **Hargadine** 1795–1857	Sarah **Cubbage** 1797–1843	Titus **Irons** 1760–1838	Mariam **Hinsley** 1798–1878

James Severson **Truax** 1811–1887

Mary **Patterson** 1819–1905

32 Samuel Emmett **Hargadine I** 1821–1895

Mariam **Irons** 1823–1903

John Severson **Truax** 1840–1868

87 Sarah **Hargadine** 1843–1922

Marriage: 1864

196 William Hargadine **Truax** 1865–1907

Here are the details about **Sarah Hargadine's** first marriage, with John Severson Truax. You can read more about Sarah on page 130.

At the age of 21, Sarah Hargadine married **John Severson Truax** on Wednesday, March 09, 1864, when he was 23 years old. By Dr. Boon. They had one son.

John Severson was born on Tuesday, June 16, 1840. He was the son of James Severson Truax and Mary Patterson.

He served in the military on October 25, 1862. Company A, 6th Delaware Infantry Regiment during the Civil War – Private. John Severson reached 27 years of age and died in Delaware, USA, on April 16, 1868. He was buried in Glenwood Cemetery, Smyrna, Kent County, Delaware (Find a Grave ID 11160883).

Son of Sarah Hargadine and John Severson Truax:

+ 196 m I. **William Hargadine Truax** was born in Delaware, USA, on January 30, 1865. He died in Delaware, USA, on January 21, 1907, at the age of 41. William Hargadine was buried in Glenwood Cemetery, Smyrna, Kent County, Delaware (Find a Grave ID 11160898).

Family of Sarah Hargadine and Joseph Hoffecker

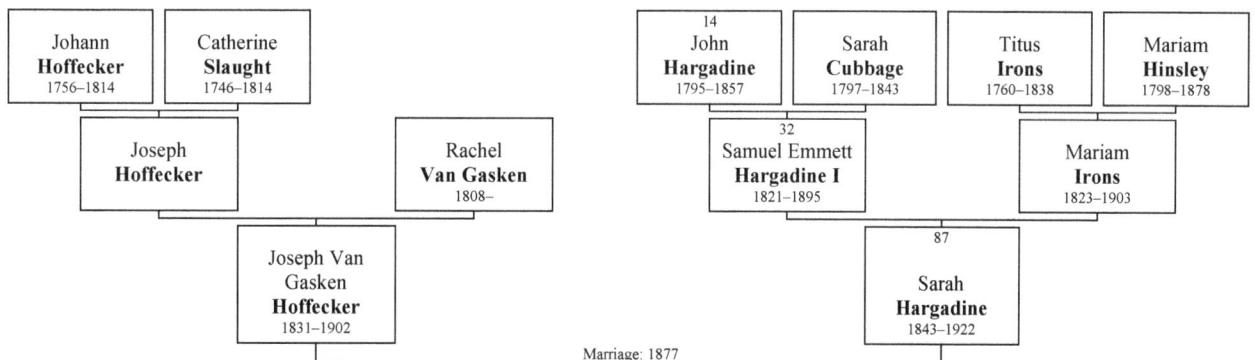

Johann **Hoffecker** 1756–1814	Catherine **Slaught** 1746–1814	14 John **Hargadine** 1795–1857	Sarah **Cubbage** 1797–1843	Titus **Irons** 1760–1838	Mariam **Hinsley** 1798–1878

Joseph **Hoffecker**

Rachel **Van Gasken** 1808–

32 Samuel Emmett **Hargadine I** 1821–1895

Mariam **Irons** 1823–1903

Joseph Van Gasken **Hoffecker** 1831–1902

87 Sarah **Hargadine** 1843–1922

Marriage: 1877

Here are the details about **Sarah Hargadine's** second marriage, with Joseph Van Gasken Hoffecker. You can read more about Sarah on page 130.

At the age of 34, Sarah Hargadine married **Joseph Van Gasken Hoffecker** on Wednesday, December 05, 1877, when he was 46 years old. By Rev. J.H. Caldwell. Joseph Van Gasken was born in Smyrna, Kent County, Delaware, on Friday, September 23, 1831. He was the son of Joseph Hoffecker and Rachel Van Gasken.

Joseph Van Gasken reached 70 years of age and died in Wilmington, New Castle County, Delaware, on April 09, 1902. He was buried in Glenwood Cemetery, Smyrna, Kent County, Delaware (Find a Grave ID 11199908).

Family of Margaret Hargadine and John Collins

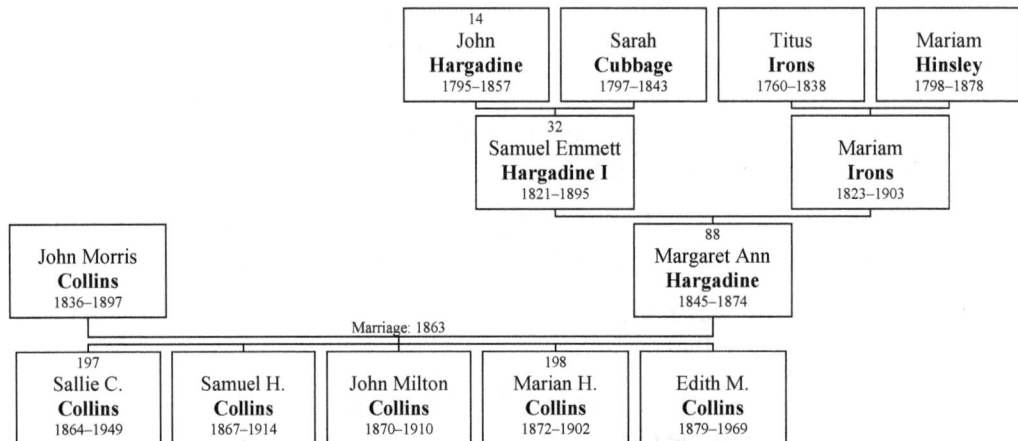

88. **Margaret Ann Hargadine** was born on Friday, January 17, 1845. She was the daughter of Samuel Emmett Hargadine I (32) and Mariam Irons.

Margaret Ann died on June 09, 1874, at the age of 29. She was buried in Glenwood Cemetery, Smyrna, Kent County, Delaware (Find a Grave ID 11169052).

At the age of 18, Margaret Ann married **John Morris Collins** on Wednesday, March 18, 1863, when he was 26 years old. By Rev. Daniel Lambden. They had five children.

John Morris was born in Delaware, USA, on Wednesday, October 26, 1836. He reached 61 years of age and died in Kent County, Delaware, on November 25, 1897. John Morris was buried in Glenwood Cemetery, Smyrna, Kent County, Delaware (Find a Grave ID 11169047).

Children of Margaret Ann Hargadine and John Morris Collins:

+   197   f   I. **Sallie C. Collins** was born in Smyrna, Kent County, Delaware, on January 28, 1864. She died in Brookfield, Linn County, Missouri, on March 31, 1949, at the age of 85. Sallie C. was buried in Rose Hill Cemetery, Brookfield, Linn County, Missouri (Find a Grave ID 80154261).

        m   II. **Samuel H. Collins** was born in Delaware, USA, in March 1867. He died in Millcreek, New Castle County, Delaware, on October 30, 1914, at the age of 47. His cause of death was pulmonary tuberculosis. He was buried on October 30, 1914.

m   III. **John Milton Collins** was born in Delaware, USA, in 1870. He died in Kent County, Delaware, on April 05, 1910, at the age of 40. His cause of death was consumption. He was buried in Glenwood Cemetery, Smyrna, Kent County, Delaware, on April 06, 1910 (Find a Grave ID 11169048).

More facts and events for John Milton Collins:

Individual Note: Machinist by trade

+ 198 f   IV. **Marian H. Collins** was born in Delaware, USA, on September 11, 1872. She died on July 23, 1902, at the age of 29. Marian H. was buried in Rose Hill Cemetery, Brookfield, Linn County, Missouri (Find a Grave ID 143227026).

f   V. **Edith M. Collins** was born on December 06, 1879. She died on December 27, 1969, at the age of 90. Edith M. was buried in Rose Hill Cemetery, Brookfield, Linn County, Missouri.

Family of Elmira Hargadine and Silas Snow

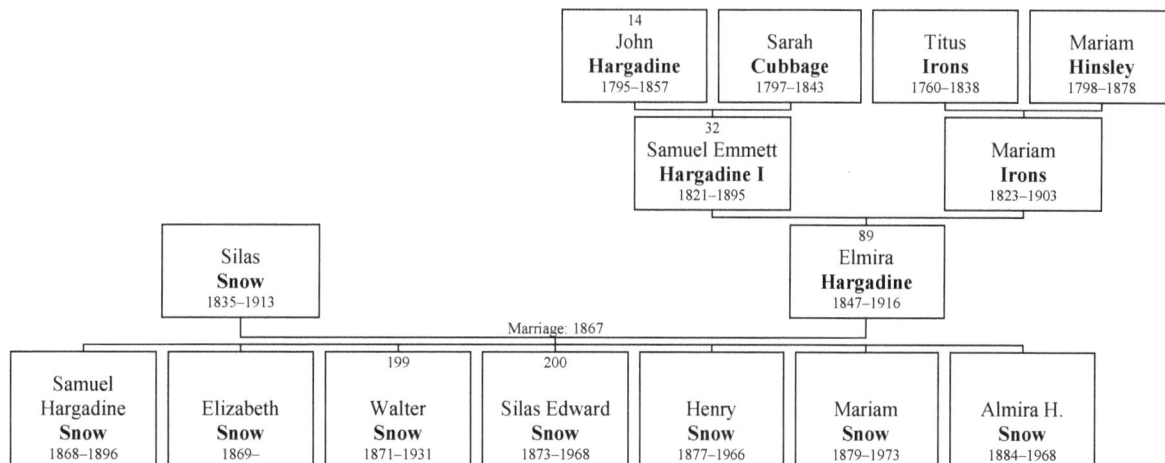

89.   **Elmira Hargadine** was born on Thursday, March 04, 1847, in Templeville, Caroline County, Maryland. She was the daughter of Samuel Emmett Hargadine I (32) and Mariam Irons. She was also known as **Ella**.

Elmira died in Brookfield, Linn County, Missouri, on April 23, 1916, at the age of 69. She was buried in Rose Hill Cemetery, Brookfield, Linn County, Missouri (Find a Grave ID 83950092).

Elmira married **Silas Snow** on Wednesday, March 06, 1867. By Rev. William Hamessly. They had seven children.

Silas was born in Duck Creek Hundred, Kent County, Delaware, in July 1835. He reached 78 years of age and died in Brookfield, Linn County, Missouri, on September 05, 1913. His cause of death was lobar pneumonia and heat exhaustion. He was buried in Rose Hill Cemetery, Brookfield, Linn County, Missouri (Find a Grave ID 83949787).

Children of Elmira Hargadine and Silas Snow:

> m   I. **Samuel Hargadine Snow** was born in Delaware, USA, on July 29, 1868. He died on May 27, 1896, at the age of 27. Samuel Hargadine was buried in Rose Hill Cemetery, Brookfield, Linn County, Missouri (Find a Grave ID 83950155).

> f   II. **Elizabeth Snow** was born in August 1869.

+ 199   m   III. **Walter Snow** was born in Leipsic, Kent County, Delaware, on August 15, 1871. He died in Lakewood, Cuyahoga County, Ohio, in 1931 at the age of 59. Walter was buried in Rose Hill Cemetery, Brookfield, Linn County, Missouri (Find a Grave ID 83950396).

+ 200   m   IV. **Silas Edward Snow** was born in Delaware, USA, on July 10, 1873. He died on April 16, 1968, at the age of 94. Silas Edward was buried in Rose Hill Cemetery, Brookfield, Linn County, Missouri (Find a Grave ID 138706333).

> m   V. **Henry Snow** was born in Delaware, USA, on April 28, 1877. He died in Missouri, USA, on February 04, 1966, at the age of 88. Henry was buried in Rose Hill Cemetery, Brookfield, Linn County, Missouri (Find a Grave ID 142847251).

> f   VI. **Mariam Snow** was born in Leipsic, Kent County, Delaware, on September 16, 1879. She was also known as **Marie M.**.
>
> Mariam died in Brookfield, Linn County, Missouri, in 1973 at the age of 93. She was buried in Rose Hill Cemetery, Brookfield, Linn County, Missouri (Find a Grave ID 122756051).

> f   VII. **Almira H. Snow** was born in Meadville, Linn County, Missouri, on March 04, 1884. She died in Missouri, USA, on April 08, 1968, at the age of 84. Almira H. was buried in Rose Hill Cemetery, Brookfield, Linn County, Missouri (Find a Grave ID 142847452).

Family of Clementine Hargadine and Joseph Palmer

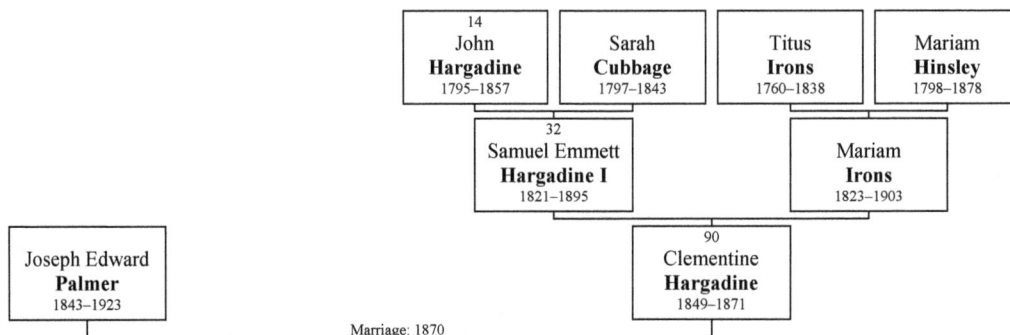

14 John **Hargadine** 1795–1857	Sarah **Cubbage** 1797–1843	Titus **Irons** 1760–1838	Mariam **Hinsley** 1798–1878
32 Samuel Emmett **Hargadine I** 1821–1895		Mariam **Irons** 1823–1903	

Joseph Edward **Palmer** 1843–1923

90 Clementine **Hargadine** 1849–1871

Marriage: 1870

90.   **Clementine Hargadine** was born on Thursday, September 13, 1849. She was the daughter of Samuel Emmett Hargadine I (32) and Mariam Irons.

Clementine died on February 07, 1871, at the age of 21. She was buried in Glenwood Cemetery, Smyrna, Kent County, Delaware (Find a Grave ID 11236609).

At the age of 20, Clementine married **Joseph Edward Palmer** on Thursday, April 21, 1870, when he was 26 years old. By Rev. E. B. Newman. Joseph Edward was born in Delaware, USA, on Tuesday, May 30, 1843.[120]

He reached 80 years of age and died in Wells County, North Dakota, on September 28, 1923.[120] Joseph Edward was buried in Hillside Cemetery, Fessenden, Wells County, North Dakota (Find a Grave ID 105054565).

Family of Mariam Hargadine and Robert Legear

91. **Mariam Celindy Hargadine** was born on Tuesday, November 12, 1850, in Maryland, USA. She was the daughter of Samuel Emmett Hargadine I (32) and Mariam Irons. She was also known as **Mellie**.

Mariam Celindy died on November 11, 1890, at the age of 39.

Mariam Celindy married **Robert Legear** in December 1880. By Rev. M. Sealy.

Family of Laura Hargadine and Samuel Schenck

---

[120] Ancestry.com, Public Member Trees (Provo, UT, USA, Ancestry.com Operations, Inc., 2006), Ancestry.com, Record for Joseph Edward Palmer. https://search.ancestry.co.uk/cgi-bin/sse.dll?db=1030&h=44357489880&indiv=try.

92. **Laura H. Hargadine** was born on Monday, February 04, 1861, in Delaware, USA.[121] She was the daughter of Samuel Emmett Hargadine I (32) and Mariam Irons.

Laura H. died in Brookfield, Linn County, Missouri, on June 26, 1933, at the age of 72. She was buried in Rose Hill Cemetery, Brookfield, Linn County, Missouri (Find a Grave ID 83488117).

At the age of 23, Laura H. married **Samuel Ogden Schenck** on Saturday, September 20, 1884, when he was 31 years old. They had two children.

Samuel Ogden was born in Essex County, New Jersey, on Monday, November 22, 1852. He reached 70 years of age and died on October 12, 1923. Samuel Ogden was buried in Rose Hill Cemetery, Brookfield, Linn County, Missouri (Find a Grave ID 83488341).

Children of Laura H. Hargadine and Samuel Ogden Schenck:

+ 201 f I. **Edna Schenck** was born in Brookfield, Linn County, Missouri, on February 14, 1886.[121] She died in Kansas City, Jackson County, Missouri, on August 19, 1948, at the age of 62.[121] Edna was buried in Floral Hills Cemetery, Kansas City, Jackson County, Missouri.[121]

　　 m II. **Virgil S. Schenck** was born on December 06, 1893.[121]

Family of Samuel Hargadine and Caroline Smith

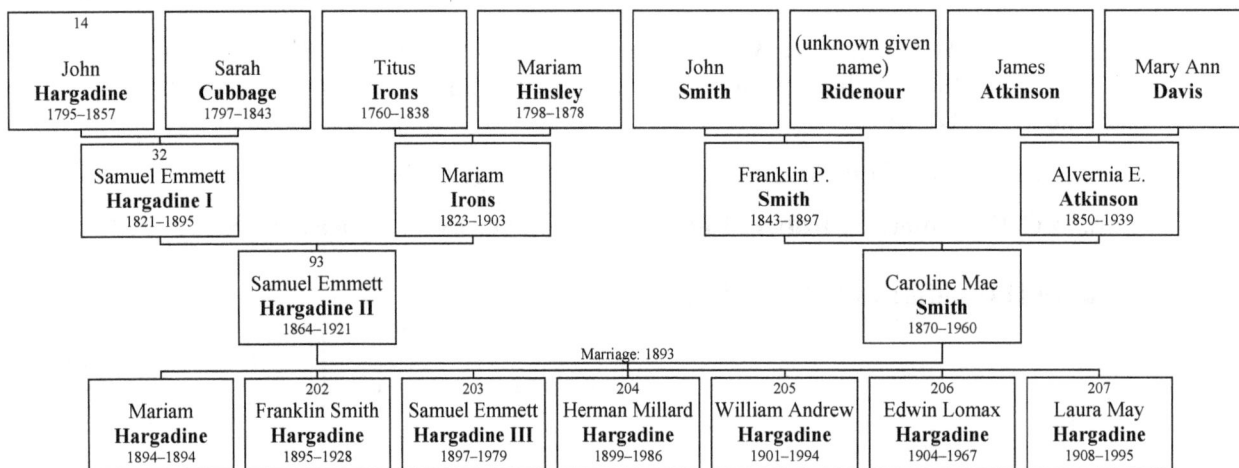

14 John **Hargadine** 1795–1857	Sarah **Cubbage** 1797–1843	Titus **Irons** 1760–1838	Mariam **Hinsley** 1798–1878	John **Smith**	(unknown given name) **Ridenour**	James **Atkinson**	Mary Ann **Davis**

32 Samuel Emmett **Hargadine I** 1821–1895	Mariam **Irons** 1823–1903	Franklin P. **Smith** 1843–1897	Alvernia E. **Atkinson** 1850–1939

93 Samuel Emmett **Hargadine II** 1864–1921	Caroline Mae **Smith** 1870–1960

Marriage: 1893

202 Mariam **Hargadine** 1894–1894	**202** Franklin Smith **Hargadine** 1895–1928	**203** Samuel Emmett **Hargadine III** 1897–1979	**204** Herman Millard **Hargadine** 1899–1986	**205** William Andrew **Hargadine** 1901–1994	**206** Edwin Lomax **Hargadine** 1904–1967	**207** Laura May **Hargadine** 1908–1995

93. **Samuel Emmett Hargadine II** was born on Tuesday, July 26, 1864, in Leipsic, Kent County, Delaware. He was the son of Samuel Emmett Hargadine I (32) and Mariam Irons.

Samuel Emmett died in Brookfield, Linn County, Missouri, on September 21, 1921, at the age of 57. His cause of death was cancer of stomach. Samuel Emmett was buried in Rose Hill Cemetery, Brookfield, Linn County, Missouri, on September 23, 1921 (Find a Grave ID 131195781).

At the age of 28, Samuel Emmett married **Caroline Mae Smith** on Tuesday, March 07, 1893. By Rev. Leonard in Brookfield, Linn County, Missouri, when she was 22 years old. They had seven children.

121　Neil Becker.FTW, Date of Import: May 19, 2004.

Caroline Mae was born in Osage, Village of Bowling Green, Wood County, Ohio, on Wednesday, September 21, 1870. She was also known as **Carrie**.

Caroline Mae reached 90 years of age and died in Brookfield, Linn County, Missouri, on November 02, 1960. She was buried on November 04, 1960, in Rose Hill Cemetery, Brookfield, Linn County, Missouri (Find a Grave ID 131195468).

She was the daughter of Franklin P. Smith and Alvernia E. Atkinson.

Children of Samuel Emmett Hargadine II and Caroline Mae Smith:

	f	I.	**Mariam Hargadine** was born in Brookfield, Linn County, Missouri, on July 26, 1894. She died in Brookfield, Linn County, Missouri, on December 27, 1894. Mariam was buried in Rose Hill Cemetery, Brookfield, Linn County, Missouri (Find a Grave ID 146981693).
+ 202	m	II.	**Franklin Smith Hargadine** was born in Brookfield, Linn County, Missouri, on October 07, 1895. He was also known as **Frank**.

> Franklin Smith died in Gillette, Campbell County, Wyoming, on March 31, 1928, at the age of 32. His cause of death was gunshot to head. Franklin Smith was buried in Rose Hill Cemetery, Brookfield, Linn County, Missouri (Find a Grave ID 131196508).

+ 203	m	III.	**Samuel Emmett Hargadine III** was born in Brookfield, Linn County, Missouri, on April 23, 1897. He died in Columbia, Boone County, Missouri, on April 06, 1979, at the age of 81. Samuel Emmett was buried in Bowling Green City Cemetery, Pike County, Missouri, on April 08, 1979 (Find a Grave ID 233241205).
+ 204	m	IV.	**Herman Millard Hargadine** was born in Brookfield, Linn County, Missouri, on April 23, 1899. He died in Kansas City, Jackson County, Missouri, on November 22, 1986, at the age of 87. Herman Millard was buried in Parklawn Memory Gardens Cemetery, Brookfield, Linn County, Missouri (Find a Grave ID 117726259).
+ 205	m	V.	**William Andrew Hargadine** was born in Brookfield, Linn County, Missouri, on June 23, 1901. He died in Brookfield Nursing Center, Linn County Missouri, on May 29, 1994, at the age of 92. William Andrew was buried in Parklawn Memory Gardens Cemetery, Brookfield, Linn County, Missouri, on May 31, 1994 (Find a Grave ID 117747166).
+ 206	m	VI.	**Edwin Lomax Hargadine** was born in Brookfield, Linn County, Missouri, on August 22, 1904. He died in Brookfield, Linn County, Missouri, on December 30, 1967, at the age of 63. His cause of death was tractor accident. He was buried in Parklawn Memory Gardens Cemetery, Brookfield, Linn County, Missouri, on January 02, 1968 (Find a Grave ID 117739893).
+ 207	f	VII.	**Laura May Hargadine** was born in Brookfield, Linn County, Missouri, on September 12, 1908. She died in Brookfield, Linn County, Missouri, on June 29, 1995, at the age of 86. Laura May was buried in Laclede Cemetery, Laclede, Linn County, Missouri (Find a Grave ID 90566613).

Family of Robert Carson and Emma Green

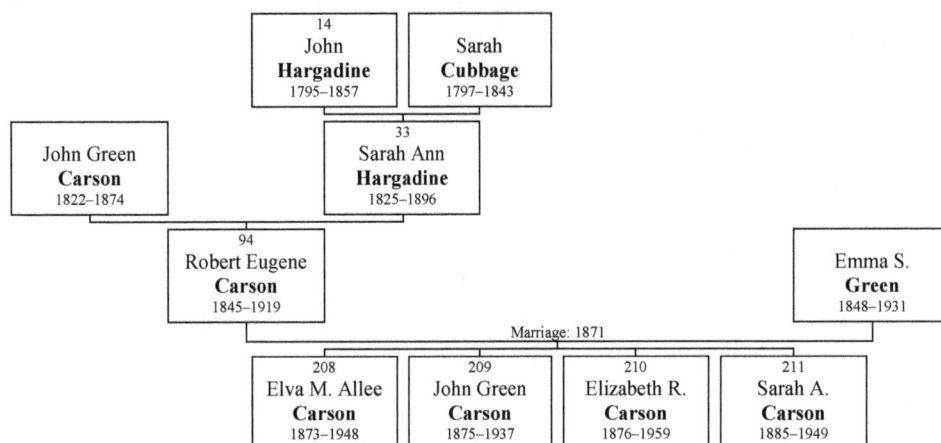

```
                        ┌─────────────┬─────────────┐
                        │     14      │    Sarah    │
                        │    John     │   Cubbage   │
                        │  Hargadine  │  1797–1843  │
                        │  1795–1857  │             │
                        └─────────────┴─────────────┘
        ┌─────────────┐      ┌─────────────┐
        │ John Green  │      │     33      │
        │   Carson    │      │  Sarah Ann  │
        │  1822–1874  │      │  Hargadine  │
        │             │      │  1825–1896  │
        └─────────────┘      └─────────────┘
               ┌─────────────┐              ┌─────────────┐
               │     94      │              │  Emma S.    │
               │Robert Eugene│              │   Green     │
               │   Carson    │              │  1848–1931  │
               │  1845–1919  │              │             │
               └─────────────┘              └─────────────┘
                          Marriage: 1871
   ┌──────────┬──────────┬──────────┬──────────┐
   │   208    │   209    │   210    │   211    │
   │Elva M. Allee│John Green│Elizabeth R.│ Sarah A. │
   │  Carson  │  Carson  │  Carson  │  Carson  │
   │ 1873–1948│ 1875–1937│ 1876–1959│ 1885–1949│
   └──────────┴──────────┴──────────┴──────────┘
```

94.   **Robert Eugene Carson** was born on Wednesday, February 05, 1845, in Dover, Kent County, Delaware. He was the son of John Green Carson and Sarah Ann Hargadine (33).

Robert Eugene died in Dover, Kent County, Delaware, on April 22, 1919, at the age of 74. He was buried in Lakeside Cemetery, Dover, Kent County, Delaware (Find a Grave ID 7588806).

At the age of 26, Robert Eugene married **Emma S. Green** on Thursday, February 23, 1871, in Delaware, USA, when she was 22 years old. They had four children.

Emma S. was born on Saturday, July 22, 1848. She reached 82 years of age and died in Dover, Kent County, Delaware, on March 31, 1931. Her cause of death was chronic myocarditis. She was buried in Lakeside Cemetery, Dover, Kent County, Delaware (Find a Grave ID 75082330).

Children of Robert Eugene Carson and Emma S. Green:

+ 208   f   I. **Elva M. Allee Carson** was born in Little Creek, Kent County, Delaware, in 1873. She was also known as **Annie**.

Elva M. Allee died in Camden, Kent County, Delaware, on May 12, 1948, at the age of 75. She was buried in Odd Fellows Cemetery, Camden, Kent County, Delaware (Find a Grave ID 111024276).

+ 209   m   II. **John Green Carson** was born on June 18, 1875. He died in Dover, Kent County, Delaware, on April 18, 1937, at the age of 61. His cause of death was automobile accident. He was buried in Lakeside Cemetery, Dover, Kent County, Delaware (Find a Grave ID 7588801).

+ 210   f   III. **Elizabeth R. Carson** was born in Little Creek, Kent County, Delaware, on December 21, 1876. She died on May 28, 1959, at the age of 82. Elizabeth R. was buried in Lakeside Cemetery, Dover, Kent County, Delaware (Find a Grave ID 7669654).

+   211   f   IV. **Sarah A. Carson** was born in May 1885. She died in 1949 at the age of 63. Sarah A. was buried in Lakeside Cemetery, Dover, Kent County, Delaware (Find a Grave ID 7677350).

Family of Anna Carson and Alfred Clark

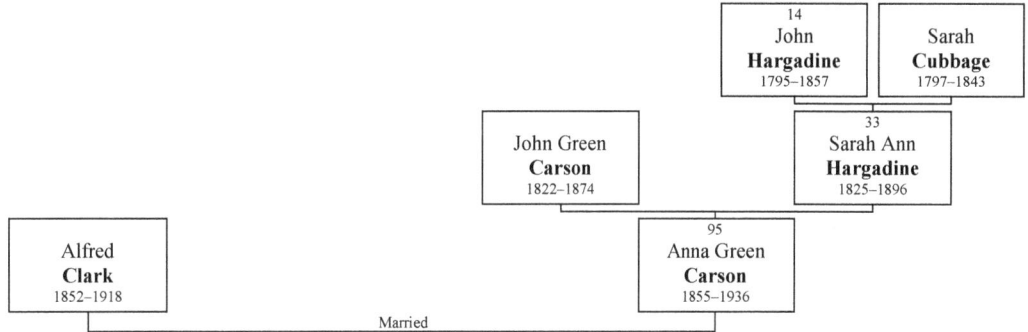

95.   **Anna Green Carson** was born on Friday, May 25, 1855, in Dover, Kent County, Delaware. She was the daughter of John Green Carson and Sarah Ann Hargadine (33).

Anna Green died in Harrington, Kent County, Delaware, on December 10, 1936, at the age of 81. She was buried in Greensboro Cemetery, Greensboro, Caroline County, Maryland (Find a Grave ID 45482606).

She married **Alfred Clark**. Alfred was born in Kent County, Delaware, on Monday, April 19, 1852.

He reached 66 years of age and died in Denton, Caroline County, Maryland, on June 18, 1918. Alfred was buried in Greensboro Cemetery, Greensboro, Caroline County, Maryland (Find a Grave ID 45481469).

Family of James Carson and Aletha Pearson

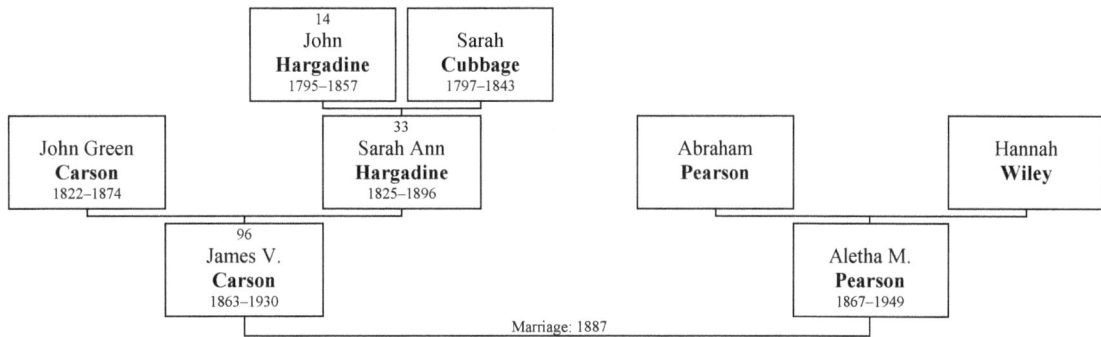

96.   **James V. Carson** was born on Friday, April 17, 1863, in Delaware, USA. He was the son of John Green Carson and Sarah Ann Hargadine (33).

James V. died in Kent County, Delaware, on March 29, 1930, at the age of 66. He was buried in Lakeside Cemetery, Dover, Kent County, Delaware (Find a Grave ID 7588798).

At the age of 23, James V. married **Aletha M. Pearson** on Tuesday, January 04, 1887, in Kent County, Delaware, when she was 19 years old. Aletha M. was born in Delaware, USA, on Wednesday, December 11, 1867. She was the daughter of Abraham Pearson and Hannah Wiley.

Aletha M. reached 81 years of age and died in Philadelphia, Philadelphia County, Pennsylvania, on July 24, 1949. She was buried in Lakeside Cemetery, Dover, Kent County, Delaware (Find a Grave ID 7588789).

Family of Willard Carson and Sallie Bickle

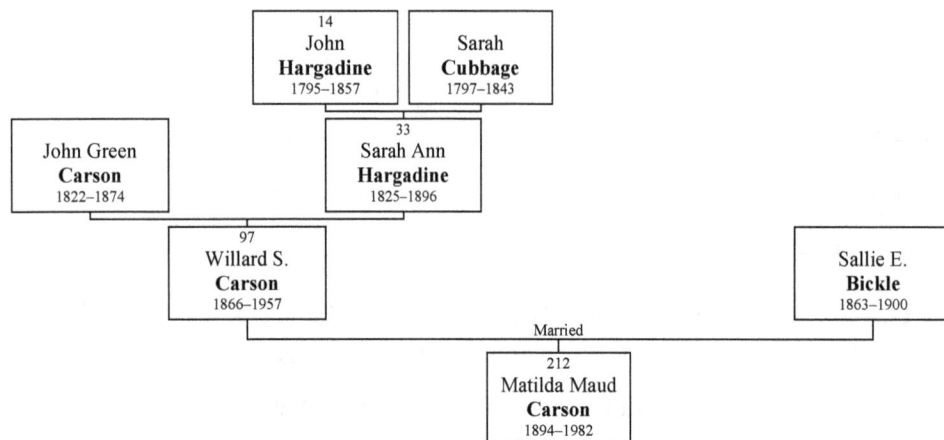

97.   **Willard S. Carson** was born on Sunday, April 22, 1866. He was the son of John Green Carson and Sarah Ann Hargadine (33).

Willard S. died on February 07, 1957, at the age of 90. He was buried in Lakeside Cemetery, Dover, Kent County, Delaware (Find a Grave ID 7588810).

He married **Sallie E. Bickle**. They had one daughter.

Sallie E. was born in Delaware, USA, in January 1863.[122] She reached 37 years of age and died in 1900.[122]

Daughter of Willard S. Carson and Sallie E. Bickle:

+   212   f   I. **Matilda Maud Carson** was born in Delaware, USA, on June 03, 1894.[122] She died in Dover, Kent County, Delaware, on May 02, 1982, at the age of 87.[122] Matilda Maud was buried in Lakeside Cemetery, Dover, Kent County, Delaware (Find a Grave ID 7596828).

122   Ancestry.com, Public Member Trees (Provo, UT, USA, Ancestry.com Operations, Inc., 2006), Ancestry.com, Record for Maude Carson. https://search.ancestry.co.uk/cgi-bin/sse.dll?db=1030&h=122145638684&indiv=try.

Family of Clementine Hargadine and William McKee

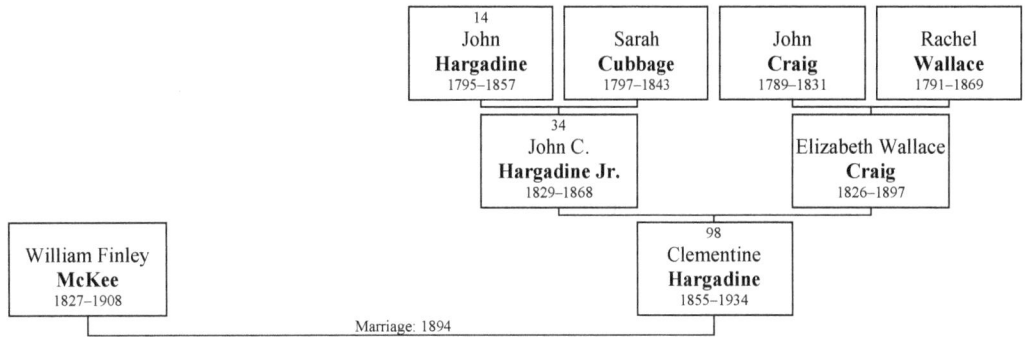

```
          14                                    
          John          Sarah          John          Rachel
          Hargadine     Cubbage        Craig         Wallace
          1795–1857     1797–1843      1789–1831     1791–1869

                    34                    
                    John C.              Elizabeth Wallace
                    Hargadine Jr.        Craig
                    1829–1868            1826–1897

                              98
  William Finley               Clementine
  McKee                        Hargadine
  1827–1908                    1855–1934
                Marriage: 1894
```

98.   **Clementine Hargadine** was born on Friday, June 15, 1855. She was the daughter of John C. Hargadine Jr. (34) and Elizabeth Wallace Craig.

Clementine died on April 03, 1934, at the age of 78. She was buried in Hargadine Family Cemetery; Dover, Kent County, Delaware (Find a Grave ID 13265875).

Clementine married **William Finley McKee** in 1894. William Finley was born on Wednesday, May 30, 1827.

He reached 81 years of age and died on August 19, 1908. William Finley was buried in Bethel Methodist Episcopal Cemetery, Cheswold, Kent County, Delaware (Find a Grave ID 11267734).

Family of Frances Hargadine and Arthur Crook

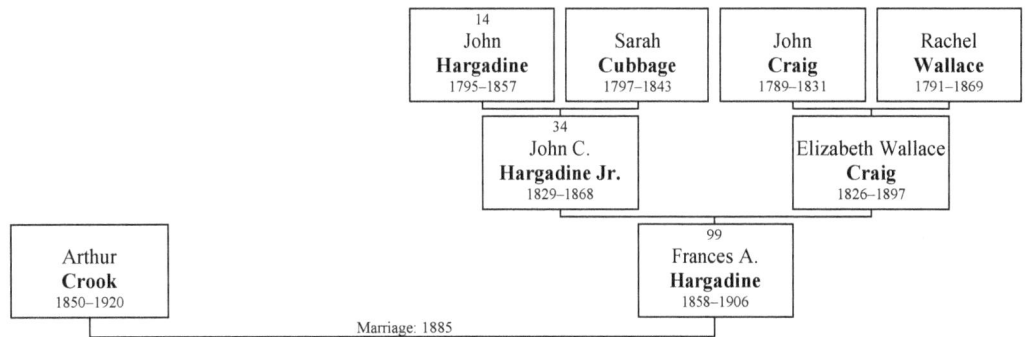

```
          14                                    
          John          Sarah          John          Rachel
          Hargadine     Cubbage        Craig         Wallace
          1795–1857     1797–1843      1789–1831     1791–1869

                    34                    
                    John C.              Elizabeth Wallace
                    Hargadine Jr.        Craig
                    1829–1868            1826–1897

                              99
  Arthur                      Frances A.
  Crook                       Hargadine
  1850–1920                   1858–1906
                Marriage: 1885
```

99.   **Frances A. Hargadine** was born on Wednesday, August 25, 1858. She was the daughter of John C. Hargadine Jr. (34) and Elizabeth Wallace Craig.

Frances A. died in Kent County, Delaware, on February 28, 1906, at the age of 47. She was buried in Hargadine Family Cemetery; Dover, Kent County, Delaware (Find a Grave ID 13265767).

At the age of 26, Frances A. married **Arthur Crook** on Thursday, January 08, 1885, in Kent County, Delaware, when he was 34 years old. Arthur was born on Thursday, August 15, 1850.

He reached 69 years of age and died in Kent County, Delaware, on January 01, 1920. Arthur was buried in Odd Fellows Cemetery.

5th Generation

Family of Robert Carson and Georgia Ann

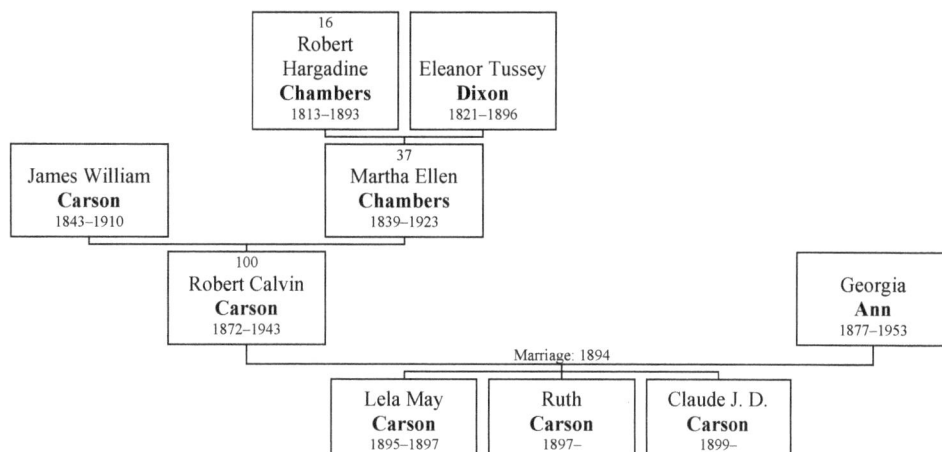

```
                    ┌──────────────┐
                    │      16      │
                    │   Robert     │┌──────────────┐
                    │  Hargadine   ││Eleanor Tussey│
                    │  Chambers    ││    Dixon     │
                    │  1813–1893   ││  1821–1896   │
                    └──────────────┘└──────────────┘
┌──────────────┐    ┌──────────────┐
│ James William│    │      37      │
│   Carson     │    │ Martha Ellen │
│  1843–1910   │    │  Chambers    │
│              │    │  1839–1923   │
└──────────────┘    └──────────────┘
        ┌──────────────┐                    ┌──────────────┐
        │     100      │                    │   Georgia    │
        │ Robert Calvin│                    │     Ann      │
        │   Carson     │                    │  1877–1953   │
        │  1872–1943   │                    │              │
        └──────────────┘                    └──────────────┘
                        Marriage: 1894
    ┌──────────────┐  ┌──────────────┐  ┌──────────────┐
    │   Lela May   │  │    Ruth      │  │  Claude J. D.│
    │   Carson     │  │   Carson     │  │   Carson     │
    │  1895–1897   │  │   1897–      │  │   1899–      │
    └──────────────┘  └──────────────┘  └──────────────┘
```

100. **Robert Calvin Carson** was born on Friday, September 27, 1872, in Clarke County, Iowa.[123] He was the son of James William Carson and Martha Ellen Chambers (37).

Robert Calvin died in Creston, Union County, Iowa, on August 06, 1943, at the age of 70.[124] He was buried in Ottawa Cemetery, Ottawa, Clarke County, Iowa (Find a Grave ID 63567476).

Robert Calvin married **Georgia Ann** in 1894. They had three children.

Georgia was born in Montgomery County, Iowa, in July 1877.[123] She reached 75 years of age and died in Creston, Union County, Iowa, on April 27, 1953.[125] Georgia was buried in Ottawa Cemetery, Ottawa, Clarke County, Iowa (Find a Grave ID 63567465).

Children of Robert Calvin Carson and Georgia Ann:

      f   I. **Lela May Carson** was born in Iowa, USA, on November 23, 1895.[125] She died in Iowa, USA, on March 27, 1897, at the age of 1.[125] Lela May was buried in Ottawa Cemetery, Ottawa, Clarke County, Iowa (Find a Grave ID 63567481).

      f   II. **Ruth Carson** was born in Iowa, USA, in May 1897.[123]

      m   III. **Claude J. D. Carson** was born in Iowa, USA, in September 1899.[123]

---

[123]   Birth month and year given in 1900 Census.

[124]   Tombstone in Ottawa Cemetery.

[125]   Tombstone.

Family of Edward Carson and Della Hill

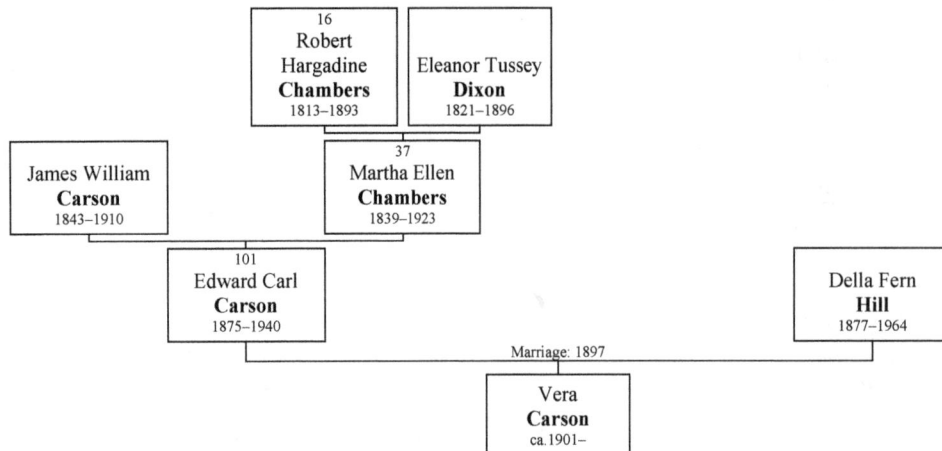

101. **Edward Carl Carson** was born on Thursday, December 23, 1875, in Ottawa, Clarke County, Iowa.[126] He was the son of James William Carson and Martha Ellen Chambers (37).

Edward Carl died in Clarke County, Iowa, on January 03, 1940, at the age of 64. He was buried in Woodburn Cemetery, Woodburn, Clarke County, Iowa (Find a Grave ID 63791573).

Edward Carl married **Della Fern Hill** on Wednesday, September 08, 1897, in Clarke, Iowa, USA. They had one daughter.

Della Fern was born in Iowa, USA, in August 1877.[126] She reached 86 years of age and died in Clarke County, Iowa, on May 02, 1964. Della Fern was buried in Woodburn Cemetery, Woodburn, Clarke County, Iowa (Find a Grave ID 63930002).

Daughter of Edward Carl Carson and Della Fern Hill:

    f   I. **Vera Carson** was born in Clarke County, Iowa, about 1901.[127]

Family of Cordelia Carson and William Cutter

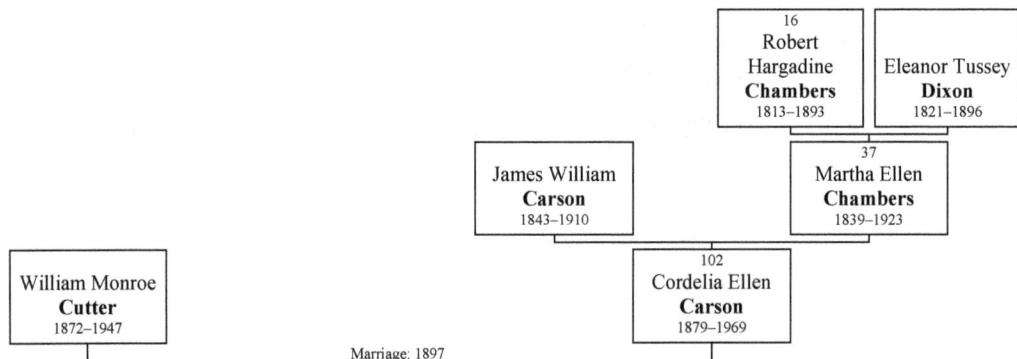

---

126   Birth month and year given in 1900 Census.

127   Age given as 19 years in 1920 Iowa Soundex.

102. **Cordelia Ellen Carson** was born on Friday, February 28, 1879, in Clarke County, Iowa.[128] She was the daughter of James William Carson and Martha Ellen Chambers (37). She was also known as **Nellie**.

Cordelia Ellen died in 1969 at the age of 89. She was buried in Snow Hill Cemetery, Lincoln Township, Page County, Iowa.

At the age of 17, Cordelia Ellen married **Mr. William Monroe Cutter** on Wednesday, February 24, 1897, in Woodburn, Clarke County, Iowa, when he was 24 years old. William Monroe was born on Thursday, December 19, 1872.

He reached 74 years of age and died on January 22, 1947. William Monroe was buried in Snow Hill Cemetery, Lincoln Township, Page County, Iowa (Find a Grave ID 53673656).

William Bruffey

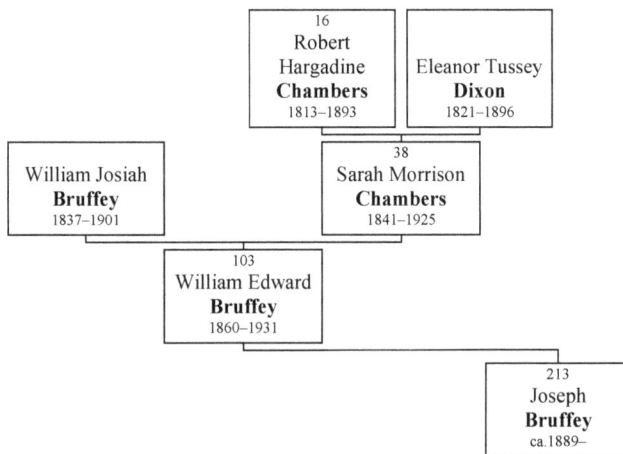

103. **William Edward Bruffey** was born on Monday, October 01, 1860, in Attica, Marion County, Iowa.[129] He was the son of William Josiah Bruffey and Sarah Morrison Chambers (38).

William Edward died in Springdale, Washington County, Arkansas, on January 05, 1931, at the age of 70. He was buried in Hillcrest Cemetery, Mountain Grove, Wright County, Missouri (Find a Grave ID 33939805).

Son of William Edward Bruffey:

+   213   m   I. **Joseph Bruffey** was born in Iowa, USA, about 1889.[130]

---

128   Age given as 1 year in 1880 Iowa Soundex.

129   Age given as 20 years in 1880 Iowa Soundex.

130   Age given as 31 years in 1920 Missouri Soundex.

Family of Lena Clark and William Underwood

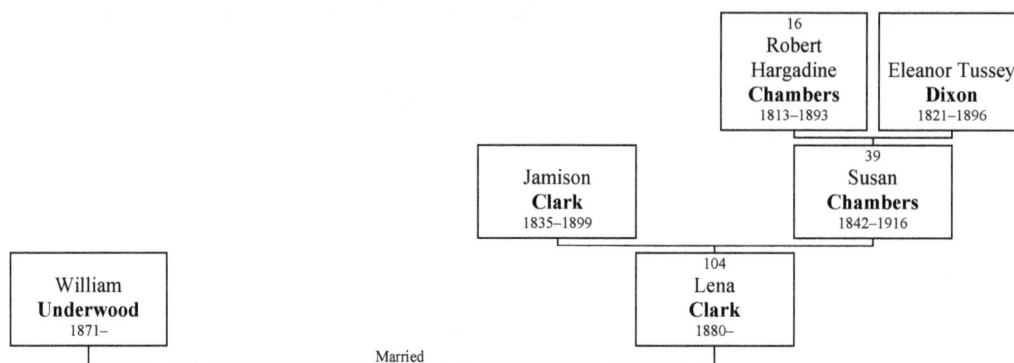

```
                                          ┌──────────────┐ ┌──────────────┐
                                          │      16      │ │              │
                                          │    Robert    │ │              │
                                          │   Hargadine  │ │Eleanor Tussey│
                                          │   Chambers   │ │    Dixon     │
                                          │  1813–1893   │ │  1821–1896   │
                                          └──────────────┘ └──────────────┘
                          ┌──────────────┐           ┌──────────────┐
                          │   Jamison    │           │      39      │
                          │    Clark     │           │    Susan     │
                          │  1835–1899   │           │   Chambers   │
                          └──────────────┘           │  1842–1916   │
         ┌──────────────┐                  └──────────────┐
         │   William    │                  │     104      │
         │  Underwood   │                  │     Lena     │
         │    1871–     │                  │    Clark     │
         └──────────────┘                  │    1880–     │
                          Married          └──────────────┘
```

104.   Lena Clark was born in July 1880 in Iowa, USA.[131] She was the daughter of Jamison Clark and Susan Chambers (39).

She married **William Underwood**. William was born in Ohio, USA, in May 1871.[132]

Family of Sarah Clark and Edward Boden

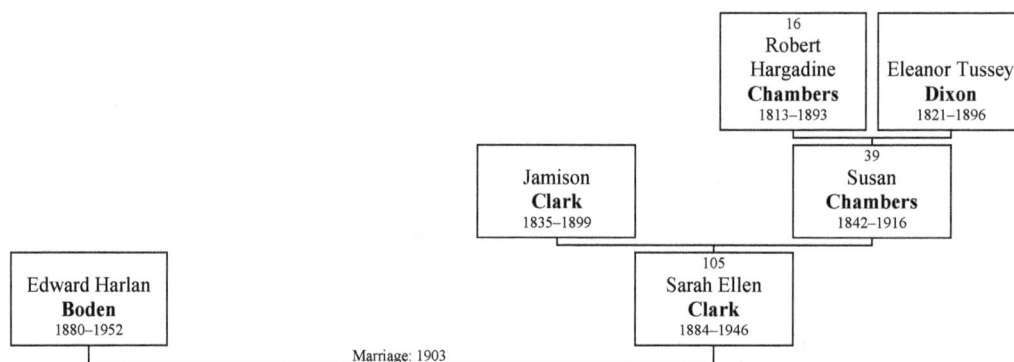

```
                                          ┌──────────────┐ ┌──────────────┐
                                          │      16      │ │              │
                                          │    Robert    │ │              │
                                          │   Hargadine  │ │Eleanor Tussey│
                                          │   Chambers   │ │    Dixon     │
                                          │  1813–1893   │ │  1821–1896   │
                                          └──────────────┘ └──────────────┘
                          ┌──────────────┐           ┌──────────────┐
                          │   Jamison    │           │      39      │
                          │    Clark     │           │    Susan     │
                          │  1835–1899   │           │   Chambers   │
                          └──────────────┘           │  1842–1916   │
         ┌──────────────┐                  ┌──────────────┐
         │ Edward Harlan│                  │     105      │
         │    Boden     │                  │  Sarah Ellen │
         │  1880–1952   │                  │    Clark     │
         └──────────────┘                  │  1884–1946   │
                    Marriage: 1903         └──────────────┘
```

105.   Sarah Ellen Clark was born on Thursday, June 19, 1884, in Murray, Clarke County, Iowa.[133, 134] She was the daughter of Jamison Clark and Susan Chambers (39).

Sarah Ellen died in Santa Cruz County, California, on May 10, 1946, at the age of 61.[133] She was buried in Golden Gate National Cemetery, San Bruno, San Mateo County, California (Find a Grave ID 3553344).[133]

At the age of 19, Sarah Ellen married **Edward Harlan Boden** on Wednesday, November 04, 1903, in Rocky Ford, Otero County, Colorado, USA, when he was 23 years old.[133] Edward Harlan was born in Woodburn, Clarke County, Iowa, on Sunday, June 20, 1880.[133]

He served in the military at U.S. Army, Spanish American War in Iowa, USA, on June 13, 1898.[133] Edward Harlan served in the military on November 02, 1899.[133]

---

131   Birth month and year given in 1900 Census.

132   Birth month and year given in 1900 Iowa Census.

133   Ancestry.com, Public Member Trees (Provo, UT, USA, Ancestry.com Operations, Inc., 2006), Ancestry.com, Record for Sarah Ellen Clark. https://search.ancestry.co.uk/cgi-bin/sse.dll?db=1030&h=162182227685&indiv=try.

134   Birth month and year given in 1900 Census.

He reached 71 years of age and died in San Diego, San Diego County, California, on February 23, 1952.[133] Edward Harlan was buried in Fort Rosecrans National Cemetery, San Diego, San Diego County, California (Find a Grave ID 3388026).[133]

Family of Walter Ball and Lenora Venable

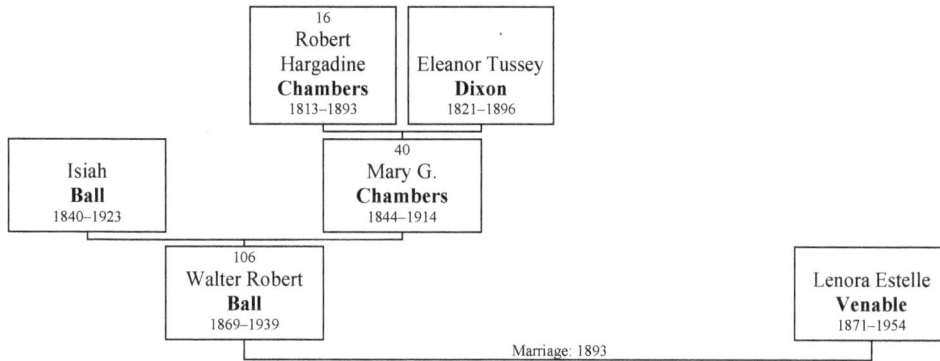

106.   **Walter Robert Ball** was born on Wednesday, June 16, 1869, in Wayne County, Indiana.[135] He was the son of Isiah Ball and Mary G. Chambers (40).

Walter Robert died in Des Moines, Polk County, Iowa, on April 19, 1939, at the age of 69.[135] He was buried in Graceland Cemetery, Knoxville, Marion County, Iowa (Find a Grave ID 135716729).

Walter Robert married **Lenora Estelle Venable** in 1893. Lenora Estelle was born in Iowa, USA, in 1871.[135] She was also known as **Nora**.

Lenora Estelle reached 83 years of age and died in 1954.[135] She was buried in Graceland Cemetery, Knoxville, Marion County, Iowa (Find a Grave ID 135716678).

Family of Blanche Ghrist and John Reese

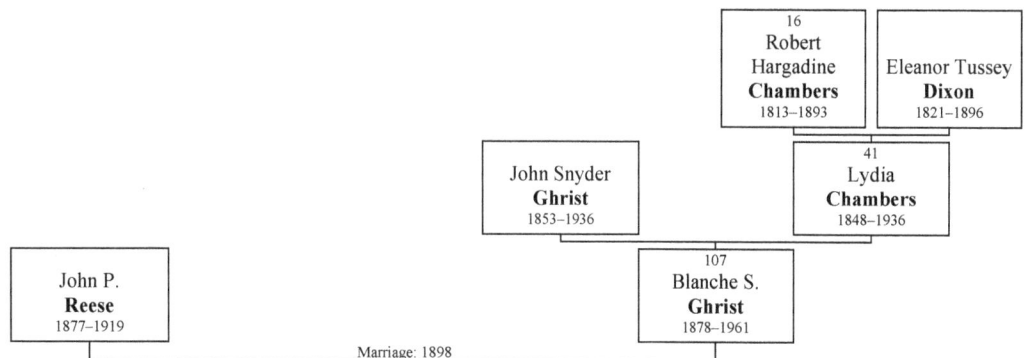

107.   **Blanche S. Ghrist** was born on Sunday, May 19, 1878, in Marion, Linn County, Iowa.[136, 137] She was the daughter of John Snyder Ghrist and Lydia Chambers (41).

---

135   Tombstone in Graceland Cemetery.

136   Ancestry.com, Public Member Trees (Provo, UT, USA, Ancestry.com Operations, Inc., 2006), Ancestry.com, Record for Blanche S. Ghrist. https://search.ancestry.co.uk/cgi-bin/sse.dll?db=1030&h=42262304840&indiv=try.

137   Age given as 2 years in 1880 Iowa Census.

Blanche S. died in Los Angeles, California, on April 05, 1961, at the age of 82.[136] She was buried in Oakview Cemetery, Albia, Monroe County, Iowa (Find a Grave ID 23193005).

At the age of 20, Blanche S. married **John P. Reese** on Wednesday, September 21, 1898, in Hiteman, Iowa, when he was 21 years old. John P. was born in Mineral Ridge, Trumbull County, Ohio, on Sunday, January 14, 1877.

He reached 42 years of age and died in Saint Louis, Saint Louis County, Missouri, on May 27, 1919. John P. was buried in Oakview Cemetery, Albia, Monroe County, Iowa (Find a Grave ID 23192860).

Family of Bertha Chambers and Albert Rowland

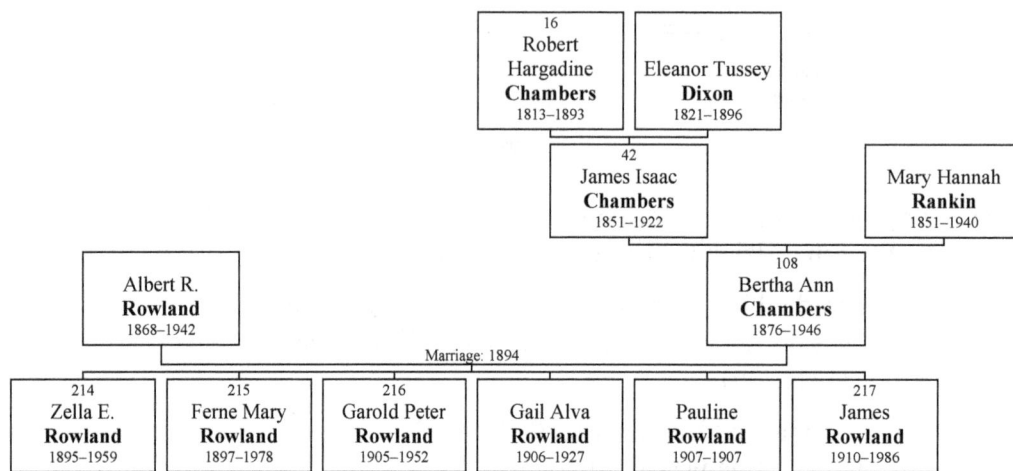

108. **Bertha Ann Chambers** was born on Monday, February 07, 1876, in Farm southeast of Knoxville, Marion County, Iowa.[138] She was the daughter of James Isaac Chambers (42) and Mary Hannah Rankin.

Bertha Ann died in Knoxville, Marion County, Iowa, on August 13, 1946, at the age of 70.[138] She was buried in Zion Cemetery, Pershing, Marion County, Iowa (Find a Grave ID 66718662).

At the age of 18, Bertha Ann married **Albert R. Rowland** on Tuesday, March 13, 1894, in Knoxville, Marion County, Iowa, when he was 25 years old.[139] They had six children.

Albert R. was born in Fayette County, Iowa, on Saturday, July 25, 1868.[138] He reached 73 years of age and died in Knoxville, Marion County, Iowa, on April 02, 1942.[138] Albert R. was buried in Zion Cemetery, Pershing, Marion County, Iowa (Find a Grave ID 58435337).

Children of Bertha Ann Chambers and Albert R. Rowland:

+ 214 f I. **Zella E. Rowland** was born in Fayette County, Iowa, on June 12, 1895. She died in Chariton, Lucas County, Iowa, on May 24, 1959, at the age of 63. Zella E. was buried in Graceland Cemetery, Knoxville, Marion County, Iowa (Find a Grave ID 132575533).

---

138 Newspaper Clipping.

139 Marion County, Iowa Marriage Records.

+   215   f   II.   **Ferne Mary Rowland** was born in Fayette County, Iowa, on April 01, 1897. She died in Albia, Monroe County, Iowa, on March 08, 1978, at the age of 80. Ferne Mary was buried in Woodlawn Cemetery, Lovilia, Monroe County, Iowa (Find a Grave ID 62739070).

+   216   m   III.   **Garold Peter Rowland** was born in Dundee, Delaware County, Iowa, on May 22, 1905.[140] He died in Knoxville, Marion County, Iowa, on June 03, 1952, at the age of 47.[140] Garold Peter was buried in Zion Cemetery, Pershing, Marion County, Iowa (Find a Grave ID 54506083).

         f   IV.   **Gail Alva Rowland** was born in Marion County, Iowa, on January 07, 1906.[140] She died in Knoxville, Marion County, Iowa, on June 14, 1927, at the age of 21.[140] Gail Alva was buried in Zion Cemetery, Pershing, Marion County, Iowa (Find a Grave ID 118999433).

         f   V.   **Pauline Rowland** was born in Marion County, Iowa, on November 29, 1907.[140] She died in Marion County, Iowa, on November 29, 1907.[140] Pauline was buried in Zion Cemetery, Pershing, Marion County, Iowa (Find a Grave ID 118999457).

+   217   m   VI.   **James Rowland** was born in Knoxville, Marion County, Iowa, on March 10, 1910. He was also known as **Lee**.

                     James died in Knoxville, Marion County, Iowa, on January 07, 1986, at the age of 75. He was buried in Graceland Cemetery, Knoxville, Marion County, Iowa (Find a Grave ID 133101145).

Family of Stella Chambers and Avery Tucker

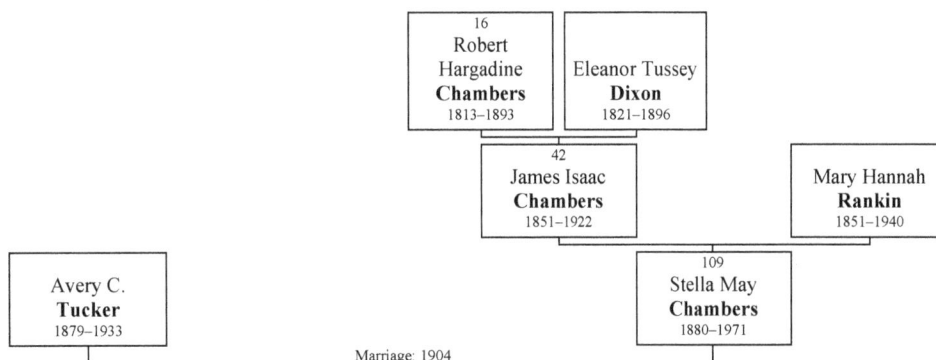

109.   **Stella May Chambers** was born on Monday, June 28, 1880, in Attica, Marion County, Iowa.[141] She was the daughter of James Isaac Chambers (42) and Mary Hannah Rankin.

Stella May died in Knoxville, Marion County, Iowa, on June 23, 1971, at the age of 90.[141] She was buried in Zion Cemetery, Pershing, Marion County, Iowa (Find a Grave ID 66774914).

---

140   Tombstone in Zion Chapel Cemetery.

141   Tombstone.

Stella May married **Avery C. Tucker** on Wednesday, April 06, 1904, in Marion County, Iowa.[142] Avery C. was born in 1879.[141]

He reached 54 years of age and died in 1933.[141]

Family of Sarah Chambers and Harold Baker

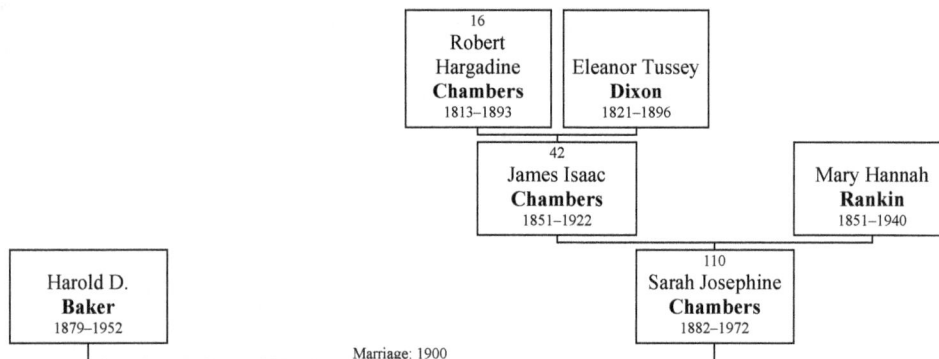

110.   **Sarah Josephine Chambers** was born on Saturday, November 18, 1882, in Indiana Township, Marion County, Iowa.[143] She was the daughter of James Isaac Chambers (42) and Mary Hannah Rankin. She was also known as **Josie**.

Sarah Josephine died in Albia, Monroe County, Iowa, on October 27, 1972, at the age of 89. She was buried in Oakview Cemetery, Albia, Monroe County, Iowa (Find a Grave ID 16350096).

At the age of 18, Sarah Josephine married **Harold D. Baker** on Monday, November 19, 1900, in Marion County, Iowa, when he was 21 years old.[144] Harold D. was born in Monroe County, Iowa, on Friday, January 03, 1879.

He reached 73 years of age and died in Albia, Monroe County, Iowa, on May 08, 1952. Harold D. was buried in Oakview Cemetery, Albia, Monroe County, Iowa (Find a Grave ID 16350043).

---

142   Marion County Iowa Marriage Records.

143   Marion County, Iowa Birth Records.

144   Marion County Marriage Records.

Family of Cameron Chambers and Susky Woody

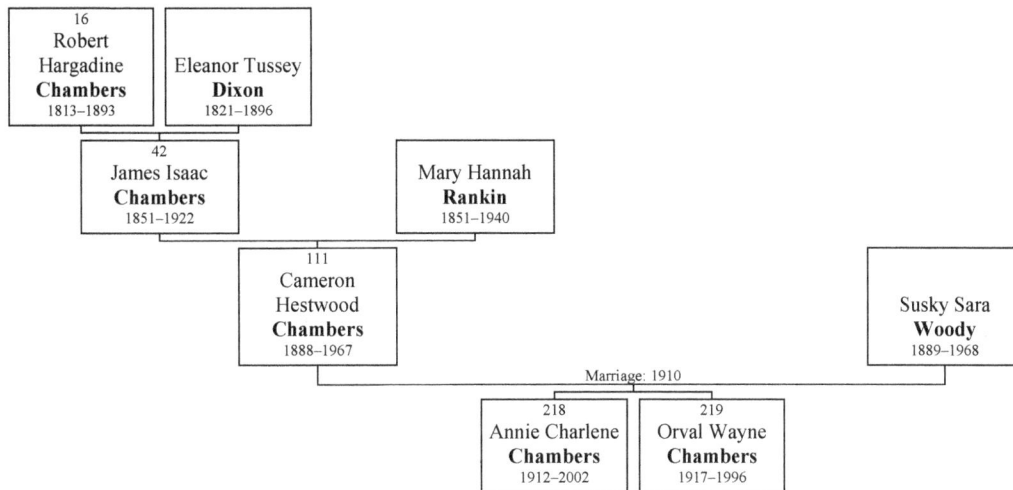

111. **Cameron Hestwood Chambers** was born on Tuesday, October 16, 1888, in Marion County, Iowa.[145] He was the son of James Isaac Chambers (42) and Mary Hannah Rankin.

Cameron Hestwood died in Knoxville, Marion County, Iowa, on September 12, 1967, at the age of 78.[145] He was buried in Breckenridge Cemetery, Harvey, Marion County, Iowa (Find a Grave ID 16456705).

At the age of 21, Cameron Hestwood married **Susky Sara Woody** on Wednesday, September 21, 1910, in Marion County, Iowa, when she was 21 years old.[146] They had two children.

Susky Sara was born in Durham, Marion County, Iowa, on Wednesday, February 13, 1889.[145] She reached 79 years of age and died in Knoxville, Marion County, Iowa, on June 06, 1968.[145] Susky Sara was buried in Breckenridge Cemetery, Harvey, Marion County, Iowa (Find a Grave ID 16481336).

Children of Cameron Hestwood Chambers and Susky Sara Woody:

+ 218 f I. **Annie Charlene Chambers** was born in Indiana Township, Marion County, Iowa, on October 25, 1912.[147] She died in Palisade, Mesa County, Colorado, on August 18, 2002, at the age of 89. Annie Charlene was buried in Memorial Gardens, Grand Junction, Mesa County, Colorado (Find a Grave ID 19231440).

+ 219 m II. **Orval Wayne Chambers** was born in Clay Township, Marion County, Iowa, on August 13, 1917.[147] He died in Clinton, Clinton County, Iowa, on October 28, 1996, at the age of 79. Orval Wayne was buried in Miles Cemetery, Miles, Jackson County, Iowa (Find a Grave ID 64850883).

---

[145] Tombstone in Breckenridge Cemetery.

[146] Marion County Marriage Records.

[147] Marion County, Iowa Birth Records.

Family of Robert Chambers and Nina Hartness

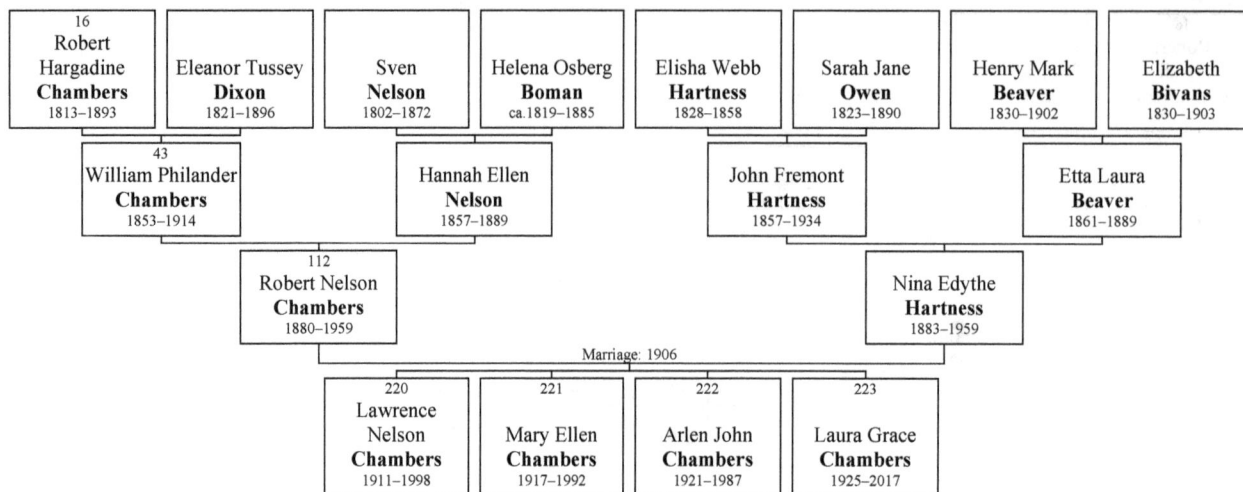

112. **Robert Nelson Chambers** was born on Wednesday, August 18, 1880, in Columbia, Marion County, Iowa.[148] He was the son of William Philander Chambers (43) and Hannah Ellen Nelson.

Robert Nelson died in Davenport, Scott County, Iowa, on December 12, 1959, at the age of 79.[149] He was buried in Graceland Cemetery, Knoxville, Marion County, Iowa (Find a Grave ID 135668230).

At the age of 25, Robert Nelson married **Nina Edythe Hartness** on Wednesday, March 21, 1906, when she was 22 years old.[150] John Fremont Hartness Home. They had four children.

Nina Edythe was born in Clay Township, Marion County, Iowa, on Monday, August 06, 1883.[151] She was the daughter of John Fremont Hartness and Etta Laura Beaver.

Nina Edythe reached 75 years of age and died in Marion County, Iowa, on May 15, 1959.[152] Her cause of death was heart failure. Nina Edythe was buried in Graceland Cemetery, Knoxville, Marion County, Iowa (Find a Grave ID 135668218).

Children of Robert Nelson Chambers and Nina Edythe Hartness:

+ 220 m I. **Lawrence Nelson Chambers** was born in Knoxville, Marion County, Iowa, on March 04, 1911.[152] He died in Davenport, Scott County, Iowa, on February 26, 1998, at the age of 86.[153] His cause of death was heart attack. He was buried in Graceland Cemetery, Knoxville, Marion County, Iowa (Find a Grave ID 135668388).

---

148   Lawrence N. Chambers and Ruth Hawks Wright.

149   Lawrence Nelson Chambers.

150   Newspaper Clipping + Marion County Mariage Records 1900-1915.

151   Marion County Iowa Birth Records.

152   Lawrence N. Chambers.

153   Attended Funeral.

+ 221 f II. **Mary Ellen Chambers** was born in Marion County, Iowa, on May 12, 1917.[154] She died in Roanoke, Roanoke County, Virginia, on September 12, 1992, at the age of 75.[155] Mary Ellen was buried in Blue Ridge Memorial Gardens, Roanoke, Roanoke County, Virginia (Find a Grave ID 137405508).

+ 222 m III. **Arlen John Chambers** was born in Marion County, Iowa, on August 08, 1921.[148] He died in Hastings, Barry County, Michigan, on January 24, 1987, at the age of 65.[156] His cause of death was suicide–gunshot. He was buried in Riverside Cemetery, Hastings, Barry County, Michigan (Find a Grave ID 22096208).

+ 223 f IV. **Laura Grace Chambers** was born in Knoxville Township, Marion County, Iowa, on November 24, 1925.[157] She died in Anamosa, Jones County, Iowa, on July 11, 2017, at the age of 91. Laura Grace was buried in Graceland Cemetery, Knoxville, Marion County, Iowa (Find a Grave ID 181280153).

Family of Jesse Chambers and Lila Pinkerton

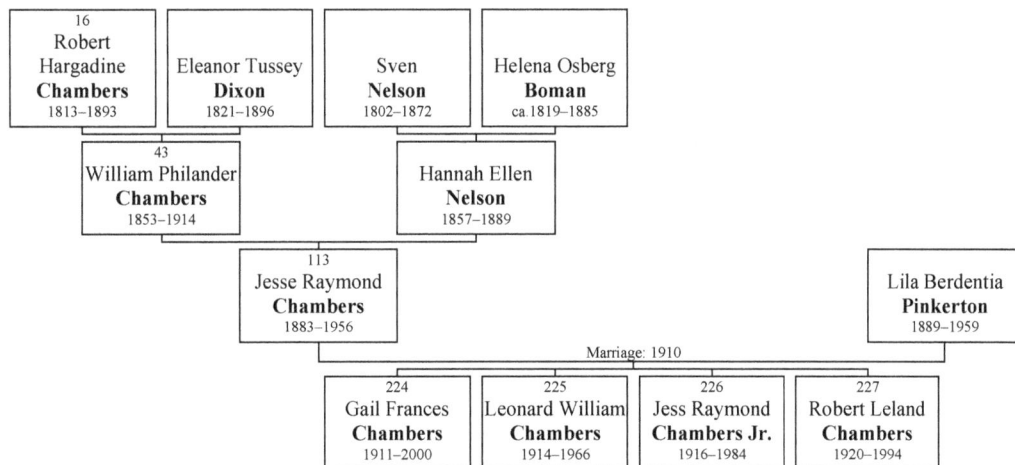

113. **Jesse Raymond Chambers** was born on Saturday, March 31, 1883, in Columbia, Marion County, Iowa.[158] He was the son of William Philander Chambers (43) and Hannah Ellen Nelson.

Jesse Raymond died in Loveland, Larimer County, Colorado, on September 14, 1956, at the age of 73.[158] He was buried in Loveland Burial Park, Loveland, Larimer County, Colorado (Find a Grave ID 150047205).

---

154 Mary Ellen Chambers.

155 Death Certificate.

156 His wife.

157 Birth Certificate.

158 Lawrence N. Chambers and Ruth Hawks Wright.

At the age of 27, Jesse Raymond married **Lila Berdentia Pinkerton** on Wednesday, April 06, 1910, in Angora, Morrill County, Nebraska, when she was 21 years old.[159] They had four children.

Lila Berdentia was born in Hemingford, Box Butte County, Nebraska, on Wednesday, January 30, 1889.[159] She reached 70 years of age and died in Loveland, Larimer County, Colorado, on June 08, 1959.[159] Lila Berdentia was buried in Loveland Burial Park, Loveland, Larimer County, Colorado (Find a Grave ID 150047371).

Children of Jesse Raymond Chambers and Lila Berdentia Pinkerton:

+ 224   f   I. **Gail Frances Chambers** was born in Alliance, Box Butte County, Nebraska, on June 30, 1911.[159] She died on November 04, 2000, at the age of 89. Gail Frances was buried in Loveland Burial Park, Loveland, Larimer County, Colorado (Find a Grave ID 154680889).

+ 225   m   II. **Leonard William Chambers** was born in Alliance, Box Butte County, Nebraska, on April 02, 1914.[160] He died in Casper, Natrona County, Wyoming, on February 12, 1966, at the age of 51.[160] Leonard William was buried in Highland Cemetery, Casper, Natrona County, Wyoming (Find a Grave ID 62089534).

+ 226   m   III. **Jess Raymond Chambers Jr.** was born in Alliance, Box Butte County, Nebraska, on November 27, 1916.[159] He died in Grand Junction, Mesa County, Colorado, on November 14, 1984, at the age of 67.[159] Jess Raymond was buried in Orchard Mesa Cemetery, Grand Junction, Mesa County, Colorado (Find a Grave ID 105025933).

+ 227   m   IV. **Robert Leland Chambers** was born in Rushville, Sheridan County, Nebraska, on May 15, 1920.[159] He died in Kansas City, Kansas, on February 24, 1994, at the age of 73.[159] Robert Leland was buried in Leavenworth National Cemetery, Leavenworth, Leavenworth County, Kansas (Find a Grave ID 481525).

Family of Pauline Chambers and Herbert Lamb

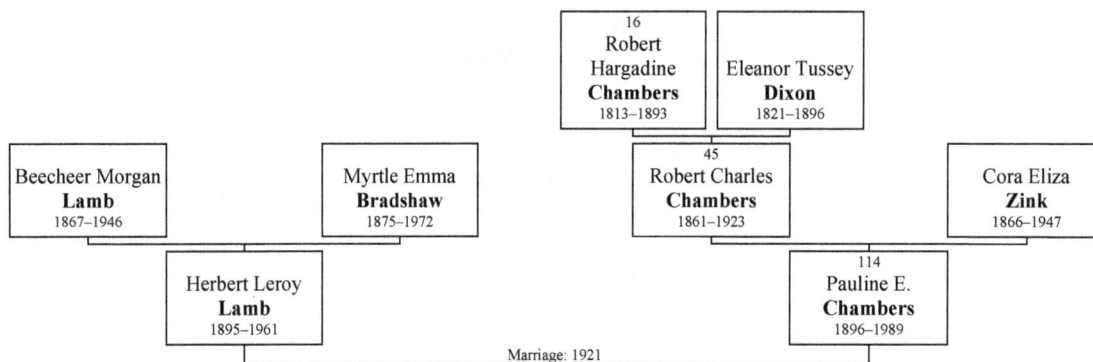

---

159   Gail Chambers Moritz.

160   Lynne Frances Chambers.

114. **Pauline E. Chambers** was born on Sunday, March 29, 1896, in Osceola, Clarke County, Iowa.[161] She was the daughter of Robert Charles Chambers (45) and Cora Eliza Zink.

Pauline E. died in 1989 at the age of 92. She was buried in Junction Township Cemetery, Grand Junction, Greene County, Iowa (Find a Grave ID 40455492).

Pauline E. married **Mr. Herbert Leroy Lamb** in June 1921 in Greene County, Iowa. Herbert Leroy was born in Iowa, USA, on Sunday, August 11, 1895. He was the son of Beecheer Morgan Lamb and Myrtle Emma Bradshaw.

He served in the military: WWI. Herbert Leroy reached 66 years of age and died in Grand Junction, Greene County, Iowa, on October 07, 1961. He was buried on October 10, 1961, in Junction Township Cemetery, Grand Junction, Greene County, Iowa (Find a Grave ID 40455494).

Family of Cora Chambers and Eli Schuelke

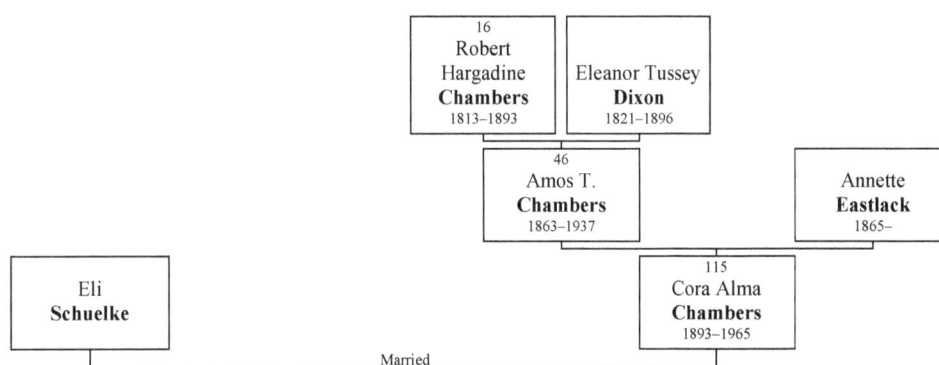

115. **Cora Alma Chambers** was born on Wednesday, March 08, 1893, in Murray, Clarke County, Iowa.[162] She was the daughter of Amos T. Chambers (46) and Annette Eastlack.

Cora Alma died in Phoenix, Maricopa County, Arizona, on September 04, 1965, at the age of 72. Her cause of death was acute coronary thrombosis with myocardial infarction, arteriosclerosis. Cora Alma was cremated on September 08, 1965 (Find a Grave ID 228140275).

She married **Eli Schuelke**.

---

[161]   Birth month and year given in 1900 Census.

[162]   From the 1900 Census Information.

Family of Fern Chambers and Royal Reisner

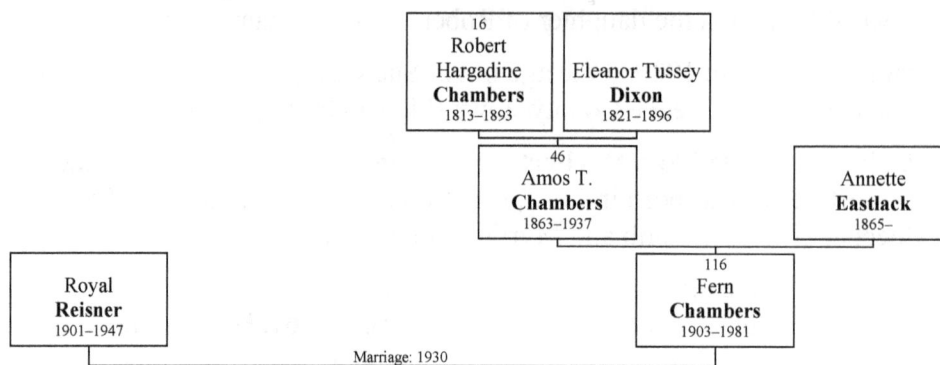

116. Fern Chambers was born in 1903. She was the daughter of Amos T. Chambers (46) and Annette Eastlack.

Fern died in 1981 at the age of 78. She was buried in Bellevue Memorial Park, Ontario, San Bernardino County, California (Find a Grave ID 151101256).

At the age of 27, Fern married **Royal Reisner** on Wednesday, July 30, 1930, at Upland Methodist Church in Upland, San Bernardino, California, when he was 28 years old. Royal was born in Illinois, USA, on Wednesday, October 23, 1901.

He reached 45 years of age and died in San Bernardino County, California, on June 29, 1947. Royal was buried in Bellevue Memorial Park, Ontario, San Bernardino County, California (Find a Grave ID 151101243).

Family of Herbert Hargadine and Mary Noel

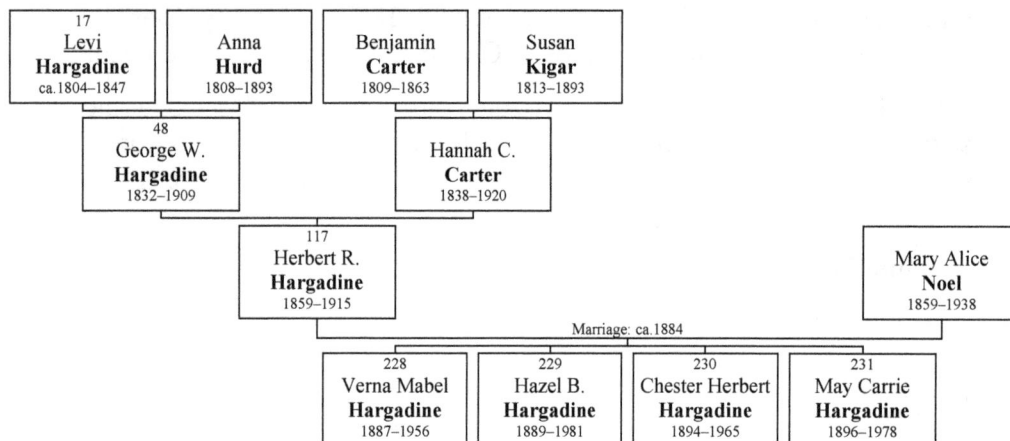

117. Herbert R. Hargadine was born on Thursday, June 23, 1859, in Illinois, USA. He was the son of George W. Hargadine (48) and Hannah C. Carter.

Herbert R. died on April 12, 1915, at the age of 55. He was buried in Ashland Cemetery, Saunders County, Nebraska (Find a Grave ID 41928399).

Herbert R. married **Mary Alice Noel** about 1884 in Burt County, Nebraska. They had four children.

Mary Alice was born in Illinois, USA, on Monday, June 20, 1859. Mary Alice reached 78 years of age and died on April 05, 1938. She was buried in Ashland Cemetery, Saunders County, Nebraska (Find a Grave ID 41928398).

Children of Herbert R. Hargadine and Mary Alice Noel:

+ 228   f   I. **Verna Mabel Hargadine** was born in Nebraska, USA, on February 23, 1887. She died in San Bernardino County, California, on May 28, 1956, at the age of 69. Verna Mabel was buried in Rose Hills Memorial Park, Whittier, Los Angeles County, California (Find a Grave ID 158734080).

+ 229   f   II. **Hazel B. Hargadine** was born in Nebraska, USA, on June 19, 1889. She died in Los Angeles, Los Angeles County, California, on August 12, 1981, at the age of 92. Hazel B. was buried in Rose Hills Memorial Park, Whittier, Los Angeles County, California (Find a Grave ID 105093056).

+ 230   m   III. **Chester Herbert Hargadine** was born in Omaha, Douglas County, Nebraska, on June 07, 1894.[163] He died in Los Angeles, Los Angeles County, California, on February 19, 1965, at the age of 70.[163] Chester Herbert was buried in Rose Hills Memorial Park, Whittier, Los Angeles County, California (Find a Grave ID 158295152).

+ 231   f   IV. **May Carrie Hargadine** was born in Nebraska, USA, on October 13, 1896. She was also known as **Carrie May**.

                      May Carrie died in Los Angeles County, California, on September 19, 1978, at the age of 81. She was buried in Rose Hills Memorial Park, Whittier, Los Angeles County, California (Find a Grave ID 252727875).

Family of Byron Hargadine and Effie Monninger

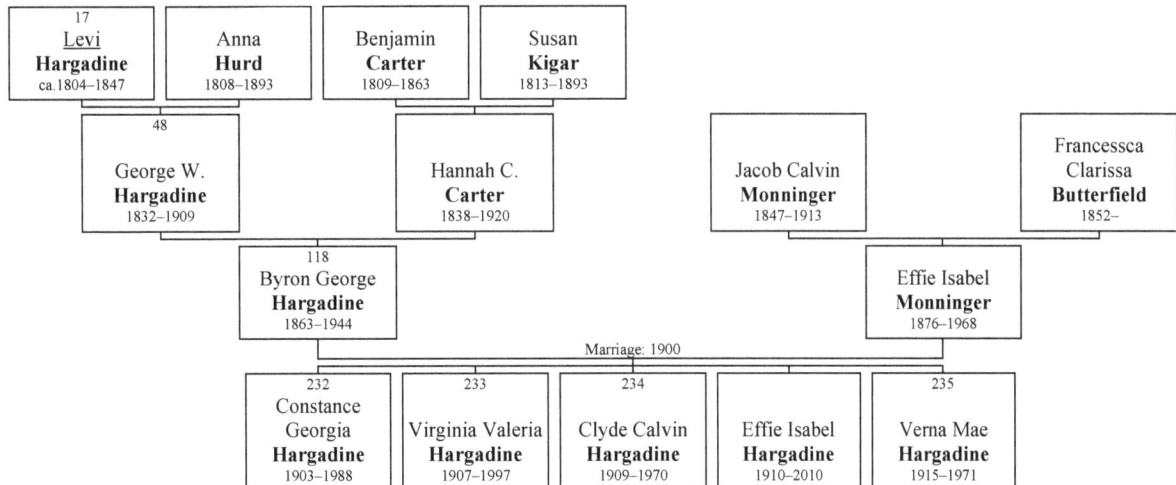

---

[163] Ancestry.com, Public Member Trees (Provo, UT, USA, Ancestry.com Operations, Inc., 2006), Ancestry.com, Record for Chester Herbert Hargadine. https://search.ancestry.co.uk/cgi-bin/sse.dll?db=1030&h=232061984725&indiv=try.

118. **Byron George Hargadine** was born in September 1863 in Lasalle County, Illinois.[164] He was the son of George W. Hargadine (48) and Hannah C. Carter.

Byron George died in Omaha, Douglas County, Nebraska, on September 10, 1944, at the age of 81.

At the age of 36, Byron George married **Effie Isabel Monninger** on Wednesday, July 11, 1900, in Omaha, Douglas County, Nebraska, when she was 24 years old. They had five children.

Effie Isabel was born in Omaha, Douglas County, Nebraska, on Monday, May 29, 1876.[165] She was the daughter of Jacob Calvin Monninger and Francessca Clarissa Butterfield.

Effie Isabel reached 92 years of age and died at Providence Hospital in Portland, Multnomah County, Oregon, on June 03, 1968.[165] Her cause of death was coronary thrombosis. Effie Isabel was buried (Find a Grave ID 205460537).

Children of Byron George Hargadine and Effie Isabel Monninger:

+ 232   f   I. **Constance Georgia Hargadine** was born in Omaha, Douglas County, Nebraska, on November 14, 1903.[166] She died in San Diego, San Diego County, California, on April 12, 1988, at the age of 84. Constance Georgia was buried in Evergreen Cemetery, El Centro, Imperial County, California (Find a Grave ID 114501079).

+ 233   f   II. **Virginia Valeria Hargadine** was born in Nebraska, USA, on April 24, 1907. She died in Hillsboro, Washington County, Oregon, on November 29, 1997, at the age of 90.

+ 234   m   III. **Clyde Calvin Hargadine** was born in Ohio, USA, on April 06, 1909. He died in Hamilton, Butler County, Ohio, on November 01, 1970, at the age of 61.

         f   IV. **Effie Isabel Hargadine** was born in Omaha, Douglas County, Nebraska, on December 05, 1910. She died in Omaha, Douglas County, Nebraska, on November 02, 2010, at the age of 99. Effie Isabel was buried in Calvary Cemetery, Omaha, Douglas County, Nebraska (Find a Grave ID 61103877).

+ 235   f   V. **Verna Mae Hargadine** was born in Douglas County, Nebraska, on February 06, 1915.[167] She died in Multnomah, Oregon, USA, on September 14, 1971, at the age of 56.[167]

---

164   1900 Census Douglas County, Nebraska Omaha City (Vol 14, ED 58, Sheet 2) June 2, 1900.

165   Social Security Death Index.

166   California Death Records.

167   Ancestry.com, Public Member Trees (Provo, UT, USA, Ancestry.com Operations, Inc., 2006), Ancestry.com, Record for Verna Mae Hargadine. https://search.ancestry.co.uk/cgi-bin/sse.dll?db=1030&h=232061989514&indiv=try.

Family of Charles Hargadine and Lillie Eby

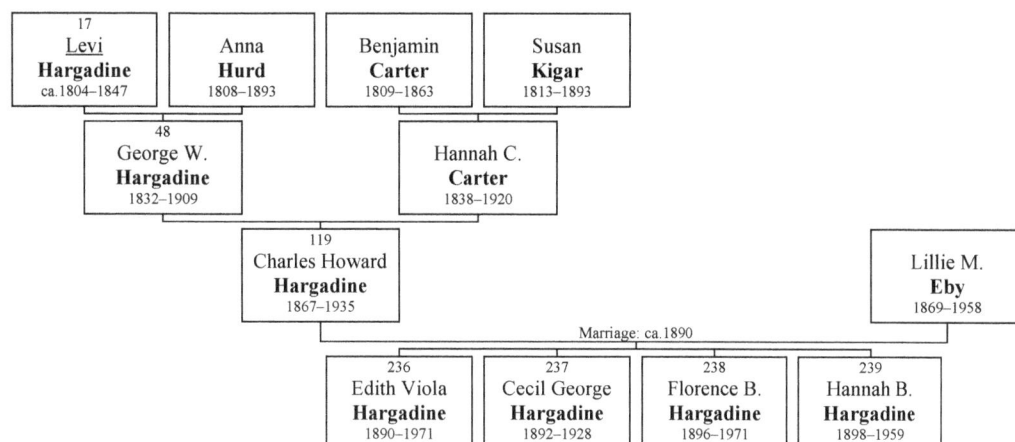

119. **Charles Howard Hargadine** was born in October 1867 in Illinois, USA. He was the son of George W. Hargadine (48) and Hannah C. Carter.

Charles Howard worked as a Controller; UP Railroad Company in 1916.[168] He died in Omaha, Douglas County, Nebraska, in April 1935 at the age of 67. Charles Howard was buried in Forest Lawn Memorial Park, Omaha, Douglas County, Nebraska, on April 10, 1935 (Find a Grave ID 136311888).

More facts and events for Charles Howard Hargadine:

Individual Note: March 29, 1921   Received patent 1,372,687 for window design

Charles Howard married **Lillie M. Eby** about 1890. They had four children.

Lillie M. was born in Iowa, USA, in December 1869. She reached 88 years of age and died in Omaha, Douglas County, Nebraska, in June 1958. Lillie M. was buried on June 05, 1958, in Forest Lawn Cemetery, Omaha, Douglas County, Nebraska (Find a Grave ID 136312037).

Children of Charles Howard Hargadine and Lillie M. Eby:

+ 236   f   I. **Edith Viola Hargadine** was born in Omaha, Douglas County, Nebraska, on September 23, 1890.[169] She died in Tekamah, Burt County, Nebraska, on July 27, 1971, at the age of 80.[169]

+ 237   m   II. **Cecil George Hargadine** was born in Nebraska, USA, in January 1892. He died on August 16, 1928, at the age of 36. Cecil George was buried in Forest Lawn Memorial Park, Omaha, Douglas County, Nebraska, on August 18, 1928 (Find a Grave ID 136311868).[170]

+ 238   f   III. **Florence B. Hargadine** was born in Nebraska, USA, on December 28, 1896. She died in Miami, Dade County, Florida, on June 11, 1971, at the

---

168   Omaha Directory County's, Omaha City Directory, 1916, 521.

169   Ancestry.com, Public Member Trees (Provo, UT, USA, Ancestry.com Operations, Inc., 2006), Ancestry.com, Record for Edith Viola Hargadine. https://search.ancestry.co.uk/cgi-bin/sse.dll?db=1030&h=24051617541&indiv=try.

170   http://www.forestlawnomaha.com/GraveIndex/IndexSummaryH.html.

age of 74.[171, 172] Florence B. was buried in Woodlawn Park North Cemetery and Mausoleum, Miami, Miami-Dade County, Florida (Find a Grave ID 205319385).

+ 239   f   IV. **Hannah B. Hargadine** was born in Omaha, Douglas County, Nebraska, on August 09, 1898.[173] She died in Omaha, Douglas County, Nebraska, on July 20, 1959, at the age of 60.[173] Hannah B. was buried in Forest Lawn Memorial Park, Omaha, Douglas County, Nebraska, on July 22, 1959 (Find a Grave ID 73050259).

Family of Bertha Hargadine and James Morton

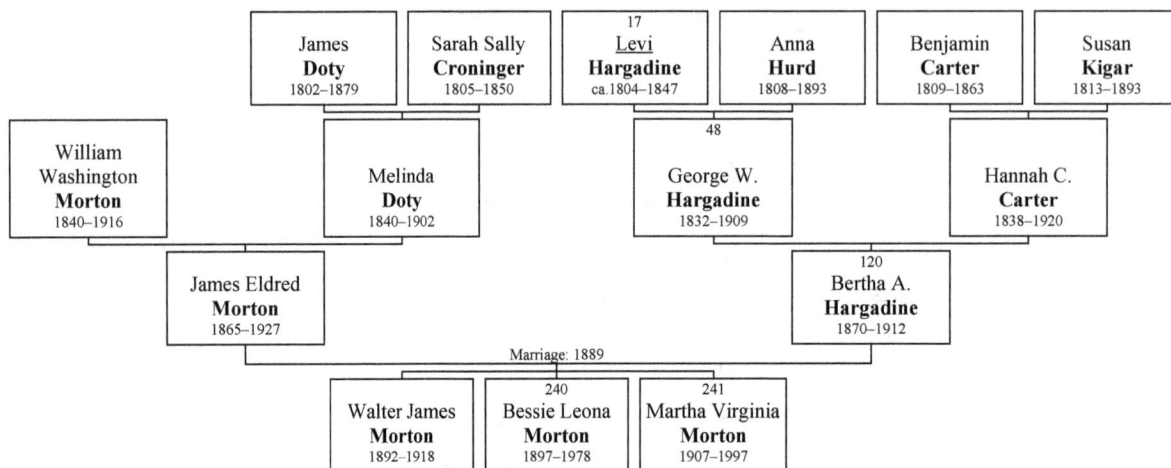

James **Doty** 1802–1879	Sarah Sally **Croninger** 1805–1850	17 Levi **Hargadine** ca.1804–1847	Anna **Hurd** 1808–1893	Benjamin **Carter** 1809–1863	Susan **Kigar** 1813–1893

William Washington **Morton** 1840–1916	Melinda **Doty** 1840–1902	48 George W. **Hargadine** 1832–1909	Hannah C. **Carter** 1838–1920

James Eldred **Morton** 1865–1927		120 Bertha A. **Hargadine** 1870–1912

Marriage: 1889

240 Walter James **Morton** 1892–1918	Bessie Leona **Morton** 1897–1978	241 Martha Virginia **Morton** 1907–1997

120.   **Bertha A. Hargadine** was born on Friday, December 02, 1870, in Chillicothe, Peoria County, Illinois. She was the daughter of George W. Hargadine (48) and Hannah C. Carter.

Bertha A. died in Spooner, Washburn County, Wisconsin, on October 28, 1912, at the age of 41. Her cause of death was carcinoma of the liver and carcinoma of the lung. Bertha A. was buried in Chillicothe, Peoria County, Illinois.

At the age of 18, Bertha A. married **James Eldred Morton** on Wednesday, July 10, 1889, in Norfolk, Madison County, Nebraska, when he was 23 years old. They had three children.

> James Eldred was born in Modale, Harrison County, Iowa, on Wednesday, October 18, 1865. James Eldred reached 61 years of age and died in Spooner, Washburn County, Wisconsin, in 1927. He was buried in Spooner Cemetery, Spooner, Washburn County, Wisconsin (Find a Grave ID 96330777). James E., who now lives in Spooner, Wisconsin, married Bertha Hargadine. His wife died in 1912, leaving him with one daughter, Martha. James E. began life when very young as a telegraph operator, in fact, lacking one month of being thirteen years of age when he received his first appointment. He has always been with the Chicago & Northwestern Railway Company, and is now division superintendent of the road, having made a remarkable record with this company.*
>
> *Source: 1915 *Harrison County Iowa History*, pp. 564, 565, 566, 567
> Provided by Tim Chambers. He was the son of William Washington Morton and Melinda Doty.

---

171   Social Security Death Index.

172   Florida Death Index 1877-1998, Certificate: 35871.

173   Ancestry.com, Public Member Trees (Provo, UT, USA, Ancestry.com Operations, Inc., 2006), Ancestry.com, Record for Hannah A Hargadine. https://search.ancestry.co.uk/cgi-bin/sse.dll?db=1030&h=150007353034&indiv=try.

Children of Bertha A. Hargadine and James Eldred Morton:

m   I.   **Walter James Morton** was born in Omaha, Douglas County, Nebraska, on March 16, 1892. He was adopted. 1900 Census shows adopted.

                Walter James died in Hopedale, Worcester County, Massachusetts, on September 27, 1918, at the age of 26. He was buried in Hopedale Village Cemetery, Hopedale, Worcester County, Massachusetts (Find a Grave ID 135708473).

+ 240   f   II.   **Bessie Leona Morton** was born in Blanchard, Page County, Iowa, on April 13, 1897.[174] They were her parents by adoption.

                She died in Spooner, Washburn County, Wisconsin, on March 05, 1978, at the age of 80. Bessie Leona was buried in Spooner Cemetery, Spooner, Washburn County, Wisconsin (Find a Grave ID 105078856).

+ 241   f   III.   **Martha Virginia Morton** was born in Omaha, Douglas County, Nebraska, on May 09, 1907. She died in Spooner, Washburn County, Wisconsin, on February 22, 1997, at the age of 89. Martha Virginia was buried in Spooner Cemetery, Spooner, Washburn County, Wisconsin (Find a Grave ID 128353853).

Family of Ralph Hargadine and Bessie Davis

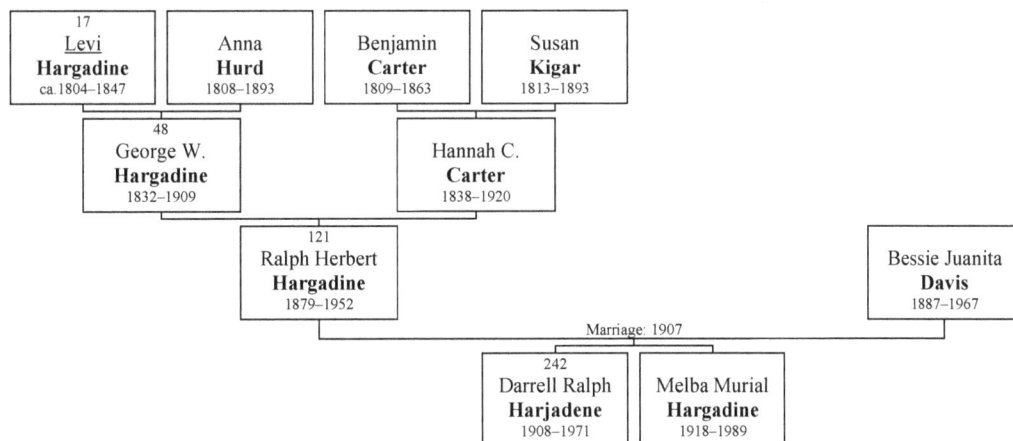

121.   **Ralph Herbert Hargadine** was born on Saturday, September 06, 1879, in Groveland Twp., LaSalle County, Illinois. He was the son of George W. Hargadine (48) and Hannah C. Carter. He was also known as **Jackson R. Davis**.

       Ralph Herbert worked as an Omaha Electric Light & Power Company in 1916.[175] He died in Long Beach, Los Angeles County, California, on March 03, 1952, at the age of 72. Ralph Herbert was buried in Forest Lawn Memorial Park, Long Beach, Los Angeles County, California (Find a Grave ID 200477703).

---

174   Ancestry.com, Public Member Trees (Provo, UT, USA, Ancestry.com Operations, Inc., 2006), Ancestry.com, Record for Bessie Morton. https://search.ancestry.co.uk/cgi-bin/sse.dll?db=1030&h=40446052398&indiv=try.

175   Omaha Directory Counties, Omaha City Directory, 1916, 521.

At the age of 27, Ralph Herbert married **Bessie Juanita Davis** on Monday, August 05, 1907, in Omaha, Douglas County, Nebraska, when she was 20 years old. They had two children.

Bessie Juanita was born in Creston, Union County, Iowa, on Sunday, May 29, 1887. She reached 79 years of age and died in Los Angeles, Los Angeles County, California, on April 08, 1967. Bessie Juanita was buried in Forest Lawn Memorial Park, Long Beach, Los Angeles County, California (Find a Grave ID 200477701).

Children of Ralph Herbert Hargadine and Bessie Juanita Davis:

+ 242 m I. **Darrell Ralph Harjadene** was born in Lincoln, Lancaster County, Nebraska, on June 03, 1908. He was also known as **Darrell Ralph Hargadine**.

Darrell Ralph died in Page, Coconino County, Arizona, on December 30, 1971, at the age of 63. He was buried in Mountain View Cemetery, Williams, Coconino County, Arizona (Find a Grave ID 62653440).

f II. **Melba Murial Hargadine** was born in Oakland, Alameda County, California, on July 21, 1918. She died in Los Angeles, Los Angeles County, California, on December 17, 1989, at the age of 71. Melba Murial was buried in Forest Lawn Memorial Park, Long Beach, Los Angeles County, California (Find a Grave ID 200477702).

Family of Mary Clyne and John Sturm

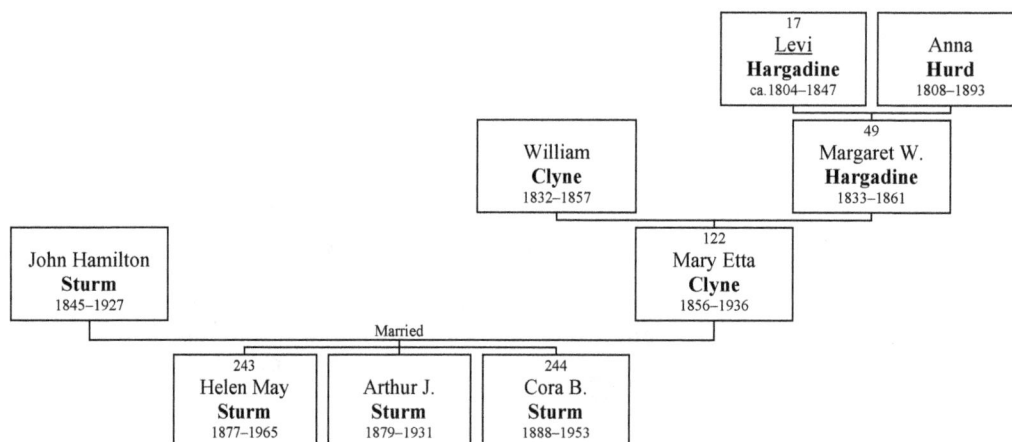

122. **Mary Etta Clyne** was born on Tuesday, June 17, 1856, in Illinois, USA. She was the daughter of William Clyne and Margaret W. Hargadine (49).

Mary Etta died in Medina, Peoria County, Illinois, on February 10, 1936, at the age of 79. Her cause of death was carcinoma of the intestines, cirrhosis of liver. Mary Etta was buried in La Salle Cemetery, Rome, Peoria County, Illinois, on February 13, 1936 (Find a Grave ID 23286807).

She married **John Hamilton Sturm**. They had three children.

John Hamilton was born in Peoria County, Illinois, in December 1845. He reached 81 years of age and died in Dunlap, Peoria County, Illinois, on March 02, 1927. John Hamilton was buried on March 05, 1927, in La Salle Cemetery, Rome, Peoria County, Illinois (Find a Grave ID 23286795).

Children of Mary Etta Clyne and John Hamilton Sturm:

+ 243 f I. **Helen May Sturm** was born in Dunlap, Peoria County, Illinois, on December 18, 1877. She died on June 10, 1965, at the age of 87. Helen May was buried in Springdale Cemetery and Mausoleum, Peoria, Peoria County, Illinois (Find a Grave ID 148218293).

  m II. **Arthur J. Sturm** was born in Illinois, USA, in October 1879. He died in Medina, Peoria County, Illinois, on April 05, 1931, at the age of 51. Arthur J. was buried in La Salle Cemetery, Rome, Peoria County, Illinois (Find a Grave ID 23286594).

+ 244 f III. **Cora B. Sturm** was born in Dunlap, Peoria County, Illinois, on March 19, 1888. She died in Edelstein, Peoria County, Illinois, in 1953 at the age of 64. Cora B. was buried in La Salle Cemetery, Rome, Peoria County, Illinois (Find a Grave ID 23269872).

Family of Nancy Van Alstine and John Mathews

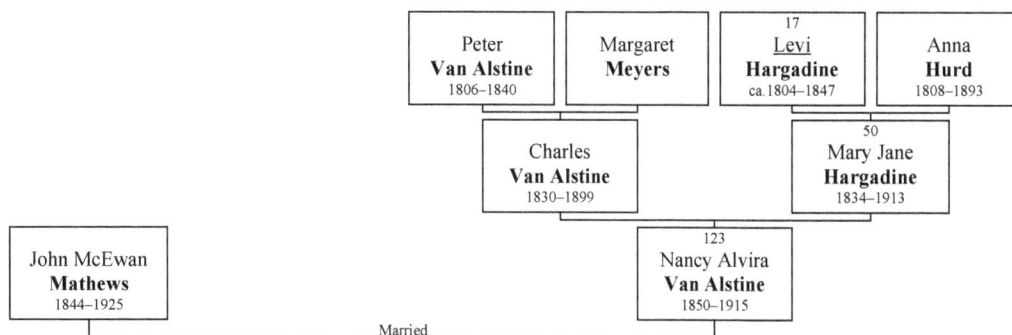

123. **Nancy Alvira Van Alstine** was born on Friday, December 27, 1850, in Olena, Henderson County, Illinois.[176] She was the daughter of Charles Van Alstine and Mary Jane Hargadine (50).

Nancy Alvira died in Omaha, Douglas County, Nebraska, on June 29, 1915, at the age of 64. She was buried in Evergreen Cemetery, Red Oak, Montgomery County, Iowa (Find a Grave ID 26152434).

---

176 Tim Chambers, Vanalstines.GED, Date of Import: Mar 11, 2001.

She married **John McEwan Mathews**. John McEwan was born in Greene County, Indiana, on Monday, December 02, 1844.

He reached 80 years of age and died in Omaha, Douglas County, Nebraska, on April 27, 1925. John McEwan was buried in Evergreen Cemetery, Red Oak, Montgomery County, Iowa (Find a Grave ID 26152421).

Family of Peter Van Alstine and Martha Charter

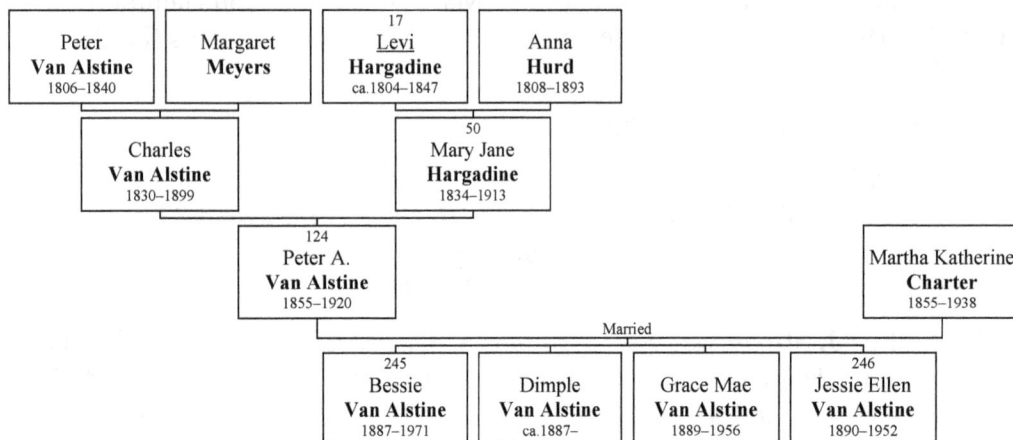

124. **Peter A. Van Alstine** was born on Monday, February 26, 1855, in Henderson County, Illinois.[177] He was the son of Charles Van Alstine and Mary Jane Hargadine (50).

Peter A. died in McDonough County, Illinois, on February 19, 1920, at the age of 64. He was buried in Mount Auburn Cemetery, Colchester, McDonough County, Illinois (Find a Grave ID 82893699).

He married **Martha Katherine Charter**. They had four daughters.

Martha Katherine was born in Henderson County, Illinois, on Thursday, September 27, 1855.[177] She reached 82 years of age and died in Illinois, USA, on January 06, 1938. Martha Katherine was buried in Mount Auburn Cemetery, Colchester, McDonough County, Illinois (Find a Grave ID 82893620).

Daughters of Peter A. Van Alstine and Martha Katherine Charter:

+ 245   f   I. **Bessie Van Alstine** was born in Taylor County, Iowa, in 1887.[177] She died in 1971 at the age of 84. Bessie was buried in Oakwood Cemetery, Macomb, McDonough County, Illinois (Find a Grave ID 128286839).

         f   II. **Dimple Van Alstine** was born in Taylor County, Iowa, about 1887.[177]

         f   III. **Grace Mae Van Alstine** was born in Montgomery County, Iowa, on January 16, 1889.[177] She died in Illinois, USA, on May 29, 1956, at the age of 67. Grace Mae was buried in Mount Auburn Cemetery, Colchester, McDonough County, Illinois (Find a Grave ID 83456874).

---

177   Tim Chambers, Vanalstines.GED, Date of Import: Mar 11, 2001.

+ 246   f   IV. **Jessie Ellen Van Alstine** was born in Taylor County, Iowa, on October 30, 1890.[177] She died on August 20, 1952, at the age of 61. Jessie Ellen was buried in Good Hope Cemetery, Good Hope, McDonough County, Illinois (Find a Grave ID 68375527).

Family of Charles Van Alstine and Nancy Kunce

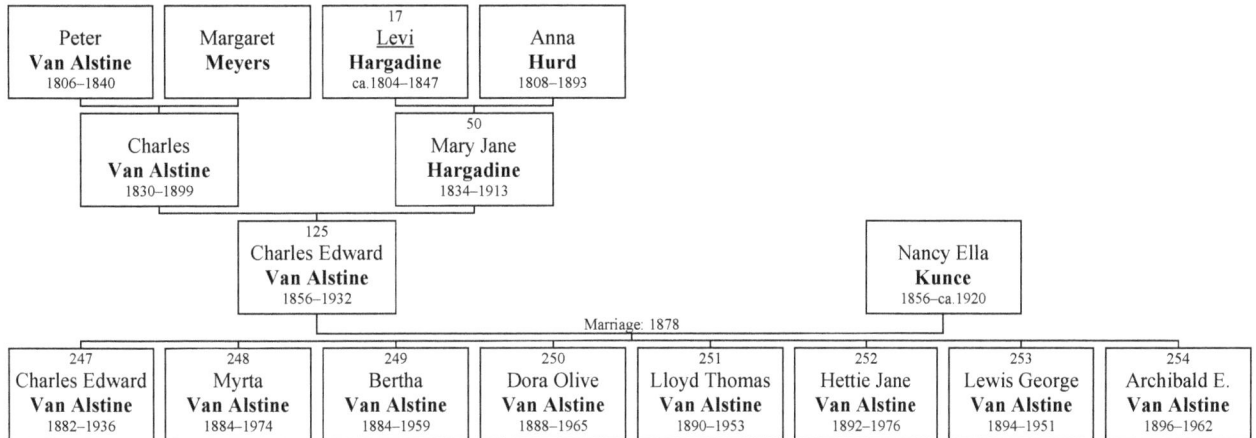

Peter **Van Alstine** 1806–1840	Margaret **Meyers**	17 <u>Levi</u> **Hargadine** ca.1804–1847	Anna **Hurd** 1808–1893

Charles **Van Alstine** 1830–1899	50 Mary Jane **Hargadine** 1834–1913

125 Charles Edward **Van Alstine** 1856–1932	Nancy Ella **Kunce** 1856–ca.1920

Marriage: 1878

247 Charles Edward **Van Alstine** 1882–1936	248 Myrta **Van Alstine** 1884–1974	249 Bertha **Van Alstine** 1884–1959	250 Dora Olive **Van Alstine** 1888–1965	251 Lloyd Thomas **Van Alstine** 1890–1953	252 Hettie Jane **Van Alstine** 1892–1976	253 Lewis George **Van Alstine** 1894–1951	254 Archibald E. **Van Alstine** 1896–1962

125.   **Charles Edward Van Alstine** was born in July 1856 in Pottawattamie County, Iowa.[178] He was the son of Charles Van Alstine and Mary Jane Hargadine (50). He was also known as **Ed**.

Charles Edward died in Nodaway, Taylor County, Iowa, on September 15, 1932, at the age of 76.

Charles Edward married **Nancy Ella Kunce** on Sunday, November 10, 1878, in Taylor County, Florida. They had eight children.

Nancy Ella was born in Illinois, USA, in March 1856.[178] She reached 63 years of age and died about 1920.

Children of Charles Edward Van Alstine and Nancy Ella Kunce:

+ 247   m   I. **Charles Edward Van Alstine** was born in Guss, Taylor County, Iowa, on February 21, 1882.[178] He died in Gravity, Taylor County, Iowa, on May 24, 1936, at the age of 54.[178–180] Charles Edward was buried in Washington Cemetery, Gravity, Taylor County, Iowa, on May 26, 1936 (Find a Grave ID 57720344).[178]

+ 248   f   II. **Myrta Van Alstine** was born in Taylor County, Iowa, on January 12, 1884.[178] She died in Jefferson County, Colorado, on September 27, 1974, at the age of 90. Myrta was buried in Crown Hill Cemetery, Wheat Ridge, Jefferson County, Colorado (Find a Grave ID 20883570).

---

178   Tim Chambers, Vanalstines.GED, Date of Import: Mar 11, 2001.

179   *Bedford Times Press* Newspaper: Bedford, Taylor County, Iowa, 28 MAY 1936.

180   *Clarinda Herald Journal* Newspaper: Clarinda, Page County, Iowa, 01 JUN 1936.

+ 249 f III. **Bertha Van Alstine** was born in Taylor County, Iowa, on September 04, 1884.[178] She died in Clarinda, Page County, Iowa, in January 1959 at the age of 74. Bertha was buried in Clarinda Cemetery, Clarinda, Page County, Iowa (Find a Grave ID 77875905).

+ 250 f IV. **Dora Olive Van Alstine** was born in Taylor County, Iowa, on October 10, 1888.[178] She died in St. James, Phelps County, Missouri, on June 17, 1965, at the age of 76. Her cause of death was myocardial infarction. She was buried in Hematite Methodist Cemetery, Hematite, Jefferson County, Missouri, on June 19, 1965 (Find a Grave ID 141154414).

+ 251 m V. **Lloyd Thomas Van Alstine** was born in Taylor County, Iowa, on August 15, 1890.[178] He died in White Salmon, Klickitat County, Washington, on June 29, 1953, at the age of 62.[178, 181] Lloyd Thomas was buried in Pine Grove Cemetery, Hood River, Hood River County, Oregon, on July 02, 1953 (Find a Grave ID 32766717).

+ 252 f VI. **Hettie Jane Van Alstine** was born in Montgomery County, Iowa, on September 27, 1892.[178, 182] She died in Clarinda, Page County, Iowa, on May 20, 1976, at the age of 83.[178, 183] Hettie Jane was buried in North Grove Cemetery, Hepburn, Page County, Iowa (Find a Grave ID 66596661).

+ 253 m VII. **Lewis George Van Alstine** was born in Montgomery County, Iowa, on March 21, 1894.[178] He died in Excelsior Springs, Clay County, Missouri, on May 30, 1951, at the age of 57.[178, 184, 185] Lewis George was buried in Clarinda Cemetery, Clarinda, Page County, Iowa (Find a Grave ID 78719424).[178]

+ 254 m VIII. **Archibald E. Van Alstine** was born in Guss, Taylor County, Iowa, on June 15, 1896.[178] He died in Concord, Contra Costa County, California, on February 12, 1962, at the age of 65.[178] Archibald E. was buried in Sunset View Cemetery, El Cerrito, Contra Costa County, California (Find a Grave ID 136603669).[178]

---

181 *Clarinda Herald Journal* Newspaper: Clarinda, Page County, Iowa, 02 JUL 1953.

182 Social Security Death Index.

183 *Clarinda Herald Journal* Newspaper: Clarinda, Page County, Iowa, 27 MAY 1976 -(#345)?.

184 *Bedford Times Press* Newspaper: Bedford, Taylor County, Iowa, 07 JUN 1951.

185 *Clarinda Herald Journal* Newspaper: Clarinda, Page County, Iowa, 05 JUN 1951.

Family of Emma Van Alstine and William Wilson

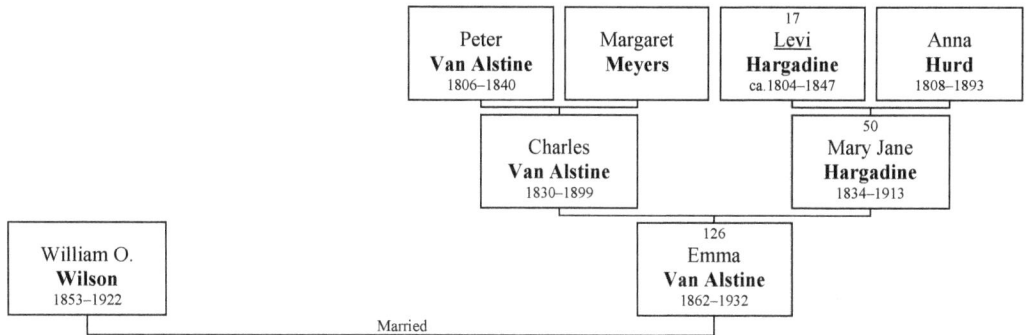

126.　**Emma Van Alstine** was born in October 1862 in Illinois, USA.[186] She was the daughter of Charles Van Alstine and Mary Jane Hargadine (50).

Emma died in Wasco County, Oregon, on September 15, 1932, at the age of 69. She was buried in Kelly Cemetery, Maupin, Wasco County, Oregon (Find a Grave ID 155713925).

She married **William O. Wilson**. William O. was born in 1853.

He reached 69 years of age and died in Douglas County, Oregon, on March 04, 1922. William O. was buried on March 04, 1922, in Kelly Cemetery, Maupin, Wasco County, Oregon (Find a Grave ID 35292558).

Family of Thomas Van Alstine and Nellie Firkins

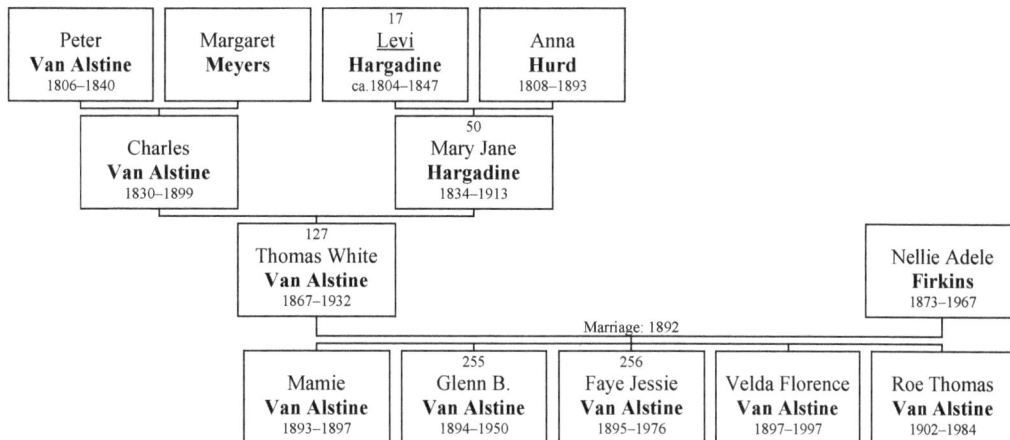

127.　**Thomas White Van Alstine** was born on Monday, June 17, 1867, in Peoria, Peoria County, Illinois.[187] He was the son of Charles Van Alstine and Mary Jane Hargadine (50).

Thomas White died in Taylor County, Iowa, on September 15, 1932, at the age of 65.[187] He was buried in Prairie Rose Cemetery, Corning, Adams County, Iowa (Find a Grave ID 80093109).[187]

186　Tim Chambers, Vanalstines.GED, Date of Import: Mar 11, 2001.

187　Tim Chambers, Vanalstines.GED, Date of Import: Mar 11, 2001.

Thomas White married **Nellie Adele Firkins** in 1892 in Taylor County, Iowa.[187] They had five children.

Nellie Adele was born in Knox County, Illinois, on Friday, February 07, 1873.[187] She reached 94 years of age and died in Taylor County, Iowa, on February 07, 1967.[187–189] Nellie Adele was buried in Prairie Rose Cemetery, Corning, Adams County, Iowa (Find a Grave ID 80093852).[187]

Children of Thomas White Van Alstine and Nellie Adele Firkins:

	f	I.	**Mamie Van Alstine** was born in Adams County, Iowa, in 1893.[187] She died in Adams County, Iowa, in 1897 at the age of 4.[187] Mamie was buried in Prairie Rose Cemetery, Corning, Adams County, Iowa (Find a Grave ID 91434334).[187]
+ 255	m	II.	**Glenn B. Van Alstine** was born in Taylor County, Iowa, on February 18, 1894.[187] He died on November 05, 1950, at the age of 56. Glenn B. was buried in Villisca Cemetery, Villisca, Montgomery County, Iowa (Find a Grave ID 94431841).
+ 256	f	III.	**Faye Jessie Van Alstine** was born in Taylor County, Iowa, on September 04, 1895.[187, 190] She died in Omaha, Douglas County, Nebraska, on June 11, 1976, at the age of 80.[187] Faye Jessie was buried in Villisca Cemetery, Villisca, Montgomery County, Iowa (Find a Grave ID 152717078).
	f	IV.	**Velda Florence Van Alstine** was born in Guss, Taylor County, Iowa, on August 12, 1897.[187] She died in Villisca, Montgomery County, Iowa, on May 27, 1997, at the age of 99. Velda Florence was buried in Villisca Cemetery, Villisca, Montgomery County, Iowa (Find a Grave ID 82743599).
	m	V.	**Roe Thomas Van Alstine** was born in Taylor County, Iowa, on February 15, 1902. He died on October 22, 1984, at the age of 82. Roe Thomas was buried in Camas Cemetery, Camas, Clark County, Washington (Find a Grave ID 64515480).

---

188   Social Security Death Index.

189   Clarinda Herald Journal Newspaper: Clarinda, Page County, Iowa, 09 FEB 1967.

190   Social Security Index.

Family of Dora Van Alstine and Arthur Lee

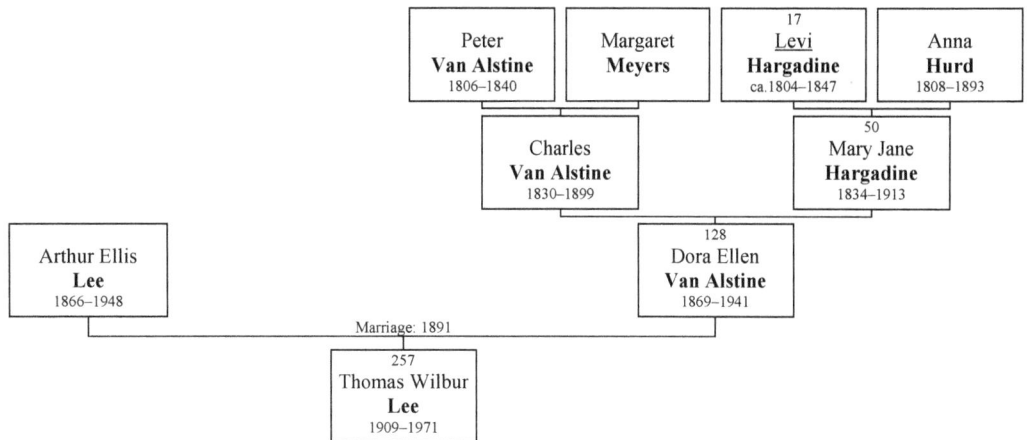

		17	
Peter **Van Alstine** 1806–1840	Margaret **Meyers**	Levi **Hargadine** ca.1804–1847	Anna **Hurd** 1808–1893

Charles **Van Alstine** 1830–1899

50 Mary Jane **Hargadine** 1834–1913

Arthur Ellis **Lee** 1866–1948

128 Dora Ellen **Van Alstine** 1869–1941

Marriage: 1891

257 Thomas Wilbur **Lee** 1909–1971

128. **Dora Ellen Van Alstine** was born on Monday, August 16, 1869, in Peoria, Peoria County, Illinois.[191] She was the daughter of Charles Van Alstine and Mary Jane Hargadine (50).

Dora Ellen died in Atkinson, Holt County, Nebraska, on April 12, 1941, at the age of 71. She was buried in Stuart Cemetery, Stuart, Holt County, Nebraska (Find a Grave ID 115024401).

At the age of 21, Dora Ellen married **Arthur Ellis Lee** on Friday, February 06, 1891, when he was 24 years old.[191] They had one son.

Arthur Ellis was born in Three Oaks, Berrien County, Michigan, on Tuesday, February 20, 1866. He reached 82 years of age and died in Rochester, Thurston County, Washington, on November 06, 1948. Arthur Ellis was buried in Stuart Cemetery, Stuart, Holt County, Nebraska (Find a Grave ID 115024313).

Son of Dora Ellen Van Alstine and Arthur Ellis Lee:

+ 257 m I. **Thomas Wilbur Lee** was born on May 09, 1909.[192] He died in August 1971 at the age of 62.[192]

Family of Lewis Van Alstine and Draxia Hanks

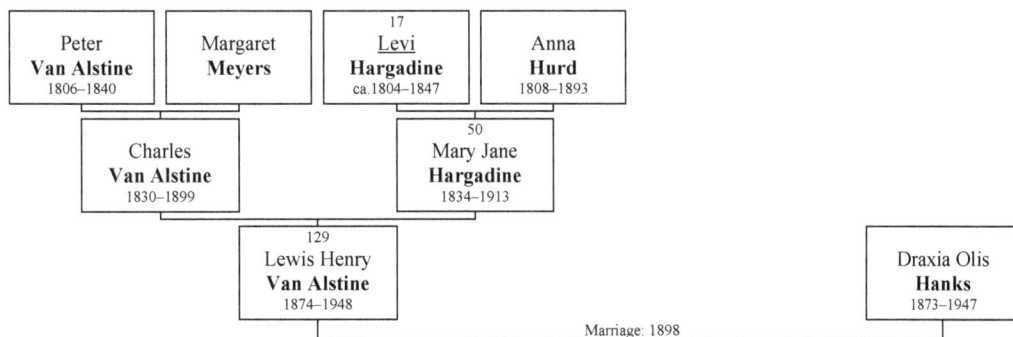

		17	
Peter **Van Alstine** 1806–1840	Margaret **Meyers**	Levi **Hargadine** ca.1804–1847	Anna **Hurd** 1808–1893

Charles **Van Alstine** 1830–1899

50 Mary Jane **Hargadine** 1834–1913

129 Lewis Henry **Van Alstine** 1874–1948

Draxia Olis **Hanks** 1873–1947

Marriage: 1898

---

191   Tim Chambers, Date of Import: Mar 11, 2001.

192   Tim Chambers, Vanalstines.GED, Date of Import: Mar 11, 2001.

129. **Lewis Henry Van Alstine** was born in June 1874 in Illinois, USA.[193] He was the son of Charles Van Alstine and Mary Jane Hargadine (50).

Lewis Henry died on October 14, 1948, at the age of 74. He was buried in Graceland Cemetery, Mitchell, Davison County, South Dakota (Find a Grave ID 105095310).

Lewis Henry married **Draxia Olis Hanks** on Wednesday, September 21, 1898, in Taylor County, Iowa. Draxia Olis was born in Kansas, USA, in July 1873.[193] She was also known as **Draxy**.

Draxia Olis reached 73 years of age and died in Mitchell, Davison County, South Dakota, in 1947. She was buried in Graceland Cemetery, Mitchell, Davison County, South Dakota (Find a Grave ID 188483871).

Family of Harriet Van Alstine and Noah Whitecotton

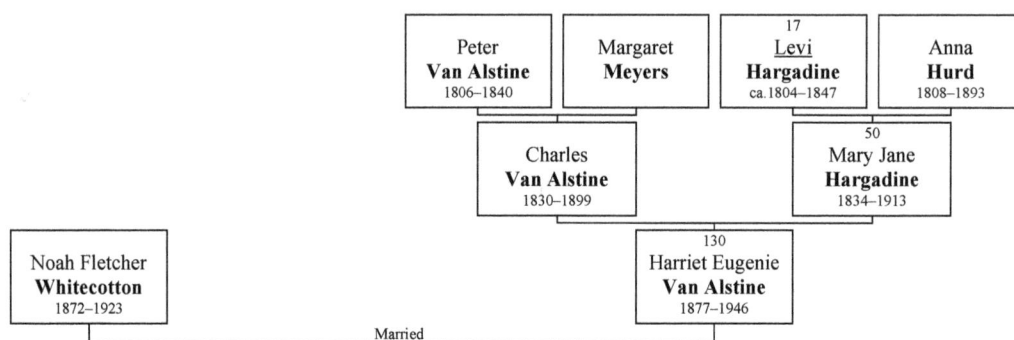

130. **Harriet Eugenie Van Alstine** was born on Sunday, May 20, 1877, in Villisca, Montgomery County, Iowa.[194] She was the daughter of Charles Van Alstine and Mary Jane Hargadine (50).

Harriet Eugenie died in Oregon, USA, on May 24, 1946, at the age of 69. She was buried in Pine Grove Cemetery, Hood River, Hood River County, Oregon (Find a Grave ID 29269441).

She married **Noah Fletcher Whitecotton**. Noah Fletcher was born in Holt, Taylor County, Iowa, on Monday, October 21, 1872. He was also known as **Richard**.

Noah Fletcher reached 50 years of age and died in Portland, Multnomah County, Oregon, on August 29, 1923. He was buried in Pine Grove Cemetery, Hood River, Hood River County, Oregon (Find a Grave ID 29269316).

---

193   Tim Chambers, Vanalstines.GED, Date of Import: Mar 11, 2001.

194   Tim Chambers, Vanalstines.GED, Date of Import: Mar 11, 2001.

Family of Martha Clifton and Charles Schroder

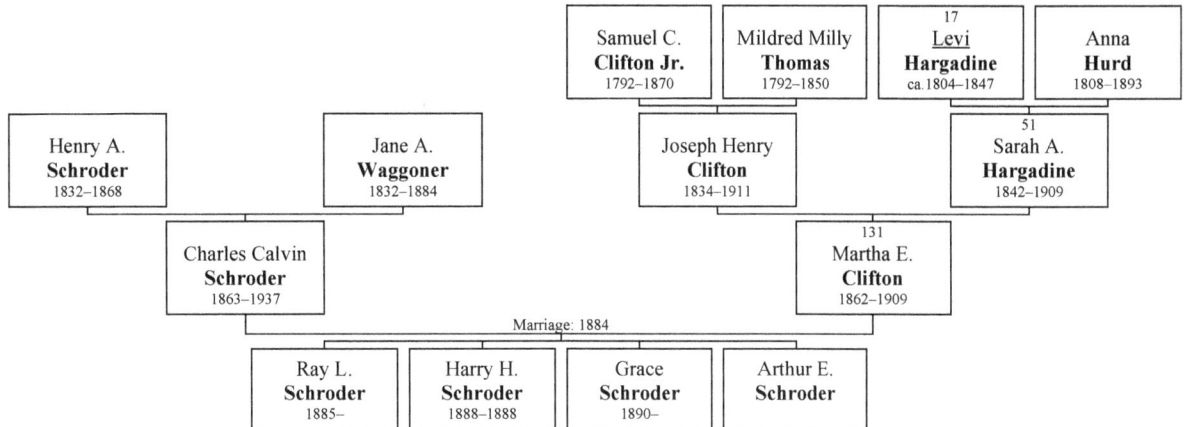

131. **Martha E. Clifton** was born on Friday, November 28, 1862, in Peoria, Peoria County, Illinois.[195] She was the daughter of Joseph Henry Clifton and Sarah A. Hargadine (51). She was also known as **Katie**.

Martha E. died in Decatur, Burt County, Nebraska, on March 18, 1909, at the age of 46.[195] She was buried in Calhoun Cemetery, Harrison County, Iowa (Find a Grave ID 232989891).

At the age of 21, Martha E. married **Charles Calvin Schroder** on Wednesday, May 07, 1884, in Harrison County, Iowa, when he was 20 years old.[195] They had four children.

Charles Calvin was born in Lewis, Lewis County, Missouri, on Wednesday, September 09, 1863.[195, 196] He was the son of Henry A. Schroder and Jane A. Waggoner.

Charles Calvin reached 74 years of age and died in Decatur, Burt County, Nebraska, on December 15, 1937.[196] He was buried in Calhoun Cemetery, Harrison County, Iowa (Find a Grave ID 232989827).[196]

Children of Martha E. Clifton and Charles Calvin Schroder:

m   I. **Ray L. Schroder** was born in Modale, Harrison County, Iowa, on March 30, 1885.[195]

m   II. **Harry H. Schroder** was born in Harrison County, Iowa, in September 1888.[195] He died in Harrison County, Iowa, on December 14, 1888.[195] Harry H. was buried in Calhoun Cemetery, Harrison County, Iowa (Find a Grave ID 138105534).[195]

f   III. **Grace Schroder** was born in Harrison County, Iowa, on July 04, 1890.

m   IV. **Arthur E. Schroder** was born in Harrison County, Iowa.

---

195   Norma Pugmire Gedcom file, Date of Import: Feb 2, 2000.

196   Ancestry.com, Public Member Trees (Provo, UT, USA, Ancestry.com Operations, Inc., 2006), Ancestry.com, Record for Henry Schroder. https://search.ancestry.co.uk/cgi-bin/sse.dll?db=1030&h=352135638848&indiv=try.

Family of William Clifton and Louie Hall

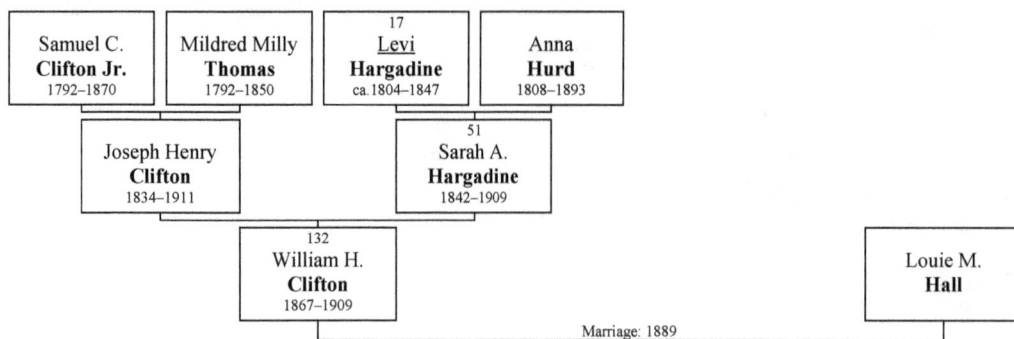

```
┌──────────────┐ ┌──────────────┐ ┌──────────────┐ ┌──────────────┐
│ Samuel C.    │ │ Mildred Milly│ │    17        │ │              │
│ Clifton Jr.  │ │   Thomas     │ │    Levi      │ │    Anna      │
│  1792-1870   │ │  1792-1850   │ │  Hargadine   │ │    Hurd      │
│              │ │              │ │ ca.1804-1847 │ │  1808-1893   │
└──────────────┘ └──────────────┘ └──────────────┘ └──────────────┘
      ┌──────────────┐               ┌──────────────┐
      │ Joseph Henry │               │     51       │
      │   Clifton    │               │  Sarah A.    │
      │  1834-1911   │               │  Hargadine   │
      │              │               │  1842-1909   │
      └──────────────┘               └──────────────┘
            ┌──────────────┐                   ┌──────────────┐
            │    132       │                   │  Louie M.    │
            │  William H.  │                   │    Hall      │
            │   Clifton    │                   │              │
            │  1867-1909   │                   │              │
            └──────────────┘                   └──────────────┘
                        Marriage: 1889
```

132.   **William H. Clifton** was born on Thursday, April 25, 1867, in Peoria, Peoria County, Illinois.[197] He was the son of Joseph Henry Clifton and Sarah A. Hargadine (51).

William H. died on March 24, 1909, at the age of 41.[197]

William H. married **Louie M. Hall** on Sunday, August 04, 1889, in Harrison County, Illinois.

Family of George Clifton and Viola West

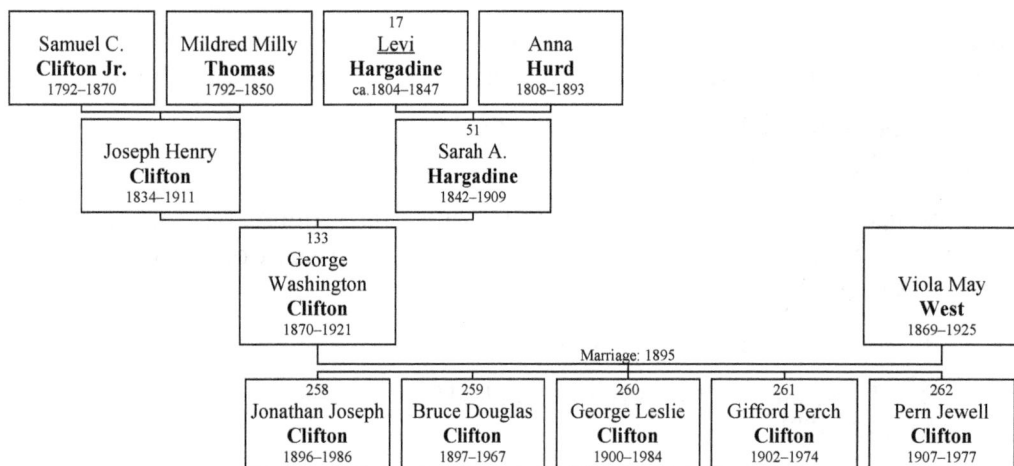

```
┌──────────────┐ ┌──────────────┐ ┌──────────────┐ ┌──────────────┐
│ Samuel C.    │ │ Mildred Milly│ │    17        │ │              │
│ Clifton Jr.  │ │   Thomas     │ │    Levi      │ │    Anna      │
│  1792-1870   │ │  1792-1850   │ │  Hargadine   │ │    Hurd      │
│              │ │              │ │ ca.1804-1847 │ │  1808-1893   │
└──────────────┘ └──────────────┘ └──────────────┘ └──────────────┘
      ┌──────────────┐               ┌──────────────┐
      │ Joseph Henry │               │     51       │
      │   Clifton    │               │  Sarah A.    │
      │  1834-1911   │               │  Hargadine   │
      │              │               │  1842-1909   │
      └──────────────┘               └──────────────┘
            ┌──────────────┐                   ┌──────────────┐
            │    133       │                   │              │
            │   George     │                   │  Viola May   │
            │  Washington  │                   │    West      │
            │   Clifton    │                   │  1869-1925   │
            │  1870-1921   │                   │              │
            └──────────────┘                   └──────────────┘
                        Marriage: 1895
```

258	259	260	261	262
Jonathan Joseph **Clifton** 1896-1986	Bruce Douglas **Clifton** 1897-1967	George Leslie **Clifton** 1900-1984	Gifford Perch **Clifton** 1902-1974	Pern Jewell **Clifton** 1907-1977

133.   **George Washington Clifton** was born on Monday, March 21, 1870, in Peoria, Peoria County, Illinois.[198] He was the son of Joseph Henry Clifton and Sarah A. Hargadine (51).

George Washington died in Wessington Springs Township, Jerauld County, South Dakota, on September 22, 1921, at the age of 51.[198] He was buried in Rose Hill Memorial Gardens, Missouri Valley, Harrison County, Iowa (Find a Grave ID 155535120).[198]

At the age of 25, George Washington married **Viola May West** on Thursday, July 11, 1895, in Modale, Harrison County, Iowa, when she was 26 years old.[198] They had five sons.

Viola May was born in Ohio, USA, on Sunday, March 14, 1869.[198] She reached 56 years of age and died in Wessington Springs Township, Jerauld County, South Dakota, on November

---

197   Norma Pugmire Gedcom file, Date of Import: Feb 2, 2000.

198   Norma Pugmire Gedcom file, Date of Import: Feb 2, 2000.

02, 1925.[198] Viola May was buried in Rose Hill Memorial Gardens, Missouri Valley, Harrison County, Iowa (Find a Grave ID 155535142).[198]

Sons of George Washington Clifton and Viola May West:

+ 258 m I. **Jonathan Joseph Clifton** was born in Modale, Harrison County, Iowa, on May 01, 1896.[198] He was also known as **Jack**.

Jonathan Joseph died in Freeman, Hutchinson County, South Dakota, on February 09, 1986, at the age of 89.[198] He was buried in Prospect Hill Cemetery, Wessington Springs , Jerauld County, South Dakota, on February 11, 1986 (Find a Grave ID 27974832).[198]

+ 259 m II. **Bruce Douglas Clifton** was born in Modale, Harrison County, Iowa, on December 17, 1897.[198] He died in Mobridge, Walworth County, South Dakota, on June 28, 1967, at the age of 69.[198] Bruce Douglas was buried in Greenwood Cemetery, Mobridge, Walworth County, South Dakota (Find a Grave ID 202268003).

+ 260 m III. **George Leslie Clifton** was born in Modale, Harrison County, Iowa, on April 26, 1900. He died in Sioux Falls, Minnehaha County, South Dakota, on May 24, 1984, at the age of 84. George Leslie was buried in Woodlawn Cemetery, Sioux Falls, Minnehaha County, South Dakota, on May 26, 1984 (Find a Grave ID 136979163).

+ 261 m IV. **Gifford Perch Clifton** was born in Modale, Harrison County, Iowa, on April 13, 1902.[198] He died in Winslow, Kitsap County, Washington, on August 30, 1974, at the age of 72.[198] Gifford Perch was buried in Kane Cemetery, Bainbridge Island, Kitsap County, Washington (Find a Grave ID 24671880).

+ 262 m V. **Pern Jewell Clifton** was born in Modale, Harrison County, Iowa, on June 05, 1907.[198] He died in Sumner, Pierce County, Washington, on May 22, 1977, at the age of 69.[198]

Family of Anna Clifton and Albert Compton

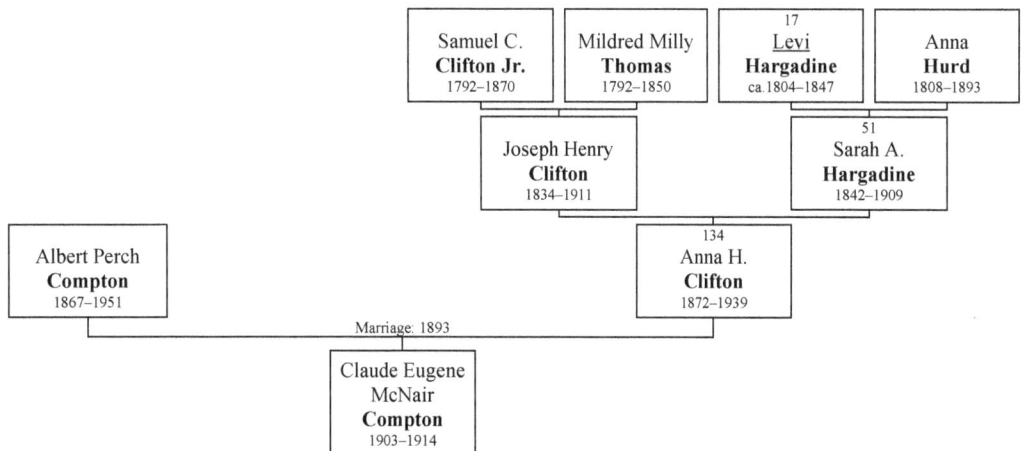

134. **Anna H. Clifton** was born on Sunday, January 14, 1872, in LaSalle, LaSalle County, Illinois.[199] She was the daughter of Joseph Henry Clifton and Sarah A. Hargadine (51).

Anna H. died at Methodist Hospital in Omaha, Douglas County, Nebraska, on December 08, 1939, at the age of 67.[199] She was buried in Blair Cemetery, Blair, Washington County, Nebraska, on December 10, 1939 (Find a Grave ID 77018111).[199]

At the age of 21, Anna H. married **Albert Perch Compton** on Wednesday, February 01, 1893, when he was 25 years old. They had one son.

Albert Perch was born in Adams County, Ohio, on Saturday, June 01, 1867. He was also known as **A.P.**.

Albert Perch reached 83 years of age and died in Blair, Washington County, Nebraska, on February 13, 1951.[199] He was buried in Blair Cemetery, Blair, Washington County, Nebraska (Find a Grave ID 77017899).

Son of Anna H. Clifton and Albert Perch Compton:

m   I. **Claude Eugene McNair Compton** was born in Blair, Washington County, Nebraska, on August 08, 1903. He died in Blair, Washington County, Nebraska, on December 23, 1914, at the age of 11. His cause of death was following surgery for acute appendicitis. He was buried in Blair Cemetery, Blair, Washington County, Nebraska (Find a Grave ID 77018308).

Family of Franklin Clifton and Elizabeth Duhigg

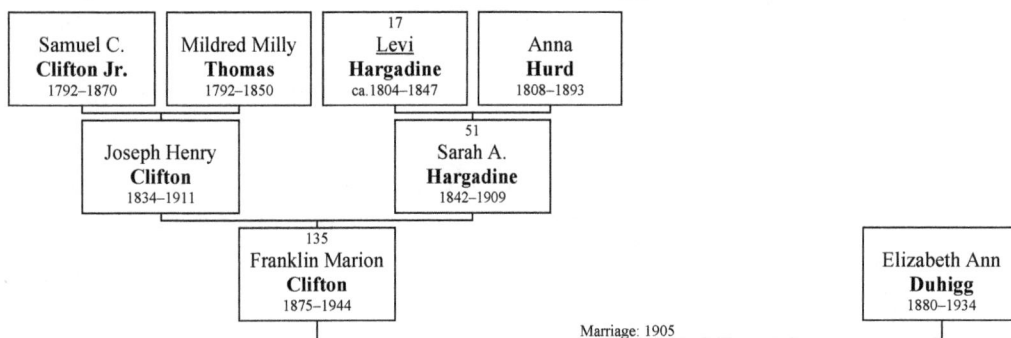

135. **Franklin Marion Clifton** was born on Monday, April 26, 1875, in Peoria, Peoria County, Illinois.[200] He was the son of Joseph Henry Clifton and Sarah A. Hargadine (51).

Franklin Marion died in Okmulgee, Okmulgee County, Oklahoma, on June 24, 1944, at the age of 69.[200] He was buried in Okmulgee Cemetery, Okmulgee, Okmulgee County, Oklahoma, on June 29, 1944 (Find a Grave ID 122913383).

Franklin Marion married **Elizabeth Ann Duhigg** on Saturday, January 28, 1905, in Blair, Washington County, Nebraska. Elizabeth Ann was born in Harrison County, Iowa, in November 1880. She was also known as **Lizzie**.

199   Norma Pugmire Gedcom file, Date of Import: Feb 2, 2000.

200   Norma Pugmire Gedcom file, Date of Import: Feb 2, 2000.

Elizabeth Ann reached 53 years of age and died in Okmulgee, Okmulgee County, Oklahoma, on July 23, 1934. She was buried on July 24, 1934, in Okmulgee Cemetery, Okmulgee, Okmulgee County, Oklahoma (Find a Grave ID 122913215).

Family of Elsie Clifton and Bert Fensler

136. **Elsie Nevada Clifton** was born on Saturday, December 23, 1876, in Adams County, Iowa.[201] She was the daughter of Joseph Henry Clifton and Sarah A. Hargadine (51).

Elsie Nevada died in Long Beach, Los Angeles County, California, on August 18, 1939, at the age of 62.[201] She was buried in Rose Hills Memorial Park, Whittier, Los Angeles County, California (Find a Grave ID 127285911).

At the age of 18, Elsie Nevada married **Bert S. Fensler** on Wednesday, August 28, 1895, in Harrison, Harrison County, Iowa, when he was 26 years old.[201] Bert S. was born in Iowa, USA, on Saturday, June 12, 1869.[201]

He reached 65 years of age and died on March 20, 1935. Bert S. was buried in Rose Hills Memorial Park, Whittier, Los Angeles County, California (Find a Grave ID 80857621).

Levi Clifton

137. **Levi Taylor Clifton** was born on Monday, December 09, 1878, in Clarks, Merrick County, Nebraska.[202] He was the son of Joseph Henry Clifton and Sarah A. Hargadine (51).

Levi Taylor died in Seattle, King County, Washington, on May 10, 1979, at the age of 100.[202] He was buried in Calvary Mausoleum, Seattle, King County, Washington, on May 12, 1979 (Find a Grave ID 76264110).[202]

Marriages with Vill Nettie Fern Fry and Maude Helen Schmidt (Page 177) are known.

---

201   Norma Pugmire Gedcom file, Date of Import: Feb 2, 2000.

202   Norma Pugmire Gedcom file, Date of Import: Feb 2, 2000.

Family of Levi Clifton and Vill Fry

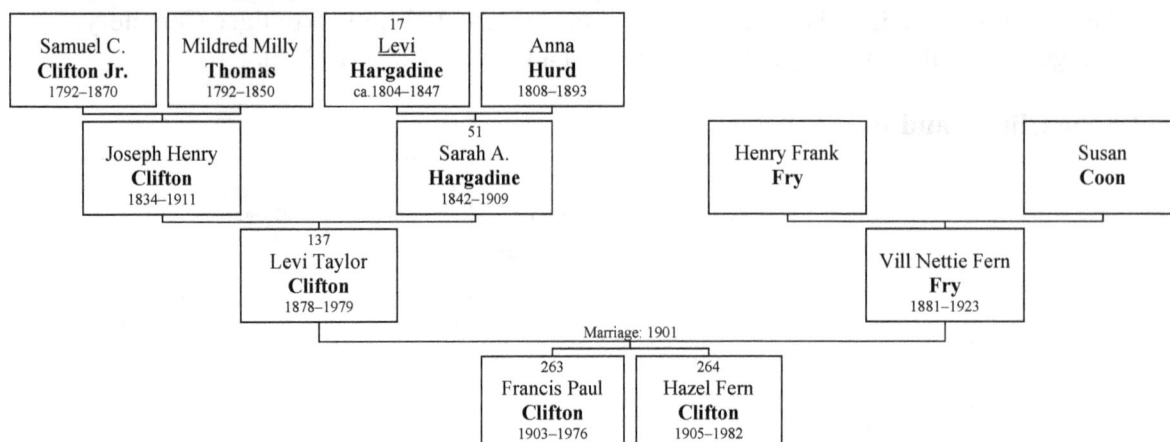

```
┌──────────────┬──────────────┬──────────────┬──────────────┐
│ Samuel C.    │ Mildred Milly│      17      │   Anna       │
│ Clifton Jr.  │   Thomas     │    Levi      │   Hurd       │
│ 1792–1870    │ 1792–1850    │  Hargadine   │  1808–1893   │
│              │              │ ca.1804–1847 │              │
└──────────────┴──────────────┴──────────────┴──────────────┘
        │                              │
   ┌──────────────┐          ┌──────────────┐     ┌──────────────┐     ┌──────────────┐
   │ Joseph Henry │          │      51      │     │ Henry Frank  │     │   Susan      │
   │  Clifton     │          │  Sarah A.    │     │    Fry       │     │   Coon       │
   │ 1834–1911    │          │  Hargadine   │     │              │     │              │
   └──────────────┘          │ 1842–1909    │     └──────────────┘     └──────────────┘
            │                └──────────────┘              │
        ┌──────────────┐                         ┌──────────────────┐
        │     137      │                         │ Vill Nettie Fern │
        │ Levi Taylor  │                         │      Fry         │
        │  Clifton     │                         │   1881–1923      │
        │ 1878–1979    │                         └──────────────────┘
        └──────────────┘
                        Marriage: 1901
           ┌──────────────┬──────────────┐
           │     263      │     264      │
           │ Francis Paul │ Hazel Fern   │
           │   Clifton    │  Clifton     │
           │ 1903–1976    │ 1905–1982    │
           └──────────────┴──────────────┘
```

Here are the details about **Levi Taylor Clifton's** first marriage, with Vill Nettie Fern Fry. You can read more about Levi Taylor on page 175.

At the age of 22, Levi Taylor Clifton married **Vill Nettie Fern Fry** on Wednesday, September 18, 1901, in Woodbine, Harrison County, Iowa, when she was 20 years old.[202] They had two children.

Vill Nettie Fern was born in Woodbine, Missouri Valley, Harrison County, Iowa, on Friday, April 08, 1881.[202] She was the daughter of Henry Frank Fry and Susan Coon.

Vill Nettie Fern reached 42 years of age and died in Long Pine, Rock County, Nebraska, on May 03, 1923.[202] She was buried on May 06, 1923, in Grandview Cemetery, Long Pine, Brown County, Nebraska (Find a Grave ID 18212405).[202]

Children of Levi Taylor Clifton and Vill Nettie Fern Fry:

+   263   m   I. **Francis Paul Clifton** was born in Missouri Valley, Harrison County, Iowa, on June 07, 1903.[202] He died in San Francisco, San Francisco County, California, on March 31, 1976, at the age of 72.[202] Francis Paul was buried in Cypress Lawn Memorial Park, Colma, San Mateo County, California, on April 12, 1976 (Find a Grave ID 76263851).[202]

+   264   f   II. **Hazel Fern Clifton** was born in Woodbine, Harrison County, Iowa, on February 21, 1905.[202] She died in Omaha, Douglas County, Nebraska, on November 20, 1982, at the age of 77.[202] Hazel Fern was buried in Evergreen Memorial Park Cemetery, Omaha, Douglas County, Nebraska, on November 23, 1982 (Find a Grave ID 94233995).[202]

Family of Levi Clifton and Maude Schmidt

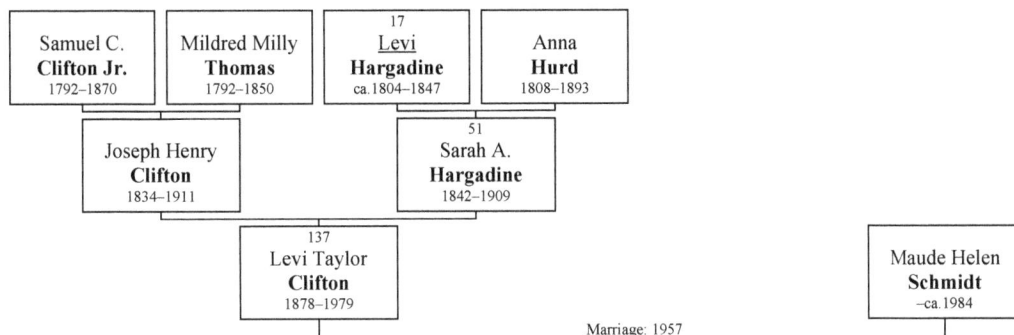

Here are the details about **Levi Taylor Clifton's** second marriage, with Maude Helen Schmidt. You can read more about Levi Taylor on page 175.

Levi Taylor Clifton married **Maude Helen Schmidt** on Monday, February 25, 1957.[202] She was also known as **Bobby**.

Maude Helen died in Seattle, King County, Washington, about February 1984.[202]

Family of Mary Clifton and Arthur Dasher

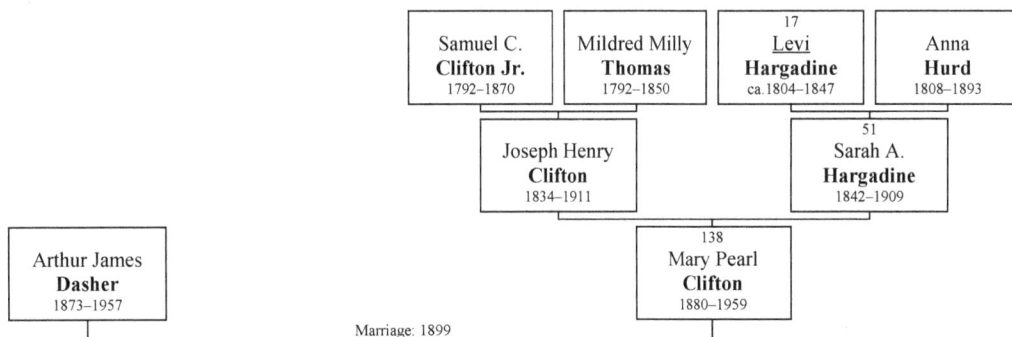

138. **Mary Pearl Clifton** was born on Friday, August 27, 1880, in Clarks, Merrick County, Nebraska.[203] She was the daughter of Joseph Henry Clifton and Sarah A. Hargadine (51).

Mary Pearl died in Los Angeles, Los Angeles County, California, on October 05, 1959, at the age of 79.[203]

At the age of 19, Mary Pearl married **Arthur James Dasher** on Tuesday, November 07, 1899, in Harrison, Harrison County, Iowa, when he was 26 years old.[203] Arthur James was born in Osborne, Osborne County, Kansas, on Wednesday, January 29, 1873.[203]

He reached 84 years of age and died in Los Angeles, Los Angeles County, California, on May 03, 1957.[203] Arthur James was buried (See notes).

203   Norma Pugmire Gedcom file, Date of Import: Feb 2, 2000.

Family of Lewis Hargadine and Josephine Medi

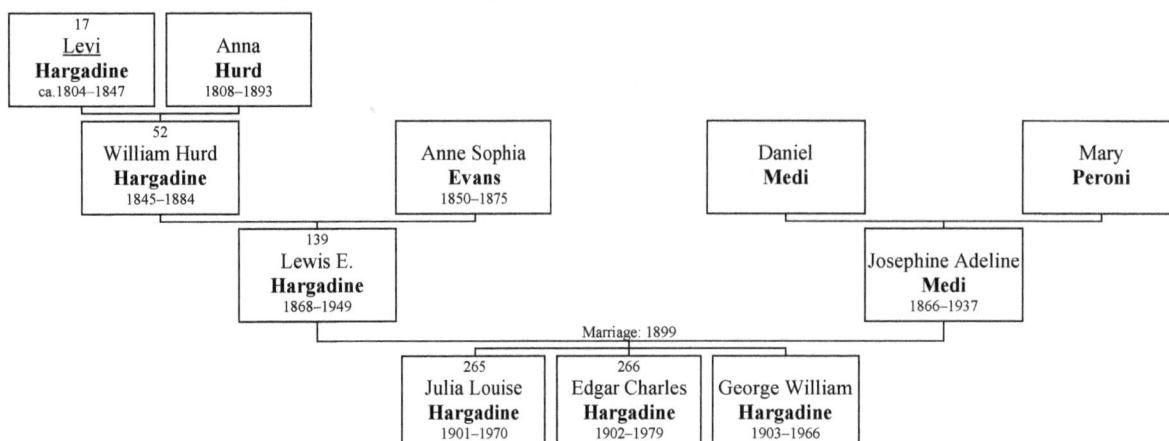

139.   **Lewis E. Hargadine** was born on Thursday, April 16, 1868, in Dunlap, Peoria County, Illinois. He was the son of William Hurd Hargadine (52) and Anne Sophia Evans. He was also known as **Lewis**.

Lewis E. died in Speer, Stark County, Illinois, on July 05, 1949, at the age of 81. He was buried in Saint Mary of the Woods Cemetery, Princeville, Peoria County, Illinois, on July 07, 1949 (Find a Grave ID 31412732).

At the age of 31, Lewis E. married **Josephine Adeline Medi** on Wednesday, December 13, 1899, in Brimfield, Peoria County, Illinois, when she was 33 years old. There is record that they obtained a marriage license. They had three children.

Josephine Adeline was born in Rosefield Township, Peoria, Peoria County, Illinois, on Tuesday, June 19, 1866. She was the daughter of Daniel Medi and Mary Peroni.

Josephine Adeline reached 71 years of age and died in Peoria County, Illinois, on November 29, 1937. She was buried in Saint Mary of the Woods Cemetery, Princeville, Peoria County, Illinois (Find a Grave ID 31412730).

Children of Lewis E. Hargadine and Josephine Adeline Medi:

+   265   f   I. **Julia Louise Hargadine** was born in Jubilee, Peoria County, Illinois, on January 14, 1901. She died in Peoria, Peoria County, Illinois, on May 30, 1970, at the age of 69. Julia Louise was buried in Saint Mary of the Woods Cemetery, Princeville, Peoria County, Illinois (Find a Grave ID 31412956).

+   266   m   II. **Edgar Charles Hargadine** was born in Jubilee Twp., Peoria County, Illinois, on June 03, 1902. He died in Marianna, Jackson County, Florida, on January 11, 1979, at the age of 76. Edgar Charles was buried in Swan Lake Memory Gardens, Peoria, Peoria County, Illinois (Find a Grave ID 167036363).

         m   III. **George William Hargadine** was born in Jubilee, Peoria County, Illinois, on August 29, 1903. He died in Peoria County, Illinois, on August 27, 1966, at the age of 62. His cause of death was heart attack. He was buried in Saint Mary of the Woods Cemetery, Princeville, Peoria County, Illinois (Find a Grave ID 31412731).

Levi Hargadine

140. **Levi Lester Hargadine** was born on Wednesday, December 20, 1871, in Medina, Peoria County, Illinois. He was the son of Levi Taylor Hargadine (53) and Louisa Jane Hurd.

Levi Lester worked as a Farmer. He died in North Chillicothe, Peoria County, Illinois, on July 31, 1947, at the age of 75. His cause of death was carcinoma of prostate with metastasis. He was buried in La Salle Cemetery, Rome, Peoria County, Illinois, on August 02, 1947 (Find a Grave ID 24825518).

Marriages with Annie Louisa Cook and Ursula Reynolds (Page 180) are known.

Family of Levi Hargadine and Annie Cook

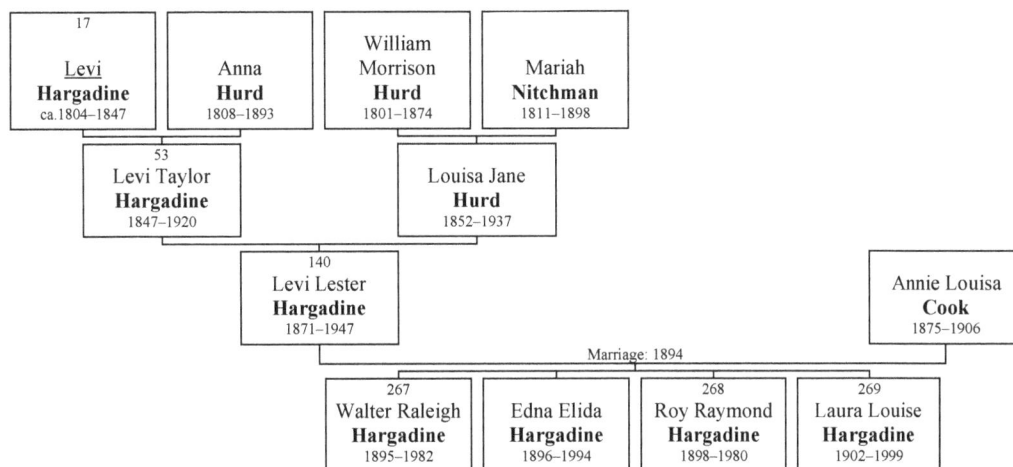

Here are the details about **Levi Lester Hargadine's** first marriage, with Annie Louisa Cook. You can read more about Levi Lester on page 179.

Levi Lester Hargadine married **Annie Louisa Cook** in April 1894. They had four children.

Annie Louisa was born in Woodford County, Illinois, on Tuesday, March 02, 1875. She reached 31 years of age and died in Medina, Peoria County, Illinois, on November 03, 1906. Annie Louisa was buried on November 06, 1906, in La Salle Cemetery, Rome, Peoria County, Illinois (Find a Grave ID 24825509).

Children of Levi Lester Hargadine and Annie Louisa Cook:

+ 267 m I. **Walter Raleigh Hargadine** was born in Medina, Peoria County, Illinois, on April 22, 1895. He died in Peoria, Peoria County, Illinois, on January 11, 1982, at the age of 86. Walter Raleigh was buried in Swan Lake Memory Gardens, Peoria, Peoria County, Illinois (Find a Grave ID 178696338).

      f II. **Edna Elida Hargadine** was born in Peoria, Peoria County, Illinois, on December 18, 1896. She died in Morton, Tazewell County, Illinois, on July 08, 1994, at the age of 97. Edna Elida was buried in Swan Lake Memory Gardens, Peoria, Peoria County, Illinois (Find a Grave ID 134023171).

+ 268 m III. **Roy Raymond Hargadine** was born in Medina, Peoria County, Illinois, on September 02, 1898. He died in Dunlap, Peoria County, Illinois, on January 12, 1980, at the age of 81. Roy Raymond was buried in Mount Hawley Cemetery, Peoria, Peoria County, Illinois (Find a Grave ID 22160135).

+ 269 f IV. **Laura Louise Hargadine** was born in Radnor Township, Peoria County, Illinois, on January 04, 1902. She died in Toulon Health Care Center, Toulon, Stark County, Illinois, on March 04, 1999, at the age of 97. Laura Louise was buried in Swan Lake Memory Gardens, Peoria, Peoria County, Illinois (Find a Grave ID 134027162).

Family of Levi Hargadine and Ursula Reynolds

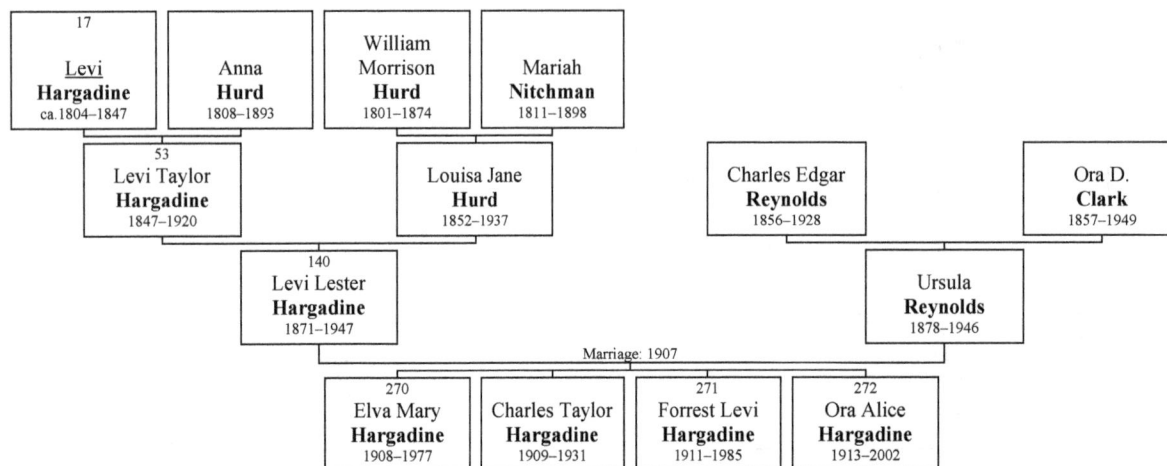

Here are the details about **Levi Lester Hargadine's** second marriage, with Ursula Reynolds. You can read more about Levi Lester on page 179.

At the age of 35, Levi Lester Hargadine married **Ursula Reynolds** on Wednesday, October 02, 1907, in Springfield, Sangamon County, Illinois, when she was 28 years old. They had four children.

Ursula was born in Princeville, Stark County, Illinois, on Saturday, December 21, 1878. She was the daughter of Charles Edgar Reynolds and Ora D. Clark.

Ursula reached 68 years of age and died in North Chillicothe, Peoria County, Illinois, on December 26, 1946. She was buried in La Salle Cemetery, Rome, Peoria County, Illinois (Find a Grave ID 44542918).

Children of Levi Lester Hargadine and Ursula Reynolds:

+ 270 f I. **Elva Mary Hargadine** was born in Dunlap, Peoria County, Illinois, on June 23, 1908. She died on December 17, 1977, at the age of 69. Elva Mary was buried in Chillicothe City Cemetery, Chillicothe, Peoria County, Illinois (Find a Grave ID 63906894).

m II. **Charles Taylor Hargadine** was born in Peoria County, Illinois, on September 03, 1909. He died in Akron Township, Peoria County, Illinois, on July 03, 1931, at the age of 21. His cause of death was: struck by a car while changing a flat tire. He was buried in La Salle Cemetery, Rome, Peoria County, Illinois (Find a Grave ID 24825513).

+ 271 m III. **Forrest Levi Hargadine** was born in Medina, Peoria County, Illinois, on March 13, 1911. He was also known as **Frosty**.

Forrest Levi died in Dunlap, Peoria County, Illinois, on January 23, 1985, at the age of 73. He was buried in Prospect Cemetery, Dunlap, Peoria County, Illinois, on January 26, 1985 (Find a Grave ID 22160966).

+ 272 f IV. **Ora Alice Hargadine** was born in Dunlap, Peoria County, Illinois, on June 11, 1913. Ursula Reynolds was her stepmother.

She died in Peoria, Peoria County, Illinois, on July 07, 2002, at the age of 89. Ora Alice was buried in Chillicothe City Cemetery, Chillicothe, Peoria County, Illinois (Find a Grave ID 59248974).

Family of John Hargadine and Sarah Grundy

141. **John Charles Hargadine** was born on Tuesday, August 22, 1876, in Medina, Peoria County, Illinois. He was the son of Levi Taylor Hargadine (53) and Louisa Jane Hurd.

John Charles died in Peoria, Peoria County, Illinois, on January 27, 1934, at the age of 57. His cause of death was: fractured skull and hemorrhage of brain due to injuries accidentally received. John Charles was buried in Prospect Cemetery, Dunlap, Peoria County, Illinois, on January 31, 1934 (Find a Grave ID 22160967).

At the age of 31, John Charles married **Sarah May Grundy** on Saturday, January 11, 1908, when she was 21 years old. They had four daughters.

Sarah May was born in Alta, Peoria County, Illinois, on Sunday, October 17, 1886. She was the daughter of Phoenix Edmond Grundy and Margaret Ann Goldsbrough.

She worked as a dietitian-Peoria Municipal Tuberculosis sanitarium. Sarah May reached 72 years of age and died in Peoria, Peoria County, Illinois, on January 06, 1959. She was buried in Prospect Cemetery, Dunlap, Peoria County, Illinois (Find a Grave ID 22160968).

Daughters of John Charles Hargadine and Sarah May Grundy:

+ 273 f I. **Margaret Louise Hargadine** was born in Peoria, Peoria County, Illinois, on August 13, 1909. She died in Stark County, Illinois, on December 16, 1970, at the age of 61. Margaret Louise was buried in Prospect Cemetery, Dunlap, Peoria County, Illinois (Find a Grave ID 22159597).

+ 274   f   II. **Lucile May Hargadine** was born in Peoria, Peoria County, Illinois, on April 08, 1912. She died in Lacon, Marshall County, Illinois, on April 18, 1993, at the age of 81. Lucile May was buried in Prospect Cemetery, Dunlap, Peoria County, Illinois (Find a Grave ID 49214782).

        f   III. **Ethel I. Hargadine** was born in Medina, Peoria County, Illinois, on October 28, 1914. She died in Toulon Health Care Center, Toulon, Stark County, Illinois, on January 12, 1997, at the age of 82. Ethel I. was buried in Prospect Cemetery, Dunlap, Peoria County, Illinois, on January 15, 1997 (Find a Grave ID 22160965).

+ 275   f   IV. **Elma Louella Hargadine** was born in Peoria, Peoria County, Illinois, on October 17, 1922.[204] She died in Dunlap, Peoria County, Illinois, on June 10, 2000, at the age of 77. Elma Louella was buried in Prospect Cemetery, Dunlap, Peoria County, Illinois (Find a Grave ID 22161209).

Family of George Yates and Mary Giles

142.   **George N. Yates** was born on Tuesday, December 06, 1859, in Peoria County, Illinois. He was the son of John Caldwell Yates and Jane Ellen Hargadine (54).

George N. died in Peoria, Peoria County, Illinois, on November 28, 1928, at the age of 68. He was buried in Mount Hawley Cemetery, Peoria, Peoria County, Illinois, on November 30, 1928 (Find a Grave ID 22160515).

George N. married **Mary Helena Giles** on Saturday, December 29, 1883.

---

204   Peoria Herald Transcript, 20 Aug 1909, pg 8. Born Friday August 13, to Mr. and Mrs. John Hargadine, a girl.

Family of Mary Yates and Samuel Smith

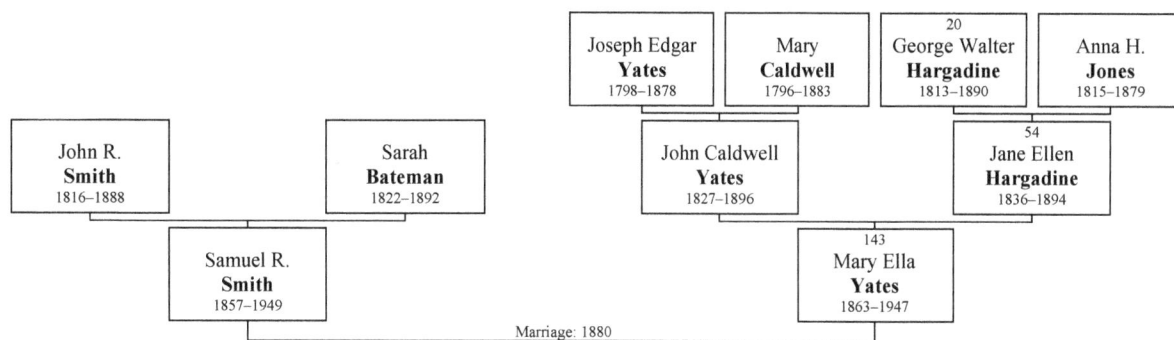

```
                              ┌──────────────┐┌──────────┐┌─────20─────┐┌──────────┐
                              │ Joseph Edgar ││   Mary   ││George Walter││  Anna H. │
                              │    Yates     ││ Caldwell ││  Hargadine  ││   Jones  │
                              │  1798–1878   ││1796–1883 ││  1813–1890  ││1815–1879 │
                              └──────────────┘└──────────┘└─────────────┘└──────────┘
┌──────────────┐┌──────────┐        ┌──────────────┐      ┌──────54──────┐
│   John R.    ││  Sarah   │        │ John Caldwell│      │  Jane Ellen  │
│    Smith     ││ Bateman  │        │    Yates     │      │  Hargadine   │
│  1816–1888   ││1822–1892 │        │  1827–1896   │      │  1836–1894   │
└──────────────┘└──────────┘        └──────────────┘      └──────────────┘
        ┌──────────────┐                     ┌─────143──────┐
        │   Samuel R.  │                     │  Mary Ella   │
        │    Smith     │                     │    Yates     │
        │  1857–1949   │                     │  1863–1947   │
        └──────────────┘                     └──────────────┘
                          Marriage: 1880
```

143.   **Mary Ella Yates** was born on Wednesday, August 12, 1863. She was the daughter of John Caldwell Yates and Jane Ellen Hargadine (54).

Mary Ella died in Filley, Gage County, Nebraska, on May 28, 1947, at the age of 83. She was buried in Filley Cemetery, Filley, Gage County, Nebraska (Find a Grave ID 59312714).

At the age of 17, Mary Ella married **Samuel R. Smith** on Thursday, November 18, 1880, in Peoria County, Illinois, when he was 23 years old. Samuel R. was born in Peoria County, Illinois, on Saturday, September 26, 1857. He was the son of John R. Smith and Sarah Bateman.

Samuel R. reached 91 years of age and died in Filley, Gage County, Nebraska, on September 03, 1949. He was buried in Filley Cemetery, Filley, Gage County, Nebraska (Find a Grave ID 59312721).

Family of Addie Yates and William Ballinger

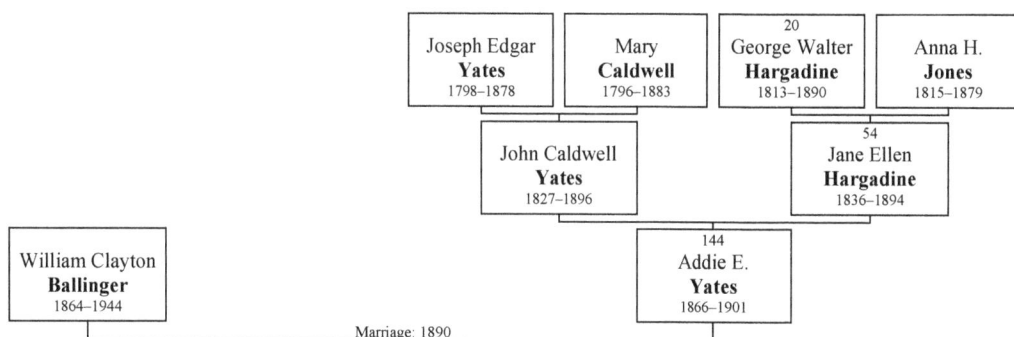

```
                              ┌──────────────┐┌──────────┐┌─────20─────┐┌──────────┐
                              │ Joseph Edgar ││   Mary   ││George Walter││  Anna H. │
                              │    Yates     ││ Caldwell ││  Hargadine  ││   Jones  │
                              │  1798–1878   ││1796–1883 ││  1813–1890  ││1815–1879 │
                              └──────────────┘└──────────┘└─────────────┘└──────────┘
                                     ┌──────────────┐      ┌──────54──────┐
                                     │ John Caldwell│      │  Jane Ellen  │
                                     │    Yates     │      │  Hargadine   │
                                     │  1827–1896   │      │  1836–1894   │
                                     └──────────────┘      └──────────────┘
┌──────────────┐                              ┌─────144──────┐
│William Clayton│                             │   Addie E.   │
│  Ballinger   │                              │    Yates     │
│  1864–1944   │                              │  1866–1901   │
└──────────────┘                              └──────────────┘
                          Marriage: 1890
```

144.   **Addie E. Yates** was born on Tuesday, June 05, 1866. She was the daughter of John Caldwell Yates and Jane Ellen Hargadine (54).

Addie E. died on August 19, 1901, at the age of 35. She was buried in Springdale Cemetery and Mausoleum, Peoria, Peoria County, Illinois (Find a Grave ID 136695218).

At the age of 24, Addie E. married **William Clayton Ballinger** on Wednesday, September 03, 1890, in McLean County, Illinois, when he was 26 years old. William Clayton was born on Wednesday, May 11, 1864.

He reached 79 years of age and died on January 21, 1944. William Clayton was buried in Lexington Cemetery, Lexington, McLean County, Illinois (Find a Grave ID 7315151).

Family of Jenny Yates and Melvin McCullough

Joseph Edgar **Yates** 1798–1878	Mary **Caldwell** 1796–1883	20 George Walter **Hargadine** 1813–1890	Anna H. **Jones** 1815–1879

John Caldwell **Yates** 1827–1896	54 Jane Ellen **Hargadine** 1836–1894

Melvin G. **McCullough** 1870–1939	145 Jenny C. **Yates** 1869–1928

Marriage: 1891

145. **Jenny C. Yates** was born on Thursday, November 18, 1869. She was the daughter of John Caldwell Yates and Jane Ellen Hargadine (54).

Jenny C. died on August 19, 1928, at the age of 58. She was buried in Smithville Cemetery, Hanna City, Peoria County, Illinois (Find a Grave ID 133133752).

At the age of 21, Jenny C. married **Melvin G. McCullough** on Wednesday, September 23, 1891, in Mc Lean County, Illinois, when he was 21 years old. Melvin G. was born on Saturday, July 16, 1870.

He reached 68 years of age and died on March 12, 1939. Melvin G. was buried in Smithville Cemetery, Hanna City, Peoria County, Illinois (Find a Grave ID 133133723).

Family of Loren Hargadine and Allice Hollingsworth

20 George Walter **Hargadine** 1813–1890	Anna H. **Jones** 1815–1879	Simeon **Sprague** 1819–1851	Elizabeth **Vanschoick** 1825–1889	James **Hollingsworth** 1815–1902	Elizabeth **Shinkle** 1819–1891

55 William Henry **Hargadine** 1841–1912	Sarah Mariah **Sprague** 1843–1928	Elias Charles **Hollingsworth** 1838–1923	Elizabeth Rebecca **Brown** 1840–1891

146 Loren Edward **Hargadine** 1861–1932	Allice Belle **Hollingsworth** 1865–1947

Marriage: 1890

276 Walter A. **Hargadine** 1891–1966	277 Loren Henry **Hargadine** 1895–1961	278 Gaylord Warren **Hargadine** 1897–1964	279 Ada Leona **Hargadine** 1903–1983

146. **Loren Edward Hargadine** was born on Thursday, October 10, 1861, in Chenoa, McLean County, Illinois. He was the son of William Henry Hargadine (55) and Sarah Mariah Sprague. He was also known as **Ed**.

Loren Edward died in Kinsley, Edwards County, Kansas, on March 15, 1932, at the age of 70. He was buried in Bethel Cemetery, Hodges, Edwards County, Kansas (Find a Grave ID 67562844).

At the age of 29, Loren Edward married **Allice Belle Hollingsworth** on Thursday, December 25, 1890, when she was 25 years old. They had four children.

Allice Belle was born on Thursday, April 27, 1865. She was the daughter of Elias Charles Hollingsworth and Elizabeth Rebecca Brown.

Allice Belle reached 81 years of age and died in 1947.[205] She was buried in Bethel Cemetery, Hodges, Edwards County, Kansas (Find a Grave ID 67562754).

Children of Loren Edward Hargadine and Allice Belle Hollingsworth:

+ 276   m   I. **Walter A. Hargadine** was born on October 15, 1891. He died on November 02, 1966, at the age of 75. Walter A. was buried in Bethel Cemetery, Hodges, Edwards County, Kansas (Find a Grave ID 67563210).

+ 277   m   II. **Loren Henry Hargadine** was born on April 27, 1895. He died on April 28, 1961, at the age of 66. Loren Henry was buried in Bethel Cemetery, Hodges, Edwards County, Kansas (Find a Grave ID 67562861).

+ 278   m   III. **Gaylord Warren Hargadine** was born in Kiowa County, Kansas, on December 21, 1897. He died in Kinsley, Edwards County, Kansas, on October 19, 1964, at the age of 66. His cause of death was heart attack. He was buried in Hillside Cemetery, Kinsley, Edwards County, Kansas (Find a Grave ID 11422744).

+ 279   f   IV. **Ada Leona Hargadine** was born on January 03, 1903. She died in Kinsley, Edwards County, Kansas, on March 23, 1983, at the age of 80. Ada Leona was buried in Hillside Cemetery, Kinsley, Edwards County, Kansas (Find a Grave ID 11636385).

Family of George Hargadine and Ethel Barnes

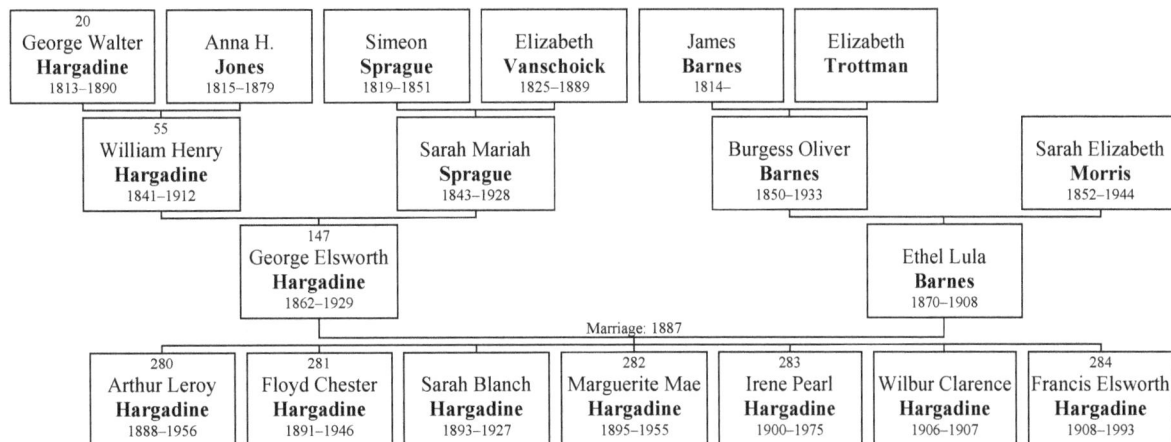

147. **George Elsworth Hargadine** was born on Wednesday, January 01, 1862, in Chenoa, McLean County, Illinois. He was the son of William Henry Hargadine (55) and Sarah Mariah Sprague.

George Elsworth died on July 22, 1929, at the age of 67. He was buried in Prairie Lawn Cemetery, Wellington, Sumner County, Kansas (Find a Grave ID 63279785).

---

205   Bethel Cemetery Records.

At the age of 25, George Elsworth married **Ethel Lula Barnes** on Thursday, October 13, 1887, in Kiowa County, Kansas, when she was 17 years old. They had seven children.

Ethel Lula was born in Rolla, Phelps County, Missouri, on Thursday, February 24, 1870. She was the daughter of Burgess Oliver Barnes and Sarah Elizabeth Morris.

Ethel Lula reached 38 years of age and died on July 21, 1908. She was buried in Bethany Cemetery, Beaver Corner, Beaver County, Oklahoma (Find a Grave ID 16572033).

Children of George Elsworth Hargadine and Ethel Lula Barnes:

+ 280 m I. **Arthur Leroy Hargadine** was born on July 06, 1888. He died in Alden, Rice County, Kansas, on March 16, 1956, at the age of 67. Arthur Leroy was buried in Alden Valley Cemetery, Alden, Rice County, Kansas (Find a Grave ID 52865637).

+ 281 m II. **Floyd Chester Hargadine** was born in Ottumwa, Wapello County, Iowa, on April 22, 1891. He died in Sheridan, Yamhill County, Oregon, on February 08, 1946, at the age of 54. Floyd Chester was buried in Evergreen Memorial Park, McMinnville, Yamhill County, Oregon, on February 12, 1946 (Find a Grave ID 193555745).

f III. **Sarah Blanch Hargadine** was born on May 30, 1893. She died on July 29, 1927, at the age of 34. Sarah Blanch was buried in Bethel Cemetery, Hodges, Edwards County, Kansas (Find a Grave ID 77359936).

+ 282 f IV. **Marguerite Mae Hargadine** was born in Competine, Wapello County, Iowa, on November 11, 1895. She died in Dalhart, Hartley County, Texas, on June 11, 1955, at the age of 59. Marguerite Mae was buried in Memorial Park Cemetery, Dalhart, Hartley County, Texas (Find A Grave ID 44923571).

+ 283 f V. **Irene Pearl Hargadine** was born in Ottumwa, Wapello County, Iowa, on June 07, 1900. She died on September 24, 1975, at the age of 75. Irene Pearl was buried in Hillcrest Cemetery, Mullinville, Kiowa County, Kansas (Find a Grave ID 34627112).

m VI. **Wilbur Clarence Hargadine** was born on November 01, 1906. He died on January 30, 1907. Wilbur Clarence was buried in Cimarron Valley Cemetery, Kingfisher County, Oklahoma (Find a Grave ID 7714192).

+ 284 m VII. **Francis Elsworth Hargadine** was born in Geary, Oklahoma, on March 03, 1908. He died in Redding, Shasta County, California, on April 12, 1993, at the age of 85. Francis Elsworth was buried in Anderson, Shasta County, California, on April 14, 1993.

Family of Cora Hargadine and Charles Scott

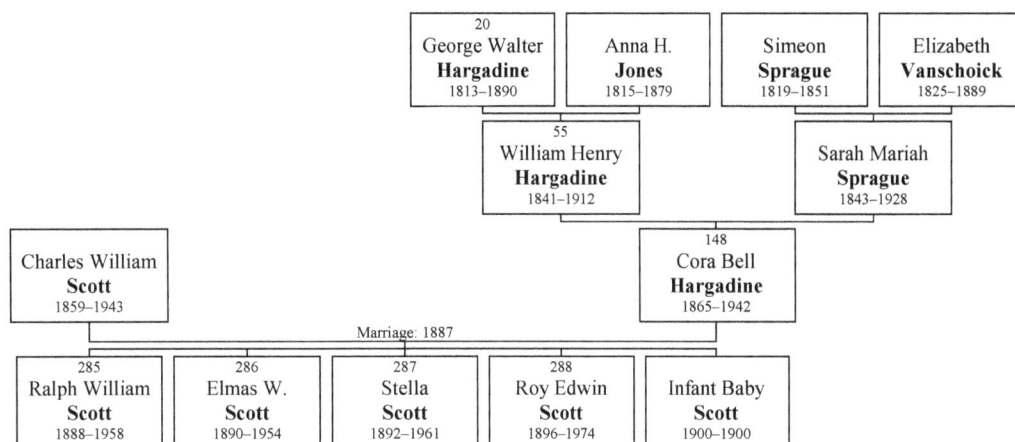

```
                          ┌─────────────┐ ┌─────────────┐ ┌─────────────┐ ┌─────────────┐
                          │      20     │ │             │ │             │ │             │
                          │George Walter│ │   Anna H.   │ │   Simeon    │ │  Elizabeth  │
                          │  Hargadine  │ │    Jones    │ │   Sprague   │ │ Vanschoick  │
                          │  1813–1890  │ │  1815–1879  │ │  1819–1851  │ │  1825–1889  │
                          └─────────────┘ └─────────────┘ └─────────────┘ └─────────────┘
                                 ┌──────────────────┐     ┌──────────────────┐
                                 │        55        │     │                  │
                                 │  William Henry   │     │  Sarah Mariah    │
                                 │    Hargadine     │     │     Sprague      │
                                 │    1841–1912     │     │    1843–1928     │
                                 └──────────────────┘     └──────────────────┘
         ┌──────────────────┐                      ┌──────────────────┐
         │  Charles William │                      │       148        │
         │      Scott       │                      │    Cora Bell     │
         │    1859–1943     │                      │    Hargadine     │
         │                  │   Marriage: 1887     │    1865–1942     │
         └──────────────────┘                      └──────────────────┘
    ┌───────────┐ ┌───────────┐ ┌───────────┐ ┌───────────┐ ┌───────────┐
    │    285    │ │    286    │ │    287    │ │    288    │ │           │
    │   Ralph   │ │  Elmas W. │ │  Stella   │ │ Roy Edwin │ │Infant Baby│
    │  William  │ │   Scott   │ │   Scott   │ │   Scott   │ │   Scott   │
    │   Scott   │ │           │ │           │ │           │ │           │
    │ 1888–1958 │ │ 1890–1954 │ │ 1892–1961 │ │ 1896–1974 │ │ 1900–1900 │
    └───────────┘ └───────────┘ └───────────┘ └───────────┘ └───────────┘
```

148. **Cora Bell Hargadine** was born on Friday, December 08, 1865, in Chenoa, McLean County, Illinois. She was the daughter of William Henry Hargadine (55) and Sarah Mariah Sprague.

Cora Bell died in Edwards County, Kansas, on August 17, 1942, at the age of 76. She was buried in Bethel Cemetery, Hodges, Edwards County, Kansas (Find a Grave ID 67570823).

Cora Bell married **Charles William Scott** on Thursday, December 08, 1887, in Kansas, USA. They had five children.

Charles William was born in Sinking Spring, Highland County, Ohio, in February 1859. He reached 83 years of age and died in Kiowa County, Kansas, in 1943. Charles William was buried in Bethel Cemetery, Hodges, Edwards County, Kansas (Find a Grave ID 67570806).

Children of Cora Bell Hargadine and Charles William Scott:

+ 285 m I. **Ralph William Scott** was born in Edwards County, Kansas, on October 23, 1888. He died in Kinsley, Edwards County, Kansas, on December 30, 1958, at the age of 70. Ralph William was buried in Bethel Cemetery, Hodges, Edwards County, Kansas (Find a Grave ID 67570932).

+ 286 m II. **Elmas W. Scott** was born in Edwards County, Kansas, on September 22, 1890. He died on October 13, 1954, at the age of 64. Elmas W. was buried in Bethel Cemetery, Hodges, Edwards County, Kansas (Find a Grave ID 67570866).

+ 287 f III. **Stella Scott** was born in Kinsley, Edwards County, Kansas, on December 27, 1892. She died in Lebanon, Linn County, Oregon, on July 11, 1961, at the age of 68. Her cause of death was myocardial infarction, coronary occlusion. She was buried in Bethel Cemetery, Hodges, Edwards County, Kansas (Find a Grave ID 28724524).

+ 288 m IV. **Roy Edwin Scott** was born in Edwards County, Kansas, on February 02, 1896. He died in Edwards County, Kansas, on July 02, 1974, at the age of 78. Roy Edwin was buried in Bethel Cemetery, Hodges, Edwards County, Kansas (Find a Grave ID 67570952).

f V. **Infant Baby Scott** was born in Edwards County, Kansas, on May 18, 1900. She died in Edwards County, Kansas, on May 18, 1900.

John Hargadine

149. **John Byron Hargadine** was born on Sunday, July 04, 1869, in Chenoa, McLean County, Illinois. He was the son of William Henry Hargadine (55) and Sarah Mariah Sprague. He was also known as **Jack**.

John Byron worked as a Minister. He died in Haviland, Kiowa County, Kansas, on May 27, 1936, at the age of 66. John Byron was buried in Bethel Cemetery, Hodges, Edwards County, Kansas (Find a Grave ID 67562830).

Marriages with Rebecca Ann Keasling and Mary Grace Copley (Page 189) are known.

Family of John Hargadine and Rebecca Keasling

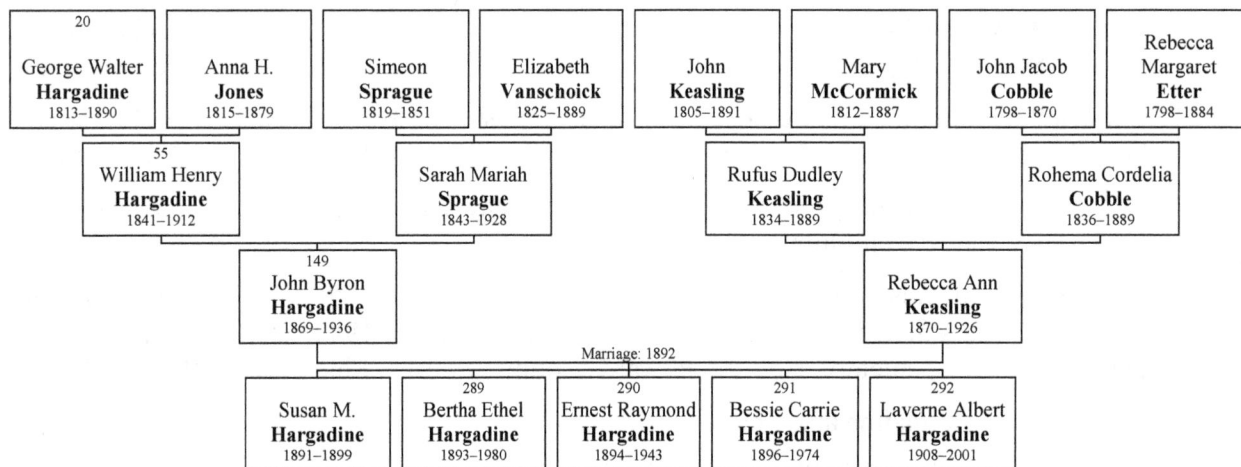

Here are the details about **John Byron Hargadine's** first marriage, with Rebecca Ann Keasling. You can read more about John Byron on page 188.

At the age of 23, John Byron Hargadine married **Rebecca Ann Keasling** on Tuesday, October 11, 1892, in Mullinville, Kiowa County, Kansas, when she was 22 years old. They had five children.

Rebecca Ann was born in Greene County, Tennessee, on Monday, March 28, 1870. She was the daughter of Rufus Dudley Keasling and Rohema Cordelia Cobble.

Rebecca Ann reached 56 years of age and died in Pratt, Pratt County, Kansas, on April 21, 1926. She was buried in Bethel Cemetery, Hodges, Edwards County, Kansas (Find a Grave ID 67563007).

Children of John Byron Hargadine and Rebecca Ann Keasling:

f I. **Susan M. Hargadine** was born on July 01, 1891. She was also known as **Susie**.

Susan M. died on August 21, 1899, at the age of 8. She was buried in Bethel Cemetery, Hodges, Edwards County, Kansas (Find a Grave ID 67563157).

+ 289   f   II. **Bertha Ethel Hargadine** was born in Mullinville, Kiowa County, Kansas, on July 24, 1893. She died in Winona, Logan County, Kansas, on October 01, 1980, at the age of 87. Bertha Ethel was buried in Winona Cemetery, Winona, Logan County, Kansas, on October 04, 1980 (Find a Grave ID 32434692).

+ 290   m   III. **Ernest Raymond Hargadine** was born in Edwards County, Kansas, on October 28, 1894. He died in Pretty Prairie, Reno County, Kansas, on January 09, 1943, at the age of 48. Ernest Raymond was buried in Farmington Cemetery, Macksville, Stafford County, Kansas (Find a Grave ID 210059584).

+ 291   f   IV. **Bessie Carrie Hargadine** was born in Kansas, USA, on April 24, 1896. She died in Arlington, Snohomish County, Washington, on November 23, 1974, at the age of 78. Bessie Carrie was buried in Acacia Memorial Park and Funeral Home, Lake Forest Park, King County, Washington (Find a Grave ID 159272581).

+ 292   m   V. **Laverne Albert Hargadine** was born in Wichita County, Kansas, on May 02, 1908. He died in Overland Park, Johnson County, Kansas, on February 07, 2001, at the age of 92. Laverne Albert was buried in Lakeside Cemetery, Hastings, Dakota County, Minnesota, on February 13, 2001 (Find a Grave ID 126025134).

Family of John Hargadine and Mary Copley

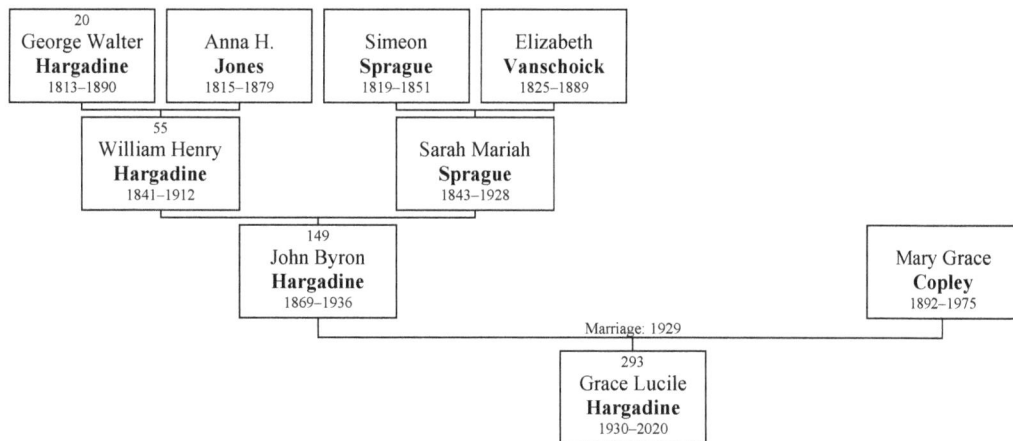

Here are the details about **John Byron Hargadine's** second marriage, with Mary Grace Copley. You can read more about John Byron on page 188.

At the age of 60, John Byron Hargadine married **Mary Grace Copley** on Tuesday, August 27, 1929, when she was 37 years old. They had one daughter.

Mary Grace was born in Kansas, USA, on Saturday, July 16, 1892. She reached 82 years of age and died in Eudora, Douglas County, Kansas, on March 15, 1975. Mary Grace was buried in Eudora City Cemetery, Eudora, Douglas County, Kansas (Find a Grave ID 11048201).

Daughter of John Byron Hargadine and Mary Grace Copley:

+ 293   f   I. **Grace Lucile Hargadine** was born in Greensburg, Kiowa County, Kansas, on November 07, 1930. She died in Orange City, Volusia County, Florida, on November 13, 2020, at the age of 90. Grace Lucile was buried in Eudora City Cemetery, Eudora, Douglas County, Kansas (Find a Grave ID 39044003).

William Hargadine

150.   **William Ezekiel Hargadine** was born on Wednesday, April 17, 1872, in Chenoa, McLean County, Illinois. He was the son of William Henry Hargadine (55) and Sarah Mariah Sprague. He was also known as **Will**.

William Ezekiel died in Edwards County, Kansas, on November 12, 1949, at the age of 77. He was buried in Bethel Cemetery, Hodges, Edwards County, Kansas (Find a Grave ID 67563044).

More facts and events for William Ezekiel Hargadine:

Individual Note: 1923   Pastor of West Bethany Free Methodist Church[206]

Marriages with Rohema Cordelia Keasling and Bessie Mae McNeece (Page 192) are known.

Family of William Hargadine and Rohema Keasling

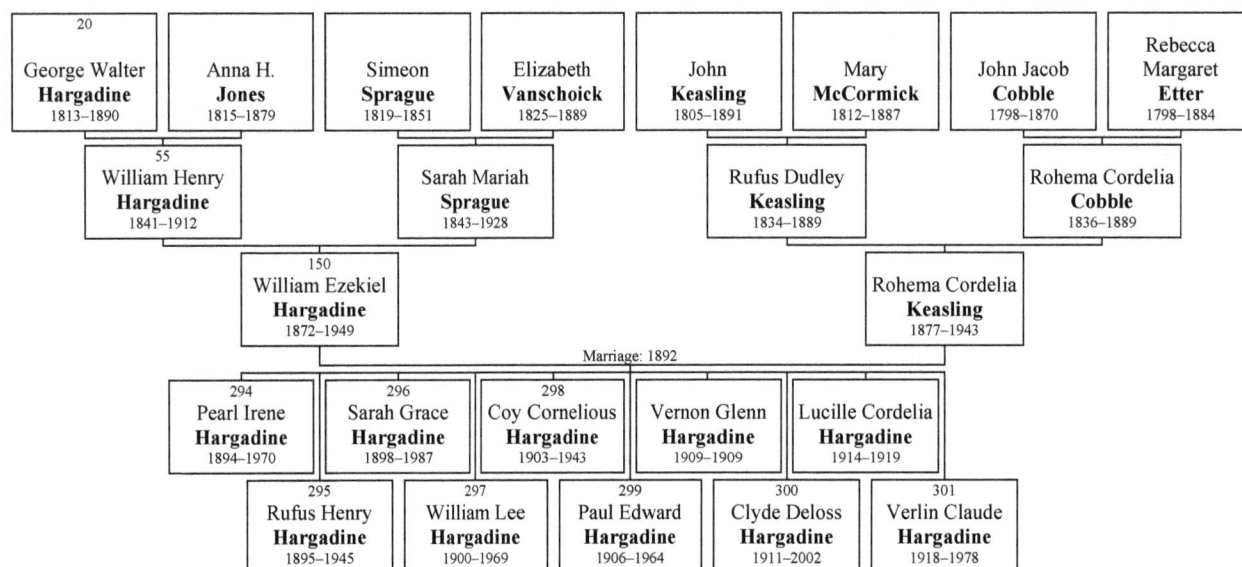

20 George Walter **Hargadine** 1813–1890	Anna H. **Jones** 1815–1879	Simeon **Sprague** 1819–1851	Elizabeth **Vanschoick** 1825–1889	John **Keasling** 1805–1891	Mary **McCormick** 1812–1887	John Jacob **Cobble** 1798–1870	Rebecca Margaret **Etter** 1798–1884

55 William Henry **Hargadine** 1841–1912 — Sarah Mariah **Sprague** 1843–1928 — Rufus Dudley **Keasling** 1834–1889 — Rohema Cordelia **Cobble** 1836–1889

150 William Ezekiel **Hargadine** 1872–1949 — Rohema Cordelia **Keasling** 1877–1943

Marriage: 1892

294 Pearl Irene **Hargadine** 1894–1970	296 Sarah Grace **Hargadine** 1898–1987	298 Coy Cornelious **Hargadine** 1903–1943	Vernon Glenn **Hargadine** 1909–1909	Lucille Cordelia **Hargadine** 1914–1919

295 Rufus Henry **Hargadine** 1895–1945	297 William Lee **Hargadine** 1900–1969	299 Paul Edward **Hargadine** 1906–1964	300 Clyde Deloss **Hargadine** 1911–2002	301 Verlin Claude **Hargadine** 1918–1978

Here are the details about **William Ezekiel Hargadine's** first marriage, with Rohema Cordelia Keasling. You can read more about William Ezekiel on page 190.

At the age of 20, William Ezekiel Hargadine married **Rohema Cordelia Keasling** on Sunday, September 18, 1892, in Martin, Kiowa County, Kansas, when she was 15 years old. They had ten children.

---

206   Wichita County History Book.

Rohema Cordelia was born in Midway, Greene County, Tennessee, on Saturday, March 10, 1877. She was the daughter of Rufus Dudley Keasling and Rohema Cordelia Cobble. She was also known as **Cordie**.

Rohema Cordelia reached 66 years of age and died in Hutchinson, Reno County, Kansas, on April 14, 1943. She was buried in Bethel Cemetery, Hodges, Edwards County, Kansas (Find a Grave ID 67563056).

Children of William Ezekiel Hargadine and Rohema Cordelia Keasling:

+ 294   f   I. **Pearl Irene Hargadine** was born in Edwards County, Kansas, on January 12, 1894. She died in Edwards County, Kansas, on June 14, 1970, at the age of 76. Pearl Irene was buried in Hillside Cemetery, Kinsley, Edwards County, Kansas, on June 16, 1970 (Find a Grave ID 67570381).

+ 295   m   II. **Rufus Henry Hargadine** was born in Kiowa, Edwards County, Kansas, on December 14, 1895. He died in Dodge City, Ford County, Kansas, on December 02, 1945, at the age of 49. Rufus Henry was buried in Bethel Cemetery, Hodges, Edwards County, Kansas, on December 05, 1945 (Find a Grave ID 67563086).

+ 296   f   III. **Sarah Grace Hargadine** was born in Kiowa, Edwards County, Kansas, on January 24, 1898. She died in Florence, Lauderdale County, Alabama, on December 30, 1987, at the age of 89. Sarah Grace was buried in Bethel Cemetery, Hodges, Edwards County, Kansas, on January 04, 1988 (Find a Grave ID 67571620).

+ 297   m   IV. **William Lee Hargadine** was born in Kiowa, Kansas, on April 04, 1900. He died in Pratt, Pratt County, Kansas, on November 19, 1969, at the age of 69. William Lee was buried in Greenlawn Cemetery, Pratt, Pratt County, Kansas, on November 21, 1969 (Find a Grave ID 76141586).

+ 298   m   V. **Coy Cornelious Hargadine** was born in Kiowa, Kansas, on August 16, 1903. He died in Winona, Logan County, Kansas, on April 01, 1943, at the age of 39. Coy Cornelious was buried in Bethel Cemetery, Hodges, Edwards County, Kansas, on April 05, 1943 (Find a Grave ID 67562812).

+ 299   m   VI. **Paul Edward Hargadine** was born in Kiowa, Barber County, Kansas, on January 15, 1906. He died in Kinsley, Edwards County, Kansas, on May 10, 1964, at the age of 58. Paul Edward was buried in Bethel Cemetery, Hodges, Edwards County, Kansas, on May 12, 1964 (Find a Grave ID 67562982).

       m   VII. **Vernon Glenn Hargadine** was born in Kiowa, Kansas, on November 28, 1909. He died on December 24, 1909. Vernon Glenn was buried in Bethel Cemetery, Hodges, Edwards County, Kansas (Find a Grave ID 67563189).

+ 300   m   VIII. **Clyde Deloss Hargadine** was born in Kiowa, Edwards County, Kansas, on June 01, 1911. He was also known as **Dee**.

         Clyde Deloss died in Overland Park Regional Medical Center, Overland Park, Johnson County, Kansas, on December 06, 2002, at the age of 91.

He was buried in Oak Hill Cemetery, Lawrence, Douglas County, Kansas, on December 11, 2002 (Find a Grave ID 23837222).

f   IX. **Lucille Cordelia Hargadine** was born in Kiowa County, Kansas, on August 23, 1914. She died in Kinsley, Edwards County, Kansas, on December 03, 1919, at the age of 5. Her cause of death was diphtheria. She was buried in Bethel Cemetery, Hodges, Edwards County, Kansas, on December 04, 1919 (Find a Grave ID 67562888).

+   301   m   X. **Verlin Claude Hargadine** was born in Kinsley, Edwards County, Kansas, on May 26, 1918. He died in Liberal, Seward County, Kansas, on September 25, 1978, at the age of 60. Verlin Claude was buried in Stafford Cemetery, Stafford, Stafford County, Kansas, on September 27, 1978 (Find a Grave ID 93811668).

Family of William Hargadine and Bessie McNeece

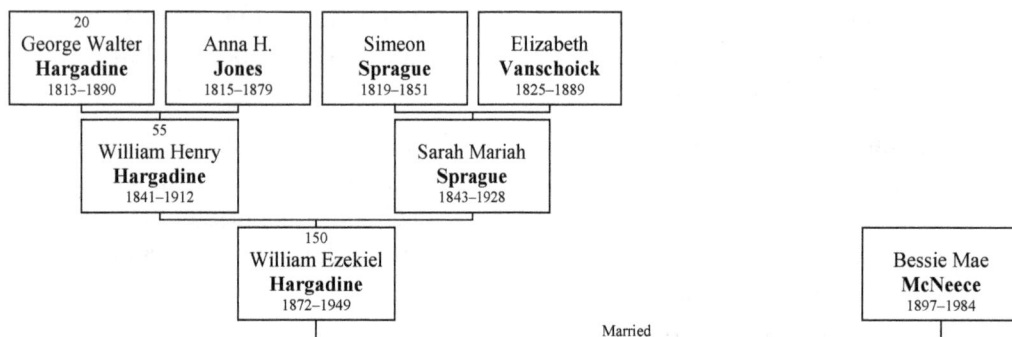

20 George Walter **Hargadine** 1813–1890	Anna H. **Jones** 1815–1879	Simeon **Sprague** 1819–1851	Elizabeth **Vanschoick** 1825–1889

55
William Henry
Hargadine
1841–1912

Sarah Mariah
Sprague
1843–1928

150
William Ezekiel
Hargadine
1872–1949

Bessie Mae
McNeece
1897–1984

Married

Here are the details about **William Ezekiel Hargadine's** second marriage, with Bessie Mae McNeece. You can read more about William Ezekiel on page 190.

William Ezekiel Hargadine married **Bessie Mae McNeece**. Bessie Mae was born in Vernon County, Missouri, on Monday, October 25, 1897.

She reached 86 years of age and died in Dodge City, Ford County, Kansas, on March 07, 1984. Bessie Mae was buried in Ford Cemetery, Ford, Ford County, Kansas (Find a Grave ID 30779536).

Family of Luella Hargadine and William LoVette

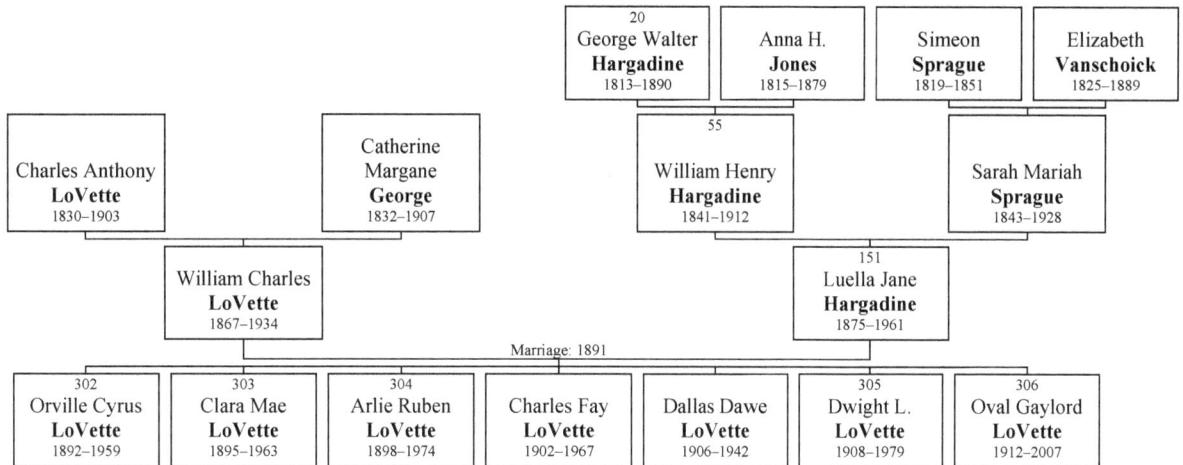

```
                                    ┌──────────┐ ┌──────────┐ ┌──────────┐ ┌──────────┐
                                    │    20    │ │  Anna H. │ │  Simeon  │ │ Elizabeth│
                                    │  George  │ │          │ │          │ │          │
                                    │  Walter  │ │  Jones   │ │ Sprague  │ │Vanschoick│
                                    │ Hargadine│ │1815–1879 │ │1819–1851 │ │1825–1889 │
                                    │1813–1890 │ └──────────┘ └──────────┘ └──────────┘
                                    └──────────┘
  ┌──────────┐   ┌──────────┐        ┌──────────┐              ┌──────────┐
  │  Charles │   │ Catherine│        │    55    │              │   Sarah  │
  │  Anthony │   │  Margane │        │  William │              │  Mariah  │
  │  LoVette │   │  George  │        │   Henry  │              │  Sprague │
  │1830–1903 │   │1832–1907 │        │ Hargadine│              │1843–1928 │
  └──────────┘   └──────────┘        │1841–1912 │              └──────────┘
         ┌──────────┐                └──────────┘
         │  William │                       ┌──────────┐
         │  Charles │                       │   151    │
         │  LoVette │                       │  Luella  │
         │1867–1934 │                       │   Jane   │
         └──────────┘                       │ Hargadine│
                            Marriage: 1891  │1875–1961 │
                                            └──────────┘
```

| 302 Orville Cyrus LoVette 1892–1959 | 303 Clara Mae LoVette 1895–1963 | 304 Arlie Ruben LoVette 1898–1974 | Charles Fay LoVette 1902–1967 | Dallas Dawe LoVette 1906–1942 | 305 Dwight L. LoVette 1908–1979 | 306 Oval Gaylord LoVette 1912–2007 |

151. Luella Jane Hargadine was born on Monday, March 01, 1875, in Chenoa, McLean County, Illinois. She was the daughter of William Henry Hargadine (55) and Sarah Mariah Sprague.

Luella Jane died in Kinsley, Edwards County, Kansas, on January 08, 1961, at the age of 85. She was buried in Hillside Cemetery, Kinsley, Edwards County, Kansas (Find a Grave ID 11471653).

Luella Jane married **William Charles LoVette** in 1891. They had seven children.

William Charles was born in Morristown, Hamblen County, Tennessee, on Tuesday, September 10, 1867. He was the son of Charles Anthony LoVette and Catherine Margane George.

William Charles reached 67 years of age and died in Kinsley, Edwards County, Kansas, on December 28, 1934. He was buried in Hillside Cemetery, Kinsley, Edwards County, Kansas (Find a Grave ID 11471672).

Children of Luella Jane Hargadine and William Charles LoVette:

+ 302   m   I. **Orville Cyrus LoVette** was born in Crescent, Kiowa County, Kansas, on September 05, 1892. He died on September 20, 1959, at the age of 67. Orville Cyrus was buried in Hillside Cemetery, Kinsley, Edwards County, Kansas (Find a Grave ID 11471657).

+ 303   f   II. **Clara Mae LoVette** was born in Kansas, USA, on January 25, 1895. She died on July 05, 1963, at the age of 68. Clara Mae was buried in Hillside Cemetery, Kinsley, Edwards County, Kansas (Find a Grave ID 11197812).

+ 304   m   III. **Arlie Ruben LoVette** was born in Kansas, USA, on May 09, 1898. He died in Lewis, Edwards County, Kansas, on July 28, 1974, at the age of 76. Arlie Ruben was buried in Wayne Cemetery, Lewis, Edwards County, Kansas (Find a Grave ID 76154958).

      m   IV. **Charles Fay LoVette** was born on May 01, 1902. He died on March 05, 1967, at the age of 64. Charles Fay was buried in Hillside Cemetery, Kinsley, Edwards County, Kansas (Find a Grave ID 11471648).

m V. **Dallas Dawe LoVette** was born on March 09, 1906. He died on July 25, 1942, at the age of 36. His cause of death was a combine accident. He was buried in Hillside Cemetery, Kinsley, Edwards County, Kansas (Find a Grave ID 11471650).

+ 305 m VI. **Dwight L. LoVette** was born on March 18, 1908. He died on December 28, 1979, at the age of 71. Dwight L. was buried in Forest Lawn Memorial Park, Hollywood Hills, Los Angeles County, California (Find a Grave ID 169489516).

+ 306 m VII. **Oval Gaylord LoVette** was born in Bison, Garfield County, Oklahoma, on August 09, 1912. He died on January 11, 2007, at the age of 94. Oval Gaylord was buried in Sierra Hills Memorial Park, Sacramento, Sacramento County, California (Find a Grave ID 155842052).

Family of Clara Hargadine and James Keasling

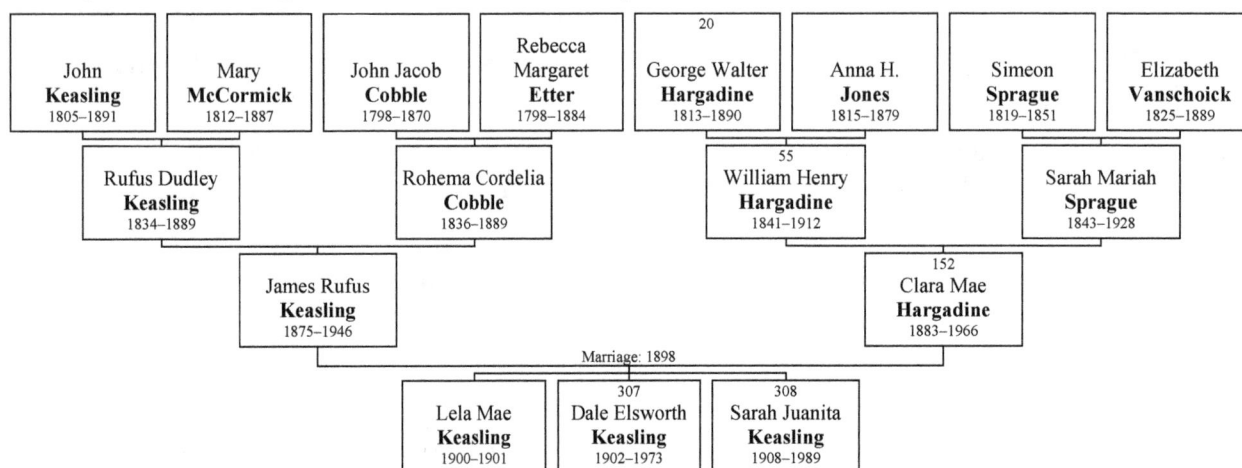

152. **Clara Mae Hargadine** was born on Wednesday, September 26, 1883, in Chenoa, McLean County, Illinois. She was the daughter of William Henry Hargadine (55) and Sarah Mariah Sprague.

Clara Mae died in Protection, Comanche County, Kansas, on October 04, 1966, at the age of 83. She was buried in Protection Cemetery, Protection, Comanche County, Kansas (Find a Grave ID 21542845).

At the age of 14, Clara Mae married **James Rufus Keasling** on Sunday, September 11, 1898, in Kiowa County, Kansas, when he was 23 years old. They had three children.

James Rufus was born in Midway, Greene County, Tennessee, on Sunday, January 24, 1875. He was the son of Rufus Dudley Keasling and Rohema Cordelia Cobble.

He worked as a Mechanic. James Rufus reached 71 years of age and died in Protection, Comanche County, Kansas, on February 04, 1946. He was buried in Protection Cemetery, Protection, Comanche County, Kansas (Find a Grave ID 21542853).

Children of Clara Mae Hargadine and James Rufus Keasling:

f	I.	**Lela Mae Keasling** was born on August 27, 1900. She died on March 25, 1901. Lela Mae was buried in Bethel Cemetery, Hodges, Edwards County, Kansas (Find a Grave ID 67563738).	
+ 307	m	II.	**Dale Elsworth Keasling** was born in Coldwater, Comanche County, Kansas, on July 09, 1902. He died in Protection, Comanche County, Kansas, on April 27, 1973, at the age of 70. Dale Elsworth was buried in Protection Cemetery, Protection, Comanche County, Kansas (Find a Grave ID 21542846).
+ 308	f	III.	**Sarah Juanita Keasling** was born on January 08, 1908. She died in Hutchinson, Reno County, Kansas, on October 18, 1989, at the age of 81. Sarah Juanita was buried in Memorial Park Cemetery, Hutchinson, Reno County, Kansas (Find a Grave ID 37388566).

Raymond Hargadine

153. **Raymond Franklin Hargadine** was born on Thursday, January 26, 1888, in Mullinville, Kiowa County, Kansas. He was the son of William Henry Hargadine (55) and Sarah Mariah Sprague.

Raymond Franklin died in Seattle, King County, Washington, on March 28, 1971, at the age of 83. He was buried in Old Carson Cemetery, Skamania County, Washington, on April 01, 1971 (Find a Grave ID 43234197).

Marriages with Jennetta Zimmerman and Orpha Janie Dane (Page 196) are known.

Family of Raymond Hargadine and Jennetta Zimmerman

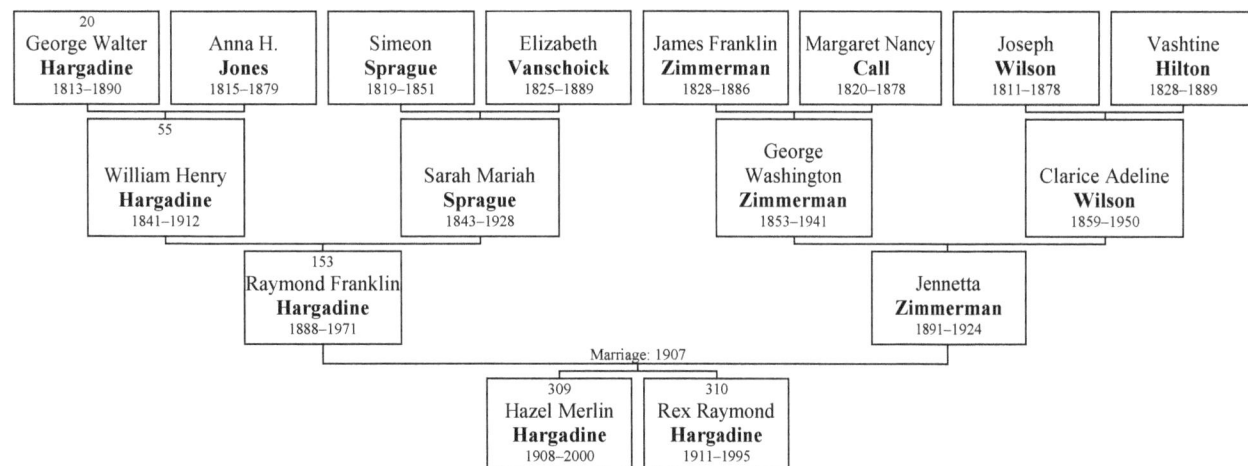

Here are the details about **Raymond Franklin Hargadine's** first marriage, with Jennetta Zimmerman. You can read more about Raymond Franklin on page 195.

At the age of 19, Raymond Franklin Hargadine married **Jennetta Zimmerman** on Sunday, July 21, 1907, in Mullinville, Kiowa County, Kansas, when she was 16 years old. They had two children.

Jennetta was born in Blackford, Jasper County, Indiana, on Tuesday, March 17, 1891. She was the daughter of George Washington Zimmerman and Clarice Adeline Wilson.

Jennetta reached 33 years of age and died in Emigrant, Park County, Montana, on August 29, 1924. She was buried in Emigrant Cemetery, Park County, Montana (Find a Grave ID 49088281).

Children of Raymond Franklin Hargadine and Jennetta Zimmerman:

+ 309 f I. **Hazel Merlin Hargadine** was born in Mullinville, Kiowa County, Kansas, on June 02, 1908. She died in Providence St. Peter Hospital, Olympia, Thurston, Washington, on August 03, 2000, at the age of 92. Her cause of death was renal failure. She was buried in Yelm Cemetery, Yelm, Thurston County, Washington, on August 07, 2000 (Find a Grave ID 39843041).

+ 310 m II. **Rex Raymond Hargadine** was born in Ematon, Stevens County, Kansas, on May 30, 1911. He died in Portland, Multnomah County, Oregon, on February 20, 1995, at the age of 83. Rex Raymond was buried in Old Carson Cemetery, Skamania County, Washington, on February 23, 1995 (Find a Grave ID 43234369).

Family of Raymond Hargadine and Orpha Dane

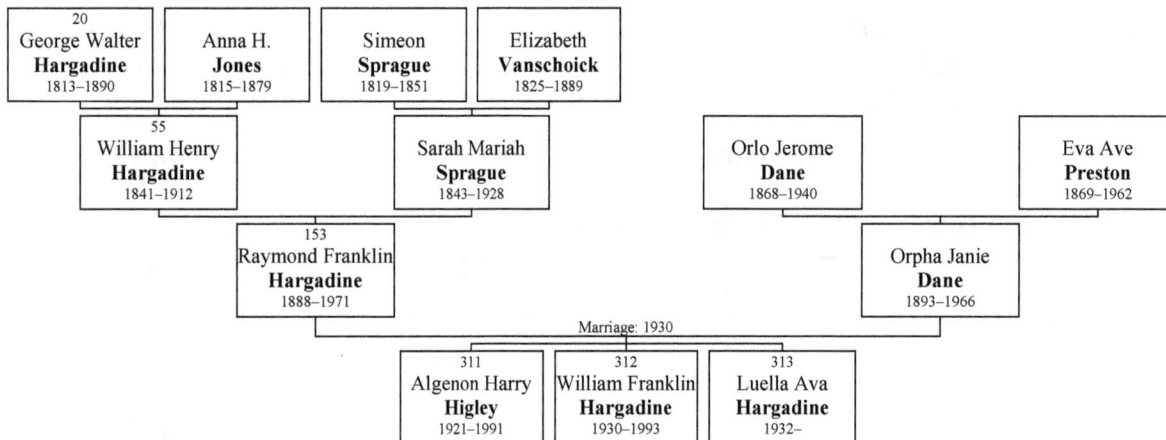

Here are the details about **Raymond Franklin Hargadine's** second marriage, with Orpha Janie Dane. You can read more about Raymond Franklin on page 195.

At the age of 42, Raymond Franklin Hargadine married **Orpha Janie Dane** on Friday, August 29, 1930, in Chelan, Chelan County, Washington, when she was 36 years old. They had three children.

Orpha Janie was born in Minnesota, USA, on Friday, September 29, 1893. She was the daughter of Orlo Jerome Dane and Eva Ave Preston.

She was buried in December 1966 in Mount Hope Cemetery, San Diego, San Diego County, California (Find a Grave ID 11344070). Orpha Janie reached 73 years of age and died in San Diego, San Diego County, California, on December 12, 1966.

Children of Raymond Franklin Hargadine and Orpha Janie Dane:

+ 311   m   I. **Algenon Harry Higley** was born in Lakeside, Chelan County, Washington, on April 21, 1921. He died in Hurricane, Washington County, Utah, on July 31, 1991, at the age of 70. Algenon Harry was buried in Kanab City Cemetery, Kanab, Kane County, Utah (Find a Grave ID 13208036).

+ 312   m   II. **William Franklin Hargadine** was born in Chelan, Chelan County, Washington, on November 15, 1930. He was also known as **Bill**.

William Franklin died in Mesa, Maricopa County, Arizona, on February 04, 1993, at the age of 62. He was buried in Willamette National Cemetery, Portland, Multnomah County, Oregon, on February 23, 1993 (Find a Grave ID 753315).

+ 313   f   III. **Luella Ava Hargadine** was born in Chelan, Chelan County, Washington, on November 08, 1932. She is also known as **Ava**.

Family of George Drommond and Mary McGinnis

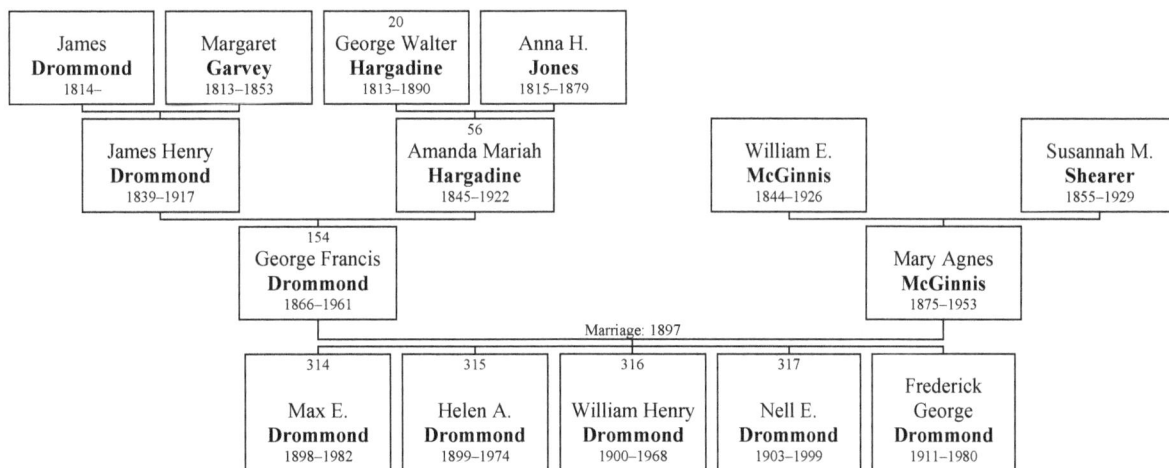

154.   **George Francis Drommond** was born on Saturday, November 17, 1866, in Peoria, Peoria County, Illinois. He was the son of James Henry Drommond and Amanda Mariah Hargadine (56).

George Francis died in Loveland, Larimer County, Colorado, on July 16, 1961, at the age of 94. He was buried in Grandview Cemetery, Wray, Yuma County, Colorado (Find a Grave ID 56943092).

At the age of 30, George Francis married **Mary Agnes McGinnis** on Wednesday, April 28, 1897, in Laird, Yuma County, Colorado, when she was 21 years old. They had five children.

Mary Agnes was born in Creston, Union County, Iowa, on Thursday, July 15, 1875. Mary Agnes reached 78 years of age and died in Laird, Yuma County, Colorado, on October 12, 1953. She was buried on October 15, 1953, in Grandview Cemetery, Wray, Yuma County, Colorado (Find a Grave ID 50355314).

GEORGE F. AND MARY AGNES DROMMOND

"That was a great day in Laird" was the comment of George F. Drommond as he would relate that for a short time on one particular day he was official guard at the railroad crossing when the Burlington Zephyr made its initial run from Chicago to Denver.

George and Agnes Drommond were not early-day settlers of eastern Yuma County but they were not strangers to it by any means as they had proved up on a homestead just east of the Colorado-Nebraska line along Highway 34, adjacent to the railroad. In the early 20s they moved to Laird when their son Bill took over operation of the farm and ranch, to be near William and Susannah McGinnis, the aging and ailing parents of Agnes.

George worked with a team of horses on the development of the irrigation ditch and by his labor acquired water rights for irrigation of his land. Agnes taught school at Wiggins, Colorado, which at that time seemed a long distance from Laird. The Drommonds were married at Laird, April 28, 1897, and began their married life in the sod house on the claim one and one half miles from the little hamlet of Sanborn, Nebraska. As their children, Max, Helen, William, Nell and Fred arrived, a frame dwelling was constructed and rooms added as needed by the growing family.

Their home at Laird was a haven for "Those away from home," as a section foreman sent to Laird stayed with them until he could get his family moved. Raleigh Clegg who came as Telegraph Operator at the depot was their guest for a time and through the years many of the Laird school teachers called the Drommond house "Home." With so many lovely young ladies from various parts of the country coming as teachers, it made a very busy household as eligible young men of the area found much of interest there, some developing into marriages.

George kept busy tending the sandy-soil garden plot which provided fresh vegetables for the "boarders" and Agnes was constantly planning or preparing tasty meals but she found time to be a faithful member of the Laird Methodist Church. They had a well dug which provided good water for all their needs and made it possible to have one of the homes in Laird considered "modern."

Agnes died October 12, 1953, at Laird. George on July 16, 1961, at Loveland. Burial of each was in the Wray Cemetery where also was buried their son William who died on June 27, 1968 and a daughter Helen (Mrs. Arthur) Hultquist on August 8, 1974.

   —A History of East Yuma County

This is a collection of general history and family histories of East Yuma County from 1868 through 1978. Pages 108. *(Written account by Nell E. Drommond Pahl, Daughter of William E. McGinnis and Susannah M. Shearer)

Children of George Francis Drommond and Mary Agnes McGinnis:

+   314   m   I. **Max E. Drommond** was born in Sanborn, Dundy County, Nebraska, on March 24, 1898. He died in Seattle, King County, Washington, on December 31, 1982, at the age of 84. Max E. was buried in Lake View Cemetery, Seattle, King County, Washington, on January 05, 1983 (Find a Grave ID).

+   315   f   II. **Helen A. Drommond** was born on May 08, 1899. She died on August 08, 1974, at the age of 75. Helen A. was buried in Grandview Cemetery, Wray, Yuma County, Colorado (Find a Grave ID 37801129).

+   316   m   III. **William Henry Drommond** was born in Sanborn, Dundy County, Nebraska, on September 10, 1900. He died in Haigler, Dundy County, Nebraska, on June 27, 1968, at the age of 67. William Henry was buried in Grandview Cemetery, Wray, Yuma County, Colorado, on June 29, 1968 (Find a Grave ID 50166367).

+ 317   f   IV. **Nell E. Drommond** was born in Sanborn, Dundy County, Nebraska, on April 12, 1903.[207] She died in Loveland, Larimer County, Colorado, on October 19, 1999, at the age of 96.[207] Nell E. was buried in Loveland Burial Park, Loveland, Larimer County, Colorado (Find a Grave ID 154832344).[207]

       m   V. **Frederick George Drommond** was born in Sanborn, Dundy County, Nebraska, on March 05, 1911. He died on January 13, 1980, at the age of 68.

Family of Lena Drommond and William Fisk

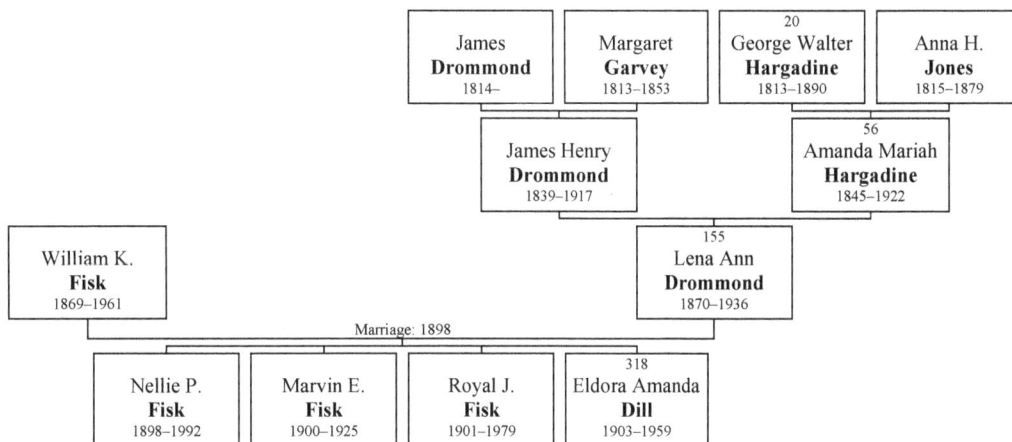

155.   **Lena Ann Drommond** was born on Sunday, January 30, 1870, in Lyman Twp., Ford County, Illinois. She was the daughter of James Henry Drommond and Amanda Mariah Hargadine (56).

Lena Ann died in 1936 at the age of 65. She was buried in Crown Hill Cemetery, Wheat Ridge, Jefferson County, Colorado (Find a Grave ID 34249816).

Lena Ann married **William K. Fisk** in 1898. They had four children.

William K. was born in 1869. He reached 92 years of age and died in 1961. William K. was buried in Crown Hill Cemetery, Wheat Ridge, Jefferson County, Colorado (Find a Grave ID 34249784).

Children of Lena Ann Drommond and William K. Fisk:

       f   I. **Nellie P. Fisk** was born in Nebraska, USA, on September 18, 1898. She died in Nevada County, California, on November 24, 1992, at the age of 94. Nellie P. was buried in Crown Hill Cemetery, Wheat Ridge, Jefferson County, Colorado.

---

207   Ancestry.com, U.S., Find a Grave® Index, 1600s-Current (Lehi, UT, USA, Ancestry.com Operations, Inc., 2012), Ancestry.com, Record for Nell E. Pahl. https://search.ancestry.co.uk/cgi-bin/sse.dll?db=60525&h=127477485&indiv=try.

m   II. **Marvin E. Fisk** was born in Haigler, Dundy County, Nebraska, on February 05, 1900.[208] He died in Jefferson County, Colorado, on August 22, 1925, at the age of 25.[208] His cause of death was drowning. He was buried in Crown Hill Cemetery, Wheat Ridge, Jefferson County, Colorado (Find a Grave ID 202776130).[208]

m   III. **Royal J. Fisk** was born in Wray, Yuma County, Colorado, on December 25, 1901. He died in Denver, Denver County, Colorado, on February 23, 1979, at the age of 77. Royal J. was buried in Arvada Cemetery, Arvada, Jefferson County, Colorado (Find a Grave ID 18917888).

+   318   f   IV. **Eldora Amanda Dill** was born in Colorado, USA, on August 30, 1903.[209, 210] She died in Los Angeles, Los Angeles County, California, on November 24, 1959, at the age of 56.[209, 210]

Family of Mary Drommond and Charles Bullard

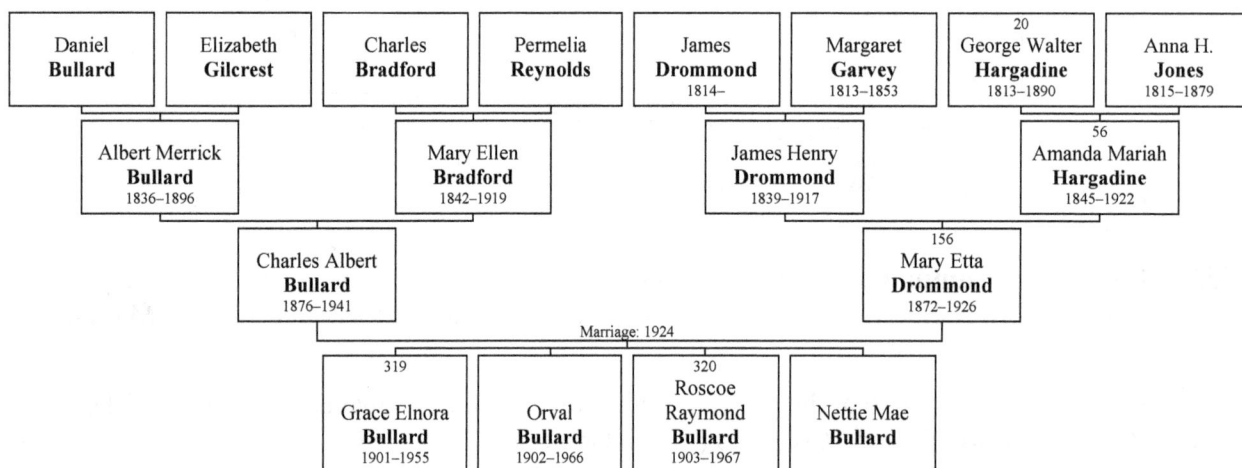

156.   **Mary Etta Drommond** was born on Friday, April 26, 1872, in Lyman Twp., Ford County, Illinois. She was the daughter of James Henry Drommond and Amanda Mariah Hargadine (56).

208   Ancestry.com, U.S., Find a Grave® Index, 1600s-Current (Lehi, UT, USA, Ancestry.com Operations, Inc., 2012), Ancestry.com, Record for Marvin E. Fisk. https://search.ancestry.co.uk/cgi-bin/sse.dll?db=60525&h=167410043&indiv=try.

209   Ancestry.com, California, U.S., Death Index, 1940-1997 (Provo, UT, USA, Ancestry.com Operations Inc, 2000), Ancestry.com, Place: Los Angeles; Date: 24 Nov 1959; Social Security: 547445629. Record for Eldora Amanda Dill. https://search.ancestry.co.uk/cgi-bin/sse.dll?db=5180&h=1879319&indiv=try.

210   Ancestry.com, Public Member Trees (Provo, UT, USA, Ancestry.com Operations, Inc., 2006), Ancestry.com, Record for Eldora Amanda Fisk. https://search.ancestry.co.uk/cgi-bin/sse.dll?db=1030&h=13896600421&indiv=try.

Mary Etta died in Englewood, Arapahoe County, Colorado, on April 03, 1926, at the age of 53. Her cause of death was accidentally killed by a truck. Mary Etta was buried in Grandview Cemetery, Wray, Yuma County, Colorado (Find a Grave ID 17059444).

At the age of 52, Mary Etta married **Charles Albert Bullard** on Sunday, June 08, 1924, in Haigler, Dundy County, Nebraska, when he was 48 years old. They had four children.

Charles Albert was born in Creston, Union County, Iowa, on Sunday, April 16, 1876. Charles Albert reached 65 years of age and died in Denver, Denver County, Colorado, on September 02, 1941. His cause of death was heart attack. Charles Albert was buried in Grandview Cemetery, Wray, Yuma County, Colorado (Find a Grave ID 50359004).

Charles and Mary Bullard

Charles Albert Bullard, son of Albert Merrick and Mary Ellen Bradford Bullard, was a lad of 10 years when he came with his parents to the area south of Laird. The trip was made in 1886 by covered wagon.
He was born in Creston, Iowa, on 16 April 1876, and died at Denver, Colorado, on 2 September 1941, following a heart attack.

Charles Bullard had a great capacity for making friends with his ready smile and friendly ways. In his younger years, he was an enthusiastic sportsman. Newspaper accounts tell of his ball playing and foot racing in stories of the new community's celebrations and harvest festivals.
The greater part of his life was spent in Yuma County as a public servant. He was elected sheriff of Yuma County in 1912 and was later employed by the Town of Wray as a marshal for several years before moving to Denver in 1924.

He and Mary Etta Drommond were married at a home wedding near Haigler, Nebraska, on 8 June 1924.

Two children died in infancy. Their other children were Mrs. Grace Gibson of California, a teacher for many years, who died in 1955. Roscoe Bullard, newspaperman, and Mrs. Nettie Mae Benson of Golden. Death of all three was attributed to cancer.

Mrs. Bullard, daughter of James and Amanda Hargadine Drommond, was born in Ford County, Illinois, on 26 April 1872. She was a talented seamstress and before her marriage, would often be a houseguest while creating a family's wardrobe.

The Bullards had lived in Denver only a little over a year when they were struck in a hit-run accident on 3 April 1926. Her death occurred at the scene. Burial was in Grandview Cemetery at Wray.

Mr. Bullard later married Mrs. Goldie Hedman. She established her home in Clay Center, Kansas, following his death in 1941. He was the son of Albert Merrick Bullard and Mary Ellen Bradford.

—*A History of East Yuma County*   This is a collection of general history and family histories of East Yuma County from 1868 through 1978.

Children of Mary Etta Drommond and Charles Albert Bullard:

+   319   f   I. **Grace Elnora Bullard** was born in Colorado Springs, El Paso County, Colorado, on November 09, 1901. She died in Torrance, Los Angeles, California, on May 26, 1955, at the age of 53. Grace Elnora was buried in Grandview Cemetery, Wray, Yuma County, Colorado (Find a Grave ID 30893177).

  m   II. **Orval Bullard** was born on June 12, 1902. He died in February 1966 at the age of 63.

\+ 320 m   III. **Roscoe Raymond Bullard** was born in Laird, Yuma County, Colorado, on November 11, 1903. He died in Denver, Denver County, Colorado, on May 12, 1967, at the age of 63. Roscoe Raymond was buried in Grandview Cemetery, Wray, Yuma County, Colorado (Find a Grave ID 17075799).

  f   IV. **Nettie Mae Bullard**.

Family of John Drommond and Hattie Steele

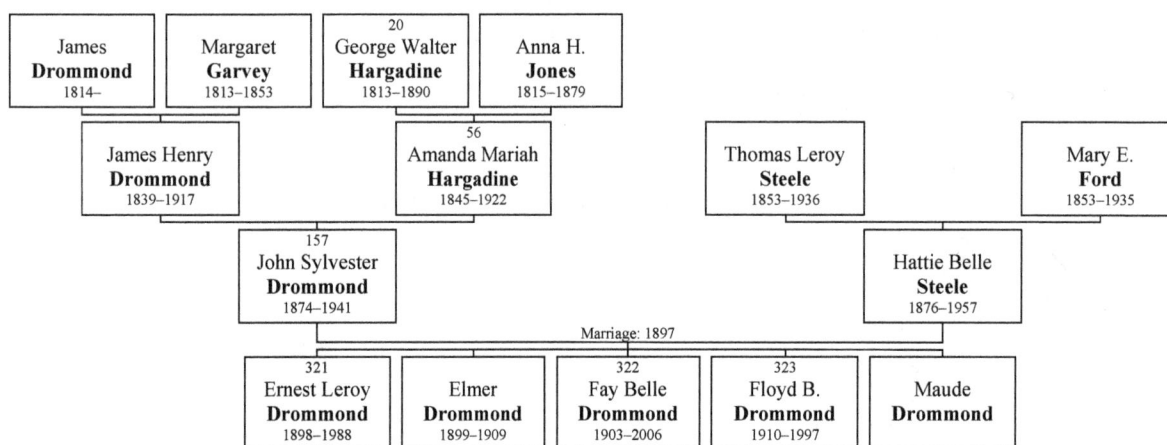

157.   **John Sylvester Drommond** was born on Monday, March 23, 1874, in Lyman Twp., Ford County, Illinois. He was the son of James Henry Drommond and Amanda Mariah Hargadine (56).

John Sylvester died in Colorado Springs, El Paso County, Colorado, on November 22, 1941, at the age of 67. He was buried in Evergreen Cemetery, Colorado Springs, El Paso County, Colorado (Find a Grave ID 34611285).

At the age of 23, John Sylvester married **Hattie Belle Steele** on Wednesday, June 23, 1897, in Laird, Yuma County, Colorado, when she was 20 years old. They had five children.

Hattie Belle was born in Illinois, USA, on Saturday, December 30, 1876. She was the daughter of Thomas Leroy Steele and Mary E. Ford.

Hattie Belle reached 80 years of age and died in Colorado Springs, El Paso County, Colorado, on March 10, 1957. She was buried on March 12, 1957, in Evergreen Cemetery, Colorado Springs, El Paso County, Colorado (Find a Grave ID 34611282).

Children of John Sylvester Drommond and Hattie Belle Steele:

+ 321   m   I. **Ernest Leroy Drommond** was born in Haigler, Dundy County, Nebraska, on March 23, 1898. He died in Colorado, USA, on May 25, 1988, at the age of 90. Ernest Leroy was buried in Memorial Gardens Cemetery and Mausoleum, Colorado Springs, El Paso County, Colorado (Find a Grave ID 49825963).

         m   II. **Elmer Drommond** was born on September 11, 1899. He died on February 08, 1909, at the age of 9. Elmer was buried in Grandview Cemetery, Wray, Yuma County, Colorado (Find a Grave ID 50355583).

+ 322   f   III. **Fay Belle Drommond** was born on September 19, 1903. She died on April 13, 2006, at the age of 102. Fay Belle was buried in Evergreen Cemetery, Colorado Springs, El Paso County, Colorado (Find a Grave ID 35152035).

+ 323   m   IV. **Floyd B. Drommond** was born in Colorado Springs, El Paso County, Colorado, on December 22, 1910. He died in Colorado Springs, El Paso County, Colorado, on July 25, 1997, at the age of 86. Floyd B. was buried in Evergreen Cemetery, Colorado Springs, El Paso County, Colorado, on August 01, 1997 (Find a Grave ID 34611284).

         f   V. **Maude Drommond.**

Family of Alva Drommond and Daisy McGinnis

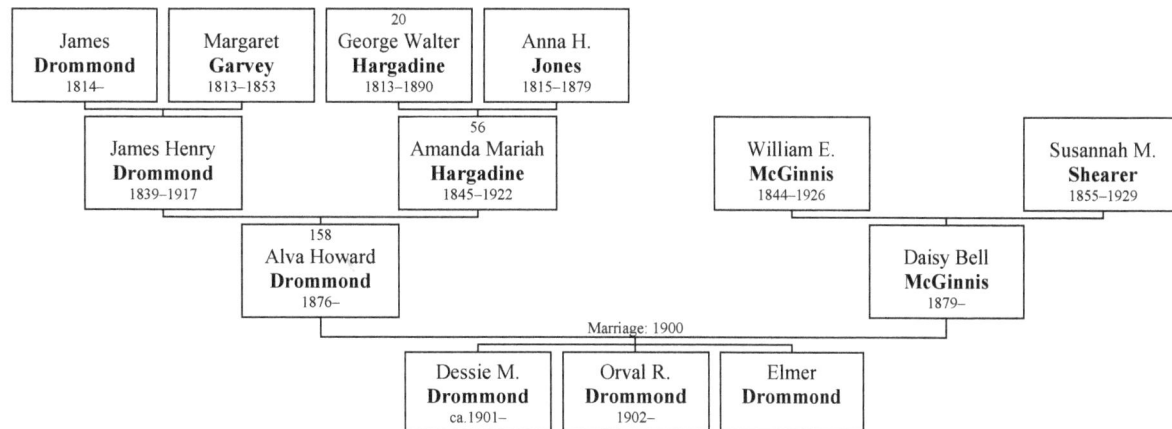

158. **Alva Howard Drommond** was born on Wednesday, December 06, 1876, in Chenoa, McLean County, Illinois. He was the son of James Henry Drommond and Amanda Mariah Hargadine (56).

At the age of 23, Alva Howard married **Daisy Bell McGinnis** on Wednesday, April 25, 1900, in Laird, Yuma County, Colorado, when she was 21 years old. They had three sons.

Daisy Bell was born in Creston, Union County, Iowa, on Tuesday, April 22, 1879. She was the daughter of William E. McGinnis and Susannah M. Shearer.

Daisy Bell was buried in Denver, Denver County, Colorado.

Sons of Alva Howard Drommond and Daisy Bell McGinnis:

m   I. **Dessie M. Drommond** was born about 1901.

m   II. **Orval R. Drommond** was born on June 12, 1902.

m   III. **Elmer Drommond**.

Family of Laura Drommond and Walter Kerns

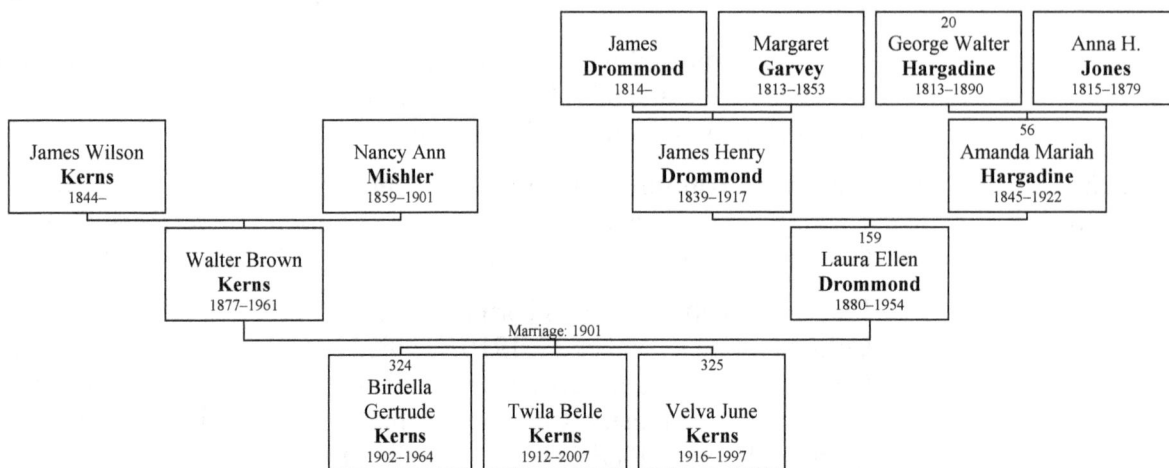

159.   **Laura Ellen Drommond** was born on Sunday, January 18, 1880, in Weston, McLean County, Illinois. She was the daughter of James Henry Drommond and Amanda Mariah Hargadine (56).

Laura Ellen died in Wray, Yuma County, Colorado, on September 26, 1954, at the age of 74. She was buried in Grandview Cemetery, Wray, Yuma County, Colorado (Find a Grave ID 9393640).

At the age of 21, Laura Ellen married **Walter Brown Kerns** on Wednesday, September 18, 1901, in Colorado Springs, El Paso County, Colorado, when he was 24 years old. They had three daughters.

Walter Brown was born in Carlinville, Macoupin County, Illinois, on Tuesday, February 20, 1877. He was the son of James Wilson Kerns and Nancy Ann Mishler.

Walter Brown reached 84 years of age and died in Wray, Yuma County, Colorado, on August 20, 1961. He was buried in Grandview Cemetery, Wray, Yuma County, Colorado (Find a Grave ID 9393631).

Daughters of Laura Ellen Drommond and Walter Brown Kerns:

+   324   f   I. **Birdella Gertrude Kerns** was born in 1902. She died on September 15, 1964, at the age of 62. Birdella Gertrude was buried in Grandview Cemetery, Wray, Yuma County, Colorado (Find a Grave ID 62637457).

          f   II. **Twila Belle Kerns** was born in Colorado, USA, on July 06, 1912. She died in Littleton, Arapahoe County, Colorado, on August 25, 2007, at the age of 95. Twila Belle was buried in Chapel Hill Memorial Gardens, Littleton, Arapahoe County, Colorado (Find a Grave ID 142345474).

+ 325   f   III. **Velva June Kerns** was born on June 11, 1916. She died on May 22, 1997, at the age of 80. Velva June was buried in San Jacinto Valley Cemetery, San Jacinto, Riverside County, California (Find a Grave ID 110414193).

Family of James Drommond and Mae Johnson

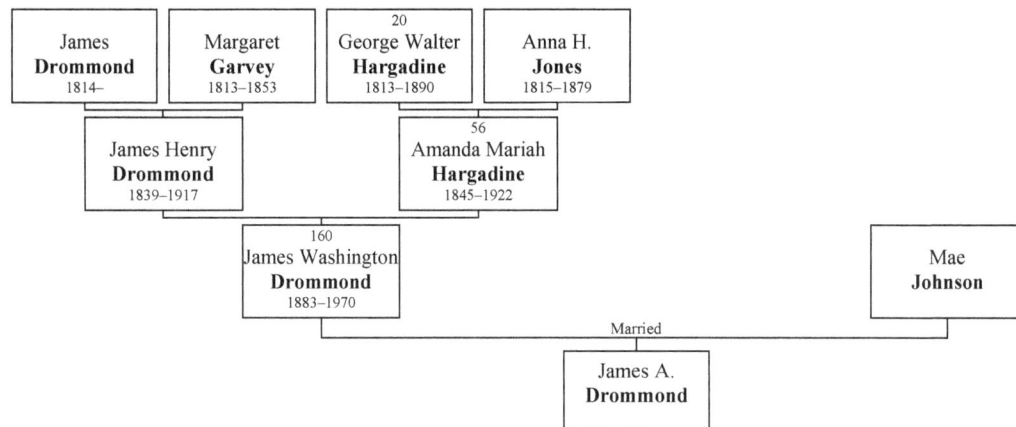

160.   **James Washington Drommond** was born on Friday, February 02, 1883, in Eppards Point Township, Livingston County, Illinois. He was the son of James Henry Drommond and Amanda Mariah Hargadine (56).

James Washington worked as a Colorado Fish and Game Department. He died in Wray, Yuma County, Colorado, on December 21, 1970, at the age of 87. James Washington was buried in Grandview Cemetery, Wray, Yuma County, Colorado, on December 23, 1970 (Find a Grave ID 50358395).

He married **Mae Johnson**. They had one son.

Son of James Washington Drommond and Mae Johnson:

      m   I. **James A. Drommond**.

Family of Roy Drommond and Amy Smith

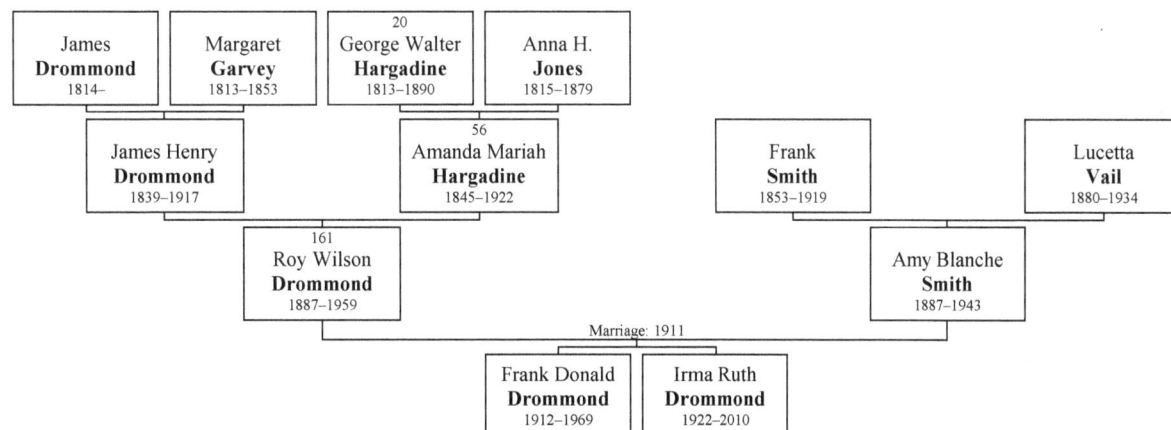

161.   **Roy Wilson Drommond** was born on Thursday, May 05, 1887, in Haigler, Dundy County, Nebraska. He was the son of James Henry Drommond and Amanda Mariah Hargadine (56).

Roy Wilson worked at Operated Drommond Meat Market in Wray with brother Earle. He died on September 30, 1959, at the age of 72. Roy Wilson was buried in Grandview Cemetery, Wray, Yuma County, Colorado (Find a Grave ID 50359537).

At the age of 24, Roy Wilson married **Amy Blanche Smith** on Thursday, June 15, 1911, when she was 24 years old. They had two children.

Amy Blanche was born in Callao, Macon County, Missouri, on Tuesday, February 15, 1887. She was the daughter of Frank Smith and Lucetta Vail.

Amy Blanche reached 56 years of age and died on December 23, 1943. She was buried in Grandview Cemetery, Wray, Yuma County, Colorado (Find a Grave ID 50359689).

Children of Roy Wilson Drommond and Amy Blanche Smith:

m   I.   **Frank Donald Drommond** was born on March 25, 1912. He served in the military: WWII, PFC, Medical Dept.

Frank Donald died on January 29, 1969, at the age of 56. He was buried in Fort Logan National Cemetery, Denver County, Colorado (Find a Grave ID 3344464).

f   II. **Irma Ruth Drommond** was born on January 18, 1922. She died in Denver, Denver County, Colorado, on January 12, 2010, at the age of 87. Irma Ruth was buried in Crown Hill Cemetery, Wheat Ridge, Jefferson County, Colorado (Find a Grave ID 48152276).

Family of Earle Drommond and Mary Cuney

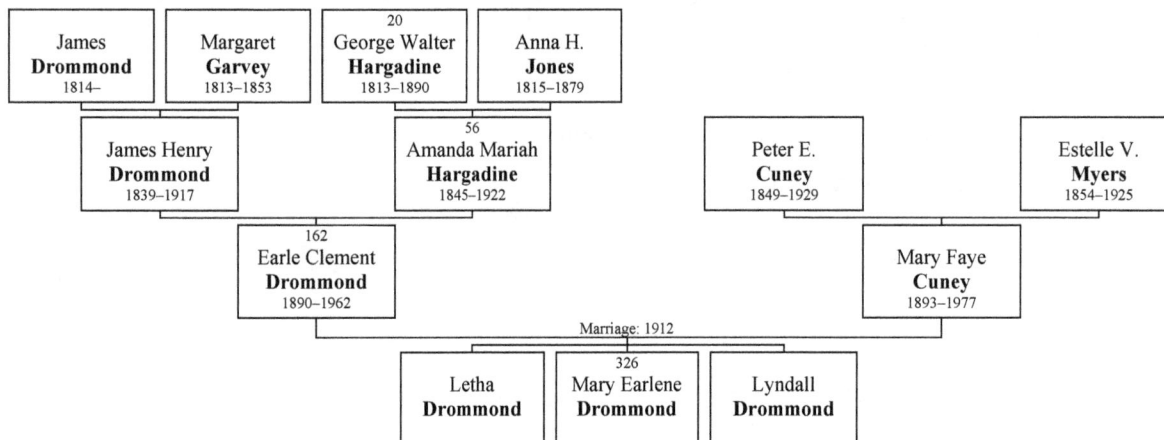

162.   **Earle Clement Drommond** was born on Thursday, July 10, 1890, in Haigler, Dundy County, Nebraska. He was the son of James Henry Drommond and Amanda Mariah Hargadine (56).

Earle Clement worked as an Operated Drommond Meat Market in Wray with brother Roy. He died in Wray, Yuma County, Colorado, on January 08, 1962, at the age of 71. Earle Clement was buried in Grandview Cemetery, Wray, Yuma County, Colorado (Find a Grave ID 50538843).

At the age of 21, Earle Clement married **Mary Faye Cuney** on Wednesday, June 05, 1912, when she was 18 years old. They had three daughters.

Mary Faye was born in Wray, Yuma County, Colorado, on Sunday, December 03, 1893. She was the daughter of Peter E. Cuney and Estelle V. Myers.

Mary Faye reached 83 years of age and died in Wray, Yuma County, Colorado, in March 1977. She was buried on March 26, 1977, in Grandview Cemetery, Wray, Yuma County, Colorado (Find a Grave ID 50538420).

Daughters of Earle Clement Drommond and Mary Faye Cuney:

		f	I. **Letha Drommond.**
+	326	f	II. **Mary Earlene Drommond.**
		f	III. **Lyndall Drommond.**

Family of George Chambers and Ella Finley

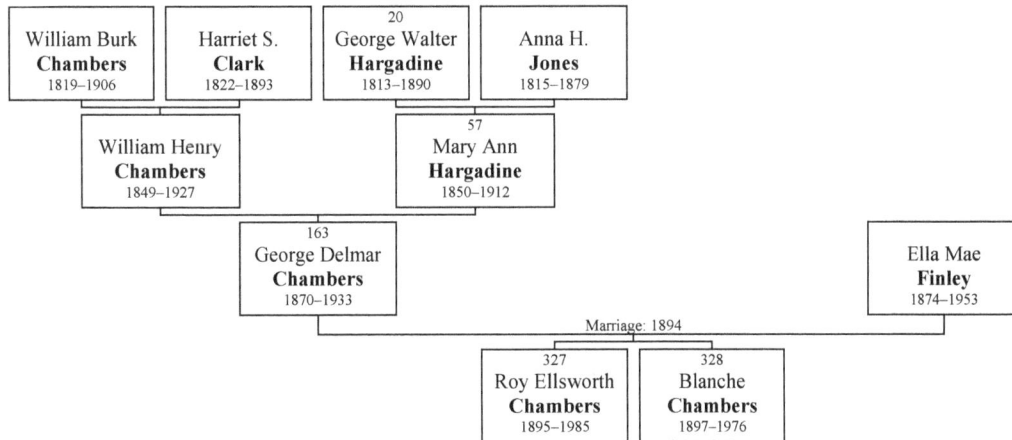

163. **George Delmar Chambers** was born on Thursday, June 16, 1870, in Chenoa, McLean County, Illinois. He was the son of William Henry Chambers and Mary Ann Hargadine (57).

His religious affiliation was Methodist. He worked as a Carpenter on June 16, 1900.[211]

George Delmar died in Bloomington, McLean County, Illinois, on December 09, 1933, at the age of 63. He was buried in Park Hill Cemetery and Mausoleum, Bloomington, McLean County, Illinois, on December 11, 1933 (Find a Grave ID 58544177).

At the age of 24, George Delmar married **Ella Mae Finley** on Saturday, October 20, 1894, in Pontiac, Livingston County, Illinois, when she was 19 years old. They had two children.

Ella Mae was born in Weston, McLean County, Illinois, on Wednesday, November 18, 1874. She reached 78 years of age and died in Columbus, Franklin County, Ohio, on April 30, 1953. Ella Mae was buried in Park Hill Cemetery and Mausoleum, Bloomington, McLean County, Illinois (Find a Grave ID 58544056).

---

[211] 1900 Census Mclean County Chenoa Township, Vol. 117 - Ed. 98 - Sheet 9 - Line 70.

Children of George Delmar Chambers and Ella Mae Finley:

+ 327 m I. **Roy Ellsworth Chambers** was born in Chenoa, McLean County, Illinois, on July 28, 1895.[212] He was also known as **Shorty**.

Roy Ellsworth died in Pompano Beach, Broward County, Florida, on July 11, 1985, at the age of 89.[212] He was buried in Park Hill Cemetery and Mausoleum, Bloomington, McLean County, Illinois, on July 16, 1985 (Find a Grave ID 58571202).

+ 328 f II. **Blanche Chambers** was born in Chenoa, McLean County, Illinois, on February 20, 1897.[213, 214] She died in Pompano Beach, Broward County, Florida, on February 13, 1976, at the age of 78.[212, 213] Blanche was buried in Forest Lawn Memorial Gardens North, Pompano Beach, Broward County, Florida (Find a Grave ID 101845641).

Family of Charles Chambers and Lelia Downing

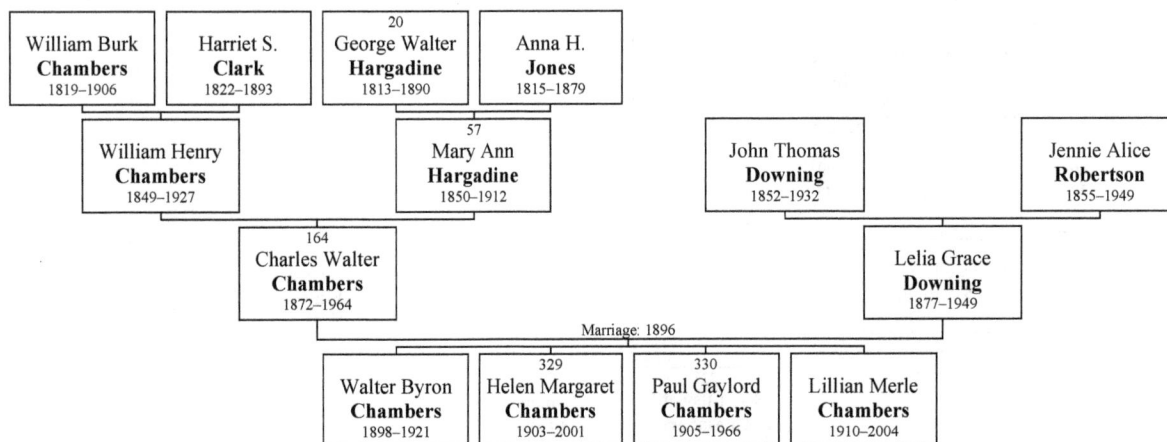

| William Burk **Chambers** 1819–1906 | Harriet S. **Clark** 1822–1893 | 20 George Walter **Hargadine** 1813–1890 | Anna H. **Jones** 1815–1879 | | | John Thomas **Downing** 1852–1932 | | Jennie Alice **Robertson** 1855–1949 |

William Henry **Chambers** 1849–1927

57 Mary Ann **Hargadine** 1850–1912

164 Charles Walter **Chambers** 1872–1964

Lelia Grace **Downing** 1877–1949

Marriage: 1896

| Walter Byron **Chambers** 1898–1921 | 329 Helen Margaret **Chambers** 1903–2001 | 330 Paul Gaylord **Chambers** 1905–1966 | Lillian Merle **Chambers** 1910–2004 |

164. **Charles Walter Chambers** was born on Friday, November 01, 1872, in Chenoa, McLean County, Illinois. He was the son of William Henry Chambers and Mary Ann Hargadine (57).

Charles Walter worked as a Painter on June 16, 1900.[215] He died in Saint Louis, Saint Louis County, Missouri, on April 13, 1964, at the age of 91. Charles Walter was buried in Park Hill Cemetery and Mausoleum, Bloomington, McLean County, Illinois, on April 15, 1964 (Find a Grave ID 58543841).

At the age of 23, Charles Walter married **Lelia Grace Downing** on Tuesday, June 23, 1896, in Bloomington, McLean County, Illinois, when she was 18 years old. They had four children.

---

212 *Bloomington Pantagraph*, Roy E. Chambers Obituary (Sunday July 15, 1985).

213 Social Security Death Index.

214 1900 Census Mclean County Chenoa Township, Vol 117 - Ed. 98 - Sheet 9 - Line 20.

215 1900 Census Mclean County Chenoa Township, Vol. 117 - Ed. 98 - Sheet 9 - Line 67.

Lelia Grace was born in Hannibal, Marion County, Missouri, on Wednesday, July 11, 1877. She was the daughter of John Thomas Downing and Jennie Alice Robertson. She was also known as **Grace Downing**.

Lelia Grace reached 72 years of age and died in Bloomington, McLean County, Illinois, on October 21, 1949. She was buried on October 22, 1949, in Park Hill Cemetery and Mausoleum, Bloomington, McLean County, Illinois (Find a Grave ID 58570277).

Children of Charles Walter Chambers and Lelia Grace Downing:

	m	I.	**Walter Byron Chambers** was born in Chenoa, McLean County, Illinois, on October 18, 1898.[216] He died in Bloomington, McLean County, Illinois, on June 29, 1921, at the age of 22. Walter Byron was buried in Park Hill Cemetery and Mausoleum, Bloomington, McLean County, Illinois (Find a Grave ID 58571306).
+ 329	f	II.	**Helen Margaret Chambers** was born in Chenoa, McLean County, Illinois, on August 13, 1903. She died in Saint Petersburg, Pinellas County, Florida, on September 15, 2001, at the age of 98. Helen Margaret was buried in Memorial Park Cemetery, Saint Petersburg, Pinellas County, Florida (Find a Grave ID 104743841).
+ 330	m	III.	**Paul Gaylord Chambers** was born in Chenoa, McLean County, Illinois, on October 19, 1905. He died in Huntington Beach, Orange County, California, on May 27, 1966, at the age of 60. His cause of death was cerebral edema due to purulent meningitis. He was buried in Good Shepherd Cemetery, Huntington Beach, Orange County, California, on May 31, 1966 (Find a Grave ID 158373146).
	f	IV.	**Lillian Merle Chambers** was born in Chenoa, McLean County, Illinois, on July 06, 1910. She died in Kirkwood, St. Louis County, Missouri, on July 08, 2004, at the age of 94. Lillian Merle was buried in Oak Hill Cemetery, Kirkwood, St. Louis County, Missouri (Find a Grave ID 158455934).

Family of Norval Chambers and Charlotte Abbott

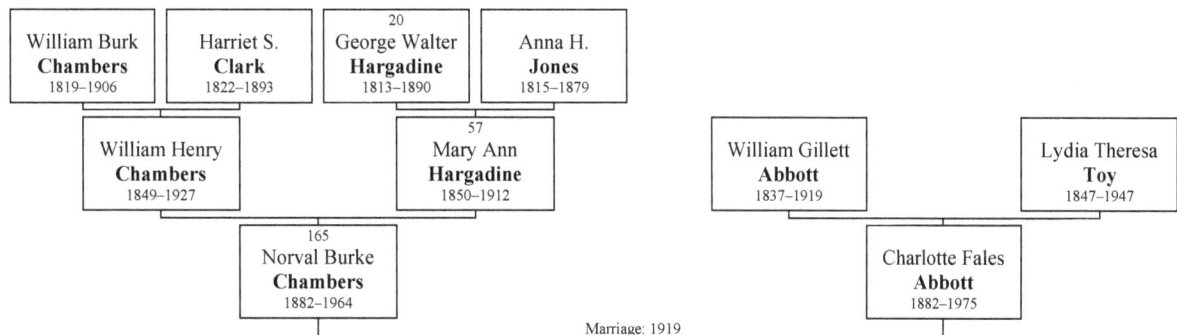

| William Burk **Chambers** 1819–1906 | Harriet S. **Clark** 1822–1893 | 20 George Walter **Hargadine** 1813–1890 | Anna H. **Jones** 1815–1879 | | William Gillett **Abbott** 1837–1919 | Lydia Theresa **Toy** 1847–1947 |

William Henry **Chambers** 1849–1927   57 Mary Ann **Hargadine** 1850–1912

165 Norval Burke **Chambers** 1882–1964

Charlotte Fales **Abbott** 1882–1975

Marriage: 1919

---

216   *The Daily Pantagraph* (Bloomington, Illinois), June 30, 1921.

165. **Norval Burke Chambers** was born on Thursday, September 21, 1882, in Chenoa, McLean County, Illinois. He was the son of William Henry Chambers and Mary Ann Hargadine (57).

Norval Burke died in Bloomington, McLean County, Illinois, on July 09, 1964, at the age of 81. He was buried in Chenoa Cemetery, McLean County, Illinois, on July 12, 1964 (Find a Grave ID 80966677).

At the age of 36, Norval Burke married **Charlotte Fales Abbott** on Tuesday, January 21, 1919, in Chenoa, McLean County, Illinois, when she was 36 years old.[217] Charlotte Fales was born in Chenoa, McLean County, Illinois, on Saturday, February 25, 1882. She was the daughter of William Gillett Abbott and Lydia Theresa Toy.

Charlotte Fales reached 93 years of age and died in Meadows, McLean County, Illinois, on December 27, 1975. She was buried on December 29, 1975, in Chenoa Cemetery, McLean County, Illinois (Find a Grave ID 80966646).

Family of Maude Nelson and Edward Murphy

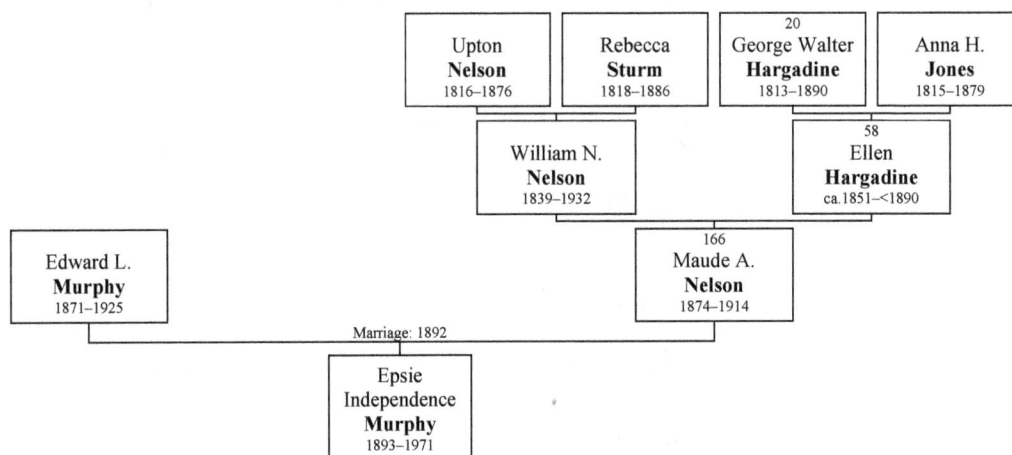

166. **Maude A. Nelson** was born in 1874 in Peoria, Peoria County, Illinois.[218] She was the daughter of William N. Nelson and Ellen Hargadine (58).

Maude A. died in Pleasanton, Linn County, Kansas, in 1914 at the age of 40. She was buried in Pleasanton Cemetery, Pleasanton, Linn County, Kansas (Find a Grave ID 62208874).

Maude A. married **Edward L. Murphy** in 1892. They had one daughter.

Edward L. was born in 1871. He reached 54 years of age and died in 1925. Edward L. was buried in Pleasanton Cemetery, Pleasanton, Linn County, Kansas (Find a Grave ID 62208779).

217 Bloomington Pantagraph, Norval B. Chambers Obituary (Friday, July 10, 1964).

218 FamilySearch.org, United States Census, 1910, FamilySearch, "United States Census, 1910," database with images, <i>FamilySearch</i> (https://familysearch.org/ark:/61903/1:1:M2CK-SS5 : accessed 23 January 2023), Maude Murphy in household of Edward Murphy, Potosi, Linn, Kansas, United States; citing enumeration district (ED) ED 122, sheet 8B, family 115, NARA microfilm publication T624 (Washington D.C.: National Archives and Records Administration, 1982), roll 445; FHL microfilm 1,374,458.

Daughter of Maude A. Nelson and Edward L. Murphy:

    f   I. **Epsie Independence Murphy** was born in Rich Hill, Bates County, Missouri, on July 04, 1893. She died in Pleasanton, Linn County, Kansas, on September 01, 1971, at the age of 78. Epsie Independence was buried in Pleasanton Cemetery, Pleasanton, Linn County, Kansas (Find a Grave ID 62208828).

Family of Della Jewell and William Craig

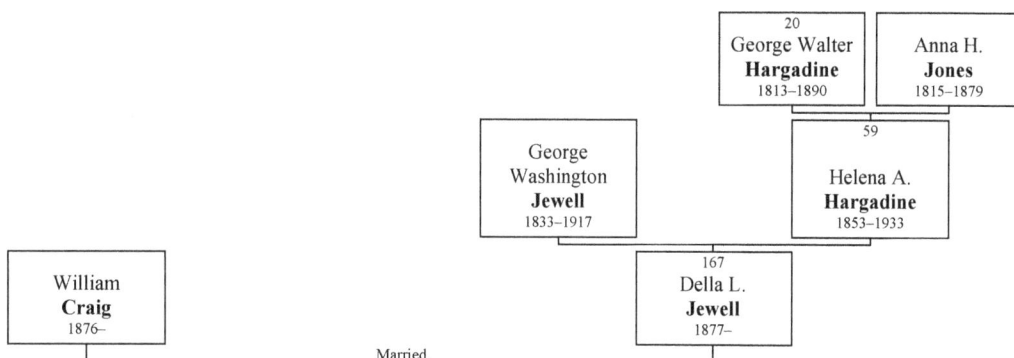

167.   **Della L. Jewell** was born in November 1877 in Pennsylvania, USA. She was the daughter of George Washington Jewell and Helena A. Hargadine (59).

She married **William Craig**. William was born in July 1876.

Family of Inez Hargadine and George Pennell

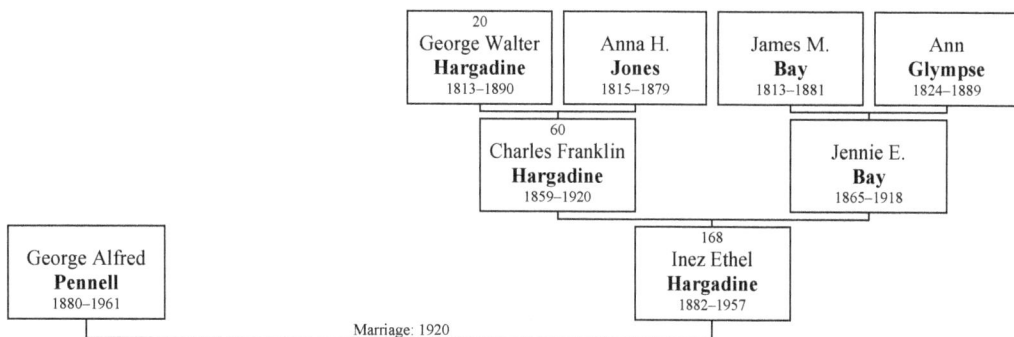

168.   **Inez Ethel Hargadine** was born on Monday, January 16, 1882, in Illinois, USA. She was the daughter of Charles Franklin Hargadine (60) and Jennie E. Bay.

Inez Ethel died in Chicago, Cook County, Illinois, on February 12, 1957, at the age of 75. She was buried in Rosehill Cemetery and Mausoleum, Chicago, Cook County, Illinois, on February 15, 1957.

At the age of 38, Inez Ethel married **George Alfred Pennell** on Wednesday, April 28, 1920, in Chicago, Cook County, Illinois, when he was 39 years old. George Alfred was born in Illinois, USA, on Saturday, October 09, 1880.

He reached 80 years of age and died in Chicago, Cook County, Illinois, on March 15, 1961.

Family of Glenna Hunter and John Foley

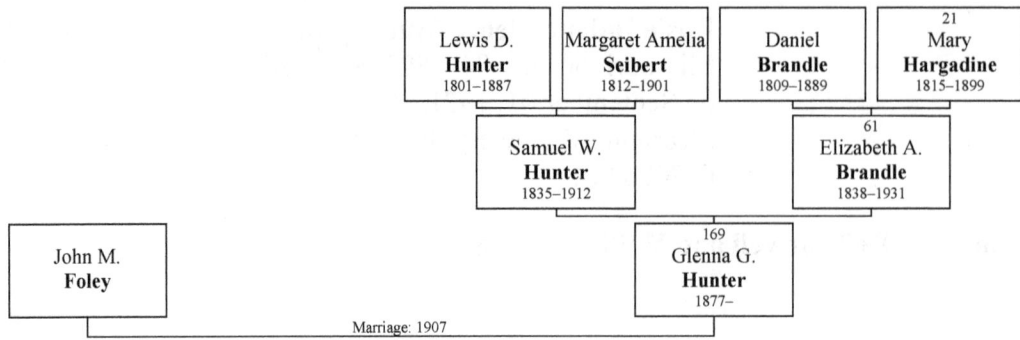

```
┌──────────┬──────────┐  ┌──────────┬──────────┐
│ Lewis D. │Margaret  │  │  Daniel  │    21    │
│  Hunter  │Amelia    │  │ Brandle  │   Mary   │
│1801–1887 │ Seibert  │  │1809–1889 │Hargadine │
│          │1812–1901 │  │          │1815–1899 │
└──────────┴──────────┘  └──────────┴──────────┘
     │   Samuel W.    │      │  Elizabeth A.  │
     │    Hunter      │      │    Brandle     │
     │   1835–1912    │      │   1838–1931    │
                    │      169      │
                    │   Glenna G.   │
                    │    Hunter     │
                    │    1877–      │
   John M.                          
    Foley                           
          Marriage: 1907
```

169. **Glenna G. Hunter** was born on Saturday, February 03, 1877, in Clark County, Ohio. She was the daughter of Samuel W. Hunter and Elizabeth A. Brandle (61).

Glenna G. married **John M. Foley** on Tuesday, August 27, 1907, in Clark County, Ohio.

Charles Luker

170. **Charles M. Luker** was born in Ohio, USA. He was the son of Caleb L. Luker and Elizabeth A. Hargadine (64).

Marriages with Mary Hutchins and Anna H. McDowell (Page 213) are known.

Family of Charles Luker and Mary Hutchins

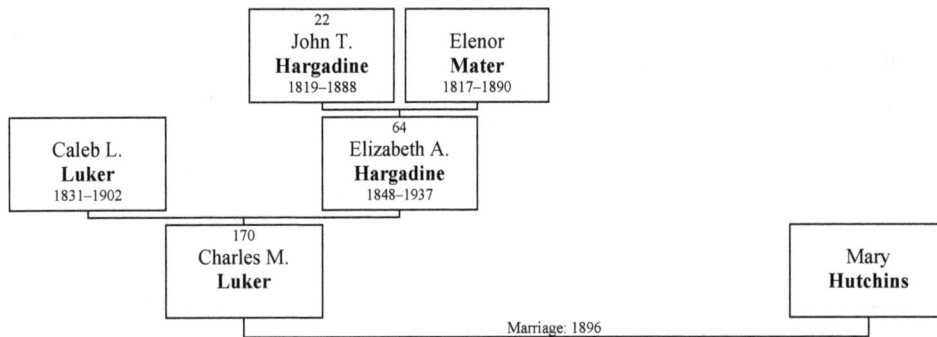

```
        ┌──────────┬──────────┐
        │    22    │          │
        │ John T.  │  Elenor  │
        │Hargadine │  Mater   │
        │1819–1888 │1817–1890 │
        └──────────┴──────────┘
┌──────────┐    │     64      │
│ Caleb L. │    │Elizabeth A. │
│  Luker   │    │ Hargadine   │
│1831–1902 │    │ 1848–1937   │
└──────────┘
        │     170      │          ┌──────────┐
        │  Charles M.  │          │   Mary   │
        │    Luker     │          │ Hutchins │
        │              │          └──────────┘
              Marriage: 1896
```

Here are the details about **Charles M. Luker's** first marriage, with Mary Hutchins. You can read more about Charles M. on page 212.

Charles M. Luker married **Mary Hutchins** in 1896 in Miami County, Ohio.

Family of Charles Luker and Anna McDowell

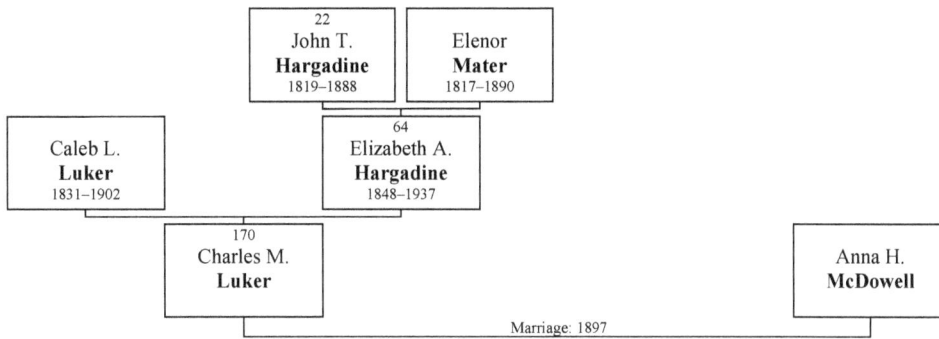

```
        ┌─────────────┐  ┌─────────────┐
        │     22      │  │             │
        │  John T.    │  │  Elenor     │
        │  Hargadine  │  │  Mater      │
        │  1819–1888  │  │  1817–1890  │
        └─────────────┘  └─────────────┘
┌─────────────┐  ┌─────────────┐
│             │  │     64      │
│  Caleb L.   │  │  Elizabeth A.│
│  Luker      │  │  Hargadine  │
│  1831–1902  │  │  1848–1937  │
└─────────────┘  └─────────────┘
        ┌─────────────┐              ┌─────────────┐
        │    170      │              │             │
        │  Charles M. │              │  Anna H.    │
        │  Luker      │              │  McDowell   │
        └─────────────┘              └─────────────┘
                        Marriage: 1897
```

Here are the details about **Charles M. Luker's** second marriage, with Anna H. McDowell. You can read more about Charles M. on page 212.

Charles M. Luker married **Anna H. McDowell** in 1897 in Miami County, Ohio.

Family of Martha Coffman and Isaac Leffler

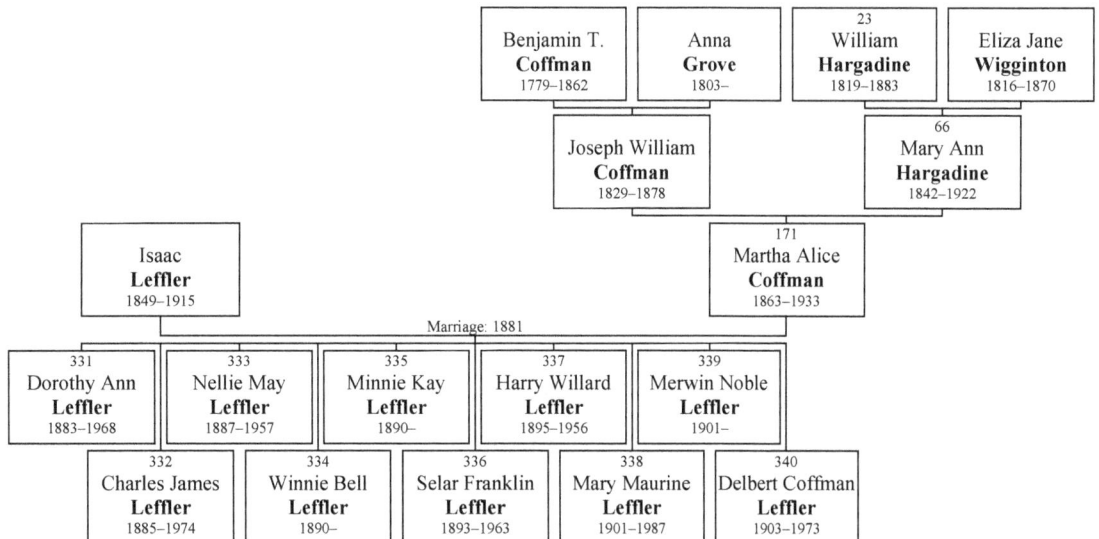

```
┌─────────────┐ ┌─────────┐ ┌─────────────┐ ┌─────────────┐
│ Benjamin T. │ │  Anna   │ │     23      │ │  Eliza Jane │
│  Coffman    │ │  Grove  │ │  William    │ │  Wigginton  │
│  1779–1862  │ │  1803–  │ │  Hargadine  │ │  1816–1870  │
└─────────────┘ └─────────┘ │  1819–1883  │ └─────────────┘
                            └─────────────┘
      ┌───────────────┐          ┌─────────────┐
      │ Joseph William│          │     66      │
      │  Coffman      │          │  Mary Ann   │
      │  1829–1878    │          │  Hargadine  │
      └───────────────┘          │  1842–1922  │
                                 └─────────────┘
                        ┌─────────────┐
                        │    171      │
                        │ Martha Alice│
                        │  Coffman    │
┌─────────────┐         │  1863–1933  │
│   Isaac     │         └─────────────┘
│  Leffler    │
│  1849–1915  │
└─────────────┘
              Marriage: 1881
```

331 Dorothy Ann Leffler 1883–1968	333 Nellie May Leffler 1887–1957	335 Minnie Kay Leffler 1890–	337 Harry Willard Leffler 1895–1956	339 Merwin Noble Leffler 1901–
332 Charles James Leffler 1885–1974	334 Winnie Bell Leffler 1890–	336 Selar Franklin Leffler 1893–1963	338 Mary Maurine Leffler 1901–1987	340 Delbert Coffman Leffler 1903–1973

171. **Martha Alice Coffman** was born on Saturday, February 28, 1863, in Lincoln, Logan County, Illinois.[219, 220] She was the daughter of Joseph William Coffman and Mary Ann Hargadine (66).

Martha Alice died in Holdrege, Phelps County, Nebraska, on April 14, 1933, at the age of 70.[219, 220] She was buried in Prairie Home Cemetery, Holdrege, Phelps County, Nebraska (Find a Grave ID 35323785).[219, 220]

At the age of 18, Martha Alice married **Isaac Leffler** on Thursday, November 03, 1881, in Lincoln, Logan County, Illinois, when he was 32 years old.[219, 220] They had ten children.

---

219   LDS Ancestral File.

220   Leffler.FTW, Date of Import: Jan 3, 2002.

Isaac was born in Canton, Stark County, Ohio, on Sunday, August 12, 1849. He worked as a Farmer on June 20, 1900.[220]

Isaac reached 65 years of age and died in Holdrege, Phelps County, Nebraska, on July 12, 1915. He was buried in Prairie Home Cemetery, Holdrege, Phelps County, Nebraska (Find a Grave ID 35323853).[220]

Children of Martha Alice Coffman and Isaac Leffler:

+ 331   f   I. **Dorothy Ann Leffler** was born in Lincoln, Logan County, Illinois, on June 25, 1883.[220] She was also known as **Dora Leffler**.

         Dorothy Ann died in Simi Valley, Ventura County, California, on April 23, 1968, at the age of 84.[220] She was buried in Palisade Cemetery, Palisade, Hitchcock County, Nebraska (Find a Grave ID 11898759).

+ 332   m   II. **Charles James Leffler** was born in Lincoln, Logan County, Illinois, on August 14, 1885.[220] He died in Imperial, Chase County, Nebraska, in November 1974 at the age of 89.[220, 221]

+ 333   f   III. **Nellie May Leffler** was born in Lincoln, Logan County, Illinois, on October 05, 1887.[220] She died on September 06, 1957, at the age of 69.[220] Nellie May was buried in Prairie Home Cemetery, Holdrege, Phelps County, Nebraska (Find a Grave ID 38370472).

+ 334   f   IV. **Winnie Bell Leffler** was born in Holdrege, Phelps County, Nebraska, on September 16, 1890.[220]

+ 335   f   V. **Minnie Kay Leffler** was born in Holdrege, Phelps County, Nebraska, on September 16, 1890.[220]

+ 336   m   VI. **Selar Franklin Leffler** was born in Nebraska, USA, on April 10, 1893.[220] He died on June 03, 1963, at the age of 70.[220, 222]

+ 337   m   VII. **Harry Willard Leffler** was born in Holdrege, Phelps County, Nebraska, on April 22, 1895.[220] He died on September 25, 1956, at the age of 61.[220]

+ 338   f   VIII. **Mary Maurine Leffler** was born in Holdrege, Phelps County, Nebraska, on September 07, 1901.[220, 223] She died in Spencer, Clay County, Iowa, on February 08, 1987, at the age of 85.[223] Mary Maurine was buried in Riverside Cemetery, Spencer, Clay County, Iowa (Find a Grave ID 189659310).

+ 339   m   IX. **Merwin Noble Leffler** was born in Nebraska, USA, on September 07, 1901.[220]

---

221   Social Security Death Index, CHARLES LEFFLER.

222   Social Security Death Index, SELAR LEFFLER.

223   Ancestry.com, Public Member Trees (Provo, UT, USA, Ancestry.com Operations, Inc., 2006), Ancestry.com, Record for Mary Maurine Leffler. https://search.ancestry.co.uk/cgi-bin/sse.dll?db=1030&h=222028657458&indiv=try.

+ 340 m   X. **Delbert Coffman Leffler** was born in Phelps County, Nebraska, on September 21, 1903.[220] He died in Holdrege, Phelps County, Nebraska, in May 1973 at the age of 69.[220, 224] Delbert Coffman was buried in Prairie Home Cemetery, Holdrege, Phelps County, Nebraska (Find a Grave ID 35323531).

Family of Benjamin Coffman and Emma Lipp

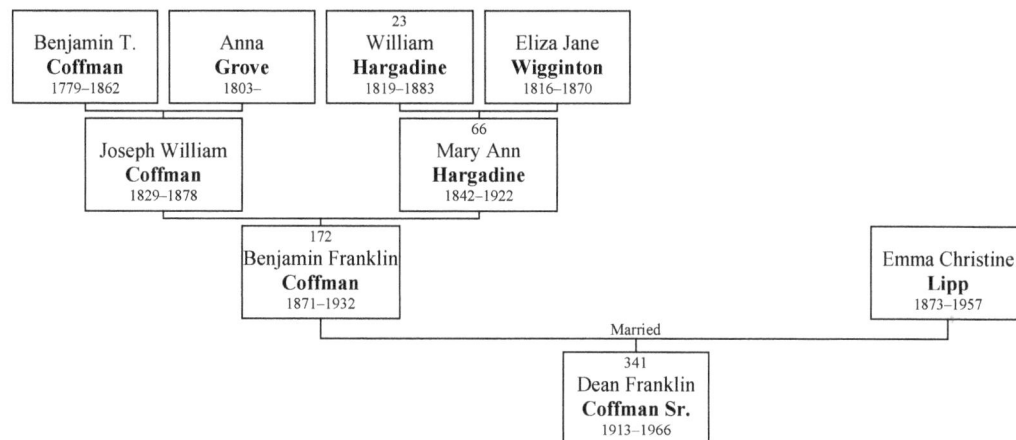

172.   **Benjamin Franklin Coffman** was born on Sunday, August 06, 1871. He was the son of Joseph William Coffman and Mary Ann Hargadine (66).

Benjamin Franklin died on June 26, 1932, at the age of 60. He was buried in Fairlawn Cemetery, Decatur, Macon County, Illinois (Find a Grave ID 64982460).

He married **Emma Christine Lipp**. They had one son.

Emma Christine was born in Lincoln, Logan County, Illinois, on Tuesday, January 28, 1873. She reached 84 years of age and died in Illinois, USA, on March 26, 1957. Emma Christine was buried in Fairlawn Cemetery, Decatur, Macon County, Illinois (Find a Grave ID 64982443).

Son of Benjamin Franklin Coffman and Emma Christine Lipp:

+ 341 m   I. **Dean Franklin Coffman Sr.** was born in Lincoln, Logan County, Illinois, on February 28, 1913. He died in Decatur, Macon County, Illinois, on May 30, 1966, at the age of 53. Dean Franklin was buried in Fairlawn Cemetery, Decatur, Macon County, Illinois (Find a Grave ID 65013002).

---

224   Social Security Death Index, DELBERT LEFFLER.

Family of Mason Merrilees and Claude Applegate

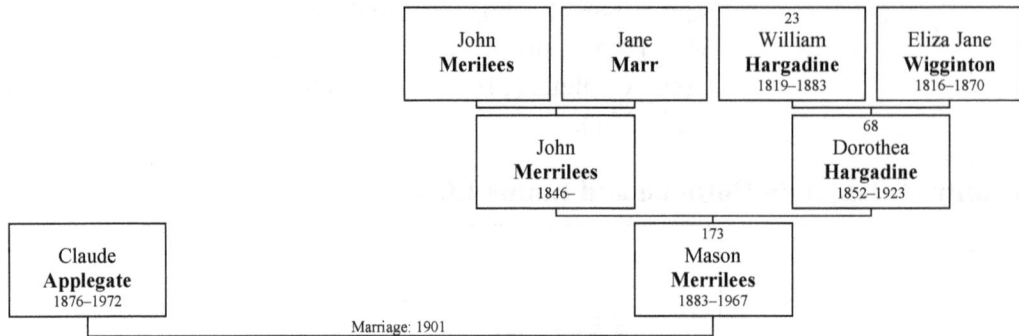

173. **Mason Merrilees** was born on Saturday, February 17, 1883. She was the daughter of John Merrilees and Dorothea Hargadine (68).

Mason died in Lincoln, Logan County, Illinois, in June 1967 at the age of 84.

At the age of 18, Mason married **Claude Applegate** on Sunday, October 27, 1901, when he was 25 years old. Claude was born in Logan County, Illinois, on Monday, January 31, 1876.

He reached 96 years of age and died in Lincoln, Logan County, Illinois, on May 29, 1972.

Laveta Hargadine

174. **Laveta M. Hargadine** was born on Tuesday, March 24, 1891, in Oregon, USA. She was the daughter of George Robert Hargadine (72) and Allie Averil.

Laveta M. died in San Bernardino, San Bernardino County, California, on December 17, 1948, at the age of 57.

Marriages with Frank Warren Megredy and Lawrence Ray Pardee (Page 217) are known.

Family of Laveta Hargadine and Frank Megredy

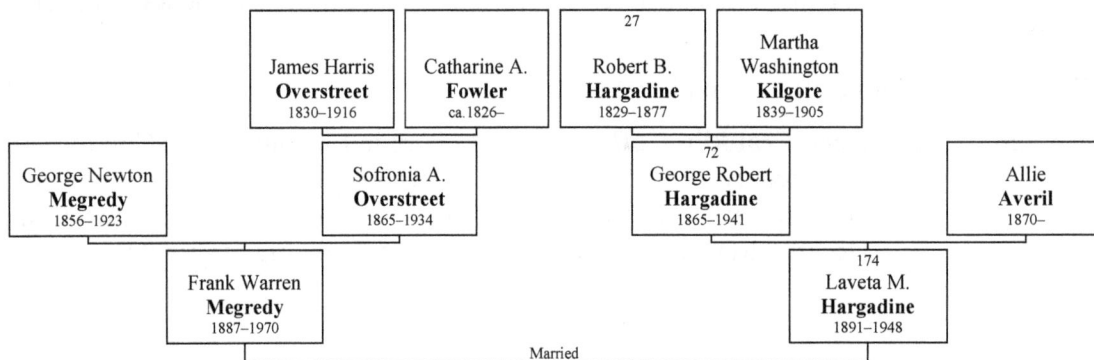

Here are the details about **Laveta M. Hargadine's** first marriage, with Frank Warren Megredy. You can read more about Laveta M. on page 216.

Laveta M. Hargadine married **Frank Warren Megredy**. Frank Warren was born in Kansas City, Jackson County, Missouri, on Friday, November 18, 1887. He was the son of George Newton Megredy and Sofronia A. Overstreet.

Frank Warren reached 82 years of age and died in Los Angeles, Los Angeles County, California, on March 27, 1970.[225] He was buried in Eternal Valley Memorial Park, Newhall, Los Angeles County, California (Find a Grave ID 51290087).

Family of Laveta Hargadine and Lawrence Pardee

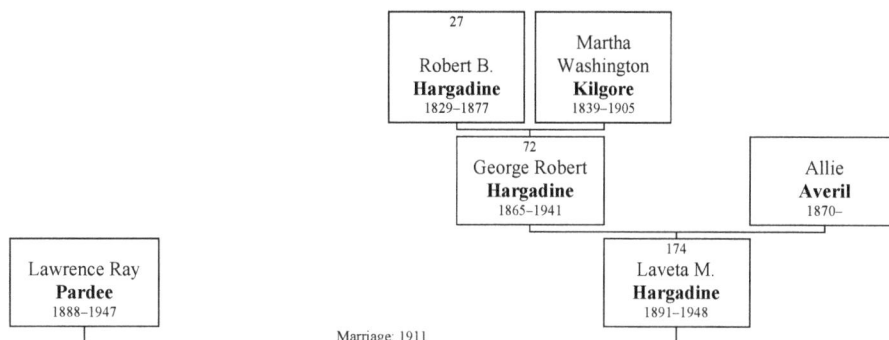

Here are the details about **Laveta M. Hargadine's** second marriage, with Lawrence Ray Pardee. You can read more about Laveta M. on page 216.

At the age of 20, Laveta M. Hargadine married **Lawrence Ray Pardee** on Wednesday, April 12, 1911, in Long Beach, Los Angeles County, California, when he was 22 years old. Lawrence Ray was born in Corwith, Hancock County, Iowa, on Monday, December 24, 1888.

He reached 58 years of age and died in Los Angeles County, California, on September 18, 1947. Lawrence Ray was buried in Forest Lawn Memorial Park, Glendale, Los Angeles County, California (Find a Grave ID 85483608).

Family of Edward Hargadine and Anna Dignan

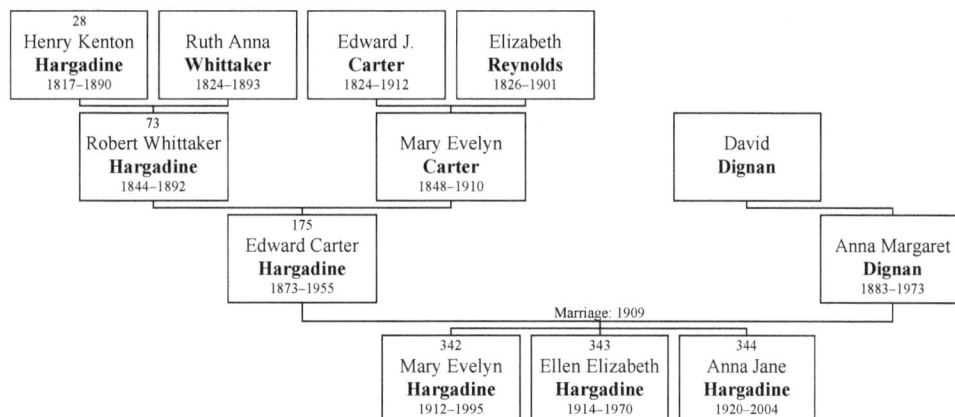

---

225   Ancestry.com. California Death Index, 1940-1997 [database on-line]. Provo, UT, USA: The Generations Network, Inc., 2000. Original data: State of California. California Death Index, 1940-1997. Sacramento, CA, USA: State of California Department of Health Services, Center for Health Statistics.

175. **Edward Carter Hargadine** was born on Saturday, November 22, 1873, in Felton, Kent County, Delaware.[226] He was the son of Robert Whittaker Hargadine (73) and Mary Evelyn Carter.

Edward Carter worked as a Great Northern Railroad. He died in Ramsey County, Minnesota, on April 29, 1955, at the age of 81.

At the age of 35, Edward Carter married **Anna Margaret Dignan** on Tuesday, August 24, 1909, in Glasgow, Valley County, Montana, when he was 25 years old. They had three daughters.

Anna Margaret was born in New York, New York, on Saturday, December 29, 1883. He was the son of David Dignan.

Anna Margaret reached 89 years of age and died in St. Paul, Ramsey County, Minnesota, in March 1973.

Daughters of Edward Carter Hargadine and Anna Margaret Dignan:

+   342   f   I. **Mary Evelyn Hargadine** was born in Glasgow, Valley County, Montana, on June 20, 1912. She died in St. Mary's Home, St. Paul, Ramsey County, Minnesota, on June 28, 1995, at the age of 83. Mary Evelyn was buried in Resurrection Cemetery, Mendota Heights, Dakota County, Minnesota (Find a Grave ID 248684450).

+   343   f   II. **Ellen Elizabeth Hargadine** was born in Glasgo, Valley County, Montana, on February 21, 1914. She was also known as **Ellen Ann Marians**.

Ellen Elizabeth died in El Paso, El Paso County, Texas, on February 24, 1970, at the age of 56. She was buried in Memory Gardens of the Valley, Santa Teresa, Doña Ana County, New Mexico (Find a Grave ID 93091528).

+   344   f   III. **Anna Jane Hargadine** was born in Glasgow, Valley County, Montana, on February 29, 1920. She died in Oregon, USA, on December 01, 2004, at the age of 84. Anna Jane was buried in Mount Calvary Cemetery, Portland, Multnomah County, Oregon (Find a Grave ID 43056303).

---

226   Death Certificate, CertID# 1955-MN-026578.

Family of Mary Hargadine and George Hurd

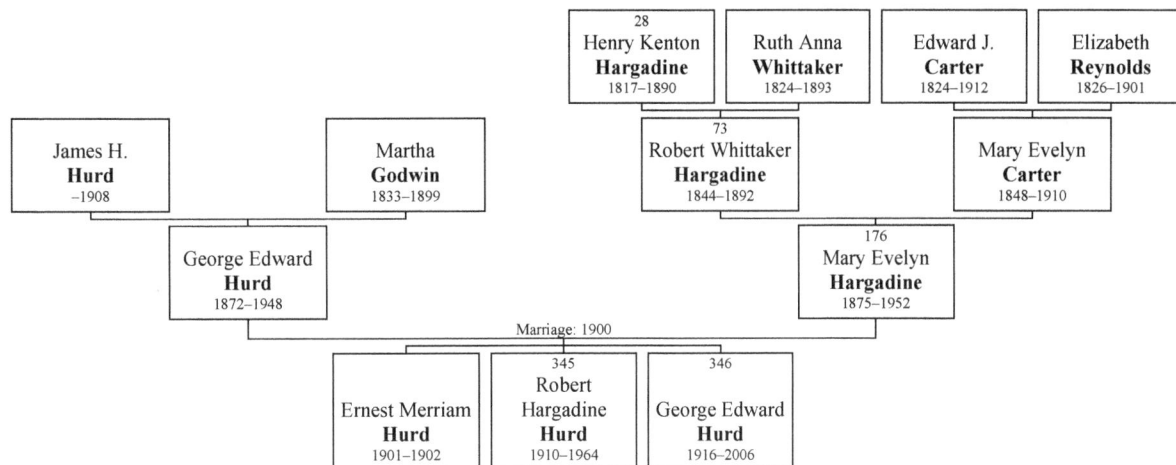

176. **Mary Evelyn Hargadine** was born on Sunday, September 12, 1875, in Felton, Kent County, Delaware. She was the daughter of Robert Whittaker Hargadine (73) and Mary Evelyn Carter.

Mary Evelyn died in Great Falls, Cascade County, Montana, on May 09, 1952, at the age of 76.[227] She was buried in Highland Cemetery, Great Falls, Cascade County, Montana (Find a Grave ID 9510564).

At the age of 25, Mary Evelyn married **George Edward Hurd** on Thursday, December 20, 1900, when he was 28 years old. They had three sons.

George Edward was born in Kent County, Delaware, on Thursday, July 11, 1872. He was the son of James H. Hurd and Martha Godwin.

George Edward reached 76 years of age and died in Great Falls, Cascade County, Montana, on December 28, 1948.[227] He was buried in Highland Cemetery, Great Falls, Cascade County, Montana (Find a Grave ID 9510539).

More facts and events for George Edward Hurd:

Individual Note: 1900   Attorney/admitted to law practice

Sons of Mary Evelyn Hargadine and George Edward Hurd:

> m   I. **Ernest Merriam Hurd** was born in Montana, USA, on November 08, 1901. He died in Montana, USA, on September 04, 1902. Ernest Merriam was buried in Barratts Chapel Cemetery, Frederica, Kent County, Delaware (Find a Grave ID 29493522).

+ 345   m   II. **Robert Hargadine Hurd** was born in Great Falls, Cascade County, Montana, on June 22, 1910. He died in San Diego, San Diego County, California, on July 26, 1964, at the age of 54. Robert Hargadine was buried in Fort Rosecrans National Cemetery, San Diego, San Diego County, California, on July 30, 1964 (Find a Grave ID 3408341).

---

227   Montana Death Index, 1907-1953.

+ 346   m   III. **George Edward Hurd** was born in Great Falls, Cascade County, Montana, on December 27, 1916. He died in Kaneohe, Honolulu County, Hawaii, on June 25, 2006, at the age of 89.

Family of Robert Hargadine and Irene O'Connor

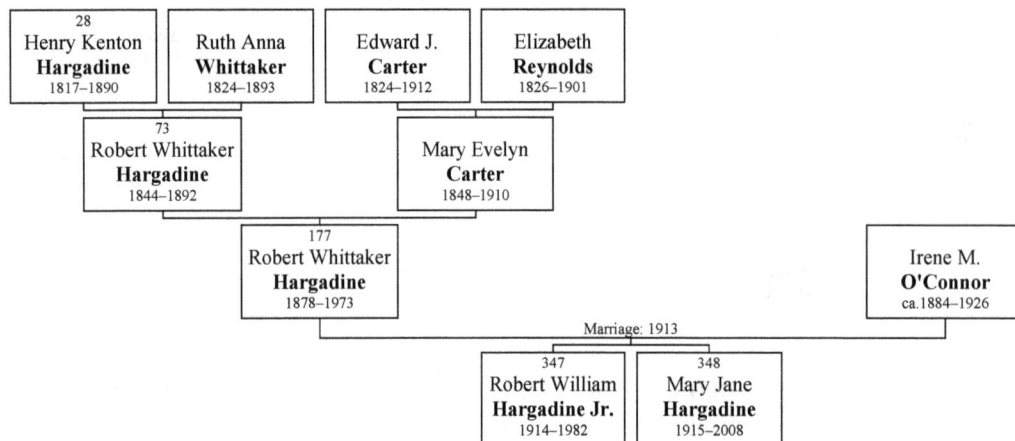

177.   **Robert Whittaker Hargadine** was born on Tuesday, December 17, 1878, in Felton, Kent County, Delaware. He was the son of Robert Whittaker Hargadine (73) and Mary Evelyn Carter. At age 18 he went to work for the Great Northern Railway in Glasgow, Montana. in 1898. He worked as a salesman; Great Lakes Land Company in 1913.[228]

Robert Whittaker died in St. Paul, Ramsey County, Minnesota, in January 1973 at the age of 94.

Robert Whittaker married **Irene M. O'Connor** on Tuesday, May 27, 1913, in St Paul, Ramsey County, Minnesota. They had two children.

Irene M. was born in Minnesota, USA, about 1884. She reached 42 years of age and died in Ramsey County, Minnesota, on March 31, 1926.[229]

Children of Robert Whittaker Hargadine and Irene M. O'Connor:

+ 347   m   I. **Robert William Hargadine Jr.** was born in Minnesota, USA, on May 29, 1914. He died in St. Paul, Ramsey County, Minnesota, on August 15, 1982, at the age of 68. Robert William was buried in Fort Snelling National Cemetery, Minneapolis, Hennepin County, Minnesota (Find a Grave ID 753313).

+ 348   f   II. **Mary Jane Hargadine** was born in Saint Paul, Ramsey County, Minnesota, on August 15, 1915. She died in Maplewood, Ramsey County, Minnesota, on November 18, 2008, at the age of 93. Mary Jane was buried in Saint Elizabeth Ann Seton Catholic Cemetery, Hastings, Dakota County, Minnesota (Find a Grave ID 31724824).

---

228   R.L. Polk & County's St. Paul City Directory, 1913, 813.

229   Death Certificate, CertID# 1926-MN-023799.

Family of Albert Hargadine and Katherine Mayhew

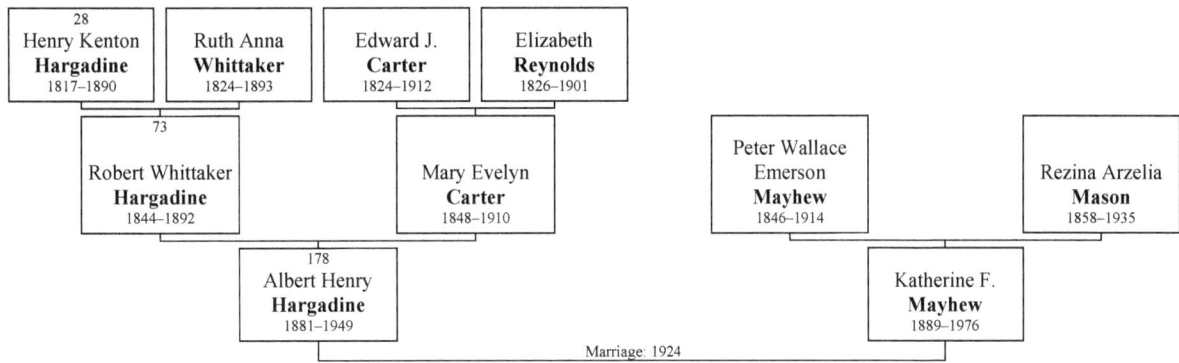

178.   **Albert Henry Hargadine** was born on Wednesday, October 05, 1881, in Felton, Kent County, Delaware. He was the son of Robert Whittaker Hargadine (73) and Mary Evelyn Carter.

Albert Henry worked as a conductor of the Great Northern Railway from 1909–1946. He died in Great Falls, Cascade County, Montana, on November 23, 1949, at the age of 68. Albert Henry was buried in Holy Cross Catholic Cemetery, Dover, Kent County, Delaware, on November 26, 1949 (Find a Grave ID 6345492).

More facts and events for Albert Henry Hargadine:

At the age of 42, Albert Henry married **Katherine F. Mayhew** on Tuesday, April 08, 1924, in Fort Benton, Chouteau County, Montana, when she was 34 years old. Katherine F. was born in Buckman, Morrison County, Minnesota, on Tuesday, September 03, 1889. She was the daughter of Peter Wallace Emerson Mayhew and Rezina Arzelia Mason.

Katherine F. reached 86 years of age and died in Washington, USA, in September 1976. She was buried in Forest Lawn Cemetery, Bremerton, Kitsap County, Washington (Find a Grave ID 13686804).

Family of Julia Hargadine and Robert McKeller

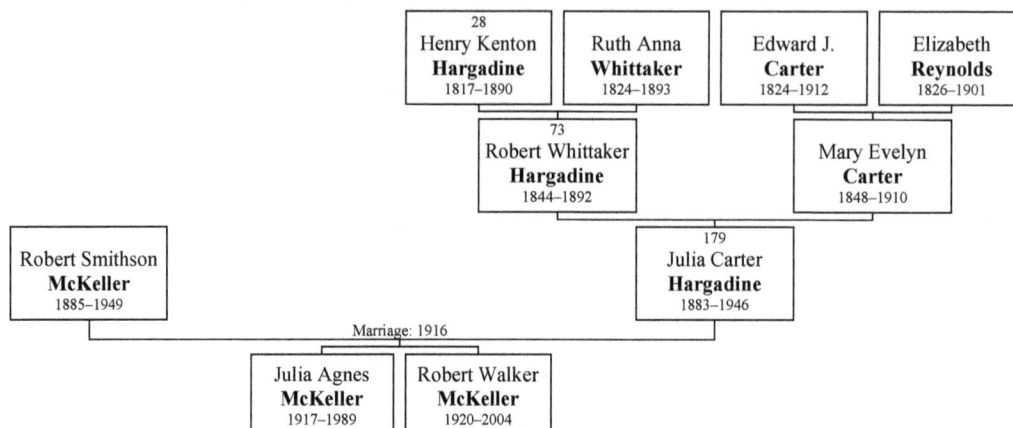

179. **Julia Carter Hargadine** was born on Sunday, August 12, 1883, in Felton, Kent County, Delaware. She was the daughter of Robert Whittaker Hargadine (73) and Mary Evelyn Carter.

Julia Carter died in Pheonix, Maricopa County, Arizona, on November 17, 1946, at the age of 63. She was buried in Saint Francis Catholic Cemetery, Phoenix, Maricopa County, Arizona, on November 21, 1946 (Find a Grave ID 70526028).

Julia Carter married **Robert Smithson McKeller** in 1916. They had two children.

Robert Smithson was born in Stillwater, Washington County, Minnesota, on Thursday, February 26, 1885. He worked as a Law partner with George Hurd (Mary Evelyn's husband).

Robert Smithson reached 64 years of age and died in Phoenix, Maricopa County, Arizona, on August 23, 1949. He was buried in Saint Francis Catholic Cemetery, Phoenix, Maricopa County, Arizona (Find a Grave ID 70528907).

Children of Julia Carter Hargadine and Robert Smithson McKeller:

f   I. **Julia Agnes McKeller** was born in Great Falls, Cascade County, Montana, on August 21, 1917. She died in Tucson, Pima County, Arizona, on June 15, 1989, at the age of 71. Julia Agnes was buried in Holy Hope Cemetery and Mausoleum, Tucson, Pima County, Arizona (Find a Grave ID 198016639).

m   II. **Robert Walker McKeller** was born in Tucson, Pima County, Arizona, on March 25, 1920. He died in Dallas, Dallas County, Texas, on December 26, 2004, at the age of 84. Robert Walker was buried in Restland Memorial Park, Dallas, Dallas County, Texas (Find a Grave ID 10185111).

Family of Aimee Hargadine and John Todd

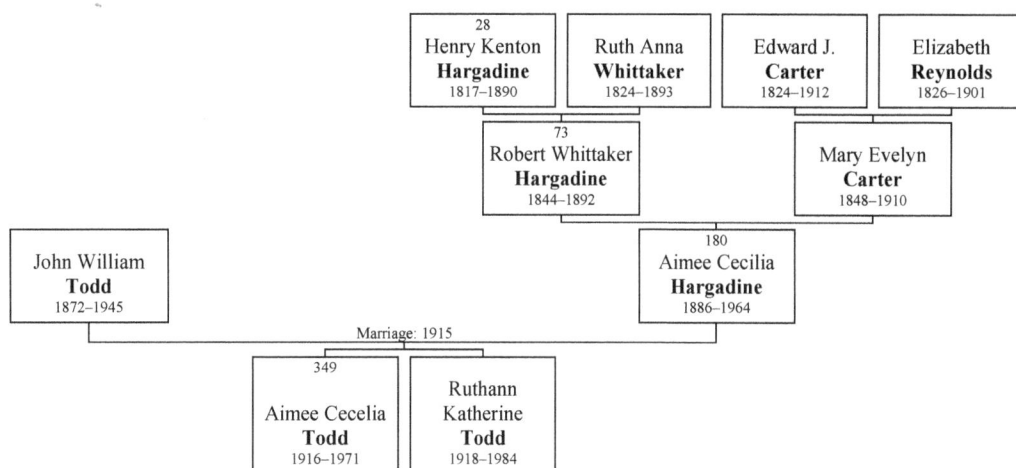

180. **Aimee Cecilia Hargadine** was born on Sunday, March 14, 1886, in Delaware, USA. She was the daughter of Robert Whittaker Hargadine (73) and Mary Evelyn Carter.

Aimee Cecilia died in Glasgow, Valley County, Montana, on January 02, 1964, at the age of 77. She was buried in Highland Cemetery, Glasgow, Valley County, Montana (Find a Grave ID 210159324).

Aimee Cecilia married **John William Todd** in 1915 in Glasgow, Valley County, Montana. They had two daughters.

John William was born in Cedar Falls, Black Hawk County, Iowa, on Friday, February 02, 1872. He worked as a Rancher.

John William reached 73 years of age and died in Glasgow, Valley County, Montana, on September 09, 1945. He was buried on September 12, 1945, in Highland Cemetery, Glasgow, Valley County, Montana (Find a Grave ID 210159118).

Census 1: 2 June 1900, South Murderkill Hundred, Kent County, Delaware (ED 80, Sht 3B)
Census 2: 1 January 1920, Glasgow City; School Dist I, Valley County, Montana (ED 223, Pg 3, Sht 3B)

Daughters of Aimee Cecilia Hargadine and John William Todd:

+ 349　　f　　I. **Aimee Cecelia Todd** was born in Glasgow, Valley County, Montana, on May 16, 1916. She died in California, USA, on December 11, 1971, at the age of 55. Aimee Cecelia was buried in Sidney Cemetery, Sidney, Richland County, Montana (Find a Grave ID 33343092).

　　　　　f　　II. **Ruthann Katherine Todd** was born in Montana, USA, on November 29, 1918. She died in Rialto, San Bernardino County, California, on February 06, 1984, at the age of 65. Ruthann Katherine was buried in Sidney Cemetery, Sidney, Richland County, Montana (Find a Grave ID 186099075).

Walter Burton

181.   **Walter Rodney Burton** was born in 1872. He was the son of Walter Burton and Mary C. Hargadine (74).

Walter Rodney died in 1936 at the age of 64. He was buried in Saint Peter's Episcopal Churchyard, Lewes, Sussex County, Delaware (Find a Grave ID 7716670).

Marriages with Emily Annan and May Johnson (Page 224) are known.

Family of Walter Burton and Emily Annan

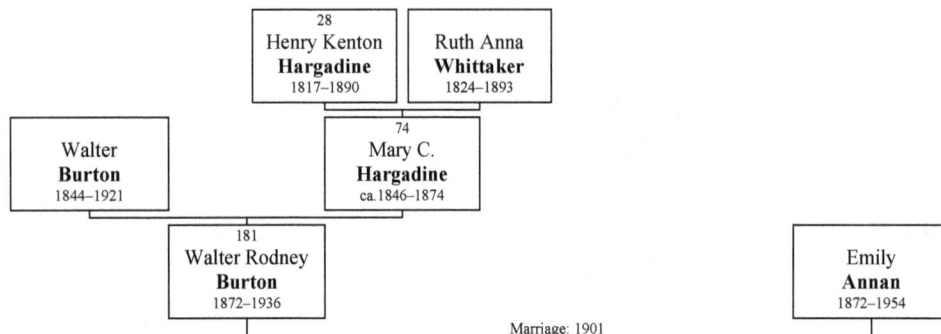

Here are the details about **Walter Rodney Burton's** first marriage, with Emily Annan. You can read more about Walter Rodney on page 224.

Walter Rodney Burton married **Emily Annan** in 1901. Emily was born in 1872.

She reached 82 years of age and died in 1954. Emily was buried in Saint Peter's Episcopal Churchyard, Lewes, Sussex County, Delaware (Find a Grave ID 7716671).

Family of Walter Burton and May Johnson

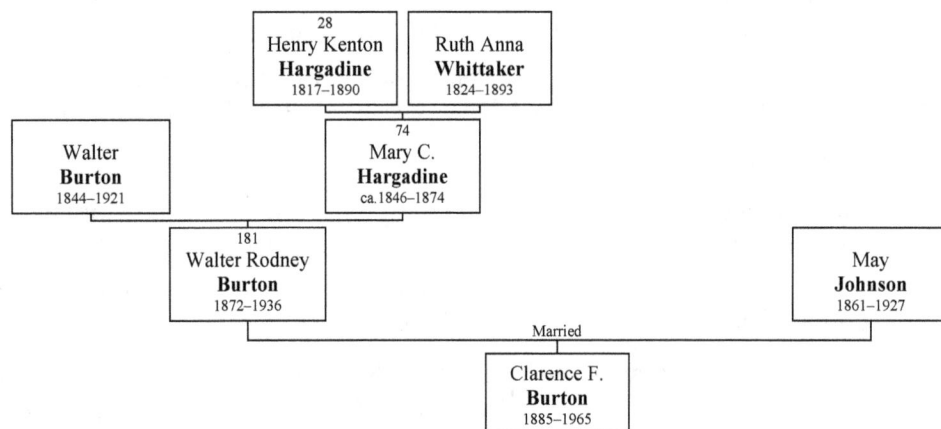

Here are the details about **Walter Rodney Burton's** second marriage, with May Johnson. You can read more about Walter Rodney on page 224.

Walter Rodney Burton married **May Johnson**. They had one son.

May was born in District of Columbia, USA, in May 1861. She reached 66 years of age and died in District of Columbia, USA, on November 02, 1927. May was buried in Oak Hill Cemetery, Washington, District of Columbia (Find a Grave ID 55674569).

Son of Walter Rodney Burton and May Johnson:

m   I. **Clarence F. Burton** was born in 1885. He died in 1965 at the age of 80. Clarence F. was buried in Oak Hill Cemetery, Washington, District of Columbia (Find a Grave ID 55681884).

Family of Mary Dill and Lewis Richards

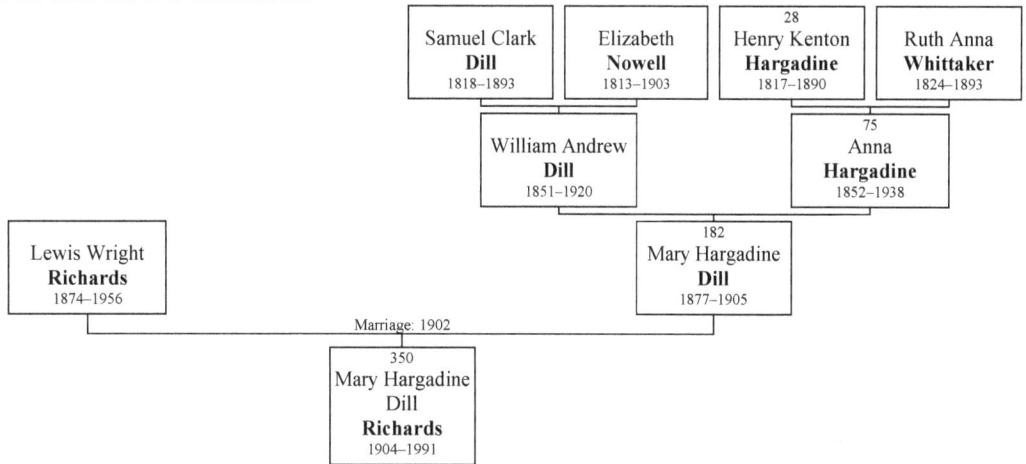

```
┌──────────────┐ ┌──────────────┐ ┌──────────────┐ ┌──────────────┐
│ Samuel Clark │ │  Elizabeth   │ │      28      │ │  Ruth Anna   │
│     Dill     │ │    Nowell    │ │ Henry Kenton │ │  Whittaker   │
│  1818–1893   │ │  1813–1903   │ │  Hargadine   │ │  1824–1893   │
└──────────────┘ └──────────────┘ │  1817–1890   │ └──────────────┘
                                   └──────────────┘
          ┌──────────────┐              ┌──────────────┐
          │William Andrew│              │      75      │
          │     Dill     │              │     Anna     │
          │  1851–1920   │              │  Hargadine   │
          └──────────────┘              │  1852–1938   │
                                        └──────────────┘
┌──────────────┐          ┌──────────────┐
│ Lewis Wright │          │     182      │
│   Richards   │          │Mary Hargadine│
│  1874–1956   │          │     Dill     │
└──────────────┘          │  1877–1905   │
                          └──────────────┘
            Marriage: 1902
          ┌──────────────┐
          │     350      │
          │Mary Hargadine│
          │     Dill     │
          │   Richards   │
          │  1904–1991   │
          └──────────────┘
```

182.   **Mary Hargadine Dill** was born on Tuesday, April 24, 1877, in Kent County, Delaware. She was the daughter of William Andrew Dill and Anna Hargadine (75).

Mary Hargadine died in Greenwood, Sussex County, Delaware, on January 20, 1905, at the age of 27. She was buried in Odd Fellows Cemetery, Camden, Kent County, Delaware (Find a Grave ID 45752389).

Mary Hargadine married **Lewis Wright Richards** in 1902. They had one daughter.

Lewis Wright was born in 1874. He reached 82 years of age and died in 1956. Lewis Wright was buried in Bridgeville Cemetery, Bridgeville, Sussex County, Delaware (Find a Grave ID 64546798).

Daughter of Mary Hargadine Dill and Lewis Wright Richards:

+   350   f   I. **Mary Hargadine Dill Richards** was born in 1904. She died in 1991 at the age of 87. Mary Hargadine Dill was buried in Odd Fellows Cemetery, Camden, Kent County, Delaware (Find a Grave ID 111022121).

William Hargadine

183.   **William Andrew Hargadine** was born on Thursday, November 08, 1877, in Delaware, USA. He was the son of Henry K. Hargadine (76) and Laura Virginia Jones.

William Andrew served in the military between 1917 and 1918. Drafted for WW I. He died in 1958 at the age of 80. William Andrew was buried in Barratts Chapel Cemetery, Frederica, Kent County, Delaware (Find a Grave ID 29366398).

Marriages with Mary Elizabeth Tharp and Bessie Wright (Page 227) are known.

Family of William Hargadine and Mary Tharp

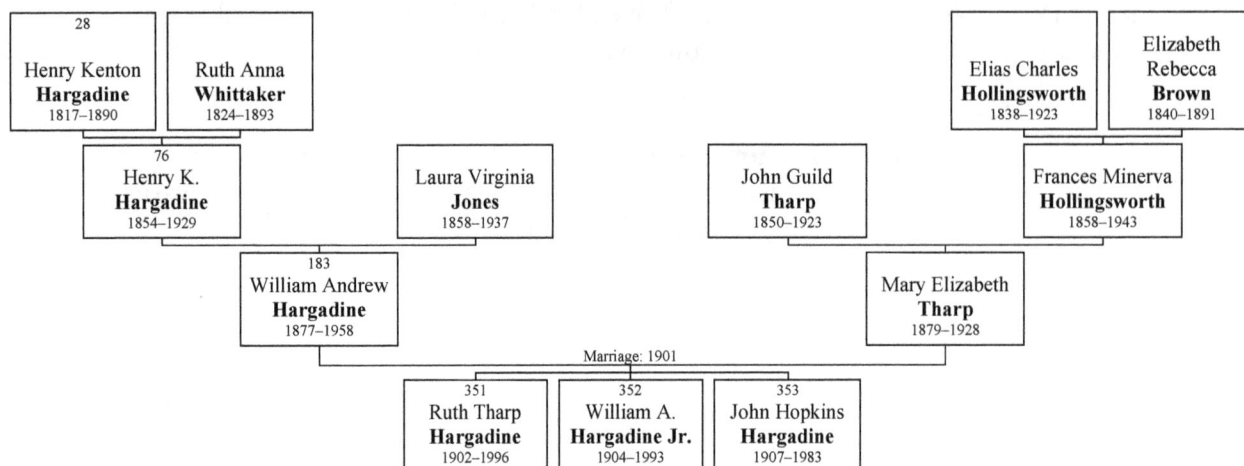

| 28 Henry Kenton **Hargadine** 1817–1890 | Ruth Anna **Whittaker** 1824–1893 | | | | Elias Charles **Hollingsworth** 1838–1923 | Elizabeth Rebecca **Brown** 1840–1891 |

| 76 Henry K. **Hargadine** 1854–1929 | Laura Virginia **Jones** 1858–1937 | John Guild **Tharp** 1850–1923 | Frances Minerva **Hollingsworth** 1858–1943 |

183
William Andrew
Hargadine
1877–1958

Mary Elizabeth
Tharp
1879–1928

Marriage: 1901

| 351 Ruth Tharp **Hargadine** 1902–1996 | 352 William A. **Hargadine Jr.** 1904–1993 | 353 John Hopkins **Hargadine** 1907–1983 |

Here are the details about **William Andrew Hargadine's** first marriage, with Mary Elizabeth Tharp. You can read more about William Andrew on page 225.

At the age of 24, William Andrew Hargadine married **Mary Elizabeth Tharp** on Wednesday, November 27, 1901, when she was 22 years old. They had three children.

Mary Elizabeth was born on Saturday, November 08, 1879. Mary Elizabeth reached 48 years of age and died in Felton, Kent County, Delaware, on March 02, 1928. She was buried in Barratts Chapel Cemetery, Frederica, Kent County, Delaware (Find a Grave ID 29366394).

The William Fleming Family

Mary Tharp (2-3-3), born November 8, 1879, married William A. Hargadine, son of Harry K. Hargadine, November 27, 1901, and lived at Felton, Delaware, till her death on the 2nd of March, 1928. Children: (1) Ruth Tharp; (2) William A.; and (3) John Hopkins.

Ruth Tharp Hargadine (2-3-3-1), born September 8, 1902, married George C. Palmer, October 4, 1919, and lives at West Chester, Pennsylvania. Children: (1) Mary Virginia; and (2) George Richard.

William A. Hargadine (2-3-3-2), born September 16, 1904, married Marjorie Hindley, December 24, 1928, lives at 286 Hampton Road, Upper Derby, Pennsylvania, and has one child, Walter William.

John Hopkins Hargadine (2-3-3-3), born January 25, 1907, married Hazel D. Helms, October 10, 1929, and lives at Felton, Delaware. His only child is Jane Helen. She was the daughter of John Guild Tharp and Frances Minerva Hollingsworth.

The history and genealogy of the William Fleming Family and other Flemings of Delaware.

Bibliographic Information: Brand, Franklin Marion. *The William Fleming Family*. Charleston, West Virginia. Mathews Ptg. & Lith County 1941 Author: Franklin Marion Brand p. 526

Children of William Andrew Hargadine and Mary Elizabeth Tharp:

+ 351 f I. **Ruth Tharp Hargadine** was born in Woodside, Kent County, Delaware, on September 08, 1902. She died on December 05, 1996, at the age of 94. Ruth Tharp was buried in Barratts Chapel Cemetery, Frederica, Kent County, Delaware (Find a Grave ID 154507803).

+ 352 m II. **William A. Hargadine Jr.** was born in Felton, Kent County, Delaware, on September 16, 1904. He died in Fayetteville, Franklin County, Pennsylvania, on September 03, 1993, at the age of 88. William A. was buried in Barratts Chapel Cemetery, Frederica, Kent County, Delaware (Find a Grave ID 154507712).

+ 353 m III. **John Hopkins Hargadine** was born in Delaware, USA, on January 25, 1907. He died in March 1983 at the age of 76. His cause of death was cancer. He was buried in Barratts Chapel Cemetery, Frederica, Kent County, Delaware (Find a Grave ID 29366390).

Family of William Hargadine and Bessie Wright

28
Henry Kenton
Hargadine
1817–1890
Ruth Anna
Whittaker
1824–1893
76
Henry K.
Hargadine
1854–1929
Laura Virginia
Jones
1858–1937
183
William Andrew
Hargadine
1877–1958
Bessie
Wright
1889–1968
Marriage: 1931

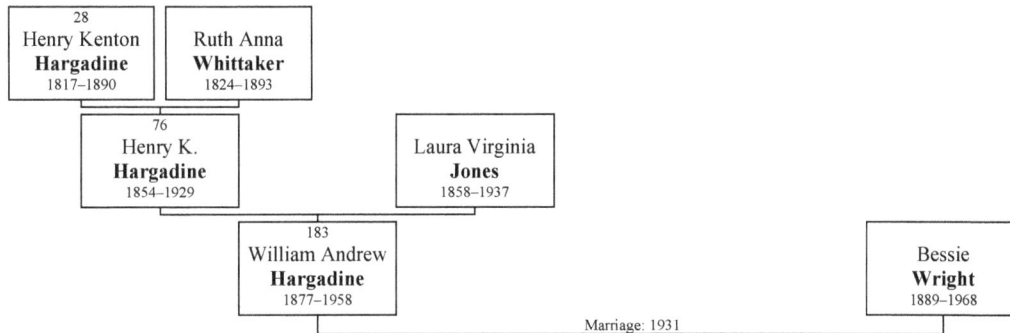

Here are the details about **William Andrew Hargadine's** second marriage, with Bessie Wright. You can read more about William Andrew on page 225.

At the age of 53, William Andrew Hargadine married **Bessie Wright** on Sunday, April 12, 1931, in Georgetown, Sussex County, Delaware, when she was 42 years old. Bessie was born in Delaware, USA, on Sunday, January 06, 1889.

She reached 79 years of age and died in Felton, Kent County, Delaware, on May 16, 1968. Bessie was buried in Barratts Chapel Cemetery, Frederica, Kent County, Delaware (Find a Grave ID 29366369).

Alice Hargadine

184. **Alice Hargadine** was born on Wednesday, October 24, 1883, in Viola, Kent County, Delaware. She was the daughter of Henry K. Hargadine (76) and Laura Virginia Jones.

Alice died on September 22, 1954, at the age of 70. She was buried in Lakeside Cemetery, Dover, Kent County, Delaware (Find a Grave ID 7802648).

Marriages with Cahall Sipple and Alexander Goodwin Wolcott (Page 228) are known.

Family of Alice Hargadine and Cahall Sipple

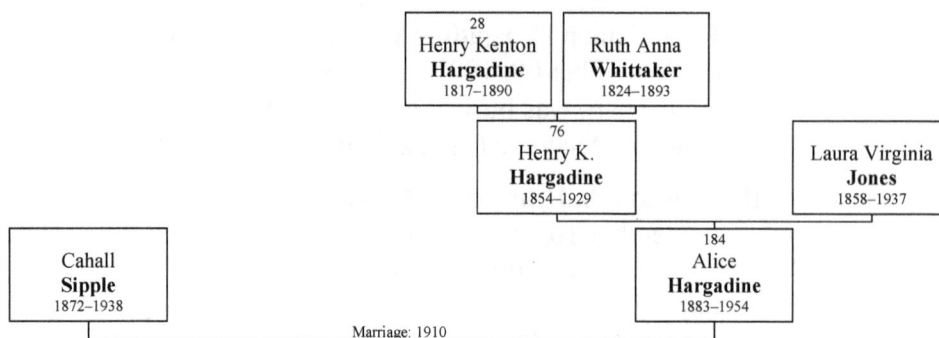

```
                    ┌──────────────┬──────────────┐
                    │      28      │              │
                    │ Henry Kenton │  Ruth Anna   │
                    │  Hargadine   │  Whittaker   │
                    │  1817–1890   │  1824–1893   │
                    └──────────────┴──────────────┘
                            │ 76                      ┌──────────────┐
                       Henry K.                       │ Laura Virginia│
                       Hargadine                      │    Jones     │
                       1854–1929                      │  1858–1937   │
                                                      └──────────────┘
   ┌──────────┐                        184
   │  Cahall  │                       Alice
   │  Sipple  │                     Hargadine
   │ 1872–1938│                     1883–1954
   └──────────┘
              Marriage: 1910
```

Here are the details about **Alice Hargadine's** first marriage, with Cahall Sipple. You can read more about Alice on page 227.

At the age of 26, Alice Hargadine married **Cahall Sipple** on Saturday, August 06, 1910, in Viola, Kent County, Delaware, when he was 37 years old. Cahall was born in Delaware, USA, on Tuesday, December 17, 1872.

He reached 65 years of age and died in Dover, Kent County, Delaware, on August 10, 1938. Cahall was buried in Barratts Chapel Cemetery, Frederica, Kent County, Delaware (Find a Grave ID 35960262).

More facts and events for Cahall Sipple:

Individual Note: Dentist

Family of Alice Hargadine and Alexander Wolcott

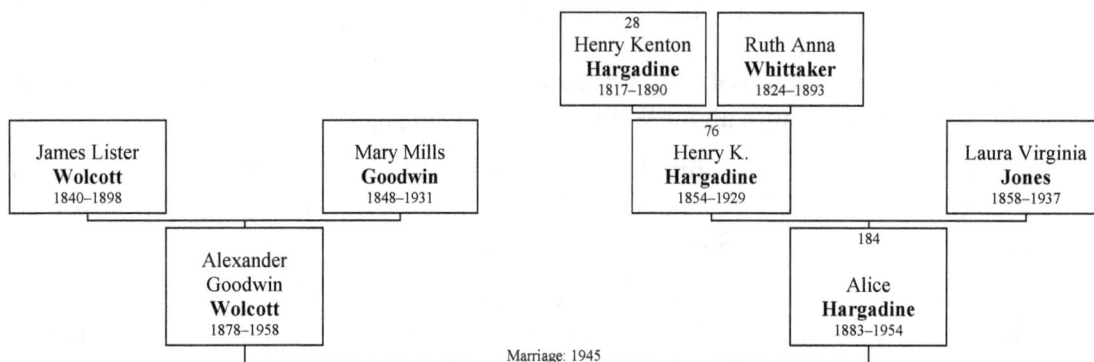

```
                              ┌──────────────┬──────────────┐
                              │      28      │              │
                              │ Henry Kenton │  Ruth Anna   │
                              │  Hargadine   │  Whittaker   │
                              │  1817–1890   │  1824–1893   │
                              └──────────────┴──────────────┘
                                      │ 76
  ┌──────────────┬──────────────┐  Henry K.         ┌──────────────┐
  │ James Lister │  Mary Mills  │  Hargadine        │Laura Virginia│
  │   Wolcott    │   Goodwin    │  1854–1929        │    Jones     │
  │  1840–1898   │  1848–1931   │                   │  1858–1937   │
  └──────────────┴──────────────┘                   └──────────────┘
          │   Alexander                      184
              Goodwin                        Alice
              Wolcott                      Hargadine
             1878–1958                     1883–1954
                          Marriage: 1945
```

Here are the details about **Alice Hargadine's** second marriage, with Alexander Goodwin Wolcott. You can read more about Alice on page 227.

At the age of 62, Alice Hargadine married **Alexander Goodwin Wolcott** on Wednesday, November 14, 1945, in Dover, Kent County, Delaware, when he was 67 years old. Alexander Goodwin was born on Monday, November 11, 1878. He was the son of James Lister Wolcott and Mary Mills Goodwin.

Alexander Goodwin reached 79 years of age and died on September 13, 1958. He was buried in Lakeside Cemetery, Dover, Kent County, Delaware (Find a Grave ID 7802637).

Family of Henry Hargadine and Edith Noble

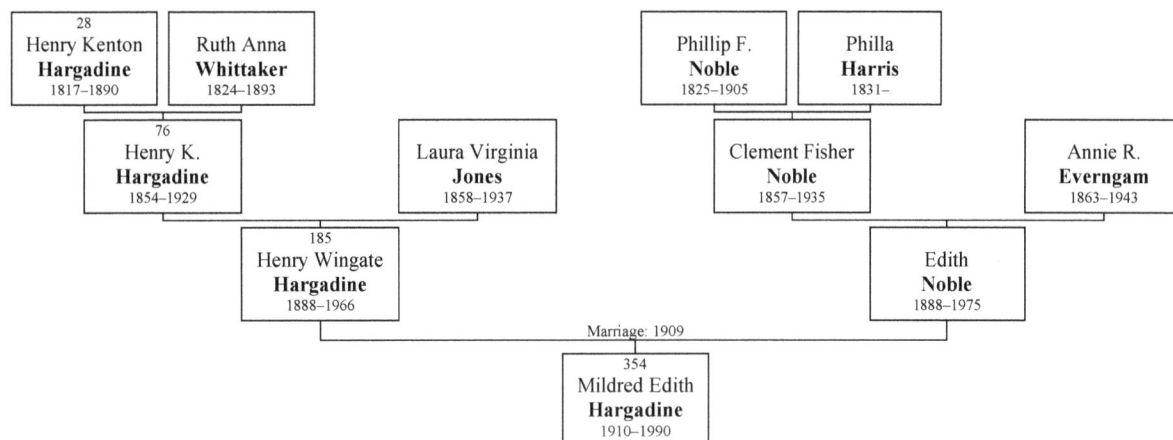

185.   **Henry Wingate Hargadine** was born on Monday, October 08, 1888, in Woodside, Kent County, Delaware. He was the son of Henry K. Hargadine (76) and Laura Virginia Jones.

Henry Wingate served in the military between 1917 and 1918. Drafted for WW I. He died on October 01, 1966, at the age of 77. Henry Wingate was buried in Barratts Chapel Cemetery, Frederica, Kent County, Delaware (Find a Grave ID 29366385).

Henry Wingate married **Edith Noble** in April 1909 in Frederica, Kent County, Delaware. They had one daughter.

Edith was born in Camden, Camden County, New Jersey, on Sunday, December 23, 1888.[230] She was the daughter of Clement Fisher Noble and Annie R. Everngam.

Edith reached 86 years of age and died in Hubert, Onslow County, North Carolina, on February 17, 1975.[230] She was buried in Barratts Chapel Cemetery, Frederica, Kent County, Delaware (Find a Grave ID 29366376).[230]

Daughter of Henry Wingate Hargadine and Edith Noble:

+   354   f   I. **Mildred Edith Hargadine** was born in Frederica, Kent County, Delaware, on August 11, 1910. She died on July 22, 1990, at the age of 79.

230   Ancestry.com, Public Member Trees (Provo, UT, USA, Ancestry.com Operations, Inc., 2006), Ancestry.com, Record for Edith Noble. https://search.ancestry.co.uk/cgi-bin/sse.dll?db=1030&h=24653929859&indiv=try.

Family of Anna Hargadine and Oscar Allen

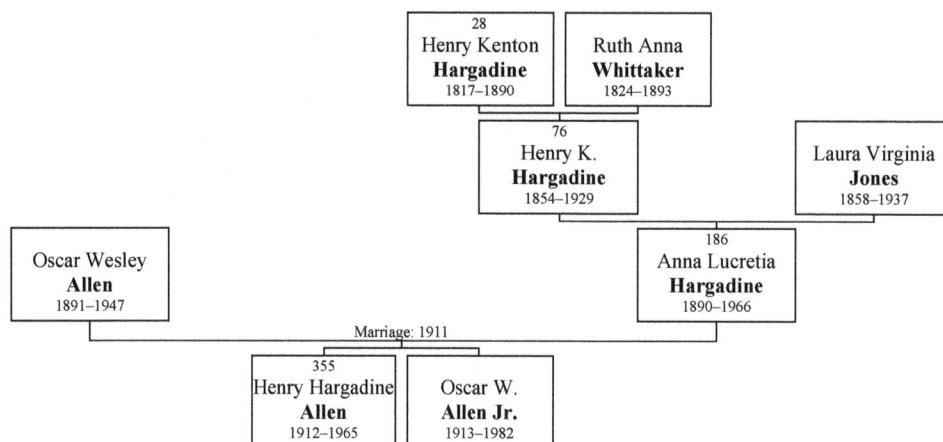

186. **Anna Lucretia Hargadine** was born on Wednesday, June 04, 1890, in Delaware, USA. She was the daughter of Henry K. Hargadine (76) and Laura Virginia Jones.

Anna Lucretia died in Seaford, Sussex County, Delaware, on July 04, 1966, at the age of 76. She was buried in Odd Fellows Cemetery, Seaford, Sussex County, Delaware, on July 06, 1966 (Find a Grave ID 86288948).

Anna Lucretia married **Oscar Wesley Allen** in 1911. They had two sons.

Oscar Wesley was born in Seaford, Sussex County, Delaware, on Friday, September 18, 1891. He worked as a railroad telegraph operator.

Oscar Wesley reached 55 years of age and died in Seaford, Sussex County, Delaware, on January 12, 1947. He was buried on January 15, 1947, in Odd Fellows Cemetery, Seaford, Sussex County, Delaware (Find a Grave ID 86289193).

Sons of Anna Lucretia Hargadine and Oscar Wesley Allen:

+ 355   m   I. **Henry Hargadine Allen** was born in Clayton, Kent County, Delaware, on January 01, 1912. He died in Wilmington, New Castle County, Delaware, on April 26, 1965, at the age of 53. Henry Hargadine was buried in Gracelawn Memorial Park, New Castle, New Castle County, Delaware (Find a Grave ID 134998535).

       m   II. **Oscar W. Allen Jr.** was born in Woodside, Kent County, Delaware, USA, on December 03, 1913. He died on September 28, 1982, at the age of 68. Oscar W. was buried in Odd Fellows Cemetery, Seaford, Sussex County, Delaware (Find a Grave ID 86289448).

Family of July Thomson and Charles Collins

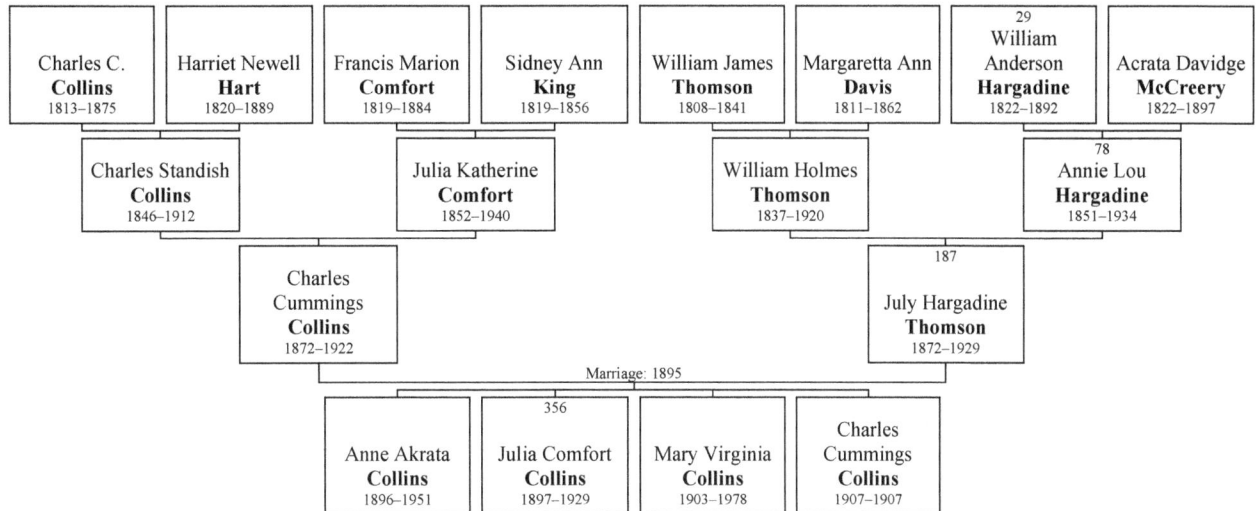

187. **July Hargadine Thomson** was born on Monday, December 09, 1872, in Saint Louis, Saint Louis County, Missouri. She was the daughter of William Holmes Thomson and Annie Lou Hargadine (78).

July Hargadine died in Saint Louis, Saint Louis County, Missouri, on October 16, 1929, at the age of 56. She was buried in Bellefontaine Cemetery, Saint Louis, St. Louis City, Missouri (Find a Grave ID 99059481).

At the age of 22, July Hargadine married **Charles Cummings Collins** on Wednesday, October 16, 1895, in Saint Louis, Saint Louis County, Missouri, when he was 23 years old. They had four children.

Charles Cummings was born in Memphis, Shelby County, Tennessee, on Saturday, July 06, 1872. Charles Cummings reached 50 years of age and died in Saint Louis, Saint Louis County, Missouri, on September 22, 1922. He was buried in Bellefontaine Cemetery, Saint Louis, St. Louis City, Missouri (Find a Grave ID 99059799).

1920 Census, St. Louis, St. Louis, Missouri, 2 Jan 1920, ED 499, Sheet 1B:

Charles C. Collins Head 47 M TN TN TN Lawyer
July   Wife 47 M MO MD MO
July C.   Dau 10 S MO TN MO
Mary Virginia   Dau 16 S MO TN MO
H. A. Gifford   Son-i-l 29 M Mass. Mass. Mass. Stock Broker
July C.   Dau   22 M MO TN MO He was the son of Charles Standish Collins and Julia
Katherine Comfort.

Children of July Hargadine Thomson and Charles Cummings Collins:

    f   I. **Anne Akrata Collins** was born in Saint Louis, Saint Louis County, Missouri, on August 26, 1896. She died on March 28, 1951, at the age of 54.

+ 356   f   II. **Julia Comfort Collins** was born in Saint Louis, Saint Louis County, Missouri, on October 29, 1897. She died in Saint Louis, Saint Louis County, Missouri, on November 11, 1929, at the age of 32. Julia Comfort was buried in Bellefontaine Cemetery, Saint Louis, St. Louis City, Missouri (Find a Grave ID 99059887).

      f   III. **Mary Virginia Collins** was born in Saint Louis, Saint Louis County, Missouri, on May 13, 1903. She died in Berkeley, Alameda County, California, on December 28, 1978, at the age of 75. Mary Virginia was buried in Bellefontaine Cemetery, Saint Louis, St. Louis City, Missouri (Find a Grave ID 99157733).

      m   IV. **Charles Cummings Collins** was born in 1907. He died in Saint Louis, Saint Louis County, Missouri, in 1907. Charles Cummings was buried in Bellefontaine Cemetery, Saint Louis, St. Louis City, Missouri (Find a Grave ID 99060131).

Family of William Thomson and Elizabeth Johnson

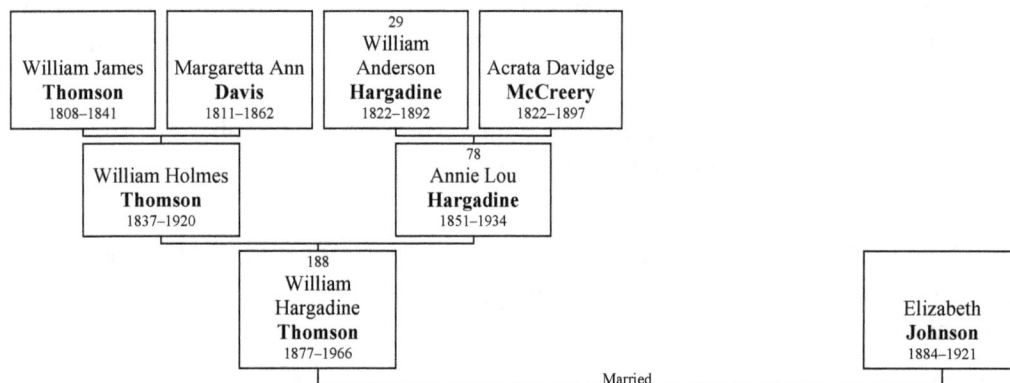

188.   **William Hargadine Thomson** was born on Thursday, July 05, 1877, in Saint Louis, Saint Louis County, Missouri. He was the son of William Holmes Thomson and Annie Lou Hargadine (78).

William Hargadine died in Dallas, Dallas County, Texas, on October 18, 1966, at the age of 89. He was buried in Sparkman Hillcrest Memorial Park, Dallas, Dallas County, Texas (Find a Grave ID 170461505).

He married **Elizabeth Johnson**. Elizabeth was born in Georgia, USA, on Tuesday, September 09, 1884.

She reached 36 years of age and died in Dallas, Dallas County, Texas, on February 25, 1921. Elizabeth was buried in Oakwood Cemetery, Corsicana, Navarro County, Texas (Find a Grave ID 104825551).

Family of Susan Thomson and Alexander Coxe

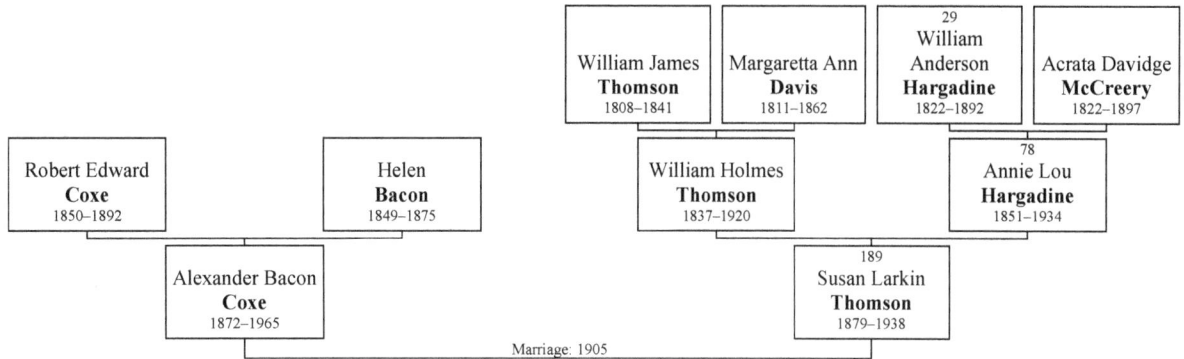

```
                                    ┌──────────────┬──────────────┬──────29──────┬──────────────┐
                                    │ William James│Margaretta Ann│   William    │Acrata Davidge│
                                    │   Thomson    │    Davis     │   Anderson   │  McCreery    │
                                    │  1808–1841   │  1811–1862   │  Hargadine   │  1822–1897   │
                                    │              │              │  1822–1892   │              │
                                    └──────────────┴──────────────┴──────────────┴──────────────┘
┌──────────────┬──────────────┐        ┌──────────────┐              ┌──────78──────┐
│ Robert Edward│    Helen     │        │William Holmes│              │  Annie Lou   │
│     Coxe     │    Bacon     │        │   Thomson    │              │  Hargadine   │
│  1850–1892   │  1849–1875   │        │  1837–1920   │              │  1851–1934   │
└──────────────┴──────────────┘        └──────────────┘              └──────────────┘
        ┌──────────────┐                      ┌──────189──────┐
        │Alexander Bacon│                     │ Susan Larkin  │
        │     Coxe     │                      │   Thomson     │
        │  1872–1965   │                      │  1879–1938    │
        └──────────────┘                      └───────────────┘
                    Marriage: 1905
```

189.   **Susan Larkin Thomson** was born on Friday, June 20, 1879, in Saint Louis, Saint Louis County, Missouri. She was the daughter of William Holmes Thomson and Annie Lou Hargadine (78).

Susan Larkin died in El Paso, El Paso County, Texas, on August 10, 1938, at the age of 59. She was buried in Arlington National Cemetery, Arlington, Arlington County, Virginia (Find a Grave ID 49171749).

At the age of 25, Susan Larkin married **Alexander Bacon Coxe** on Wednesday, January 25, 1905, when he was 32 years old. Alexander Bacon was born in Santa Fe County, New Mexico, on Tuesday, December 03, 1872. He was the son of Robert Edward Coxe and Helen Bacon.

He served in the military: Colonel; U.S. Army. Alexander Bacon reached 92 years of age and died in Marin County, California, on March 12, 1965. He was buried in Arlington National Cemetery, Arlington, Arlington County, Virginia (Find a Grave ID 49171744).

Family of Virginia Thomson and George Tracy

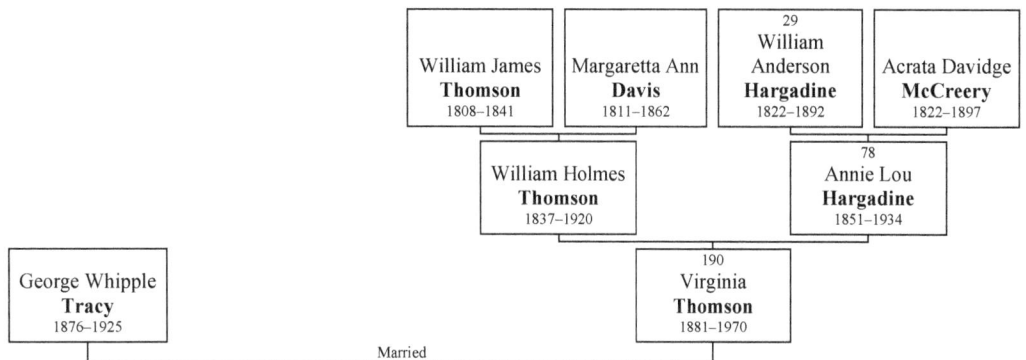

```
                                    ┌──────────────┬──────────────┬──────29──────┬──────────────┐
                                    │ William James│Margaretta Ann│   William    │Acrata Davidge│
                                    │   Thomson    │    Davis     │   Anderson   │  McCreery    │
                                    │  1808–1841   │  1811–1862   │  Hargadine   │  1822–1897   │
                                    │              │              │  1822–1892   │              │
                                    └──────────────┴──────────────┴──────────────┴──────────────┘
                                       ┌──────────────┐              ┌──────78──────┐
                                       │William Holmes│              │  Annie Lou   │
                                       │   Thomson    │              │  Hargadine   │
                                       │  1837–1920   │              │  1851–1934   │
                                       └──────────────┘              └──────────────┘
┌──────────────┐                              ┌──────190──────┐
│George Whipple│                              │   Virginia    │
│    Tracy     │                              │   Thomson     │
│  1876–1925   │                              │  1881–1970    │
└──────────────┘                              └───────────────┘
              Married
```

190.   **Virginia Thomson** was born on Tuesday, January 11, 1881, in Saint Louis, Saint Louis County, Missouri. She was the daughter of William Holmes Thomson and Annie Lou Hargadine (78).

Virginia died in Saint Louis, Saint Louis County, Missouri, in February 1970 at the age of 89. She was buried in Bellefontaine Cemetery, Saint Louis, St. Louis City, Missouri (Find a Grave ID 99078737).

She married **George Whipple Tracy**. George Whipple was born in Kirkwood, St. Louis County, Missouri, on Thursday, December 07, 1876.

He reached 48 years of age and died in Richmond Heights, St. Louis County, Missouri, on June 05, 1925. George Whipple was buried in Bellefontaine Cemetery, Saint Louis, St. Louis City, Missouri (Find a Grave ID 99078618).

Family of Holmes Thomson and Eugene Funsten

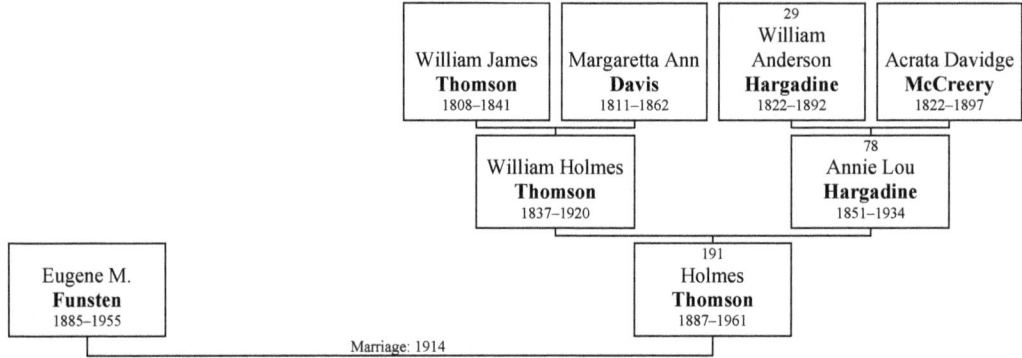

191. **Holmes Thomson** was born on Sunday, November 06, 1887. She was the daughter of William Holmes Thomson and Annie Lou Hargadine (78).

Holmes died on May 13, 1961, at the age of 73. She was buried in Bellefontaine Cemetery, Saint Louis, St. Louis City, Missouri (Find a Grave ID 99077730).

At the age of 26, Holmes married **Eugene M. Funsten** on Sunday, June 14, 1914, in Saint Louis, Saint Louis County, Missouri, when he was 28 years old. Eugene M. was born in Saint Louis, Saint Louis County, Missouri, on Thursday, August 06, 1885.

He reached 70 years of age and died in Saint Louis, Saint Louis County, Missouri, on September 19, 1955. Eugene M. was buried in Bellefontaine Cemetery, Saint Louis, St. Louis City, Missouri (Find a Grave ID 99076658).

Family of William Glasgow and Yvonne Merrill

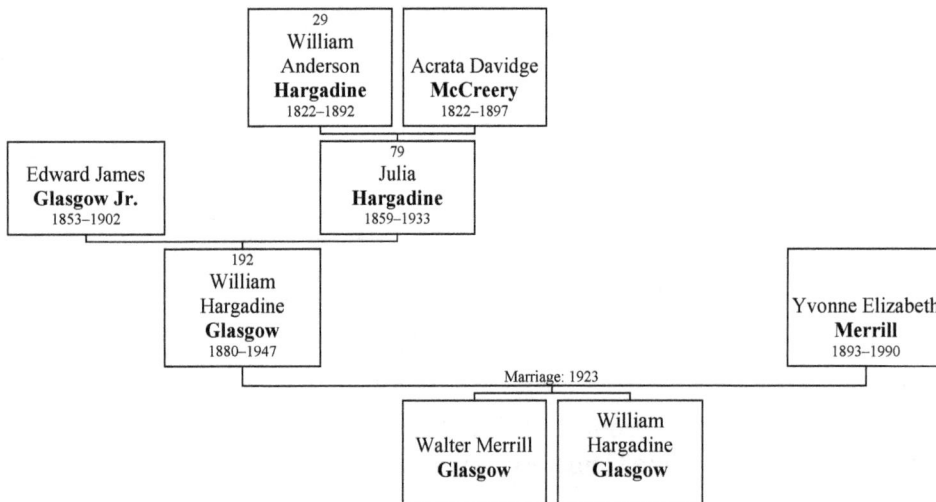

192. **William Hargadine Glasgow** was born on Tuesday, November 09, 1880, in Saint Louis, Saint Louis County, Missouri. He was the son of Edward James Glasgow Jr. and Julia Hargadine (79).

William Hargadine died on June 21, 1947, at the age of 66. He was buried in Bellefontaine Cemetery, Saint Louis, St. Louis City, Missouri (Find a Grave ID 99080462).

At the age of 42, William Hargadine married **Yvonne Elizabeth Merrill** on Saturday, August 11, 1923, when she was 29 years old. They had two sons.

Yvonne Elizabeth was born on Thursday, August 17, 1893. She reached 97 years of age and died on September 10, 1990.

Sons of William Hargadine Glasgow and Yvonne Elizabeth Merrill:

> m   I. **Walter Merrill Glasgow**.

> m   II. **William Hargadine Glasgow**.

Family of Atreus Von Schrader and Mary Leffingwell

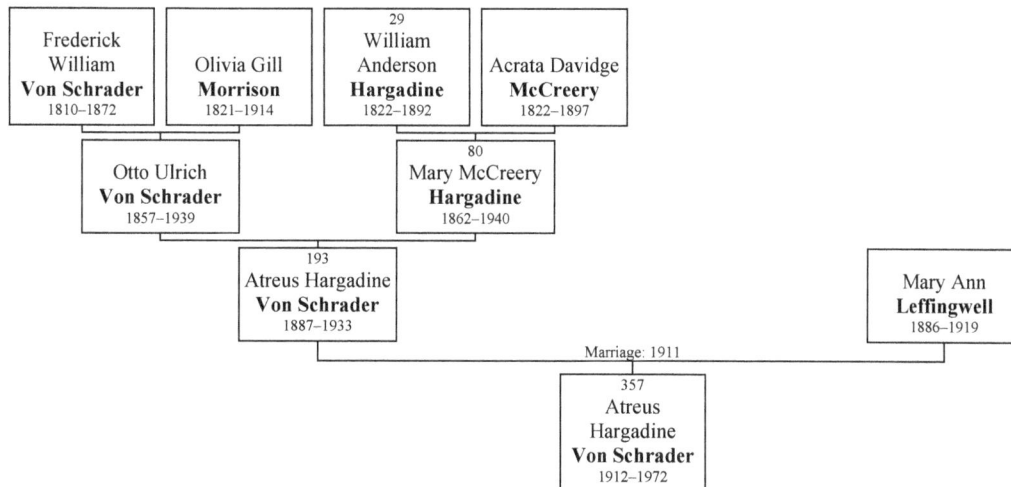

193. **Atreus Hargadine Von Schrader** was born on Sunday, November 06, 1887. He was the son of Otto Ulrich Von Schrader and Mary McCreery Hargadine (80).

Atreus Hargadine died on October 06, 1933, at the age of 45. He was buried in Bellefontaine Cemetery, Saint Louis, St. Louis City, Missouri (Find a Grave ID 99079007).

Atreus Hargadine married **Mary Ann Leffingwell** in May 1911. They had one son.

Mary Ann was born in 1886. She reached 33 years of age and died in 1919.

Son of Atreus Hargadine Von Schrader and Mary Ann Leffingwell:

+   357   m   I. **Atreus Hargadine Von Schrader** was born in Saint Louis, Saint Louis County, Missouri, on January 01, 1912. He died in Bar Harbor, Hancock County, Maine, on August 09, 1972, at the age of 60. Atreus Hargadine was buried in Oakwood Cemetery, Syracuse, Onondaga County, New York (Find a Grave ID 77270957).

Family of William Hall and Margaret Johnson

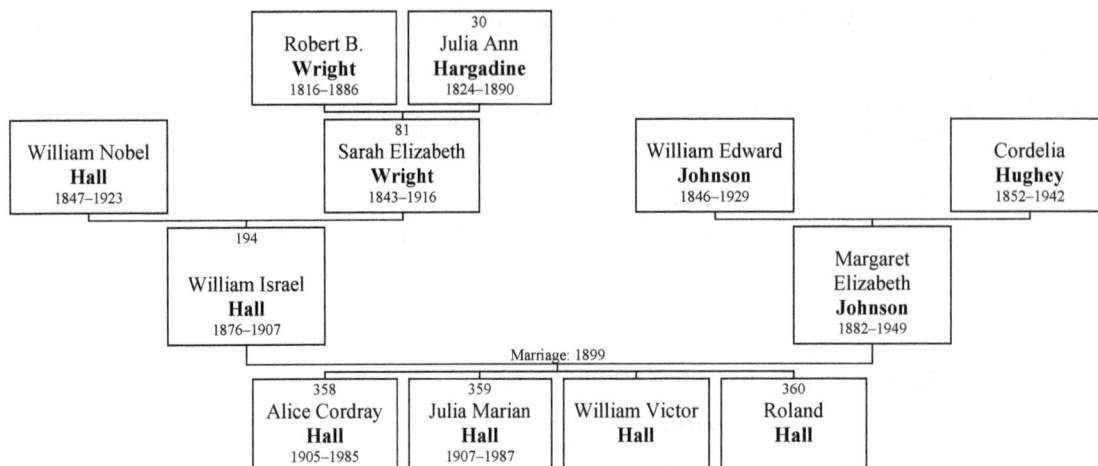

```
                    ┌─────────────┬─────────────┐
                    │ Robert B.   │     30      │
                    │   Wright    │  Julia Ann  │
                    │  1816–1886  │  Hargadine  │
                    │             │  1824–1890  │
                    └─────────────┴─────────────┘
```

	30
Robert B. **Wright** 1816–1886	Julia Ann **Hargadine** 1824–1890

| William Nobel **Hall** 1847–1923 | 81 Sarah Elizabeth **Wright** 1843–1916 | | William Edward **Johnson** 1846–1929 | Cordelia **Hughey** 1852–1942 |

| 194 William Israel **Hall** 1876–1907 | Margaret Elizabeth **Johnson** 1882–1949 |

Marriage: 1899

| 358 Alice Cordray **Hall** 1905–1985 | 359 Julia Marian **Hall** 1907–1987 | William Victor **Hall** | 360 Roland **Hall** |

194. **William Israel Hall** was born on Monday, June 12, 1876. He was the son of William Nobel Hall and Sarah Elizabeth Wright (81).

William Israel died in New Castle County, Delaware, on September 15, 1907, at the age of 31. His cause of death was: railroad accident. William Israel was buried in Lakeside Cemetery, Dover, Kent County, Delaware (Find a Grave ID 198356405).

At the age of 23, William Israel married **Margaret Elizabeth Johnson** on Wednesday, October 11, 1899, in Kent County, Delaware, when she was 17 years old. They had four children.

Margaret Elizabeth was born in Dover, Kent County, Delaware, on Sunday, February 12, 1882. She was the daughter of William Edward Johnson and Cordelia Hughey.

Margaret Elizabeth reached 67 years of age and died in Wilmington, New Castle County, Delaware, on June 15, 1949.

Children of William Israel Hall and Margaret Elizabeth Johnson:

+ 358   f   I. **Alice Cordray Hall** was born on March 17, 1905. She died in April 1985 at the age of 80.

+ 359   f   II. **Julia Marian Hall** was born on February 14, 1907. She died on April 21, 1987, at the age of 80.

         m   III. **William Victor Hall**.

+ 360   m   IV. **Roland Hall**.

Family of Harry Wright and Mary McBride

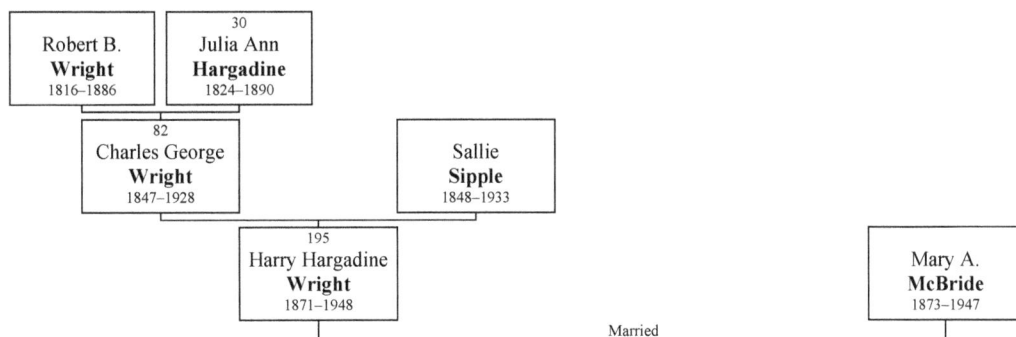

195.   **Harry Hargadine Wright** was born in 1871 in Delaware, USA. He was the son of Charles George Wright (82) and Sallie Sipple.

Harry Hargadine died in Wilmington, New Castle County, Delaware, in 1948 at the age of 77. He was buried in Silverbrook Cemetery and Memorial Park, Wilmington, New Castle County, Delaware (Find a Grave ID 116979676).

He married **Mary A. McBride**. Mary A. was born in Chester, Delaware County, Pennsylvania, in 1873.

She reached 74 years of age and died in Wilmington, New Castle County, Delaware, in 1947. Mary A. was buried in Silverbrook Cemetery and Memorial Park, Wilmington, New Castle County, Delaware (Find a Grave ID 116979658).

Family of William Truax and Katherine Brott

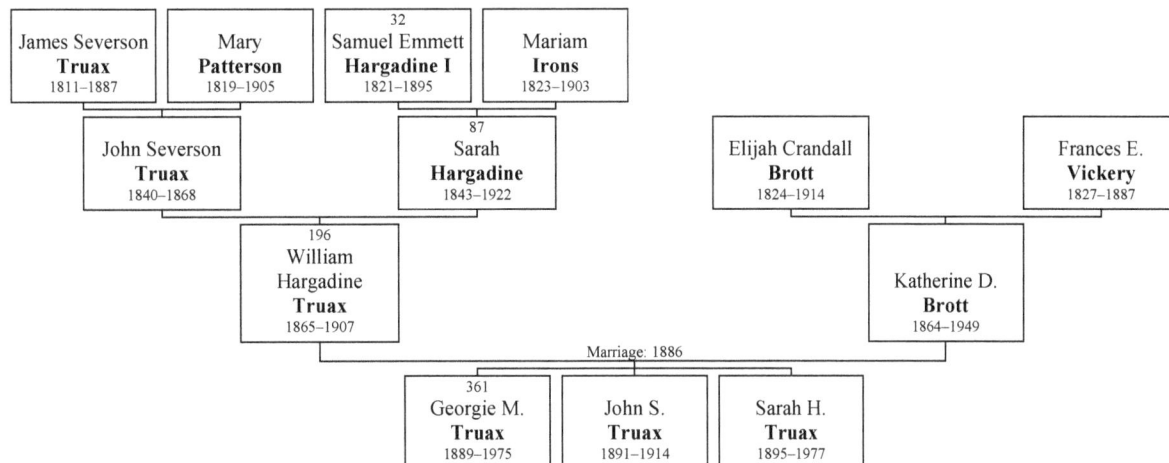

196.   **William Hargadine Truax** was born on Monday, January 30, 1865, in Delaware, USA. He was the son of John Severson Truax and Sarah Hargadine (87).

William Hargadine died in Delaware, USA, on January 21, 1907, at the age of 41. He was buried in Glenwood Cemetery, Smyrna, Kent County, Delaware (Find a Grave ID 11160898).

At the age of 21, William Hargadine married **Katherine D. Brott** on Thursday, May 27, 1886, in Brookfield, Linn County, Missouri, when she was 21 years old. They had three children.

Katherine D. was born in Tennessee, USA, on Wednesday, December 28, 1864. She was the daughter of Elijah Crandall Brott and Frances E. Vickery.

Katherine D. reached 84 years of age and died in Delaware, USA, on August 16, 1949. She was buried in Glenwood Cemetery, Smyrna, Kent County, Delaware (Find a Grave ID 11160885).

Children of William Hargadine Truax and Katherine D. Brott:

+ 361   f   I. **Georgie M. Truax** was born in Missouri, USA, on June 13, 1889. She died in Wilmington, New Castle County, Delaware, on July 25, 1975, at the age of 86. Georgie M. was buried in Silverbrook Cemetery and Memorial Park, Wilmington, New Castle County, Delaware (Find a Grave ID 137029595).

      m   II. **John S. Truax** was born in Missouri, USA, on March 10, 1891. He died in Delaware, USA, on October 13, 1914, at the age of 23. John S. was buried in Glenwood Cemetery, Smyrna, Kent County, Delaware (Find a Grave ID 11160884).

      f   III. **Sarah H. Truax** was born in Missouri, USA, on September 24, 1895. She died in Wilmington, New Castle County, Delaware, in July 1977 at the age of 81.

Family of Sallie Collins and Marvin Post

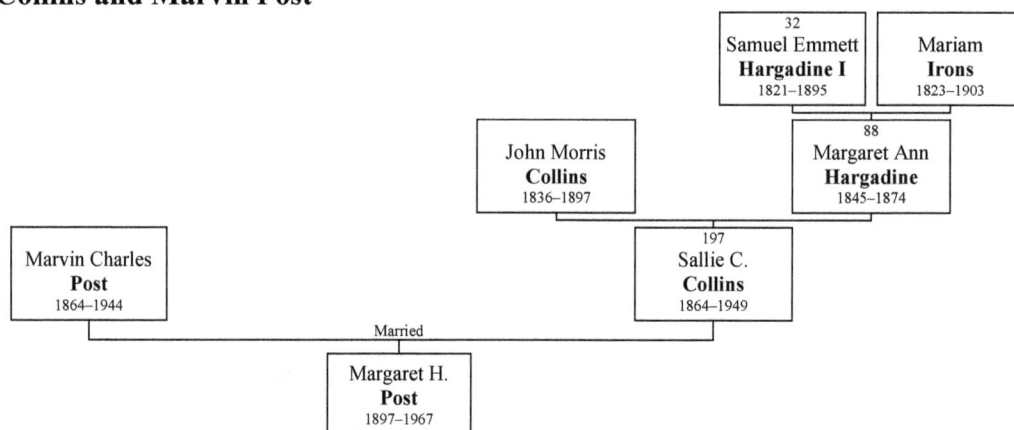

197.   Sallie C. Collins was born on Thursday, January 28, 1864, in Smyrna, Kent County, Delaware. She was the daughter of John Morris Collins and Margaret Ann Hargadine (88).

Sallie C. died in Brookfield, Linn County, Missouri, on March 31, 1949, at the age of 85. She was buried in Rose Hill Cemetery, Brookfield, Linn County, Missouri (Find a Grave ID 80154261).

She married **Marvin Charles Post**. They had one daughter.

Marvin Charles was born in Fond du Lac County, Wisconsin, on Friday, March 18, 1864. He reached 80 years of age and died in Brookfield, Linn County, Missouri, on November

18, 1944. Marvin Charles was buried in Rose Hill Cemetery, Brookfield, Linn County, Missouri (Find a Grave ID 80154111).

Daughter of Sallie C. Collins and Marvin Charles Post:

f   I. **Margaret H. Post** was born in Brookfield, Linn County, Missouri, in September 1897. She died in 1967 at the age of 69. Margaret H. was buried in Rose Hill Cemetery, Brookfield, Linn County, Missouri (Find a Grave ID 138949516).

Family of Marian Collins and Herman Craig

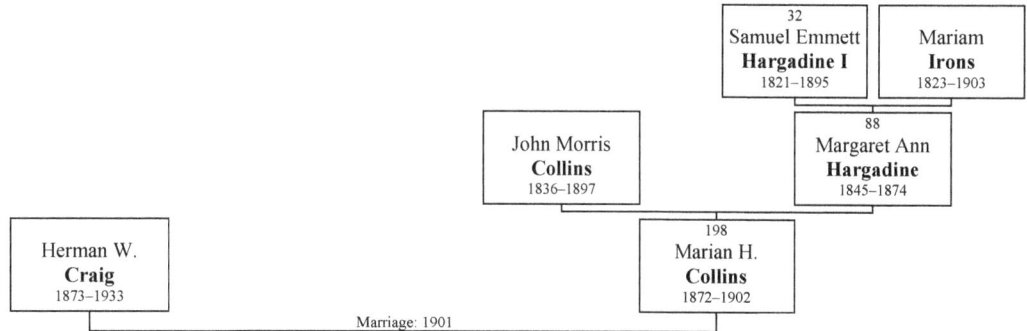

198.   **Marian H. Collins** was born on Wednesday, September 11, 1872, in Delaware, USA. She was the daughter of John Morris Collins and Margaret Ann Hargadine (88).

Marian H. died on July 23, 1902, at the age of 29. She was buried in Rose Hill Cemetery, Brookfield, Linn County, Missouri (Find a Grave ID 143227026).

Marian H. married **Herman W. Craig** in 1901. Herman W. was born in Linneus, Linn County, Missouri, on Tuesday, February 18, 1873.

He reached 60 years of age and died in Brookfield, Linn County, Missouri, on December 06, 1933. Herman W. was buried in Rose Hill Cemetery, Brookfield, Linn County, Missouri (Find a Grave ID 143226914).

Family of Walter Snow and Edith Terwilliger

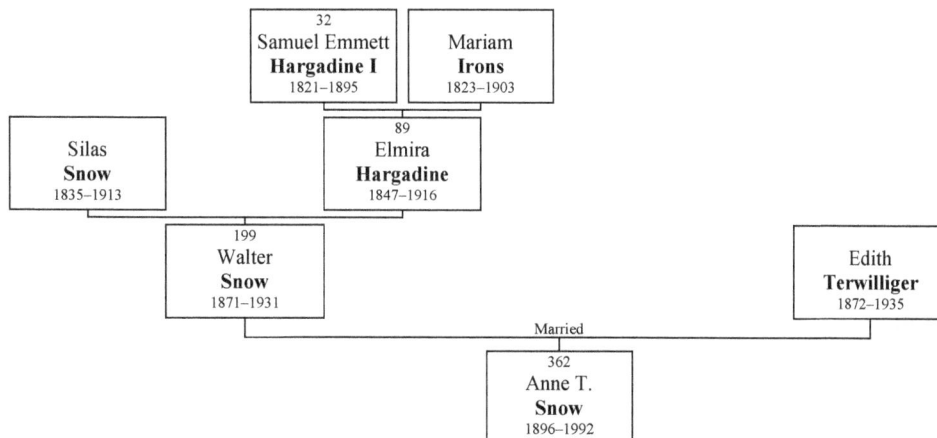

199. **Walter Snow** was born on Tuesday, August 15, 1871, in Leipsic, Kent County, Delaware. He was the son of Silas Snow and Elmira Hargadine (89).

Walter died in Lakewood, Cuyahoga County, Ohio, in 1931 at the age of 59. He was buried in Rose Hill Cemetery, Brookfield, Linn County, Missouri (Find a Grave ID 83950396).

He married **Edith Terwilliger**. They had one daughter.

Edith was born in Linn County, Missouri, in 1872. She reached 63 years of age and died in Ohio, USA, in 1935. Edith was buried in Rose Hill Cemetery, Brookfield, Linn County, Missouri (Find a Grave ID 83950424).

Daughter of Walter Snow and Edith Terwilliger:

+ 362   f   I. **Anne T. Snow** was born in 1896. She died in 1992 at the age of 96. Anne T. was buried in Rose Hill Cemetery, Brookfield, Linn County, Missouri (Find a Grave ID 192067411).

Family of Silas Snow and Nannie Givens

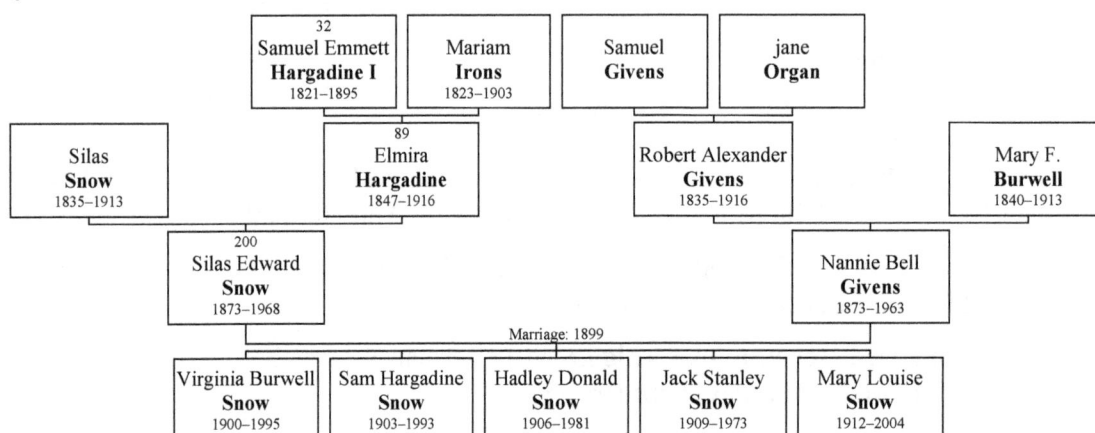

200. **Silas Edward Snow** was born on Thursday, July 10, 1873, in Delaware, USA. He was the son of Silas Snow and Elmira Hargadine (89).

Silas Edward died on April 16, 1968, at the age of 94. He was buried in Rose Hill Cemetery, Brookfield, Linn County, Missouri (Find a Grave ID 138706333).

At the age of 26, Silas Edward married **Nannie Bell Givens** on Saturday, October 14, 1899, in Brookfield, Linn County, Missouri, when she was 26 years old. They had five children.

Nannie Bell was born in Missouri, USA, on Monday, March 10, 1873. She was the daughter of Robert Alexander Givens and Mary F. Burwell.

Nannie Bell reached 90 years of age and died on March 18, 1963. She was buried in Rose Hill Cemetery, Brookfield, Linn County, Missouri (Find a Grave ID 138706213).

Children of Silas Edward Snow and Nannie Bell Givens:

     f   I. **Virginia Burwell Snow** was born in Cameron, Missouri, on August 30, 1900. She died in Chicago, Cook County, Illinois, on June 16, 1995, at the age of 94. Virginia Burwell was buried in Rose Hill Cemetery, Brookfield, Linn County, Missouri, on July 03, 2004 (Find a Grave ID 138706418).

m   II. **Sam Hargadine Snow** was born in 1903. He died in 1993 at the age of 90. Sam Hargadine was buried in Rose Hill Cemetery, Brookfield, Linn County, Missouri (Find a Grave ID 138706266).

m   III. **Hadley Donald Snow** was born in Brookfield, Linn County, Missouri, on August 19, 1906. He died in Illinois, USA, on June 24, 1981, at the age of 74. Hadley Donald was buried in Rose Hill Cemetery, Brookfield, Linn County, Missouri (Find a Grave ID 135838605).

m   IV. **Jack Stanley Snow** was born in Brookfield, Linn County, Missouri, on August 08, 1909. He died in Illinois, USA, on November 18, 1973, at the age of 64. Jack Stanley was buried in Rose Hill Cemetery, Brookfield, Linn County, Missouri (Find a Grave ID 122752590).

f   V. **Mary Louise Snow** was born in Missouri, USA, on July 11, 1912. She died in Chicago, Cook County, Illinois, on May 22, 2004, at the age of 91. Mary Louise was buried in Rose Hill Cemetery, Brookfield, Linn County, Missouri, on July 03, 2004 (Find a Grave ID 138706143).

Family of Edna Schenck and George Sayles

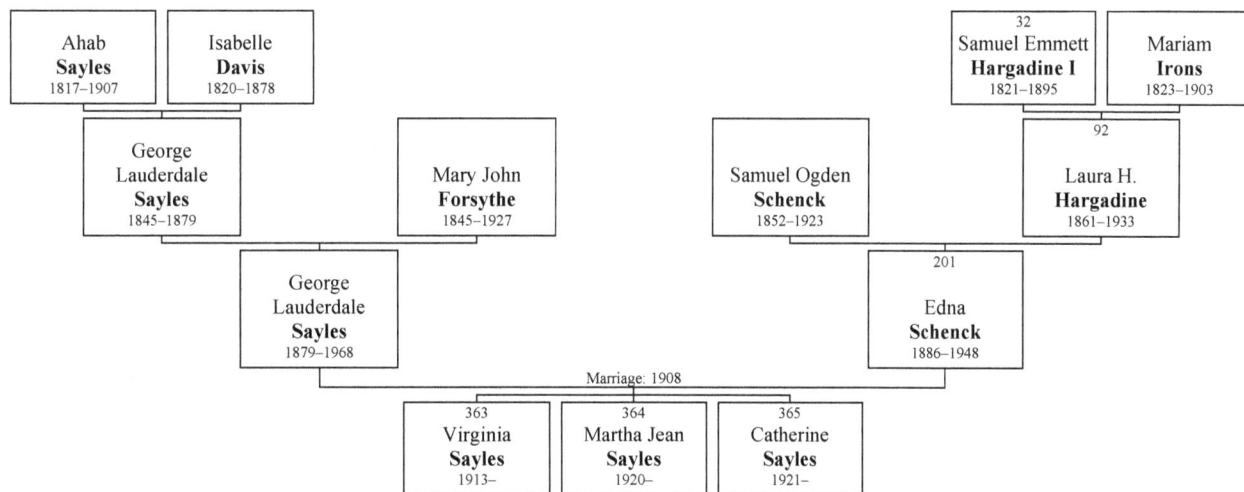

201.   **Edna Schenck** was born on Sunday, February 14, 1886, in Brookfield, Linn County, Missouri.[231] She was the daughter of Samuel Ogden Schenck and Laura H. Hargadine (92).

Edna died in Kansas City, Jackson County, Missouri, on August 19, 1948, at the age of 62.[231] She was buried in Floral Hills Cemetery, Kansas City, Jackson County, Missouri.[231]

At the age of 21, Edna married **George Lauderdale Sayles** on Wednesday, January 15, 1908, in Oklahoma City, Oklahoma County, Oklahoma, when he was 28 years old.[231] They had three daughters.

George Lauderdale was born in Winfield, Henry County, Iowa, on Saturday, June 28, 1879.[231] He was the son of George Lauderdale Sayles and Mary John Forsythe.

---

[231]   Neil Becker.FTW, Date of Import: May 19, 2004.

He worked as a salesman.[231] George Lauderdale reached 88 years of age and died in Kansas City, Jackson County, Missouri, on February 17, 1968.[231] He was buried on February 19, 1968, in Floral Hills Cemetery, Kansas City, Jackson County, Missouri (Find a Grave ID 198823447).[231]

Daughters of Edna Schenck and George Lauderdale Sayles:

+ 363   f   I. **Virginia Sayles** was born on December 29, 1913.[231]

+ 364   f   II. **Martha Jean Sayles** was born in Arkansas City, Cowley County, Kansas, on March 13, 1920.[231]

+ 365   f   III. **Catherine Sayles** was born on November 15, 1921.[231]

Family of Franklin Hargadine and Jennie Johnson

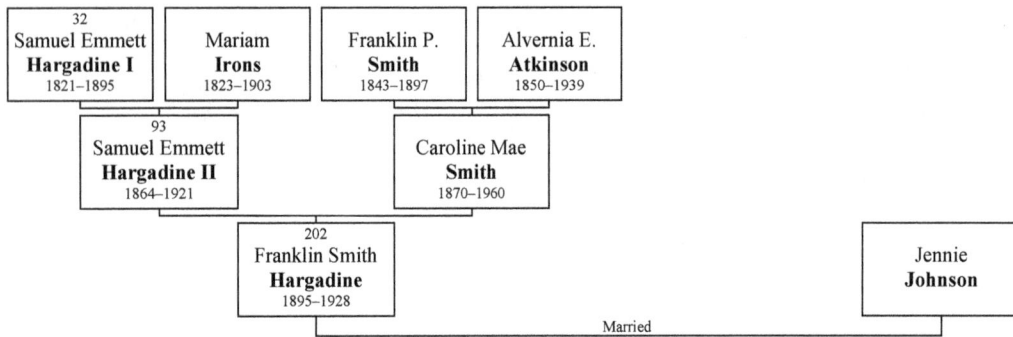

202.   **Franklin Smith Hargadine** was born on Monday, October 07, 1895, in Brookfield, Linn County, Missouri. He was the son of Samuel Emmett Hargadine II (93) and Caroline Mae Smith. He was also known as **Frank**.

Franklin Smith served in the military: WWI. He died in Gillette, Campbell County, Wyoming, on March 31, 1928, at the age of 32. His cause of death was gunshot to head. He was buried in Rose Hill Cemetery, Brookfield, Linn County, Missouri (Find a Grave ID 131196508).

He married **Jennie Johnson**.

Family of Samuel Hargadine and Viola Cox

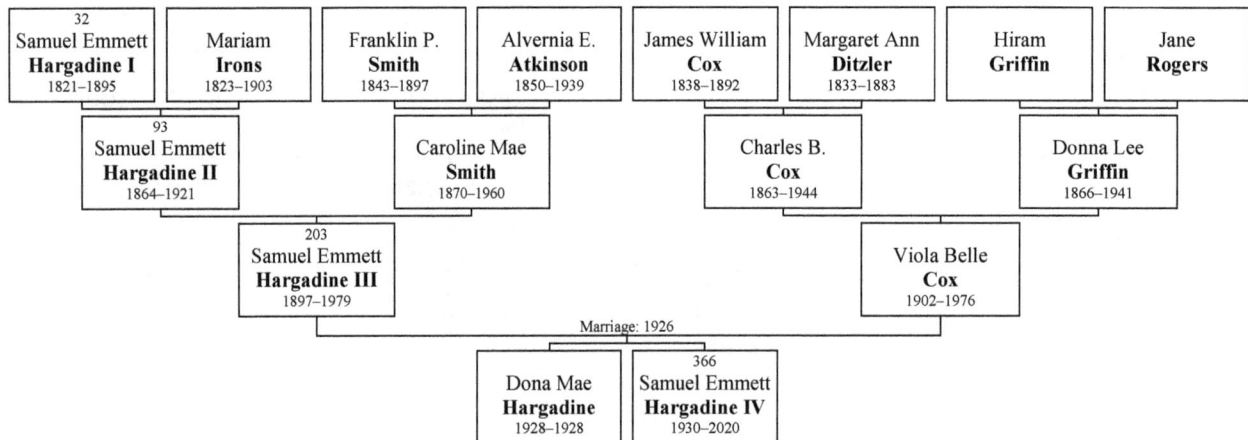

203. **Samuel Emmett Hargadine III** was born on Friday, April 23, 1897, in Brookfield, Linn County, Missouri. He was the son of Samuel Emmett Hargadine II (93) and Caroline Mae Smith.

Samuel Emmett served in the military: WWI Veteran. He died in Columbia, Boone County, Missouri, on April 06, 1979, at the age of 81. Samuel Emmett was buried in Bowling Green City Cemetery, Pike County, Missouri, on April 08, 1979 (Find a Grave ID 233241205).

At the age of 29, Samuel Emmett married **Viola Belle Cox** on Wednesday, June 02, 1926. By Rev. Smith in Columbia, Boone County, Missouri, when she was 24 years old. They had two children.

Viola Belle was born in Fayette, Howard County, Missouri, on Saturday, March 29, 1902. She was the daughter of Charles B. Cox and Donna Lee Griffin.

She worked as an Awarded Advanced Teachers Certificate for teaching piano on September 18, 1924. Viola Belle reached 74 years of age and died in Bowling Green, Pike County, Missouri, on July 04, 1976. She was buried on July 07, 1976, in Bowling Green City Cemetery, Pike County, Missouri (Find a Grave ID 217986780).

Children of Samuel Emmett Hargadine III and Viola Belle Cox:

	f	I.	**Dona Mae Hargadine** was born in Bowling Green, Pike County, Missouri, on September 14, 1928. She died in Bowling Green, Pike County, Missouri, on September 14, 1928. Her cause of death was: stillborn. She was buried in Bowling Green City Cemetery, Pike County, Missouri (Find a Grave ID 250051559).
+ 366	m	II.	**Samuel Emmett Hargadine IV** was born in Bowling Green, Pike County, Missouri, on June 05, 1930. He died in Saint Louis, Saint Louis County, Missouri, on June 27, 2020, at the age of 90. Samuel Emmett was buried in Memorial Gardens Cemetery, Bowling Green, Pike County, Missouri, on October 23, 2021 (Find a Grave ID 211927637).

Family of Herman Hargadine and Lola Armstrong

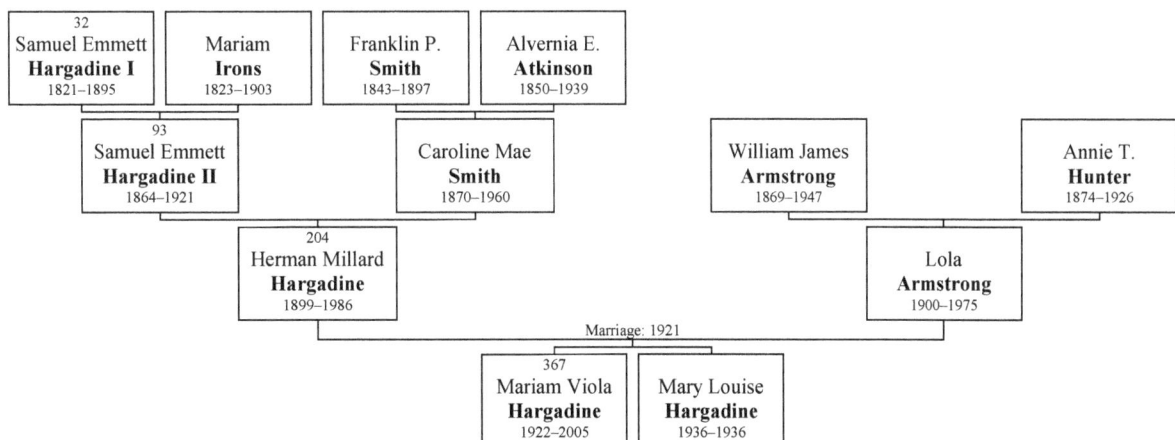

32 Samuel Emmett **Hargadine I** 1821–1895	Mariam **Irons** 1823–1903	Franklin P. **Smith** 1843–1897	Alvernia E. **Atkinson** 1850–1939	William James **Armstrong** 1869–1947	Annie T. **Hunter** 1874–1926

93 Samuel Emmett **Hargadine II** 1864–1921 — Caroline Mae **Smith** 1870–1960

Lola **Armstrong** 1900–1975

204 Herman Millard **Hargadine** 1899–1986

Marriage: 1921

367 Mariam Viola **Hargadine** 1922–2005	Mary Louise **Hargadine** 1936–1936

204. **Herman Millard Hargadine** was born on Sunday, April 23, 1899, in Brookfield, Linn County, Missouri. He was the son of Samuel Emmett Hargadine II (93) and Caroline Mae Smith.

Herman Millard died in Kansas City, Jackson County, Missouri, on November 22, 1986, at the age of 87. He was buried in Parklawn Memory Gardens Cemetery, Brookfield, Linn County, Missouri (Find a Grave ID 117726259).

At the age of 22, Herman Millard married **Lola Armstrong** on Monday, October 03, 1921, in Brookfield, Linn County, Missouri, when she was 20 years old. They had two daughters.

Lola was born in Purdin, Linn County, Missouri, on Wednesday, October 10, 1900. She was the daughter of William James Armstrong and Annie T. Hunter.

Lola reached 74 years of age and died in Brookfield, Linn County, Missouri, on September 14, 1975. She was buried on September 16, 1975, in Parklawn Memory Gardens Cemetery, Brookfield, Linn County, Missouri (Find a Grave ID 117726223).

Daughters of Herman Millard Hargadine and Lola Armstrong:

+ 367 f I. **Mariam Viola Hargadine** was born in Brookfield, Linn County, Missouri, on August 02, 1922. She died in Overland Park, Johnson County, Kansas, on June 26, 2005, at the age of 82. Mariam Viola was buried in Maple Hill Cemetery, Kansas City, Wyandotte County, Kansas, on June 29, 2005 (Find a Grave ID 71923221).

  f II. **Mary Louise Hargadine** was born in Brookfield, Linn County, Missouri, on August 03, 1936. She died in Brookfield, Linn County, Missouri, on August 03, 1936. Mary Louise was buried in Rose Hill Cemetery, Brookfield, Linn County, Missouri, on August 04, 1936 (Find a Grave ID 146950270).

William Hargadine

205. **William Andrew Hargadine** was born on Sunday, June 23, 1901, in Brookfield, Linn County, Missouri. He was the son of Samuel Emmett Hargadine II (93) and Caroline Mae Smith.

William Andrew died in Brookfield Nursing Center, Linn County Missouri, on May 29, 1994, at the age of 92. He was buried in Parklawn Memory Gardens Cemetery, Brookfield, Linn County, Missouri, on May 31, 1994 (Find a Grave ID 117747166).

Marriages with Jennie Mae Ogle and Mildred Juanita Batye (Page 246) are known.

Family of William Hargadine and Jennie Ogle

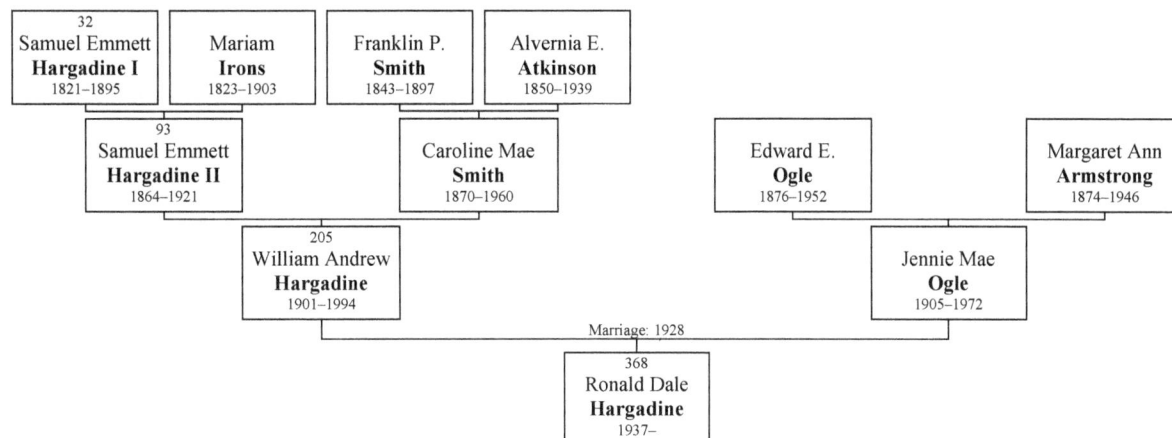

Here are the details about **William Andrew Hargadine's** first marriage, with Jennie Mae Ogle. You can read more about William Andrew on page 244.

At the age of 26, William Andrew Hargadine married **Jennie Mae Ogle** on Tuesday, March 20, 1928, in Brookfield, Linn County, Missouri, when she was 22 years old. They had one son.

Jennie Mae was born in Linn County, Missouri, on Tuesday, April 11, 1905.[232–234] She was the daughter of Edward E. Ogle and Margaret Ann Armstrong.

Jennie Mae reached 67 years of age and died in Brookfield, Linn County, Missouri, on May 06, 1972. She was buried in Parklawn Memory Gardens Cemetery, Brookfield, Linn County, Missouri (Find a Grave ID 117747080).

Son of William Andrew Hargadine and Jennie Mae Ogle:

+   368   m   I. **Ronald Dale Hargadine** was born on August 24, 1937.

Family of William Hargadine and Mildred Batye

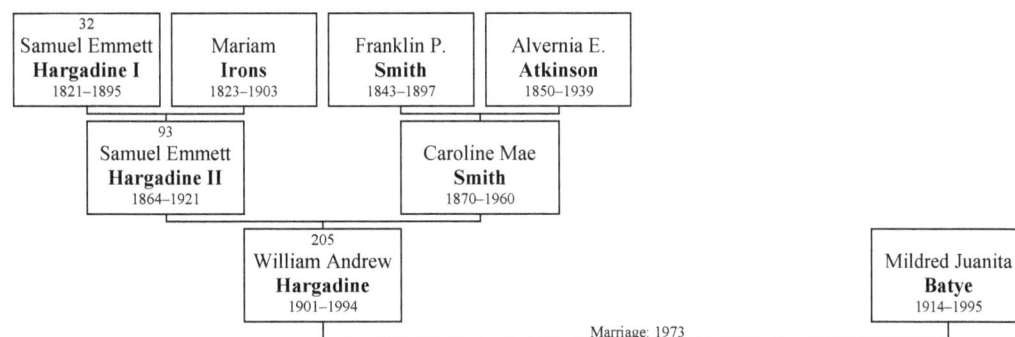

232   FamilySearch.org, United States Census, 1940, FamilySearch, "United States Census, 1940." <i>FamilySearch</i> (https://www.familysearch.org/ark:/61903/1:1:K77Q-ZR3 : Wed Nov 22 11:10:58 UTC 2023), Entry for William Hargadine and Jenny Hargadine, 1940.

233   FamilySearch.org, United States Census, 1910, FamilySearch, "United States Census, 1910." <i>FamilySearch</i> (https://www.familysearch.org/ark:/61903/1:1:M2B9-41H : Tue Oct 03 21:07:35 UTC 2023), Entry for Ed Ogle and Margret A Ogle, 1910.

234   FamilySearch.org, United States Census, 1920, FamilySearch, "United States Census, 1920." <i>FamilySearch</i> (https://www.familysearch.org/ark:/61903/1:1:M8CS-T38 : Fri Nov 10 07:09:10 UTC 2023), Entry for Edward Ogle and Margret Ogle, 1920.

Here are the details about **William Andrew Hargadine's** second marriage, with Mildred Juanita Batye. You can read more about William Andrew on page 244.

At the age of 71, William Andrew Hargadine married **Mildred Juanita Batye** on Tuesday, February 27, 1973, when she was 58 years old. Mildred Juanita was born in Chariton County, Missouri, on Monday, March 23, 1914.

She reached 81 years of age and died in Brookfield, Linn County, Missouri, on April 07, 1995. Mildred Juanita was buried in McCullough Cemetery, Triplett Township, Chariton County, Missouri (Find a Grave ID 31836099).

Family of Edwin Hargadine and Winifred Buswell

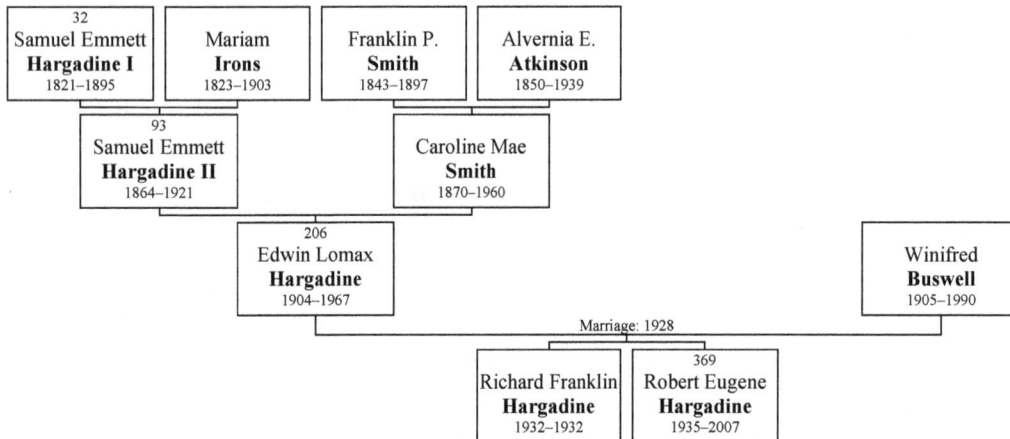

206. **Edwin Lomax Hargadine** was born on Monday, August 22, 1904, in Brookfield, Linn County, Missouri. He was the son of Samuel Emmett Hargadine II (93) and Caroline Mae Smith.

Edwin Lomax died in Brookfield, Linn County, Missouri, on December 30, 1967, at the age of 63. His cause of death wasa tractor accident. Edwin Lomax was buried in Parklawn Memory Gardens Cemetery, Brookfield, Linn County, Missouri, on January 02, 1968 (Find a Grave ID 117739893).

At the age of 23, Edwin Lomax married **Winifred Buswell** on Tuesday, March 20, 1928, when she was 23 years old. They had two sons.

Winifred was born in Brookfield, Linn County, Missouri, on Wednesday, February 08, 1905. She reached 85 years of age and died in Brookfield, Linn County, Missouri, on May 29, 1990. Winifred was buried in Parklawn Memory Gardens Cemetery, Brookfield, Linn County, Missouri (Find a Grave ID 117739141).

Sons of Edwin Lomax Hargadine and Winifred Buswell:

m   I. **Richard Franklin Hargadine** was born in Linn County, Missouri, on October 23, 1932. He died in Brussells, Lincoln County, Missouri, on November 03, 1932. His cause of death was cerebral hemorrhage. He was buried in Rose Hill Cemetery, Brookfield, Linn County, Missouri, on November 04, 1932 (Find a Grave ID 146977870).

+ 369 m II. **Robert Eugene Hargadine** was born in Brookfield, Linn County, Missouri, on July 25, 1935. He was also known as **Bob**.

Robert Eugene died in Pershing Memorial Hospital, Brookfield, Linn County, Missouri, on March 23, 2007, at the age of 71. His cause of death was cancer of the blood. Robert Eugene was buried in Parklawn Memory Gardens Cemetery, Brookfield, Linn County, Missouri, on March 26, 2007 (Find a Grave ID 155138339).

Family of Laura Hargadine and Paul Harbaugh

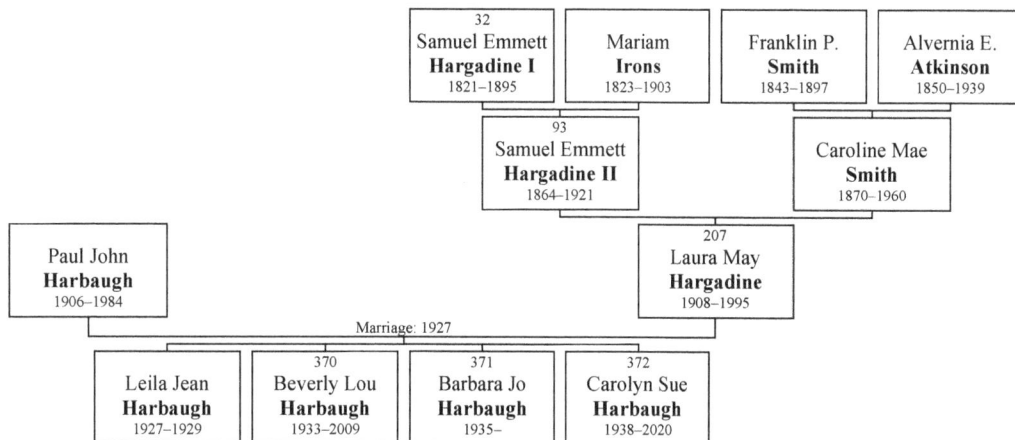

207. **Laura May Hargadine** was born on Saturday, September 12, 1908, in Brookfield, Linn County, Missouri. She was the daughter of Samuel Emmett Hargadine II (93) and Caroline Mae Smith.

Laura May died in Brookfield, Linn County, Missouri, on June 29, 1995, at the age of 86. She was buried in Laclede Cemetery, Laclede, Linn County, Missouri (Find a Grave ID 90566613).

At the age of 18, Laura May married **Paul John Harbaugh** on Thursday, January 20, 1927, when he was 20 years old. They had four daughters.

Paul John was born in Laclede, Linn County, Missouri, on Wednesday, February 28, 1906. He reached 78 years of age and died in Laclede, Linn County, Missouri, on August 23, 1984. Paul John was buried in Laclede Cemetery, Laclede, Linn County, Missouri (Find a Grave ID 90566585).

Daughters of Laura May Hargadine and Paul John Harbaugh:

f I. **Leila Jean Harbaugh** was born in Brookfield, Linn County, Missouri, on October 09, 1927. She died in Brookfield, Linn County, Missouri, on February 10, 1929, at the age of 1. Her cause of death was acute meningitis. She was buried in Rose Hill Cemetery, Brookfield, Linn County, Missouri (Find a Grave ID 146981388).

+ 370 f II. **Beverly Lou Harbaugh** was born on November 16, 1933. She died on April 10, 2009, at the age of 75. Beverly Lou was buried in Laclede Cemetery, Laclede, Linn County, Missouri (Find a Grave ID 85610180).

+   371   f   III. **Barbara Jo Harbaugh** was born on October 23, 1935.

+   372   f   IV. **Carolyn Sue Harbaugh** was born in Laclede, Linn County, Missouri, on January 24, 1938. She died in Saint Peters, St. Charles County, Missouri, on December 19, 2020, at the age of 82. Carolyn Sue was buried in Jefferson Barracks National Cemetery, Lemay, St. Louis County, Missouri, on December 29, 2020 (Find a Grave ID 220130791).

Family of Elva Carson and Edward O'Day

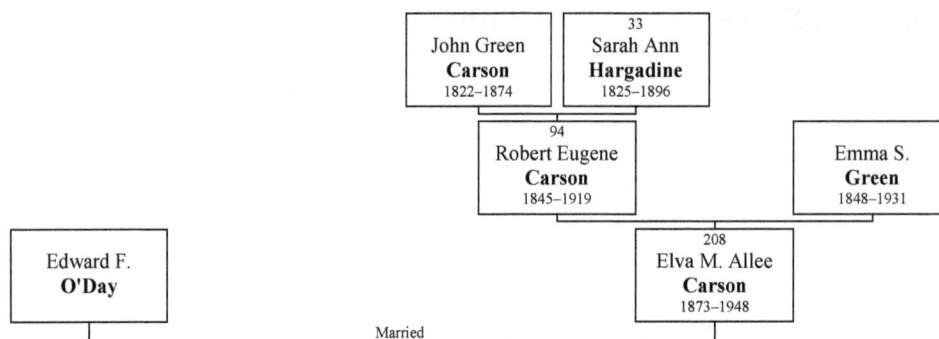

208.   **Elva M. Allee Carson** was born in 1873 in Little Creek, Kent County, Delaware. She was the daughter of Robert Eugene Carson (94) and Emma S. Green. She was also known as **Annie**.

Elva M. Allee died in Camden, Kent County, Delaware, on May 12, 1948, at the age of 75. She was buried in Odd Fellows Cemetery, Camden, Kent County, Delaware (Find a Grave ID 111024276).

She married **Edward F. O'Day**. They had no children.

Family of John Carson and Harriett Buckson

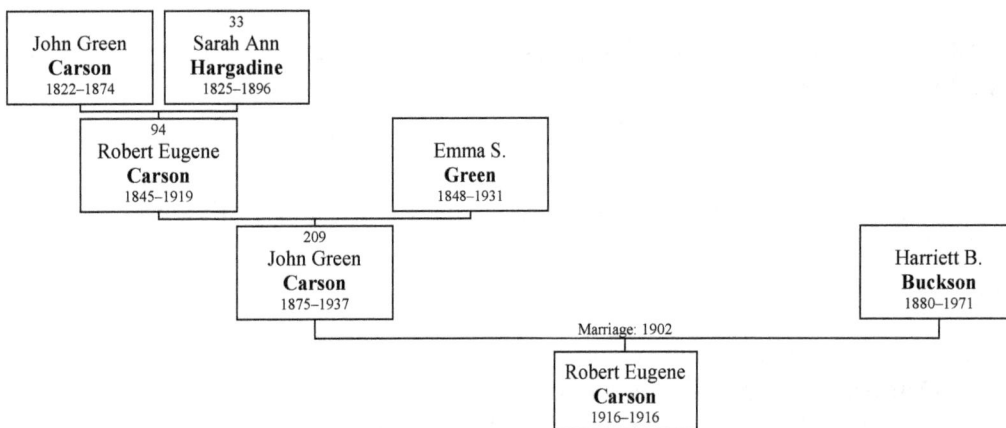

209.   **John Green Carson** was born on Friday, June 18, 1875. He was the son of Robert Eugene Carson (94) and Emma S. Green.

John Green died in Dover, Kent County, Delaware, on April 18, 1937, at the age of 61. His cause of death was an automobile accident. John Green was buried in Lakeside Cemetery, Dover, Kent County, Delaware (Find a Grave ID 7588801).

At the age of 26, John Green married **Harriett B. Buckson** on Wednesday, January 01, 1902, in Little Creek, Kent County, Delaware, when she was 21 years old. They had one son.

Harriett B. was born in Little Creek, Kent County, Delaware, on Saturday, May 15, 1880. She was also known as **Hattie**.

Harriett B. reached 91 years of age and died in Dover, Kent County, Delaware, on December 14, 1971. She was buried in Lakeside Cemetery, Dover, Kent County, Delaware (Find a Grave ID 7588797). They had seven children.

Son of John Green Carson and Harriett B. Buckson:

m   I. **Robert Eugene Carson** was born in Little Creek, Kent County, Delaware, on March 23, 1916. He died in Dover, Kent County, Delaware, on May 26, 1916. Robert Eugene was buried in Lakeside Cemetery, Dover, Kent County, Delaware (Find a Grave ID 55245985).

Family of Elizabeth Carson and Walter Muncy

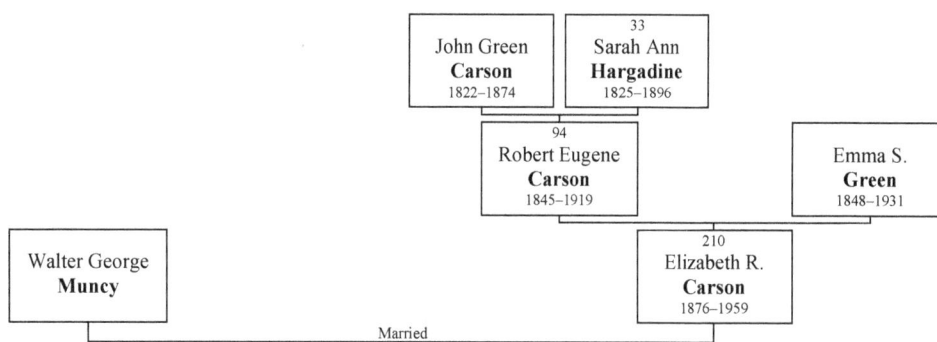

```
                                    ┌──────────┬──────────┐
                                    │John Green│    33    │
                                    │  Carson  │ Sarah Ann│
                                    │1822–1874 │ Hargadine│
                                    │          │1825–1896 │
                                    └──────────┴──────────┘
                                          │
                                    ┌──────────┐            ┌──────────┐
                                    │    94    │            │ Emma S.  │
                                    │  Robert  │            │  Green   │
                                    │  Eugene  │            │1848–1931 │
                                    │  Carson  │            │          │
                                    │1845–1919 │            └──────────┘
                                    └──────────┘
                                          │
                ┌──────────┐        ┌──────────┐
                │  Walter  │        │   210    │
                │  George  │        │Elizabeth │
                │  Muncy   │        │   R.     │
                │          │        │ Carson   │
                └──────────┘        │1876–1959 │
                      └────Married──┴──────────┘
```

210.   **Elizabeth R. Carson** was born on Thursday, December 21, 1876, in Little Creek, Kent County, Delaware. She was the daughter of Robert Eugene Carson (94) and Emma S. Green.

Elizabeth R. died on May 28, 1959, at the age of 82. She was buried in Lakeside Cemetery, Dover, Kent County, Delaware (Find a Grave ID 7669654).

She married **Walter George Muncy**. They had no children.

Family of Sarah Carson and William Paradee

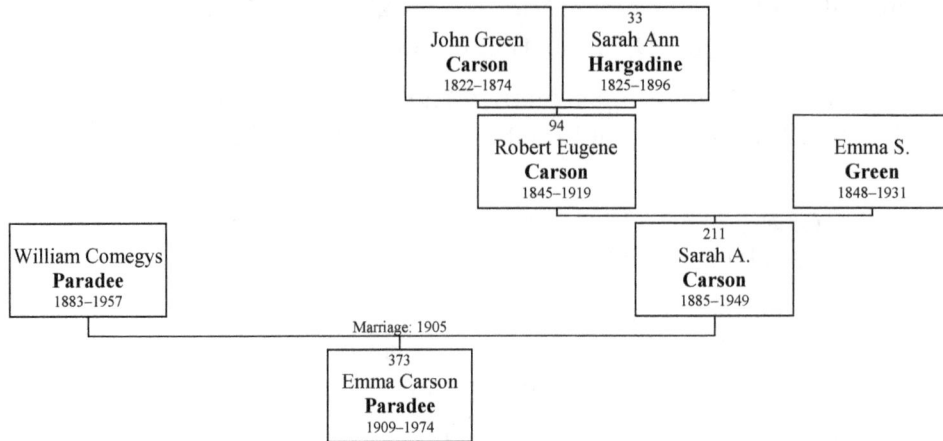

211.   **Sarah A. Carson** was born in May 1885. She was the daughter of Robert Eugene Carson (94) and Emma S. Green.

Sarah A. died in 1949 at the age of 63. She was buried in Lakeside Cemetery, Dover, Kent County, Delaware (Find a Grave ID 7677350).

Sarah A. married **William Comegys Paradee** in 1905. They had one daughter.

William Comegys was born on Monday, July 09, 1883. He reached 73 years of age and died in 1957. William Comegys was buried in Lakeside Cemetery, Dover, Kent County, Delaware (Find a Grave ID 7677354).

Daughter of Sarah A. Carson and William Comegys Paradee:

+   373   f   I. **Emma Carson Paradee** was born on November 26, 1909. She died in Frederica, Kent County, Delaware, in November 1974 at the age of 64. Emma Carson was buried in Barratts Chapel Cemetery, Frederica, Kent County, Delaware (Find a Grave ID 30369051).

Family of Matilda Carson and James Coudright

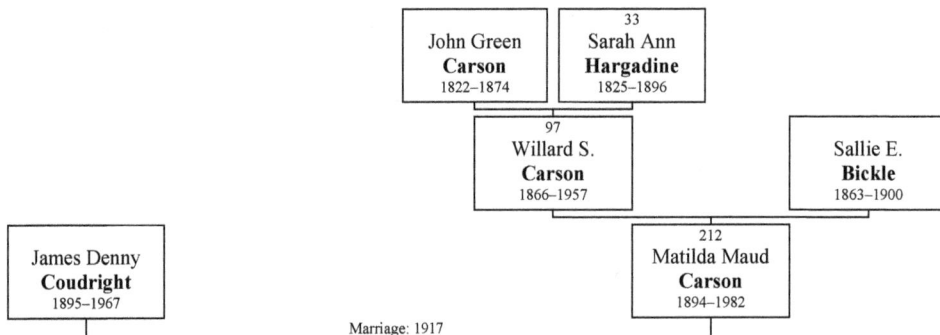

212. **Matilda Maud Carson** was born on Sunday, June 03, 1894, in Delaware, USA.[235] She was the daughter of Willard S. Carson (97) and Sallie E. Bickle.

Matilda Maud died in Dover, Kent County, Delaware, on May 02, 1982, at the age of 87.[235] She was buried in Lakeside Cemetery, Dover, Kent County, Delaware (Find a Grave ID 7596828).

At the age of 23, Matilda Maud married **James Denny Coudright** on Saturday, December 08, 1917, in Wilmington, New Castle County, Delaware, when he was 22 years old.[235] James Denny was born in Camden, Kent County, Delaware, on Wednesday, January 23, 1895.[235]

He reached 72 years of age and died on January 25, 1967.[235] James Denny was buried in Lakeside Cemetery, Dover, Kent County, Delaware (Find a Grave ID 7596823).[235]

---

235   Ancestry.com, Public Member Trees (Provo, UT, USA, Ancestry.com Operations, Inc., 2006), Ancestry.com, Record for Maude Carson. https://search.ancestry.co.uk/cgi-bin/sse.dll?db=1030&h=122145638684&indiv=try.

6th Generation

Family of Joseph Bruffey and Callie Tucker

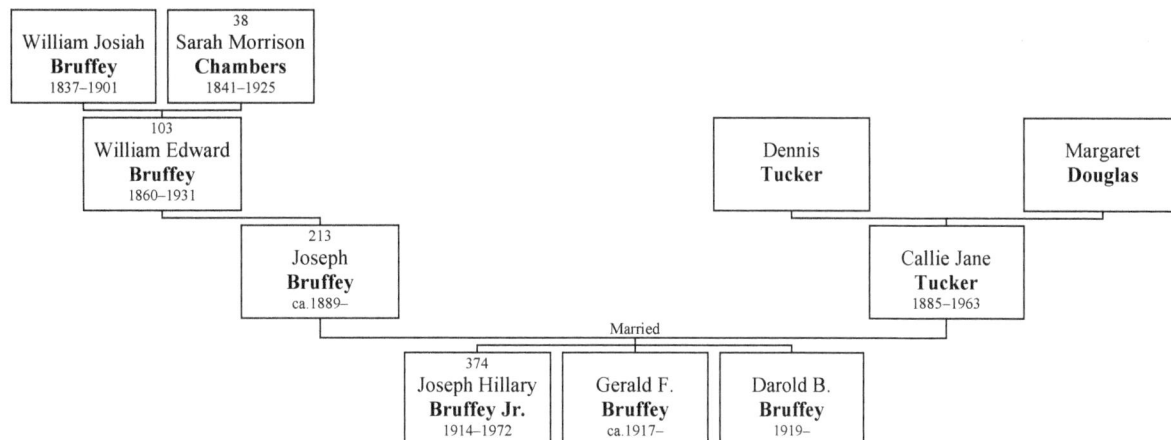

213. **Joseph Bruffey** was born about 1889 in Iowa, USA.[236] He was the son of William Edward Bruffey (103).

He married **Callie Jane Tucker**. They had three sons.

Callie Jane was born in Texas County, Missouri, on Friday, June 12, 1885.[237] She was the daughter of Dennis Tucker and Margaret Douglas.

Callie Jane reached 77 years of age and died at Burge Protestant Hospital in Springfield, Greene County, Missouri, on June 03, 1963. Her cause of death was carcinoma of the breast. Callie Jane was buried in Seymour Masonic Cemetery, Seymour, Webster County, Missouri (Find a Grave ID 27332351).

Sons of Joseph Bruffey and Callie Jane Tucker:

+ 374   m   I. **Joseph Hillary Bruffey Jr.** was born in Missouri, USA, on November 15, 1914.[238] He died on October 15, 1972, at the age of 57. Joseph Hillary was buried in Howell Memorial Park Cemetery, Pomona, Howell County, Missouri (Find a Grave ID 126446769).

       m   II. **Gerald F. Bruffey** was born in Missouri, USA, about 1917.[239]

       m   III. **Darold B. Bruffey** was born in Missouri, USA, in 1919.[240]

---

236   Age given as 31 years in 1920 Missouri Soundex.

237   Age given as 34 years in 1920 Missouri Soundex.

238   Age given as 5 years in 1920 Missouri Soundex.

239   Age given as 3 years in 1920 Missouri Soundex.

240   Age given as 10 months in 1920 Missouri Soundex.

Family of Zella Rowland and Jesse Reeves

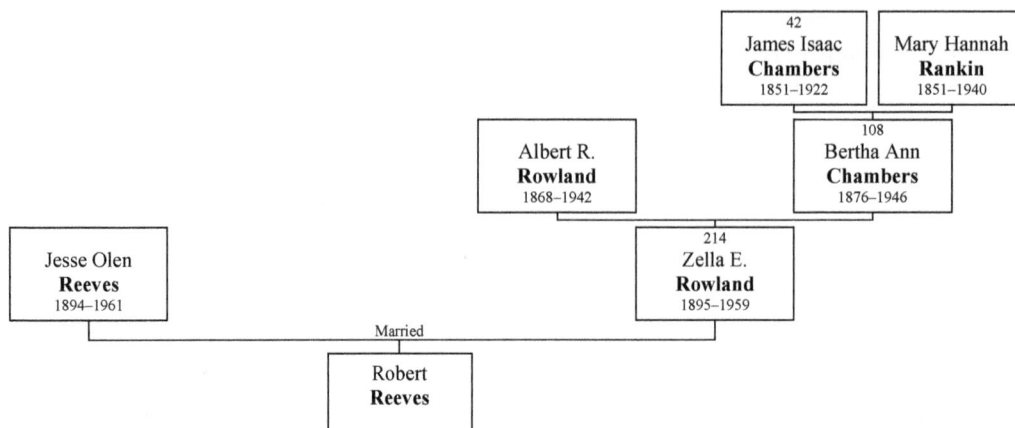

```
                                              ┌──────────────┬──────────────┐
                                              │      42      │              │
                                              │ James Isaac  │ Mary Hannah  │
                                              │  Chambers    │   Rankin     │
                                              │  1851–1922   │  1851–1940   │
                          ┌──────────────┐    └──────────────┴──────────────┘
                          │  Albert R.   │    ┌──────────────┐
                          │  Rowland     │    │     108      │
                          │  1868–1942   │    │  Bertha Ann  │
                          └──────────────┘    │  Chambers    │
       ┌──────────────┐                       │  1876–1946   │
       │ Jesse Olen   │                       └──────────────┘
       │  Reeves      │          ┌──────────────┐
       │  1894–1961   │          │     214      │
       └──────────────┘          │  Zella E.    │
                                 │  Rowland     │
                                 │  1895–1959   │
                        Married  └──────────────┘
              ┌──────────────┐
              │   Robert     │
              │   Reeves     │
              └──────────────┘
```

214.   **Zella E. Rowland** was born on Wednesday, June 12, 1895, in Fayette County, Iowa. She was the daughter of Albert R. Rowland and Bertha Ann Chambers (108).

Zella E. died in Chariton, Lucas County, Iowa, on May 24, 1959, at the age of 63. She was buried in Graceland Cemetery, Knoxville, Marion County, Iowa (Find a Grave ID 132575533).

She married **Jesse Olen Reeves**. They had one son.

Jesse Olen was born in Attica, Marion County, Iowa, on Tuesday, May 29, 1894. He reached 66 years of age and died in Knoxville, Marion County, Iowa, on May 24, 1961. Jesse Olen was buried in Graceland Cemetery, Knoxville, Marion County, Iowa (Find a Grave ID 132575509).

Son of Zella E. Rowland and Jesse Olen Reeves:

    m   I. **Robert Reeves**.

Family of Ferne Rowland and Frank Etcher

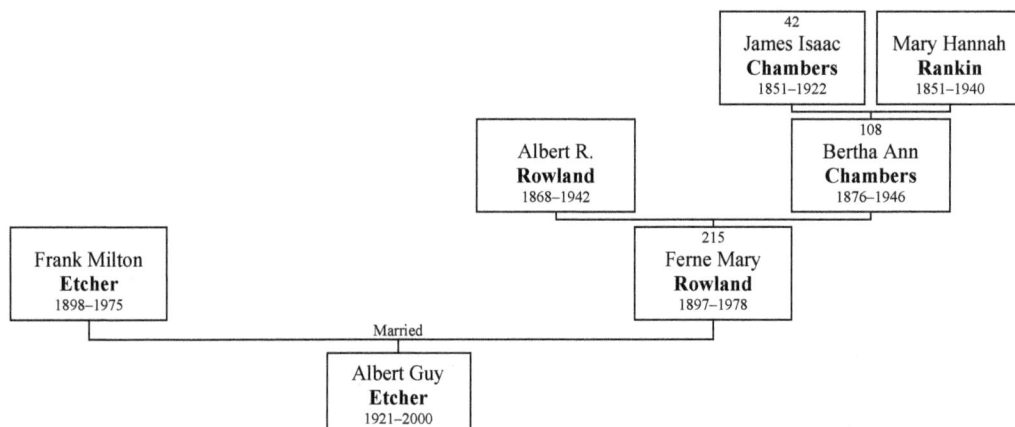

```
                                              ┌──────────────┬──────────────┐
                                              │      42      │              │
                                              │ James Isaac  │ Mary Hannah  │
                                              │  Chambers    │   Rankin     │
                                              │  1851–1922   │  1851–1940   │
                          ┌──────────────┐    └──────────────┴──────────────┘
                          │  Albert R.   │    ┌──────────────┐
                          │  Rowland     │    │     108      │
                          │  1868–1942   │    │  Bertha Ann  │
                          └──────────────┘    │  Chambers    │
       ┌──────────────┐                       │  1876–1946   │
       │ Frank Milton │                       └──────────────┘
       │  Etcher      │          ┌──────────────┐
       │  1898–1975   │          │     215      │
       └──────────────┘          │  Ferne Mary  │
                                 │  Rowland     │
                                 │  1897–1978   │
                        Married  └──────────────┘
              ┌──────────────┐
              │ Albert Guy   │
              │   Etcher     │
              │  1921–2000   │
              └──────────────┘
```

215.   **Ferne Mary Rowland** was born on Thursday, April 01, 1897, in Fayette County, Iowa. She was the daughter of Albert R. Rowland and Bertha Ann Chambers (108).

Ferne Mary died in Albia, Monroe County, Iowa, on March 08, 1978, at the age of 80. She was buried in Woodlawn Cemetery, Lovilia, Monroe County, Iowa (Find a Grave ID 62739070).

She married **Frank Milton Etcher**. They had one son.

Frank Milton was born in Monroe, Jasper County, Iowa, on Monday, September 19, 1898. He reached 77 years of age and died in Albia, Monroe County, Iowa, on December 21, 1975. Frank Milton was buried in Woodlawn Cemetery, Lovilia, Monroe County, Iowa (Find a Grave ID 62739071).

Son of Ferne Mary Rowland and Frank Milton Etcher:

m   I. **Albert Guy Etcher** was born in Lovilia, Monroe County, Iowa, on January 28, 1921. He died in Des Moines, Polk County, Iowa, on March 03, 2000, at the age of 79. Albert Guy was buried in Woodlawn Cemetery, Lovilia, Monroe County, Iowa (Find a Grave ID 62739069).

Family of Garold Rowland and Majorie Mitchell

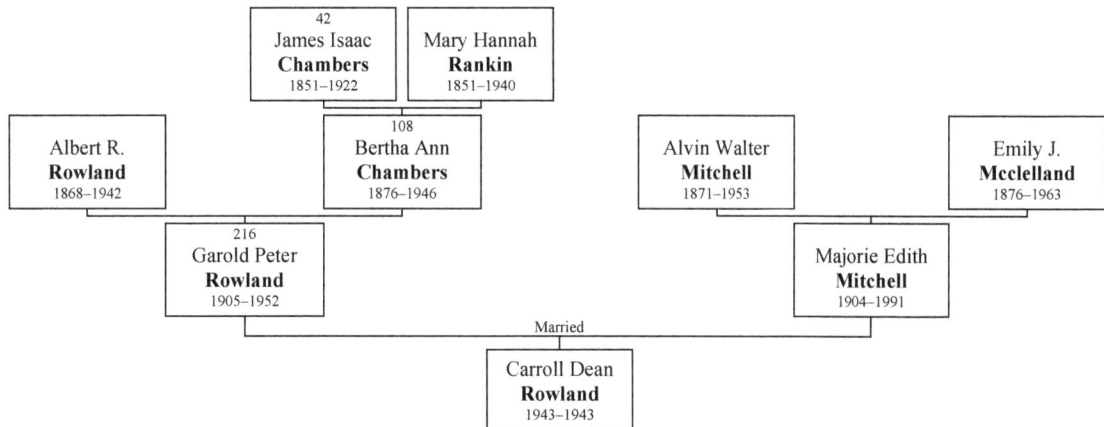

216. **Garold Peter Rowland** was born on Monday, May 22, 1905, in Dundee, Delaware County, Iowa.[241] He was the son of Albert R. Rowland and Bertha Ann Chambers (108).

Garold Peter died in Knoxville, Marion County, Iowa, on June 03, 1952, at the age of 47.[241] He was buried in Zion Cemetery, Pershing, Marion County, Iowa (Find a Grave ID 54506083).

He married **Majorie Edith Mitchell**. They had one son.

Majorie Edith was born in Yorktown, Page County, Iowa, on Sunday, January 10, 1904.[241] She was the daughter of Alvin Walter Mitchell and Emily J. Mcclelland.

Majorie Edith reached 87 years of age and died in Knoxville, Marion County, Iowa, on June 30, 1991. She was buried in Zion Cemetery, Pershing, Marion County, Iowa (Find a Grave ID 54505921).

---

[241]   Tombstone in Zion Chapel Cemetery.

Son of Garold Peter Rowland and Majorie Edith Mitchell:

m   I. **Carroll Dean Rowland** was born on November 28, 1943.[241] He died on November 29, 1943.[241] Carroll Dean was buried in Zion Cemetery, Pershing, Marion County, Iowa (Find a Grave ID 117593982).

Family of James Rowland and Myreeta Harvey

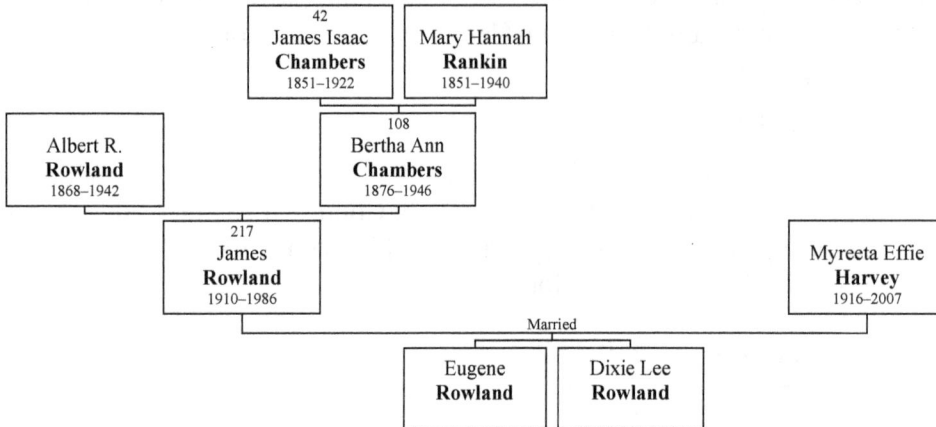

217. **James Rowland** was born on Thursday, March 10, 1910, in Knoxville, Marion County, Iowa. He was the son of Albert R. Rowland and Bertha Ann Chambers (108). He was also known as **Lee**.

James died in Knoxville, Marion County, Iowa, on January 07, 1986, at the age of 75. He was buried in Graceland Cemetery, Knoxville, Marion County, Iowa (Find a Grave ID 133101145).

He married **Myreeta Effie Harvey**. They had two children.

Myreeta Effie was born in Marion County, Iowa, on Thursday, July 27, 1916. She reached 90 years of age and died in Knoxville, Marion County, Iowa, on January 22, 2007. Myreeta Effie was buried in Graceland Cemetery, Knoxville, Marion County, Iowa (Find a Grave ID 133101161).

Children of James Rowland and Myreeta Effie Harvey:

m   I. **Eugene Rowland**.

f   II. **Dixie Lee Rowland**.

Annie Chambers

218. **Annie Charlene Chambers** was born on Friday, October 25, 1912, in Indiana Township, Marion County, Iowa.[242] She was the daughter of Cameron Hestwood Chambers (111) and Susky Sara Woody.

---

[242]   Marion County, Iowa Birth Records.

Annie Charlene died in Palisade, Mesa County, Colorado, on August 18, 2002, at the age of 89. She was buried in Memorial Gardens, Grand Junction, Mesa County, Colorado (Find a Grave ID 19231440).

Marriages with Titus Albert Giebler and Kenneth Bernard Lilly (Page 258) are known.

Family of Annie Chambers and Titus Giebler

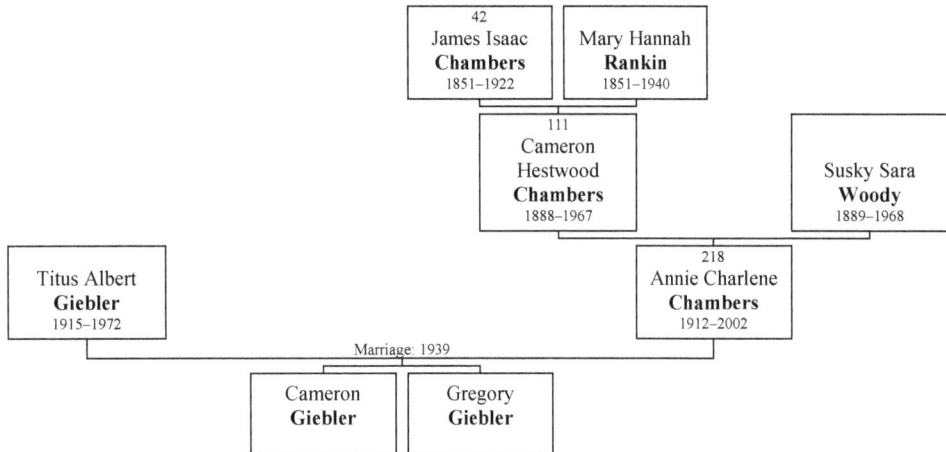

Here are the details about **Annie Charlene Chambers's** first marriage, with Titus Albert Giebler. You can read more about Annie Charlene on page 256.

Annie Charlene Chambers married **Titus Albert Giebler** in 1939. They had two sons.

Titus Albert was born in Kit Carson, Cheyenne County, Colorado, on Monday, January 04, 1915. He reached 57 years of age and died in Rifle, Garfield County, Colorado, in April 1972. Titus Albert was buried in Memorial Gardens, Grand Junction, Mesa County, Colorado (Find a Grave ID 16481856).

Sons of Annie Charlene Chambers and Titus Albert Giebler:

m   I. **Cameron Giebler** was born in Grand Junction, Mesa County, Colorado.

m   II. **Gregory Giebler** was born in Grand Junction, Mesa County, Colorado.

Family of Annie Chambers and Kenneth Lilly

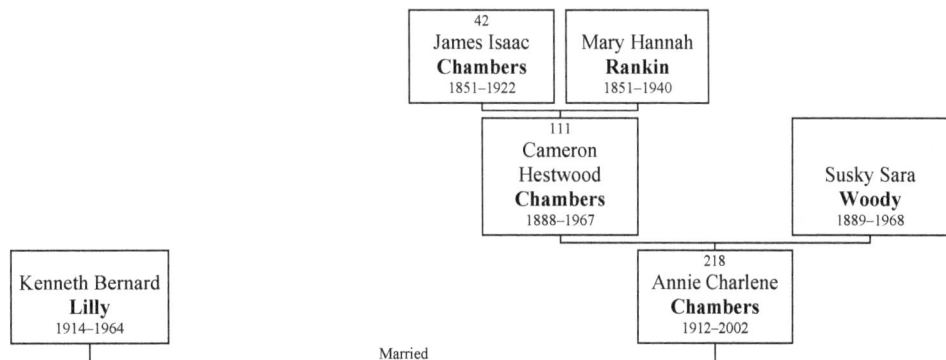

Here are the details about **Annie Charlene Chambers's** second marriage, with Kenneth Bernard Lilly. You can read more about Annie Charlene on page 256.

Annie Charlene Chambers married **Kenneth Bernard Lilly**. Kenneth Bernard was born in Whiting, Monona County, Iowa, on Wednesday, March 18, 1914.

He reached 50 years of age and died in Clayton County, Georgia, on June 29, 1964. Kenneth Bernard was buried in Masonic Cemetery, Des Moines, Polk County, Iowa (Find a Grave ID 87407244).

Family of Orval Chambers and Goldie Furgison

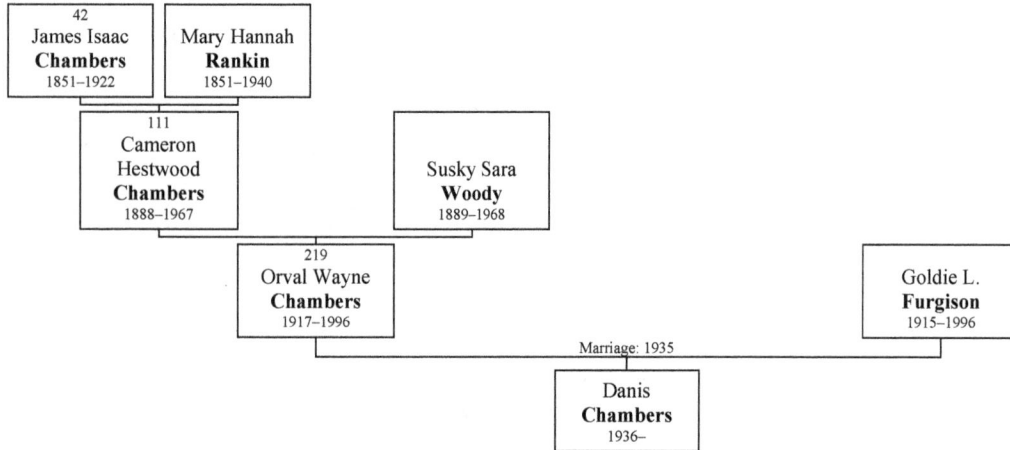

219. **Orval Wayne Chambers** was born on Monday, August 13, 1917, in Clay Township, Marion County, Iowa.[243] He was the son of Cameron Hestwood Chambers (111) and Susky Sara Woody.

Orval Wayne died in Clinton, Clinton County, Iowa, on October 28, 1996, at the age of 79. He was buried in Miles Cemetery, Miles, Jackson County, Iowa (Find a Grave ID 64850883).

At the age of 17, Orval Wayne married **Goldie L. Furgison** on Wednesday, May 22, 1935, in Oskaloosa, Mahaska County, Iowa, when she was 19 years old. They had one daughter.

Goldie L. was born in Lynnville, Jasper County, Iowa, on Saturday, September 11, 1915. She reached 80 years of age and died in Pella, Marion County, Iowa, on June 11, 1996. Goldie L. was buried in Ollie Cemetery, Ollie, Keokuk County, Iowa (Find a Grave ID 59894821).

Daughter of Orval Wayne Chambers and Goldie L. Furgison:

    f   I. **Danis Chambers** was born on March 01, 1936.

---

243   Marion County, Iowa Birth Records.

Family of Lawrence Chambers and Johanna Myre

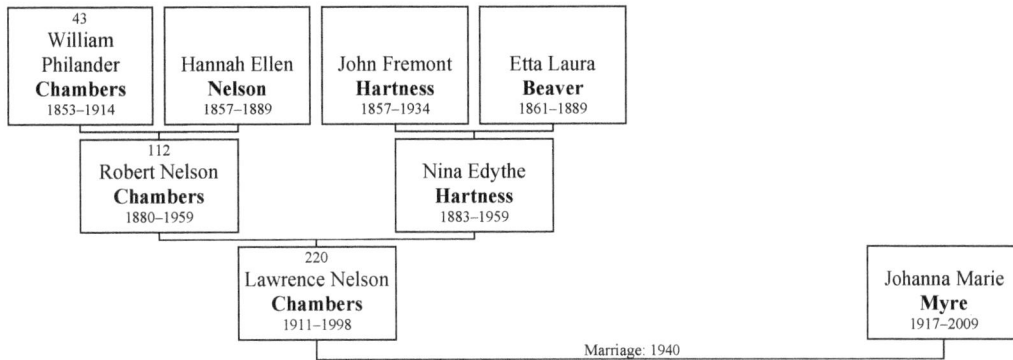

220. **Lawrence Nelson Chambers** was born on Saturday, March 04, 1911, in Knoxville, Marion County, Iowa.[244] He was the son of Robert Nelson Chambers (112) and Nina Edythe Hartness.

Lawrence Nelson died in Davenport, Scott County, Iowa, on February 26, 1998, at the age of 86.[245] His cause of death was heart attack. Lawrence Nelson was buried in Graceland Cemetery, Knoxville, Marion County, Iowa (Find a Grave ID 135668388).

At the age of 29, Lawrence Nelson married **Johanna Marie Myre** on Saturday, September 07, 1940, in Pekin, Tazewell County, Illinois, when she was 23 years old.[246] Johanna Marie was born in Pekin, Tazewell County, Illinois, on Tuesday, August 14, 1917.[246]

She reached 91 years of age and died in Davenport, Scott County, Iowa, on June 19, 2009. Johanna Marie was buried in Graceland Cemetery, Knoxville, Marion County, Iowa (Find a Grave ID 135668408).

Family of Mary Chambers and Robert Kaylor

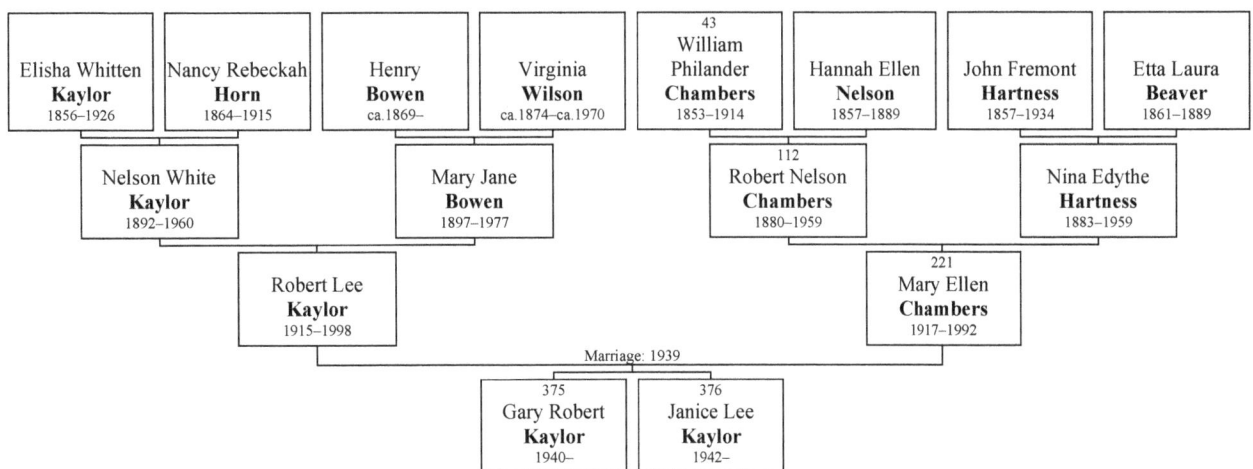

---

244   Lawrence N. Chambers.

245   Attended Funeral.

246   Marie Myre Chambers.

221. **Mary Ellen Chambers** was born on Saturday, May 12, 1917, in Marion County, Iowa.[247] She was the daughter of Robert Nelson Chambers (112) and Nina Edythe Hartness.

Mary Ellen died in Roanoke, Roanoke County, Virginia, on September 12, 1992, at the age of 75.[248] She was buried in Blue Ridge Memorial Gardens, Roanoke, Roanoke County, Virginia (Find a Grave ID 137405508).

At the age of 22, Mary Ellen married **Robert Lee Kaylor** on Friday, December 29, 1939, in Santa Anna, Orange County, California, when he was 24 years old.[249] They had two children.

Robert Lee was born in Buchanan County, Virginia, on Wednesday, June 09, 1915.[250] He was the son of Nelson White Kaylor and Mary Jane Bowen.

Robert Lee reached 82 years of age and died in Roanoke County, Virginia, on May 05, 1998.[248] He was buried in Blue Ridge Memorial Gardens, Roanoke, Roanoke County, Virginia (Find a Grave ID 137405493).

Children of Mary Ellen Chambers and Robert Lee Kaylor:

+ 375 m I. **Gary Robert Kaylor** was born in Clinchco, Dickenson County, Virginia, on December 02, 1940.[251]

+ 376 f II. **Janice Lee Kaylor** was born in Jefferson Hospital, Roanoke, Virginia, on May 08, 1942.[250]

Family of Arlen Chambers and Evelynne Parker

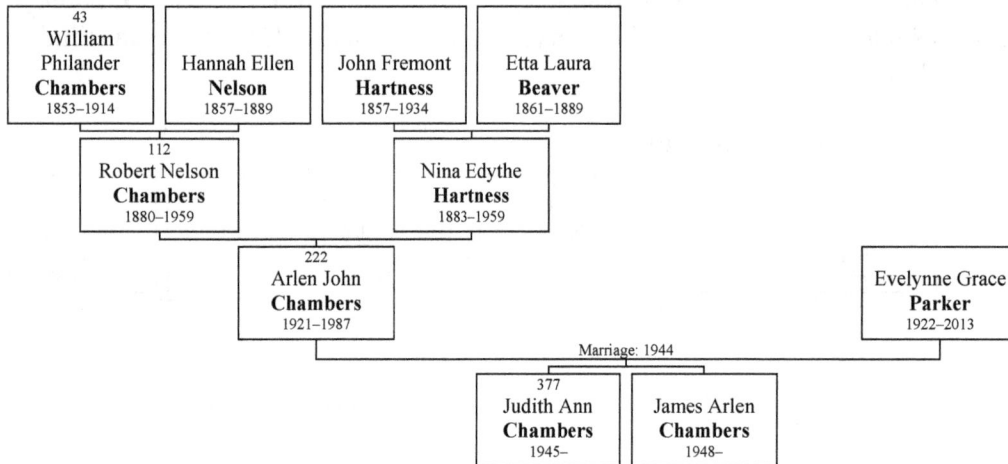

222. **Arlen John Chambers** was born on Monday, August 08, 1921, in Marion County, Iowa.[252] He was the son of Robert Nelson Chambers (112) and Nina Edythe Hartness.

---

247   Mary Ellen Chambers.

248   Death Certificate.

249   Robert Lee Kaylor.

250   Birth Certificate.

251   Virginia Birth Certificate.

252   Lawrence N. Chambers and Ruth Hawks Wright.

Arlen John died in Hastings, Barry County, Michigan, on January 24, 1987, at the age of 65.[253] His cause of death was: suicide-gunshot. Arlen John was buried in Riverside Cemetery, Hastings, Barry County, Michigan (Find a Grave ID 22096208).

At the age of 22, Arlen John married **Evelynne Grace Parker** on Saturday, June 10, 1944, in Hastings, Barry County, Michigan, when she was 21 years old.[252] They had two children.

Evelynne Grace was born in Flint, Genesee County, Michigan, on Sunday, August 20, 1922.[254] She reached 90 years of age and died in Hastings, Barry County, Michigan, on February 14, 2013. Evelynne Grace was buried in Riverside Cemetery, Hastings, Barry County, Michigan (Find a Grave ID 105272245).

Children of Arlen John Chambers and Evelynne Grace Parker:

+ 377   f   I. **Judith Ann Chambers** was born on March 29, 1945.

      m   II. **James Arlen Chambers** was born on November 17, 1948.[252]

Family of Laura Chambers and Charles Calhoun

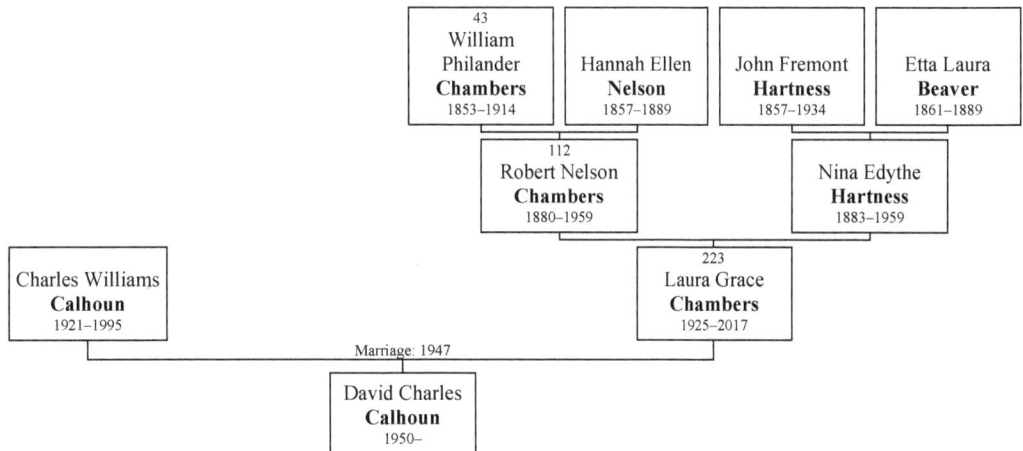

223.   **Laura Grace Chambers** was born on Tuesday, November 24, 1925, in Knoxville Township, Marion County, Iowa.[255] She was the daughter of Robert Nelson Chambers (112) and Nina Edythe Hartness.

Laura Grace died in Anamosa, Jones County, Iowa, on July 11, 2017, at the age of 91. She was buried in Graceland Cemetery, Knoxville, Marion County, Iowa (Find a Grave ID 181280153).

At the age of 21, Laura Grace married **Charles Williams Calhoun** on Saturday, April 12, 1947, in Knoxville, Marion County, Iowa, when he was 26 years old.[256] They had one son.

---

253   His wife.

254   Lawrence Chambers from his father Robert Nelson Chambers.

255   Birth Certificate.

256   Lawrence N. Chambers and Ruth Hawks Wright.

Charles Williams was born in Melcher, Marion County, Iowa, on Wednesday, February 09, 1921. He reached 74 years of age and died in Anamosa, Jones County, Iowa, on December 24, 1995.

Son of Laura Grace Chambers and Charles Williams Calhoun:

> m   I. **David Charles Calhoun** was born in Estherville, Emmet County, Iowa, on November 08, 1950.[257]

Family of Gail Chambers and Irvin Moritz

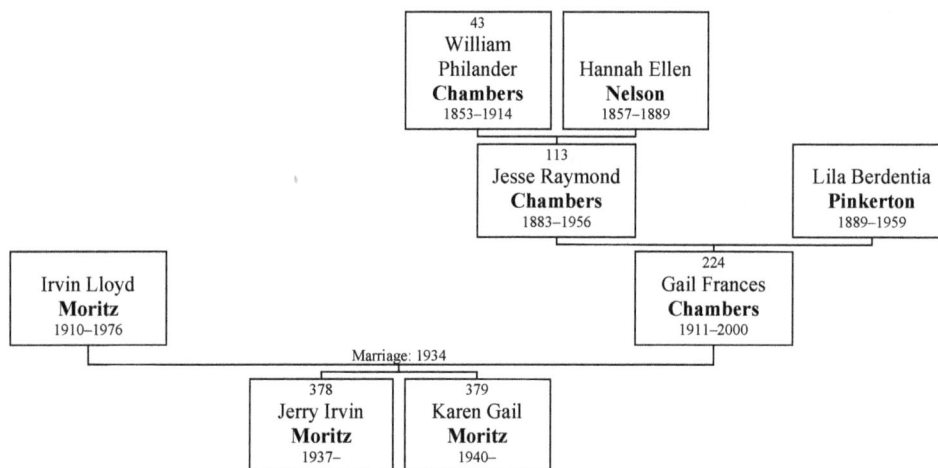

224.   **Gail Frances Chambers** was born on Friday, June 30, 1911, in Alliance, Box Butte County, Nebraska.[258] She was the daughter of Jesse Raymond Chambers (113) and Lila Berdentia Pinkerton.

Gail Frances died on November 04, 2000, at the age of 89. She was buried in Loveland Burial Park, Loveland, Larimer County, Colorado (Find a Grave ID 154680889).

At the age of 22, Gail Frances married **Irvin Lloyd Moritz** on Sunday, April 15, 1934, in Rushville, Sheridan County, Nebraska, when he was 24 years old.[258] They had two children.

Irvin Lloyd was born in Tilden, Nebraska, on Friday, April 01, 1910.[258] He reached 66 years of age and died in Brownsboro, Henderson County, Texas, on December 20, 1976.[258] Irvin Lloyd was buried in Loveland Burial Park, Loveland, Larimer County, Colorado (Find a Grave ID 154682633).

Children of Gail Frances Chambers and Irvin Lloyd Moritz:

+   378   m   I. **Jerry Irvin Moritz** was born in Rushville, Sheridan County, Nebraska, on May 07, 1937.[258]

+   379   f   II. **Karen Gail Moritz** was born in Rushville, Sheridan County, Nebraska, on February 27, 1940.[258]

---

257   Laura Chambers Calhoun.

258   Gail Chambers Moritz.

Family of Leonard Chambers and Frances Nylen

225. **Leonard William Chambers** was born on Thursday, April 02, 1914, in Alliance, Box Butte County, Nebraska.[259] He was the son of Jesse Raymond Chambers (113) and Lila Berdentia Pinkerton.

Leonard William died in Casper, Natrona County, Wyoming, on February 12, 1966, at the age of 51.[259] He was buried in Highland Cemetery, Casper, Natrona County, Wyoming (Find a Grave ID 62089534).

At the age of 22, Leonard William married **Frances Elizabeth Nylen** on Monday, May 25, 1936, in Chadron, Dawes County, Nebraska, when she was 22 years old.[259] They had two children.

Frances Elizabeth was born in Hot Springs, Fall River County, South Dakota, on Saturday, June 07, 1913.[259] She reached 70 years of age and died in Casper, Natrona County, Wyoming, on July 06, 1983.[259] Frances Elizabeth was buried in Highland Cemetery, Casper, Natrona County, Wyoming (Find a Grave ID 62089478).

Children of Leonard William Chambers and Frances Elizabeth Nylen:

+ 380   f   I. **Lynne Frances Chambers** was born in Chadron, Dawes County, Nebraska, on July 02, 1942.[259] She died in Mapleton, Utah County, Utah, on April 02, 2009, at the age of 66. Lynne Frances was buried in Lyman City Cemetery, Lyman, Uinta County, Wyoming (Find a Grave ID 163470986).

        m   II. **Craig Warren Chambers** was born in Powell, Park County, Wyoming, on October 04, 1947.[260] He died in Casper, Natrona County, Wyoming, on October 18, 1997, at the age of 50.[260] Craig Warren was buried in Highland Cemetery, Casper, Natrona County, Wyoming (Find a Grave ID 62089616).

---

259   Lynne Frances Chambers.

260   Jennifer Laub Davidson.

Family of Jess Chambers and Gene McNutt

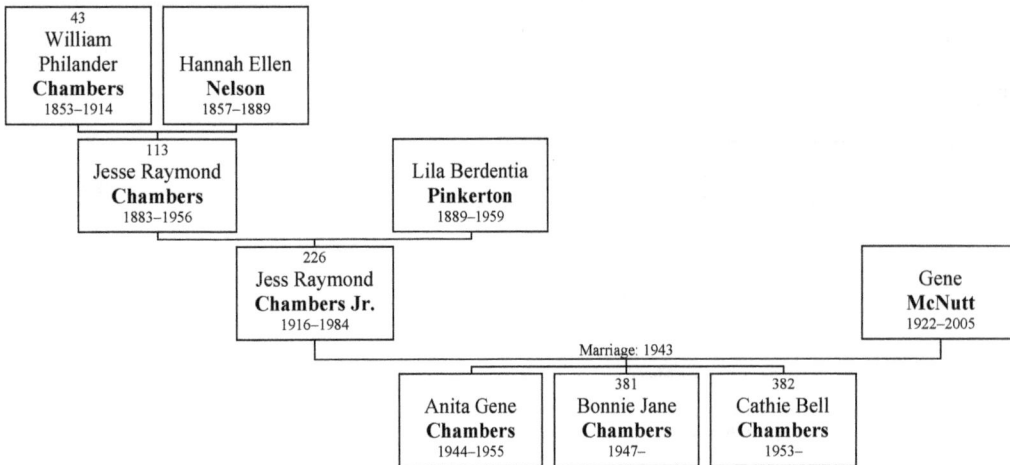

```
┌──────────────┐  ┌──────────────┐
│      43      │  │              │
│   William    │  │ Hannah Ellen │
│  Philander   │  │   Nelson     │
│  Chambers    │  │  1857–1889   │
│  1853–1914   │  │              │
└──────────────┘  └──────────────┘
   ┌──────────────┐       ┌──────────────┐
   │     113      │       │ Lila Berdentia│
   │ Jesse Raymond│       │  Pinkerton   │
   │  Chambers    │       │  1889–1959   │
   │  1883–1956   │       │              │
   └──────────────┘       └──────────────┘
      ┌──────────────┐                    ┌──────────────┐
      │     226      │                    │    Gene      │
      │ Jess Raymond │                    │   McNutt     │
      │ Chambers Jr. │                    │  1922–2005   │
      │  1916–1984   │                    │              │
      └──────────────┘                    └──────────────┘
                    Marriage: 1943
   ┌──────────────┐ ┌──────────────┐ ┌──────────────┐
   │ Anita Gene   │ │     381      │ │     382      │
   │  Chambers    │ │ Bonnie Jane  │ │ Cathie Bell  │
   │  1944–1955   │ │  Chambers    │ │  Chambers    │
   │              │ │   1947–      │ │   1953–      │
   └──────────────┘ └──────────────┘ └──────────────┘
```

226.   **Jess Raymond Chambers Jr.** was born on Monday, November 27, 1916, in Alliance, Box Butte County, Nebraska.[261] He was the son of Jesse Raymond Chambers (113) and Lila Berdentia Pinkerton.

Jess Raymond died in Grand Junction, Mesa County, Colorado, on November 14, 1984, at the age of 67.[261] He was buried in Orchard Mesa Cemetery, Grand Junction, Mesa County, Colorado (Find a Grave ID 105025933).

At the age of 27, Jess Raymond married **Gene McNutt** on Monday, December 13, 1943, in Denver, Denver County, Colorado, when she was 21 years old.[262] They had three daughters.

Gene was born in Otero County, Colorado, on Saturday, January 28, 1922.[262] She reached 83 years of age and died on June 09, 2005. Gene was buried in Orchard Mesa Cemetery, Grand Junction, Mesa County, Colorado (Find a Grave ID 105025852).

Daughters of Jess Raymond Chambers Jr. and Gene McNutt:

       f   I. **Anita Gene Chambers** was born in Fort Hays, Ellis County, Kansas, on October 15, 1944.[262] She died in Grand Junction, Mesa County, Colorado, on November 15, 1955, at the age of 11.[262] Anita Gene was buried in Orchard Mesa Cemetery, Grand Junction, Mesa County, Colorado (Find a Grave ID 105025618).

+ 381   f   II. **Bonnie Jane Chambers** was born in Fort Collins, Larimer County, Colorado, on July 15, 1947.[262]

+ 382   f   III. **Cathie Bell Chambers** was born in Grand Junction, Mesa County, Colorado, on March 17, 1953.[262]

---

261   Gail Chambers Moritz.

262   Gene McNutt Chambers.

Family of Robert Chambers and June Eads

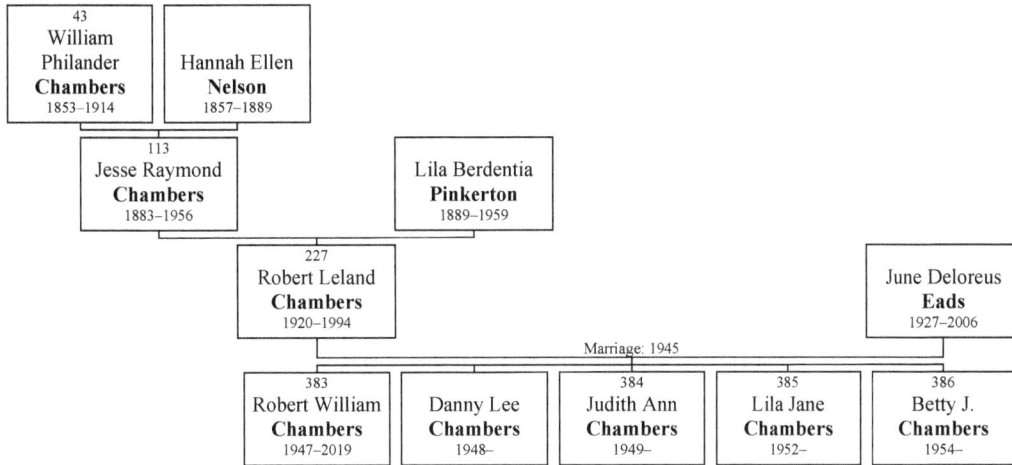

227. **Robert Leland Chambers** was born on Saturday, May 15, 1920, in Rushville, Sheridan County, Nebraska.[263] He was the son of Jesse Raymond Chambers (113) and Lila Berdentia Pinkerton.

Robert Leland died at Veterans Hospital in Kansas City, Kansas, on February 24, 1994, at the age of 73.[263] He was buried in Leavenworth National Cemetery, Leavenworth, Leavenworth County, Kansas (Find a Grave ID 481525).

At the age of 25, Robert Leland married **June Deloreus Eads** on Saturday, November 17, 1945, in Loveland, Larimer County, Colorado, when she was 18 years old.[264] They had five children.

June Deloreus was born in Detroit, Wayne County, Michigan, on Wednesday, June 01, 1927.[263] She reached 78 years of age and died in Detroit, Jackson County, Michigan, on April 12, 2006. June Deloreus was buried in Floral Hills Cemetery, Kansas City, Jackson County, Missouri (Find a Grave ID 200536931).

Children of Robert Leland Chambers and June Deloreus Eads:

+   383   m   I. **Robert William Chambers** was born in Fort Collins, Larimer County, Colorado, on August 07, 1947.[263] He died in Reeds Spring, Stone County, Missouri, on March 17, 2019, at the age of 71. Robert William was buried in Eisenhour Cemetery, Spokane, Christian County, Missouri (Find a Grave ID 215376652).

                m   II. **Danny Lee Chambers** was born in Denver, Denver County, Colorado, on August 27, 1948.[263]

+   384   f   III. **Judith Ann Chambers** was born in Omaha, Douglas County, Nebraska, on December 16, 1949.[263]

+   385   f   IV. **Lila Jane Chambers** was born in Colorado Springs, El Paso County, Colorado, on January 09, 1952.[263]

---

[263]   Gail Chambers Moritz.

[264]   June Eads Chambers.

+ 386 f V. **Betty J. Chambers** was born in Loveland, Larimer County, Colorado, on March 13, 1954.[263]

Family of Verna Hargadine and Leroy Kelley

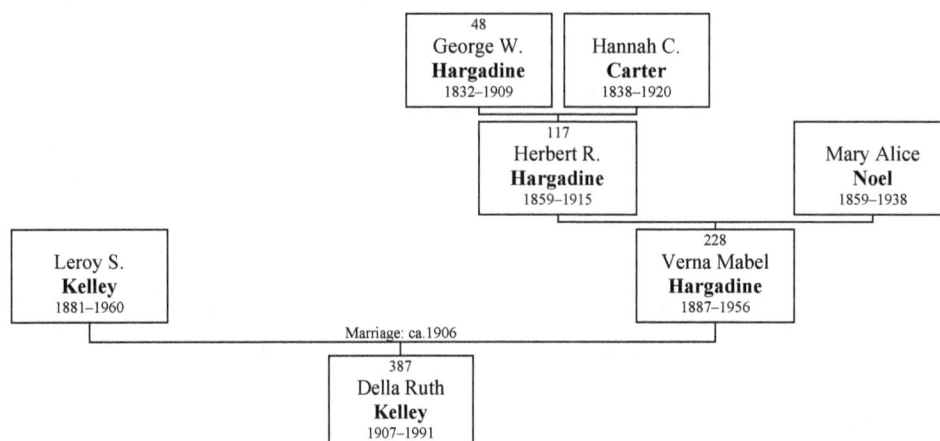

228. **Verna Mabel Hargadine** was born on Wednesday, February 23, 1887, in Nebraska, USA. She was the daughter of Herbert R. Hargadine (117) and Mary Alice Noel.

Verna Mabel died in San Bernardino County, California, on May 28, 1956, at the age of 69. She was buried in Rose Hills Memorial Park, Whittier, Los Angeles County, California (Find a Grave ID 158734080).

Verna Mabel married **Leroy S. Kelley** about 1906. They had one daughter.

Leroy S. was born in Iowa, USA, on Sunday, March 13, 1881. He reached 79 years of age and died on May 21, 1960. Leroy S. was buried in Rose Hills Memorial Park, Whittier, Los Angeles County, California (Find a Grave ID 158673938).

Daughter of Verna Mabel Hargadine and Leroy S. Kelley:

+ 387 f I. **Della Ruth Kelley** was born in Ashland, Boone County, Nebraska, on August 11, 1907.[265] She died in Los Angeles, Los Angeles County, California, on October 23, 1991, at the age of 84.[265] Della Ruth was buried in Rose Hills Memorial Park, Whittier, Los Angeles County, California (Find a Grave ID 104952668).[265]

---

265 Ancestry.com, Public Member Trees (Provo, UT, USA, Ancestry.com Operations, Inc., 2006), Ancestry.com, Record for Della Ruth Kelley. https://search.ancestry.co.uk/cgi-bin/sse.dll?db=1030&h=25125634030&indiv=try.

Family of Hazel Hargadine and Ray Blackman

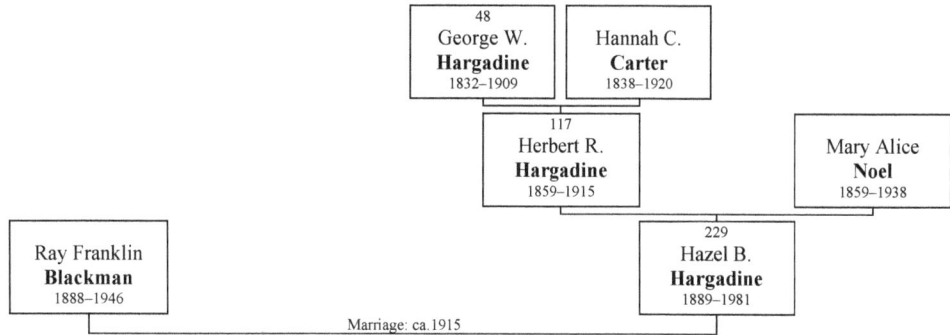

229.   **Hazel B. Hargadine** was born on Wednesday, June 19, 1889, in Nebraska, USA. She was the daughter of Herbert R. Hargadine (117) and Mary Alice Noel.

Hazel B. died in Los Angeles, Los Angeles County, California, on August 12, 1981, at the age of 92. She was buried in Rose Hills Memorial Park, Whittier, Los Angeles County, California (Find a Grave ID 105093056).

Hazel B. married **Ray Franklin Blackman** about 1915. Ray Franklin was born in Nebraska, USA, on Monday, September 10, 1888.

He reached 57 years of age and died in Los Angeles County, California, on July 06, 1946. Ray Franklin was buried in Rose Hills Memorial Park, Whittier, Los Angeles County, California (Find a Grave ID 105092795).

Family of Chester Hargadine and Donella Wilson

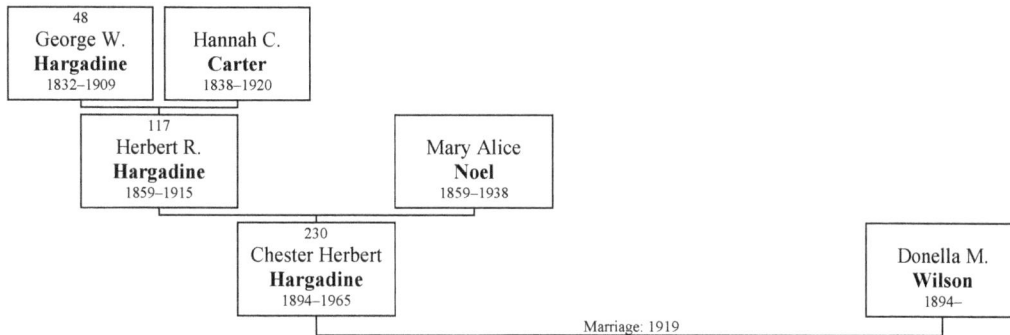

230.   **Chester Herbert Hargadine** was born on Thursday, June 07, 1894, in Omaha, Douglas County, Nebraska.[266] He was the son of Herbert R. Hargadine (117) and Mary Alice Noel.

Chester Herbert served in the military: WWI, Quartermaster Corps. He died in Los Angeles, Los Angeles County, California, on February 19, 1965, at the age of 70.[266] Chester Herbert was buried in Rose Hills Memorial Park, Whittier, Los Angeles County, California (Find a Grave ID 158295152).

266   Ancestry.com, Public Member Trees (Provo, UT, USA, Ancestry.com Operations, Inc., 2006), Ancestry.com, Record for Chester Herbert Hargadine. https://search.ancestry.co.uk/cgi-bin/sse.dll?db=1030&h=232061984725&indiv=try.

Chester Herbert married **Donella M. Wilson** on Thursday, May 15, 1919, in Louisville, Jefferson County, Kentucky.[266] Donella M. was born in Indiana, USA, in 1894.[266] She was also known as **Donna**.

May Hargadine

231.   **May Carrie Hargadine** was born on Tuesday, October 13, 1896, in Nebraska, USA. She was the daughter of Herbert R. Hargadine (117) and Mary Alice Noel. She was also known as **Carrie May**.

May Carrie died in Los Angeles County, California, on September 19, 1978, at the age of 81. She was buried in Rose Hills Memorial Park, Whittier, Los Angeles County, California (Find a Grave ID 252727875).

Marriages with Charles Edward Beer and Charles Alonzo Burch (Page 269) are known.

Family of May Hargadine and Charles Beer

Here are the details about **May Carrie Hargadine's** first marriage, with Charles Edward Beer. You can read more about May Carrie on page 268.

May Carrie Hargadine married **Charles Edward Beer** in 1916. Charles Edward was born on Wednesday, August 10, 1887.

He reached 51 years of age and died on March 25, 1939. Charles Edward was buried in Rose Hills Memorial Park, Whittier, Los Angeles County, California (Find a Grave ID 130708142).

Family of May Hargadine and Charles Burch

Here are the details about **May Carrie Hargadine's** second marriage, with Charles Alonzo Burch. You can read more about May Carrie on page 268.

May Carrie Hargadine married **Charles Alonzo Burch** in 1947. Charles Alonzo was born in Kansas, USA, on Sunday, December 06, 1885.

He reached 84 years of age and died in Los Angeles, Los Angeles County, California, on July 23, 1970. Charles Alonzo was buried in Sunset Hill Cemetery, Corning, Tehama County, California (Find a Grave ID 7954323).

Family of Constance Hargadine and Benjamin Wright

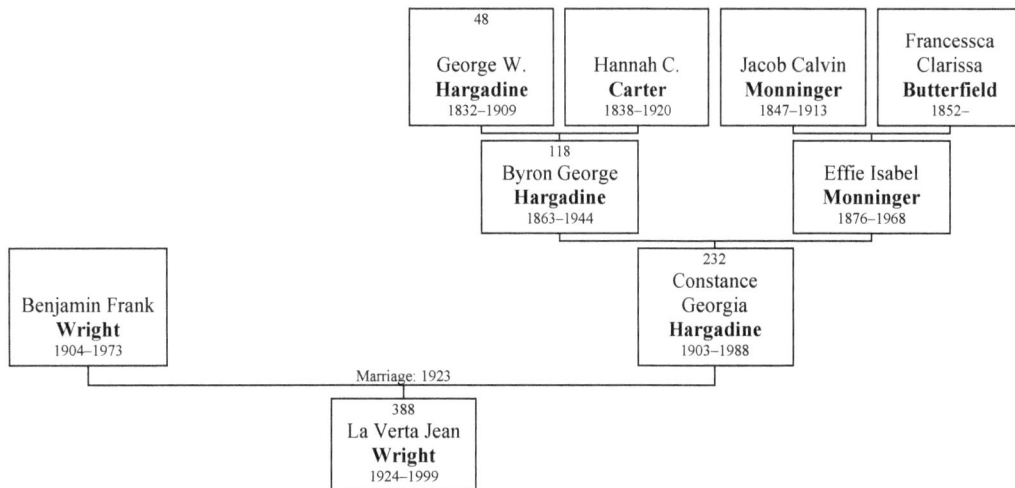

```
                                    ┌──────────────┐  ┌──────────┐  ┌──────────────┐  ┌──────────────┐
                                    │      48      │  │          │  │              │  │  Francessca  │
                                    │  George W.   │  │ Hannah C.│  │ Jacob Calvin │  │   Clarissa   │
                                    │  Hargadine   │  │  Carter  │  │  Monninger   │  │  Butterfield │
                                    │  1832–1909   │  │1838–1920 │  │  1847–1913   │  │    1852–     │
                                    └──────────────┘  └──────────┘  └──────────────┘  └──────────────┘
                                         ┌──────────────┐              ┌──────────────┐
                                         │     118      │              │              │
                                         │ Byron George │              │ Effie Isabel │
                                         │  Hargadine   │              │  Monninger   │
                                         │  1863–1944   │              │  1876–1968   │
                                         └──────────────┘              └──────────────┘
                                                    ┌──────────────┐
                                                    │     232      │
                                                    │  Constance   │
                                                    │   Georgia    │
                                                    │  Hargadine   │
                                                    │  1903–1988   │
   ┌──────────────┐                                 └──────────────┘
   │              │
   │Benjamin Frank│
   │    Wright    │
   │  1904–1973   │
   └──────────────┘
           Marriage: 1923
                  ┌──────────────┐
                  │     388      │
                  │ La Verta Jean│
                  │    Wright    │
                  │  1924–1999   │
                  └──────────────┘
```

232. **Constance Georgia Hargadine** was born on Saturday, November 14, 1903, in Omaha, Douglas County, Nebraska.[267] She was the daughter of Byron George Hargadine (118) and Effie Isabel Monninger.

Constance Georgia died in San Diego, San Diego County, California, on April 12, 1988, at the age of 84. She was buried in Evergreen Cemetery, El Centro, Imperial County, California (Find a Grave ID 114501079).

Constance Georgia married **Benjamin Frank Wright** in 1923 in Nebraska, USA. They had one daughter.

Benjamin Frank was born in Omaha, Douglas County, Nebraska, on Sunday, January 03, 1904. He reached 69 years of age and died in Imperial County, California, on April 01, 1973. Benjamin Frank was buried in Evergreen Cemetery, El Centro, Imperial County, California (Find a Grave ID 114501081).

Daughter of Constance Georgia Hargadine and Benjamin Frank Wright:

+   388   f   I. **La Verta Jean Wright** was born in Douglas County, Nebraska, on December 17, 1924. She died in San Diego, California, on June 10, 1999, at the age of 74.

---

267   California Death Records.

Family of Virginia Hargadine and John Stuhldreier

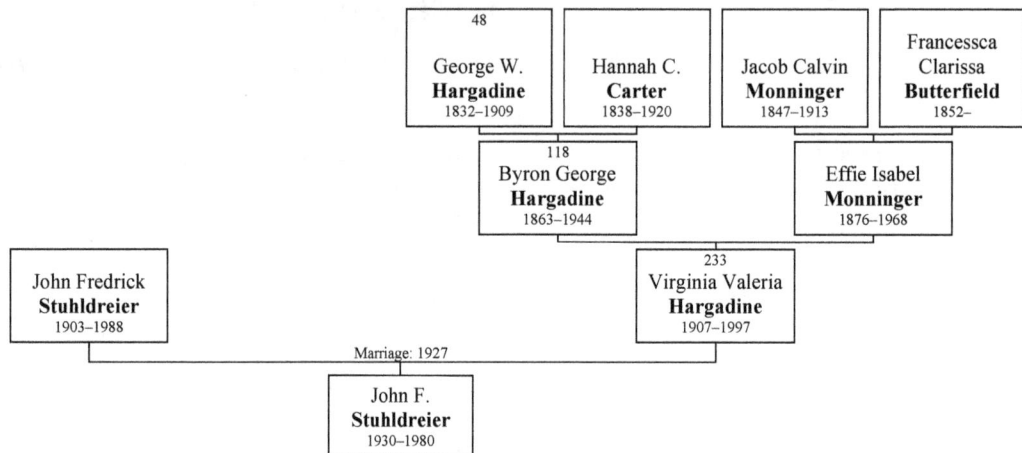

233. **Virginia Valeria Hargadine** was born on Wednesday, April 24, 1907, in Nebraska, USA. She was the daughter of Byron George Hargadine (118) and Effie Isabel Monninger.

Virginia Valeria died in Hillsboro, Washington County, Oregon, on November 29, 1997, at the age of 90.

At the age of 20, Virginia Valeria married **John Fredrick Stuhldreier** on Saturday, September 17, 1927, in Nebraska City, Otoe County, Nebraska, when he was 24 years old. They had one son.

John Fredrick was born in Nebraska, USA, on Friday, June 12, 1903. He reached 85 years of age and died in Washington County, Oregon, on October 10, 1988.

Son of Virginia Valeria Hargadine and John Fredrick Stuhldreier:

m   I. **John F. Stuhldreier** was born in Omaha, Douglas County, Nebraska, on August 02, 1930.[268] He died in Washington County, Oregon, on May 24, 1980, at the age of 49.[268]

---

[268] Ancestry.com, U.S., Social Security Death Index, 1935-2014 (Provo, UT, USA, Ancestry.com Operations Inc, 2014), Ancestry.com, Social Security Administration; Washington D.C., USA; Social Security Death Index, Master File. Record for John Stuhldreier. https://search.ancestry.co.uk/cgi-bin/sse.dll?db=3693&h=60676593&indiv=try.

Family of Clyde Hargadine and Mildred Higgins

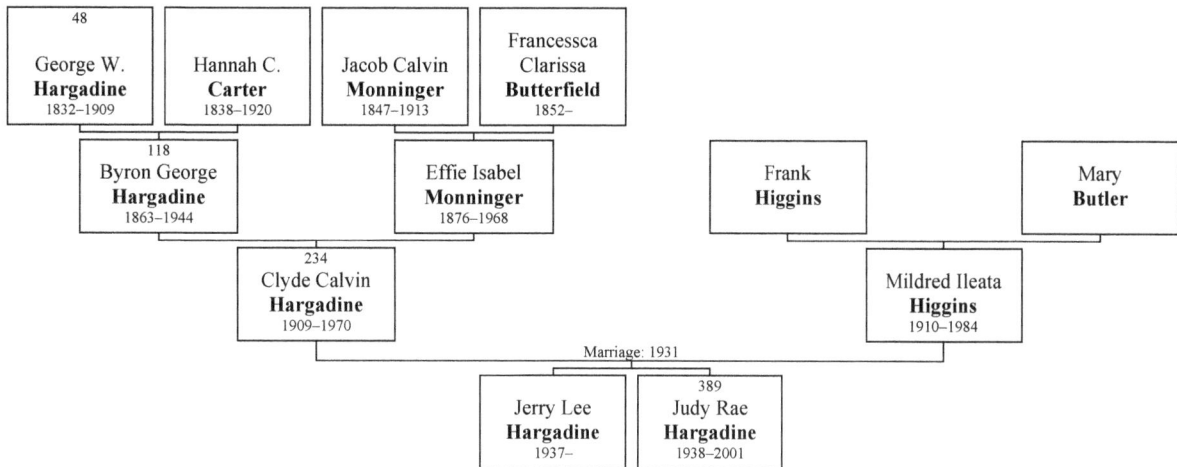

234. **Clyde Calvin Hargadine** was born on Tuesday, April 06, 1909, in Ohio, USA. He was the son of Byron George Hargadine (118) and Effie Isabel Monninger.

Clyde Calvin died in Hamilton, Butler County, Ohio, on November 01, 1970, at the age of 61.

Clyde Calvin married **Mildred Ileata Higgins** in 1931. They had two children.

Mildred Ileata was born in Sloan, Woodbury County, Iowa, on Sunday, June 26, 1910. She was the daughter of Frank Higgins and Mary Butler.

Mildred Ileata reached 74 years of age and died in Sacramento County, California, on November 15, 1984. She was buried on November 19, 1984, in Hillcrest Cemetery, Omaha, Douglas County, Nebraska.

Children of Clyde Calvin Hargadine and Mildred Ileata Higgins:

     m   I. **Jerry Lee Hargadine** was born in Douglas, Otoe County, Nebraska, on April 01, 1937.

           More facts and events for Jerry Lee Hargadine:

           Individual Note: July 10, 1938 Fairview Presbyterian Church, Omaha, Nebraska
                        Baptism

+ 389 f   II. **Judy Rae Hargadine** was born in Omaha, Douglas County, Nebraska, on December 08, 1938. She died in Bellaire, Harris County, Texas, on April 01, 2001, at the age of 62.[269] Judy Rae was buried on April 04, 2001.

---

269 Social Security Death Index, JUDY HARGADINE.

Family of Verna Hargadine and Fritz Burke

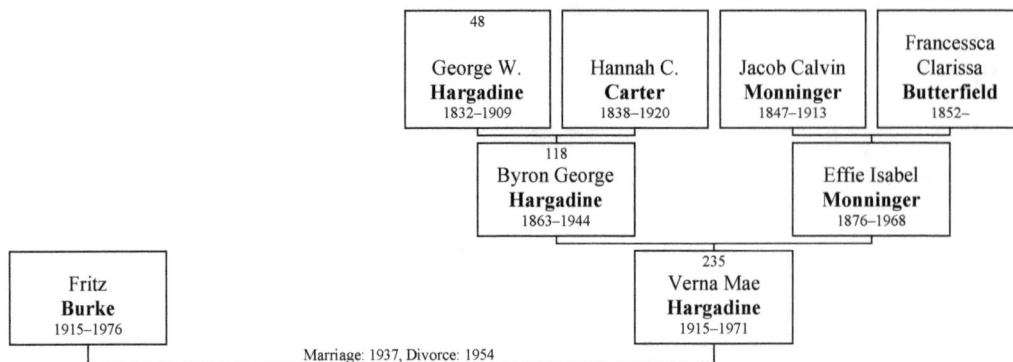

```
                                          ┌──────────┐ ┌──────────┐ ┌──────────┐ ┌──────────────┐
                                          │    48    │ │          │ │          │ │  Francessca  │
                                          │George W. │ │ Hannah C.│ │  Jacob   │ │   Clarissa   │
                                          │Hargadine │ │  Carter  │ │ Calvin   │ │  Butterfield │
                                          │1832–1909 │ │1838–1920 │ │Monninger │ │    1852–     │
                                          │          │ │          │ │1847–1913 │ │              │
                                          └──────────┘ └──────────┘ └──────────┘ └──────────────┘
                                              ┌───────────────┐        ┌───────────────┐
                                              │      118      │        │  Effie Isabel │
                                              │  Byron George │        │   Monninger   │
                                              │   Hargadine   │        │   1876–1968   │
                                              │   1863–1944   │        │               │
                                              └───────────────┘        └───────────────┘
         ┌──────────┐                               ┌───────────────┐
         │  Fritz   │                               │      235      │
         │  Burke   │                               │  Verna Mae    │
         │1915–1976 │                               │  Hargadine    │
         │          │                               │  1915–1971    │
         └──────────┘                               └───────────────┘
                          Marriage: 1937, Divorce: 1954
```

235. **Verna Mae Hargadine** was born on Saturday, February 06, 1915, in Douglas County, Nebraska.[270] She was the daughter of Byron George Hargadine (118) and Effie Isabel Monninger.

Verna Mae died in Multnomah, Oregon, USA, on September 14, 1971, at the age of 56.[270]

At the age of 22, Verna Mae married **Fritz Burke** on Wednesday, June 09, 1937, when he was 22 years old.[271] They were divorced on June 03, 1954. Multnomah, Oregon.

Fritz was born in Lincoln, Antelope County, Nebraska, on Wednesday, April 14, 1915. He reached 61 years of age and died in Multnomah County, Oregon, on August 19, 1976. Fritz was buried in Skyline Memorial Gardens, Portland, Multnomah County, Oregon (Find a Grave ID 182846823).

Family of Edith Hargadine and George Roth

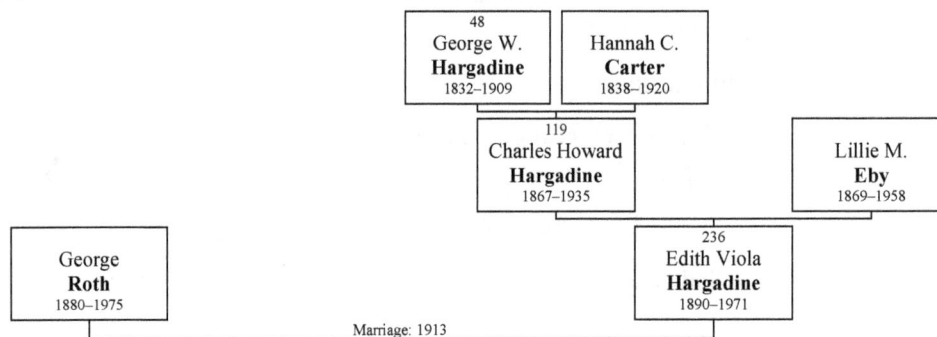

```
                                    ┌──────────┐ ┌──────────┐
                                    │    48    │ │          │
                                    │George W. │ │ Hannah C.│
                                    │Hargadine │ │  Carter  │
                                    │1832–1909 │ │1838–1920 │
                                    └──────────┘ └──────────┘
                                       ┌───────────────┐        ┌──────────┐
                                       │      119      │        │ Lillie M.│
                                       │Charles Howard │        │   Eby    │
                                       │   Hargadine   │        │1869–1958 │
                                       │   1867–1935   │        │          │
                                       └───────────────┘        └──────────┘
         ┌──────────┐                        ┌───────────────┐
         │  George  │                        │      236      │
         │   Roth   │                        │  Edith Viola  │
         │1880–1975 │                        │   Hargadine   │
         │          │                        │   1890–1971   │
         └──────────┘                        └───────────────┘
                          Marriage: 1913
```

236. **Edith Viola Hargadine** was born on Tuesday, September 23, 1890, in Omaha, Douglas County, Nebraska.[272] She was the daughter of Charles Howard Hargadine (119) and Lillie M. Eby.

Edith Viola died in Tekamah, Burt County, Nebraska, on July 27, 1971, at the age of 80.[272]

---

270   Ancestry.com, Public Member Trees (Provo, UT, USA, Ancestry.com Operations, Inc., 2006), Ancestry.com, Record for Verna Mae Hargadine. https://search.ancestry.co.uk/cgi-bin/sse.dll?db=1030&h=232061989514&indiv=try.

271   State of Oregon Divorces, File number 2638, Docket Number 218540. Divorced 3 Jun 1954.

272   Ancestry.com, Public Member Trees (Provo, UT, USA, Ancestry.com Operations, Inc., 2006), Ancestry.com, Record for Edith Viola Hargadine. https://search.ancestry.co.uk/cgi-bin/sse.dll?db=1030&h=24051617541&indiv=try.

At the age of 22, Edith Viola married **George Roth** on Thursday, June 05, 1913, in Omaha, Douglas County, Nebraska, when he was 32 years old.[272] George was born in Tekamah, Burt County, Nebraska, on Tuesday, August 17, 1880.[272]

He reached 95 years of age and died in Tekamah, Burt County, Nebraska, on October 24, 1975.[272] George was buried in Omaha, Douglas County, Nebraska.[272]

Family of Cecil Hargadine and Pauline Sorensen

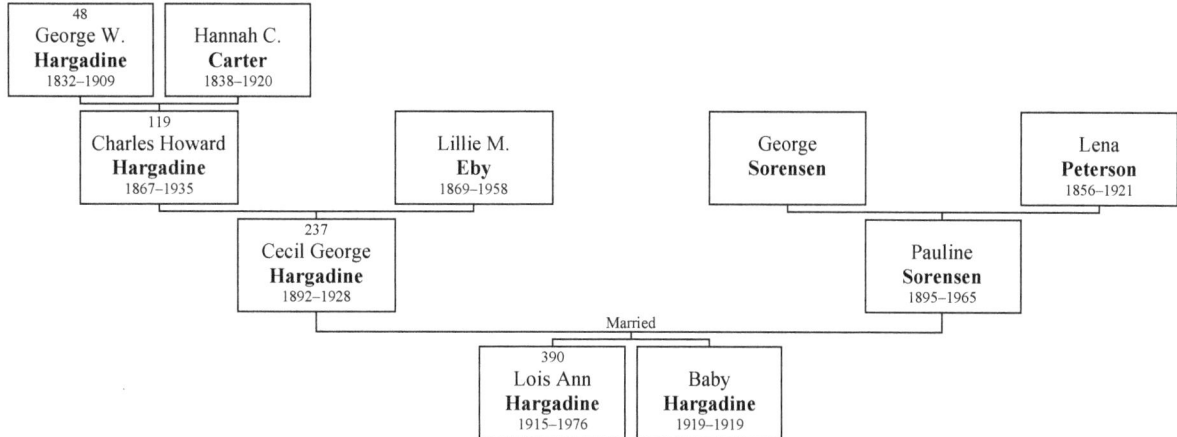

237. Cecil George Hargadine was born in January 1892 in Nebraska, USA. He was the son of Charles Howard Hargadine (119) and Lillie M. Eby.

Cecil George worked as a Clerk; UP Railroad Company in 1916.[273] He died on August 16, 1928, at the age of 36. Cecil George was buried in Forest Lawn Memorial Park, Omaha, Douglas County, Nebraska, on August 18, 1928 (Find a Grave ID 136311868).[274]

He married **Pauline Sorensen**. They had two children.

Pauline was born in Nebraska, USA, in 1895. She was the daughter of George Sorensen and Lena Peterson.

Pauline reached 70 years of age and died on May 22, 1965. She was buried in Forest Lawn Memorial Park, Omaha, Douglas County, Nebraska (Find a Grave ID 37001629).

Children of Cecil George Hargadine and Pauline Sorensen:

+ 390 f I. **Lois Ann Hargadine** was born in Omaha, Douglas County, Nebraska, on July 28, 1915. She died in Omaha, Douglas County, Nebraska, in July 1976 at the age of 60. Lois Ann was buried in Forest Lawn Memorial Park, Omaha, Douglas County, Nebraska, on August 02, 1976 (Find a Grave ID 182103299).

II. **Baby Hargadine** was born in 1919. He or she died on October 30, 1919. Baby was buried in Forest Lawn Memorial Park, Omaha, Douglas County, Nebraska (Find a Grave ID 136311930).

---

273 Omaha Directory County's, Omaha City Directory, 1916, 521.

274 http://www.forestlawnomaha.com/GraveIndex/IndexSummaryH.html.

Family of Florence Hargadine and William Dewey

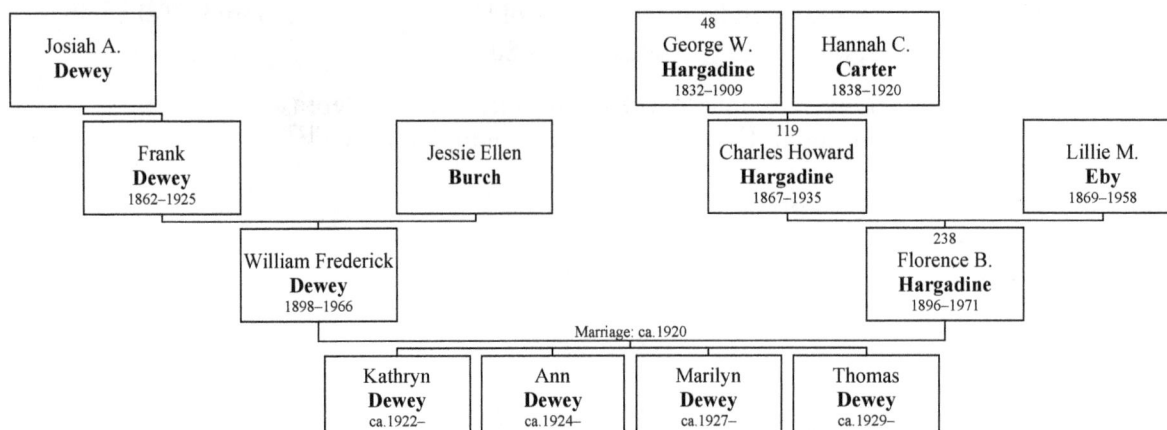

238. **Florence B. Hargadine** was born on Monday, December 28, 1896, in Nebraska, USA. She was the daughter of Charles Howard Hargadine (119) and Lillie M. Eby.

Florence B. died in Miami, Dade County, Florida, on June 11, 1971, at the age of 74.[275, 276] She was buried in Woodlawn Park North Cemetery and Mausoleum, Miami, Miami-Dade County, Florida (Find a Grave ID 205319385).

Florence B. married **William Frederick Dewey** about 1920. They had four children.

William Frederick was born on Sunday, January 16, 1898. He was the son of Frank Dewey and Jessie Ellen Burch.

William Frederick reached 68 years of age and died in Miami, Dade County, Florida, in February 1966.[275] He was buried in Woodlawn Park North Cemetery and Mausoleum, Miami, Miami-Dade County, Florida (Find a Grave ID 205319384).

Children of Florence B. Hargadine and William Frederick Dewey:

    f   I. **Kathryn Dewey** was born about 1922.

    f   II. **Ann Dewey** was born about 1924.

    f   III. **Marilyn Dewey** was born about 1927.

    m   IV. **Thomas Dewey** was born about 1929.

---

275   Social Security Death Index.

276   Florida Death Index 1877-1998, Certificate: 35871.

Family of Hannah Hargadine and Edwin Peck

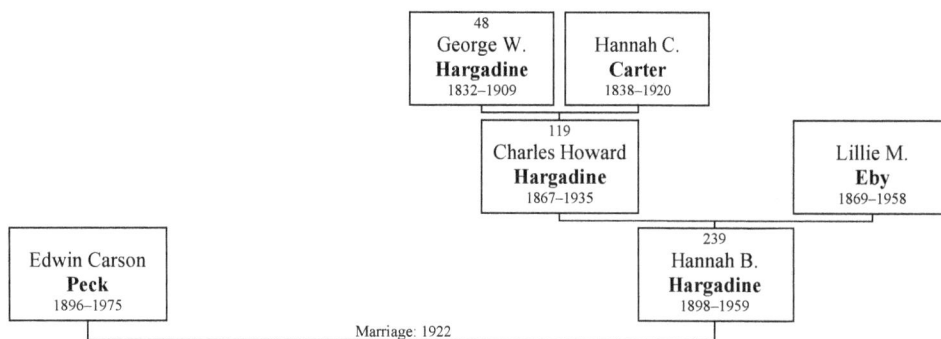

```
                                    48
                              George W.        Hannah C.
                              Hargadine          Carter
                              1832–1909        1838–1920
                                      119
                                Charles Howard                Lillie M.
                                  Hargadine                     Eby
                                  1867–1935                   1869–1958
                                               239
              Edwin Carson                  Hannah B.
                 Peck                       Hargadine
              1896–1975                     1898–1959
                              Marriage: 1922
```

239.   Hannah B. Hargadine was born on Tuesday, August 09, 1898, in Omaha, Douglas County, Nebraska.[277] She was the daughter of Charles Howard Hargadine (119) and Lillie M. Eby.

Hannah B. died in Omaha, Douglas County, Nebraska, on July 20, 1959, at the age of 60.[277] She was buried in Forest Lawn Memorial Park, Omaha, Douglas County, Nebraska, on July 22, 1959 (Find a Grave ID 73050259).

Hannah B. married **Edwin Carson Peck** in 1922. Edwin Carson was born in Chicago, Cook County, Illinois, on Monday, August 31, 1896.[277]

He served in the military on December 10, 1917.[277] U.S Army, Sgt. Edwin Carson reached 78 years of age and died in Tavares, Lake County, Florida, on June 26, 1975.[277] He was buried on July 01, 1975, in Forest Lawn Memorial Park, Omaha, Douglas County, Nebraska (Find a Grave ID 73050253).

Family of Bessie Morton and Alfred Nystrom

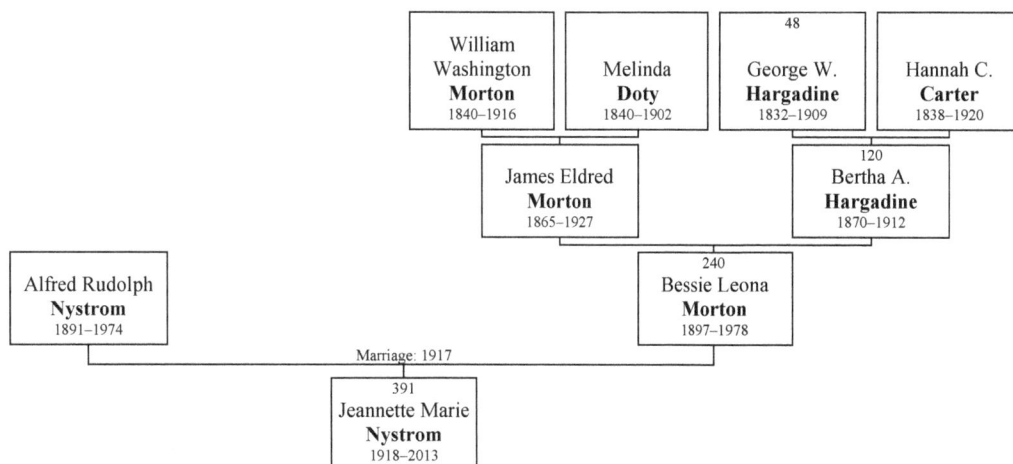

```
                                                                    48
          William
          Washington       Melinda        George W.       Hannah C.
           Morton           Doty          Hargadine         Carter
          1840–1916       1840–1902       1832–1909       1838–1920
                                                  120
               James Eldred                  Bertha A.
                 Morton                       Hargadine
                 1865–1927                    1870–1912
                                     240
         Alfred Rudolph             Bessie Leona
            Nystrom                   Morton
           1891–1974                 1897–1978
                           Marriage: 1917
                                   391
                            Jeannette Marie
                               Nystrom
                               1918–2013
```

277   Ancestry.com, Public Member Trees (Provo, UT, USA, Ancestry.com Operations, Inc., 2006), Ancestry.com, Record for Hannah A Hargadine. https://search.ancestry.co.uk/cgi-bin/sse.dll?db=1030&h=150007353034&indiv=try.

240. **Bessie Leona Morton** was born on Tuesday, April 13, 1897, in Blanchard, Page County, Iowa.[278] She was the daughter of James Eldred Morton and Bertha A. Hargadine (120). They were her parents by adoption. Bessie Leona was adopted. Birth name: Leona McKee.

She died in Spooner, Washburn County, Wisconsin, on March 05, 1978, at the age of 80. Bessie Leona was buried in Spooner Cemetery, Spooner, Washburn County, Wisconsin (Find a Grave ID 105078856).

At the age of 19, Bessie Leona married **Alfred Rudolph Nystrom** on Wednesday, April 11, 1917, in Washburn County, Wisconsin, when he was 25 years old. They had one daughter.

Alfred Rudolph was born in Cumberland, Barron County, Wisconsin, on Wednesday, September 30, 1891.[278] He reached 83 years of age and died in Spooner, Washburn County, Wisconsin, on November 27, 1974. Alfred Rudolph was buried in Spooner Cemetery, Spooner, Washburn County, Wisconsin (Find a Grave ID 105078799).

Daughter of Bessie Leona Morton and Alfred Rudolph Nystrom:

+ 391 f I. **Jeannette Marie Nystrom** was born in Spooner, Washburn County, Wisconsin, on May 02, 1918. She died in Spooner, Washburn County, Wisconsin, on February 08, 2013, at the age of 94. Jeannette Marie was buried in Spooner Cemetery, Spooner, Washburn County, Wisconsin (Find a Grave ID 105078624).

Family of Martha Morton and Harry Dahl

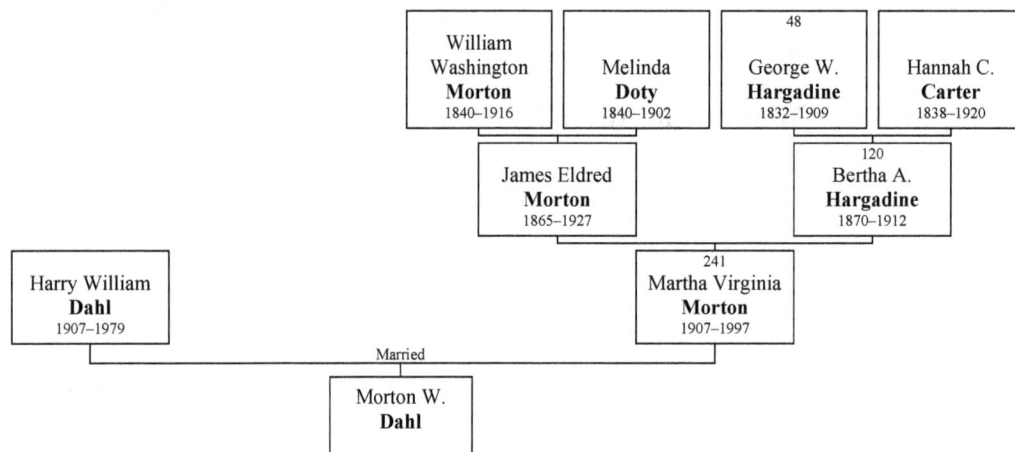

241. **Martha Virginia Morton** was born on Thursday, May 09, 1907, in Omaha, Douglas County, Nebraska. She was the daughter of James Eldred Morton and Bertha A. Hargadine (120).

Martha Virginia died in Spooner, Washburn County, Wisconsin, on February 22, 1997, at the age of 89. She was buried in Spooner Cemetery, Spooner, Washburn County, Wisconsin (Find a Grave ID 128353853).

She married **Harry William Dahl**. They had one son.

---

278 Ancestry.com, Public Member Trees (Provo, UT, USA, Ancestry.com Operations, Inc., 2006), Ancestry.com, Record for Bessie Morton. https://search.ancestry.co.uk/cgi-bin/sse.dll?db=1030&h=40446052398&indiv=try.

Harry William was born in Trego, Washburn County, Wisconsin, on Monday, February 11, 1907. He reached 72 years of age and died in Duluth, St. Louis County, Minnesota, on May 10, 1979. Harry William was buried in Spooner Cemetery, Spooner, Washburn County, Wisconsin (Find a Grave ID 128354114).

Son of Martha Virginia Morton and Harry William Dahl:

m   I. **Morton W. Dahl.**

Darrell Harjadene

242.   **Darrell Ralph Harjadene** was born on Wednesday, June 03, 1908, in Lincoln, Lancaster County, Nebraska. He was the son of Ralph Herbert Hargadine (121) and Bessie Juanita Davis. He was also known as **Darrell Ralph Hargadine**.

Darrell Ralph served in the military at WWII, USMC, PFC in New York, USA, on July 18, 1944. He died in Page, Coconino County, Arizona, on December 30, 1971, at the age of 63. Darrell Ralph was buried in Mountain View Cemetery, Williams, Coconino County, Arizona (Find a Grave ID 62653440).

Marriages with Kathleen Eva Duggan and Florence M. Gavin (Page 278) are known.

Family of Darrell Harjadene and Kathleen Duggan

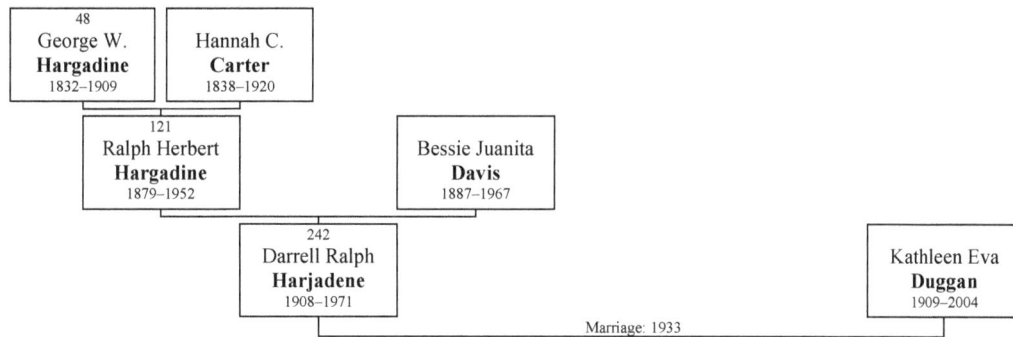

Here are the details about **Darrell Ralph Harjadene's** first marriage, with Kathleen Eva Duggan. You can read more about Darrell Ralph on page 277.

At the age of 25, Darrell Ralph Harjadene married **Kathleen Eva Duggan** on Thursday, November 30, 1933, in Vancouver, Clark County, Washington, when she was 24 years old.[279] Kathleen Eva was born in Lockport, Niagara County, New York, on Friday, July 02, 1909.

She reached 95 years of age and died in Oxnard, Ventura County, California, on November 23, 2004. Kathleen Eva was buried in Conejo Mountain Memorial Park, Camarillo, Ventura County, California (Find a Grave ID 76421100).

---

279   Vancouver, Clark County Certificate of Marriage, The name on the marriage certificate says Jack R. Harjadene.

Family of Darrell Harjadene and Florence Gavin

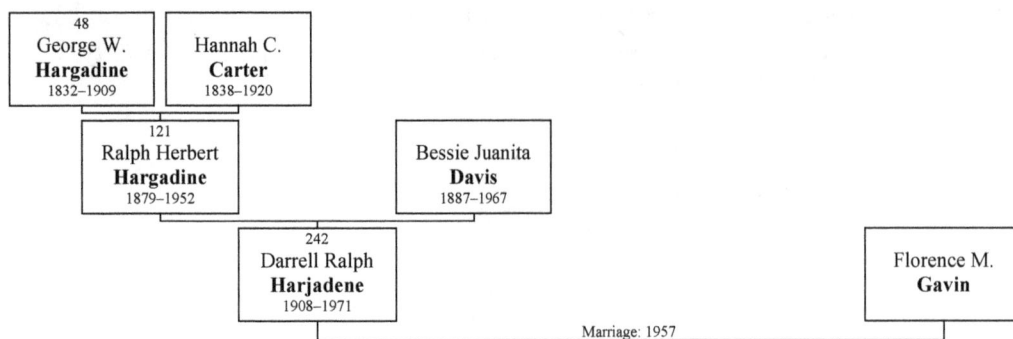

```
┌─────────────┐ ┌─────────────┐
│     48      │ │             │
│ George W.   │ │ Hannah C.   │
│ Hargadine   │ │ Carter      │
│ 1832–1909   │ │ 1838–1920   │
└─────────────┘ └─────────────┘
      ┌─────────────┐ ┌─────────────┐
      │    121      │ │             │
      │ Ralph Herbert│ │ Bessie Juanita│
      │ Hargadine   │ │ Davis       │
      │ 1879–1952   │ │ 1887–1967   │
      └─────────────┘ └─────────────┘
            ┌─────────────┐          ┌─────────────┐
            │    242      │          │             │
            │ Darrell Ralph│          │ Florence M. │
            │ Harjadene   │          │ Gavin       │
            │ 1908–1971   │          │             │
            └─────────────┘          └─────────────┘
                    Marriage: 1957
```

Here are the details about **Darrell Ralph Harjadene's** second marriage, with Florence M. Gavin. You can read more about Darrell Ralph on page 277.

Darrell Ralph Harjadene married **Florence M. Gavin** on Tuesday, January 08, 1957, in Clark County, Nevada.

Family of Helen Sturm and Arthur Ruse

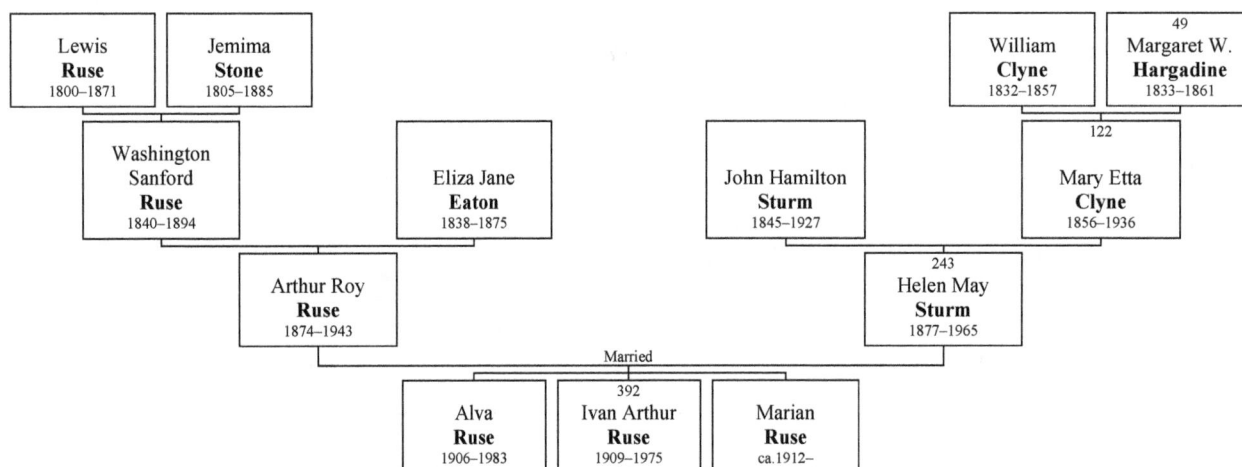

```
┌─────────────┐ ┌─────────────┐              ┌─────────────┐ ┌─────────────┐
│ Lewis       │ │ Jemima      │              │ William     │ │     49      │
│ Ruse        │ │ Stone       │              │ Clyne       │ │ Margaret W. │
│ 1800–1871   │ │ 1805–1885   │              │ 1832–1857   │ │ Hargadine   │
└─────────────┘ └─────────────┘              └─────────────┘ │ 1833–1861   │
                                                             └─────────────┘
   ┌─────────────┐ ┌─────────────┐   ┌─────────────┐   ┌─────────────┐
   │ Washington  │ │ Eliza Jane  │   │ John Hamilton│   │    122      │
   │ Sanford     │ │ Eaton       │   │ Sturm       │   │ Mary Etta   │
   │ Ruse        │ │ 1838–1875   │   │ 1845–1927   │   │ Clyne       │
   │ 1840–1894   │ └─────────────┘   └─────────────┘   │ 1856–1936   │
   └─────────────┘                                     └─────────────┘
      ┌─────────────┐                       ┌─────────────┐
      │ Arthur Roy  │                       │    243      │
      │ Ruse        │                       │ Helen May   │
      │ 1874–1943   │                       │ Sturm       │
      └─────────────┘                       │ 1877–1965   │
                    Married                  └─────────────┘
        ┌─────────────┐ ┌─────────────┐ ┌─────────────┐
        │ Alva        │ │    392      │ │ Marian      │
        │ Ruse        │ │ Ivan Arthur │ │ Ruse        │
        │ 1906–1983   │ │ Ruse        │ │ ca.1912–    │
        └─────────────┘ │ 1909–1975   │ └─────────────┘
                        └─────────────┘
```

243. **Helen May Sturm** was born on Tuesday, December 18, 1877, in Dunlap, Peoria County, Illinois. She was the daughter of John Hamilton Sturm and Mary Etta Clyne (122).

Helen May died on June 10, 1965, at the age of 87. She was buried in Springdale Cemetery and Mausoleum, Peoria, Peoria County, Illinois (Find a Grave ID 148218293).

She married **Arthur Roy Ruse**. They had three children.

Arthur Roy was born in Pennsylvania, USA, on Saturday, January 24, 1874. He was the son of Washington Sanford Ruse and Eliza Jane Eaton.

Arthur Roy reached 69 years of age and died in Peoria, Peoria County, Illinois, on August 19, 1943. He was buried in Springdale Cemetery and Mausoleum, Peoria, Peoria County, Illinois (Find a Grave ID 119232907).

Children of Helen May Sturm and Arthur Roy Ruse:

       m   I. **Alva Ruse** was born in Illinois, USA, on March 20, 1906. He died in Edelstein, Peoria County, Illinois, in January 1983 at the age of 76.

+   392   m   II. **Ivan Arthur Ruse** was born in Dunlap, Peoria County, Illinois, on January 16, 1909. He died in Penn Township, Stark County, Illinois, on February 17, 1975, at the age of 66. Ivan Arthur was buried in Prospect Cemetery, Dunlap, Peoria County, Illinois (Find a Grave ID 22159596).

       f   III. **Marian Ruse** was born about 1912.

Family of Cora Sturm and Ernest Aby

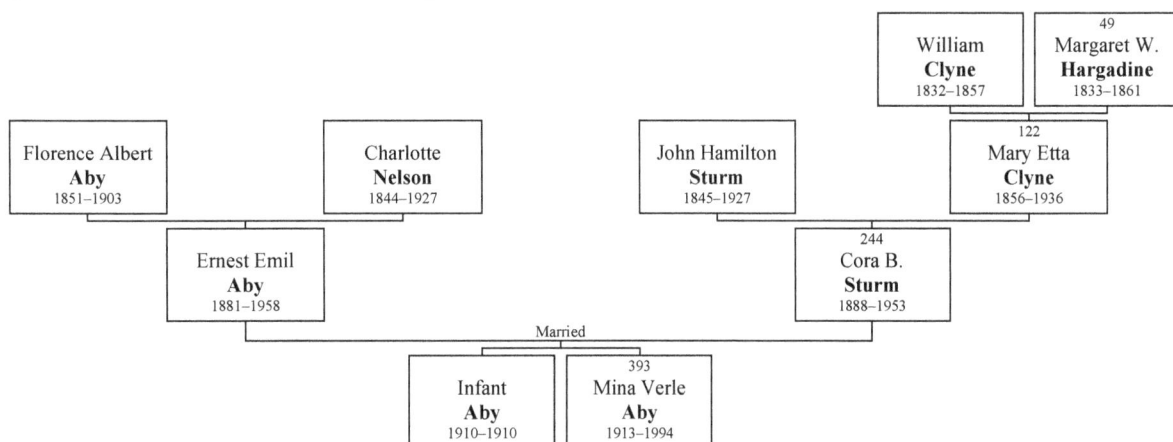

244.   **Cora B. Sturm** was born on Monday, March 19, 1888, in Dunlap, Peoria County, Illinois. She was the daughter of John Hamilton Sturm and Mary Etta Clyne (122).

Cora B. died in Edelstein, Peoria County, Illinois, in 1953 at the age of 64. She was buried in La Salle Cemetery, Rome, Peoria County, Illinois (Find a Grave ID 23269872).

She married **Ernest Emil Aby**. They had two daughters.

Ernest Emil was born in Elsmore, Allen County, Kansas, on Wednesday, July 13, 1881. He was the son of Florence Albert Aby and Charlotte Nelson.

Ernest Emil reached 76 years of age and died in 1958. He was buried in La Salle Cemetery, Rome, Peoria County, Illinois (Find a Grave ID 23269883).

Daughters of Cora B. Sturm and Ernest Emil Aby:

       f   I. **Infant Aby** was born in Peoria, Peoria County, Illinois, on June 11, 1910. She died in Peoria, Peoria County, Illinois, on June 11, 1910. Infant was buried in La Salle Cemetery, Rome, Peoria County, Illinois (Find a Grave ID 23269892).

+   393   f   II. **Mina Verle Aby** was born in Dunlap, Peoria County, Illinois, on September 04, 1913. She died in Toulon, Stark County, Illinois, on February 07, 1994, at the age of 80. Mina Verle was buried in La Salle Cemetery, Rome, Peoria County, Illinois (Find a Grave ID 44542886).

Family of Bessie Van Alstine and Roy Griffith

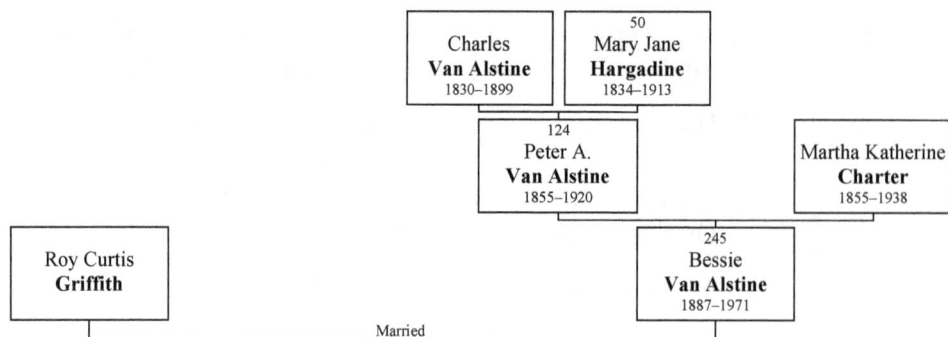

```
                    ┌──────────┬──────────┐
                    │ Charles  │    50    │
                    │Van Alstine│Mary Jane │
                    │1830–1899 │Hargadine │
                    │          │1834–1913 │
                    └──────────┴──────────┘
                         ┌──────────┐              ┌──────────────┐
                         │   124    │              │Martha Katherine│
                         │ Peter A. │              │   Charter    │
                         │Van Alstine│              │  1855–1938   │
                         │1855–1920 │              └──────────────┘
                         └──────────┘
   ┌──────────┐              ┌──────────┐
   │Roy Curtis│              │   245    │
   │ Griffith │              │  Bessie  │
   │          │              │Van Alstine│
   │          │              │1887–1971 │
   └──────────┘   Married    └──────────┘
```

245.   **Bessie Van Alstine** was born in 1887 in Taylor County, Iowa.[280] She was the daughter of Peter A. Van Alstine (124) and Martha Katherine Charter.

Bessie died in 1971 at the age of 84. She was buried in Oakwood Cemetery, Macomb, McDonough County, Illinois (Find a Grave ID 128286839).

She married **Roy Curtis Griffith**. Roy Curtis was buried (Find a Grave ID 128286817).

Family of Jessie Van Alstine and Sherman Hall

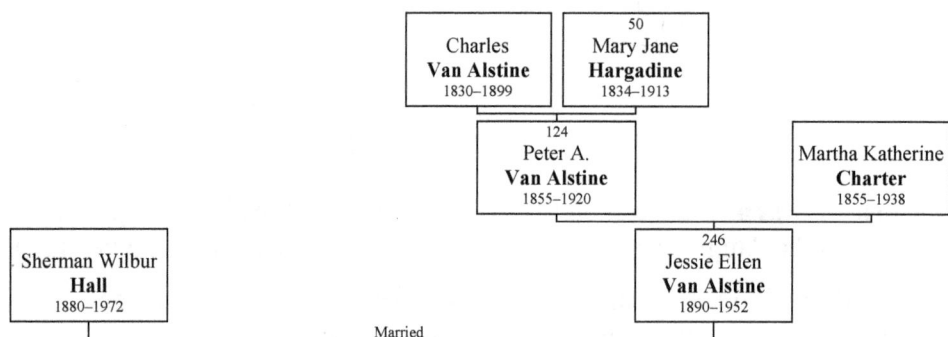

```
                    ┌──────────┬──────────┐
                    │ Charles  │    50    │
                    │Van Alstine│Mary Jane │
                    │1830–1899 │Hargadine │
                    │          │1834–1913 │
                    └──────────┴──────────┘
                         ┌──────────┐              ┌──────────────┐
                         │   124    │              │Martha Katherine│
                         │ Peter A. │              │   Charter    │
                         │Van Alstine│              │  1855–1938   │
                         │1855–1920 │              └──────────────┘
                         └──────────┘
   ┌──────────────┐           ┌──────────┐
   │Sherman Wilbur│           │   246    │
   │    Hall      │           │Jessie Ellen│
   │  1880–1972   │           │Van Alstine│
   │              │           │1890–1952 │
   └──────────────┘  Married  └──────────┘
```

246.   **Jessie Ellen Van Alstine** was born on Thursday, October 30, 1890, in Taylor County, Iowa.[281] She was the daughter of Peter A. Van Alstine (124) and Martha Katherine Charter.

Jessie Ellen died on August 20, 1952, at the age of 61. She was buried in Good Hope Cemetery, Good Hope, McDonough County, Illinois (Find a Grave ID 68375527).

She married **Sherman Wilbur Hall**. Sherman Wilbur was born in Sciota, McDonough County, Illinois, on Friday, July 16, 1880.

He reached 92 years of age and died in December 1972. Sherman Wilbur was buried in Good Hope Cemetery, Good Hope, McDonough County, Illinois (Find a Grave ID 68375510).

---

[280]   Tim Chambers, Vanalstines.GED, Date of Import: Mar 11, 2001.

[281]   Tim Chambers, Vanalstines.GED, Date of Import: Mar 11, 2001.

Family of Charles Van Alstine and Emma Shum

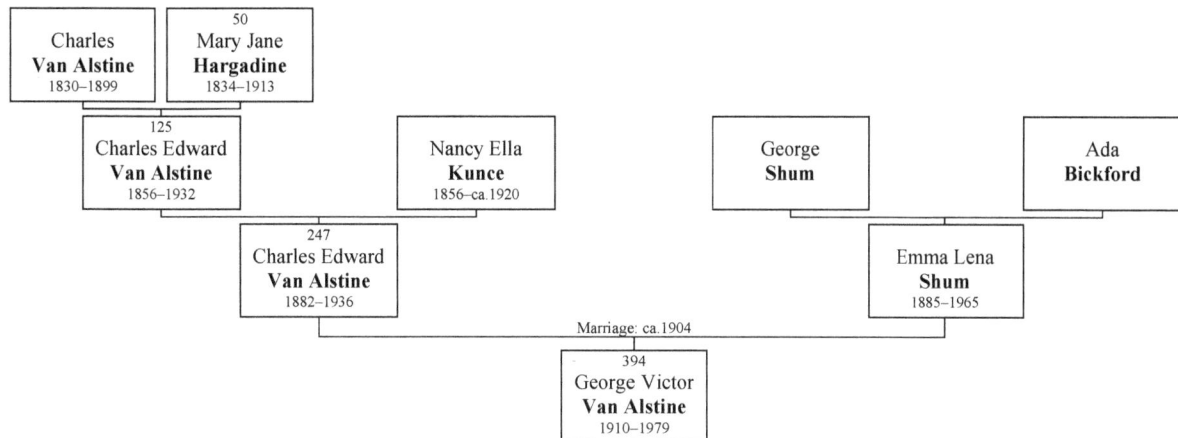

247. **Charles Edward Van Alstine** was born on Tuesday, February 21, 1882, in Guss, Taylor County, Iowa.[282] He was the son of Charles Edward Van Alstine (125) and Nancy Ella Kunce.

Charles Edward died in Gravity, Taylor County, Iowa, on May 24, 1936, at the age of 54.[282–284] He was buried in Washington Cemetery, Gravity, Taylor County, Iowa, on May 26, 1936 (Find a Grave ID 57720344).[282]

Charles Edward married **Emma Lena Shum** about December 1904 in Iowa, USA.[282, 285] They had one son.

Emma Lena was born in Greenleaf, Washington County, Kansas, on Thursday, July 30, 1885.[282] She was the daughter of George Shum and Ada Bickford.

Emma Lena reached 79 years of age and died at Skyline Hospital, White Salmon, Klickitat County, Washington in Bingen, Klickitat County, Washington, on January 22, 1965.[282, 286] Her cause of death was myocardial infarction. Emma Lena was buried on January 26, 1965, in West Klickitat Cemetery, District No. 1, White Salmon, Klickitat County, Washington (Find a Grave ID 37208600).[282]

Son of Charles Edward Van Alstine and Emma Lena Shum:

+ 394 m I. **George Victor Van Alstine** was born in Washington Township, Taylor County, Iowa, on July 11, 1910.[282, 287] He died in White Salmon, Klickitat County, Washington, on August 07, 1979, at the age of 69.[282] George Victor was buried in West Klickitat Cemetery, District No. 1, White Salmon, Klickitat County, Washington, on August 09, 1979 (Find a Grave ID 37766210).[282]

---

282 Tim Chambers, Vanalstines.GED, Date of Import: Mar 11, 2001.

283 *Bedford Times Press* Newspaper: Bedford, Taylor County, Iowa, 28 MAY 1936.

284 *Clarinda Herald* Journal Newspaper: Clarinda, Page County, Iowa, 01 JUN 1936.

285 *Bedford Free Press* Newspaper: Bedford, Taylor County, Iowa, 29 DEC 1904.

286 *Clarinda Herald Journal* Newspaper: Clarinda, Page County, Iowa, 25 JAN 1965.

287 *The Enterprise* Newspaper -White Salmon, Klickitat County, Washington, 16 AUG 1979, Pg. 4.

Family of Myrta Van Alstine and George Wilcox

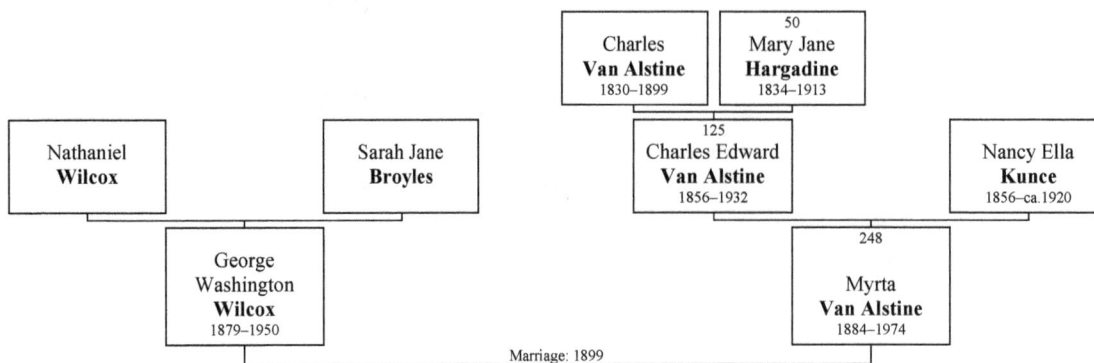

248. **Myrta Van Alstine** was born on Saturday, January 12, 1884, in Taylor County, Iowa.[288] She was the daughter of Charles Edward Van Alstine (125) and Nancy Ella Kunce.

Myrta died in Jefferson County, Colorado, on September 27, 1974, at the age of 90. She was buried in Crown Hill Cemetery, Wheat Ridge, Jefferson County, Colorado (Find a Grave ID 20883570).

At the age of 15, Myrta married **George Washington Wilcox** on Wednesday, July 19, 1899, in Page County, Iowa, when he was 19 years old.[288, 289] George Washington was born in Taylor County, Iowa, on Sunday, December 07, 1879.[288] He was the son of Nathaniel Wilcox and Sarah Jane Broyles.

George Washington reached 70 years of age and died on April 12, 1950. He was buried in Crown Hill Cemetery, Wheat Ridge, Jefferson County, Colorado (Find a Grave ID 208630324).

Bertha Van Alstine

249. **Bertha Van Alstine** was born on Thursday, September 04, 1884, in Taylor County, Iowa.[290] She was the daughter of Charles Edward Van Alstine (125) and Nancy Ella Kunce.

Bertha died in Clarinda, Page County, Iowa, in January 1959 at the age of 74. She was buried in Clarinda Cemetery, Clarinda, Page County, Iowa (Find a Grave ID 77875905).

Marriages with Gomer Henry McKinley, William Earl Mack (Page 284) and Emmett Bartley (Page 284) are known.

---

288   Tim Chambers, Vanalstines.GED, Date of Import: Mar 11, 2001.

289   *Page County Democrat* Newspaper: Page County, Iowa, 20 JUL 1899.

290   Tim Chambers, Vanalstines.GED, Date of Import: Mar 11, 2001.

Family of Bertha Van Alstine and Gomer McKinley

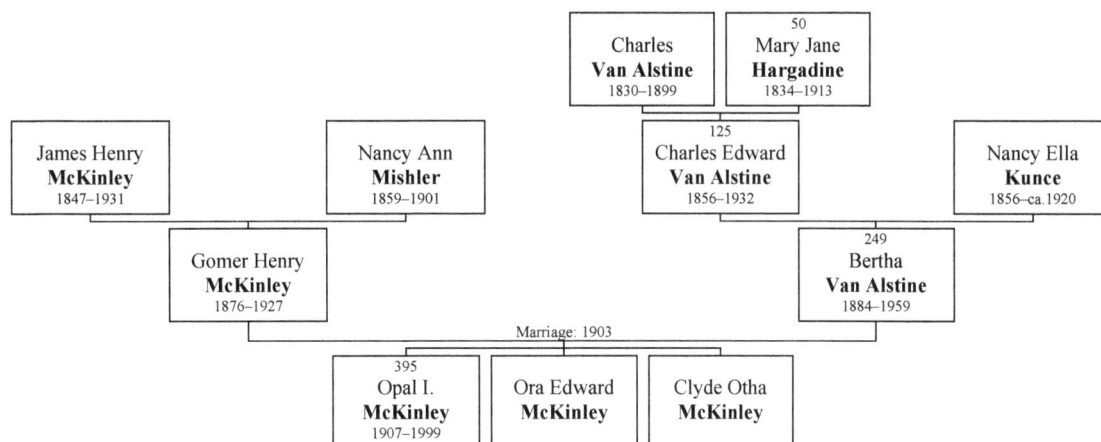

```
                                            ┌─────────┬─────────┐
                                            │ Charles │   50    │
                                            │Van Alstine│Mary Jane│
                                            │1830–1899│Hargadine│
                                            │         │1834–1913│
┌──────────┐         ┌──────────┐           ├─────────┴─────────┤         ┌──────────┐
│James Henry│         │Nancy Ann │           │        125        │         │Nancy Ella│
│ McKinley  │         │ Mishler  │           │   Charles Edward  │         │  Kunce   │
│1847–1931  │         │1859–1901 │           │    Van Alstine    │         │1856–ca.1920│
└──────────┘         └──────────┘           │     1856–1932     │         └──────────┘
      └──────┬──────────────┘               └─────────┬─────────┘              │
       ┌──────────┐                              ┌─────────────┐
       │Gomer Henry│                             │     249     │
       │ McKinley  │                             │   Bertha    │
       │1876–1927  │                             │ Van Alstine │
       └──────────┘                              │  1884–1959  │
              │         Marriage: 1903           └─────────────┘
              └─────────────────┬─────────────────────┘
         ┌──────────┐     ┌──────────┐     ┌──────────┐
         │   395    │     │Ora Edward│     │Clyde Otha│
         │  Opal I. │     │ McKinley │     │ McKinley │
         │ McKinley │     └──────────┘     └──────────┘
         │1907–1999 │
         └──────────┘
```

Here are the details about **Bertha Van Alstine's** first marriage, with Gomer Henry McKinley. You can read more about Bertha on page 282.

At the age of 18, Bertha Van Alstine married **Gomer Henry McKinley** on Monday, March 16, 1903, in Page County, Iowa, when he was 26 years old.[290–292] They had three children.

Gomer Henry was born in Boone County, Iowa, on Wednesday, June 07, 1876.[290] He was the son of James Henry McKinley and Nancy Ann Mishler.

Gomer Henry reached 51 years of age and died at Clarinda State Hospital in Clarinda, Page County, Iowa, on August 15, 1927.[290, 293] His cause of death was pernicious anemia w/ alcoholic psychosis. Gomer Henry was buried on August 17, 1927, in Memory Cemetery, Page County, Iowa (Find a Grave ID 70659301).[290]

Children of Bertha Van Alstine and Gomer Henry McKinley:

+ 395   f   I. **Opal I. McKinley** was born in Villisca, Montgomery County, Iowa, on March 18, 1907.[294] She died in Clearmont, Nodaway County, Missouri, on July 25, 1999, at the age of 92.[294] Opal I. was buried in Clarinda Cemetery, Clarinda, Page County, Iowa.[294]

       m   II. **Ora Edward McKinley**.

       m   III. **Clyde Otha McKinley**.

---

[291]   *Shenandoah World* Newspaper: Shenandoah, Page County, Iowa, 24 MAR 1903.

[292]   *Page County Democrat* Newspaper: Page County, Iowa, 26 MAR 1903.

[293]   *Clarinda Herald* Newspaper: Clarinda, Page County, Iowa, 18 AUG 1927.

[294]   Ancestry.com, Public Member Trees (Provo, UT, USA, Ancestry.com Operations, Inc., 2006), Ancestry.com, Record for Opal Icie McKinley. https://search.ancestry.co.uk/cgi-bin/sse.dll?db=1030&h=412064400747&indiv=try.

Family of Bertha Van Alstine and William Mack

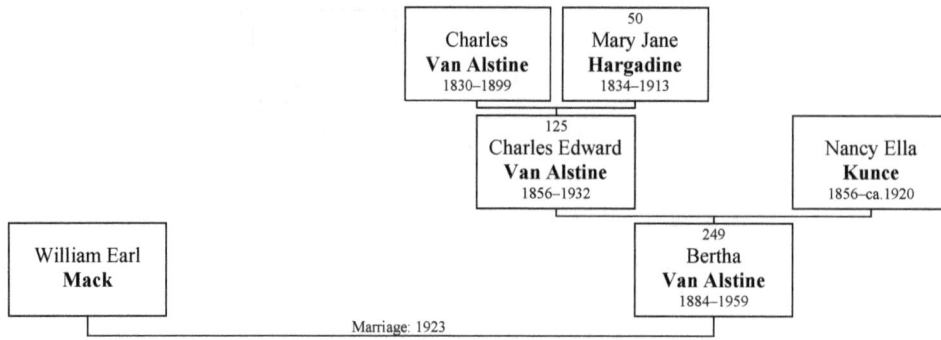

```
                                    ┌──────────┬──────────┐
                                    │ Charles  │    50    │
                                    │Van Alstine│Mary Jane│
                                    │ 1830–1899│Hargadine │
                                    │          │1834–1913 │
                                    └──────────┴──────────┘
                                    ┌──────────────────┐
                                    │       125        │    ┌──────────────┐
                                    │ Charles Edward   │    │  Nancy Ella  │
                                    │  Van Alstine     │    │    Kunce     │
                                    │   1856–1932      │    │ 1856–ca.1920 │
                                    └──────────────────┘    └──────────────┘
┌──────────────┐                          ┌──────────────┐
│ William Earl │                          │     249      │
│     Mack     │                          │   Bertha     │
│              │                          │ Van Alstine  │
│              │                          │  1884–1959   │
└──────────────┘                          └──────────────┘
                         Marriage: 1923
```

Here are the details about **Bertha Van Alstine's** second marriage, with William Earl Mack. You can read more about Bertha on page 282.

Bertha Van Alstine married **William Earl Mack** on Saturday, May 12, 1923, in Shambaugh, Page County, Iowa.

Family of Bertha Van Alstine and Emmett Bartley

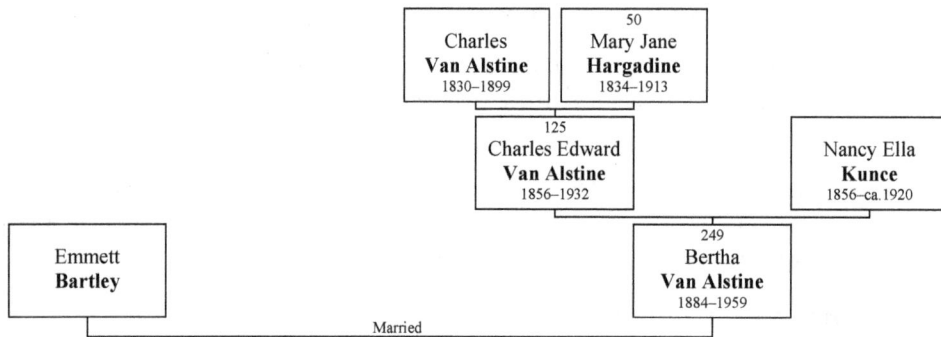

```
                                    ┌──────────┬──────────┐
                                    │ Charles  │    50    │
                                    │Van Alstine│Mary Jane│
                                    │ 1830–1899│Hargadine │
                                    │          │1834–1913 │
                                    └──────────┴──────────┘
                                    ┌──────────────────┐
                                    │       125        │    ┌──────────────┐
                                    │ Charles Edward   │    │  Nancy Ella  │
                                    │  Van Alstine     │    │    Kunce     │
                                    │   1856–1932      │    │ 1856–ca.1920 │
                                    └──────────────────┘    └──────────────┘
┌──────────────┐                          ┌──────────────┐
│   Emmett     │                          │     249      │
│   Bartley    │                          │   Bertha     │
│              │                          │ Van Alstine  │
│              │                          │  1884–1959   │
└──────────────┘                          └──────────────┘
                           Married
```

Here are the details about **Bertha Van Alstine's** third marriage, with Emmett Bartley. You can read more about Bertha on page 282.

Bertha Van Alstine married **Emmett Bartley**.

Family of Dora Van Alstine and Nathan Swallow

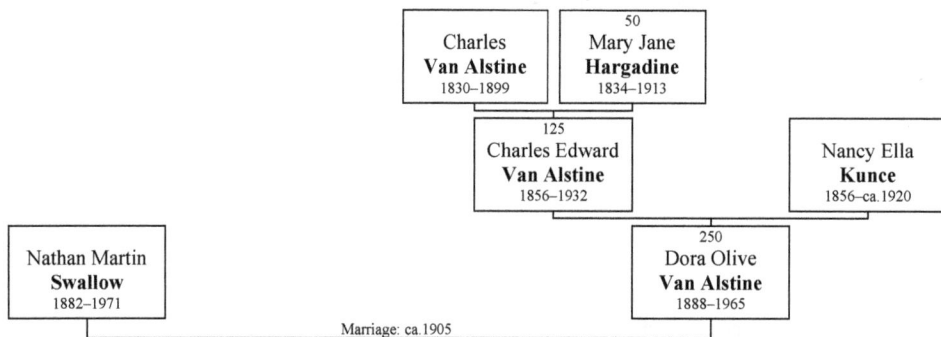

```
                                    ┌──────────┬──────────┐
                                    │ Charles  │    50    │
                                    │Van Alstine│Mary Jane│
                                    │ 1830–1899│Hargadine │
                                    │          │1834–1913 │
                                    └──────────┴──────────┘
                                    ┌──────────────────┐
                                    │       125        │    ┌──────────────┐
                                    │ Charles Edward   │    │  Nancy Ella  │
                                    │  Van Alstine     │    │    Kunce     │
                                    │   1856–1932      │    │ 1856–ca.1920 │
                                    └──────────────────┘    └──────────────┘
┌──────────────┐                          ┌──────────────┐
│Nathan Martin │                          │     250      │
│   Swallow    │                          │ Dora Olive   │
│  1882–1971   │                          │ Van Alstine  │
│              │                          │  1888–1965   │
└──────────────┘                          └──────────────┘
                       Marriage: ca.1905
```

250. **Dora Olive Van Alstine** was born on Wednesday, October 10, 1888, in Taylor County, Iowa.[295] She was the daughter of Charles Edward Van Alstine (125) and Nancy Ella Kunce.

Dora Olive died in St. James, Phelps County, Missouri, on June 17, 1965, at the age of 76. Her cause of death was myocardial infarction. Dora Olive was buried in Hematite Methodist Cemetery, Hematite, Jefferson County, Missouri, on June 19, 1965 (Find a Grave ID 141154414).

Dora Olive married **Nathan Martin Swallow** about April 14, 1905.[295, 296] Nathan Martin was born in Taylor County, Iowa, on Sunday, July 16, 1882.[295] He was also known as **Nate**.

Nathan Martin reached 89 years of age and died in Benton, Franklin County, Illinois, on October 22, 1971. He was buried in Hematite Methodist Cemetery, Hematite, Jefferson County, Missouri (Find a Grave ID 141154444).

Lloyd Van Alstine

251. **Lloyd Thomas Van Alstine** was born on Friday, August 15, 1890, in Taylor County, Iowa.[297] He was the son of Charles Edward Van Alstine (125) and Nancy Ella Kunce.

Lloyd Thomas died at Skyline Hospital, White Salmon, Klickitat County, Washington in White Salmon, Klickitat County, Washington, on June 29, 1953, at the age of 62.[297, 298] He was buried in Pine Grove Cemetery, Hood River, Hood River County, Oregon, on July 02, 1953 (Find a Grave ID 32766717).

Marriages with Maude Olive Neeley and Mae Shum (Page 286) are known.

Family of Lloyd Van Alstine and Maude Neeley

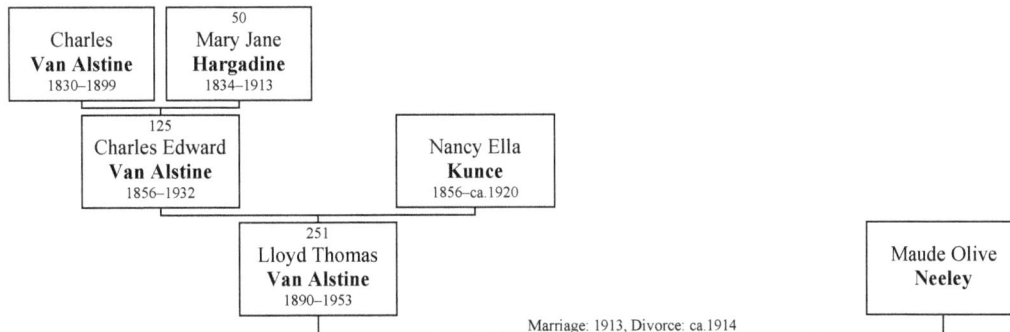

Here are the details about **Lloyd Thomas Van Alstine's** first marriage, with Maude Olive Neeley. You can read more about Lloyd Thomas on page 285.

295   Tim Chambers, Vanalstines.GED, Date of Import: Mar 11, 2001.

296   *Shenandoah World* Newspaper: Shenandoah, Page County, Iowa, 14 APR & 18 APR 1905.

297   Tim Chambers, Vanalstines.GED, Date of Import: Mar 11, 2001.

298   *Clarinda Herald Journal* Newspaper: Clarinda, Page County, Iowa, 02 JUL 1953.

Lloyd Thomas Van Alstine married **Maude Olive Neeley** on Saturday, November 08, 1913, in Clarinda, Page County, Iowa.[297, 299] They were divorced in Clarinda, Page County, Iowa, about November 1914.[297, 300]

Family of Lloyd Van Alstine and Mae Shum

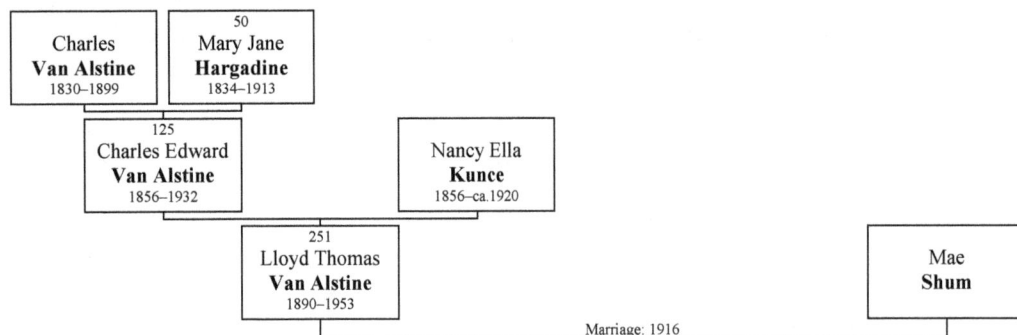

Here are the details about **Lloyd Thomas Van Alstine's** second marriage, with Mae Shum. You can read more about Lloyd Thomas on page 285.

Lloyd Thomas Van Alstine married **Mae Shum** on Wednesday, September 27, 1916, in Dallas Twp., Taylor County, Iowa.[297, 301]

Family of Hettie Van Alstine and William Orme

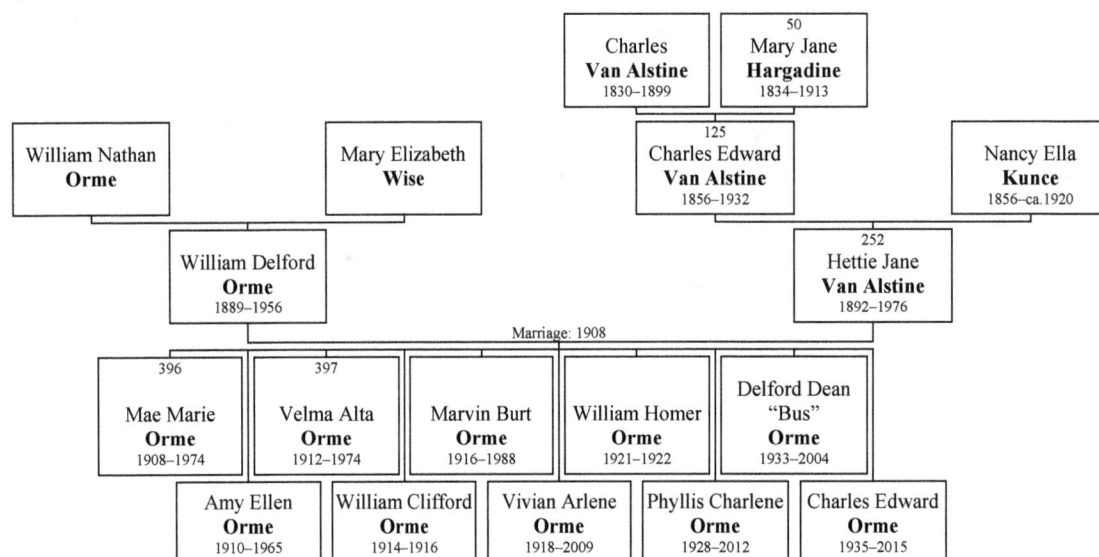

---

299   *Clarinda Herald* Newspaper: Clarinda, Page County, Iowa, 13 NOV 1913.

300   *Clarinda Herald* Newspaper: Clarinda, Page County, Iowa, 19 NOV 1914.

301   *Bedford Free Press* Newspaper: Bedford, Taylor County, Iowa, 03 OCT & 10 OCT 1916.

252.   **Hettie Jane Van Alstine** was born on Tuesday, September 27, 1892, in Montgomery County, Iowa.[302, 303] She was the daughter of Charles Edward Van Alstine (125) and Nancy Ella Kunce.

Hettie Jane died in Clarinda, Page County, Iowa, on May 20, 1976, at the age of 83.[303, 304] She was buried in North Grove Cemetery, Hepburn, Page County, Iowa (Find a Grave ID 66596661).

At the age of 15, Hettie Jane married **William Delford Orme** on Wednesday, January 22, 1908, when he was 18 years old.[303, 305] They had ten children.

William Delford was born in Taylor County, Iowa, on Sunday, February 03, 1889.[303] He was the son of William Nathan Orme and Mary Elizabeth Wise.

William Delford reached 67 years of age and died in Iowa City, Johnson County, Iowa, on March 08, 1956.[303, 306] He was buried in North Grove Cemetery, Hepburn, Page County, Iowa (Find a Grave ID 66596672).[303]

Children of Hettie Jane Van Alstine and William Delford Orme:

+   396   f   I. **Mae Marie Orme** was born in Page County, Iowa, on January 28, 1908.[303, 307] She died in Clarinda, Page County, Iowa, on April 18, 1974, at the age of 66.[303, 308] Mae Marie was buried in Clarinda Cemetery, Clarinda, Page County, Iowa (Find a Grave ID 83650420).

         f   II. **Amy Ellen Orme** was born in Page County, Iowa, on February 04, 1910. She died in Omaha, Douglas County, Nebraska, in February 1965 at the age of 54. Amy Ellen was buried in Clarinda Cemetery, Clarinda, Page County, Iowa (Find a Grave ID 71573700).

+   397   f   III. **Velma Alta Orme** was born in Hawleyville, Page County, Iowa, on February 05, 1912.[303, 307] She died in Clarinda, Page County, Iowa, on April 06, 1974, at the age of 62.[303, 309] Velma Alta was buried in Clarinda Cemetery, Clarinda, Page County, Iowa, on April 09, 1974 (Find a Grave ID 83627050).[303]

         m   IV. **William Clifford Orme** was born in Page County, Iowa, on August 24, 1914. He died in Page County, Iowa, on October 05, 1916, at the age of 2. William Clifford was buried in North Grove Cemetery, Hepburn, Page County, Iowa (Find a Grave ID 67791744).

         m   V. **Marvin Burt Orme** was born in Page County, Iowa, on July 15, 1916.[302, 303] He died in Shenandoah, Page County, Iowa, on July 17, 1988, at the age of 72.[303] Marvin Burt was buried in Guss Cemetery, Guss, Taylor County, Iowa (Find a Grave ID 50755954).

302   Social Security Death Index.

303   Tim Chambers, Vanalstines.GED, Date of Import: Mar 11, 2001.

304   *Clarinda Herald Journal* Newspaper: Clarinda, Page County, Iowa, 27 MAY 1976 -(#345)?.

305   *Bedford Free Press* Newspaper: Bedford, Taylor County, Iowa, 23 JAN 1908 (2).

306   *Clarinda Herald Journal* Newspaper: Clarinda, Page County, Iowa, 09 APR 1956.

307   Social Security Index.

308   *Clarinda Herald Journal* Newspaper: Clarinda, Page County, Iowa, 18 APR 1974.

309   *Clarinda Herald Journal* Newspaper: Clarinda, Page County, Iowa, 08 APR 1974.

f   VI. **Vivian Arlene Orme** was born in Page County, Iowa, on December 11, 1918.[303, 310] She died in Villisca, Montgomery County, Iowa, on May 12, 2009, at the age of 90. Vivian Arlene was buried in Villisca Cemetery, Villisca, Montgomery County, Iowa (Find a Grave ID 73310906).

m   VII. **William Homer Orme** was born in Page County, Iowa, on February 15, 1921. He died in Page County, Iowa, on December 29, 1922, at the age of 1. William Homer was buried in North Grove Cemetery, Hepburn, Page County, Iowa (Find a Grave ID 67791916).

f   VIII. **Phyllis Charlene Orme** was born in Clarinda, Page County, Iowa, on April 06, 1928.[303, 311] She died in Clarinda, Page County, Iowa, on February 18, 2012, at the age of 83. Phyllis Charlene was buried in North Grove Cemetery, Hepburn, Page County, Iowa (Find a Grave ID 190983808).

m   IX. **Delford Dean "Bus" Orme** was born in Clarinda, Page County, Iowa, on February 23, 1933. He died in Clarinda, Page County, Iowa, on April 11, 2004, at the age of 71. Delford Dean "Bus" was buried in Union Grove Cemetery, Northboro, Page County, Iowa (Find a Grave ID 47472117).

m   X. **Charles Edward Orme** was born in Clarinda, Page County, Iowa, on September 26, 1935. He died in Lincoln, Lancaster County, Nebraska, on June 02, 2015, at the age of 79. Charles Edward was buried in Union Grove Cemetery, Northboro, Page County, Iowa (Find a Grave ID 148603787).

Family of Lewis Van Alstine and Bertha Sollars

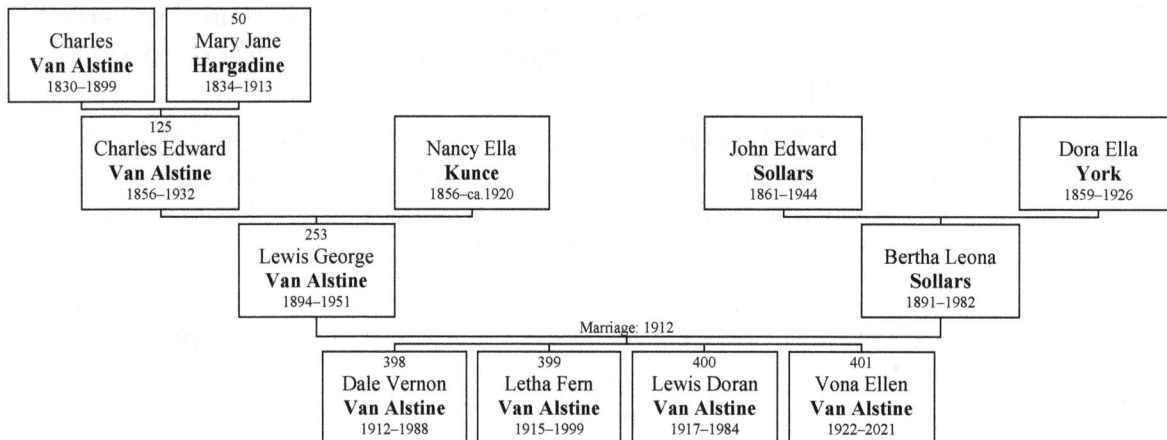

253.   **Lewis George Van Alstine** was born on Wednesday, March 21, 1894, in Montgomery County, Iowa.[312] He was the son of Charles Edward Van Alstine (125) and Nancy Ella Kunce.

---

310   *Clarinda Herald* Newspaper: Clarinda, Page County, Iowa, 27 FEB 1919.

311   *Clarinda Herald* Newspaper: Clarinda, Page County, Iowa, 07 MAY 1928.

312   Tim Chambers, Vanalstines.GED, Date of Import: Mar 11, 2001.

Lewis George died in Excelsior Springs, Clay County, Missouri, on May 30, 1951, at the age of 57.[312–314] He was buried in Clarinda Cemetery, Clarinda, Page County, Iowa (Find a Grave ID 78719424).[312]

At the age of 17, Lewis George married **Bertha Leona Sollars** on Wednesday, February 21, 1912, in Dallas Twp., Taylor County, Iowa, when she was 20 years old.[312, 315–317] They had four children.

Bertha Leona was born in Kansas, USA, on Thursday, July 30, 1891.[312] She was the daughter of John Edward Sollars and Dora Ella York.

Bertha Leona reached 90 years of age and died in Clarinda, Page County, Iowa, on June 13, 1982.[312, 318] She was buried in Clarinda Cemetery, Clarinda, Page County, Iowa (Find a Grave ID 78719543).[312]

Children of Lewis George Van Alstine and Bertha Leona Sollars:

+ 398 m   I. **Dale Vernon Van Alstine** was born in Taylor County, Iowa, on December 30, 1912. He died in Yuma, Yuma County, Arizona, on March 26, 1988, at the age of 75. Dale Vernon was buried in Clarinda Cemetery, Clarinda, Page County, Iowa (Find a Grave ID 80489337).

+ 399 f   II. **Letha Fern Van Alstine** was born in Taylor County, Iowa, on March 05, 1915.[312] She died in White Salmon, Klickitat County, Washington, on July 07, 1999, at the age of 84. Letha Fern was buried in West Klickitat Cemetery, District No. 1, White Salmon, Klickitat County, Washington (Find a Grave ID 36316760).

+ 400 m   III. **Lewis Doran Van Alstine** was born in New Market, Taylor County, Iowa, on November 29, 1917.[312, 319] He died in Stuart, Adair County, Iowa, on August 26, 1984, at the age of 66.[312, 320] Lewis Doran was buried in Clarinda Cemetery, Clarinda, Page County, Iowa (Find a Grave ID 79274588).[312]

+ 401 f   IV. **Vona Ellen Van Alstine** was born in Nodaway, Page County, Iowa, on February 27, 1922.[312, 321] She died in Iowa City, Johnson County, Iowa, on March 28, 2021, at the age of 99. Vona Ellen was buried in Oakland Cemetery, Iowa City, Johnson County, Iowa (Find a Grave ID 225111194).

---

313   *Bedford Times Press* Newspaper: Bedford, Taylor County, Iowa, 07 JUN 1951.

314   *Clarinda Herald Journal* Newspaper: Clarinda, Page County, Iowa, 05 JUN 1951.

315   *Bedford Times Republican* Newspaper: Bedford, Taylor County, Iowa, 22 FEB 1912.

316   *Bedford Free Press Newspaper*: Bedford, Taylor County, Iowa, 22 FEB 1912.

317   *Clarinda Herald* Newspaper: Clarinda, Page County, Iowa, 29 FEB 1912.

318   *Clarinda Herald Journal* Newspaper: Clarinda, Page County, Iowa, 14 JUN 1982.

319   Social Security Death Index.

320   *Clarinda Herald Journal* Newspaper: Clarinda, Page County, Iowa, 30 AUG 1984.

321   *Clarinda Herald* Newspaper: Clarinda, Page County, Iowa, 16 MAR 1922.

Family of Archibald Van Alstine and Myrtle Wallace

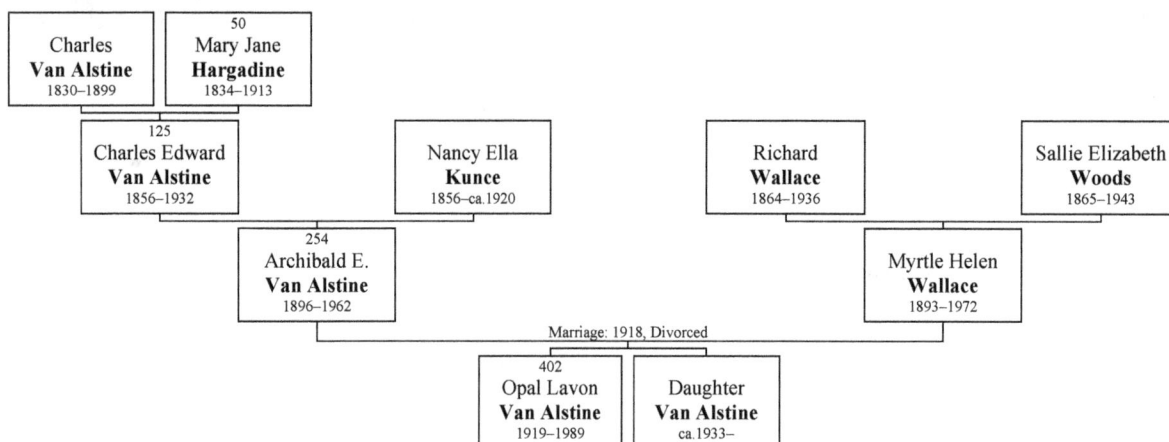

```
┌─────────────┐ ┌─────────────┐
│   Charles   │ │     50      │
│ Van Alstine │ │ Mary Jane   │
│  1830–1899  │ │  Hargadine  │
│             │ │  1834–1913  │
└─────────────┘ └─────────────┘
```

┌──────────────────┐   ┌──────────────┐   ┌──────────────┐   ┌──────────────────┐
│   125   │   │   │   │   │   │   │
│ Charles Edward   │   │ Nancy Ella   │   │   Richard   │   │ Sallie Elizabeth │
│ Van Alstine   │   │   Kunce   │   │   Wallace   │   │   Woods   │
│ 1856–1932   │   │ 1856–ca.1920 │   │ 1864–1936   │   │   1865–1943   │
└──────────────────┘   └──────────────┘   └──────────────┘   └──────────────────┘

┌──────────────┐   ┌──────────────┐
│   254   │   │ Myrtle Helen │
│ Archibald E. │   │   Wallace   │
│ Van Alstine │   │ 1893–1972   │
│ 1896–1962   │   └──────────────┘
└──────────────┘

Marriage: 1918, Divorced

┌──────────────┐ ┌──────────────┐
│   402   │ │   │
│ Opal Lavon   │ │ Daughter   │
│ Van Alstine │ │ Van Alstine │
│ 1919–1989   │ │   ca.1933–   │
└──────────────┘ └──────────────┘

254. Archibald E. Van Alstine was born on Monday, June 15, 1896, in Guss, Taylor County, Iowa.[322] He was the son of Charles Edward Van Alstine (125) and Nancy Ella Kunce.

Archibald E. died in Concord, Contra Costa County, California, on February 12, 1962, at the age of 65.[322] He was buried in Sunset View Cemetery, El Cerrito, Contra Costa County, California (Find a Grave ID 136603669).[322]

At the age of 22, Archibald E. married **Myrtle Helen Wallace** on Wednesday, July 17, 1918, in Clarinda, Page County, Iowa, when she was 25 years old.[322–326] They had two daughters. They later divorced.

Myrtle Helen was born in Missouri, USA, on Monday, March 13, 1893.[322] She was the daughter of Richard Wallace and Sallie Elizabeth Woods.

Myrtle Helen reached 79 years of age and died in Richmond, Madison County, Kentucky, on November 15, 1972. She was buried in Richmond Cemetery, Richmond, Madison County, Kentucky (Find a Grave ID 88890463).

Daughters of Archibald E. Van Alstine and Myrtle Helen Wallace:

+ 402   f   I. **Opal Lavon Van Alstine** was born in New Market, Taylor County, Iowa, on July 29, 1919.[322] She died on October 28, 1989, at the age of 70. Opal Lavon was buried in Valley View Cemetery, Sutherlin, Douglas County, Oregon (Find a Grave ID 129953448).

       f   II. **Daughter Van Alstine** was born about June 15, 1933.[322, 327]

---

322   Tim Chambers, Vanalstines.GED, Date of Import: Mar 11, 2001.

323   *Clarinda Herald* Newspaper: Clarinda, Page County, Iowa, 18 JUL 1918 & 25 JUL 1918.

324   *Bedford Times Press* Newspaper: Bedford, Taylor County, Iowa, 06 NOV 1941.

325   *Taylor County Herald* Newspaper: Bedford, Taylor County, Iowa, 06 NOV 1941.

326   *New Market Herald* New Market Newspaper: Taylor County, Iowa, 25 JUL 1918.

327   *Clarinda Herald Journal* Newspaper: Clarinda, Page County, Iowa, 15 JUN 1933.

Family of Glenn Van Alstine and Faye Miller

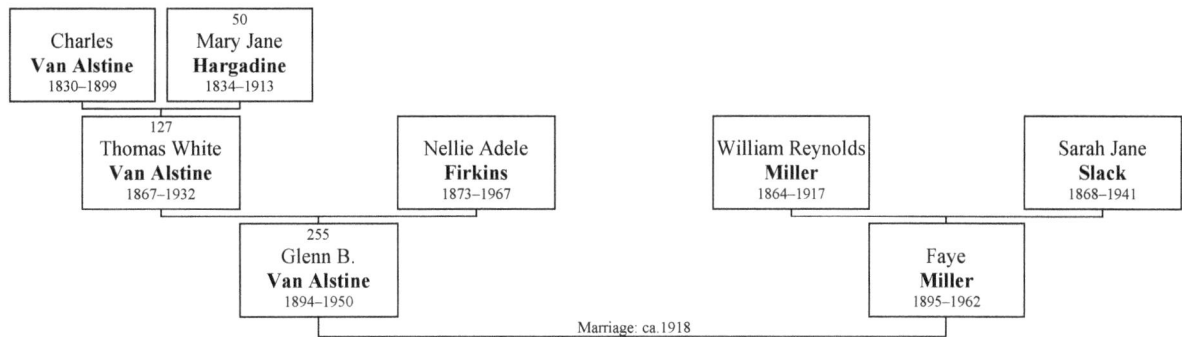

255.   **Glenn B. Van Alstine** was born on Sunday, February 18, 1894, in Taylor County, Iowa.[328] He was the son of Thomas White Van Alstine (127) and Nellie Adele Firkins.

Glenn B. died on November 05, 1950, at the age of 56. He was buried in Villisca Cemetery, Villisca, Montgomery County, Iowa (Find a Grave ID 94431841).

Glenn B. married **Faye Miller** about July 04, 1918 in Corning, Adams County, Iowa.[328, 329] Faye was born on Wednesday, November 13, 1895.[328] She was the daughter of William Reynolds Miller and Sarah Jane Slack.

Faye reached 66 years of age and died in October 1962.[328]

Family of Faye Van Alstine and Lonnie Milligan

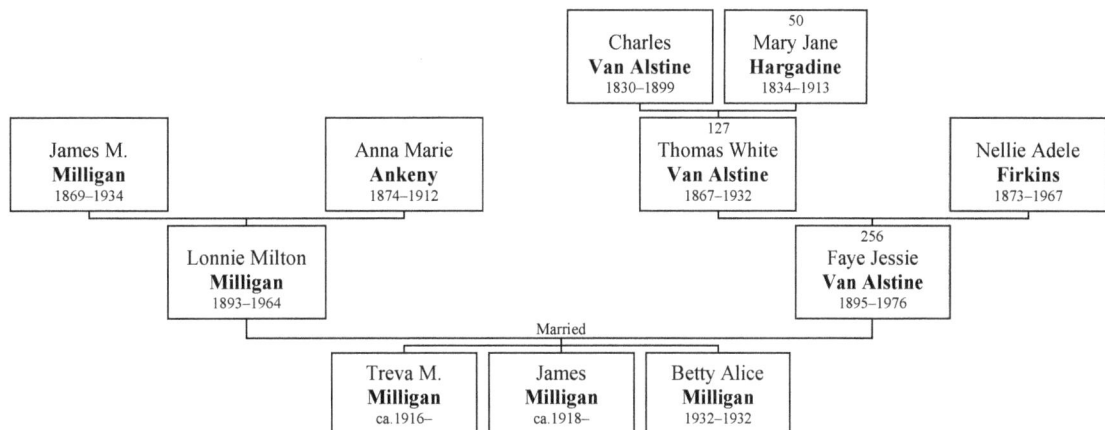

256.   **Faye Jessie Van Alstine** was born on Wednesday, September 04, 1895, in Taylor County, Iowa.[330, 331] She was the daughter of Thomas White Van Alstine (127) and Nellie Adele Firkins.

---

328   Tim Chambers, Vanalstines.GED, Date of Import: Mar 11, 2001.

329   *Bedford Times Republican* Newspaper: Bedford, Taylor County, Iowa, 04 JUL 1918.

330   Social Security Index.

331   Tim Chambers, Vanalstines.GED, Date of Import: Mar 11, 2001.

Faye Jessie died in Omaha, Douglas County, Nebraska, on June 11, 1976, at the age of 80.[331] She was buried in Villisca Cemetery, Villisca, Montgomery County, Iowa (Find a Grave ID 152717078).

She married **Lonnie Milton Milligan**. They had three children.

Lonnie Milton was born on Friday, August 25, 1893.[330, 331] He was the son of James M. Milligan and Anna Marie Ankeny. He was also known as **Lon**.

Lonnie Milton reached 70 years of age and died in Corning, Adams County, Iowa, in February 1964.[331, 332] He was buried in Villisca Cemetery, Villisca, Montgomery County, Iowa (Find a Grave ID 152717095).[331]

Children of Faye Jessie Van Alstine and Lonnie Milton Milligan:

       f   I. **Treva M. Milligan** was born about 1916.[331]

      m   II. **James Milligan** was born about 1918.[331]

      f   III. **Betty Alice Milligan** was born on November 01, 1932.[331] She died in Villisca, Montgomery County, Iowa, on November 03, 1932.[331]

Thomas Lee

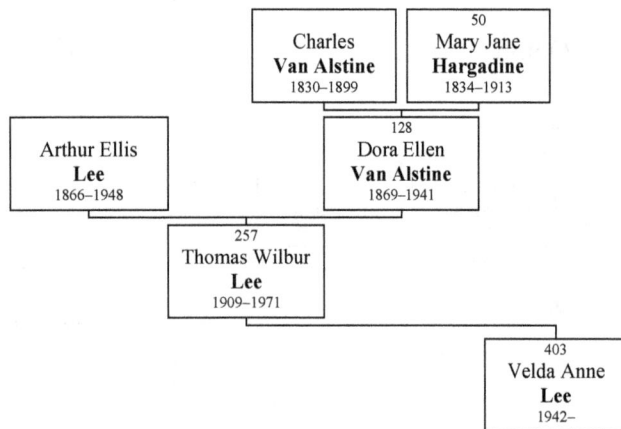

257.   **Thomas Wilbur Lee** was born on Sunday, May 09, 1909.[333] He was the son of Arthur Ellis Lee and Dora Ellen Van Alstine (128).

Thomas Wilbur died in August 1971 at the age of 62.[333]

Daughter of Thomas Wilbur Lee:

+   403   f   I. **Velda Anne Lee** was born on April 29, 1942.[333]

332   *Clarinda Herald Journal* Newspaper: Clarinda, Page County, Iowa, 17 FEB 1964.

333   Tim Chambers, Vanalstines.GED, Date of Import: Mar 11, 2001.

Family of Jonathan Clifton and Fern McFarling

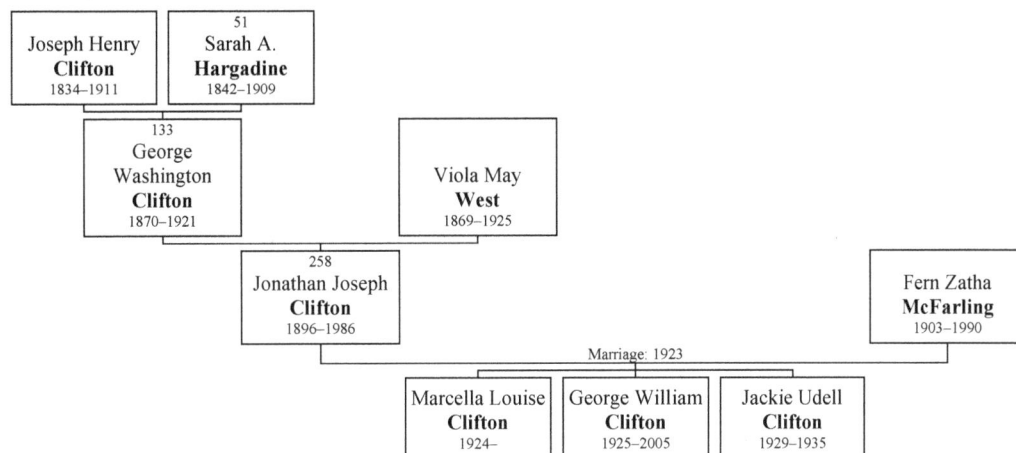

258. **Jonathan Joseph Clifton** was born on Friday, May 01, 1896, in Modale, Harrison County, Iowa.[334] He was the son of George Washington Clifton (133) and Viola May West. He was also known as **Jack**.

Jonathan Joseph served in the military: WWI, US Army, Private. He died in Freeman, Hutchinson County, South Dakota, on February 09, 1986, at the age of 89.[334] Jonathan Joseph was buried in Prospect Hill Cemetery, Wessington Springs , Jerauld County, South Dakota, on February 11, 1986 (Find a Grave ID 27974832).[334]

At the age of 26, Jonathan Joseph married **Fern Zatha McFarling** on Monday, March 05, 1923, in Plankinton, Aurora, South Dakota, when she was 20 years old.[334] They had three children.

Fern Zatha was born in Ottumwa, Wapello County, Iowa, on Tuesday, March 03, 1903.[334] She reached 87 years of age and died in Wessington Springs Township, Jerauld County, South Dakota, on August 02, 1990.[334] Fern Zatha was buried on August 06, 1990, in Prospect Hill Cemetery, Wessington Springs , Jerauld County, South Dakota (Find a Grave ID 27974877).[334]

Children of Jonathan Joseph Clifton and Fern Zatha McFarling:

f   I. **Marcella Louise Clifton** was born in Modale, Harrison County, Iowa, on February 01, 1924.

m   II. **George William Clifton** was born in Wessington Springs, Jerauld County, South Dakota, on October 18, 1925. He served in the military: WWII Veteran.

        George William died on August 31, 2005, at the age of 79. He was buried in Restlawn Memory Gardens, Huron, Beadle County, South Dakota (Find a Grave ID 27980535).

m   III. **Jackie Udell Clifton** was born in Wessington Springs Township, Jerauld County, South Dakota, on January 06, 1929. He died in Wessington Springs

---

334   Norma Pugmire Gedcom file, Date of Import: Feb 2, 2000.

Township, Jerauld County, South Dakota, on December 14, 1935, at the age of 6. Jackie Udell was buried in Prospect Hill Cemetery, Wessington Springs, Jerauld County, South Dakota (Find a Grave ID 27974778).

Family of Bruce Clifton and Jessie Burger

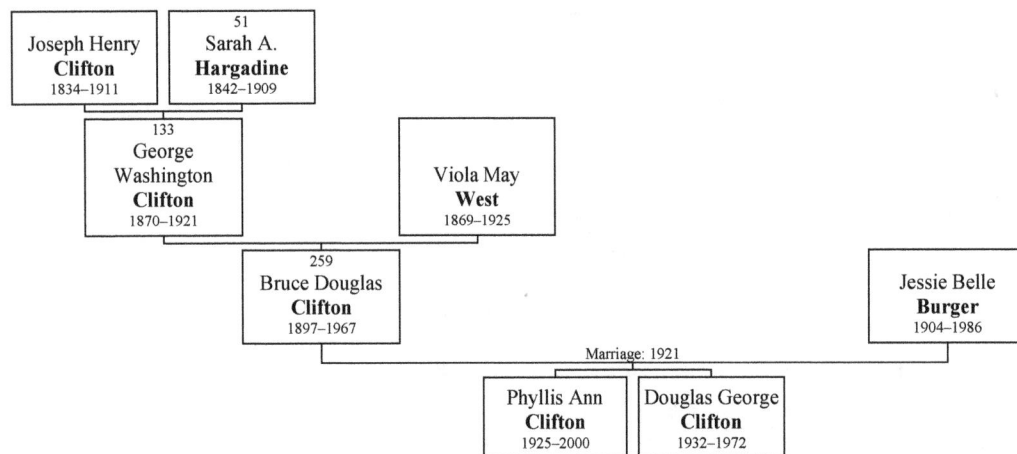

259. **Bruce Douglas Clifton** was born on Friday, December 17, 1897, in Modale, Harrison County, Iowa.[335] He was the son of George Washington Clifton (133) and Viola May West.

Bruce Douglas died in Mobridge, Walworth County, South Dakota, on June 28, 1967, at the age of 69.[335] He was buried in Greenwood Cemetery, Mobridge, Walworth County, South Dakota (Find a Grave ID 202268003).

At the age of 23, Bruce Douglas married **Jessie Belle Burger** on Tuesday, March 08, 1921, in Wessington Springs Township, Jerauld County, South Dakota, when she was 16 years old.[335] They had two children.

Jessie Belle was born in Wessington Springs Township, Jerauld County, South Dakota, on Sunday, March 27, 1904.[335] She reached 82 years of age and died in Mobridge, Walworth County, South Dakota, on May 29, 1986.[335] Jessie Belle was buried in Greenwood Cemetery, Mobridge, Walworth County, South Dakota (Find a Grave ID 202267980).[335]

Children of Bruce Douglas Clifton and Jessie Belle Burger:

f   I. **Phyllis Ann Clifton** was born in Wessington Springs Township, Jerauld County, South Dakota, on September 15, 1925. She died in Bismarck, Burleigh County, North Dakota, on May 04, 2000, at the age of 74. Phyllis Ann was buried in Greenwood Cemetery, Mobridge, Walworth County, South Dakota, on May 08, 2000 (Find a Grave ID 201929499).

m   II. **Douglas George Clifton** was born in Woonsocket, Sanborn County, South Dakota, on March 28, 1932. He died in Olivia, Renville County, Minnesota, on November 18, 1972, at the age of 40. Douglas George was buried in Greenwood Cemetery, Mobridge, Walworth County, South Dakota (Find a Grave ID 202268032).

---

335   Norma Pugmire Gedcom file, Date of Import: Feb 2, 2000.

George Clifton

260. **George Leslie Clifton** was born on Thursday, April 26, 1900, in Modale, Harrison County, Iowa. He was the son of George Washington Clifton (133) and Viola May West.

George Leslie died in Sioux Falls, Minnehaha County, South Dakota, on May 24, 1984, at the age of 84. He was buried in Woodlawn Cemetery, Sioux Falls, Minnehaha County, South Dakota, on May 26, 1984 (Find a Grave ID 136979163).

Marriages with Naomi Beltch and Florence O. Peterson (Page 295) are known.

Family of George Clifton and Naomi Beltch

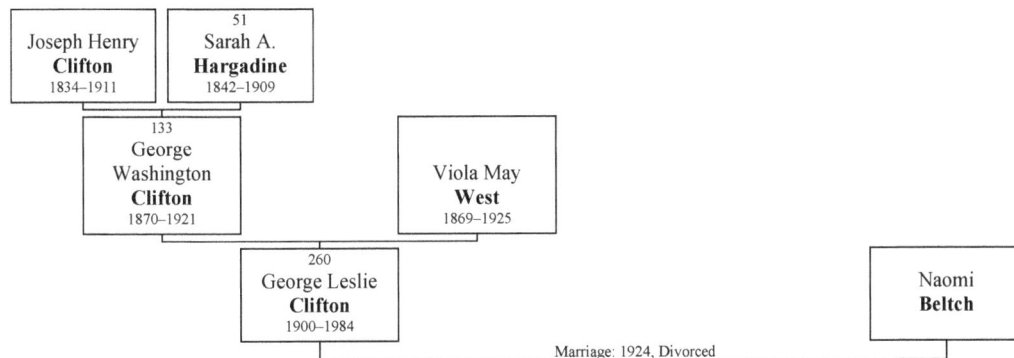

Here are the details about **George Leslie Clifton's** first marriage, with Naomi Beltch. You can read more about George Leslie on page 295.

George Leslie Clifton married **Naomi Beltch** on Monday, July 28, 1924. They are divorced. Unknown date.

Family of George Clifton and Florence Peterson

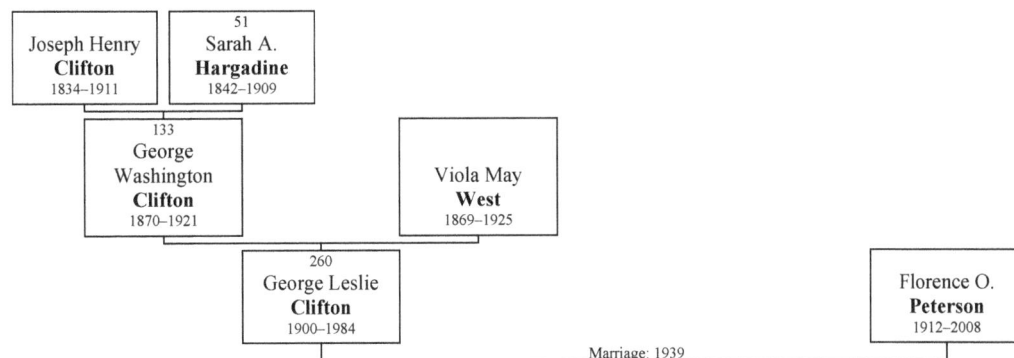

Here are the details about **George Leslie Clifton's** second marriage, with Florence O. Peterson. You can read more about George Leslie on page 295.

George Leslie Clifton married **Florence O. Peterson** in 1939. Florence O. was born in Lyons, Minnehaha County, South Dakota, on Sunday, January 28, 1912.

She reached 96 years of age and died in Sioux Falls, Minnehaha County, South Dakota, on October 17, 2008. Florence O. was buried in Woodlawn Cemetery, Sioux Falls, Minnehaha County, South Dakota (Find a Grave ID 136979062).

Gifford Clifton

261. **Gifford Perch Clifton** was born on Sunday, April 13, 1902, in Modale, Harrison County, Iowa.[336] He was the son of George Washington Clifton (133) and Viola May West.

Gifford Perch died in Winslow, Kitsap County, Washington, on August 30, 1974, at the age of 72.[336] He was buried in Kane Cemetery, Bainbridge Island, Kitsap County, Washington (Find a Grave ID 24671880).

Marriages with Evalyn Eggers and Sylvia Gough (Page 296) are known.

Family of Gifford Clifton and Evalyn Eggers

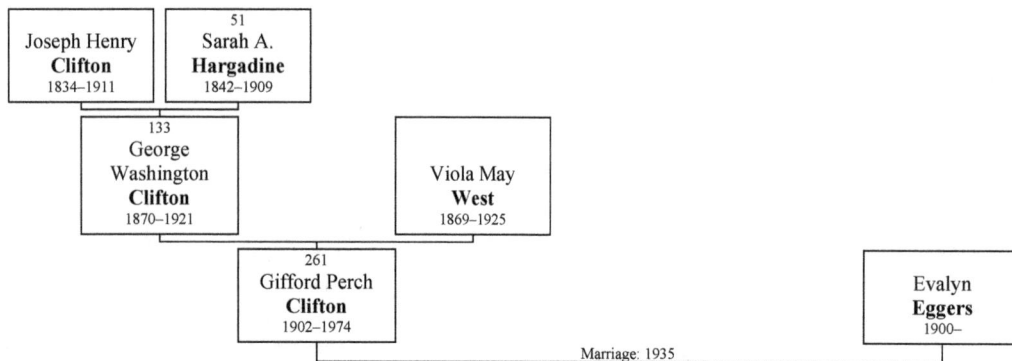

Here are the details about **Gifford Perch Clifton's** first marriage, with Evalyn Eggers. You can read more about Gifford Perch on page 296.

Gifford Perch Clifton married **Evalyn Eggers** on Friday, July 19, 1935, in Sioux Falls, Minnehaha County, South Dakota. Evalyn was born in Huron, Beadle County, South Dakota, in 1900.

Family of Gifford Clifton and Sylvia Gough

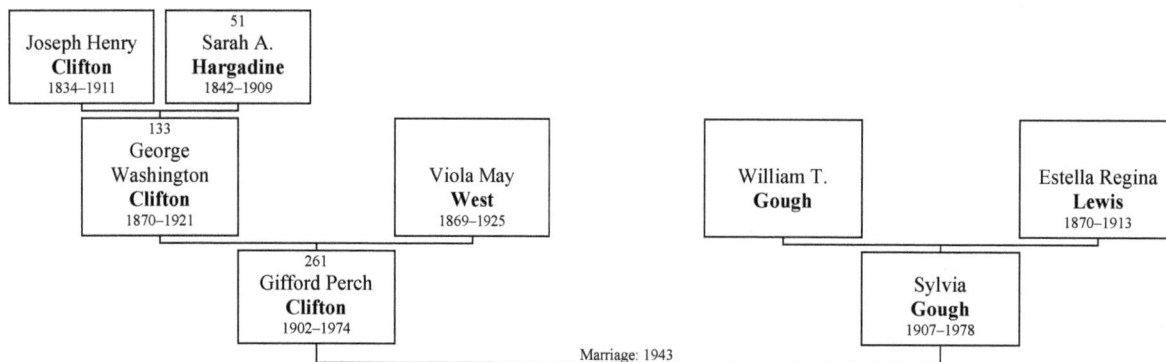

Here are the details about **Gifford Perch Clifton's** second marriage, with Sylvia Gough. You can read more about Gifford Perch on page 296.

At the age of 40, Gifford Perch Clifton married **Sylvia Gough** on Wednesday, January 20, 1943, in Seattle, King County, Washington, when she was 35 years old.[336] Sylvia was born

---

336   Norma Pugmire Gedcom file, Date of Import: Feb 2, 2000.

in Adrian, Nobles County, Minnesota, on Sunday, March 10, 1907.[336] She was the daughter of William T. Gough and Estella Regina Lewis.

Sylvia reached 71 years of age and died in Winslow, Kitsap County, Washington, on March 23, 1978.[336] She was buried in Kane Cemetery, Bainbridge Island, Kitsap County, Washington (Find a Grave ID 53173993).

Family of Pern Clifton and Elsie Johanson

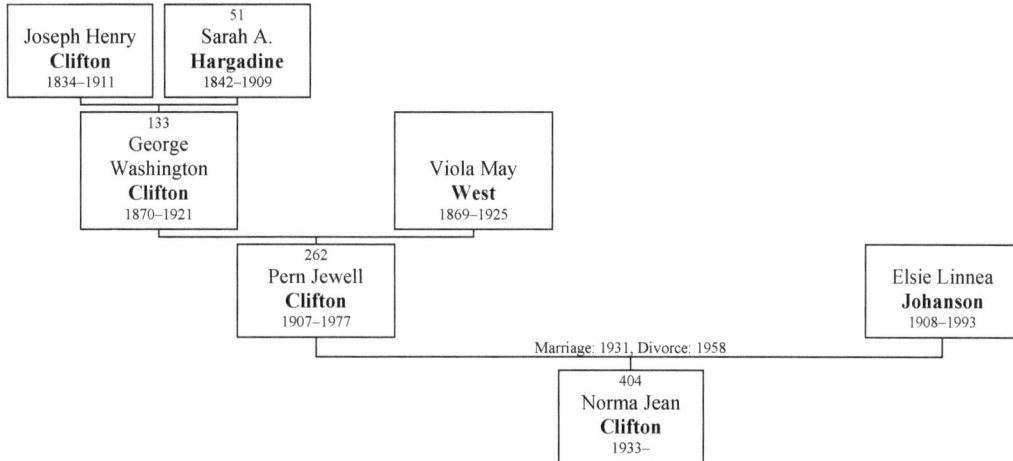

262. **Pern Jewell Clifton** was born on Wednesday, June 05, 1907, in Modale, Harrison County, Iowa.[337] He was the son of George Washington Clifton (133) and Viola May West.

Pern Jewell died in Sumner, Pierce County, Washington, on May 22, 1977, at the age of 69.[337] His body was cremated after May 22, 1977.

At the age of 23, Pern Jewell married **Elsie Linnea Johanson** on Thursday, April 02, 1931, in Tacoma, Pierce County, Washington, when she was 22 years old.[337] They were divorced in 1958. They had one daughter.

Elsie Linnea was born in Gamlakarleby, Vassa, Finland, on Tuesday, August 18, 1908.[337] She reached 85 years of age and died in Tacoma, Pierce County, Washington, on December 28, 1993.[337] Elsie Linnea was buried on December 31, 1993, in Port Blakely Cemetery, Bainbridge Island, Kitsap County, Washington (Find a Grave ID 30418208).[337]

Daughter of Pern Jewell Clifton and Elsie Linnea Johanson:

+ 404 f   I. **Norma Jean Clifton** was born in Seattle, King County, Washington, on April 07, 1933.

---

337 Norma Pugmire Gedcom file, Date of Import: Feb 2, 2000.

Family of Francis Clifton and Mildred Allred

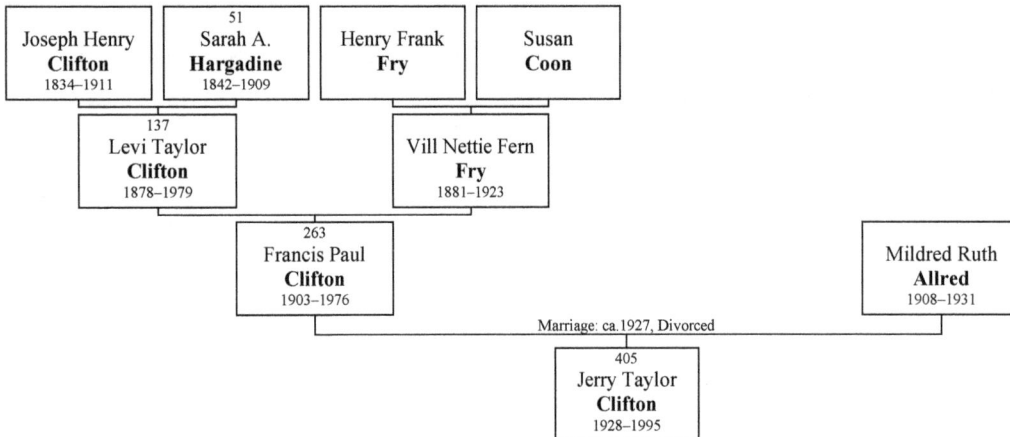

263.   **Francis Paul Clifton** was born on Sunday, June 07, 1903, in Missouri Valley, Harrison County, Iowa.[338] He was the son of Levi Taylor Clifton (137) and Vill Nettie Fern Fry.

Francis Paul died in San Francisco, San Francisco County, California, on March 31, 1976, at the age of 72.[338] He was buried in Cypress Lawn Memorial Park, Colma, San Mateo County, California, on April 12, 1976 (Find a Grave ID 76263851).[338]

Francis Paul married **Mildred Ruth Allred** about 1927 in Okmulgee County, Oklahoma.[338] They were divorced, date unknown. They had one son.

Mildred Ruth was born in Morris, Okmulgee County, Oklahoma, on Monday, April 27, 1908.[338] She reached 23 years of age and died in Long Pine, Brown County, Nebraska, on August 11, 1931.[338] Mildred Ruth was buried in Blanchard Cemetery, Blanchard, McClain County, Oklahoma (Find a Grave ID 75529678).[338]

Son of Francis Paul Clifton and Mildred Ruth Allred:

+   405   m   I. **Jerry Taylor Clifton** was born in Tulsa, Tulsa County, Oklahoma, on June 09, 1928. He died in Las Vegas, Clark County, Nevada, on September 04, 1995, at the age of 67. Jerry Taylor was buried in Bunkers Memory Gardens Cemetery, Las Vegas, Clark County, Nevada (Find a Grave ID 23317842).

Hazel Clifton

264.   **Hazel Fern Clifton** was born on Tuesday, February 21, 1905, in Woodbine, Harrison County, Iowa.[339] She was the daughter of Levi Taylor Clifton (137) and Vill Nettie Fern Fry.

Hazel Fern died in Omaha, Douglas County, Nebraska, on November 20, 1982, at the age of 77.[339] She was buried in Evergreen Memorial Park Cemetery, Omaha, Douglas County, Nebraska, on November 23, 1982 (Find a Grave ID 94233995).[339]

Marriages with Ernest Homer Mockbee and James R. Ford (Page 299) are known.

---

338   Norma Pugmire Gedcom file, Date of Import: Feb 2, 2000.

339   Norma Pugmire Gedcom file, Date of Import: Feb 2, 2000.

Family of Hazel Clifton and Ernest Mockbee

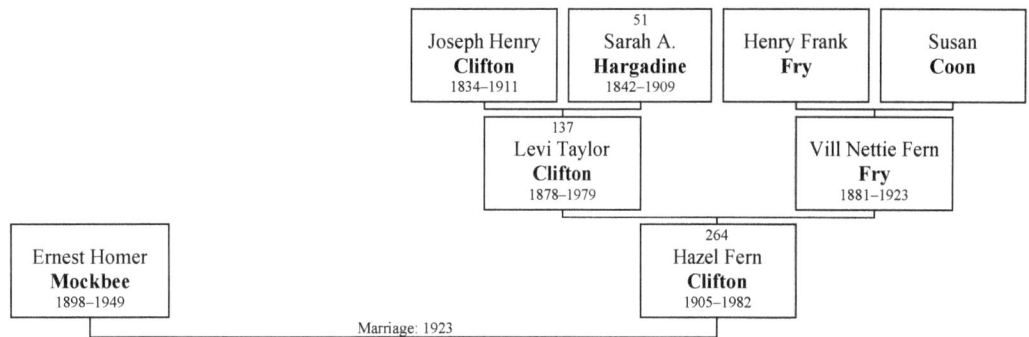

```
┌──────────────┐ ┌──────────────┐ ┌──────────────┐ ┌──────────────┐
│              │ │      51      │ │              │ │              │
│ Joseph Henry │ │  Sarah A.    │ │ Henry Frank  │ │   Susan      │
│  Clifton     │ │  Hargadine   │ │    Fry       │ │   Coon       │
│  1834–1911   │ │  1842–1909   │ │              │ │              │
└──────────────┘ └──────────────┘ └──────────────┘ └──────────────┘
          ┌──────────────┐            ┌──────────────┐
          │     137      │            │Vill Nettie Fern│
          │ Levi Taylor  │            │    Fry       │
          │  Clifton     │            │  1881–1923   │
          │  1878–1979   │            └──────────────┘
          └──────────────┘
                    ┌──────────────┐
┌──────────────┐    │     264      │
│Ernest Homer  │    │ Hazel Fern   │
│  Mockbee     │    │  Clifton     │
│  1898–1949   │    │  1905–1982   │
└──────────────┘    └──────────────┘
         Marriage: 1923
```

Here are the details about **Hazel Fern Clifton's** first marriage, with Ernest Homer Mockbee. You can read more about Hazel Fern on page 298.

At the age of 18, Hazel Fern Clifton married **Ernest Homer Mockbee** on Friday, August 17, 1923, in Council Bluffs, Pottawattamie County, Iowa, when he was 24 years old. Ernest Homer was born in Niantic, Macon County, Illinois, on Tuesday, September 27, 1898.

He reached 50 years of age and died in Winnebago, Illinois, on August 14, 1949.

Mockbee - Clifton 1923

> Ernest Mockbee and Miss Hazel Clifton, both of this city were married Friday, August 17, at Council Bluffs, Ia. Miss Clifton is the daughter of Mr. and Mrs. L. T. Clifton and is a popular and accomplished young lady and was graduate with the class of 1923 from Long Pine high school. Mr. Mockbee is a machinist's helper at the round house. Mrs. Mockbee is now visiting Missouri while Mr. Mockbee has returned to this city to resume his duties. Their plans are not announced, but it is expected they will make their home here. *The Journal* extends congratulations.

Family of Hazel Clifton and James Ford

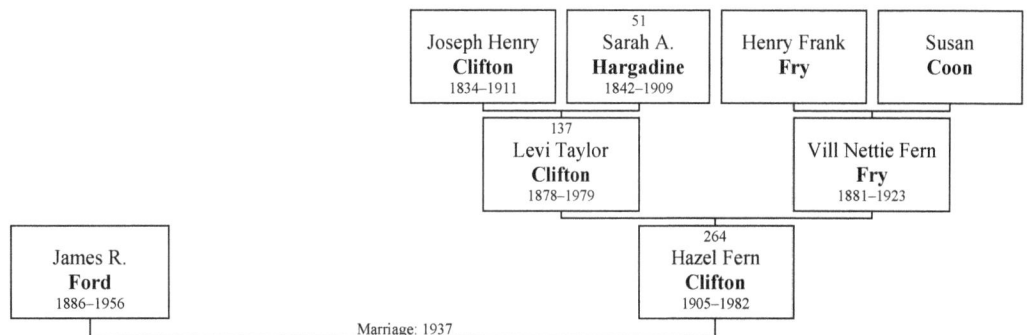

```
┌──────────────┐ ┌──────────────┐ ┌──────────────┐ ┌──────────────┐
│              │ │      51      │ │              │ │              │
│ Joseph Henry │ │  Sarah A.    │ │ Henry Frank  │ │   Susan      │
│  Clifton     │ │  Hargadine   │ │    Fry       │ │   Coon       │
│  1834–1911   │ │  1842–1909   │ │              │ │              │
└──────────────┘ └──────────────┘ └──────────────┘ └──────────────┘
          ┌──────────────┐            ┌──────────────┐
          │     137      │            │Vill Nettie Fern│
          │ Levi Taylor  │            │    Fry       │
          │  Clifton     │            │  1881–1923   │
          │  1878–1979   │            └──────────────┘
          └──────────────┘
                    ┌──────────────┐
┌──────────────┐    │     264      │
│  James R.    │    │ Hazel Fern   │
│   Ford       │    │  Clifton     │
│  1886–1956   │    │  1905–1982   │
└──────────────┘    └──────────────┘
         Marriage: 1937
```

Here are the details about **Hazel Fern Clifton's** second marriage, with James R. Ford. You can read more about Hazel Fern on page 298.

Hazel Fern Clifton married **James R. Ford** in 1937. James R. was born in Rapid City, Pennington County, South Dakota, on Monday, January 04, 1886.[339]

He reached 70 years of age and died in Omaha, Douglas County, Nebraska, on May 18, 1956.[339] James R. was buried in Greenwood Cemetery, Chadron, Dawes County, Nebraska (Find a Grave ID 109553297).

Family of Julia Hargadine and Michael Morrissey

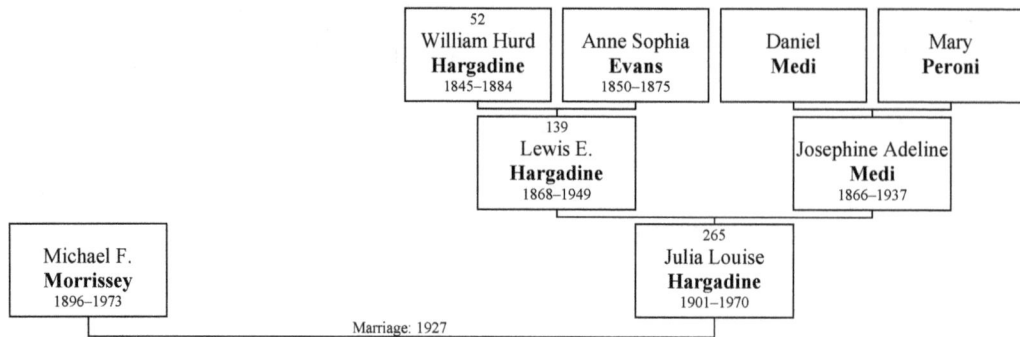

52 William Hurd **Hargadine** 1845–1884	Anne Sophia **Evans** 1850–1875	Daniel **Medi**	Mary **Peroni**

139 Lewis E. **Hargadine** 1868–1949	Josephine Adeline **Medi** 1866–1937

Michael F. **Morrissey** 1896–1973	265 Julia Louise **Hargadine** 1901–1970

Marriage: 1927

265.   **Julia Louise Hargadine** was born on Monday, January 14, 1901, in Jubilee, Peoria County, Illinois. She was the daughter of Lewis E. Hargadine (139) and Josephine Adeline Medi.

Julia Louise died in Peoria, Peoria County, Illinois, on May 30, 1970, at the age of 69. She was buried in Saint Mary of the Woods Cemetery, Princeville, Peoria County, Illinois (Find a Grave ID 31412956).

At the age of 26, Julia Louise married **Michael F. Morrissey** on Wednesday, February 16, 1927, when he was 30 years old. Michael F. was born in Peoria County, Illinois, on Tuesday, August 04, 1896.

He reached 76 years of age and died in Stark County, Illinois, on April 30, 1973. Michael F. was buried in Saint Mary of the Woods Cemetery, Princeville, Peoria County, Illinois (Find a Grave ID 31412957).

Family of Edgar Hargadine and Zella Bliss

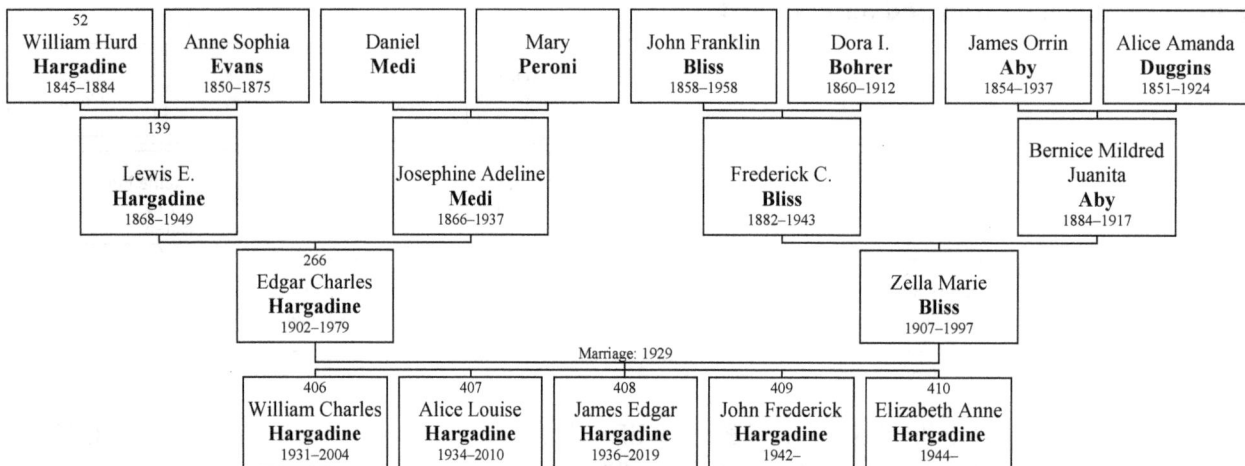

52 William Hurd **Hargadine** 1845–1884	Anne Sophia **Evans** 1850–1875	Daniel **Medi**	Mary **Peroni**	John Franklin **Bliss** 1858–1958	Dora I. **Bohrer** 1860–1912	James Orrin **Aby** 1854–1937	Alice Amanda **Duggins** 1851–1924

139 Lewis E. **Hargadine** 1868–1949	Josephine Adeline **Medi** 1866–1937	Frederick C. **Bliss** 1882–1943	Bernice Mildred Juanita **Aby** 1884–1917

266 Edgar Charles **Hargadine** 1902–1979	Zella Marie **Bliss** 1907–1997

Marriage: 1929

406 William Charles **Hargadine** 1931–2004	407 Alice Louise **Hargadine** 1934–2010	408 James Edgar **Hargadine** 1936–2019	409 John Frederick **Hargadine** 1942–	410 Elizabeth Anne **Hargadine** 1944–

266.   **Edgar Charles Hargadine** was born on Tuesday, June 03, 1902, in Jubilee Twp., Peoria County, Illinois. He was the son of Lewis E. Hargadine (139) and Josephine Adeline Medi.

Edgar Charles died in Marianna, Jackson County, Florida, on January 11, 1979, at the age of 76. He was buried in Swan Lake Memory Gardens, Peoria, Peoria County, Illinois (Find a Grave ID 167036363).

At the age of 27, Edgar Charles married **Zella Marie Bliss** on Thursday, August 29, 1929, in Lacon, Marshall County, Illinois, when she was 22 years old. They had five children.

Zella Marie was born in Princeville, Peoria County, Illinois, on Saturday, July 20, 1907. She was the daughter of Frederick C. Bliss and Bernice Mildred Juanita Aby.

Zella Marie reached 90 years of age and died in Marianna, Jackson County, Florida, on September 28, 1997. She was buried in Swan Lake Memory Gardens, Peoria, Peoria County, Illinois (Find a Grave ID 145586279).

Children of Edgar Charles Hargadine and Zella Marie Bliss:

+ 406 m I. **William Charles Hargadine** was born in Princeville, Peoria County, Illinois, on May 18, 1931. He died in Dellwood, Pinellas County, Florida, on October 28, 2004, at the age of 73. William Charles was buried in Evergreen Memorial Gardens, Kewanee, Henry County, Illinois (Find a Grave ID 145824166).

+ 407 f II. **Alice Louise Hargadine** was born in Toulon, Stark County, Illinois, on May 22, 1934. She died in Jackson, Hinds County, Mississippi, on January 06, 2010, at the age of 75. Alice Louise was buried in Toulon Cemetery, Toulon, Stark County, Illinois (Find a Grave ID 46749179).

+ 408 m III. **James Edgar Hargadine** was born in Toulon, Stark County, Illinois, on March 20, 1936. He died in New Port Richey, Pasco County, Florida, on March 04, 2019, at the age of 82. James Edgar was buried in Rienzi Cemetery, Fond du Lac, Fond du Lac County, Wisconsin, on March 09, 2019 (Find a Grave ID 197358202).

+ 409 m IV. **John Frederick Hargadine** was born in Peoria, Peoria County, Illinois, on June 30, 1942.

+ 410 f V. **Elizabeth Anne Hargadine** was born in Peoria, Peoria County, Illinois, on December 13, 1944.

Family of Walter Hargadine and Francis Budde

267. **Walter Raleigh Hargadine** was born on Monday, April 22, 1895, in Medina, Peoria County, Illinois. He was the son of Levi Lester Hargadine (140) and Annie Louisa Cook.

Walter Raleigh died in Peoria, Peoria County, Illinois, on January 11, 1982, at the age of 86. He was buried in Swan Lake Memory Gardens, Peoria, Peoria County, Illinois (Find a Grave ID 178696338).

At the age of 47, Walter Raleigh married **Francis Viola Budde** on Saturday, March 20, 1943, in Lincoln, Logan County, Illinois, when she was 32 years old. Francis Viola was born in Princeville, Stark County, Illinois, on Tuesday, August 09, 1910.

She reached 79 years of age and died in Peoria, Peoria County, Illinois, on May 05, 1990. Francis Viola was buried in Swan Lake Memory Gardens, Peoria, Peoria County, Illinois (Find a Grave ID 178696314).

Roy Hargadine

268. **Roy Raymond Hargadine** was born on Friday, September 02, 1898, in Medina, Peoria County, Illinois. He was the son of Levi Lester Hargadine (140) and Annie Louisa Cook.

Roy Raymond died in Dunlap, Peoria County, Illinois, on January 12, 1980, at the age of 81. He was buried in Mount Hawley Cemetery, Peoria, Peoria County, Illinois (Find a Grave ID 22160135).

Marriages with Cora D. Flinner and Lola B. Williams (Page 303) are known.

Family of Roy Hargadine and Cora Flinner

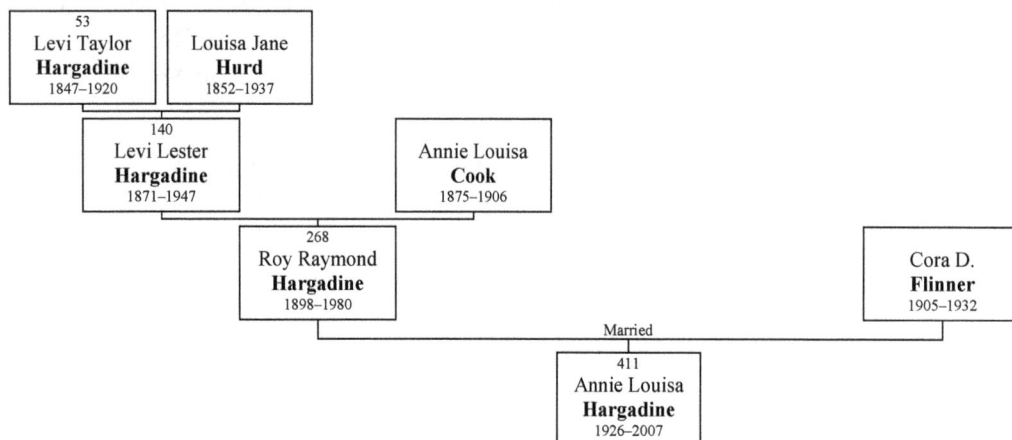

Here are the details about **Roy Raymond Hargadine's** first marriage, with Cora D. Flinner. You can read more about Roy Raymond on page 302.

Roy Raymond Hargadine married **Cora D. Flinner**. They had one daughter.

Cora D. was born in Secor, Woodford County, Illinois, on Tuesday, October 24, 1905. She reached 26 years of age and died in Hallock Township, Peoria County, Illinois, on February 03, 1932. Cora D. was buried in La Salle Cemetery, Rome, Peoria County, Illinois (Find a Grave ID 44542914).

Daughter of Roy Raymond Hargadine and Cora D. Flinner:

+ 411 f I. **Annie Louisa Hargadine** was born in Chillicothe, Peoria County, Illinois, on April 07, 1926. She was also known as **Toots**.

Annie Louisa died in Chillicothe, Peoria County, Illinois, on July 04, 2007, at the age of 81. She was buried in Chillicothe City Cemetery, Chillicothe, Peoria County, Illinois (Find a Grave ID 59248759).

Family of Roy Hargadine and Lola Williams

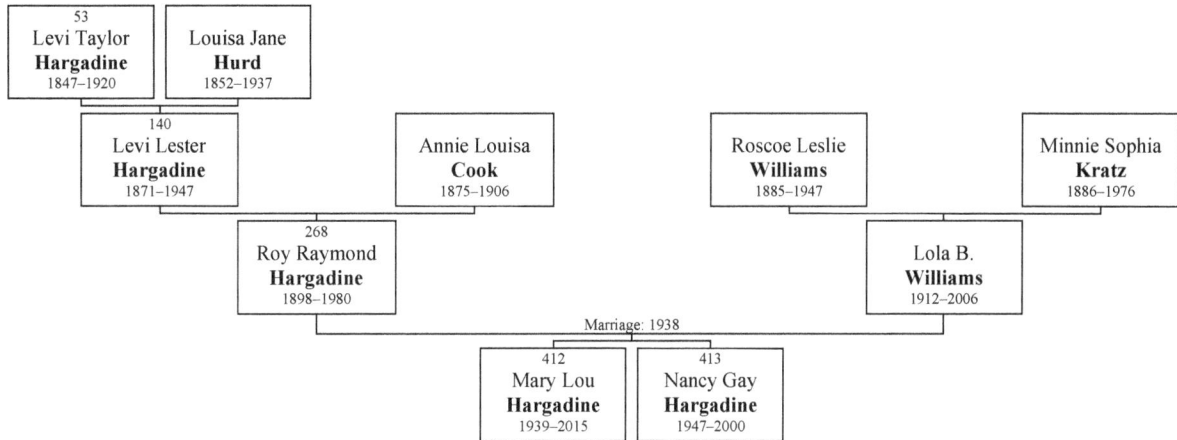

Here are the details about **Roy Raymond Hargadine's** second marriage, with Lola B. Williams. You can read more about Roy Raymond on page 302.

Roy Raymond Hargadine married **Lola B. Williams** in 1938 in Davenport, Scott County, Iowa. They had two daughters.

Lola B. was born in Marshall County, Illinois, on Saturday, March 23, 1912. She was the daughter of Roscoe Leslie Williams and Minnie Sophia Kratz.

Lola B. reached 94 years of age and died in Peoria, Peoria County, Illinois, on June 10, 2006. She was buried in Mount Hawley Cemetery, Peoria, Peoria County, Illinois (Find a Grave ID 22160134).

Daughters of Roy Raymond Hargadine and Lola B. Williams:

+ 412 f I. **Mary Lou Hargadine** was born in Alta, Peoria County, Illinois, on October 17, 1939. She died in Peoria, Peoria County, Illinois, on April 30, 2015, at the age of 75. Mary Lou was buried in Mount Hawley Cemetery, Peoria, Peoria County, Illinois (Find a Grave ID 145910274).

+ 413 f II. **Nancy Gay Hargadine** was born in Peoria, Peoria County, Illinois, on November 09, 1947. She died in Peoria, Peoria County, Illinois, on August 18, 2000, at the age of 52. Nancy Gay was buried in Mount Hawley Cemetery, Peoria, Peoria County, Illinois, on August 22, 2000 (Find a Grave ID 22160313).

Family of Laura Hargadine and Otto Mangold

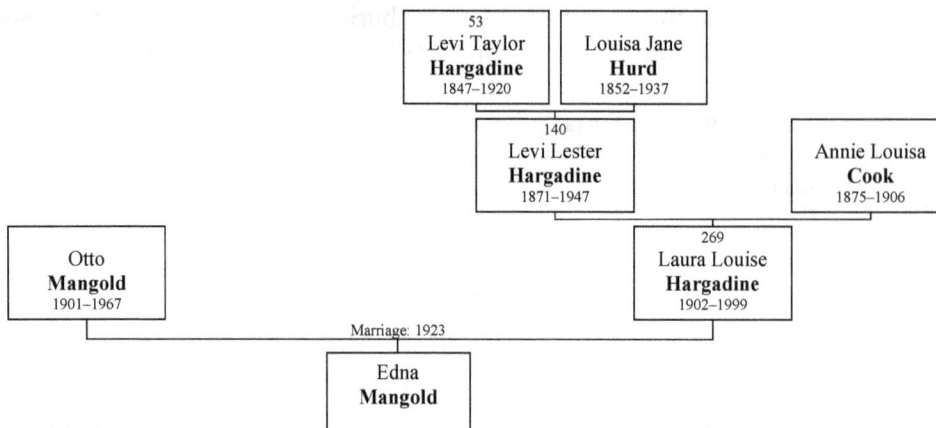

```
                    ┌──────────────┬──────────────┐
                    │ 53           │ Louisa Jane  │
                    │ Levi Taylor  │ Hurd         │
                    │ Hargadine    │ 1852–1937    │
                    │ 1847–1920    │              │
                    └──────────────┴──────────────┘
                         ┌──────────────┐           ┌──────────────┐
                         │ 140          │           │ Annie Louisa │
                         │ Levi Lester  │           │ Cook         │
                         │ Hargadine    │           │ 1875–1906    │
                         │ 1871–1947    │           └──────────────┘
                         └──────────────┘
  ┌──────────┐              ┌──────────────┐
  │ Otto     │              │ 269          │
  │ Mangold  │              │ Laura Louise │
  │ 1901–1967│              │ Hargadine    │
  └──────────┘              │ 1902–1999    │
                            └──────────────┘
              Marriage: 1923
              ┌──────────┐
              │ Edna     │
              │ Mangold  │
              └──────────┘
```

269. **Laura Louise Hargadine** was born on Saturday, January 04, 1902, in Radnor Township, Peoria County, Illinois. She was the daughter of Levi Lester Hargadine (140) and Annie Louisa Cook.

Laura Louise died in Toulon Health Care Center, Toulon, Stark County, Illinois, on March 04, 1999, at the age of 97. She was buried in Swan Lake Memory Gardens, Peoria, Peoria County, Illinois (Find a Grave ID 134027162).

At the age of 21, Laura Louise married **Otto Mangold** on Thursday, November 08, 1923, in Peoria, Peoria County, Illinois, when he was 22 years old. They had one daughter.

Otto was born in Akron Township, Peoria County, Illinois, on Tuesday, February 05, 1901. He reached 66 years of age and died in Wyoming, Stark County, Illinois, on April 08, 1967. Otto was buried in Swan Lake Memory Gardens, Peoria, Peoria County, Illinois (Find a Grave ID 169681941).

Daughter of Laura Louise Hargadine and Otto Mangold:

    f   I. **Edna Mangold**.

Family of Elva Hargadine and John Gray

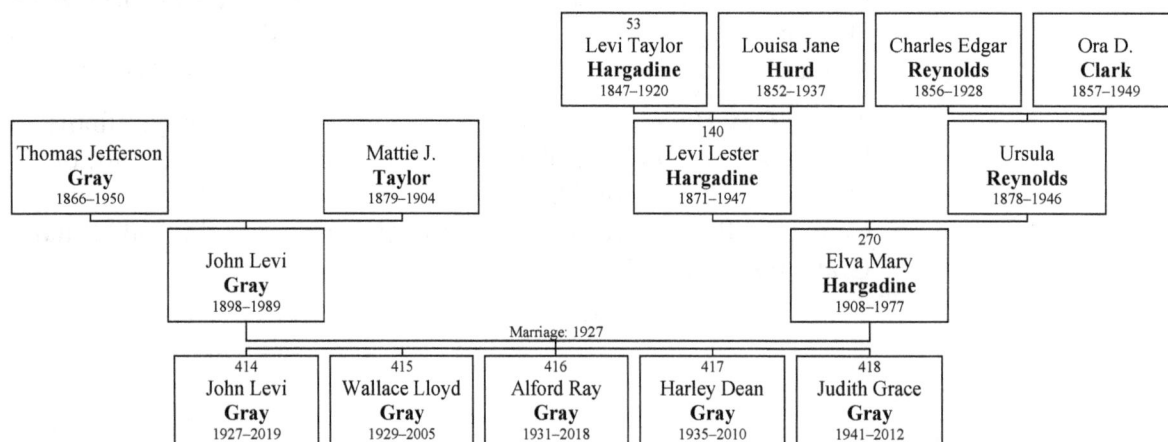

```
                              ┌────────────┬────────────┬────────────┬──────────┐
                              │ 53         │ Louisa Jane│ Charles    │ Ora D.   │
                              │ Levi Taylor│ Hurd       │ Edgar      │ Clark    │
                              │ Hargadine  │ 1852–1937  │ Reynolds   │ 1857–1949│
                              │ 1847–1920  │            │ 1856–1928  │          │
                              └────────────┴────────────┴────────────┴──────────┘
                                   ┌──────────────┐        ┌──────────────┐
┌──────────────┐   ┌──────────┐    │ 140          │        │ Ursula       │
│ Thomas       │   │ Mattie J.│    │ Levi Lester  │        │ Reynolds     │
│ Jefferson    │   │ Taylor   │    │ Hargadine    │        │ 1878–1946    │
│ Gray         │   │ 1879–1904│    │ 1871–1947    │        └──────────────┘
│ 1866–1950    │   └──────────┘    └──────────────┘
└──────────────┘
         ┌──────────┐                  ┌──────────────┐
         │ John Levi│                  │ 270          │
         │ Gray     │                  │ Elva Mary    │
         │ 1898–1989│                  │ Hargadine    │
         └──────────┘                  │ 1908–1977    │
                                       └──────────────┘
                       Marriage: 1927
  ┌────────┬────────┬────────┬────────┬────────┐
  │ 414    │ 415    │ 416    │ 417    │ 418    │
  │John Levi│Wallace │Alford  │Harley  │Judith  │
  │Gray    │Lloyd   │Ray     │Dean    │Grace   │
  │1927–2019│Gray   │Gray    │Gray    │Gray    │
  │        │1929–2005│1931–2018│1935–2010│1941–2012│
  └────────┴────────┴────────┴────────┴────────┘
```

270. **Elva Mary Hargadine** was born on Tuesday, June 23, 1908, in Dunlap, Peoria County, Illinois. She was the daughter of Levi Lester Hargadine (140) and Ursula Reynolds.

Elva Mary died on December 17, 1977, at the age of 69. She was buried in Chillicothe City Cemetery, Chillicothe, Peoria County, Illinois (Find a Grave ID 63906894).

At the age of 18, Elva Mary married **John Levi Gray** on Sunday, January 30, 1927, in Peoria, Peoria County, Illinois, when he was 29 years old. They had five children.

John Levi was born in Putnam, Putnam County, Illinois, on Tuesday, January 11, 1898. He was the son of Thomas Jefferson Gray and Mattie J. Taylor.

John Levi reached 91 years of age and died in Peoria, Peoria County, Illinois, on January 29, 1989. He was buried in Chillicothe City Cemetery, Chillicothe, Peoria County, Illinois (Find a Grave ID 63906896).

Children of Elva Mary Hargadine and John Levi Gray:

+ 414　m　I. **John Levi Gray** was born in Chillicothe, Peoria County, Illinois, on August 02, 1927. He was also known as **Jr.**.

John Levi died in La Salle, La Salle County, Illinois, on January 23, 2019, at the age of 91. He was buried in Chillicothe City Cemetery, Chillicothe, Peoria County, Illinois (Find a Grave ID 196357292).

+ 415　m　II. **Wallace Lloyd Gray** was born in Marshall County, Illinois, on July 18, 1929. He was also known as **Wally**.

Wallace Lloyd died in Peoria, Peoria County, Illinois, on September 18, 2005, at the age of 76. He was buried in Chillicothe City Cemetery, Chillicothe, Peoria County, Illinois (Find a Grave ID 59249049).

+ 416　m　III. **Alford Ray Gray** was born in Henry, Marshall County, Illinois, on December 30, 1931. He was also known as **Tote**.

Alford Ray died in Peoria, Peoria County, Illinois, on March 11, 2018, at the age of 86. He was buried in Chillicothe City Cemetery, Chillicothe, Peoria County, Illinois (Find a Grave ID 187980993).

+ 417　m　IV. **Harley Dean Gray** was born in Marshall County, Illinois, on January 30, 1935. He died in Peoria, Peoria County, Illinois, on September 20, 2010, at the age of 75. Harley Dean was buried in Chillicothe City Cemetery, Chillicothe, Peoria County, Illinois (Find a Grave ID 59036502).

+ 418　f　V. **Judith Grace Gray** was born in Henry, Marshall County, Illinois, on December 05, 1941. She died in East Peoria, Tazewell County, Illinois, on August 15, 2012, at the age of 70. Judith Grace was buried in Chillicothe City Cemetery, Chillicothe, Peoria County, Illinois (Find a Grave ID 95893159).

Forrest Hargadine

271. **Forrest Levi Hargadine** was born on Monday, March 13, 1911, in Medina, Peoria County, Illinois. He was the son of Levi Lester Hargadine (140) and Ursula Reynolds. He was also known as **Frosty**.

Forrest Levi died in Dunlap, Peoria County, Illinois, on January 23, 1985, at the age of 73. He was buried in Prospect Cemetery, Dunlap, Peoria County, Illinois, on January 26, 1985 (Find a Grave ID 22160966).

Marriages with Aletha Maude Oldfield and Dora E. Mercer (Page 307) are known.

Family of Forrest Hargadine and Aletha Oldfield

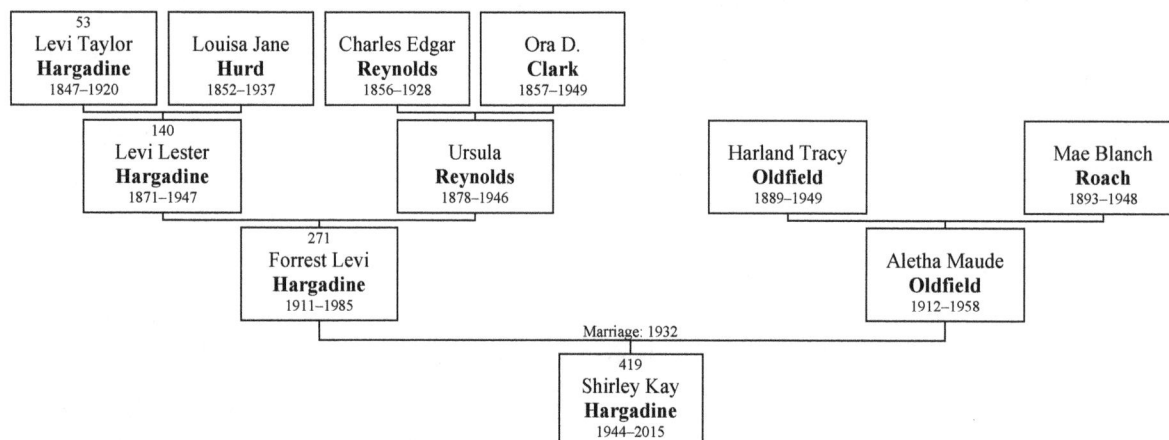

Here are the details about **Forrest Levi Hargadine's** first marriage, with Aletha Maude Oldfield. You can read more about Forrest Levi on page 305.

At the age of 21, Forrest Levi Hargadine married **Aletha Maude Oldfield** on Thursday, March 24, 1932, when she was 20 years old. They had one daughter.

Aletha Maude was born in Farmington, Fulton County, Illinois, on Wednesday, March 06, 1912. She was the daughter of Harland Tracy Oldfield and Mae Blanch Roach. She was also known as **Letha**.

Aletha Maude reached 45 years of age and died in Dunlap, Peoria County, Illinois, on January 12, 1958. She was buried on January 15, 1958, in Swan Lake Memory Gardens, Peoria, Peoria County, Illinois.

Daughter of Forrest Levi Hargadine and Aletha Maude Oldfield:

+ 419   f   I. **Shirley Kay Hargadine** was born in Peoria, Peoria County, Illinois, on September 02, 1944. Aletha Maude Oldfield was her stepmother.

                She died on November 13, 2015, at the age of 71. Shirley Kay was buried in Mason City Cemetery, Mason City, Mason County, Illinois (Find a Grave ID 155012039).

Family of Forrest Hargadine and Dora Mercer

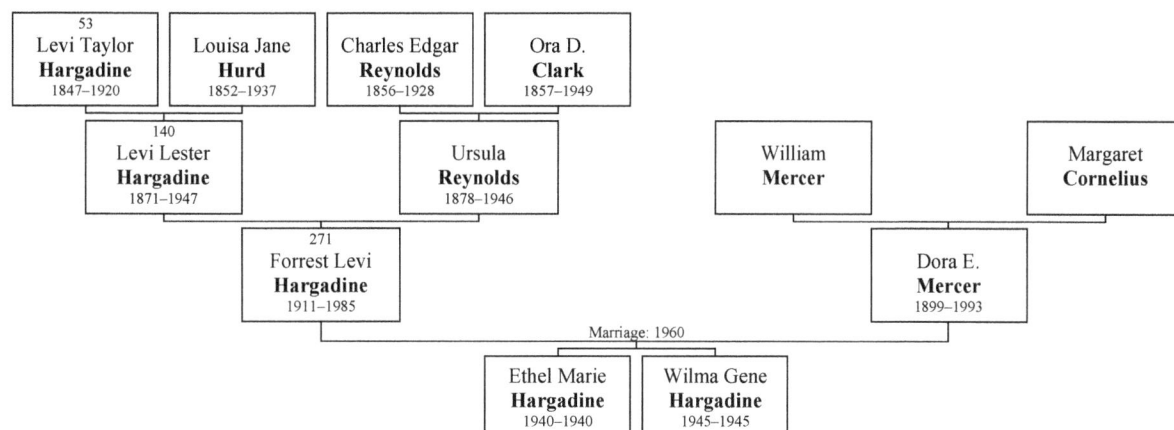

Here are the details about **Forrest Levi Hargadine's** second marriage, with Dora E. Mercer. You can read more about Forrest Levi on page 305.

At the age of 49, Forrest Levi Hargadine married **Dora E. Mercer** on Saturday, August 27, 1960, when she was 61 years old. They had two daughters.

Dora E. was born in Chickasaw Nation Indian Territory, Oklahoma, on Thursday, February 09, 1899. She was the daughter of William Mercer and Margaret Cornelius.

Dora E. reached 93 years of age and died in Peoria County, Illinois, on February 05, 1993. She was buried in Prospect Cemetery, Dunlap, Peoria County, Illinois (Find a Grave ID 22160964).

Daughters of Forrest Levi Hargadine and Dora E. Mercer:

f   I.   **Ethel Marie Hargadine** was born in Peoria, Peoria County, Illinois, on November 02, 1940. She died in Peoria, Peoria County, Illinois, on November 02, 1940. Her cause of death was: stillborn. She was buried in La Salle Cemetery, Rome, Peoria County, Illinois, on November 04, 1940 (Find a Grave ID 44542915).

f   II. **Wilma Gene Hargadine** was born in Peoria, Peoria County, Illinois, on November 28, 1945. She died in Peoria, Peoria County, Illinois, on November 28, 1945. Her cause of death was: stillborn. She was buried in La Salle Cemetery, Rome, Peoria County, Illinois (Find a Grave ID 44542920).

Ora Hargadine

272.   **Ora Alice Hargadine** was born on Wednesday, June 11, 1913, in Dunlap, Peoria County, Illinois. She was the daughter of Levi Lester Hargadine (140) and Ursula Reynolds. Ursula Reynolds was her stepmother.

Ora Alice died in Peoria, Peoria County, Illinois, on July 07, 2002, at the age of 89. She was buried in Chillicothe City Cemetery, Chillicothe, Peoria County, Illinois (Find a Grave ID 59248974).

Marriages with Arthur S. Fahay and Hal Predmore (Page 308) are known.

Family of Ora Hargadine and Arthur Fahay

```
                    ┌──────────┬──────────┐ ┌──────────┬──────────┐
                    │    53    │          │ │          │          │
                    │Levi Taylor│Louisa Jane│ │Charles Edgar│ Ora D. │
                    │Hargadine │   Hurd   │ │ Reynolds │  Clark   │
                    │1847–1920 │1852–1937 │ │1856–1928 │1857–1949 │
                    └──────────┴──────────┘ └──────────┴──────────┘
                          ┌──────────┐           ┌──────────┐
                          │   140    │           │          │
                          │Levi Lester│           │  Ursula  │
                          │Hargadine │           │ Reynolds │
                          │1871–1947 │           │1878–1946 │
                          └──────────┘           └──────────┘
      ┌──────────┐                    ┌──────────┐
      │Arthur S. │                    │   272    │
      │  Fahay   │                    │Ora Alice │
      │1907–1985 │                    │Hargadine │
      └──────────┘                    │1913–2002 │
                  Marriage: 1950      └──────────┘
```

Here are the details about **Ora Alice Hargadine's** first marriage, with Arthur S. Fahay. You can read more about Ora Alice on page 307.

At the age of 36, Ora Alice Hargadine married **Arthur S. Fahay** on Saturday, March 18, 1950, in Chillicothe, Peoria County, Illinois, when he was 42 years old. Arthur S. was born on Saturday, November 23, 1907.

He reached 77 years of age and died on June 20, 1985. Arthur S. was buried in Chillicothe City Cemetery, Chillicothe, Peoria County, Illinois (Find a Grave ID 63906698).

Family of Ora Hargadine and Hal Predmore

```
                    ┌──────────┬──────────┐ ┌──────────┬──────────┐
                    │    53    │          │ │          │          │
                    │Levi Taylor│Louisa Jane│ │Charles Edgar│ Ora D. │
                    │Hargadine │   Hurd   │ │ Reynolds │  Clark   │
                    │1847–1920 │1852–1937 │ │1856–1928 │1857–1949 │
                    └──────────┴──────────┘ └──────────┴──────────┘
                          ┌──────────┐           ┌──────────┐
                          │   140    │           │          │
                          │Levi Lester│           │  Ursula  │
                          │Hargadine │           │ Reynolds │
                          │1871–1947 │           │1878–1946 │
                          └──────────┘           └──────────┘
      ┌──────────┐                    ┌──────────┐
      │   Hal    │                    │   272    │
      │ Predmore │                    │Ora Alice │
      │1892–1972 │                    │Hargadine │
      └──────────┘                    │1913–2002 │
                      Married         └──────────┘
              ┌──────────┐
              │   420    │
              │Harold Lester│
              │ Predmore │
              │1930–1989 │
              └──────────┘
```

Here are the details about **Ora Alice Hargadine's** second marriage, with Hal Predmore. You can read more about Ora Alice on page 307.

Ora Alice Hargadine married **Hal Predmore**. They had one son.

Hal was born in Walworth, Custer County, Nebraska, on Tuesday, October 11, 1892. He served in the military: WWI Veteran.

Hal reached 80 years of age and died in Peoria, Peoria County, Illinois, on December 15, 1972. He was buried in Swan Lake Memory Gardens, Peoria, Peoria County, Illinois (Find a Grave ID 7019487).

Son of Ora Alice Hargadine and Hal Predmore:

+   420   m   I. **Harold Lester Predmore** was born in Edelstein, Peoria County, Illinois, on December 16, 1930. He died in Peoria, Peoria County, Illinois, on May 16, 1989, at the age of 58. Harold Lester was buried in Swan Lake Memory Gardens, Peoria, Peoria County, Illinois (Find a Grave ID 7019494).

Family of Margaret Hargadine and Ivan Ruse

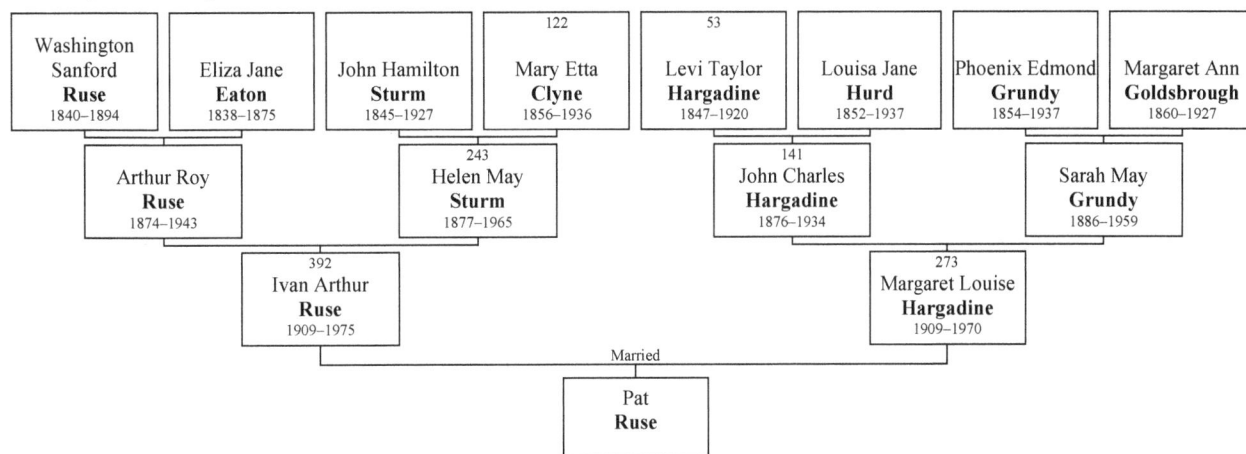

273.   **Margaret Louise Hargadine** was born on Friday, August 13, 1909, in Peoria, Peoria County, Illinois. She was the daughter of John Charles Hargadine (141) and Sarah May Grundy.

Margaret Louise died in Stark County, Illinois, on December 16, 1970, at the age of 61. She was buried in Prospect Cemetery, Dunlap, Peoria County, Illinois (Find a Grave ID 22159597).

She married **Ivan Arthur Ruse**. They had one daughter.

Ivan Arthur was born in Dunlap, Peoria County, Illinois, on Saturday, January 16, 1909. Ivan Arthur reached 66 years of age and died in Penn Township, Stark County, Illinois, on February 17, 1975.

This family is duplicated because of common ancestors. See person reference number 392 on page 417.

Daughter of Margaret Louise Hargadine and Ivan Arthur Ruse:

        f   I. **Pat Ruse**.

Family of Lucile Hargadine and Lester Streitmatter

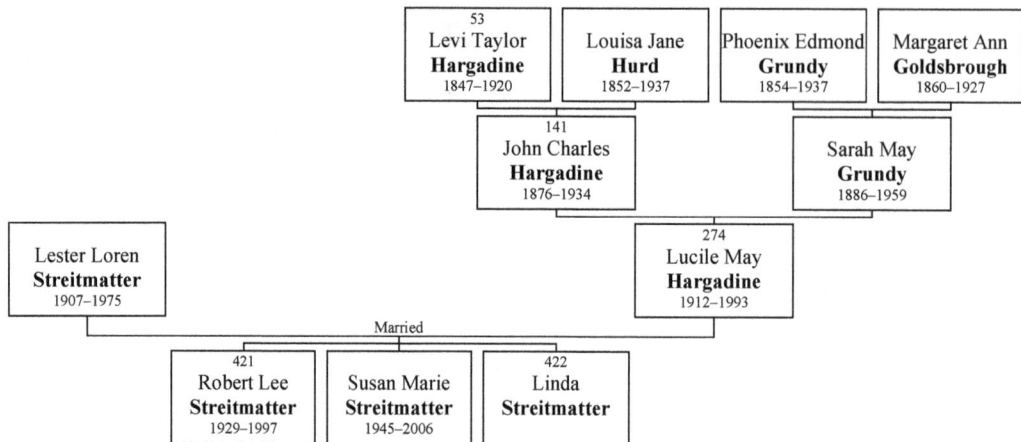

274. **Lucile May Hargadine** was born on Monday, April 08, 1912, in Peoria, Peoria County, Illinois. She was the daughter of John Charles Hargadine (141) and Sarah May Grundy.

Lucile May died in Lacon, Marshall County, Illinois, on April 18, 1993, at the age of 81. She was buried in Prospect Cemetery, Dunlap, Peoria County, Illinois (Find a Grave ID 49214782).

Lucile May married **Lester Loren Streitmatter** in Lacon, Marshall County, Illinois. They had three children.

Lester Loren was born in Peoria County, Illinois, on Monday, September 23, 1907. He was also known as **Bill**.

Lester Loren reached 68 years of age and died in Peoria, Peoria County, Illinois, on October 11, 1975. He was buried in Prospect Cemetery, Dunlap, Peoria County, Illinois (Find a Grave ID 22159729).

Children of Lucile May Hargadine and Lester Loren Streitmatter:

+ 421 m I. **Robert Lee Streitmatter** was born in Peoria County, Illinois, on November 01, 1929. He died in Chillicothe, Peoria County, Illinois, on July 08, 1997, at the age of 67. Robert Lee was buried in Prospect Cemetery, Dunlap, Peoria County, Illinois (Find a Grave ID 22159734).

f II. **Susan Marie Streitmatter** was born in Edelstein, Peoria County, Illinois, on December 27, 1945. She died in West Peoria, Peoria County, Illinois, on October 16, 2006, at the age of 60. Susan Marie was cremated (Find a Grave ID 175480538).

+ 422 f III. **Linda Streitmatter**.

Family of Elma Hargadine and Donald Langloss

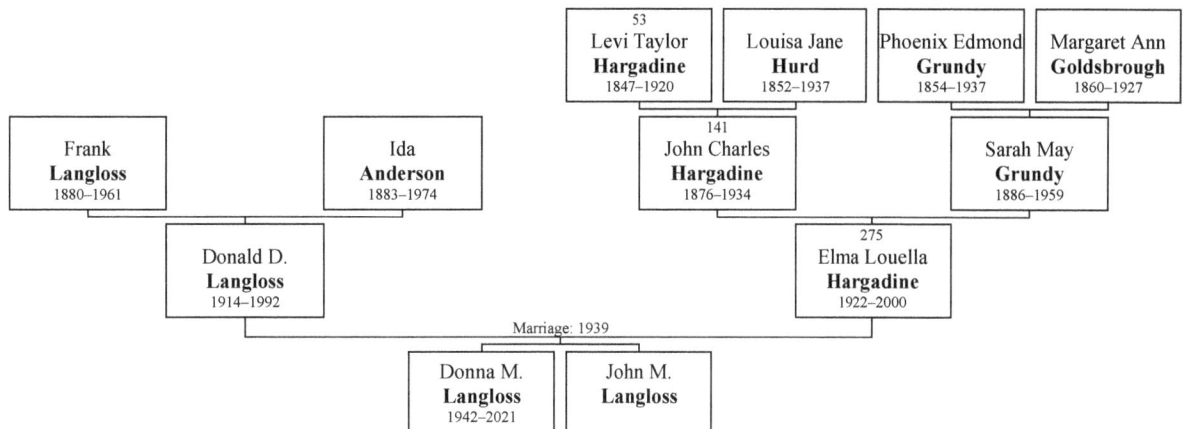

```
                                        ┌─────────────┐ ┌─────────────┐ ┌──────────────┐ ┌──────────────┐
                                        │     53      │ │             │ │Phoenix Edmond│ │ Margaret Ann │
                                        │ Levi Taylor │ │ Louisa Jane │ │    Grundy    │ │ Goldsbrough  │
                                        │  Hargadine  │ │    Hurd     │ │  1854–1937   │ │  1860–1927   │
                                        │  1847–1920  │ │  1852–1937  │ └──────────────┘ └──────────────┘
                                        └─────────────┘ └─────────────┘
┌─────────────┐      ┌─────────────┐       ┌─────────────┐             ┌─────────────┐
│    Frank    │      │     Ida     │       │     141     │             │  Sarah May  │
│   Langloss  │      │   Anderson  │       │ John Charles│             │    Grundy   │
│  1880–1961  │      │  1883–1974  │       │  Hargadine  │             │  1886–1959  │
└─────────────┘      └─────────────┘       │  1876–1934  │             └─────────────┘
          ┌─────────────┐                  └─────────────┘       ┌─────────────┐
          │  Donald D.  │                                        │     275     │
          │   Langloss  │                                        │ Elma Louella│
          │  1914–1992  │                                        │  Hargadine  │
          └─────────────┘         Marriage: 1939                 │  1922–2000  │
                                                                 └─────────────┘
                         ┌─────────────┐ ┌─────────────┐
                         │  Donna M.   │ │  John M.    │
                         │   Langloss  │ │   Langloss  │
                         │  1942–2021  │ │             │
                         └─────────────┘ └─────────────┘
```

275. **Elma Louella Hargadine** was born on Tuesday, October 17, 1922, in Peoria, Peoria County, Illinois.[340] She was the daughter of John Charles Hargadine (141) and Sarah May Grundy.

Elma Louella died in Dunlap, Peoria County, Illinois, on June 10, 2000, at the age of 77. She was buried in Prospect Cemetery, Dunlap, Peoria County, Illinois (Find a Grave ID 22161209).

At the age of 16, Elma Louella married **Donald D. Langloss** on Saturday, August 19, 1939, in Davenport, Scott County, Iowa, when he was 25 years old. They had two children.

Donald D. was born in Portage, Nebraska, on Tuesday, July 14, 1914. He was the son of Frank Langloss and Ida Anderson.

Donald D. reached 78 years of age and died in Dunlap, Peoria County, Illinois, on September 07, 1992. He was buried in Prospect Cemetery, Dunlap, Peoria County, Illinois (Find a Grave ID 22161208).

Children of Elma Louella Hargadine and Donald D. Langloss:

f I. **Donna M. Langloss** was born in Peoria, Peoria County, Illinois, on January 13, 1942. She died in Peoria, Peoria County, Illinois, on September 17, 2021, at the age of 79. Donna M. was buried in Prospect Cemetery, Dunlap, Peoria County, Illinois (Find a Grave ID 232301985).

m II. **John M. Langloss**.

---

340 *Peoria Herald* Transcript, 20 Aug 1909, pg 8. Born Friday August 13, to Mr. and Mrs. John Hargadine, a girl.

Family of Walter Hargadine and Lula Wilkerson

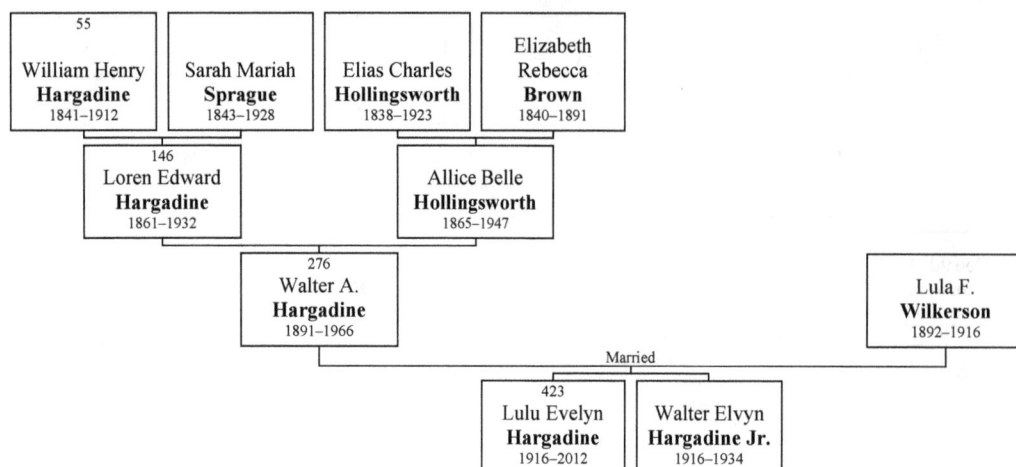

```
┌──────────────┬──────────────┬──────────────┬──────────────┐
│      55      │              │              │  Elizabeth   │
│ William Henry│ Sarah Mariah │ Elias Charles│  Rebecca     │
│  Hargadine   │   Sprague    │Hollingsworth │   Brown      │
│  1841–1912   │  1843–1928   │  1838–1923   │  1840–1891   │
└──────────────┴──────────────┴──────────────┴──────────────┘
        ┌──────────────┐      ┌──────────────┐
        │     146      │      │ Allice Belle │
        │ Loren Edward │      │Hollingsworth │
        │  Hargadine   │      │  1865–1947   │
        │  1861–1932   │      └──────────────┘
        └──────────────┘
             ┌──────────────┐              ┌──────────────┐
             │     276      │              │   Lula F.    │
             │  Walter A.   │              │  Wilkerson   │
             │  Hargadine   │              │  1892–1916   │
             │  1891–1966   │              └──────────────┘
             └──────────────┘
                        Married
             ┌──────────────┬──────────────┐
             │     423      │              │
             │ Lulu Evelyn  │ Walter Elvyn │
             │  Hargadine   │ Hargadine Jr.│
             │  1916–2012   │  1916–1934   │
             └──────────────┴──────────────┘
```

276.   **Walter A. Hargadine** was born on Thursday, October 15, 1891. He was the son of Loren Edward Hargadine (146) and Allice Belle Hollingsworth.

Walter A. served in the military: World War I, Private, 4 Co 164 Depot Brigade. He died on November 02, 1966, at the age of 75. Walter A. was buried in Bethel Cemetery, Hodges, Edwards County, Kansas (Find a Grave ID 67563210).

He married **Lula F. Wilkerson**. They had two children.

Lula F. was born on Wednesday, November 02, 1892. She reached 23 years of age and died on February 17, 1916. Lula F. was buried in Bethel Cemetery, Hodges, Edwards County, Kansas (Find a Grave ID 77360308).

Children of Walter A. Hargadine and Lula F. Wilkerson:

+ 423   f   I. **Lulu Evelyn Hargadine** was born in Kiowa County, Kansas, on January 23, 1916. She died in Stafford, Stafford County, Kansas, on December 16, 2012, at the age of 96. Lulu Evelyn was buried in Stafford Cemetery, Stafford, Stafford County, Kansas (Find a Grave ID 102433229).

          m   II. **Walter Elvyn Hargadine Jr.** was born in Kiowa County, Kansas, on January 23, 1916. He died on August 03, 1934, at the age of 18. Walter Elvyn was buried in Bethel Cemetery, Hodges, Edwards County, Kansas (Find a Grave ID 67563284).

Family of Loren Hargadine and Rella Stevens

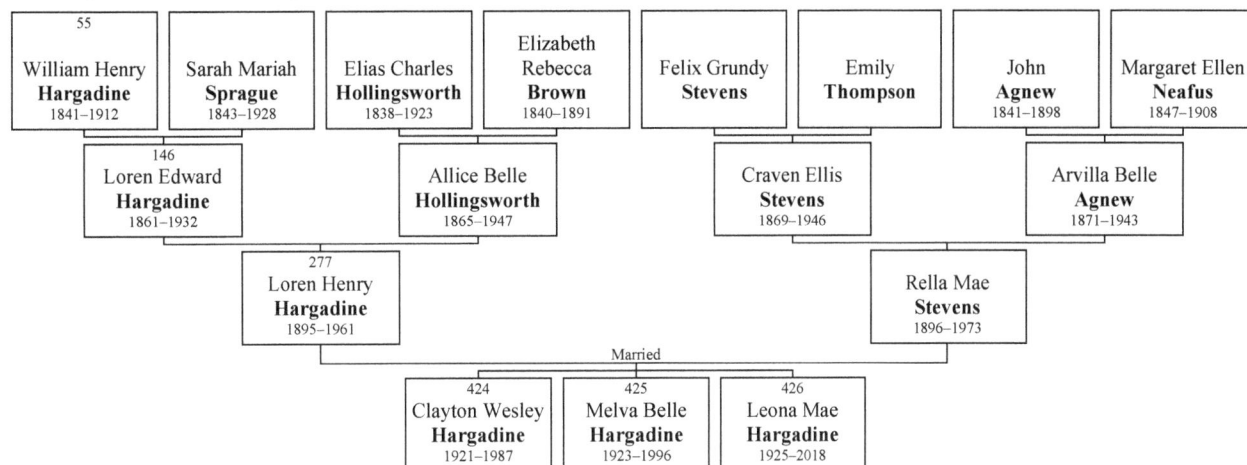

277. **Loren Henry Hargadine** was born on Saturday, April 27, 1895. He was the son of Loren Edward Hargadine (146) and Allice Belle Hollingsworth.

Loren Henry died on April 28, 1961, at the age of 66. He was buried in Bethel Cemetery, Hodges, Edwards County, Kansas (Find a Grave ID 67562861).

He married **Rella Mae Stevens**. They had three children.

Rella Mae was born in Corydon, Harrison County, Indiana, on Wednesday, May 13, 1896. She was the daughter of Craven Ellis Stevens and Arvilla Belle Agnew.

Rella Mae reached 77 years of age and died in Greensburg, Kiowa County, Kansas, on September 24, 1973. She was buried on September 27, 1973, in Bethel Cemetery, Hodges, Edwards County, Kansas (Find a Grave ID 67563033).

Children of Loren Henry Hargadine and Rella Mae Stevens:

+ 424   m   I. **Clayton Wesley Hargadine** was born in Kiowa County, Kansas, on January 12, 1921. He died in Wichita, Sedgwick County, Kansas, on December 19, 1987, at the age of 66. His cause of death was heart attack. He was buried in Hillcrest Cemetery, Mullinville, Kiowa County, Kansas (Find a Grave ID 119318359).

+ 425   f   II. **Melva Belle Hargadine** was born on December 03, 1923. She died in Wichita, Sedgwick County, Kansas, on September 06, 1996, at the age of 72. Melva Belle was buried in Lakeview Cemetery & Mausoleum, Wichita, Sedgwick County, Kansas (Find a Grave ID 71277097).

+ 426   f   III. **Leona Mae Hargadine** was born in Mullinville, Kiowa County, Kansas, on December 09, 1925. She died in Emporia, Lyon County, Kansas, on March 31, 2018, at the age of 92. Leona Mae was buried in Maplewood Memorial Lawn Cemetery, Emporia, Lyon County, Kansas, on April 06, 2018 (Find a Grave ID 91010250).

Gaylord Hargadine

278. **Gaylord Warren Hargadine** was born on Tuesday, December 21, 1897, in Kiowa County, Kansas. He was the son of Loren Edward Hargadine (146) and Allice Belle Hollingsworth.

Gaylord Warren died in Kinsley, Edwards County, Kansas, on October 19, 1964, at the age of 66. His cause of death was heart attack. Gaylord Warren was buried in Hillside Cemetery, Kinsley, Edwards County, Kansas (Find a Grave ID 11422744).

Marriages with Anna Adeline Riley and Roxie Isabell Branstetter (Page 315) are known.

Family of Gaylord Hargadine and Anna Riley

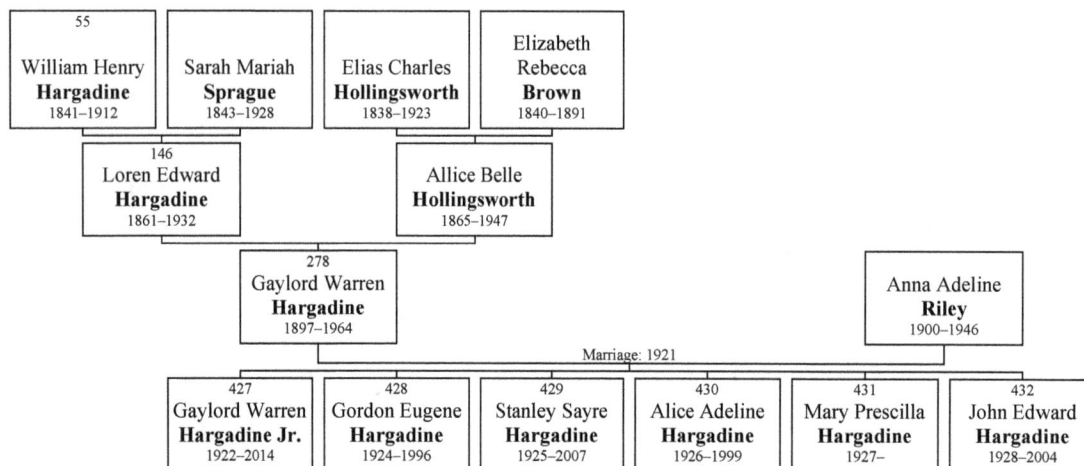

Here are the details about **Gaylord Warren Hargadine's** first marriage, with Anna Adeline Riley. You can read more about Gaylord Warren on page 314.

Gaylord Warren Hargadine married **Anna Adeline Riley** in 1921. They had six children.

Anna Adeline was born in Kinsley, Edwards County, Kansas, on Sunday, September 30, 1900. She reached 45 years of age and died on February 11, 1946. Her cause of death was cancer. She was buried in Hillside Cemetery, Kinsley, Edwards County, Kansas (Find a Grave ID 11422742).

Children of Gaylord Warren Hargadine and Anna Adeline Riley:

+ 427 m I. **Gaylord Warren Hargadine Jr.** was born in Edwards County, Kansas, on September 14, 1922. He was also known as **Gayle**.

Gaylord Warren died in Southlake, Tarrant County, Texas, on January 26, 2014, at the age of 91. He was buried in Bluebonnet Hills Memorial Park, Colleyville, Tarrant County, Texas (Find a Grave ID 124324658).

+ 428 m II. **Gordon Eugene Hargadine** was born in Mullinville, Kiowa County, Kansas, on February 02, 1924. He died on December 21, 1996, at the age of 72. Gordon Eugene was buried in Fort Logan National Cemetery, Denver County, Colorado, on August 13, 1997 (Find a Grave ID 753312).

+ 429 m III. **Stanley Sayre Hargadine** was born in Kiowa, Barber County, Kansas, on February 12, 1925. He died in Wenatchee, Chelan County, Washington, on May 19, 2007, at the age of 82.

+ 430 f IV. **Alice Adeline Hargadine** was born in Mullinville, Kiowa County, Kansas, on July 29, 1926. She died in Coquille, Coos County, Oregon, on December 25, 1999, at the age of 73. Alice Adeline was cremated.

+ 431 f V. **Mary Prescilla Hargadine** was born in Mullinville, Kiowa County, Kansas, on October 23, 1927.

+ 432 m VI. **John Edward Hargadine** was born in Mullinville, Kiowa County, Kansas, on November 24, 1928. He died in Fort Collins, Larimer County, Colorado, on July 28, 2004, at the age of 75.

Family of Gaylord Hargadine and Roxie Branstetter

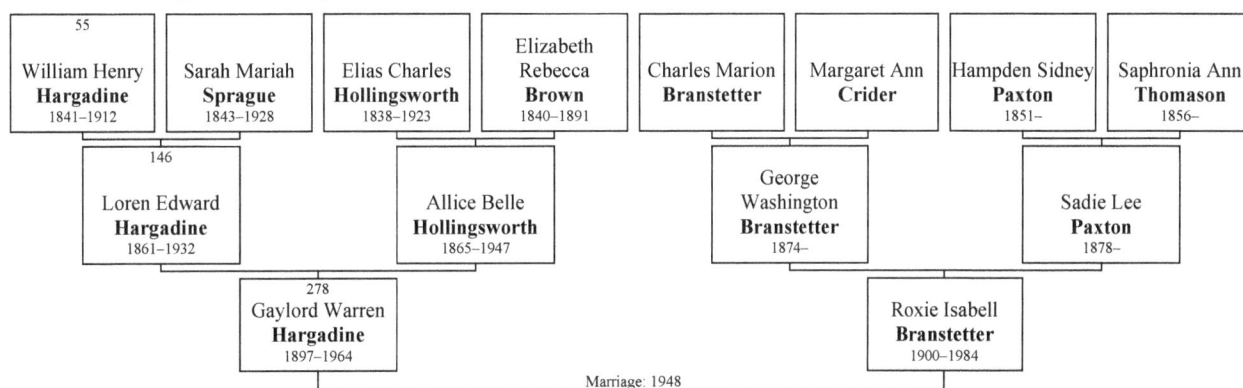

55							
William Henry **Hargadine** 1841–1912	Sarah Mariah **Sprague** 1843–1928	Elias Charles **Hollingsworth** 1838–1923	Elizabeth Rebecca **Brown** 1840–1891	Charles Marion **Branstetter**	Margaret Ann **Crider**	Hampden Sidney **Paxton** 1851–	Saphronia Ann **Thomason** 1856–

146 Loren Edward **Hargadine** 1861–1932	Allice Belle **Hollingsworth** 1865–1947	George Washington **Branstetter** 1874–	Sadie Lee **Paxton** 1878–

278 Gaylord Warren **Hargadine** 1897–1964	Roxie Isabell **Branstetter** 1900–1984

Marriage: 1948

Here are the details about **Gaylord Warren Hargadine's** second marriage, with Roxie Isabell Branstetter. You can read more about Gaylord Warren on page 314.

At the age of 50, Gaylord Warren Hargadine married **Roxie Isabell Branstetter** on Sunday, May 02, 1948, when she was 48 years old. Roxie Isabell was born in Mansfield, Wright County, Missouri, on Wednesday, January 03, 1900. She was the daughter of George Washington Branstetter and Sadie Lee Paxton.

Roxie Isabell reached 84 years of age and died in Greensburg, Kiowa County, Kansas, on January 17, 1984. She was buried in Fairview Cemetery, Greensburg, Kiowa County, Kansas (Find a Grave ID 155943941).

Family of Ada Hargadine and George Tieperman

279.   **Ada Leona Hargadine** was born on Saturday, January 03, 1903. She was the daughter of Loren Edward Hargadine (146) and Allice Belle Hollingsworth.

Ada Leona died in Kinsley, Edwards County, Kansas, on March 23, 1983, at the age of 80. She was buried in Hillside Cemetery, Kinsley, Edwards County, Kansas (Find a Grave ID 11636385).

At the age of 21, Ada Leona married **George Ernest Tieperman** on Tuesday, November 18, 1924, when he was 26 years old. They had one son.

George Ernest was born in Ellinwood, Barton County, Kansas, on Wednesday, January 12, 1898. He reached 72 years of age and died in Kinsley, Edwards County, Kansas, on April 27, 1970. George Ernest was buried on April 29, 1970, in Hillside Cemetery, Kinsley, Edwards County, Kansas (Find a Grave ID 11636392).

Son of Ada Leona Hargadine and George Ernest Tieperman:

m   I. **Louis E. Tieperman** was born in Kinsley, Edwards County, Kansas, on November 10, 1931. He died in Kinsley, Edwards County, Kansas, on October 16, 2022, at the age of 90. Louis E. was buried in Hillside Cemetery, Kinsley, Edwards County, Kansas (Find a Grave ID 244807255).

Family of Arthur Hargadine and Mintie Barnes

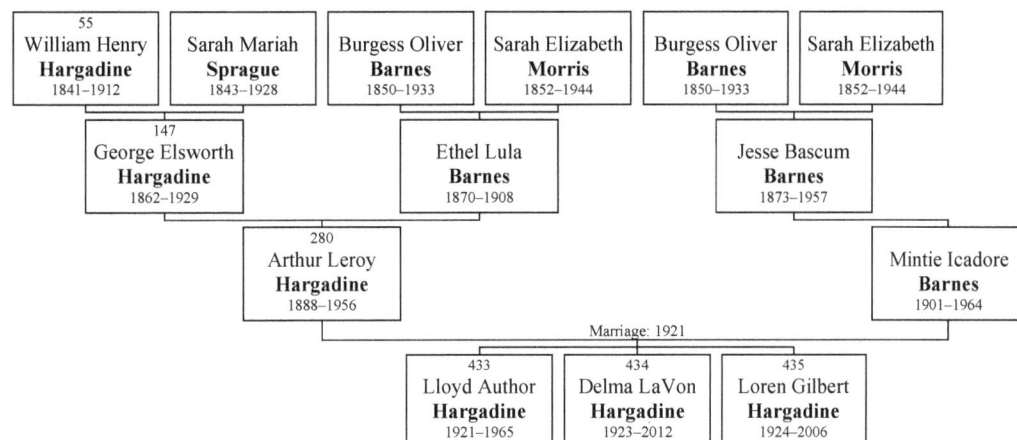

280. **Arthur Leroy Hargadine** was born on Friday, July 06, 1888. He was the son of George Elsworth Hargadine (147) and Ethel Lula Barnes.

Arthur Leroy served in the military: WWI PFC, Co F 32, Engineers. He died in Alden, Rice County, Kansas, on March 16, 1956, at the age of 67. Arthur Leroy was buried in Alden Valley Cemetery, Alden, Rice County, Kansas (Find a Grave ID 52865637).

At the age of 33, Arthur Leroy married **Mintie Icadore Barnes** on Wednesday, July 27, 1921, when she was 20 years old. They had three children.

Mintie Icadore was born on Tuesday, June 25, 1901. She was the daughter of Jesse Bascum Barnes.

Mintie Icadore reached 62 years of age and died on March 04, 1964. She was buried in Alden Valley Cemetery, Alden, Rice County, Kansas (Find a Grave ID 52866031).

Children of Arthur Leroy Hargadine and Mintie Icadore Barnes:

+ 433 m I. **Lloyd Author Hargadine** was born on June 17, 1921. He died on September 13, 1965, at the age of 44. Lloyd Author was buried in Alden Valley Cemetery, Alden, Rice County, Kansas (Find a Grave ID 52865939).

+ 434 f II. **Delma LaVon Hargadine** was born in Alden, Rice County, Kansas, on February 17, 1923. She died in Buhler, Reno County, Kansas, on November 25, 2012, at the age of 89. Delma LaVon was buried in Memorial Park Cemetery, Hutchinson, Reno County, Kansas, on November 30, 2012 (Find a Grave ID 101350449).

+ 435 m III. **Loren Gilbert Hargadine** was born in Alden, Rice County, Kansas, on January 31, 1924. He died in Alden, Rice County, Kansas, on September 04, 2006, at the age of 82. Loren Gilbert was buried in Alden Valley Cemetery, Alden, Rice County, Kansas (Find a Grave ID 65498459).

Family of Floyd Hargadine and Belle Liggett

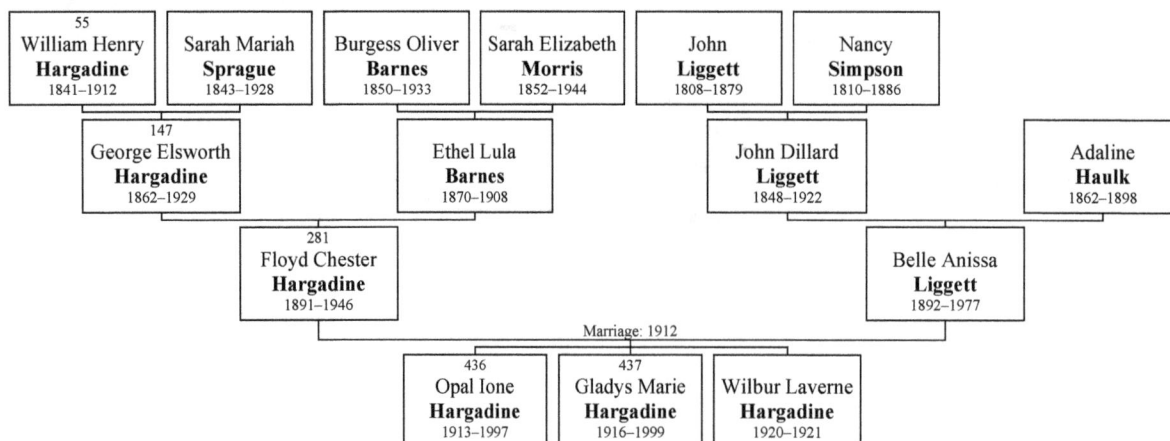

281. **Floyd Chester Hargadine** was born on Wednesday, April 22, 1891, in Ottumwa, Wapello County, Iowa. He was the son of George Elsworth Hargadine (147) and Ethel Lula Barnes.

Floyd Chester died in Sheridan, Yamhill County, Oregon, on February 08, 1946, at the age of 54. He was buried in Evergreen Memorial Park, McMinnville, Yamhill County, Oregon, on February 12, 1946 (Find a Grave ID 193555745).

At the age of 21, Floyd Chester married **Belle Anissa Liggett** on Sunday, September 01, 1912, when she was 19 years old. They had three children.

Belle Anissa was born in Mullinville, Kiowa County, Kansas, on Friday, December 16, 1892. She was the daughter of John Dillard Liggett and Adaline Haulk. She was also known as **Anna Belle**.

Belle Anissa reached 84 years of age and died in McMinnville, Yamhill County, Oregon, on August 09, 1977. She was buried in Evergreen Memorial Park, McMinnville, Yamhill County, Oregon (Find a Grave ID 193555724).

Children of Floyd Chester Hargadine and Belle Anissa Liggett:

+ 436 f I. **Opal Ione Hargadine** was born in Greensburg, Kiowa County, Kansas, on July 08, 1913. She died in Camarillo, Ventura County, California, on October 11, 1997, at the age of 84. Opal Ione was buried in Conejo Mountain Memorial Park, Camarillo, Ventura County, California (Find a Grave ID 76421198).

+ 437 f II. **Gladys Marie Hargadine** was born in Mullinville, Kiowa County, Kansas, on December 04, 1916. She died in McMinnville, Yamhill County, Oregon, on May 19, 1999, at the age of 82. Gladys Marie was buried in Evergreen Memorial Park, McMinnville, Yamhill County, Oregon (Find a Grave ID 34509535).

m III. **Wilbur Laverne Hargadine** was born in Greensburg, Kiowa County, Kansas, on May 28, 1920. He died on January 16, 1921. Wilbur Laverne was buried in Bethel Cemetery, Hodges, Edwards County, Kansas (Find a Grave ID 67563412).

Family of Marguerite Hargadine and Alvin Clinkenbeard

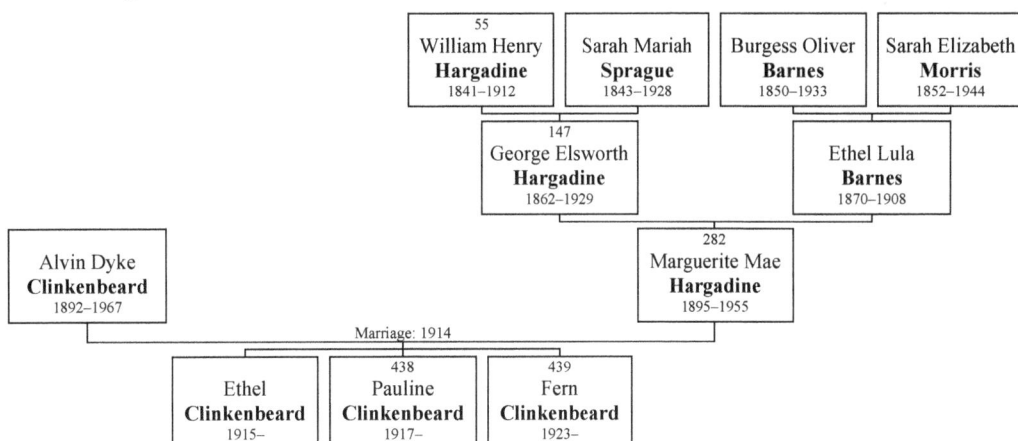

282. **Marguerite Mae Hargadine** was born on Monday, November 11, 1895, in Competine, Wapello County, Iowa. She was the daughter of George Elsworth Hargadine (147) and Ethel Lula Barnes.

Marguerite Mae died in Dalhart, Hartley County, Texas, on June 11, 1955, at the age of 59. She was buried in Memorial Park Cemetery, Dalhart, Hartley County, Texas (Find A Grave ID 44923571).

At the age of 18, Marguerite Mae married **Alvin Dyke Clinkenbeard** on Wednesday, August 19, 1914, when he was 22 years old. They had three daughters.

Alvin Dyke was born in Laclede County, Missouri, on Saturday, March 26, 1892. He reached 75 years of age and died in Dalhart, Hartley County, Texas, on July 16, 1967. Alvin Dyke was buried in Memorial Park Cemetery, Dalhart, Dallam County, Texas (Find a Grave ID 104335882).

Daughters of Marguerite Mae Hargadine and Alvin Dyke Clinkenbeard:

		f		
		f	I.	**Ethel Clinkenbeard** was born on August 19, 1915.
+	438	f	II.	**Pauline Clinkenbeard** was born on June 14, 1917.
+	439	f	III.	**Fern Clinkenbeard** was born on June 17, 1923.

Family of Irene Hargadine and Luther Miller

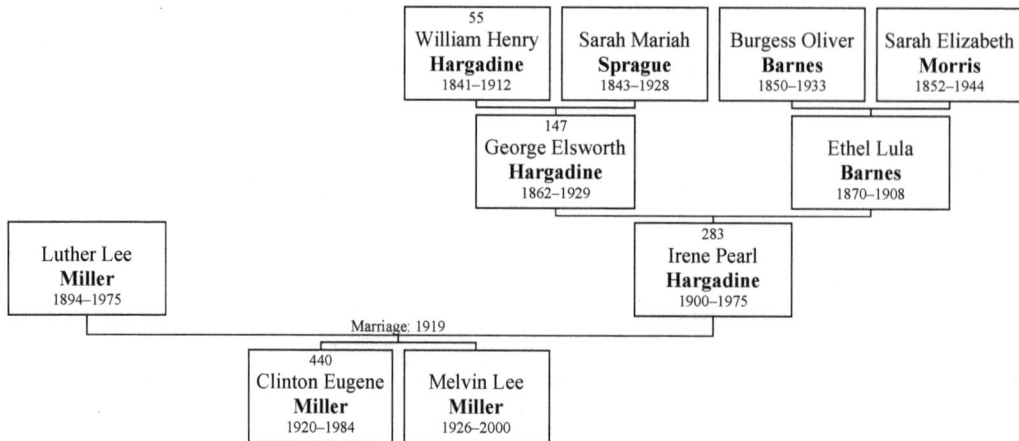

```
                    ┌──────────────┬──────────────┐┌──────────────┬──────────────┐
                    │      55      │              ││              │              │
                    │William Henry │ Sarah Mariah ││Burgess Oliver│Sarah Elizabeth│
                    │  Hargadine   │   Sprague    ││   Barnes     │    Morris    │
                    │  1841–1912   │  1843–1928   ││  1850–1933   │  1852–1944   │
                    └──────────────┴──────────────┘└──────────────┴──────────────┘
                           ┌──────────────────┐         ┌──────────────────┐
                           │       147        │         │                  │
                           │George Elsworth   │         │   Ethel Lula     │
                           │   Hargadine      │         │     Barnes       │
                           │   1862–1929      │         │   1870–1908      │
                           └──────────────────┘         └──────────────────┘
                                   ┌──────────────────┐
     ┌──────────────┐              │       283        │
     │ Luther Lee   │              │  Irene Pearl     │
     │   Miller     │              │   Hargadine      │
     │  1894–1975   │              │   1900–1975      │
     └──────────────┘              └──────────────────┘
                    Marriage: 1919
              ┌──────────────────┬──────────────┐
              │       440        │              │
              │ Clinton Eugene   │  Melvin Lee  │
              │    Miller        │   Miller     │
              │   1920–1984      │  1926–2000   │
              └──────────────────┴──────────────┘
```

283.   **Irene Pearl Hargadine** was born on Thursday, June 07, 1900, in Ottumwa, Wapello County, Iowa. She was the daughter of George Elsworth Hargadine (147) and Ethel Lula Barnes.

Irene Pearl died on September 24, 1975, at the age of 75. She was buried in Hillcrest Cemetery, Mullinville, Kiowa County, Kansas (Find a Grave ID 34627112).

At the age of 19, Irene Pearl married **Luther Lee Miller** on Thursday, September 11, 1919, when he was 24 years old. They had two sons.

Luther Lee was born on Friday, November 23, 1894. He reached 80 years of age and died on January 01, 1975. Luther Lee was buried in Hillcrest Cemetery, Mullinville, Kiowa County, Kansas (Find a Grave ID 34627066).

Sons of Irene Pearl Hargadine and Luther Lee Miller:

+   440   m   I.   **Clinton Eugene Miller** was born on September 20, 1920. He died in Minneola, Clark County, Kansas, on June 20, 1984, at the age of 63. Clinton Eugene was buried in Appleton Township Cemetery, Minneola, Clark County, Kansas (Find a Grave ID 69140064).

           m   II.   **Melvin Lee Miller** was born in Kiowa County, Kansas, on August 23, 1926. He died in Via Christi Regional Medical Center, Wichita, Sedgwick County, Kansas, on September 28, 2000, at the age of 74. Melvin Lee was buried in Hillcrest Cemetery, Mullinville, Kiowa County, Kansas (Find a Grave ID 34627021).

Family of Francis Hargadine and Bessie Evans

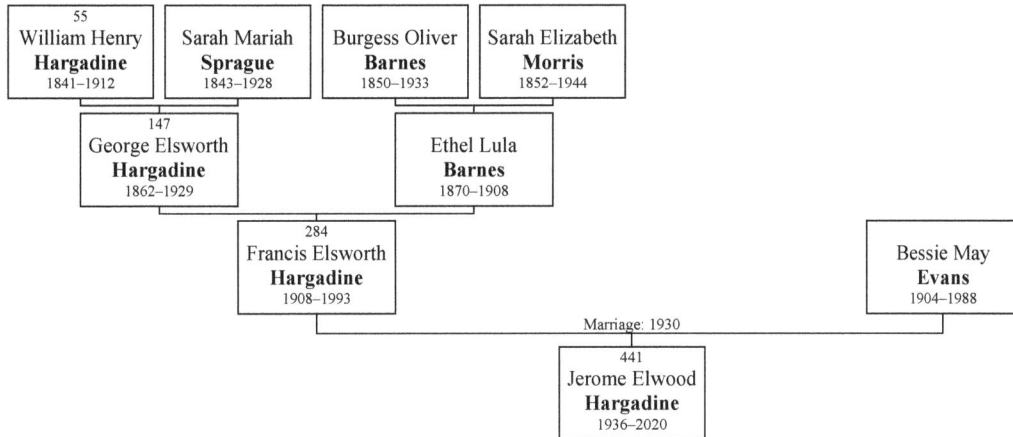

```
┌──────────────┐ ┌──────────────┐ ┌──────────────┐ ┌──────────────┐
│      55      │ │ Sarah Mariah │ │Burgess Oliver│ │Sarah Elizabeth│
│William Henry │ │   Sprague    │ │   Barnes     │ │   Morris     │
│  Hargadine   │ │  1843–1928   │ │  1850–1933   │ │  1852–1944   │
│  1841–1912   │ └──────────────┘ └──────────────┘ └──────────────┘
└──────────────┘
    ┌──────────────┐            ┌──────────────┐
    │     147      │            │  Ethel Lula  │
    │George Elsworth│           │   Barnes     │
    │  Hargadine   │            │  1870–1908   │
    │  1862–1929   │            └──────────────┘
    └──────────────┘
            ┌──────────────┐                          ┌──────────────┐
            │     284      │                          │  Bessie May  │
            │Francis Elsworth│                        │    Evans     │
            │  Hargadine   │                          │  1904–1988   │
            │  1908–1993   │                          └──────────────┘
            └──────────────┘
                        Marriage: 1930
                    ┌──────────────┐
                    │     441      │
                    │Jerome Elwood │
                    │  Hargadine   │
                    │  1936–2020   │
                    └──────────────┘
```

284. **Francis Elsworth Hargadine** was born on Tuesday, March 03, 1908, in Geary, Oklahoma. He was the son of George Elsworth Hargadine (147) and Ethel Lula Barnes.

Francis Elsworth died in Redding, Shasta County, California, on April 12, 1993, at the age of 85. He was buried in Anderson, Shasta County, California, on April 14, 1993.

At the age of 22, Francis Elsworth married **Bessie May Evans** on Sunday, May 11, 1930, in Bucklin, Ford County, Kansas, when she was 25 years old. They had one son.

Bessie May was born in Russell, Russell County, Kansas, on Wednesday, August 03, 1904. She reached 84 years of age and died in Anderson, Shasta County, California, on October 18, 1988.

Son of Francis Elsworth Hargadine and Bessie May Evans:

+ 441 m I. **Jerome Elwood Hargadine** was born in Kinsley, Edwards County, Kansas, on January 25, 1936. He was also known as **Jerry**.

Jerome Elwood died in Paris, Lamar County, Texas, on October 10, 2020, at the age of 84. He was cremated (Find a Grave ID 216699191).

Family of Ralph Scott and Lula Barnes

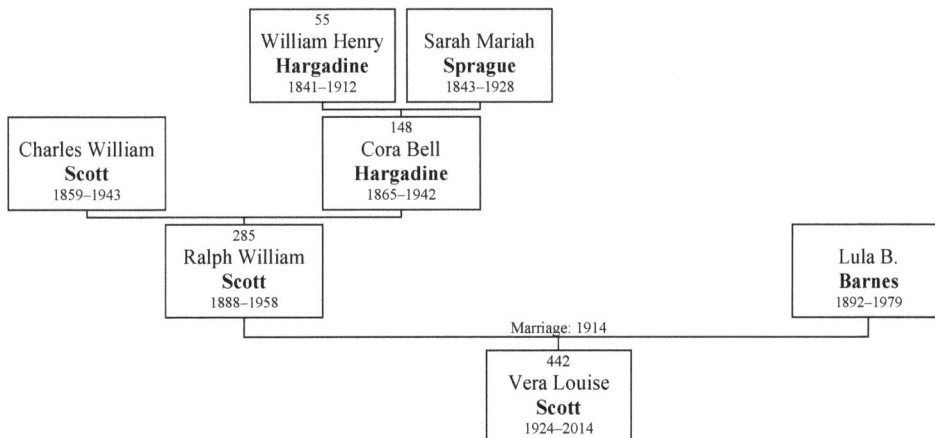

```
                ┌──────────────┐ ┌──────────────┐
                │      55      │ │ Sarah Mariah │
                │William Henry │ │   Sprague    │
                │  Hargadine   │ │  1843–1928   │
                │  1841–1912   │ └──────────────┘
                └──────────────┘
┌──────────────┐     ┌──────────────┐
│Charles William│    │     148      │
│    Scott      │    │  Cora Bell   │
│  1859–1943    │    │  Hargadine   │
└──────────────┘     │  1865–1942   │
                     └──────────────┘
        ┌──────────────┐                          ┌──────────────┐
        │     285      │                          │   Lula B.    │
        │Ralph William │                          │   Barnes     │
        │    Scott     │                          │  1892–1979   │
        │  1888–1958   │                          └──────────────┘
        └──────────────┘
                        Marriage: 1914
                    ┌──────────────┐
                    │     442      │
                    │ Vera Louise  │
                    │    Scott     │
                    │  1924–2014   │
                    └──────────────┘
```

285. **Ralph William Scott** was born on Tuesday, October 23, 1888, in Edwards County, Kansas. He was the son of Charles William Scott and Cora Bell Hargadine (148).

Ralph William died in Kinsley, Edwards County, Kansas, on December 30, 1958, at the age of 70. He was buried in Bethel Cemetery, Hodges, Edwards County, Kansas (Find a Grave ID 67570932).

Ralph William married **Lula B. Barnes** in March 1914. They had one daughter.

Lula B. was born in Edwards County, Kansas, on Thursday, March 03, 1892. She reached 86 years of age and died in Edwards County, Kansas, on March 02, 1979. Lula B. was buried in Bethel Cemetery, Hodges, Edwards County, Kansas (Find a Grave ID 67570893).

Daughter of Ralph William Scott and Lula B. Barnes:

+ 442   f   I. **Vera Louise Scott** was born in Hodges, Edwards County, Kansas, on August 03, 1924. She died in Kinsley, Edwards County, Kansas, on December 07, 2014, at the age of 90. Vera Louise was buried in Hillside Cemetery, Kinsley, Edwards County, Kansas (Find a Grave ID 142438452).

Family of Elmas Scott and Dora Smith

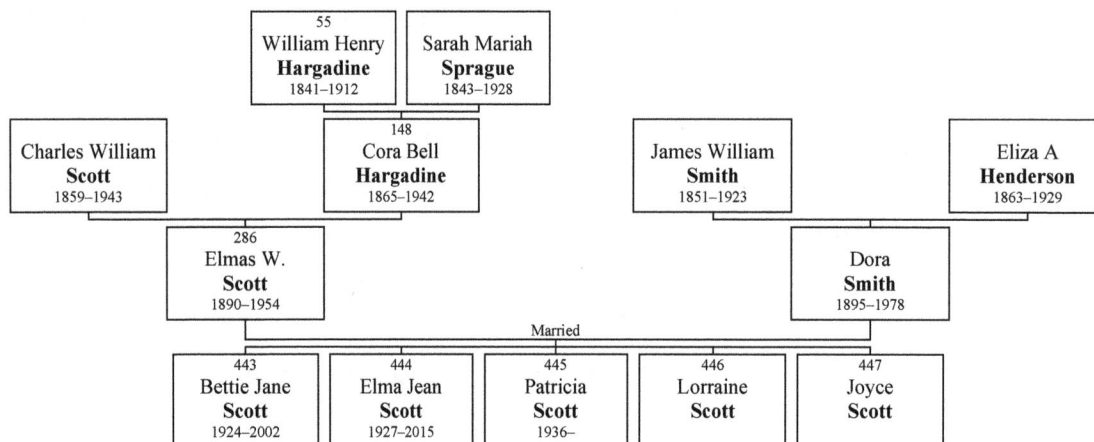

286. **Elmas W. Scott** was born on Monday, September 22, 1890, in Edwards County, Kansas. He was the son of Charles William Scott and Cora Bell Hargadine (148).

Elmas W. died on October 13, 1954, at the age of 64. He was buried in Bethel Cemetery, Hodges, Edwards County, Kansas (Find a Grave ID 67570866).

He married **Dora Smith**. They had five children.

Dora was born on Monday, April 15, 1895. She was the daughter of James William Smith and Eliza A Henderson.

Dora reached 83 years of age and died in Kansas, USA, in December 1978. She was buried in Bethel Cemetery, Hodges, Edwards County, Kansas (Find a Grave ID 67570845).

Children of Elmas W. Scott and Dora Smith:

+ 443 f I. **Bettie Jane Scott** was born in Kinsley, Edwards County, Kansas, on March 09, 1924.[341] She died in Topeka, Shawnee County, Kansas, on February 23, 2002, at the age of 77.[341] Bettie Jane was buried in Atwood Fairview Cemetery, Atwood, Rawlins County, Kansas (Find a Grave ID 103811456).[341]

+ 444 f II. **Elma Jean Scott** was born in Mullinville, Kiowa County, Kansas, on October 26, 1927. She died in Leonardville, Riley County, Kansas, on September 09, 2015, at the age of 87. Elma Jean was buried in Fancy Creek Randolph Cemetery, Randolph, Riley County, Kansas (Find a Grave ID 152127556).

+ 445 f III. **Patricia Scott** was born in Kansas, USA, in 1936.

+ 446 m IV. **Lorraine Scott.**

+ 447 f V. **Joyce Scott.**

Family of Stella Scott and Paul Baker

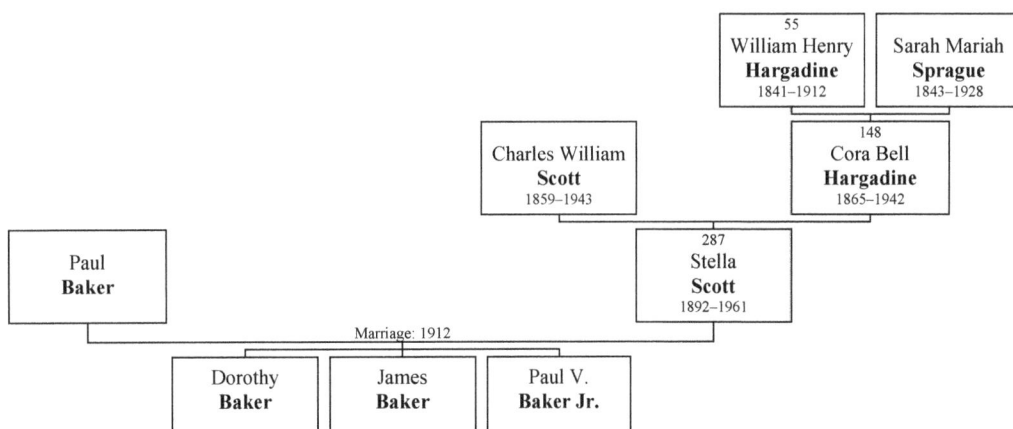

287. **Stella Scott** was born on Tuesday, December 27, 1892, in Kinsley, Edwards County, Kansas. She was the daughter of Charles William Scott and Cora Bell Hargadine (148).

Stella died in Lebanon, Linn County, Oregon, on July 11, 1961, at the age of 68. Her cause of death was myocardial Infarction, coronary occlusion. Stella was buried in Bethel Cemetery, Hodges, Edwards County, Kansas (Find a Grave ID 28724524).

Stella married **Paul Baker** on Sunday, May 12, 1912. They had three children.

Children of Stella Scott and Paul Baker:

f I. **Dorothy Baker.**

m II. **James Baker.**

m III. **Paul V. Baker Jr..**

---

341 Ancestry.com, U.S., Find a Grave® Index, 1600s-Current (Lehi, UT, USA, Ancestry.com Operations, Inc., 2012), Ancestry.com, Record for Bettie Jane Bergling. https://search.ancestry.co.uk/cgi-bin/sse.dll?db=60525&h=55387407&indiv=try.

Family of Roy Scott and Myrtle Seely

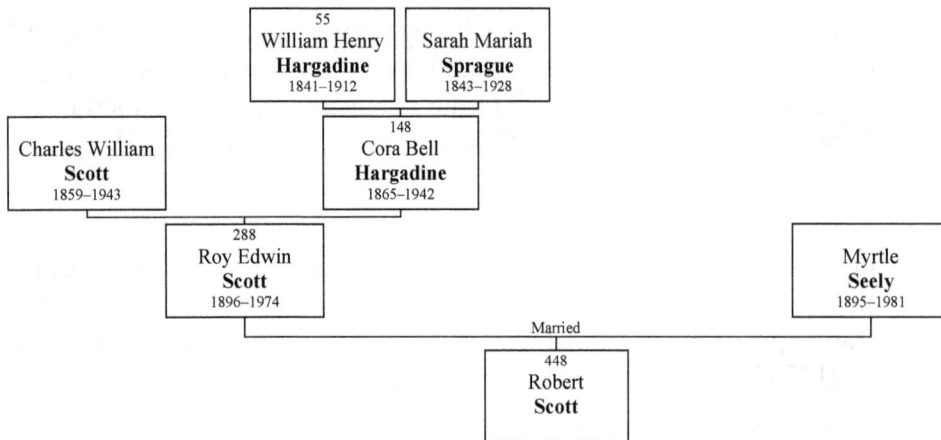

288. **Roy Edwin Scott** was born on Sunday, February 02, 1896, in Edwards County, Kansas. He was the son of Charles William Scott and Cora Bell Hargadine (148).

Roy Edwin died in Edwards County, Kansas, on July 02, 1974, at the age of 78. He was buried in Bethel Cemetery, Hodges, Edwards County, Kansas (Find a Grave ID 67570952).

He married **Myrtle Seely**. They had one son.

Myrtle was born on Saturday, March 30, 1895. She reached 86 years of age and died in September 1981. Myrtle was buried in Bethel Cemetery, Hodges, Edwards County, Kansas (Find a Grave ID 67570911).

Son of Roy Edwin Scott and Myrtle Seely:

+ 448 m I. **Robert Scott**.

Family of Bertha Hargadine and Charles Marsteller

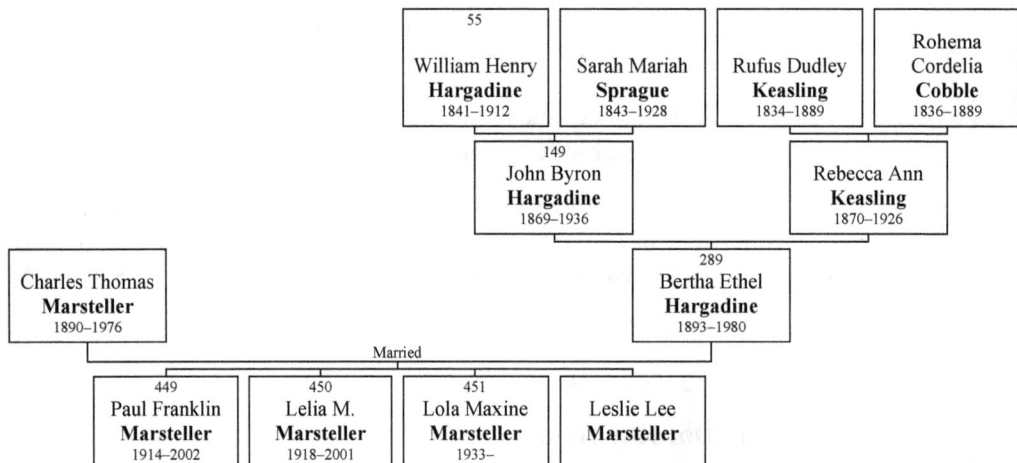

289. **Bertha Ethel Hargadine** was born on Monday, July 24, 1893, in Mullinville, Kiowa County, Kansas. She was the daughter of John Byron Hargadine (149) and Rebecca Ann Keasling.

Bertha Ethel died in Winona, Logan County, Kansas, on October 01, 1980, at the age of 87. She was buried in Winona Cemetery, Winona, Logan County, Kansas, on October 04, 1980 (Find a Grave ID 32434692).

She married **Charles Thomas Marsteller**. They had four children.

Charles Thomas was born in Winona, Logan County, Kansas, on Wednesday, February 05, 1890. He reached 86 years of age and died in Colby, Thomas County, Kansas, on July 11, 1976. Charles Thomas was buried in Winona Cemetery, Winona, Logan County, Kansas (Find a Grave ID 32434698).

Children of Bertha Ethel Hargadine and Charles Thomas Marsteller:

+   449   m   I. **Paul Franklin Marsteller** was born in Edwards County, Kansas, on June 04, 1914. He died in Dighton, Lane County, Kansas, on March 12, 2002, at the age of 87. Paul Franklin was buried in Dighton Cemetery, Dighton, Lane County, Kansas (Find a Grave ID 81738405).

+   450   f   II. **Lelia M. Marsteller** was born in Mullinville, Kiowa, Kansas, USA, on February 24, 1918.[342] Lelia M. was buried in Winona Cemetery, Winona, Logan County, Kansas, in April 2001 (Find a Grave ID 32420971).[342] She died in Oakley, Logan, Kansas, USA, on April 17, 2001, at the age of 83.[342]

+   451   f   III. **Lola Maxine Marsteller** was born on January 30, 1933.

            f   IV. **Leslie Lee Marsteller**. Leslie Lee died in Winina, Logan County, Kansas.

Family of Ernest Hargadine and Alice Davison

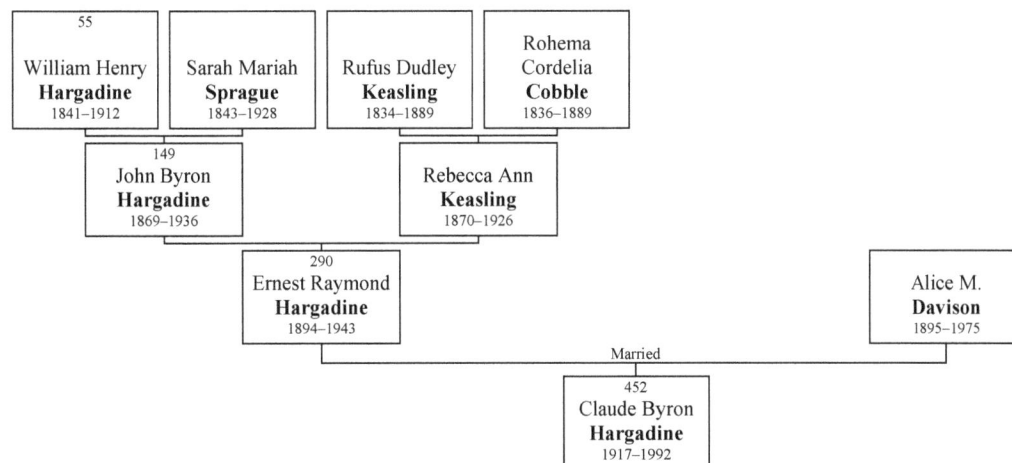

290.   **Ernest Raymond Hargadine** was born on Sunday, October 28, 1894, in Edwards County, Kansas. He was the son of John Byron Hargadine (149) and Rebecca Ann Keasling.

---

342   Ancestry.com, Public Member Trees (Provo, UT, USA, Ancestry.com Operations, Inc., 2006), Ancestry.com, Record for Boyd Clyde Craik. https://search.ancestry.co.uk/cgi-bin/sse.dll?db=1030&h=110039168410&indiv=try.

Ernest Raymond died in Pretty Prairie, Reno County, Kansas, on January 09, 1943, at the age of 48. He was buried in Farmington Cemetery, Macksville, Stafford County, Kansas (Find a Grave ID 210059584).

He married **Alice M. Davison**. They had one son.

Alice M. was born in Kansas, USA, on Friday, September 20, 1895. She reached 80 years of age and died on September 21, 1975. Alice M. was buried in Farmington Cemetery, Macksville, Stafford County, Kansas (Find a Grave ID 197047419).

Son of Ernest Raymond Hargadine and Alice M. Davison:

+ 452 m I. **Claude Byron Hargadine** was born on May 25, 1917. He died in Rogers, Benton County, Arkansas, on February 08, 1992, at the age of 74. Claude Byron was buried in Lone Star Cemetery, Pretty Prairie, Reno County, Kansas (Find a Grave ID 22002088).

Bessie Hargadine

291. **Bessie Carrie Hargadine** was born on Friday, April 24, 1896, in Kansas, USA. She was the daughter of John Byron Hargadine (149) and Rebecca Ann Keasling.

Bessie Carrie died in Arlington, Snohomish County, Washington, on November 23, 1974, at the age of 78. She was buried in Acacia Memorial Park and Funeral Home, Lake Forest Park, King County, Washington (Find a Grave ID 159272581).

Marriages with Raymond Earl Freeman, Guy Homer Hogg (Page 327) and William Anderson (Page 328) are known.

Family of Bessie Hargadine and Raymond Freeman

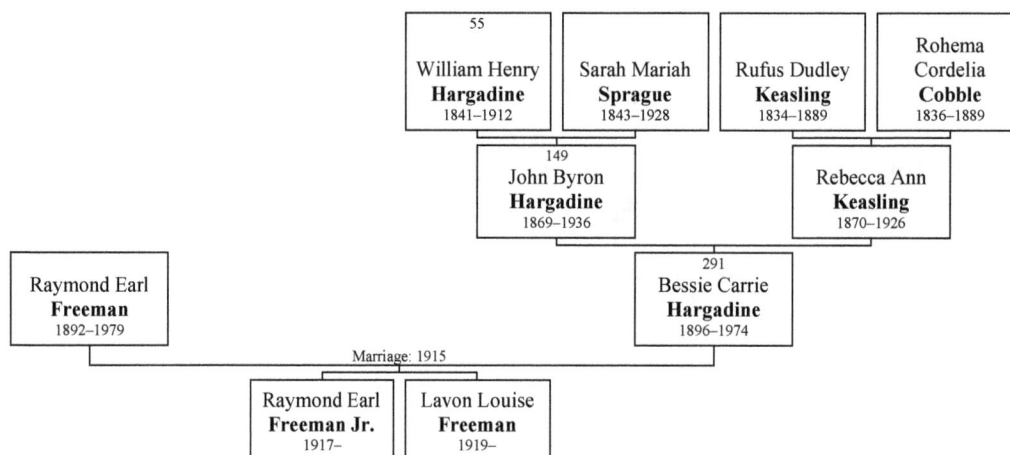

| 55 | | | Rohema |
| William Henry **Hargadine** 1841–1912 | Sarah Mariah **Sprague** 1843–1928 | Rufus Dudley **Keasling** 1834–1889 | Cordelia **Cobble** 1836–1889 |

| 149 John Byron **Hargadine** 1869–1936 | Rebecca Ann **Keasling** 1870–1926 |

| Raymond Earl **Freeman** 1892–1979 | 291 Bessie Carrie **Hargadine** 1896–1974 |

Marriage: 1915

| Raymond Earl **Freeman Jr.** 1917– | Lavon Louise **Freeman** 1919– |

Here are the details about **Bessie Carrie Hargadine's** first marriage, with Raymond Earl Freeman. You can read more about Bessie Carrie on page 326.

At the age of 19, Bessie Carrie Hargadine married **Raymond Earl Freeman** on Sunday, May 09, 1915, when he was 22 years old. They had two children.

Raymond Earl was born in Edwards County, Kansas, on Sunday, July 24, 1892.[343, 344] He reached 86 years of age and died in Sabetha, Nemaha County, Kansas, on May 08, 1979.[343, 344] Raymond Earl was buried in Sabetha, Nemaha County, Kansas.[344]

Children of Bessie Carrie Hargadine and Raymond Earl Freeman:

m   I. **Raymond Earl Freeman Jr.** was born on September 11, 1917.

f   II. **Lavon Louise Freeman** was born on December 28, 1919.

Family of Bessie Hargadine and Guy Hogg

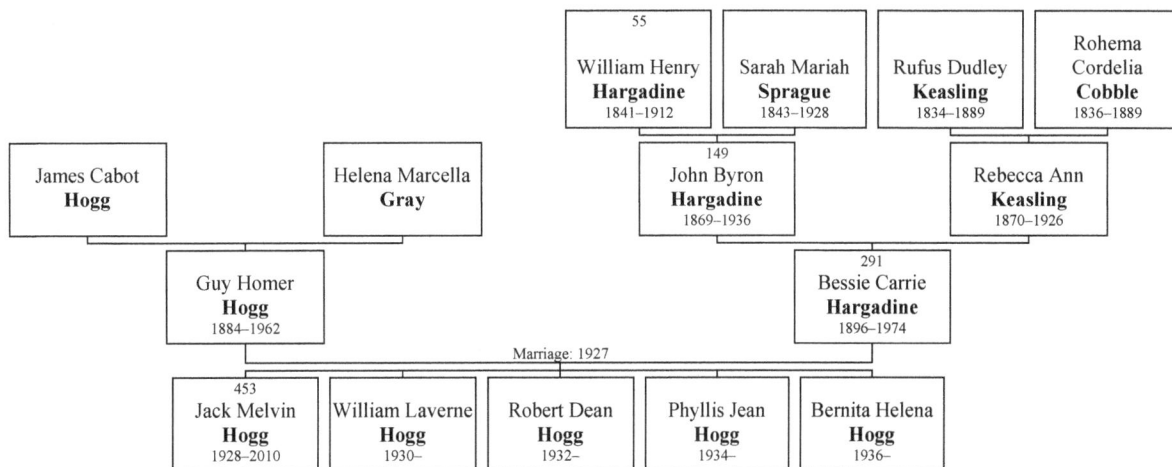

Here are the details about **Bessie Carrie Hargadine's** second marriage, with Guy Homer Hogg. You can read more about Bessie Carrie on page 326.

At the age of 31, Bessie Carrie Hargadine married **Guy Homer Hogg** on Wednesday, June 22, 1927, when he was 42 years old. They had five children.

Guy Homer was born in Wichita, Sedgwick County, Kansas, on Wednesday, October 01, 1884. He was the son of James Cabot Hogg and Helena Marcella Gray.

Guy Homer reached 77 years of age and died in Seattle, King County, Washington, on May 07, 1962. He was buried on May 11, 1962, in Acacia Memorial Park and Funeral Home, Lake Forest Park, King County, Washington (Find a Grave ID 159272593).

Children of Bessie Carrie Hargadine and Guy Homer Hogg:

+ 453   m   I. **Jack Melvin Hogg** was born in Kinsley, Edwards County, Kansas, on April 27, 1928. He died in Washington, USA, on August 19, 2010, at the age of 82. Jack Melvin was buried (Find a Grave ID 99196320).

         m   II. **William Laverne Hogg** was born on September 28, 1930.

         m   III. **Robert Dean Hogg** was born on September 12, 1932.

343   Ancestry.com, Public Member Trees (Provo, UT, USA, Ancestry.com Operations, Inc., 2006), Ancestry.com, Record for Raymond Earle Freeman. https://search.ancestry.co.uk/cgi-bin/sse.dll?db=1030&h=130174729942&indiv=try.

344   Ancestry.com, U.S., Find a Grave® Index, 1600s-Current (Lehi, UT, USA, Ancestry.com Operations, Inc., 2012), Ancestry.com, Record for Raymond Earl Freeman. https://search.ancestry.co.uk/cgi-bin/sse.dll?db=60525&h=51813906&indiv=try.

f   IV. **Phyllis Jean Hogg** was born on November 15, 1934.

f   V. **Bernita Helena Hogg** was born on February 12, 1936.

Family of Bessie Hargadine and William Anderson

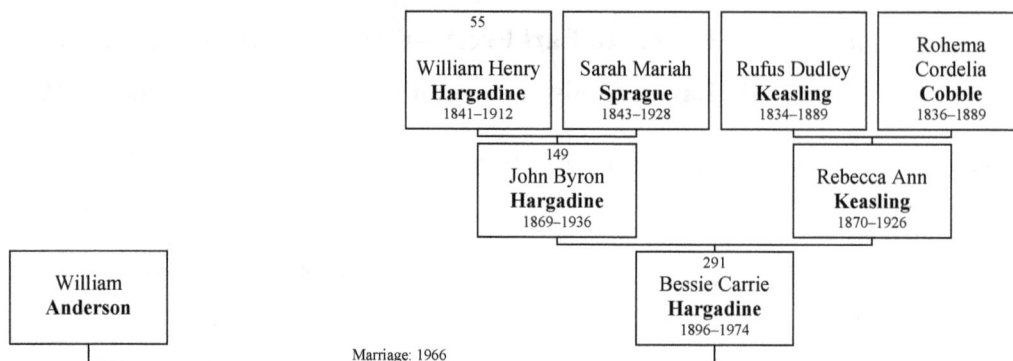

Here are the details about **Bessie Carrie Hargadine's** third marriage, with William Anderson. You can read more about Bessie Carrie on page 326.

Bessie Carrie Hargadine married **William Anderson** on Friday, January 21, 1966.

Family of Laverne Hargadine and Lois Harmon

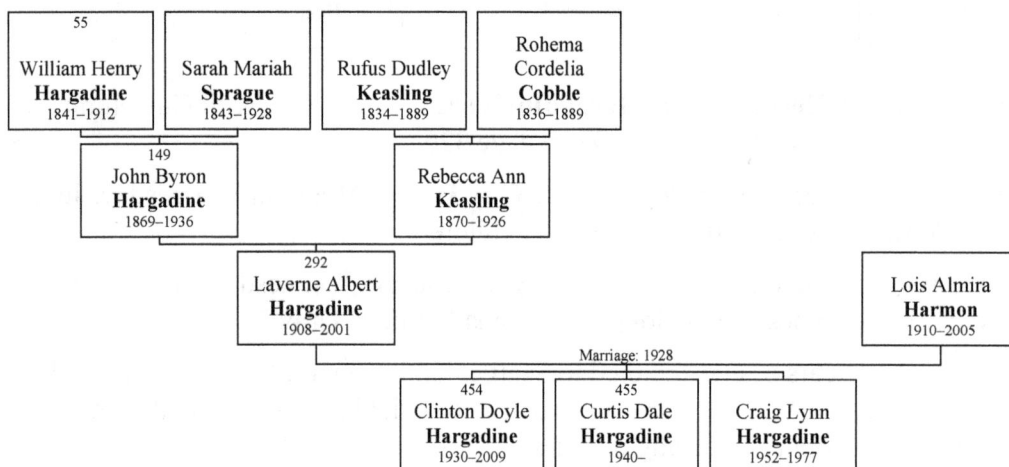

292.   **Laverne Albert Hargadine** was born on Saturday, May 02, 1908, in Wichita County, Kansas. He was the son of John Byron Hargadine (149) and Rebecca Ann Keasling.

Laverne Albert died in Overland Park, Johnson County, Kansas, on February 07, 2001, at the age of 92. He was buried in Lakeside Cemetery, Hastings, Dakota County, Minnesota, on February 13, 2001 (Find a Grave ID 126025134).

At the age of 20, Laverne Albert married **Lois Almira Harmon** on Thursday, August 30, 1928, when she was 18 years old. They had three sons.

Lois Almira was born in Beloit, Mitchell County, Kansas, on Sunday, August 14, 1910. She reached 94 years of age and died in Prairie Village, Overland Park, Johnson County. Kansas, on July 21, 2005. Lois Almira was buried in Lakeside Cemetery, Hastings, Dakota County, Minnesota (Find a Grave ID 135696487).

Sons of Laverne Albert Hargadine and Lois Almira Harmon:

+ 454 m I. **Clinton Doyle Hargadine** was born in Salina, Saline County, Kansas, on February 25, 1930. He died in Prairie Village, Overland Park, Johnson County. Kansas, on March 08, 2009, at the age of 79. Clinton Doyle was buried in Corinth Cemetery, Prairie Village, Johnson County, Kansas (Find a Grave ID 124358667).

+ 455 m II. **Curtis Dale Hargadine** was born in McPherson, McPherson County, Kansas, on June 04, 1940.

  m III. **Craig Lynn Hargadine** was born in McPherson, McPherson County, Kansas, on August 18, 1952. He died in Dakota, Winona County, Minnesota, on May 15, 1977, at the age of 24. Craig Lynn was buried in Lakeside Cemetery, Hastings, Dakota County, Minnesota (Find a Grave ID 126025135).

Family of Grace Hargadine and John Eisele

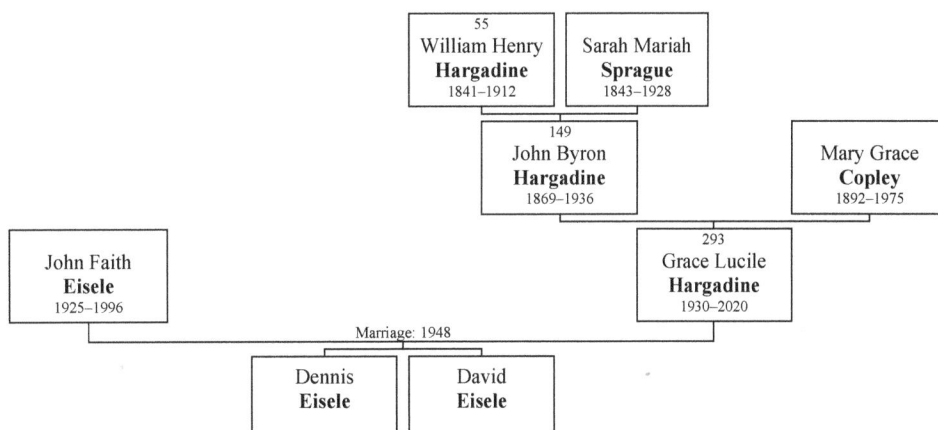

293. **Grace Lucile Hargadine** was born on Friday, November 07, 1930, in Greensburg, Kiowa County, Kansas. She was the daughter of John Byron Hargadine (149) and Mary Grace Copley.

Grace Lucile died in Orange City, Volusia County, Florida, on November 13, 2020, at the age of 90. She was buried in Eudora City Cemetery, Eudora, Douglas County, Kansas (Find a Grave ID 39044003).

At the age of 17, Grace Lucile married **John Faith Eisele** on Sunday, July 18, 1948, in Alba, Jasper County, Missouri, when he was 23 years old. They had two sons.

John Faith was born in Eudora, Douglas County, Kansas, on Monday, March 16, 1925. He reached 71 years of age and died in Deltona, Volusia County, Florida, on September 11, 1996. John Faith was buried in Eudora City Cemetery, Eudora, Douglas County, Kansas (Find a Grave ID 39043927).

Sons of Grace Lucile Hargadine and John Faith Eisele:

m   I. **Dennis Eisele.**

m   II. **David Eisele.**

Family of Pearl Hargadine and Adam Parton

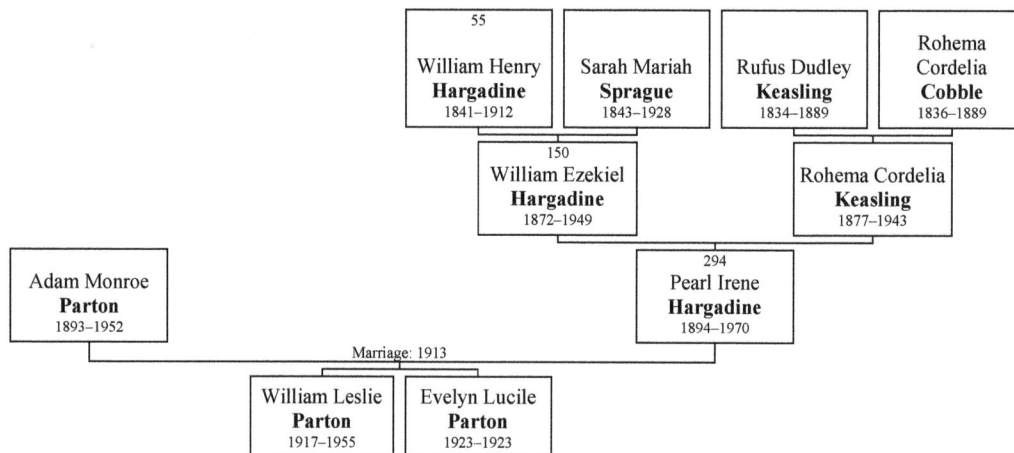

294. **Pearl Irene Hargadine** was born on Friday, January 12, 1894, in Edwards County, Kansas. She was the daughter of William Ezekiel Hargadine (150) and Rohema Cordelia Keasling.

Pearl Irene died in Edwards County, Kansas, on June 14, 1970, at the age of 76. She was buried in Hillside Cemetery, Kinsley, Edwards County, Kansas, on June 16, 1970 (Find a Grave ID 67570381).

At the age of 19, Pearl Irene married **Adam Monroe Parton** on Wednesday, June 11, 1913, when he was 19 years old. They had two children.

Adam Monroe was born in Sevierville, Sevier County, Tennessee, on Friday, July 28, 1893. He reached 58 years of age and died in Wichita, Sedgwick County, Kansas, on May 24, 1952. Adam Monroe was buried in Bethel Cemetery, Hodges, Edwards County, Kansas (Find a Grave ID 67570381).

Children of Pearl Irene Hargadine and Adam Monroe Parton:

m   I. **William Leslie Parton** was born on November 07, 1917. He died in Oklahoma, USA, on May 24, 1955, at the age of 37. William Leslie was buried in Greensburg, Kiowa County, Kansas, on May 27, 1955.

f   II. **Evelyn Lucile Parton** was born in Kinsley, Edwards County, Kansas, on June 21, 1923.[345] She died on June 21, 1923.

---

345   Kinsley Library, http://www.kinsleylibrary.info/birthrec/recordp.htm.

Family of Rufus Hargadine and Bernice Seevers

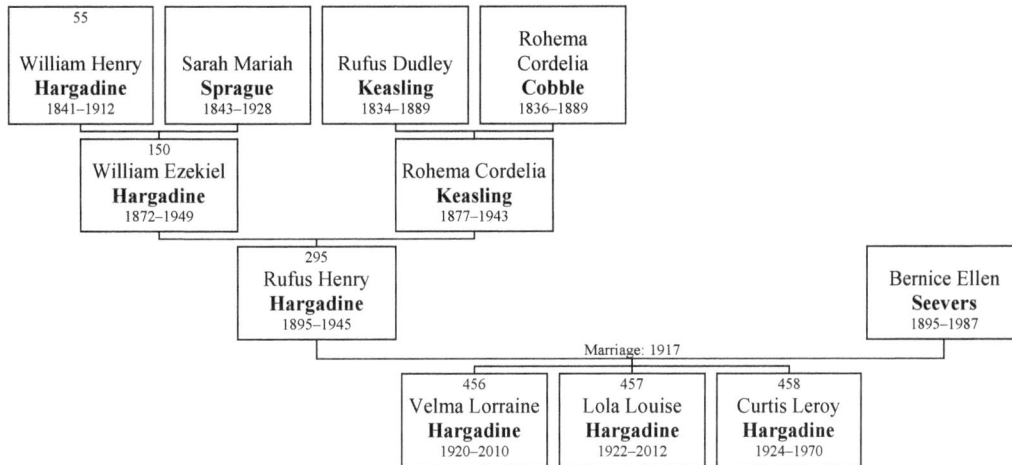

295. **Rufus Henry Hargadine** was born on Saturday, December 14, 1895, in Kiowa, Edwards County, Kansas. He was the son of William Ezekiel Hargadine (150) and Rohema Cordelia Keasling.

Rufus Henry served in the military: CPL HO All American Div. WWI. He died in Dodge City, Ford County, Kansas, on December 02, 1945, at the age of 49. Rufus Henry was buried in Bethel Cemetery, Hodges, Edwards County, Kansas, on December 05, 1945 (Find a Grave ID 67563086).

At the age of 21, Rufus Henry married **Bernice Ellen Seevers** on Wednesday, March 14, 1917, in Kiowa County, Kansas, when she was 21 years old. They had three children.

Bernice Ellen was born in Osage County, Kansas, on Wednesday, December 11, 1895. She reached 91 years of age and died in Greensburg, Kiowa County, Kansas, in May 1987. Bernice Ellen was buried in Bethel Cemetery, Hodges, Edwards County, Kansas (Find a Grave ID 67562798).

Children of Rufus Henry Hargadine and Bernice Ellen Seevers:

+ 456 f I. **Velma Lorraine Hargadine** was born in Mullinville, Kiowa County, Kansas, on July 21, 1920. She died on August 16, 2010, at the age of 90. Velma Lorraine was buried in Hillside Cemetery, Kinsley, Edwards County, Kansas (Find a Grave ID 119453896).

+ 457 f II. **Lola Louise Hargadine** was born in Kiowa County, Kansas, on May 17, 1922. She died in Illinois, USA, on May 17, 2012, at the age of 90. Lola Louise was buried in Hillcrest Cemetery, Mullinville, Kiowa County, Kansas (Find a Grave ID 160311413).

+ 458 m III. **Curtis Leroy Hargadine** was born in Edwards County, Kansas, on September 14, 1924. He died in Mullinville, Kiowa County, Kansas, on October 06, 1970, at the age of 46. Curtis Leroy was buried in Hillcrest Cemetery, Mullinville, Kiowa County, Kansas, on October 10, 1970 (Find a Grave ID 119318961).

Family of Sarah Hargadine and Wilbur Stevens

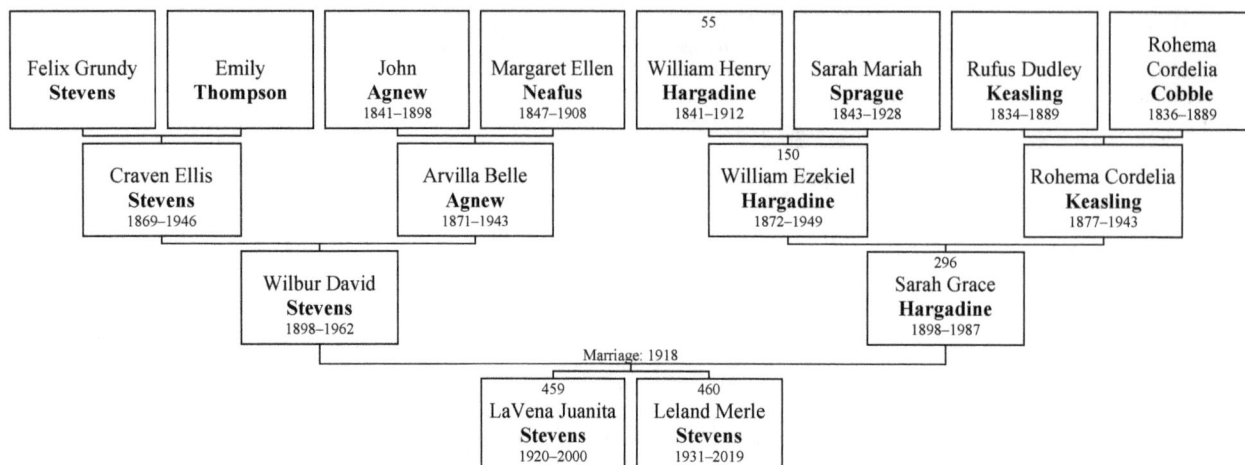

| Felix Grundy **Stevens** | Emily **Thompson** | John **Agnew** 1841–1898 | Margaret Ellen **Neafus** 1847–1908 | 55 William Henry **Hargadine** 1841–1912 | Sarah Mariah **Sprague** 1843–1928 | Rufus Dudley **Keasling** 1834–1889 | Rohema Cordelia **Cobble** 1836–1889 |

Craven Ellis **Stevens** 1869–1946

Arvilla Belle **Agnew** 1871–1943

150 William Ezekiel **Hargadine** 1872–1949

Rohema Cordelia **Keasling** 1877–1943

Wilbur David **Stevens** 1898–1962

296 Sarah Grace **Hargadine** 1898–1987

Marriage: 1918

459 LaVena Juanita **Stevens** 1920–2000

460 Leland Merle **Stevens** 1931–2019

296.   **Sarah Grace Hargadine** was born on Monday, January 24, 1898, in Kiowa, Edwards County, Kansas. She was the daughter of William Ezekiel Hargadine (150) and Rohema Cordelia Keasling.

Sarah Grace died in Florence, Lauderdale County, Alabama, on December 30, 1987, at the age of 89. She was buried in Bethel Cemetery, Hodges, Edwards County, Kansas, on January 04, 1988 (Find a Grave ID 67571620).

At the age of 20, Sarah Grace married **Wilbur David Stevens** on Wednesday, September 04, 1918, when he was 20 years old. They had two children.

Wilbur David was born in Harrison County, Indiana, on Saturday, February 05, 1898. He was the son of Craven Ellis Stevens and Arvilla Belle Agnew.

Wilbur David reached 64 years of age and died in Edwards County, Kansas, on May 23, 1962. He was buried in Bethel Cemetery, Hodges, Edwards County, Kansas (Find a Grave ID 67571642).

Children of Sarah Grace Hargadine and Wilbur David Stevens:

+   459   f   I. **LaVena Juanita Stevens** was born in Kinsley, Edwards County, Kansas, on July 23, 1920. She died in Thibodaux, Lafourche Parish, Louisiana, on March 16, 2000, at the age of 79. LaVena Juanita was buried in Bethel Cemetery, Hodges, Edwards County, Kansas (Find a Grave ID 67563788).

+   460   m   II. **Leland Merle Stevens** was born on October 03, 1931. He died on June 07, 2019, at the age of 87. Leland Merle was buried in Bethel Cemetery, Hodges, Edwards County, Kansas (Find a Grave ID 199899994).

Family of William Hargadine and Bessie Burcher

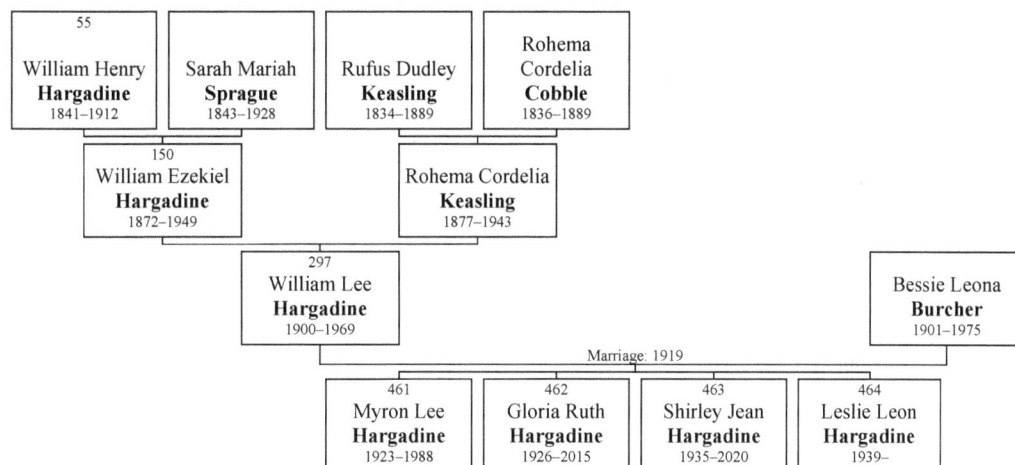

297. **William Lee Hargadine** was born on Wednesday, April 04, 1900, in Kiowa, Kansas. He was the son of William Ezekiel Hargadine (150) and Rohema Cordelia Keasling. He was the pastor of West Bethany Free Methodist Church[346] from 1937-1940.

William Lee died in Pratt, Pratt County, Kansas, on November 19, 1969, at the age of 69. He was buried in Greenlawn Cemetery, Pratt, Pratt County, Kansas, on November 21, 1969 (Find a Grave ID 76141586).

At the age of 19, William Lee married **Bessie Leona Burcher** on Saturday, August 30, 1919, in Kinsley, Edwards County, Kansas, when she was 18 years old. They had four children.

Bessie Leona was born in Hutchinson, Reno County, Kansas, on Wednesday, January 16, 1901.[347] She reached 74 years of age and died in Pratt, Pratt County, Kansas, on January 25, 1975.[347] Bessie Leona was buried on January 28, 1975, in Greenlawn Cemetery, Pratt, Pratt County, Kansas (Find a Grave ID 76141585). Burial documentation: http://skyways.lib.ks.us/genweb/pratt/greenlawn7.html

Children of William Lee Hargadine and Bessie Leona Burcher:

+ 461 m I. **Myron Lee Hargadine** was born in Kinsley, Edwards County, Kansas, on October 04, 1923. He died in Dodge City, Ford County, Kansas, on October 11, 1988, at the age of 65. Myron Lee was buried in Maple Grove Cemetery, Dodge City, Ford County, Kansas (Find a Grave ID 112013915).

+ 462 f II. **Gloria Ruth Hargadine** was born in Lewis, Edwards County, Kansas, on February 07, 1926. She died in Springdale, Washington County, Arkansas, on June 13, 2015, at the age of 89. Gloria Ruth was buried in Rosedale Cemetery, Ada, Pontotoc County, Oklahoma (Find a Grave ID 147933603).

---

[346] Wichita County History Book.

[347] Ancestry.com, U.S., Social Security Death Index, 1935-2014 (Provo, UT, USA, Ancestry.com Operations Inc, 2014), Ancestry.com, Social Security Administration; Washington D.C., USA; Social Security Death Index, Master File. Record for Bessie Hargadine. https://search.ancestry.co.uk/cgi-bin/sse.dll?db=3693&h=25534244&indiv=try.

+ 463 f III. **Shirley Jean Hargadine** was born in Kinsley, Edwards County, Kansas, on October 06, 1935. She died on March 16, 2020, at the age of 84. Shirley Jean was buried in Greenlawn Cemetery, Pratt, Pratt County, Kansas (Find a Grave ID 208769908).

+ 464 m IV. **Leslie Leon Hargadine** was born in Winona, Logan County, Kansas, on January 12, 1939.

Family of Coy Hargadine and Gladys Carlile

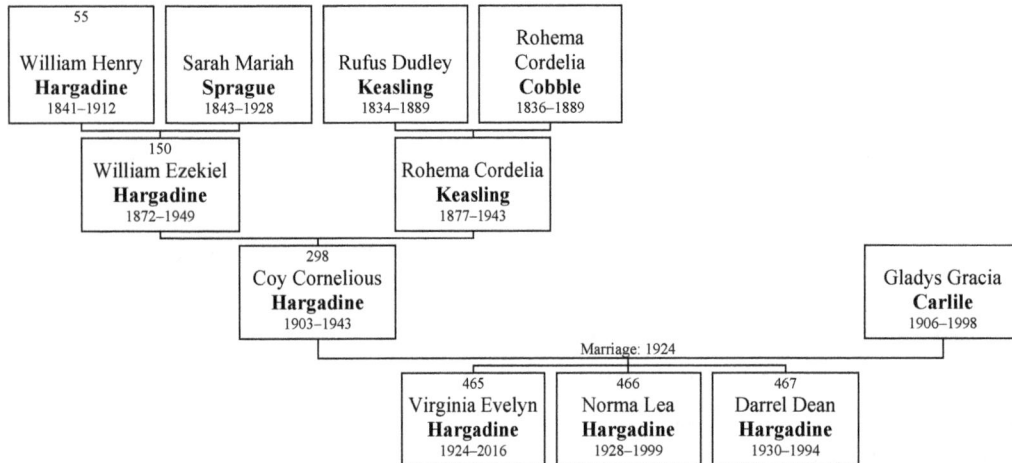

298. **Coy Cornelious Hargadine** was born on Sunday, August 16, 1903, in Kiowa, Kansas. He was the son of William Ezekiel Hargadine (150) and Rohema Cordelia Keasling.

Coy Cornelious died in Winona, Logan County, Kansas, on April 01, 1943, at the age of 39. He was buried in Bethel Cemetery, Hodges, Edwards County, Kansas, on April 05, 1943 (Find a Grave ID 67562812).

At the age of 20, Coy Cornelious married **Gladys Gracia Carlile** on Wednesday, July 23, 1924, in Meade, Weld County, Kansas, when she was 17 years old. They had three children.

Gladys Gracia was born on Thursday, August 23, 1906. She reached 91 years of age and died on July 10, 1998. Gladys Gracia was buried in Winona Cemetery, Winona, Logan County, Kansas (Find a Grave ID 31160063).

Children of Coy Cornelious Hargadine and Gladys Gracia Carlile:

+ 465 f I. **Virginia Evelyn Hargadine** was born in Winona, Logan County, Kansas, on December 21, 1924. She died in Covington, St. Tammany Parish, Louisiana, on April 19, 2016, at the age of 91. Virginia Evelyn was buried in Rochester Cemetery, Topeka, Shawnee County, Kansas (Find a Grave ID 211313117).

+ 466 f II. **Norma Lea Hargadine** was born in Winona, Logan County, Kansas, on September 13, 1928. She died in Loveland, Larimer County, Colorado, on June 19, 1999, at the age of 70. Norma Lea was buried in Genoa Community Cemetery, Genoa, Lincoln County, Colorado (Find a Grave ID 56924247).

+   467   m   III. **Darrel Dean Hargadine** was born in Winona, Logan County, Kansas, on February 20, 1930. He died in Colby, Thomas County, Kansas, on May 11, 1994, at the age of 64. Darrel Dean was buried in Goodland Cemetery, Goodland, Sherman County, Kansas, on May 13, 1994 (Find a Grave ID 97936230).

Paul Hargadine

299.   **Paul Edward Hargadine** was born on Monday, January 15, 1906, in Kiowa, Barber County, Kansas. He was the son of William Ezekiel Hargadine (150) and Rohema Cordelia Keasling.

Paul Edward died in Kinsley, Edwards County, Kansas, on May 10, 1964, at the age of 58. He was buried in Bethel Cemetery, Hodges, Edwards County, Kansas, on May 12, 1964 (Find a Grave ID 67562982).

Marriages with Alice Alveria Schroeder and Murrel Hazel Nelson (Page 336) are known.

Family of Paul Hargadine and Alice Schroeder

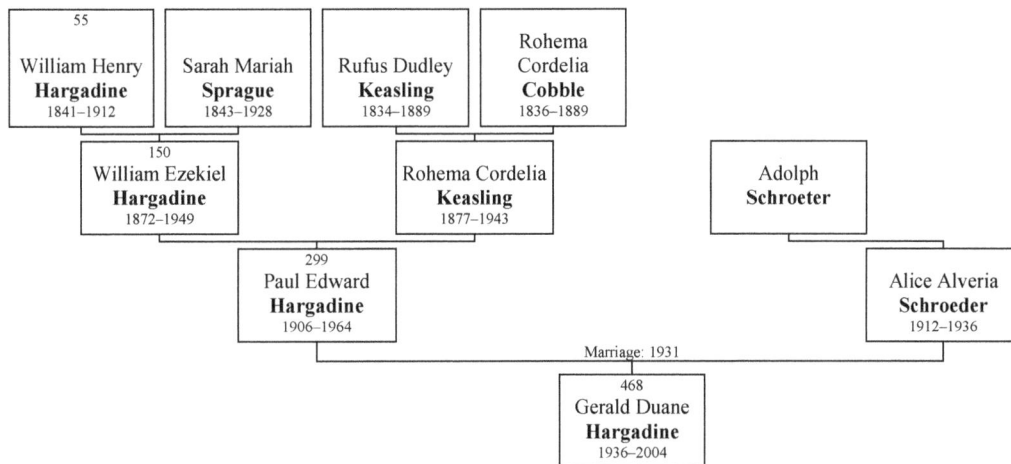

	55			
	William Henry **Hargadine** 1841–1912	Sarah Mariah **Sprague** 1843–1928	Rufus Dudley **Keasling** 1834–1889	Rohema Cordelia **Cobble** 1836–1889

150
William Ezekiel
Hargadine
1872–1949

Rohema Cordelia
Keasling
1877–1943

Adolph
Schroeter

299
Paul Edward
Hargadine
1906–1964

Alice Alveria
Schroeder
1912–1936

Marriage: 1931

468
Gerald Duane
Hargadine
1936–2004

Here are the details about **Paul Edward Hargadine's** first marriage, with Alice Alveria Schroeder. You can read more about Paul Edward on page 335.

At the age of 25, Paul Edward Hargadine married **Alice Alveria Schroeder** on Tuesday, April 14, 1931, when she was 18 years old. They had one son.

Alice Alveria was born in Raymond, Rice County, Kansas, on Tuesday, September 17, 1912. She was the daughter of Adolph Schroeter.

Alice Alveria reached 23 years of age and died in Dodge City, Ford County, Kansas, on March 09, 1936. She was buried in Bethel Cemetery, Hodges, Edwards County, Kansas (Find a Grave ID 67562772).

Son of Paul Edward Hargadine and Alice Alveria Schroeder:

+ 468 m I. **Gerald Duane Hargadine** was born in Kiowa County, Kansas, on January 05, 1936. He was also known as **Jerry**.

Gerald Duane died in Manhattan, Riley County, Kansas, on July 08, 2004, at the age of 68. He was buried in Czech-Moravian Cemetery, Swede Creek Township, Riley County, Kansas (Find a Grave ID 9087778).

Family of Paul Hargadine and Murrel Nelson

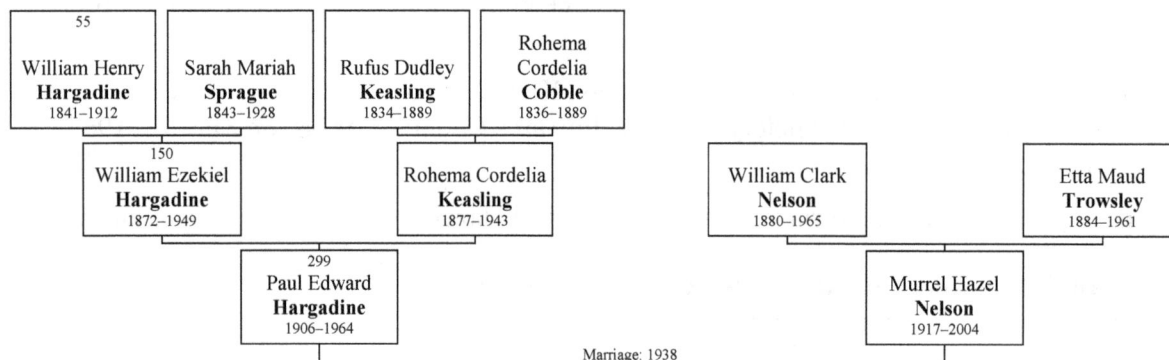

55 William Henry **Hargadine** 1841–1912	Sarah Mariah **Sprague** 1843–1928	Rufus Dudley **Keasling** 1834–1889	Rohema Cordelia **Cobble** 1836–1889

150
William Ezekiel
Hargadine
1872–1949

Rohema Cordelia
Keasling
1877–1943

William Clark
Nelson
1880–1965

Etta Maud
Trowsley
1884–1961

299
Paul Edward
Hargadine
1906–1964

Murrel Hazel
Nelson
1917–2004

Marriage: 1938

Here are the details about **Paul Edward Hargadine's** second marriage, with Murrel Hazel Nelson. You can read more about Paul Edward on page 335.

At the age of 32, Paul Edward Hargadine married **Murrel Hazel Nelson** on Thursday, June 02, 1938, when she was 21 years old. Murrel Hazel was born in Kismet, Seward County, Kansas, on Thursday, May 10, 1917. She was the daughter of William Clark Nelson and Etta Maud Trowsley.

Murrel Hazel reached 87 years of age and died in Kinsley, Edwards County, Kansas, on September 18, 2004. She was buried on September 22, 2004, in Bethel Cemetery, Hodges, Edwards County, Kansas (Find a Grave ID 77415908).

Family of Clyde Hargadine and Emma Gaddis

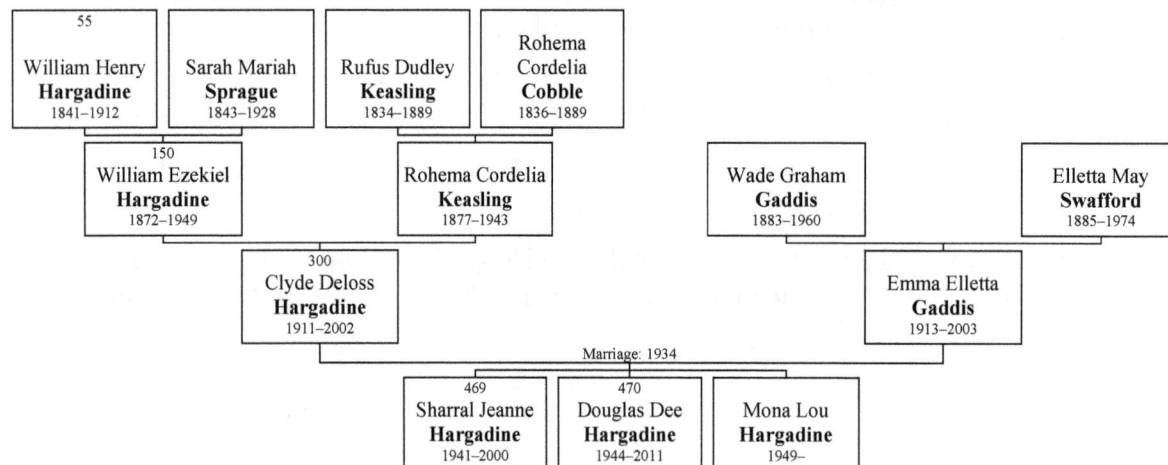

55
William Henry
Hargadine
1841–1912

Sarah Mariah
Sprague
1843–1928

Rufus Dudley
Keasling
1834–1889

Rohema
Cordelia
Cobble
1836–1889

150
William Ezekiel
Hargadine
1872–1949

Rohema Cordelia
Keasling
1877–1943

Wade Graham
Gaddis
1883–1960

Elletta May
Swafford
1885–1974

300
Clyde Deloss
Hargadine
1911–2002

Emma Elletta
Gaddis
1913–2003

Marriage: 1934

469
Sharral Jeanne
Hargadine
1941–2000

470
Douglas Dee
Hargadine
1944–2011

Mona Lou
Hargadine
1949–

300. **Clyde Deloss Hargadine** was born on Thursday, June 01, 1911, in Kiowa, Edwards County, Kansas. He was the son of William Ezekiel Hargadine (150) and Rohema Cordelia Keasling. He was also known as **Dee**.

Clyde Deloss worked as an Educator. He died in Overland Park Regional Medical Center, Overland Park, Johnson County, Kansas, on December 06, 2002, at the age of 91. Clyde Deloss was buried in Oak Hill Cemetery, Lawrence, Douglas County, Kansas, on December 11, 2002 (Find a Grave ID 23837222).

More facts and events for Clyde Deloss Hargadine:

Individual Note: One of the original Hargadine researchers with the Kansas line.

At the age of 22, Clyde Deloss married **Emma Elletta Gaddis** on Monday, May 21, 1934, in Kinsley, Edwards County, Kansas, when she was 21 years old. They had three children.

Emma Elletta was born in Stevens County, Kansas, on Tuesday, January 14, 1913. She was the daughter of Wade Graham Gaddis and Elletta May Swafford.

Emma Elletta reached 90 years of age and died in Overland Park, Johnson County, Kansas, on January 20, 2003. She was buried on January 22, 2003, in Oak Hill Cemetery, Lawrence, Douglas County, Kansas (Find a Grave ID 23837226).

Children of Clyde Deloss Hargadine and Emma Elletta Gaddis:

+ 469   f   I. **Sharral Jeanne Hargadine** was born in Ashland, Clark County, Kansas, on March 27, 1941. She died in Kansas City, Wyandotte County, Kansas, on August 06, 2000, at the age of 59. Her cause of death was head injuries after accidental fall. She was buried in Vinland Cemetery, Vinland, Douglas County, Kansas, on August 10, 2000 (Find a Grave ID 23260293).

+ 470   m   II. **Douglas Dee Hargadine** was born in Hutchinson, Reno County, Kansas, on January 07, 1944. He died in Overland Park, Johnson County, Kansas, on November 05, 2011, at the age of 67. Douglas Dee was buried in Oak Hill Cemetery, Lawrence, Douglas County, Kansas (Find a Grave ID 147817957).

         f   III. **Mona Lou Hargadine** was born in Montezuma, Gray County, Kansas, on August 05, 1949.

Family of Verlin Hargadine and Dorothy Taylor

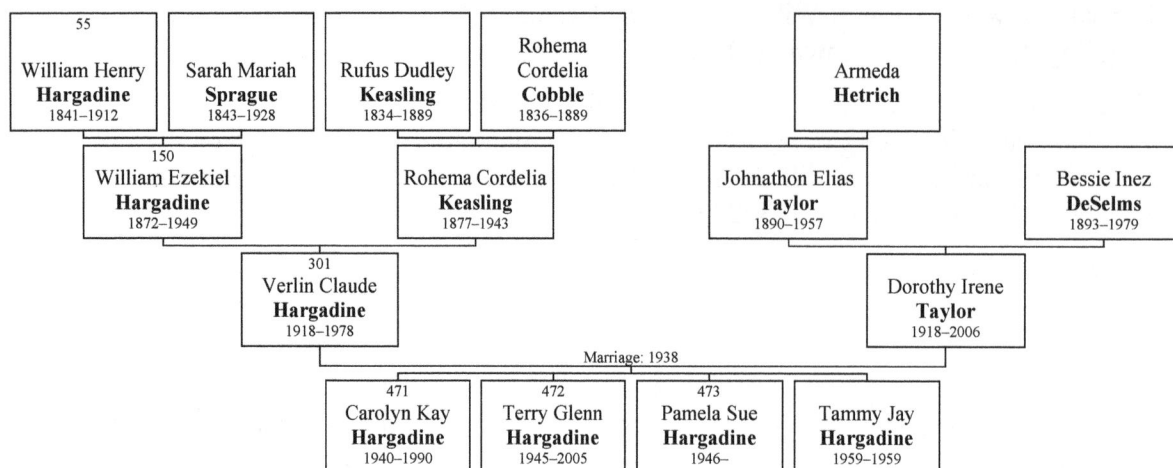

55	

```
┌──────────────┬──────────────┬──────────────┬──────────────┐          ┌──────────────┐
│      55      │              │              │   Rohema     │          │              │
│ William Henry│ Sarah Mariah │ Rufus Dudley │   Cordelia   │          │   Armeda     │
│  Hargadine   │   Sprague    │   Keasling   │    Cobble     │          │   Hetrich    │
│  1841–1912   │  1843–1928   │  1834–1889   │  1836–1889    │          │              │
└──────────────┴──────────────┴──────────────┴──────────────┘          └──────────────┘
        └──────┬───────┘              └──────┬───────┘
    ┌──────────────────┐          ┌──────────────────┐      ┌──────────────┐          ┌──────────────┐
    │       150        │          │                  │      │Johnathon Elias│         │  Bessie Inez │
    │ William Ezekiel  │          │ Rohema Cordelia  │      │    Taylor     │         │   DeSelms    │
    │   Hargadine      │          │    Keasling      │      │  1890–1957    │         │  1893–1979   │
    │   1872–1949      │          │   1877–1943      │      └──────────────┘          └──────────────┘
    └──────────────────┘          └──────────────────┘              └──────────┬──────────┘
              └────────────┬────────────┘                            ┌──────────────────┐
                  ┌──────────────────┐                               │ Dorothy Irene    │
                  │       301        │                               │    Taylor        │
                  │  Verlin Claude   │                               │   1918–2006      │
                  │   Hargadine      │                               └──────────────────┘
                  │   1918–1978      │
                  └──────────────────┘
                            Marriage: 1938
```

471	472	473	
Carolyn Kay **Hargadine** 1940–1990	Terry Glenn **Hargadine** 1945–2005	Pamela Sue **Hargadine** 1946–	Tammy Jay **Hargadine** 1959–1959

301. **Verlin Claude Hargadine** was born on Sunday, May 26, 1918, in Kinsley, Edwards County, Kansas. He was the son of William Ezekiel Hargadine (150) and Rohema Cordelia Keasling.

Verlin Claude died in Liberal, Seward County, Kansas, on September 25, 1978, at the age of 60. He was buried in Stafford Cemetery, Stafford, Stafford County, Kansas, on September 27, 1978 (Find a Grave ID 93811668).

At the age of 20, Verlin Claude married **Dorothy Irene Taylor** on Thursday, November 24, 1938, when she was 20 years old. They had four children.

Dorothy Irene was born in Stafford County, Kansas, on Wednesday, May 15, 1918. She was the daughter of Johnathon Elias Taylor and Bessie Inez DeSelms.

Dorothy Irene reached 88 years of age and died in Stafford, Stafford County, Kansas, on July 31, 2006. She was buried in Stafford Cemetery, Stafford, Stafford County, Kansas (Find a Grave ID 93811708).

Children of Verlin Claude Hargadine and Dorothy Irene Taylor:

+ 471   f   I. **Carolyn Kay Hargadine** was born in Stafford, Stafford County, Kansas, on February 22, 1940. She died in Queen City, Cass County, Texas, on January 29, 1990, at the age of 49. Carolyn Kay was buried in Sardis Cemetery, Shelbyville, Shelby County, Texas, on February 02, 1990 (Find a Grave ID 14814819).

+ 472   m   II. **Terry Glenn Hargadine** was born in Stafford County, Kansas, on April 02, 1945. He died in Queen City, Cass County, Texas, on June 05, 2005, at the age of 60. Terry Glenn was buried in Chapelwood Memorial Gardens and Mausoleum, Wake Village, Bowie County, Texas (Find a Grave ID 136785300).

+ 473   f   III. **Pamela Sue Hargadine** was born on June 22, 1946.

        f   IV. **Tammy Jay Hargadine** was born on June 03, 1959. She died on June 03, 1959. Tammy Jay was buried in Stafford Cemetery, Stafford, Stafford County, Kansas (Find a Grave ID 93820368).

Family of Orville LoVette and Jaunita Whitcomb

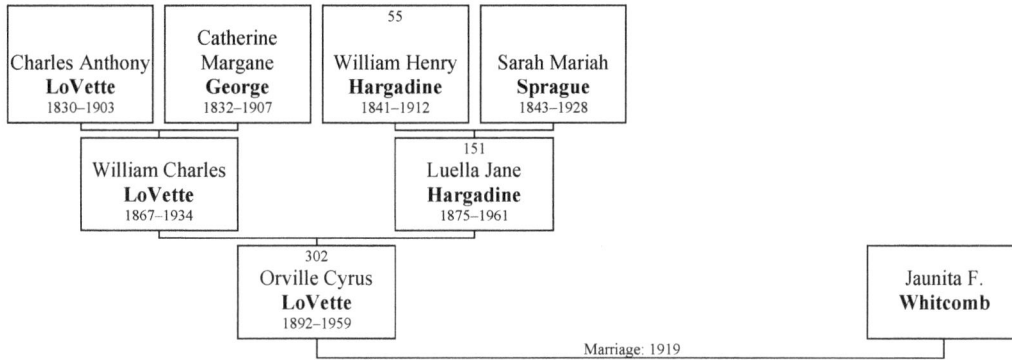

		55	
Charles Anthony **LoVette** 1830–1903	Catherine Margane **George** 1832–1907	William Henry **Hargadine** 1841–1912	Sarah Mariah **Sprague** 1843–1928

William Charles **LoVette** 1867–1934

151
Luella Jane **Hargadine** 1875–1961

302
Orville Cyrus **LoVette** 1892–1959

Jaunita F. **Whitcomb**

Marriage: 1919

302. **Orville Cyrus LoVette** was born on Monday, September 05, 1892, in Crescent, Kiowa County, Kansas. He was the son of William Charles LoVette and Luella Jane Hargadine (151).

Orville Cyrus died on September 20, 1959, at the age of 67. He was buried in Hillside Cemetery, Kinsley, Edwards County, Kansas (Find a Grave ID 11471657).

Orville Cyrus married **Jaunita F. Whitcomb** in August 1919.

Family of Clara LoVette and Everett Bitner

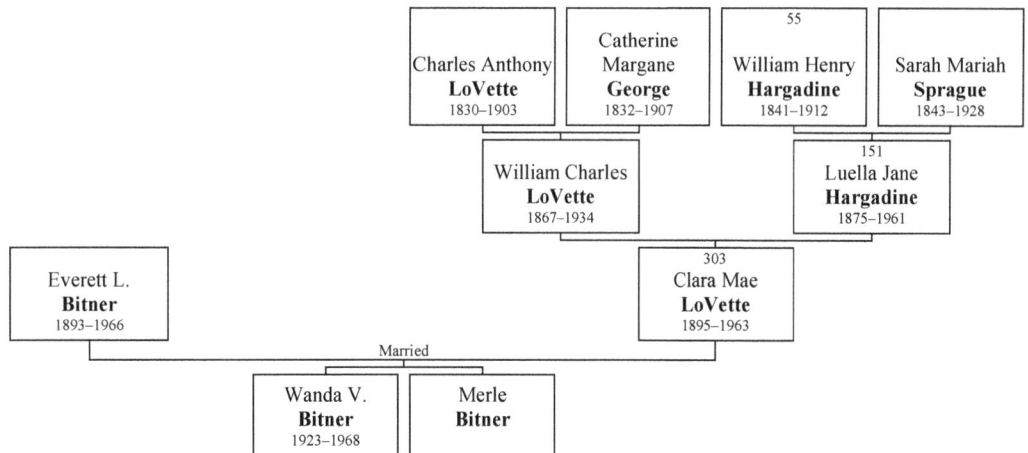

		55	
Charles Anthony **LoVette** 1830–1903	Catherine Margane **George** 1832–1907	William Henry **Hargadine** 1841–1912	Sarah Mariah **Sprague** 1843–1928

William Charles **LoVette** 1867–1934

151
Luella Jane **Hargadine** 1875–1961

Everett L. **Bitner** 1893–1966

303
Clara Mae **LoVette** 1895–1963

Married

Wanda V. **Bitner** 1923–1968

Merle **Bitner**

303. **Clara Mae LoVette** was born on Friday, January 25, 1895, in Kansas, USA. She was the daughter of William Charles LoVette and Luella Jane Hargadine (151).

Clara Mae died on July 05, 1963, at the age of 68. She was buried in Hillside Cemetery, Kinsley, Edwards County, Kansas (Find a Grave ID 11197812).

She married **Everett L. Bitner**. They had two children.

Everett L. was born on Wednesday, September 13, 1893. He reached 72 years of age and died on August 22, 1966. Everett L. was buried in Hillside Cemetery, Kinsley, Edwards County, Kansas (Find a Grave ID 11197814).

Children of Clara Mae LoVette and Everett L. Bitner:

f   I. **Wanda V. Bitner** was born on May 28, 1923.[348] She died on September 30, 1968, at the age of 45.[348] Wanda V. was buried in Hillside Cemetery, Kinsley, Edwards County, Kansas (Find a Grave ID 11197821).[348]

m   II. **Merle Bitner**.

Family of Arlie LoVette and Lottie Abrams

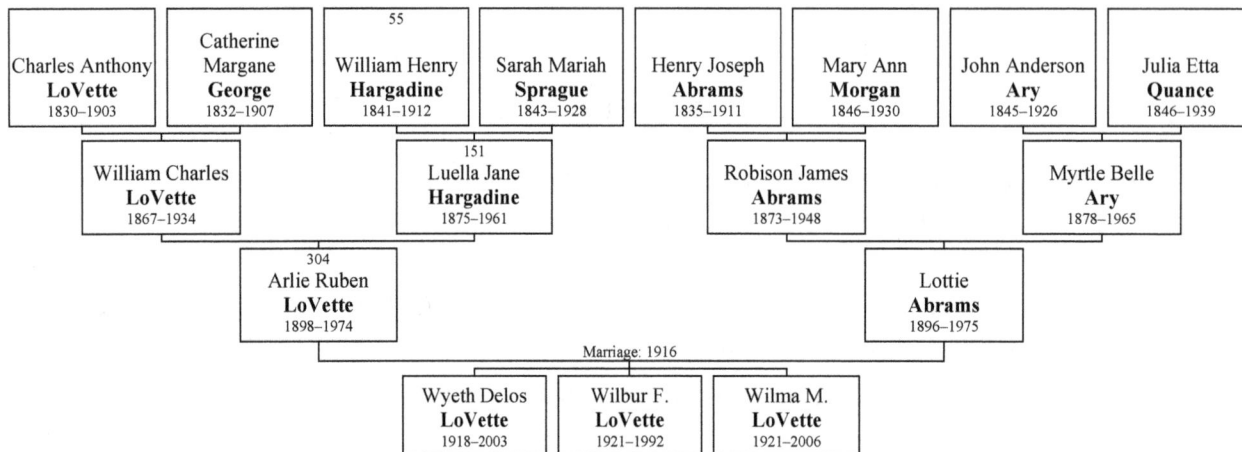

304. **Arlie Ruben LoVette** was born on Monday, May 09, 1898, in Kansas, USA. He was the son of William Charles LoVette and Luella Jane Hargadine (151).

Arlie Ruben died in Lewis, Edwards County, Kansas, on July 28, 1974, at the age of 76. He was buried in Wayne Cemetery, Lewis, Edwards County, Kansas (Find a Grave ID 76154958).

At the age of 17, Arlie Ruben married **Lottie Abrams** on Saturday, March 18, 1916, in Kansas, USA, when she was 19 years old. They had three children.

Lottie was born on Wednesday, August 26, 1896. She was the daughter of Robison James Abrams and Myrtle Belle Ary.

Lottie reached 79 years of age and died in Lewis, Edwards County, Kansas, on November 09, 1975. She was buried in Wayne Cemetery, Lewis, Edwards County, Kansas (Find a Grave ID 76154899).

Children of Arlie Ruben LoVette and Lottie Abrams:

m   I. **Wyeth Delos LoVette** was born in Edwards, Wyandotte County, Kansas, on December 16, 1918. He served in the military: WWII, U.S. Army-Purple Heart.

Wyeth Delos died in Edwards, Wyandotte County, Kansas, on April 12, 2003, at the age of 84. He was buried in Wayne Cemetery, Lewis, Edwards County, Kansas (Find a Grave ID 76156706).

---

348   Ancestry.com, U.S., Find a Grave® Index, 1600s-Current (Lehi, UT, USA, Ancestry.com Operations, Inc., 2012), Ancestry.com, Record for Wanda V. Bitner. https://search.ancestry.co.uk/cgi-bin/sse.dll?db=60525&h=104140842&indiv=try.

m   II. **Wilbur F. LoVette** was born on June 03, 1921. He died on December 20, 1992, at the age of 71. Wilbur F. was buried in Hillside Cemetery, Kinsley, Edwards County, Kansas (Find a Grave ID 11471669).

f   III. **Wilma M. LoVette** was born on June 03, 1921. She died in Hutchinson, Reno County, Kansas, on August 09, 2006, at the age of 85. Wilma M. was buried in Wayne Cemetery, Lewis, Edwards County, Kansas (Find a Grave ID 76152489).

Family of Dwight LoVette and Gladys Huffman

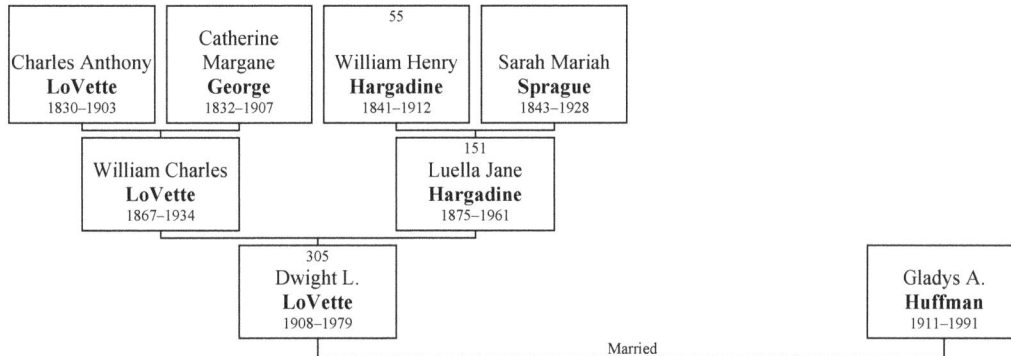

305.   Dwight L. LoVette was born on Wednesday, March 18, 1908. He was the son of William Charles LoVette and Luella Jane Hargadine (151).

Dwight L. served in the military: U.S. Navy. He died on December 28, 1979, at the age of 71. Dwight L. was buried in Forest Lawn Memorial Park, Hollywood Hills, Los Angeles County, California (Find a Grave ID 169489516).

He married **Gladys A. Huffman**. Gladys A. was born in 1911.

She reached 80 years of age and died in 1991. Gladys A. was buried in Forest Lawn Memorial Park, Hollywood Hills, Los Angeles County, California (Find a Grave ID 169489639).

Family of Oval LoVette and Elizabeth Sterrett

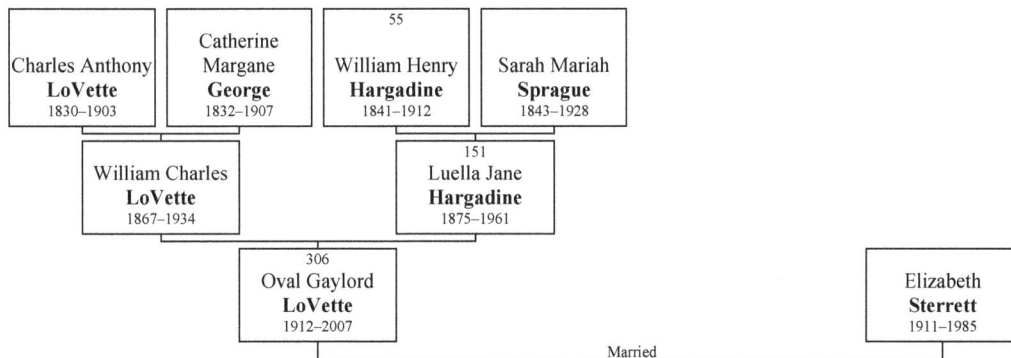

306.   Oval Gaylord LoVette was born on Friday, August 09, 1912, in Bison, Garfield County, Oklahoma. He was the son of William Charles LoVette and Luella Jane Hargadine (151).

Oval Gaylord served in the military between 1944 and 1946. He died on January 11, 2007, at the age of 94. Oval Gaylord was buried in Sierra Hills Memorial Park, Sacramento, Sacramento County, California (Find a Grave ID 155842052).

He married **Elizabeth Sterrett**. Elizabeth was born in 1911.

She reached 74 years of age and died in 1985. Elizabeth was buried in Sierra Hills Memorial Park, Sacramento, Sacramento County, California (Find a Grave ID 155842043).

Family of Dale Keasling and Irene Barnes

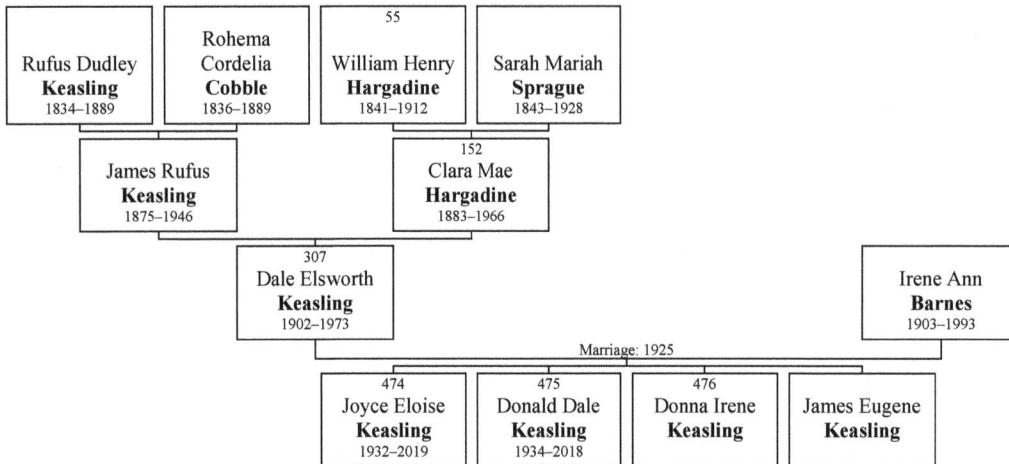

307. **Dale Elsworth Keasling** was born on Wednesday, July 09, 1902, in Coldwater, Comanche County, Kansas. He was the son of James Rufus Keasling and Clara Mae Hargadine (152).

Dale Elsworth died in Protection, Comanche County, Kansas, on April 27, 1973, at the age of 70. He was buried in Protection Cemetery, Protection, Comanche County, Kansas (Find a Grave ID 21542846).

At the age of 23, Dale Elsworth married **Irene Ann Barnes** on Sunday, September 20, 1925, in Florence, Fremont County, Colorado, when she was 22 years old. They had four children.

Irene Ann was born in Coldwater, Comanche County, Kansas, on Thursday, June 25, 1903. She reached 90 years of age and died in Buffalo, Harper County, Oklahoma, on July 05, 1993. Irene Ann was buried in Protection Cemetery, Protection, Comanche County, Kansas (Find a Grave ID 21542848).

Children of Dale Elsworth Keasling and Irene Ann Barnes:

+ 474   f   I. **Joyce Eloise Keasling** was born in Protection, Comanche County, Kansas, on June 19, 1932. She died on December 13, 2019, at the age of 87. Joyce Eloise was buried in Highland Cemetery, Center Township, Clark County, Kansas (Find a Grave ID 210126968).

+ 475   m   II. **Donald Dale Keasling** was born in Protection, Comanche County, Kansas, on July 06, 1934. He died on June 16, 2018, at the age of 83. Donald Dale was buried in Memorial Park Cemetery, Hutchinson, Reno County, Kansas (Find a Grave ID 247911819).

+ 476   f   III. **Donna Irene Keasling**.

          m   IV. **James Eugene Keasling**.

Family of Sarah Keasling and Ermon Haag

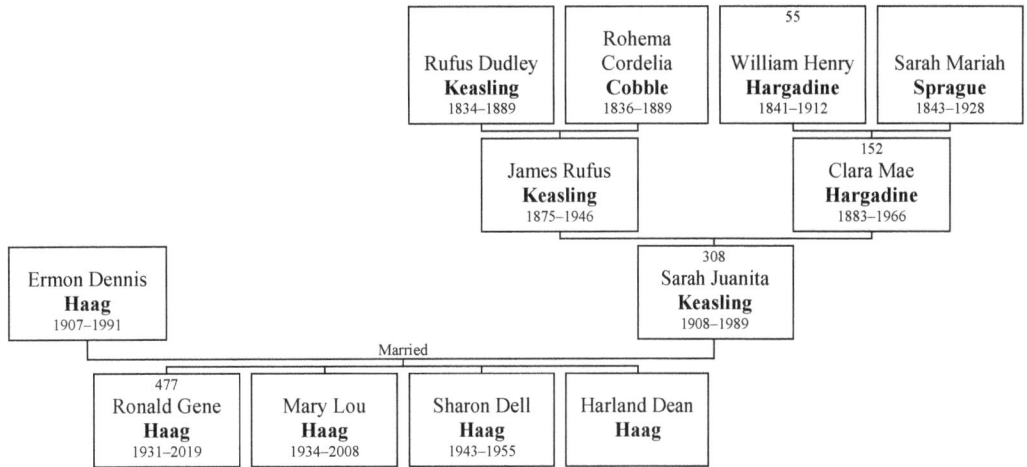

308.   **Sarah Juanita Keasling** was born on Wednesday, January 08, 1908. She was the daughter of James Rufus Keasling and Clara Mae Hargadine (152).

Sarah Juanita died in Hutchinson, Reno County, Kansas, on October 18, 1989, at the age of 81. She was buried in Memorial Park Cemetery, Hutchinson, Reno County, Kansas (Find a Grave ID 37388566).

She married **Ermon Dennis Haag**. They had four children.

Ermon Dennis was born on Thursday, December 19, 1907. He reached 83 years of age and died on February 15, 1991. Ermon Dennis was buried in Memorial Park Cemetery, Hutchinson, Reno County, Kansas (Find a Grave ID 37388565).

Children of Sarah Juanita Keasling and Ermon Dennis Haag:

+ 477   m   I. **Ronald Gene Haag** was born in Larned, Pawnee County, Kansas, on October 09, 1931. He died in Hutchinson, Reno County, Kansas, on May 05, 2019, at the age of 87. Ronald Gene was buried in Abbyville Cemetery, Abbyville, Reno County, Kansas (Find a Grave ID 199977143).

          f   II. **Mary Lou Haag** was born on December 31, 1934. She died on December 02, 2008, at the age of 73. Mary Lou was buried in Memorial Park Cemetery, Hutchinson, Reno County, Kansas (Find a Grave ID 84792649).

          f   III. **Sharon Dell Haag** was born on September 20, 1943. She died on December 13, 1955, at the age of 12. Sharon Dell was buried in Memorial Park Cemetery, Hutchinson, Reno County, Kansas (Find a Grave ID 37388567).

          m   IV. **Harland Dean Haag**.

Hazel Hargadine

309. **Hazel Merlin Hargadine** was born on Tuesday, June 02, 1908, in Mullinville, Kiowa County, Kansas. She was the daughter of Raymond Franklin Hargadine (153) and Jennetta Zimmerman.

Hazel Merlin died in Providence St. Peter Hospital, Olympia, Thurston, Washington, on August 03, 2000, at the age of 92. Her cause of death was renal failure. Hazel Merlin was buried in Yelm Cemetery, Yelm, Thurston County, Washington, on August 07, 2000 (Find a Grave ID 39843041).

Marriages with Harry William Reed and Charles Frederick Klontz (Page 345) are known.

Family of Hazel Hargadine and Harry Reed

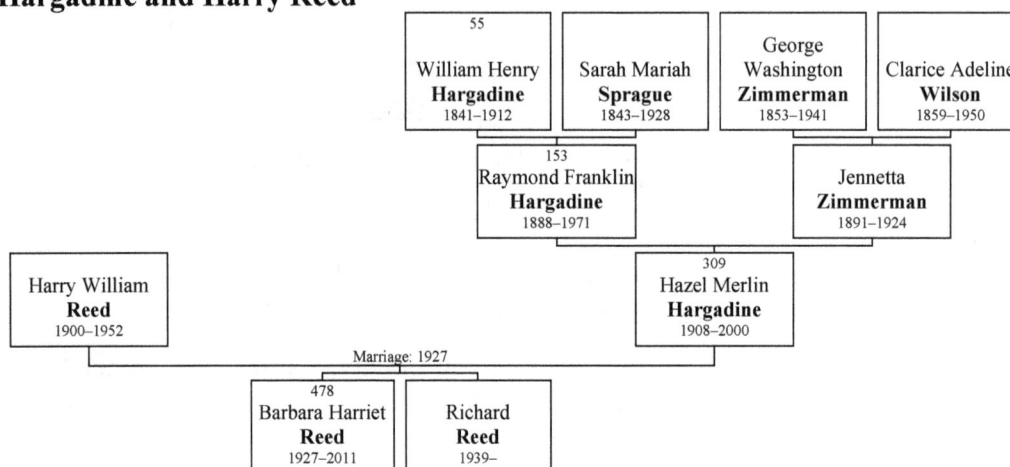

```
┌─────────────┐ ┌─────────────┐ ┌─────────────┐ ┌─────────────┐
│     55      │ │             │ │   George    │ │   Clarice   │
│William Henry│ │Sarah Mariah │ │ Washington  │ │  Adeline    │
│  Hargadine  │ │  Sprague    │ │ Zimmerman   │ │   Wilson    │
│  1841–1912  │ │  1843–1928  │ │  1853–1941  │ │  1859–1950  │
└─────────────┘ └─────────────┘ └─────────────┘ └─────────────┘
        ┌─────────────┐              ┌─────────────┐
        │    153      │              │             │
        │Raymond      │              │  Jennetta   │
        │Franklin     │              │  Zimmerman  │
        │Hargadine    │              │  1891–1924  │
        │1888–1971    │              └─────────────┘
        └─────────────┘
┌─────────────┐                  ┌─────────────┐
│Harry William│                  │    309      │
│    Reed     │                  │Hazel Merlin │
│  1900–1952  │                  │ Hargadine   │
└─────────────┘   Marriage: 1927 │  1908–2000  │
                                 └─────────────┘
        ┌─────────────┐ ┌─────────────┐
        │    478      │ │             │
        │Barbara      │ │  Richard    │
        │Harriet Reed │ │   Reed      │
        │  1927–2011  │ │   1939–     │
        └─────────────┘ └─────────────┘
```

Here are the details about **Hazel Merlin Hargadine's** first marriage, with Harry William Reed. You can read more about Hazel Merlin on page 344.

At the age of 19, Hazel Merlin Hargadine married **Harry William Reed** on Monday, June 20, 1927, at Harry A. Bell Minister in Wenatchee, Chelan County, Washington, when he was 26 years old. They had two children.

Harry William was born in Fergus Falls, Otter Tail County, Minnesota, on Tuesday, August 14, 1900. He served in the military between 1917 and 1919. WWI, US Army, Private Medical Corp.

Harry William reached 51 years of age and died in Seattle, King County, Washington, on May 27, 1952. His cause of death was: fracture base of skull, cerebral concussion; accidental fall. Harry William was buried on May 29, 1952, in Washington Memorial Park, Seattle, King County, Washington.

Children of Hazel Merlin Hargadine and Harry William Reed:

+   478   f   I. **Barbara Harriet Reed** was born in Seattle, King County, Washington, on April 11, 1927. She died in Yelm, Thurston County, Washington, on February 11, 2011, at the age of 83. Barbara Harriet was buried in Yelm Cemetery, Yelm, Thurston County, Washington (Find a Grave ID 88387449).

         m   II. **Richard Reed** was born in 1939.

Family of Hazel Hargadine and Charles Klontz

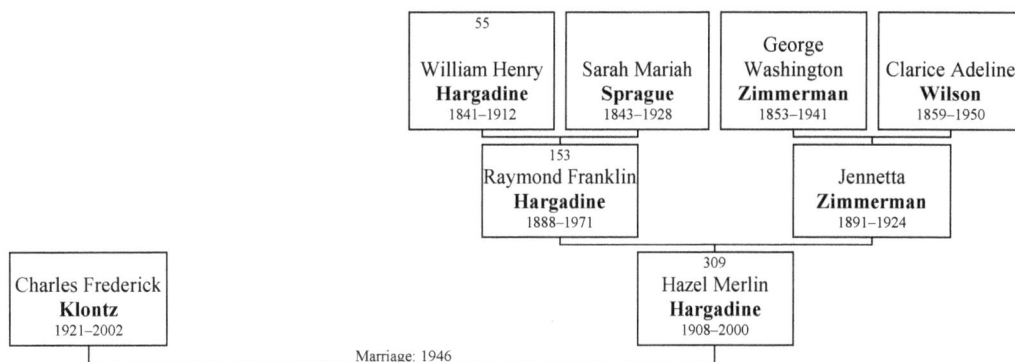

Here are the details about **Hazel Merlin Hargadine's** second marriage, with Charles Frederick Klontz. You can read more about Hazel Merlin on page 344.

At the age of 38, Hazel Merlin Hargadine married **Charles Frederick Klontz** on Monday, December 02, 1946, at Guy B. Knott, Justice of the Peace in Seattle, King County, Washington, when he was 25 years old. Charles Frederick was born in Needles, Canada, on Friday, March 11, 1921.

He reached 81 years of age and died in Yelm, Thurston County, Washington, on October 14, 2002. Charles Frederick was buried on October 19, 2002.

Rex Hargadine

310.   **Rex Raymond Hargadine** was born on Tuesday, May 30, 1911, in Ematon, Stevens County, Kansas. He was the son of Raymond Franklin Hargadine (153) and Jennetta Zimmerman.

Rex Raymond worked as a Plumber; Carson, Washington. He died in Portland, Multnomah County, Oregon, on February 20, 1995, at the age of 83. Rex Raymond was buried in Old Carson Cemetery, Skamania County, Washington, on February 23, 1995 (Find a Grave ID 43234369).

Marriages with Daisy Mae Fleming and Hazel Evine Erickson (Page 347) are known.

Family of Rex Hargadine and Daisy Fleming

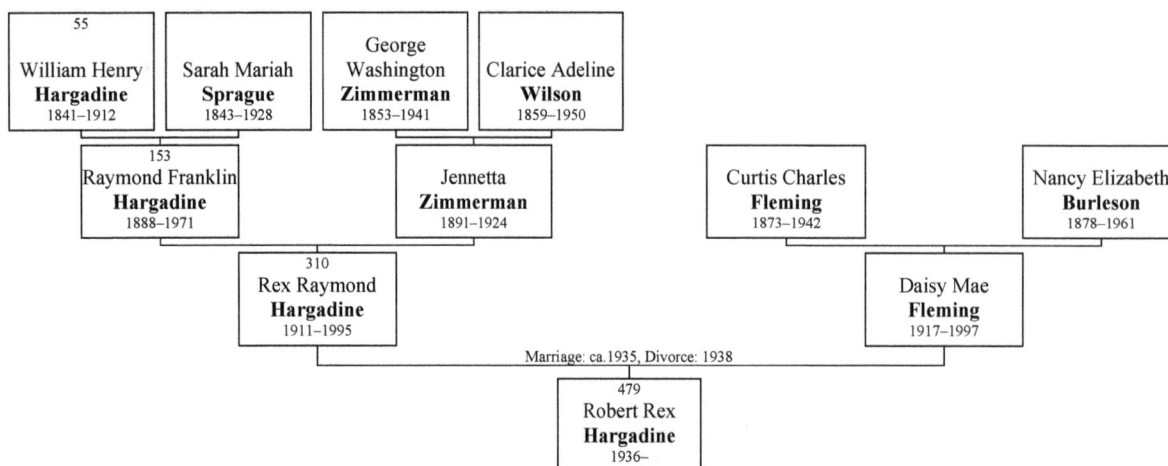

```
┌──────────────┐  ┌──────────────┐  ┌──────────────┐  ┌──────────────┐
│      55      │  │ Sarah Mariah │  │    George    │  │    Clarice   │
│William Henry │  │   Sprague    │  │  Washington  │  │   Adeline    │
│  Hargadine   │  │  1843–1928   │  │  Zimmerman   │  │    Wilson    │
│  1841–1912   │  │              │  │  1853–1941   │  │  1859–1950   │
└──────────────┘  └──────────────┘  └──────────────┘  └──────────────┘
```

Boxes: William Henry **Hargadine** 1841–1912 (55); Sarah Mariah **Sprague** 1843–1928; George Washington **Zimmerman** 1853–1941; Clarice Adeline **Wilson** 1859–1950

Raymond Franklin **Hargadine** 1888–1971 (153); Jennetta **Zimmerman** 1891–1924

Curtis Charles **Fleming** 1873–1942; Nancy Elizabeth **Burleson** 1878–1961

Rex Raymond **Hargadine** 1911–1995 (310)

Daisy Mae **Fleming** 1917–1997

Marriage: ca.1935, Divorce: 1938

Robert Rex **Hargadine** 1936– (479)

Here are the details about **Rex Raymond Hargadine's** first marriage, with Daisy Mae Fleming. You can read more about Rex Raymond on page 345.

Rex Raymond Hargadine married **Daisy Mae Fleming** about August 1935 in Chelan, Chelan County, Washington. They were divorced in Chelan, Chelan County, Washington, on December 10, 1938. They had one son.

Daisy Mae was born in Glendive, Dawson County, Montana, on Saturday, June 16, 1917. She was the daughter of Curtis Charles Fleming and Nancy Elizabeth Burleson.

Daisy Mae reached 79 years of age and died in Moscow, Latah County, Idaho, on January 23, 1997. She was buried in Chelan, Chelan County, Washington (Find a Grave ID 24301998).

Son of Rex Raymond Hargadine and Daisy Mae Fleming:

+ 479   m   I. **Robert Rex Hargadine** was born in Chelan, Chelan County, Washington, on October 10, 1936. He is also known as **Robert Rex Nichols**.

Family of Rex Hargadine and Hazel Erickson

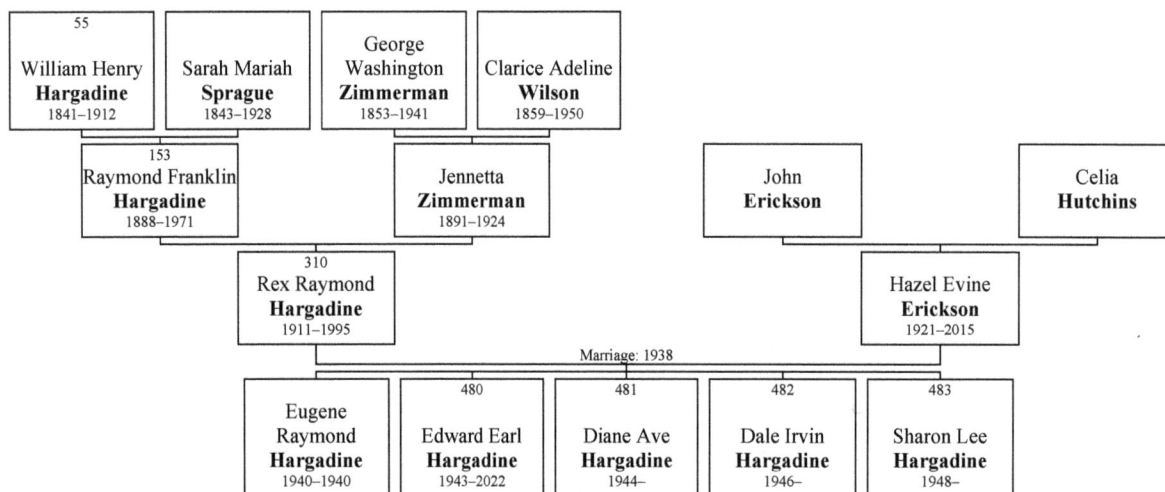

Boxes: William Henry **Hargadine** 1841–1912 (55); Sarah Mariah **Sprague** 1843–1928; George Washington **Zimmerman** 1853–1941; Clarice Adeline **Wilson** 1859–1950

Raymond Franklin **Hargadine** 1888–1971 (153); Jennetta **Zimmerman** 1891–1924

John **Erickson**; Celia **Hutchins**

Rex Raymond **Hargadine** 1911–1995 (310)

Hazel Evine **Erickson** 1921–2015

Marriage: 1938

Eugene Raymond **Hargadine** 1940–1940; Edward Earl **Hargadine** 1943–2022 (480); Diane Ave **Hargadine** 1944– (481); Dale Irvin **Hargadine** 1946– (482); Sharon Lee **Hargadine** 1948– (483)

Here are the details about **Rex Raymond Hargadine's** second marriage, with Hazel Evine Erickson. You can read more about Rex Raymond on page 345.

At the age of 27, Rex Raymond Hargadine married **Hazel Evine Erickson** on Saturday, July 16, 1938, in Chelan, Chelan County, Washington, when she was 17 years old. They had five children.

Hazel Evine was born in Hibbing, Saint Louis County, Minnesota, on Saturday, March 26, 1921. She was the daughter of John Erickson and Celia Hutchins.

Hazel Evine reached 94 years of age and died in Carson, Skamania County, Washington, on August 07, 2015. She was buried in Old Carson Cemetery, Skamania County, Washington (Find a Grave ID 213284235).

Children of Rex Raymond Hargadine and Hazel Evine Erickson:

	m	I.	**Eugene Raymond Hargadine** was born in Wenatchee, Chelan County, Washington, on August 11, 1940. He died in Wenatchee, Chelan County, Washington, on August 11, 1940. Eugene Raymond was buried in Fraternal Cemetery, Chelan, Chelan County, Washington (Find a Grave ID 24310015).
+ 480	m	II.	**Edward Earl Hargadine** was born in Portland, Multnomah County, Oregon, on January 19, 1943. He died in Carson, Skamania County, Washington, on September 21, 2022, at the age of 79.
+ 481	f	III.	**Diane Ave Hargadine** was born in White Salmon, Klickitat County, Washington, on June 01, 1944.
+ 482	m	IV.	**Dale Irvin Hargadine** was born in White Salmon, Klickitat County, Washington, on November 29, 1946.
+ 483	f	V.	**Sharon Lee Hargadine** was born in White Salmon, Klickitat County, Washington, on December 29, 1948. She is also known as **Shari**.

Family of Algenon Higley and Helen O'Neil

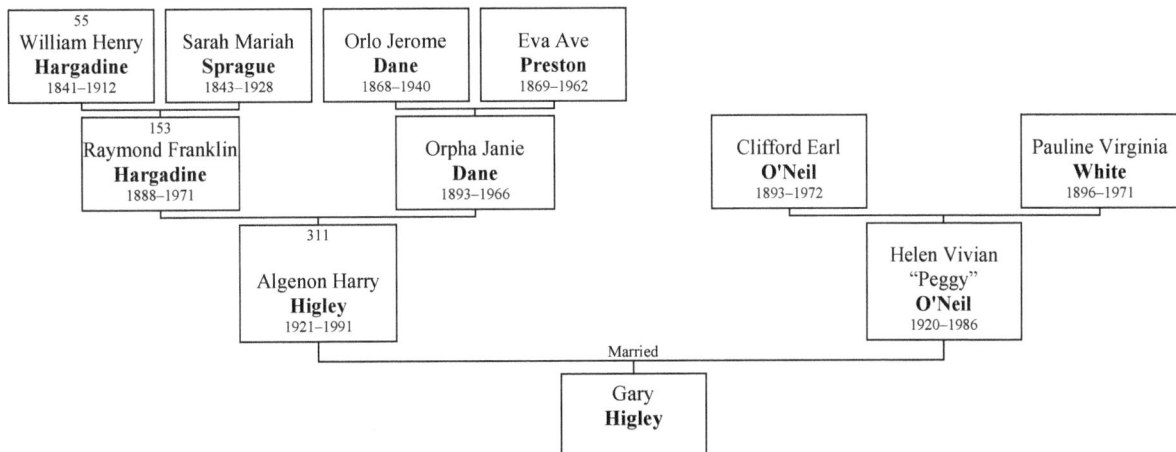

311. **Algenon Harry Higley** was born on Thursday, April 21, 1921, in Lakeside, Chelan County, Washington. He was the son of Raymond Franklin Hargadine (153) and Orpha Janie Dane.

Algenon Harry died in Hurricane, Washington County, Utah, on July 31, 1991, at the age of 70. He was buried in Kanab City Cemetery, Kanab, Kane County, Utah (Find a Grave ID 13208036).

He married **Helen Vivian "Peggy" O'Neil**. They had one son.

Helen Vivian "Peggy" was born in Moundsville, Marshall County, West Virginia, on Tuesday, March 23, 1920. She was the daughter of Clifford Earl O'Neil and Pauline Virginia White.

Helen Vivian "Peggy" reached 66 years of age and died in Kanab, Kane County, Utah, on September 18, 1986. She was buried in Kanab City Cemetery, Kanab, Kane County, Utah (Find a Grave ID 13208041).

Son of Algenon Harry Higley and Helen Vivian "Peggy" O'Neil:

> m   I. **Gary Higley**.

Family of William Hargadine and Carol Neil

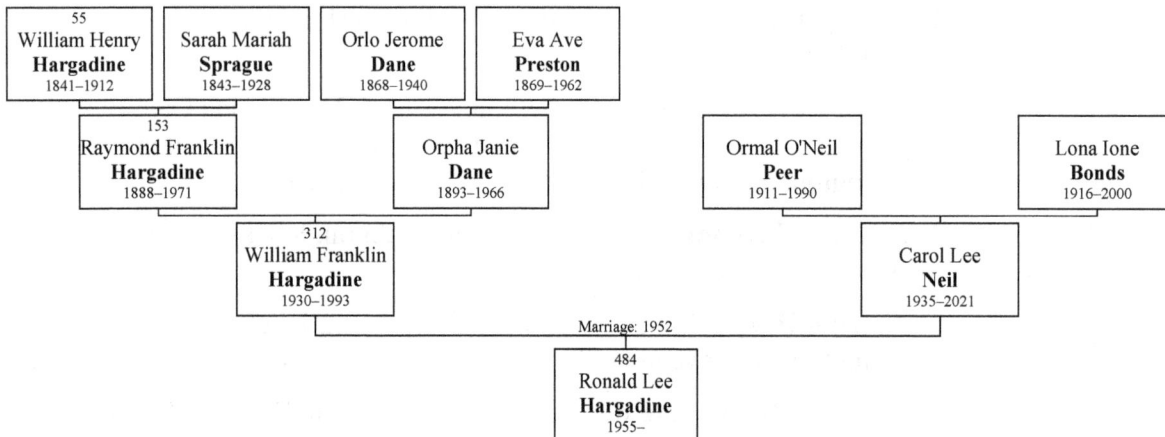

312. **William Franklin Hargadine** was born on Saturday, November 15, 1930, in Chelan, Chelan County, Washington. He was the son of Raymond Franklin Hargadine (153) and Orpha Janie Dane. He was also known as **Bill**.

William Franklin served in the military between March 15, 1951 and December 14, 1954. US Air Force, SSGT. He died in Mesa, Maricopa County, Arizona, on February 04, 1993, at the age of 62. William Franklin was buried in Willamette National Cemetery, Portland, Multnomah County, Oregon, on February 23, 1993 (Find a Grave ID 753315).

At the age of 21, William Franklin married **Carol Lee Neil** on Sunday, April 20, 1952, in Riverside, Riverside County, California, when she was 17 years old. They had one son.

Carol Lee was born on Monday, April 15, 1935. She was the daughter of Ormal O'Neil Peer and Lona Ione Bonds.

Carol Lee reached 86 years of age and died on December 27, 2021. Her cause of death was Lewy body dementia. Carol Lee was buried on September 08, 2022, in Willamette National Cemetery, Portland, Multnomah County, Oregon (Find a Grave ID 243310718).

Son of William Franklin Hargadine and Carol Lee Neil:

+ 484   m   I. **Ronald Lee Hargadine** was born in January 1955.

Family of Luella Hargadine and Richard O'Keefe

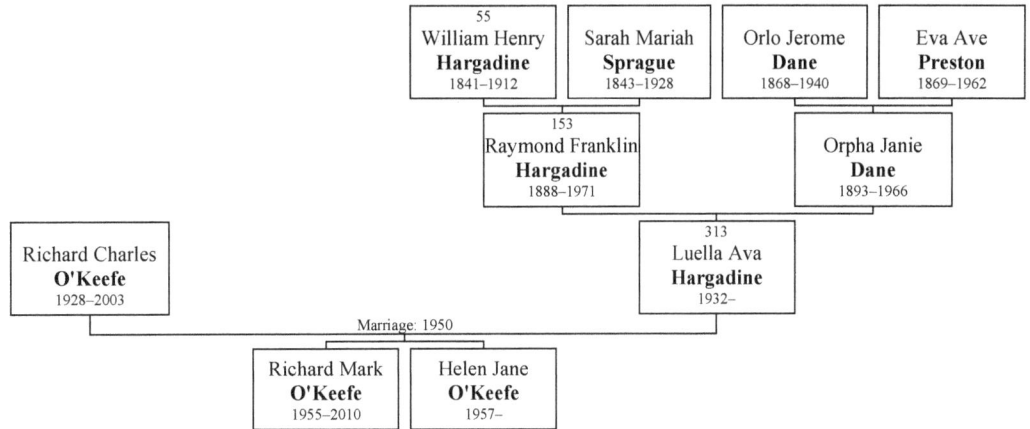

313.   **Luella Ava Hargadine** was born on Tuesday, November 08, 1932, in Chelan, Chelan County, Washington. She is the daughter of Raymond Franklin Hargadine (153) and Orpha Janie Dane. She is also known as **Ava**.

At the age of 17, Luella Ava married **Richard Charles O'Keefe** on Wednesday, August 30, 1950, in Carson, Skamania County, Washington, when he was 22 years old. They had two children.

Richard Charles was born in Los Angeles, Los Angeles County, California, on Wednesday, August 01, 1928. He reached 74 years of age and died in Maricopa, Pinal County, Arizona, on May 17, 2003.

Children of Luella Ava Hargadine and Richard Charles O'Keefe:

    m   I. **Richard Mark O'Keefe** was born in December 1955. He was also known as **Ricky**.

                Richard Mark died in Clatsop County, Oregon, in July 2010 at the age of 54.

    f   II. **Helen Jane O'Keefe** was born in October 1957.

Family of Max Drommond and Italia E

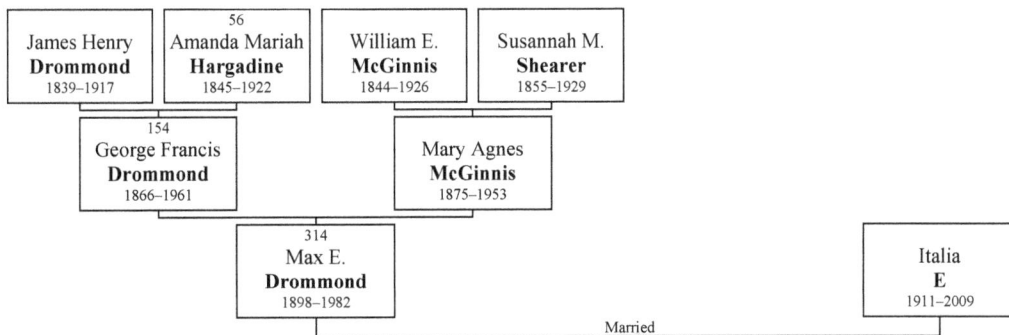

314. **Max E. Drommond** was born on Thursday, March 24, 1898, in Sanborn, Dundy County, Nebraska. He was the son of George Francis Drommond (154) and Mary Agnes McGinnis.

Max E. served in the military on December 14, 1917. Served in WWI and WWII, Retired as Colonel. He died in Seattle, King County, Washington, on December 31, 1982, at the age of 84. Max E. was buried in Lake View Cemetery, Seattle, King County, Washington, on January 05, 1983 (Find a Grave ID).

He married **Italia E**. Italia was born in July 1911.

She reached 97 years of age and died in King County, Washington, in 2009. Italia was buried in Lake View Cemetery, Seattle, King County, Washington (Find a Grave ID 89893470).

Family of Helen Drommond and Arthur Hultquist

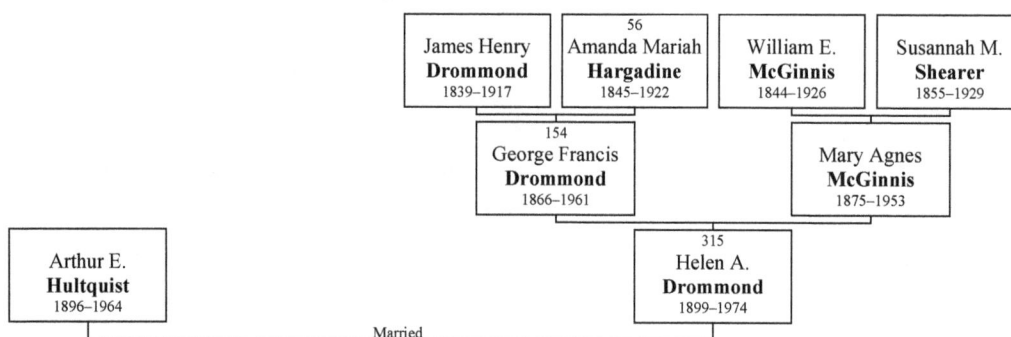

315. **Helen A. Drommond** was born on Monday, May 08, 1899. She was the daughter of George Francis Drommond (154) and Mary Agnes McGinnis.

Helen A. died on August 08, 1974, at the age of 75. She was buried in Grandview Cemetery, Wray, Yuma County, Colorado (Find a Grave ID 37801129).

She married **Arthur E. Hultquist**. Arthur E. was born on Saturday, May 30, 1896.

He reached 68 years of age and died on July 09, 1964. Arthur E. was buried in Grandview Cemetery, Wray, Yuma County, Colorado (Find a Grave ID 37801019).

Family of William Drommond and Velma Seward

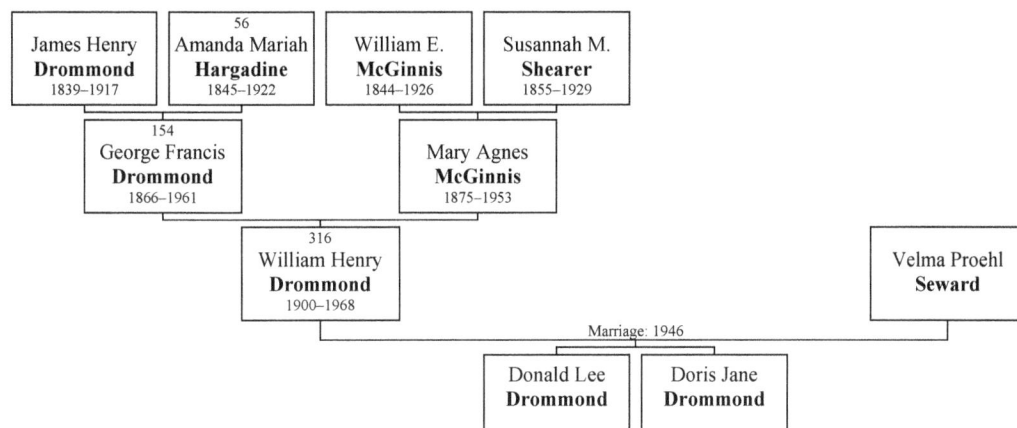

316. **William Henry Drommond** was born on Monday, September 10, 1900, in Sanborn, Dundy County, Nebraska. He was the son of George Francis Drommond (154) and Mary Agnes McGinnis.

William Henry died in Haigler, Dundy County, Nebraska, on June 27, 1968, at the age of 67. He was buried in Grandview Cemetery, Wray, Yuma County, Colorado, on June 29, 1968 (Find a Grave ID 50166367).

William Henry married **Velma Proehl Seward** on Saturday, January 05, 1946. They had two children.

Children of William Henry Drommond and Velma Proehl Seward:

    m   I. **Donald Lee Drommond**.

    f   II. **Doris Jane Drommond**.

Family of Nell Drommond and Philip Pahl

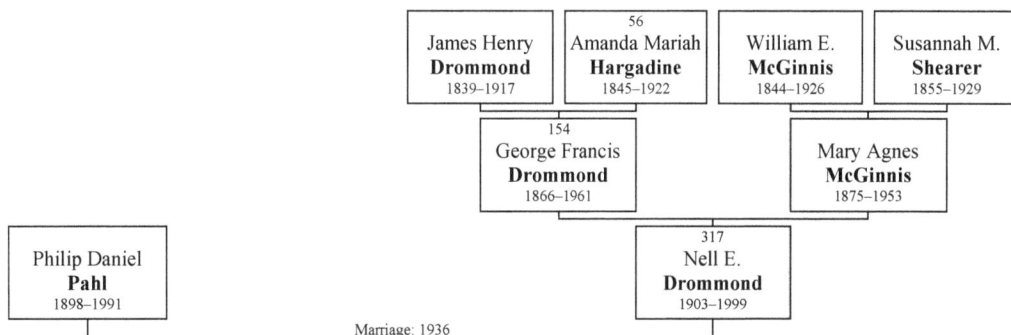

317. **Nell E. Drommond** was born on Sunday, April 12, 1903, in Sanborn, Dundy County, Nebraska.[349] She was the daughter of George Francis Drommond (154) and Mary Agnes McGinnis.

---

349   Ancestry.com, U.S., Find a Grave® Index, 1600s-Current (Lehi, UT, USA, Ancestry.com Operations, Inc., 2012), Ancestry.com, Record for Nell E. Pahl. https://search.ancestry.co.uk/cgi-bin/sse.dll?db=60525&h=127477485&indiv=try.

Nell E. died in Loveland, Larimer County, Colorado, on October 19, 1999, at the age of 96.[349] She was buried in Loveland Burial Park, Loveland, Larimer County, Colorado (Find a Grave ID 154832344).[349]

At the age of 33, Nell E. married **Philip Daniel Pahl** on Friday, July 17, 1936, when he was 37 years old. Philip Daniel was born in Swanton, Saline County, Nebraska, on Sunday, August 07, 1898.[349]

He reached 93 years of age and died in Loveland, Larimer County, Colorado, on September 10, 1991.[349] Philip Daniel was buried in Loveland Burial Park, Loveland, Larimer County, Colorado (Find a Grave ID 154832401).[349]

Family of Eldora Dill and Robert Dill

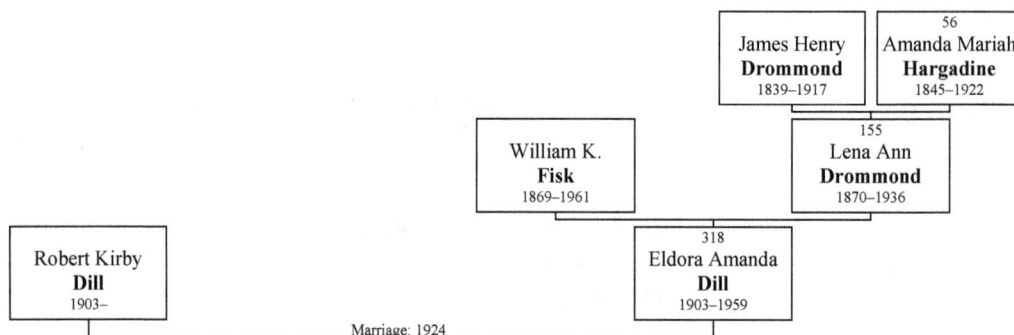

318. **Eldora Amanda Dill** was born on Sunday, August 30, 1903, in Colorado, USA.[350, 351] She was the daughter of William K. Fisk and Lena Ann Drommond (155).

Eldora Amanda died in Los Angeles, Los Angeles County, California, on November 24, 1959, at the age of 56.[350, 351]

Eldora Amanda married **Robert Kirby Dill** on Saturday, December 27, 1924, in Denver, Denver County, Colorado. Robert Kirby was born in Illinois, USA, in 1903.[351]

---

350 Ancestry.com, California, U.S., Death Index, 1940-1997 (Provo, UT, USA, Ancestry.com Operations Inc, 2000), Ancestry.com, Place: Los Angeles; Date: 24 Nov 1959; Social Security: 547445629. Record for Eldora Amanda Dill. https://search.ancestry.co.uk/cgi-bin/sse.dll?db=5180&h=1879319&indiv=try.

351 Ancestry.com, Public Member Trees (Provo, UT, USA, Ancestry.com Operations, Inc., 2006), Ancestry.com, Record for Eldora Amanda Fisk. https://search.ancestry.co.uk/cgi-bin/sse.dll?db=1030&h=13896600421&indiv=try.

Family of Grace Bullard and Clarence Gibson

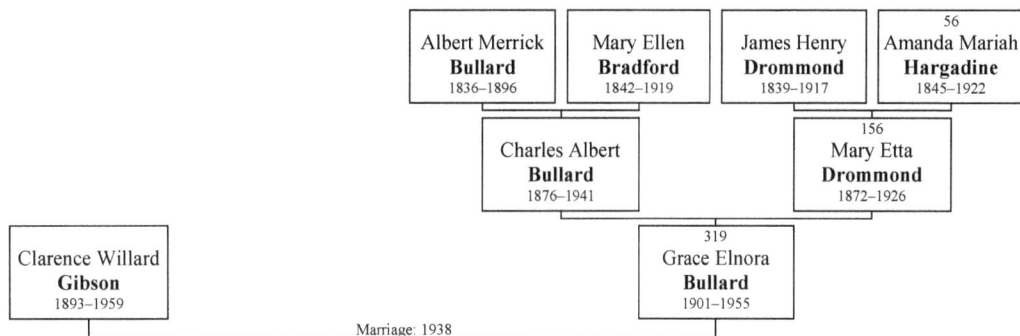

319. **Grace Elnora Bullard** was born on Saturday, November 09, 1901, in Colorado Springs, El Paso County, Colorado. She was the daughter of Charles Albert Bullard and Mary Etta Drommond (156).

Grace Elnora died in Torrance, Los Angeles, California, on May 26, 1955, at the age of 53. She was buried in Grandview Cemetery, Wray, Yuma County, Colorado (Find a Grave ID 30893177).

At the age of 36, Grace Elnora married **Clarence Willard Gibson** on Sunday, June 05, 1938, in Colorado Springs, Denver, Colorado, when he was 44 years old. Clarence Willard was born in Mississippi, USA, on Saturday, July 29, 1893.

He reached 65 years of age and died in North Las Vegas, Clark County, Nevada, on January 15, 1959. Clarence Willard was buried in Green Hills Memorial Park, Rancho Palos Verdes, Los Angeles County, California (Find a Grave ID 38541786).

Family of Roscoe Bullard and Nellie Miller

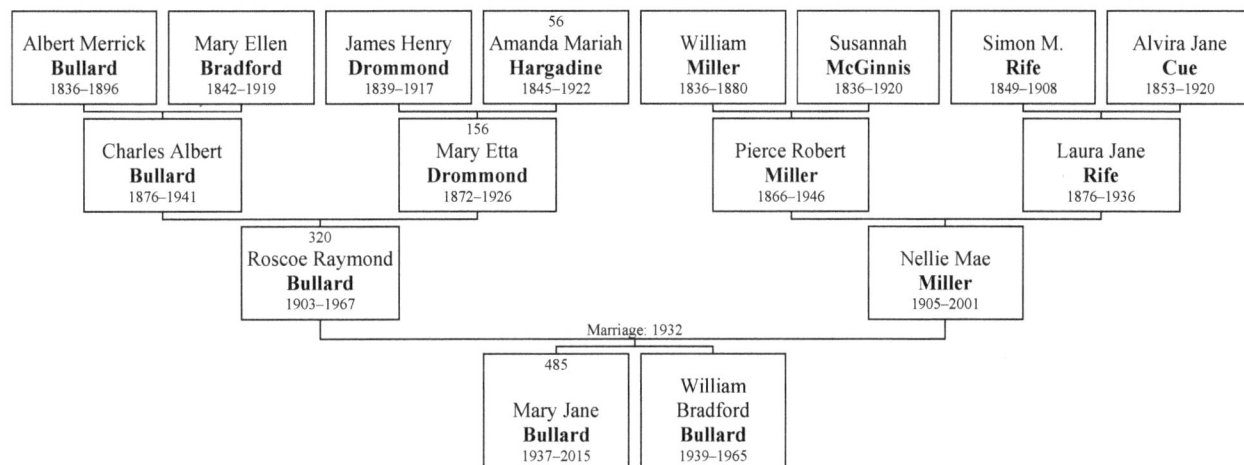

320. **Roscoe Raymond Bullard** was born on Wednesday, November 11, 1903, in Laird, Yuma County, Colorado. He was the son of Charles Albert Bullard and Mary Etta Drommond (156).

Roscoe Raymond worked as an editor and later owner *Wray Gazette.* He died in Denver, Denver County, Colorado, on May 12, 1967, at the age of 63. Roscoe Raymond was buried in Grandview Cemetery, Wray, Yuma County, Colorado (Find a Grave ID 17075799).

At the age of 28, Roscoe Raymond married **Nellie Mae Miller** on Sunday, September 25, 1932, in McDonald, Rawlins County, Kansas, when she was 26 years old. They had two children.

Nellie Mae was born in Laird, Yuma County, Colorado, on Tuesday, December 05, 1905.

Nellie Mae reached 95 years of age and died in 2001. She was buried in Grandview Cemetery, Wray, Yuma County, Colorado (Find a Grave ID 17059460).

ROSCOE AND NELL BULLARD

"The only newspaper in the world whose chief interest is *Wray*" - these words on the masthead of the *Wray Gazette* best reflected the life and journalistic philosophy of Roscoe Bullard. His entire life, with the exception of seven years, was spent in Yuma County where he was born 11 November, 1903, at the homestead home of his grandparents south of Laird.

He was an apprentice at the *Wray Rattler* during high school days and later was employed by the *Denver Post* for one year. Roscoe returned to Wray in 1926 and became editor of the *Wray Gazette* for the owner, Leo M. Simpson, until 1935. After one year at the *Delta Tribune* and five with the *Yuma Pioneer*, he formed a partnership with John Graves to purchase the *Gazette* from G. M. MacGinnis.
He and his wife Nellie Miller, published the weekly paper until 1966 when he became ill with cancer. He died in Denver on 12 May 1967. Burial was in Grandview Cemetery at Wray.

Mr. Bullard was extremely proud of the title "Country Editor." People were his hobby and he enjoyed the confidence and respect of both his advertisers and his subscribers. His column "Wray-vings by R. B." was a popular feature of the paper.

He was active in the Chamber of Commerce (as secretary for many years), Rotary, Volunteer Fire Department, the School Board and the Republican Charter Committee for the Town of Wray and was president of the Colorado Press Association in 1947.

Nell Bullard, also born in Yuma county, taught in the county high school for five years before her marriage on 25 September, 1932. She then shared the responsibilities of the newspaper until its sale in 1966.

The Bullards and their children were members of the United Methodist Church. A daughter, Mary Jane, is married to William B. Groves. The son, William Bradford, was a casualty in an Eastern Airline crash in 1965 while in service and stationed in Georgia.

The family home was at 556 Grant in Wray.

A History of East Yuma County
This is a collection of general history and family histories of East Yuma County from 1868 through 1978. Page 68. Nell was the daughter of Pierce Robert Miller and Laura Jane Rife.

Children of Roscoe Raymond Bullard and Nellie Mae Miller:

+ 485   f   I. **Mary Jane Bullard** was born in Yuma, Yuma County, Colorado, on April 23, 1937. She died in Loveland, Larimer County, Colorado, on February 20, 2015, at the age of 77. Mary Jane was cremated—Ashes scattered (Find a Grave ID 143428396).

       m   II. **William Bradford Bullard** was born in Yuma, Yuma County, Colorado, on March 01, 1939. He died at Died in an Eastern Airlines crash while a Private in the U.S. Army in Jones Beach State Park, New York, on February 08, 1965, at the age of 25. His cause of death was airplane crash. He was buried in Grandview Cemetery, Wray, Yuma County, Colorado (Find a Grave ID 8283064).

Family of Ernest Drommond and Iva Spears

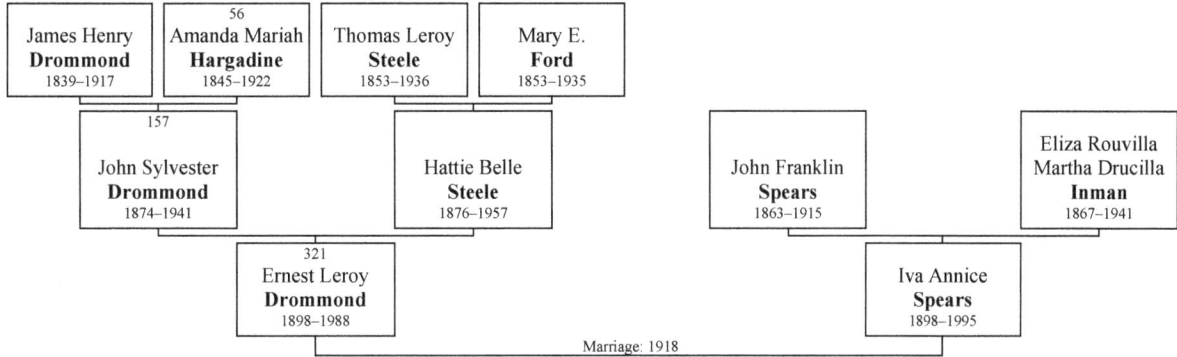

321.   **Ernest Leroy Drommond** was born on Wednesday, March 23, 1898, in Haigler, Dundy County, Nebraska. He was the son of John Sylvester Drommond (157) and Hattie Belle Steele.

Ernest Leroy died in Colorado, USA, on May 25, 1988, at the age of 90. He was buried in Memorial Gardens Cemetery and Mausoleum, Colorado Springs, El Paso County, Colorado (Find a Grave ID 49825963).

At the age of 20, Ernest Leroy married **Iva Annice Spears** on Wednesday, May 01, 1918, in Squirrel Creek, Colorado, when she was 19 years old. Iva Annice was born in Hutton Valley, Howell County, Missouri, on Monday, December 12, 1898. She was the daughter of John Franklin Spears and Eliza Rouvilla Martha Drucilla Inman.

Iva Annice reached 96 years of age and died in Colorado Springs, El Paso County, Colorado, on October 09, 1995. She was buried in Memorial Gardens Cemetery and Mausoleum, Colorado Springs, El Paso County, Colorado (Find a Grave ID 49824668).

Family of Fay Drommond and Edgar Spears

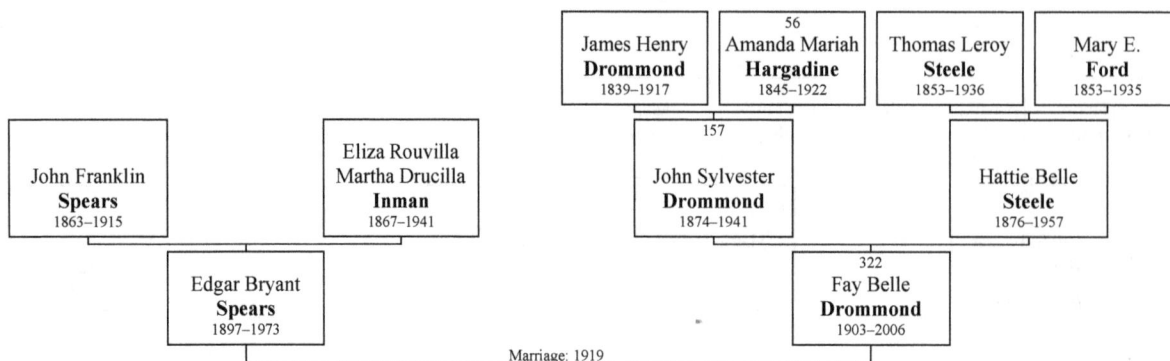

			56				
		James Henry **Drommond** 1839–1917	Amanda Mariah **Hargadine** 1845–1922	Thomas Leroy **Steele** 1853–1936	Mary E. **Ford** 1853–1935		

John Franklin **Spears** 1863–1915

Eliza Rouvilla Martha Drucilla **Inman** 1867–1941

157
John Sylvester **Drommond** 1874–1941

Hattie Belle **Steele** 1876–1957

Edgar Bryant **Spears** 1897–1973

322
Fay Belle **Drommond** 1903–2006

Marriage: 1919

322. **Fay Belle Drommond** was born on Saturday, September 19, 1903. She was the daughter of John Sylvester Drommond (157) and Hattie Belle Steele.

Fay Belle died on April 13, 2006, at the age of 102. She was buried in Evergreen Cemetery, Colorado Springs, El Paso County, Colorado (Find a Grave ID 35152035).

Fay Belle married **Edgar Bryant Spears** in 1919. Edgar Bryant was born in Hutton Valley, Howell County, Missouri, on Monday, January 25, 1897. He was the son of John Franklin Spears and Eliza Rouvilla Martha Drucilla Inman.

Edgar Bryant reached 76 years of age and died in Colorado Springs, El Paso County, Colorado, on July 03, 1973. He was buried on July 06, 1973, in Evergreen Cemetery, Colorado Springs, El Paso County, Colorado (Find a Grave ID 35152033).

Family of Floyd Drommond and Ellen VanDusen

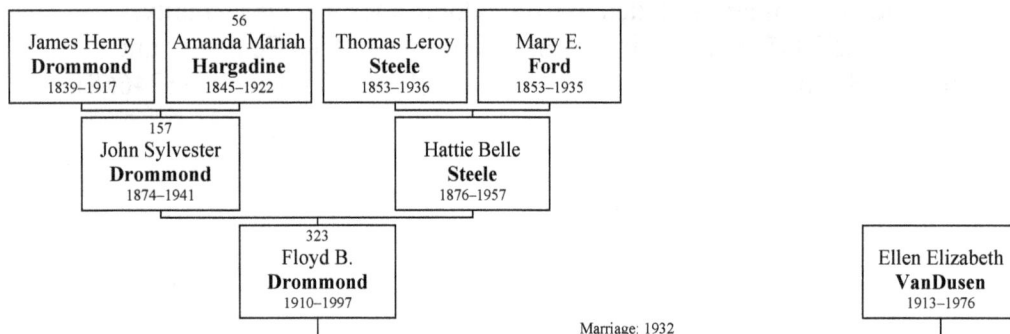

James Henry **Drommond** 1839–1917	56 Amanda Mariah **Hargadine** 1845–1922	Thomas Leroy **Steele** 1853–1936	Mary E. **Ford** 1853–1935

157
John Sylvester **Drommond** 1874–1941

Hattie Belle **Steele** 1876–1957

323
Floyd B. **Drommond** 1910–1997

Ellen Elizabeth **VanDusen** 1913–1976

Marriage: 1932

323. **Floyd B. Drommond** was born on Thursday, December 22, 1910, in Colorado Springs, El Paso County, Colorado. He was the son of John Sylvester Drommond (157) and Hattie Belle Steele.

Floyd B. died in Colorado Springs, El Paso County, Colorado, on July 25, 1997, at the age of 86. He was buried in Evergreen Cemetery, Colorado Springs, El Paso County, Colorado, on August 01, 1997 (Find a Grave ID 34611284).

At the age of 21, Floyd B. married **Ellen Elizabeth VanDusen** on Wednesday, December 14, 1932, in Colorado Springs, El Paso County, Colorado, when she was 19 years old. Ellen Elizabeth was born on Saturday, October 04, 1913.

She reached 63 years of age and died in Colorado Springs, El Paso County, Colorado, on November 12, 1976. Ellen Elizabeth was buried on November 16, 1976, in Evergreen Cemetery, Colorado Springs, El Paso County, Colorado (Find a Grave ID 34611283).

Family of Birdella Kerns and Ray Ralph

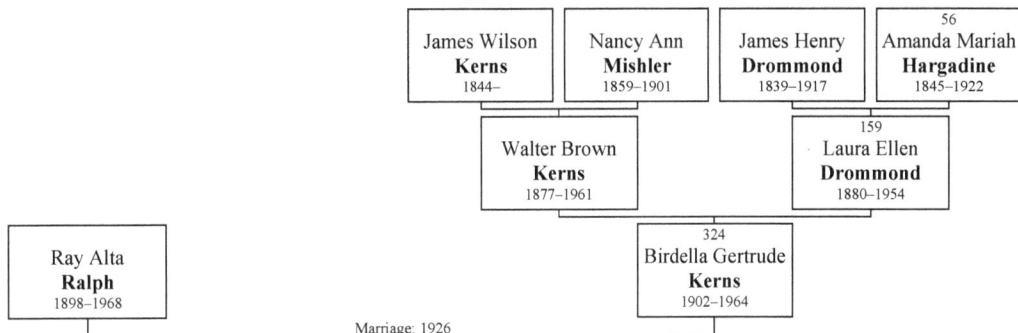

324. **Birdella Gertrude Kerns** was born in 1902. She was the daughter of Walter Brown Kerns and Laura Ellen Drommond (159).

Birdella Gertrude died on September 15, 1964, at the age of 62. She was buried in Grandview Cemetery, Wray, Yuma County, Colorado (Find a Grave ID 62637457).

Birdella Gertrude married **Ray Alta Ralph** in 1926. Ray Alta was born in Red Cloud, Webster County, Nebraska, on Saturday, July 16, 1898.

He reached 70 years of age and died in Yuma County, Colorado, in September 1968. Ray Alta was buried in Grandview Cemetery, Wray, Yuma County, Colorado (Find a Grave ID 62637633).

Family of Velva Kerns and Earl Chapman

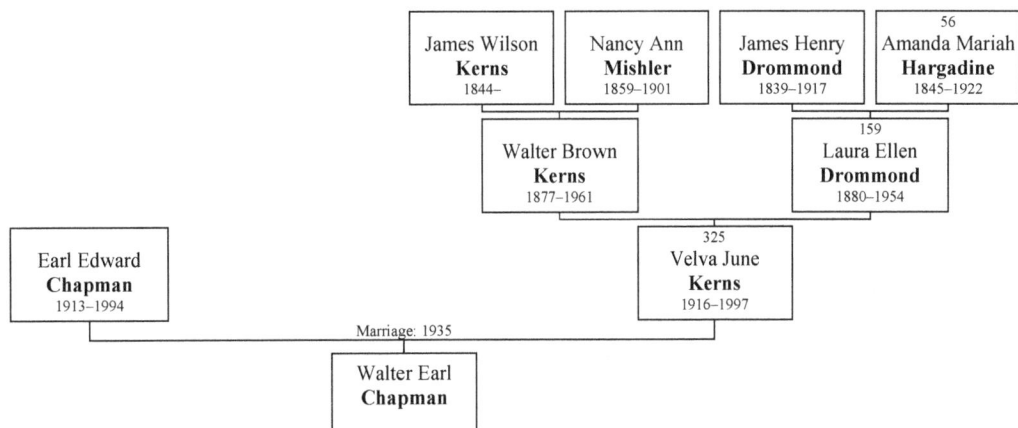

325. **Velva June Kerns** was born on Sunday, June 11, 1916. She was the daughter of Walter Brown Kerns and Laura Ellen Drommond (159).

Velva June died on May 22, 1997, at the age of 80. She was buried in San Jacinto Valley Cemetery, San Jacinto, Riverside County, California (Find a Grave ID 110414193).

At the age of 19, Velva June married **Earl Edward Chapman** on Friday, August 02, 1935, when he was 21 years old. They had one son.

Earl Edward was born in Edison, Furnas County, Nebraska, on Tuesday, November 18, 1913. He was also known as **Buck**.

Earl Edward reached 80 years of age and died on October 16, 1994. He was buried in San Jacinto Valley Cemetery, San Jacinto, Riverside County, California (Find a Grave ID 110414145).

Son of Velva June Kerns and Earl Edward Chapman:

m   I. **Walter Earl Chapman**.

Family of Mary Drommond and Harold Whyte

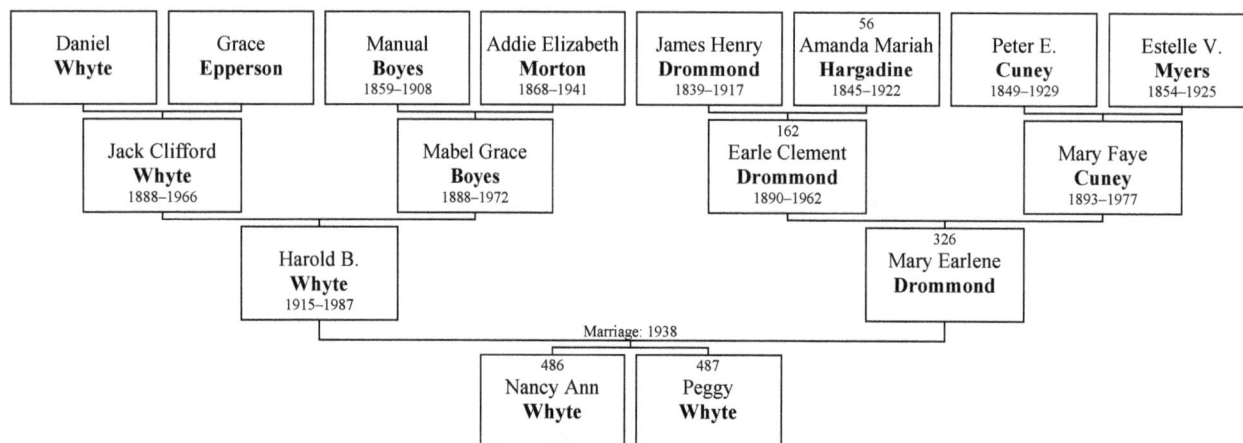

326.   **Mary Earlene Drommond**. She was the daughter of Earle Clement Drommond (162) and Mary Faye Cuney.

Mary Earlene married **Harold B. Whyte** in March 1938. They had two daughters.

Harold B. was born on Friday, January 08, 1915. He was also known as **Hy**.

Harold B. reached 72 years of age and died on December 29, 1987.

H. B. (HY) AND EARLENE WHYTE

Harold B. Whyte nicknamed "Hy" by his Uncle Lowery Boyes, arrived in Wray January 8, 1915 in the home of J. C. (Jack) and Mabel Whyte. The address 531 W. 4th St. "This Old House" was built by Hy's wife's uncle, Charles Bullard. In 1947 Hy and his wife Earlene bought the house from Roy Cuney, another uncle of Earlene's. It is still "Home Sweet Home."

When Harold was three, his folks moved to the farm, 7 miles south of Wray on the Beecher Island road. Hy's Dad taught him to love horses, farm, care of machinery, but gave him a dislike to milking cows. His mother taught him many household chores (he is still a good dishwasher) so he was eager to be a big boy to go with his dad.

Hy attended Wray Schools. In March 1938, he married Mary Earlene Drommond. Earlene was a native Wrayite, daughter of Earle and Mary Drommond. Their marriage life began on the farm. At the outbreak of World War II, Hy and Earlene moved to Denver. They were employed at Remington Arms plant until Hy enlisted in the Navy Construction Battalion in 1942. Hy spent 2-1/2 years in New Guinea and the Philippines, driving heavy equipment. In 1945 he received his military discharge. Hy and Earlene returned to Wray and got employment with Royal Lynam, the Conoco distributor.

Hy was hired as Wray City Manager in March 1952. One year of city problems caused ulcers so back to the farm. Wheat farming left idle winter months so Hy again took the challenge of being city manager in March 1954. He survived and loved his work till he retired in March 1975.

During the time he served as Wray Fire Chief 10 years, president of Commercial Club, Colorado District Municipalities, Wray Country Club, Commander of Legion and V. F. W. He also served as trustee in the Presbyterian Church.

Hy and Earlene have two daughters. Nancy Ann resides in Aurora with husband Patrolman Randell Pennington and son John Whyte, known as J. W.

Peggy Lee and husband, John Lynch with sons Shawn and Chad live in Ranier, Minnesota. They operate a fishing resort "The Musket Inn" on Rainy Lake in the summer. Winters are busy with running their "Pickle Barrel Pub."   By Earlene Whyte

A History of East Yuma County
This is a collection of general history and family histories of East Yuma County from 1868 through 1978. Pages 303. He was the son of Jack Clifford Whyte and Mabel Grace Boyes.

Daughters of Mary Earlene Drommond and Harold B. Whyte:

+　486　　f　　　I. **Nancy Ann Whyte**.

+　487　　f　　　II. **Peggy Whyte**.

Family of Roy Chambers and Gladys Kinney

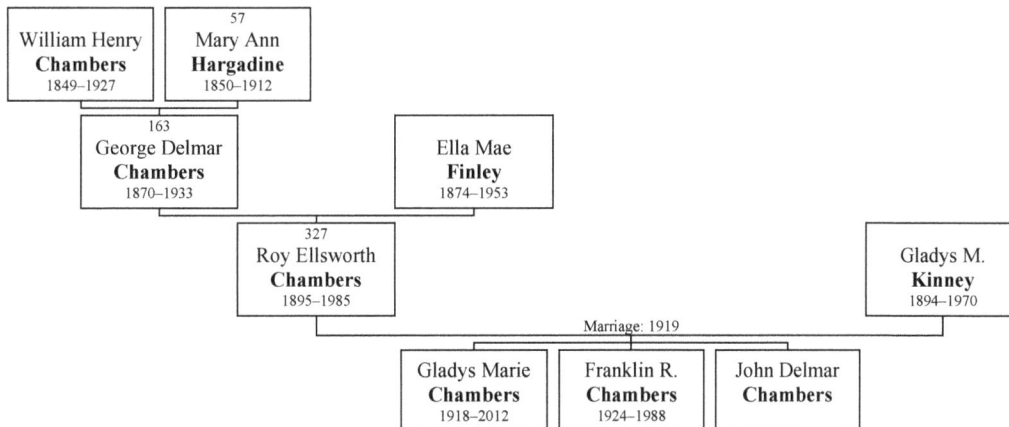

327.　　**Roy Ellsworth Chambers** was born on Sunday, July 28, 1895, in Chenoa, McLean County, Illinois.[352] He was the son of George Delmar Chambers (163) and Ella Mae Finley. He was also known as **Shorty**.

Roy Ellsworth died in Pompano Beach, Broward County, Florida, on July 11, 1985, at the age of 89.[352] He was buried in Park Hill Cemetery and Mausoleum, Bloomington, McLean County, Illinois, on July 16, 1985 (Find a Grave ID 58571202).

At the age of 23, Roy Ellsworth married **Gladys M. Kinney** on Thursday, May 15, 1919, in Champaign, Champaign County, Illinois, when she was 24 years old.[352] They had three children.

352　　*Bloomington Pantagraph*, Roy E. Chambers Obituary (Sunday July 15, 1985).

Gladys M. was born in Milan, Erie County, Ohio, on Monday, July 02, 1894.[353] She reached 75 years of age and died in Bloomington, McLean County, Illinois, on March 13, 1970.[352] Gladys M. was buried on March 16, 1970, in Park Hill Cemetery and Mausoleum, Bloomington, McLean County, Illinois (Find a Grave ID 58544288).

Children of Roy Ellsworth Chambers and Gladys M. Kinney:

f   I. **Gladys Marie Chambers** was born in Normal, McLean County, Illinois, on September 13, 1918. She died in Bloomington, McLean County, Illinois, on May 19, 2012, at the age of 93. Gladys Marie was buried in Friends Cemetery, Bentown, McLean County, Illinois (Find a Grave ID 90541433).

m   II. **Franklin R. Chambers** was born in Pennsylvania, USA, on November 29, 1924. He died in St. Petersburg, Pinellas County, Florida, on June 09, 1988, at the age of 63.[354]

m   III. **John Delmar Chambers**.

Family of Blanche Chambers and Ray Stretch

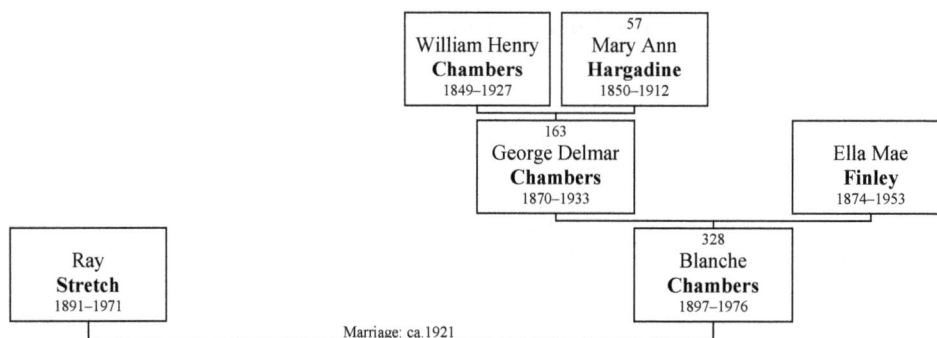

328.   Blanche Chambers was born on Saturday, February 20, 1897, in Chenoa, McLean County, Illinois.[355, 356] She was the daughter of George Delmar Chambers (163) and Ella Mae Finley.

Blanche died in Pompano Beach, Broward County, Florida, on February 13, 1976, at the age of 78.[355, 357] She was buried in Forest Lawn Memorial Gardens North, Pompano Beach, Broward County, Florida (Find a Grave ID 101845641).

Blanche married **Ray Stretch** about 1921. Ray was born in Lafayette, Tippecanoe County, Indiana, on Saturday, October 03, 1891.[355]

He reached 79 years of age and died in Pompano Beach, Broward County, Florida, on February 27, 1971.[355] Ray was buried in Forest Lawn Memorial Gardens North, Pompano Beach, Broward County, Florida (Find a Grave ID 101845635).

353   *Bloomington Pantagraph*, Mrs. Gladys Chambers Obituary (March 15, 1970).

354   Social Security Death Index.

355   Social Security Death Index.

356   1900 Census Mclean County Chenoa Township, Vol 117 - Ed. 98 - Sheet 9 - Line 20.

357   *Bloomington Pantagraph*, Roy E. Chambers Obituary (Sunday July 15, 1985).

Family of Helen Chambers and Herbert Rediger

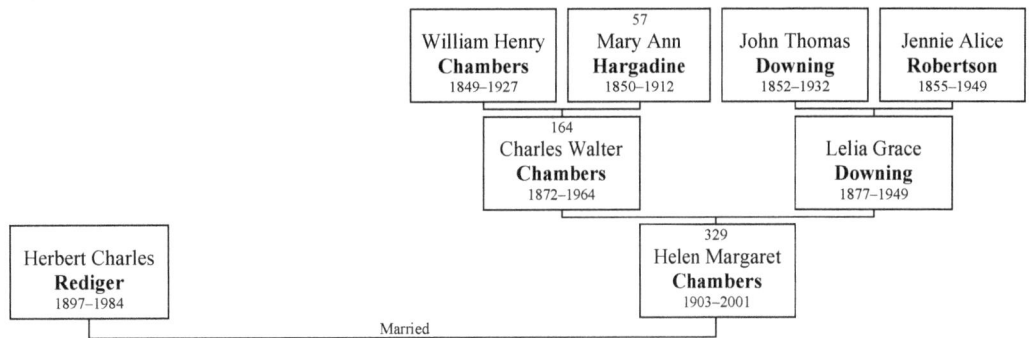

```
                    ┌──────────┬─────57─────┬──────────┬──────────┐
                    │ William  │  Mary Ann  │   John   │  Jennie  │
                    │  Henry   │ Hargadine  │  Thomas  │  Alice   │
                    │ Chambers │ 1850-1912  │ Downing  │ Robertson│
                    │1849-1927 │            │1852-1932 │1855-1949 │
                    └──────────┴──────┬─────┴─────┬────┴──────────┘
                         ┌─────164────┴──┐   ┌────┴──────────┐
                         │ Charles Walter│   │  Lelia Grace  │
                         │   Chambers    │   │   Downing     │
                         │   1872-1964   │   │   1877-1949   │
                         └───────┬───────┘   └───────┬───────┘
    ┌──────────────┐          ┌──┴─────329────────┴──┐
    │   Herbert    │          │    Helen Margaret     │
    │   Charles    │          │      Chambers         │
    │   Rediger    │          │      1903-2001        │
    │  1897-1984   │          └───────────────────────┘
    └──────┬───────┘                     │
           └──────────────Married────────┘
```

329.   **Helen Margaret Chambers** was born on Thursday, August 13, 1903, in Chenoa, McLean County, Illinois. She was the daughter of Charles Walter Chambers (164) and Lelia Grace Downing.

Helen Margaret died in Saint Petersburg, Pinellas County, Florida, on September 15, 2001, at the age of 98. She was buried in Memorial Park Cemetery, Saint Petersburg, Pinellas County, Florida (Find a Grave ID 104743841).

She married **Herbert Charles Rediger**. Herbert Charles was born in Bloomington, McLean County, Illinois, on Tuesday, May 18, 1897. He was also known as **Herbert (Mick) Rediger**.

Herbert Charles reached 87 years of age and died in Bay Pines, Pinellas County, Florida, on December 31, 1984. He was buried on January 02, 1985, in Memorial Park Cemetery, Saint Petersburg, Pinellas County, Florida (Find a Grave ID 104743814).

Paul Chambers

330.   **Paul Gaylord Chambers** was born on Thursday, October 19, 1905, in Chenoa, McLean County, Illinois. He was the son of Charles Walter Chambers (164) and Lelia Grace Downing.

Paul Gaylord worked as a decorator, Cook & Meyer Company (window displays) about 1960. He died in Huntington Beach, Orange County, California, on May 27, 1966, at the age of 60. His cause of death was cerebral edema due to purulent meningitis. He was buried in Good Shepherd Cemetery, Huntington Beach, Orange County, California, on May 31, 1966 (Find a Grave ID 158373146).

Marriages with Mabel E. Campbell and Elouise Geraldine Smith (Page 362) are known.

Family of Paul Chambers and Mabel Campbell

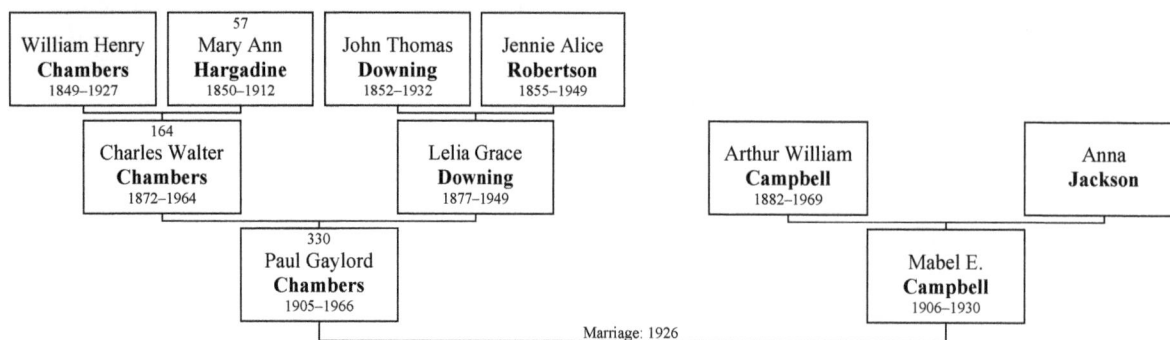

	57		
William Henry **Chambers** 1849–1927	Mary Ann **Hargadine** 1850–1912	John Thomas **Downing** 1852–1932	Jennie Alice **Robertson** 1855–1949

164	
Charles Walter **Chambers** 1872–1964	Lelia Grace **Downing** 1877–1949

Arthur William **Campbell** 1882–1969	Anna **Jackson**

330
Paul Gaylord **Chambers** 1905–1966

Mabel E. **Campbell** 1906–1930

Marriage: 1926

Here are the details about **Paul Gaylord Chambers's** first marriage, with Mabel E. Campbell. You can read more about Paul Gaylord on page 361.

At the age of 20, Paul Gaylord Chambers married **Mabel E. Campbell** on Tuesday, August 03, 1926, in Bloomington, McLean County, Illinois, when she was 19 years old.[358] Mabel E. was born in Fremont, Lake County, Illinois, on Thursday, December 06, 1906. She was the daughter of Arthur William Campbell and Anna Jackson.

Mabel E. reached 23 years of age and died in Bloomington, McLean County, Illinois, on January 29, 1930. She was buried in Park Hill Cemetery and Mausoleum, Bloomington, McLean County, Illinois (Find a Grave ID 58570715).

Family of Paul Chambers and Elouise Smith

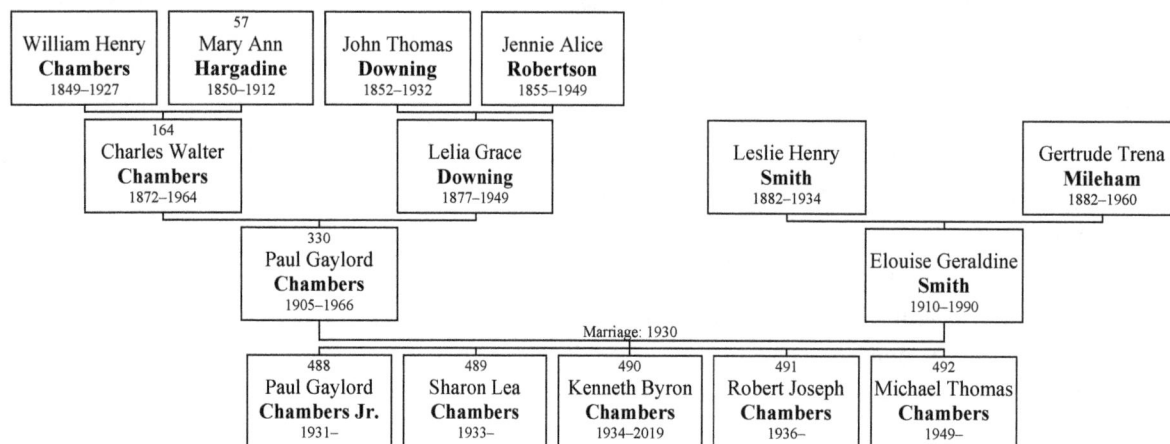

	57		
William Henry **Chambers** 1849–1927	Mary Ann **Hargadine** 1850–1912	John Thomas **Downing** 1852–1932	Jennie Alice **Robertson** 1855–1949

164	
Charles Walter **Chambers** 1872–1964	Lelia Grace **Downing** 1877–1949

Leslie Henry **Smith** 1882–1934	Gertrude Trena **Mileham** 1882–1960

330
Paul Gaylord **Chambers** 1905–1966

Elouise Geraldine **Smith** 1910–1990

Marriage: 1930

488	489	490	491	492
Paul Gaylord **Chambers Jr.** 1931–	Sharon Lea **Chambers** 1933–	Kenneth Byron **Chambers** 1934–2019	Robert Joseph **Chambers** 1936–	Michael Thomas **Chambers** 1949–

Here are the details about **Paul Gaylord Chambers's** second marriage, with Elouise Geraldine Smith. You can read more about Paul Gaylord on page 361.

At the age of 25, Paul Gaylord Chambers married **Elouise Geraldine Smith** on Wednesday, December 10, 1930, in Eureka, Woodford County, Illinois, when she was 20 years old. They had five children.

---

[358] *Chenoa Clipper Times*, Obituary (William Henry Chambers) (May 12, 1927).

Elouise Geraldine was born in Dawson, Sangamon County, Illinois, on Wednesday, July 06, 1910.[359] She was the daughter of Leslie Henry Smith and Gertrude Trena Mileham.

Elouise Geraldine reached 79 years of age and died in Escondido, San Diego County, California, on April 26, 1990. Her cause of death was congestive heart failure. Elouise Geraldine was buried on April 30, 1990, in Good Shepherd Cemetery, Huntington Beach, Orange County, California (Find a Grave ID 158373295).

Children of Paul Gaylord Chambers and Elouise Geraldine Smith:

+   488   m   I. **Paul Gaylord Chambers Jr.** was born in Bloomington, McLean County, Illinois, on July 25, 1931. He is also known as **Bud Chambers**.

+   489   f   II. **Sharon Lea Chambers** was born in Bloomington, McLean County, Illinois, on January 31, 1933.

+   490   m   III. **Kenneth Byron Chambers** was born in Terre Haute, Vigo County, Indiana, on July 03, 1934. He was also known as **Kenneth James**.

                                        Kenneth Byron died in Munster Lake County, Indiana, on January 06, 2019, at the age of 84. He was buried in Skyline Memorial Park, Monee, Will County, Illinois (Cremated).

+   491   m   IV. **Robert Joseph Chambers** was born in Terre Haute, Vigo County, Indiana, on October 23, 1936.

+   492   m   V. **Michael Thomas Chambers** was born in Chicago Heights, Cook County, Illinois, on July 14, 1949.

Dorothy Leffler

331.   **Dorothy Ann Leffler** was born on Monday, June 25, 1883, in Lincoln, Logan County, Illinois.[360] She was the daughter of Isaac Leffler and Martha Alice Coffman (171). She was also known as **Dora Leffler**.

Dorothy Ann died in Simi Valley, Ventura County, California, on April 23, 1968, at the age of 84.[360] She was buried in Palisade Cemetery, Palisade, Hitchcock County, Nebraska (Find a Grave ID 11898759).

Marriages with Francis Paul Young and Howard Young (Page 365) are known.

---

359   1910 Sangamon County - Village of Dawson - Census.

360   Leffler.FTW, Date of Import: Jan 3, 2002.

Family of Dorothy Leffler and Francis Young

```
                                                    ┌──────────────┬──────────────┐
                                                    │ Joseph William│    66        │
                                                    │   Coffman     │  Mary Ann    │
                                                    │  1829–1878    │  Hargadine   │
                                                    │               │  1842–1922   │
                          ┌──────────────┐          └──────────────┴──────────────┘
                          │    Isaac      │          ┌──────────────┐
                          │   Leffler     │          │    171        │
                          │  1849–1915    │          │ Martha Alice  │
                          │               │          │   Coffman     │
                          └──────────────┘          │  1863–1933    │
   ┌──────────────┐                      ┌──────────────┐
   │ Francis Paul  │                     │    331        │
   │   Young       │                     │ Dorothy Ann   │
   │  1873–1955    │                     │   Leffler     │
   │               │                     │  1883–1968    │
   └──────────────┘    Marriage: 1903   └──────────────┘
```

| Clifford Aresene Young 1907–2000 | Robert Paul Young 1910–2001 | Clarence Laverne Young 1916–1994 | Fern Ramona Young 1919–2001 |

Here are the details about **Dorothy Ann Leffler's** first marriage, with Francis Paul Young. You can read more about Dorothy Ann on page 363.

At the age of 19, Dorothy Ann Leffler married **Francis Paul Young** on Wednesday, June 10, 1903, in Holdrege, Phelps County, Nebraska, when he was 29 years old.[360] They had four children.

Francis Paul was born in Waterloo, Black Hawk County, Iowa, on Tuesday, August 12, 1873.[360] He was also known as **Frank**.

Francis Paul reached 81 years of age and died on February 26, 1955. He was buried in Palisade Cemetery, Palisade, Hitchcock County, Nebraska (Find a Grave ID 11898753).

Children of Dorothy Ann Leffler and Francis Paul Young:

m   I. **Clifford Aresene Young** was born in Holdrege, Phelps County, Nebraska, on June 13, 1907. He was also known as **Cliff**.

          Clifford Aresene died in Spokane, Spokane County, Washington, on September 12, 2000, at the age of 93. He was buried in East Lawn Palms Cemetery and Mortuary, Tucson, Pima County, Arizona (Find a Grave ID 46061359).

m   II. **Robert Paul Young** was born on July 26, 1910. He died on October 16, 2001, at the age of 91. Robert Paul was buried in Palisade Cemetery, Palisade, Hitchcock County, Nebraska (Find a Grave ID 11898831).

m   III. **Clarence Laverne Young** was born on April 29, 1916. He died on September 04, 1994, at the age of 78. Clarence Laverne was buried in Hayes Center Cemetery, Hayes Center, Hayes County, Nebraska (Find a Grave ID 57737988).

f   IV. **Fern Ramona Young** was born in Hitchcock County, Nebraska, on April 27, 1919. She died in Hood County, Texas, on February 06, 2001, at the age of 81. Fern Ramona was buried in Pierce Brothers Valley Oaks Memorial Park, Westlake Village, Los Angeles County, California (Find a Grave ID 74186074).

Family of Dorothy Leffler and Howard Young

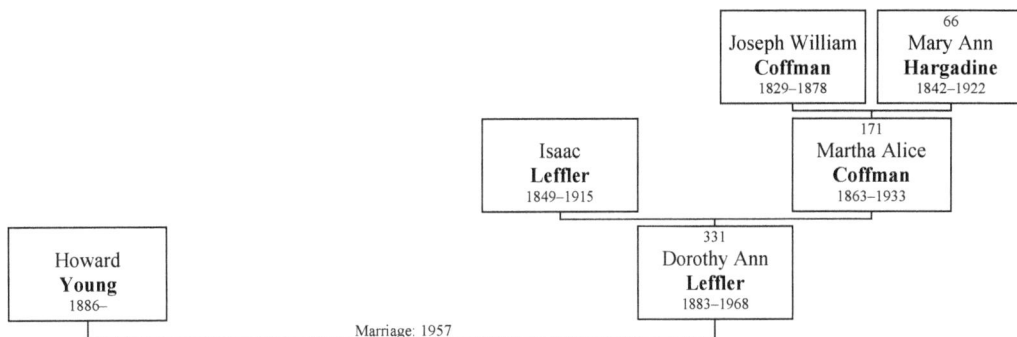

Here are the details about **Dorothy Ann Leffler's** second marriage, with Howard Young. You can read more about Dorothy Ann on page 363.

At the age of 74, Dorothy Ann Leffler married **Howard Young** on Friday, September 06, 1957, in Culbertson, Hitchcock County, Nebraska, when he was 71 years old.[360] Howard was born in Danbury, Woodbury County, Iowa, on Sunday, January 24, 1886.[360]

Family of Charles Leffler and Nellie Cannon

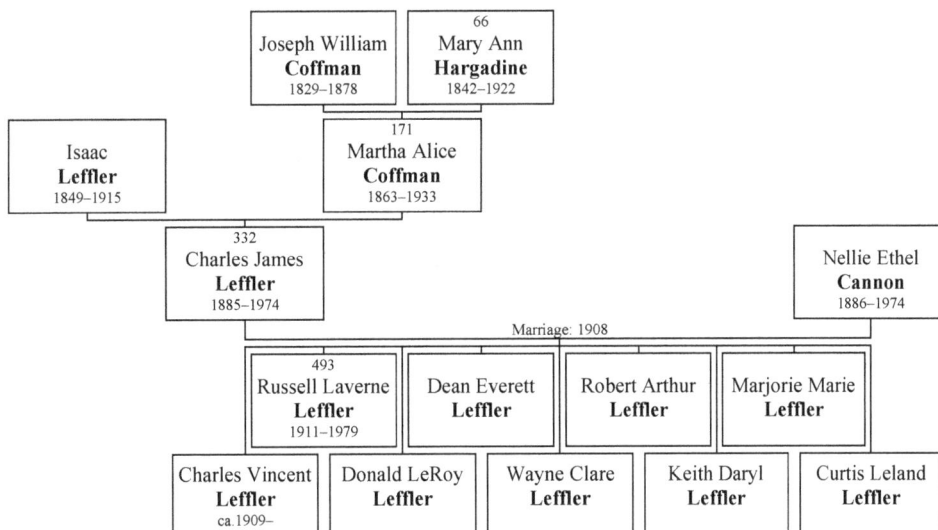

332. **Charles James Leffler** was born on Friday, August 14, 1885, in Lincoln, Logan County, Illinois.[361] He was the son of Isaac Leffler and Martha Alice Coffman (171).

Charles James worked as a Farmer on May 04, 1910.[361] He died in Imperial, Chase County, Nebraska, in November 1974 at the age of 89.[361, 362]

At the age of 22, Charles James married **Nellie Ethel Cannon** on Wednesday, February 05, 1908, when she was 21 years old.[361] They had nine children.

---

361   Leffler.FTW, Date of Import: Jan 3, 2002.

362   Social Security Death Index, CHARLES LEFFLER.

Nellie Ethel was born in Chestnut, Logan County, Illinois, on Tuesday, April 06, 1886.[361] She reached 87 years of age and died in Imperial, Chase County, Nebraska, in April 1974.[361, 363]

Children of Charles James Leffler and Nellie Ethel Cannon:

| | m | I. | **Charles Vincent Leffler** was born in Nebraska, USA, about 1909.[361] |

+ 493 m   II. **Russell Laverne Leffler** was born in Holdrege, Phelps County, Nebraska, on February 02, 1911.[364, 365] He died in Orange County, Florida, on June 17, 1979, at the age of 68.[364]

    m   III. **Donald LeRoy Leffler.**

    m   IV. **Dean Everett Leffler.**

    m   V. **Wayne Clare Leffler.**

    m   VI. **Robert Arthur Leffler.**

    m   VII. **Keith Daryl Leffler.**

    f   VIII. **Marjorie Marie Leffler.**

    m   IX. **Curtis Leland Leffler.**

Nellie Leffler

333. **Nellie May Leffler** was born on Wednesday, October 05, 1887, in Lincoln, Logan County, Illinois.[366] She was the daughter of Isaac Leffler and Martha Alice Coffman (171).

Nellie May died on September 06, 1957, at the age of 69.[366] She was buried in Prairie Home Cemetery, Holdrege, Phelps County, Nebraska (Find a Grave ID 38370472).

Marriages with William Harrison Cain and Orval Chester Randall (Page 367) are known.

363   Social Security Death Index, NELLIE LEFFLER.

364   Ancestry.com, U.S., Social Security Death Index, 1935-2014 (Provo, UT, USA, Ancestry.com Operations Inc, 2014), Ancestry.com, Social Security Administration; Washington D.C., USA; Social Security Death Index, Master File. Record for Russell Leffler. https://search.ancestry.co.uk/cgi-bin/sse.dll?db=3693&h=36092214&indiv=try.

365   Ancestry.com, Virginia, U.S., Marriage Records, 1936-2014 (Lehi, UT, USA, Ancestry.com Operations, Inc., 2015), Ancestry.com, Virginia Department of Health; Richmond, Virginia; Virginia, Marriages, 1936-2014; Roll: 101166970. Record for Russell Laverne Leffler. https://search.ancestry.co.uk/cgi-bin/sse.dll?db=9279&h=10966770&indiv=try.

366   Leffler.FTW, Date of Import: Jan 3, 2002.

Family of Nellie Leffler and William Cain

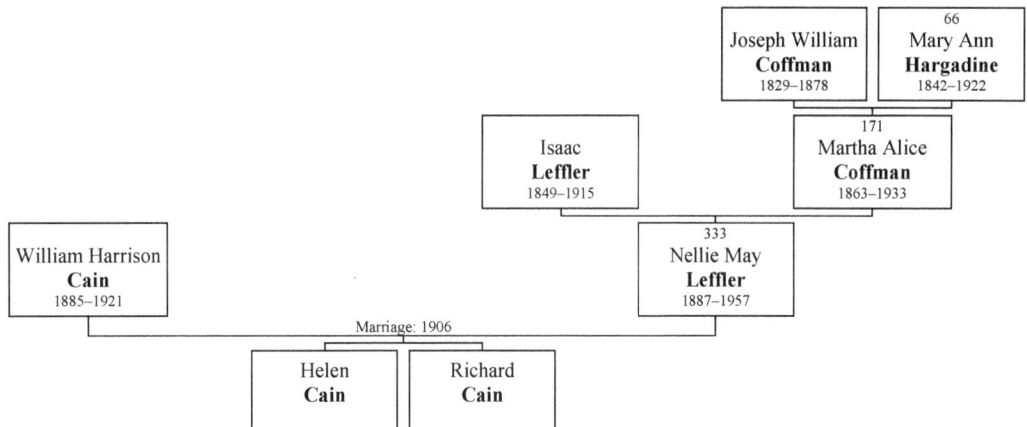

Here are the details about **Nellie May Leffler's** first marriage, with William Harrison Cain. You can read more about Nellie May on page 366.

At the age of 18, Nellie May Leffler married **William Harrison Cain** on Wednesday, June 06, 1906, when he was 21 years old.[366] They had two children.

William Harrison was born on Wednesday, May 20, 1885. He reached 35 years of age and died on January 22, 1921.[366] William Harrison was buried in Prairie Home Cemetery, Holdrege, Phelps County, Nebraska (Find a Grave ID 35322146).

Children of Nellie May Leffler and William Harrison Cain:

f   I. **Helen Cain**.

m   II. **Richard Cain**.

Family of Nellie Leffler and Orval Randall

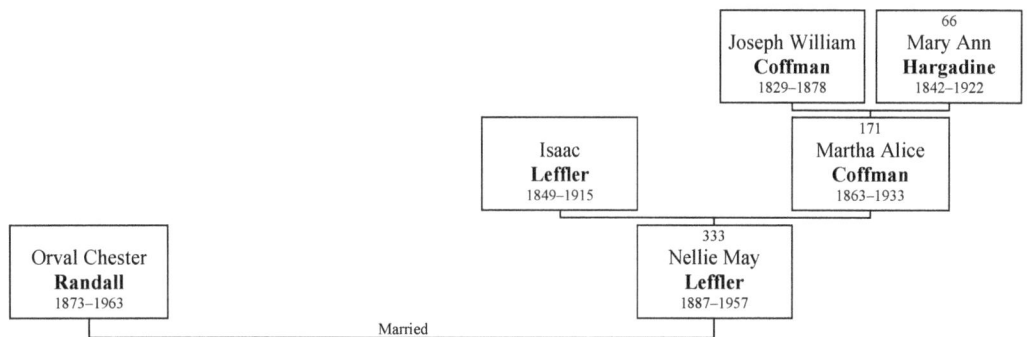

Here are the details about **Nellie May Leffler's** second marriage, with Orval Chester Randall. You can read more about Nellie May on page 366.

Nellie May Leffler married **Orval Chester Randall**. Orval Chester was born in Bowen, Hancock County, Illinos, on Saturday, September 06, 1873.[366]

He reached 89 years of age and died in Holdrege, Phelps County, Nebraska, on June 03, 1963.[366] Orval Chester was buried in Prairie Home Cemetery, Holdrege, Phelps County, Nebraska (Find a Grave ID 7219293).

More facts and events for Orval Chester Randall:

Individual Note: 1929 - 1931 Member, Nebraska House of Representatives

Family of Winnie Leffler and James Cannon

334. **Winnie Bell Leffler** was born on Tuesday, September 16, 1890, in Holdrege, Phelps County, Nebraska.[367] She was the daughter of Isaac Leffler and Martha Alice Coffman (171).

At the age of 23, Winnie Bell married **James H. Cannon** on Wednesday, June 03, 1914, when he was 35 years old.[367] They had four sons.

James H. was born on Wednesday, January 01, 1879.[367]

Sons of Winnie Bell Leffler and James H. Cannon:

m	I.	**James Herschel Cannon.**
m	II.	**Jack Clayton Cannon.**
m	III.	**Stanley LeRoy Cannon.**
m	IV.	**Phillip Ray Cannon.**

---

367   Leffler.FTW, Date of Import: Jan 3, 2002.

Family of Minnie Leffler and Park Talbott

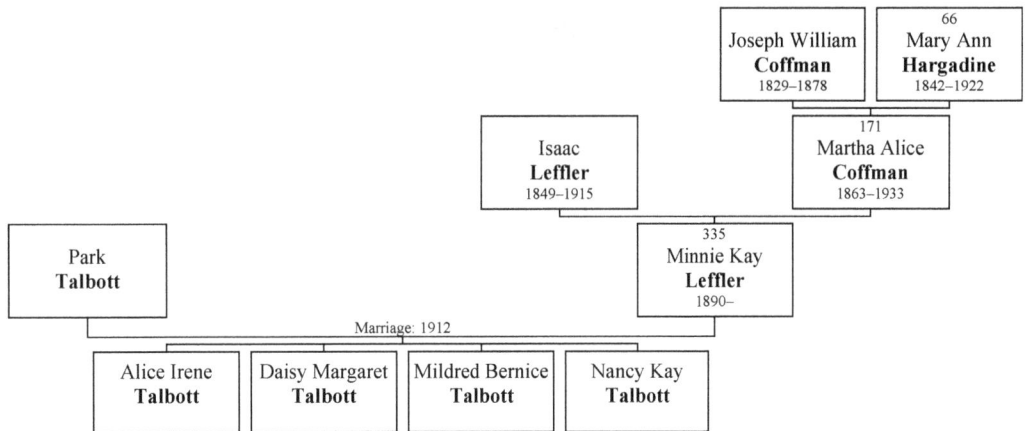

335. **Minnie Kay Leffler** was born on Tuesday, September 16, 1890, in Holdrege, Phelps County, Nebraska.[368] She was the daughter of Isaac Leffler and Martha Alice Coffman (171).

Minnie Kay married **Park Talbott** on Monday, February 12, 1912, in Holdrege, Phelps County, Nebraska.[368] They had four daughters.

Daughters of Minnie Kay Leffler and Park Talbott:

f	I.	**Alice Irene Talbott.**
f	II.	**Daisy Margaret Talbott.**
f	III.	**Mildred Bernice Talbott.**
f	IV.	**Nancy Kay Talbott.**

Family of Selar Leffler and Clara Nelson

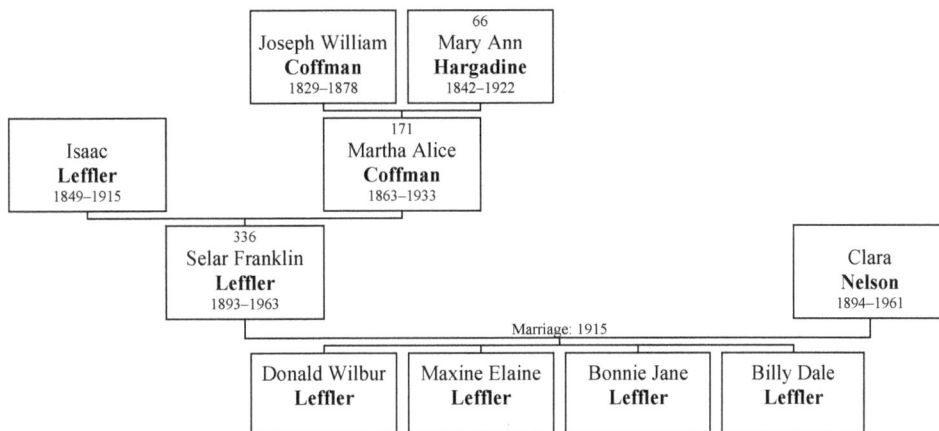

336. **Selar Franklin Leffler** was born on Monday, April 10, 1893, in Nebraska, USA.[369] He was the son of Isaac Leffler and Martha Alice Coffman (171).

---

368   Leffler.FTW, Date of Import: Jan 3, 2002.

369   Leffler.FTW, Date of Import: Jan 3, 2002.

Selar Franklin died on June 03, 1963, at the age of 70.[369, 370]

At the age of 22, Selar Franklin married **Clara Nelson** on Tuesday, October 05, 1915, when she was 21 years old.[369] They had four children.

Clara was born on Friday, July 13, 1894.[369] She reached 67 years of age and died on November 16, 1961.[369]

Children of Selar Franklin Leffler and Clara Nelson:

m	I.	**Donald Wilbur Leffler**.
f	II.	**Maxine Elaine Leffler**.
f	III.	**Bonnie Jane Leffler**.
m	IV.	**Billy Dale Leffler**.

Family of Harry Leffler and Ramona Moore

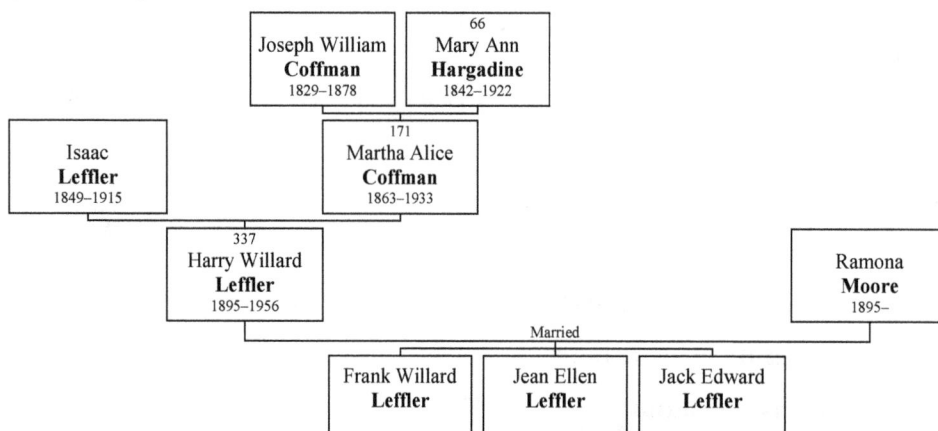

337. **Harry Willard Leffler** was born on Monday, April 22, 1895, in Holdrege, Phelps County, Nebraska.[371] He was the son of Isaac Leffler and Martha Alice Coffman (171).

Harry Willard died on September 25, 1956, at the age of 61.[371]

He married **Ramona Moore**. They had three children.

Ramona was born in Holdrege, Phelps County, Nebraska, on Monday, July 08, 1895.[371]

Children of Harry Willard Leffler and Ramona Moore:

m	I.	**Frank Willard Leffler**.
f	II.	**Jean Ellen Leffler**.
m	III.	**Jack Edward Leffler**.

---

370   Social Security Death Index, SELAR LEFFLER.

371   Leffler.FTW, Date of Import: Jan 3, 2002.

Family of Mary Leffler and Edward Jensen

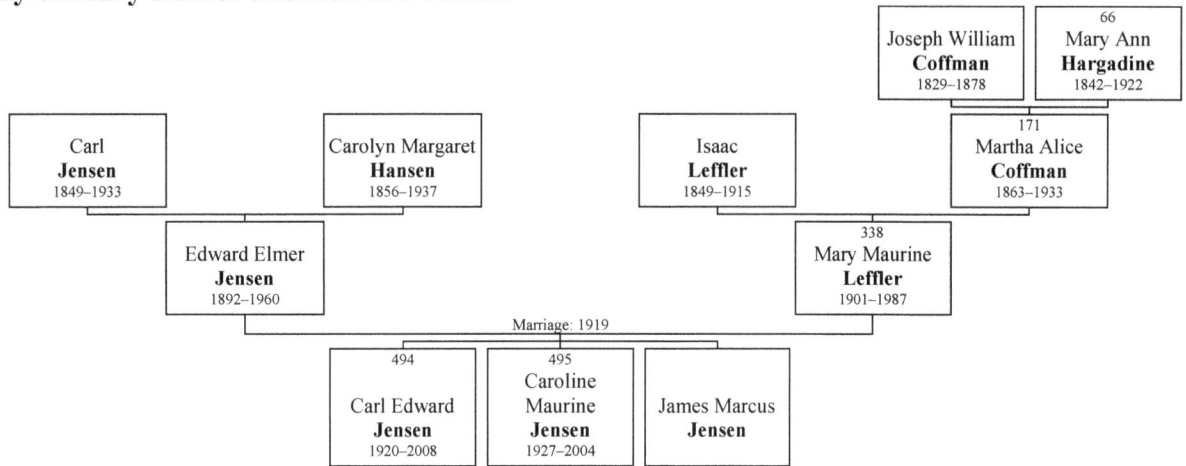

338. **Mary Maurine Leffler** was born on Saturday, September 07, 1901, in Holdrege, Phelps County, Nebraska.[372, 373] She was the daughter of Isaac Leffler and Martha Alice Coffman (171).

Mary Maurine died in Spencer, Clay County, Iowa, on February 08, 1987, at the age of 85.[372] She was buried in Riverside Cemetery, Spencer, Clay County, Iowa (Find a Grave ID 189659310).

At the age of 18, Mary Maurine married **Edward Elmer Jensen** on Tuesday, September 16, 1919, when he was 27 years old.[373] They had three children.

Edward Elmer was born in Chicago, Cook County, Illinois, on Monday, April 25, 1892.[373] He was the son of Carl Jensen and Carolyn Margaret Hansen.

Edward Elmer reached 68 years of age and died in Excelsior Springs, Clay County, Missouri, on May 31, 1960. His cause of death was coronary heart disease. Edward Elmer was buried on June 03, 1960, in Spencer, Clay County, Iowa (Exact cemetery is unknown).

Children of Mary Maurine Leffler and Edward Elmer Jensen:

+ 494 m I. **Carl Edward Jensen** was born in McCook, Red Willow County, Nebraska, on September 01, 1920. He was also known as **Ed**.

   Carl Edward died in Spencer, Clay County, Iowa, on April 30, 2008, at the age of 87.[372] He was buried in Riverside Cemetery, Spencer, Clay County, Iowa (Find a Grave ID 114959794).

+ 495 f II. **Caroline Maurine Jensen** was born in McCook, Red Willow County, Nebraska, on September 05, 1927.[374] She died on August 25, 2004, at the age of 76.[374]

   m III. **James Marcus Jensen**.

---

372 Ancestry.com, Public Member Trees (Provo, UT, USA, Ancestry.com Operations, Inc., 2006), Ancestry.com, Record for Mary Maurine Leffler. https://search.ancestry.co.uk/cgi-bin/sse.dll?db=1030&h=222028657458&indiv=try.

373 Leffler.FTW, Date of Import: Jan 3, 2002.

374 Ancestry.com, U.S., Social Security Death Index, 1935-2014 (Provo, UT, USA, Ancestry.com Operations Inc, 2014), Ancestry.com, Social Security Administration; Washington D.C., USA; Social Security Death Index, Master File. Record for Carolyn Maurine Furst. https://search.ancestry.co.uk/cgi-bin/sse.dll?db=3693&h=73678343&indiv=try.

Family of Merwin Leffler and Ruth McFarland

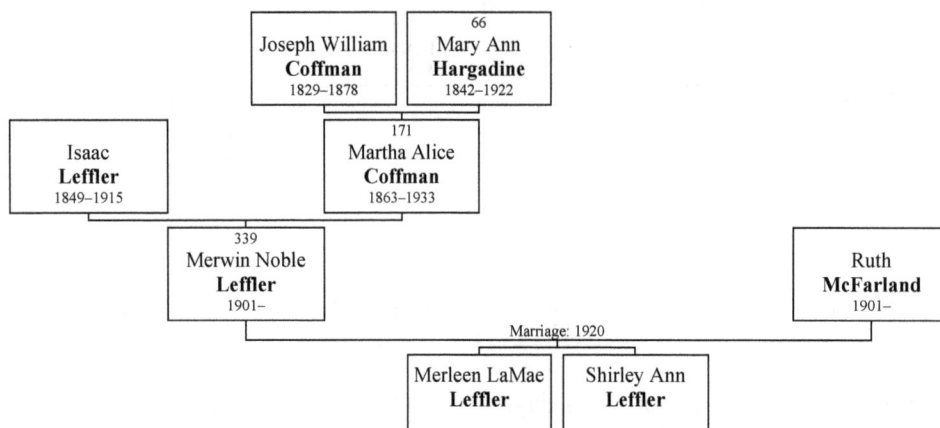

339. **Merwin Noble Leffler** was born on Saturday, September 07, 1901, in Nebraska, USA.[375] He was the son of Isaac Leffler and Martha Alice Coffman (171).

At the age of 18, Merwin Noble married **Ruth McFarland** on Wednesday, September 01, 1920, when she was 19 years old.[375] They had two daughters.

Ruth was born in Grand Island, Hall County, Nebraska, on Friday, March 22, 1901.[375]

Daughters of Merwin Noble Leffler and Ruth McFarland:

  f   I. **Merleen LaMae Leffler**.

  f   II. **Shirley Ann Leffler**.

Delbert Leffler

340. **Delbert Coffman Leffler** was born on Monday, September 21, 1903, in Phelps County, Nebraska.[376] He was the son of Isaac Leffler and Martha Alice Coffman (171).

Delbert Coffman died in Holdrege, Phelps County, Nebraska, in May 1973 at the age of 69.[376, 377] He was buried in Prairie Home Cemetery, Holdrege, Phelps County, Nebraska (Find a Grave ID 35323531).

Marriages with Stella Ann Huff and Margaret Ella O'Rourke (Page 374) are known.

---

375 Leffler.FTW, Date of Import: Jan 3, 2002.

376 Leffler.FTW, Date of Import: Jan 3, 2002.

377 Social Security Death Index, DELBERT LEFFLER.

Family of Delbert Leffler and Stella Huff

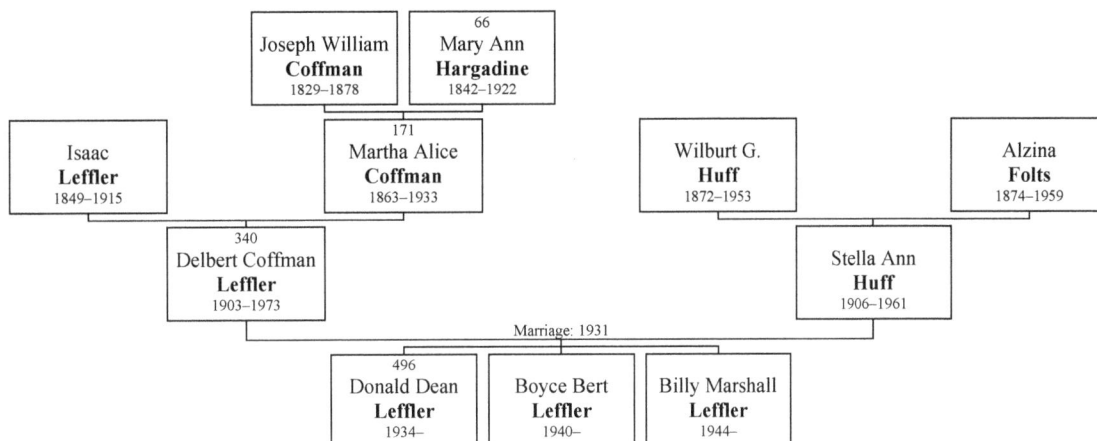

```
                    ┌──────────────┬──────────────┐
                    │ Joseph William│      66      │
                    │   Coffman     │  Mary Ann    │
                    │  1829–1878    │  Hargadine   │
                    │               │  1842–1922   │
          ┌─────────┴───────┬───────┴──────────────┘
   ┌──────────┐      ┌──────────────┐         ┌──────────┐           ┌──────────┐
   │  Isaac   │      │     171      │         │ Wilburt G.│          │  Alzina  │
   │  Leffler │      │Martha Alice  │         │   Huff    │          │  Folts   │
   │ 1849–1915│      │  Coffman     │         │ 1872–1953 │          │1874–1959 │
   └────┬─────┘      │  1863–1933   │         └─────┬────┘           └────┬─────┘
        └──────┬─────┴──────┘                       └────────┬───────────┘
          ┌──────────────┐                           ┌──────────────┐
          │     340      │                           │ Stella Ann   │
          │Delbert Coffman│                          │    Huff      │
          │   Leffler    │                           │  1906–1961   │
          │  1903–1973   │                           └──────────────┘
          └──────┬───────┘        Marriage: 1931
                 └──────────────────────┬─────────────────┐
           ┌──────────┐   ┌──────────┐   ┌──────────────┐
           │   496    │   │Boyce Bert│   │Billy Marshall│
           │Donald Dean│  │ Leffler  │   │   Leffler    │
           │  Leffler │   │  1940–   │   │   1944–      │
           │  1934–   │   └──────────┘   └──────────────┘
           └──────────┘
```

Here are the details about **Delbert Coffman Leffler's** first marriage, with Stella Ann Huff. You can read more about Delbert Coffman on page 372.

At the age of 27, Delbert Coffman Leffler married **Stella Ann Huff** on Friday, March 20, 1931, in Hays, Ellis County, Kansas, when she was 24 years old.[376] They had three sons.

Stella Ann was born in Sacramento, Phelps County, Nebraska, on Saturday, September 01, 1906. She was the daughter of Wilburt G. Huff and Alzina Folts.

Stella Ann reached 54 years of age and died in Nebraska, USA, on April 21, 1961.[376] She was buried in Prairie Home Cemetery, Holdrege, Phelps County, Nebraska (Find a Grave ID 35323565).

Sons of Delbert Coffman Leffler and Stella Ann Huff:

+ 496   m   I. **Donald Dean Leffler** was born in Holdrege, Phelps County, Nebraska, on February 02, 1934.[376]

        m   II. **Boyce Bert Leffler** was born in Holdrege, Phelps County, Nebraska, on September 18, 1940.[376]

        m   III. **Billy Marshall Leffler** was born in Holdrege, Phelps County, Nebraska, on February 12, 1944.[376]

Family of Delbert Leffler and Margaret O'Rourke

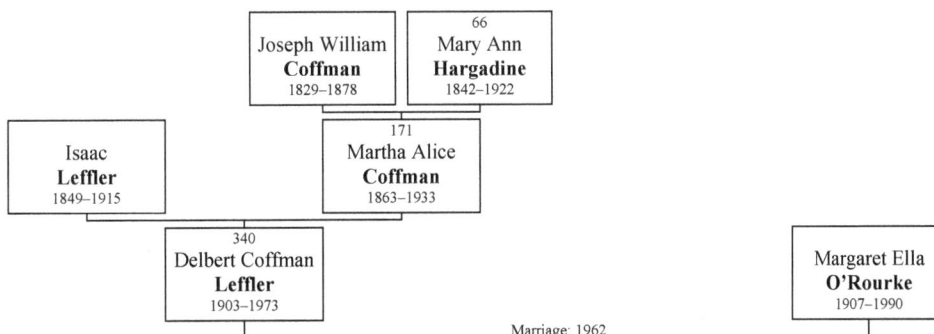

```
                    ┌──────────────┬──────────────┐
                    │ Joseph William│     66       │
                    │   Coffman     │  Mary Ann    │
                    │  1829–1878    │  Hargadine   │
                    │               │  1842–1922   │
          ┌─────────┴──────┬────────┴──────────────┘
   ┌──────────┐      ┌──────────────┐
   │  Isaac   │      │     171      │
   │  Leffler │      │Martha Alice  │
   │ 1849–1915│      │  Coffman     │
   └────┬─────┘      │  1863–1933   │
        └─────┬──────┴──────┘                      ┌──────────────┐
          ┌──────────────┐                         │Margaret Ella │
          │     340      │                         │  O'Rourke    │
          │Delbert Coffman│                        │  1907–1990   │
          │   Leffler    │                         └──────────────┘
          │  1903–1973   │        Marriage: 1962
          └──────────────┘
```

Here are the details about **Delbert Coffman Leffler's** second marriage, with Margaret Ella O'Rourke. You can read more about Delbert Coffman on page 372.

At the age of 58, Delbert Coffman Leffler married **Margaret Ella O'Rourke** on Wednesday, August 22, 1962, when she was 55 years old.[376] Margaret Ella was born in Creston, Union County, Iowa, on Saturday, August 17, 1907.[378]

She reached 82 years of age and died in Holdrege, Phelps County, Nebraska, on January 18, 1990.[378] Margaret Ella was buried in Prairie Home Cemetery, Holdrege, Phelps County, Nebraska (Find a Grave ID 35323609).[378]

Family of Dean Coffman and Melva Arnold

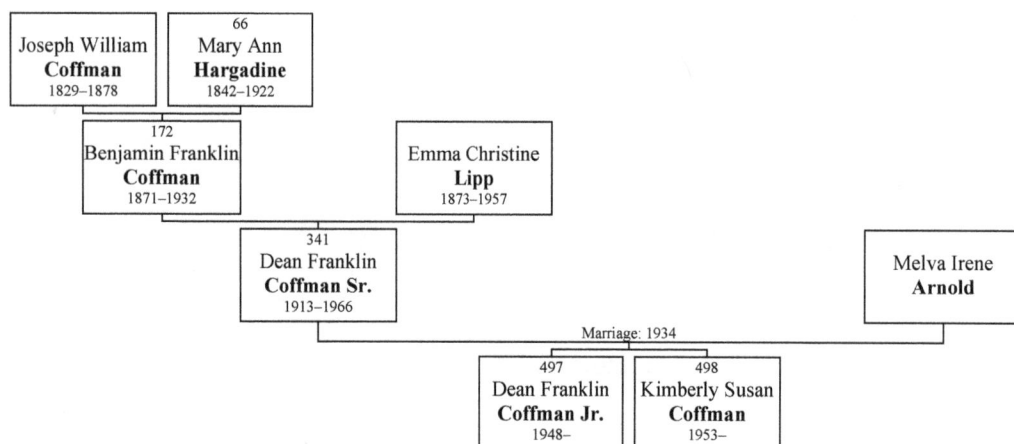

```
┌──────────────┐ ┌──────────────┐
│Joseph William│ │     66       │
│  Coffman     │ │  Mary Ann    │
│  1829–1878   │ │  Hargadine   │
│              │ │  1842–1922   │
└──────────────┘ └──────────────┘
    ┌──────────────────┐   ┌──────────────┐
    │       172        │   │Emma Christine│
    │Benjamin Franklin │   │    Lipp      │
    │    Coffman       │   │  1873–1957   │
    │   1871–1932      │   │              │
    └──────────────────┘   └──────────────┘
         ┌──────────────┐              ┌──────────────┐
         │     341      │              │  Melva Irene │
         │Dean Franklin │              │    Arnold    │
         │ Coffman Sr.  │              │              │
         │  1913–1966   │              │              │
         └──────────────┘              └──────────────┘
                      Marriage: 1934
         ┌──────────────┐ ┌──────────────┐
         │     497      │ │     498      │
         │Dean Franklin │ │Kimberly Susan│
         │ Coffman Jr.  │ │   Coffman    │
         │   1948–      │ │   1953–      │
         └──────────────┘ └──────────────┘
```

341.   **Dean Franklin Coffman Sr.** was born on Friday, February 28, 1913, in Lincoln, Logan County, Illinois. He was the son of Benjamin Franklin Coffman (172) and Emma Christine Lipp.

Dean Franklin served in the military: US Army, WWII Sergeant, Military Police. He died in Decatur, Macon County, Illinois, on May 30, 1966, at the age of 53. Dean Franklin was buried in Fairlawn Cemetery, Decatur, Macon County, Illinois (Find a Grave ID 65013002).

Dean Franklin married **Melva Irene Arnold** on Saturday, April 14, 1934, in Decatur, Macon County, Illinois. They had two children.

Children of Dean Franklin Coffman Sr. and Melva Irene Arnold:

+   497   m   I.   **Dean Franklin Coffman Jr.** was born in Decatur, Macon County, Illinois, on June 29, 1948. He is also known as **Frank**.

+   498   f   II.   **Kimberly Susan Coffman** was born in Decatur, Macon County, Illinois, on March 07, 1953.

378   Ancestry.com, Public Member Trees (Provo, UT, USA, Ancestry.com Operations, Inc., 2006), Ancestry.com, Record for Margaret Ella O'Rourke. https://search.ancestry.co.uk/cgi-bin/sse.dll?db=1030&h=252222639893&indiv=try.

Family of Mary Hargadine and Everett Faltesek

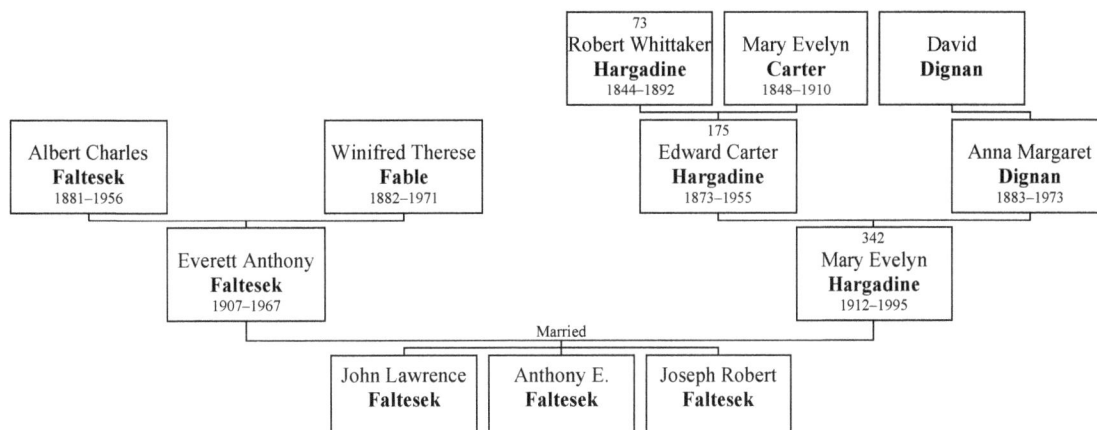

```
                                    ┌─────────────┐ ┌─────────────┐  ┌─────────────┐
                                    │      73     │ │ Mary Evelyn │  │    David    │
                                    │Robert Whittaker│ │   Carter   │  │   Dignan    │
                                    │  Hargadine  │ │  1848–1910  │  │             │
                                    │  1844–1892  │ └─────────────┘  └─────────────┘
                                    └─────────────┘
┌─────────────┐  ┌─────────────┐      ┌─────────────┐       ┌─────────────┐
│Albert Charles│ │Winifred Therese│    │     175     │       │Anna Margaret│
│   Faltesek  │ │    Fable    │      │ Edward Carter│       │   Dignan    │
│  1881–1956  │ │  1882–1971  │      │  Hargadine  │       │  1883–1973  │
└─────────────┘ └─────────────┘      │  1873–1955  │       └─────────────┘
                                     └─────────────┘
       ┌─────────────┐                      ┌─────────────┐
       │Everett Anthony│                     │     342     │
       │   Faltesek  │                      │ Mary Evelyn │
       │  1907–1967  │                      │  Hargadine  │
       └─────────────┘                      │  1912–1995  │
                                            └─────────────┘
                            Married
          ┌─────────────┐ ┌─────────────┐ ┌─────────────┐
          │John Lawrence│ │ Anthony E.  │ │Joseph Robert│
          │   Faltesek  │ │  Faltesek   │ │  Faltesek   │
          └─────────────┘ └─────────────┘ └─────────────┘
```

342. **Mary Evelyn Hargadine** was born on Thursday, June 20, 1912, in Glasgow, Valley County, Montana. She was the daughter of Edward Carter Hargadine (175) and Anna Margaret Dignan.

Mary Evelyn died in St. Mary's Home, St. Paul, Ramsey County, Minnesota, on June 28, 1995, at the age of 83. She was buried in Resurrection Cemetery, Mendota Heights, Dakota County, Minnesota (Find a Grave ID 248684450).

She married **Everett Anthony Faltesek**. They had three sons.

Everett Anthony was born in St. Croix County, Wisconsin, on Monday, April 29, 1907. He was the son of Albert Charles Faltesek and Winifred Therese Fable.

Everett Anthony reached 60 years of age and died on May 21, 1967. He was buried in Resurrection Cemetery, Mendota Heights, Dakota County, Minnesota (Find a Grave ID 24868439).

Sons of Mary Evelyn Hargadine and Everett Anthony Faltesek:

> m   I. **John Lawrence Faltesek**.
>
> m   II. **Anthony E. Faltesek**.
>
> m   III. **Joseph Robert Faltesek**.

Family of Ellen Hargadine and Abraham Marians

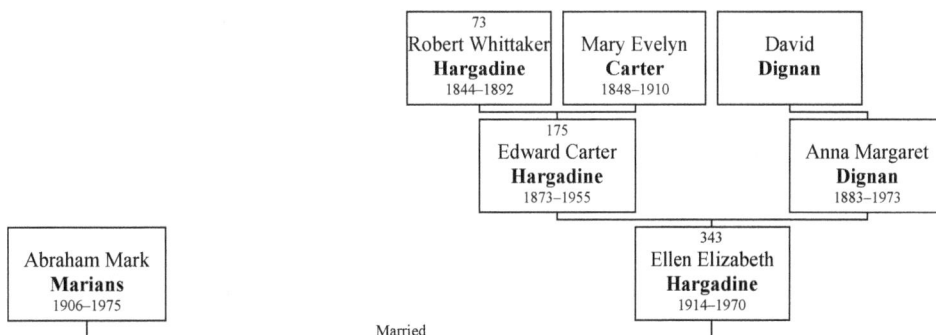

```
                                    ┌─────────────┐ ┌─────────────┐  ┌─────────────┐
                                    │      73     │ │ Mary Evelyn │  │    David    │
                                    │Robert Whittaker│ │   Carter   │  │   Dignan    │
                                    │  Hargadine  │ │  1848–1910  │  │             │
                                    │  1844–1892  │ └─────────────┘  └─────────────┘
                                    └─────────────┘
                                     ┌─────────────┐       ┌─────────────┐
                                     │     175     │       │Anna Margaret│
                                     │ Edward Carter│       │   Dignan    │
                                     │  Hargadine  │       │  1883–1973  │
                                     │  1873–1955  │       └─────────────┘
                                     └─────────────┘
┌─────────────┐                            ┌─────────────┐
│Abraham Mark │                            │     343     │
│   Marians   │                            │Ellen Elizabeth│
│  1906–1975  │                            │  Hargadine  │
└─────────────┘                            │  1914–1970  │
                            Married        └─────────────┘
```

343. **Ellen Elizabeth Hargadine** was born on Saturday, February 21, 1914, in Glasgo, Valley County, Montana. She was the daughter of Edward Carter Hargadine (175) and Anna Margaret Dignan. She was also known as **Ellen Ann Marians**.

Ellen Elizabeth died in El Paso, El Paso County, Texas, on February 24, 1970, at the age of 56. She was buried in Memory Gardens of the Valley, Santa Teresa, Doña Ana County, New Mexico (Find a Grave ID 93091528).

She married **Abraham Mark Marians**. Abraham Mark was born in Manhattan, New York City, New York, on Monday, February 26, 1906.[379]

He reached 68 years of age and died in 1975.[379]

Family of Anna Hargadine and Thomas Culhane

344. **Anna Jane Hargadine** was born on Sunday, February 29, 1920, in Glasgow, Valley County, Montana. She was the daughter of Edward Carter Hargadine (175) and Anna Margaret Dignan.

Anna Jane died in Oregon, USA, on December 01, 2004, at the age of 84. She was buried in Mount Calvary Cemetery, Portland, Multnomah County, Oregon (Find a Grave ID 43056303).

At the age of 25, Anna Jane married **Thomas Lincoln Culhane** on Monday, October 22, 1945, in Prince George, Virginia, when he was 28 years old. Thomas Lincoln was born in Minneapolis, Hennepin County, Minnesota, on Thursday, October 26, 1916.

He reached 86 years of age and died in Lake Oswego, Oregon, on October 02, 2003. Thomas Lincoln was buried in Mount Calvary Cemetery, Portland, Multnomah County, Oregon (Find a Grave ID 43056304).

379   Ancestry.com, Public Member Trees (Provo, UT, USA, Ancestry.com Operations, Inc., 2006), Ancestry.com, Record for Abraham Mark Marians. https://search.ancestry.co.uk/cgi-bin/sse.dll?db=1030&h=232200105118&indiv=try.

Family of Robert Hurd and Violet Miloshus

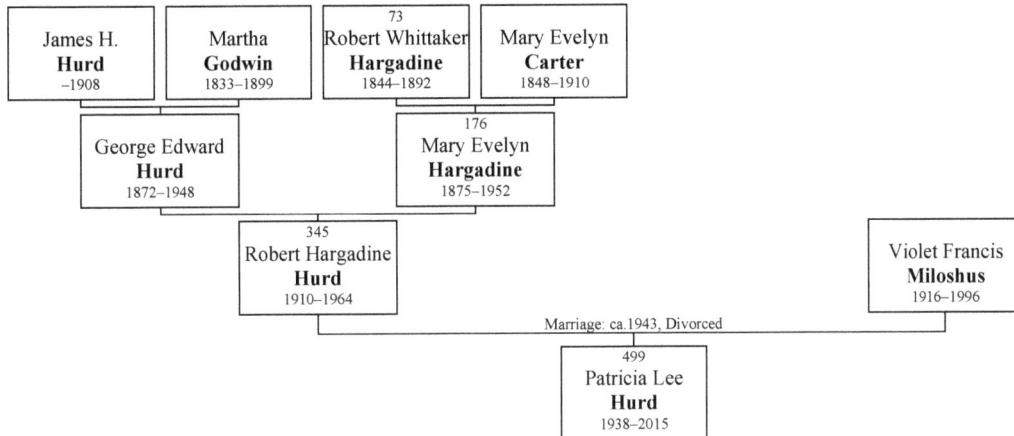

345. **Robert Hargadine Hurd** was born on Wednesday, June 22, 1910, in Great Falls, Cascade County, Montana. He was the son of George Edward Hurd and Mary Evelyn Hargadine (176).

Robert Hargadine served in the military: SSGT 89 CML SVC CO CWS. He died in San Diego, San Diego County, California, on July 26, 1964, at the age of 54. Robert Hargadine was buried in Fort Rosecrans National Cemetery, San Diego, San Diego County, California, on July 30, 1964 (Find a Grave ID 3408341).

Robert Hargadine married **Violet Francis Miloshus** about 1943. They later divorced. They had one daughter.

Violet Francis was born in Chicago, Cook County, Illinois, on Tuesday, March 21, 1916. She reached 80 years of age and died in Miami Springs, Miami-Dade County, Florida, on March 27, 1996.

Daughter of Robert Hargadine Hurd and Violet Francis Miloshus:

+ 499   f   I. **Patricia Lee Hurd** was born in Chicago, Cook County, Illinois, on December 01, 1938. She died in Hollywood, Dade County, Florida, on April 19, 2015, at the age of 76. Patricia Lee was buried in Vista Memorial Gardens, Miami Lakes, Miami-Dade County, Florida.

Family of George Hurd and Katherine Strain

James H. **Hurd** –1908	**Martha** **Godwin** 1833–1899

73
Robert Whittaker **Hargadine** 1844–1892

Mary Evelyn **Carter** 1848–1910

George Edward **Hurd** 1872–1948

176
Mary Evelyn **Hargadine** 1875–1952

346
George Edward **Hurd** 1916–2006

Katherine Lee **Strain** 1918–1990

Marriage: 1940

Douglass **Hurd**

Kathleen **Hurd**

346.   **George Edward Hurd** was born on Wednesday, December 27, 1916, in Great Falls, Cascade County, Montana. He was the son of George Edward Hurd and Mary Evelyn Hargadine (176).

George Edward died in Kaneohe, Honolulu County, Hawaii, on June 25, 2006, at the age of 89.

At the age of 23, George Edward married **Katherine Lee Strain** on Thursday, November 21, 1940, in Great Falls, Cascade, Montana, when she was 22 years old. They had two children.

Katherine Lee was born in Great Falls, Cascade County, Montana, on Wednesday, March 06, 1918. She reached 72 years of age and died in Kailua, Hawaii, on August 13, 1990. Katherine Lee was cremated.

Children of George Edward Hurd and Katherine Lee Strain:

> m   I. **Douglass Hurd**.
>
> f   II. **Kathleen Hurd**.

Family of Robert Hargadine and Ruth Ellit

73
Robert Whittaker **Hargadine** 1844–1892

Mary Evelyn **Carter** 1848–1910

177
Robert Whittaker **Hargadine** 1878–1973

Irene M. **O'Connor** ca.1884–1926

Louis Frederick **Christian** **Ellit** 1875–1952

Aloysia **Kropf** 1877–1948

347
Robert William **Hargadine Jr.** 1914–1982

Ruth Louise **Ellit** 1917–1992

Married

| 500 **Shannon Louise** **Hargadine** 1943–2023 | 501 **Noreen Loy** **Hargadine** 1947– | 502 **Robert Ellit** **Hargadine** 1949–2017 | **Bridgit Mary** **Hargadine** 1951– | **Michael Girard** **Hargadine** 1955– | 503 **Keith William** **Hargadine** 1959– | **Kathleen Ann** **Hargadine** 1959– | **Meegan Marie** **Hargadine** 1962– |

347. **Robert William Hargadine Jr.** was born on Friday, May 29, 1914, in Minnesota, USA. He was the son of Robert Whittaker Hargadine (177) and Irene M. O'Connor.

Robert William served in the military between 1942 and 1945. U.S. Navy, WWII. He died in St. Paul, Ramsey County, Minnesota, on August 15, 1982, at the age of 68. Robert William was buried in Fort Snelling National Cemetery, Minneapolis, Hennepin County, Minnesota (Find a Grave ID 753313).

He married **Ruth Louise Ellit**. They had eight children.

Ruth Louise was born in Minnesota, USA, on Saturday, December 15, 1917. She was the daughter of Louis Frederick Christian Ellit and Aloysia Kropf.

Ruth Louise reached 74 years of age and died in Saint Paul, Ramsey County, Minnesota, on July 20, 1992. She was buried on July 23, 1992, in Fort Snelling National Cemetery, Minneapolis, Hennepin County, Minnesota (Find a Grave ID 753314).

Children of Robert William Hargadine Jr. and Ruth Louise Ellit:

+ 500   f   I. **Shannon Louise Hargadine** was born in Ramsey, Anoka County, Minnesota, on June 07, 1943. She died in Ramsey, Anoka County, Minnesota, on August 24, 2023, at the age of 80.

+ 501   f   II. **Noreen Loy Hargadine** was born in Ramsey, Anoka County, Minnesota, on February 06, 1947.

+ 502   m   III. **Robert Ellit Hargadine** was born in Ramsey, Anoka County, Minnesota, on October 02, 1949. He died in Ely, St Louis County, Minnesota, on October 23, 2017, at the age of 68. Robert Ellit was buried on November 03, 2017.

             f   IV. **Bridgit Mary Hargadine** was born in Ramsey, Anoka County, Minnesota, on May 05, 1951.

             m   V. **Michael Girard Hargadine** was born in Ramsey, Anoka County, Minnesota, on February 24, 1955.

+ 503   m   VI. **Keith William Hargadine** was born in Ramsey, Anoka County, Minnesota, on January 17, 1959.

             f   VII. **Kathleen Ann Hargadine** was born in Ramsey, Anoka County, Minnesota, on January 17, 1959.

             f   VIII. **Meegan Marie Hargadine** was born in Ramsey, Anoka County, Minnesota, on May 19, 1962.

Family of Mary Hargadine and Eugene Radabaugh

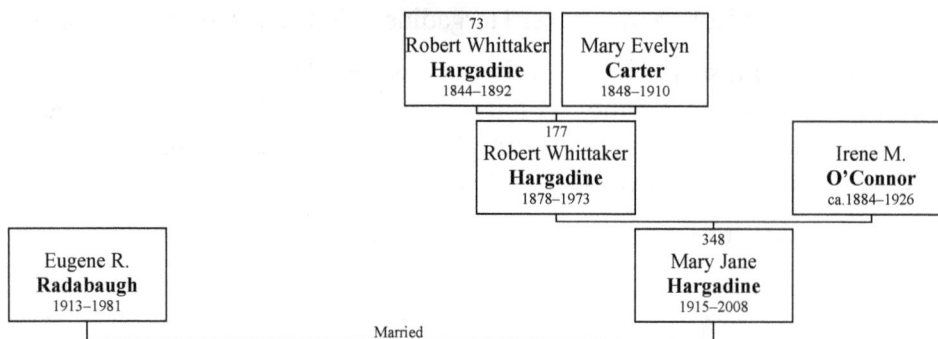

```
                              ┌──────────────┬──────────────┐
                              │      73      │              │
                              │Robert Whittaker│ Mary Evelyn │
                              │  Hargadine   │    Carter    │
                              │  1844–1892   │  1848–1910   │
                              └──────────────┴──────────────┘
                              ┌──────────────┐        ┌──────────────┐
                              │     177      │        │   Irene M.   │
                              │Robert Whittaker│       │   O'Connor   │
                              │  Hargadine   │        │ ca.1884–1926 │
                              │  1878–1973   │        └──────────────┘
                              └──────────────┘
                                          ┌──────────────┐
┌──────────────┐                          │     348      │
│  Eugene R.   │                          │  Mary Jane   │
│  Radabaugh   │                          │  Hargadine   │
│  1913–1981   │                          │  1915–2008   │
└──────────────┘          Married         └──────────────┘
```

348. **Mary Jane Hargadine** was born on Sunday, August 15, 1915, in Saint Paul, Ramsey County, Minnesota. She was the daughter of Robert Whittaker Hargadine (177) and Irene M. O'Connor.

Mary Jane died in Maplewood, Ramsey County, Minnesota, on November 18, 2008, at the age of 93. She was buried in Saint Elizabeth Ann Seton Catholic Cemetery, Hastings, Dakota County, Minnesota (Find a Grave ID 31724824).

She married **Eugene R. Radabaugh**. Eugene R. was born in Saint Paul, Ramsey County, Minnesota, in 1913.

He reached 68 years of age and died in Hastings, Dakota County, Minnesota, in 1981. Eugene R. was buried in Saint Elizabeth Ann Seton Catholic Cemetery, Hastings, Dakota County, Minnesota (Find a Grave ID 129748850).

Family of Aimee Todd and Reginald Gorder

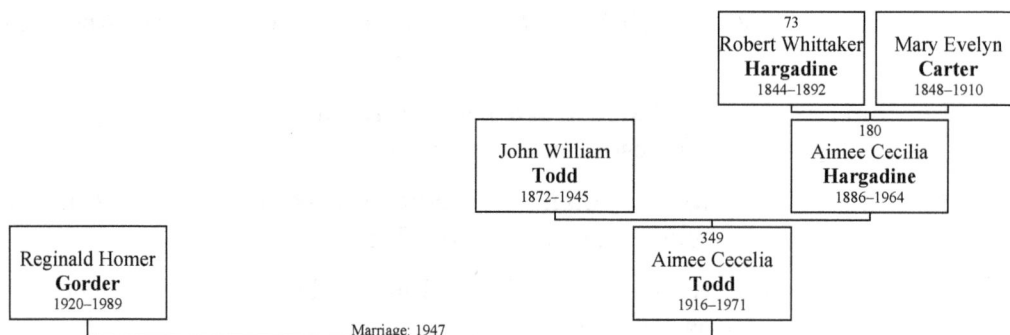

```
                                        ┌──────────────┬──────────────┐
                                        │      73      │              │
                                        │Robert Whittaker│ Mary Evelyn │
                                        │  Hargadine   │    Carter    │
                                        │  1844–1892   │  1848–1910   │
                                        └──────────────┴──────────────┘
                          ┌──────────────┐        ┌──────────────┐
                          │ John William │        │     180      │
                          │     Todd     │        │ Aimee Cecilia│
                          │  1872–1945   │        │  Hargadine   │
                          └──────────────┘        │  1886–1964   │
                                        ┌──────────────┐
┌──────────────┐                        │     349      │
│Reginald Homer│                        │ Aimee Cecilia│
│    Gorder    │                        │     Todd     │
│  1920–1989   │                        │  1916–1971   │
└──────────────┘        Marriage: 1947  └──────────────┘
```

349. **Aimee Cecelia Todd** was born on Tuesday, May 16, 1916, in Glasgow, Valley County, Montana. She was the daughter of John William Todd and Aimee Cecilia Hargadine (180).

Aimee Cecelia died in California, USA, on December 11, 1971, at the age of 55. She was buried in Sidney Cemetery, Sidney, Richland County, Montana (Find a Grave ID 33343092).

Aimee Cecelia married **Reginald Homer Gorder** in 1947 in Cincinnati, Hamilton County, Ohio. Reginald Homer was born in Starbuck, Pope County, Minnesota, on Wednesday, December 01, 1920.

He reached 68 years of age and died in Choteau, Teton County, Montana, on January 09, 1989. Reginald Homer was buried in Sidney Cemetery, Sidney, Richland County, Montana (Find a Grave ID 115966109).

Family of Mary Richards and Purnal Friedel

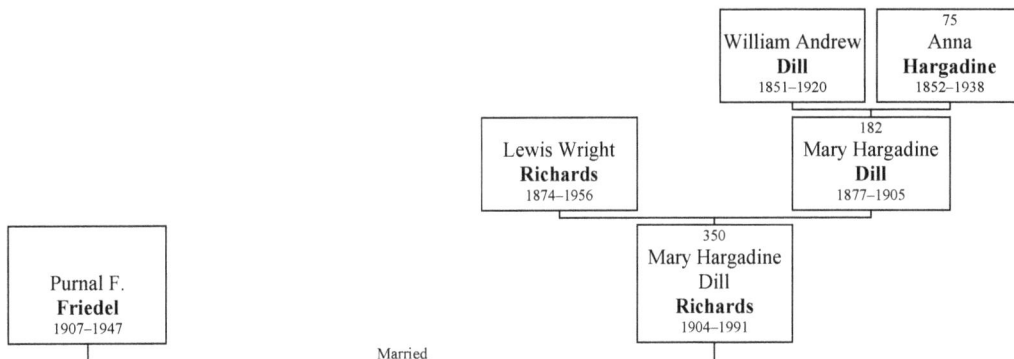

350. **Mary Hargadine Dill Richards** was born in 1904. She was the daughter of Lewis Wright Richards and Mary Hargadine Dill (182).

Mary Hargadine Dill died in 1991 at the age of 87. She was buried in Odd Fellows Cemetery, Camden, Kent County, Delaware (Find a Grave ID 111022121).

She married **Purnal F. Friedel**. Purnal F. was born in 1907.

He reached 40 years of age and died in 1947. Purnal F. was buried in Odd Fellows Cemetery, Camden, Kent County, Delaware (Find a Grave ID 111022122).

Family of Ruth Hargadine and George Palmer

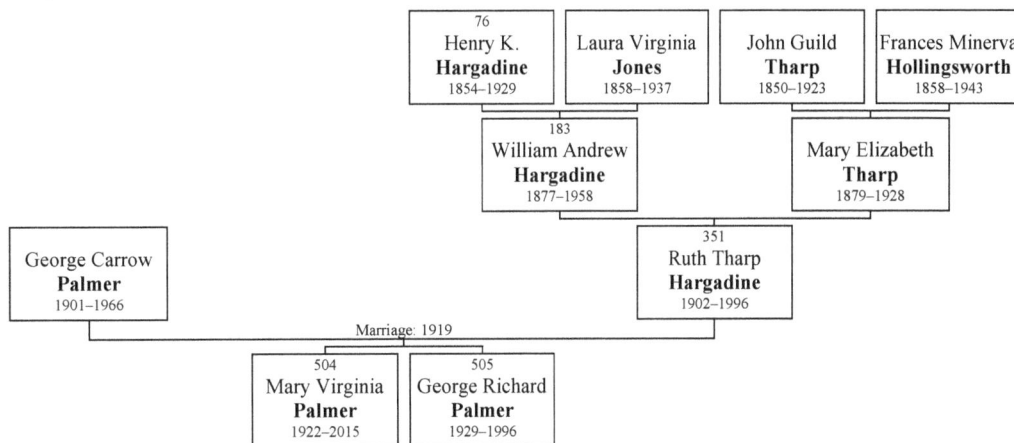

351. **Ruth Tharp Hargadine** was born on Monday, September 08, 1902, in Woodside, Kent County, Delaware. She was the daughter of William Andrew Hargadine (183) and Mary Elizabeth Tharp.

Ruth Tharp died on December 05, 1996, at the age of 94. She was buried in Barratts Chapel Cemetery, Frederica, Kent County, Delaware (Find a Grave ID 154507803).

At the age of 17, Ruth Tharp married **George Carrow Palmer** on Saturday, October 04, 1919, in Frederica, Kent County, Delaware, when he was 18 years old. They had two children.

George Carrow was born in Frederica, Kent County, Delaware, on Wednesday, March 13, 1901. He reached 64 years of age and died in 1966. George Carrow was buried in Barratts Chapel Cemetery, Frederica, Kent County, Delaware (Find a Grave ID 30844794).

Children of Ruth Tharp Hargadine and George Carrow Palmer:

+ 504   f   I. **Mary Virginia Palmer** was born in Milford, Sussex County, Delaware, on January 25, 1922. She was also known as **Ginny**.

                     Mary Virginia died in West Melbourne, Brevard County, Florida, on May 23, 2015, at the age of 93. She was buried in Arlington National Cemetery, Arlington, Arlington County, Virginia (Find a Grave ID 147362939).

+ 505   m   II. **George Richard Palmer** was born in West Chester, Chester, Pennsylvania, on February 14, 1929. He died on December 05, 1996, at the age of 67. George Richard was buried in Barratts Chapel Cemetery, Frederica, Kent County, Delaware (Find a Grave ID 30844798 & 33315217).

William Hargadine

352.   **William A. Hargadine Jr.** was born on Friday, September 16, 1904, in Felton, Kent County, Delaware. He was the son of William Andrew Hargadine (183) and Mary Elizabeth Tharp.

William A. died in Fayetteville, Franklin County, Pennsylvania, on September 03, 1993, at the age of 88. He was buried in Barratts Chapel Cemetery, Frederica, Kent County, Delaware (Find a Grave ID 154507712).

Marriages with Marjorie Hindley and Isabel Ferguson (Page 383) are known.

Family of William Hargadine and Marjorie Hindley

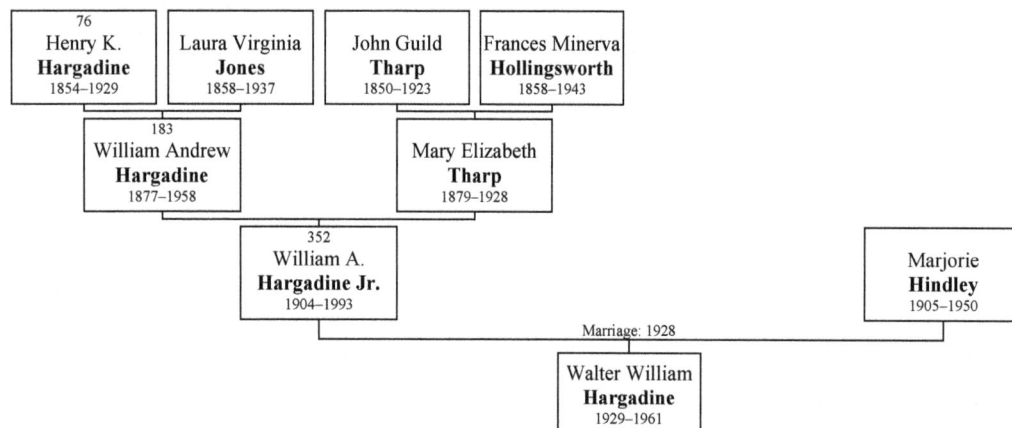

Here are the details about **William A. Hargadine Jr.'s** first marriage, with Marjorie Hindley. You can read more about William A. on page 382.

At the age of 24, William A. Hargadine Jr. married **Marjorie Hindley** on Monday, December 24, 1928, when she was 23 years old. They had one son.

Marjorie was born in Ashton Under Lyne, Lancashire, England, on Wednesday, June 21, 1905. She reached 44 years of age and died in Philadelphia, Philadelphia County, Pennsylvania, on March 21, 1950. Marjorie was buried on March 25, 1950, in Northwood Cemetery, West Oak Lane, Philadelphia County, Pennsylvania (Find a Grave ID 149138789).

Son of William A. Hargadine Jr. and Marjorie Hindley:

m   I. **Walter William Hargadine** was born in Pennsylvania, USA, on December 28, 1929. He served in the military: Captain USMC.

Walter William died on February 15, 1961, at the age of 31. He was buried in Barratts Chapel Cemetery, Frederica, Kent County, Delaware (Find a Grave ID 83823603).

Family of William Hargadine and Isabel Ferguson

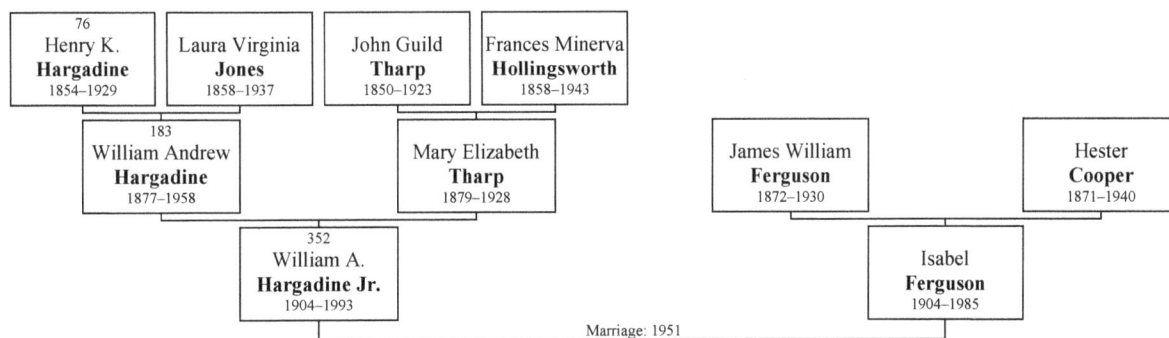

76 Henry K. **Hargadine** 1854–1929	Laura Virginia **Jones** 1858–1937	John Guild **Tharp** 1850–1923	Frances Minerva **Hollingsworth** 1858–1943		James William **Ferguson** 1872–1930	Hester **Cooper** 1871–1940

183
William Andrew **Hargadine** 1877–1958

Mary Elizabeth **Tharp** 1879–1928

Isabel **Ferguson** 1904–1985

352
William A. **Hargadine Jr.** 1904–1993

Marriage: 1951

Here are the details about **William A. Hargadine Jr.'s** second marriage, with Isabel Ferguson. You can read more about William A. on page 382.

At the age of 46, William A. Hargadine Jr. married **Isabel Ferguson** on Saturday, May 05, 1951, at by Ramond Davis, Episcopal Church in Fairfax County, Virginia, when she was 46 years old. Isabel was born in Waynesville Township, Haywood County, North Carolina, on Wednesday, June 22, 1904. She was the daughter of James William Ferguson and Hester Cooper.

Isabel reached 81 years of age and died in Fayetteville, Franklin County, Pennsylvania, on August 11, 1985. She was buried in Green Hill Cemetery, Waynesville, Haywood County, North Carolina (Find a Grave ID 33377573).

Family of John Hargadine and Hazel Helm

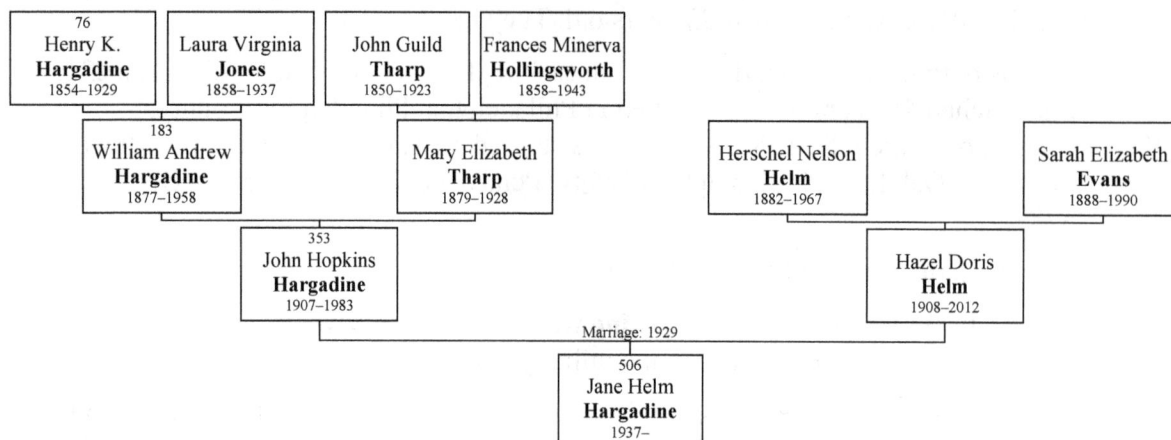

```
┌─────────────┐ ┌─────────────┐ ┌─────────────┐ ┌──────────────┐
│     76      │ │Laura Virginia│ │ John Guild  │ │Frances Minerva│
│  Henry K.   │ │    Jones    │ │   Tharp     │ │Hollingsworth │
│ Hargadine   │ │  1858–1937  │ │  1850–1923  │ │  1858–1943   │
│  1854–1929  │ │             │ │             │ │              │
└─────────────┘ └─────────────┘ └─────────────┘ └──────────────┘
```

183 William Andrew **Hargadine** 1877–1958		Mary Elizabeth **Tharp** 1879–1928	Herschel Nelson **Helm** 1882–1967	Sarah Elizabeth **Evans** 1888–1990

353 John Hopkins **Hargadine** 1907–1983

Hazel Doris **Helm** 1908–2012

Marriage: 1929

506 Jane Helm **Hargadine** 1937–

353. **John Hopkins Hargadine** was born on Friday, January 25, 1907, in Delaware, USA. He was the son of William Andrew Hargadine (183) and Mary Elizabeth Tharp.

John Hopkins died in March 1983 at the age of 76. His cause of death was cancer. John Hopkins was buried in Barratts Chapel Cemetery, Frederica, Kent County, Delaware (Find a Grave ID 29366390).

At the age of 22, John Hopkins married **Hazel Doris Helm** on Thursday, October 10, 1929, when she was 21 years old. They had one daughter.

Hazel Doris was born in Clarksville, Sussex County, Delaware, on Sunday, September 13, 1908. She was the daughter of Herschel Nelson Helm and Sarah Elizabeth Evans.

Hazel Doris reached 103 years of age and died in Port Charlotte, Charlotte County, Florida, on August 11, 2012. She was buried in Barratts Chapel Cemetery, Frederica, Kent County, Delaware (Find a Grave ID 29366379).

Daughter of John Hopkins Hargadine and Hazel Doris Helm:

+ 506 f I. **Jane Helm Hargadine** was born on August 25, 1937.

Family of Mildred Hargadine and Maxwell Harrington

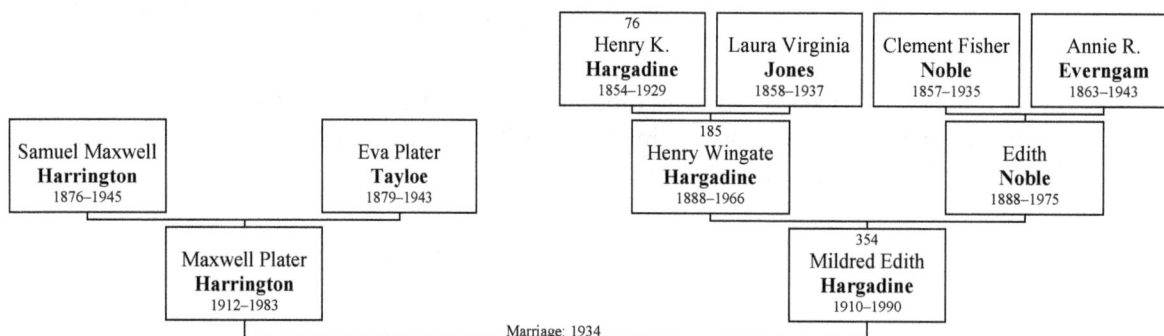

```
                              ┌─────────────┐ ┌─────────────┐ ┌──────────────┐ ┌──────────────┐
                              │     76      │ │Laura Virginia│ │Clement Fisher│ │  Annie R.    │
                              │  Henry K.   │ │    Jones    │ │    Noble     │ │  Everngam    │
                              │ Hargadine   │ │  1858–1937  │ │  1857–1935   │ │  1863–1943   │
                              │  1854–1929  │ │             │ │              │ │              │
                              └─────────────┘ └─────────────┘ └──────────────┘ └──────────────┘
```

Samuel Maxwell **Harrington** 1876–1945	Eva Plater **Tayloe** 1879–1943	**185** Henry Wingate **Hargadine** 1888–1966	Edith **Noble** 1888–1975

Maxwell Plater **Harrington** 1912–1983

354 Mildred Edith **Hargadine** 1910–1990

Marriage: 1934

354. **Mildred Edith Hargadine** was born on Thursday, August 11, 1910, in Frederica, Kent County, Delaware. She was the daughter of Henry Wingate Hargadine (185) and Edith Noble.

Mildred Edith died on July 22, 1990, at the age of 79.

At the age of 24, Mildred Edith married **Maxwell Plater Harrington** on Saturday, November 17, 1934, in Wilmington, New Castle County, Delaware, when he was 22 years old. Maxwell Plater was born in Wilmington, New Castle County, Delaware, on Friday, August 02, 1912.[380]

He served in the military between 1942 and 1946. U.S. Army, WWII. Maxwell Plater served in the military on May 19, 1942.[380]

Maxwell P. reached 70 years of age and died in Myrtle Beach, Horry County, South Carolina, on February 14, 1983.[380]

Her husband, Maxwell P. Harrington, was a graduate of the University of Delaware. He was in the Class of 1950 although he was a returning student (having studied here for two years in the early 1930s). During his freshman year, he was listed in the 1931-1932 student annual (yearbook) as being from Dover, Delaware and was a member of the Rifle Club. He resumed his college education in 1947 and graduated in 1950 when he was 38 years old.

Very little is known about either of the Harringtons except the information that Mrs. Harrington told development officers when they met with her prior to the execution of her estate plan and in later visits and phone conversations. Most of the information that I am sending you was gleaned from "contact reports" which were written following each contact with Mrs. Harrington.

She was very interested in hearing about the work in the University's College of Marine Studies. A generous bequest came to the University of Delaware at her death to set up an endowed fund known as the Maxwell Plater Harrington and Mildred Hargadine Harrington Fund. In her will she specified that "the net income from such fund is . . . for the general enrichment of the educational programs of the College of Marine Studies."

You already have the names of Mrs. Harrington parents. They apparently lived on "The Strand" in New Castle, Delaware from 1940 until 1966. Following the death of Mr. Hargadine in 1966, Mrs. Hargadine went to Myrtle Beach, South Carolina to live with Mrs. Maxwell. Before they moved to New Castle, they (the Hargadines) lived briefly in Wilmington, Delaware and, before that, in Frederica, Delaware.

In the late 1940s to the mid-1950s, Mrs. Maxwell operated an antique shop in the old Court House building in New Castle. She apparently had some significant pieces of antique furniture which she collected over the years. Some may have been family pieces although the notes do not specify this. According to a contact report, she discussed, and was concerned about, the proper place for these pieces following her death. It appeared that they were going to be devised to a museum but I note that there is no mention of them in her will so they were apparently sold with the residue of her estate.

She said that Mr. Harrington's grandfather started the railroad in Delaware (no indication of which railroad), and, that Harrington, Delaware, was named for him. The founder of the family in Delaware, John Harrington, came to Kent County from Dorchester County, Maryland in 1741. His son, also named John, "moved to what is now Harrington, Delaware, about fifty years later" according to H. Clay Reed in his 1950 book, *Delaware: A History of the First State*.

Our alumni records indicate that Mr. and Mrs. Harrington were married in 1934 and that they had no children. He worked for the federal government.

Mrs. Harrington died on July 22, 1990. There was no funeral service as she requested. One of our notes indicates that at the time of her death, her cousin, Mary Virginia Burton (and her husband) were staying at Mrs. Harrington's condominium. The Burtons were from Winter Springs, Florida.

Mrs. Harrington left bequests to two cemeteries for the perpetual care of specific lots including the preservation of the grave markers and monuments.

---

380   Ancestry.com, Public Member Trees (Provo, UT, USA, Ancestry.com Operations, Inc., 2006), Ancestry.com, Record for Maxwell Plater Harrington. https://search.ancestry.co.uk/cgi-bin/sse.dll?db=1030&h=362068076925&indiv=try.

The following were so specified in her will:

1. Barretts Chapel Cemetery in Frederica, Delaware (lots 1065, 1066, 1067 and 1068 of section 5, Center Front; and,
2. Odd Fellows Cemetery, Milford, Delaware (general cemetery care and lot 460).

> Hopefully, you are able to get some "leads" from this information.
> John M. Clayton, Jr.
> Assistant Director of Planned Giving University of Delaware.

M.P. Harrington was the son of Samuel Maxwell Harrington and Eva Plater Tayloe.

Family of Henry Allen and Frances Figgs

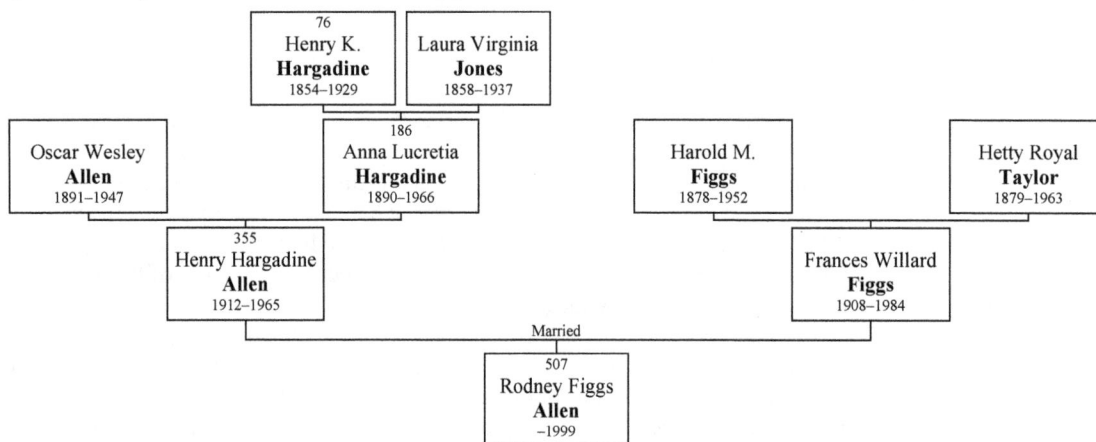

355. **Henry Hargadine Allen** was born on Monday, January 01, 1912, in Clayton, Kent County, Delaware. He was the son of Oscar Wesley Allen and Anna Lucretia Hargadine (186).

Henry Hargadine died in Wilmington, New Castle County, Delaware, on April 26, 1965, at the age of 53. He was buried in Gracelawn Memorial Park, New Castle, New Castle County, Delaware (Find a Grave ID 134998535).

He married **Frances Willard Figgs**. They had one son.

Frances Willard was born in Accomack County, Virginia, on Tuesday, May 26, 1908. She was the daughter of Harold M. Figgs and Hetty Royal Taylor.

She worked as a School teacher. Frances Willard reached 75 years of age and died in Leon County, Florida, on February 28, 1984. She was buried in Parksley Cemetery, Parksley, Accomack County, Virginia (Find a Grave ID 164437114).

Son of Henry Hargadine Allen and Frances Willard Figgs:

+ 507 m I. **Rodney Figgs Allen**. Rodney Figgs died in 1999.

Julia Collins

356. **Julia Comfort Collins** was born on Friday, October 29, 1897, in Saint Louis, Saint Louis County, Missouri. She was the daughter of Charles Cummings Collins and July Hargadine Thomson (187).

Julia Comfort died in Saint Louis, Saint Louis County, Missouri, on November 11, 1929, at the age of 32. She was buried in Bellefontaine Cemetery, Saint Louis, St. Louis City, Missouri (Find a Grave ID 99059887).

Marriages with Humphrey Almy Gifford and Stewart Anderson (Page 388) are known.

Family of Julia Collins and Humphrey Gifford

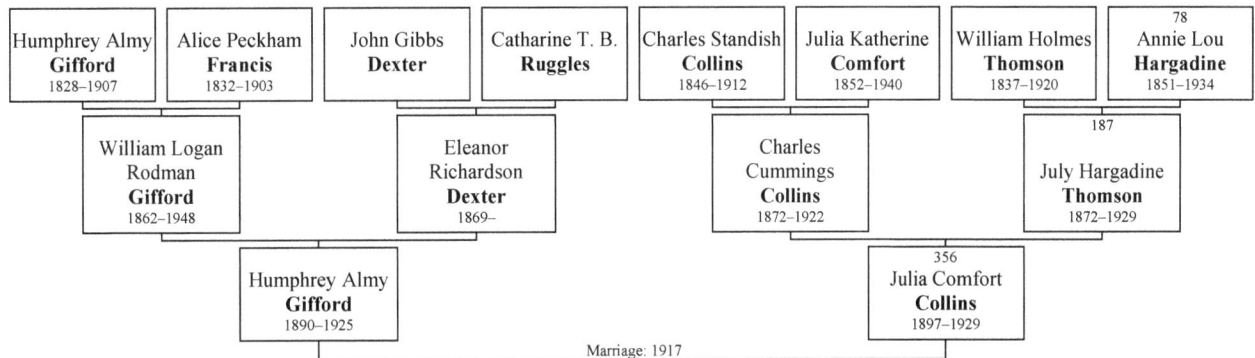

| Humphrey Almy **Gifford** 1828–1907 | Alice Peckham **Francis** 1832–1903 | John Gibbs **Dexter** | Catharine T. B. **Ruggles** | Charles Standish **Collins** 1846–1912 | Julia Katherine **Comfort** 1852–1940 | William Holmes **Thomson** 1837–1920 | 78 Annie Lou **Hargadine** 1851–1934 |

| William Logan Rodman **Gifford** 1862–1948 | | Eleanor Richardson **Dexter** 1869– | | Charles Cummings **Collins** 1872–1922 | | 187 July Hargadine **Thomson** 1872–1929 | |

| | Humphrey Almy **Gifford** 1890–1925 | | | | 356 Julia Comfort **Collins** 1897–1929 | | |

Marriage: 1917

Here are the details about **Julia Comfort Collins's** first marriage, with Humphrey Almy Gifford. You can read more about Julia Comfort on page 387.

At the age of 20, Julia Comfort Collins married **Humphrey Almy Gifford** on Saturday, December 08, 1917, when he was 27 years old. Humphrey Almy was born in Massachusetts, USA, on Saturday, November 15, 1890. He was the son of William Logan Rodman Gifford and Eleanor Richardson Dexter.

Humphrey Almy reached 34 years of age and died in Saint Louis, Saint Louis County, Missouri, on July 21, 1925. He was cremated (Find a Grave ID 136703351).

Family of Julia Collins and Stewart Anderson

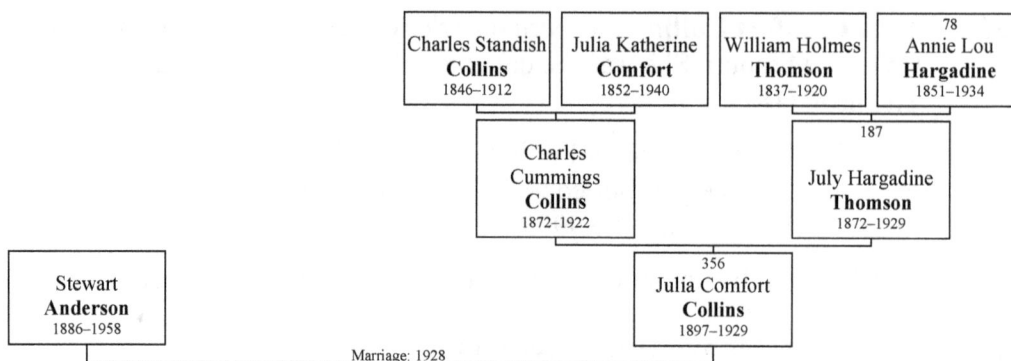

			78
Charles Standish **Collins** 1846–1912	Julia Katherine **Comfort** 1852–1940	William Holmes **Thomson** 1837–1920	Annie Lou **Hargadine** 1851–1934

	187
Charles Cummings **Collins** 1872–1922	July Hargadine **Thomson** 1872–1929

Stewart **Anderson** 1886–1958	356 Julia Comfort **Collins** 1897–1929

Marriage: 1928

Here are the details about **Julia Comfort Collins's** second marriage, with Stewart Anderson. You can read more about Julia Comfort on page 387.

Julia Comfort Collins married **Stewart Anderson** in 1928. Stewart was born in Cincinnati, Hamilton County, Ohio, on Saturday, June 12, 1886.

He reached 72 years of age and died in Saint Louis, Saint Louis County, Missouri, on August 02, 1958. Stewart was buried in Bellefontaine Cemetery, Saint Louis, St. Louis City, Missouri (Find a Grave ID 136702592).

Family of Atreus Von Schrader and Caroline King

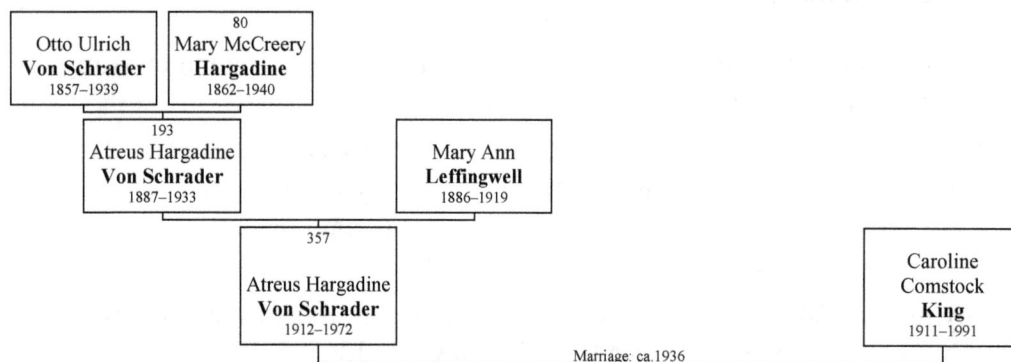

	80
Otto Ulrich **Von Schrader** 1857–1939	Mary McCreery **Hargadine** 1862–1940

193	
Atreus Hargadine **Von Schrader** 1887–1933	Mary Ann **Leffingwell** 1886–1919

357 Atreus Hargadine **Von Schrader** 1912–1972	Caroline Comstock **King** 1911–1991

Marriage: ca.1936

357. **Atreus Hargadine Von Schrader** was born on Monday, January 01, 1912, in Saint Louis, Saint Louis County, Missouri. He was the son of Atreus Hargadine Von Schrader (193) and Mary Ann Leffingwell.

Atreus Hargadine served in the military on May 19, 1942. US Army. He died in Bar Harbor, Hancock County, Maine, on August 09, 1972, at the age of 60. Atreus Hargadine was buried in Oakwood Cemetery, Syracuse, Onondaga County, New York (Find a Grave ID 77270957).

Atreus Hargadine married **Caroline Comstock King** about January 1936. Caroline Comstock was born in Syracuse, Onondaga County, New York, on Saturday, June 03, 1911.

She reached 80 years of age and died in Syracuse, Onondaga County, New York, on November 22, 1991. Caroline Comstock was buried in Oakwood Cemetery, Syracuse, Onondaga County, New York (Find a Grave ID 77270999).

Family of Alice Hall and Anthony Hayden

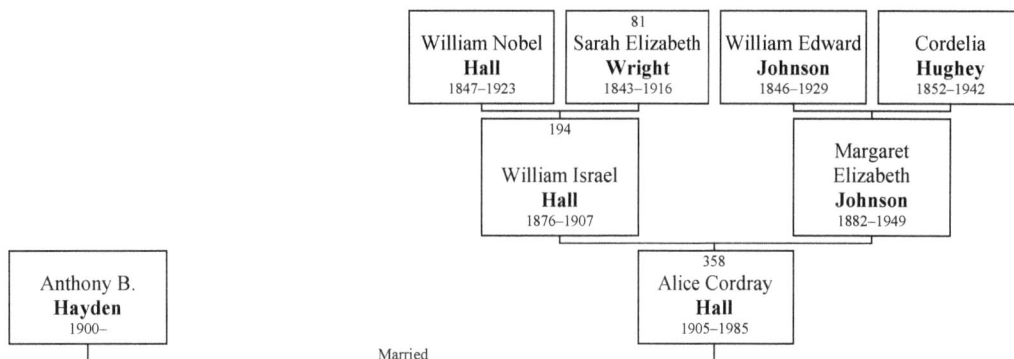

	81		
William Nobel **Hall** 1847–1923	Sarah Elizabeth **Wright** 1843–1916	William Edward **Johnson** 1846–1929	Cordelia **Hughey** 1852–1942

194
William Israel **Hall** 1876–1907

Margaret Elizabeth **Johnson** 1882–1949

Anthony B. **Hayden** 1900–

358
Alice Cordray **Hall** 1905–1985

Married

358. **Alice Cordray Hall** was born on Friday, March 17, 1905. She was the daughter of William Israel Hall (194) and Margaret Elizabeth Johnson.

Alice Cordray died in April 1985 at the age of 80.

She married **Anthony B. Hayden**. Anthony B. was born on Wednesday, March 14, 1900.

Family of Julia Hall and Millard Passwater

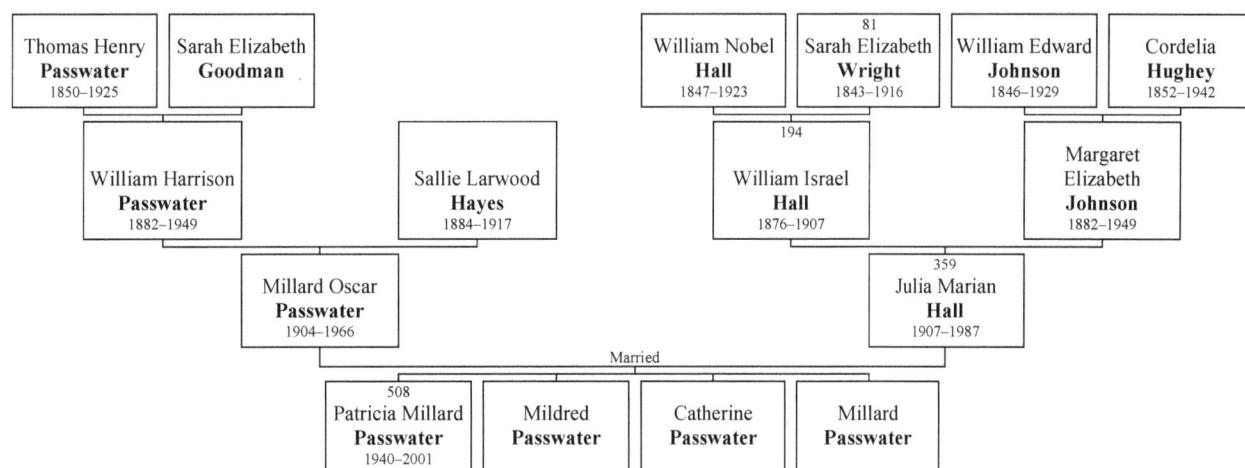

Thomas Henry **Passwater** 1850–1925	Sarah Elizabeth **Goodman**			William Nobel **Hall** 1847–1923	Sarah Elizabeth **Wright** 1843–1916	William Edward **Johnson** 1846–1929	Cordelia **Hughey** 1852–1942

William Harrison **Passwater** 1882–1949

Sallie Larwood **Hayes** 1884–1917

194
William Israel **Hall** 1876–1907

Margaret Elizabeth **Johnson** 1882–1949

Millard Oscar **Passwater** 1904–1966

359
Julia Marian **Hall** 1907–1987

Married

508 Patricia Millard **Passwater** 1940–2001	Mildred **Passwater**	Catherine **Passwater**	Millard **Passwater**

359. **Julia Marian Hall** was born on Thursday, February 14, 1907. She was the daughter of William Israel Hall (194) and Margaret Elizabeth Johnson.

Julia Marian died on April 21, 1987, at the age of 80.

She married **Millard Oscar Passwater**. They had four children.

Millard Oscar was born in Wilmington, New Castle County, Delaware, on Monday, September 26, 1904. He was the son of William Harrison Passwater and Sallie Larwood Hayes.

Millard Oscar reached 62 years of age and died in Bear, New Castle County, Delaware, on November 04, 1966. He was buried on November 08, 1966, in Silverbrook Cemetery and Memorial Park, Wilmington, New Castle County, Delaware.

Children of Julia Marian Hall and Millard Oscar Passwater:

+ 508   f   I. **Patricia Millard Passwater** was born on September 19, 1940. She died in Clayton, Kent County, Delaware, on May 31, 2001, at the age of 60. Patricia Millard was buried in Lakeside Cemetery, Dover, Kent County, Delaware, on June 05, 2001 (Find a Grave ID 141801874).

       f   II. **Mildred Passwater**.

       f   III. **Catherine Passwater**.

       m   IV. **Millard Passwater**.

Family of Roland Hall and Margaret Hurley

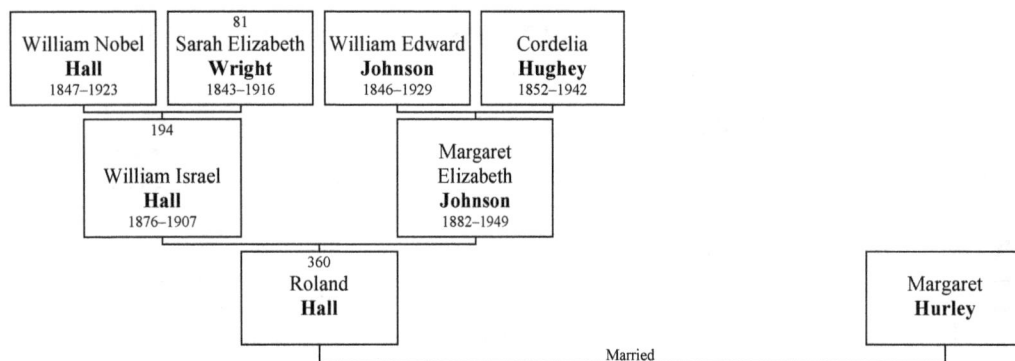

360.   **Roland Hall**. He was the son of William Israel Hall (194) and Margaret Elizabeth Johnson.

He married **Margaret Hurley**.

Family of Georgie Truax and Frederic Warrington

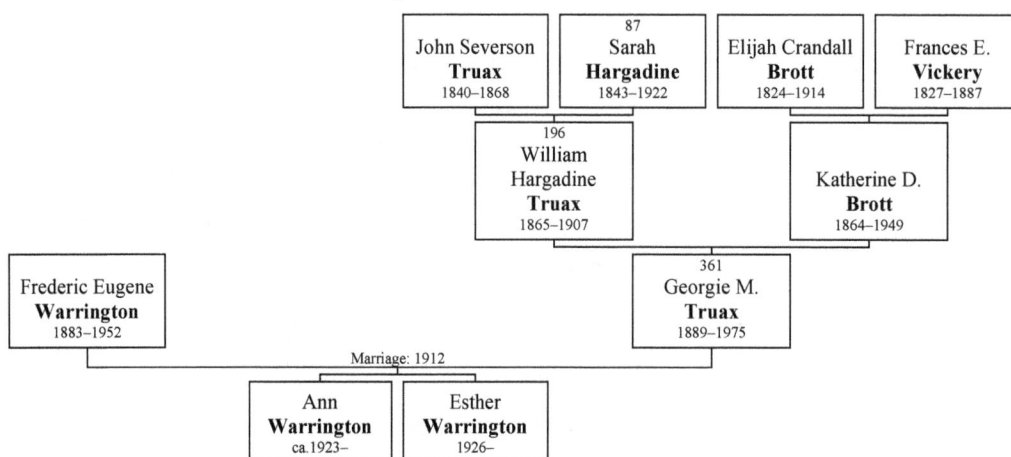

361.   **Georgie M. Truax** was born on Thursday, June 13, 1889, in Missouri, USA. She was the daughter of William Hargadine Truax (196) and Katherine D. Brott.

Georgie M. died in Wilmington, New Castle County, Delaware, on July 25, 1975, at the age of 86. She was buried in Silverbrook Cemetery and Memorial Park, Wilmington, New Castle County, Delaware (Find a Grave ID 137029595).

Georgie M. married **Frederic Eugene Warrington** in 1912. They had two daughters.

Frederic Eugene was born in Dagsboro, Sussex County, Delaware, on Thursday, October 25, 1883. He was also known as **Fred**.

Frederic Eugene reached 68 years of age and died in Wilmington, New Castle County, Delaware, on August 23, 1952. He was buried in Silverbrook Cemetery and Memorial Park, Wilmington, New Castle County, Delaware (Find a Grave ID 137029533).

Daughters of Georgie M. Truax and Frederic Eugene Warrington:

f   I. **Ann Warrington** was born in Delaware, USA, about 1923.

f   II. **Esther Warrington** was born in Wilmington, New Castle County, Delaware, on December 01, 1926. She was buried in Gracelawn Memorial Park, New Castle, New Castle County, Delaware (Find a Grave ID 134997762).

Family of Anne Snow and Harry Kimball

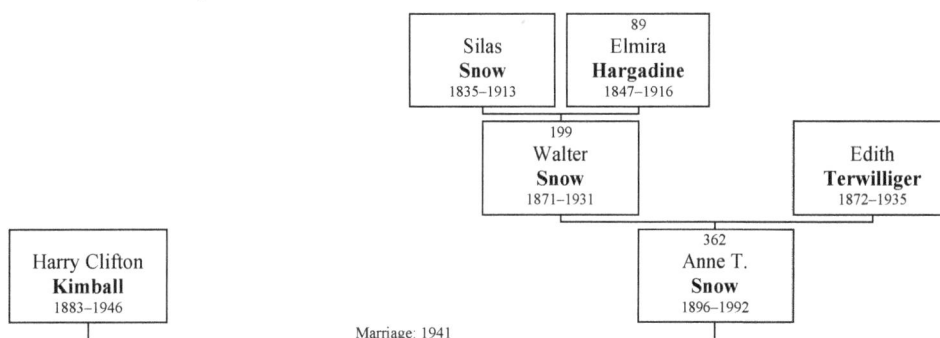

362.   **Anne T. Snow** was born in 1896. She was the daughter of Walter Snow (199) and Edith Terwilliger.

Anne T. died in 1992 at the age of 96. She was buried in Rose Hill Cemetery, Brookfield, Linn County, Missouri (Find a Grave ID 192067411).

At the age of 45, Anne T. married **Harry Clifton Kimball** on Saturday, June 28, 1941, in Cuyahoga County, Ohio, when he was 57 years old. Harry Clifton was born in Skowhegan, Somerset County, Maine, on Monday, September 10, 1883.

He reached 63 years of age and died in Bay Village, Cuyahoga County, Ohio, on November 18, 1946. Harry Clifton was buried in Lakewood Park Cemetery, Rocky River, Cuyahoga County, Ohio (Find a Grave ID 157863676).

Family of Virginia Sayles and Glenn Crosby

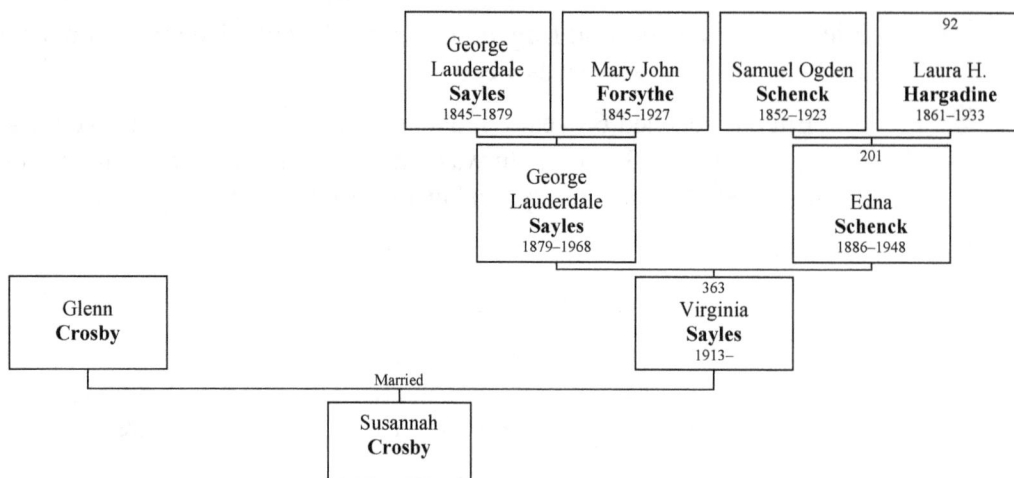

			92
George Lauderdale **Sayles** 1845–1879	Mary John **Forsythe** 1845–1927	Samuel Ogden **Schenck** 1852–1923	Laura H. **Hargadine** 1861–1933

George Lauderdale **Sayles** 1879–1968

201
Edna **Schenck** 1886–1948

Glenn **Crosby**

363
Virginia **Sayles** 1913–

Married

Susannah **Crosby**

363. **Virginia Sayles** was born on Monday, December 29, 1913.[381] She was the daughter of George Lauderdale Sayles and Edna Schenck (201).

She married **Glenn Crosby**. They had one daughter.

Daughter of Virginia Sayles and Glenn Crosby:

    f   I. **Susannah Crosby**.

Family of Martha Sayles and Norman Becker

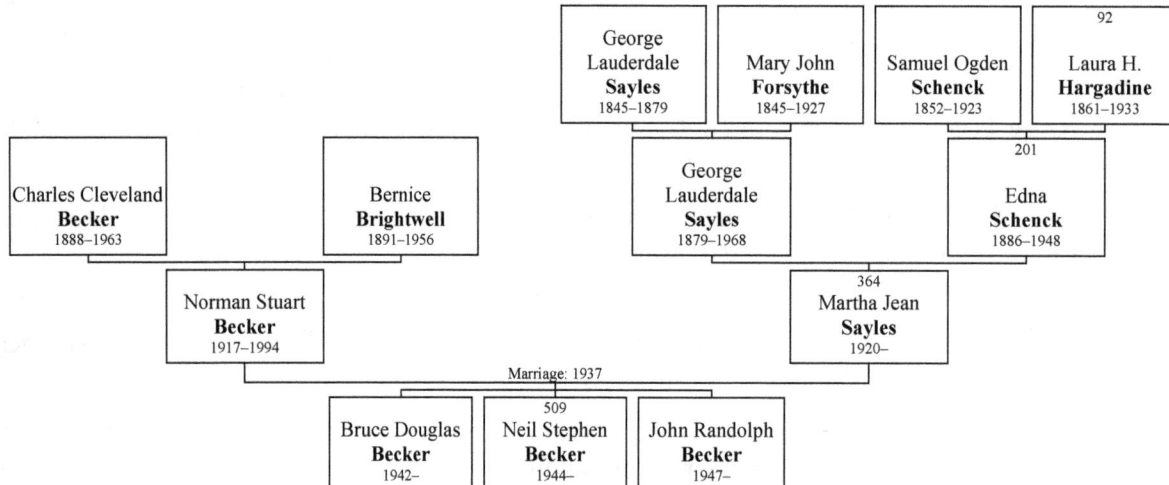

			92
George Lauderdale **Sayles** 1845–1879	Mary John **Forsythe** 1845–1927	Samuel Ogden **Schenck** 1852–1923	Laura H. **Hargadine** 1861–1933

Charles Cleveland **Becker** 1888–1963

Bernice **Brightwell** 1891–1956

George Lauderdale **Sayles** 1879–1968

201
Edna **Schenck** 1886–1948

Norman Stuart **Becker** 1917–1994

364
Martha Jean **Sayles** 1920–

Marriage: 1937

Bruce Douglas **Becker** 1942–

509
Neil Stephen **Becker** 1944–

John Randolph **Becker** 1947–

364. **Martha Jean Sayles** was born on Saturday, March 13, 1920, in Arkansas City, Cowley County, Kansas.[382] She is the daughter of George Lauderdale Sayles and Edna Schenck (201).

---

381   Neil Becker.FTW, Date of Import: May 19, 2004.

382   Neil Becker.FTW, Date of Import: May 19, 2004.

At the age of 17, Martha Jean married **Norman Stuart Becker** on Friday, May 14, 1937, in Olathe, Johnson County, Kansas, when he was 19 years old.[382] They had three sons.

Norman Stuart was born in Kansas City, Clay County, Missouri, on Wednesday, November 14, 1917.[382] He was the son of Charles Cleveland Becker and Bernice Brightwell.

Norman Stuart reached 76 years of age and died in Kansas City, Clay County, Missouri, in 1994.[382]

Sons of Martha Jean Sayles and Norman Stuart Becker:

m	I.	**Bruce Douglas Becker** was born on July 26, 1942.[382]
+ 509	m	II. **Neil Stephen Becker** was born in Kansas City, Jackson County, Missouri, on October 12, 1944.[382]
	m	III. **John Randolph Becker** was born on December 15, 1947.[382]

Family of Catherine Sayles and Carlton Wetzell

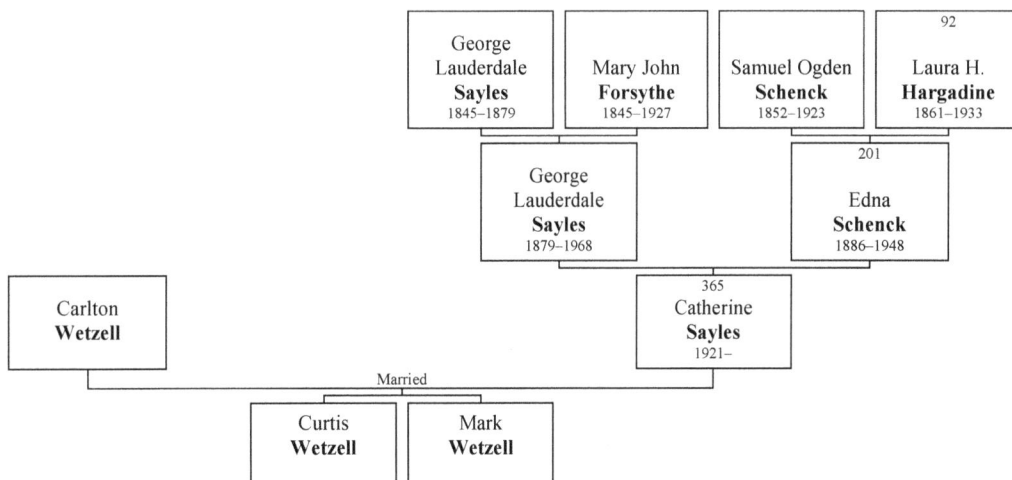

365. **Catherine Sayles** was born on Tuesday, November 15, 1921.[383] She is the daughter of George Lauderdale Sayles and Edna Schenck (201).

She married **Carlton Wetzell**. They had two sons.

Sons of Catherine Sayles and Carlton Wetzell:

m	I.	**Curtis Wetzell**.
m	II.	**Mark Wetzell**.

Samuel Hargadine

366. **Samuel Emmett Hargadine IV** was born on Thursday, June 05, 1930, in Bowling Green, Pike County, Missouri. He was the son of Samuel Emmett Hargadine III (203) and Viola Belle Cox.

---

[383] Neil Becker.FTW, Date of Import: May 19, 2004.

Samuel Emmett served in the military on April 21, 1953: US Army; Korean War Conflict, Corporal. He died in Saint Louis, Saint Louis County, Missouri, on June 27, 2020, at the age of 90. Samuel Emmett was buried in Memorial Gardens Cemetery, Bowling Green, Pike County, Missouri, on October 23, 2021 (Find a Grave ID 211927637).

More facts and events for Samuel Emmett Hargadine IV:

Individual Note: March 10, 1969   Received Medal for Civilian Service in Vietnam

Marriages with Georganna Myers, Eileen Olivia Howell (Page 395) and Regina J. Mandour (Page 395) are known.

Family of Samuel Hargadine and Georganna Myers

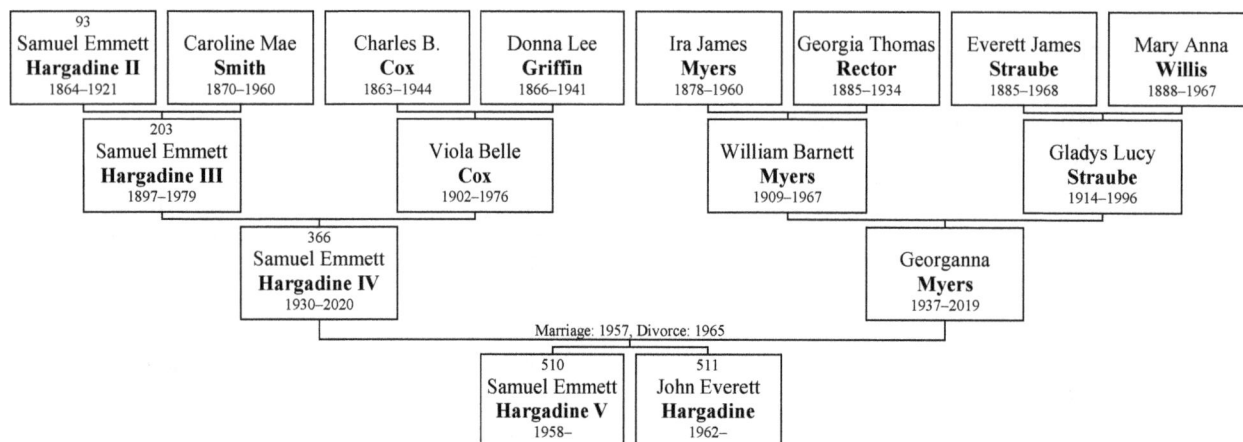

93 Samuel Emmett **Hargadine II** 1864–1921	Caroline Mae **Smith** 1870–1960	Charles B. **Cox** 1863–1944	Donna Lee **Griffin** 1866–1941	Ira James **Myers** 1878–1960	Georgia Thomas **Rector** 1885–1934	Everett James **Straube** 1885–1968	Mary Anna **Willis** 1888–1967

203 Samuel Emmett **Hargadine III** 1897–1979	Viola Belle **Cox** 1902–1976	William Barnett **Myers** 1909–1967	Gladys Lucy **Straube** 1914–1996

366 Samuel Emmett **Hargadine IV** 1930–2020	Georganna **Myers** 1937–2019

Marriage: 1957, Divorce: 1965

510 Samuel Emmett **Hargadine V** 1958–	511 John Everett **Hargadine** 1962–

Here are the details about **Samuel Emmett Hargadine IV's** first marriage, with Georganna Myers. You can read more about Samuel Emmett on page 393.

At the age of 27, Samuel Emmett Hargadine IV married **Georganna Myers** on Sunday, August 25, 1957, in Bowling Green, Pike County, Missouri, when she was 19 years old. They were divorced in Fairfax, Fairfax County, Virginia, on October 03, 1965. They had two sons.

Georganna was born in Bowling Green, Pike County, Missouri, on Thursday, December 30, 1937. She was the daughter of William Barnett Myers and Gladys Lucy Straube.

Georganna reached 81 years of age and died at Capitol Region Hospital in Jefferson City, Cole County, Missouri, on May 15, 2019. She was buried on May 20, 2019, in Memorial Gardens Cemetery, Bowling Green, Pike County, Missouri (Find a Grave ID 199157394).

Sons of Samuel Emmett Hargadine IV and Georganna Myers:

+ 510   m   I. **Samuel Emmett Hargadine V** was born in Columbia, Boone County, Missouri, on August 10, 1958.

+ 511   m   II. **John Everett Hargadine** was born in Washington D.C. on March 21, 1962.

Family of Samuel Hargadine and Eileen Howell

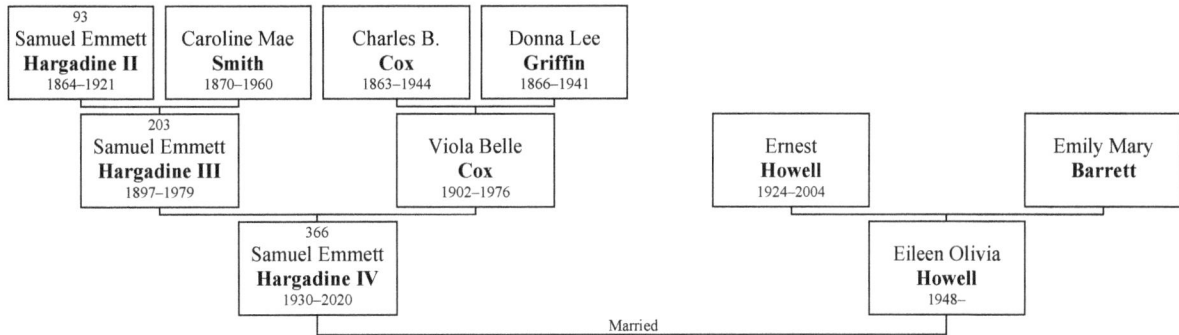

| 93 Samuel Emmett **Hargadine II** 1864–1921 | Caroline Mae **Smith** 1870–1960 | Charles B. **Cox** 1863–1944 | Donna Lee **Griffin** 1866–1941 |

203 Samuel Emmett **Hargadine III** 1897–1979 — Viola Belle **Cox** 1902–1976

Ernest **Howell** 1924–2004 — Emily Mary **Barrett**

366 Samuel Emmett **Hargadine IV** 1930–2020

Eileen Olivia **Howell** 1948–

Married

Here are the details about **Samuel Emmett Hargadine IV's** second marriage, with Eileen Olivia Howell. You can read more about Samuel Emmett on page 393.

Samuel Emmett Hargadine IV married **Eileen Olivia Howell**. Eileen Olivia was born in Harris County, Texas, on Saturday, December 11, 1948. She is the daughter of Ernest Howell and Emily Mary Barrett.

Family of Samuel Hargadine and Regina Mandour

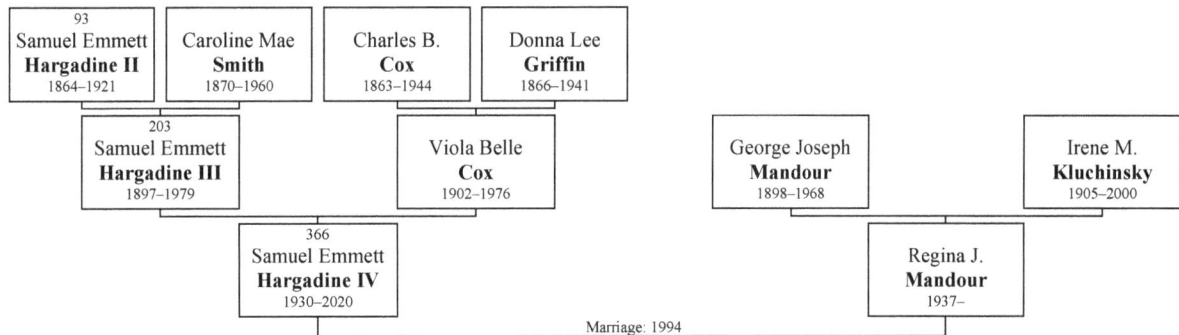

| 93 Samuel Emmett **Hargadine II** 1864–1921 | Caroline Mae **Smith** 1870–1960 | Charles B. **Cox** 1863–1944 | Donna Lee **Griffin** 1866–1941 |

203 Samuel Emmett **Hargadine III** 1897–1979 — Viola Belle **Cox** 1902–1976

George Joseph **Mandour** 1898–1968 — Irene M. **Kluchinsky** 1905–2000

366 Samuel Emmett **Hargadine IV** 1930–2020

Regina J. **Mandour** 1937–

Marriage: 1994

Here are the details about **Samuel Emmett Hargadine IV's** third marriage, with Regina J. Mandour. You can read more about Samuel Emmett on page 393.

At the age of 63, Samuel Emmett Hargadine IV married **Regina J. Mandour** on Friday, February 11, 1994, in Bisbee, Cochise County, Arizona, when she was 56 years old. Regina J. was born in Hometown, Schuylkill County, Pennsylvania, on Friday, February 12, 1937. She is the daughter of George Joseph Mandour and Irene M. Kluchinsky.

Mariam Hargadine

367. **Mariam Viola Hargadine** was born on Wednesday, August 02, 1922, in Brookfield, Linn County, Missouri. She was the daughter of Herman Millard Hargadine (204) and Lola Armstrong.

Mariam Viola died in Overland Park, Johnson County, Kansas, on June 26, 2005, at the age of 82. She was buried in Maple Hill Cemetery, Kansas City, Wyandotte County, Kansas, on June 29, 2005 (Find a Grave ID 71923221).

Marriages with Carl Francis Farrar and Julius H. Haase (Page 397) are known.

Family of Mariam Hargadine and Carl Farrar

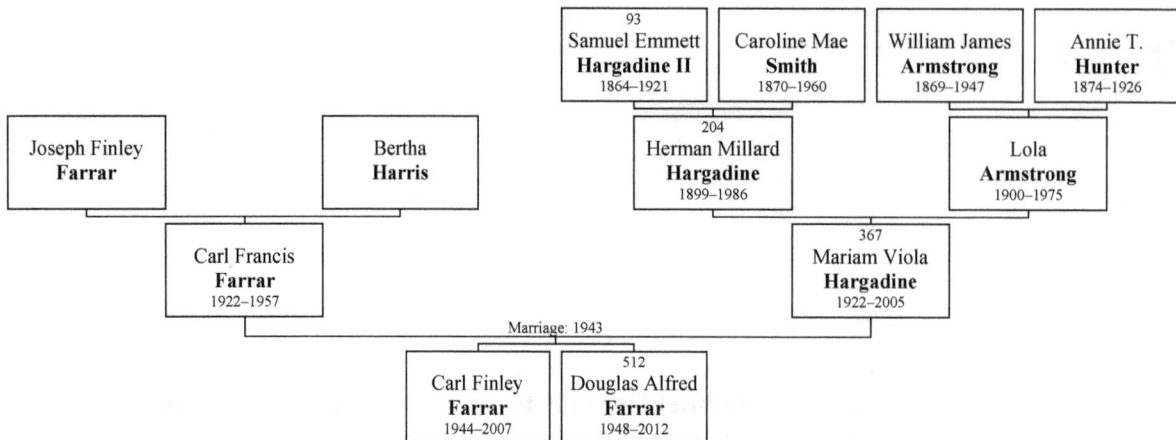

```
                                    ┌─────────────┐ ┌─────────────┐ ┌─────────────┐ ┌─────────────┐
                                    │     93      │ │             │ │             │ │             │
                                    │Samuel Emmett│ │Caroline Mae │ │William James│ │  Annie T.   │
                                    │ Hargadine II│ │   Smith     │ │ Armstrong   │ │   Hunter    │
                                    │  1864–1921  │ │  1870–1960  │ │  1869–1947  │ │  1874–1926  │
                                    └─────────────┘ └─────────────┘ └─────────────┘ └─────────────┘
  ┌─────────────┐      ┌─────────────┐      ┌─────────────┐          ┌─────────────┐
  │Joseph Finley│      │   Bertha    │      │     204     │          │    Lola     │
  │   Farrar    │      │   Harris    │      │Herman Millard│         │  Armstrong  │
  │             │      │             │      │  Hargadine  │          │  1900–1975  │
  └─────────────┘      └─────────────┘      │  1899–1986  │          └─────────────┘
          ┌─────────────┐                   └─────────────┘
          │Carl Francis │                          ┌─────────────┐
          │   Farrar    │                          │     367     │
          │  1922–1957  │                          │ Mariam Viola│
          └─────────────┘                          │  Hargadine  │
                          Marriage: 1943            │  1922–2005  │
                                                    └─────────────┘
                      ┌─────────────┐ ┌─────────────┐
                      │ Carl Finley │ │     512     │
                      │   Farrar    │ │Douglas Alfred│
                      │  1944–2007  │ │   Farrar    │
                      └─────────────┘ │  1948–2012  │
                                      └─────────────┘
```

Here are the details about **Mariam Viola Hargadine's** first marriage, with Carl Francis Farrar. You can read more about Mariam Viola on page 395.

At the age of 21, Mariam Viola Hargadine married **Carl Francis Farrar** on Monday, September 20, 1943, in Laclede, Linn County, Missouri, when he was 21 years old. They had two sons.

Carl Francis was born in Laclede, Linn County, Missouri, on Wednesday, March 01, 1922. He was the son of Joseph Finley Farrar and Bertha Harris.

He served in the military: US Army, WWI, PFC. Carl Francis reached 35 years of age and died on July 01, 1957. He was buried in Maple Hill Cemetery, Kansas City, Wyandotte County, Kansas (Find a Grave ID 71923181).

Sons of Mariam Viola Hargadine and Carl Francis Farrar:

m   I. **Carl Finley Farrar** was born on September 10, 1944. He served in the military: U.S. Air Force, Master Sergeant, Vietnam.

Carl Finley died on November 09, 2007, at the age of 63. He was buried in Leavenworth National Cemetery, Leavenworth, Leavenworth County, Kansas (Find a Grave ID 24703639).

+ 512 m   II. **Douglas Alfred Farrar** was born in Brookfield, Linn County, Missouri, on February 19, 1948. He was also known as **Doug**.

Douglas Alfred died in Overland Park, Johnson County, Kansas, on May 29, 2012, at the age of 64. He was buried in Maple Hill Cemetery, Kansas City, Wyandotte County, Kansas (Find a Grave ID 91051829).

Family of Mariam Hargadine and Julius Haase

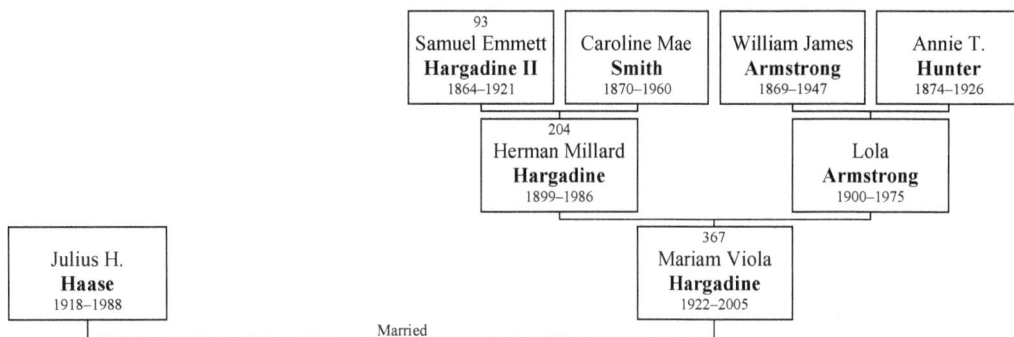

	93 Samuel Emmett **Hargadine II** 1864–1921	Caroline Mae **Smith** 1870–1960	William James **Armstrong** 1869–1947	Annie T. **Hunter** 1874–1926

	204 Herman Millard **Hargadine** 1899–1986		Lola **Armstrong** 1900–1975

Julius H. **Haase** 1918–1988		367 Mariam Viola **Hargadine** 1922–2005

Married

Here are the details about **Mariam Viola Hargadine's** second marriage, with Julius H. Haase. You can read more about Mariam Viola on page 395.

Mariam Viola Hargadine married **Julius H. Haase**. Julius H. was born on Thursday, October 24, 1918.

He served in the military: US Army, WWI, SSGT. Julius H. reached 69 years of age and died on June 01, 1988. He was buried in Maple Hill Cemetery, Kansas City, Wyandotte County, Kansas (Find a Grave ID 71923262).

Family of Ronald Hargadine and Marlyn Detwiller

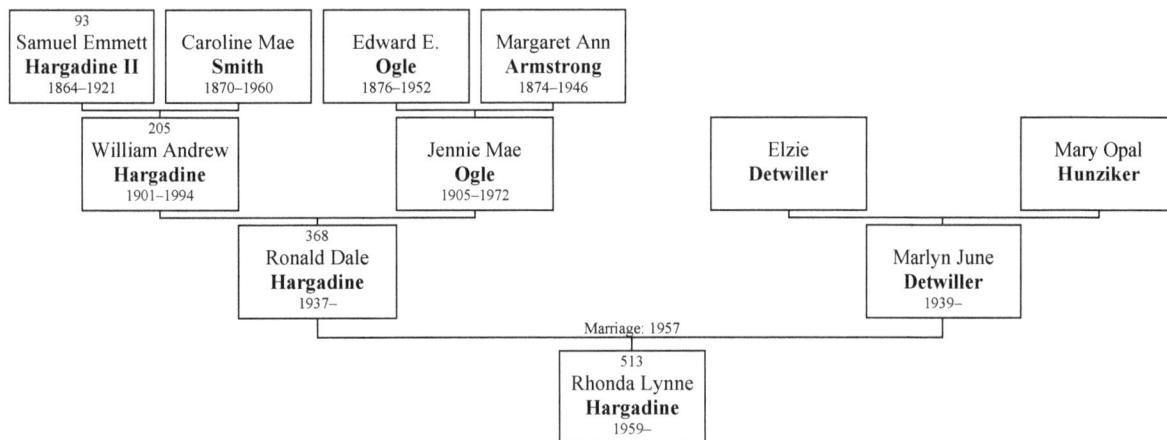

93 Samuel Emmett **Hargadine II** 1864–1921	Caroline Mae **Smith** 1870–1960	Edward E. **Ogle** 1876–1952	Margaret Ann **Armstrong** 1874–1946		

205 William Andrew **Hargadine** 1901–1994		Jennie Mae **Ogle** 1905–1972		Elzie **Detwiller**	Mary Opal **Hunziker**

	368 Ronald Dale **Hargadine** 1937–			Marlyn June **Detwiller** 1939–

Marriage: 1957

	513 Rhonda Lynne **Hargadine** 1959–

368. **Ronald Dale Hargadine** was born on Tuesday, August 24, 1937. He is the son of William Andrew Hargadine (205) and Jennie Mae Ogle.

At the age of 20, Ronald Dale married **Marlyn June Detwiller** on Friday, September 20, 1957, at Park Baptist Church in Brookfield, Linn County, Missouri, when she was 18 years old. They have one daughter.

Marlyn June was born on Saturday, July 15, 1939. She is the daughter of Elzie Detwiller and Mary Opal Hunziker.

Daughter of Ronald Dale Hargadine and Marlyn June Detwiller:

+ 513 f I. **Rhonda Lynne Hargadine** was born on January 02, 1959.

Family of Robert Hargadine and Mary Meneely

93 Samuel Emmett **Hargadine II** 1864–1921	Caroline Mae **Smith** 1870–1960

Frank Logan **Meneely** 1867–1945	Emma Matilda **Bergstrum** 1870–1955

Jefferson Davis **Molloy** 1861–1936	Mary **Hayes** 1875–1964

206 Edwin Lomax **Hargadine** 1904–1967	Winifred **Buswell** 1905–1990

James Edward
Meneely
1903–2001

Blanche Mary
Molloy
1912–1997

369
Robert Eugene
Hargadine
1935–2007

Mary Annabeth
Meneely
1937–2015

Marriage: 1955

514 Jim Edwin **Hargadine** 1956–	**515** Richard Craig **Hargadine** 1959–	**516** Loren Dale **Hargadine** 1964–

369. **Robert Eugene Hargadine** was born on Thursday, July 25, 1935, in Brookfield, Linn County, Missouri. He was the son of Edwin Lomax Hargadine (206) and Winifred Buswell. He was also known as **Bob**.

Robert Eugene served in the military between 1953 and 1957: U.S. Air Force. He died in Pershing Memorial Hospital, Brookfield, Linn County, Missouri, on March 23, 2007, at the age of 71. His cause of death was cancer of the blood. He was buried in Parklawn Memory Gardens Cemetery, Brookfield, Linn County, Missouri, on March 26, 2007 (Find a Grave ID 155138339).

At the age of 20, Robert Eugene married **Mary Annabeth Meneely** on Sunday, October 09, 1955, in Meadville, Linn County, Missouri, when she was 18 years old. They had three sons.

Mary Annabeth was born in Laclede, Linn County, Missouri, on Tuesday, June 22, 1937. She was the daughter of James Edward Meneely and Blanche Mary Molloy.

Mary Annabeth reached 78 years of age and died at Boone Hospital Center in Columbia, Boone County, Missouri, on July 26, 2015. Her cause of death was cancer. Mary Annabeth was buried on July 30, 2015, in Parklawn Memory Gardens Cemetery, Brookfield, Linn County, Missouri (Find a Grave ID 149963134).

Sons of Robert Eugene Hargadine and Mary Annabeth Meneely:

+   514   m   I. **Jim Edwin Hargadine** was born in Denver, Denver County, Colorado, on September 06, 1956.

+   515   m   II. **Richard Craig Hargadine** was born in Brookfield, Linn County, Missouri, on August 01, 1959.

+   516   m   III. **Loren Dale Hargadine** was born in Brookfield, Linn County, Missouri, on November 18, 1964.

Family of Beverly Harbaugh and Darrell Spidle

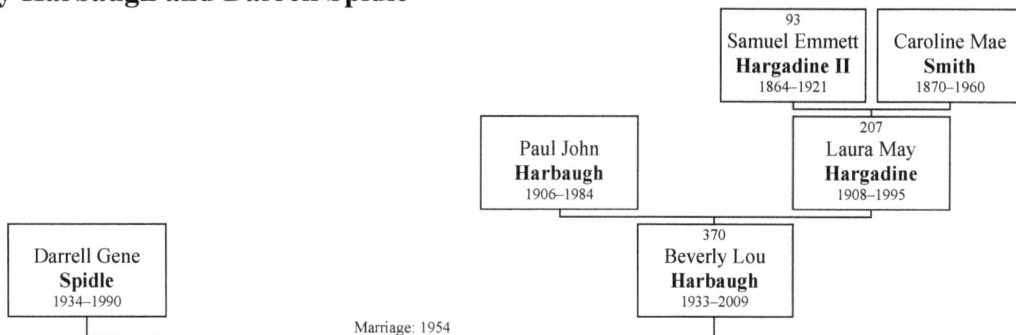

370. **Beverly Lou Harbaugh** was born on Thursday, November 16, 1933. She was the daughter of Paul John Harbaugh and Laura May Hargadine (207).

Beverly Lou died on April 10, 2009, at the age of 75. She was buried in Laclede Cemetery, Laclede, Linn County, Missouri (Find a Grave ID 85610180).

Beverly Lou married **Darrell Gene Spidle** in 1954. Darrell Gene was born on Thursday, November 22, 1934.

He reached 55 years of age and died on June 14, 1990. Darrell Gene was buried in Laclede Cemetery, Laclede, Linn County, Missouri (Find a Grave ID 90566543).

Family of Barbara Harbaugh and Dale Beach

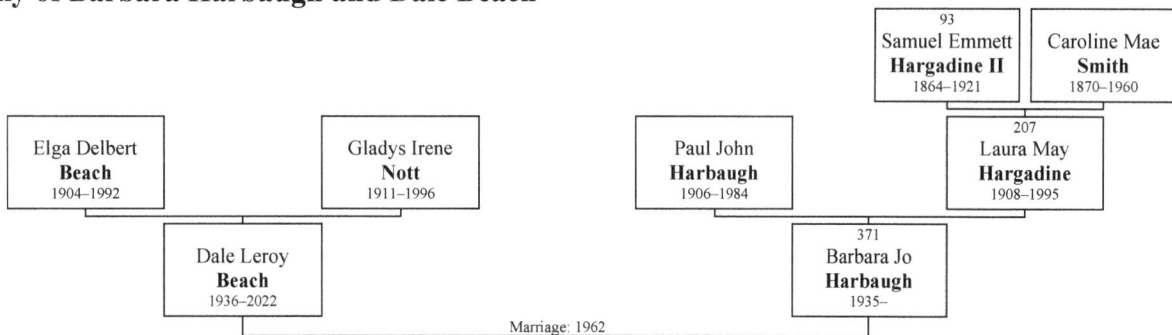

371. **Barbara Jo Harbaugh** was born on Wednesday, October 23, 1935. She is the daughter of Paul John Harbaugh and Laura May Hargadine (207).

At the age of 27, Barbara Jo married **Dale Leroy Beach** on Saturday, November 17, 1962, in Laclede, Linn County, Missouri, when he was 26 years old. Dale Leroy was born in Onaga, Pottawatomie County, Kansas, on Monday, August 03, 1936.[384] He was the son of Elga Delbert Beach and Gladys Irene Nott.

Dale Leroy reached 85 years of age and died in Lawrence, Douglas County, Kansas, on March 05, 2022.[384] He was buried on March 19, 2022, in Parklawn Memory Gardens Cemetery, Brookfield, Linn County, Missouri.[384]

---

384 Ancestry.com, Public Member Trees (Provo, UT, USA, Ancestry.com Operations, Inc., 2006), Ancestry.com, Record for Dale Leroy Beach. https://search.ancestry.co.uk/cgi-bin/sse.dll?db=1030&h=402438788178&indiv=try.

Family of Carolyn Harbaugh and Charles Fitzgerald

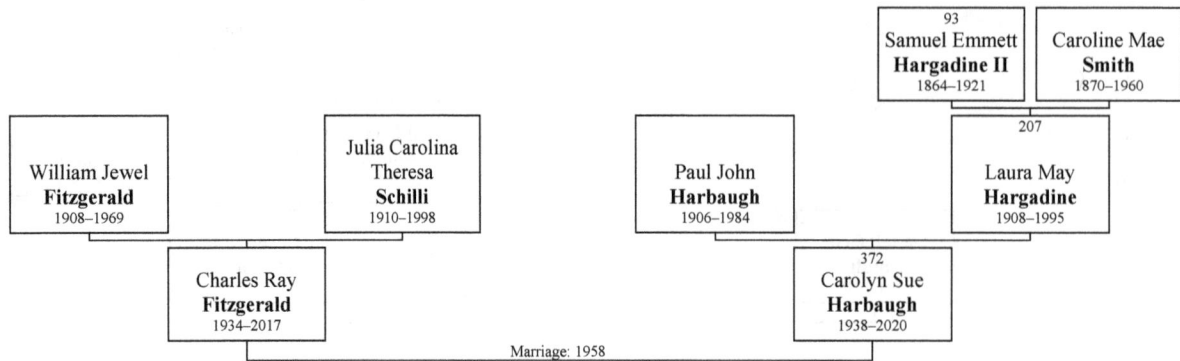

	93 Samuel Emmett **Hargadine II** 1864–1921	Caroline Mae **Smith** 1870–1960

William Jewel **Fitzgerald** 1908–1969	Julia Carolina Theresa **Schilli** 1910–1998	Paul John **Harbaugh** 1906–1984	207 Laura May **Hargadine** 1908–1995

Charles Ray **Fitzgerald** 1934–2017	372 Carolyn Sue **Harbaugh** 1938–2020

Marriage: 1958

372. **Carolyn Sue Harbaugh** was born on Monday, January 24, 1938, in Laclede, Linn County, Missouri. She was the daughter of Paul John Harbaugh and Laura May Hargadine (207).

Carolyn Sue died in Saint Peters, St. Charles County, Missouri, on December 19, 2020, at the age of 82. She was buried in Jefferson Barracks National Cemetery, Lemay, St. Louis County, Missouri, on December 29, 2020 (Find a Grave ID 220130791).

At the age of 20, Carolyn Sue married **Charles Ray Fitzgerald** on Sunday, June 15, 1958, when he was 24 years old. Charles Ray was born in Saint Louis, Saint Louis County, Missouri, on Tuesday, June 12, 1934. He was the son of William Jewel Fitzgerald and Julia Carolina Theresa Schilli.

Charles Ray reached 83 years of age and died in Saint Louis, Saint Louis County, Missouri, on October 12, 2017. He was buried in Jefferson Barracks National Cemetery, Lemay, St. Louis County, Missouri (Find a Grave ID 184343098).

Family of Emma Paradee and James McIlvaine

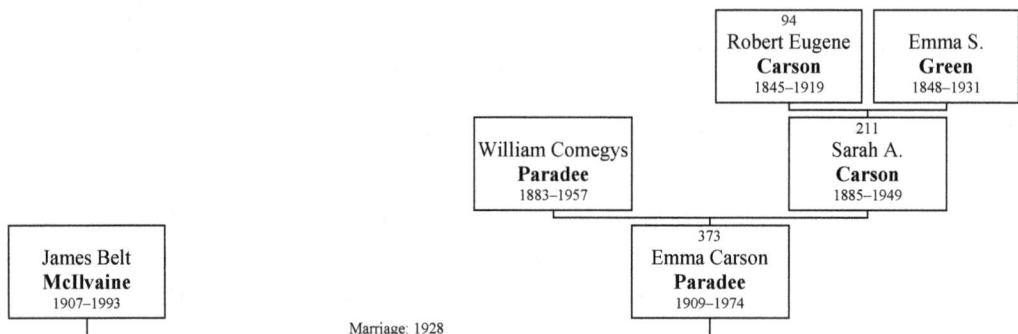

	94 Robert Eugene **Carson** 1845–1919	Emma S. **Green** 1848–1931

William Comegys **Paradee** 1883–1957	211 Sarah A. **Carson** 1885–1949

James Belt **McIlvaine** 1907–1993	373 Emma Carson **Paradee** 1909–1974

Marriage: 1928

373. **Emma Carson Paradee** was born on Friday, November 26, 1909. She was the daughter of William Comegys Paradee and Sarah A. Carson (211).

Emma Carson died in Frederica, Kent County, Delaware, in November 1974 at the age of 64. She was buried in Barratts Chapel Cemetery, Frederica, Kent County, Delaware (Find a Grave ID 30369051).

Emma Carson married **James Belt McIlvaine** in 1928. James Belt was born in 1907.

He reached 86 years of age and died in August 1993. James Belt was buried in Barratts Chapel Cemetery, Frederica, Kent County, Delaware (Find a Grave ID 30369113). They had no children.

7th Generation

Family of Joseph Bruffey and Lillie Chaney

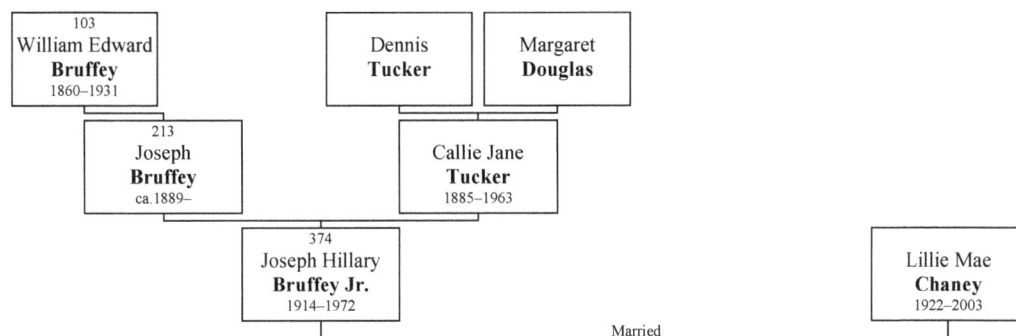

```
┌──────────────┐
│     103      │
│William Edward│      ┌──────────┐  ┌──────────┐
│   Bruffey    │      │  Dennis  │  │ Margaret │
│  1860–1931   │      │  Tucker  │  │ Douglas  │
└──────────────┘      └──────────┘  └──────────┘
   ┌──────────────┐      ┌──────────────┐
   │     213      │      │  Callie Jane │
   │    Joseph    │      │    Tucker    │
   │   Bruffey    │      │  1885–1963   │
   │   ca.1889–   │      └──────────────┘
   └──────────────┘
      ┌──────────────┐                    ┌──────────────┐
      │     374      │                    │  Lillie Mae  │
      │Joseph Hillary│                    │    Chaney    │
      │  Bruffey Jr. │                    │  1922–2003   │
      │  1914–1972   │                    └──────────────┘
      └──────────────┘        Married
```

374. **Joseph Hillary Bruffey Jr.** was born on Sunday, November 15, 1914, in Missouri, USA.[385] He was the son of Joseph Bruffey (213) and Callie Jane Tucker.

Joseph Hillary served in the military between February 1943 and April 1943: U.S. Army. He died on October 15, 1972, at the age of 57. Joseph Hillary was buried in Howell Memorial Park Cemetery, Pomona, Howell County, Missouri (Find a Grave ID 126446769).

He married **Lillie Mae Chaney**. Lillie Mae was born in Arkansas, USA, on Wednesday, November 15, 1922.

She reached 80 years of age and died in West Plains, Howell County, Missouri, on May 05, 2003. Lillie Mae was buried in Howell Memorial Park Cemetery, Pomona, Howell County, Missouri (Find a Grave ID 126444654).

Gary Kaylor

375. **Gary Robert Kaylor** was born on Monday, December 02, 1940, in Clinchco, Dickenson County, Virginia.[386] He is the son of Robert Lee Kaylor and Mary Ellen Chambers (221).

Marriages with Charlene Eleanor Fite and Sheila Faye Wilbanks (Page 405) are known.

---

[385]   Age given as 5 years in 1920 Missouri Soundex.

[386]   Virginia Birth Certificate.

Family of Gary Kaylor and Charlene Fite

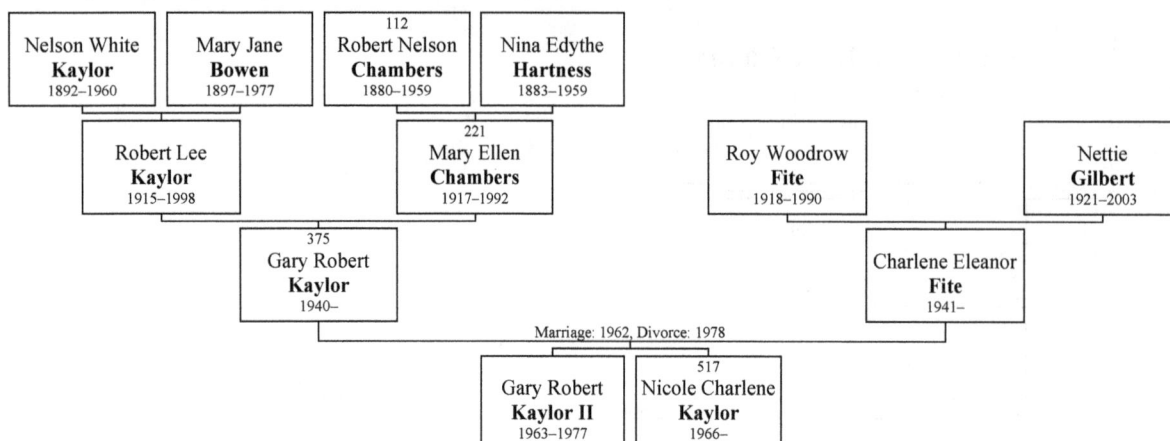

Here are the details about **Gary Robert Kaylor's** first marriage, with Charlene Eleanor Fite. You can read more about Gary Robert on page 403.

At the age of 21, Gary Robert Kaylor married **Charlene Eleanor Fite** on Saturday, June 16, 1962, in Garden City Baptist Church, Roanoke, Virginia, when she was 20 years old.[387] They were divorced in March 1978. They had two children.

Charlene Eleanor was born in Tolar, Pike County, Kentucky, on Sunday, August 10, 1941. She is the daughter of Roy Woodrow Fite and Nettie Gilbert.

Children of Gary Robert Kaylor and Charlene Eleanor Fite:

m   I. **Gary Robert Kaylor II** was born at Methodist Hospital in Houston, Texas, on June 17, 1963.[388] He was also known as **Bobby**.

Gary Robert died in Greenville, Greenville County, South Carolina, on December 20, 1977, at the age of 14.[389] He was buried in Blue Ridge Memorial Gardens, Roanoke, Roanoke County, Virginia (Find a Grave ID 166440147).

+   517   f   II. **Nicole Charlene Kaylor** was born in Houston, Texas, on July 13, 1966.[388]

---

387   Marriage Certificate.

388   Birth Certificate.

389   Gary Robert Kaylor.

Family of Gary Kaylor and Sheila Wilbanks

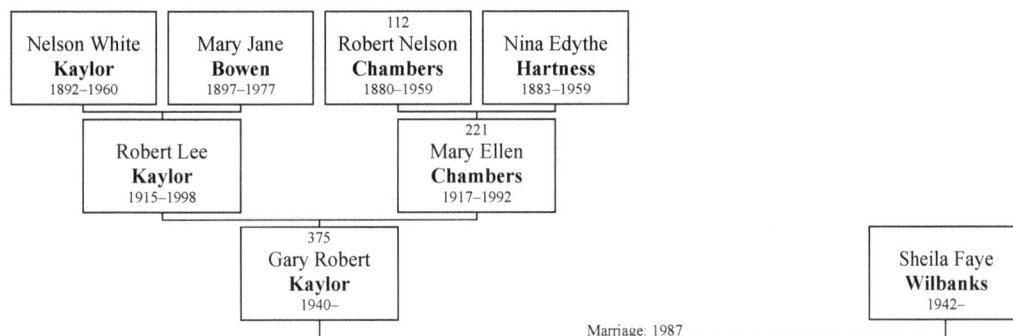

Here are the details about **Gary Robert Kaylor's** second marriage, with Sheila Faye Wilbanks. You can read more about Gary Robert on page 403.

At the age of 46, Gary Robert Kaylor married **Sheila Faye Wilbanks** on Saturday, October 10, 1987, in Powhatan, Powhatan County, Virginia, when she was 45 years old.[387] Sheila Faye was born in Tallassee, Alabama, on Tuesday, June 02, 1942.

Family of Janice Kaylor and William Stout

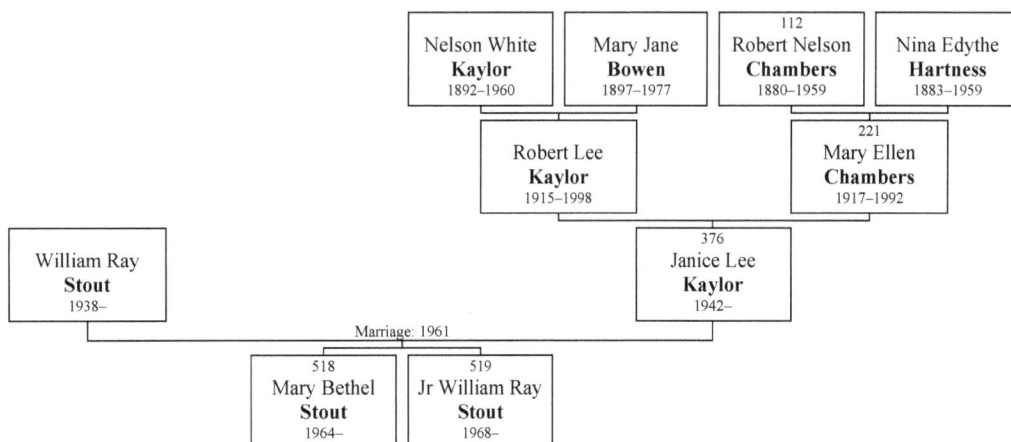

376. **Janice Lee Kaylor** was born on Friday, May 08, 1942, in Jefferson Hospital, Roanoke, Virginia.[390] She is the daughter of Robert Lee Kaylor and Mary Ellen Chambers (221).

At the age of 19, Janice Lee married **William Ray Stout** on Saturday, August 12, 1961, in Garden City Baptist Church, Roanoke, Virginia, when he was 23 years old.[391] They have two children.

William Ray was born in Beckley, Raleigh County, West Virginia, on Sunday, July 31, 1938.[392]

---

390   Birth Certificate.

391   Janice Lee Kaylor Stout.

392   William R. Stout.

Children of Janice Lee Kaylor and William Ray Stout:

+ 518   f   I. **Mary Bethel Stout** was born in Roanoke, Roanoke County, Virginia, on March 13, 1964.[393]

+ 519   m   II. **Jr William Ray Stout** was born in Roanoke, Roanoke County, Virginia, on July 26, 1968.[391]

Family of Judith Chambers and David Beh

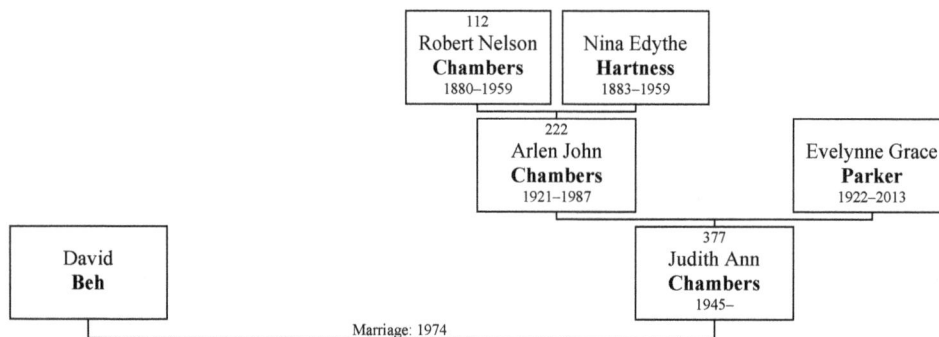

377.   **Judith Ann Chambers** was born on Thursday, March 29, 1945. She is the daughter of Arlen John Chambers (222) and Evelynne Grace Parker.

Judith Ann married **David Beh** on Saturday, March 02, 1974, in Detroit, Wayne County, Michigan.[394]

Family of Jerry Moritz and Johnie Costello

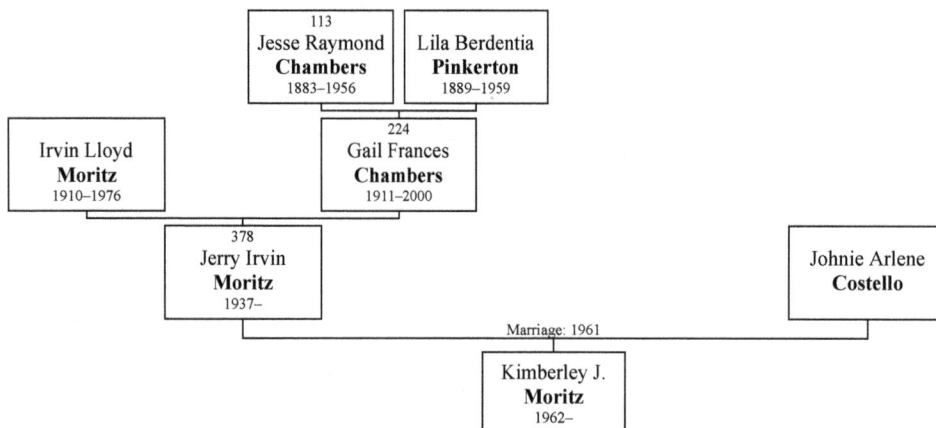

378.   **Jerry Irvin Moritz** was born on Friday, May 07, 1937, in Rushville, Sheridan County, Nebraska.[395] He is the son of Irvin Lloyd Moritz and Gail Frances Chambers (224).

Jerry Irvin married **Johnie Arlene Costello** on Saturday, June 24, 1961.[395] They have one daughter.

---

393   Mary Bethel Stout.

394   Ruth Hawks Wright.

395   Gail Chambers Moritz.

Daughter of Jerry Irvin Moritz and Johnie Arlene Costello:

f   I. **Kimberley J. Moritz** was born on September 14, 1962.[395]

Family of Karen Moritz and Earl McGuire

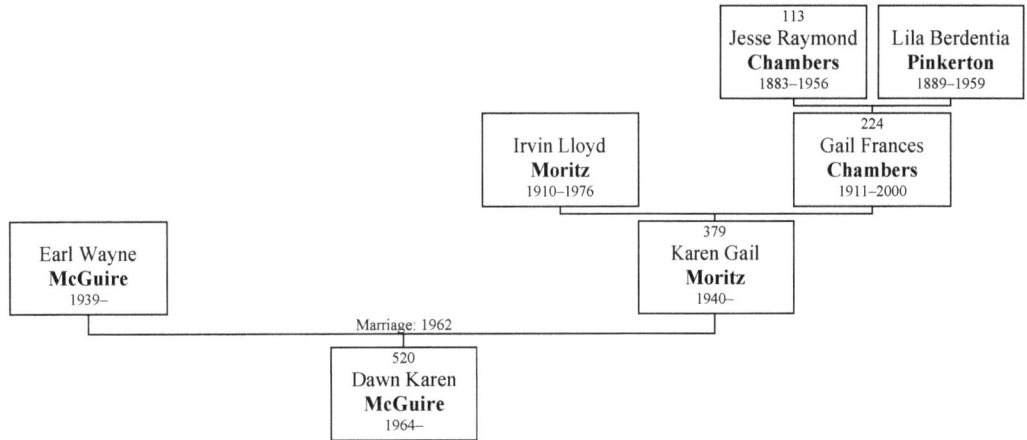

379.   **Karen Gail Moritz** was born on Tuesday, February 27, 1940, in Rushville, Sheridan County, Nebraska.[396] She is the daughter of Irvin Lloyd Moritz and Gail Frances Chambers (224).

At the age of 22, Karen Gail married **Earl Wayne McGuire** on Saturday, May 05, 1962, in Alliance, Box Butte County, Nebraska, when he was 22 years old.[397] They have one daughter.

Earl Wayne was born in Alliance, Box Butte County, Nebraska, on Saturday, October 21, 1939.[397]

Daughter of Karen Gail Moritz and Earl Wayne McGuire:

+   520   f   I. **Dawn Karen McGuire** was born in Colorado Springs, El Paso County, Colorado, on July 23, 1964.[397]

---

396   Gail Chambers Moritz.

397   Karen Moritz McGuire.

Family of Lynne Chambers and Allen Davidson

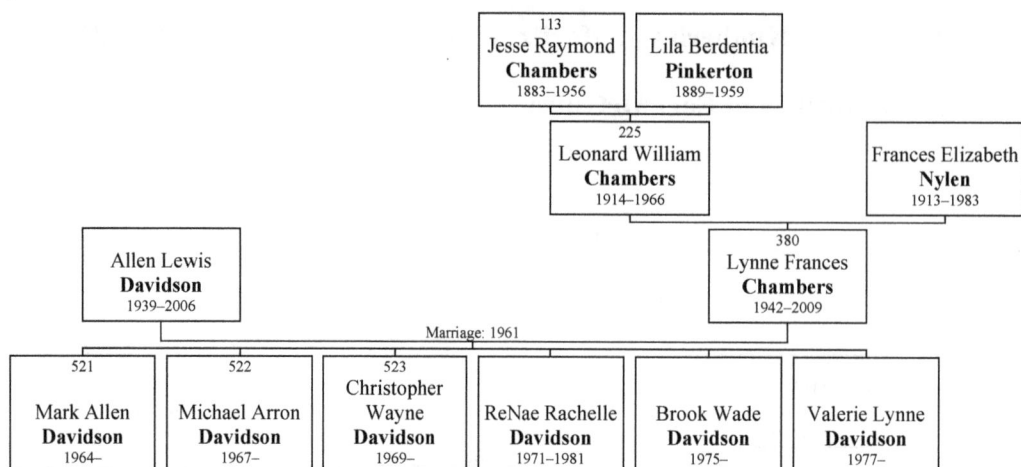

380. **Lynne Frances Chambers** was born on Thursday, July 02, 1942, in Chadron, Dawes County, Nebraska.[398] She was the daughter of Leonard William Chambers (225) and Frances Elizabeth Nylen.

Lynne Frances died in Mapleton, Utah County, Utah, on April 02, 2009, at the age of 66. She was buried in Lyman City Cemetery, Lyman, Uinta County, Wyoming (Find a Grave ID 163470986).

At the age of 18, Lynne Frances married **Allen Lewis Davidson** on Saturday, June 10, 1961, in Casper, Natrona County, Wyoming, when he was 22 years old.[399] They had six children.

Allen Lewis was born in Lyman, Uinta County, Wyoming, on Saturday, April 22, 1939.[398] He reached 66 years of age and died in Mapleton, Utah County, Utah, on February 04, 2006. Allen Lewis was buried in Lyman City Cemetery, Lyman, Uinta County, Wyoming (Find a Grave ID 39290907).

Children of Lynne Frances Chambers and Allen Lewis Davidson:

+ 521   m   I. **Mark Allen Davidson** was born in Rawlins, Carbon County, Wyoming, on November 04, 1964.[399]

+ 522   m   II. **Michael Arron Davidson** was born in Rawlins, Carbon County, Wyoming, on September 02, 1967.[398]

+ 523   m   III. **Christopher Wayne Davidson** was born in Rawlins, Carbon County, Wyoming, on November 09, 1969.[399]

        f   IV. **ReNae Rachelle Davidson** was born in Rawlins, Carbon County, Wyoming, on February 26, 1971.[398] She died in Rawlins, Carbon County, Wyoming, on May 07, 1981, at the age of 10.[398] ReNae Rachelle was buried in Lyman City Cemetery, Lyman, Uinta County, Wyoming (Find a Grave ID 163471362).

---

398   Lynne Frances Chambers.

399   Jennifer Laub Davidson.

f   V. **Brook Wade Davidson** was born in Rawlins, Carbon County, Wyoming, on November 04, 1975.[398]

f   VI. **Valerie Lynne Davidson** was born in Rawlins, Carbon County, Wyoming, on November 19, 1977.[398]

Family of Bonnie Chambers and James Spehar

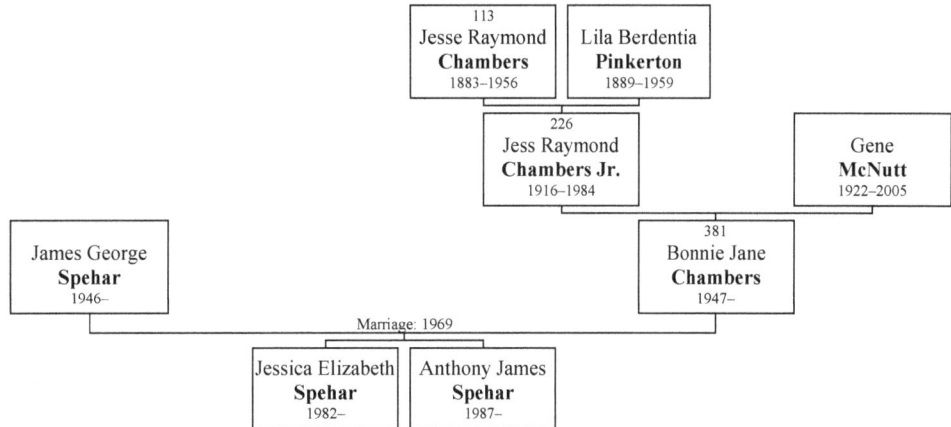

```
                    ┌────────────────┬────────────────┐
                    │     113        │                │
                    │ Jesse Raymond  │ Lila Berdentia │
                    │   Chambers     │   Pinkerton    │
                    │   1883–1956    │   1889–1959    │
                    └────────────────┴────────────────┘
                        ┌──────────────────┐          ┌──────────────┐
                        │      226         │          │              │
                        │  Jess Raymond    │          │    Gene      │
                        │  Chambers Jr.    │          │   McNutt     │
                        │   1916–1984      │          │  1922–2005   │
                        └──────────────────┘          └──────────────┘
   ┌──────────────┐                     ┌──────────────┐
   │              │                     │     381      │
   │ James George │                     │ Bonnie Jane  │
   │   Spehar     │                     │  Chambers    │
   │   1946–      │                     │   1947–      │
   └──────────────┘                     └──────────────┘
                    Marriage: 1969
              ┌──────────────────┬──────────────┐
              │ Jessica Elizabeth│ Anthony James│
              │     Spehar       │   Spehar     │
              │     1982–        │   1987–      │
              └──────────────────┴──────────────┘
```

381.   **Bonnie Jane Chambers** was born on Tuesday, July 15, 1947, in Fort Collins, Larimer County, Colorado.[400] She is the daughter of Jess Raymond Chambers Jr. (226) and Gene McNutt.

At the age of 22, Bonnie Jane married **James George Spehar** on Saturday, August 09, 1969, in St. Joseph's Catholic Church in Grand Junction, Colorado, when he was 22 years old.[400] They have two children.

James George was born in Grand Junction, Mesa County, Colorado, on Tuesday, August 20, 1946.[400]

Children of Bonnie Jane Chambers and James George Spehar:

f   I. **Jessica Elizabeth Spehar** was born in Grand Junction, Mesa County, Colorado, on April 23, 1982.[400]

m   II. **Anthony James Spehar** was born in Grand Junction, Mesa County, Colorado, on April 21, 1987.[400]

---

[400]   Gene McNutt Chambers.

Family of Cathie Chambers and Robert Zarlingo

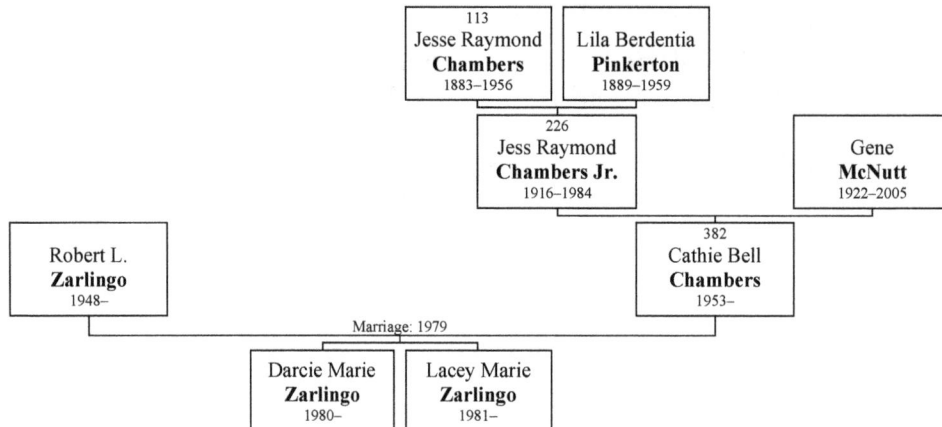

382. **Cathie Bell Chambers** was born on Tuesday, March 17, 1953, in Grand Junction, Mesa County, Colorado.[401] She is the daughter of Jess Raymond Chambers Jr. (226) and Gene McNutt.

At the age of 26, Cathie Bell married **Robert L. Zarlingo** on Sunday, October 07, 1979, in Glade Park, Colorado, when he was 31 years old.[401] They have two daughters.

Robert L. was born on Monday, July 26, 1948.[401]

Daughters of Cathie Bell Chambers and Robert L. Zarlingo:

f   I. **Darcie Marie Zarlingo** was born in Grand Junction, Mesa County, Colorado, on August 08, 1980.[401]

f   II. **Lacey Marie Zarlingo** was born in Grand Junction, Mesa County, Colorado, on December 21, 1981.[401]

Robert Chambers

383. **Robert William Chambers** was born on Thursday, August 07, 1947, in Fort Collins, Larimer County, Colorado.[402] He was the son of Robert Leland Chambers (227) and June Deloreus Eads.

Robert William died in Reeds Spring, Stone County, Missouri, on March 17, 2019, at the age of 71. He was buried in Eisenhour Cemetery, Spokane, Christian County, Missouri (Find a Grave ID 215376652).

Marriages with Andrea J. Davis and (unknown given name) Ann (Page 411) are known.

---

401   Gene McNutt Chambers.

402   Gail Chambers Moritz.

Family of Robert Chambers and Andrea Davis

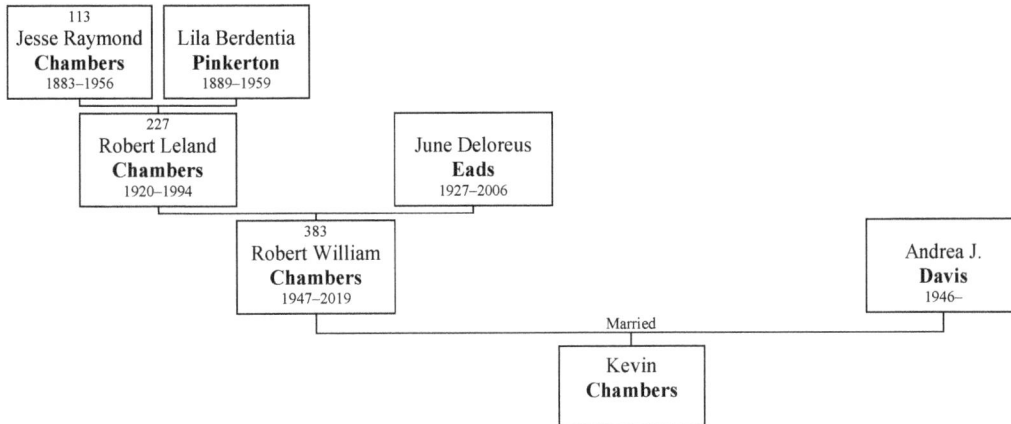

```
113                                                          Andrea J.
Jesse Raymond    Lila Berdentia                               Davis
  Chambers        Pinkerton                                   1946–
  1883–1956        1889–1959
          227                       June Deloreus
     Robert Leland                     Eads
       Chambers                       1927–2006
       1920–1994
             383
        Robert William
          Chambers
          1947–2019
                          Married
                   Kevin
                  Chambers
```

Here are the details about **Robert William Chambers's** first marriage, with Andrea J. Davis. You can read more about Robert William on page 410.

Robert William Chambers married **Andrea J. Davis**. They had one son.

Andrea J. was born on Saturday, July 27, 1946.

Son of Robert William Chambers and Andrea J. Davis:

m   I. **Kevin Chambers**.

Family of Robert Chambers and Ann

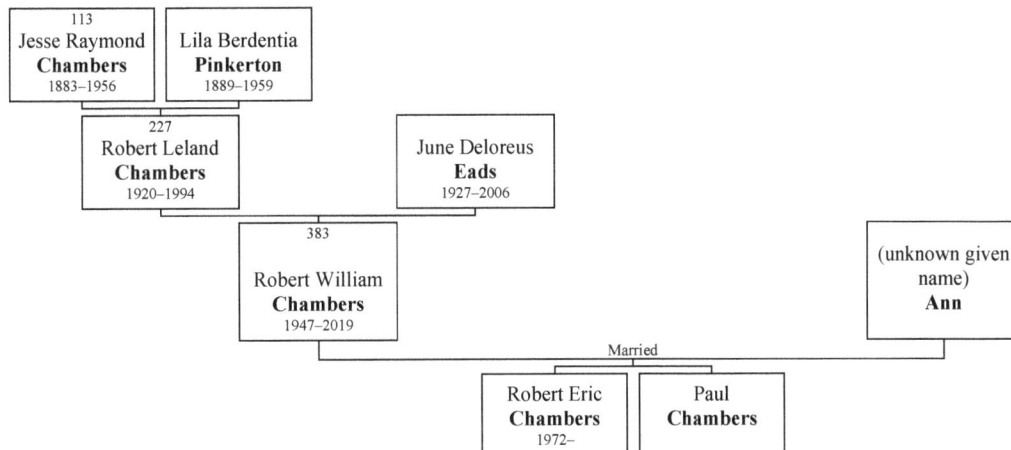

```
113                                                      (unknown given
Jesse Raymond    Lila Berdentia                              name)
  Chambers        Pinkerton                                   Ann
  1883–1956        1889–1959
          227                       June Deloreus
     Robert Leland                     Eads
       Chambers                       1927–2006
       1920–1994
             383
        Robert William
          Chambers
          1947–2019
                          Married
            Robert Eric        Paul
             Chambers        Chambers
             1972–
```

Here are the details about **Robert William Chambers's** second marriage, with (unknown given name) Ann. You can read more about Robert William on page 410.

Robert William Chambers married **(unknown given name) Ann**. They had two sons.

Sons of Robert William Chambers and (unknown given name) Ann:

m   I. **Robert Eric Chambers** was born in Missouri, USA, on July 17, 1972.[403]

m   II. **Paul Chambers**.

Family of Judith Chambers and Larry Williams

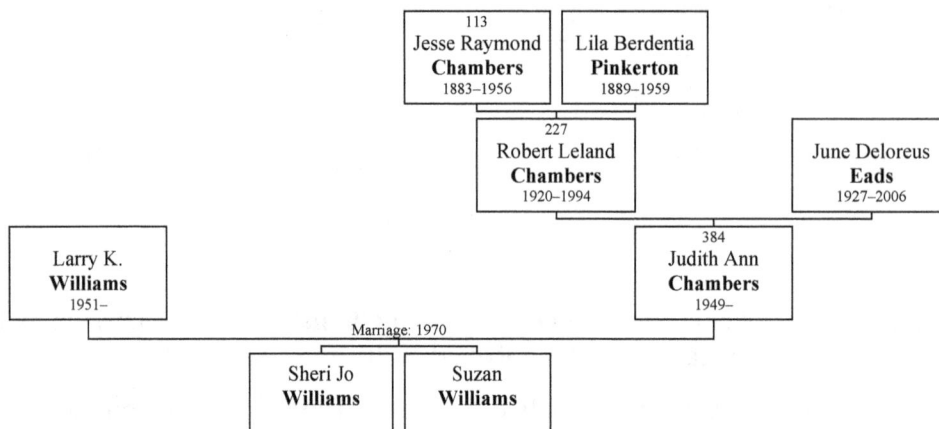

384.   **Judith Ann Chambers** was born on Friday, December 16, 1949, in Omaha, Douglas County, Nebraska.[404] She is the daughter of Robert Leland Chambers (227) and June Deloreus Eads.

Judith Ann married **Mr. Larry K. Williams** in 1970. They have two daughters.

Larry K. was born in Kansas City, Missouri, on Friday, November 02, 1951.

Daughters of Judith Ann Chambers and Larry K. Williams:

f   I. **Sheri Jo Williams**.

f   II. **Suzan Williams**.

403   Ancestry.com, Missouri, U.S., Birth Registers, 1847-2002 (Lehi, UT, USA, Ancestry.com Operations, Inc., 2007), Ancestry.com, Missouri State Archives; Jefferson City, MO, USA; Birth Index, 1920-1999. Record for Robert Eric Chambers. https://search.ancestry.co.uk/cgi-bin/sse.dll?db=1170&h=18015975&indiv=try.

404   Gail Chambers Moritz.

Family of Lila Chambers and James Anderson

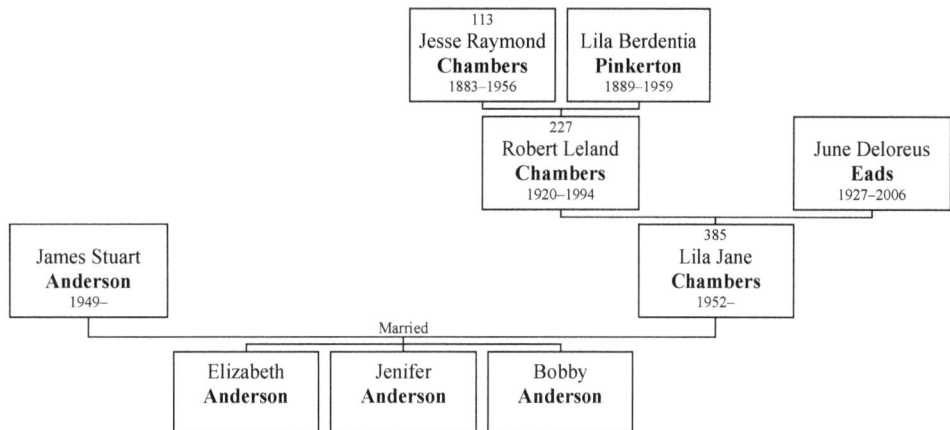

```
                        ┌──────────────┬──────────────┐
                        │     113      │Lila Berdentia│
                        │Jesse Raymond │  Pinkerton   │
                        │  Chambers    │  1889–1959   │
                        │  1883–1956   │              │
                        └──────┬───────┴──────────────┘
                        ┌──────┴───────┐         ┌──────────────┐
                        │     227      │         │June Deloreus │
                        │Robert Leland │         │    Eads      │
                        │  Chambers    │         │  1927–2006   │
                        │  1920–1994   │         └──────┬───────┘
                        └──────────────┴────────────────┘
                                       ┌──────────────┐
                                       │     385      │
                                       │  Lila Jane   │
                                       │  Chambers    │
                                       │   1952–      │
┌──────────────┐                       └──────────────┘
│ James Stuart │
│  Anderson    │
│   1949–      │
└──────┬───────┘
       └──────────Married──────────┘
   ┌──────────┬──────────┬──────────┐
   │Elizabeth │ Jenifer  │  Bobby   │
   │ Anderson │ Anderson │ Anderson │
   └──────────┴──────────┴──────────┘
```

385. **Lila Jane Chambers** was born on Wednesday, January 09, 1952, in Colorado Springs, El Paso County, Colorado.[405] She is the daughter of Robert Leland Chambers (227) and June Deloreus Eads.

She married **James Stuart Anderson**. They have three children.

James Stuart was born in Independence, Jackson County, Missouri, on Monday, May 02, 1949.[406]

Children of Lila Jane Chambers and James Stuart Anderson:

    f   I. **Elizabeth Anderson**.

    f   II. **Jenifer Anderson**.

    m   III. **Bobby Anderson**.

Family of Betty Chambers and Dale Fredrickson

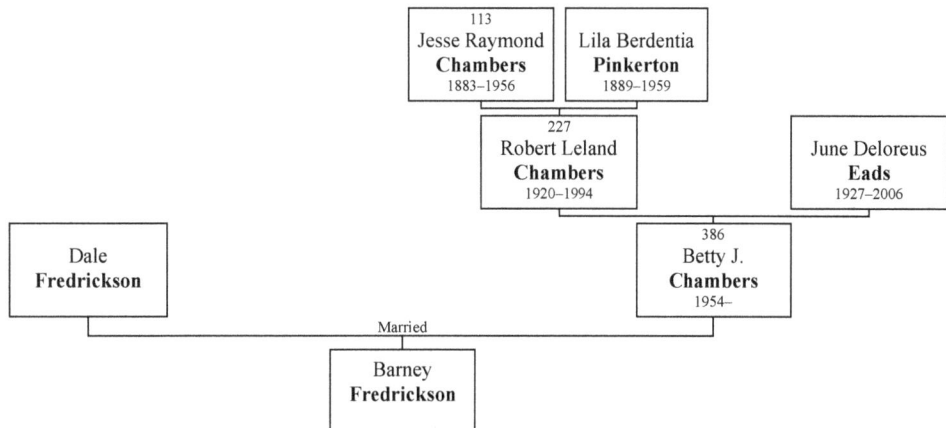

```
                        ┌──────────────┬──────────────┐
                        │     113      │Lila Berdentia│
                        │Jesse Raymond │  Pinkerton   │
                        │  Chambers    │  1889–1959   │
                        │  1883–1956   │              │
                        └──────┬───────┴──────────────┘
                        ┌──────┴───────┐         ┌──────────────┐
                        │     227      │         │June Deloreus │
                        │Robert Leland │         │    Eads      │
                        │  Chambers    │         │  1927–2006   │
                        │  1920–1994   │         └──────┬───────┘
                        └──────────────┴────────────────┘
                                       ┌──────────────┐
                                       │     386      │
                                       │  Betty J.    │
                                       │  Chambers    │
                                       │   1954–      │
┌──────────────┐                       └──────────────┘
│    Dale      │
│ Fredrickson  │
└──────┬───────┘
       └──────────Married──────────┘
          ┌──────────────┐
          │   Barney     │
          │ Fredrickson  │
          └──────────────┘
```

---

405   Gail Chambers Moritz.

406   Karen Moritz McGuire.

386. **Betty J. Chambers** was born on Saturday, March 13, 1954, in Loveland, Larimer County, Colorado.[407] She is the daughter of Robert Leland Chambers (227) and June Deloreus Eads.

She married **Dale Fredrickson**. They have one son.

Son of Betty J. Chambers and Dale Fredrickson:

     m   I. **Barney Fredrickson**.

Family of Della Kelley and Harry Larson

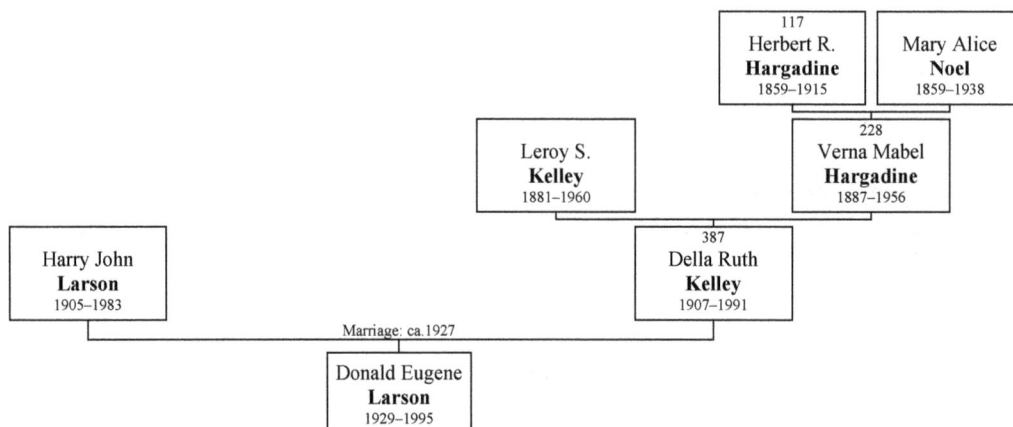

387. **Della Ruth Kelley** was born on Sunday, August 11, 1907, in Ashland, Boone County, Nebraska.[408] She was the daughter of Leroy S. Kelley and Verna Mabel Hargadine (228).

Della Ruth died in Los Angeles, Los Angeles County, California, on October 23, 1991, at the age of 84.[408] She was buried in Rose Hills Memorial Park, Whittier, Los Angeles County, California (Find a Grave ID 104952668).[408]

Della Ruth married **Harry John Larson** about 1927. They had one son.

Harry John was born in Illinois, USA, on Saturday, November 04, 1905.[408] He reached 78 years of age and died in Laguna Hills, Orange, California, on November 12, 1983.[408] Harry John was buried in Rose Hills Memorial Park, Whittier, Los Angeles County, California (Find a Grave ID 104954167).[408]

Son of Della Ruth Kelley and Harry John Larson:

     m   I. **Donald Eugene Larson** was born in Los Angeles, California, on October 14, 1929.[408] He died on January 08, 1995, at the age of 65.[408] Donald Eugene was buried in Green Hills Memorial Park, Rancho Palos Verdes, Los Angeles County, California (Find a Grave ID 15645939).

---

407   Gail Chambers Moritz.

408   Ancestry.com, Public Member Trees (Provo, UT, USA, Ancestry.com Operations, Inc., 2006), Ancestry.com, Record for Della Ruth Kelley. https://search.ancestry.co.uk/cgi-bin/sse.dll?db=1030&h=25125634030&indiv=try.

Family of La Wright and Harold Gedenberg

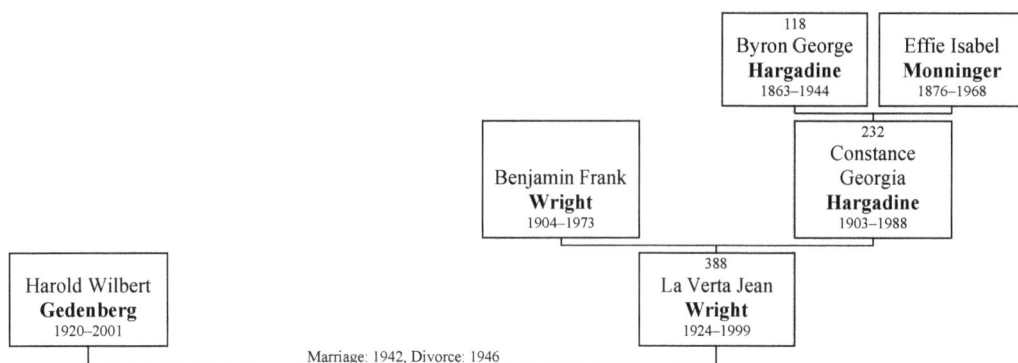

388. **La Verta Jean Wright** was born on Wednesday, December 17, 1924, in Douglas County, Nebraska. She was the daughter of Benjamin Frank Wright and Constance Georgia Hargadine (232).

La Verta Jean died in San Diego, California, on June 10, 1999, at the age of 74.

At the age of 17, La Verta Jean married **Harold Wilbert Gedenberg** on Friday, July 10, 1942, in Pacific, Washington, when he was 21 years old.[409] They were divorced in Multnomah County, Oregon, on September 04, 1946.

Harold Wilbert was born on Wednesday, December 01, 1920. He reached 80 years of age and died on February 23, 2001. Harold Wilbert was buried in Greenwood Cemetery, Astoria, Clatsop County, Oregon (Find a Grave ID 146804391).

Family of Judy Hargadine and William Mackey

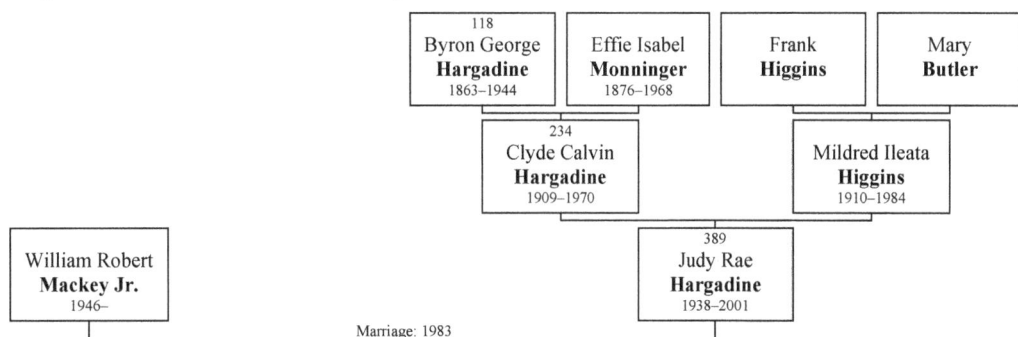

389. **Dr. Judy Rae Hargadine** was born on Thursday, December 08, 1938, in Omaha, Douglas County, Nebraska. She was the daughter of Clyde Calvin Hargadine (234) and Mildred Ileata Higgins.

Judy Rae worked as a Neurological Surgeon. She died in Bellaire, Harris County, Texas, on April 01, 2001, at the age of 62.[410] Judy Rae was buried on April 04, 2001.

---

409 Ancestry.com, Washington, U.S., Marriage Records, 1854-2013 (Provo, UT, USA, Ancestry.com Operations, Inc., 2012), Ancestry.com, Washington State Archives; Olympia, Washington; Washington Marriage Records, 1854-2013; Reference Number: sw-325-02-001-v8-000605.tiff. Record for Laverta Jeanne Wright. https://search.ancestry.co.uk/cgi-bin/sse.dll?db=2378&h=3451328&indiv=try.

410 Social Security Death Index, JUDY HARGADINE.

More facts and events for Judy Rae Hargadine:

Individual Note: Medical Doctor - Neurosurgeon

Judy Rae married **William Robert Mackey Jr.** on Sunday, February 20, 1983, in Alameda, California. William Robert was born in May 1946.

Family of Lois Hargadine and Edward Holyoke

119
Charles Howard
Hargadine
1867–1935
Lillie M.
Eby
1869–1958
George
Sorensen
Lena
Peterson
1856–1921
237
Cecil George
Hargadine
1892–1928
Pauline
Sorensen
1895–1965
Edward Augustus
Holyoke
1908–2001
390
Lois Ann
Hargadine
1915–1976
Marriage: 1940

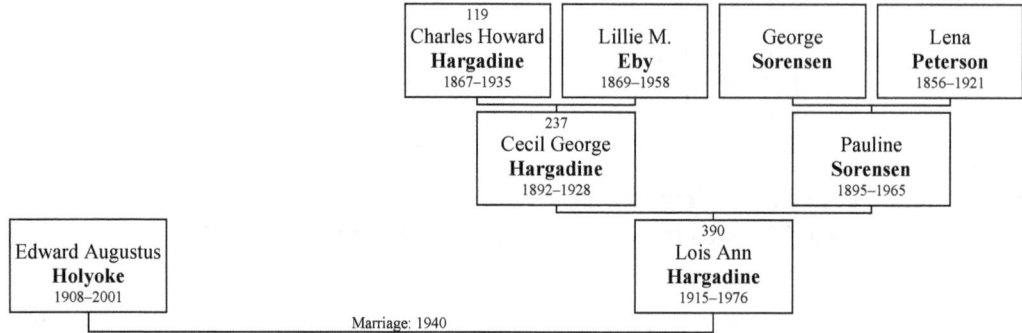

390. **Lois Ann Hargadine** was born on Wednesday, July 28, 1915, in Omaha, Douglas County, Nebraska. She was the daughter of Cecil George Hargadine (237) and Pauline Sorensen.

Lois Ann died in Omaha, Douglas County, Nebraska, in July 1976 at the age of 60. She was buried in Forest Lawn Memorial Park, Omaha, Douglas County, Nebraska, on August 02, 1976 (Find a Grave ID 182103299).

Lois Ann married **Edward Augustus Holyoke** in July 1940 in Omaha, Douglas County, Nebraska. Edward Augustus was born in Madrid, Perkins County, Nebraska, on Tuesday, March 10, 1908. He was also known as **Ed**.

Edward Augustus reached 93 years of age and died in Omaha, Douglas County, Nebraska, on August 20, 2001. He was buried in Forest Lawn Memorial Park, Omaha, Douglas County, Nebraska (Find a Grave ID 182103232).

Family of Jeannette Nystrom and Lester Olson

James Eldred
Morton
1865–1927
120
Bertha A.
Hargadine
1870–1912
Alfred Rudolph
Nystrom
1891–1974
240
Bessie Leona
Morton
1897–1978
Lester J.
Olson
1916–1994
391
Jeannette Marie
Nystrom
1918–2013
Marriage: 1942
Greg
Olson
ca.1954–

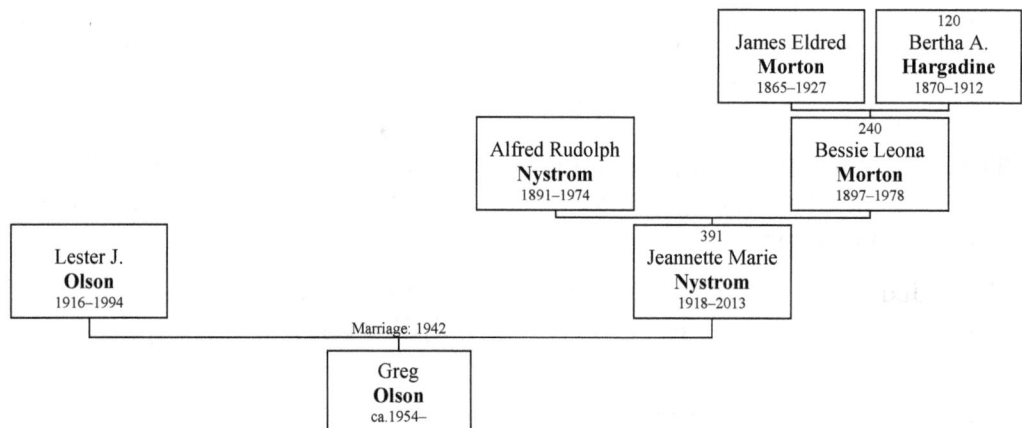

391. **Jeannette Marie Nystrom** was born on Thursday, May 02, 1918, in Spooner, Washburn County, Wisconsin. She was the daughter of Alfred Rudolph Nystrom and Bessie Leona Morton (240).

Jeannette Marie died in Spooner, Washburn County, Wisconsin, on February 08, 2013, at the age of 94. She was buried in Spooner Cemetery, Spooner, Washburn County, Wisconsin (Find a Grave ID 105078624).

At the age of 24, Jeannette Marie married **Lester J. Olson** on Wednesday, June 17, 1942, at Methodist Episcopal Church in Spooner, Washburn County, Wisconsin, when he was 26 years old. They had one son.

Lester J. was born in Minneapolis, Hennepin County, Minnesota, on Tuesday, April 25, 1916. He reached 78 years of age and died in Spooner, Washburn County, Wisconsin, on August 25, 1994.

Son of Jeannette Marie Nystrom and Lester J. Olson:

    m   I. **Greg Olson** was born about 1954.

Family of Ivan Ruse and Margaret Hargadine

392. **Ivan Arthur Ruse** was born on Saturday, January 16, 1909, in Dunlap, Peoria County, Illinois. He was the son of Arthur Roy Ruse and Helen May Sturm (243).

Ivan Arthur died in Penn Township, Stark County, Illinois, on February 17, 1975, at the age of 66. He was buried in Prospect Cemetery, Dunlap, Peoria County, Illinois (Find a Grave ID 22159596).

He married **Margaret Louise Hargadine**. They had one daughter.

Margaret Louise was born in Peoria, Peoria County, Illinois, on Friday, August 13, 1909. Margaret Louise reached 61 years of age and died in Stark County, Illinois, on December 16, 1970.

This family is duplicated because of common ancestors. For further details see person reference number 273 on page 309.

Family of Mina Aby and Earl Fitzpatrick

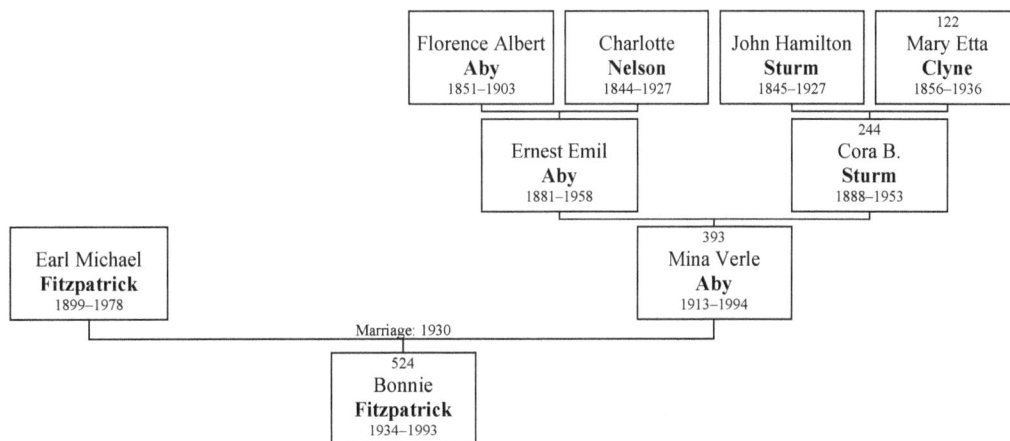

393. **Mina Verle Aby** was born on Thursday, September 04, 1913, in Dunlap, Peoria County, Illinois. She was the daughter of Ernest Emil Aby and Cora B. Sturm (244).

Mina Verle died in Toulon, Stark County, Illinois, on February 07, 1994, at the age of 80. She was buried in La Salle Cemetery, Rome, Peoria County, Illinois (Find a Grave ID 44542886).

At the age of 17, Mina Verle married **Earl Michael Fitzpatrick** on Saturday, December 20, 1930, in Peoria, Peoria County, Illinois, when he was 31 years old. They had one daughter.

Earl Michael was born in Dunlap, Peoria County, Illinois, on Friday, June 02, 1899. He reached 79 years of age and died in Edelstein, Peoria County, Illinois, on November 10, 1978. Earl Michael was buried in La Salle Cemetery, Rome, Peoria County, Illinois (Find a Grave ID 25646260).

Daughter of Mina Verle Aby and Earl Michael Fitzpatrick:

+ 524   f   I. **Bonnie Fitzpatrick** was born on July 26, 1934. She died in Dunlap, Peoria County, Illinois, on January 27, 1993, at the age of 58. Bonnie was buried in La Salle Cemetery, Rome, Peoria County, Illinois (Find a Grave ID 22159383).

Family of George Van Alstine and Helen Masters

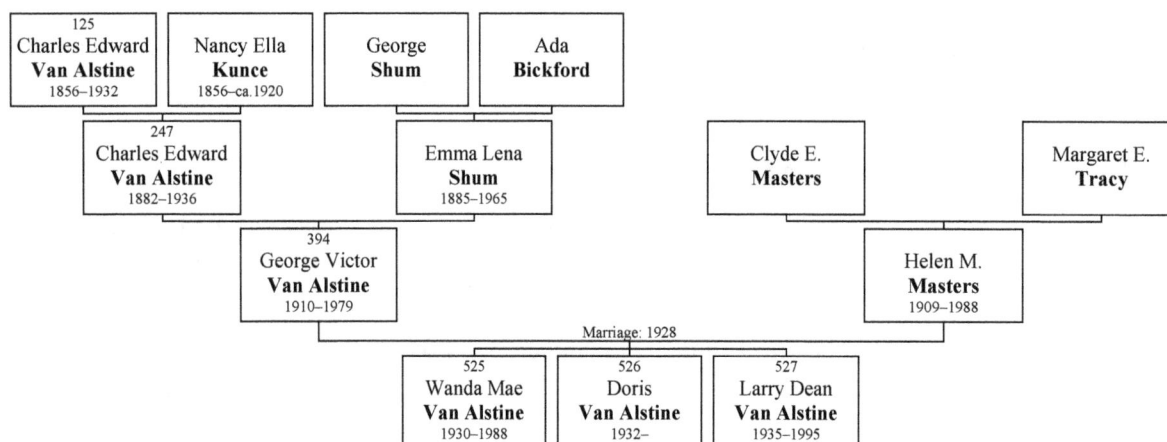

394. **George Victor Van Alstine** was born on Monday, July 11, 1910, in Washington Township, Taylor County, Iowa.[411, 412] He was the son of Charles Edward Van Alstine (247) and Emma Lena Shum.

George Victor died in White Salmon, Klickitat County, Washington, on August 07, 1979, at the age of 69.[412] He was buried in West Klickitat Cemetery, District No. 1, White Salmon, Klickitat County, Washington, on August 09, 1979 (Find a Grave ID 37766210).[412]

At the age of 18, George Victor married **Helen M. Masters** on Tuesday, December 25, 1928, in Iowa, USA, when she was 19 years old.[412, 413] They had three children.

---

411   *The Enterprise* Newspaper -White Salmon, Klickitat County, Washington, 16 AUG 1979, Pg. 4.

412   Tim Chambers, Vanalstines.GED, Date of Import: Mar 11, 2001.

413   *Bedford Times Republican* Newspaper: Bedford, Taylor County, Iowa, 27 DEC 1928.

Helen M. was born in Bedford, Taylor County, Iowa, on Saturday, April 24, 1909.[412, 414] She was the daughter of Clyde E. Masters and Margaret E. Tracy.

Helen M. reached 79 years of age and died in Vancouver, Clark County, Washington, on November 30, 1988.[412] She was buried on December 05, 1988, in West Klickitat Cemetery, District No. 1, White Salmon, Klickitat County, Washington (Find a Grave ID 37766247).[412]

Children of George Victor Van Alstine and Helen M. Masters:

+ 525   f   I. **Wanda Mae Van Alstine** was born in Gravity, Taylor County, Iowa, on July 08, 1930.[412, 415] She died in The Dalles, Wasco County, Oregon, on October 05, 1988, at the age of 58.[412] Wanda Mae was buried in West Klickitat Cemetery, District No. 1, White Salmon, Klickitat County, Washington, on October 10, 1988 (Find a Grave ID 38956606).[412]

+ 526   f   II. **Doris Van Alstine** was born in Taylor County, Iowa, on August 18, 1932.[416]

+ 527   m   III. **Larry Dean Van Alstine** was born in Iowa City, Johnson County, Iowa, on July 21, 1935.[412, 417, 418] He died in Vancouver, Clark County, Washington, on January 26, 1995, at the age of 59.[412] Larry Dean was buried in West Klickitat Cemetery, District No. 1, White Salmon, Klickitat County, Washington (Find a Grave ID 37766229).[412]

Family of Opal McKinley and William Mack

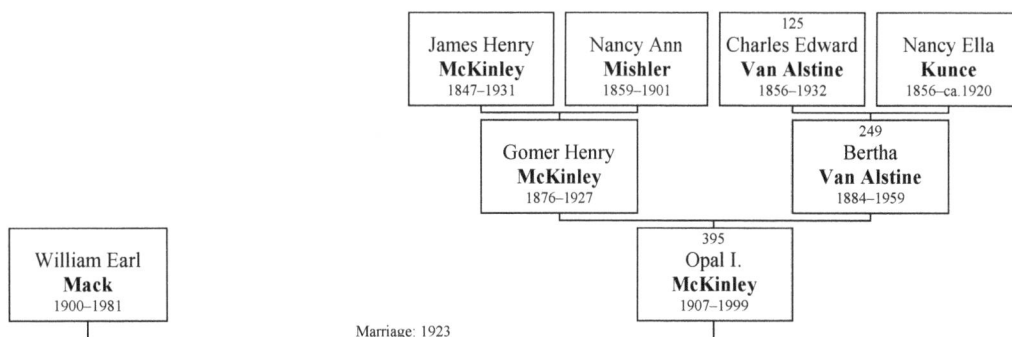

```
┌─────────────┐ ┌─────────────┐ ┌─────125─────┐ ┌─────────────┐
│ James Henry │ │ Nancy Ann   │ │Charles Edward│ │ Nancy Ella  │
│ McKinley    │ │ Mishler     │ │ Van Alstine │ │ Kunce       │
│ 1847–1931   │ │ 1859–1901   │ │ 1856–1932   │ │ 1856–ca.1920│
└─────────────┘ └─────────────┘ └─────────────┘ └─────────────┘
        ┌───────────────┐           ┌─────249─────┐
        │ Gomer Henry   │           │ Bertha      │
        │ McKinley      │           │ Van Alstine │
        │ 1876–1927     │           │ 1884–1959   │
        └───────────────┘           └─────────────┘
┌─────────────┐           ┌─────395─────┐
│ William Earl│           │ Opal I.     │
│ Mack        │           │ McKinley    │
│ 1900–1981   │           │ 1907–1999   │
└─────────────┘           └─────────────┘
              Marriage: 1923
```

395. **Opal I. McKinley** was born on Monday, March 18, 1907, in Villisca, Montgomery County, Iowa.[419] She was the daughter of Gomer Henry McKinley and Bertha Van Alstine (249).

414   *The Enterprise* Newspaper -White Salmon, Klickitat County, Washington, 8 DEC 1988, Pg. 5.

415   *The Enterprise* Newspaper -White Salmon, Klickitat County, Washington, 13 OCT 1988, Pg. 18.

416   Ancestry.com, Iowa, U.S., Births (series) 1880-1904, 1921-1944 and Delayed Births (series), 1856-1940 (Lehi, UT, USA, Ancestry.com Operations, Inc., 2017), Ancestry.com, State Historical Society of Iowa; Des Moines, Iowa; Title: Iowa Birth Records, 1888-1904. Record for Doris Jean Van Alstine. https://search.ancestry.co.uk/cgi-bin/sse.dll?db=61441&h=535105&indiv=try.

417   *The Enterprise* Newspaper -White Salmon, Klickitat County, Washington, 02 FEB 1995, Pg. 16.

418   *Bedford Times Press* Newspaper: Bedford, Taylor County, Iowa, 01 AUG 1935.

419   Ancestry.com, Public Member Trees (Provo, UT, USA, Ancestry.com Operations, Inc., 2006), Ancestry.com, Record for Opal Icie McKinley. https://search.ancestry.co.uk/cgi-bin/sse.dll?db=1030&h=412064400747&indiv=try.

Opal I. died in Clearmont, Nodaway County, Missouri, on July 25, 1999, at the age of 92.[419] She was buried in Clarinda Cemetery, Clarinda, Page County, Iowa.[419]

At the age of 16, Opal I. married **William Earl Mack** on Saturday, May 12, 1923, in Shambaugh, Page County, Iowa, when he was 22 years old.[419] William Earl was born in Carbon, Adams County, Iowa, on Thursday, July 19, 1900.[419]

He served in the military on October 24, 1945.[419] William Earl reached 80 years of age and died in Clarinda, Page County, Iowa, on February 15, 1981.[419] He was buried in Clarinda Cemetery, Clarinda, Page County, Iowa (Find a Grave ID 70052249).[419]

Mae Orme

396.　**Mae Marie Orme** was born on Tuesday, January 28, 1908, in Page County, Iowa.[420, 421] She was the daughter of William Delford Orme and Hettie Jane Van Alstine (252).

Mae Marie died in Clarinda, Page County, Iowa, on April 18, 1974, at the age of 66.[421, 422] She was buried in Clarinda Cemetery, Clarinda, Page County, Iowa (Find a Grave ID 83650420).

Marriages with Melvin Howard Scott and Lewis Parsons (Page 421) are known.

Family of Mae Orme and Melvin Scott

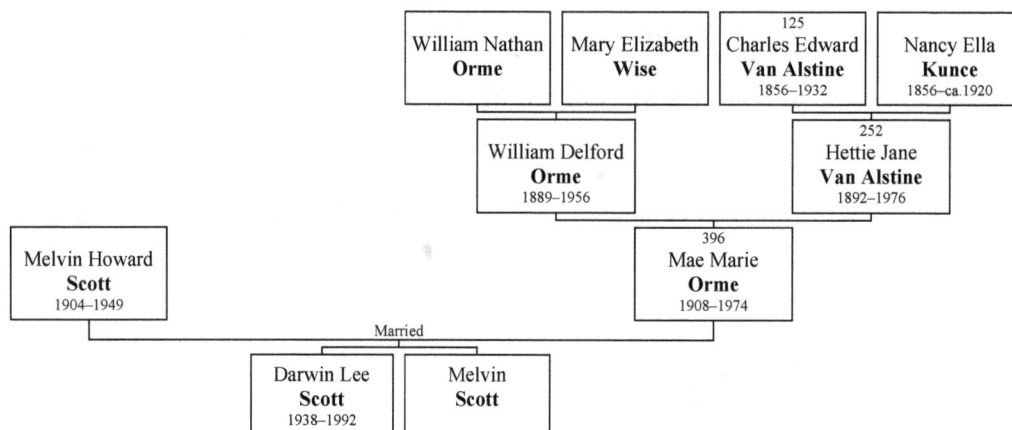

Here are the details about **Mae Marie Orme's** first marriage, with Melvin Howard Scott. You can read more about Mae Marie on page 420.

Mae Marie Orme married **Melvin Howard Scott**. They had two sons.

Melvin Howard was born in Clarinda, Page County, Iowa, on Sunday, August 14, 1904. He reached 44 years of age and died in Omaha, Douglas County, Nebraska, on April 16, 1949. Melvin Howard was buried in Clarinda Cemetery, Clarinda, Page County, Iowa (Find a Grave ID 77849822).

420　Social Security Index.

421　Tim Chambers, Vanalstines.GED, Date of Import: Mar 11, 2001.

422　*Clarinda Herald Journal* Newspaper: Clarinda, Page County, Iowa, 18 APR 1974.

Sons of Mae Marie Orme and Melvin Howard Scott:

m   I. **Darwin Lee Scott** was born in Clarinda, Page County, Iowa, on March 05, 1938. He died in Antioch, Contra Costa County, California, on August 08, 1992, at the age of 54. Darwin Lee was buried in Oak View Memorial Park, Antioch, Contra Costa County, California (Find a Grave ID 174005698).

m   II. **Melvin Scott**.

Family of Mae Orme and Lewis Parsons

Here are the details about **Mae Marie Orme's** second marriage, with Lewis Parsons. You can read more about Mae Marie on page 420.

Mae Marie Orme married **Lewis Parsons** on Tuesday, September 13, 1966.[421]

Velma Orme

397.   **Velma Alta Orme** was born on Monday, February 05, 1912, in Hawleyville, Page County, Iowa.[423, 424] She was the daughter of William Delford Orme and Hettie Jane Van Alstine (252).

Velma Alta died in Clarinda, Page County, Iowa, on April 06, 1974, at the age of 62.[424, 425] She was buried in Clarinda Cemetery, Clarinda, Page County, Iowa, on April 09, 1974 (Find a Grave ID 83627050).[424]

Marriages with Harold Lowell Brown and Ogden Lofgren (Page 423) are known.

423   Social Security Index.

424   Tim Chambers, Vanalstines.GED, Date of Import: Mar 11, 2001.

425   *Clarinda Herald Journal* Newspaper: Clarinda, Page County, Iowa, 08 APR 1974.

Family of Velma Orme and Harold Brown

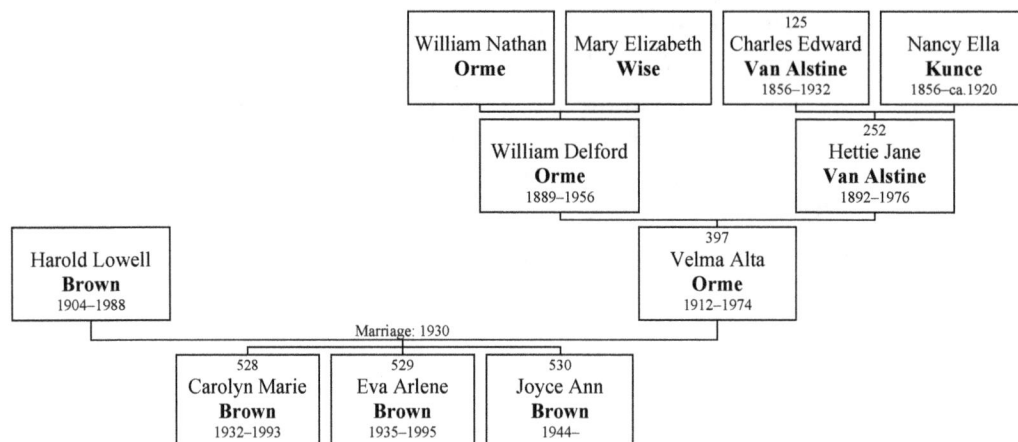

Here are the details about **Velma Alta Orme's** first marriage, with Harold Lowell Brown. You can read more about Velma Alta on page 421.

At the age of 18, Velma Alta Orme married **Harold Lowell Brown** on Friday, May 02, 1930, in Shambaugh, Page County, Iowa, when he was 26 years old. They had three daughters.

Harold Lowell was born in Shambaugh, Page County, Iowa, on Tuesday, January 26, 1904. He reached 83 years of age and died in Clarinda, Page County, Iowa, on January 11, 1988. Harold Lowell was buried in Clarinda Cemetery, Clarinda, Page County, Iowa (Find a Grave ID 79728720).

Daughters of Velma Alta Orme and Harold Lowell Brown:

+ 528　　f　　I. **Carolyn Marie Brown** was born in Clarinda, Page County, Iowa, on August 29, 1932. She died in Dickson, Dickson County, Iowa, on October 26, 1993, at the age of 61. Carolyn Marie was buried in Clarinda Cemetery, Clarinda, Page County, Iowa.

+ 529　　f　　II. **Eva Arlene Brown** was born in Shambaugh, Page County, Iowa, on May 05, 1935. She died in San Bernardino, San Bernardino County, California, on April 14, 1995, at the age of 59. Eva Arlene was buried in Clarinda Cemetery, Clarinda, Page County, Iowa (Find a Grave ID 195385891).

+ 530　　f　　III. **Joyce Ann Brown** was born in Clarinda, Page County, Iowa, on March 07, 1944.

Family of Velma Orme and Ogden Lofgren

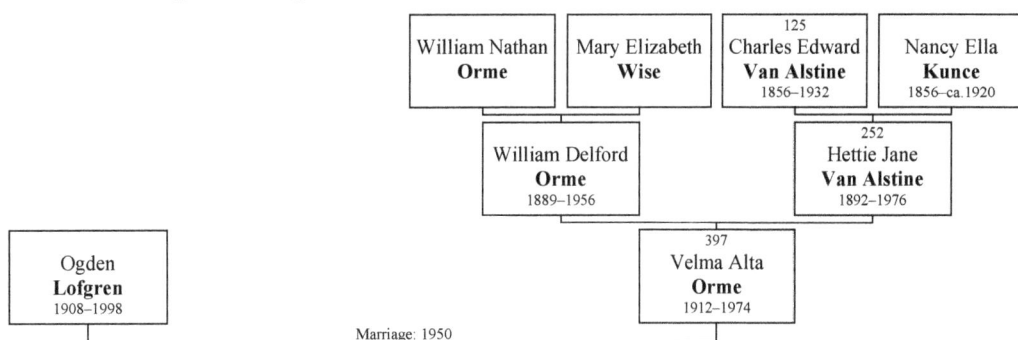

```
┌──────────────┬──────────────┬──────────────┬──────────────┐
│William Nathan│Mary Elizabeth│     125      │  Nancy Ella  │
│     Orme     │     Wise     │Charles Edward│    Kunce     │
│              │              │ Van Alstine  │ 1856–ca.1920 │
│              │              │  1856–1932   │              │
└──────────────┴──────────────┴──────────────┴──────────────┘
        William Delford              252
            Orme                  Hettie Jane
          1889–1956               Van Alstine
                                   1892–1976
                      397
                  Velma Alta
                     Orme
                   1912–1974
  Ogden
  Lofgren
  1908–1998
              Marriage: 1950
```

Here are the details about **Velma Alta Orme's** second marriage, with Ogden Lofgren. You can read more about Velma Alta on page 421.

At the age of 38, Velma Alta Orme married **Ogden Lofgren** on Wednesday, December 20, 1950, when he was 42 years old.[424] Ogden was born on Sunday, March 22, 1908.[423, 424]

He reached 90 years of age and died on September 28, 1998.[424]

Dale Van Alstine

398.   **Dale Vernon Van Alstine** was born on Monday, December 30, 1912, in Taylor County, Iowa. He was the son of Lewis George Van Alstine (253) and Bertha Leona Sollars.

Dale Vernon died in Yuma, Yuma County, Arizona, on March 26, 1988, at the age of 75. He was buried in Clarinda Cemetery, Clarinda, Page County, Iowa (Find a Grave ID 80489337).

Marriages with Margaret Rose Lack and Gladys Lucille Williamson (Page 424) are known.

Family of Dale Van Alstine and Margaret Lack

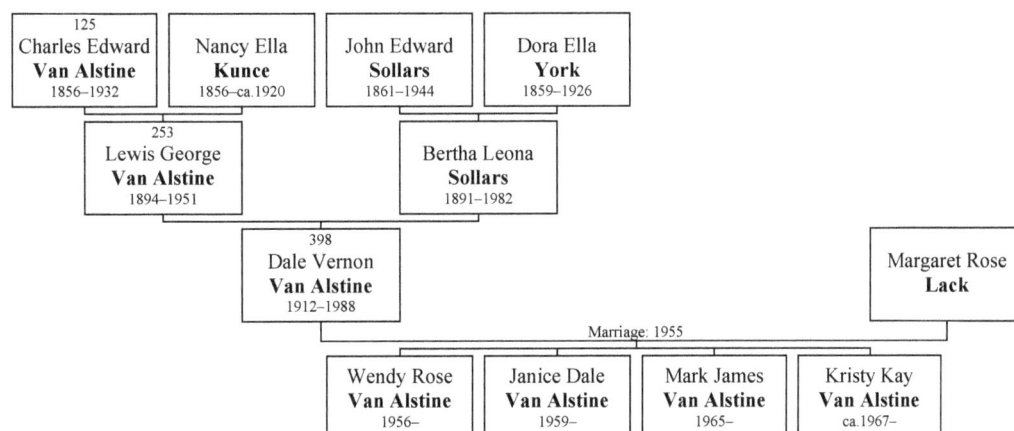

```
┌──────────────┬──────────────┬──────────────┬──────────────┐
│     125      │  Nancy Ella  │ John Edward  │  Dora Ella   │
│Charles Edward│    Kunce     │   Sollars    │    York      │
│ Van Alstine  │ 1856–ca.1920 │  1861–1944   │  1859–1926   │
│  1856–1932   │              │              │              │
└──────────────┴──────────────┴──────────────┴──────────────┘
        253                      Bertha Leona
    Lewis George                   Sollars
    Van Alstine                   1891–1982
     1894–1951
                      398
                  Dale Vernon                    Margaret Rose
                  Van Alstine                        Lack
                   1912–1988
                              Marriage: 1955
  Wendy Rose    Janice Dale    Mark James    Kristy Kay
  Van Alstine   Van Alstine    Van Alstine   Van Alstine
    1956–         1959–          1965–         ca.1967–
```

Here are the details about **Dale Vernon Van Alstine's** first marriage, with Margaret Rose Lack. You can read more about Dale Vernon on page 423.

Dale Vernon Van Alstine married **Margaret Rose Lack** on Saturday, July 23, 1955, in Beaconsfield Terrace, Rusden, England.[426, 427] They had four children.

Children of Dale Vernon Van Alstine and Margaret Rose Lack:

f	I.	**Wendy Rose Van Alstine** was born in Red Oak, Montgomery County, Iowa, on August 04, 1956.[427]
f	II.	**Janice Dale Van Alstine** was born in Clarinda, Page County, Iowa, on February 18, 1959.[427]
m	III.	**Mark James Van Alstine** was born on July 01, 1965.[427]
f	IV.	**Kristy Kay Van Alstine** was born about October 26, 1967.[427]

Family of Dale Van Alstine and Gladys Williamson

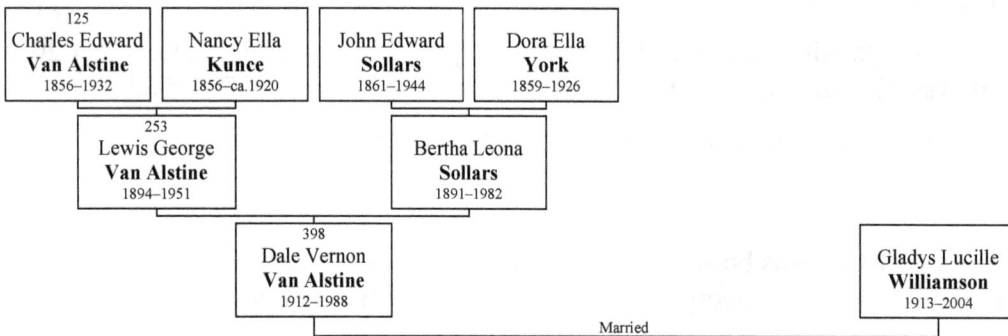

125 Charles Edward **Van Alstine** 1856–1932	Nancy Ella **Kunce** 1856–ca.1920	John Edward **Sollars** 1861–1944	Dora Ella **York** 1859–1926

253
Lewis George
Van Alstine
1894–1951

Bertha Leona
Sollars
1891–1982

398
Dale Vernon
Van Alstine
1912–1988

Gladys Lucille
Williamson
1913–2004

Married

Here are the details about **Dale Vernon Van Alstine's** second marriage, with Gladys Lucille Williamson. You can read more about Dale Vernon on page 423.

Dale Vernon Van Alstine married **Gladys Lucille Williamson**. Gladys Lucille was born in Nodaway County, Missouri, on Sunday, June 29, 1913.

She reached 90 years of age and died in Villisca, Montgomery County, Iowa, on April 21, 2004. Gladys Lucille was buried in Clarinda Cemetery, Clarinda, Page County, Iowa (Find a Grave ID 236665276).

---

426   *Clarinda Herald Journal* Newspaper: Clarinda, Page County, Iowa, 29 SEP 1955.

427   Tim Chambers, Vanalstines.GED, Date of Import: Mar 11, 2001.

Family of Letha Van Alstine and Max Williamson

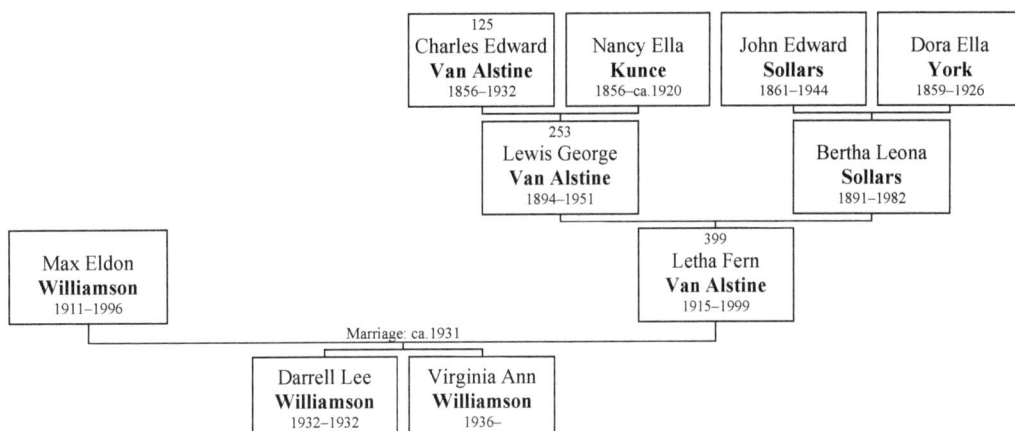

399. **Letha Fern Van Alstine** was born on Friday, March 05, 1915, in Taylor County, Iowa.[428] She was the daughter of Lewis George Van Alstine (253) and Bertha Leona Sollars.

Letha Fern died in White Salmon, Klickitat County, Washington, on July 07, 1999, at the age of 84. She was buried in West Klickitat Cemetery, District No. 1, White Salmon, Klickitat County, Washington (Find a Grave ID 36316760).

Letha Fern married **Max Eldon Williamson** about January 1931.[428, 429] They had two children.

Max Eldon was born in Hopkins, Nodaway County, Missouri, on Tuesday, March 21, 1911. He reached 85 years of age and died in Vancouver, Clark County, Washington, on November 24, 1996. Max Eldon was buried in West Klickitat Cemetery, District No. 1, White Salmon, Klickitat County, Washington (Find a Grave ID 36316751).

Children of Letha Fern Van Alstine and Max Eldon Williamson:

m   I. **Darrell Lee Williamson** was born in Taylor County, Iowa, on March 25, 1932. He died in Iowa City, Johnson County, Iowa, on November 28, 1932. Darrell Lee was buried in Dallas Center Cemetery, New Market, Taylor County, Iowa, on December 01, 1932 (Find a Grave ID 57942220).

f   II. **Virginia Ann Williamson** was born in Amity, Page County, Iowa, on July 21, 1936.

Lewis Van Alstine

400. **Lewis Doran Van Alstine** was born on Thursday, November 29, 1917, in New Market, Taylor County, Iowa.[430, 431] He was the son of Lewis George Van Alstine (253) and Bertha Leona Sollars.

---

428   Tim Chambers, Vanalstines.GED, Date of Import: Mar 11, 2001.

429   *Clarinda Journal* Newspaper: Clarinda, Page County, Iowa, 22 JAN 1931.

430   Social Security Death Index.

431   Tim Chambers, Vanalstines.GED, Date of Import: Mar 11, 2001.

Lewis Doran died in Stuart, Adair County, Iowa, on August 26, 1984, at the age of 66.[431, 432] He was buried in Clarinda Cemetery, Clarinda, Page County, Iowa (Find a Grave ID 79274588).[431]

Marriages with Virginia Helen Waxmonsky and Orpha Carolyn Passick (Page 427) are known.

Family of Lewis Van Alstine and Virginia Waxmonsky

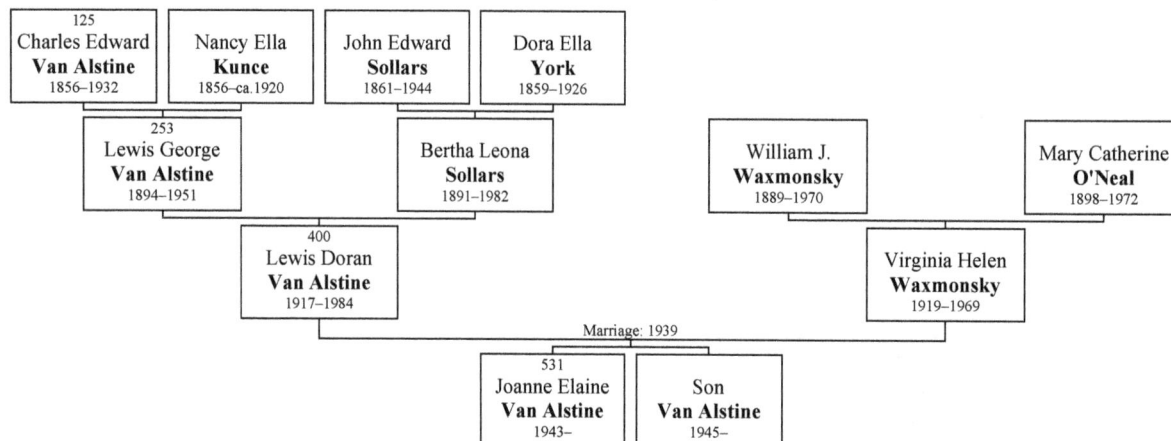

Here are the details about **Lewis Doran Van Alstine's** first marriage, with Virginia Helen Waxmonsky. You can read more about Lewis Doran on page 425.

Lewis Doran Van Alstine married **Virginia Helen Waxmonsky** on Sunday, April 09, 1939, in Clarinda, Page County, Iowa.[431, 433] They had two children.

Virginia Helen was born in 1919.[431] She was the daughter of William J. Waxmonsky and Mary Catherine O'Neal.

Virginia Helen reached 50 years of age and died in Adel, Dallas County, Iowa, on December 04, 1969.[431, 434] She was buried in Clarinda Cemetery, Clarinda, Page County, Iowa (Find a Grave ID 79274634).[431]

Children of Lewis Doran Van Alstine and Virginia Helen Waxmonsky:

+ 531   f   I. **Joanne Elaine Van Alstine** was born in Clarinda, Page County, Iowa, on December 28, 1943.[431, 435, 436]

       m   II. **Son Van Alstine** was born on September 27, 1945.[431, 437]

---

432   *Clarinda Herald Journal* Newspaper: Clarinda, Page County, Iowa, 30 AUG 1984.

433   *Clarinda Herald Journal* Newspaper: Clarinda, Page County, Iowa, 06 APR & 13 APR 1939.

434   *Clarinda Herald Journal* Newspaper: Clarinda, Page County, Iowa, 04 DEC 1969.

435   *Bedford Times Press* Newspaper: Bedford, Taylor County, Iowa, 06 JAN 1944.

436   *Clarinda Herald Journal* Newspaper: Clarinda, Page County, Iowa, 30 DEC 1943 & 03 JAN 1944.

437   *Clarinda Herald Journal* Newspaper: Clarinda, Page County, Iowa, 01 OCT 1945.

Family of Lewis Van Alstine and Orpha Passick

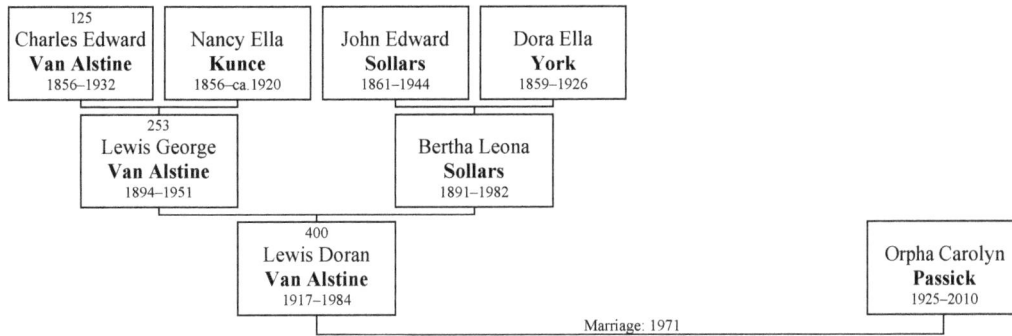

Here are the details about **Lewis Doran Van Alstine's** second marriage, with Orpha Carolyn Passick. You can read more about Lewis Doran on page 425.

At the age of 53, Lewis Doran Van Alstine married **Orpha Carolyn Passick** on Saturday, October 02, 1971, in Earlham, Madison County, Iowa, when she was 46 years old.[431, 438] Orpha Carolyn was born in Arcadia Township, Carroll County, Iowa, on Saturday, January 31, 1925.

She reached 85 years of age and died in Iowa, USA, on October 18, 2010. Orpha Carolyn was buried in Earlham Cemetery, Earlham, Madison County, Iowa (Find a Grave ID 73166801).

Family of Vona Van Alstine and Howard Robertson

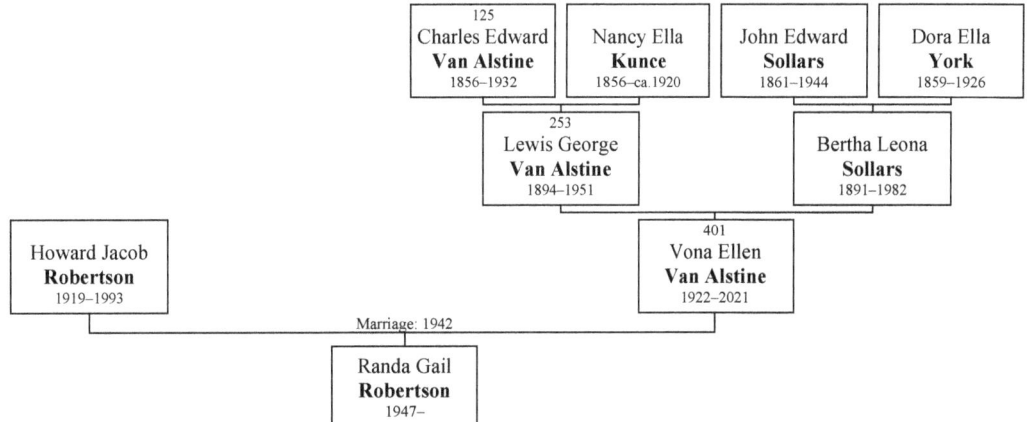

401. **Vona Ellen Van Alstine** was born on Monday, February 27, 1922, in Nodaway, Page County, Iowa.[439, 440] She was the daughter of Lewis George Van Alstine (253) and Bertha Leona Sollars.

---

438   *Clarinda Herald Journal* Newspaper: Clarinda, Page County, Iowa, 11 OCT 1971.

439   *Clarinda Herald* Newspaper: Clarinda, Page County, Iowa, 16 MAR 1922.

440   Tim Chambers, Vanalstines.GED, Date of Import: Mar 11, 2001.

Vona Ellen died in Iowa City, Johnson County, Iowa, on March 28, 2021, at the age of 99. She was buried in Oakland Cemetery, Iowa City, Johnson County, Iowa (Find a Grave ID 225111194).

At the age of 20, Vona Ellen married **Howard Jacob Robertson** on Sunday, June 07, 1942, in Clarinda, Page County, Iowa, when he was 22 years old.[440, 441] They had one son.

Howard Jacob was born in Confidence, Wayne County, Iowa, on Tuesday, November 18, 1919. He reached 73 years of age and died in Iowa City, Johnson County, Iowa, on July 20, 1993. Howard Jacob was buried in Oakland Cemetery, Iowa City, Johnson County, Iowa (Find a Grave ID 14710452).

Son of Vona Ellen Van Alstine and Howard Jacob Robertson:

m   I. **Randa Gail Robertson** was born in Iowa City, Johnson County, Iowa, on March 13, 1947.[440, 442]

Family of Opal Van Alstine and Herman Shum

402.   **Opal Lavon Van Alstine** was born on Tuesday, July 29, 1919, in New Market, Taylor County, Iowa.[443] She was the daughter of Archibald E. Van Alstine (254) and Myrtle Helen Wallace.

Opal Lavon died on October 28, 1989, at the age of 70. She was buried in Valley View Cemetery, Sutherlin, Douglas County, Oregon (Find a Grave ID 129953448).

Opal Lavon married **Herman Shum** on Sunday, October 02, 1938, in Bingen, Skamania County, Washington.

441   *Clarinda Herald Journal* Newspaper: Clarinda, Page County, Iowa, 11 JUN 1942.

442   *Clarinda Herald Journal* Newspaper: Clarinda, Page County, Iowa, 20 MAR 1947.

443   Tim Chambers, Vanalstines.GED, Date of Import: Mar 11, 2001.

Family of Velda Lee and Gary Roe

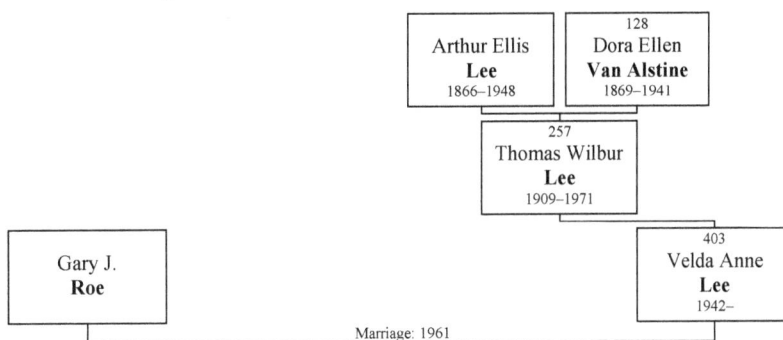

```
                    ┌─────────────┬──────────────┐
                    │ Arthur Ellis│     128      │
                    │    Lee      │  Dora Ellen  │
                    │  1866–1948  │ Van Alstine  │
                    │             │  1869–1941   │
                    └──────┬──────┴──────────────┘
                           │      257
                           │ Thomas Wilbur
                           │     Lee
                           │  1909–1971
                           └──────────┐
  ┌─────────────┐              ┌──────┴──────┐
  │   Gary J.   │              │     403     │
  │     Roe     │              │ Velda Anne  │
  │             │              │    Lee      │
  │             │              │   1942–     │
  └──────┬──────┴──────────────┴─────────────┘
       Marriage: 1961
```

403.   Velda Anne Lee was born on Wednesday, April 29, 1942.[444] She is the daughter of Thomas Wilbur Lee (257).

Velda Anne married **Gary J. Roe** on Wednesday, December 27, 1961.[444]

Family of Norma Clifton and Harold Pugmire

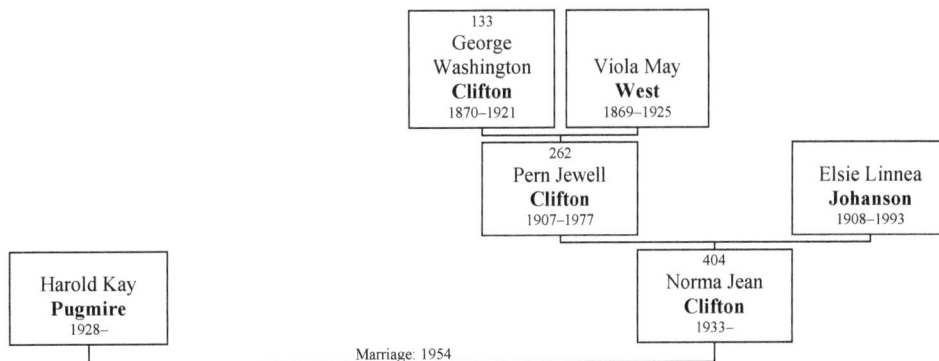

```
                    ┌─────────────┬──────────────┐
                    │    133      │              │
                    │  George     │  Viola May   │
                    │ Washington  │    West      │
                    │  Clifton    │  1869–1925   │
                    │  1870–1921  │              │
                    └──────┬──────┴──────────────┘
                           │  262
                           │ Pern Jewell        ┌─────────────┐
                           │   Clifton          │ Elsie Linnea│
                           │  1907–1977         │  Johanson   │
                           └──────────┐         │  1908–1993  │
                                      │         └──────┬──────┘
  ┌─────────────┐              ┌──────┴──────┐
  │ Harold Kay  │              │     404     │
  │  Pugmire    │              │ Norma Jean  │
  │   1928–     │              │  Clifton    │
  │             │              │   1933–     │
  └──────┬──────┴──────────────┴─────────────┘
       Marriage: 1954
```

404.   Norma Jean Clifton was born on Friday, April 07, 1933, in Seattle, King County, Washington. She is the daughter of Pern Jewell Clifton (262) and Elsie Linnea Johanson.

At the age of 21, Norma Jean married **Harold Kay Pugmire** on Wednesday, October 13, 1954, in Idaho Falls, Bannock County, Idaho, when he was 25 years old.[445] Harold Kay was born in Pocatello, Bannock County, Idaho, on Thursday, November 01, 1928.

---

444   Tim Chambers, Vanalstines.GED, Date of Import: Mar 11, 2001.

445   Marriage Certificate No. 303887.

Family of Jerry Clifton and Annalou Flowers

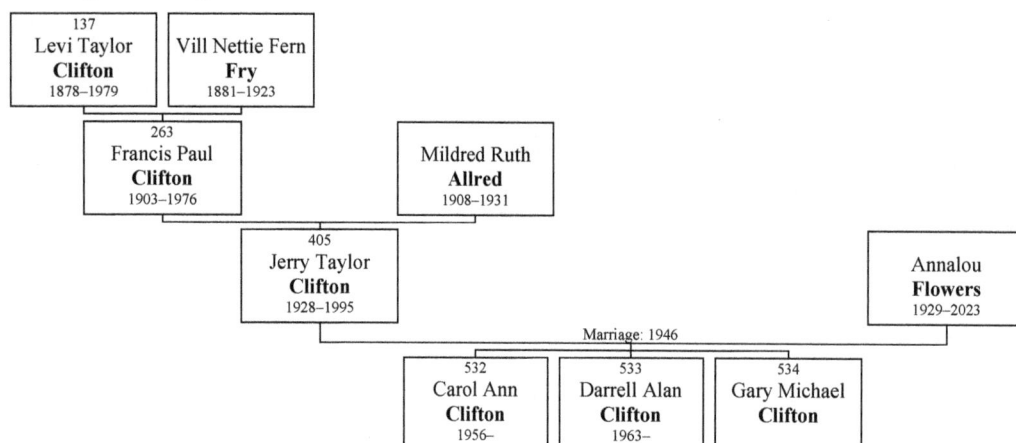

405. **Dr. Jerry Taylor Clifton** was born on Saturday, June 09, 1928, in Tulsa, Tulsa County, Oklahoma. He was the son of Francis Paul Clifton (263) and Mildred Ruth Allred.

Jerry Taylor died in Las Vegas, Clark County, Nevada, on September 04, 1995, at the age of 67. He was buried in Bunkers Memory Gardens Cemetery, Las Vegas, Clark County, Nevada (Find a Grave ID 23317842).

Jerry Taylor married **Annalou Flowers** in 1946. They had three children.

Annalou was born in Erick Township, Beckham County, Oklahoma, on Tuesday, June 18, 1929.[446] She was also known as **Dute**.

Annalou reached 93 years of age and died in Santa Clarita, Los Angeles County, California, on April 04, 2023.[446] She was buried in Bunkers Memory Gardens Cemetery, Las Vegas, Clark County, Nevada (Find a Grave ID 251994271).[446]

Children of Jerry Taylor Clifton and Annalou Flowers:

+ 532   f   I. **Carol Ann Clifton** was born in November 1956.

+ 533   m   II. **Darrell Alan Clifton** was born in August 1963.

+ 534   m   III. **Gary Michael Clifton.**

William Hargadine

406. **William Charles Hargadine** was born on Monday, May 18, 1931, in Princeville, Peoria County, Illinois. He was the son of Edgar Charles Hargadine (266) and Zella Marie Bliss.

William Charles served in the military: U.S. Air Force, Bronze Star & Korean Service Medal. He died in Dellwood, Pinellas County, Florida, on October 28, 2004, at the age of 73. William Charles was buried in Evergreen Memorial Gardens, Kewanee, Henry County, Illinois (Find a Grave ID 145824166).

Marriages with Lela V. Morrison and Edythe Conger (Page 431) are known.

---

446   Ancestry.com, U.S., Find a Grave® Index, 1600s-Current (Lehi, UT, USA, Ancestry.com Operations, Inc., 2012), Ancestry.com, Record for Annalou Clifton. https://search.ancestry.co.uk/cgi-bin/sse.dll?db=60525&h=226360552&indiv=try.

Family of William Hargadine and Lela Morrison

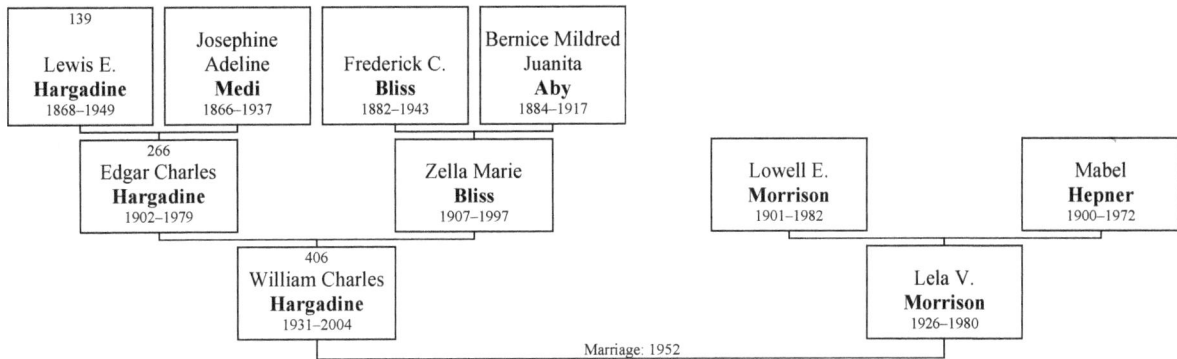

139	Josephine		Bernice Mildred			
Lewis E. **Hargadine** 1868–1949	Adeline **Medi** 1866–1937	Frederick C. **Bliss** 1882–1943	Juanita **Aby** 1884–1917			

266 Edgar Charles **Hargadine** 1902–1979

Zella Marie **Bliss** 1907–1997

Lowell E. **Morrison** 1901–1982

Mabel **Hepner** 1900–1972

406 William Charles **Hargadine** 1931–2004

Lela V. **Morrison** 1926–1980

Marriage: 1952

Here are the details about **William Charles Hargadine's** first marriage, with Lela V. Morrison. You can read more about William Charles on page 430.

At the age of 21, William Charles Hargadine married **Lela V. Morrison** on Sunday, June 22, 1952, in Kewanee, Henry County, Illinois, when she was 25 years old. Lela V. was born in Illinois, USA, on Saturday, July 03, 1926. She was the daughter of Lowell E. Morrison and Mabel Hepner.

Lela V. reached 53 years of age and died in Kewanee, Henry County, Illinois, on February 25, 1980. She was buried in Evergreen Memorial Gardens, Kewanee, Henry County, Illinois (Find a Grave ID 144926326).

Family of William Hargadine and Edythe Conger

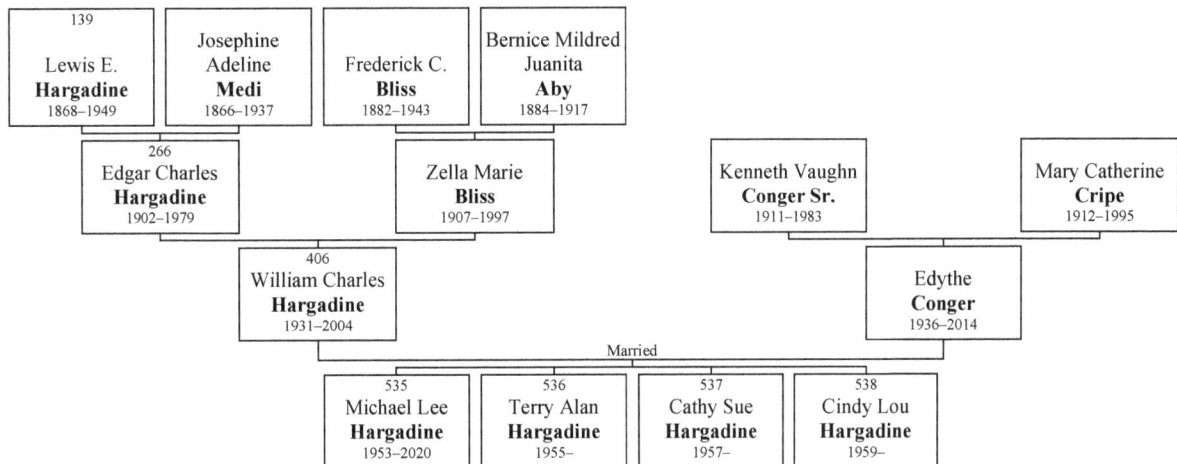

139	Josephine		Bernice Mildred			
Lewis E. **Hargadine** 1868–1949	Adeline **Medi** 1866–1937	Frederick C. **Bliss** 1882–1943	Juanita **Aby** 1884–1917			

266 Edgar Charles **Hargadine** 1902–1979

Zella Marie **Bliss** 1907–1997

Kenneth Vaughn **Conger Sr.** 1911–1983

Mary Catherine **Cripe** 1912–1995

406 William Charles **Hargadine** 1931–2004

Edythe **Conger** 1936–2014

Married

535	536	537	538
Michael Lee **Hargadine** 1953–2020	Terry Alan **Hargadine** 1955–	Cathy Sue **Hargadine** 1957–	Cindy Lou **Hargadine** 1959–

Here are the details about **William Charles Hargadine's** second marriage, with Edythe Conger. You can read more about William Charles on page 430.

William Charles Hargadine married **Edythe Conger**. They had four children.

Edythe was born in Peoria, Peoria County, Illinois, on Friday, April 17, 1936. She was the daughter of Kenneth Vaughn Conger Sr. and Mary Catherine Cripe. She was also known as **Ede**.

Edythe reached 77 years of age and died on March 30, 2014.

Children of William Charles Hargadine and Edythe Conger:

+ 535   m   I. **Michael Lee Hargadine** was born in Kewanee, Henry County, Illinois, on October 14, 1953. He died in Polk, Florida, USA, on October 11, 2020, at the age of 66.

+ 536   ´ m   II. **Terry Alan Hargadine** was born in Kewanee, Henry County, Illinois, on May 07, 1955.

+ 537   f   III. **Cathy Sue Hargadine** was born in Kewanee, Henry County, Illinois, on June 28, 1957.

+ 538   f   IV. **Cindy Lou Hargadine** was born in Kewanee, Henry County, Illinois, on January 21, 1959.

Alice Hargadine

407.   **Alice Louise Hargadine** was born on Tuesday, May 22, 1934, in Toulon, Stark County, Illinois. She was the daughter of Edgar Charles Hargadine (266) and Zella Marie Bliss.

Alice Louise died in Jackson, Hinds County, Mississippi, on January 06, 2010, at the age of 75. She was buried in Toulon Cemetery, Toulon, Stark County, Illinois (Find a Grave ID 46749179).

Marriages with Lloyd Russell Phillips and Richard Jones (Page 433) are known.

Family of Alice Hargadine and Lloyd Phillips

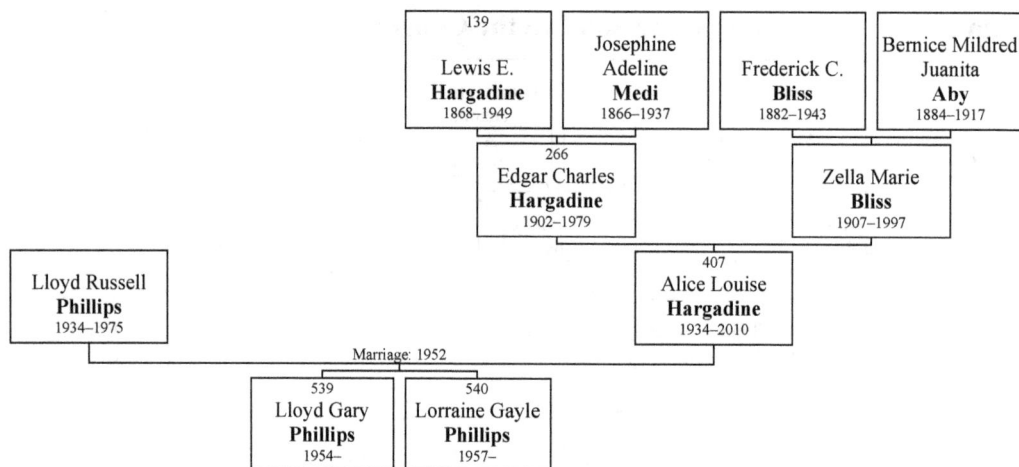

Here are the details about **Alice Louise Hargadine's** first marriage, with Lloyd Russell Phillips. You can read more about Alice Louise on page 432.

At the age of 18, Alice Louise Hargadine married **Lloyd Russell Phillips** on Sunday, November 30, 1952, when he was 18 years old. They had two children.

Lloyd Russell was born in West Jersey, Stark County, Illinois, on Thursday, May 17, 1934. He reached 40 years of age and died in Marianna, Jackson County, Florida, on February 01, 1975. Lloyd Russell was buried in Toulon Cemetery, Toulon, Stark County, Illinois (Find a Grave ID 64827939).

Children of Alice Louise Hargadine and Lloyd Russell Phillips:

+ 539 m I. **Lloyd Gary Phillips** was born in Kewanee, Henry County, Illinois, on September 16, 1954.

+ 540 f II. **Lorraine Gayle Phillips** was born in Kewanee, Henry County, Illinois, on August 27, 1957.

Family of Alice Hargadine and Richard Jones

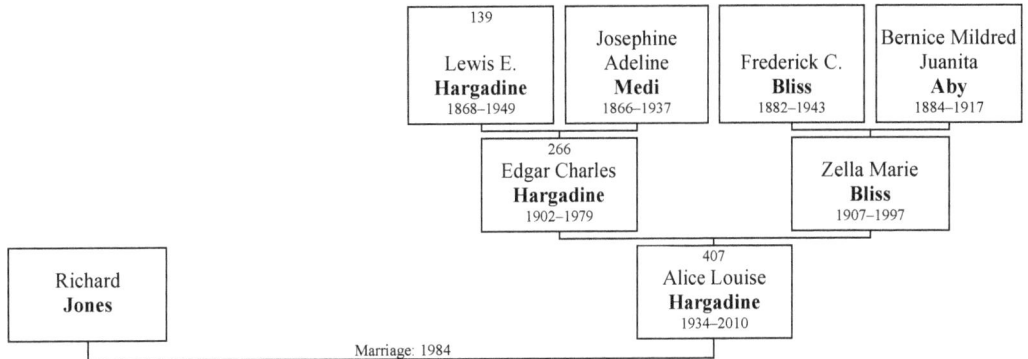

Here are the details about **Alice Louise Hargadine's** second marriage, with Richard Jones. You can read more about Alice Louise on page 432.

Alice Louise Hargadine married **Richard Jones** on Thursday, December 27, 1984.

Family of James Hargadine and Patricia Gray

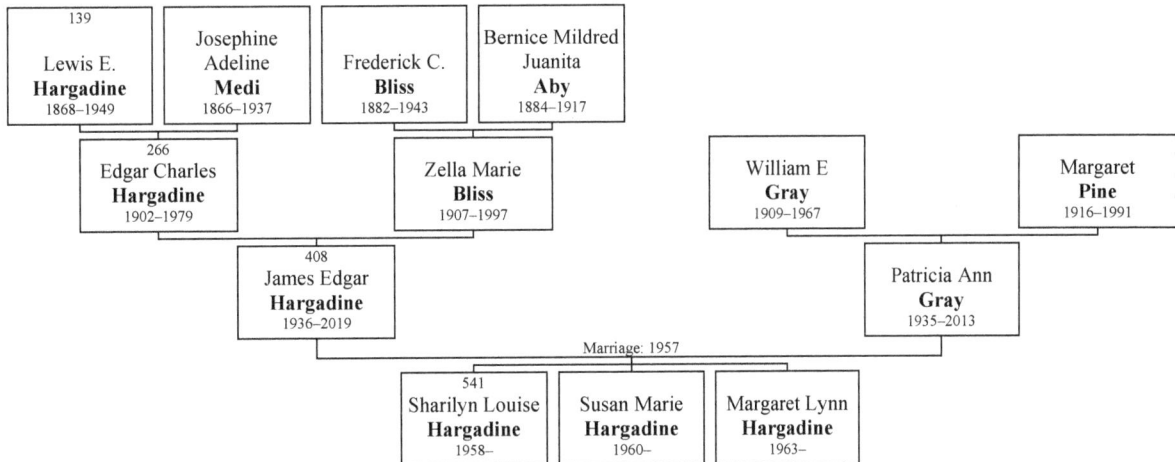

408. **James Edgar Hargadine** was born on Friday, March 20, 1936, in Toulon, Stark County, Illinois. He was the son of Edgar Charles Hargadine (266) and Zella Marie Bliss.

James Edgar died in New Port Richey, Pasco County, Florida, on March 04, 2019, at the age of 82. He was buried in Rienzi Cemetery, Fond du Lac, Fond du Lac County, Wisconsin, on March 09, 2019 (Find a Grave ID 197358202).

James Edgar married **Patricia Ann Gray** on Saturday, July 13, 1957, in Macomb, McDonough County, Illinois. They had three daughters.

Patricia Ann was born in 1935. She was the daughter of William E Gray and Margaret Pine.

Patricia Ann reached 78 years of age and died on March 04, 2013. She was buried in Rienzi Cemetery, Fond du Lac, Fond du Lac County, Wisconsin (Find a Grave ID 161362900).

Daughters of James Edgar Hargadine and Patricia Ann Gray:

+ 541   f   I. **Sharilyn Louise Hargadine** was born in Peoria, Peoria County, Illinois, on December 30, 1958.[447]

    f   II. **Susan Marie Hargadine** was born in Kewanee, Henry County, Illinois, on November 27, 1960.

    f   III. **Margaret Lynn Hargadine** was born in Milwaukee, Milwaukee County, Wisconsin, on December 11, 1963.

John Hargadine

409. **John Frederick Hargadine** was born on Tuesday, June 30, 1942, in Peoria, Peoria County, Illinois. He is the son of Edgar Charles Hargadine (266) and Zella Marie Bliss.

Marriages with Margaret Hadfield, Jane Marlene Woodhouse (Page 435) and Jane M. Trigg (Page 435) are known.

Family of John Hargadine and Margaret Hadfield

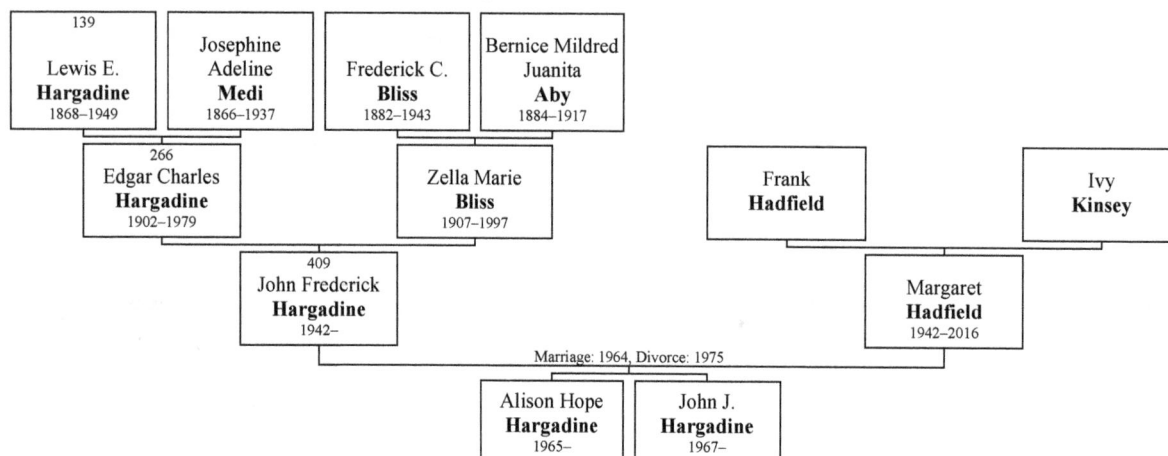

Here are the details about **John Frederick Hargadine's** first marriage, with Margaret Hadfield. You can read more about John Frederick on page 434.

At the age of 22, John Frederick Hargadine married **Margaret Hadfield** on Saturday, October 10, 1964, in Wayne County, North Carolina, when she was 22 years old. They were divorced in San Bernardino, San Bernardino County, California, in August 1975. They had two children.

Margaret was born in Stockport, England, on Sunday, February 08, 1942. She was the daughter of Frank Hadfield and Ivy Kinsey.

---

447   Ancestry.com, Wisconsin, U.S., Marriage Index, 1973-1997 (Provo, UT, USA, Ancestry.com Operations Inc, 2005), Ancestry.com, Record for Sharlyn Louise Hargadine. https://search.ancestry.co.uk/cgi-bin/sse.dll?db=8744&h=1600421&indiv=try.

Margaret reached 74 years of age and died in Durham, Durham County, North Carolina, on October 04, 2016.

Children of John Frederick Hargadine and Margaret Hadfield:

f   I. **Alison Hope Hargadine** was born in Pensacola, Escambia County, Florida, on April 28, 1965.

m   II. **John J. Hargadine** was born in Mountain Home, Elmore County, Idaho, on January 11, 1967.

Family of John Hargadine and Jane Woodhouse

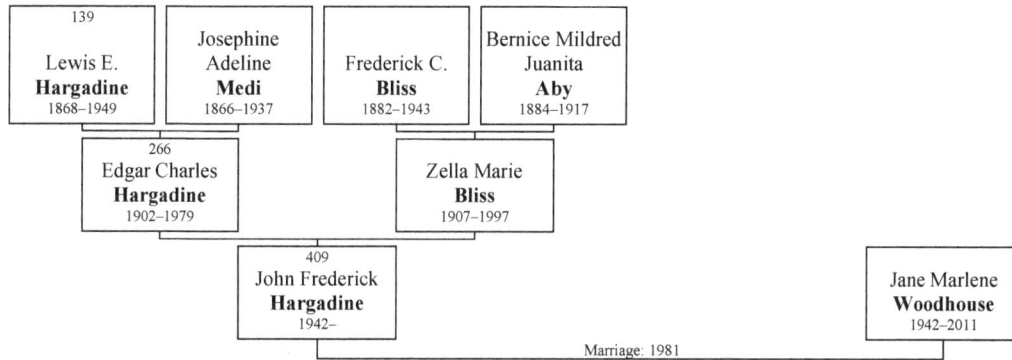

Here are the details about **John Frederick Hargadine's** second marriage, with Jane Marlene Woodhouse. You can read more about John Frederick on page 434.

At the age of 39, John Frederick Hargadine married **Jane Marlene Woodhouse** on Wednesday, September 02, 1981, in Reno, Washoe County, Nevada, when she was 39 years old. Jane Marlene was born on Saturday, June 06, 1942.

She reached 68 years of age and died in Riverside County, California, on May 08, 2011.

Family of John Hargadine and Jane Trigg

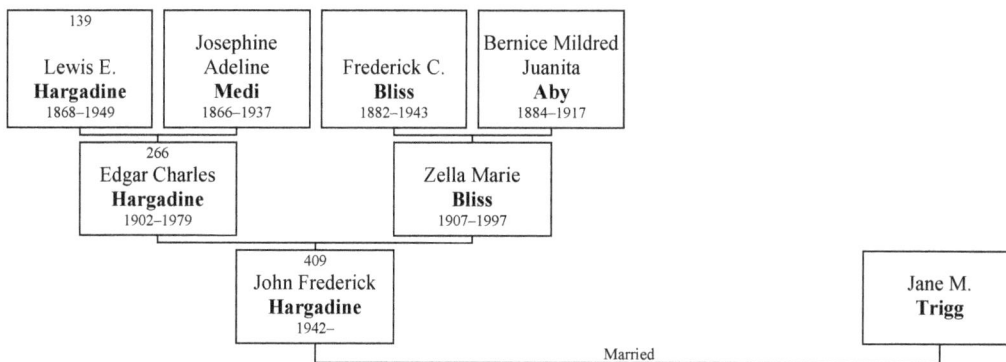

Here are the details about **John Frederick Hargadine's** third marriage, with Jane M. Trigg. You can read more about John Frederick on page 434.

John Frederick Hargadine married **Jane M. Trigg**.

Family of Elizabeth Hargadine and Jerry McCord

410. **Elizabeth Anne Hargadine** was born on Wednesday, December 13, 1944, in Peoria, Peoria County, Illinois. She is the daughter of Edgar Charles Hargadine (266) and Zella Marie Bliss.

Elizabeth Anne married **Jerry Lynn McCord** on Sunday, November 08, 1964. They later divorced. They have three daughters.

Daughters of Elizabeth Anne Hargadine and Jerry Lynn McCord:

> f   I. **Jennifer Lynn McCord** was born in Peoria, Peoria County, Illinois, on December 11, 1965.

> f   II. **Julie Anne McCord** was born in Peoria, Peoria County, Illinois, on May 01, 1968.

> f   III. **Jeanna Louise McCord** was born in Peoria, Peoria County, Illinois, on September 26, 1969.

Family of Annie Hargadine and Gerald Arndt

411. **Annie Louisa Hargadine** was born on Wednesday, April 07, 1926, in Chillicothe, Peoria County, Illinois. She was the daughter of Roy Raymond Hargadine (268) and Cora D. Flinner. She was also known as **Toots**.

Annie Louisa died in Chillicothe, Peoria County, Illinois, on July 04, 2007, at the age of 81. She was buried in Chillicothe City Cemetery, Chillicothe, Peoria County, Illinois (Find a Grave ID 59248759).

At the age of 23, Annie Louisa married **Gerald R. Arndt** on Sunday, August 14, 1949, when he was 21 years old. Gerald R. was born in Freeport, Stephenson County, Illinois, on Wednesday, August 24, 1927. He was also known as **Jerry**.

Gerald R. reached 71 years of age and died in Peoria, Peoria County, Illinois, on November 21, 1998. He was buried in Chillicothe City Cemetery, Chillicothe, Peoria County, Illinois (Find a Grave ID 59248760).

Mary Hargadine

412.   **Mary Lou Hargadine** was born on Tuesday, October 17, 1939, in Alta, Peoria County, Illinois. She was the daughter of Roy Raymond Hargadine (268) and Lola B. Williams.·

Mary Lou died in Peoria, Peoria County, Illinois, on April 30, 2015, at the age of 75. She was buried in Mount Hawley Cemetery, Peoria, Peoria County, Illinois (Find a Grave ID 145910274).

Marriages with Al Behymer and Richard Erwin Hagemann (Page 438) are known.

Family of Mary Hargadine and Al Behymer

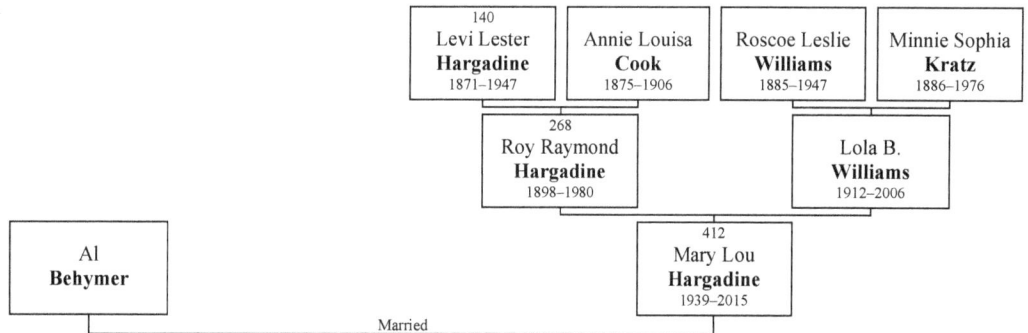

Here are the details about **Mary Lou Hargadine's** first marriage, with Al Behymer. You can read more about Mary Lou on page 437.

Mary Lou Hargadine married **Al Behymer**.

Family of Mary Hargadine and Richard Hagemann

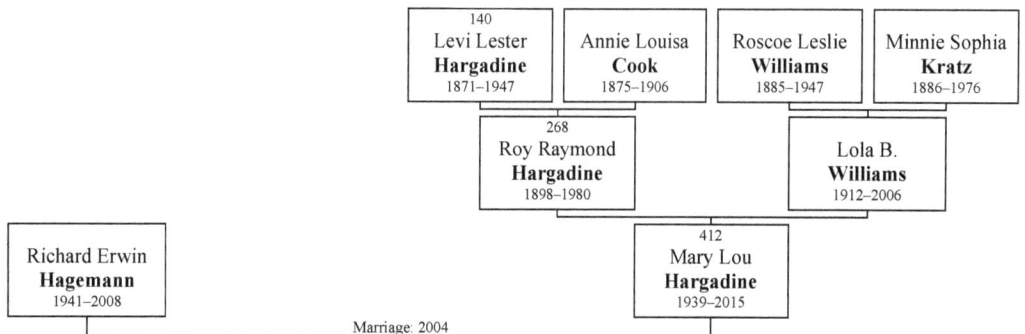

Here are the details about **Mary Lou Hargadine's** second marriage, with Richard Erwin Hagemann. You can read more about Mary Lou on page 437.

Mary Lou Hargadine married **Richard Erwin Hagemann** in 2004. Richard Erwin was born in Winfred, Lake County, South Dakota, on Saturday, July 05, 1941.

He reached 66 years of age and died in Peoria, Peoria County, Illinois, on May 04, 2008. Richard Erwin was buried in Mount Hawley Cemetery, Peoria, Peoria County, Illinois (Find a Grave ID 26814490).

Family of Nancy Hargadine and Terry Moran

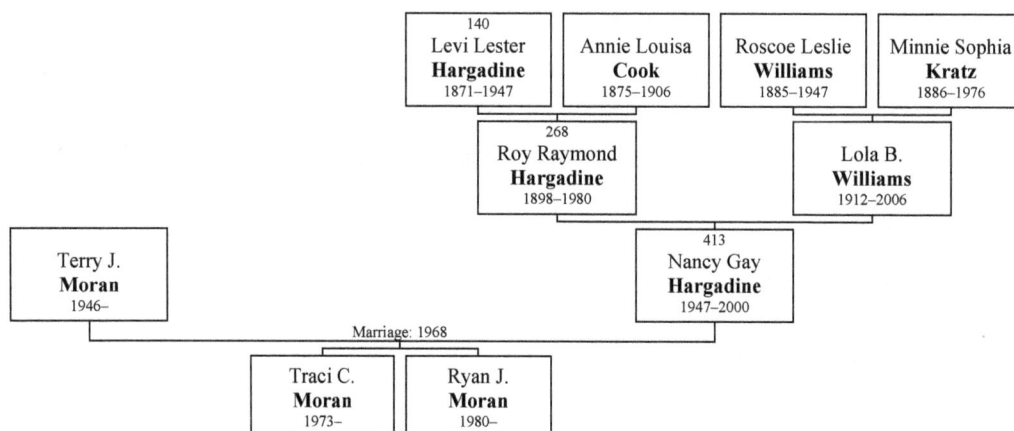

140 Levi Lester **Hargadine** 1871–1947	Annie Louisa **Cook** 1875–1906	Roscoe Leslie **Williams** 1885–1947	Minnie Sophia **Kratz** 1886–1976

268 Roy Raymond **Hargadine** 1898–1980

Lola B. **Williams** 1912–2006

413 Nancy Gay **Hargadine** 1947–2000

Terry J. **Moran** 1946–

Marriage: 1968

Traci C. **Moran** 1973–

Ryan J. **Moran** 1980–

413. **Nancy Gay Hargadine** was born on Sunday, November 09, 1947, in Peoria, Peoria County, Illinois. She was the daughter of Roy Raymond Hargadine (268) and Lola B. Williams.

Nancy Gay died in Peoria, Peoria County, Illinois, on August 18, 2000, at the age of 52. She was buried in Mount Hawley Cemetery, Peoria, Peoria County, Illinois, on August 22, 2000 (Find a Grave ID 22160313).

At the age of 21, Nancy Gay married **Terry J. Moran** on Saturday, December 14, 1968, in Peoria, Peoria County, Illinois, when he was 22 years old.[448] They had two children.

Terry J. was born on Tuesday, July 09, 1946.

Children of Nancy Gay Hargadine and Terry J. Moran:

    f   I. **Traci C. Moran** was born on April 14, 1973.

    m   II. **Ryan J. Moran** was born on April 25, 1980.

John Gray

414. **John Levi Gray** was born on Tuesday, August 02, 1927, in Chillicothe, Peoria County, Illinois. He was the son of John Levi Gray and Elva Mary Hargadine (270). He was also known as **Jr.**.

---

[448] Obituary of Nancy Hargadine Moran (Peoria J-Star, August 20, 2000, B-4).

John Levi died in La Salle, La Salle County, Illinois, on January 23, 2019, at the age of 91. He was buried in Chillicothe City Cemetery, Chillicothe, Peoria County, Illinois (Find a Grave ID 196357292).

Marriages with Marilyn A. Wagel and Barbara J. Worthington (Page 439) are known.

Family of John Gray and Marilyn Wagel

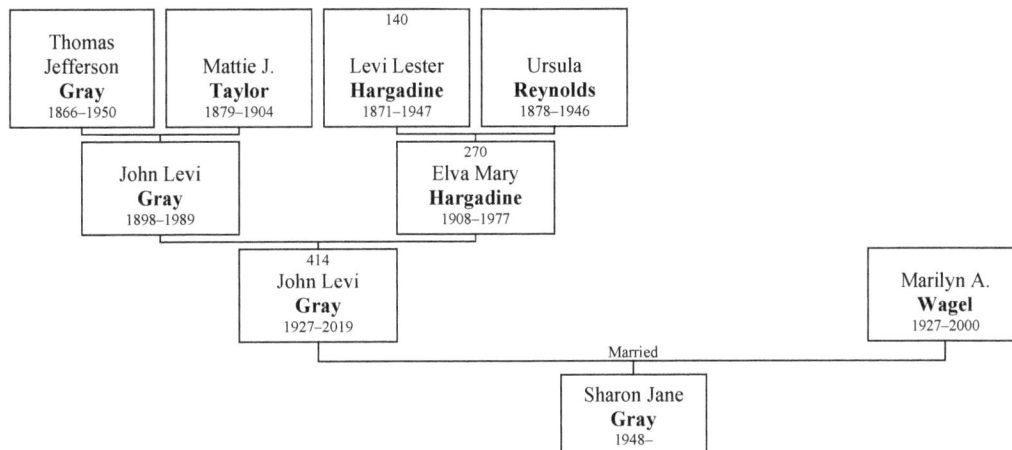

Here are the details about **John Levi Gray's** first marriage, with Marilyn A. Wagel. You can read more about John Levi on page 438.

John Levi Gray married **Marilyn A. Wagel**. They had one daughter.

Marilyn A. was born in Illinois, USA, in 1927. She reached 73 years of age and died in May 2000.

Daughter of John Levi Gray and Marilyn A. Wagel:

    f   I. **Sharon Jane Gray** was born on October 06, 1948.

Family of John Gray and Barbara Worthington

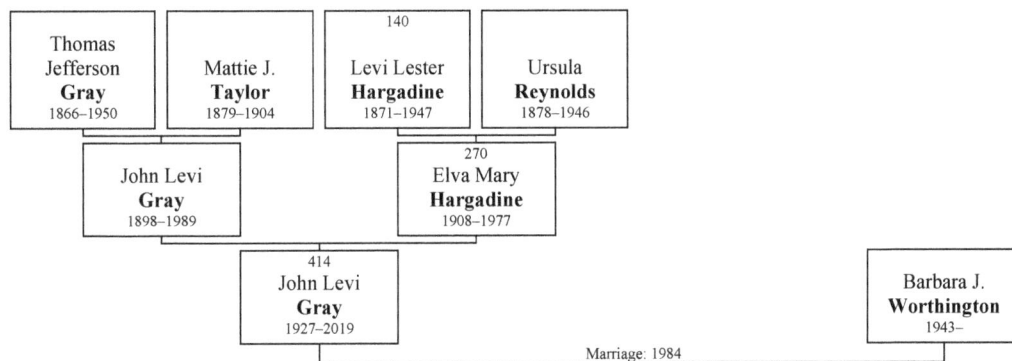

Here are the details about **John Levi Gray's** second marriage, with Barbara J. Worthington. You can read more about John Levi on page 438.

John Levi Gray married **Barbara J. Worthington** on Friday, November 02, 1984, in Chillicothe, Peoria County, Illinois. Barbara J. was born in June 1943.

Wallace Gray

415. **Wallace Lloyd Gray** was born on Thursday, July 18, 1929, in Marshall County, Illinois. He was the son of John Levi Gray and Elva Mary Hargadine (270). He was also known as **Wally**.

Wallace Lloyd died in Peoria, Peoria County, Illinois, on September 18, 2005, at the age of 76. He was buried in Chillicothe City Cemetery, Chillicothe, Peoria County, Illinois (Find a Grave ID 59249049).

Marriages with Dorthey Hancher and Doris Rosella Bailey (Page 441) are known.

Family of Wallace Gray and Dorthey Hancher

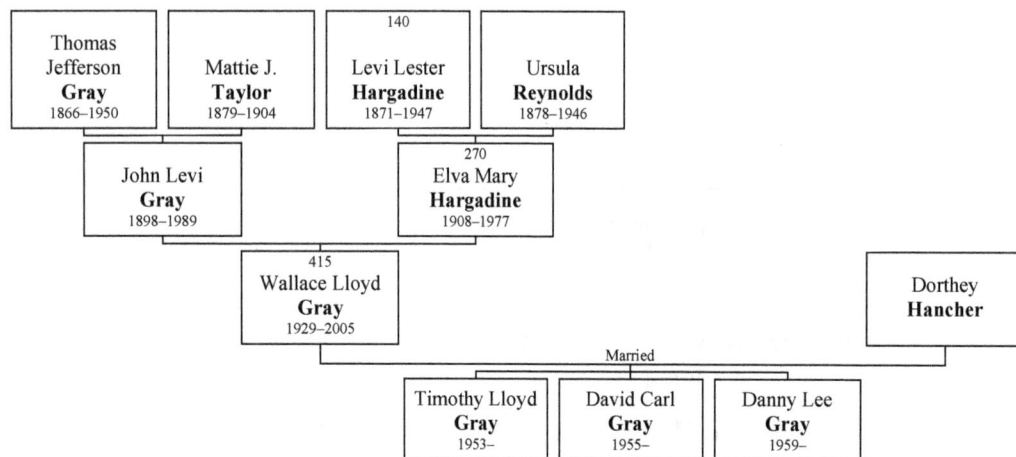

Here are the details about **Wallace Lloyd Gray's** first marriage, with Dorthey Hancher. You can read more about Wallace Lloyd on page 440.

Wallace Lloyd Gray married **Dorthey Hancher**. They had three sons.

Sons of Wallace Lloyd Gray and Dorthey Hancher:

m   I.   **Timothy Lloyd Gray** was born on April 23, 1953.

m   II.   **David Carl Gray** was born on March 26, 1955.

m   III.   **Danny Lee Gray** was born on November 04, 1959.

Family of Wallace Gray and Doris Bailey

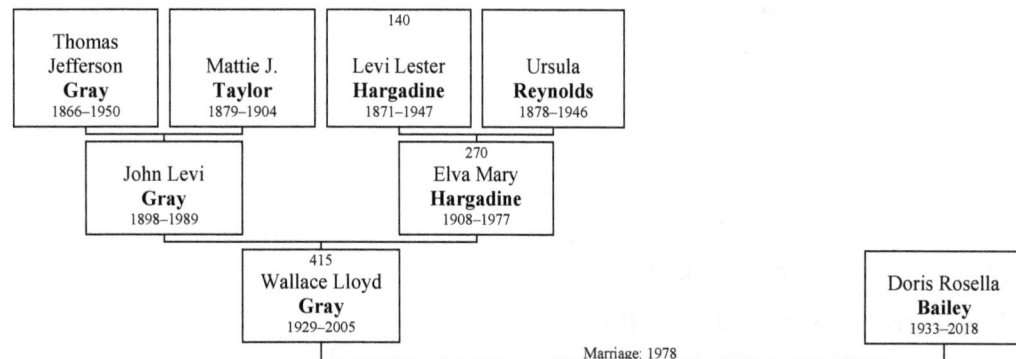

Here are the details about **Wallace Lloyd Gray's** second marriage, with Doris Rosella Bailey. You can read more about Wallace Lloyd on page 440.

At the age of 49, Wallace Lloyd Gray married **Doris Rosella Bailey** on Tuesday, October 03, 1978, in Kahoka, Clark County, Missouri, when she was 45 years old. Doris Rosella was born in Fort Madison, Lee County, Iowa, on Thursday, March 16, 1933. She was also known as **Rosie**.

Doris Rosella reached 85 years of age and died in Burlington, Des Moines County, Iowa, on June 07, 2018. She was buried in Chillicothe City Cemetery, Chillicothe, Peoria County, Illinois (Find a Grave ID 190408909).

Family of Alford Gray and Shirley Ford

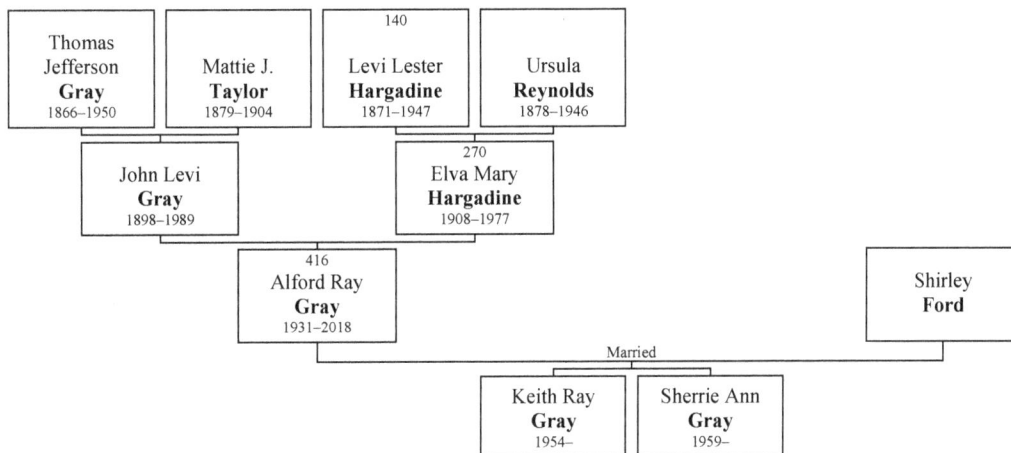

416. **Alford Ray Gray** was born on Wednesday, December 30, 1931, in Henry, Marshall County, Illinois. He was the son of John Levi Gray and Elva Mary Hargadine (270). He was also known as **Tote**.

Alford Ray died in Peoria, Peoria County, Illinois, on March 11, 2018, at the age of 86. He was buried in Chillicothe City Cemetery, Chillicothe, Peoria County, Illinois (Find a Grave ID 187980993).

He married **Shirley Ford**. They had two children.

Children of Alford Ray Gray and Shirley Ford:

m   I. **Keith Ray Gray** was born on February 22, 1954.

f   II. **Sherrie Ann Gray** was born on April 25, 1959.

Family of Harley Gray and Judith Weitz

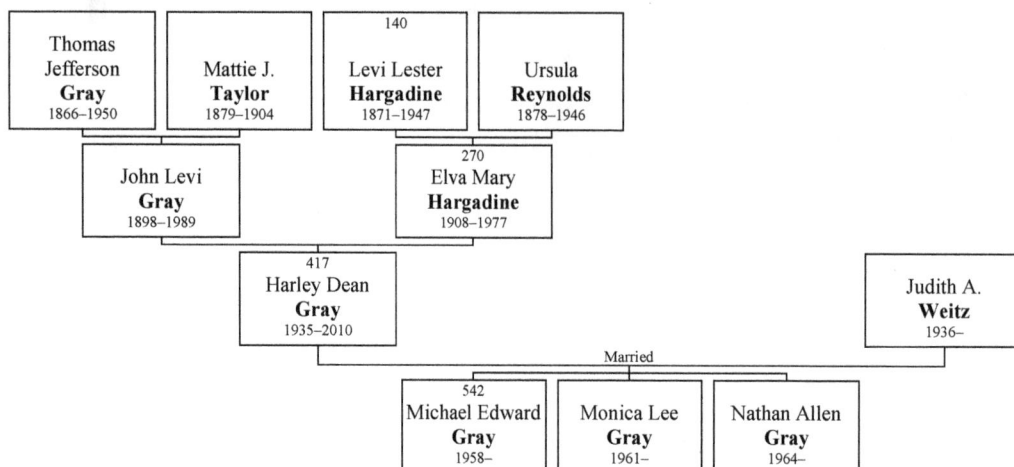

```
┌─────────────┐ ┌─────────────┐ ┌──────140────┐ ┌─────────────┐
│   Thomas    │ │             │ │             │ │             │
│  Jefferson  │ │  Mattie J.  │ │ Levi Lester │ │   Ursula    │
│    Gray     │ │   Taylor    │ │  Hargadine  │ │  Reynolds   │
│  1866–1950  │ │  1879–1904  │ │  1871–1947  │ │  1878–1946  │
└─────────────┘ └─────────────┘ └─────────────┘ └─────────────┘
      ┌───────────────┐         ┌──────270──────┐
      │  John Levi    │         │  Elva Mary    │
      │    Gray       │         │  Hargadine    │
      │  1898–1989    │         │  1908–1977    │
      └───────────────┘         └───────────────┘
              ┌──────417──────┐              ┌─────────────┐
              │  Harley Dean  │              │  Judith A.  │
              │    Gray       │              │   Weitz     │
              │  1935–2010    │              │   1936–     │
              └───────────────┘              └─────────────┘
                        Married
   ┌──────542──────┐ ┌─────────────┐ ┌─────────────┐
   │Michael Edward │ │ Monica Lee  │ │ Nathan Allen│
   │    Gray       │ │    Gray     │ │    Gray     │
   │   1958–       │ │   1961–     │ │   1964–     │
   └───────────────┘ └─────────────┘ └─────────────┘
```

417. **Harley Dean Gray** was born on Wednesday, January 30, 1935, in Marshall County, Illinois. He was the son of John Levi Gray and Elva Mary Hargadine (270).

Harley Dean died in Peoria, Peoria County, Illinois, on September 20, 2010, at the age of 75. He was buried in Chillicothe City Cemetery, Chillicothe, Peoria County, Illinois (Find a Grave ID 59036502).

He married **Judith A. Weitz**. They had three children.

Judith A. was born on Monday, August 17, 1936.[449]

Children of Harley Dean Gray and Judith A. Weitz:

+ 542   m   I. **Michael Edward Gray** was born on December 09, 1958.

        f   II. **Monica Lee Gray** was born on May 09, 1961.

        m   III. **Nathan Allen Gray** was born on November 19, 1964.

Family of Judith Gray and Duke Secrest

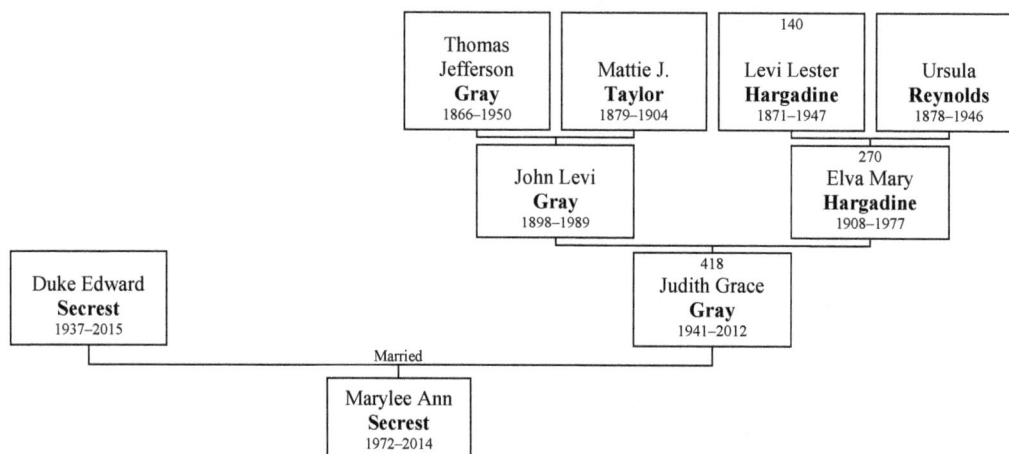

```
                    ┌─────────────┐ ┌─────────────┐ ┌──────140────┐ ┌─────────────┐
                    │   Thomas    │ │             │ │             │ │             │
                    │  Jefferson  │ │  Mattie J.  │ │ Levi Lester │ │   Ursula    │
                    │    Gray     │ │   Taylor    │ │  Hargadine  │ │  Reynolds   │
                    │  1866–1950  │ │  1879–1904  │ │  1871–1947  │ │  1878–1946  │
                    └─────────────┘ └─────────────┘ └─────────────┘ └─────────────┘
                          ┌───────────────┐         ┌──────270──────┐
                          │  John Levi    │         │  Elva Mary    │
                          │    Gray       │         │  Hargadine    │
                          │  1898–1989    │         │  1908–1977    │
                          └───────────────┘         └───────────────┘
   ┌─────────────┐                    ┌──────418──────┐
   │Duke Edward  │                    │ Judith Grace  │
   │  Secrest    │                    │    Gray       │
   │  1937–2015  │                    │  1941–2012    │
   └─────────────┘                    └───────────────┘
                        Married
              ┌─────────────┐
              │ Marylee Ann │
              │   Secrest   │
              │  1972–2014  │
              └─────────────┘
```

---

449   Ancestry.com, U.S., Public Records Index, 1950-1993, Volume 2 (Lehi, UT, USA, Ancestry.com Operations, Inc., 2010), Ancestry.com, Record for Judith A Gray. https://search.ancestry.co.uk/cgi-bin/sse.dll?db=1732&h=58533869&indiv=try.

418. **Judith Grace Gray** was born on Friday, December 05, 1941, in Henry, Marshall County, Illinois. She was the daughter of John Levi Gray and Elva Mary Hargadine (270).

Judith Grace died in East Peoria, Tazewell County, Illinois, on August 15, 2012, at the age of 70. She was buried in Chillicothe City Cemetery, Chillicothe, Peoria County, Illinois (Find a Grave ID 95893159).

She married **Duke Edward Secrest**. They had one daughter.

Duke Edward was born in Beeville, Bee County, Texas, on Wednesday, January 06, 1937.[450] He reached 77 years of age and died in Peoria, Peoria County, Illinois, on January 02, 2015.[450] Duke Edward was buried in Lutheran Cemetery, Peoria, Peoria County, Illinois (Find a Grave ID 140893706).[450]

Daughter of Judith Grace Gray and Duke Edward Secrest:

f   I. **Marylee Ann Secrest** was born in Peoria, Peoria County, Illinois, on March 16, 1972. She died in Peoria, Peoria County, Illinois, on September 16, 2014, at the age of 42. Marylee Ann was cremated (Find a Grave ID 136758370).

Shirley Hargadine

419. **Shirley Kay Hargadine** was born on Saturday, September 02, 1944, in Peoria, Peoria County, Illinois. She was the daughter of Forrest Levi Hargadine (271) and Aletha Maude Oldfield. Aletha Maude Oldfield was her stepmother.

Shirley Kay died on November 13, 2015, at the age of 71. She was buried in Mason City Cemetery, Mason City, Mason County, Illinois (Find a Grave ID 155012039).

Marriages with Billy Don Miller and Wesley Eugene Bowersock (Page 444) are known.

Family of Shirley Hargadine and Billy Miller

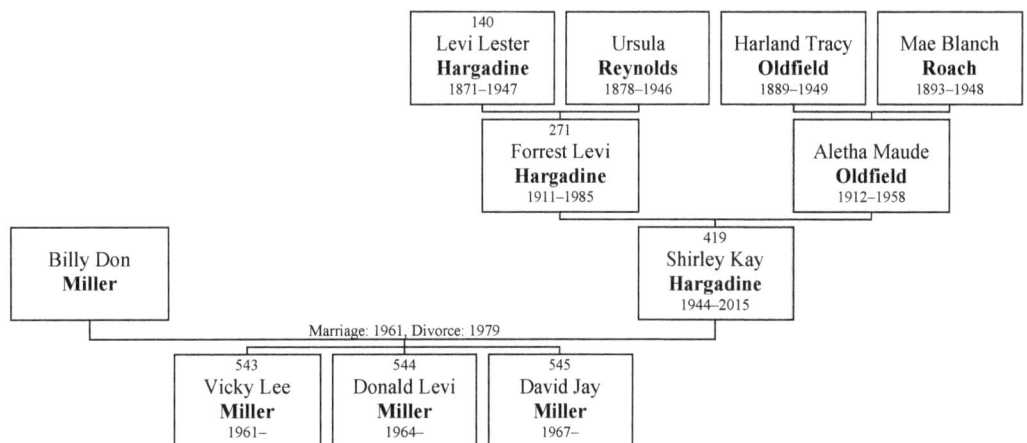

---

450   Ancestry.com, U.S., Find a Grave® Index, 1600s-Current (Lehi, UT, USA, Ancestry.com Operations, Inc., 2012), Ancestry.com, Record for Duke Edward Secrest. https://search.ancestry.co.uk/cgi-bin/sse.dll?db=60525&h=115988877&indiv=try.

Here are the details about **Shirley Kay Hargadine's** first marriage, with Billy Don Miller. You can read more about Shirley Kay on page 443.

Shirley Kay Hargadine married **Billy Don Miller** on Monday, April 03, 1961, in Angleton, Brazoria County, Texas. They were divorced in February 1979. They had three children.

Children of Shirley Kay Hargadine and Billy Don Miller:

+   543   f   I. **Vicky Lee Miller** was born in Athens, Athens County, Ohio, on August 22, 1961.

+   544   m   II. **Donald Levi Miller** was born in Peoria, Peoria County, Illinois, on August 30, 1964.

+   545   m   III. **David Jay Miller** was born in Peoria, Peoria County, Illinois, on July 10, 1967.

Family of Shirley Hargadine and Wesley Bowersock

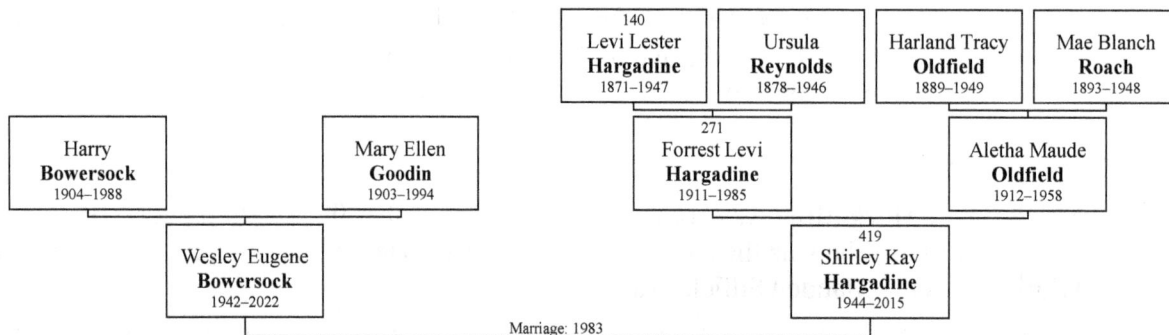

Here are the details about **Shirley Kay Hargadine's** second marriage, with Wesley Eugene Bowersock. You can read more about Shirley Kay on page 443.

At the age of 39, Shirley Kay Hargadine married **Wesley Eugene Bowersock** on Saturday, November 12, 1983, in Peoria, Peoria County, Illinois, when he was 41 years old. Wesley Eugene was born in Mason City, Mason County, Illinois, on Friday, February 13, 1942. He was the son of Harry Bowersock and Mary Ellen Goodin.

Wesley Eugene reached 80 years of age and died in Peoria, Peoria County, Illinois, on March 29, 2022. He was buried in Mason City Cemetery, Mason City, Mason County, Illinois (Find a Grave ID 238358701).

Family of Harold Predmore and Mary Taft

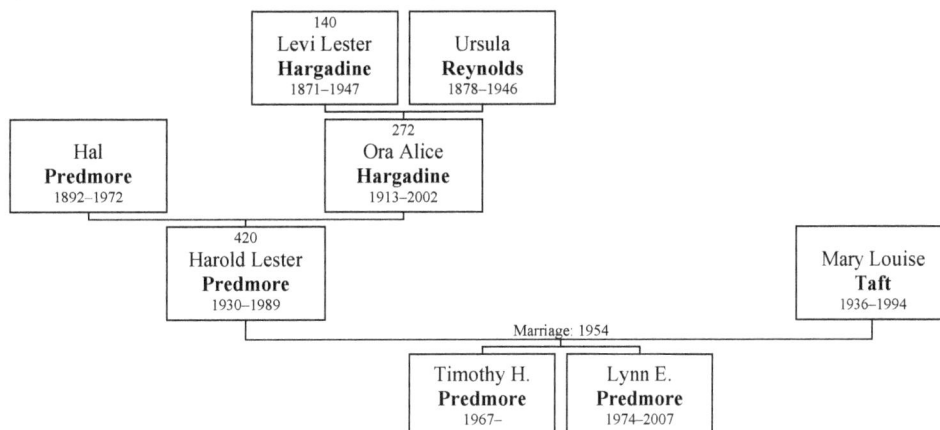

420. **Harold Lester Predmore** was born on Tuesday, December 16, 1930, in Edelstein, Peoria County, Illinois. He was the son of Hal Predmore and Ora Alice Hargadine (272).

Harold Lester died in Peoria, Peoria County, Illinois, on May 16, 1989, at the age of 58. He was buried in Swan Lake Memory Gardens, Peoria, Peoria County, Illinois (Find a Grave ID 7019494).

At the age of 23, Harold Lester married **Mary Louise Taft** on Sunday, July 04, 1954, in Peoria, Peoria County, Illinois, when she was 17 years old. They had two children.

Mary Louise was born in Peoria, Peoria County, Illinois, on Sunday, September 06, 1936. She reached 57 years of age and died in Peoria, Peoria County, Illinois, on April 29, 1994. Mary Louise was buried in Swan Lake Memory Gardens, Peoria, Peoria County, Illinois (Find a Grave ID 27811926).

Children of Harold Lester Predmore and Mary Louise Taft:

m   I. **Timothy H. Predmore** was born in September 1967.

f   II. **Lynn E. Predmore** was born in Peoria, Peoria County, Illinois, on April 12, 1974. She died in Peoria, Peoria County, Illinois, on October 03, 2007, at the age of 33. Lynn E. was cremated (Find a Grave ID 21983764).

Family of Robert Streitmatter and Alice Arbogast

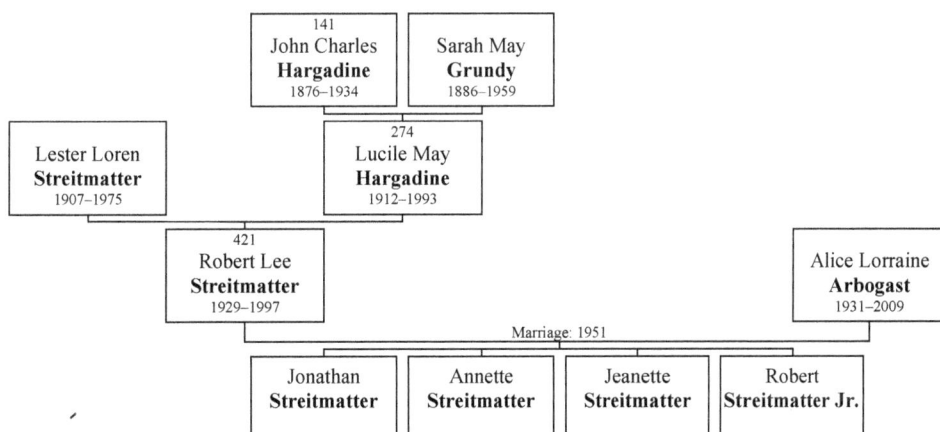

421. **Robert Lee Streitmatter** was born on Friday, November 01, 1929, in Peoria County, Illinois. He was the son of Lester Loren Streitmatter and Lucile May Hargadine (274).

Robert Lee died in Chillicothe, Peoria County, Illinois, on July 08, 1997, at the age of 67. He was buried in Prospect Cemetery, Dunlap, Peoria County, Illinois (Find a Grave ID 22159734).

At the age of 22, Robert Lee married **Alice Lorraine Arbogast** on Thursday, November 01, 1951, in Bossier City, Louisiana, when she was 20 years old. They had four children.

Alice Lorraine was born in Peoria, Peoria County, Illinois, on Tuesday, October 27, 1931. She reached 77 years of age and died in Peoria, Peoria County, Illinois, on March 15, 2009. Alice Lorraine was buried in Prospect Cemetery, Dunlap, Peoria County, Illinois (Find a Grave ID 127153410).

Children of Robert Lee Streitmatter and Alice Lorraine Arbogast:

m   I. **Jonathan Streitmatter**.

f   II. **Annette Streitmatter**.

f   III. **Jeanette Streitmatter**.

m   IV. **Robert Streitmatter Jr.**.

Family of Linda Streitmatter and Jim Feurer

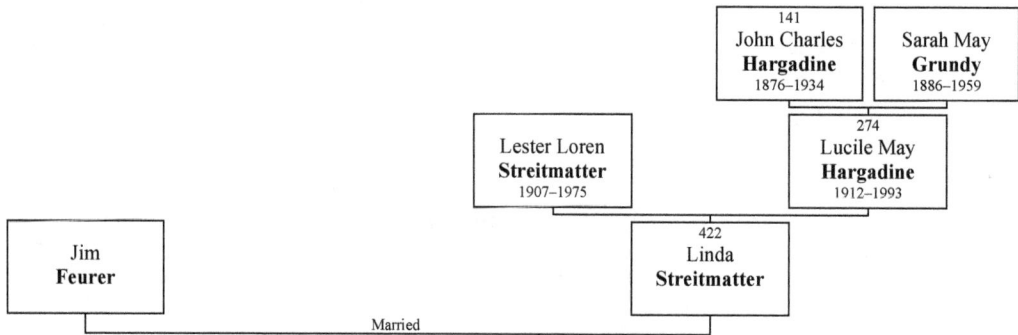

422. **Linda Streitmatter**. She was the daughter of Lester Loren Streitmatter and Lucile May Hargadine (274).

She married **Jim Feurer**.

Family of Lulu Hargadine and Donald Harrison

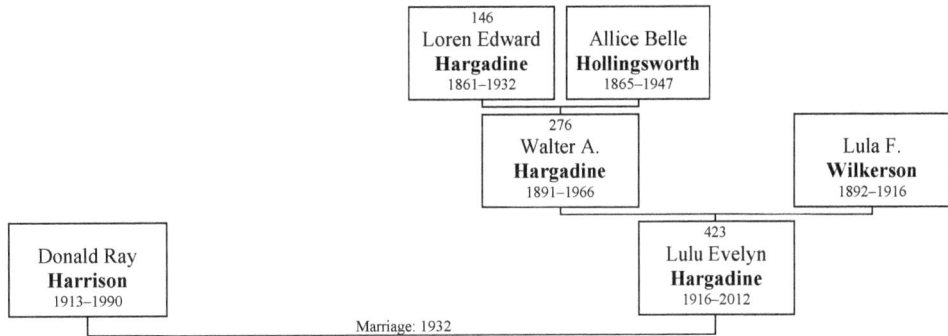

```
                    ┌──────────────┐ ┌──────────────┐
                    │      146     │ │              │
                    │ Loren Edward │ │ Allice Belle │
                    │  Hargadine   │ │Hollingsworth │
                    │  1861–1932   │ │  1865–1947   │
                    └──────────────┘ └──────────────┘
                         ┌──────────────┐        ┌──────────────┐
                         │      276     │        │    Lula F.   │
                         │   Walter A.  │        │  Wilkerson   │
                         │  Hargadine   │        │  1892–1916   │
                         │  1891–1966   │        └──────────────┘
                         └──────────────┘
┌──────────────┐                  ┌──────────────┐
│ Donald Ray   │                  │      423     │
│  Harrison    │                  │ Lulu Evelyn  │
│  1913–1990   │                  │  Hargadine   │
└──────────────┘                  │  1916–2012   │
         Marriage: 1932           └──────────────┘
```

423. **Lulu Evelyn Hargadine** was born on Sunday, January 23, 1916, in Kiowa County, Kansas. She was the daughter of Walter A. Hargadine (276) and Lula F. Wilkerson.

Lulu Evelyn died in Stafford, Stafford County, Kansas, on December 16, 2012, at the age of 96. She was buried in Stafford Cemetery, Stafford, Stafford County, Kansas (Find a Grave ID 102433229).

At the age of 16, Lulu Evelyn married **Donald Ray Harrison** on Monday, March 14, 1932, when he was 18 years old. Donald Ray was born in Arkansas, USA, on Tuesday, July 22, 1913.

He reached 76 years of age and died on January 10, 1990. Donald Ray was buried in Stafford Cemetery, Stafford, Stafford County, Kansas (Find a Grave ID 93847038).

Family of Clayton Hargadine and Eleanor McElwaine

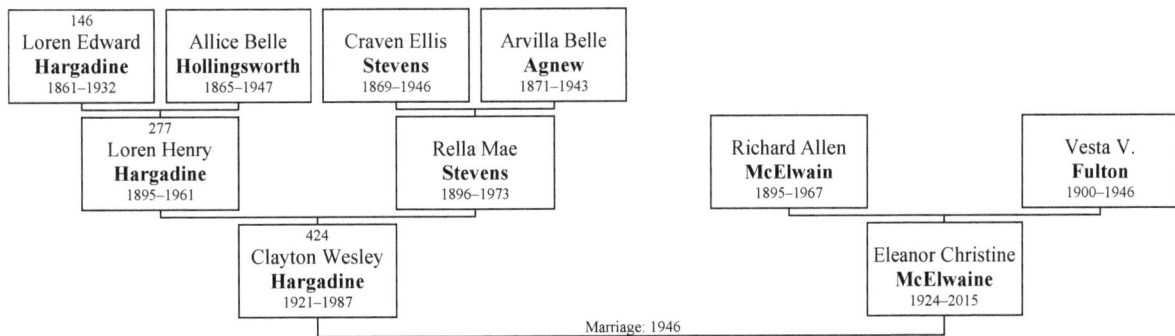

```
┌──────────────┐┌──────────────┐┌──────────────┐┌──────────────┐
│      146     ││              ││ Craven Ellis ││ Arvilla Belle│
│ Loren Edward ││ Allice Belle ││   Stevens    ││    Agnew     │
│  Hargadine   ││Hollingsworth ││  1869–1946   ││  1871–1943   │
│  1861–1932   ││  1865–1947   │└──────────────┘└──────────────┘
└──────────────┘└──────────────┘
  ┌──────────────┐      ┌──────────────┐   ┌──────────────┐     ┌──────────────┐
  │      277     │      │  Rella Mae   │   │ Richard Allen│     │   Vesta V.   │
  │ Loren Henry  │      │   Stevens    │   │  McElwain    │     │   Fulton     │
  │  Hargadine   │      │  1896–1973   │   │  1895–1967   │     │  1900–1946   │
  │  1895–1961   │      └──────────────┘   └──────────────┘     └──────────────┘
  └──────────────┘
        ┌──────────────┐              ┌──────────────┐
        │      424     │              │   Eleanor    │
        │Clayton Wesley│              │  Christine   │
        │  Hargadine   │              │  McElwaine   │
        │  1921–1987   │              │  1924–2015   │
        └──────────────┘              └──────────────┘
                    Marriage: 1946
```

424. **Clayton Wesley Hargadine** was born on Wednesday, January 12, 1921, in Kiowa County, Kansas. He was the son of Loren Henry Hargadine (277) and Rella Mae Stevens.

Clayton Wesley died in Wichita, Sedgwick County, Kansas, on December 19, 1987, at the age of 66. His cause of death was heart attack. Clayton Wesley was buried in Hillcrest Cemetery, Mullinville, Kiowa County, Kansas (Find a Grave ID 119318359).

At the age of 25, Clayton Wesley married **Eleanor Christine McElwaine** on Sunday, March 31, 1946, in Mullinville, Kiowa County, Kansas, when she was 21 years old. Eleanor Christine was born in Hutchinson, Reno County, Kansas, on Tuesday, July 01, 1924. She was the daughter of Richard Allen McElwain and Vesta V. Fulton.

Eleanor Christine reached 90 years of age and died in Pratt, Pratt County, Kansas, on February 17, 2015. She was buried in Hillcrest Cemetery, Mullinville, Kiowa County, Kansas (Find a Grave ID 142911527).

Family of Melva Hargadine and Willis Webster

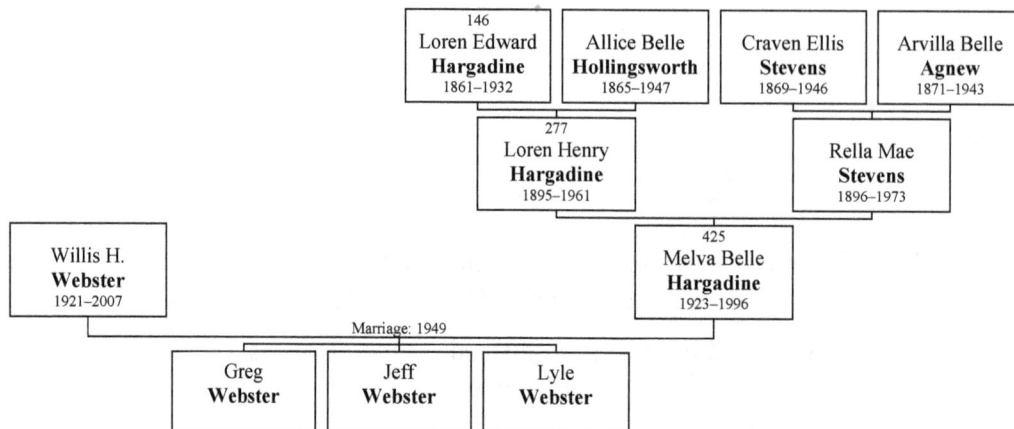

425. **Melva Belle Hargadine** was born on Monday, December 03, 1923. She was the daughter of Loren Henry Hargadine (277) and Rella Mae Stevens.

Melva Belle died in Wichita, Sedgwick County, Kansas, on September 06, 1996, at the age of 72. She was buried in Lakeview Cemetery & Mausoleum, Wichita, Sedgwick County, Kansas (Find a Grave ID 71277097).

At the age of 25, Melva Belle married **Willis H. Webster** on Saturday, July 16, 1949, when he was 28 years old. They had three sons.

Willis H. was born on Thursday, April 21, 1921. He was also known as **Bill**.

Willis H. reached 86 years of age and died on July 03, 2007. He was buried in Lakeview Cemetery & Mausoleum, Wichita, Sedgwick County, Kansas (Find a Grave ID 71277150).

Sons of Melva Belle Hargadine and Willis H. Webster:

m	I. **Greg Webster**.
m	II. **Jeff Webster**.
m	III. **Lyle Webster**.

Family of Leona Hargadine and David Travis

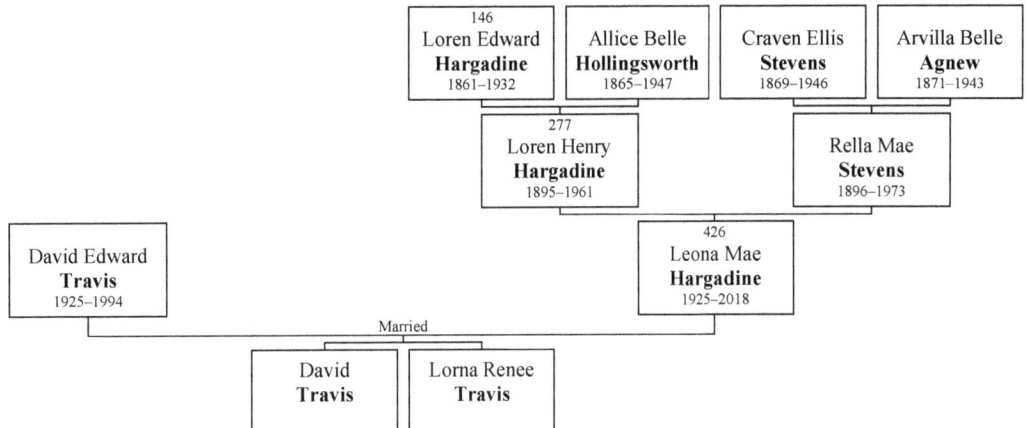

426. **Leona Mae Hargadine** was born on Wednesday, December 09, 1925, in Mullinville, Kiowa County, Kansas. She was the daughter of Loren Henry Hargadine (277) and Rella Mae Stevens.

Leona Mae died in Emporia, Lyon County, Kansas, on March 31, 2018, at the age of 92. She was buried in Maplewood Memorial Lawn Cemetery, Emporia, Lyon County, Kansas, on April 06, 2018 (Find a Grave ID 91010250).

She married **David Edward Travis**. They had two children.

David Edward was born in Bloom, Ford County, Kansas, on Tuesday, March 31, 1925. He reached 69 years of age and died in Emporia, Lyon County, Kansas, on December 24, 1994. David Edward was buried in Maplewood Memorial Lawn Cemetery, Emporia, Lyon County, Kansas (Find a Grave ID 91010224).

Children of Leona Mae Hargadine and David Edward Travis:

  m I. **David Travis.**

  f II. **Lorna Renee Travis.**

Family of Gaylord Hargadine and Eloise Sloan

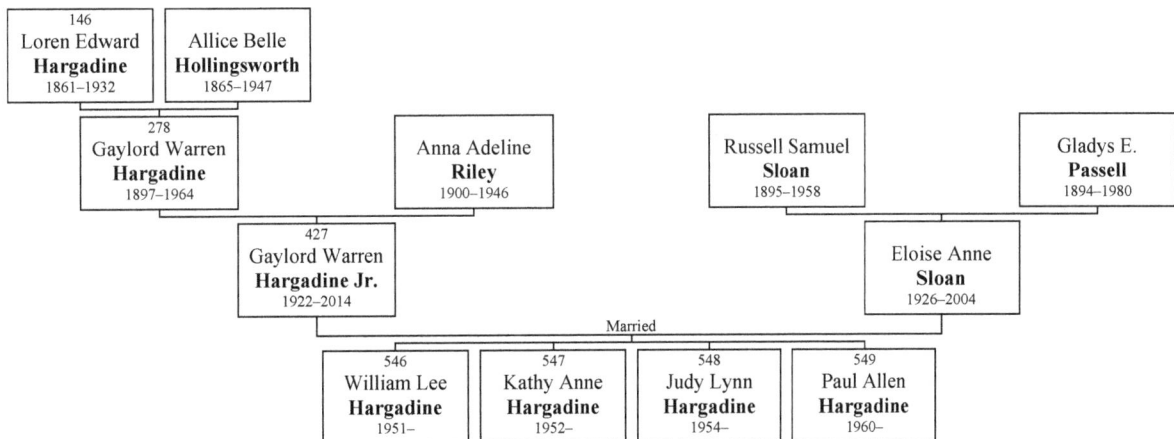

427. **Gaylord Warren Hargadine Jr.** was born on Thursday, September 14, 1922, in Edwards County, Kansas. He was the son of Gaylord Warren Hargadine (278) and Anna Adeline Riley. He was also known as **Gayle**.

Gaylord Warren died in Southlake, Tarrant County, Texas, on January 26, 2014, at the age of 91. He was buried in Bluebonnet Hills Memorial Park, Colleyville, Tarrant County, Texas (Find a Grave ID 124324658).

He married **Eloise Anne Sloan**. They had four children.

Eloise Anne was born in Colby, Thomas County, Kansas, on Wednesday, April 21, 1926.[451] She was the daughter of Russell Samuel Sloan and Gladys E. Passell.

Eloise Anne reached 78 years of age and died in Bedford, Tarrant County, Texas, on December 19, 2004.[451] She was buried in Bluebonnet Hills Memorial Park, Colleyville, Tarrant County, Texas (Find a Grave ID 153635643).[451]

Children of Gaylord Warren Hargadine Jr. and Eloise Anne Sloan:

+ 546　m　　I. **William Lee Hargadine** was born in El Paso County, Texas, on January 10, 1951.

+ 547　f　　II. **Kathy Anne Hargadine** was born in Harris County, Texas, on October 20, 1952.

+ 548　f　　III. **Judy Lynn Hargadine** was born in Dallas County, Texas, on October 22, 1954.

+ 549　m　　IV. **Paul Allen Hargadine** was born in Dallas County, Texas, on October 16, 1960.

Family of Gordon Hargadine and Marjorie Dozier

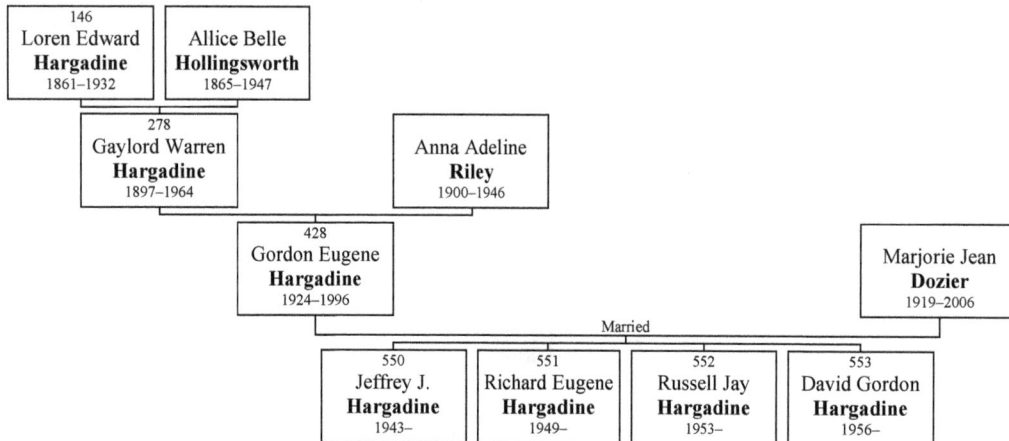

428. **Gordon Eugene Hargadine** was born on Saturday, February 02, 1924, in Mullinville, Kiowa County, Kansas. He was the son of Gaylord Warren Hargadine (278) and Anna Adeline Riley.

451　Ancestry.com, Public Member Trees (Provo, UT, USA, Ancestry.com Operations, Inc., 2006), Ancestry.com, Record for Eloise Anne Sloan. https://search.ancestry.co.uk/cgi-bin/sse.dll?db=1030&h=420085835009&indiv=try.

Gordon Eugene served in the military: US Navy. He died on December 21, 1996, at the age of 72. Gordon Eugene was buried in Fort Logan National Cemetery, Denver County, Colorado, on August 13, 1997 (Find a Grave ID 753312).

He married **Marjorie Jean Dozier**. They had four sons.

Marjorie Jean was born in Monte Vista, Colorado, on Thursday, April 03, 1919. She reached 86 years of age and died in Grand County, Colorado, on March 27, 2006.

Sons of Gordon Eugene Hargadine and Marjorie Jean Dozier:

+   550   m   I. **Jeffrey J. Hargadine** was born on September 08, 1943.

+   551   m   II. **Richard Eugene Hargadine** was born on September 21, 1949.

+   552   m   III. **Russell Jay Hargadine** was born on February 19, 1953.

+   553   m   IV. **David Gordon Hargadine** was born on October 02, 1956.

Stanley Hargadine

429.   **Stanley Sayre Hargadine** was born on Thursday, February 12, 1925, in Kiowa, Barber County, Kansas. He was the son of Gaylord Warren Hargadine (278) and Anna Adeline Riley.

Stanley Sayre died in Wenatchee, Chelan County, Washington, on May 19, 2007, at the age of 82.

Marriages with Clara Lou Cook and Dolores Zerenella Carpenter (Page 452) are known.

Family of Stanley Hargadine and Clara Cook

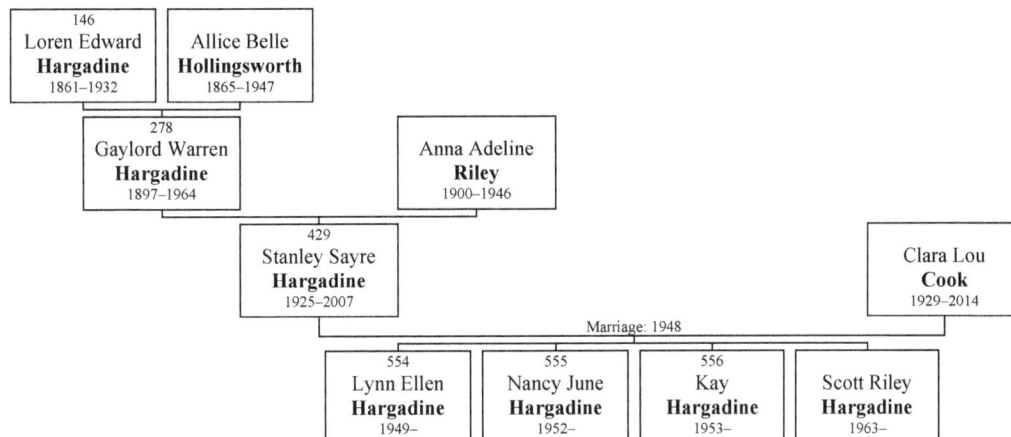

Here are the details about **Stanley Sayre Hargadine's** first marriage, with Clara Lou Cook. You can read more about Stanley Sayre on page 451.

At the age of 23, Stanley Sayre Hargadine married **Clara Lou Cook** on Monday, August 23, 1948, in Great Bend, Barton County, Kansas, when she was 18 years old.[452] They had four children.

---

[452]   Idaho Divorce Record, Docket No. 26045. Spouse of Stanley found because of a divorce record. Divorce granted on May 19, 1966. http://ancestry.com/.

Clara Lou was born in Wichita, Sedgwick County, Kansas, on Saturday, October 12, 1929. She reached 84 years of age and died in Boulder City, Clark County, Nevada, on June 10, 2014. Clara Lou was buried in Heber Springs City Cemetery, Heber Springs, Cleburne County, Arkansas (Find a Grave ID 132648755).

Children of Stanley Sayre Hargadine and Clara Lou Cook:

+ 554 f I. **Lynn Ellen Hargadine** was born on October 02, 1949.[453]

+ 555 f II. **Nancy June Hargadine** was born on September 17, 1952.

+ 556 f III. **Kay Hargadine** was born on December 23, 1953.

      m IV. **Scott Riley Hargadine** was born on November 20, 1963.

Family of Stanley Hargadine and Dolores Carpenter

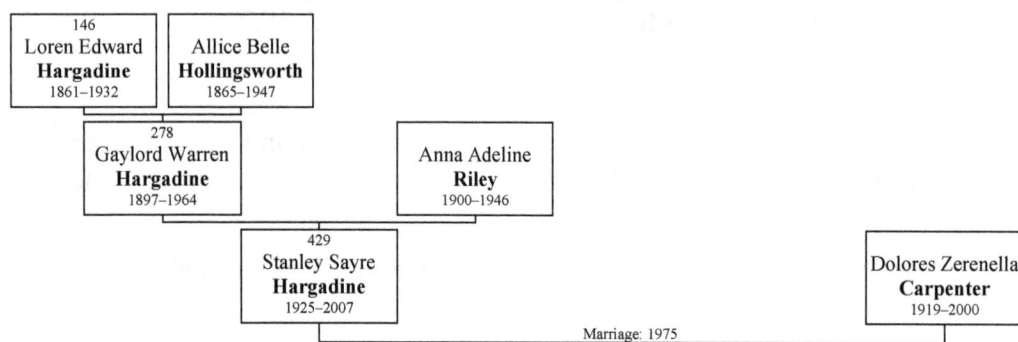

Here are the details about **Stanley Sayre Hargadine's** second marriage, with Dolores Zerenella Carpenter. You can read more about Stanley Sayre on page 451.

At the age of 50, Stanley Sayre Hargadine married **Dolores Zerenella Carpenter** on Sunday, September 14, 1975, in Spokane, Spokane County, Washington, when she was 56 years old. Dolores Zerenella was born in LaGrange, Troup County, Georgia, on Saturday, May 31, 1919.

She reached 81 years of age and died in Spokane, Spokane County, Washington, on September 20, 2000.

---

453   Ancestry.com, Arkansas, Marriage Certificates, 1917-1972 (Lehi, UT, USA, Ancestry.com Operations, Inc., 2019), Ancestry.com, Arkansas Department of Vital Records; Little Rock, Arkansas; Marriage Certificates; Year: 1968; Film: #4. Record for Lynn Hargadine. https://search.ancestry.co.uk/cgi-bin/sse.dll?db=61775&h=90011501&indiv=try.

Family of Alice Hargadine and Karl Grossarth

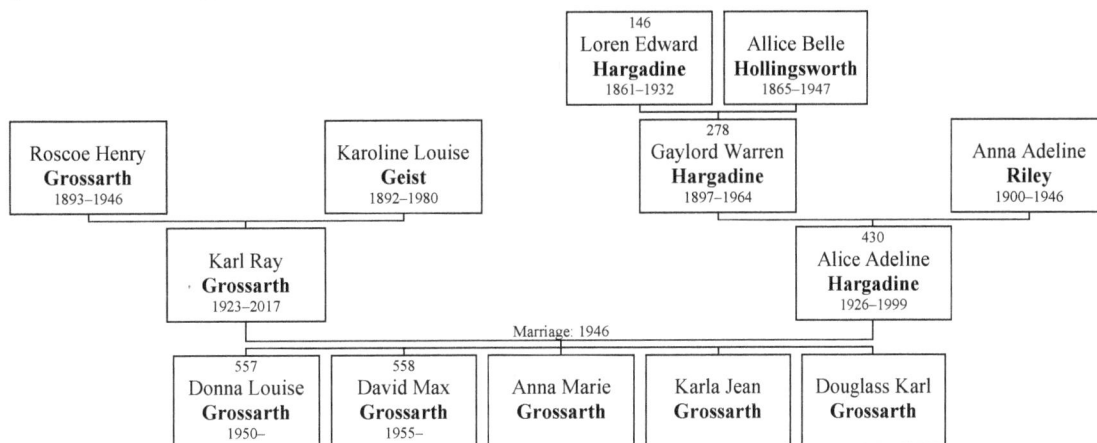

430. **Alice Adeline Hargadine** was born on Thursday, July 29, 1926, in Mullinville, Kiowa County, Kansas. She was the daughter of Gaylord Warren Hargadine (278) and Anna Adeline Riley.

Alice Adeline died in Coquille, Coos County, Oregon, on December 25, 1999, at the age of 73. Her body was cremated. Source: Gaylord W. Hargadine Jr.

At the age of 20, Alice Adeline married **Karl Ray Grossarth** on Thursday, December 12, 1946, in Kinsley, Edwards County, Kansas, when he was 23 years old. They had five children.

Karl Ray was born in Hutchinson, Reno County, Kansas, on Thursday, January 04, 1923. He was the son of Roscoe Henry Grossarth and Karoline Louise Geist.

Karl Ray reached 94 years of age and died in Benton County, Washington, on November 19, 2017.

Children of Alice Adeline Hargadine and Karl Ray Grossarth:

+ 557 f I. **Donna Louise Grossarth** was born in Kansas, USA, on March 01, 1950.

+ 558 m II. **David Max Grossarth** was born on February 08, 1955.

        f III. **Anna Marie Grossarth**.

        f IV. **Karla Jean Grossarth**.

        m V. **Douglass Karl Grossarth**.

Mary Hargadine

431. **Mary Prescilla Hargadine** was born on Sunday, October 23, 1927, in Mullinville, Kiowa County, Kansas. She is the daughter of Gaylord Warren Hargadine (278) and Anna Adeline Riley.

Marriages with Jack Wayne Phillips, John Eugene Moore (Page 454) and Abel G. Gomez (Page 455) are known.

Family of Mary Hargadine and Jack Phillips

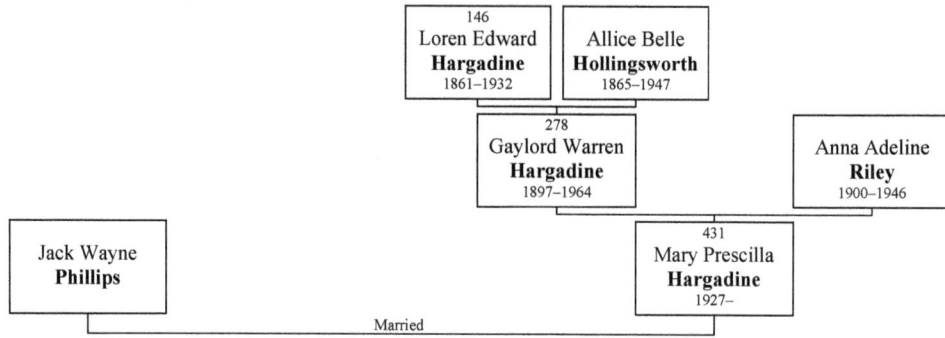

```
                                    ┌──────────────┬──────────────┐
                                    │     146      │ Allice Belle │
                                    │ Loren Edward │ Hollingsworth│
                                    │  Hargadine   │  1865–1947   │
                                    │  1861–1932   │              │
                                    └──────────────┴──────────────┘
                                    ┌──────────────┐        ┌──────────────┐
                                    │     278      │        │ Anna Adeline │
                                    │ Gaylord Warren│       │    Riley     │
                                    │  Hargadine   │        │  1900–1946   │
                                    │  1897–1964   │        │              │
                                    └──────────────┘        └──────────────┘
    ┌──────────────┐                        ┌──────────────┐
    │ Jack Wayne   │                        │     431      │
    │  Phillips    │                        │Mary Prescilla│
    │              │                        │  Hargadine   │
    │              │                        │    1927–     │
    └──────────────┘        Married         └──────────────┘
```

Here are the details about **Mary Prescilla Hargadine's** first marriage, with Jack Wayne Phillips. You can read more about Mary Prescilla on page 453.

Mary Prescilla Hargadine married **Jack Wayne Phillips**.

Family of Mary Hargadine and John Moore

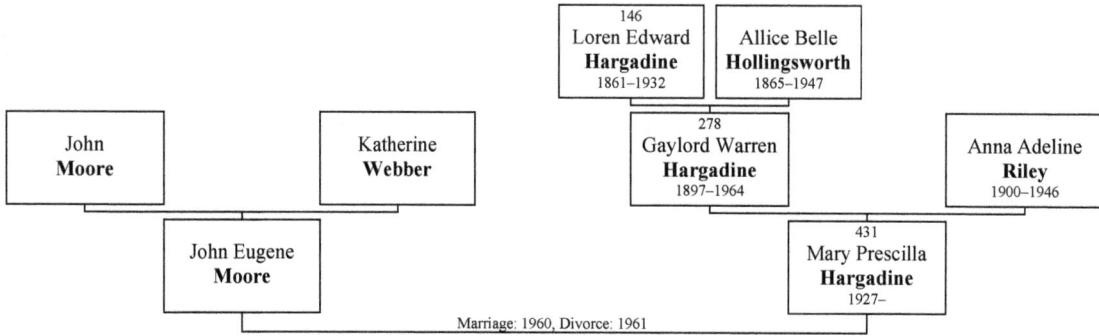

```
                                    ┌──────────────┬──────────────┐
                                    │     146      │ Allice Belle │
                                    │ Loren Edward │ Hollingsworth│
                                    │  Hargadine   │  1865–1947   │
                                    │  1861–1932   │              │
                                    └──────────────┴──────────────┘
    ┌──────────┐     ┌──────────┐   ┌──────────────┐        ┌──────────────┐
    │  John    │     │Katherine │   │     278      │        │ Anna Adeline │
    │  Moore   │     │ Webber   │   │Gaylord Warren│        │    Riley     │
    │          │     │          │   │  Hargadine   │        │  1900–1946   │
    │          │     │          │   │  1897–1964   │        │              │
    └──────────┘     └──────────┘   └──────────────┘        └──────────────┘
         ┌──────────────┐                   ┌──────────────┐
         │ John Eugene  │                   │     431      │
         │    Moore     │                   │Mary Prescilla│
         │              │                   │  Hargadine   │
         │              │                   │    1927–     │
         └──────────────┘ Marriage: 1960, Divorce: 1961 └──────────────┘
```

Here are the details about **Mary Prescilla Hargadine's** second marriage, with John Eugene Moore. You can read more about Mary Prescilla on page 453.

Mary Prescilla Hargadine married **John Eugene Moore** on Saturday, October 01, 1960, at William Kopach, Justice of the Peace in Silver Bow, Montana. They were divorced in Silver Bow County, Montana, on August 14, 1961.

John Eugene was born in Sturgis, Meade County, South Dakota. He is the son of John Moore and Katherine Webber.

Family of Mary Hargadine and Abel Gomez

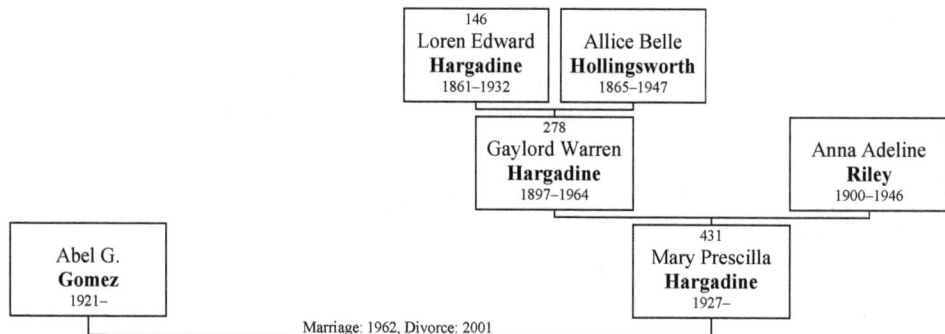

```
                                    ┌──────────────┬──────────────┐
                                    │     146      │ Allice Belle │
                                    │ Loren Edward │ Hollingsworth│
                                    │  Hargadine   │  1865–1947   │
                                    │  1861–1932   │              │
                                    └──────────────┴──────────────┘
                                    ┌──────────────┐        ┌──────────────┐
                                    │     278      │        │ Anna Adeline │
                                    │Gaylord Warren│        │    Riley     │
                                    │  Hargadine   │        │  1900–1946   │
                                    │  1897–1964   │        │              │
                                    └──────────────┘        └──────────────┘
    ┌──────────────┐                        ┌──────────────┐
    │   Abel G.    │                        │     431      │
    │    Gomez     │                        │Mary Prescilla│
    │    1921–     │                        │  Hargadine   │
    │              │                        │    1927–     │
    └──────────────┘ Marriage: 1962, Divorce: 2001 └──────────────┘
```

Here are the details about **Mary Prescilla Hargadine's** third marriage, with Abel G. Gomez. You can read more about Mary Prescilla on page 453.

Mary Prescilla Hargadine married **Abel G. Gomez** on Monday, July 16, 1962, in Coeur d'Alene, Kootenai County, Idaho. They were divorced in Benton, Washington, on March 08, 2001.

Abel G. was born in August 1921.

Family of John Hargadine and Carol Tackitt

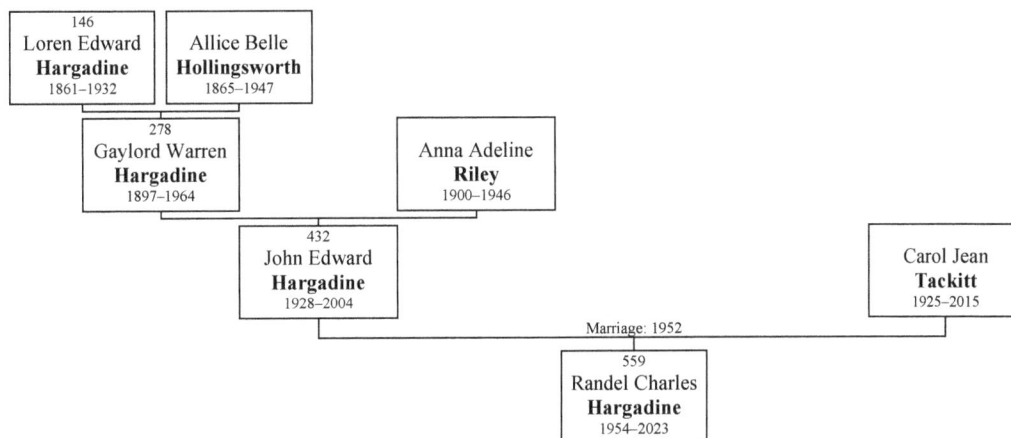

432. **John Edward Hargadine** was born on Saturday, November 24, 1928, in Mullinville, Kiowa County, Kansas. He was the son of Gaylord Warren Hargadine (278) and Anna Adeline Riley.

John Edward died in Fort Collins, Larimer County, Colorado, on July 28, 2004, at the age of 75.

John Edward married **Carol Jean Tackitt** on Wednesday, November 26, 1952, in Denver, Denver County, Colorado. They had one son.

Carol Jean was born in 1925. She reached 90 years of age and died on April 13, 2015.

Son of John Edward Hargadine and Carol Jean Tackitt:

+ 559 m I. **Randel Charles Hargadine** was born in Colorado, USA, on February 17, 1954. He died on August 30, 2023, at the age of 69.

Family of Lloyd Hargadine and Agnes Bankey

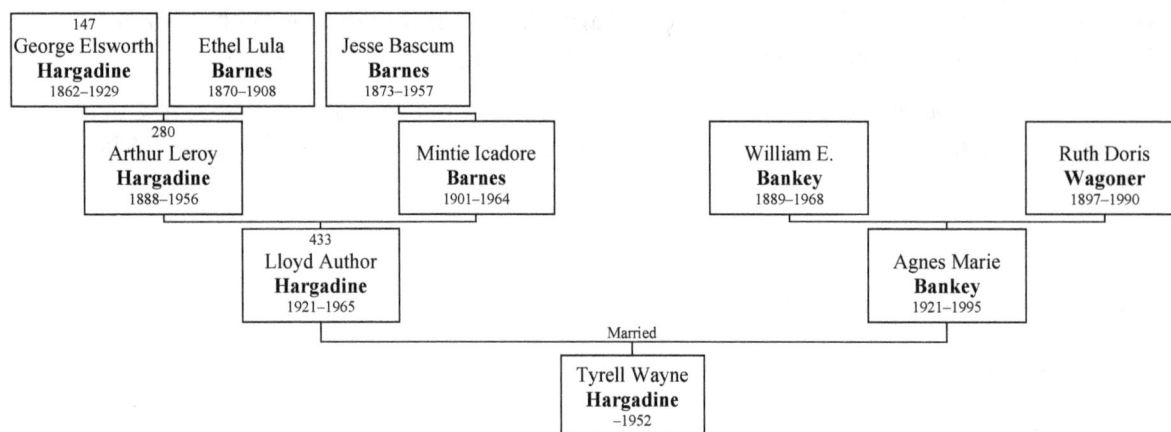

433. **Lloyd Author Hargadine** was born on Friday, June 17, 1921. He was the son of Arthur Leroy Hargadine (280) and Mintie Icadore Barnes.

Lloyd Author served in the military between 1942 and 1945: WWII, Tech, 3HQ Btry 961 Field Arty BN 9 KS. He died on September 13, 1965, at the age of 44. Lloyd Author was buried in Alden Valley Cemetery, Alden, Rice County, Kansas (Find a Grave ID 52865939).

He married **Agnes Marie Bankey**. They had one son.

Agnes Marie was born in Eureka, Greenwood County, Kansas, on Monday, March 28, 1921. She was the daughter of William E. Bankey and Ruth Doris Wagoner.

Agnes Marie reached 73 years of age and died in Alden, Rice County, Kansas, on January 02, 1995. She was buried on January 05, 1995, in Alden Valley Cemetery, Alden, Rice County, Kansas (Find a Grave ID 159839943).

Son of Lloyd Author Hargadine and Agnes Marie Bankey:

> m   I. **Tyrell Wayne Hargadine**. He was also known as **Skeeter**.
>
> Tyrell Wayne died on September 04, 1952. He was buried in Alden Valley Cemetery, Alden, Rice County, Kansas (Find a Grave ID 52866106).

Delma Hargadine

434. **Delma LaVon Hargadine** was born on Saturday, February 17, 1923, in Alden, Rice County, Kansas. She was the daughter of Arthur Leroy Hargadine (280) and Mintie Icadore Barnes.

Delma LaVon died in Buhler, Reno County, Kansas, on November 25, 2012, at the age of 89. She was buried in Memorial Park Cemetery, Hutchinson, Reno County, Kansas, on November 30, 2012 (Find a Grave ID 101350449).

Marriages with Maurice Daily and James M. Parker (Page 458) are known.

Family of Delma Hargadine and Maurice Daily

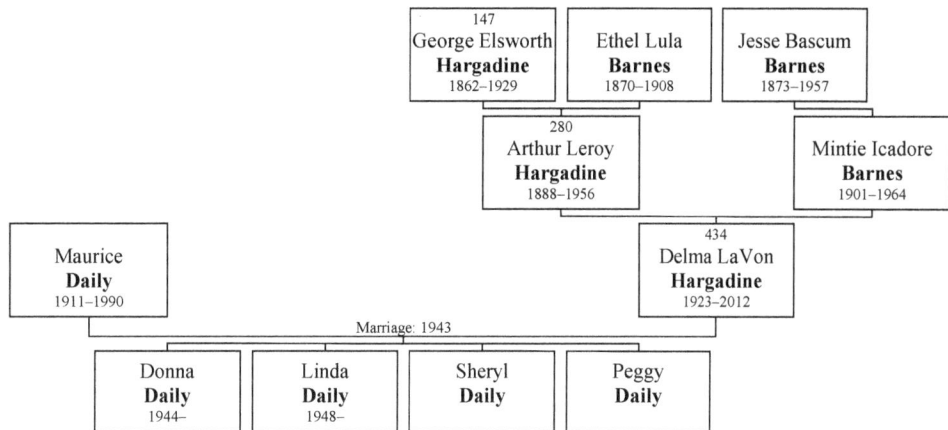

Here are the details about **Delma LaVon Hargadine's** first marriage, with Maurice Daily. You can read more about Delma LaVon on page 456.

At the age of 20, Delma LaVon Hargadine married **Maurice Daily** on Sunday, October 10, 1943, in McPherson, McPherson County, Kansas, when he was 31 years old. They had four daughters.

Maurice was born in Harveyville, Wabaunsee County, Kansas, on Saturday, October 28, 1911. He reached 78 years of age and died in Hutchinson, Reno County, Kansas, on August 16, 1990. Maurice was buried in Memorial Park Cemetery, Hutchinson, Reno County, Kansas (Find a Grave ID 37147654).

Daughters of Delma LaVon Hargadine and Maurice Daily:

f   I. **Donna Daily** was born in August 1944.

f   II. **Linda Daily** was born in Kansas, USA, in 1948.

f   III. **Sheryl Daily**.

f   IV. **Peggy Daily**.

Family of Delma Hargadine and James Parker

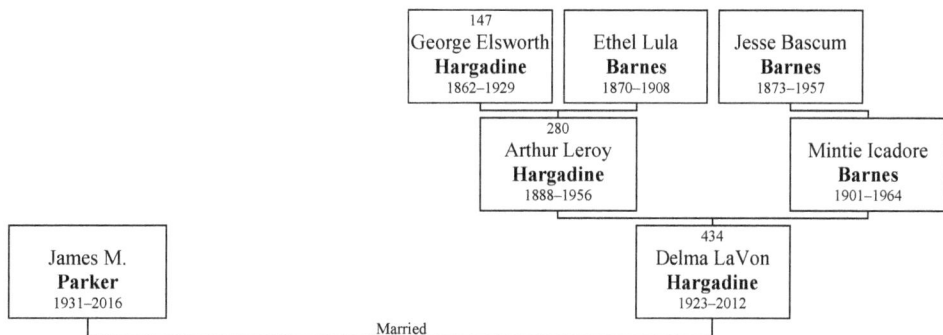

Here are the details about **Delma LaVon Hargadine's** second marriage, with James M. Parker. You can read more about Delma LaVon on page 456.

Delma LaVon Hargadine married **James M. Parker**. James M. was born in Newton, Harvey County, Kansas, on Thursday, April 16, 1931.

He reached 84 years of age and died in Buhler, Reno County, Kansas, on March 18, 2016. James M. was buried in Star Cemetery, Patterson, Harvey County, Kansas (Find a Grave ID 159836505).

Family of Loren Hargadine and Virginia Newell

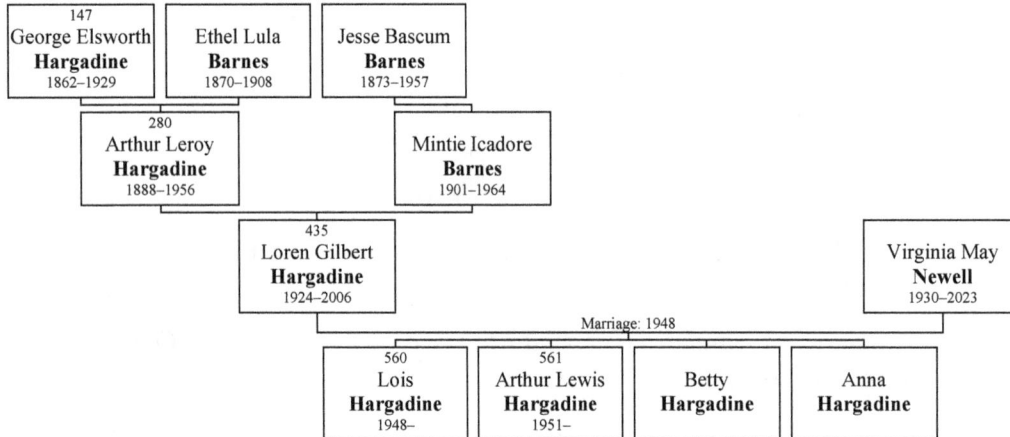

435. **Loren Gilbert Hargadine** was born on Thursday, January 31, 1924, in Alden, Rice County, Kansas. He was the son of Arthur Leroy Hargadine (280) and Mintie Icadore Barnes.

Loren Gilbert died in Alden, Rice County, Kansas, on September 04, 2006, at the age of 82. He was buried in Alden Valley Cemetery, Alden, Rice County, Kansas (Find a Grave ID 65498459).

At the age of 23, Loren Gilbert married **Virginia May Newell** on Monday, January 12, 1948, in Alden, Rice County, Kansas, when she was 17 years old. They had four children.

Virginia May was born in Stafford, Stafford County, Kansas, on Wednesday, June 04, 1930. She reached 93 years of age and died in Little River, Rice County, Kansas, on June 23, 2023. Virginia May was buried in Alden Valley Cemetery, Alden, Rice County, Kansas (Find a Grave ID 255856013).

Children of Loren Gilbert Hargadine and Virginia May Newell:

+ 560 f I. **Lois Hargadine** was born on September 01, 1948.

+ 561 m II. **Arthur Lewis Hargadine** was born on November 13, 1951.

      f III. **Betty Hargadine**.

      f IV. **Anna Hargadine**.

Opal Hargadine

436. **Opal Ione Hargadine** was born on Tuesday, July 08, 1913, in Greensburg, Kiowa County, Kansas. She was the daughter of Floyd Chester Hargadine (281) and Belle Anissa Liggett.

Opal Ione died in Camarillo, Ventura County, California, on October 11, 1997, at the age of 84. She was buried in Conejo Mountain Memorial Park, Camarillo, Ventura County, California (Find a Grave ID 76421198).

Marriages with Thomas Ethel Darbison and Derrall F. Bucknam (Page 459) are known.

Family of Opal Hargadine and Thomas Darbison

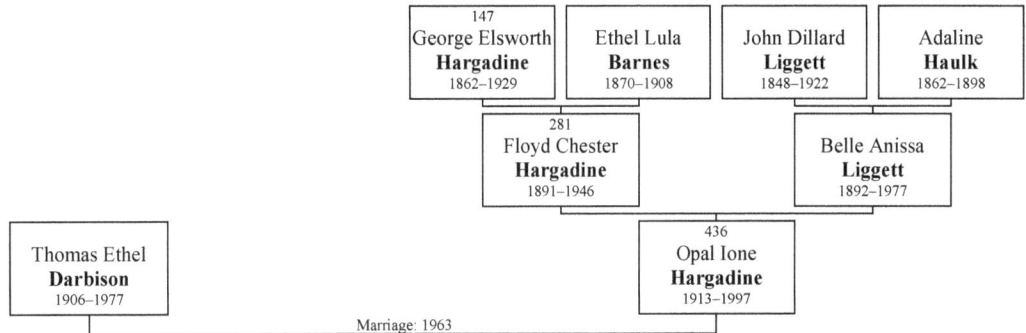

147 George Elsworth **Hargadine** 1862–1929	Ethel Lula **Barnes** 1870–1908	John Dillard **Liggett** 1848–1922	Adaline **Haulk** 1862–1898

281 Floyd Chester **Hargadine** 1891–1946	Belle Anissa **Liggett** 1892–1977

Thomas Ethel **Darbison** 1906–1977

436 Opal Ione **Hargadine** 1913–1997

Marriage: 1963

Here are the details about **Opal Ione Hargadine's** first marriage, with Thomas Ethel Darbison. You can read more about Opal Ione on page 458.

Opal Ione Hargadine married **Thomas Ethel Darbison** in 1963. Thomas Ethel was born in Hobart, Meade County, Kansas, on Thursday, December 27, 1906.

He reached 70 years of age and died in Oxnard, Ventura County, California, on June 29, 1977. Thomas Ethel was buried in Conejo Mountain Memorial Park, Camarillo, Ventura County, California (Find a Grave ID 76421199).

Family of Opal Hargadine and Derrall Bucknam

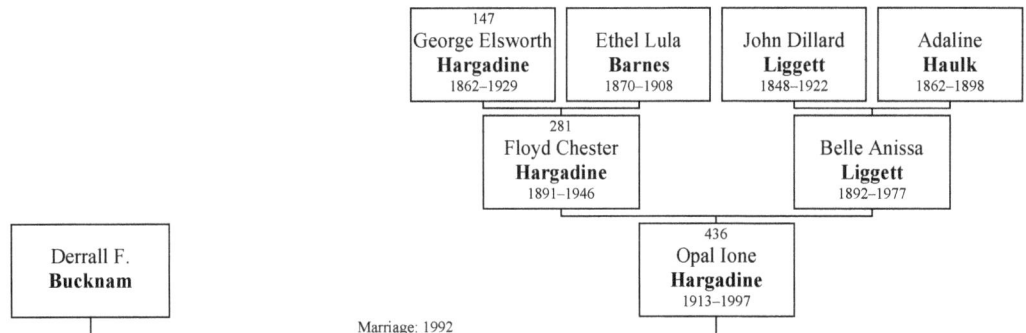

147 George Elsworth **Hargadine** 1862–1929	Ethel Lula **Barnes** 1870–1908	John Dillard **Liggett** 1848–1922	Adaline **Haulk** 1862–1898

281 Floyd Chester **Hargadine** 1891–1946	Belle Anissa **Liggett** 1892–1977

Derrall F. **Bucknam**

436 Opal Ione **Hargadine** 1913–1997

Marriage: 1992

Here are the details about **Opal Ione Hargadine's** second marriage, with Derrall F. Bucknam. You can read more about Opal Ione on page 458.

Opal Ione Hargadine married **Derrall F. Bucknam** on Tuesday, May 19, 1992, in Clark County, Nevada.

Family of Gladys Hargadine and Rumohr Hendrichs

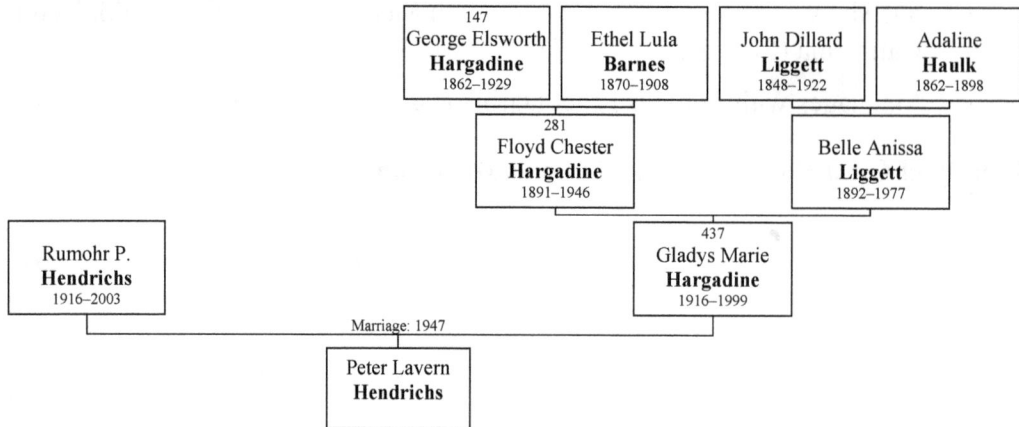

437. **Gladys Marie Hargadine** was born on Monday, December 04, 1916, in Mullinville, Kiowa County, Kansas. She was the daughter of Floyd Chester Hargadine (281) and Belle Anissa Liggett.

Gladys Marie died in McMinnville, Yamhill County, Oregon, on May 19, 1999, at the age of 82. She was buried in Evergreen Memorial Park, McMinnville, Yamhill County, Oregon (Find a Grave ID 34509535).

At the age of 30, Gladys Marie married **Rumohr P. Hendrichs** on Sunday, June 08, 1947, in Salem, Marion County, Oregon, when he was 31 years old. They had one son.

Rumohr P. was born in Alexander, McKenzie County, North Dakota, on Tuesday, May 02, 1916. He was also known as **Butch**.

Rumohr P. reached 87 years of age and died in McMinnville, Yamhill County, Oregon, on May 14, 2003. He was buried in Evergreen Memorial Park, McMinnville, Yamhill County, Oregon (Find a Grave ID 20120072).

Son of Gladys Marie Hargadine and Rumohr P. Hendrichs:

    m   I. **Peter Lavern Hendrichs**.

Family of Pauline Clinkenbeard and Ed Reilman

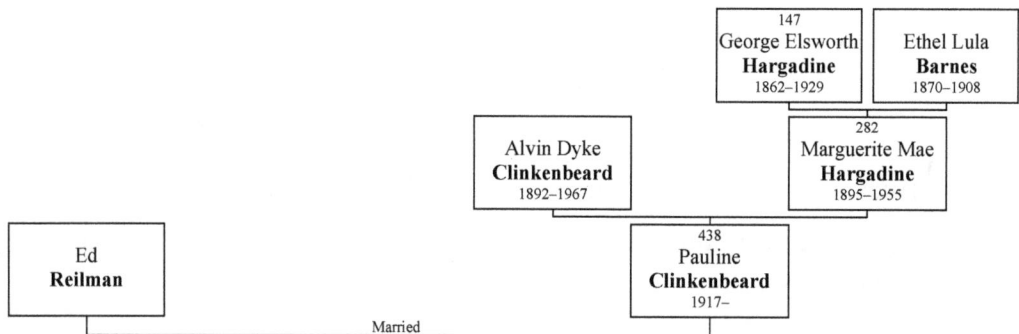

438. **Pauline Clinkenbeard** was born on Thursday, June 14, 1917. She is the daughter of Alvin Dyke Clinkenbeard and Marguerite Mae Hargadine (282).

She married **Ed Reilman**.

Family of Fern Clinkenbeard and Bennie Kirkwood

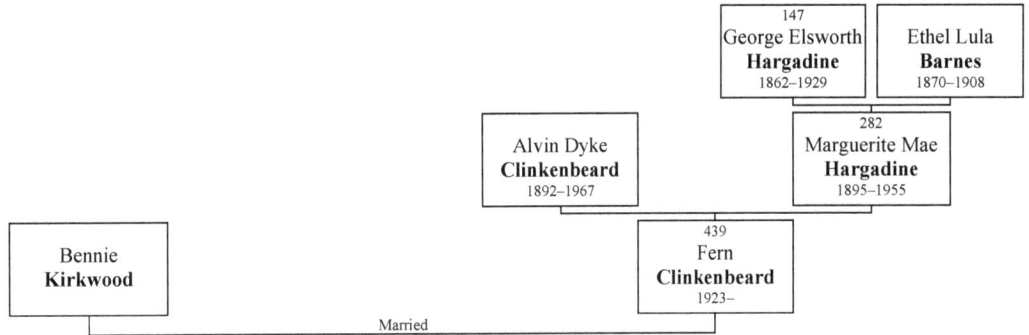

439. **Fern Clinkenbeard** was born on Sunday, June 17, 1923. She is the daughter of Alvin Dyke Clinkenbeard and Marguerite Mae Hargadine (282).

She married **Bennie Kirkwood**.

Family of Clinton Miller and Emma Neier

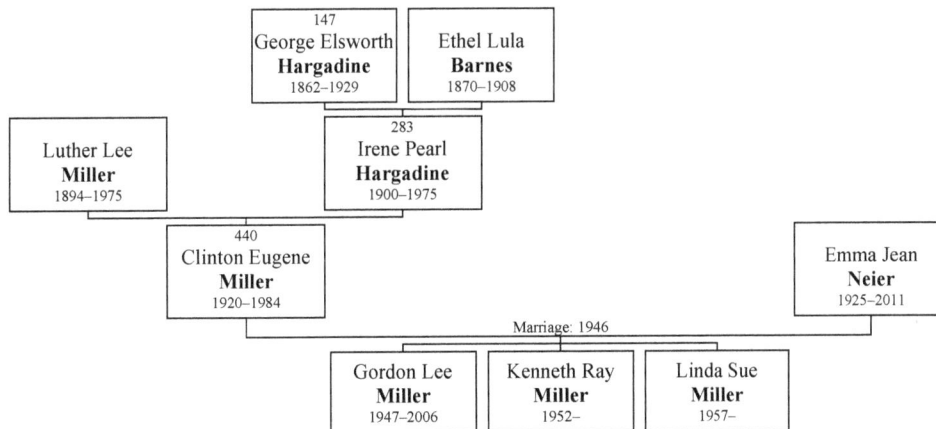

440. **Clinton Eugene Miller** was born on Monday, September 20, 1920. He was the son of Luther Lee Miller and Irene Pearl Hargadine (283).

Clinton Eugene served in the military between 1942 and 1945: U.S. Army. He died in Minneola, Clark County, Kansas, on June 20, 1984, at the age of 63. Clinton Eugene was buried in Appleton Township Cemetery, Minneola, Clark County, Kansas (Find a Grave ID 69140064).

Clinton Eugene married **Emma Jean Neier** in 1946. They had three children.

Emma Jean was born in Mullinville, Kiowa County, Kansas, on Sunday, January 18, 1925. She was also known as **Jean**.

Emma Jean reached 86 years of age and died in Minneola, Clark County, Kansas, on April 24, 2011. She was buried in Appleton Township Cemetery, Minneola, Clark County, Kansas (Find a Grave ID 68942189).

Children of Clinton Eugene Miller and Emma Jean Neier:

m   I. **Gordon Lee Miller** was born on February 03, 1947. He died in Clark, Kansas, USA, on August 05, 2006, at the age of 59. Gordon Lee was buried in Fairview Cemetery, Greensburg, Kiowa County, Kansas (Find a Grave ID 30551235).

m   II. **Kenneth Ray Miller** was born in January 1952.

f   III. **Linda Sue Miller** was born in August 1957.

Family of Jerome Hargadine and Wanda Williams

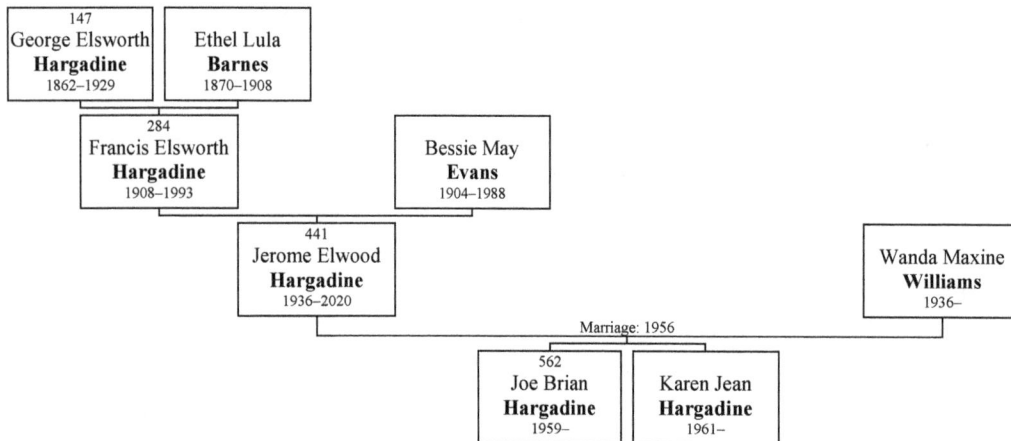

441. **Jerome Elwood Hargadine** was born on Saturday, January 25, 1936, in Kinsley, Edwards County, Kansas. He was the son of Francis Elsworth Hargadine (284) and Bessie May Evans. He was also known as **Jerry**.

Jerome Elwood died in Paris, Lamar County, Texas, on October 10, 2020, at the age of 84. He was cremated (Find a Grave ID 216699191).

At the age of 20, Jerome Elwood married **Wanda Maxine Williams** on Sunday, November 04, 1956, in Anderson, Shasta County, California, when she was 19 years old. They had two children.

Wanda Maxine was born on Sunday, December 20, 1936.[454]

Children of Jerome Elwood Hargadine and Wanda Maxine Williams:

+ 562   m   I. **Joe Brian Hargadine** was born in Shasta County, California, on January 20, 1959.

f   II. **Karen Jean Hargadine** was born in Shasta County, California, on April 10, 1961.

---

454 Ancestry.com, California, U.S., Marriage Index, 1949-1959 (Provo, UT, USA, Ancestry.com Operations, Inc., 2013), Ancestry.com, Record for Wanda M Williams. https://search.ancestry.co.uk/cgi-bin/sse.dll?db=5186&h=21407368&indiv=try.

Family of Vera Scott and Buford Broadbeck

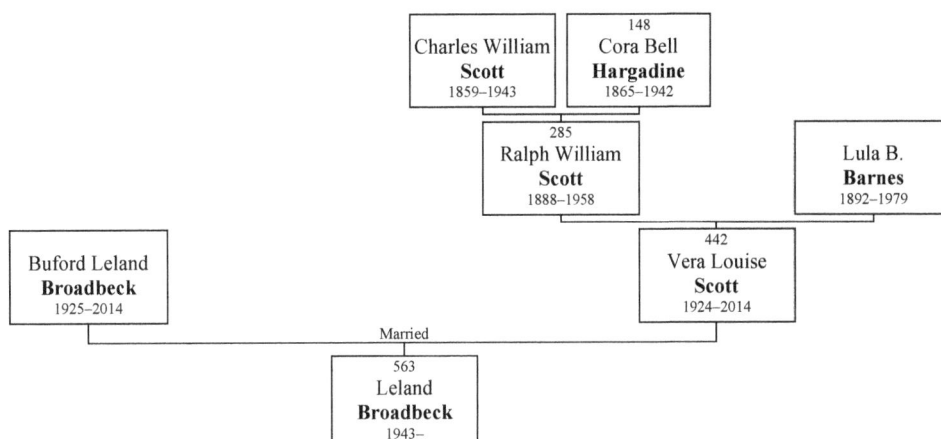

442. **Vera Louise Scott** was born on Sunday, August 03, 1924, in Hodges, Edwards County, Kansas. She was the daughter of Ralph William Scott (285) and Lula B. Barnes.

Vera Louise died in Kinsley, Edwards County, Kansas, on December 07, 2014, at the age of 90. She was buried in Hillside Cemetery, Kinsley, Edwards County, Kansas (Find a Grave ID 142438452).

She married **Buford Leland Broadbeck**. They had one son.

Buford Leland was born in Kinsley, Edwards County, Kansas, on Monday, May 11, 1925. He reached 89 years of age and died in Wichita, Sedgwick County, Kansas, on November 19, 2014. Buford Leland was buried in Hillside Cemetery, Kinsley, Edwards County, Kansas (Find a Grave ID 142436012).

More facts and events for Buford Leland Broadbeck:

Individual Note: 1955 - 2005   Fire Chief

Son of Vera Louise Scott and Buford Leland Broadbeck:

+   563   m   I. **Leland Broadbeck** was born in 1943.[455]

---

[455]   Ancestry.com, U.S., Newspapers.com™ Marriage Index, 1800s-current (Lehi, UT, USA, Ancestry.com Operations Inc, 2020), Ancestry.com, *The Hays Daily News*; Publication Date: 6/ Aug/ 1961; Publication Place: Hays, Kansas, USA; URL: https://www.newspapers.com/image/1389921/?article=ce50a66a-9c4c-43f2-8c3a-9157ef6fe1da/4b239523-4a70-41cb-b1c1-ec07d151d9ff&focus=0.013420457,0.60109,0.13575448,0.6805659&xid=3398. Record for Leland Brodbeck. https://search.ancestry.co.uk/cgi-bin/sse.dll?db=62116&h=331428808&indiv=try.

Family of Bettie Scott and Howard Koch

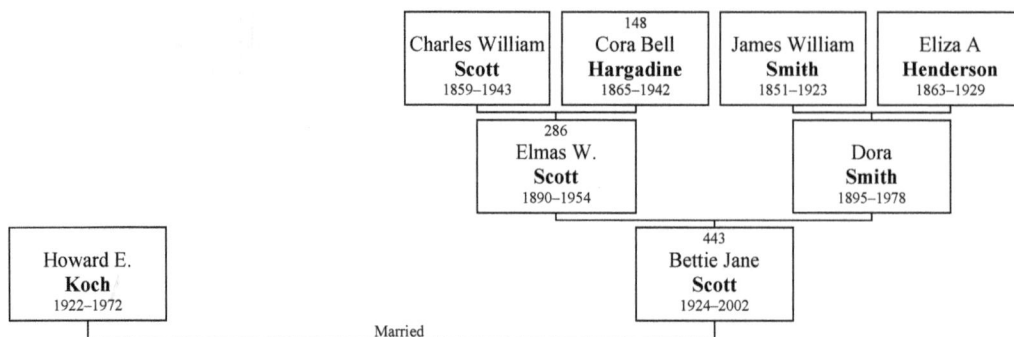

	148		
Charles William **Scott** 1859–1943	Cora Bell **Hargadine** 1865–1942	James William **Smith** 1851–1923	Eliza A **Henderson** 1863–1929

286
Elmas W. **Scott** 1890–1954

Dora **Smith** 1895–1978

Howard E. **Koch** 1922–1972

443
Bettie Jane **Scott** 1924–2002

Married

443. **Bettie Jane Scott** was born on Sunday, March 09, 1924, in Kinsley, Edwards County, Kansas.[456] She was the daughter of Elmas W. Scott (286) and Dora Smith.

Bettie Jane died in Topeka, Shawnee County, Kansas, on February 23, 2002, at the age of 77.[456] She was buried in Atwood Fairview Cemetery, Atwood, Rawlins County, Kansas (Find a Grave ID 103811456).[456]

She married **Howard E. Koch**. Howard E. was born on Monday, January 23, 1922.[456]

He reached 50 years of age and died on July 21, 1972.[456] Howard E. was buried in Atwood Fairview Cemetery, Atwood, Rawlins County, Kansas (Find a Grave ID 106907539).[456]

Family of Elma Scott and Earl Wendland

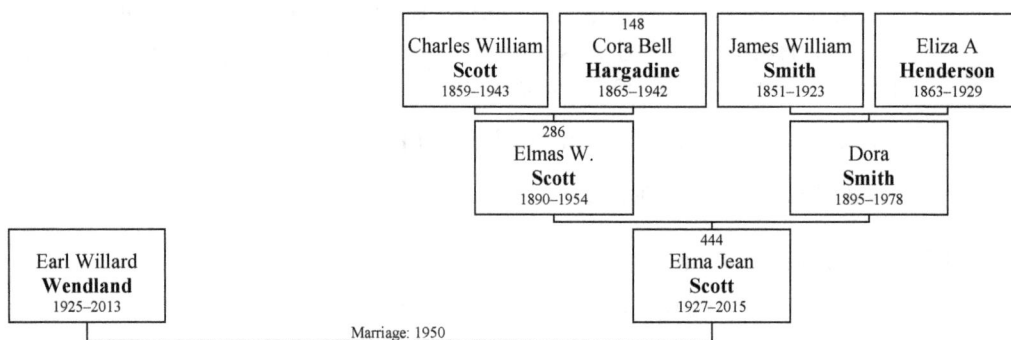

	148		
Charles William **Scott** 1859–1943	Cora Bell **Hargadine** 1865–1942	James William **Smith** 1851–1923	Eliza A **Henderson** 1863–1929

286
Elmas W. **Scott** 1890–1954

Dora **Smith** 1895–1978

Earl Willard **Wendland** 1925–2013

444
Elma Jean **Scott** 1927–2015

Marriage: 1950

444. **Elma Jean Scott** was born on Wednesday, October 26, 1927, in Mullinville, Kiowa County, Kansas. She was the daughter of Elmas W. Scott (286) and Dora Smith.

Elma Jean died in Leonardville, Riley County, Kansas, on September 09, 2015, at the age of 87. She was buried in Fancy Creek Randolph Cemetery, Randolph, Riley County, Kansas (Find a Grave ID 152127556).

At the age of 22, Elma Jean married **Earl Willard Wendland** on Friday, September 01, 1950, in Kinsley, Edwards County, Kansas, when he was 25 years old. Earl Willard was born in Riley County, Kansas, on Monday, May 11, 1925.

456 Ancestry.com, U.S., Find a Grave® Index, 1600s-Current (Lehi, UT, USA, Ancestry.com Operations, Inc., 2012), Ancestry.com, Record for Bettie Jane Bergling. https://search.ancestry.co.uk/cgi-bin/sse.dll?db=60525&h=55387407&indiv=try.

He reached 87 years of age and died in Leonardville, Riley County, Kansas, on April 09, 2013. Earl Willard was buried in Fancy Creek Randolph Cemetery, Randolph, Riley County, Kansas (Find a Grave ID 108552037).

Family of Patricia Scott and Don Allison

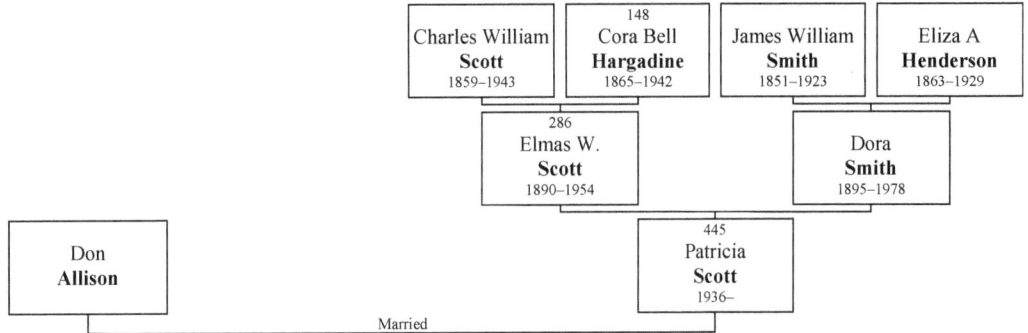

445. **Patricia Scott** was born in 1936 in Kansas, USA. She is the daughter of Elmas W. Scott (286) and Dora Smith.

She married **Don Allison**.

Family of Lorraine Scott and Stacy Graff

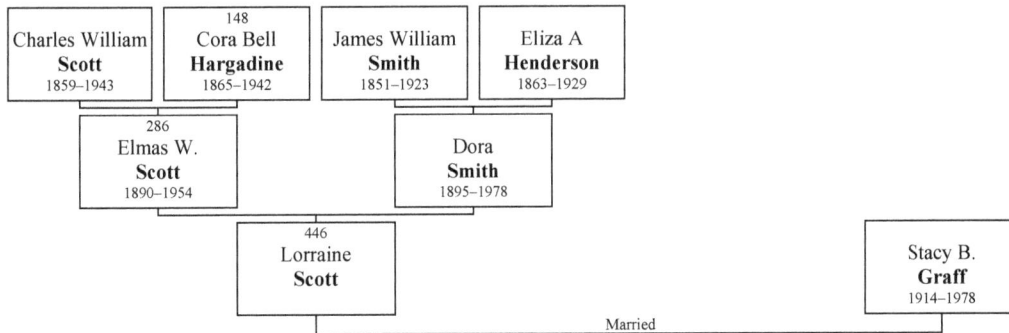

446. **Lorraine Scott**. He was the son of Elmas W. Scott (286) and Dora Smith.

He married **Stacy B. Graff**. Stacy B. was born on Wednesday, November 18, 1914.

She reached 63 years of age and died on March 13, 1978. Stacy B. was buried in Hillside Cemetery, Kinsley, Edwards County, Kansas (Find a Grave ID 11421739).

Family of Joyce Scott and Gale Carney

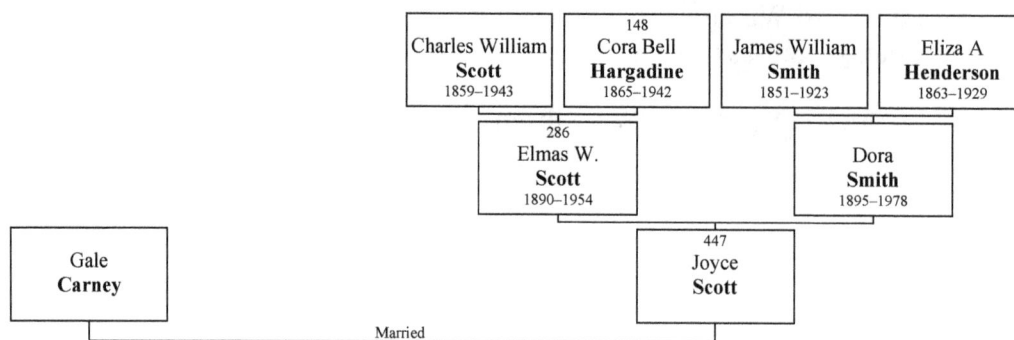

	148		
Charles William **Scott** 1859–1943	Cora Bell **Hargadine** 1865–1942	James William **Smith** 1851–1923	Eliza A **Henderson** 1863–1929

286
Elmas W. **Scott** 1890–1954

Dora **Smith** 1895–1978

Gale **Carney**

447
Joyce **Scott**

Married

447. **Joyce Scott**. She was the daughter of Elmas W. Scott (286) and Dora Smith.

She married **Gale Carney**.

Family of Robert Scott and Betty Priest

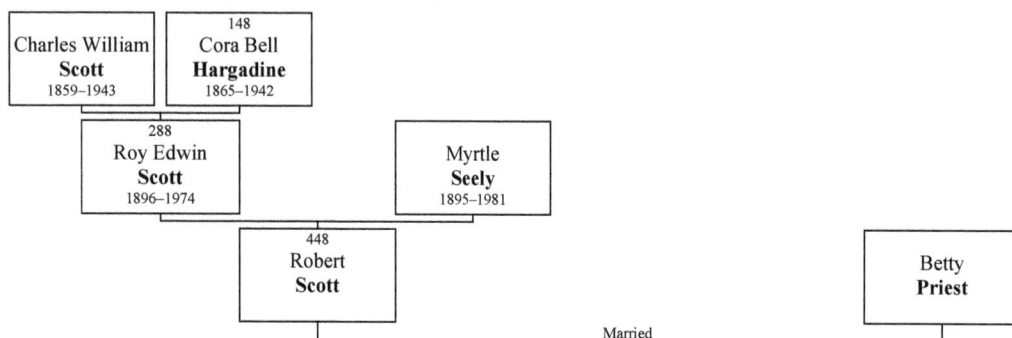

Charles William **Scott** 1859–1943	148 Cora Bell **Hargadine** 1865–1942

288
Roy Edwin **Scott** 1896–1974

Myrtle **Seely** 1895–1981

448
Robert **Scott**

Betty **Priest**

Married

448. **Robert Scott**. He was the son of Roy Edwin Scott (288) and Myrtle Seely.

He married **Betty Priest**.

Family of Paul Marsteller and Jeanne Strobel

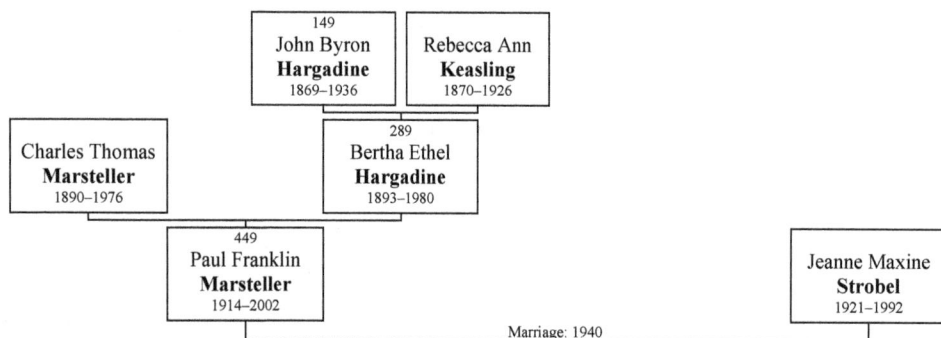

149
John Byron **Hargadine** 1869–1936

Rebecca Ann **Keasling** 1870–1926

Charles Thomas **Marsteller** 1890–1976

289
Bertha Ethel **Hargadine** 1893–1980

449
Paul Franklin **Marsteller** 1914–2002

Jeanne Maxine **Strobel** 1921–1992

Marriage: 1940

449. **Paul Franklin Marsteller** was born on Thursday, June 04, 1914, in Edwards County, Kansas. He was the son of Charles Thomas Marsteller and Bertha Ethel Hargadine (289).

Paul Franklin worked as Lane County Sheriff and Dighton Police Chief. He died in Dighton, Lane County, Kansas, on March 12, 2002, at the age of 87. Paul Franklin was buried in Dighton Cemetery, Dighton, Lane County, Kansas (Find a Grave ID 81738405).

At the age of 26, Paul Franklin married **Jeanne Maxine Strobel** on Saturday, July 06, 1940, when she was 19 years old. Jeanne Maxine was born in Healy, Lane County, Kansas, on Sunday, June 12, 1921.

She reached 70 years of age and died in Garden City, Finney County, Kansas, on April 23, 1992. Jeanne Maxine was buried in Dighton Cemetery, Dighton, Lane County, Kansas (Find a Grave ID 105900699).

Family of Lelia Marsteller and Clyde Craik

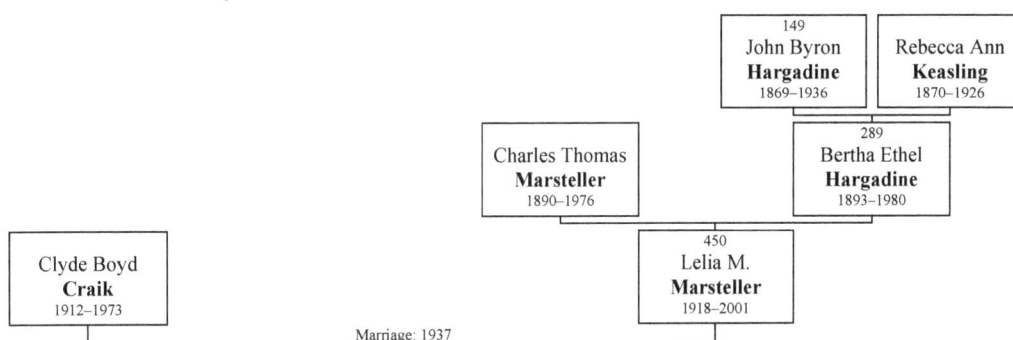

```
                                                                    ┌─────────────┬─────────────┐
                                                                    │     149     │             │
                                                                    │ John Byron  │ Rebecca Ann │
                                                                    │ Hargadine   │  Keasling   │
                                                                    │  1869–1936  │  1870–1926  │
                                                                    └─────────────┴─────────────┘
                                              ┌──────────────┐            ┌─────────────┐
                                              │ Charles Thomas│           │     289     │
                                              │  Marsteller   │           │ Bertha Ethel│
                                              │  1890–1976    │           │ Hargadine   │
                                              └──────────────┘            │  1893–1980  │
                  ┌──────────────┐                  ┌─────────────┐
                  │ Clyde Boyd   │                  │    450      │
                  │   Craik      │                  │  Lelia M.   │
                  │  1912–1973   │                  │ Marsteller  │
                  └──────────────┘                  │  1918–2001  │
                              Marriage: 1937
```

450. **Lelia M. Marsteller** was born on Sunday, February 24, 1918, in Mullinville, Kiowa, Kansas, USA.[457] She was the daughter of Charles Thomas Marsteller and Bertha Ethel Hargadine (289).

She was buried in Winona Cemetery, Winona, Logan County, Kansas, in April 2001 (Find a Grave ID 32420971).[457] Lelia M. died in Oakley, Logan, Kansas, USA, on April 17, 2001, at the age of 83.[457]

At the age of 19, Lelia M. married **Clyde Boyd Craik** on Saturday, November 06, 1937, when he was 24 years old.[457] Clyde Boyd was born in Kansas, USA, on Saturday, December 14, 1912.[457] He was also known as **Bus**.

He was buried in March 1973 in Winona Cemetery, Winona, Logan County, Kansas (Find a Grave ID 32420978).[457] Clyde Boyd reached 60 years of age and died on March 09, 1973.[457]

Family of Lola Marsteller and Lindy Bretz

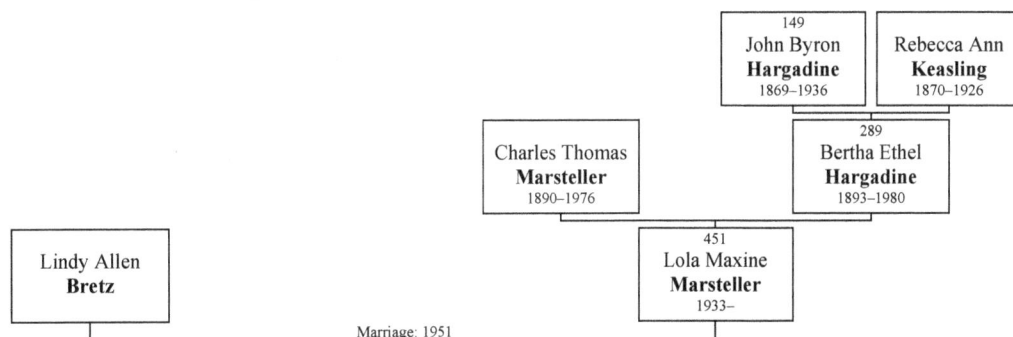

```
                                                                    ┌─────────────┬─────────────┐
                                                                    │     149     │             │
                                                                    │ John Byron  │ Rebecca Ann │
                                                                    │ Hargadine   │  Keasling   │
                                                                    │  1869–1936  │  1870–1926  │
                                                                    └─────────────┴─────────────┘
                                              ┌──────────────┐            ┌─────────────┐
                                              │ Charles Thomas│           │     289     │
                                              │  Marsteller   │           │ Bertha Ethel│
                                              │  1890–1976    │           │ Hargadine   │
                                              └──────────────┘            │  1893–1980  │
                  ┌──────────────┐                  ┌─────────────┐
                  │ Lindy Allen  │                  │    451      │
                  │   Bretz      │                  │ Lola Maxine │
                  └──────────────┘                  │ Marsteller  │
                                                    │   1933–     │
                              Marriage: 1951
```

457   Ancestry.com, Public Member Trees (Provo, UT, USA, Ancestry.com Operations, Inc., 2006), Ancestry.com, Record for Boyd Clyde Craik. https://search.ancestry.co.uk/cgi-bin/sse.dll?db=1030&h=110039168410&indiv=try.

451. **Lola Maxine Marsteller** was born on Monday, January 30, 1933. She is the daughter of Charles Thomas Marsteller and Bertha Ethel Hargadine (289).

Lola Maxine married **Lindy Allen Bretz** on Wednesday, January 10, 1951.

Family of Claude Hargadine and Francine Hosey

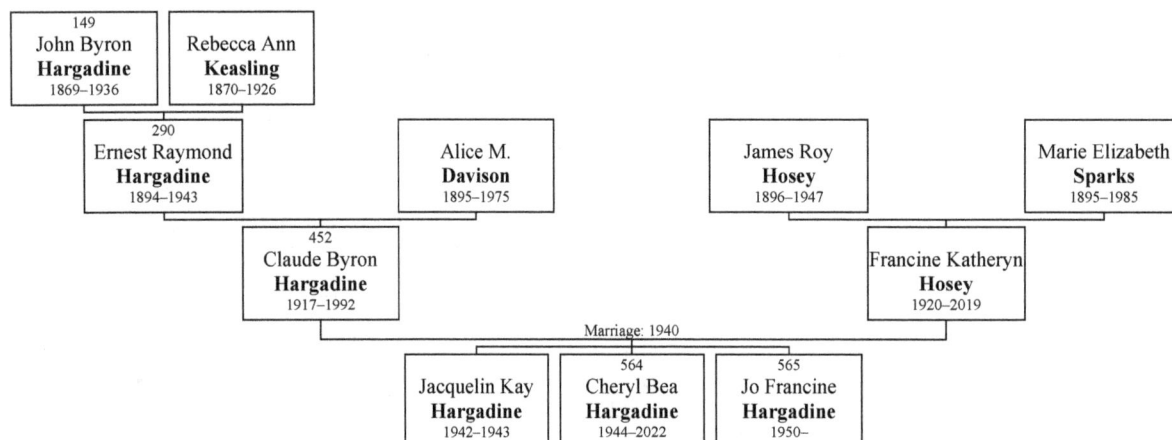

452. **Claude Byron Hargadine** was born on Friday, May 25, 1917. He was the son of Ernest Raymond Hargadine (290) and Alice M. Davison.

Claude Byron served in the military: US Army; WWII. He died in Rogers, Benton County, Arkansas, on February 08, 1992, at the age of 74. Claude Byron was buried in Lone Star Cemetery, Pretty Prairie, Reno County, Kansas (Find a Grave ID 22002088).

At the age of 23, Claude Byron married **Francine Katheryn Hosey** on Sunday, November 10, 1940, when she was 19 years old. They had three daughters.

Francine Katheryn was born in Blackwell, Kay County, Oklahoma, on Wednesday, December 29, 1920. She was the daughter of James Roy Hosey and Marie Elizabeth Sparks. She was also known as **Fran**.

Francine Katheryn reached 98 years of age and died on October 19, 2019. She was buried on November 16, 2019, in Lone Star Cemetery, Pretty Prairie, Reno County, Kansas (Find a Grave ID 34007766).

Daughters of Claude Byron Hargadine and Francine Katheryn Hosey:

		f	I.	**Jacquelin Kay Hargadine** was born on October 01, 1942. She died on April 22, 1943. Jacquelin Kay was buried in Lone Star Cemetery, Pretty Prairie, Reno County, Kansas (Find a Grave ID 22002115).
+	564	f	II.	**Cheryl Bea Hargadine** was born on August 11, 1944. She died in Kansas, USA, on May 12, 2022, at the age of 77. Her cause of death was Alzheimer's. She was cremated (Find a Grave ID 248049336).
+	565	f	III.	**Jo Francine Hargadine** was born in February 1950.

Family of Jack Hogg and Joan Nopp

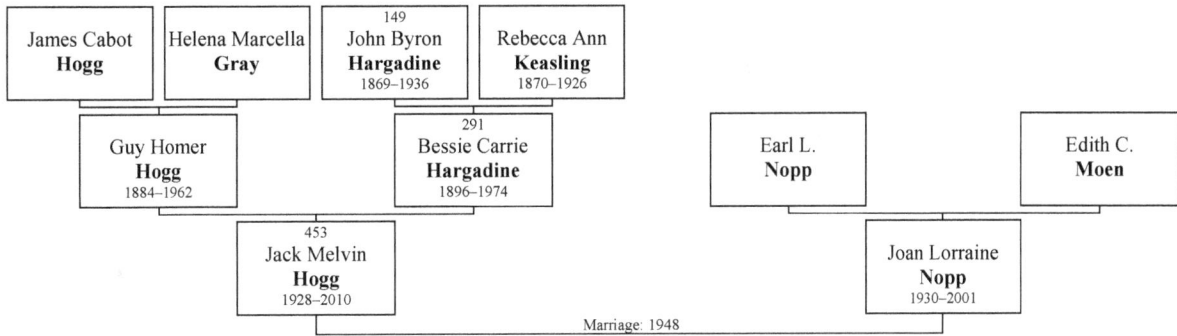

		149				
James Cabot **Hogg**	Helena Marcella **Gray**	John Byron **Hargadine** 1869–1936	Rebecca Ann **Keasling** 1870–1926		Earl L. **Nopp**	Edith C. **Moen**

Guy Homer **Hogg** 1884–1962

291
Bessie Carrie **Hargadine** 1896–1974

453
Jack Melvin **Hogg** 1928–2010

Joan Lorraine **Nopp** 1930–2001

Marriage: 1948

453. **Jack Melvin Hogg** was born on Friday, April 27, 1928, in Kinsley, Edwards County, Kansas. He was the son of Guy Homer Hogg and Bessie Carrie Hargadine (291).

Jack Melvin died in Washington, USA, on August 19, 2010, at the age of 82. He was buried (Find a Grave ID 99196320).

At the age of 20, Jack Melvin married **Joan Lorraine Nopp** on Thursday, July 01, 1948, in Seattle, King County, Washington, when she was 18 years old. Joan Lorraine was born in Lethbridge, Alberta, Canada, on Thursday, February 06, 1930. She was the daughter of Earl L. Nopp and Edith C. Moen.

Joan Lorraine reached 70 years of age and died in Benton, Washington, USA, on January 12, 2001.

Family of Clinton Hargadine and Dortha Emery

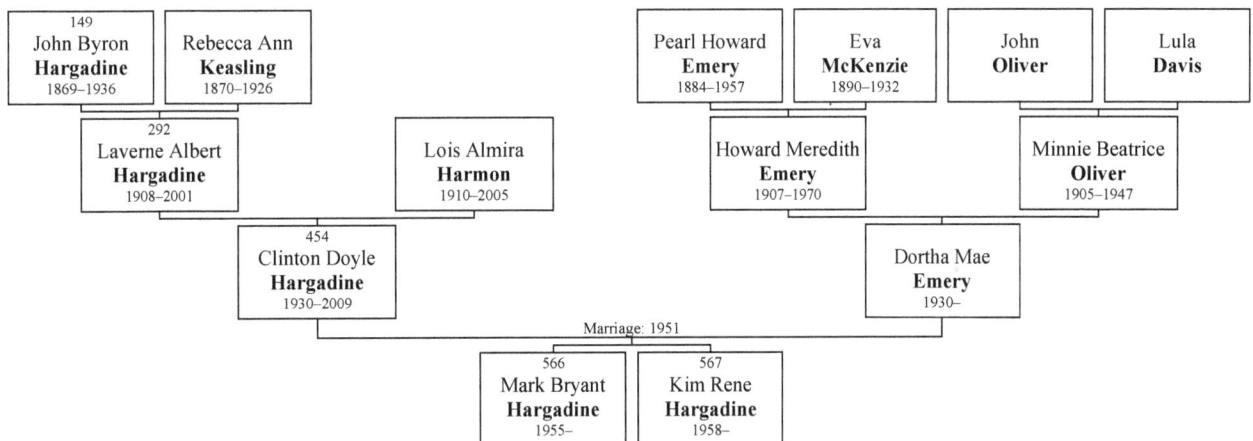

149 John Byron **Hargadine** 1869–1936	Rebecca Ann **Keasling** 1870–1926			Pearl Howard **Emery** 1884–1957	Eva **McKenzie** 1890–1932	John **Oliver**	Lula **Davis**

292
Laverne Albert **Hargadine** 1908–2001

Lois Almira **Harmon** 1910–2005

Howard Meredith **Emery** 1907–1970

Minnie Beatrice **Oliver** 1905–1947

454
Clinton Doyle **Hargadine** 1930–2009

Dortha Mae **Emery** 1930–

Marriage: 1951

566
Mark Bryant **Hargadine** 1955–

567
Kim Rene **Hargadine** 1958–

454. **Clinton Doyle Hargadine** was born on Tuesday, February 25, 1930, in Salina, Saline County, Kansas. He was the son of Laverne Albert Hargadine (292) and Lois Almira Harmon.

Clinton Doyle died in Prairie Village, Overland Park, Johnson County. Kansas, on March 08, 2009, at the age of 79. He was buried in Corinth Cemetery, Prairie Village, Johnson County, Kansas (Find a Grave ID 124358667).

At the age of 20, Clinton Doyle married **Dortha Mae Emery** on Sunday, January 28, 1951, when she was 20 years old. They had two children.

Dortha Mae was born on Wednesday, April 16, 1930. She was the daughter of Howard Meredith Emery and Minnie Beatrice Oliver.

Dortha Mae was buried in Corinth Cemetery, Prairie Village, Johnson County, Kansas (Find a Grave ID 256342024).

Children of Clinton Doyle Hargadine and Dortha Mae Emery:

+ 566   m   I. **Mark Bryant Hargadine** was born on May 10, 1955.

+ 567   f   II. **Kim Rene Hargadine** was born on February 13, 1958.

Curtis Hargadine

455.   **Curtis Dale Hargadine** was born on Tuesday, June 04, 1940, in McPherson, McPherson County, Kansas. He is the son of Laverne Albert Hargadine (292) and Lois Almira Harmon.

Marriages with Carol K. Klinger and Janice Ley Zimmerman (Page 471) are known.

Family of Curtis Hargadine and Carol Klinger

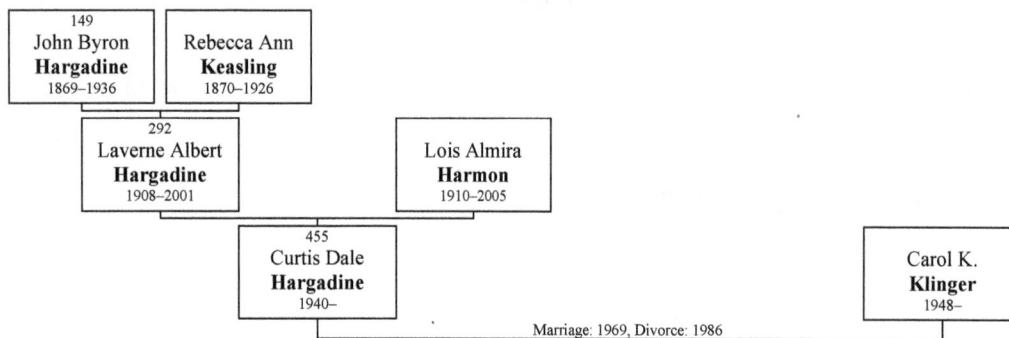

Here are the details about **Curtis Dale Hargadine's** first marriage, with Carol K. Klinger. You can read more about Curtis Dale on page 470.

Curtis Dale Hargadine married **Carol K. Klinger** in 1969 in Minnesota, USA.[458] They were divorced at Ramsey County, Minnesota, on March 14, 1986.

Carol Klinger was born in 1948.

---

458   Minnesota Divorce Index, Divorced Carol A. Hargadine 14 Mar 1986, Ramsey County, MN.

Family of Curtis Hargadine and Janice Zimmerman

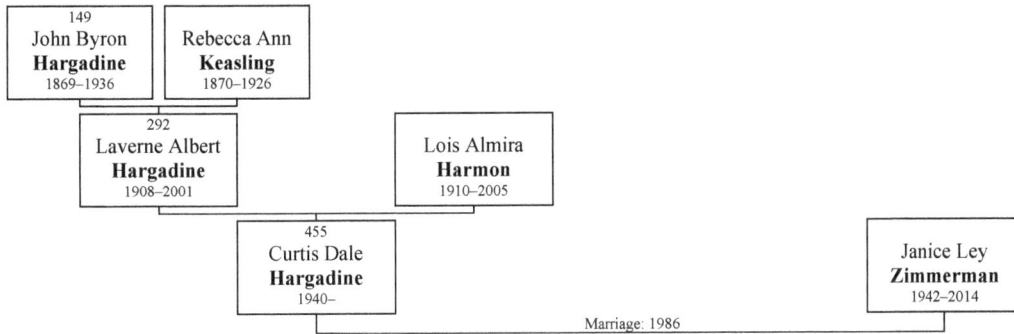

```
┌──────────┐ ┌──────────┐
│   149    │ │          │
│John Byron│ │Rebecca Ann│
│Hargadine │ │ Keasling │
│1869–1936 │ │1870–1926 │
└──────────┘ └──────────┘
     ┌──────────┐            ┌──────────┐
     │   292    │            │          │
     │Laverne Albert│        │Lois Almira│
     │ Hargadine │           │  Harmon  │
     │1908–2001 │            │1910–2005 │
     └──────────┘            └──────────┘
          ┌──────────┐                          ┌──────────┐
          │   455    │                          │Janice Ley│
          │Curtis Dale│                         │Zimmerman │
          │ Hargadine │                         │1942–2014 │
          │  1940–   │                          └──────────┘
          └──────────┘    Marriage: 1986
```

Here are the details about **Curtis Dale Hargadine's** second marriage, with Janice Ley Zimmerman. You can read more about Curtis Dale on page 470.

At the age of 46, Curtis Dale Hargadine married **Janice Ley Zimmerman** on Saturday, June 28, 1986, in Hennepin County, Minnesota, when she was 44 years old. Janice Ley was born in Cherokee, Cherokee County, Iowa, on Friday, March 06, 1942.

She reached 72 years of age and died in Oakdale, Washington County, Minnesota, on May 26, 2014. Janice Ley was buried in Lakeside Cemetery, Hastings, Dakota County, Minnesota (Find a Grave ID 130589926).

Family of Velma Hargadine and William Adams

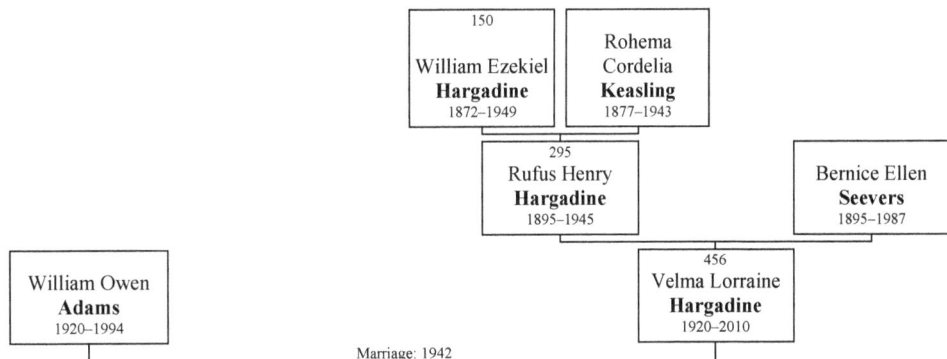

```
                              ┌──────────┐ ┌──────────┐
                              │   150    │ │ Rohema   │
                              │William Ezekiel│ Cordelia│
                              │ Hargadine │ │ Keasling │
                              │1872–1949 │ │1877–1943 │
                              └──────────┘ └──────────┘
                                   ┌──────────┐      ┌──────────┐
                                   │   295    │      │Bernice Ellen│
                                   │Rufus Henry│      │  Seevers │
                                   │ Hargadine │      │1895–1987 │
                                   │1895–1945 │      └──────────┘
                                        ┌──────────┐
                                        │   456    │
┌──────────┐                            │Velma Lorraine│
│William Owen│                          │ Hargadine │
│  Adams   │                            │1920–2010 │
│1920–1994 │                            └──────────┘
└──────────┘         Marriage: 1942
```

456. **Velma Lorraine Hargadine** was born on Wednesday, July 21, 1920, in Mullinville, Kiowa County, Kansas. She was the daughter of Rufus Henry Hargadine (295) and Bernice Ellen Seevers.

Velma Lorraine died on August 16, 2010, at the age of 90. She was buried in Hillside Cemetery, Kinsley, Edwards County, Kansas (Find a Grave ID 119453896).

At the age of 22, Velma Lorraine married **William Owen Adams** on Sunday, September 06, 1942, when he was 22 years old. William Owen was born in Leadmine, Dallas County, Missouri, on Wednesday, August 11, 1920.

He reached 73 years of age and died in Mullinville, Kiowa County, Kansas, on April 16, 1994. William Owen was buried in Hillcrest Cemetery, Mullinville, Kiowa County, Kansas (Find a Grave ID 119408322).

Family of Lola Hargadine and Elbert Brensing

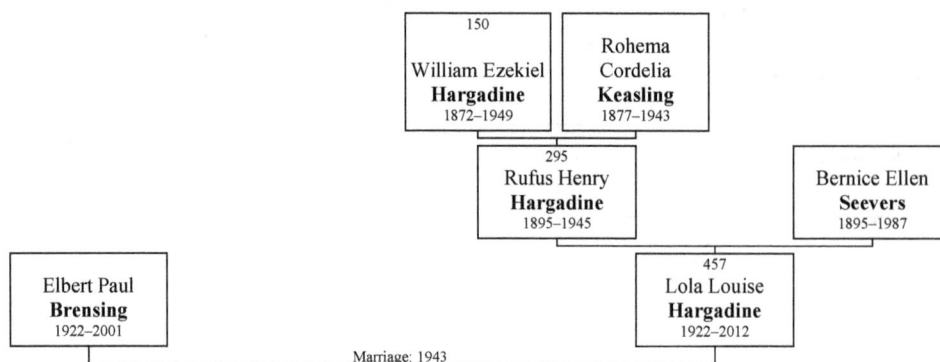

	150 William Ezekiel **Hargadine** 1872–1949	Rohema Cordelia **Keasling** 1877–1943		
		295 Rufus Henry **Hargadine** 1895–1945		Bernice Ellen **Seevers** 1895–1987
Elbert Paul **Brensing** 1922–2001			457 Lola Louise **Hargadine** 1922–2012	

Marriage: 1943

457. **Lola Louise Hargadine** was born on Wednesday, May 17, 1922, in Kiowa County, Kansas. She was the daughter of Rufus Henry Hargadine (295) and Bernice Ellen Seevers.

Lola Louise died in Illinois, USA, on May 17, 2012, at the age of 90. She was buried in Hillcrest Cemetery, Mullinville, Kiowa County, Kansas (Find a Grave ID 160311413).

At the age of 21, Lola Louise married **Elbert Paul Brensing** on Thursday, November 25, 1943, in Santa Clara County, California, when he was 21 years old.[459] Elbert Paul was born on Friday, April 21, 1922.

He reached 78 years of age and died on February 01, 2001. Elbert Paul was buried in Hillcrest Cemetery, Mullinville, Kiowa County, Kansas (Find a Grave ID 52092068).

Family of Curtis Hargadine and Emma Sloan

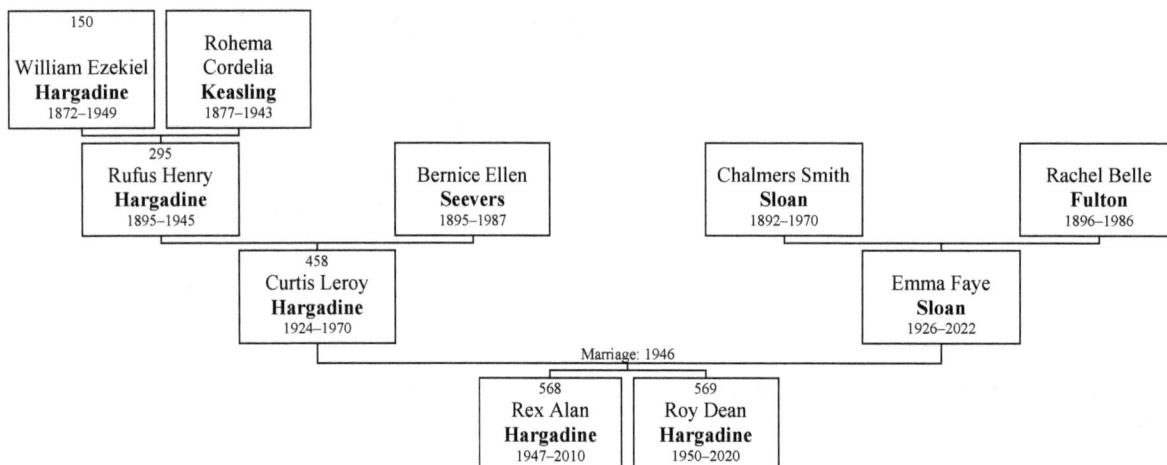

150 William Ezekiel **Hargadine** 1872–1949	Rohema Cordelia **Keasling** 1877–1943				
295 Rufus Henry **Hargadine** 1895–1945		Bernice Ellen **Seevers** 1895–1987	Chalmers Smith **Sloan** 1892–1970		Rachel Belle **Fulton** 1896–1986
	458 Curtis Leroy **Hargadine** 1924–1970			Emma Faye **Sloan** 1926–2022	

Marriage: 1946

568 Rex Alan **Hargadine** 1947–2010	569 Roy Dean **Hargadine** 1950–2020

458. **Curtis Leroy Hargadine** was born on Sunday, September 14, 1924, in Edwards County, Kansas. He was the son of Rufus Henry Hargadine (295) and Bernice Ellen Seevers.

Curtis Leroy died in Mullinville, Kiowa County, Kansas, on October 06, 1970, at the age of 46. He was buried in Hillcrest Cemetery, Mullinville, Kiowa County, Kansas, on October 10, 1970 (Find a Grave ID 119318961).

---

459   Santa Clara County California, Marriage records BRE-BRI, http://ftp.rootsweb.com/pub/usgenweb/ca/santaclara/vitals/marriages/bre-bri. Certificate # 4301731.

At the age of 21, Curtis Leroy married **Emma Faye Sloan** on Sunday, September 01, 1946, when she was 19 years old. They had two sons.

Emma Faye was born in Mullinville, Kiowa County, Kansas, on Thursday, October 14, 1926. She was the daughter of Chalmers Smith Sloan and Rachel Belle Fulton.

She worked as a Former County Treasurer of Kiowa, County, Kansas. Emma Faye reached 95 years of age and died at Hill Top House in Bucklin, Ford County, Kansas, on February 10, 2022. She was buried in Hillcrest Cemetery, Mullinville, Kiowa County, Kansas (Find a Grave ID 237577240).

Sons of Curtis Leroy Hargadine and Emma Faye Sloan:

+ 568 m I. **Rex Alan Hargadine** was born in Spearville, Ford County, Kansas, on November 12, 1947. He died in Dodge City, Ford County, Kansas, on April 26, 2010, at the age of 62. Rex Alan was buried in Kansas Veterans Cemetery at Fort Dodge, Dodge City, Ford County, Kansas (Find a Grave ID 52221554).

+ 569 m II. **Roy Dean Hargadine** was born in Greensburg, Kiowa County, Kansas, on August 15, 1950. He died in Wichita, Sedgwick County, Kansas, on July 11, 2020, at the age of 69. Roy Dean was buried in Hillcrest Cemetery, Mullinville, Kiowa County, Kansas (Find a Grave ID 212953167).

Family of LaVena Stevens and Charles Keys

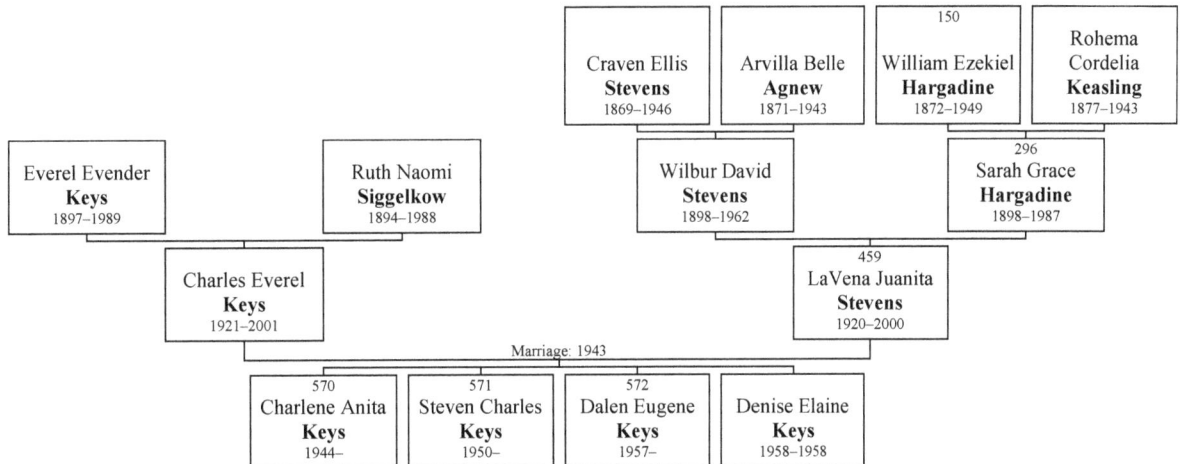

459. **LaVena Juanita Stevens** was born on Friday, July 23, 1920, in Kinsley, Edwards County, Kansas. She was the daughter of Wilbur David Stevens and Sarah Grace Hargadine (296).

LaVena Juanita died in Thibodaux, Lafourche Parish, Louisiana, on March 16, 2000, at the age of 79. She was buried in Bethel Cemetery, Hodges, Edwards County, Kansas (Find a Grave ID 67563788).

At the age of 23, LaVena Juanita married **Dr. Charles Everel Keys** on Saturday, September 04, 1943, in Camp Roberts, San Luis Obispo County, California, when he was 22 years old. They had four children.

Charles Everel was born in Richland Center, Richland County, Wisconsin, on Tuesday, May 10, 1921. He was the son of Everel Evender Keys and Ruth Naomi Siggelkow.

Charles Everel reached 80 years of age and died in Thibodaux, Lafourche Parish, Louisiana, on November 01, 2001. He was buried in Bethel Cemetery, Hodges, Edwards County, Kansas (Find a Grave ID 67563772).

Children of LaVena Juanita Stevens and Charles Everel Keys:

+ 570   f   I. **Charlene Anita Keys** was born in Dodge City, Ford County, Kansas, on October 16, 1944.

+ 571   m   II. **Steven Charles Keys** was born in Lawrence, Douglas County, Kansas, on June 28, 1950.

+ 572   m   III. **Dalen Eugene Keys** was born in Rochester, Monroe County, New York, on April 09, 1957.

         f   IV. **Denise Elaine Keys** was born in Rochester, Monroe County, New York, on July 03, 1958. She died in Rochester, Monroe County, New York, on July 03, 1958.

Family of Leland Stevens and Ester Anderson

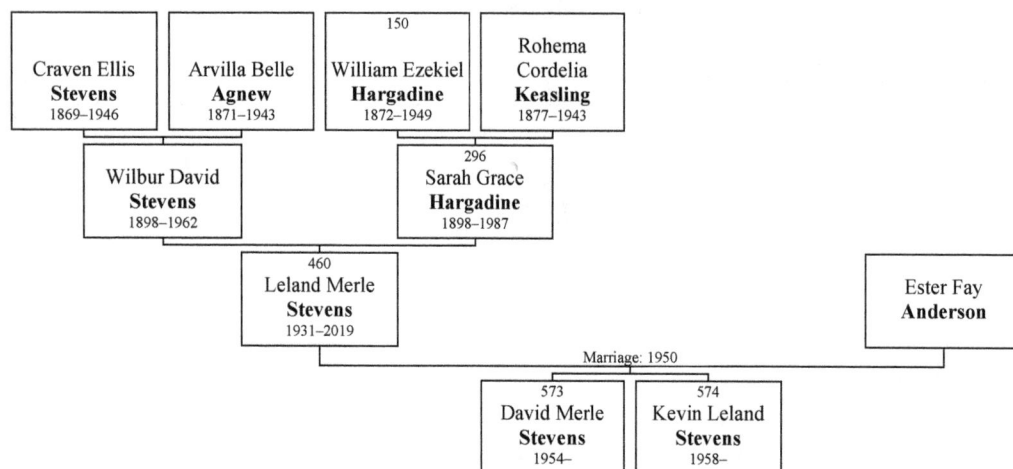

460.   **Leland Merle Stevens** was born on Saturday, October 03, 1931. He was the son of Wilbur David Stevens and Sarah Grace Hargadine (296).

Leland Merle died on June 07, 2019, at the age of 87. He was buried in Bethel Cemetery, Hodges, Edwards County, Kansas (Find a Grave ID 199899994).

Leland Merle married **Ester Fay Anderson** on Sunday, August 20, 1950. They had two sons.

Sons of Leland Merle Stevens and Ester Fay Anderson:

+ 573   m   I. **David Merle Stevens** was born in Kinsley, Edwards County, Kansas, on May 18, 1954.

+ 574   m   II. **Kevin Leland Stevens** was born on March 05, 1958.

Myron Hargadine

461. **Myron Lee Hargadine** was born on Thursday, October 04, 1923, in Kinsley, Edwards County, Kansas. He was the son of William Lee Hargadine (297) and Bessie Leona Burcher.

Myron Lee died in Dodge City, Ford County, Kansas, on October 11, 1988, at the age of 65. He was buried in Maple Grove Cemetery, Dodge City, Ford County, Kansas (Find a Grave ID 112013915).

Marriages with Virginia Rae Pritchett and Patricia L. Lensch (Page 476) are known.

Family of Myron Hargadine and Virginia Pritchett

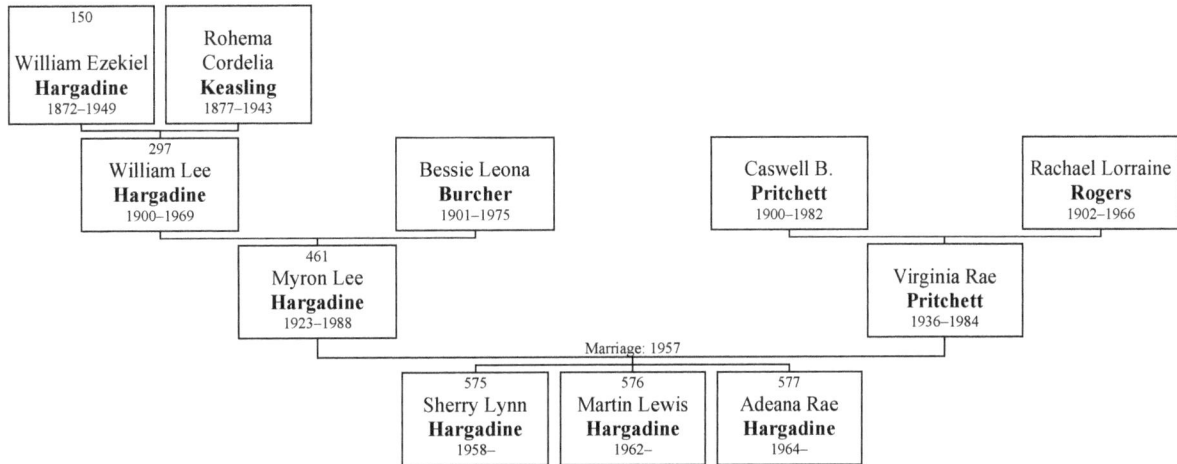

Here are the details about **Myron Lee Hargadine's** first marriage, with Virginia Rae Pritchett. You can read more about Myron Lee on page 475.

At the age of 33, Myron Lee Hargadine married **Virginia Rae Pritchett** on Wednesday, April 03, 1957, when she was 20 years old. They had three children.

Virginia Rae was born in Glasco, Cloud County, Kansas, on Saturday, September 12, 1936.[460] She was the daughter of Caswell B. Pritchett and Rachael Lorraine Rogers. She was also known as **Ginnty**.

Virginia Rae reached 48 years of age and died in Council Grove, Morris County, Kansas, on December 26, 1984.[460] She was buried in Glasco Cemetery, Glasco, Cloud County, Kansas (Find a Grave ID 98301566).

Children of Myron Lee Hargadine and Virginia Rae Pritchett:

+   575   f   I. **Sherry Lynn Hargadine** was born in June 1958.

+   576   m   II. **Martin Lewis Hargadine** was born in June 1962.

+   577   f   III. **Adeana Rae Hargadine** was born in August 1964.

---

460   Ancestry.com, U.S., Social Security Death Index, 1935-2014 (Provo, UT, USA, Ancestry.com Operations Inc, 2014), Ancestry.com, Social Security Administration; Washington D.C., USA; Social Security Death Index, Master File. Record for Virginia Dragoo. https://search.ancestry.co.uk/cgi-bin/sse.dll?db=3693&h=16410405&indiv=try.

Family of Myron Hargadine and Patricia Lensch

```
            ┌─────────────┐ ┌─────────────┐
            │     150     │ │   Rohema    │
            │William Ezekiel│ │  Cordelia   │
            │  Hargadine  │ │  Keasling   │
            │  1872–1949  │ │  1877–1943  │
            └─────────────┘ └─────────────┘
                 ┌─────────────┐ ┌─────────────┐
                 │     297     │ │ Bessie Leona│
                 │ William Lee │ │   Burcher   │
                 │  Hargadine  │ │  1901–1975  │
                 │  1900–1969  │ └─────────────┘
                 └─────────────┘
                      ┌─────────────┐          ┌─────────────┐
                      │     461     │          │ Patricia L. │
                      │  Myron Lee  │          │   Lensch    │
                      │  Hargadine  │          │  1928–1995  │
                      │  1923–1988  │          └─────────────┘
                      └─────────────┘
                            Marriage: 1973
```

Here are the details about **Myron Lee Hargadine's** second marriage, with Patricia L. Lensch. You can read more about Myron Lee on page 475.

Myron Lee Hargadine married **Patricia L. Lensch** in 1973. Patricia L. was born in New York, USA, on Monday, May 21, 1928. She was also known as **Pat**.

Patricia L. reached 66 years of age and died in Wichita, Sedgwick County, Kansas, on January 16, 1995. She was buried on January 20, 1995, in Dodge City, Ford County, Kansas (Find a Grave ID 161959868).

Family of Gloria Hargadine and Raymond Horne

```
                    ┌─────────────┐ ┌─────────────┐
                    │     150     │ │   Rohema    │
                    │William Ezekiel│ │  Cordelia   │
                    │  Hargadine  │ │  Keasling   │
                    │  1872–1949  │ │  1877–1943  │
                    └─────────────┘ └─────────────┘
                         ┌─────────────┐ ┌─────────────┐
                         │     297     │ │ Bessie Leona│
                         │ William Lee │ │   Burcher   │
                         │  Hargadine  │ │  1901–1975  │
                         │  1900–1969  │ └─────────────┘
                         └─────────────┘
    ┌─────────────┐           ┌─────────────┐
    │Raymond Stanley│          │     462     │
    │    Horne    │           │ Gloria Ruth │
    │  1924–2002  │           │  Hargadine  │
    └─────────────┘           │  1926–2015  │
                Marriage: 1951 └─────────────┘
       ┌─────────────┐ ┌─────────────┐ ┌─────────────┐
       │     578     │ │     579     │ │     580     │
       │David Lawrence│ │ Cynthia Lynn│ │Richard Norris│
       │    Horne    │ │    Horne    │ │    Horne    │
       │    1953–    │ │    1956–    │ │    1961–    │
       └─────────────┘ └─────────────┘ └─────────────┘
```

462. **Gloria Ruth Hargadine** was born on Sunday, February 07, 1926, in Lewis, Edwards County, Kansas. She was the daughter of William Lee Hargadine (297) and Bessie Leona Burcher.

Gloria Ruth died in Springdale, Washington County, Arkansas, on June 13, 2015, at the age of 89. She was buried in Rosedale Cemetery, Ada, Pontotoc County, Oklahoma (Find a Grave ID 147933603).

At the age of 25, Gloria Ruth married **Raymond Stanley Horne** on Sunday, December 30, 1951, in Pratt, Pratt County, Kansas, when he was 27 years old. They had three children.

Raymond Stanley was born in Ada, Pontotoc County, Oklahoma, on Tuesday, March 18, 1924.[461] He served in the military: WWII, US Army.

Raymond Stanley reached 78 years of age and died in Pontotoc, Oklahoma, USA, on June 28, 2002. He was buried in Rosedale Cemetery, Ada, Pontotoc County, Oklahoma (Find a Grave ID 123139517).

Children of Gloria Ruth Hargadine and Raymond Stanley Horne:

+ 578 m I. **David Lawrence Horne** was born in Ada, Pontotoc County, Oklahoma, on January 08, 1953.

+ 579 f II. **Cynthia Lynn Horne** was born in July 1956.

+ 580 m III. **Richard Norris Horne** was born in February 1961.

Family of Shirley Hargadine and Joe Dean

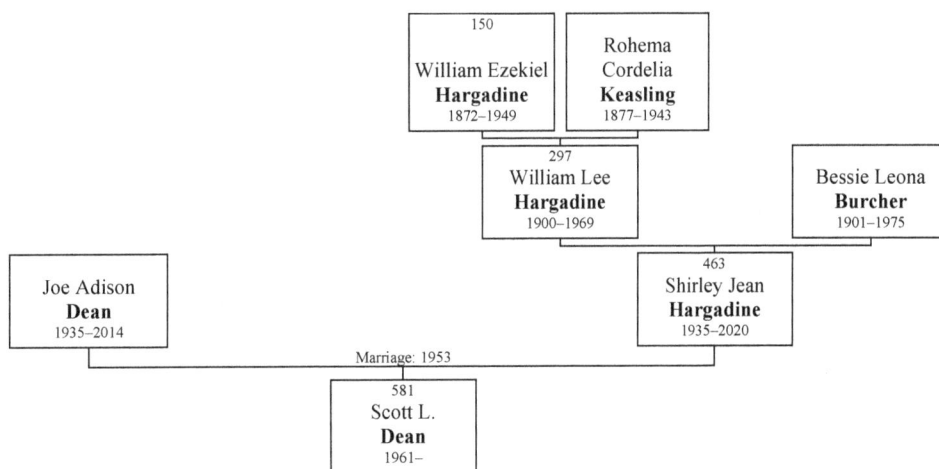

463. **Shirley Jean Hargadine** was born on Sunday, October 06, 1935, in Kinsley, Edwards County, Kansas. She was the daughter of William Lee Hargadine (297) and Bessie Leona Burcher.

Shirley Jean died on March 16, 2020, at the age of 84. She was buried in Greenlawn Cemetery, Pratt, Pratt County, Kansas (Find a Grave ID 208769908).

At the age of 18, Shirley Jean married **Joe Adison Dean** on Monday, December 28, 1953, when he was 18 years old. They had one son.

Joe Adison was born in Dewey County, Oklahoma, on Saturday, December 14, 1935. He reached 78 years of age and died in Pratt, Pratt County, Kansas, on June 07, 2014. Joe Adison was buried in Greenlawn Cemetery, Pratt, Pratt County, Kansas (Find a Grave ID 131040882).

---

461 Bottoms Family Tree, 2 of 6.

Son of Shirley Jean Hargadine and Joe Adison Dean:

+ 581 m I. **Scott L. Dean** was born on February 28, 1961.[462] He is also known as **Scooter**.

Family of Leslie Hargadine and Margie Sowers

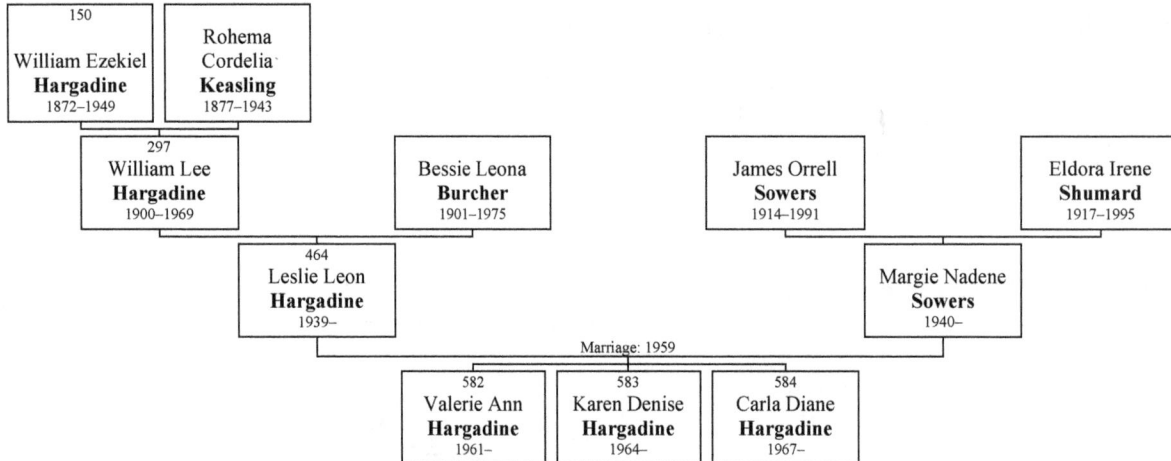

464. **Leslie Leon Hargadine** was born on Thursday, January 12, 1939, in Winona, Logan County, Kansas. He is the son of William Lee Hargadine (297) and Bessie Leona Burcher.

At the age of 20, Leslie Leon married **Margie Nadene Sowers** on Sunday, July 12, 1959, in Leota, Wichita County, Kansas, when she was 18 years old. They have three daughters.

Margie Nadene was born on Saturday, November 23, 1940. She is the daughter of James Orrell Sowers and Eldora Irene Shumard. She is also known as **Margie Nadene Shumard**.

Daughters of Leslie Leon Hargadine and Margie Nadene Sowers:

+ 582 f I. **Valerie Ann Hargadine** was born in Moundridge, McPherson County, Kansas, on March 19, 1961.

+ 583 f II. **Karen Denise Hargadine** was born in Moundridge, McPherson County, Kansas, on February 29, 1964.

+ 584 f III. **Carla Diane Hargadine** was born in Moundridge, McPherson County, Kansas, on February 17, 1967.

---

462 Ancestry.com, U.S., Public Records Index, 1950-1993, Volume 1 (Lehi, UT, USA, Ancestry.com Operations, Inc., 2010), Ancestry.com, Record for Scott L Dean. https://search.ancestry.co.uk/cgi-bin/sse.dll?db=1788&h=299346887&indiv=try.

Family of Virginia Hargadine and Melvin McCabe

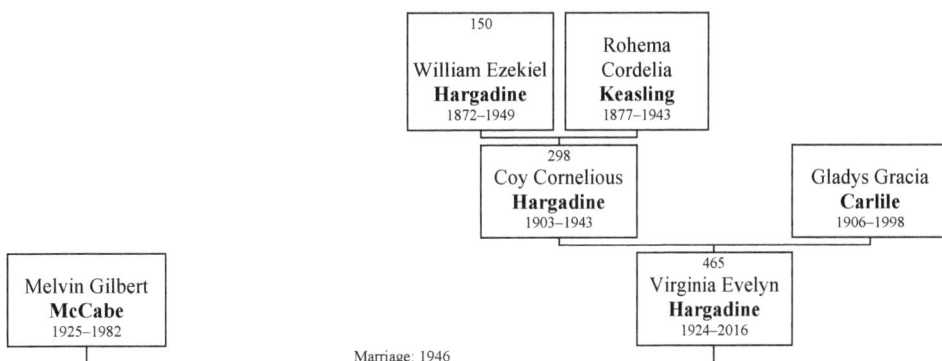

```
                            ┌──────────────┬──────────────┐
                            │     150      │   Rohema     │
                            │William Ezekiel│  Cordelia    │
                            │  Hargadine   │  Keasling    │
                            │  1872–1949   │  1877–1943   │
                            └──────────────┴──────────────┘
                                    ┌──────────────┐        ┌──────────────┐
                                    │     298      │        │ Gladys Gracia│
                                    │Coy Cornelious│        │   Carlile    │
                                    │  Hargadine   │        │  1906–1998   │
                                    │  1903–1943   │        └──────────────┘
                                    └──────────────┘   ┌──────────────┐
        ┌──────────────┐                               │     465      │
        │Melvin Gilbert│                               │Virginia Evelyn│
        │   McCabe     │                               │  Hargadine   │
        │  1925–1982   │                               │  1924–2016   │
        └──────────────┘        Marriage: 1946         └──────────────┘
```

465.   **Virginia Evelyn Hargadine** was born on Sunday, December 21, 1924, in Winona, Logan County, Kansas. She was the daughter of Coy Cornelious Hargadine (298) and Gladys Gracia Carlile.

Virginia Evelyn died in Covington, St. Tammany Parish, Louisiana, on April 19, 2016, at the age of 91. She was buried in Rochester Cemetery, Topeka, Shawnee County, Kansas (Find a Grave ID 211313117).

At the age of 21, Virginia Evelyn married **Melvin Gilbert McCabe** on Sunday, August 11, 1946, when he was 21 years old. Melvin Gilbert was born on Thursday, February 19, 1925. He was also known as **Putt**.

Melvin Gilbert reached 57 years of age and died in Kansas, USA, on May 03, 1982. He was buried in Rochester Cemetery, Topeka, Shawnee County, Kansas (Find a Grave ID 68577141).

Family of Norma Hargadine and Rollie David

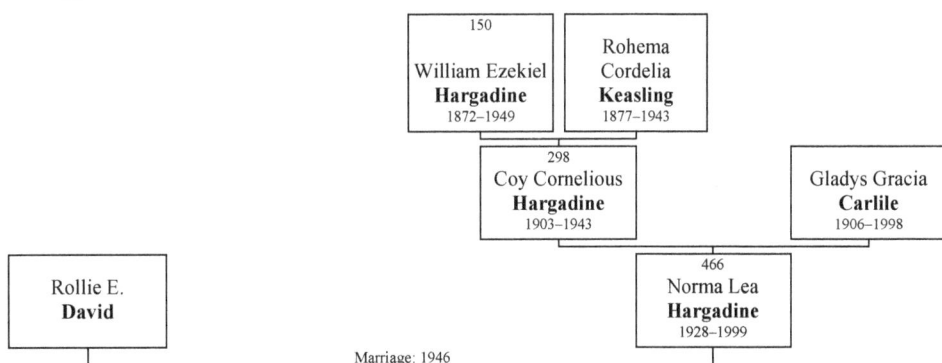

```
                            ┌──────────────┬──────────────┐
                            │     150      │   Rohema     │
                            │William Ezekiel│  Cordelia    │
                            │  Hargadine   │  Keasling    │
                            │  1872–1949   │  1877–1943   │
                            └──────────────┴──────────────┘
                                    ┌──────────────┐        ┌──────────────┐
                                    │     298      │        │ Gladys Gracia│
                                    │Coy Cornelious│        │   Carlile    │
                                    │  Hargadine   │        │  1906–1998   │
                                    │  1903–1943   │        └──────────────┘
                                    └──────────────┘   ┌──────────────┐
        ┌──────────────┐                               │     466      │
        │  Rollie E.   │                               │  Norma Lea   │
        │   David      │                               │  Hargadine   │
        │              │                               │  1928–1999   │
        └──────────────┘        Marriage: 1946         └──────────────┘
```

466.   **Norma Lea Hargadine** was born on Thursday, September 13, 1928, in Winona, Logan County, Kansas. She was the daughter of Coy Cornelious Hargadine (298) and Gladys Gracia Carlile.

Norma Lea died in Loveland, Larimer County, Colorado, on June 19, 1999, at the age of 70. She was buried in Genoa Community Cemetery, Genoa, Lincoln County, Colorado (Find a Grave ID 56924247).

Norma Lea married **Rollie E. David** on Sunday, June 09, 1946.

Family of Darrel Hargadine and Esta Crouse

467. **Darrel Dean Hargadine** was born on Thursday, February 20, 1930, in Winona, Logan County, Kansas. He was the son of Coy Cornelious Hargadine (298) and Gladys Gracia Carlile.

Darrel Dean served in the military: US Navy, Korea. He died in Colby, Thomas County, Kansas, on May 11, 1994, at the age of 64. Darrel Dean was buried in Goodland Cemetery, Goodland, Sherman County, Kansas, on May 13, 1994 (Find a Grave ID 97936230).

At the age of 27, Darrel Dean married **Esta Ruth Crouse** on Sunday, July 07, 1957, in Winona, Logan County, Kansas, when she was 19 years old. They had two children.

Esta Ruth was born in Page City, Logan County, Kansas, on Thursday, September 09, 1937. She was the daughter of Floyd E Crouse and Ruth Ellen Taylor.

Esta Ruth reached 79 years of age and died in Goodland, Sherman County, Kansas, on June 07, 2017. She was buried in Goodland Cemetery, Goodland, Sherman County, Kansas (Find a Grave ID 190534117).

Children of Darrel Dean Hargadine and Esta Ruth Crouse:

m   I. **Daren Coy Hargadine** was born in Kansas, USA, on April 21, 1958. He died in San Diego, San Diego County, California, on November 16, 1995, at the age of 37. Daren Coy was buried in Goodland Cemetery, Goodland, Sherman County, Kansas (Find a Grave ID 97936199).

f   II. **Becky Sue Hargadine** was born on September 01, 1960.

Family of Gerald Hargadine and Delores Austin

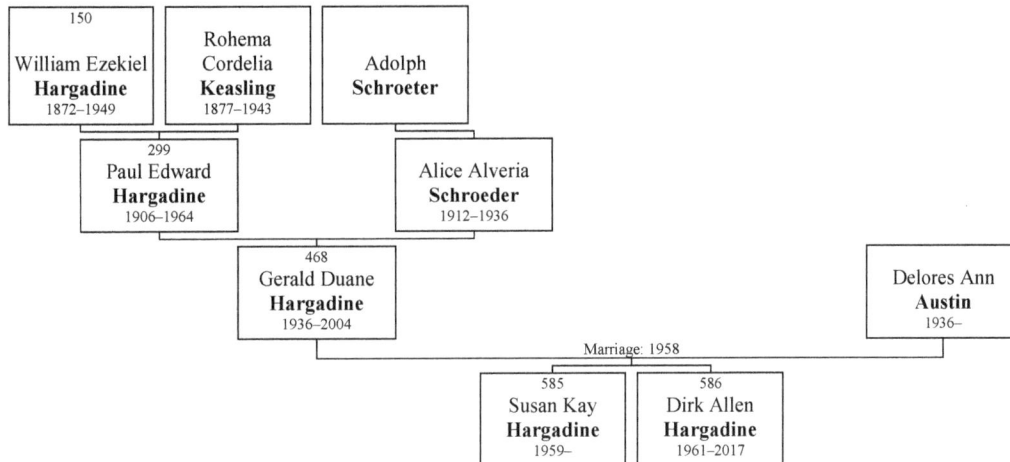

468. **Gerald Duane Hargadine** was born on Sunday, January 05, 1936, in Kiowa County, Kansas. He was the son of Paul Edward Hargadine (299) and Alice Alveria Schroeder. He was also known as **Jerry**.

Gerald Duane died in Manhattan, Riley County, Kansas, on July 08, 2004, at the age of 68. He was buried in Czech-Moravian Cemetery, Swede Creek Township, Riley County, Kansas (Find a Grave ID 9087778).

Gerald Duane married **Delores Ann Austin** on Tuesday, May 27, 1958. They had two children.

Delores Ann was born in January 1936.

Children of Gerald Duane Hargadine and Delores Ann Austin:

+ 585 f I. **Susan Kay Hargadine** was born in September 1959.

+ 586 m II. **Dirk Allen Hargadine** was born in Manhattan, Riley County, Kansas, on December 13, 1961. He died in Blue Rapids, Marshall County, Kansas, on January 03, 2017, at the age of 55. Dirk Allen was buried in Czech-Moravian Cemetery, Swede Creek Township, Riley County, Kansas (Find a Grave ID 175214373).

Sharral Hargadine

469. **Sharral Jeanne Hargadine** was born on Thursday, March 27, 1941, in Ashland, Clark County, Kansas. She was the daughter of Clyde Deloss Hargadine (300) and Emma Elletta Gaddis.

Sharral Jeanne died in Kansas City, Wyandotte County, Kansas, on August 06, 2000, at the age of 59. Her cause of death was head injuries after accidental fall. Sharral Jeanne was buried in Vinland Cemetery, Vinland, Douglas County, Kansas, on August 10, 2000 (Find a Grave ID 23260293).

Marriages with Rex Allen Gentry and Wayne Andrews (Page 482) are known.

Family of Sharral Hargadine and Rex Gentry

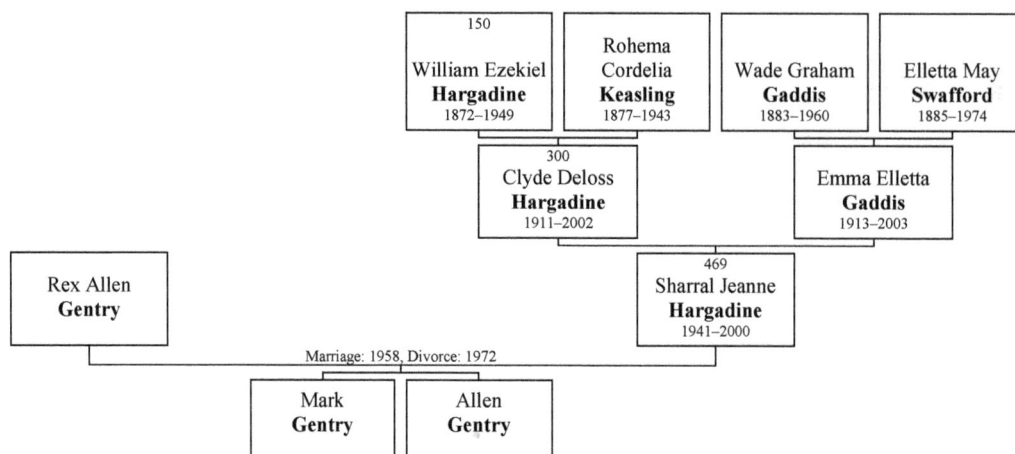

150 William Ezekiel **Hargadine** 1872–1949	Rohema Cordelia **Keasling** 1877–1943	Wade Graham **Gaddis** 1883–1960	Elletta May **Swafford** 1885–1974

300
Clyde Deloss **Hargadine** 1911–2002

Emma Elletta **Gaddis** 1913–2003

Rex Allen **Gentry**

469
Sharral Jeanne **Hargadine** 1941–2000

Marriage: 1958, Divorce: 1972

Mark **Gentry**

Allen **Gentry**

Here are the details about **Sharral Jeanne Hargadine's** first marriage, with Rex Allen Gentry. You can read more about Sharral Jeanne on page 481.

Sharral Jeanne Hargadine married **Rex Allen Gentry** on Friday, June 13, 1958, in Winchester, Jefferson County, Kansas. They were divorced in 1972. They had two sons.

Sons of Sharral Jeanne Hargadine and Rex Allen Gentry:

m   I. **Mark Gentry**.

m   II. **Allen Gentry**.

Family of Sharral Hargadine and Wayne Andrews

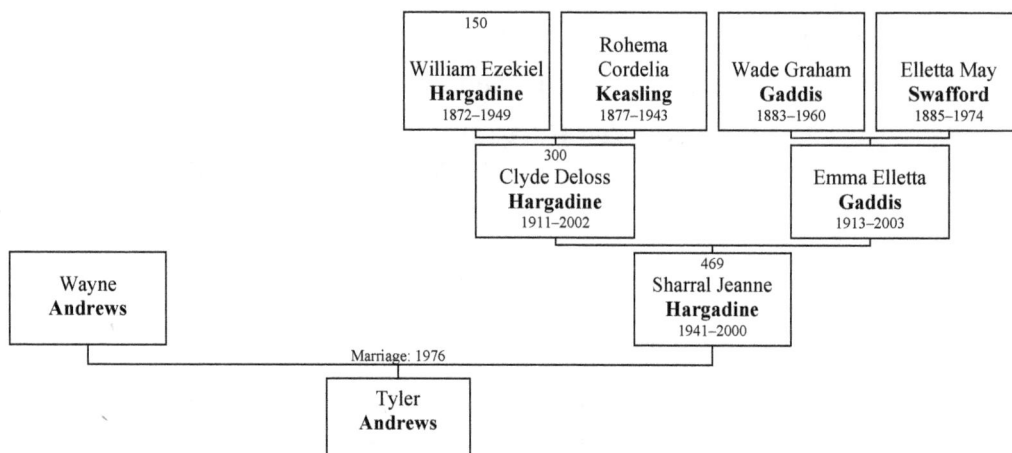

150 William Ezekiel **Hargadine** 1872–1949	Rohema Cordelia **Keasling** 1877–1943	Wade Graham **Gaddis** 1883–1960	Elletta May **Swafford** 1885–1974

300
Clyde Deloss **Hargadine** 1911–2002

Emma Elletta **Gaddis** 1913–2003

Wayne **Andrews**

469
Sharral Jeanne **Hargadine** 1941–2000

Marriage: 1976

Tyler **Andrews**

Here are the details about **Sharral Jeanne Hargadine's** second marriage, with Wayne Andrews. You can read more about Sharral Jeanne on page 481.

Sharral Jeanne Hargadine married **Wayne Andrews** on Monday, December 27, 1976, in Miami, Ottawa County, Oklahoma. They had one son.

Son of Sharral Jeanne Hargadine and Wayne Andrews:

> m   I. **Tyler Andrews**. Tyler was adopted. From first marriage of Wayne Andrews.

Family of Douglas Hargadine and Gaylene Williamson

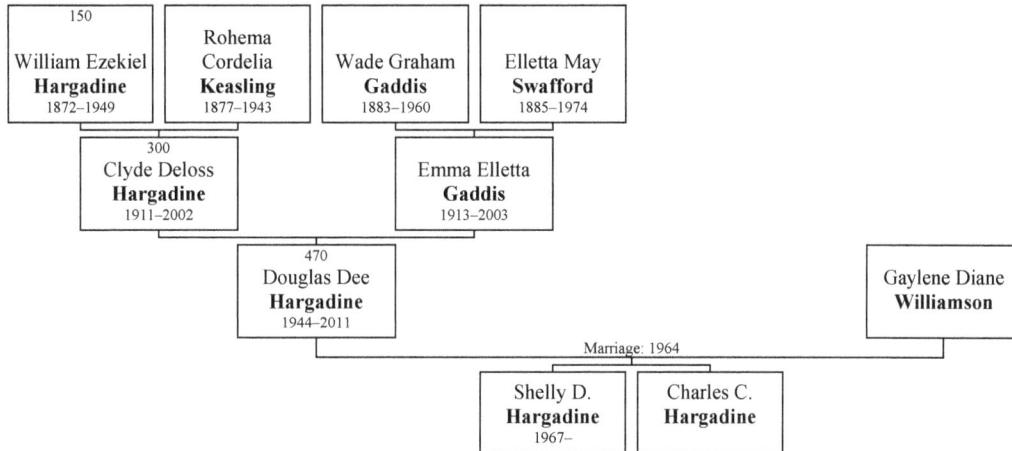

470.   **Douglas Dee Hargadine** was born on Friday, January 07, 1944, in Hutchinson, Reno County, Kansas. He was the son of Clyde Deloss Hargadine (300) and Emma Elletta Gaddis.

Douglas Dee died in Overland Park, Johnson County, Kansas, on November 05, 2011, at the age of 67. He was buried in Oak Hill Cemetery, Lawrence, Douglas County, Kansas (Find a Grave ID 147817957).

Douglas Dee married **Gaylene Diane Williamson** on Friday, December 04, 1964, in Lawrence, Douglas County, Kansas. They had two children.

Children of Douglas Dee Hargadine and Gaylene Diane Williamson:

> f   I. **Shelly D. Hargadine** was born in 1967.
>
> m   II. **Charles C. Hargadine**.

Carolyn Hargadine

471.   **Carolyn Kay Hargadine** was born on Thursday, February 22, 1940, in Stafford, Stafford County, Kansas. She was the daughter of Verlin Claude Hargadine (301) and Dorothy Irene Taylor.

Carolyn Kay died in Queen City, Cass County, Texas, on January 29, 1990, at the age of 49. She was buried in Sardis Cemetery, Shelbyville, Shelby County, Texas, on February 02, 1990 (Find a Grave ID 14814819).

Marriages with Steve Marvin Keith and Lonzo Barton (Page 485) are known.

Family of Carolyn Hargadine and Steve Keith

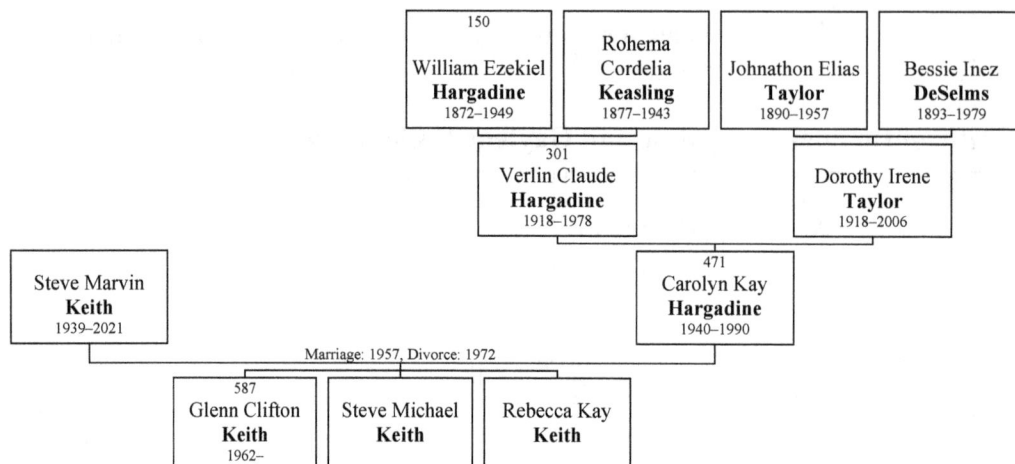

150			
William Ezekiel **Hargadine** 1872–1949	Rohema Cordelia **Keasling** 1877–1943	Johnathon Elias **Taylor** 1890–1957	Bessie Inez **DeSelms** 1893–1979

301 Verlin Claude **Hargadine** 1918–1978

Dorothy Irene **Taylor** 1918–2006

Steve Marvin **Keith** 1939–2021

471 Carolyn Kay **Hargadine** 1940–1990

Marriage: 1957, Divorce: 1972

587 Glenn Clifton **Keith** 1962–

Steve Michael **Keith**

Rebecca Kay **Keith**

Here are the details about **Carolyn Kay Hargadine's** first marriage, with Steve Marvin Keith. You can read more about Carolyn Kay on page 483.

Carolyn Kay Hargadine married **Steve Marvin Keith** in December 1957. They were divorced in Union County, Oregon, on February 24, 1972. They had three children.

Steve Marvin was born on Saturday, September 23, 1939. He reached 82 years of age and died on October 14, 2021.

Children of Carolyn Kay Hargadine and Steve Marvin Keith:

+ 587   m   I. **Glenn Clifton Keith** was born in Kansas, USA, in 1962.[463]

         m   II. **Steve Michael Keith**.

         f   III. **Rebecca Kay Keith**.

Family of Carolyn Hargadine and Lonzo Barton

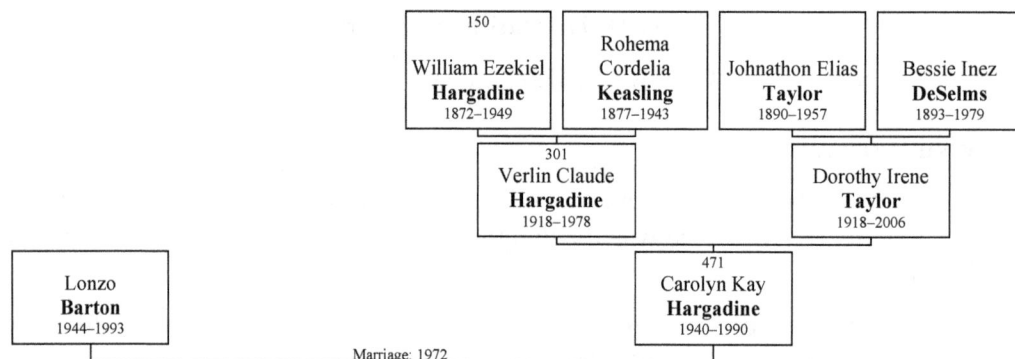

150			
William Ezekiel **Hargadine** 1872–1949	Rohema Cordelia **Keasling** 1877–1943	Johnathon Elias **Taylor** 1890–1957	Bessie Inez **DeSelms** 1893–1979

301 Verlin Claude **Hargadine** 1918–1978

Dorothy Irene **Taylor** 1918–2006

Lonzo **Barton** 1944–1993

471 Carolyn Kay **Hargadine** 1940–1990

Marriage: 1972

Here are the details about **Carolyn Kay Hargadine's** second marriage, with Lonzo Barton. You can read more about Carolyn Kay on page 483.

---

[463] Ancestry.com, Indiana, U.S., Marriage Certificates, 1960-2012 (Lehi, UT, USA, Ancestry.com Operations, Inc., 2016), Ancestry.com, Indiana Archives and Records Administration; Indianapolis, IN, USA; Records of Marriage 1961-2005; Roll Number: NA. Record for Glen Clifton Keith. https://search.ancestry.co.uk/cgi-bin/sse.dll?db=61009&h=71234&indiv=try.

At the age of 32, Carolyn Kay Hargadine married **Lonzo Barton** on Friday, December 08, 1972, when he was 28 years old. Lonzo was born in Center, Shelby County, Texas, on Thursday, February 24, 1944.

He reached 49 years of age and died in Queen City, Cass County, Texas, on December 18, 1993. Lonzo was buried in Sardis Cemetery, Shelbyville, Shelby County, Texas (Find a Grave ID 14814943).

Terry Hargadine

472. **Terry Glenn Hargadine** was born on Monday, April 02, 1945, in Stafford County, Kansas. He was the son of Verlin Claude Hargadine (301) and Dorothy Irene Taylor.

Terry Glenn died in Queen City, Cass County, Texas, on June 05, 2005, at the age of 60. He was buried in Chapelwood Memorial Gardens and Mausoleum, Wake Village, Bowie County, Texas (Find a Grave ID 136785300).

Marriages with Madlyn Carrol Kellogg and Elaine Jacqueline Vallois (Page 486) are known.

Family of Terry Hargadine and Madlyn Kellogg

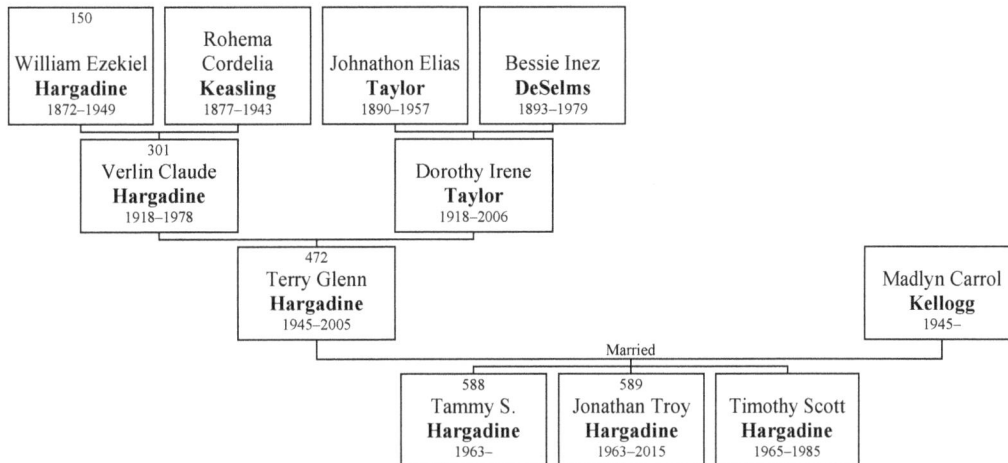

Here are the details about **Terry Glenn Hargadine's** first marriage, with Madlyn Carrol Kellogg. You can read more about Terry Glenn on page 485.

Terry Glenn Hargadine married **Madlyn Carrol Kellogg**. They had three children.

Madlyn Carrol was born in Hutchinson County, Texas, on Wednesday, September 05, 1945.

Children of Terry Glenn Hargadine and Madlyn Carrol Kellogg:

+ 588   f   I. **Tammy S. Hargadine** was born in 1963.

+ 589   m   II. **Jonathan Troy Hargadine** was born in Liberal, Seward County, Kansas, on May 02, 1963. He died in Clarksville, Montgomery County, Tennessee, on June 14, 2015, at the age of 52. His cause of death was car crash. He was buried in Kentucky Veterans Cemetery West, Hopkinsville, Christian County, Kentucky, on June 22, 2015 (Find a Grave ID 147932041).

m III. **Timothy Scott Hargadine** was born in Liberal, Seward County, Kansas, on December 27, 1965. He died in Wichita, Sedgwick County, Kansas, on August 31, 1985, at the age of 19. His cause of death was homicide; gunshot wound. He was buried in Lakeview Cemetery & Mausoleum, Wichita, Sedgwick County, Kansas, on September 04, 1985 (Find a Grave ID 61486071).

Family of Terry Hargadine and Elaine Vallois

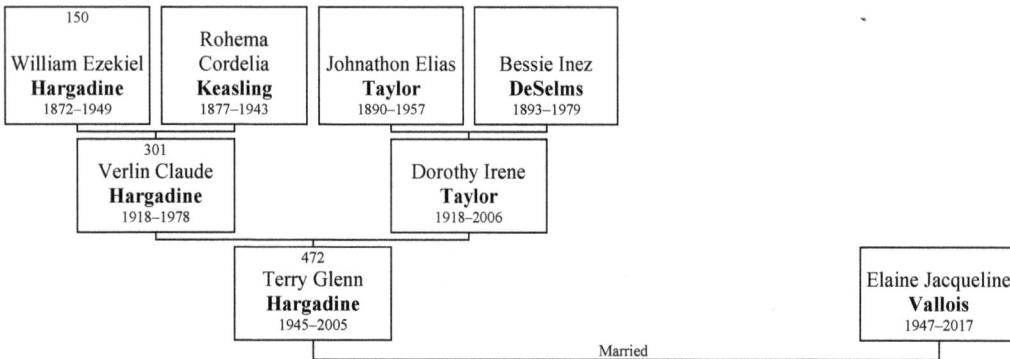

150			
William Ezekiel **Hargadine** 1872–1949	Rohema Cordelia **Keasling** 1877–1943	Johnathon Elias **Taylor** 1890–1957	Bessie Inez **DeSelms** 1893–1979

301
Verlin Claude **Hargadine** 1918–1978

Dorothy Irene **Taylor** 1918–2006

472
Terry Glenn **Hargadine** 1945–2005

Elaine Jacqueline **Vallois** 1947–2017

Married

Here are the details about **Terry Glenn Hargadine's** second marriage, with Elaine Jacqueline Vallois. You can read more about Terry Glenn on page 485.

Terry Glenn Hargadine married **Elaine Jacqueline Vallois**. Elaine Jacqueline was born in Poitiers, Vienne, France, on Monday, February 03, 1947.

She reached 70 years of age and died in Texarkana, Bowie County, Texas, on November 24, 2017. Elaine Jacqueline was buried in Chapelwood Memorial Gardens and Mausoleum, Wake Village, Bowie County, Texas (Find a Grave ID 185486422).

Family of Pamela Hargadine and Jack Dorris

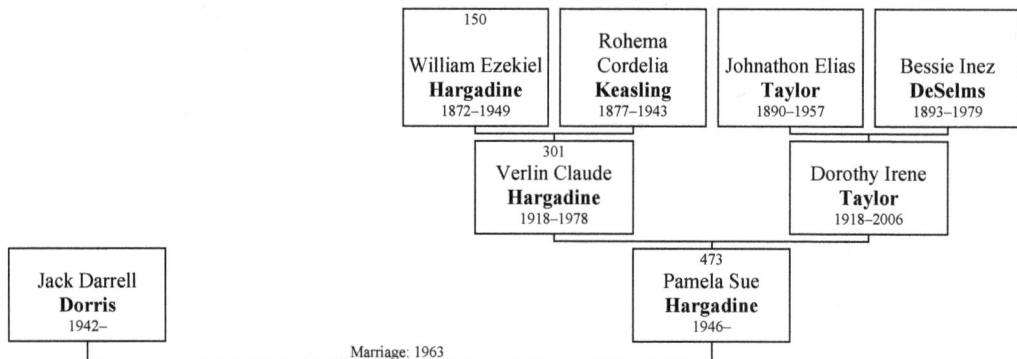

150			
William Ezekiel **Hargadine** 1872–1949	Rohema Cordelia **Keasling** 1877–1943	Johnathon Elias **Taylor** 1890–1957	Bessie Inez **DeSelms** 1893–1979

301
Verlin Claude **Hargadine** 1918–1978

Dorothy Irene **Taylor** 1918–2006

Jack Darrell **Dorris** 1942–

473
Pamela Sue **Hargadine** 1946–

Marriage: 1963

473. **Pamela Sue Hargadine** was born on Saturday, June 22, 1946. She is the daughter of Verlin Claude Hargadine (301) and Dorothy Irene Taylor.

Pamela Sue married **Jack Darrell Dorris** on Sunday, March 31, 1963, in Liberal, Seward County, Kansas. Jack Darrell was born in October 1942. He is also known as **Jackie**.

Family of Joyce Keasling and Richard Theander

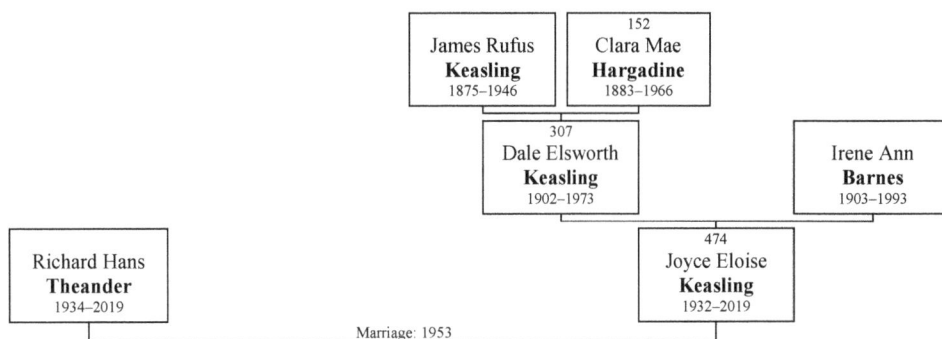

474.   **Joyce Eloise Keasling** was born on Sunday, June 19, 1932, in Protection, Comanche County, Kansas. She was the daughter of Dale Elsworth Keasling (307) and Irene Ann Barnes.

Joyce Eloise died on December 13, 2019, at the age of 87. She was buried in Highland Cemetery, Center Township, Clark County, Kansas (Find a Grave ID 210126968).

At the age of 21, Joyce Eloise married **Richard Hans Theander** on Sunday, August 16, 1953, at Ashland Methodist Church in Ashland, Clark County, Kansas, when he was 19 years old. Richard Hans was born in Matfield Green, Chase County, Kansas, on Wednesday, July 04, 1934.

He reached 85 years of age and died in Kingman, Kingman County, Kansas, on November 25, 2019. Richard Hans was buried in Highland Cemetery, Center Township, Clark County, Kansas (Find a Grave ID 210127067).

Family of Donald Keasling and Marjorie Vinso

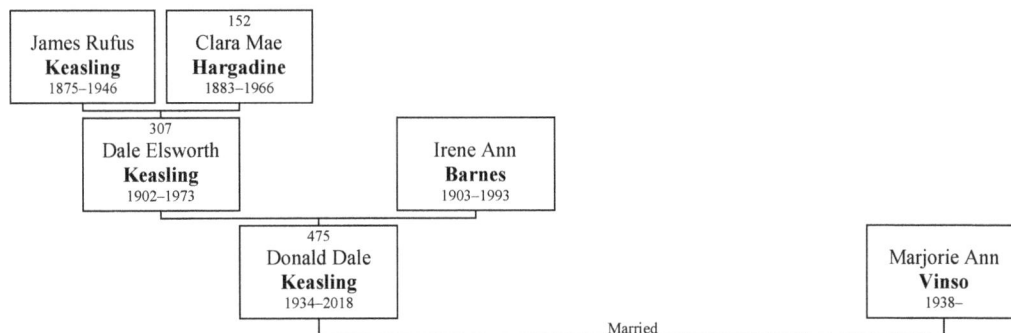

475.   **Donald Dale Keasling** was born on Friday, July 06, 1934, in Protection, Comanche County, Kansas. He was the son of Dale Elsworth Keasling (307) and Irene Ann Barnes.

Donald Dale died on June 16, 2018, at the age of 83. He was buried in Memorial Park Cemetery, Hutchinson, Reno County, Kansas (Find a Grave ID 247911819).

He married **Marjorie Ann Vinso**. Marjorie Ann was born in March 1938. She is also known as **Mary Joyce**.

Family of Donna Keasling and Dean Graff

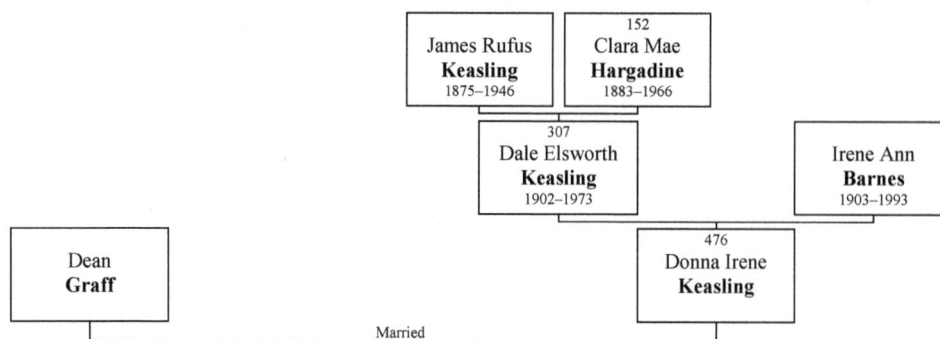

476. **Donna Irene Keasling**. She was the daughter of Dale Elsworth Keasling (307) and Irene Ann Barnes.

She married **Dean Graff**.

Family of Ronald Haag and Milbry Bridgeman

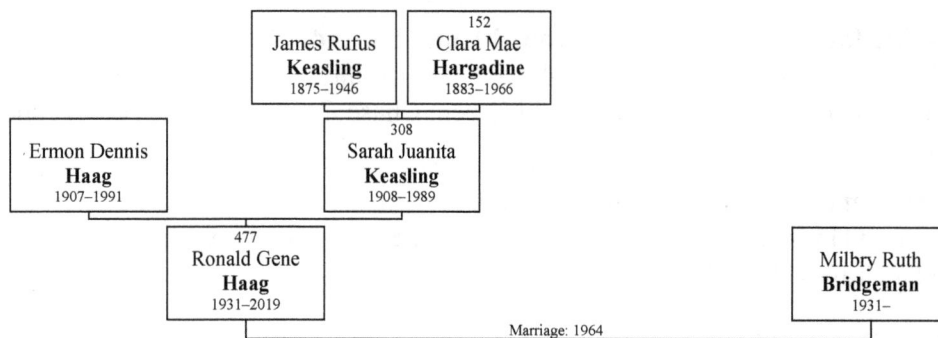

477. **Ronald Gene Haag** was born on Friday, October 09, 1931, in Larned, Pawnee County, Kansas. He was the son of Ermon Dennis Haag and Sarah Juanita Keasling (308).

Ronald Gene died in Hutchinson, Reno County, Kansas, on May 05, 2019, at the age of 87. He was buried in Abbyville Cemetery, Abbyville, Reno County, Kansas (Find a Grave ID 199977143).

At the age of 32, Ronald Gene married **Milbry Ruth Bridgeman** on Saturday, May 16, 1964, in South Hutchinson, Reno County, Kansas, when she was 32 years old. Milbry Ruth was born on Monday, September 07, 1931.

Barbara Reed

478. **Barbara Harriet Reed** was born on Monday, April 11, 1927, in Seattle, King County, Washington. She was the daughter of Harry William Reed and Hazel Merlin Hargadine (309).

Barbara Harriet died in Yelm, Thurston County, Washington, on February 11, 2011, at the age of 83. She was buried in Yelm Cemetery, Yelm, Thurston County, Washington (Find a Grave ID 88387449).

Marriages with Alton Vernoy Archer and Willard Meril Parsons (Page 490) are known.

Family of Barbara Reed and Alton Archer

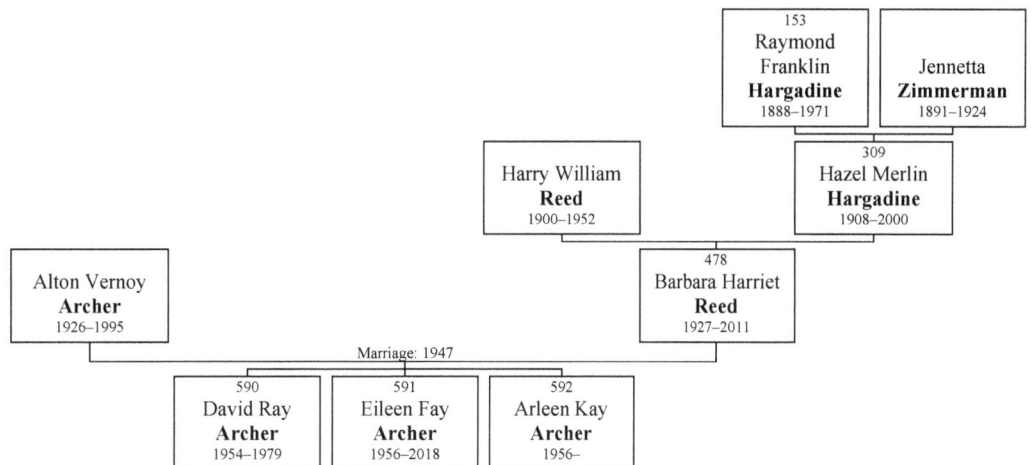

Here are the details about **Barbara Harriet Reed's** first marriage, with Alton Vernoy Archer. You can read more about Barbara Harriet on page 488.

Barbara Harriet Reed married **Alton Vernoy Archer** in 1947. They had three children.

Alton Vernoy was born in Altus, Jackson County, Oklahoma, on Sunday, November 28, 1926. He was also known as **Corky**.

Alton Vernoy reached 68 years of age and died in Prescott, Yavapai County, Arizona, on June 23, 1995. He was buried in Heritage Memorial Park, Dewey, Yavapai County, Arizona (Find a Grave ID 120917176).

Children of Barbara Harriet Reed and Alton Vernoy Archer:

+ 590   m   I. **David Ray Archer** was born in Seattle, King County, Washington, on October 15, 1954. He died in Tucson, Pima County, Arizona, on July 13, 1979, at the age of 24. David Ray was buried in Holy Hope Cemetery and Mausoleum, Tucson, Pima County, Arizona (Find a Grave ID 62310431).

+ 591   f   II. **Eileen Fay Archer** was born in Renton, King County, Washington, on June 26, 1956. She died on April 17, 2018, at the age of 61. Eileen Fay was cremated (Find a Grave ID 188911161).

+ 592   f   III. **Arleen Kay Archer** was born on June 26, 1956.

Family of Barbara Reed and Willard Parsons

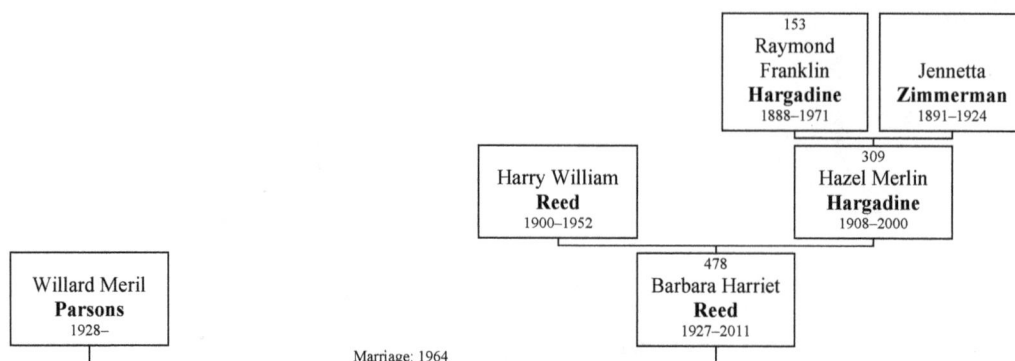

```
                                        ┌─────────────┐  ┌─────────────┐
                                        │     153     │  │             │
                                        │  Raymond    │  │             │
                                        │  Franklin   │  │  Jennetta   │
                                        │ Hargadine   │  │ Zimmerman   │
                                        │  1888–1971  │  │  1891–1924  │
                                        └─────────────┘  └─────────────┘
                        ┌──────────────┐            ┌─────────────┐
                        │ Harry William│            │     309     │
                        │    Reed      │            │ Hazel Merlin│
                        │  1900–1952   │            │  Hargadine  │
                        └──────────────┘            │  1908–2000  │
        ┌──────────────┐            ┌─────────────┐ └─────────────┘
        │ Willard Meril│            │     478      │
        │   Parsons    │            │ Barbara Harriet
        │    1928–     │            │     Reed     │
        └──────────────┘            │  1927–2011   │
                        Marriage: 1964
```

Here are the details about **Barbara Harriet Reed's** second marriage, with Willard Meril Parsons. You can read more about Barbara Harriet on page 488.

At the age of 37, Barbara Harriet Reed married **Willard Meril Parsons** on Tuesday, September 01, 1964, in Seattle, King County, Washington, when he was 35 years old. Willard Meril was born on Sunday, September 30, 1928.

Robert Hargadine

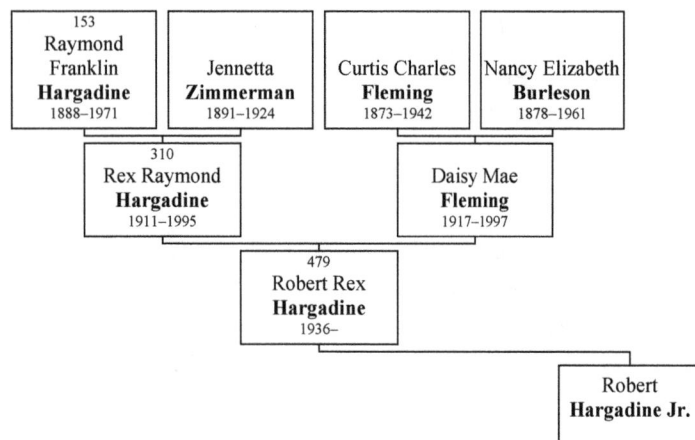

```
┌─────────────┐ ┌─────────────┐ ┌─────────────┐ ┌─────────────────┐
│     153     │ │             │ │             │ │                 │
│  Raymond    │ │             │ │ Curtis Charles│ │ Nancy Elizabeth │
│  Franklin   │ │  Jennetta   │ │   Fleming   │ │    Burleson     │
│ Hargadine   │ │ Zimmerman   │ │  1873–1942  │ │    1878–1961    │
│  1888–1971  │ │  1891–1924  │ └─────────────┘ └─────────────────┘
└─────────────┘ └─────────────┘
     ┌─────────────┐            ┌─────────────┐
     │     310     │            │  Daisy Mae  │
     │ Rex Raymond │            │   Fleming   │
     │  Hargadine  │            │  1917–1997  │
     │  1911–1995  │            └─────────────┘
     └─────────────┘
            ┌─────────────┐
            │     479     │
            │ Robert Rex  │
            │  Hargadine  │
            │    1936–    │
            └─────────────┘
                   ┌─────────────┐
                   │   Robert    │
                   │Hargadine Jr.│
                   └─────────────┘
```

479. **Robert Rex Hargadine** was born on Saturday, October 10, 1936, in Chelan, Chelan County, Washington. He is the son of Rex Raymond Hargadine (310) and Daisy Mae Fleming. He is also known as **Robert Rex Nichols**. Robert Rex was adopted in 1938 by Al and Floy Nichols.

Son of Robert Rex Hargadine:

  m   I. **Robert Hargadine Jr.** was born in Chelan, Chelan County, Washington.

Edward Hargadine

480. **Edward Earl Hargadine** was born on Tuesday, January 19, 1943, in Portland, Multnomah County, Oregon. He was the son of Rex Raymond Hargadine (310) and Hazel Evine Erickson.

Edward Earl died in Carson, Skamania County, Washington, on September 21, 2022, at the age of 79.

Marriages with Billie Louise DuBoise, Ruby R. Craig (Page 492), Kathryn Jean Graham (Page 492), Christine Rae Ford (Page 493) and Martha Parrott (Page 493) are known.

Family of Edward Hargadine and Billie DuBoise

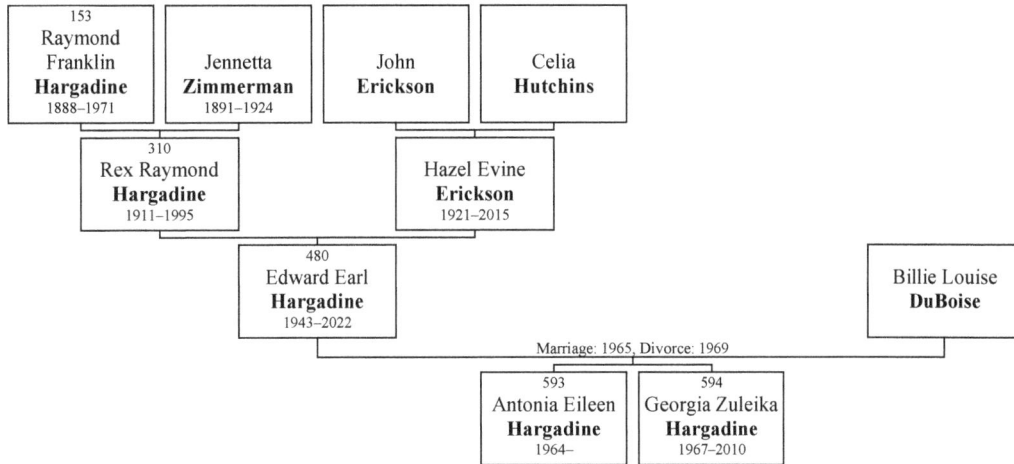

Here are the details about **Edward Earl Hargadine's** first marriage, with Billie Louise DuBoise. You can read more about Edward Earl on page 490.

Edward Earl Hargadine married **Billie Louise DuBoise** on Saturday, November 20, 1965, in Seattle, King County, Washington.[464] They were divorced on June 23, 1969. They had two daughters.

Daughters of Edward Earl Hargadine and Billie Louise DuBoise:

+ 593   f   I. **Antonia Eileen Hargadine** was born in Seattle, King County, Washington, on December 17, 1964.

+ 594   f   II. **Georgia Zuleika Hargadine** was born in Seattle, King County, Washington, on November 16, 1967. She died on January 24, 2010, at the age of 42.

---

464   King, Washington Divorce Records, Divorced 23 Jun 1969 with two children.

Family of Edward Hargadine and Ruby Craig

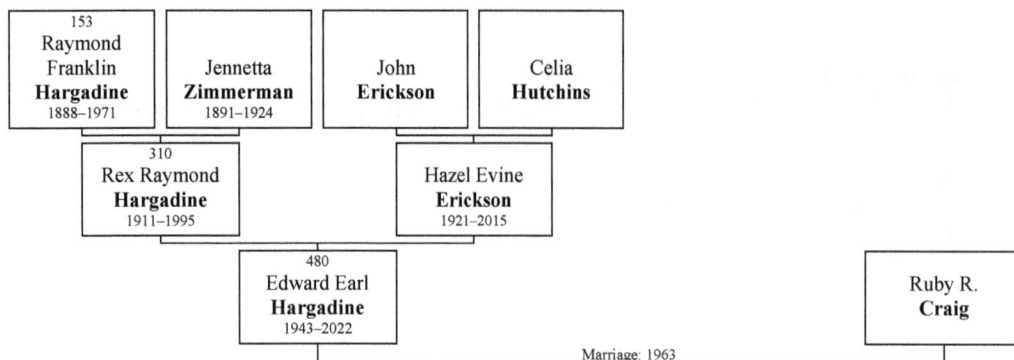

| 153 Raymond Franklin **Hargadine** 1888–1971 | Jennetta **Zimmerman** 1891–1924 | John **Erickson** | Celia **Hutchins** |

310 Rex Raymond **Hargadine** 1911–1995

Hazel Evine **Erickson** 1921–2015

480 Edward Earl **Hargadine** 1943–2022

Ruby R. **Craig**

Marriage: 1963

Here are the details about **Edward Earl Hargadine's** second marriage, with Ruby R. Craig. You can read more about Edward Earl on page 490.

Edward Earl Hargadine married **Ruby R. Craig** in June 1963. Applied for marriage license.

Family of Edward Hargadine and Kathryn Graham

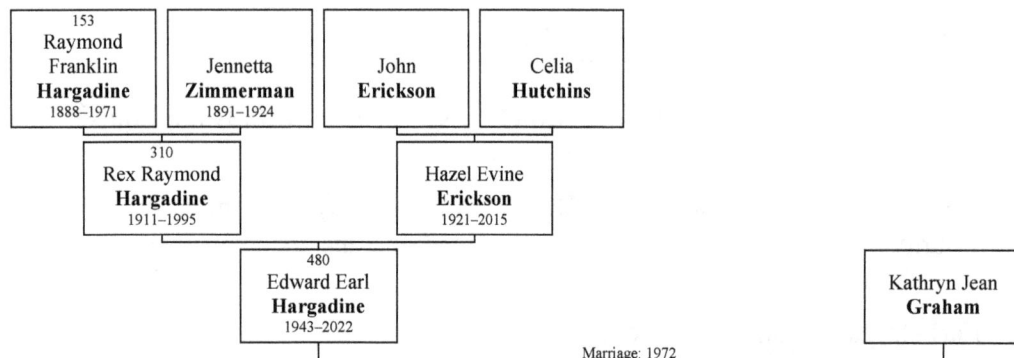

| 153 Raymond Franklin **Hargadine** 1888–1971 | Jennetta **Zimmerman** 1891–1924 | John **Erickson** | Celia **Hutchins** |

310 Rex Raymond **Hargadine** 1911–1995

Hazel Evine **Erickson** 1921–2015

480 Edward Earl **Hargadine** 1943–2022

Kathryn Jean **Graham**

Marriage: 1972

Here are the details about **Edward Earl Hargadine's** third marriage, with Kathryn Jean Graham. You can read more about Edward Earl on page 490.

Edward Earl Hargadine married **Kathryn Jean Graham** on Saturday, December 30, 1972, at Married by District Court Judge in Whatcom County, Washington.

Family of Edward Hargadine and Christine Ford

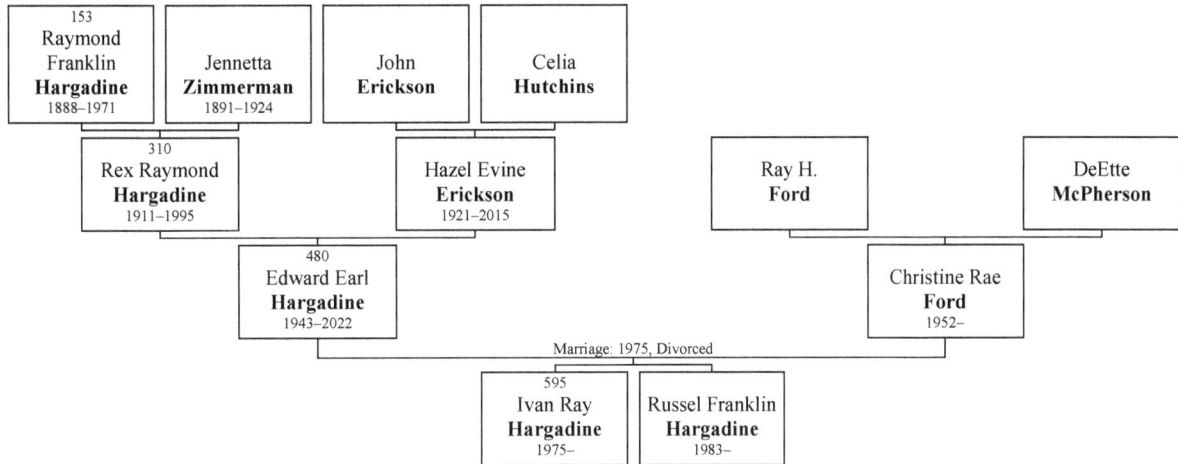

Here are the details about **Edward Earl Hargadine's** fourth marriage, with Christine Rae Ford. You can read more about Edward Earl on page 490.

Edward Earl Hargadine married **Christine Rae Ford** in April 1975. Applied for marriage license. They are divorced. Unknown. They had two sons.

Christine Rae was born in Vancouver, Clark County, Washington, on Saturday, July 26, 1952. She is the daughter of Ray H. Ford and DeEtte McPherson.

Sons of Edward Earl Hargadine and Christine Rae Ford:

+ 595   m   I. **Ivan Ray Hargadine** was born on November 09, 1975.

          m   II. **Russel Franklin Hargadine** was born on December 23, 1983.

Family of Edward Hargadine and Martha Parrott

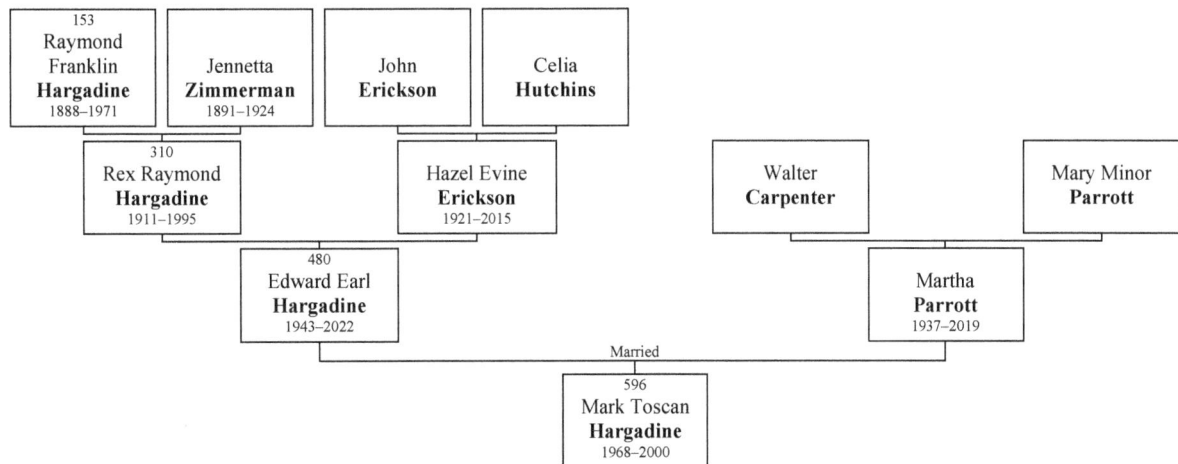

Here are the details about **Edward Earl Hargadine's** fifth marriage, with Martha Parrott. You can read more about Edward Earl on page 490.

Edward Earl Hargadine married **Martha Parrott**. They had one son.

Martha was born in East Grand Rapids, Michigan, on Wednesday, December 15, 1937. She was the daughter of Walter Carpenter and Mary Minor Parrott. She was also known as **Molly**.

Martha reached 81 years of age and died in Utah, USA, on February 18, 2019. She was buried in Lindquist Memorial Park, Layton, Davis County, Utah (Find a Grave ID 197008734).

Son of Edward Earl Hargadine and Martha Parrott:

+ 596 m I. **Mark Toscan Hargadine** was born in Lynnwood, Snohomish County, Washington, on February 14, 1968. He died in Burleson, Texas, on June 02, 2000, at the age of 32. His cause of death was auto accident. He was buried in Lindquist Memorial Park, Layton, Davis County, Utah (Find a Grave ID 108015711).

Diane Hargadine

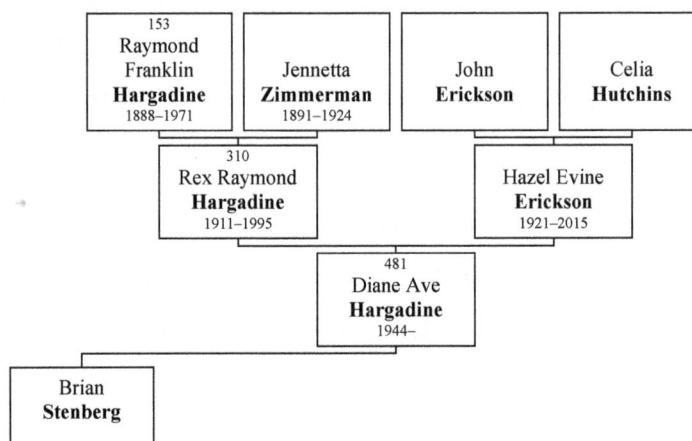

481. **Diane Ave Hargadine** was born on Thursday, June 01, 1944, in White Salmon, Klickitat County, Washington. She is the daughter of Rex Raymond Hargadine (310) and Hazel Evine Erickson.

Son of Diane Ave Hargadine:

m I. **Brian Stenberg**.

Dale Hargadine

482. **Dale Irvin Hargadine** was born on Friday, November 29, 1946, in White Salmon, Klickitat County, Washington. He is the son of Rex Raymond Hargadine (310) and Hazel Evine Erickson.

Dale Irvin served in the military: February 18, 1966; U.S.M.C. during the Vietnam War. Discharged July 9, 1969 at the rank of Corporal.

Marriages with Kathleen Marie Cameron and Linda Kay Patrick (Page 496) are known.

Family of Dale Hargadine and Kathleen Cameron

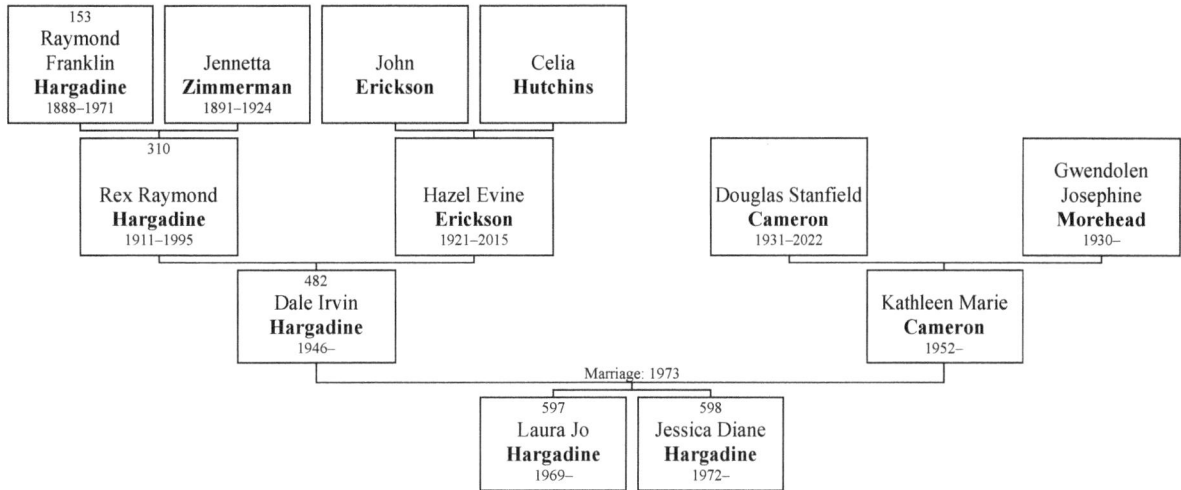

Here are the details about **Dale Irvin Hargadine's** first marriage, with Kathleen Marie Cameron. You can read more about Dale Irvin on page 494.

At the age of 26, Dale Irvin Hargadine married **Kathleen Marie Cameron** on Saturday, May 19, 1973, in Carson, Skamania County, Washington, when she was 21 years old. They have two daughters.

Kathleen Marie was born on Wednesday, January 02, 1952. She is the daughter of Douglas Stanfield Cameron and Gwendolen Josephine Morehead.

More facts and events for Kathleen Marie Cameron:

Individual Note: Step-daughter of Robert William Bent

Daughters of Dale Irvin Hargadine and Kathleen Marie Cameron:

+   597   f   I. **Laura Jo Hargadine** was born in Vancouver, Clark County, Washington, on May 29, 1969. Dale Irvin Hargadine is her stepfather. She is also known as **Laura Jo Cameron**.

+   598   f   II. **Jessica Diane Hargadine** was born in White Salmon, Klickitat County, Washington, on December 16, 1972.

Family of Dale Hargadine and Linda Patrick

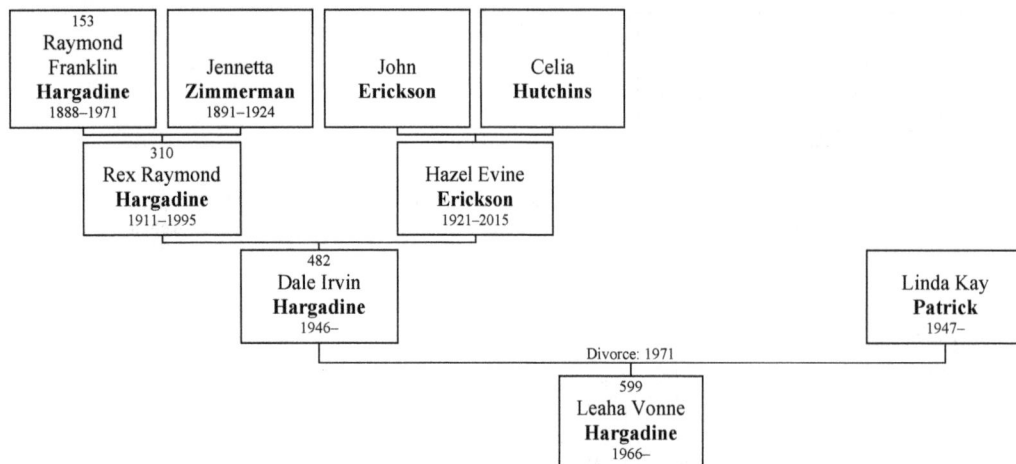

```
┌─────────────┐ ┌─────────────┐ ┌─────────────┐ ┌─────────────┐
│     153     │ │             │ │             │ │             │
│   Raymond   │ │             │ │             │ │             │
│   Franklin  │ │  Jennetta   │ │    John     │ │    Celia    │
│  Hargadine  │ │  Zimmerman  │ │  Erickson   │ │  Hutchins   │
│  1888–1971  │ │  1891–1924  │ │             │ │             │
└─────────────┘ └─────────────┘ └─────────────┘ └─────────────┘
     ┌──────────────────┐           ┌──────────────────┐
     │       310        │           │   Hazel Evine    │
     │  Rex Raymond     │           │    Erickson      │
     │   Hargadine      │           │   1921–2015      │
     │   1911–1995      │           └──────────────────┘
     └──────────────────┘
              ┌──────────────────┐        ┌──────────────┐
              │       482        │        │  Linda Kay   │
              │   Dale Irvin     │        │   Patrick    │
              │   Hargadine      │        │    1947–     │
              │     1946–        │        └──────────────┘
              └──────────────────┘
                         Divorce: 1971
                   ┌──────────────────┐
                   │       599        │
                   │   Leaha Vonne    │
                   │   Hargadine      │
                   │     1966–        │
                   └──────────────────┘
```

Here are the details about **Dale Irvin Hargadine's** second marriage, with Linda Kay Patrick. You can read more about Dale Irvin on page 494.

Dale Irvin Hargadine married **Linda Kay Patrick**. They were divorced in Clark, Washington, on October 12, 1971. They had one daughter.

Linda Kay was born on Tuesday, October 21, 1947.

Daughter of Dale Irvin Hargadine and Linda Kay Patrick:

+ 599 f I. **Leaha Vonne Hargadine** was born in Iowa City, Johnson County, Iowa, on October 30, 1966.

Sharon Hargadine

483. **Sharon Lee Hargadine** was born on Wednesday, December 29, 1948, in White Salmon, Klickitat County, Washington. She is the daughter of Rex Raymond Hargadine (310) and Hazel Evine Erickson. She is also known as **Shari**.

Marriages with William Joseph Dolan, Donald J. Sandifur (Page 497) and David Paul Schmidt (Page 498) are known.

Family of Sharon Hargadine and William Dolan

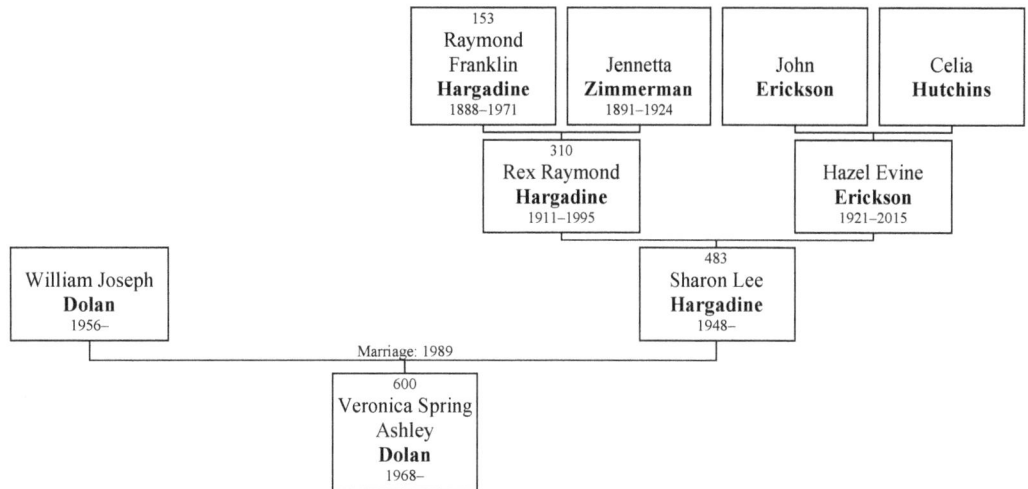

Here are the details about **Sharon Lee Hargadine's** first marriage, with William Joseph Dolan. You can read more about Sharon Lee on page 496.

At the age of 40, Sharon Lee Hargadine married **William Joseph Dolan** on Friday, June 16, 1989, in Stevenson, Skamania County, Washington, when he was 32 years old. They have one daughter.

William Joseph was born in The Dalles, Wasco County, Oregon, on Sunday, July 01, 1956.

Daughter of Sharon Lee Hargadine and William Joseph Dolan:

+ 600 f I. **Veronica Spring Ashley Dolan** was born in White Salmon, Klickitat County, Washington, on August 21, 1968. William Joseph Dolan is her stepfather.

Family of Sharon Hargadine and Donald Sandifur

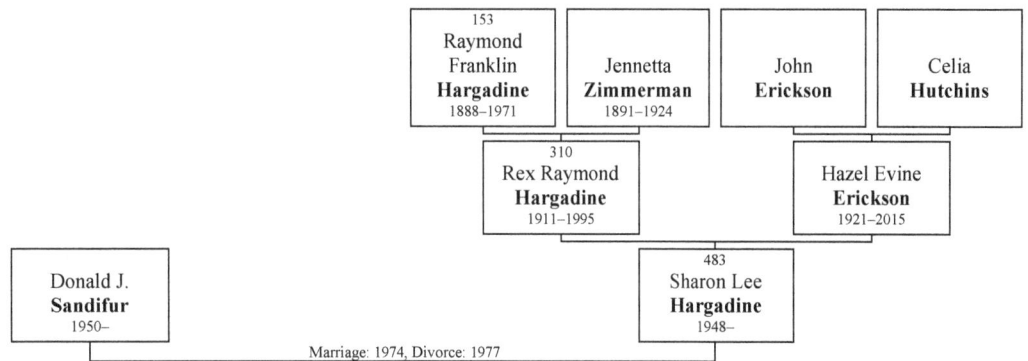

Here are the details about **Sharon Lee Hargadine's** second marriage, with Donald J. Sandifur. You can read more about Sharon Lee on page 496.

At the age of 25, Sharon Lee Hargadine married **Donald J. Sandifur** on Saturday, August 10, 1974, in Carson, Skamania County, Washington, when he was 24 years old. They divorced in Skamania County, Washington, on December 15, 1977.

Donald J. was born on Wednesday, April 12, 1950.

Family of Sharon Hargadine and David Schmidt

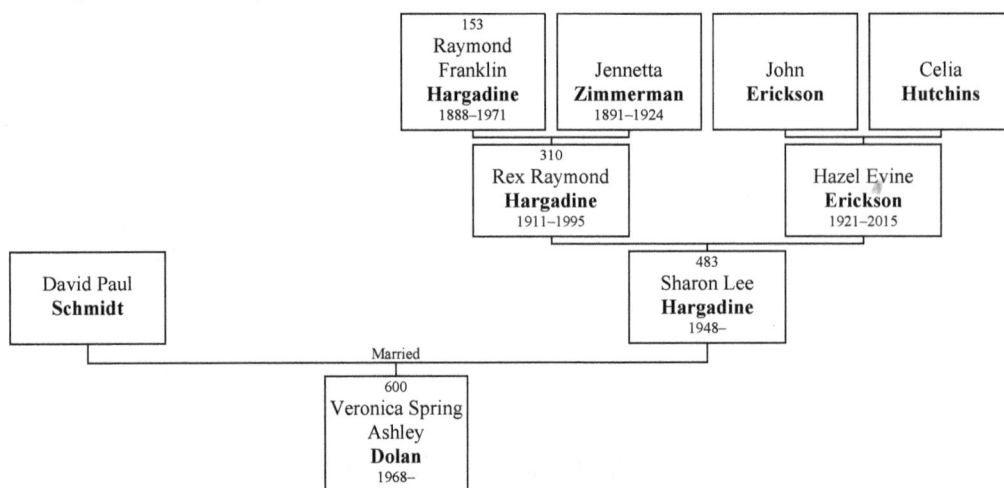

```
┌─────────────┐ ┌─────────────┐ ┌─────────────┐ ┌─────────────┐
│     153     │ │             │ │             │ │             │
│   Raymond   │ │   Jennetta  │ │    John     │ │    Celia    │
│   Franklin  │ │  Zimmerman  │ │   Erickson  │ │   Hutchins  │
│  Hargadine  │ │  1891–1924  │ │             │ │             │
│  1888–1971  │ │             │ │             │ │             │
└─────────────┘ └─────────────┘ └─────────────┘ └─────────────┘
        ┌─────────────┐                 ┌─────────────┐
        │     310     │                 │             │
        │     Rex     │                 │  Hazel Evine│
        │   Raymond   │                 │   Erickson  │
        │  Hargadine  │                 │  1921–2015  │
        │  1911–1995  │                 │             │
        └─────────────┘                 └─────────────┘
                          ┌─────────────┐
                          │     483     │
                          │  Sharon Lee │
                          │  Hargadine  │
                          │    1948–    │
                          └─────────────┘
┌─────────────┐
│ David Paul  │
│   Schmidt   │
└─────────────┘
           Married
        ┌─────────────┐
        │     600     │
        │Veronica Spring
        │   Ashley    │
        │    Dolan    │
        │    1968–    │
        └─────────────┘
```

Here are the details about **Sharon Lee Hargadine's** third marriage, with David Paul Schmidt. You can read more about Sharon Lee on page 496.

Sharon Lee Hargadine married **David Paul Schmidt**. They had one daughter.

Daughter of Sharon Lee Hargadine and David Paul Schmidt:

+ 600 f I. **Veronica Spring Ashley Dolan** was born in White Salmon, Klickitat County, Washington, on August 21, 1968. David Paul Schmidt is her stepfather.

Family of Ronald Hargadine and Gale Youngmeyers

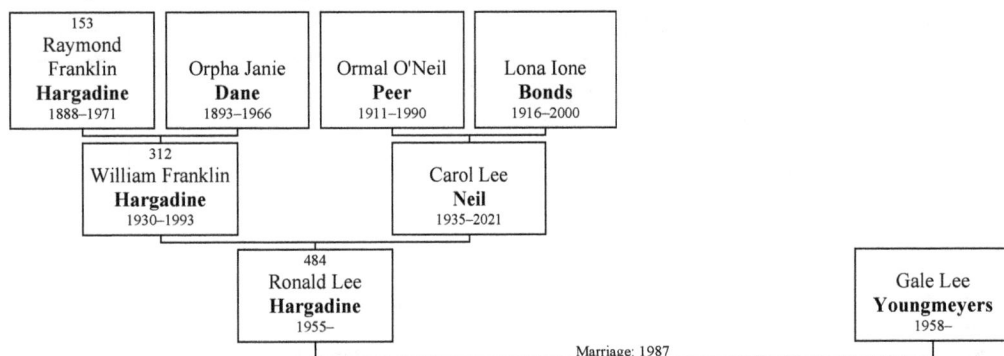

```
┌─────────────┐ ┌─────────────┐ ┌─────────────┐ ┌─────────────┐
│     153     │ │  Orpha Janie│ │ Ormal O'Neil│ │  Lona Ione  │
│   Raymond   │ │    Dane     │ │    Peer     │ │    Bonds    │
│   Franklin  │ │  1893–1966  │ │  1911–1990  │ │  1916–2000  │
│  Hargadine  │ │             │ │             │ │             │
│  1888–1971  │ │             │ │             │ │             │
└─────────────┘ └─────────────┘ └─────────────┘ └─────────────┘
  ┌─────────────┐               ┌─────────────┐
  │     312     │               │  Carol Lee  │
  │   William   │               │    Neil     │
  │   Franklin  │               │  1935–2021  │
  │  Hargadine  │               │             │
  │  1930–1993  │               │             │
  └─────────────┘               └─────────────┘
        ┌─────────────┐                      ┌─────────────┐
        │     484     │                      │  Gale Lee   │
        │  Ronald Lee │                      │ Youngmeyers │
        │  Hargadine  │                      │    1958–    │
        │    1955–    │                      │             │
        └─────────────┘                      └─────────────┘
                    Marriage: 1987
```

484. **Ronald Lee Hargadine** was born in January 1955. He is the son of William Franklin Hargadine (312) and Carol Lee Neil.

Ronald Lee married **Gale Lee Youngmeyers** on Saturday, March 07, 1987, in Clackamas, Oregon. Gale Lee was born in December 1958.

Family of Mary Bullard and William Groves

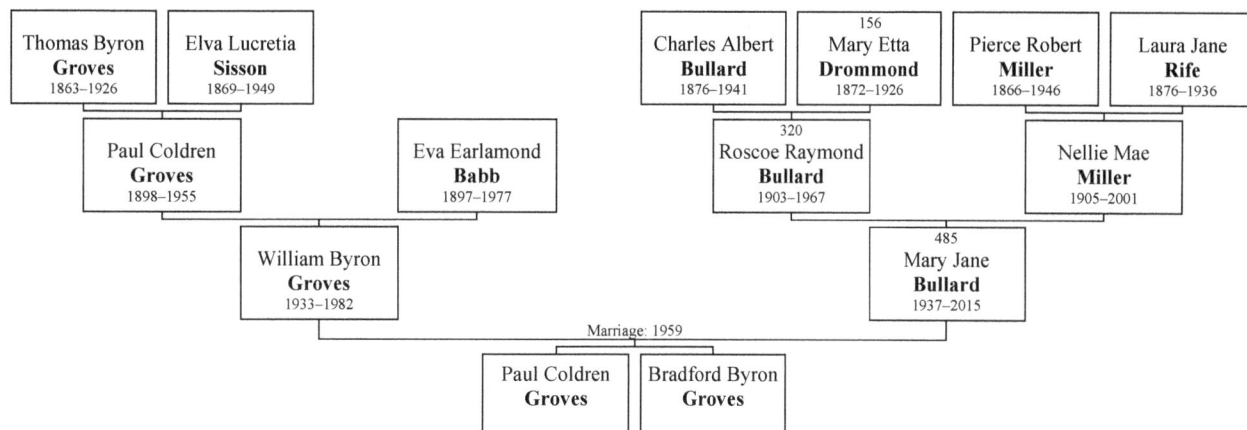

Thomas Byron **Groves** 1863–1926	Elva Lucretia **Sisson** 1869–1949

Paul Coldren **Groves** 1898–1955

Eva Earlamond **Babb** 1897–1977

Charles Albert **Bullard** 1876–1941	156 Mary Etta **Drommond** 1872–1926	Pierce Robert **Miller** 1866–1946	Laura Jane **Rife** 1876–1936

320 Roscoe Raymond **Bullard** 1903–1967

Nellie Mae **Miller** 1905–2001

William Byron **Groves** 1933–1982

485 Mary Jane **Bullard** 1937–2015

Marriage: 1959

Paul Coldren **Groves**

Bradford Byron **Groves**

485. Mary Jane Bullard was born on Friday, April 23, 1937, in Yuma, Yuma County, Colorado. She was the daughter of Roscoe Raymond Bullard (320) and Nellie Mae Miller.

Mary Jane died in Loveland, Larimer County, Colorado, on February 20, 2015, at the age of 77. She was cremated with ashes scattered (Find a Grave ID 143428396).

Mary Jane married **William Byron Groves** in 1959. They had two sons.

William Byron was born in Wray, Yuma County, Colorado, on Monday, May 29, 1933. William Byron reached 49 years of age and died in Wray, Yuma County, Colorado, on November 19, 1982. He was cremated—Ashes scattered on Groves Ranch, Yuma, Colorado (Find a Grave ID 186903759).

William and Mary Jane Groves

William and Mary Jane Groves represent the fourth generation of the early pioneers of Yuma County. William is the grandson of Byron and Elva Groves who each homesteaded west of Wray in the late 1880s and married in 1889. He is also a great grandson of Elva's father, Francis Sisson who founded the F. M. Sisson clothing Store.

Mary Jane is the granddaughter of Pierce and Laura Miller who came from Iowa by 1890 to acquire land under the Homestead Act. She is a great-granddaughter of Simon Rife who came to the Laird community in the late 1880s.

Following his college days at Colorado A&M in Fort Collins, William became associated with T. B. Groves County in 1955. Following Mary Jane's graduation from CU in Boulder, the couple was married at a holiday wedding in 1959. They lived in Colorado Springs where Mrs. Groves was librarian at the Air Force Academy high school, returning to Wray that summer to make their home. She was the librarian in the Wray Public Schools until the birth of their first son.

In 1963, Bill and his mother, Eva Groves Heindel, purchased the interest of the other family partners in T. B. Groves County and continued the business from its original location at Fourth and Adams. This half-block was sold to the First National Bank for a new bank site in 1968 and a new John Deere building was erected at the corner of U. S. 34 and 385. In 1973 the implement business was sold to Hadley-Fix and Bill has concentrated on the development of irrigation and the Hereford cattle herd on his sandhill ranch. Groves Ranch was one of the first to install irrigation wells and sprinklers north of Wray.

Both have been active in community life. He has been president of the CSU Alumni and Chamber of Commerce, chief of the Volunteer Fire Department, master of the Masonic Lodge, and a trustee of the Methodist Church. Mary Jane served two terms on the Northeast Regional Library board for Yuma County and also two terms on the Wray Public Library board at the time of the building of the new library. She is also a Methodist and P. E. O.

They are the parents of two teenage sons, Paul Coldren and Bradford Byron, and therefore support youth activities. They have been MYF sponsors, 4-H leaders, and Scout leaders as well as supporting the athletic programs of the local schools. All of the family enjoy entertaining in their home at 433 Adams and boating and water skiing at nearby Bonny Dam.

A History of East Yuma County This is a collection of general history and family histories of East Yuma County from 1868 through 1978.
Page 139. He was the son of Paul Coldren Groves and Eva Earlamond Babb.

Sons of Mary Jane Bullard and William Byron Groves:

m I. **Paul Coldren Groves**.

m II. **Bradford Byron Groves**.

Family of Nancy Whyte and Randell Pennington

486. **Nancy Ann Whyte**. She was the daughter of Harold B. Whyte and Mary Earlene Drommond (326).

She married **Randell Pennington**. They had one son.

Son of Nancy Ann Whyte and Randell Pennington:

m I. **John Whyte Pennington**.

Family of Peggy Whyte and John Lynch

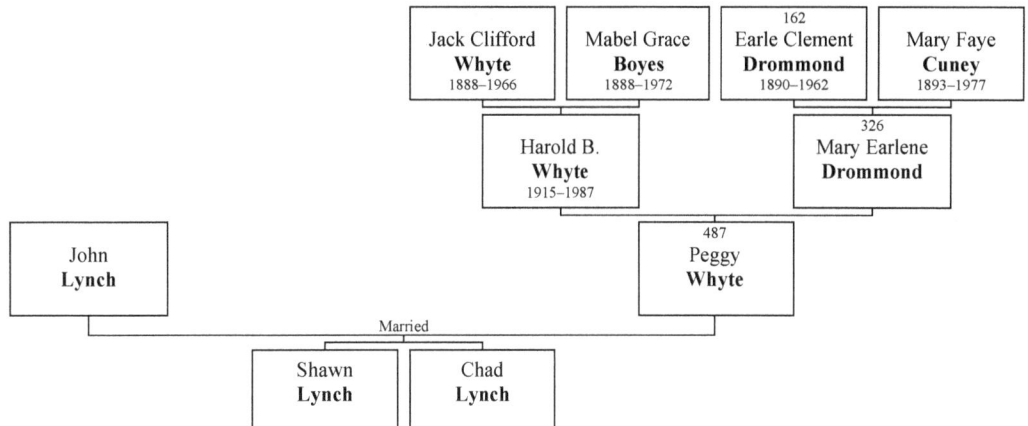

487. **Peggy Whyte**. She was the daughter of Harold B. Whyte and Mary Earlene Drommond (326).

She married **John Lynch**. They had two sons.

Sons of Peggy Whyte and John Lynch:

m   I. **Shawn Lynch**.

m   II. **Chad Lynch**.

Paul Chambers

488. **Paul Gaylord Chambers Jr.** was born on Saturday, July 25, 1931, in Bloomington, McLean County, Illinois. He is the son of Paul Gaylord Chambers (330) and Elouise Geraldine Smith. He is also known as **Bud Chambers**.

Paul Gaylord worked at Cambro Manufacturing–Huntington Beach, CA.

Marriages with Mary Bettie Jones and Sarah Carroll (Page 502) are known.

Family of Paul Chambers and Mary Jones

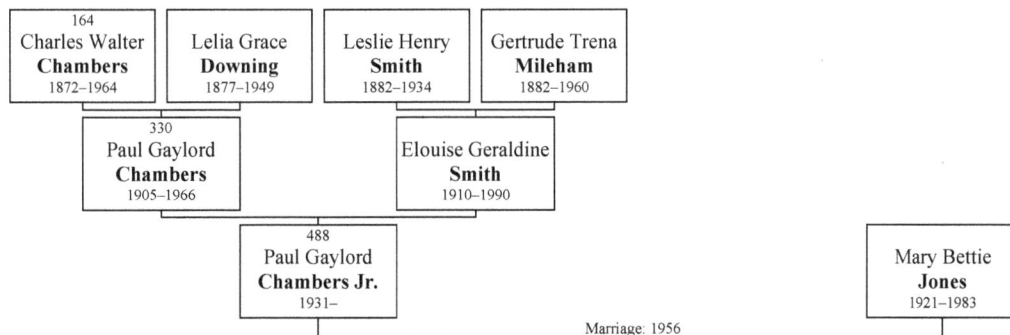

Here are the details about **Paul Gaylord Chambers Jr.'s** first marriage, with Mary Bettie Jones. You can read more about Paul Gaylord on page 501.

At the age of 24, Paul Gaylord Chambers Jr. married **Mary Bettie Jones** on Friday, March 09, 1956, in Los Angeles, Los Angeles County, California, when she was 34 years old.

Mary Bettie was born in Hutchinson, Reno County, Kansas, on Friday, December 02, 1921. She was also known as **Mary "Bettie" Jones**.

Mary Bettie reached 61 years of age and died in Huntington Beach, Orange County, California, on May 26, 1983. She was buried on May 31, 1983, in Good Shepherd Cemetery, Huntington Beach, Orange County, California (Find a Grave ID 158373449).

Family of Paul Chambers and Sarah Carroll

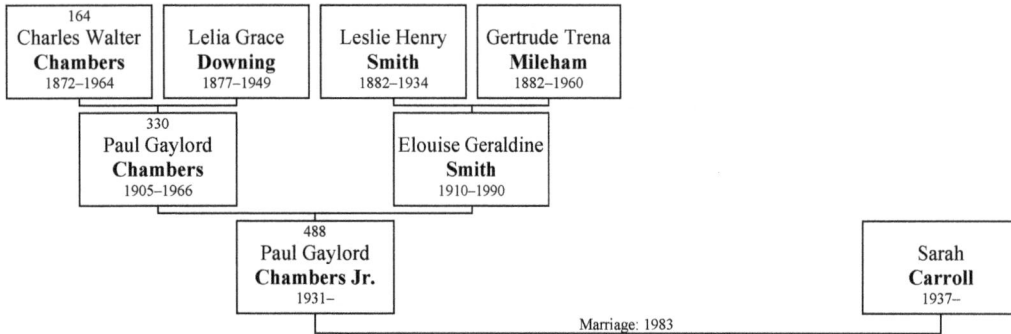

Here are the details about **Paul Gaylord Chambers Jr.'s** second marriage, with Sarah Carroll. You can read more about Paul Gaylord on page 501.

At the age of 52, Paul Gaylord Chambers Jr. married **Sarah Carroll** on Thursday, September 15, 1983, when she was 46 years old. Sarah was born in Huntington Beach, Orange County, California, on Sunday, February 21, 1937. She is also known as **Carol Chambers**.

Family of Sharon Chambers and Barry Boyens

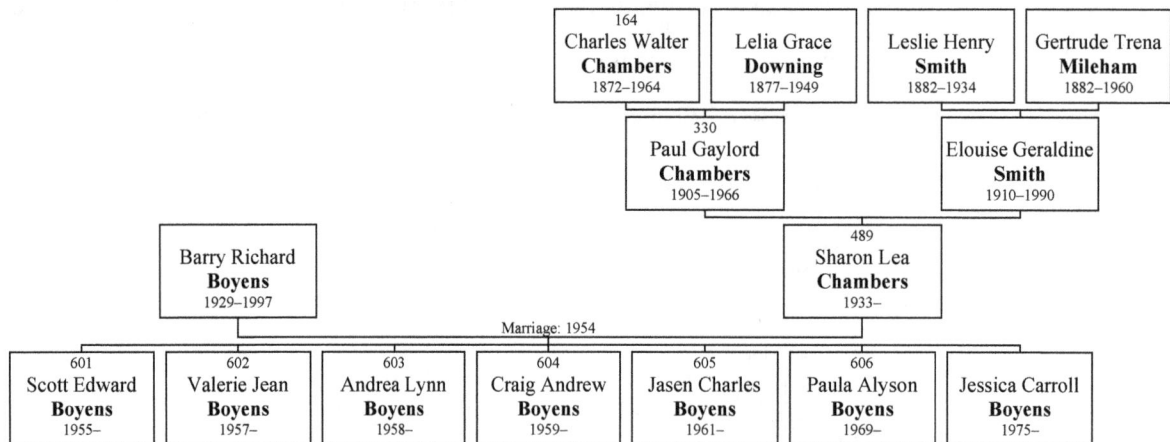

489. **Sharon Lea Chambers** was born on Tuesday, January 31, 1933, in Bloomington, McLean County, Illinois. She is the daughter of Paul Gaylord Chambers (330) and Elouise Geraldine Smith.

At the age of 21, Sharon Lea married **Barry Richard Boyens** on Saturday, February 13, 1954, in Chicago, Cook County, Illinois, when he was 24 years old. They had seven children.

Barry Richard was born in Harvey, Cook County, Illinois, on Sunday, October 20, 1929. He served in the military: U.S. Navy, QM1.

Barry Richard reached 67 years of age and died in San Marcos, San Diego County, California, on January 02, 1997. His cause of death was lung cancer. Barry Richard was buried in Fort Rosecrans National Cemetery, San Diego, San Diego County, California (Find a Grave ID 396633).

Children of Sharon Lea Chambers and Barry Richard Boyens:

+ 601 m I. **Scott Edward Boyens** was born in Harvey, Cook County, Illinois, on November 03, 1955.

+ 602 f II. **Valerie Jean Boyens** was born in Harvey, Cook County, Illinois, on February 26, 1957.

+ 603 f III. **Andrea Lynn Boyens** was born in Harvey, Cook County, Illinois, on February 05, 1958.

+ 604 m IV. **Craig Andrew Boyens** was born in Harvey, Cook County, Illinois, on September 01, 1959.

+ 605 m V. **Jasen Charles Boyens** was born in Peoria, Peoria County, Illinois, on November 30, 1961.

+ 606 f VI. **Paula Alyson Boyens** was born in Harvey, Cook County, Illinois, on September 22, 1969.

f VII. **Jessica Carroll Boyens** was born in Escondido, San Diego County, California, on March 19, 1975.

Family of Kenneth Chambers and Geraldine Gemler

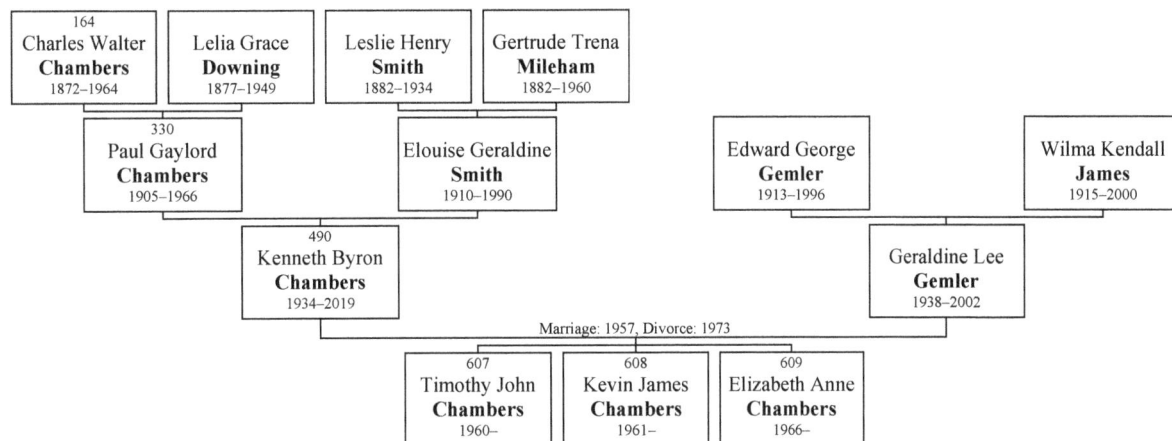

490. **Kenneth Byron Chambers** was born on Tuesday, July 03, 1934, in Terre Haute, Vigo County, Indiana. He was the son of Paul Gaylord Chambers (330) and Elouise Geraldine Smith. He was also known as **Kenneth James**.

Kenneth Byron died at Franciscan Hospital in Munster Lake County, Indiana, on January 06, 2019, at the age of 84. His ashes were interred in Skyline Memorial Park, Monee, Will County, Illinois (Cremated).

At the age of 23, Kenneth Byron married **Geraldine Lee Gemler** on Saturday, September 07, 1957, in Merrionette Park, Cook County, Illinois, when she was 19 years old. They were divorced in Country Club Hills, Cook County, Illinois, on June 05, 1973. They had three children.

Geraldine Lee was born in Chicago, Cook County, Illinois, on Saturday, January 22, 1938. She was the daughter of Edward George Gemler and Wilma Kendall James.

Geraldine Lee reached 64 years of age and died in Crestwood, Cook County, Illinois, on September 15, 2002. She was buried in Skyline Memorial Park, Monee, Will County, Illinois (Find a Grave ID 87165219).

Children of Kenneth Byron Chambers and Geraldine Lee Gemler:

+ 607 m I. **Timothy John Chambers** was born in Harvey, Cook County, Illinois, on March 01, 1960.

+ 608 m II. **Kevin James Chambers** was born in Harvey, Cook County, Illinois, on April 01, 1961.

+ 609 f III. **Elizabeth Anne Chambers** was born in Harvey, Cook County, Illinois, on January 06, 1966.

Robert Chambers

491. **Robert Joseph Chambers** was born on Friday, October 23, 1936, in Terre Haute, Vigo County, Indiana. He is the son of Paul Gaylord Chambers (330) and Elouise Geraldine Smith.

Marriages with Judith Ann Mary Carney and Ann Louise Thompson (Page 505) are known.

Family of Robert Chambers and Judith Carney

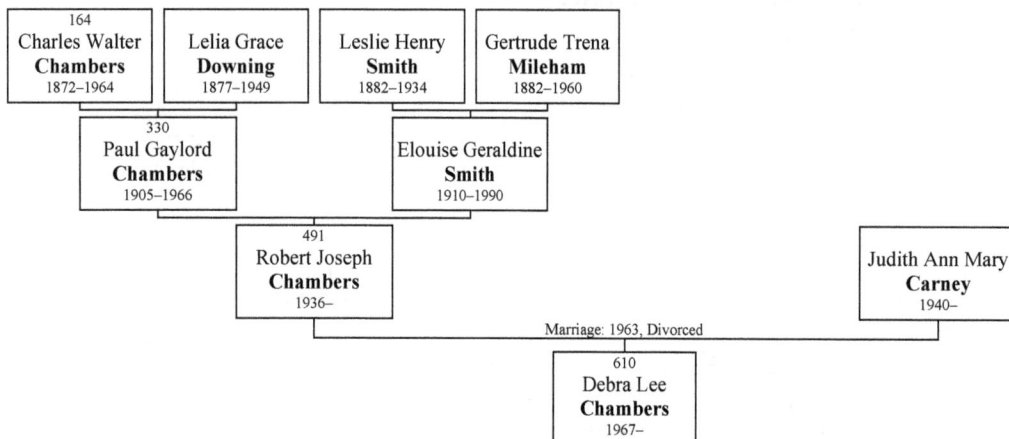

Here are the details about **Robert Joseph Chambers's** first marriage, with Judith Ann Mary Carney. You can read more about Robert Joseph on page 504.

At the age of 26, Robert Joseph Chambers married **Judith Ann Mary Carney** on Saturday, February 09, 1963, in Los Angeles, Los Angeles County, California, when she was 22 years old. They later divorced. They have one daughter.

Judith Ann Mary was born on Friday, December 13, 1940.

Daughter of Robert Joseph Chambers and Judith Ann Mary Carney:

+ 610 f I. **Debra Lee Chambers** was born in Santa Monica, Los Angeles County, California, on March 05, 1967.

Family of Robert Chambers and Ann Thompson

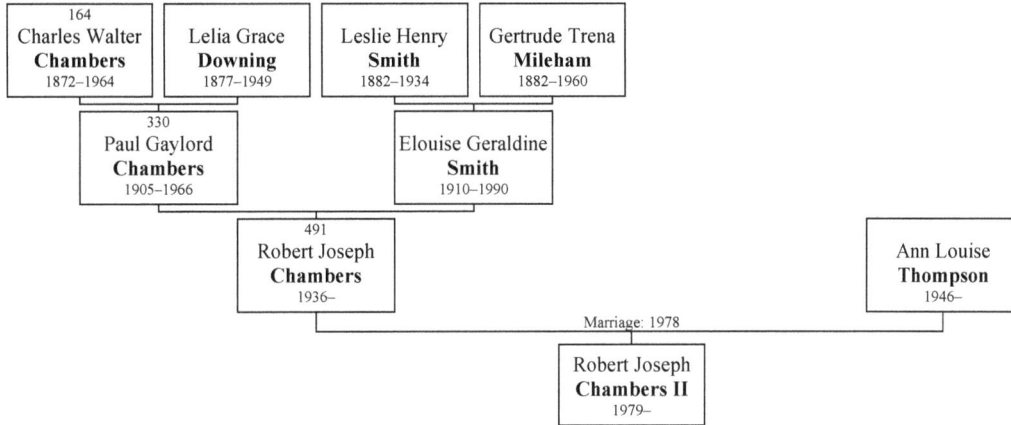

Here are the details about **Robert Joseph Chambers's** second marriage, with Ann Louise Thompson. You can read more about Robert Joseph on page 504.

At the age of 41, Robert Joseph Chambers married **Ann Louise Thompson** on Friday, October 13, 1978, in Garden Grove, Orange County, California, when she was 31 years old. They have one son.

Ann Louise was born in Los Angeles, Los Angeles County, California, on Saturday, November 02, 1946.

Son of Robert Joseph Chambers and Ann Louise Thompson:

m I. **Robert Joseph Chambers II** was born in Orange City, Orange County, California, on November 21, 1979.

Family of Michael Chambers and Alison Dong

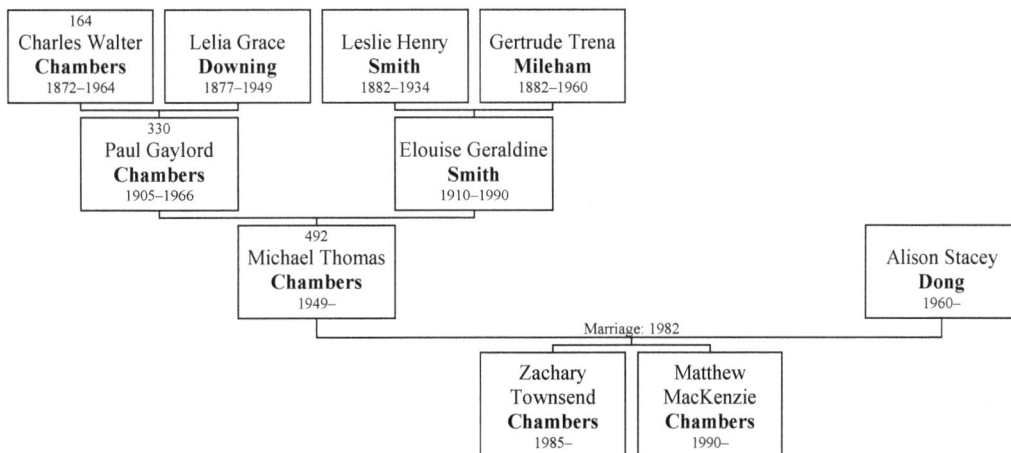

492. **Michael Thomas Chambers** was born on Thursday, July 14, 1949, in Chicago Heights, Cook County, Illinois. He is the son of Paul Gaylord Chambers (330) and Elouise Geraldine Smith.

At the age of 33, Michael Thomas married **Alison Stacey Dong** on Friday, December 24, 1982, in Las Vegas, Clark County, Nevada, when she was 22 years old. They have two sons.

Alison Stacey was born in Oakland, Alameda County, California, on Tuesday, August 02, 1960.

Sons of Michael Thomas Chambers and Alison Stacey Dong:

m   I. **Zachary Townsend Chambers** was born in Pittsfield, Berkshire County, Massachusetts, on February 22, 1985.

m   II. **Matthew MacKenzie Chambers** was born in Newport Beach, California, on December 22, 1990.

Family of Russell Leffler and Vivian Yoakum

493. **Russell Laverne Leffler** was born on Thursday, February 02, 1911, in Holdrege, Phelps County, Nebraska.[465, 466] He was the son of Charles James Leffler (332) and Nellie Ethel Cannon.

Russell Laverne died in Orange County, Florida, on June 17, 1979, at the age of 68.[465]

Russell Laverne married **Vivian Irene Yoakum** on Friday, September 22, 1944, in Nansemond County, Virginia.[466] They obtained a marriage license in Nansemond County, Virginia.[466]

Vivian Irene was born in 1922.[466]

465   Ancestry.com, U.S., Social Security Death Index, 1935-2014 (Provo, UT, USA, Ancestry.com Operations Inc, 2014), Ancestry.com, Social Security Administration; Washington D.C., USA; Social Security Death Index, Master File. Record for Russell Leffler. https://search.ancestry.co.uk/cgi-bin/sse.dll?db=3693&h=36092214&indiv=try.

466   Ancestry.com, Virginia, U.S., Marriage Records, 1936-2014 (Lehi, UT, USA, Ancestry.com Operations, Inc., 2015), Ancestry.com, Virginia Department of Health; Richmond, Virginia; Virginia, Marriages, 1936-2014; Roll: 101166970. Record for Russell Laverne Leffler. https://search.ancestry.co.uk/cgi-bin/sse.dll?db=9279&h=10966770&indiv=try.

Family of Carl Jensen and Phyllis Kabrick

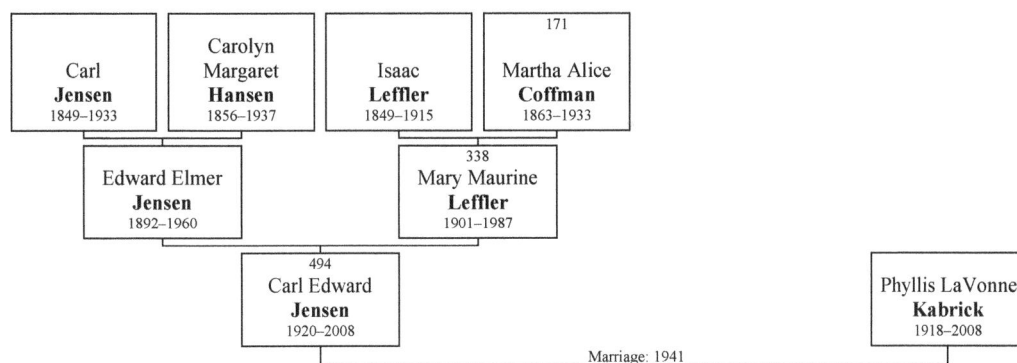

494. **Carl Edward Jensen** was born on Wednesday, September 01, 1920, in McCook, Red Willow County, Nebraska. He was the son of Edward Elmer Jensen and Mary Maurine Leffler (338). He was also known as **Ed**.

Carl Edward served in the military between 1944 and 1946. U.S. Army, WWII, Tec 5. He died in Spencer, Clay County, Iowa, on April 30, 2008, at the age of 87.[467] Carl Edward was buried in Riverside Cemetery, Spencer, Clay County, Iowa (Find a Grave ID 114959794).

At the age of 20, Carl Edward married **Phyllis LaVonne Kabrick** on Saturday, May 10, 1941, in Ponca, Dixon County, Nebraska, when she was 22 years old. Phyllis LaVonne was born in Spencer, Clay County, Iowa, on Saturday, November 16, 1918.

She reached 89 years of age and died in Spencer, Clay County, Iowa, on January 31, 2008. Phyllis LaVonne was buried in Riverside Cemetery, Spencer, Clay County, Iowa (Find a Grave ID 114959980).

Family of Caroline Jensen and Dean Shatto

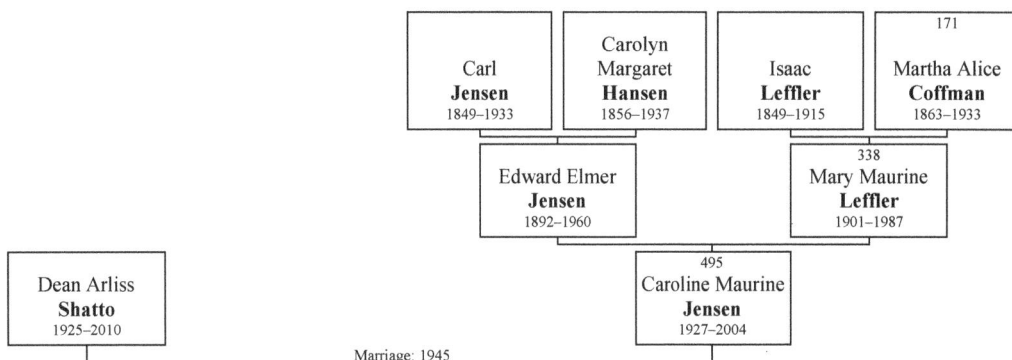

467   Ancestry.com, Public Member Trees (Provo, UT, USA, Ancestry.com Operations, Inc., 2006), Ancestry.com, Record for Mary Maurine Leffler. https://search.ancestry.co.uk/cgi-bin/sse.dll?db=1030&h=222028657458&indiv=try.

495. **Caroline Maurine Jensen** was born on Monday, September 05, 1927, in McCook, Red Willow County, Nebraska.[468] She was the daughter of Edward Elmer Jensen and Mary Maurine Leffler (338).

Caroline Maurine died on August 25, 2004, at the age of 76.[468]

At the age of 17, Caroline Maurine married **Dean Arliss Shatto** on Monday, April 23, 1945, in Spencer, Clay County, Iowa, when he was 19 years old. Dean Arliss was born in Spencer, Clay County, Iowa, on Tuesday, September 01, 1925.

He served in the military: U.S. Navy. Dean Arliss reached 85 years of age and died on September 02, 2010. (Find a Grave ID 58211230).

Family of Donald Leffler and Sue Philpot

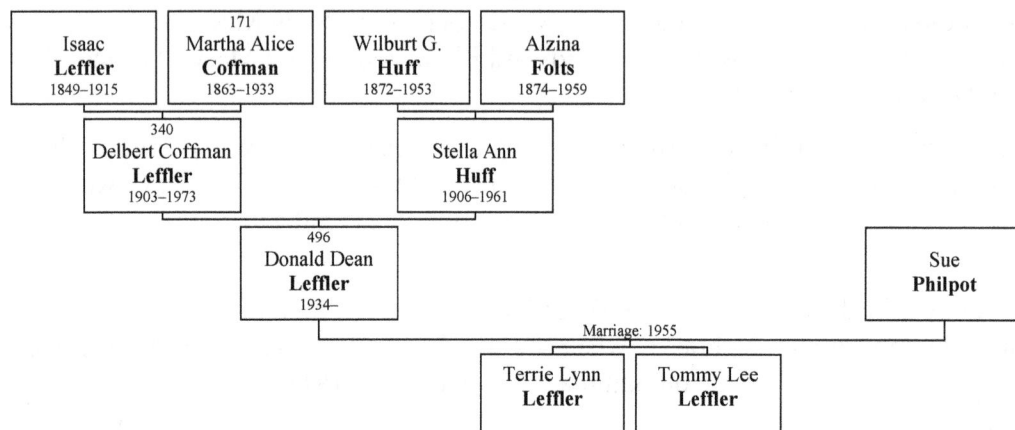

496. **Donald Dean Leffler** was born on Friday, February 02, 1934, in Holdrege, Phelps County, Nebraska.[469] He is the son of Delbert Coffman Leffler (340) and Stella Ann Huff.

Donald Dean married **Sue Philpot** on Friday, March 04, 1955.[469] They have two children.

Children of Donald Dean Leffler and Sue Philpot:

    f   I. **Terrie Lynn Leffler.**

    m   II. **Tommy Lee Leffler.**

468 Ancestry.com, U.S., Social Security Death Index, 1935-2014 (Provo, UT, USA, Ancestry.com Operations Inc, 2014), Ancestry.com, Social Security Administration; Washington D.C., USA; Social Security Death Index, Master File. Record for Carolyn Maurine Furst. https://search.ancestry.co.uk/cgi-bin/sse.dll?db=3693&h=73678343&indiv=try.

469 Leffler.FTW, Date of Import: Jan 3, 2002.

Family of Dean Coffman and Diana Heckler

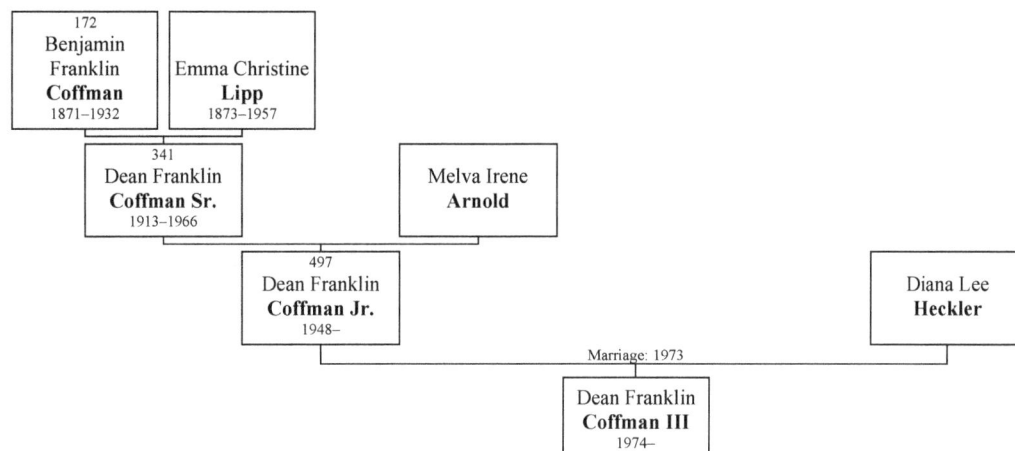

497.   **Dean Franklin Coffman Jr.** was born on Tuesday, June 29, 1948, in Decatur, Macon County, Illinois. He is the son of Dean Franklin Coffman Sr. (341) and Melva Irene Arnold. He is also known as **Frank**.

Dean Franklin married **Diana Lee Heckler** on Saturday, August 18, 1973. They have one son.

Son of Dean Franklin Coffman Jr. and Diana Lee Heckler:

> m   I. **Dean Franklin Coffman III** was born in Pekin, Tazewell County, Illinois, on December 28, 1974.

Family of Kimberly Coffman and Frank Forestiere

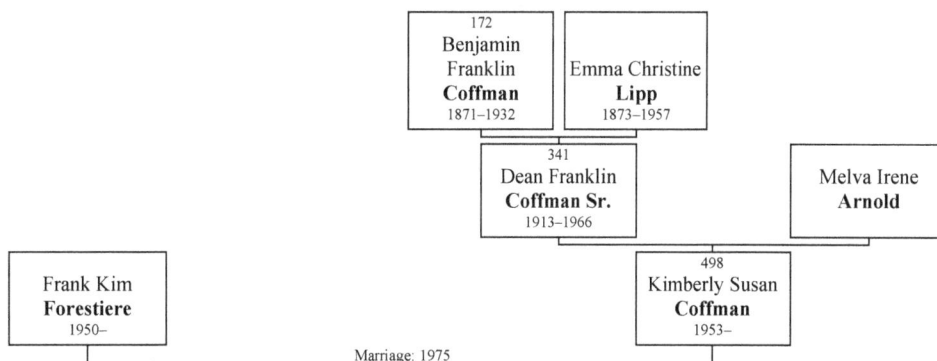

498.   **Kimberly Susan Coffman** was born on Saturday, March 07, 1953, in Decatur, Macon County, Illinois. She is the daughter of Dean Franklin Coffman Sr. (341) and Melva Irene Arnold.

Kimberly Susan married **Frank Kim Forestiere** on Saturday, May 17, 1975. Frank Kim was born in November 1950.

Patricia Hurd

499.   **Patricia Lee Hurd** was born on Thursday, December 01, 1938, in Chicago, Cook County, Illinois. She was the daughter of Robert Hargadine Hurd (345) and Violet Francis Miloshus.

Patricia Lee died in Hollywood, Dade County, Florida, on April 19, 2015, at the age of 76. She was buried in Vista Memorial Gardens, Miami Lakes, Miami-Dade County, Florida.

Marriages with James Stephen Doyle and Edward James Nolan (Page 511) are known.

Family of Patricia Hurd and James Doyle

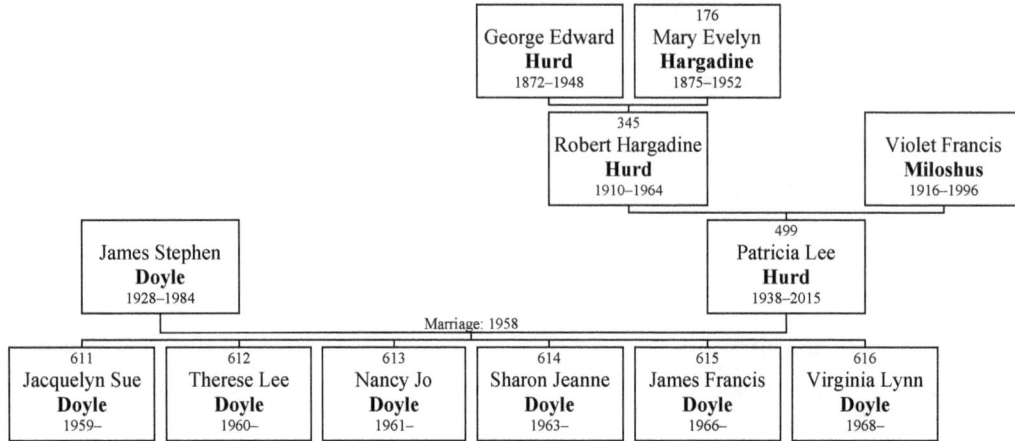

Here are the details about **Patricia Lee Hurd's** first marriage, with James Stephen Doyle. You can read more about Patricia Lee on page 509.

At the age of 19, Patricia Lee Hurd married **James Stephen Doyle** on Wednesday, November 19, 1958, at St. Leo's Catholic Church in Chicago, Cook County, Illinois, when he was 30 years old. They had six children.

James Stephen was born in Chicago, Cook County, Illinois, on Saturday, August 11, 1928. He reached 55 years of age and died in Miami, Dade County, Florida, on June 18, 1984. James Stephen was buried in Vista Memorial Gardens, Miami Lakes, Miami-Dade County, Florida.

Children of Patricia Lee Hurd and James Stephen Doyle:

+ 611   f   I. **Jacquelyn Sue Doyle** was born on July 31, 1959. She is also known as **Jacki**.

+ 612   f   II. **Therese Lee Doyle** was born on August 11, 1960. She is also known as **Teri**.

+ 613   f   III. **Nancy Jo Doyle** was born on October 09, 1961.

+ 614   f   IV. **Sharon Jeanne Doyle** was born on August 01, 1963.

+ 615   m   V. **James Francis Doyle** was born on December 30, 1966.

+ 616   f   VI. **Virginia Lynn Doyle** was born on June 03, 1968.

Family of Patricia Hurd and Edward Nolan

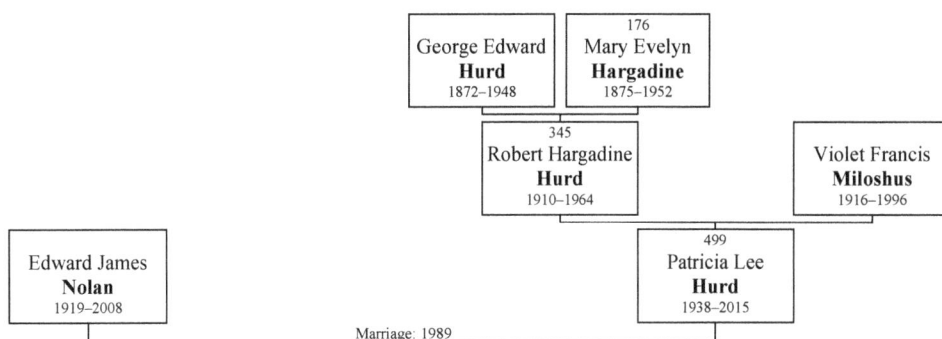

```
                              ┌─────────────┐┌─────────────┐
                              │George Edward││     176     │
                              │    Hurd     ││ Mary Evelyn │
                              │  1872-1948  ││  Hargadine  │
                              │             ││  1875-1952  │
                              └─────────────┘└─────────────┘
                                   ┌─────────────┐
                                   │     345     │           ┌─────────────┐
                                   │Robert Hargadine│        │Violet Francis│
                                   │    Hurd     │           │  Miloshus   │
                                   │  1910-1964  │           │  1916-1996  │
                                   └─────────────┘           └─────────────┘
     ┌─────────────┐                          ┌─────────────┐
     │Edward James │                          │     499     │
     │    Nolan    │                          │ Patricia Lee│
     │  1919-2008  │                          │    Hurd     │
     │             │                          │  1938-2015  │
     └─────────────┘                          └─────────────┘
              Marriage: 1989
```

Here are the details about **Patricia Lee Hurd's** second marriage, with Edward James Nolan. You can read more about Patricia Lee on page 509.

At the age of 50, Patricia Lee Hurd married **Edward James Nolan** on Tuesday, January 31, 1989, when he was 69 years old. Edward James was born in East Haven, New Haven, Connecticut, on Monday, August 11, 1919.[470, 471]

He reached 88 years of age and died in Hollywood, Broward, Florida, on May 04, 2008.[470, 471] Edward James was buried in Woodlawn Park North Cemetery and Mausoleum, Miami, Miami-Dade County, Florida (Find a Grave ID 105678875).[470]

Family of Shannon Hargadine and Jeffrey Arnold

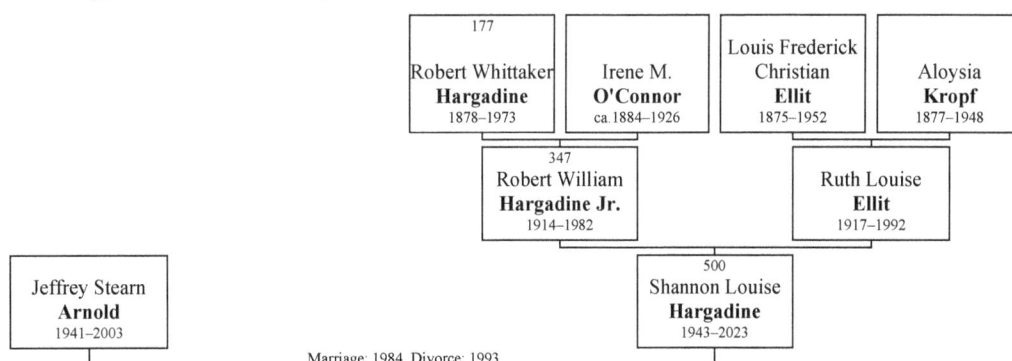

```
              ┌─────────────┐┌─────────────┐┌─────────────┐┌─────────────┐
              │     177     ││  Irene M.   ││Louis Frederick││           │
              │Robert Whittaker││ O'Connor  ││ Christian   ││  Aloysia    │
              │  Hargadine  ││ ca.1884-1926││   Ellit     ││   Kropf     │
              │  1878-1973  ││             ││  1875-1952  ││  1877-1948  │
              └─────────────┘└─────────────┘└─────────────┘└─────────────┘
                   ┌─────────────┐              ┌─────────────┐
                   │     347     │              │ Ruth Louise │
                   │Robert William│             │    Ellit    │
                   │Hargadine Jr.│              │  1917-1992  │
                   │  1914-1982  │              └─────────────┘
                   └─────────────┘
     ┌─────────────┐              ┌─────────────┐
     │Jeffrey Stearn│             │     500     │
     │   Arnold    │             │Shannon Louise│
     │  1941-2003  │             │  Hargadine  │
     │             │             │  1943-2023  │
     └─────────────┘             └─────────────┘
              Marriage: 1984, Divorce: 1993
```

500. **Shannon Louise Hargadine** was born on Monday, June 07, 1943, in Ramsey, Anoka County, Minnesota. She was the daughter of Robert William Hargadine Jr. (347) and Ruth Louise Ellit.

Shannon Louise died in Ramsey, Anoka County, Minnesota, on August 24, 2023, at the age of 80.

---

470 Ancestry.com, Public Member Trees (Provo, UT, USA, Ancestry.com Operations, Inc., 2006), Ancestry.com, Record for Edward James Nolan. https://search.ancestry.co.uk/cgi-bin/sse.dll?db=1030&h=162311914262&indiv=try.

471 Ancestry.com, U.S., Social Security Death Index, 1935-2014 (Provo, UT, USA, Ancestry.com Operations Inc, 2014), Ancestry.com, Social Security Administration; Washington D.C., USA; Social Security Death Index, Master File. Record for Edward Nolan. https://search.ancestry.co.uk/cgi-bin/sse.dll?db=3693&h=82494098&indiv=try.

At the age of 41, Shannon Louise married **Jeffrey Stearn Arnold** on Tuesday, December 18, 1984, when he was 43 years old.[472] They were divorced in Ramsey County, Minnesota, on February 03, 1993.

Jeffrey Stearn was born in Saint Paul, Ramsey County, Minnesota, on Sunday, June 29, 1941.[473, 474] He reached 62 years of age and died at University Good Samaritan Center in Minneapolis, Hennepin County, Minnesota, on November 22, 2003.[473] His cause of death was Huntington's Disease. His body was cremated on November 25, 2003.[473] Metropolitan Crematory.

Family of Noreen Hargadine and Michael Hoff

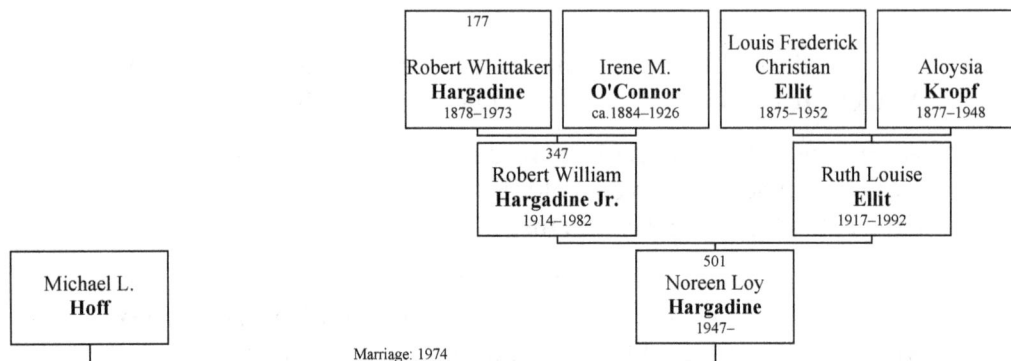

501.   **Noreen Loy Hargadine** was born on Thursday, February 06, 1947, in Ramsey, Anoka County, Minnesota. She is the daughter of Robert William Hargadine Jr. (347) and Ruth Louise Ellit.

Noreen Loy married **Michael L. Hoff** on Saturday, October 05, 1974, in Minnesota, USA.

Family of Robert Hargadine and Angina Schlavin

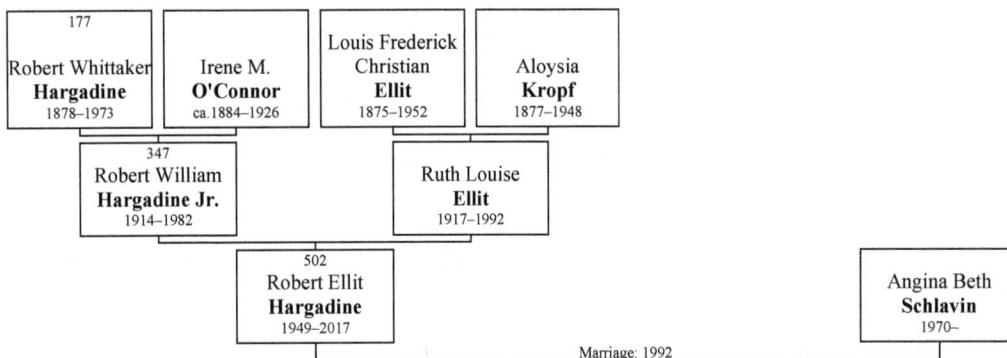

---

472   Minnesota Divorce Index, Divorced Feb. 3, 1993 Ramsey County, MN.

473   Ancestry.com, Minnesota, U.S., Death Index, 1908-2017 (Lehi, UT, USA, Ancestry.com Operations Inc, 2001), Ancestry.com, Minnesota Department of Health; St Paul, Minnesota, USA; Minnesota, Death Index, 1908-2017. Record for Jeffrey Stearn Arnold. https://search.ancestry.co.uk/cgi-bin/sse.dll?db=7316&h=3201387&indiv=try.

474   Ancestry.com, Minnesota, U.S., Marriage Index, 1958-2001 (Provo, UT, USA, Ancestry.com Operations Inc, 2007), Ancestry.com, Record for Jeffrey S Arnold. https://search.ancestry.co.uk/cgi-bin/sse.dll?db=8721&h=10151680&indiv=try.

502.   **Robert Ellit Hargadine** was born on Sunday, October 02, 1949, in Ramsey, Anoka County, Minnesota. He was the son of Robert William Hargadine Jr. (347) and Ruth Louise Ellit.

Robert Ellit died at Boundary Waters Care Center in Ely, St. Louis County, Minnesota, on October 23, 2017, at the age of 68. He was buried on November 03, 2017.

At the age of 43, Robert Ellit married **Angina Beth Schlavin** on Saturday, October 31, 1992, in St Louis, Minnesota, USA, when she was 21 years old. Angina Beth was born in Chisago City, Chisago County, Minnesota, on Friday, December 11, 1970.

Family of Keith Hargadine and Jennifer Thull

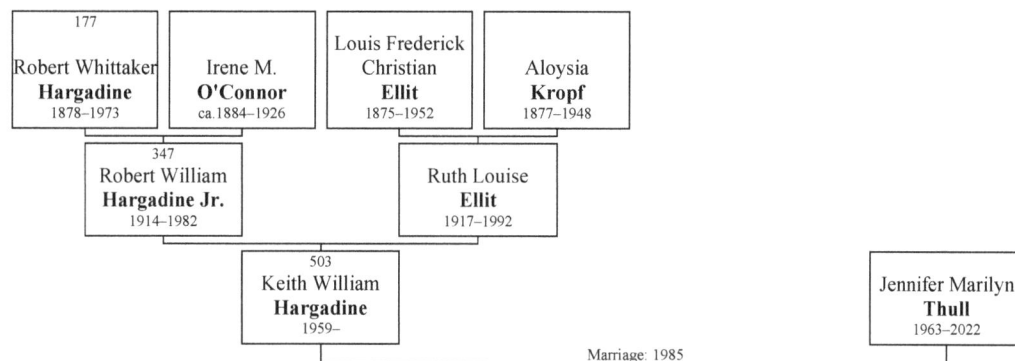

503.   **Keith William Hargadine** was born on Saturday, January 17, 1959, in Ramsey, Anoka County, Minnesota. He is the son of Robert William Hargadine Jr. (347) and Ruth Louise Ellit.

Keith William married **Jennifer Marilyn Thull** in 1985. Jennifer Marilyn was born on Sunday, August 25, 1963.

She reached 59 years of age and died in Dakota County, Minnesota, on November 01, 2022. Jennifer Marilyn was buried in Saint Elizabeth Ann Seton Catholic Cemetery, Hastings, Dakota County, Minnesota (Find a Grave ID 261085807).

Family of Mary Palmer and Edward Burton

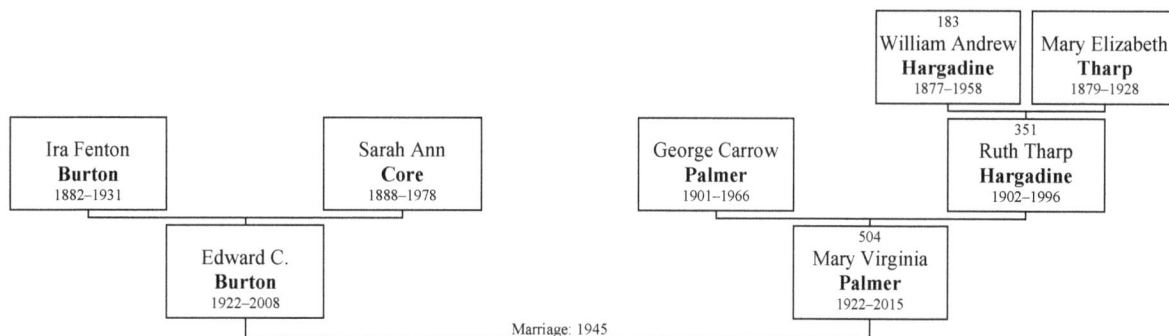

504.   **Mary Virginia Palmer** was born on Wednesday, January 25, 1922, in Milford, Sussex County, Delaware. She was the daughter of George Carrow Palmer and Ruth Tharp Hargadine (351). She was also known as **Ginny**.

Mary Virginia served in the military: U.S.M.C., WWII, Staff Sergeant. She died in West Melbourne, Brevard County, Florida, on May 23, 2015, at the age of 93. Mary Virginia was buried in Arlington National Cemetery, Arlington, Arlington County, Virginia (Find a Grave ID 147362939).

At the age of 23, Mary Virginia married **Edward C. Burton** on Sunday, April 15, 1945, at Pyote Army Air Field Chapel, Pyote Texas in Pyote, Ward County, Texas, when he was 23 years old. Edward C. was born in Wachapreague, Accomack County, Virginia, on Friday, January 27, 1922. He was the son of Ira Fenton Burton and Sarah Ann Core.

He served in the military: Served in WWII, Korea and Viet Nam, Retired as LTC. Edward C. reached 86 years of age and died in West Melbourne, Brevard County, Florida, on October 01, 2008. He was buried in Arlington National Cemetery, Arlington, Arlington County, Virginia (Find a Grave ID 30286859).

Family of George Palmer and Elizabeth Sayers

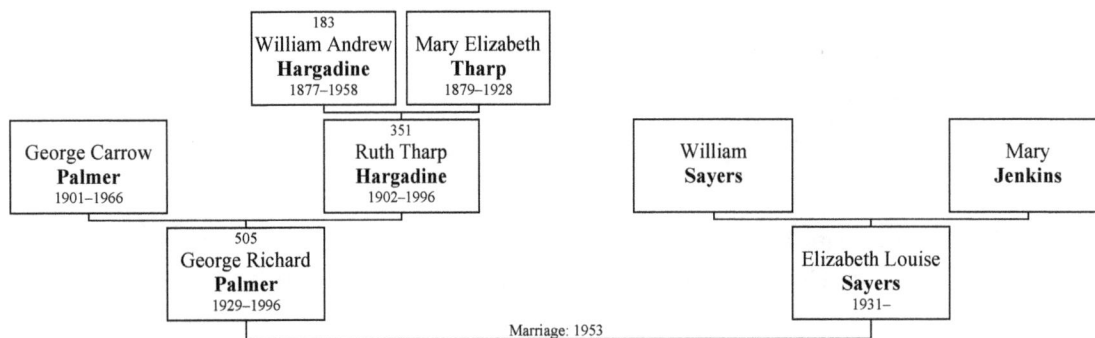

```
                    ┌──────────────┬──────────────┐
                    │     183      │              │
                    │William Andrew│Mary Elizabeth│
                    │  Hargadine   │    Tharp     │
                    │  1877–1958   │  1879–1928   │
                    └──────────────┴──────────────┘
┌──────────────┐        ┌──────────────┐      ┌──────────────┐        ┌──────────────┐
│              │        │     351      │      │              │        │              │
│George Carrow │        │  Ruth Tharp  │      │   William    │        │    Mary      │
│   Palmer     │        │  Hargadine   │      │   Sayers     │        │   Jenkins    │
│  1901–1966   │        │  1902–1996   │      │              │        │              │
└──────────────┘        └──────────────┘      └──────────────┘        └──────────────┘
          ┌──────────────┐                              ┌──────────────┐
          │     505      │                              │              │
          │George Richard│                              │Elizabeth Louise│
          │   Palmer     │                              │   Sayers     │
          │  1929–1996   │                              │   1931–      │
          └──────────────┘                              └──────────────┘
                         Marriage: 1953
```

505. **George Richard Palmer** was born on Thursday, February 14, 1929, in West Chester, Chester, Pennsylvania. He was the son of George Carrow Palmer and Ruth Tharp Hargadine (351).

George Richard died on December 05, 1996, at the age of 67. He was buried in Barratts Chapel Cemetery, Frederica, Kent County, Delaware (Find a Grave ID 30844798 & 33315217).

At the age of 24, George Richard married **Elizabeth Louise Sayers** on Saturday, June 20, 1953, at License #4538 in Centerville, New Castle, Delaware, when she was 21 years old. Elizabeth Louise was born in Wilmington, New Castle County, Delaware, on Monday, October 19, 1931. She is the daughter of William Sayers and Mary Jenkins.

Family of Jane Hargadine and Gerald Layton

```
                                    ┌──183──────┐ ┌──────────┐ ┌──────────────┐ ┌──────────────┐
                                    │William Andrew│ │Mary Elizabeth│ │Herschel Nelson│ │Sarah Elizabeth│
                                    │ Hargadine │ │   Tharp   │ │    Helm    │ │    Evans    │
                                    │ 1877–1958 │ │ 1879–1928 │ │ 1882–1967  │ │ 1888–1990   │
                                    └───────────┘ └──────────┘ └────────────┘ └─────────────┘
                                         ┌──353──────┐           ┌──────────┐
                                         │John Hopkins│           │Hazel Doris│
                                         │ Hargadine │           │   Helm    │
                                         │ 1907–1983 │           │ 1908–2012 │
                                         └───────────┘           └──────────┘
                  ┌──────────┐                    ┌──506──────┐
                  │Gerald Frank│                    │ Jane Helm │
                  │  Layton   │                    │ Hargadine │
                  │ 1935–2020 │                    │   1937–   │
                  └───────────┘                    └───────────┘
                            Marriage: 1961
```

506. **Jane Helm Hargadine** was born on Wednesday, August 25, 1937. She is the daughter of John Hopkins Hargadine (353) and Hazel Doris Helm.

At the age of 23, Jane Helm married **Gerald Frank Layton** on Monday, June 19, 1961, at Mariner's Bethel Methodist Church, Ocean View in Dagsboro, Sussex County, Delaware, when he was 26 years old. Gerald Frank was born in Frankford, Sussex County, Delaware, on Friday, May 17, 1935.

He reached 85 years of age and died in Bethany Beach, Sussex County, Delaware, on August 04, 2020. Gerald Frank was buried (Find a Grave ID 214342911).

Rodney Allen

```
┌──────────┐ ┌──186──────┐ ┌──────────┐ ┌──────────┐
│Oscar Wesley│ │Anna Lucretia│ │Harold M. │ │Hetty Royal│
│   Allen   │ │ Hargadine  │ │  Figgs   │ │  Taylor   │
│ 1891–1947 │ │ 1890–1966  │ │1878–1952 │ │ 1879–1963 │
└───────────┘ └────────────┘ └──────────┘ └───────────┘
     ┌──355──────┐              ┌──────────┐
     │Henry Hargadine│          │Frances Willard│
     │   Allen   │              │   Figgs   │
     │ 1912–1965 │              │ 1908–1984 │
     └───────────┘              └───────────┘
              ┌──507──────┐
              │Rodney Figgs│
              │   Allen   │
              │   –1999   │
              └───────────┘
                   ┌──────────┐
                   │Rodney Figgs│
                   │ Allen Jr. │
                   └───────────┘
```

507. **Rodney Figgs Allen**. He was the son of Henry Hargadine Allen (355) and Frances Willard Figgs.

Rodney Figgs died in 1999.

Son of Rodney Figgs Allen:

  m   I. **Rodney Figgs Allen Jr.**.

Patricia Passwater

508. **Patricia Millard Passwater** was born on Thursday, September 19, 1940. She was the daughter of Millard Oscar Passwater and Julia Marian Hall (359).

Patricia Millard died in Clayton, Kent County, Delaware, on May 31, 2001, at the age of 60. She was buried in Lakeside Cemetery, Dover, Kent County, Delaware, on June 05, 2001 (Find a Grave ID 141801874).

Marriages with Theodore A. Frederick and Leroy Walter Meekins (Page 517) are known.

Family of Patricia Passwater and Theodore Frederick

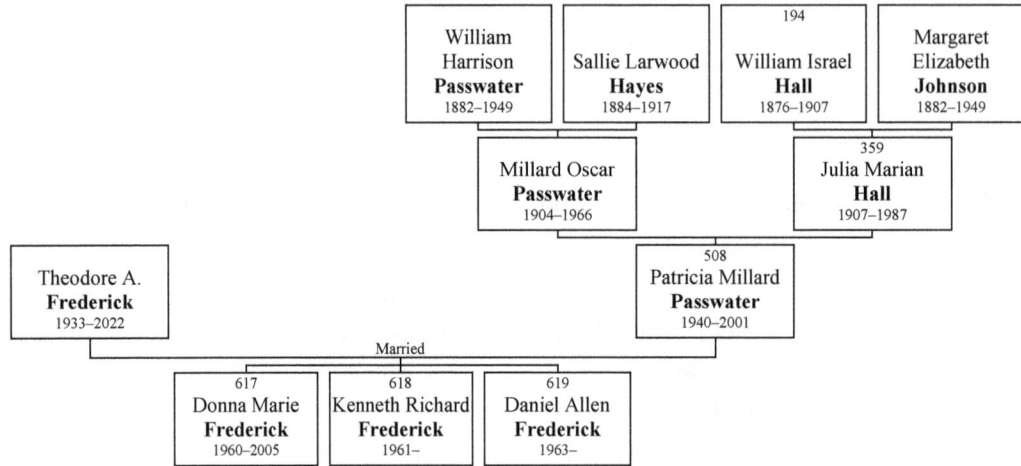

```
                              ┌──────────┐ ┌──────────┐  ┌────194────┐ ┌──────────┐
                              │ William  │ │          │  │ William   │ │ Margaret │
                              │ Harrison │ │  Sallie  │  │  Israel   │ │Elizabeth │
                              │Passwater │ │ Larwood  │  │   Hall    │ │ Johnson  │
                              │1882–1949 │ │  Hayes   │  │ 1876–1907 │ │1882–1949 │
                              │          │ │1884–1917 │  │           │ │          │
                              └──────────┘ └──────────┘  └───────────┘ └──────────┘
                                  ┌──────────────┐          ┌───359────┐
                                  │ Millard Oscar│          │   Julia  │
                                  │  Passwater   │          │  Marian  │
                                  │  1904–1966   │          │   Hall   │
                                  │              │          │1907–1987 │
                                  └──────────────┘          └──────────┘
  ┌──────────┐                          ┌───508────┐
  │Theodore A.│                         │ Patricia │
  │ Frederick │                         │ Millard  │
  │ 1933–2022 │                         │Passwater │
  │           │                         │1940–2001 │
  └──────────┘         Married          └──────────┘
           ┌───617────┐ ┌───618────┐ ┌───619────┐
           │  Donna   │ │ Kenneth  │ │  Daniel  │
           │  Marie   │ │ Richard  │ │  Allen   │
           │Frederick │ │Frederick │ │Frederick │
           │1960–2005 │ │  1961–   │ │  1963–   │
           └──────────┘ └──────────┘ └──────────┘
```

Here are the details about **Patricia Millard Passwater's** first marriage, with Theodore A. Frederick. You can read more about Patricia Millard on page 515.

Patricia Millard Passwater married **Theodore A. Frederick**. They had three children.

Theodore A. was born in Delaware, USA, on Thursday, December 14, 1933. He served in the military: US Navy.

Theodore A. reached 88 years of age and died in Newark, New Castle County, Delaware, on February 26, 2022. He was buried on April 01, 2022, in Delaware Veterans Memorial Cemetery, Bear, New Castle County, Delaware (Find a Grave ID 237401781).

Children of Patricia Millard Passwater and Theodore A. Frederick:

+   617   f   I. **Donna Marie Frederick** was born on May 16, 1960. She died on January 29, 2005, at the age of 44. Donna Marie was buried in Cathedral Cemetery, Wilmington, New Castle County, Delaware (Find a Grave ID 22909132).

+   618   m   II. **Kenneth Richard Frederick** was born on June 09, 1961.

+   619   m   III. **Daniel Allen Frederick** was born on April 12, 1963.

Family of Patricia Passwater and Leroy Meekins

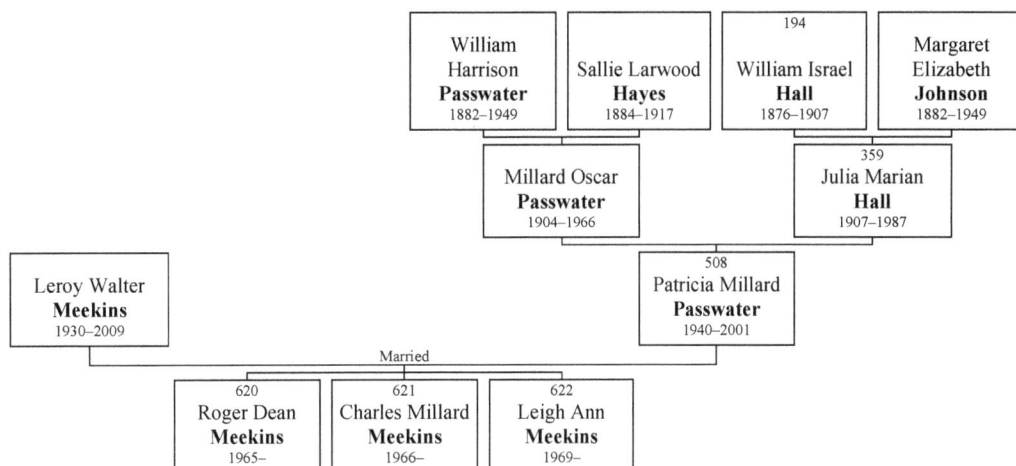

Here are the details about **Patricia Millard Passwater's** second marriage, with Leroy Walter Meekins. You can read more about Patricia Millard on page 515.

Patricia Millard Passwater married **Leroy Walter Meekins**. They had three children.

Leroy Walter was born in Chestertown, Kent County, Maryland, on Wednesday, August 20, 1930. He reached 79 years of age and died in Smyrna, Kent County, Delaware, on December 23, 2009. Leroy Walter was buried in Chester Cemetery, Chestertown, Kent County, Maryland (Find a Grave ID 67052069).

Children of Patricia Millard Passwater and Leroy Walter Meekins:

+ 620   m   I. **Roger Dean Meekins** was born in December 1965.

+ 621   m   II. **Charles Millard Meekins** was born on November 30, 1966.

+ 622   f   III. **Leigh Ann Meekins** was born on July 10, 1969.

Neil Becker

509.   **Neil Stephen Becker** was born on Thursday, October 12, 1944, in Kansas City, Jackson County, Missouri.[475] He is the son of Norman Stuart Becker and Martha Jean Sayles (364).

Marriages with Neta Rae Dull, Connie Mae Tomich (Page 519) and Peggy Lou Bradford (Page 519) are known.

---

475   Neil Becker.FTW, Date of Import: May 19, 2004.

Family of Neil Becker and Neta Dull

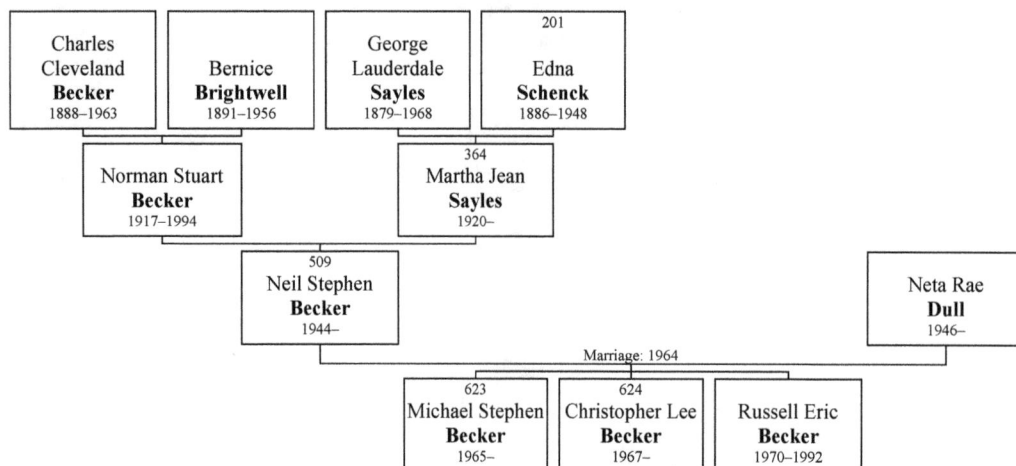

Here are the details about **Neil Stephen Becker's** first marriage, with Neta Rae Dull. You can read more about Neil Stephen on page 517.

At the age of 20, Neil Stephen Becker married **Neta Rae Dull** on Saturday, October 24, 1964, in Kansas City, Wyandotte County, Kansas, when she was 18 years old.[475] They had three sons.

Neta Rae was born in Kansas City, Jackson County, Missouri, on Saturday, April 20, 1946.[475]

Sons of Neil Stephen Becker and Neta Rae Dull:

+ 623   m   I. **Michael Stephen Becker** was born in Independence, Jackson County, Missouri, on May 08, 1965.[475]

+ 624   m   II. **Christopher Lee Becker** was born in Independence, Jackson County, Missouri, on October 13, 1967.[475]

       m   III. **Russell Eric Becker** was born in Kansas City, Jackson County, Missouri, on August 11, 1970.[475] He died in Kansas City, Jackson County, Missouri, on January 15, 1992, at the age of 21.[475]

Family of Neil Becker and Connie Tomich

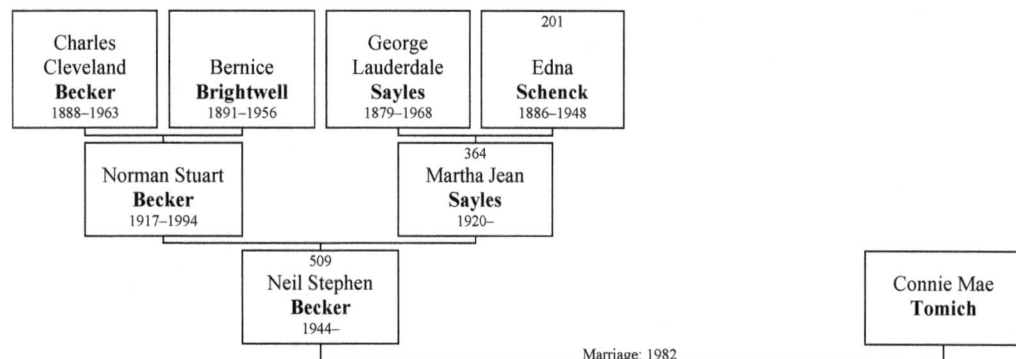

Here are the details about **Neil Stephen Becker's** second marriage, with Connie Mae Tomich. You can read more about Neil Stephen on page 517.

Neil Stephen Becker married **Connie Mae Tomich** on Thursday, January 21, 1982, in Unity Village, Jackson County, Missouri.[475]

Family of Neil Becker and Peggy Bradford

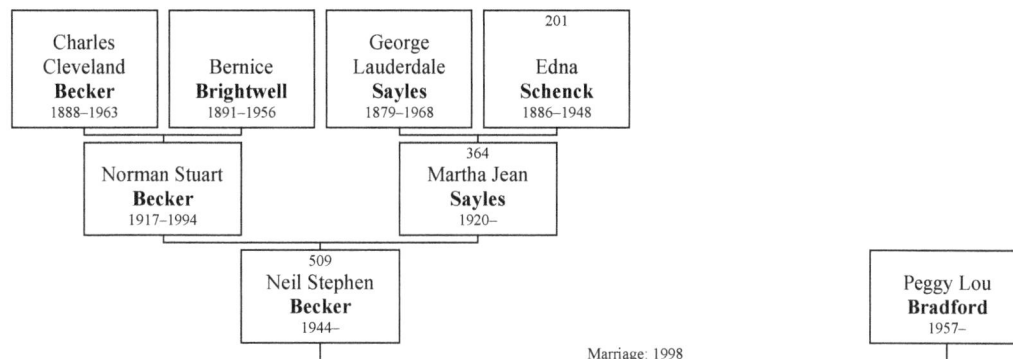

Charles Cleveland **Becker** 1888–1963	Bernice **Brightwell** 1891–1956	George Lauderdale **Sayles** 1879–1968	201 Edna **Schenck** 1886–1948

Norman Stuart **Becker** 1917–1994	364 Martha Jean **Sayles** 1920–

509 Neil Stephen **Becker** 1944–	Peggy Lou **Bradford** 1957–

Marriage: 1998

Here are the details about **Neil Stephen Becker's** third marriage, with Peggy Lou Bradford. You can read more about Neil Stephen on page 517.

At the age of 53, Neil Stephen Becker married **Peggy Lou Bradford** on Saturday, January 24, 1998, in Kansas City, Clay County, Missouri, when she was 40 years old.[475] Peggy Lou was born in Kansas City, Jackson County, Missouri, on Thursday, May 23, 1957.[475]

Samuel Hargadine

510. **Samuel Emmett Hargadine V** was born on Sunday, August 10, 1958, in Columbia, Boone County, Missouri. He is the son of Samuel Emmett Hargadine IV (366) and Georganna Myers.

Samuel Emmett served in the military between August 12, 1976 and August 12, 1979: US Army.

Marriages with Sheri Lynn Palmerton and Annette Sue Peddicord (Page 520) are known.

Family of Samuel Hargadine and Sheri Palmerton

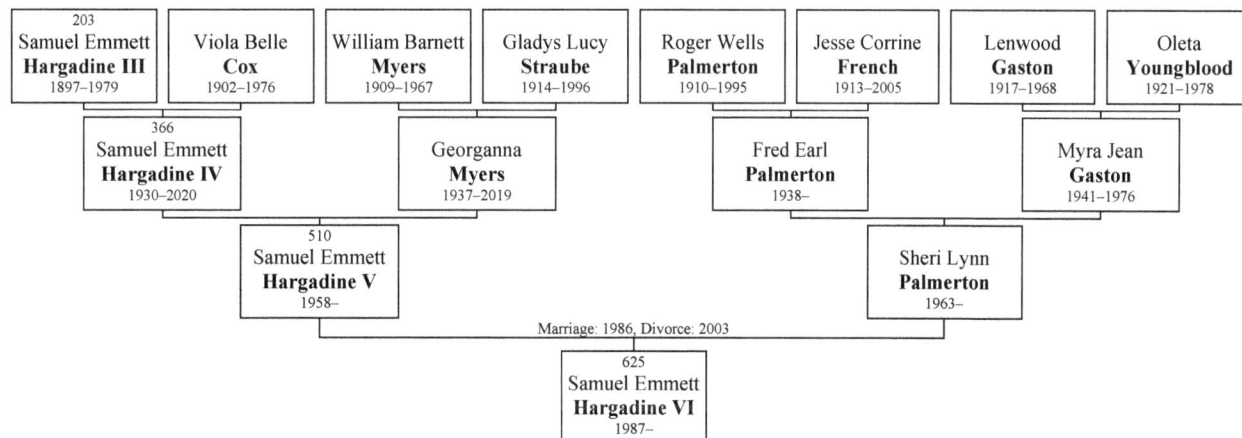

203 Samuel Emmett **Hargadine III** 1897–1979	Viola Belle **Cox** 1902–1976	William Barnett **Myers** 1909–1967	Gladys Lucy **Straube** 1914–1996	Roger Wells **Palmerton** 1910–1995	Jesse Corrine **French** 1913–2005	Lenwood Gaston **Gaston** 1917–1968	Oleta **Youngblood** 1921–1978

366 Samuel Emmett **Hargadine IV** 1930–2020	Georganna **Myers** 1937–2019	Fred Earl **Palmerton** 1938–	Myra Jean **Gaston** 1941–1976

510 Samuel Emmett **Hargadine V** 1958–	Sheri Lynn **Palmerton** 1963–

Marriage: 1986, Divorce: 2003

625 Samuel Emmett **Hargadine VI** 1987–

Here are the details about **Samuel Emmett Hargadine V's** first marriage, with Sheri Lynn Palmerton. You can read more about Samuel Emmett on page 519.

At the age of 28, Samuel Emmett Hargadine V married **Sheri Lynn Palmerton** on Saturday, September 13, 1986, in Columbia, Boone County, Missouri, when she was 23 years old. They were divorced in Howard County, Missouri, on November 06, 2003. They have one son.

Sheri Lynn was born in St. Charles, St. Charles County, Missouri, on Wednesday, January 09, 1963. She is the daughter of Fred Earl Palmerton and Myra Jean Gaston.

Son of Samuel Emmett Hargadine V and Sheri Lynn Palmerton:

+ 625   m   I. **Samuel Emmett Hargadine VI** was born in Columbia, Boone County, Missouri, on July 23, 1987. He is also known as **Sammy**.

Family of Samuel Hargadine and Annette Peddicord

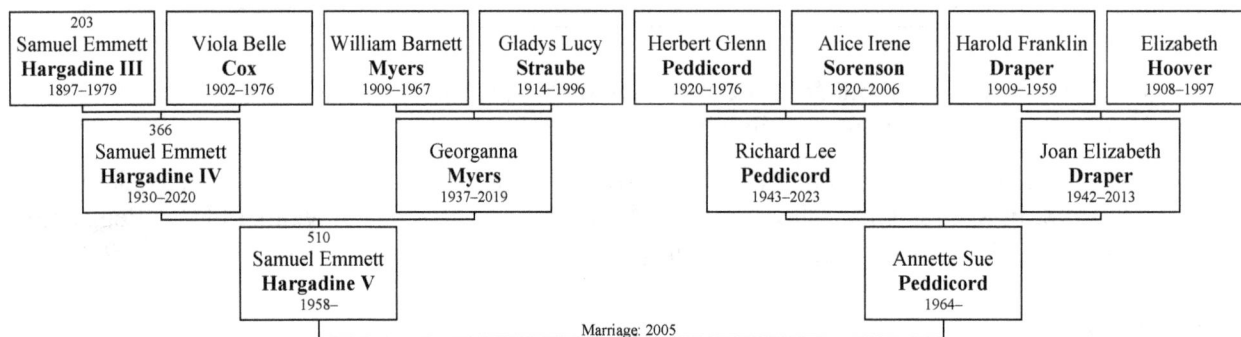

203 Samuel Emmett **Hargadine III** 1897–1979	Viola Belle **Cox** 1902–1976	William Barnett **Myers** 1909–1967	Gladys Lucy **Straube** 1914–1996	Herbert Glenn **Peddicord** 1920–1976	Alice Irene **Sorenson** 1920–2006	Harold Franklin **Draper** 1909–1959	Elizabeth **Hoover** 1908–1997

366 Samuel Emmett **Hargadine IV** 1930–2020 — Georganna **Myers** 1937–2019

Richard Lee **Peddicord** 1943–2023 — Joan Elizabeth **Draper** 1942–2013

510 Samuel Emmett **Hargadine V** 1958–

Annette Sue **Peddicord** 1964–

Marriage: 2005

Here are the details about **Samuel Emmett Hargadine V's** second marriage, with Annette Sue Peddicord. You can read more about Samuel Emmett on page 519.

At the age of 47, Samuel Emmett Hargadine V married **Annette Sue Peddicord** on Friday, August 19, 2005, in Columbia, Boone County, Missouri, when she was 41 years old. Annette Sue was born in Belmond, Wright County, Iowa, on Friday, January 10, 1964.[476] She is the daughter of Richard Lee Peddicord and Joan Elizabeth Draper.

John Hargadine

511.   **John Everett Hargadine** was born on Wednesday, March 21, 1962, at George Washington University Hospital in Washington D.C.. He is the son of Samuel Emmett Hargadine IV (366) and Georganna Myers.

Marriages with Monelle Schriewer, Patricia A. Lehman (Page 521) and Mary Anne Elizabeth Niemeyer (Page 522) are known.

---

476   Ancestry.com, U.S., Index to Public Records, 1994-2019 (Lehi, UT, USA, Ancestry.com Operations, Inc., 2020), Ancestry.com.

Family of John Hargadine and Monelle Schriewer

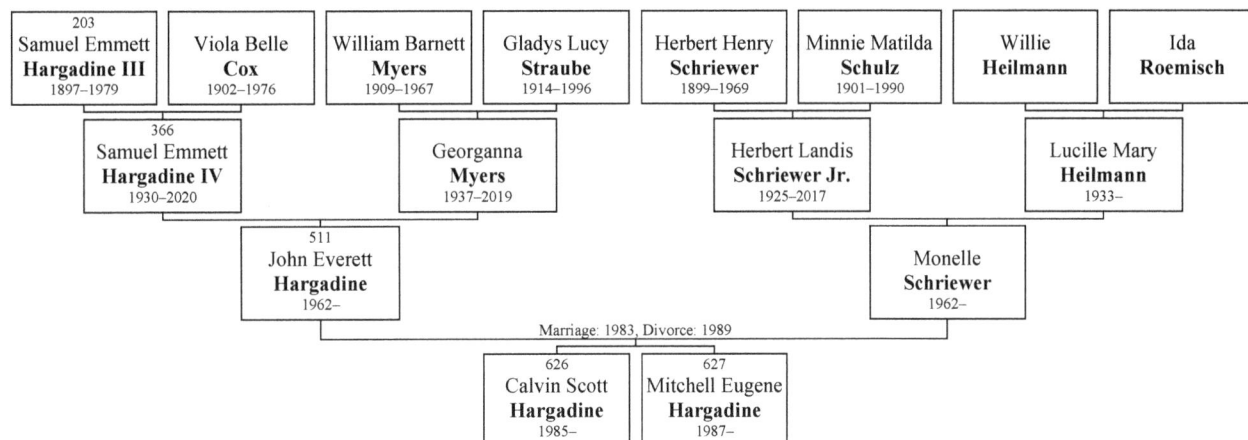

Here are the details about **John Everett Hargadine's** first marriage, with Monelle Schriewer. You can read more about John Everett on page 520.

At the age of 21, John Everett Hargadine married **Monelle Schriewer** on Thursday, September 29, 1983, in Warrensburg, Johnson County, Missouri, when she was 21 years old. They were divorced in Columbia, Boone County, Missouri, in April 1989. They have two sons.

Monelle was born in New Braunfels, Comal County, Texas, on Tuesday, January 23, 1962. She is the daughter of Herbert Landis Schriewer Jr. and Lucille Mary Heilmann.

Sons of John Everett Hargadine and Monelle Schriewer:

+ 626 m I. **Calvin Scott Hargadine** was born in Sedalia, Pettis County, Missouri, on October 22, 1985.

+ 627 m II. **Mitchell Eugene Hargadine** was born in Columbia, Boone County, Missouri, on September 17, 1987.

Family of John Hargadine and Patricia Lehman

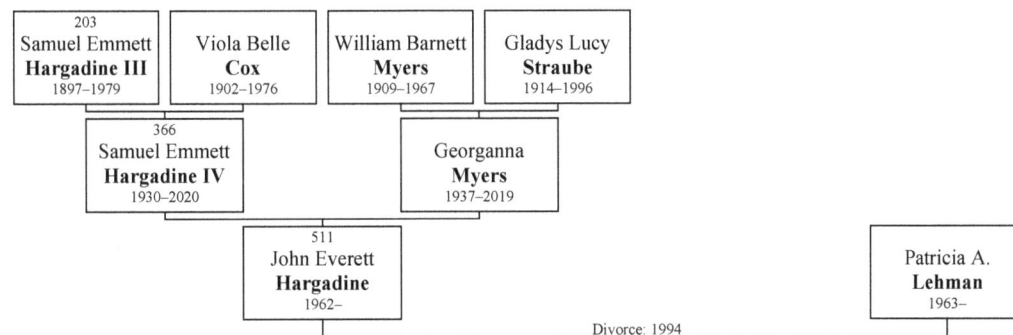

Here are the details about **John Everett Hargadine's** second marriage, with Patricia A. Lehman. You can read more about John Everett on page 520.

John Everett Hargadine married **Patricia A. Lehman**. They were divorced in Boone County, Missouri, on September 15, 1994.

Patricia A. was born in September 1963.

Family of John Hargadine and Mary Niemeyer

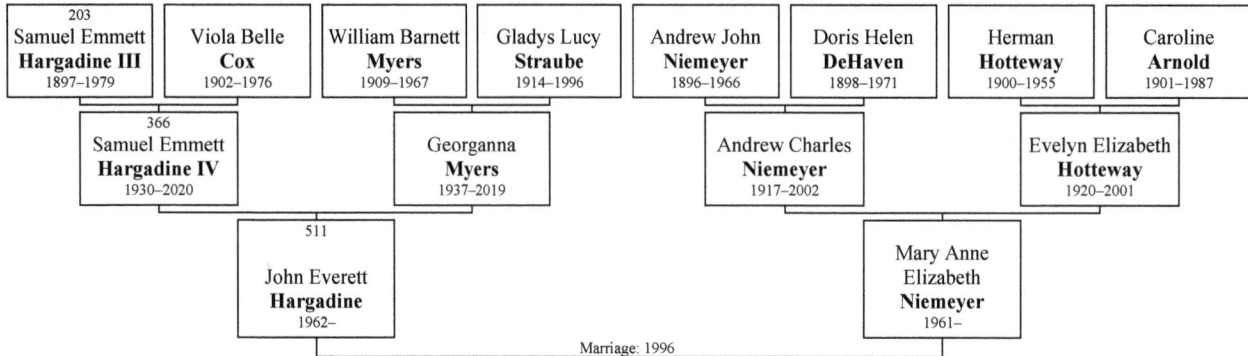

Here are the details about **John Everett Hargadine's** third marriage, with Mary Anne Elizabeth Niemeyer. You can read more about John Everett on page 520.

At the age of 34, John Everett Hargadine married **Mary Anne Elizabeth Niemeyer** on Saturday, September 28, 1996, in Saint Louis, Saint Louis County, Missouri, when she was 34 years old. Mary Anne Elizabeth was born in Saint Louis, Saint Louis County, Missouri, on Monday, October 09, 1961. She is the daughter of Andrew Charles Niemeyer and Evelyn Elizabeth Hotteway.

Family of Douglas Farrar and Karen Smith

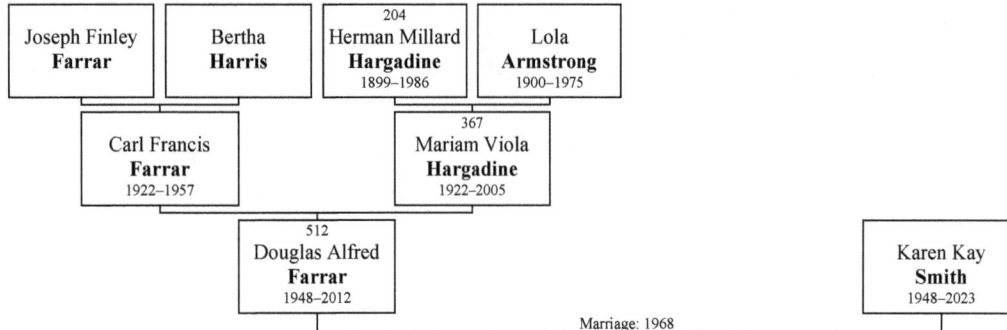

512.   **Douglas Alfred Farrar** was born on Thursday, February 19, 1948, in Brookfield, Linn County, Missouri. He was the son of Carl Francis Farrar and Mariam Viola Hargadine (367). He was also known as **Doug**.

Douglas Alfred died in Overland Park, Johnson County, Kansas, on May 29, 2012, at the age of 64. He was buried in Maple Hill Cemetery, Kansas City, Wyandotte County, Kansas (Find a Grave ID 91051829).

Douglas Alfred married **Karen Kay Smith** in 1968. Karen Kay was born in Toppenish, Yakima County, Washington, on Monday, November 01, 1948.

She reached 74 years of age and died in Olathe, Johnson County, Kansas, on August 10, 2023. Karen Kay was buried in Maple Hill Cemetery, Kansas City, Wyandotte County, Kansas (Find a Grave ID 257724360).

Family of Rhonda Hargadine and Larry Head

513. **Rhonda Lynne Hargadine** was born on Friday, January 02, 1959. She is the daughter of Ronald Dale Hargadine (368) and Marlyn June Detwiller.

Rhonda Lynne married **Larry Michael Head** on Friday, August 03, 1984, in Kirksville, Adair County, Missouri. They have two sons.

Sons of Rhonda Lynne Hargadine and Larry Michael Head:

m   I. **Michael Head**.

m   II. **Jeremy Head**.

Family of Jim Hargadine and Marla Hines

514. **Jim Edwin Hargadine** was born on Thursday, September 06, 1956, in Denver, Denver County, Colorado. He is the son of Robert Eugene Hargadine (369) and Mary Annabeth Meneely.

At the age of 26, Jim Edwin married **Marla Jeanine Hines** on Friday, July 29, 1983, in Brookfield, Linn County, Missouri, when she was 22 years old. They have one daughter.

Marla Jeanine was born in Brookfield, Linn County, Missouri, on Saturday, August 20, 1960. She is the daughter of Charles Albert Hines and Jeanette Anspaugh.

Daughter of Jim Edwin Hargadine and Marla Jeanine Hines:

+ 628   f   I. **Mary Jeanette Hargadine** was born in Brookfield, Linn County, Missouri, on September 12, 1984.

Family of Richard Hargadine and Karen Harrell

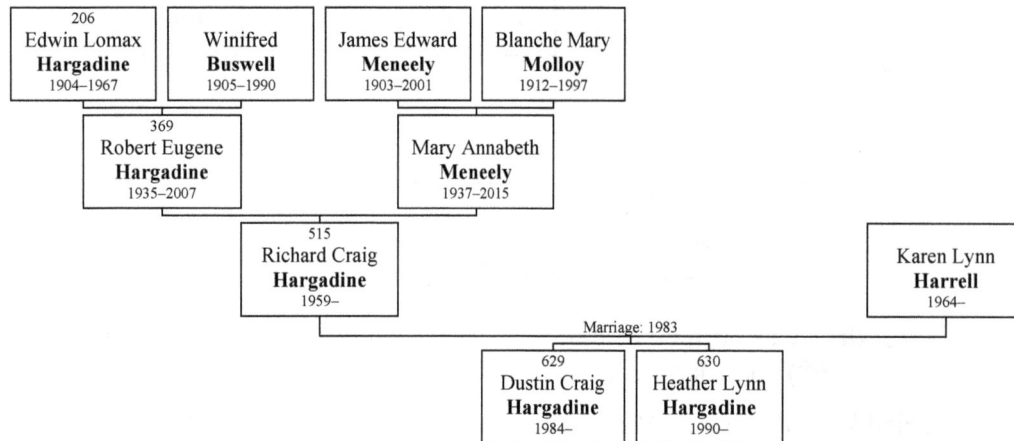

515.   **Richard Craig Hargadine** was born on Saturday, August 01, 1959, in Brookfield, Linn County, Missouri. He is the son of Robert Eugene Hargadine (369) and Mary Annabeth Meneely.

At the age of 24, Richard Craig married **Karen Lynn Harrell** on Saturday, September 03, 1983, in Brookfield, Linn County, Missouri, when she was 19 years old. They have two children.

Karen Lynn was born in Saint Louis, Saint Louis County, Missouri, on Wednesday, July 29, 1964.

Children of Richard Craig Hargadine and Karen Lynn Harrell:

+ 629   m   I. **Dustin Craig Hargadine** was born in Chillicothe, Livingston County, Missouri, on October 10, 1984.

+ 630   f   II. **Heather Lynn Hargadine** was born in Chillicothe, Livingston County, Missouri, on April 10, 1990.

Family of Loren Hargadine and Vaga Jenkins

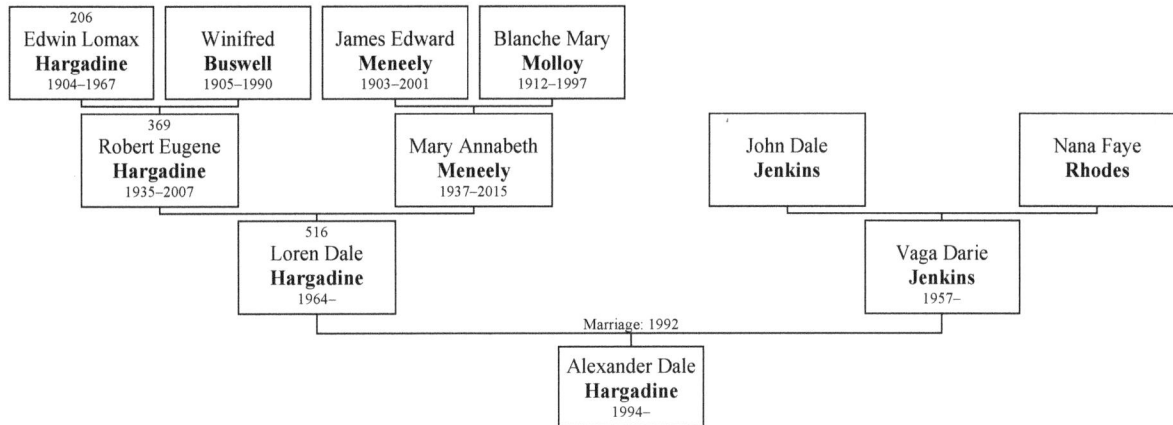

516. **Loren Dale Hargadine** was born on Wednesday, November 18, 1964, in Brookfield, Linn County, Missouri. He is the son of Robert Eugene Hargadine (369) and Mary Annabeth Meneely.

At the age of 27, Loren Dale married **Vaga Darie Jenkins** on Saturday, March 21, 1992, in Brunswick, Chariton County, Missouri, when she was 35 years old. They have one son.

Vaga Darie was born in Brookfield, Linn County, Missouri, on Wednesday, January 23, 1957. She is the daughter of John Dale Jenkins and Nana Faye Rhodes.

Son of Loren Dale Hargadine and Vaga Darie Jenkins:

  m   I. **Alexander Dale Hargadine** was born in Moberly, Randolph County, Missouri, on February 28, 1994.

8th Generation

Family of Nicole Kaylor and Timothy Wicker

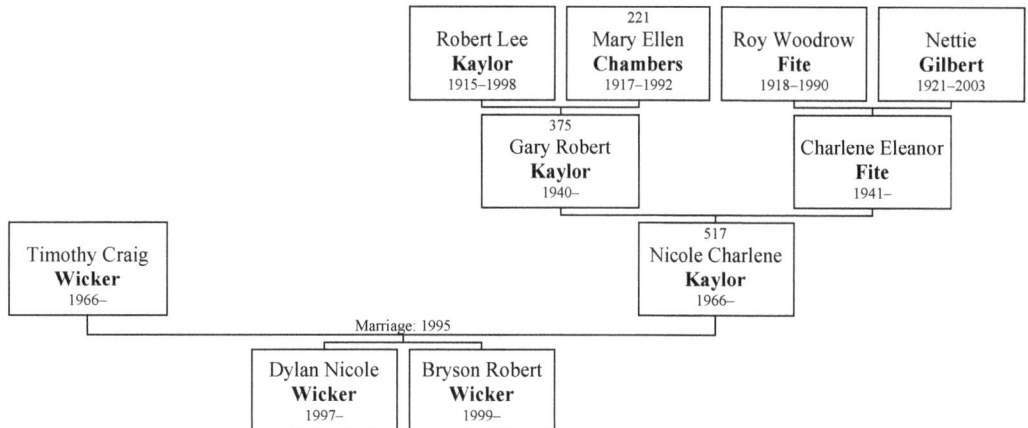

517. **Nicole Charlene Kaylor** was born on Wednesday, July 13, 1966, at Methodist Hospital in Houston, Texas.[477] She is the daughter of Gary Robert Kaylor (375) and Charlene Eleanor Fite.

At the age of 29, Nicole Charlene married **Timothy Craig Wicker** on Sunday, October 15, 1995, in Raleigh, Wake County, North Carolina, when he was 29 years old.[478] They have two children.

Timothy Craig was born in Raleigh, Wake County, North Carolina, on Wednesday, July 13, 1966.[478]

Children of Nicole Charlene Kaylor and Timothy Craig Wicker:

f   I. **Dylan Nicole Wicker** was born in Raleigh, Wake County, North Carolina, on June 27, 1997.[478]

m   II. **Bryson Robert Wicker** was born at Rex Hospital in Raleigh, North Carolina, on July 30, 1999.[478]

Family of Mary Stout and Robert Ballou

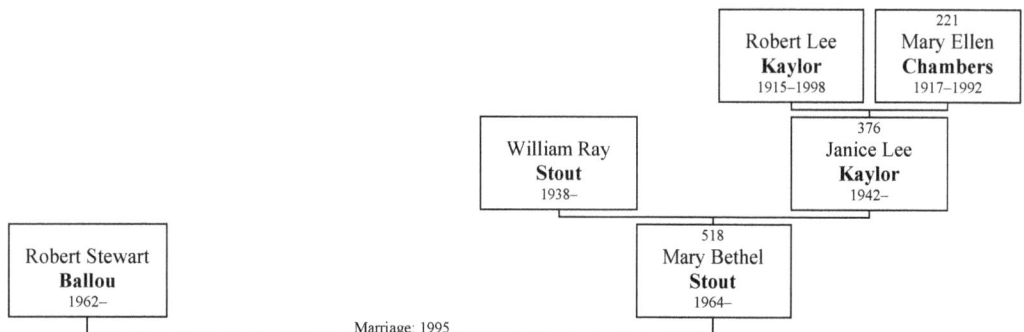

---

477   Birth Certificate.

478   Nicole Kaylor Wicker.

518. **Mary Bethel Stout** was born on Friday, March 13, 1964, in Roanoke, Roanoke County, Virginia.[479] She is the daughter of William Ray Stout and Janice Lee Kaylor (376).

At the age of 30, Mary Bethel married **Robert Stewart Ballou** on Saturday, February 25, 1995, in Roanoke, Roanoke County, Virginia, when he was 33 years old.[479] Robert Stewart was born in Roanoke, Roanoke County, Virginia, on Wednesday, January 10, 1962.[480]

Family of Jr Stout and Tia Shelton

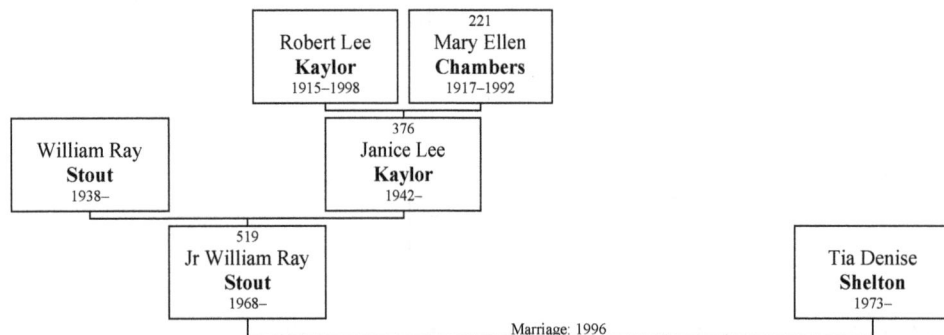

```
                        ┌─────────────┬─────────────┐
                        │ Robert Lee  │    221      │
                        │   Kaylor    │ Mary Ellen  │
                        │  1915–1998  │  Chambers   │
                        │             │  1917–1992  │
                        └─────────────┴─────────────┘
      ┌─────────────┐         ┌─────────────┐
      │ William Ray │         │    376      │
      │    Stout    │         │ Janice Lee  │
      │   1938–     │         │   Kaylor    │
      │             │         │   1942–     │
      └─────────────┘         └─────────────┘
            ┌─────────────┐                    ┌─────────────┐
            │    519      │                    │ Tia Denise  │
            │ Jr William  │                    │   Shelton   │
            │ Ray Stout   │                    │   1973–     │
            │   1968–     │                    │             │
            └─────────────┘                    └─────────────┘
                          Marriage: 1996
```

519. **Jr William Ray Stout** was born on Friday, July 26, 1968, in Roanoke, Roanoke County, Virginia.[481] He is the son of William Ray Stout and Janice Lee Kaylor (376).

At the age of 28, Jr William Ray married **Tia Denise Shelton** on Saturday, August 10, 1996, in Powhatan, Powhatan County, Virginia, when she was 22 years old.[482] Tia Denise was born in Norfolk, Virginia, on Thursday, October 04, 1973.

Family of Dawn McGuire and Robert Hoffman

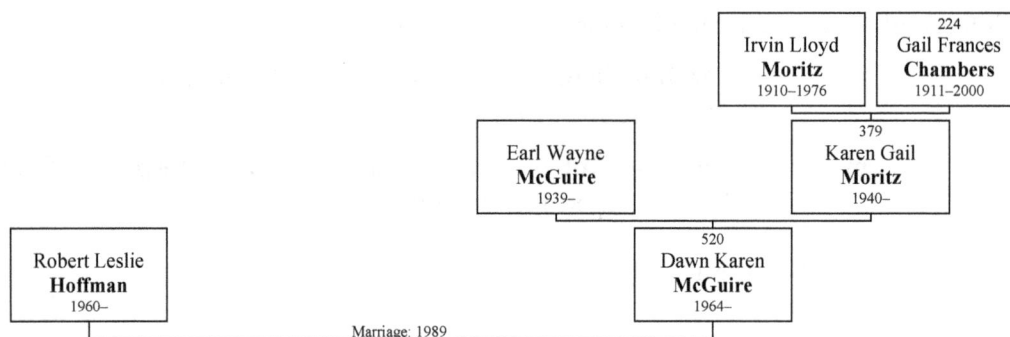

```
                                      ┌─────────────┬─────────────┐
                                      │ Irvin Lloyd │    224      │
                                      │   Moritz    │ Gail Frances│
                                      │  1910–1976  │  Chambers   │
                                      │             │  1911–2000  │
                                      └─────────────┴─────────────┘
                      ┌─────────────┐        ┌─────────────┐
                      │ Earl Wayne  │        │    379      │
                      │  McGuire    │        │ Karen Gail  │
                      │   1939–     │        │   Moritz    │
                      │             │        │   1940–     │
                      └─────────────┘        └─────────────┘
      ┌─────────────┐              ┌─────────────┐
      │ Robert Leslie│             │    520      │
      │   Hoffman   │              │ Dawn Karen  │
      │   1960–     │              │  McGuire    │
      │             │              │   1964–     │
      └─────────────┘              └─────────────┘
                      Marriage: 1989
```

520. **Dawn Karen McGuire** was born on Thursday, July 23, 1964, at Air Force Academy Hospital in Colorado Springs, El Paso County, Colorado.[483] She is the daughter of Earl Wayne McGuire and Karen Gail Moritz (379).

479   Mary Bethel Stout.

480   Robert Stewart Ballou.

481   Janice Lee Kaylor Stout.

482   William R. Stout, Jr.

483   Karen Moritz McGuire.

At the age of 24, Dawn Karen married **Robert Leslie Hoffman** on Thursday, January 12, 1989, in Broomfield, Broomfield County, Colorado, when he was 28 years old.[483] Robert Leslie was born in Sioux Falls, Minnehaha County, South Dakota, on Tuesday, September 20, 1960.[483]

Family of Mark Davidson and Jennifer Laub

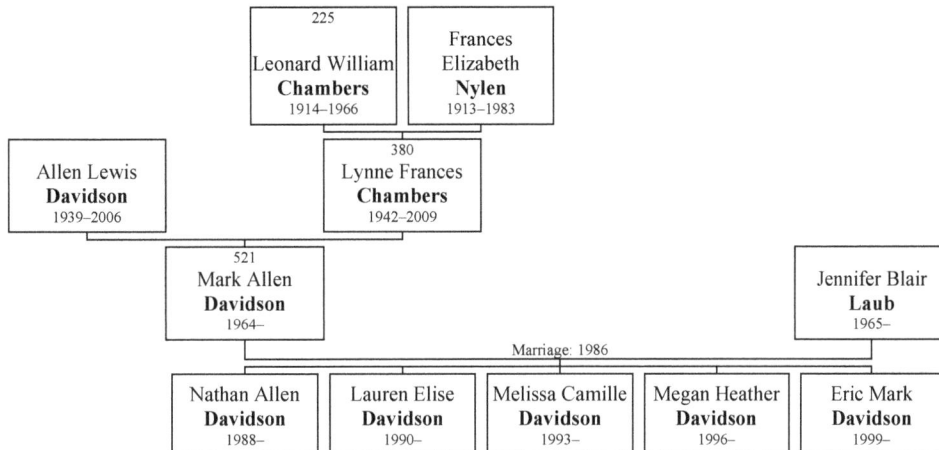

521.   **Mark Allen Davidson** was born on Wednesday, November 04, 1964, in Rawlins, Carbon County, Wyoming.[484] He is the son of Allen Lewis Davidson and Lynne Frances Chambers (380).

At the age of 21, Mark Allen married **Jennifer Blair Laub** on Saturday, May 24, 1986, in Salt Lake City, Salt Lake County, Utah, when she was 21 years old.[484] They have five children.

Jennifer Blair was born in Salt Lake City, Salt Lake County, Utah, on Saturday, February 20, 1965.[484]

Children of Mark Allen Davidson and Jennifer Blair Laub:

m   I. **Nathan Allen Davidson** was born in Orem, Utah County, Utah, on January 22, 1988.[484]

f   II. **Lauren Elise Davidson** was born in Orem, Utah County, Utah, on May 24, 1990.[484]

f   III. **Melissa Camille Davidson** was born in Fort Collins, Larimer County, Colorado, on May 01, 1993.[484]

f   IV. **Megan Heather Davidson** was born in Afton, Lincoln County, Wyoming, on July 16, 1996.[484]

m   V. **Eric Mark Davidson** was born in Prescott, Yavapai County, Arizona, on May 11, 1999.[484]

---

484   Jennifer Laub Davidson.

Family of Michael Davidson and Mary Hall

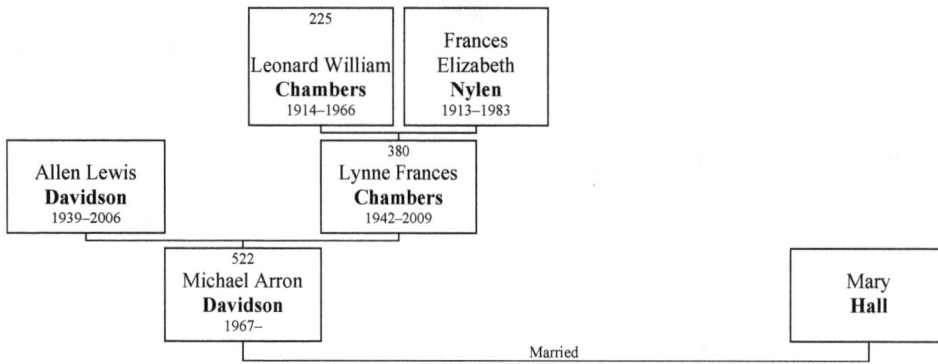

```
              ┌─────────────┬─────────────┐
              │     225     │   Frances   │
              │Leonard William│ Elizabeth  │
              │  Chambers   │    Nylen    │
              │  1914–1966  │  1913–1983  │
              └─────────────┴─────────────┘
   ┌─────────────┐   ┌─────────────┐
   │ Allen Lewis │   │     380     │
   │  Davidson   │   │Lynne Frances│
   │  1939–2006  │   │  Chambers   │
   │             │   │  1942–2009  │
   └─────────────┘   └─────────────┘
        ┌─────────────┐              ┌─────────────┐
        │     522     │              │             │
        │Michael Arron│              │    Mary     │
        │  Davidson   │              │    Hall     │
        │    1967–    │              │             │
        └─────────────┘              └─────────────┘
                        Married
```

522.   Michael Arron Davidson was born on Saturday, September 02, 1967, in Rawlins, Carbon County, Wyoming.[485] He is the son of Allen Lewis Davidson and Lynne Frances Chambers (380).

He married **Mary Hall**.

Christopher Davidson

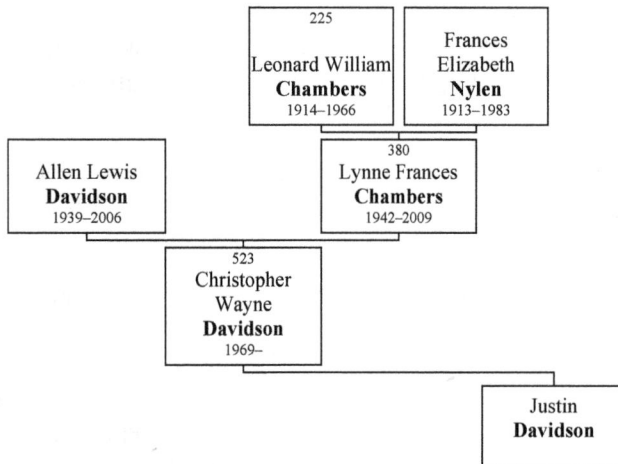

```
              ┌─────────────┬─────────────┐
              │     225     │   Frances   │
              │Leonard William│ Elizabeth  │
              │  Chambers   │    Nylen    │
              │  1914–1966  │  1913–1983  │
              └─────────────┴─────────────┘
   ┌─────────────┐   ┌─────────────┐
   │ Allen Lewis │   │     380     │
   │  Davidson   │   │Lynne Frances│
   │  1939–2006  │   │  Chambers   │
   │             │   │  1942–2009  │
   └─────────────┘   └─────────────┘
        ┌─────────────┐
        │     523     │
        │ Christopher │
        │    Wayne    │
        │  Davidson   │
        │    1969–    │
        └─────────────┘
                    ┌─────────────┐
                    │   Justin    │
                    │  Davidson   │
                    └─────────────┘
```

523.   Christopher Wayne Davidson was born on Sunday, November 09, 1969, in Rawlins, Carbon County, Wyoming.[486] He is the son of Allen Lewis Davidson and Lynne Frances Chambers (380).

Daughter of Christopher Wayne Davidson:

f   I. **Justin Davidson**.

---

485   Lynne Frances Chambers.

486   Jennifer Laub Davidson.

Family of Bonnie Fitzpatrick and Thomas Moore

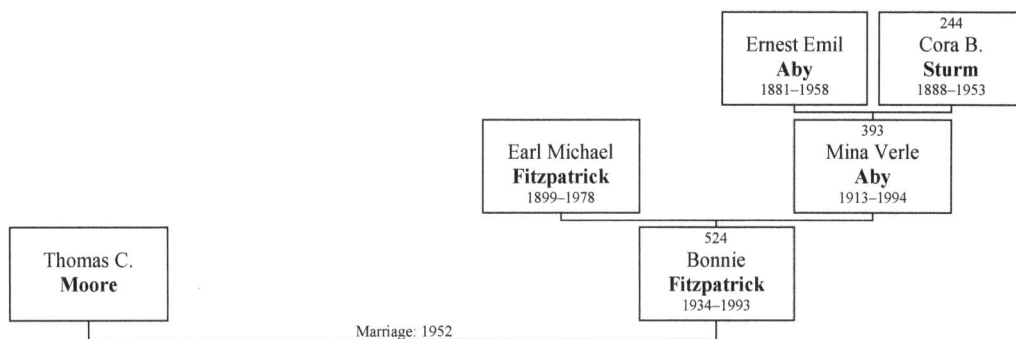

524. **Bonnie Fitzpatrick** was born on Thursday, July 26, 1934. She was the daughter of Earl Michael Fitzpatrick and Mina Verle Aby (393).

Bonnie died in Dunlap, Peoria County, Illinois, on January 27, 1993, at the age of 58. She was buried in La Salle Cemetery, Rome, Peoria County, Illinois (Find a Grave ID 22159383).

Bonnie married **Thomas C. Moore** on Saturday, November 15, 1952, in Palmyra, Marion County, Missouri.

Family of Wanda Van Alstine and Bill Barker

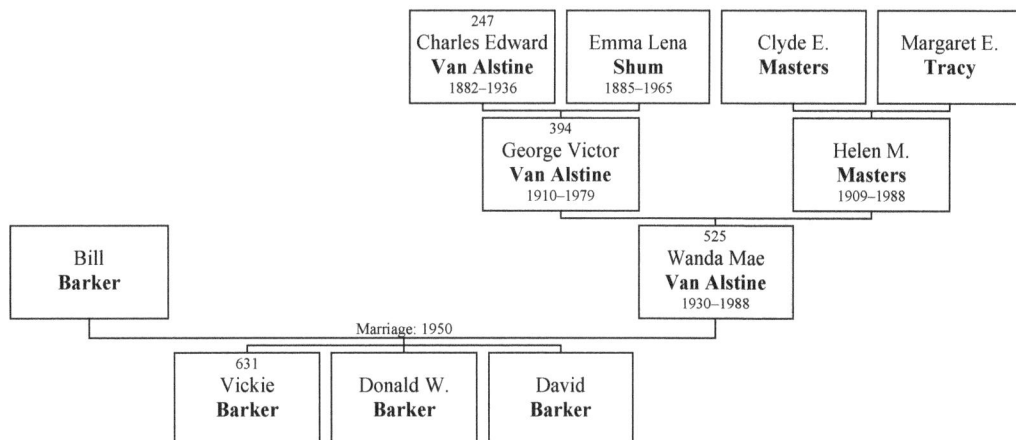

525. **Wanda Mae Van Alstine** was born on Tuesday, July 08, 1930, in Gravity, Taylor County, Iowa.[487, 488] She was the daughter of George Victor Van Alstine (394) and Helen M. Masters.

Wanda Mae died in The Dalles, Wasco County, Oregon, on October 05, 1988, at the age of 58.[488] She was buried in West Klickitat Cemetery, District No. 1, White Salmon, Klickitat County, Washington, on October 10, 1988 (Find a Grave ID 38956606).[488]

Wanda Mae married **Bill Barker** in 1950.[488] They had three children.

---

487   The Enterprise Newspaper -White Salmon, Klickitat County, Washington, 13 OCT 1988, Pg. 18.

488   Tim Chambers, Vanalstines.GED, Date of Import: Mar 11, 2001.

Children of Wanda Mae Van Alstine and Bill Barker:

+   631   f   I. **Vickie Barker.**

           m   II. **Donald W. Barker.**

           m   III. **David Barker.**

Family of Doris Van Alstine and James Frankfather

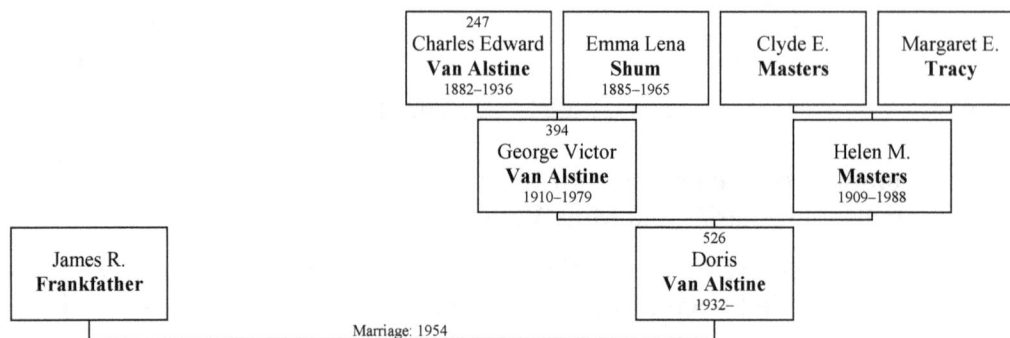

```
┌─────────────────┬─────────────┐   ┌─────────────┬──────────────┐
│     247         │  Emma Lena  │   │  Clyde E.   │  Margaret E. │
│ Charles Edward  │    Shum     │   │  Masters    │    Tracy     │
│  Van Alstine    │  1885–1965  │   │             │              │
│   1882–1936     │             │   │             │              │
└─────────────────┴─────────────┘   └─────────────┴──────────────┘
         ┌──────────────────┐         ┌──────────────────┐
         │      394         │         │    Helen M.      │
         │  George Victor   │         │    Masters       │
         │   Van Alstine    │         │   1909–1988      │
         │    1910–1979     │         │                  │
         └──────────────────┘         └──────────────────┘
                         ┌──────────────────┐
                         │       526        │
┌──────────────┐        │      Doris       │
│   James R.   │        │   Van Alstine    │
│  Frankfather │        │      1932–       │
└──────────────┘        └──────────────────┘
          Marriage: 1954
```

526.   **Doris Van Alstine** was born on Thursday, August 18, 1932, in Taylor County, Iowa.[489] She is the daughter of George Victor Van Alstine (394) and Helen M. Masters.

Doris married **James R. Frankfather** on Friday, May 07, 1954, in White Salmon, Klickitat County, Washington.[490]

Larry Van Alstine

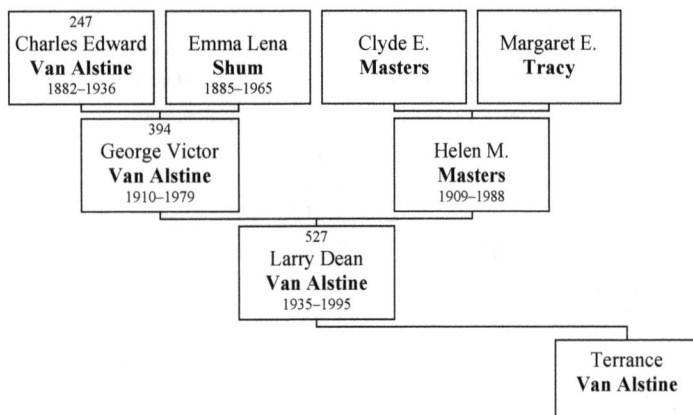

```
┌─────────────────┬─────────────┐   ┌─────────────┬──────────────┐
│     247         │  Emma Lena  │   │  Clyde E.   │  Margaret E. │
│ Charles Edward  │    Shum     │   │  Masters    │    Tracy     │
│  Van Alstine    │  1885–1965  │   │             │              │
│   1882–1936     │             │   │             │              │
└─────────────────┴─────────────┘   └─────────────┴──────────────┘
         ┌──────────────────┐         ┌──────────────────┐
         │      394         │         │    Helen M.      │
         │  George Victor   │         │    Masters       │
         │   Van Alstine    │         │   1909–1988      │
         │    1910–1979     │         │                  │
         └──────────────────┘         └──────────────────┘
                   ┌──────────────────┐
                   │       527        │
                   │   Larry Dean     │
                   │   Van Alstine    │
                   │    1935–1995     │
                   └──────────────────┘
                          ┌──────────────────┐
                          │    Terrance      │
                          │   Van Alstine    │
                          └──────────────────┘
```

489   Ancestry.com, Iowa, U.S., Births (series) 1880-1904, 1921-1944 and Delayed Births (series), 1856-1940 (Lehi, UT, USA, Ancestry.com Operations, Inc., 2017), Ancestry.com, State Historical Society of Iowa; Des Moines, Iowa; Title: Iowa Birth Records, 1888-1904. Record for Doris Jean Van Alstine. https://search.ancestry.co.uk/cgi-bin/sse.dll?db=61441&h=535105&indiv=try.

490   Ancestry.com, Washington, U.S., Marriage Records, 1854-2013 (Provo, UT, USA, Ancestry.com Operations, Inc., 2012), Ancestry.com, Washington State Archives; Olympia, Washington; Washington Marriage Records, 1854-2013; Reference Number: ceklkmarcert0007187. Record for Doris Jean Van Alstine. https://search.ancestry.co.uk/cgi-bin/sse.dll?db=2378&h=3450652&indiv=try.

527. **Larry Dean Van Alstine** was born on Sunday, July 21, 1935, in Iowa City, Johnson County, Iowa.[491–493] He was the son of George Victor Van Alstine (394) and Helen M. Masters.

Larry Dean died in Vancouver, Clark County, Washington, on January 26, 1995, at the age of 59.[493] He was buried in West Klickitat Cemetery, District No. 1, White Salmon, Klickitat County, Washington (Find a Grave ID 37766229).[493]

Son of Larry Dean Van Alstine:

     m   I. **Terrance Van Alstine**.

Carolyn Brown

528. **Carolyn Marie Brown** was born on Monday, August 29, 1932, in Clarinda, Page County, Iowa. She was the daughter of Harold Lowell Brown and Velma Alta Orme (397).

Carolyn Marie died in Dickson, Dickson County, Iowa, on October 26, 1993, at the age of 61. She was buried in Clarinda Cemetery, Clarinda, Page County, Iowa.

Marriages with (unknown given name) Christensen and John E. Fisher (Page 534) are known.

Family of Carolyn Brown and Christensen

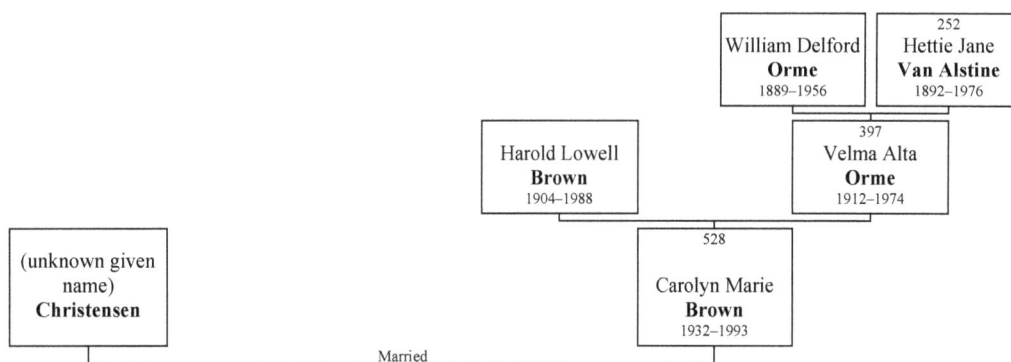

Here are the details about **Carolyn Marie Brown's** first marriage, with (unknown given name) Christensen. You can read more about Carolyn Marie on page 533.

Carolyn Marie Brown married **(unknown given name) Christensen**.

---

491   The Enterprise Newspaper -White Salmon, Klickitat County, Washington, 02 FEB 1995, Pg. 16.

492   Bedford Times Press Newspaper: Bedford, Taylor County, Iowa, 01 AUG 1935.

493   Tim Chambers, Vanalstines.GED, Date of Import: Mar 11, 2001.

Family of Carolyn Brown and John Fisher

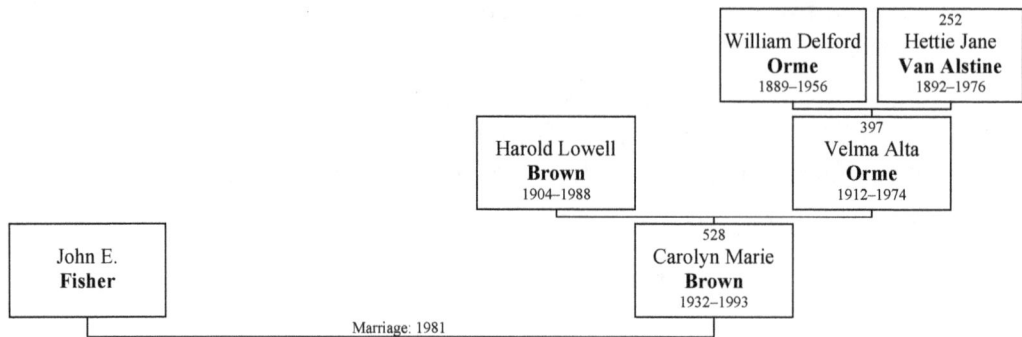

```
                                    ┌──────────────┬──────────────┐
                                    │William Delford│     252      │
                                    │    Orme      │ Hettie Jane  │
                                    │  1889–1956   │ Van Alstine  │
                                    │              │  1892–1976   │
                    ┌──────────────┐└──────────────┴──────────────┘
                    │Harold Lowell │        ┌──────────────┐
                    │    Brown     │        │     397      │
                    │  1904–1988   │        │ Velma Alta   │
                    │              │        │    Orme      │
    ┌──────────────┐└──────────────┘        │  1912–1974   │
    │   John E.    │        ┌──────────────┐└──────────────┘
    │   Fisher     │        │     528      │
    │              │        │Carolyn Marie │
    │              │        │    Brown     │
    └──────────────┘        │  1932–1993   │
           Marriage: 1981   └──────────────┘
```

Here are the details about **Carolyn Marie Brown's** second marriage, with John E. Fisher. You can read more about Carolyn Marie on page 533.

Carolyn Marie Brown married **John E. Fisher** in 1981.[494]

Family of Eva Brown and Kenneth Moody

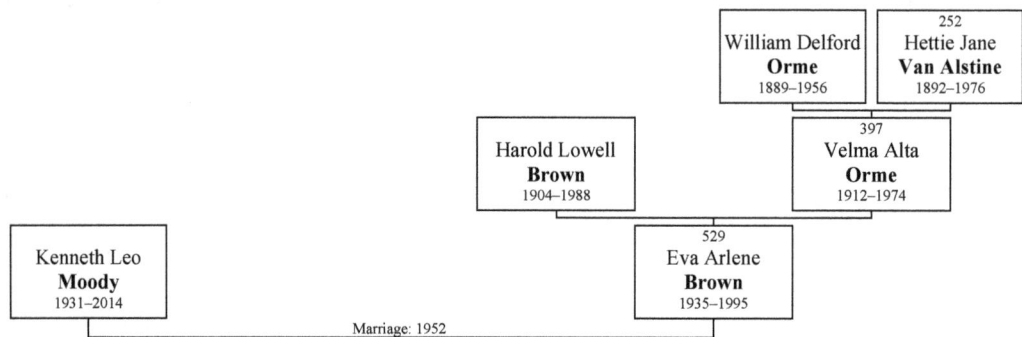

```
                                    ┌──────────────┬──────────────┐
                                    │William Delford│     252      │
                                    │    Orme      │ Hettie Jane  │
                                    │  1889–1956   │ Van Alstine  │
                                    │              │  1892–1976   │
                    ┌──────────────┐└──────────────┴──────────────┘
                    │Harold Lowell │        ┌──────────────┐
                    │    Brown     │        │     397      │
                    │  1904–1988   │        │ Velma Alta   │
                    │              │        │    Orme      │
    ┌──────────────┐└──────────────┘        │  1912–1974   │
    │ Kenneth Leo  │        ┌──────────────┐└──────────────┘
    │    Moody     │        │     529      │
    │  1931–2014   │        │  Eva Arlene  │
    │              │        │    Brown     │
    └──────────────┘        │  1935–1995   │
           Marriage: 1952   └──────────────┘
```

529. **Eva Arlene Brown** was born on Sunday, May 05, 1935, in Shambaugh, Page County, Iowa. She was the daughter of Harold Lowell Brown and Velma Alta Orme (397).

Eva Arlene died in San Bernardino, San Bernardino County, California, on April 14, 1995, at the age of 59. She was buried in Clarinda Cemetery, Clarinda, Page County, Iowa (Find a Grave ID 195385891).

Eva Arlene married **Kenneth Leo Moody** in 1952. Kenneth Leo was born in Farragut, Fremont County, Iowa, on Monday, May 04, 1931. He was also known as **Kenney**.

Kenneth Leo reached 82 years of age and died in Stockton, San Joaquin County, California, on February 02, 2014. He was buried in Clarinda Cemetery, Clarinda, Page County, Iowa (Find a Grave ID 195385711).

---

494 Ancestry.com, U.S., Newspapers.com™ Marriage Index, 1800s-current (Lehi, UT, USA, Ancestry.com Operations Inc, 2020), Ancestry.com, *The Gazette*; Publication Date: 28/ Aug/ 1981; Publication Place: Cedar Rapids, Iowa, USA; URL: https://www.newspapers.com/image/549989896/?article=b2d717d1-6783-4a1c-9b9b-84b0ae3ac4a6/c107dc95-de9d-45c2-8871-5249f96a5084&focus=0.8069349,0.18741877,0.96762705,0.38577008&xid=3398. Record for Carolyn M. Christensen. https://search.ancestry.co.uk/cgi-bin/sse.dll?db=62116&h=294748459&indiv=try.

Family of Joyce Brown and Don Porter

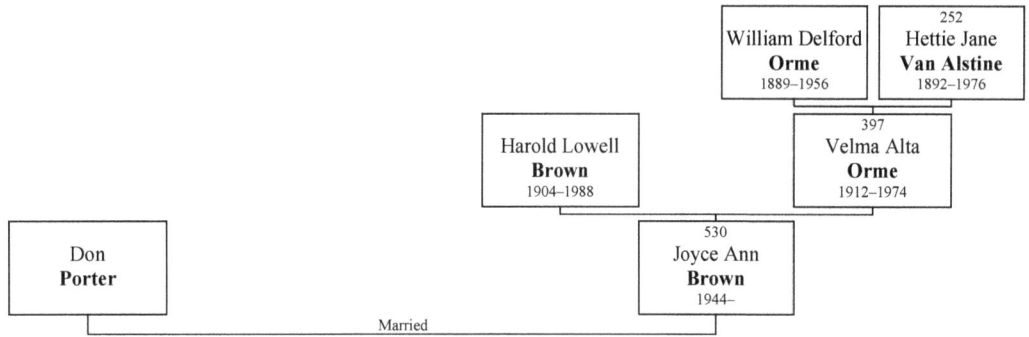

```
                                                    ┌─────────────────┬─────────────────┐
                                                    │ William Delford │       252       │
                                                    │      Orme       │   Hettie Jane   │
                                                    │    1889–1956    │   Van Alstine   │
                                                    │                 │    1892–1976    │
                                                    └─────────────────┴─────────────────┘
                                 ┌─────────────────┐        ┌─────────────────┐
                                 │  Harold Lowell  │        │       397       │
                                 │      Brown      │        │   Velma Alta    │
                                 │    1904–1988    │        │      Orme       │
                                 │                 │        │    1912–1974    │
                                 └─────────────────┘        └─────────────────┘
              ┌─────────────────┐              ┌─────────────────┐
              │       Don       │              │       530       │
              │     Porter      │              │   Joyce Ann     │
              │                 │              │     Brown       │
              │                 │              │     1944–       │
              └─────────────────┘              └─────────────────┘
                                Married
```

530. **Joyce Ann Brown** was born on Tuesday, March 07, 1944, in Clarinda, Page County, Iowa. She is the daughter of Harold Lowell Brown and Velma Alta Orme (397).

She married **Don Porter**.

Joanne Van Alstine

531. **Joanne Elaine Van Alstine** was born on Tuesday, December 28, 1943, in Clarinda, Page County, Iowa.[495–497] She is the daughter of Lewis Doran Van Alstine (400) and Virginia Helen Waxmonsky.

Marriages with David Lee Winchester and Larry Nulph (Page 536) are known.

Family of Joanne Van Alstine and David Winchester

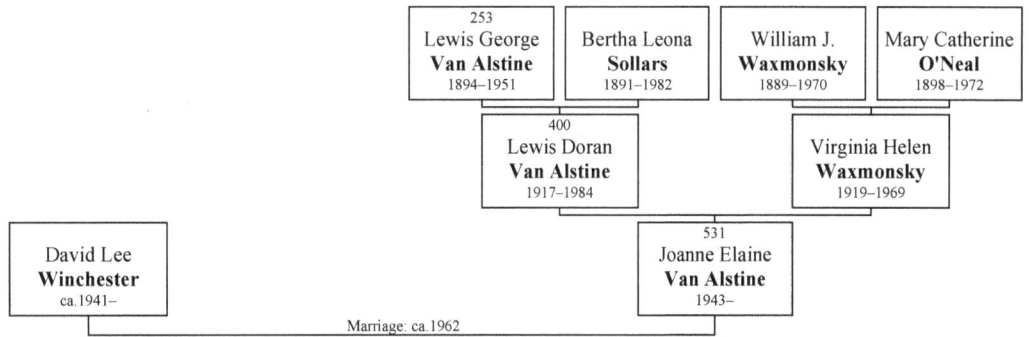

```
                    ┌─────────────────┬─────────────────┬─────────────────┬─────────────────┐
                    │       253       │  Bertha Leona   │   William J.    │ Mary Catherine  │
                    │  Lewis George   │     Sollars     │   Waxmonsky     │     O'Neal      │
                    │  Van Alstine    │    1891–1982    │    1889–1970    │    1898–1972    │
                    │    1894–1951    │                 │                 │                 │
                    └─────────────────┴─────────────────┴─────────────────┴─────────────────┘
                              ┌─────────────────┐        ┌─────────────────┐
                              │       400       │        │ Virginia Helen  │
                              │   Lewis Doran   │        │   Waxmonsky     │
                              │  Van Alstine    │        │    1919–1969    │
                              │    1917–1984    │        │                 │
                              └─────────────────┘        └─────────────────┘
           ┌─────────────────┐              ┌─────────────────┐
           │   David Lee     │              │       531       │
           │  Winchester     │              │  Joanne Elaine  │
           │    ca.1941–     │              │  Van Alstine    │
           │                 │              │     1943–       │
           └─────────────────┘              └─────────────────┘
                         Marriage: ca.1962
```

Here are the details about **Joanne Elaine Van Alstine's** first marriage, with David Lee Winchester. You can read more about Joanne Elaine on page 535.

Joanne Elaine Van Alstine married **David Lee Winchester** about June 21, 1962.[497, 498] David Lee was born about 1941.[497]

---

[495] Bedford Times Press Newspaper: Bedford, Taylor County, Iowa, 06 JAN 1944.

[496] Clarinda Herald Journal Newspaper: Clarinda, Page County, Iowa, 30 DEC 1943 & 03 JAN 1944.

[497] Tim Chambers, Vanalstines.GED, Date of Import: Mar 11, 2001.

[498] Clarinda Herald Journal Newspaper: Clarinda, Page County, Iowa, 21 JUN 1962.

Family of Joanne Van Alstine and Larry Nulph

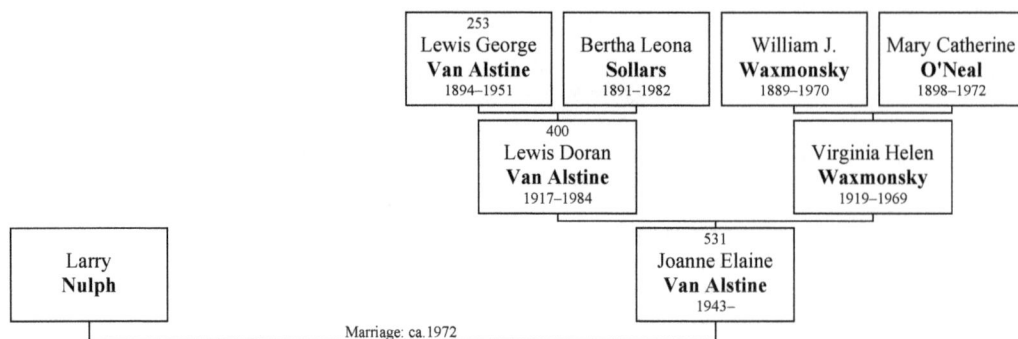

253 Lewis George **Van Alstine** 1894–1951	Bertha Leona **Sollars** 1891–1982

William J. **Waxmonsky** 1889–1970	Mary Catherine **O'Neal** 1898–1972

400
Lewis Doran
Van Alstine
1917–1984

Virginia Helen
Waxmonsky
1919–1969

Larry
Nulph

531
Joanne Elaine
Van Alstine
1943–

Marriage: ca.1972

Here are the details about **Joanne Elaine Van Alstine's** second marriage, with Larry Nulph. You can read more about Joanne Elaine on page 535.

Joanne Elaine Van Alstine married **Larry Nulph** about July 1972 in Las Vegas, Clark County, Nevada.[497, 499]

Family of Carol Clifton and Richard Lynds

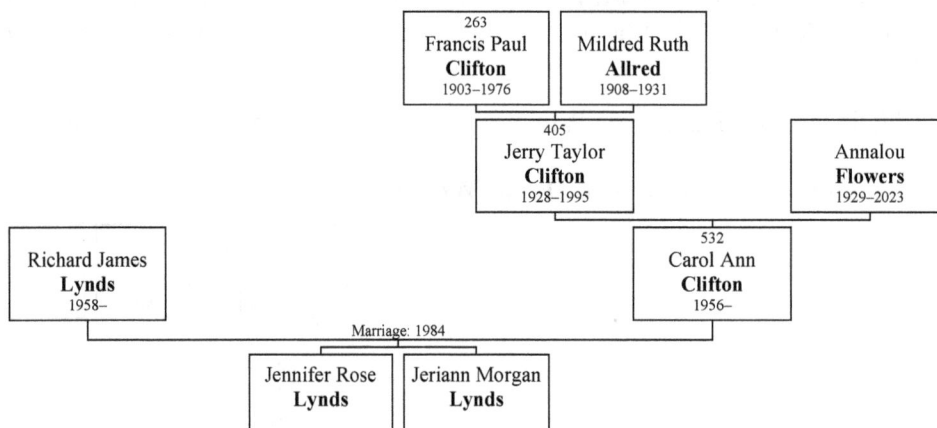

263
Francis Paul
Clifton
1903–1976

Mildred Ruth
Allred
1908–1931

405
Jerry Taylor
Clifton
1928–1995

Annalou
Flowers
1929–2023

Richard James
Lynds
1958–

532
Carol Ann
Clifton
1956–

Marriage: 1984

Jennifer Rose
Lynds

Jeriann Morgan
Lynds

532. **Carol Ann Clifton** was born in November 1956. She is the daughter of Jerry Taylor Clifton (405) and Annalou Flowers.

At the age of 27, Carol Ann married **Richard James Lynds** on Saturday, August 25, 1984, in Los Angeles, Los Angeles County, California, when he was 26 years old. They have two daughters.

Richard James was born on Saturday, April 05, 1958.

Daughters of Carol Ann Clifton and Richard James Lynds:

  f   I. **Jennifer Rose Lynds**.

  f   II. **Jeriann Morgan Lynds**.

---

499 *Clarinda Herald Journal* Newspaper: Clarinda, Page County, Iowa, 27 JUL 1972.

Family of Darrell Clifton and Sandra Quiroz

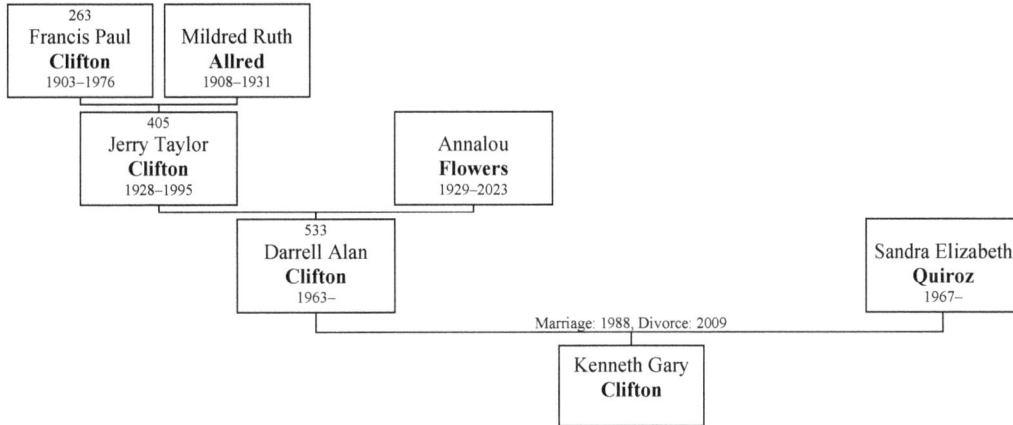

533. **Darrell Alan Clifton** was born in August 1963. He is the son of Jerry Taylor Clifton (405) and Annalou Flowers.

At the age of 24, Darrell Alan married **Sandra Elizabeth Quiroz** on Sunday, June 26, 1988, in Washoe County, Nevada, when she was 20 years old. They were divorced (Case No. DV07-00412) in Washoe County, Nevada, on July 08, 2009. They have one son.

Sandra Elizabeth was born on Monday, August 28, 1967.

Son of Darrell Alan Clifton and Sandra Elizabeth Quiroz:

> m I. **Kenneth Gary Clifton**.

Gary Clifton

534. **Gary Michael Clifton**. He was the son of Jerry Taylor Clifton (405) and Annalou Flowers.

Marriages with Kathleen Ann Girardin and Lori Eileen Albinet (Page 538) are known.

Family of Gary Clifton and Kathleen Girardin

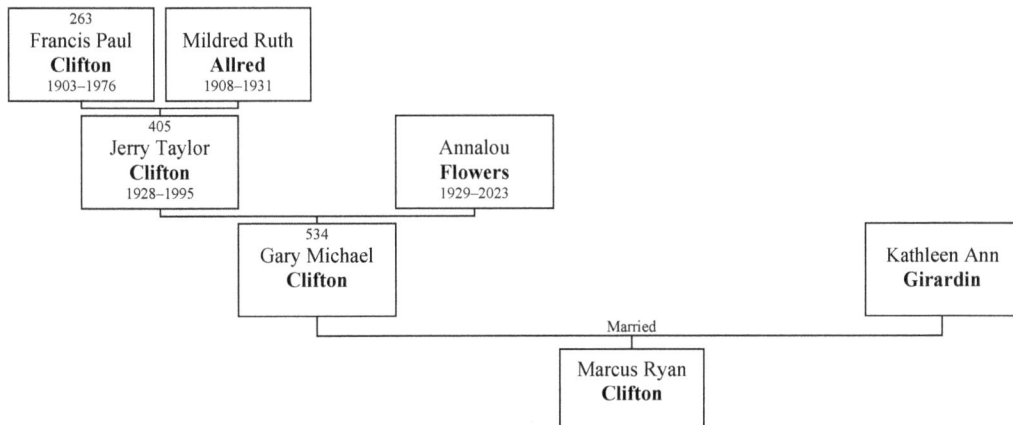

Here are the details about **Gary Michael Clifton's** first marriage, with Kathleen Ann Girardin. You can read more about Gary Michael on page 537.

Gary Michael Clifton married **Kathleen Ann Girardin**. They had one son.

Son of Gary Michael Clifton and Kathleen Ann Girardin:

    m   I. **Marcus Ryan Clifton**.

Family of Gary Clifton and Lori Albinet

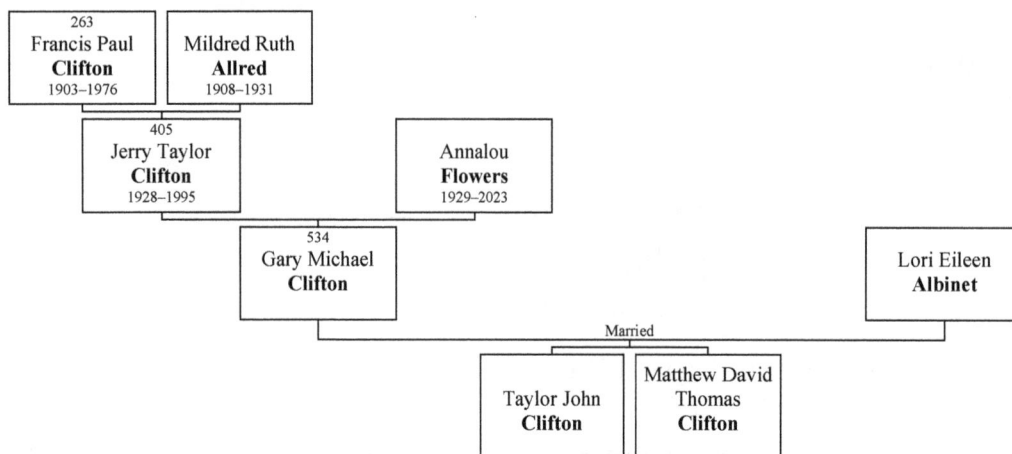

Here are the details about **Gary Michael Clifton's** second marriage, with Lori Eileen Albinet. You can read more about Gary Michael on page 537.

Gary Michael Clifton married **Lori Eileen Albinet**. They had two sons.

Sons of Gary Michael Clifton and Lori Eileen Albinet:

    m   I. **Taylor John Clifton**.

    m   II. **Matthew David Thomas Clifton**.

Family of Michael Hargadine and Edna Hepner

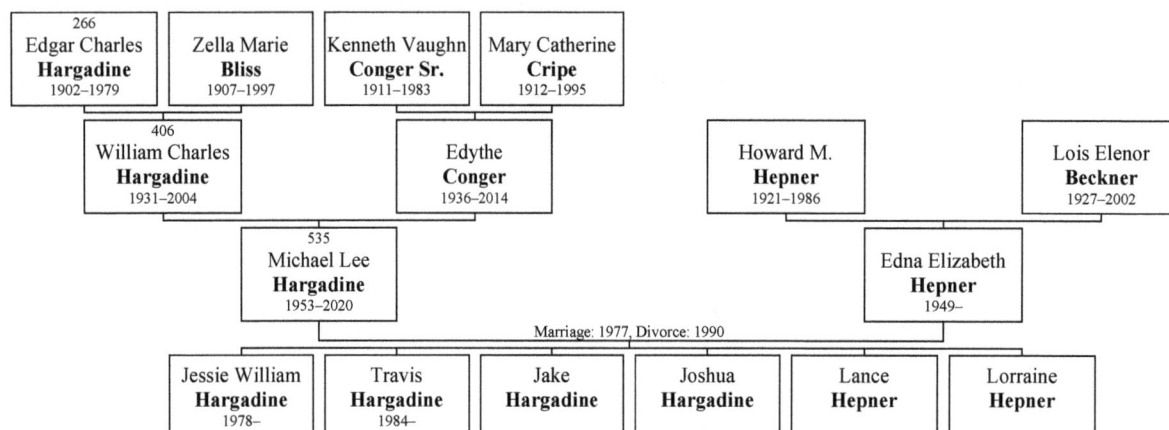

535.   **Michael Lee Hargadine** was born on Wednesday, October 14, 1953, in Kewanee, Henry County, Illinois. He was the son of William Charles Hargadine (406) and Edythe Conger.

Michael Lee died in Polk, Florida, USA, on October 11, 2020, at the age of 66.

At the age of 24, Michael Lee married **Edna Elizabeth Hepner** on Friday, December 16, 1977, when she was 28 years old. They were divorced (Certificate# 044701) in Pinellas County, Florida, on July 18, 1990. They had six children.

Edna Elizabeth was born on Thursday, July 07, 1949. She is the daughter of Howard M. Hepner and Lois Elenor Beckner.

Children of Michael Lee Hargadine and Edna Elizabeth Hepner:

> m   I. **Jessie William Hargadine** was born in June 1978.

> m   II. **Travis Hargadine** was born in July 1984.

> m   III. **Jake Hargadine**.

> m   IV. **Joshua Hargadine**.

> m   V. **Lance Hepner**.

> f   VI. **Lorraine Hepner**.

Family of Terry Hargadine and Michelle Bolen

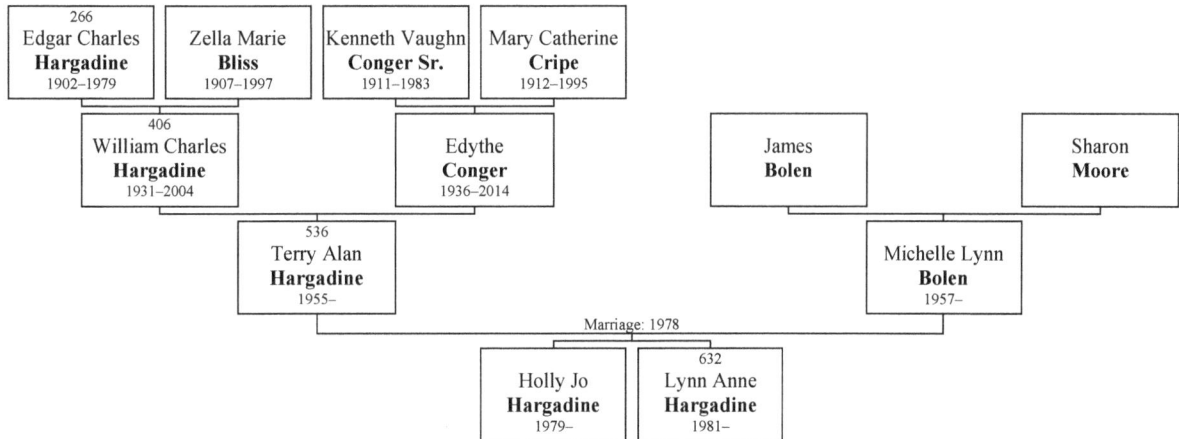

536.   **Terry Alan Hargadine** was born on Saturday, May 07, 1955, in Kewanee, Henry County, Illinois. He is the son of William Charles Hargadine (406) and Edythe Conger.

At the age of 23, Terry Alan married **Michelle Lynn Bolen** on Saturday, July 01, 1978, when she was 21 years old. They have two daughters.

Michelle Lynn was born on Thursday, January 03, 1957. She is the daughter of James Bolen and Sharon Moore.

Daughters of Terry Alan Hargadine and Michelle Lynn Bolen:

> f .   I. **Holly Jo Hargadine** was born on January 21, 1979.

> +   632   f   II. **Lynn Anne Hargadine** was born on February 24, 1981.

Family of Cathy Hargadine and Gary Morrison

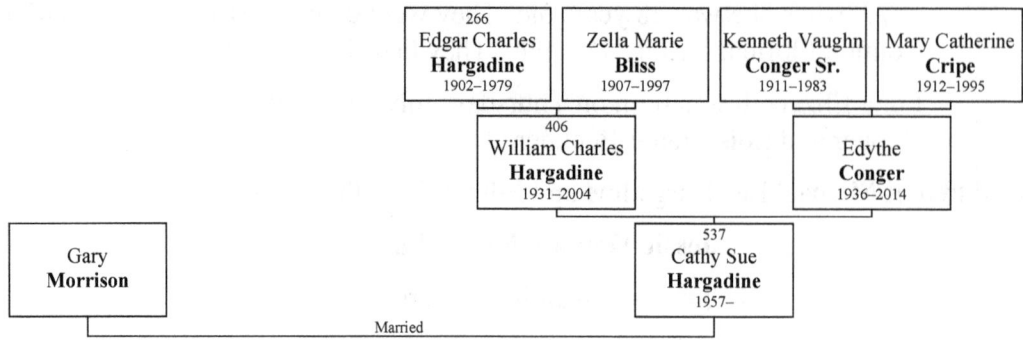

| 266
Edgar Charles
Hargadine
1902–1979 | Zella Marie
Bliss
1907–1997 | Kenneth Vaughn
Conger Sr.
1911–1983 | Mary Catherine
Cripe
1912–1995 |

| 406
William Charles
Hargadine
1931–2004 | Edythe
Conger
1936–2014 |

| Gary
Morrison | 537
Cathy Sue
Hargadine
1957– |

Married

537. **Cathy Sue Hargadine** was born on Friday, June 28, 1957, in Kewanee, Henry County, Illinois. She is the daughter of William Charles Hargadine (406) and Edythe Conger.

She married **Gary Morrison**.

Family of Cindy Hargadine and Dave Ramsey

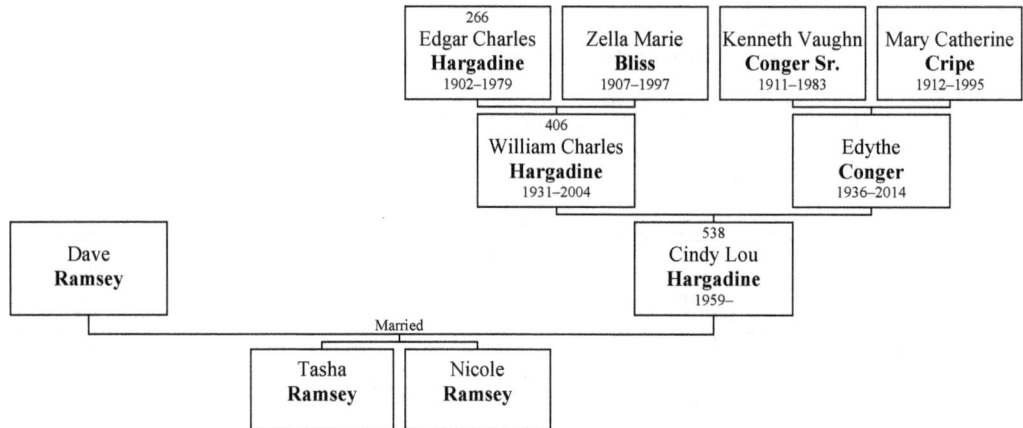

| 266
Edgar Charles
Hargadine
1902–1979 | Zella Marie
Bliss
1907–1997 | Kenneth Vaughn
Conger Sr.
1911–1983 | Mary Catherine
Cripe
1912–1995 |

| 406
William Charles
Hargadine
1931–2004 | Edythe
Conger
1936–2014 |

| Dave
Ramsey | 538
Cindy Lou
Hargadine
1959– |

Married

| Tasha
Ramsey | Nicole
Ramsey |

538. **Cindy Lou Hargadine** was born on Wednesday, January 21, 1959, in Kewanee, Henry County, Illinois. She is the daughter of William Charles Hargadine (406) and Edythe Conger.

She married **Dave Ramsey**. They have two daughters.

Daughters of Cindy Lou Hargadine and Dave Ramsey:

 f I. **Tasha Ramsey**.

 f II. **Nicole Ramsey**.

Family of Lloyd Phillips and Barbara Mayer

```
                    ┌─────────────────┬─────────────────┐
                    │      266        │   Zella Marie   │
                    │  Edgar Charles  │     Bliss       │
                    │   Hargadine     │   1907–1997     │
                    │   1902–1979     │                 │
                    └─────────────────┴─────────────────┘
                              │
    ┌─────────────────┐  ┌─────────────────┐
    │  Lloyd Russell  │  │      407        │
    │    Phillips     │  │  Alice Louise   │
    │   1934–1975     │  │   Hargadine     │
    │                 │  │   1934–2010     │
    └─────────────────┘  └─────────────────┘
              │
        ┌─────────────────┐                        ┌─────────────────┐
        │      539        │                        │ Barbara Joanne  │
        │  Lloyd Gary     │                        │     Mayer       │
        │    Phillips     │                        │                 │
        │     1954–       │                        │                 │
        └─────────────────┘──────Marriage: 1979────└─────────────────┘
```

539. **Lloyd Gary Phillips** was born on Thursday, September 16, 1954, in Kewanee, Henry County, Illinois. He is the son of Lloyd Russell Phillips and Alice Louise Hargadine (407).

Lloyd Gary married **Barbara Joanne Mayer** on Saturday, August 25, 1979, in Sturgis, St. Joseph County, Michigan.

Family of Lorraine Phillips and Robert Fontenot

```
                                              ┌─────────────────┬─────────────────┐
                                              │      266        │   Zella Marie   │
                                              │  Edgar Charles  │     Bliss       │
                                              │   Hargadine     │   1907–1997     │
                                              │   1902–1979     │                 │
                                              └─────────────────┴─────────────────┘
                                                        │
  ┌─────────────────┐  ┌─────────────────┐   ┌─────────────────┐  ┌─────────────────┐
  │ Robert Stephan  │  │     Susie       │   │  Lloyd Russell  │  │      407        │
  │    Fontenot     │  │    Baronet      │   │    Phillips     │  │  Alice Louise   │
  │                 │  │                 │   │   1934–1975     │  │   Hargadine     │
  │                 │  │                 │   │                 │  │   1934–2010     │
  └─────────────────┴──┴─────────────────┘   └─────────────────┴──┴─────────────────┘
            │                                           │
      ┌─────────────────┐                         ┌─────────────────┐
      │ Robert Stephan  │                         │      540        │
      │    Fontenot     │                         │  Lorraine Gayle │
      │     1958–       │                         │    Phillips     │
      │                 │                         │     1957–       │
      └─────────────────┘────Marriage: 1981───────└─────────────────┘
         ┌─────────────────┬─────────────────┬─────────────────┐
         │  Sarah Ashley   │  Kristin Nicole │ Phillips Stephen│
         │    Fontenot     │    Fontenot     │    Fontenot     │
         │     1984–       │     1987–       │     1998–       │
         └─────────────────┴─────────────────┴─────────────────┘
```

540. **Lorraine Gayle Phillips** was born on Tuesday, August 27, 1957, in Kewanee, Henry County, Illinois. She is the daughter of Lloyd Russell Phillips and Alice Louise Hargadine (407).

At the age of 23, Lorraine Gayle married **Robert Stephan Fontenot** on Saturday, February 21, 1981, in Marianna, Jackson County, Florida, when he was 22 years old. They have three daughters.

Robert Stephan was born in Greenville, Washington County, Mississippi, on Saturday, August 30, 1958. He is the son of Robert Stephan Fontenot and Susie Baronet.

Daughters of Lorraine Gayle Phillips and Robert Stephan Fontenot:

f I. **Sarah Ashley Fontenot** was born in Indianola, Sunflower County, Mississippi, on January 21, 1984.

f II. **Kristin Nicole Fontenot** was born in Indianola, Sunflower County, Mississippi, on March 06, 1987.

f   III. **Phillips Stephen Fontenot** was born in Indianola, Sunflower County, Mississippi, on December 10, 1998.

Family of Sharilyn Hargadine and Steven Smith

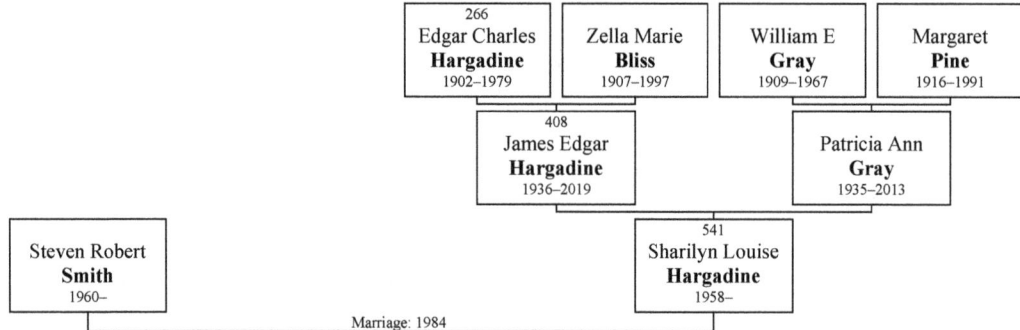

	266 Edgar Charles **Hargadine** 1902–1979	Zella Marie **Bliss** 1907–1997	William E **Gray** 1909–1967	Margaret **Pine** 1916–1991

	408 James Edgar **Hargadine** 1936–2019		Patricia Ann **Gray** 1935–2013

Steven Robert **Smith** 1960–	541 Sharilyn Louise **Hargadine** 1958–

Marriage: 1984

541.   **Sharilyn Louise Hargadine** was born on Tuesday, December 30, 1958, in Peoria, Peoria County, Illinois.[500] She is the daughter of James Edgar Hargadine (408) and Patricia Ann Gray.

Sharilyn Louise married **Steven Robert Smith** on Saturday, June 09, 1984, in Milwaukee, Milwaukee County, Wisconsin.[500] Steven Robert was born in 1960.[500]

Michael Gray

John Levi **Gray** 1898–1989	270 Elva Mary **Hargadine** 1908–1977		

417 Harley Dean **Gray** 1935–2010		Judith A. **Weitz** 1936–

542 Michael Edward **Gray** 1958–

Travis **Gray**	Tyler **Gray**

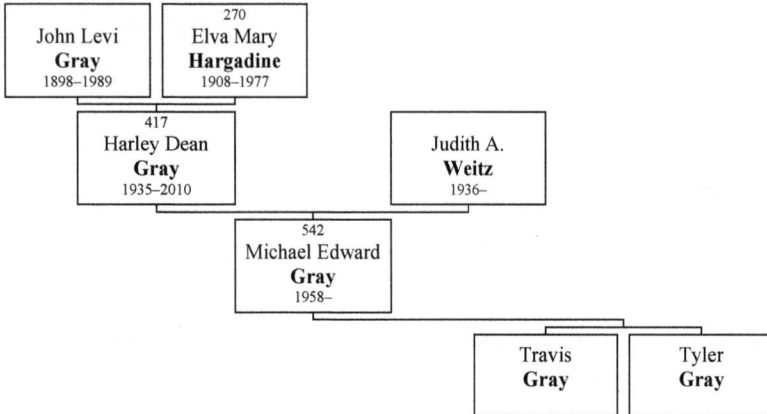

542.   **Michael Edward Gray** was born on Tuesday, December 09, 1958. He is the son of Harley Dean Gray (417) and Judith A. Weitz.

Sons of Michael Edward Gray:

m   I. **Travis Gray**.

m   II. **Tyler Gray**.

---

500   Ancestry.com, Wisconsin, U.S., Marriage Index, 1973-1997 (Provo, UT, USA, Ancestry.com Operations Inc, 2005), Ancestry.com, Record for Sharlyn Louise Hargadine. https://search.ancestry.co.uk/cgi-bin/sse.dll?db=8744&h=1600421&indiv=try.

Vicky Miller

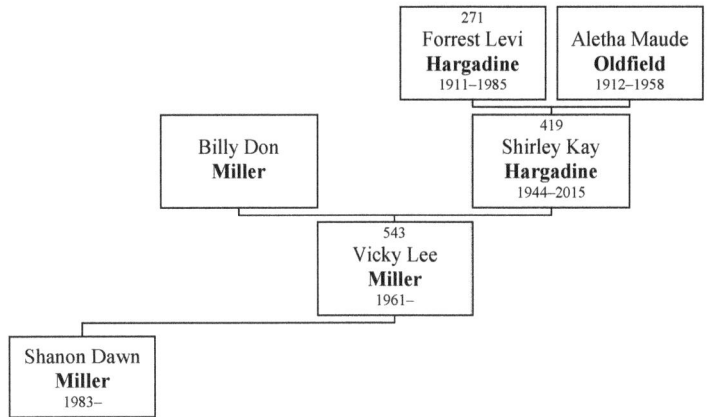

543. **Vicky Lee Miller** was born on Tuesday, August 22, 1961, in Athens, Athens County, Ohio. She is the daughter of Billy Don Miller and Shirley Kay Hargadine (419).

Daughter of Vicky Lee Miller:

     f   I. **Shanon Dawn Miller** was born on June 24, 1983.

Family of Donald Miller and Lisa Dickinson

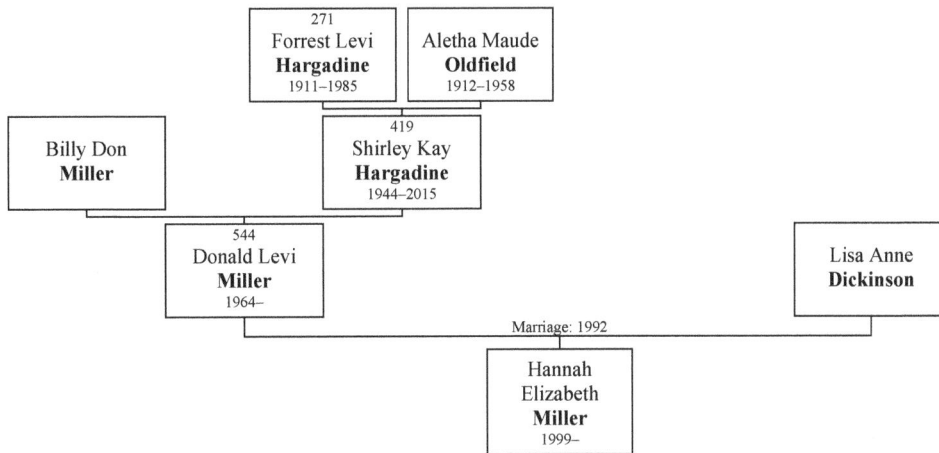

544. **Donald Levi Miller** was born on Sunday, August 30, 1964, in Peoria, Peoria County, Illinois. He is the son of Billy Don Miller and Shirley Kay Hargadine (419).

Donald Levi married **Lisa Anne Dickinson** on Friday, July 03, 1992, in Tampa, Hillsborough County, Florida. They have one daughter.

Daughter of Donald Levi Miller and Lisa Anne Dickinson:

     f   I. **Hannah Elizabeth Miller** was born on May 16, 1999.

Family of David Miller and Nancy Mayfield

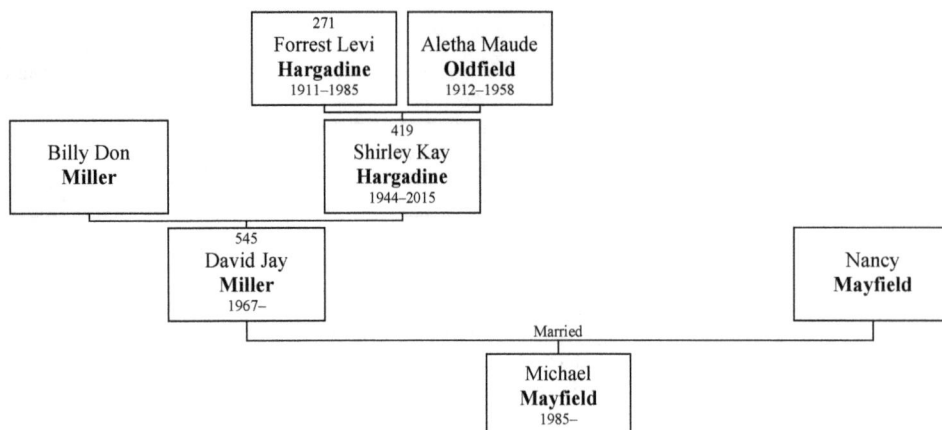

```
                    ┌─────────────────┬─────────────────┐
                    │      271        │                 │
                    │  Forrest Levi   │  Aletha Maude   │
                    │   Hargadine     │    Oldfield     │
                    │   1911–1985     │   1912–1958     │
                    └─────────────────┴─────────────────┘
  ┌─────────────┐            ┌─────────────────┐
  │  Billy Don  │            │      419        │
  │   Miller    │            │  Shirley Kay    │
  │             │            │   Hargadine     │
  │             │            │   1944–2015     │
  └─────────────┘            └─────────────────┘
            ┌─────────────────┐
            │      545        │                      ┌─────────────┐
            │  David Jay      │                      │    Nancy    │
            │   Miller        │                      │  Mayfield   │
            │   1967–         │                      │             │
            └─────────────────┘                      └─────────────┘
                            Married
                        ┌─────────────────┐
                        │    Michael      │
                        │   Mayfield      │
                        │    1985–        │
                        └─────────────────┘
```

545.   **David Jay Miller** was born on Monday, July 10, 1967, in Peoria, Peoria County, Illinois. He is the son of Billy Don Miller and Shirley Kay Hargadine (419).

He married **Nancy Mayfield**. They have one son.

Son of David Jay Miller and Nancy Mayfield:

      m   I. **Michael Mayfield** was born on September 30, 1985.

Family of William Hargadine and Holly Worsham

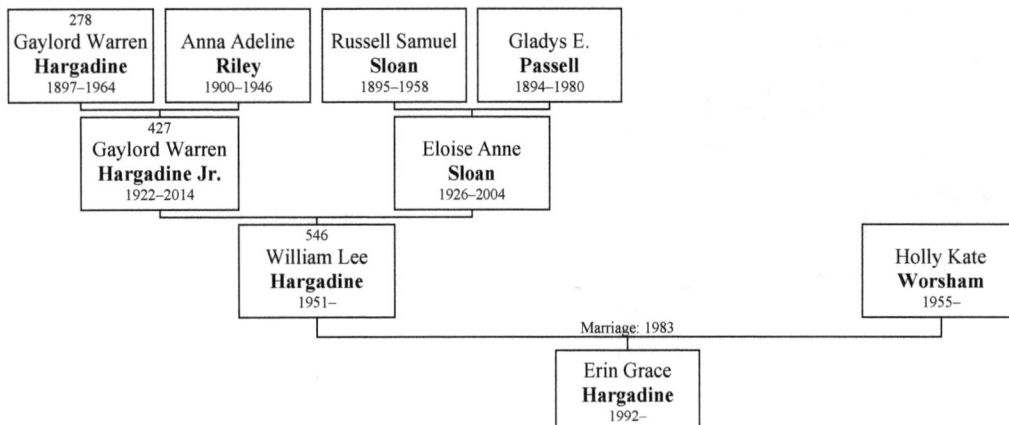

```
┌─────────────────┬─────────────────┐   ┌─────────────────┬─────────────────┐
│      278        │                 │   │                 │                 │
│ Gaylord Warren  │  Anna Adeline   │   │ Russell Samuel  │   Gladys E.     │
│   Hargadine     │     Riley       │   │     Sloan       │    Passell      │
│   1897–1964     │   1900–1946     │   │   1895–1958     │   1894–1980     │
└─────────────────┴─────────────────┘   └─────────────────┴─────────────────┘
┌─────────────────┐                   ┌─────────────────┐
│      427        │                   │  Eloise Anne    │
│ Gaylord Warren  │                   │     Sloan       │
│  Hargadine Jr.  │                   │   1926–2004     │
│   1922–2014     │                   │                 │
└─────────────────┘                   └─────────────────┘
        ┌─────────────────┐                      ┌─────────────┐
        │      546        │                      │  Holly Kate │
        │  William Lee    │                      │   Worsham   │
        │   Hargadine     │                      │   1955–     │
        │    1951–        │                      │             │
        └─────────────────┘                      └─────────────┘
                        Marriage: 1983
                    ┌─────────────────┐
                    │   Erin Grace    │
                    │   Hargadine     │
                    │    1992–        │
                    └─────────────────┘
```

546.   **William Lee Hargadine** was born on Wednesday, January 10, 1951, in El Paso County, Texas. He is the son of Gaylord Warren Hargadine Jr. (427) and Eloise Anne Sloan.

At the age of 32, William Lee married **Holly Kate Worsham** on Saturday, August 20, 1983, in Travis County, Texas, when she was 27 years old. They have one daughter.

Holly Kate was born on Thursday, September 15, 1955.

Daughter of William Lee Hargadine and Holly Kate Worsham:

      f   I. **Erin Grace Hargadine** was born in Dallas County, Texas, on October 23, 1992.

Family of Kathy Hargadine and Thomas Srokosz

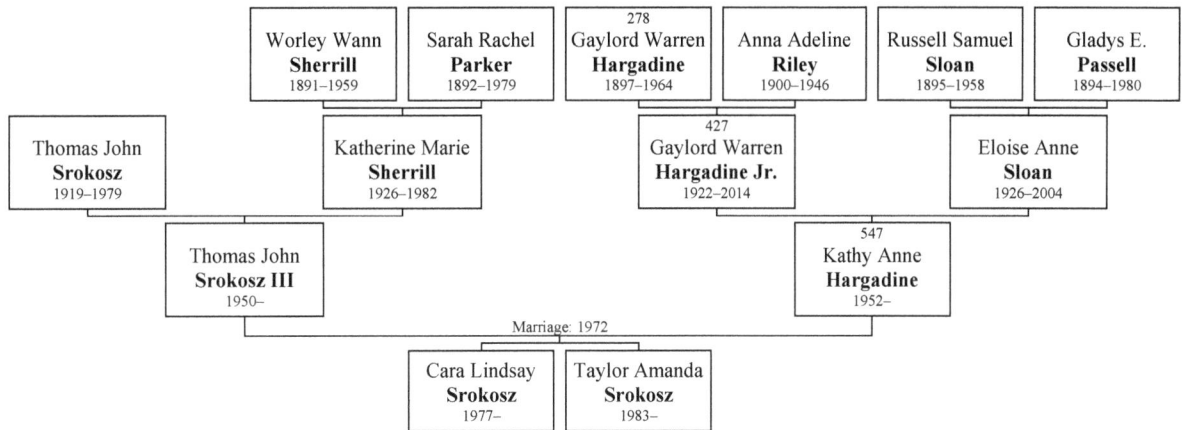

547. **Kathy Anne Hargadine** was born on Monday, October 20, 1952, in Harris County, Texas. She is the daughter of Gaylord Warren Hargadine Jr. (427) and Eloise Anne Sloan.

At the age of 19, Kathy Anne married **Thomas John Srokosz III** on Friday, August 04, 1972, in Grapevine, Tarrant County, Texas, when he was 22 years old. They have two daughters.

Thomas John was born in Denton, Denton County, Texas, on Saturday, June 03, 1950. He is the son of Thomas John Srokosz and Katherine Marie Sherrill.

Daughters of Kathy Anne Hargadine and Thomas John Srokosz III:

 f   I. **Cara Lindsay Srokosz** was born in Irving, Dallas County, Texas, on May 18, 1977.

 f   II. **Taylor Amanda Srokosz** was born in Dallas, Dallas County, Texas, on April 10, 1983.

Family of Judy Hargadine and Jerry Lehew

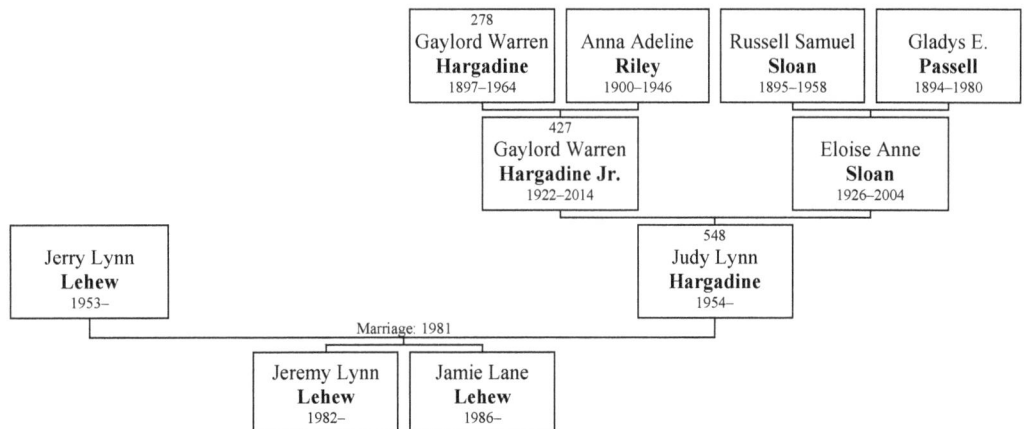

548. **Judy Lynn Hargadine** was born on Friday, October 22, 1954, in Dallas County, Texas. She is the daughter of Gaylord Warren Hargadine Jr. (427) and Eloise Anne Sloan.

At the age of 27, Judy Lynn married **Jerry Lynn Lehew** on Thursday, December 03, 1981, in Celina, Collin County, Texas, when he was 28 years old. They have two sons.

Jerry Lynn was born in Houston, Houston County, Texas, on Saturday, October 17, 1953.

Sons of Judy Lynn Hargadine and Jerry Lynn Lehew:

m   I.   **Jeremy Lynn Lehew** was born in Plano, Denton County, Texas, on December 23, 1982.

m   II.   **Jamie Lane Lehew** was born in Plano, Denton County, Texas, on August 13, 1986.

Family of Paul Hargadine and Karen Kubiak

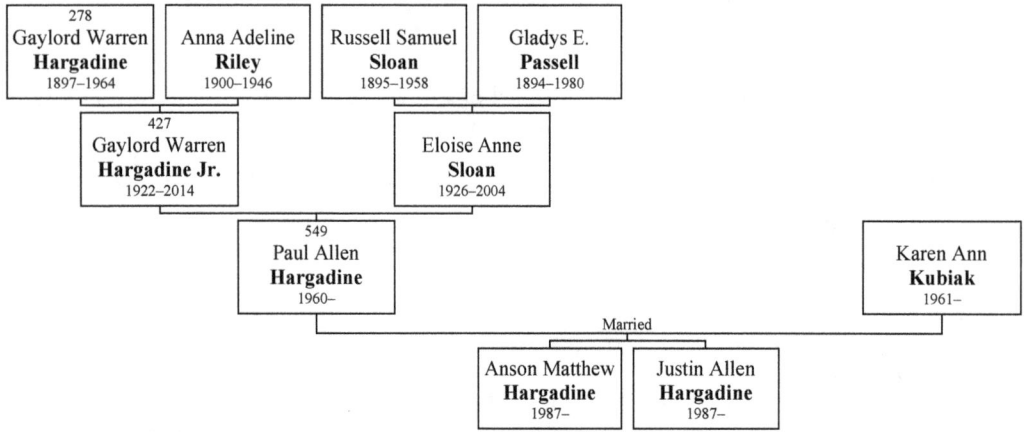

278 Gaylord Warren **Hargadine** 1897–1964	Anna Adeline **Riley** 1900–1946	Russell Samuel **Sloan** 1895–1958	Gladys E. **Passell** 1894–1980

427 Gaylord Warren **Hargadine Jr.** 1922–2014	Eloise Anne **Sloan** 1926–2004

549 Paul Allen **Hargadine** 1960–

Karen Ann **Kubiak** 1961–

Married

Anson Matthew **Hargadine** 1987–	Justin Allen **Hargadine** 1987–

549.   **Paul Allen Hargadine** was born on Sunday, October 16, 1960, in Dallas County, Texas. He is the son of Gaylord Warren Hargadine Jr. (427) and Eloise Anne Sloan.

He married **Karen Ann Kubiak**. They have two sons.

Karen Ann was born in Clearfield, Davis County, Colorado, on Sunday, September 17, 1961.

Sons of Paul Allen Hargadine and Karen Ann Kubiak:

m   I.   **Anson Matthew Hargadine** was born in Mills County, Texas, on May 27, 1987.

m   II.   **Justin Allen Hargadine** was born in Mills County, Texas, on May 27, 1987.

Jeffrey Hargadine

550.   **Jeffrey J. Hargadine** was born on Wednesday, September 08, 1943. Adopted after father died in WWII. He is the son of Gordon Eugene Hargadine (428) and Marjorie Jean Dozier.

Marriages with an unknown partner and Judy C. Oliver (Page 547) are known.

Jeffrey Hargadine

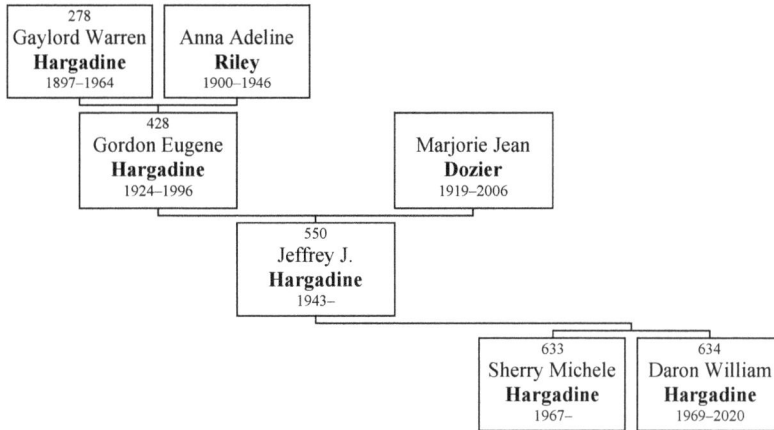

Here are the details about **Jeffrey J. Hargadine's** first marriage, with an unknown partner. You can read more about Jeffrey J. on page 546.

Children of Jeffrey J. Hargadine:

+ 633 f I. **Sherry Michele Hargadine** was born on July 27, 1967.

+ 634 m II. **Daron William Hargadine** was born in Englewood, Arapahoe County, Colorado, on May 06, 1969. He died in Phoenix, Maricopa County, Arizona, on January 02, 2020, at the age of 50. Daron William was cremated (Find a Grave ID 206084830).

Family of Jeffrey Hargadine and Judy Oliver

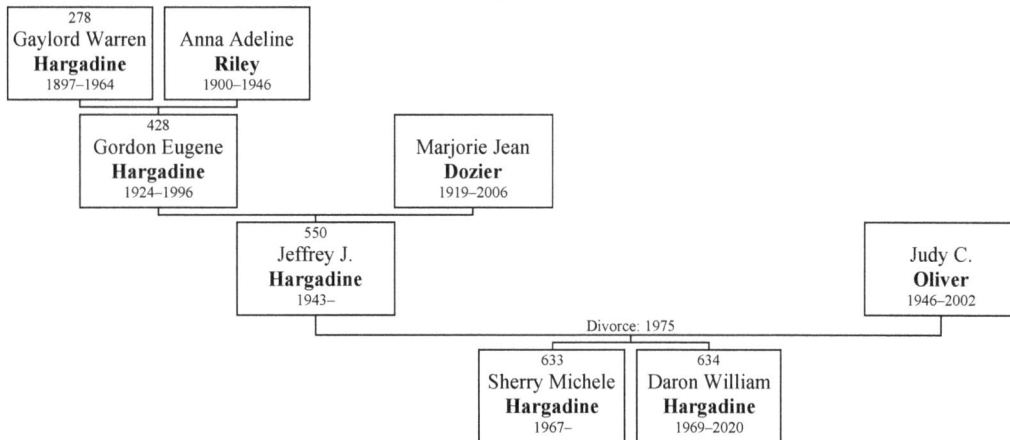

Here are the details about **Jeffrey J. Hargadine's** second marriage, with Judy C. Oliver. You can read more about Jeffrey J. on page 546.

Jeffrey J. Hargadine married **Judy C. Oliver**. They were divorced in El Paso County, Colorado, on March 19, 1975. They had two children.

Judy C. was born on Wednesday, November 13, 1946.[501] She reached 55 years of age and died on September 09, 2002.[501]

Children of Jeffrey J. Hargadine and Judy C. Oliver:

+   633   f   I.   **Sherry Michele Hargadine** was born on July 27, 1967.

+   634   m   II.   **Daron William Hargadine** was born in Englewood, Arapahoe County, Colorado, on May 06, 1969. He died in Phoenix, Maricopa County, Arizona, on January 02, 2020, at the age of 50. Daron William was cremated (Find a Grave ID 206084830).

Richard Hargadine

551.   **Richard Eugene Hargadine** was born on Wednesday, September 21, 1949. He is the son of Gordon Eugene Hargadine (428) and Marjorie Jean Dozier.

Marriages with Karen M. Carlson and Vikki Marie Miller (Page 549) are known.

Family of Richard Hargadine and Karen Carlson

Here are the details about **Richard Eugene Hargadine's** first marriage, with Karen M. Carlson. You can read more about Richard Eugene on page 548.

Richard Eugene Hargadine married **Karen M. Carlson**. Karen M. was born on Tuesday, December 18, 1951.

Family of Richard Hargadine and Vikki Miller

501   Ancestry.com, U.S., Social Security Death Index, 1935-2014 (Provo, UT, USA, Ancestry.com Operations Inc, 2014), Ancestry.com, Social Security Administration; Washington D.C., USA; Social Security Death Index, Master File. Record for Judy C. Hargadine. https://search.ancestry.co.uk/cgi-bin/sse.dll?db=3693&h=25534211&indiv=try.

Here are the details about **Richard Eugene Hargadine's** second marriage, with Vikki Marie Miller. You can read more about Richard Eugene on page 548.

Richard Eugene Hargadine married **Vikki Marie Miller** on Saturday, June 16, 1984, in Denver, Denver County, Colorado.

Family of Russell Hargadine and Mary Bradder

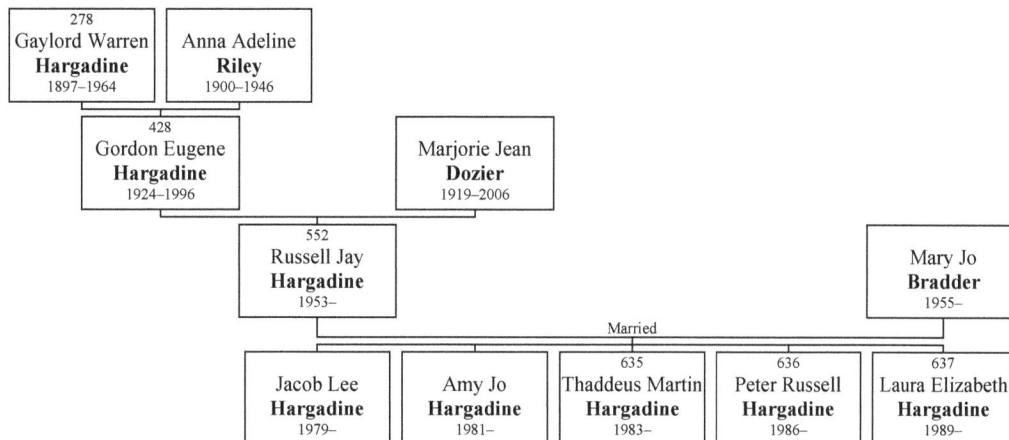

552.   **Russell Jay Hargadine** was born on Thursday, February 19, 1953. He is the son of Gordon Eugene Hargadine (428) and Marjorie Jean Dozier.

He married **Mary Jo Bradder**. They have five children.

Mary Jo was born in June 1955.

Children of Russell Jay Hargadine and Mary Jo Bradder:

	m	I.	**Jacob Lee Hargadine** was born on April 04, 1979.
	f	II.	**Amy Jo Hargadine** was born in Lakewood, Jefferson County, Colorado, on July 22, 1981.
+ 635	m	III.	**Thaddeus Martin Hargadine** was born on December 07, 1983.
+ 636	m	IV.	**Peter Russell Hargadine** was born in July 1986.
+ 637	f	V.	**Laura Elizabeth Hargadine** was born in 1989.

Family of David Hargadine and Deborah Russell

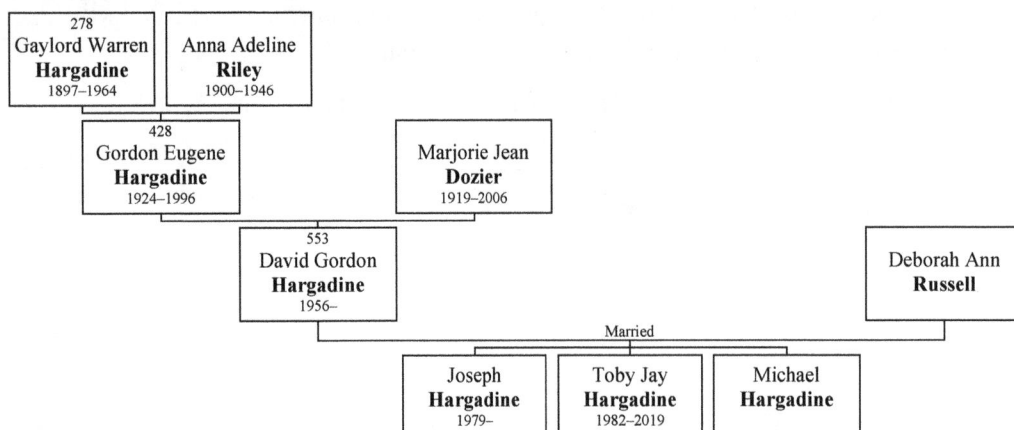

```
┌──────────────┬──────────────┐
│ 278          │ Anna Adeline │
│ Gaylord Warren│    Riley    │
│  Hargadine   │  1900–1946   │
│  1897–1964   │              │
└──────────────┴──────────────┘
        ┌──────────────┐      ┌──────────────┐
        │ 428          │      │ Marjorie Jean│
        │ Gordon Eugene│      │    Dozier    │
        │  Hargadine   │      │  1919–2006   │
        │  1924–1996   │      │              │
        └──────────────┘      └──────────────┘
              ┌──────────────┐        ┌──────────────┐
              │ 553          │        │ Deborah Ann  │
              │ David Gordon │        │   Russell    │
              │  Hargadine   │        │              │
              │  1956–       │        │              │
              └──────────────┘        └──────────────┘
                        Married
        ┌──────────┬──────────┬──────────┐
        │ Joseph   │ Toby Jay │ Michael  │
        │Hargadine │Hargadine │Hargadine │
        │ 1979–    │1982–2019 │          │
        └──────────┴──────────┴──────────┘
```

553. **David Gordon Hargadine** was born on Tuesday, October 02, 1956. He is the son of Gordon Eugene Hargadine (428) and Marjorie Jean Dozier.

He married **Deborah Ann Russell**. They had three sons.

Sons of David Gordon Hargadine and Deborah Ann Russell:

- m   I. **Joseph Hargadine** was born on November 12, 1979.

- m   II. **Toby Jay Hargadine** was born in Broken Bow, Custer County, Nebraska, USA, on January 03, 1982. He died in Kremmling, Grand County, Colorado, USA, on January 03, 2019, at the age of 37. His cause of death was truck crash.

- m   III. **Michael Hargadine**.

Family of Lynn Hargadine and Jerry Sartain

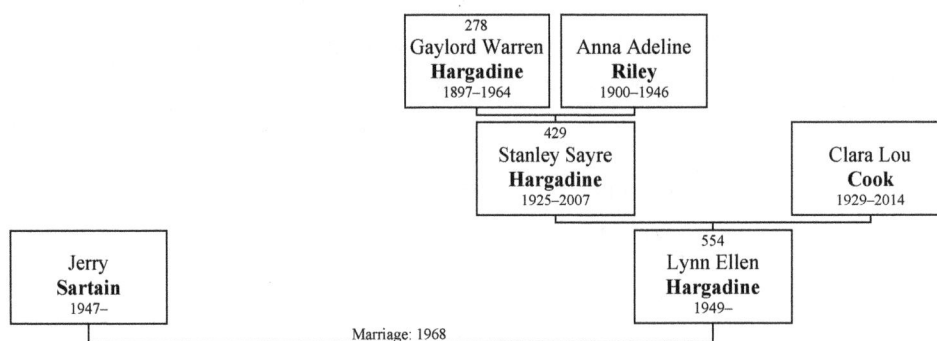

```
┌──────────────┬──────────────┐
│ 278          │ Anna Adeline │
│ Gaylord Warren│    Riley    │
│  Hargadine   │  1900–1946   │
│  1897–1964   │              │
└──────────────┴──────────────┘
        ┌──────────────┐      ┌──────────────┐
        │ 429          │      │ Clara Lou    │
        │ Stanley Sayre│      │    Cook      │
        │  Hargadine   │      │  1929–2014   │
        │  1925–2007   │      │              │
        └──────────────┘      └──────────────┘
        ┌──────────────┐        ┌──────────────┐
        │ Jerry        │        │ 554          │
        │  Sartain     │        │ Lynn Ellen   │
        │  1947–       │        │  Hargadine   │
        │              │        │  1949–       │
        └──────────────┘        └──────────────┘
                   Marriage: 1968
```

554. **Lynn Ellen Hargadine** was born on Sunday, October 02, 1949.[502] She is the daughter of Stanley Sayre Hargadine (429) and Clara Lou Cook.

---

502   Ancestry.com, Arkansas, Marriage Certificates, 1917-1972 (Lehi, UT, USA, Ancestry.com Operations, Inc., 2019), Ancestry.com, Arkansas Department of Vital Records; Little Rock, Arkansas; Marriage Certificates; Year: 1968; Film: #4. Record for Lynn Hargadine. https://search.ancestry.co.uk/cgi-bin/sse.dll?db=61775&h=90011501&indiv=try.

At the age of 18, Lynn Ellen married **Jerry Sartain** on Sunday, August 11, 1968, in Drasco, Cleburne County, Arkansas, when he was 20 years old.[502] Jerry was born in Arkansas, USA, on Wednesday, October 15, 1947.[502]

Family of Nancy Hargadine and Mike Kearney

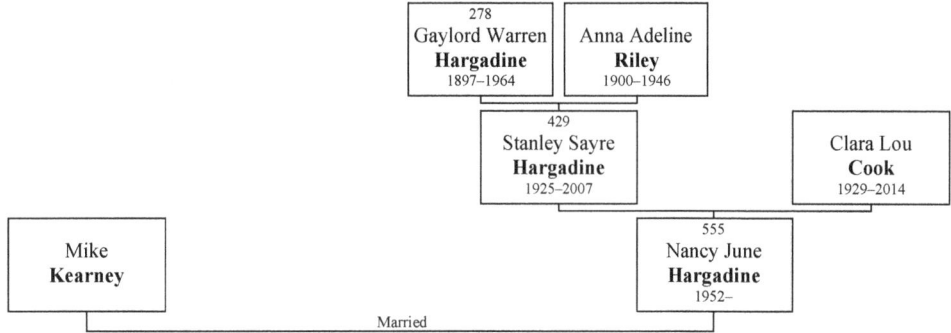

555.   **Nancy June Hargadine** was born on Wednesday, September 17, 1952. She is the daughter of Stanley Sayre Hargadine (429) and Clara Lou Cook.

She married **Mike Kearney**.

Family of Kay Hargadine and Owens

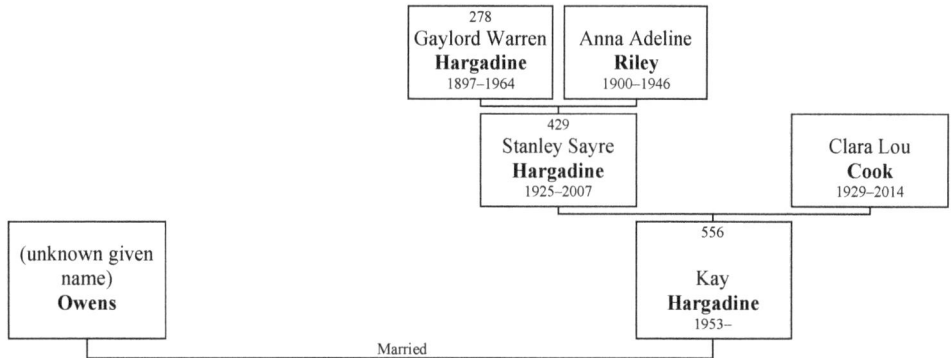

556.   **Kay Hargadine** was born on Wednesday, December 23, 1953. She is the daughter of Stanley Sayre Hargadine (429) and Clara Lou Cook.

She married **(unknown given name) Owens**.

Family of Donna Grossarth and Creige Scribner

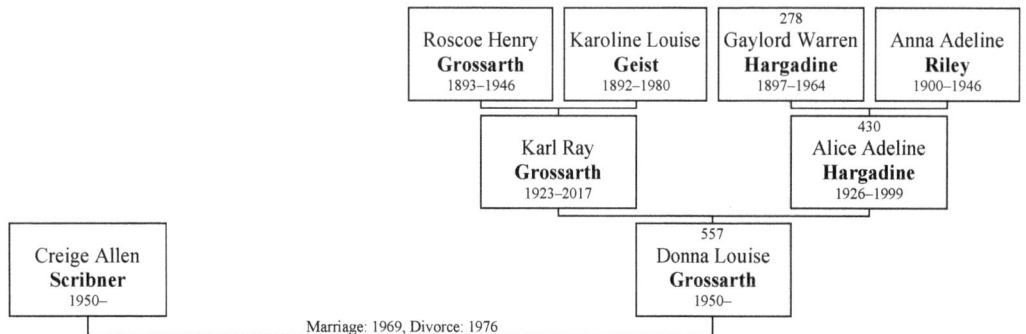

557. **Donna Louise Grossarth** was born on Wednesday, March 01, 1950, in Kansas, USA. She is the daughter of Karl Ray Grossarth and Alice Adeline Hargadine (430).

At the age of 19, Donna Louise married **Creige Allen Scribner** on Saturday, June 07, 1969, in San Juan County, Washington, when he was 19 years old. They were divorced in San Juan County, Washington, on September 28, 1976.

Creige Allen was born in Washington, USA, on Sunday, January 22, 1950.

Family of David Grossarth and Rita Morrill

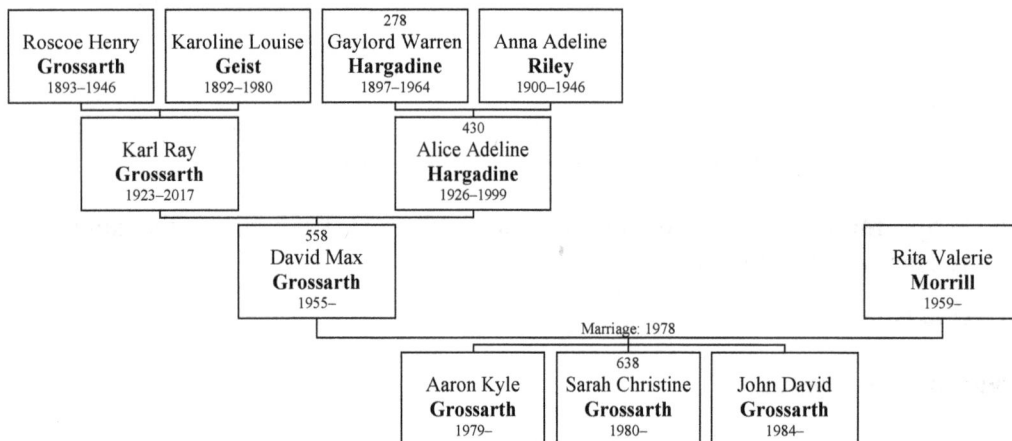

558. **David Max Grossarth** was born on Tuesday, February 08, 1955. He is the son of Karl Ray Grossarth and Alice Adeline Hargadine (430).

At the age of 23, David Max married **Rita Valerie Morrill** on Saturday, June 10, 1978, when she was 18 years old. They have three children.

Rita Valerie was born on Sunday, December 27, 1959.

Children of David Max Grossarth and Rita Valerie Morrill:

	m	I.	**Aaron Kyle Grossarth** was born on March 21, 1979.
+	638	f	II.	**Sarah Christine Grossarth** was born on December 18, 1980.
	m	III.	**John David Grossarth** was born on July 30, 1984.

Family of Randel Hargadine and Karen Campbell

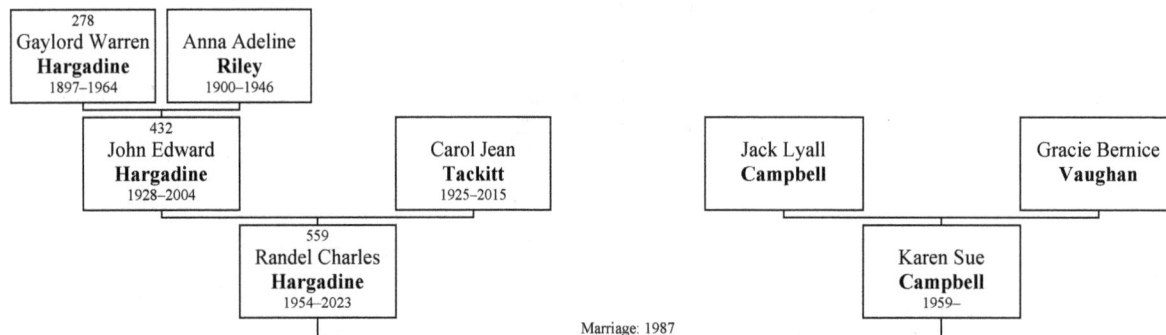

559. **Randel Charles Hargadine** was born on Wednesday, February 17, 1954, in Colorado, USA. He was the son of John Edward Hargadine (432) and Carol Jean Tackitt.

Randel Charles died on August 30, 2023, at the age of 69.

At the age of 33, Randel Charles married **Karen Sue Campbell** on Saturday, August 29, 1987, at Antioch Baptist Church in Sandston, Henrico County, Virginia, when she was 27 years old. Karen Sue was born in Virginia, USA, on Tuesday, September 22, 1959. She is the daughter of Jack Lyall Campbell and Gracie Bernice Vaughan.

Family of Lois Hargadine and Philip Chiles

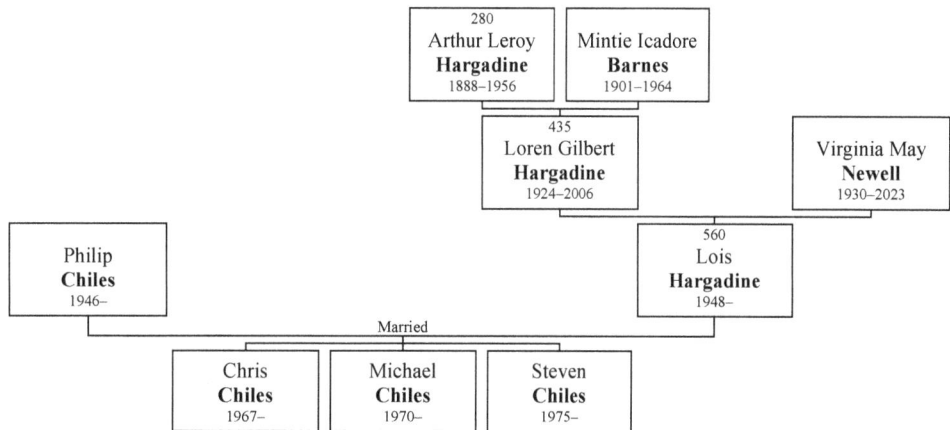

560. **Lois Hargadine** was born on Wednesday, September 01, 1948. She is the daughter of Loren Gilbert Hargadine (435) and Virginia May Newell.

She married **Philip Chiles**. They have three sons.

Philip was born on Sunday, November 10, 1946.

Sons of Lois Hargadine and Philip Chiles:

    m   I. **Chris Chiles** was born on October 04, 1967.

    m   II. **Michael Chiles** was born on August 24, 1970.

    m   III. **Steven Chiles** was born on April 26, 1975.

Family of Arthur Hargadine and Jody Hancock

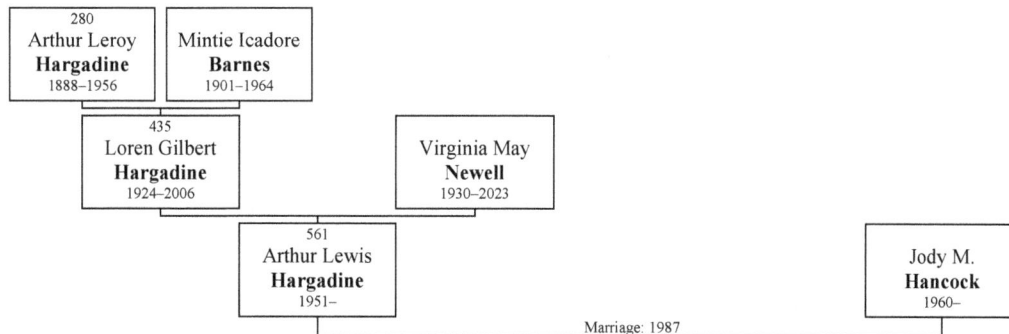

561. **Arthur Lewis Hargadine** was born on Tuesday, November 13, 1951. He is the son of Loren Gilbert Hargadine (435) and Virginia May Newell.

Arthur Lewis married **Jody M. Hancock** on Saturday, April 04, 1987. Jody M. was born in April 1960.

Joe Hargadine

562. **Joe Brian Hargadine** was born on Tuesday, January 20, 1959, in Shasta County, California.

Marriages with Janie Kell and Tammy Luann Jones (Page 554) are known.

Family of Joe Hargadine and Janie Kell

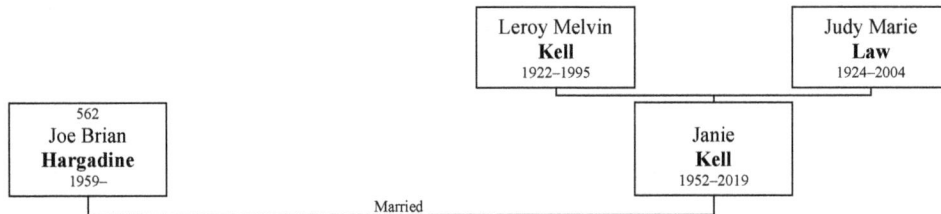

Here are the details about **Joe Brian Hargadine's** first marriage, with Janie Kell. You can read more about Joe Brian on page 554.

Joe Brian Hargadine married **Janie Kell**. Janie was born in Licking, Texas County, Missouri, on Friday, January 04, 1952. She was the daughter of Leroy Melvin Kell and Judy Marie Law.

Janie reached 67 years of age and died in Broken Bow, McCurtain County, Oklahoma, on May 24, 2019. She was cremated (Find a Grave ID 199420116).

Family of Joe Hargadine and Tammy Jones

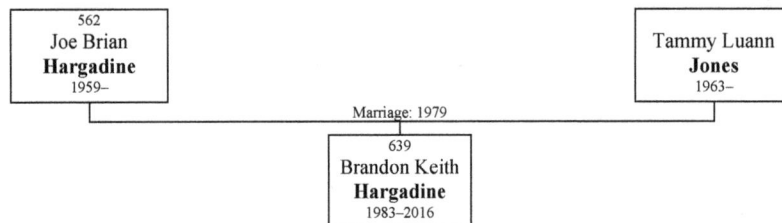

Here are the details about **Joe Brian Hargadine's** second marriage, with Tammy Luann Jones. You can read more about Joe Brian on page 554.

Joe Brian Hargadine married **Tammy Luann Jones** on Saturday, May 12, 1979, in Chelan, Washington. They had one son.

Tammy Luann was born in May 1963. She is also known as **Tammy Lee Anne Jones**.

Son of Joe Brian Hargadine and Tammy Luann Jones:

+ 639 m I. **Brandon Keith Hargadine** was born in Paris, Lamar County, Texas, on November 09, 1983. He died in Clarksville, Red River County, Texas, on

December 31, 2016, at the age of 33. His cause of death was spina bifida. He was buried (Find a Grave ID 174800325).

Family of Leland Broadbeck and Vicki January

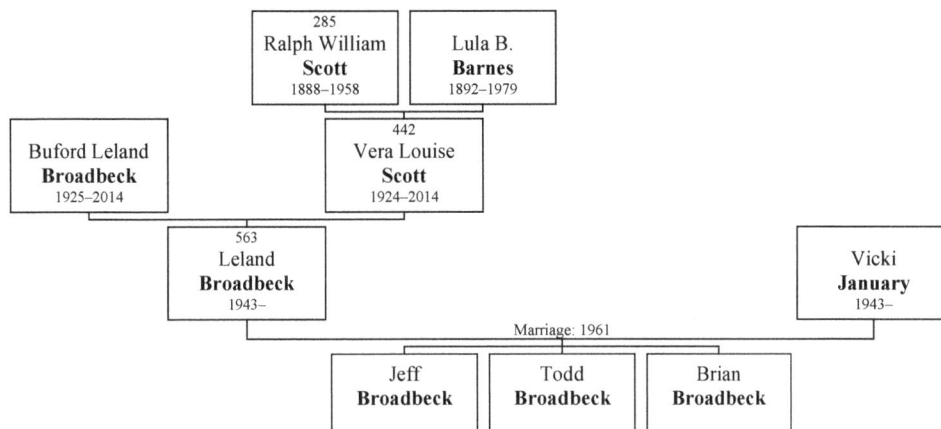

563. **Leland Broadbeck** was born in 1943.[503] He is the son of Buford Leland Broadbeck and Vera Louise Scott (442).

Leland married **Vicki January** in 1961.[503] They have three sons.

Vicki was born in 1943.[503]

Sons of Leland Broadbeck and Vicki January:

m   I. **Jeff Broadbeck**.

m   II. **Todd Broadbeck**.

m   III. **Brian Broadbeck**.

Family of Cheryl Hargadine and Dale Downing

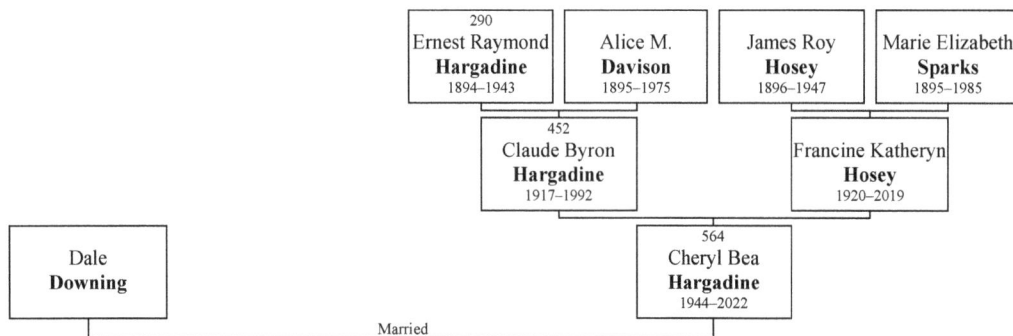

503   Ancestry.com, U.S., Newspapers.com™ Marriage Index, 1800s-current (Lehi, UT, USA, Ancestry.com Operations Inc, 2020), Ancestry.com, *The Hays Daily News*; Publication Date: 6/ Aug/ 1961; Publication Place: Hays, Kansas, USA; URL: https://www.newspapers.com/image/1389921/?article=ce50a66a-9c4c-43f2-8c3a-9157ef6fe1da/4b239523-4a70-41cb-b1c1-ec07d151d9ff&focus=0.013420457,0.60109,0.13575448,0.6805659&xid=3398. Record for Leland Brodbeck. https://search.ancestry.co.uk/cgi-bin/sse.dll?db=62116&h=331428808&indiv=try.

564. **Cheryl Bea Hargadine** was born on Friday, August 11, 1944. She was the daughter of Claude Byron Hargadine (452) and Francine Katheryn Hosey.

Cheryl Bea died in Kansas, USA, on May 12, 2022, at the age of 77. Her cause of death was Alzheimer's. Cheryl Bea was buried in Cremated- (Find a Grave ID 248049336).

She married **Dale Downing**.

Family of Jo Hargadine and Randall Kopsa

565. **Jo Francine Hargadine** was born in February 1950. She is the daughter of Claude Byron Hargadine (452) and Francine Katheryn Hosey.

Jo Francine married **Randall Lee Kopsa** on Saturday, August 08, 1970. Randall Lee was born in August 1950.

Family of Mark Hargadine and Becky Wilson

566. **Mark Bryant Hargadine** was born on Tuesday, May 10, 1955. He is the son of Clinton Doyle Hargadine (454) and Dortha Mae Emery.

He married **Becky Sue Wilson**. They have two children.

Becky Sue was born in March 1960.

Children of Mark Bryant Hargadine and Becky Sue Wilson:

| f | I. | **Jennifer Lynn Hargadine** was born in July 1981. |
| m | II. | **Travis Lee Hargadine** was born in July 1984. |

Family of Kim Hargadine and Stephen Doyle

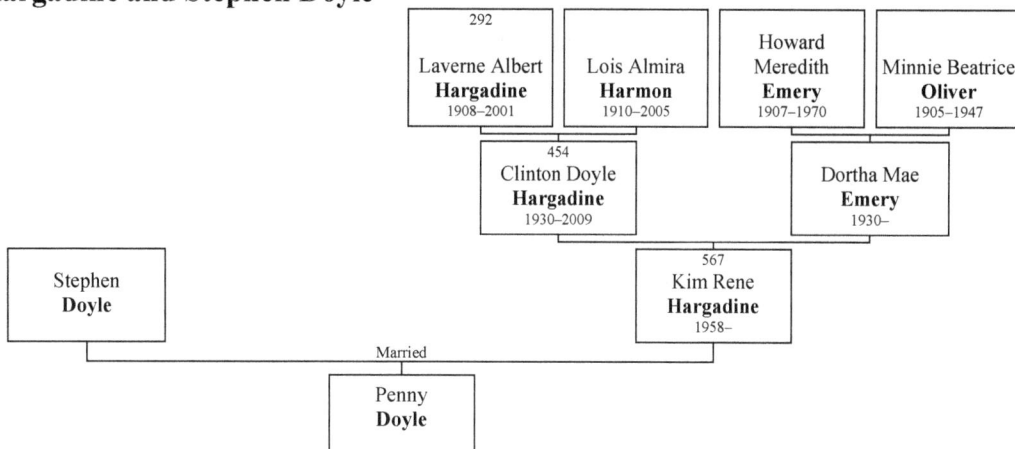

```
                                    ┌──────────┐┌──────────┐ ┌──────────┐┌──────────┐
                                    │   292    ││          │ │  Howard  ││  Minnie  │
                                    │ Laverne  ││Lois Almira││ Meredith ││ Beatrice │
                                    │  Albert  ││  Harmon  │ │  Emery   ││  Oliver  │
                                    │Hargadine ││1910–2005 │ │1907–1970 ││1905–1947 │
                                    │1908–2001 ││          │ │          ││          │
                                    └──────────┘└──────────┘ └──────────┘└──────────┘
                                         └────────┬────────┘      └─────────┬────────┘
                                         ┌──────────┐          ┌──────────┐
                                         │   454    │          │ Dortha   │
                                         │  Clinton │          │   Mae    │
                                         │  Doyle   │          │  Emery   │
                                         │Hargadine │          │  1930–   │
                                         │1930–2009 │          │          │
                                         └──────────┘          └──────────┘
                                              └─────────┬───────────┘
                                              ┌──────────┐
                                              │   567    │
                                              │  Kim Rene│
  ┌──────────┐                                │Hargadine │
  │ Stephen  │                                │  1958–   │
  │  Doyle   │                                └──────────┘
  └──────────┘
       └──────────────Married──────────────────────┘
                 ┌──────────┐
                 │  Penny   │
                 │  Doyle   │
                 └──────────┘
```

567. Kim Rene Hargadine was born on Thursday, February 13, 1958. She is the daughter of Clinton Doyle Hargadine (454) and Dortha Mae Emery.

She married **Stephen Doyle**. They have one daughter.

Daughter of Kim Rene Hargadine and Stephen Doyle:

f   I. **Penny Doyle**.

Family of Rex Hargadine and Barbara Jantz

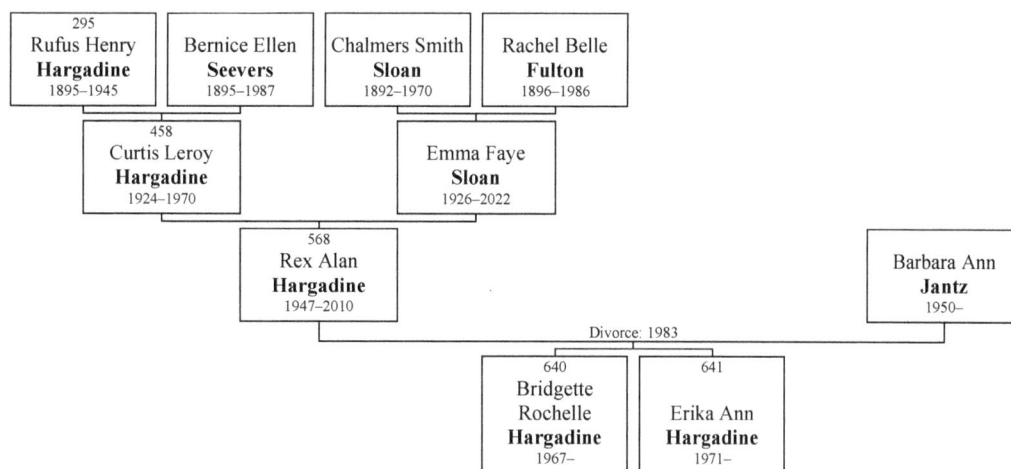

```
┌──────────┐┌──────────┐ ┌──────────┐┌──────────┐
│   295    ││          │ │ Chalmers ││  Rachel  │
│  Rufus   ││  Bernice │ │  Smith   ││  Belle   │
│  Henry   ││   Ellen  │ │  Sloan   ││  Fulton  │
│Hargadine ││  Seevers │ │1892–1970 ││1896–1986 │
│1895–1945 ││1895–1987 │ │          ││          │
└──────────┘└──────────┘ └──────────┘└──────────┘
     └────────┬────────┘      └────────┬────────┘
     ┌──────────┐              ┌──────────┐
     │   458    │              │ Emma Faye│
     │  Curtis  │              │  Sloan   │
     │  Leroy   │              │1926–2022 │
     │Hargadine │              └──────────┘
     │1924–1970 │
     └──────────┘
          └──────────┬────────────┘
          ┌──────────┐                      ┌──────────┐
          │   568    │                      │  Barbara │
          │ Rex Alan │                      │   Ann    │
          │Hargadine │                      │  Jantz   │
          │1947–2010 │                      │  1950–   │
          └──────────┘                      └──────────┘
               └──────Divorce: 1983──────────────┘
          ┌──────────┐┌──────────┐
          │   640    ││   641    │
          │ Bridgette││          │
          │ Rochelle ││ Erika Ann│
          │Hargadine ││Hargadine │
          │  1967–   ││  1971–   │
          └──────────┘└──────────┘
```

568. Rex Alan Hargadine was born on Wednesday, November 12, 1947, in Spearville, Ford County, Kansas. He was the son of Curtis Leroy Hargadine (458) and Emma Faye Sloan.

Rex Alan served in the military between January 1970 and February 2000. Colonel; U.S. Army. He died in Dodge City, Ford County, Kansas, on April 26, 2010, at the age of 62. Rex Alan was buried in Kansas Veterans Cemetery at Fort Dodge, Dodge City, Ford County, Kansas (Find a Grave ID 52221554).

He married **Barbara Ann Jantz**. They were divorced in Pierce, Washington, USA, on November 07, 1983. They had two daughters.

Barbara Ann was born in Kansas, USA, in 1950.

Daughters of Rex Alan Hargadine and Barbara Ann Jantz:

+   640   f   I. **Bridgette Rochelle Hargadine** was born on January 07, 1967.

+   641   f   II. **Erika Ann Hargadine** was born on July 28, 1971.

Family of Roy Hargadine and Shirley Thompson

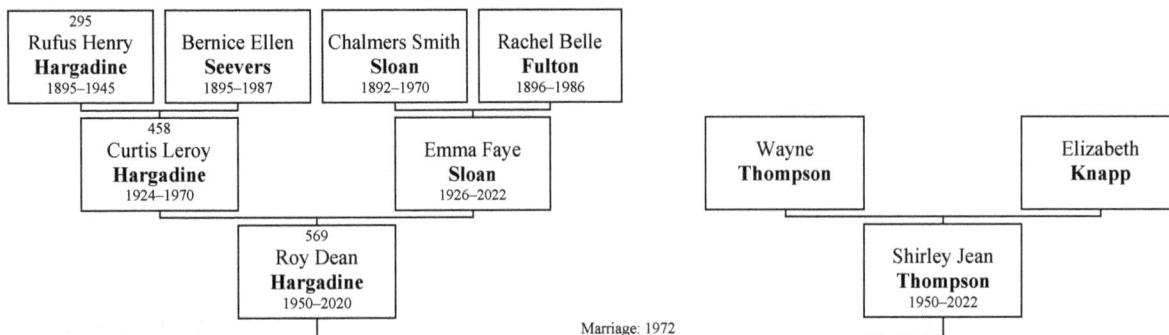

569.   **Roy Dean Hargadine** was born on Tuesday, August 15, 1950, in Greensburg, Kiowa County, Kansas. He was the son of Curtis Leroy Hargadine (458) and Emma Faye Sloan.

Roy Dean worked as a Teacher; Jetmore, Kansas. He died in Wichita, Sedgwick County, Kansas, on July 11, 2020, at the age of 69. Roy Dean was buried in Hillcrest Cemetery, Mullinville, Kiowa County, Kansas (Find a Grave ID 212953167).

At the age of 21, Roy Dean married **Shirley Jean Thompson** on Saturday, August 05, 1972, in Mullinville, Kiowa County, Kansas, when she was 21 years old. Shirley Jean was born at St. Catherine Hospital, Centura Health in Dodge City, Ford County, Kansas, on Wednesday, November 15, 1950. She was the daughter of Wayne Thompson and Elizabeth Knapp.

Shirley Jean reached 71 years of age and died in Dodge City, Ford County, Kansas, on June 25, 2022. She was buried in Hillcrest Cemetery, Mullinville, Kiowa County, Kansas (Find a Grave ID 241000594).

Family of Charlene Keys and Richard Elmore

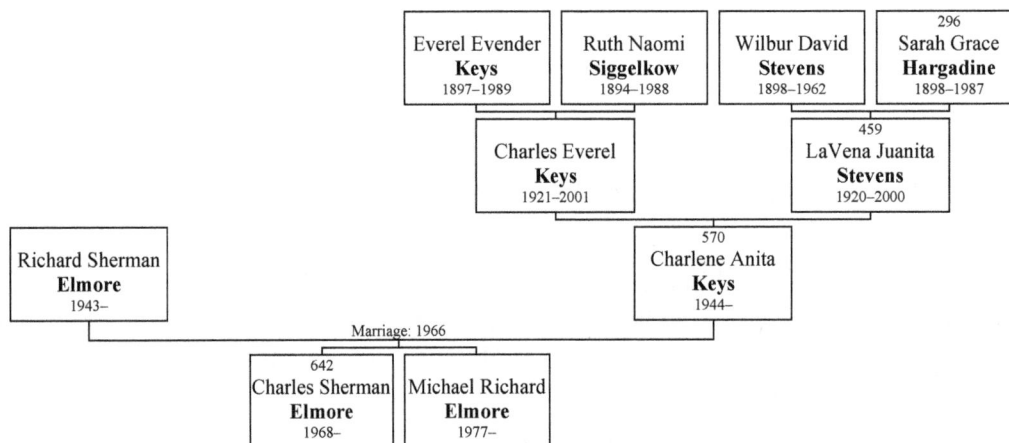

570.   **Charlene Anita Keys** was born on Monday, October 16, 1944, in Dodge City, Ford County, Kansas. She is the daughter of Charles Everel Keys and LaVena Juanita Stevens (459).

At the age of 21, Charlene Anita married **Richard Sherman Elmore** on Friday, July 01, 1966, in Florence, Lauderdale County, Alabama, when he was 23 years old. They have two sons.

Richard Sherman was born in Hillsboro, Montgomery County, Illinois, on Thursday, April 22, 1943. He works as a Retired Lieutenant Colonel; U.S. Army.

Sons of Charlene Anita Keys and Richard Sherman Elmore:

+ 642 m I. **Charles Sherman Elmore** was born in Greenville, Bond County, Illinois, on September 12, 1968.

          m II. **Michael Richard Elmore** was born in Homestead AFB, Florida, on October 05, 1977.

Family of Steven Keys and Nancy Bullamore

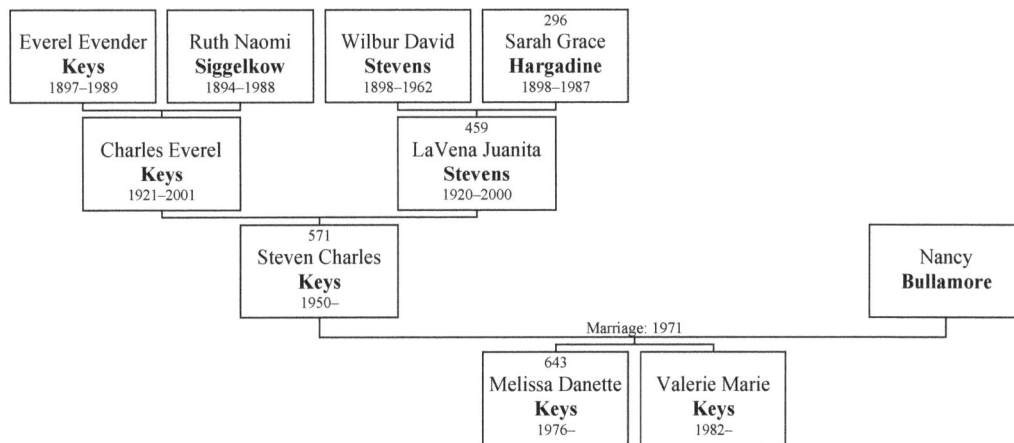

571. **Steven Charles Keys** was born on Wednesday, June 28, 1950, in Lawrence, Douglas County, Kansas. He is the son of Charles Everel Keys and LaVena Juanita Stevens (459).

Steven Charles married **Nancy Bullamore** on Friday, July 02, 1971. They have two daughters.

Daughters of Steven Charles Keys and Nancy Bullamore:

+ 643 f I. **Melissa Danette Keys** was born on April 11, 1976.

          f II. **Valerie Marie Keys** was born on March 26, 1982.

Family of Dalen Keys and Mitzie Bruce

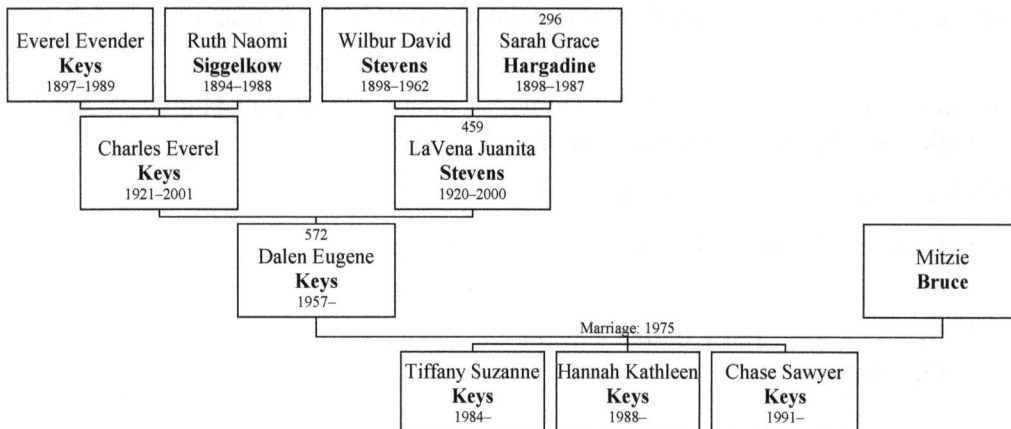

572. **Dalen Eugene Keys** was born on Tuesday, April 09, 1957, in Rochester, Monroe County, New York. He is the son of Charles Everel Keys and LaVena Juanita Stevens (459).

Dalen Eugene married **Mitzie Bruce** on Wednesday, December 31, 1975, in Sheffield, Colbert County, Alabama. They have three children.

Children of Dalen Eugene Keys and Mitzie Bruce:

    f   I.   **Tiffany Suzanne Keys** was born on December 17, 1984.

    f   II.   **Hannah Kathleen Keys** was born on June 24, 1988.

    m   III.   **Chase Sawyer Keys** was born on June 24, 1991.

Family of David Stevens and Betty E

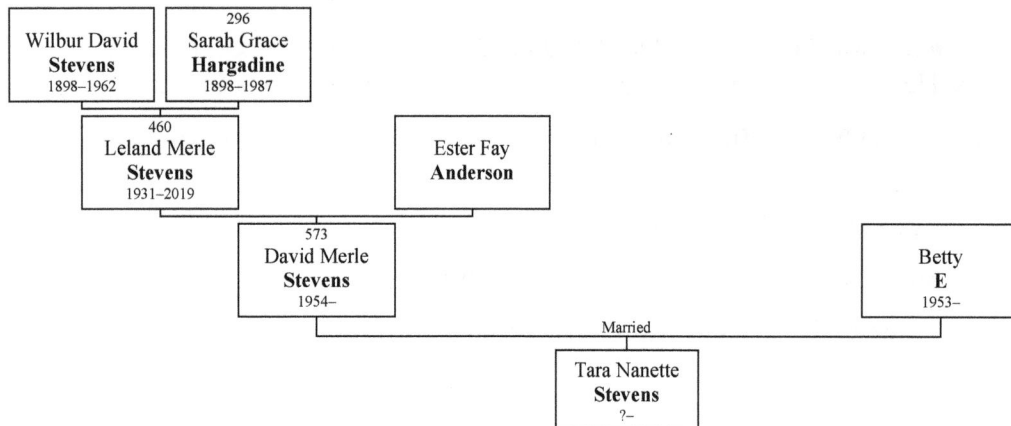

573. **David Merle Stevens** was born on Tuesday, May 18, 1954, in Kinsley, Edwards County, Kansas. He is the son of Leland Merle Stevens (460) and Ester Fay Anderson.

He married **Betty E**. They have one daughter.

Betty was born in September 1953.

Daughter of David Merle Stevens and Betty E:

    f   I.   **Tara Nanette Stevens** was born on January 14.

Family of Kevin Stevens and Anne Marie

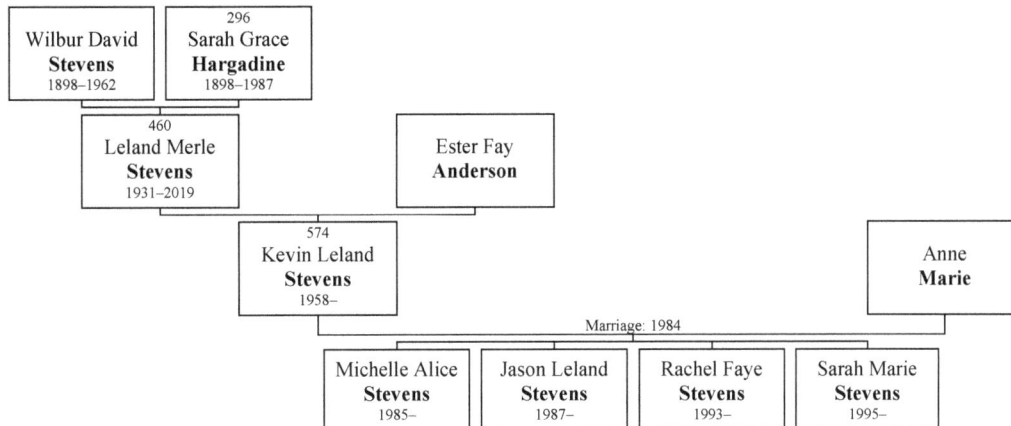

```
┌──────────────┐ ┌──────────────┐
│ Wilbur David │ │     296      │
│              │ │ Sarah Grace  │
│   Stevens    │ │  Hargadine   │
│  1898–1962   │ │  1898–1987   │
└──────────────┘ └──────────────┘
       ┌──────────────┐        ┌──────────────┐
       │     460      │        │  Ester Fay   │
       │ Leland Merle │        │  Anderson    │
       │   Stevens    │        │              │
       │  1931–2019   │        └──────────────┘
       └──────────────┘
              ┌──────────────┐                      ┌──────────────┐
              │     574      │                      │              │
              │ Kevin Leland │                      │    Anne      │
              │   Stevens    │                      │    Marie     │
              │    1958–     │                      │              │
              └──────────────┘                      └──────────────┘
                           Marriage: 1984
     ┌──────────────┐ ┌──────────────┐ ┌──────────────┐ ┌──────────────┐
     │Michelle Alice│ │ Jason Leland │ │ Rachel Faye  │ │ Sarah Marie  │
     │   Stevens    │ │   Stevens    │ │   Stevens    │ │   Stevens    │
     │    1985–     │ │    1987–     │ │    1993–     │ │    1995–     │
     └──────────────┘ └──────────────┘ └──────────────┘ └──────────────┘
```

574. **Kevin Leland Stevens** was born on Wednesday, March 05, 1958. He is the son of Leland Merle Stevens (460) and Ester Fay Anderson.

Kevin Leland married **Anne Marie** on Saturday, July 28, 1984. They have four children.

Children of Kevin Leland Stevens and Anne Marie:

    f   I. **Michelle Alice Stevens** was born on May 14, 1985.

    m   II. **Jason Leland Stevens** was born on March 09, 1987.

    f   III. **Rachel Faye Stevens** was born on December 02, 1993.

    f   IV. **Sarah Marie Stevens** was born on June 01, 1995.

Family of Sherry Hargadine and Edward Harbert

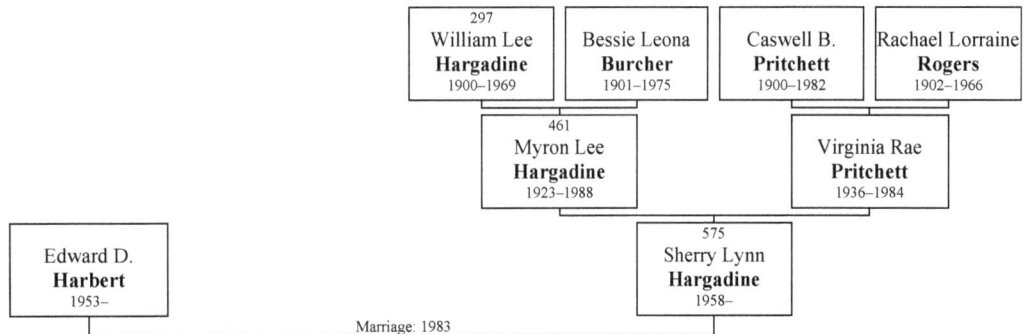

```
┌──────────────┐ ┌──────────────┐ ┌──────────────┐ ┌──────────────┐
│     297      │ │ Bessie Leona │ │  Caswell B.  │ │Rachael Lorraine│
│ William Lee  │ │   Burcher    │ │  Pritchett   │ │   Rogers     │
│  Hargadine   │ │  1901–1975   │ │  1900–1982   │ │  1902–1966   │
│  1900–1969   │ │              │ │              │ │              │
└──────────────┘ └──────────────┘ └──────────────┘ └──────────────┘
          ┌──────────────┐              ┌──────────────┐
          │     461      │              │ Virginia Rae │
          │  Myron Lee   │              │  Pritchett   │
          │  Hargadine   │              │  1936–1984   │
          │  1923–1988   │              └──────────────┘
          └──────────────┘
  ┌──────────────┐               ┌──────────────┐
  │  Edward D.   │               │     575      │
  │   Harbert    │               │ Sherry Lynn  │
  │    1953–     │               │  Hargadine   │
  └──────────────┘               │    1958–     │
                                 └──────────────┘
                  Marriage: 1983
```

575. **Sherry Lynn Hargadine** was born in June 1958. She is the daughter of Myron Lee Hargadine (461) and Virginia Rae Pritchett.

Sherry Lynn married **Edward D. Harbert** in 1983.[504] Edward D. was born in October 1953.

---

[504] Ancestry.com, U.S., Newspapers.com™ Marriage Index, 1800s-current (Lehi, UT, USA, Ancestry.com Operations Inc, 2020), Ancestry.com, *Council Grove Republican*; Publication Date: 17/ Aug/ 1983; Publication Place: Council Grove, Kansas, USA; URL: https://www.newspapers.com/image/344386600/?article=4a340a93-f981-4234-aff2-afbc63e9fa85&focus=0.2718573,0.7157939,0.38888702,0.75509226&xid=3398. Record for Sherry Hargadine. https://search.ancestry.co.uk/cgi-bin/sse.dll?db=62116&h=95515521&indiv=try.

Family of Martin Hargadine and Janet Fulk

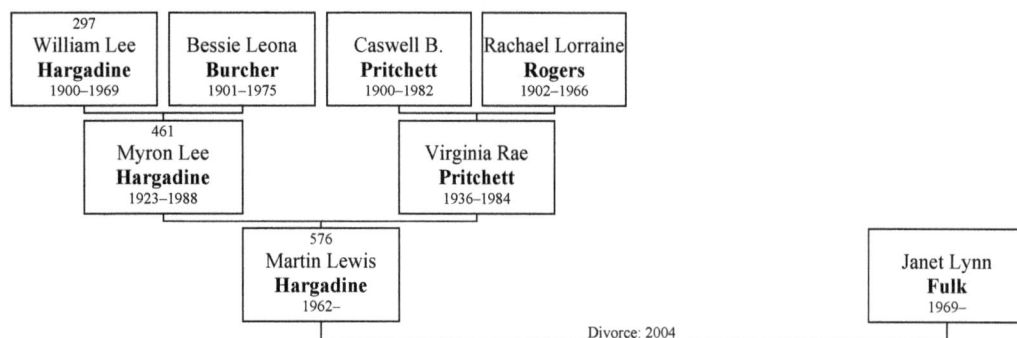

576. **Martin Lewis Hargadine** was born in June 1962. He is the son of Myron Lee Hargadine (461) and Virginia Rae Pritchett.

He married **Janet Lynn Fulk**. They were divorced in Emmet, Iowa, USA, on February 25, 2004.

Janet Lynn was born in August 1969.

Family of Adeana Hargadine and Roy DeHoff

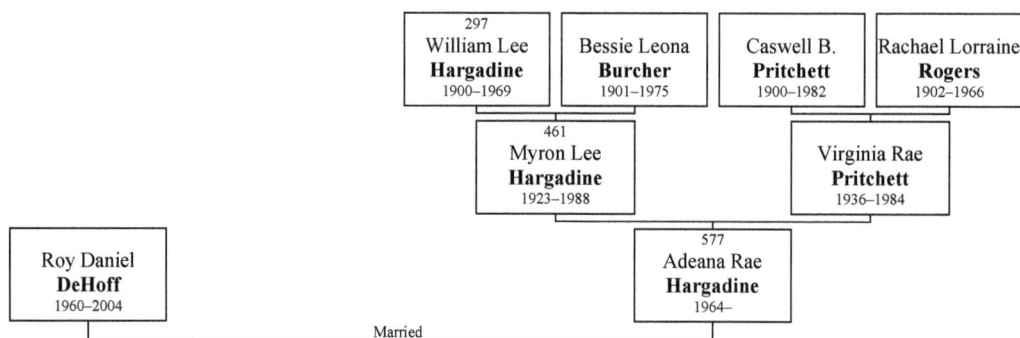

577. **Adeana Rae Hargadine** was born in August 1964. She is the daughter of Myron Lee Hargadine (461) and Virginia Rae Pritchett.

She married **Roy Daniel DeHoff**. Roy Daniel was born on Tuesday, February 09, 1960.

He reached 44 years of age and died in Council Grove, Morris County, Kansas, on July 24, 2004. Roy Daniel was buried in Sunnyslope Memorial Gardens, Council Grove, Morris County, Kansas (Find a Grave ID 35273774).

Family of David Horne and Pamela Bottoms

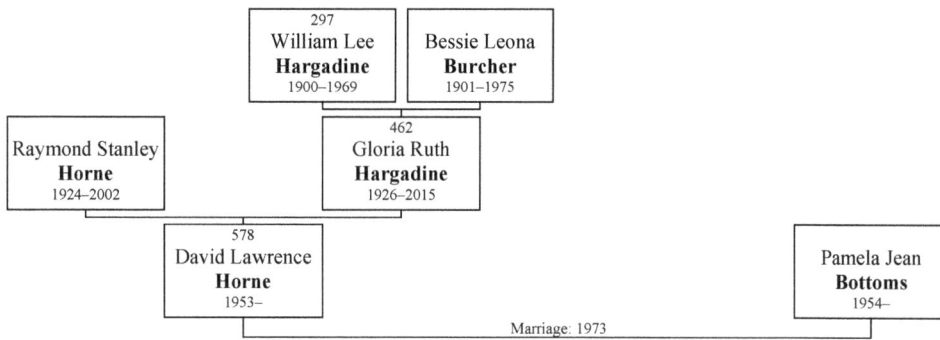

578. **David Lawrence Horne** was born on Thursday, January 08, 1953, in Ada, Pontotoc County, Oklahoma. He is the son of Raymond Stanley Horne and Gloria Ruth Hargadine (462).

At the age of 20, David Lawrence married **Pamela Jean Bottoms** on Saturday, May 26, 1973, in Ada, Pontotoc County, Oklahoma, when she was 19 years old. Pamela Jean was born in Ada, Pontotoc County, Oklahoma, on Thursday, January 07, 1954.

Family of Cynthia Horne and David Jones

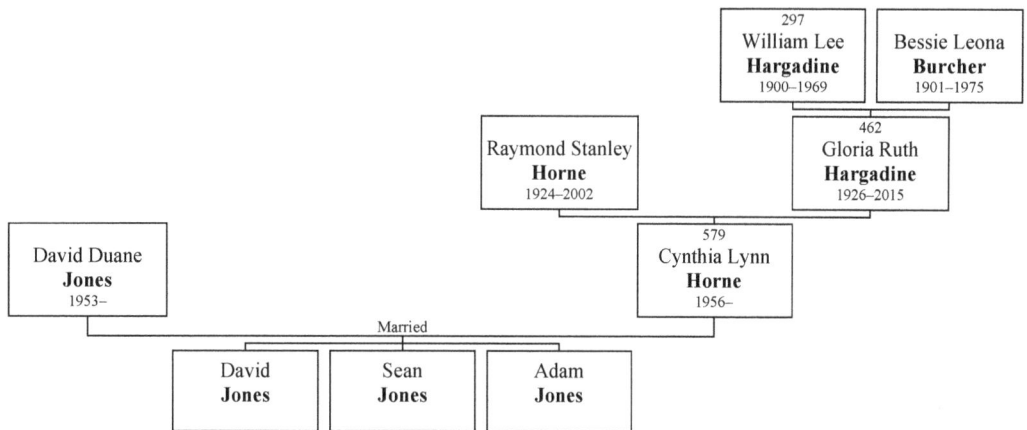

579. **Cynthia Lynn Horne** was born in July 1956. She is the daughter of Raymond Stanley Horne and Gloria Ruth Hargadine (462).

She married **David Duane Jones**. They have three sons.

David Duane was born in June 1953.

Sons of Cynthia Lynn Horne and David Duane Jones:

   m I. **David Jones**.

   m II. **Sean Jones**.

   m III. **Adam Jones**.

Family of Richard Horne and Ginger Murphy

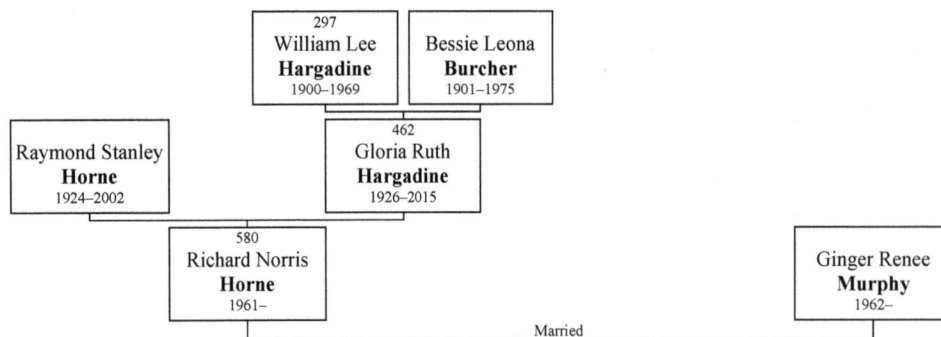

580. **Richard Norris Horne** was born in February 1961. He is the son of Raymond Stanley Horne and Gloria Ruth Hargadine (462).

He married **Ginger Renee Murphy**. Ginger Renee was born in September 1962.

Family of Scott Dean and Brenda Frantz

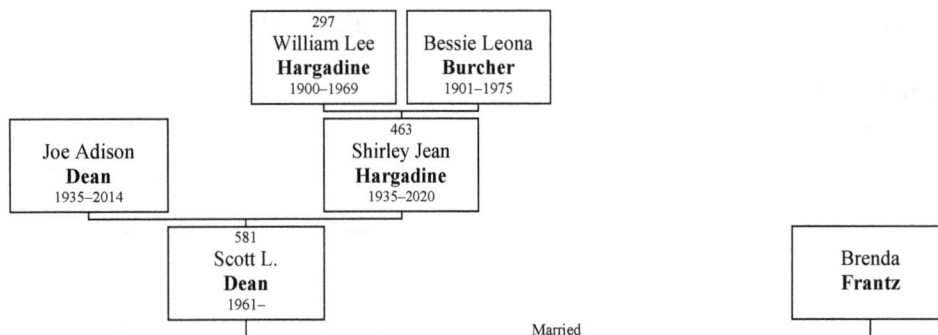

581. **Scott L. Dean** was born on Tuesday, February 28, 1961.[505] He is the son of Joe Adison Dean and Shirley Jean Hargadine (463). He is also known as **Scooter**.

He married **Brenda Frantz**.

Valerie Hargadine

582. **Valerie Ann Hargadine** was born on Sunday, March 19, 1961, in Moundridge, McPherson County, Kansas. She is the daughter of Leslie Leon Hargadine (464) and Margie Nadene Sowers.

Marriages with David Hannon and Gary Lee Cranwell (Page 565) are known.

---

505   Ancestry.com, U.S., Public Records Index, 1950-1993, Volume 1 (Lehi, UT, USA, Ancestry.com Operations, Inc., 2010), Ancestry.com, Record for Scott L Dean. https://search.ancestry.co.uk/cgi-bin/sse.dll?db=1788&h=299346887&indiv=try.

Family of Valerie Hargadine and David Hannon

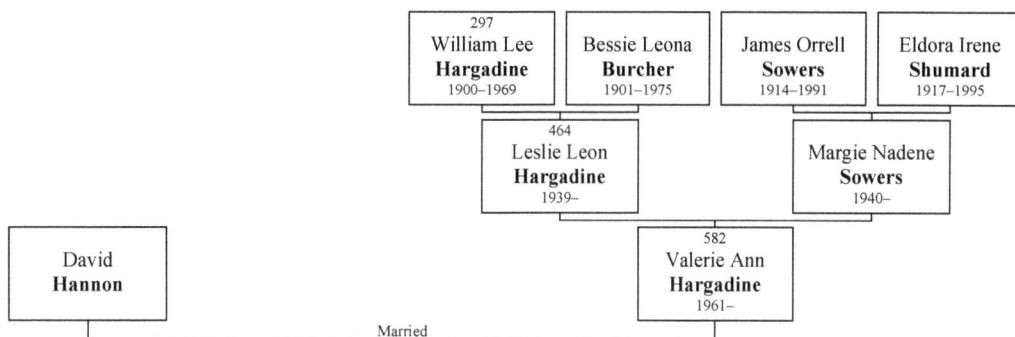

Here are the details about **Valerie Ann Hargadine's** first marriage, with David Hannon. You can read more about Valerie Ann on page 564.

Valerie Ann Hargadine married **David Hannon**.

Family of Valerie Hargadine and Gary Cranwell

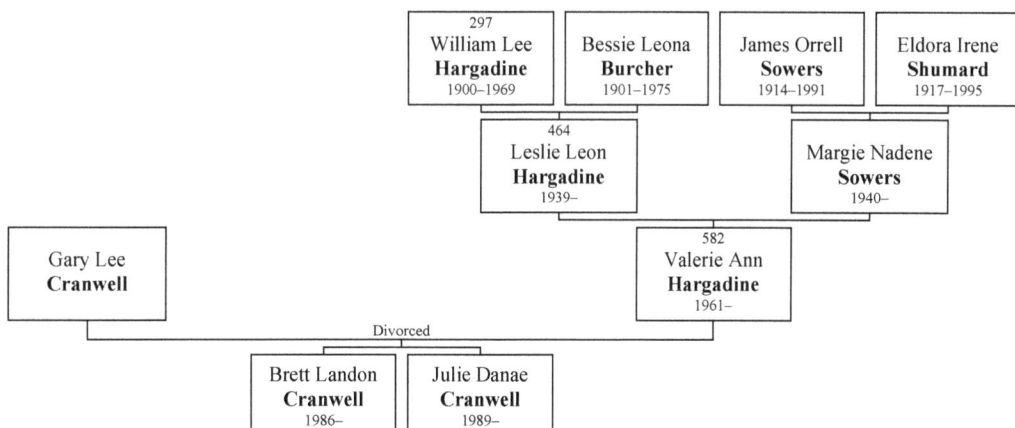

Here are the details about **Valerie Ann Hargadine's** second marriage, with Gary Lee Cranwell. You can read more about Valerie Ann on page 564.

Valerie Ann Hargadine married **Gary Lee Cranwell**. They later divorced. They have two children.

Children of Valerie Ann Hargadine and Gary Lee Cranwell:

m	I.	**Brett Landon Cranwell** was born on May 21, 1986.
f	II.	**Julie Danae Cranwell** was born on January 26, 1989.

Karen Hargadine

583. **Karen Denise Hargadine** was born on Saturday, February 29, 1964, in Moundridge, McPherson County, Kansas. She is the daughter of Leslie Leon Hargadine (464) and Margie Nadene Sowers.

Marriages with Steven Wade Henson and Steve Rolly Beck (Page 566) are known.

Family of Karen Hargadine and Steven Henson

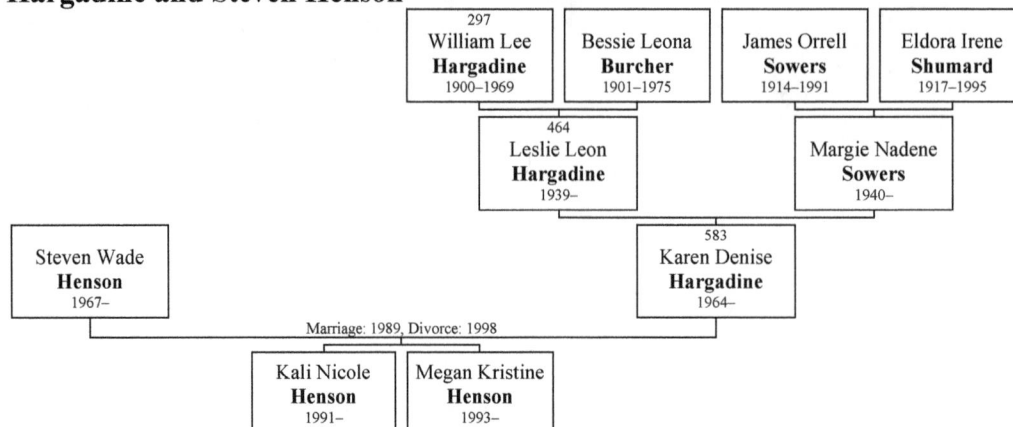

297 William Lee **Hargadine** 1900–1969	Bessie Leona **Burcher** 1901–1975	James Orrell **Sowers** 1914–1991	Eldora Irene **Shumard** 1917–1995

464 Leslie Leon **Hargadine** 1939–

Margie Nadene **Sowers** 1940–

Steven Wade **Henson** 1967–

583 Karen Denise **Hargadine** 1964–

Marriage: 1989, Divorce: 1998

Kali Nicole **Henson** 1991–	Megan Kristine **Henson** 1993–

Here are the details about **Karen Denise Hargadine's** first marriage, with Steven Wade Henson. You can read more about Karen Denise on page 565.

At the age of 25, Karen Denise Hargadine married **Steven Wade Henson** on Saturday, December 09, 1989, in McPherson, McPherson County, Kansas, when he was 22 years old. They were divorced in Hutchinson, Reno County, Kansas, on September 08, 1998. They have two daughters.

Steven Wade was born on Sunday, July 16, 1967.[506]

Daughters of Karen Denise Hargadine and Steven Wade Henson:

f   I. **Kali Nicole Henson** was born in Hutchinson, Reno County, Kansas, on February 17, 1991.

f   II. **Megan Kristine Henson** was born in Hutchinson, Reno County, Kansas, on December 30, 1993.

Family of Karen Hargadine and Steve Beck

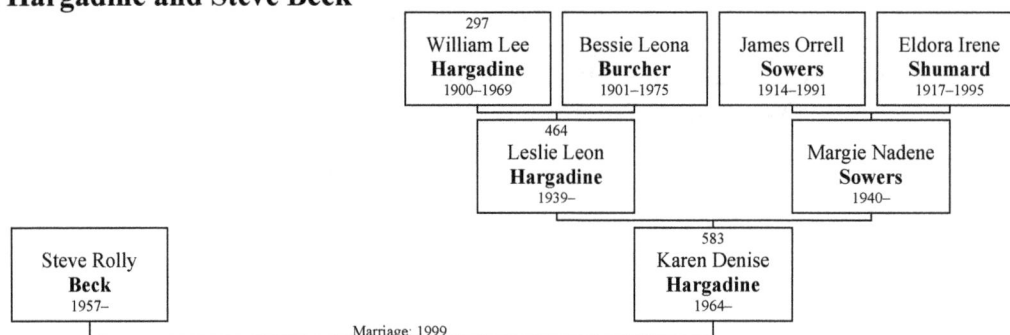

297 William Lee **Hargadine** 1900–1969	Bessie Leona **Burcher** 1901–1975	James Orrell **Sowers** 1914–1991	Eldora Irene **Shumard** 1917–1995

464 Leslie Leon **Hargadine** 1939–

Margie Nadene **Sowers** 1940–

Steve Rolly **Beck** 1957–

583 Karen Denise **Hargadine** 1964–

Marriage: 1999

Here are the details about **Karen Denise Hargadine's** second marriage, with Steve Rolly Beck. You can read more about Karen Denise on page 565.

Karen Denise Hargadine married **Steve Rolly Beck** on Tuesday, September 07, 1999, in Hutchinson, Reno County, Kansas. Steve Rolly was born in February 1957.

---

506   Ancestry.com, U.S., Public Records Index, 1950-1993, Volume 2 (Lehi, UT, USA, Ancestry.com Operations, Inc., 2010), Ancestry.com, Record for Steven W Henson. https://search.ancestry.co.uk/cgi-bin/sse.dll?db=1732&h=79966507&indiv=try.

Family of Carla Hargadine and David Hall

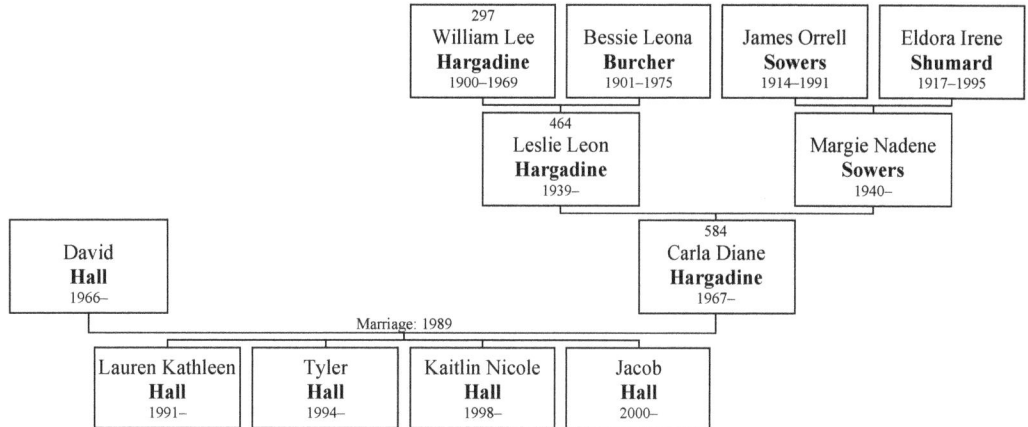

297 William Lee **Hargadine** 1900–1969	Bessie Leona **Burcher** 1901–1975	James Orrell **Sowers** 1914–1991	Eldora Irene **Shumard** 1917–1995

464
Leslie Leon
Hargadine
1939–

Margie Nadene
Sowers
1940–

David
Hall
1966–

584
Carla Diane
Hargadine
1967–

Marriage: 1989

| Lauren Kathleen
Hall
1991– | Tyler
Hall
1994– | Kaitlin Nicole
Hall
1998– | Jacob
Hall
2000– |

584. **Carla Diane Hargadine** was born on Friday, February 17, 1967, in Moundridge, McPherson County, Kansas. She is the daughter of Leslie Leon Hargadine (464) and Margie Nadene Sowers.

At the age of 22, Carla Diane married **David Hall** on Saturday, July 22, 1989, when he was 23 years old. They have four children.

David was born on Saturday, April 23, 1966.

Children of Carla Diane Hargadine and David Hall:

f   I. **Lauren Kathleen Hall** was born on August 13, 1991.

m   II. **Tyler Hall** was born on June 11, 1994.

f   III. **Kaitlin Nicole Hall** was born on February 15, 1998.

m   IV. **Jacob Hall** was born on December 26, 2000.

Family of Susan Hargadine and Robert Lytle

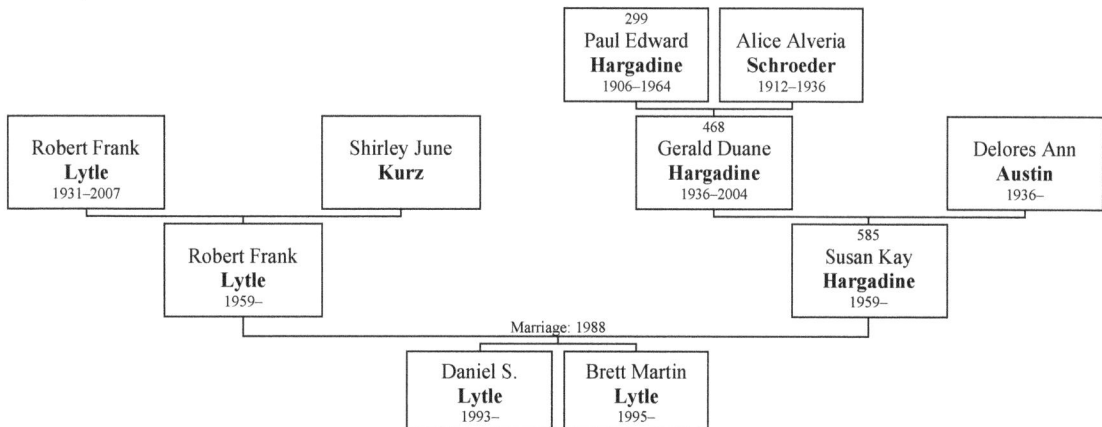

299
Paul Edward
Hargadine
1906–1964

Alice Alveria
Schroeder
1912–1936

Robert Frank
Lytle
1931–2007

Shirley June
Kurz

468
Gerald Duane
Hargadine
1936–2004

Delores Ann
Austin
1936–

Robert Frank
Lytle
1959–

585
Susan Kay
Hargadine
1959–

Marriage: 1988

| Daniel S.
Lytle
1993– | Brett Martin
Lytle
1995– |

585. **Susan Kay Hargadine** was born in September 1959. She is the daughter of Gerald Duane Hargadine (468) and Delores Ann Austin.

Susan Kay married **Robert Frank Lytle** on Saturday, July 09, 1988, in Topeka, Shawnee County, Kansas. They have two sons.

Robert Frank was born in November 1959. He is the son of Robert Frank Lytle and Shirley June Kurz.

Sons of Susan Kay Hargadine and Robert Frank Lytle:

    m   I. **Daniel S. Lytle** was born in December 1993.

    m   II. **Brett Martin Lytle** was born in October 1995.

Family of Dirk Hargadine and Vicki Smerchek

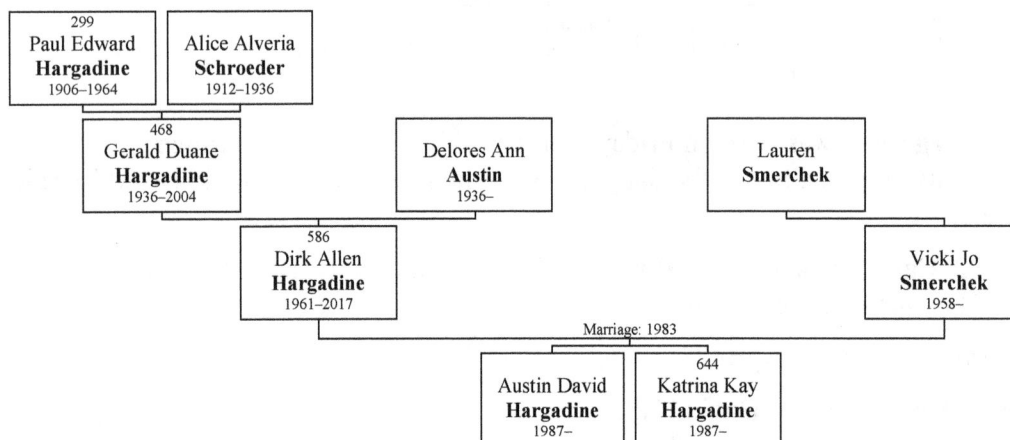

586.   **Dirk Allen Hargadine** was born on Wednesday, December 13, 1961, in Manhattan, Riley County, Kansas. He was the son of Gerald Duane Hargadine (468) and Delores Ann Austin.

Dirk Allen died in Blue Rapids, Marshall County, Kansas, on January 03, 2017, at the age of 55. He was buried in Czech-Moravian Cemetery, Swede Creek Township, Riley County, Kansas (Find a Grave ID 175214373).

Dirk Allen married **Vicki Jo Smerchek** on Friday, March 11, 1983, at Blue Rapids United Methodist Church in Blue Rapids, Marshall County, Kansas. They had two children.

Vicki Jo was born in February 1958. She is the daughter of Lauren Smerchek.

Children of Dirk Allen Hargadine and Vicki Jo Smerchek:

    m   I. **Austin David Hargadine** was born in August 1987.

+   644   f   II. **Katrina Kay Hargadine** was born in August 1987.

Family of Glenn Keith and Sheila Lamb

587. **Glenn Clifton Keith** was born in 1962 in Kansas, USA.[507] He is the son of Steve Marvin Keith and Carolyn Kay Hargadine (471).

Glenn Clifton married **Sheila Sue Lamb** on Saturday, September 17, 1983, in Indianapolis, Marion County, Indiana.[507] Sheila Sue was born in Indiana, USA, in 1966.[507]

Family of Tammy Hargadine and James Killion

588. **Tammy S. Hargadine** was born in 1963. She is the daughter of Terry Glenn Hargadine (472) and Madlyn Carrol Kellogg.

Tammy S. married **James R. Killion** on Friday, October 08, 1982. First Church of the Brethren.

---

507 Ancestry.com, Indiana, U.S., Marriage Certificates, 1960-2012 (Lehi, UT, USA, Ancestry.com Operations, Inc., 2016), Ancestry.com, Indiana Archives and Records Administration; Indianapolis, IN, USA; Records of Marriage 1961-2005; Roll Number: NA. Record for Glen Clifton Keith. https://search.ancestry.co.uk/cgi-bin/sse.dll?db=61009&h=71234&indiv=try.

Family of Jonathan Hargadine and Annette Crespo

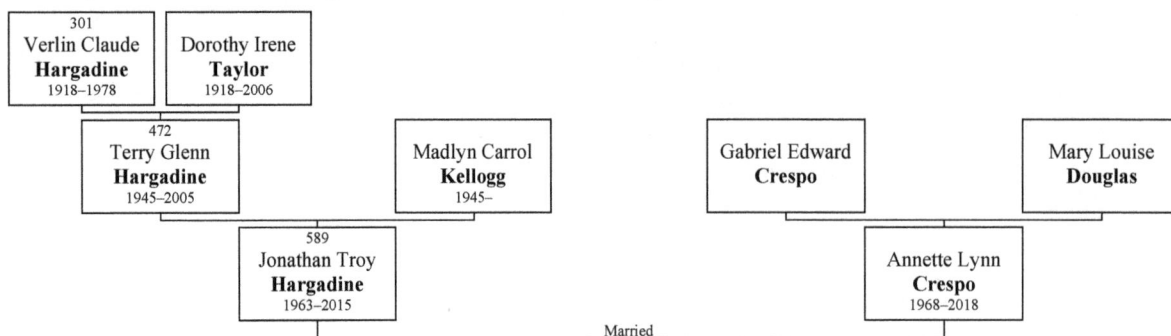

```
┌──────────────┬──────────────┐
│     301      │              │
│ Verlin Claude│ Dorothy Irene│
│  Hargadine   │    Taylor    │
│  1918–1978   │  1918–2006   │
└──────────────┴──────────────┘
        ┌──────────────┐         ┌──────────────┐         ┌──────────────┐
        │     472      │         │              │         │              │
        │ Terry Glenn  │ Madlyn Carrol │    Gabriel Edward   │  Mary Louise │
        │  Hargadine   │   Kellogg    │      Crespo      │    Douglas   │
        │  1945–2005   │    1945–     │              │              │
        └──────────────┴──────────────┘         └──────────────┴──────────────┘
               ┌──────────────┐              ┌──────────────┐
               │     589      │              │              │
               │Jonathan Troy │              │ Annette Lynn │
               │  Hargadine   │              │    Crespo    │
               │  1963–2015   │              │  1968–2018   │
               └──────────────┘   Married    └──────────────┘
```

589.   **Jonathan Troy Hargadine** was born on Thursday, May 02, 1963, in Liberal, Seward County, Kansas. He was the son of Terry Glenn Hargadine (472) and Madlyn Carrol Kellogg.

Jonathan Troy served in the military: US Army. He died in Clarksville, Montgomery County, Tennessee, on June 14, 2015, at the age of 52. His cause of death was car crash. He was buried in Kentucky Veterans Cemetery West, Hopkinsville, Christian County, Kentucky, on June 22, 2015 (Find a Grave ID 147932041).

He married **Annette Lynn Crespo**. Annette Lynn was born in Los Angeles, Los Angeles County, California, on Tuesday, May 28, 1968. She was the daughter of Gabriel Edward Crespo and Mary Louise Douglas.

Annette Lynn reached 49 years of age and died in Nashville, Davidson County, Tennessee, on March 02, 2018. She was buried on March 07, 2018, in Kentucky Veterans Cemetery West, Hopkinsville, Christian County, Kentucky (Find a Grave ID 187884308).

Family of David Archer and Francine Cruz

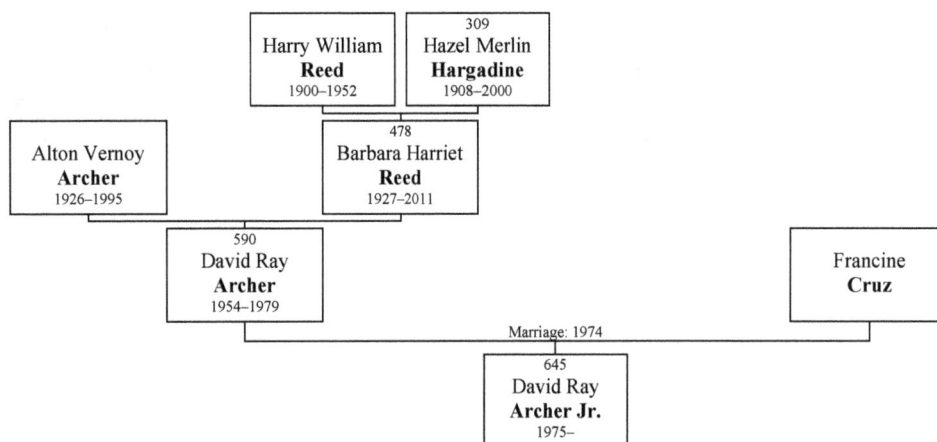

```
                    ┌──────────────┬──────────────┐
                    │ Harry William│     309      │
                    │     Reed     │ Hazel Merlin │
                    │  1900–1952   │  Hargadine   │
                    │              │  1908–2000   │
                    └──────────────┴──────────────┘
  ┌──────────────┐          ┌──────────────┐
  │              │          │     478      │
  │ Alton Vernoy │          │Barbara Harriet│
  │   Archer     │          │     Reed     │
  │  1926–1995   │          │  1927–2011   │
  └──────────────┘          └──────────────┘
          ┌──────────────┐                          ┌──────────────┐
          │     590      │                          │              │
          │  David Ray   │                          │   Francine   │
          │   Archer     │                          │     Cruz     │
          │  1954–1979   │        Marriage: 1974    │              │
          └──────────────┘                          └──────────────┘
                      ┌──────────────┐
                      │     645      │
                      │  David Ray   │
                      │  Archer Jr.  │
                      │    1975–     │
                      └──────────────┘
```

590.   **David Ray Archer** was born on Friday, October 15, 1954, in Seattle, King County, Washington. He was the son of Alton Vernoy Archer and Barbara Harriet Reed (478).

David Ray died in Tucson, Pima County, Arizona, on July 13, 1979, at the age of 24. He was buried in Holy Hope Cemetery and Mausoleum, Tucson, Pima County, Arizona (Find a Grave ID 62310431).

David Ray married **Francine Cruz** on Saturday, June 08, 1974, in Arizonia, USA. They had one son.

Son of David Ray Archer and Francine Cruz:

+ 645 m I. **David Ray Archer Jr.** was born on December 04, 1975.

Family of Eileen Archer and Gaylen Irvine

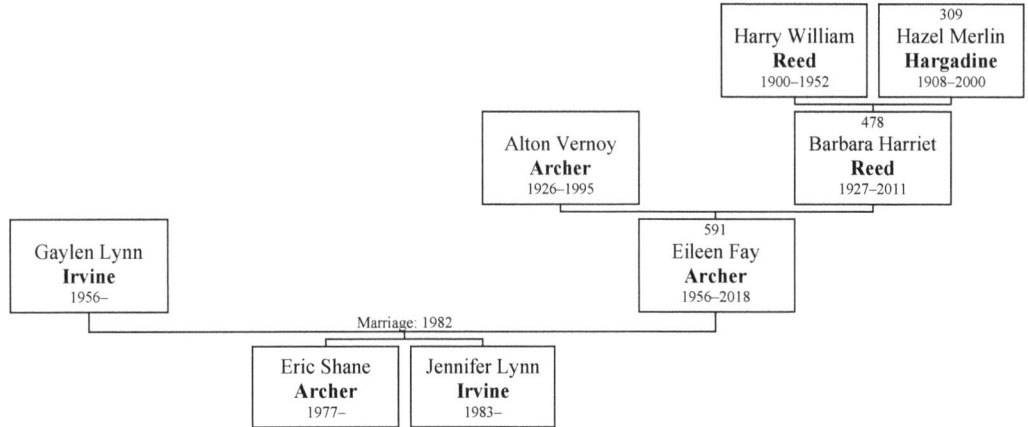

591. **Eileen Fay Archer** was born on Tuesday, June 26, 1956, in Renton, King County, Washington. She was the daughter of Alton Vernoy Archer and Barbara Harriet Reed (478).

Eileen Fay died on April 17, 2018, at the age of 61. She was cremated (Find a Grave ID 188911161).

At the age of 26, Eileen Fay married **Gaylen Lynn Irvine** on Saturday, July 24, 1982, when he was 26 years old. They had two children.

Gaylen Lynn was born in Texas, USA, on Monday, April 02, 1956.

Children of Eileen Fay Archer and Gaylen Lynn Irvine:

m I. **Eric Shane Archer** was born in Texas, USA, on March 20, 1977.

f II. **Jennifer Lynn Irvine** was born in Texas, USA, on April 29, 1983.

Family of Arleen Archer and Douglas Padley

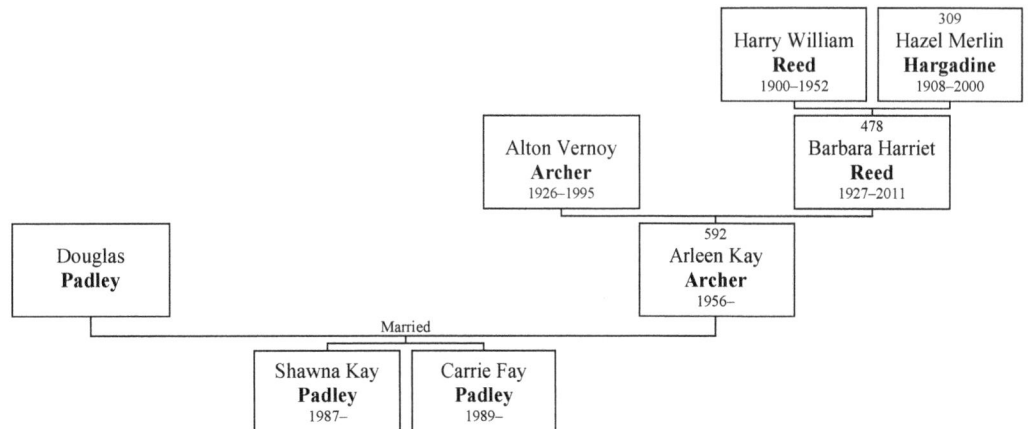

592. **Arleen Kay Archer** was born on Tuesday, June 26, 1956. She is the daughter of Alton Vernoy Archer and Barbara Harriet Reed (478).

She married **Douglas Padley**. They have two daughters.

Daughters of Arleen Kay Archer and Douglas Padley:

> f   I. **Shawna Kay Padley** was born on March 08, 1987.

> f   II. **Carrie Fay Padley** was born on November 17, 1989.

Family of Antonia Hargadine and Robert Osterhout

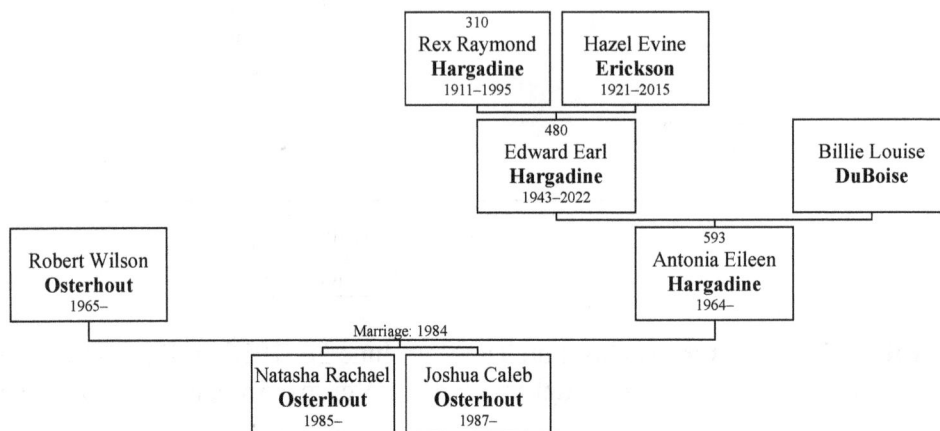

593. **Antonia Eileen Hargadine** was born on Thursday, December 17, 1964, in Seattle, King County, Washington. She is the daughter of Edward Earl Hargadine (480) and Billie Louise DuBoise.

At the age of 19, Antonia Eileen married **Robert Wilson Osterhout** on Tuesday, September 18, 1984, in Portland, Multnomah County, Oregon, when he was 19 years old. They have two children.

Robert Wilson was born in San Leandro, Alameda County, California, on Saturday, May 22, 1965.

Children of Antonia Eileen Hargadine and Robert Wilson Osterhout:

> f   I. **Natasha Rachael Osterhout** was born in Portland, Multnomah County, Oregon, on October 28, 1985.

> m   II. **Joshua Caleb Osterhout** was born in Portland, Multnomah County, Oregon, on March 17, 1987.

Family of Georgia Hargadine and Lee Taylor

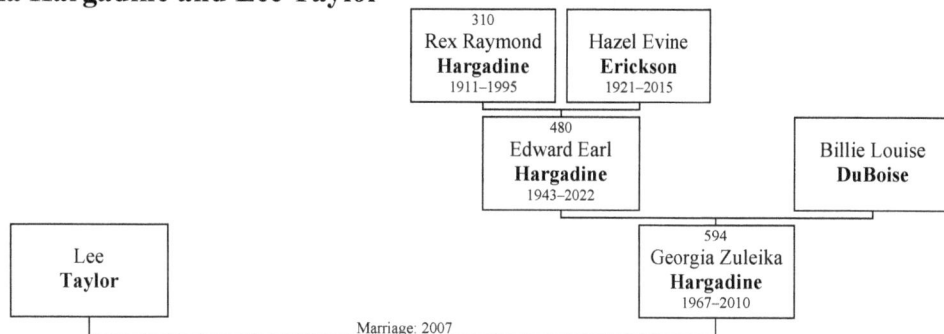

594. **Georgia Zuleika Hargadine** was born on Thursday, November 16, 1967, in Seattle, King County, Washington. She was the daughter of Edward Earl Hargadine (480) and Billie Louise DuBoise.

Georgia Zuleika died on January 24, 2010, at the age of 42.

Georgia Zuleika married **Lee Taylor** on Saturday, July 21, 2007.

Ivan Hargadine

595. **Ivan Ray Hargadine** was born on Sunday, November 09, 1975. He is the son of Edward Earl Hargadine (480) and Christine Rae Ford.

Marriages with Jaclyn Marie Runyon and Jessica A. Joseph (Page 574) are known.

Family of Ivan Hargadine and Jaclyn Runyon

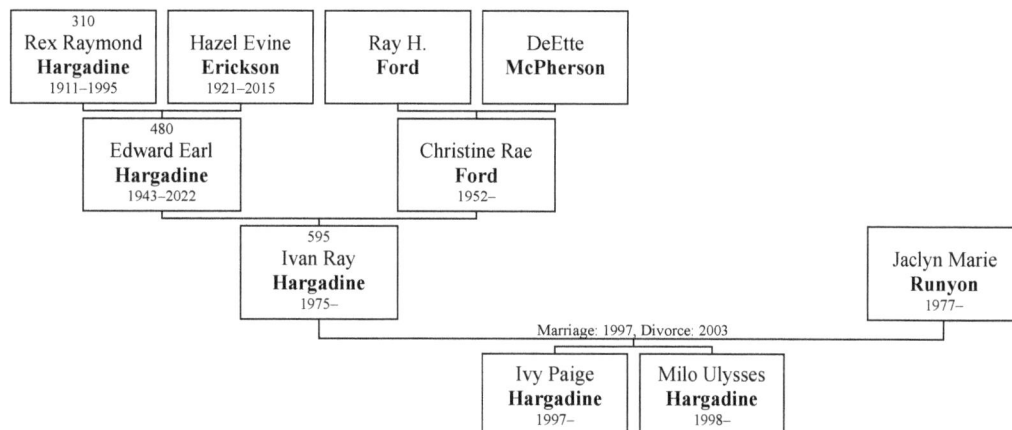

Here are the details about **Ivan Ray Hargadine's** first marriage, with Jaclyn Marie Runyon. You can read more about Ivan Ray on page 573.

At the age of 21, Ivan Ray Hargadine married **Jaclyn Marie Runyon** on Tuesday, February 04, 1997, in Vancouver, Clark County, Washington, when she was 19 years old.[508] They were divorced in Clark County, Washington, on July 07, 2003. They have two children.

Jaclyn Marie was born on Friday, July 08, 1977.

---

[508] Washington Divorce Index, Divorced 7/7/2003.

Children of Ivan Ray Hargadine and Jaclyn Marie Runyon:

f   I. **Ivy Paige Hargadine** was born in Vancouver, Clark County, Washington, on January 21, 1997.

m   II. **Milo Ulysses Hargadine** was born in Vancouver, Clark County, Washington, on May 10, 1998.

Family of Ivan Hargadine and Jessica Joseph

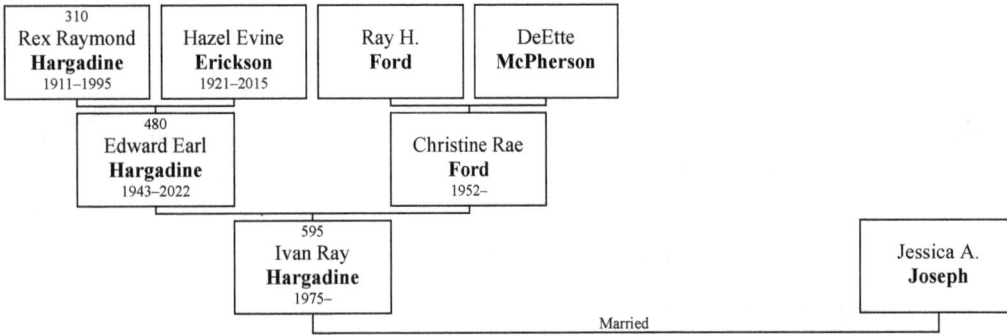

310 Rex Raymond **Hargadine** 1911–1995	Hazel Evine **Erickson** 1921–2015	Ray H. **Ford**	DeEtte **McPherson**

480 Edward Earl **Hargadine** 1943–2022

Christine Rae **Ford** 1952–

595 Ivan Ray **Hargadine** 1975–

Jessica A. **Joseph**

Married

Here are the details about **Ivan Ray Hargadine's** second marriage, with Jessica A. Joseph. You can read more about Ivan Ray on page 573.

Ivan Ray Hargadine married **Jessica A. Joseph** in Clark County, Washington.

Mark Hargadine

596.   **Mark Toscan Hargadine** was born on Wednesday, February 14, 1968, in Lynnwood, Snohomish County, Washington. He was the son of Edward Earl Hargadine (480) and Martha Parrott.

Mark Toscan died in Burleson, Texas, on June 02, 2000, at the age of 32. His cause of death was Auto Accident. Mark Toscan was buried in Lindquist Memorial Park, Layton, Davis County, Utah (Find a Grave ID 108015711).

Marriages with LaDonna F. Joiner and Wendy Storm (Page 575) are known.

Family of Mark Hargadine and LaDonna Joiner

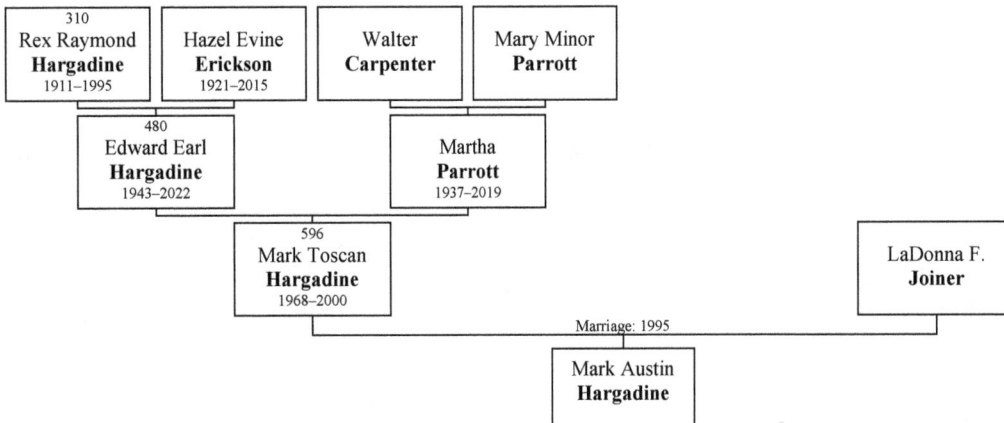

310 Rex Raymond **Hargadine** 1911–1995	Hazel Evine **Erickson** 1921–2015	Walter **Carpenter**	Mary Minor **Parrott**

480 Edward Earl **Hargadine** 1943–2022

Martha **Parrott** 1937–2019

596 Mark Toscan **Hargadine** 1968–2000

LaDonna F. **Joiner**

Marriage: 1995

Mark Austin **Hargadine**

Here are the details about **Mark Toscan Hargadine's** first marriage, with LaDonna F. Joiner. You can read more about Mark Toscan on page 574.

Mark Toscan Hargadine married **LaDonna F. Joiner** on Saturday, August 12, 1995, in Tarrant County, Texas. They had one son.

Son of Mark Toscan Hargadine and LaDonna F. Joiner:

    m   I. **Mark Austin Hargadine**.

Family of Mark Hargadine and Wendy Storm

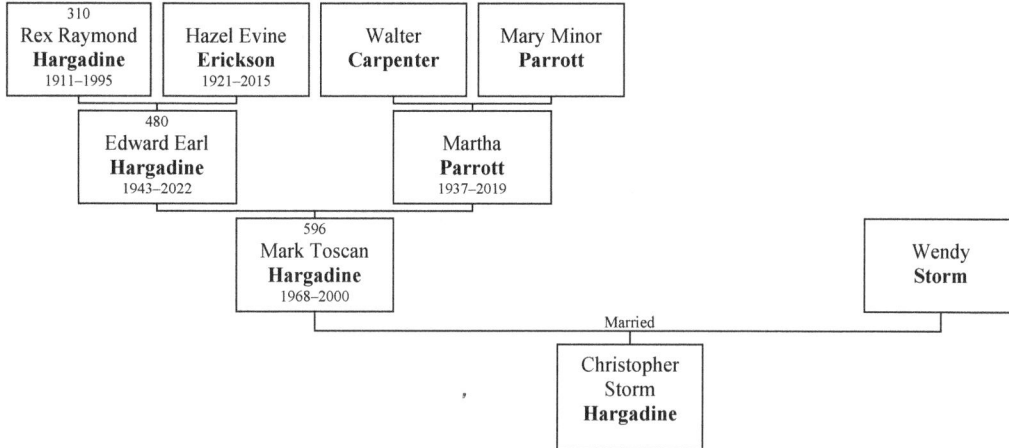

```
┌──────────────┐ ┌──────────────┐ ┌──────────────┐ ┌──────────────┐
│     310      │ │ Hazel Evine  │ │   Walter     │ │ Mary Minor   │
│ Rex Raymond  │ │  Erickson    │ │  Carpenter   │ │   Parrott    │
│  Hargadine   │ │  1921–2015   │ │              │ │              │
│  1911–1995   │ │              │ │              │ │              │
└──────────────┘ └──────────────┘ └──────────────┘ └──────────────┘
       ┌──────────────┐              ┌──────────────┐
       │     480      │              │   Martha     │
       │ Edward Earl  │              │   Parrott    │
       │  Hargadine   │              │  1937–2019   │
       │  1943–2022   │              │              │
       └──────────────┘              └──────────────┘
              ┌──────────────┐                      ┌──────────────┐
              │     596      │                      │              │
              │ Mark Toscan  │                      │    Wendy     │
              │  Hargadine   │                      │    Storm     │
              │  1968–2000   │                      │              │
              └──────────────┘      Married         └──────────────┘
                      ┌──────────────┐
                      │ Christopher  │
                      │    Storm     │
                      │  Hargadine   │
                      └──────────────┘
```

Here are the details about **Mark Toscan Hargadine's** second marriage, with Wendy Storm. You can read more about Mark Toscan on page 574.

Mark Toscan Hargadine married **Wendy Storm**. They had one son.

Son of Mark Toscan Hargadine and Wendy Storm:

    m   I. **Christopher Storm Hargadine**.

Family of Laura Hargadine and Majid Sadki

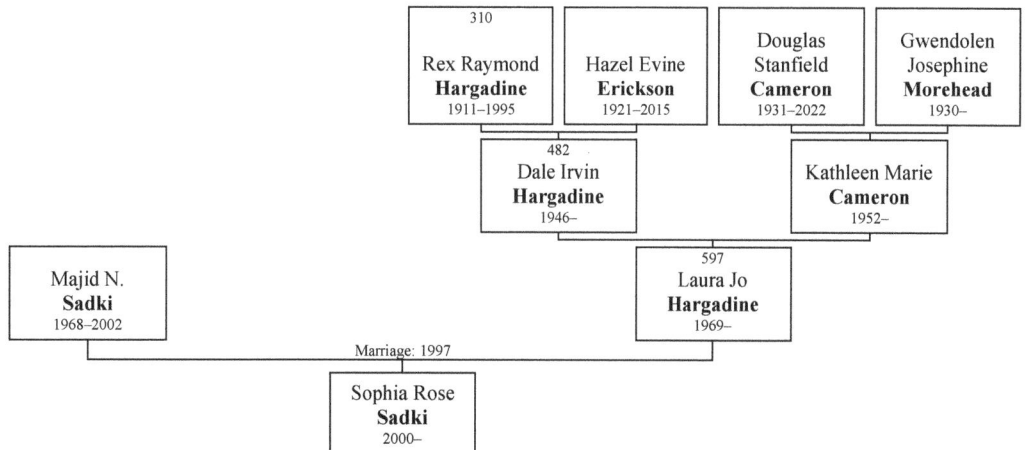

```
                              ┌──────────────┐ ┌──────────────┐ ┌──────────────┐ ┌──────────────┐
                              │     310      │ │ Hazel Evine  │ │  Douglas     │ │ Gwendolen    │
                              │ Rex Raymond  │ │  Erickson    │ │  Stanfield   │ │ Josephine    │
                              │  Hargadine   │ │  1921–2015   │ │  Cameron     │ │ Morehead     │
                              │  1911–1995   │ │              │ │  1931–2022   │ │  1930–       │
                              └──────────────┘ └──────────────┘ └──────────────┘ └──────────────┘
                                     ┌──────────────┐              ┌──────────────┐
                                     │     482      │              │ Kathleen Marie│
                                     │ Dale Irvin   │              │  Cameron     │
                                     │  Hargadine   │              │  1952–       │
                                     │  1946–       │              │              │
                                     └──────────────┘              └──────────────┘
     ┌──────────────┐                        ┌──────────────┐
     │  Majid N.    │                        │     597      │
     │   Sadki      │                        │  Laura Jo    │
     │  1968–2002   │                        │  Hargadine   │
     │              │                        │  1969–       │
     └──────────────┘       Marriage: 1997   └──────────────┘
                     ┌──────────────┐
                     │ Sophia Rose  │
                     │    Sadki     │
                     │   2000–      │
                     └──────────────┘
```

597. **Laura Jo Hargadine** was born on Thursday, May 29, 1969, in Vancouver, Clark County, Washington. She is the daughter of Dale Irvin Hargadine (482) and Kathleen Marie Cameron. Dale Irvin Hargadine is her stepfather. She is also known as **Laura Jo Cameron**.

At the age of 27, Laura Jo married **Majid N. Sadki** on Friday, April 11, 1997, in Stevenson, Skamania County, Washington, when he was 28 years old. They had one daughter.

Majid N. was born on Friday, April 12, 1968.[509, 510] He reached 34 years of age and died on April 17, 2002.[510]

Daughter of Laura Jo Hargadine and Majid N. Sadki:

  f   I. **Sophia Rose Sadki** was born in Portland, Multnomah County, Oregon, on November 05, 2000.

Family of Jessica Hargadine and Gary Daubenspeck

598. **Jessica Diane Hargadine** was born on Saturday, December 16, 1972, in White Salmon, Klickitat County, Washington. She is the daughter of Dale Irvin Hargadine (482) and Kathleen Marie Cameron.

Jessica Diane married **Gary R. Daubenspeck** on Saturday, July 22, 1995, in Stevenson, Skamania County, Washington.[511] They were divorced in Skamania, Skamania County, Washington, on August 07, 2008.

509 Ancestry.com, Washington, U.S., Marriage Records, 1854-2013 (Provo, UT, USA, Ancestry.com Operations, Inc., 2012), Ancestry.com, Washington State Archives; Olympia, Washington; Washington Marriage Records, 1854-2013. Record for Majid Sadki. https://search.ancestry.co.uk/cgi-bin/sse.dll?db=2378&h=4740429&indiv=try.

510 Ancestry.com, U.S., Social Security Death Index, 1935-2014 (Provo, UT, USA, Ancestry.com Operations Inc, 2014), Ancestry.com, Social Security Administration; Washington D.C., USA; Social Security Death Index, Master File. Record for Majid N. Sadki. https://search.ancestry.co.uk/cgi-bin/sse.dll?db=3693&h=54191643&indiv=try.

511 State of Washington Divorce Index, Both filed. Divorced August 7, 2008.

Family of Leaha Hargadine and Carl Medearis

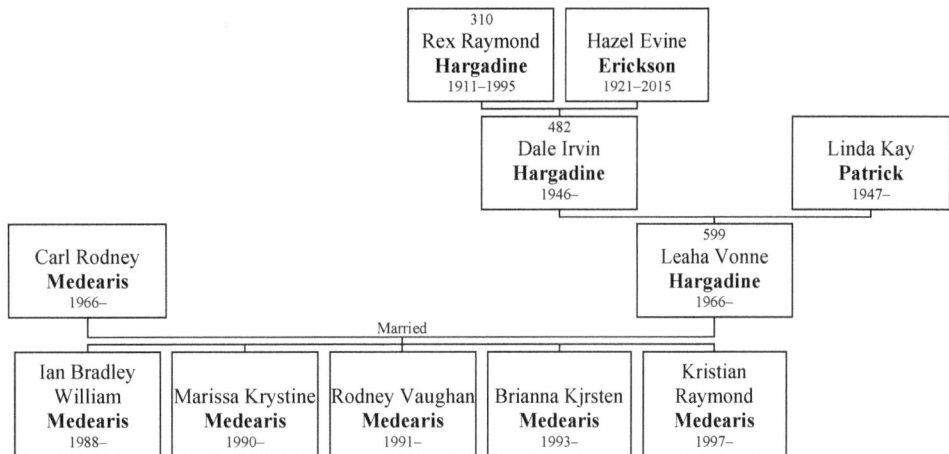

```
                              ┌──────────────┬──────────────┐
                              │     310      │  Hazel Evine │
                              │  Rex Raymond │   Erickson   │
                              │  Hargadine   │   1921–2015  │
                              │   1911–1995  │              │
                              └──────────────┴──────────────┘
                                      │
                              ┌──────────────┐           ┌──────────────┐
                              │     482      │           │  Linda Kay   │
                              │  Dale Irvin  │           │   Patrick    │
                              │  Hargadine   │           │    1947–     │
                              │    1946–     │           │              │
                              └──────────────┘           └──────────────┘
                                          │                    │
┌──────────────┐                    ┌──────────────┐
│ Carl Rodney  │                    │     599      │
│   Medearis   │                    │  Leaha Vonne │
│    1966–     │                    │  Hargadine   │
│              │     Married        │    1966–     │
└──────────────┘                    └──────────────┘
   │
┌───────────┬─────────────┬─────────────┬─────────────┬─────────────┐
│Ian Bradley│  Marissa    │  Rodney     │  Brianna    │  Kristian   │
│  William  │  Krystine   │  Vaughan    │  Kjrsten    │  Raymond    │
│  Medearis │  Medearis   │  Medearis   │  Medearis   │  Medearis   │
│   1988–   │   1990–     │   1991–     │   1993–     │   1997–     │
└───────────┴─────────────┴─────────────┴─────────────┴─────────────┘
```

599. **Leaha Vonne Hargadine** was born on Sunday, October 30, 1966, in Iowa City, Johnson County, Iowa. She is the daughter of Dale Irvin Hargadine (482) and Linda Kay Patrick. Leaha Vonne was adopted. Name changed to Isaacson prior to marriage.

She married **Carl Rodney Medearis**. They have five children.

Carl Rodney was born in Hood River, Hood River County, Oregon, on Saturday, June 11, 1966.

Children of Leaha Vonne Hargadine and Carl Rodney Medearis:

m   I. **Ian Bradley William Medearis** was born in Rexburg, Madison County, Idaho, on October 26, 1988.

f   II. **Marissa Krystine Medearis** was born in Oakland, Alameda County, California, on May 02, 1990.

m   III. **Rodney Vaughan Medearis** was born in Oakland, Alameda County, California, on October 05, 1991.

f   IV. **Brianna Kjrsten Medearis** was born in Rexburg, Madison County, Idaho, on November 21, 1993.

f   V. **Kristian Raymond Medearis** was born in Beaufort, Beaufort County, South Carolina, on November 03, 1997.

Family of Veronica Dolan and Michael Sharpe

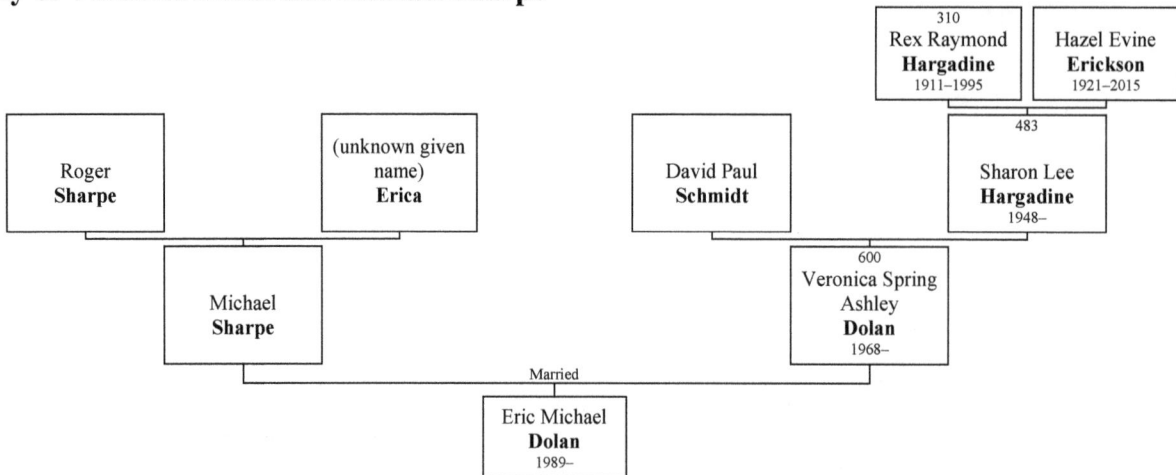

```
                                                        ┌──────────┬──────────┐
                                                        │   310    │          │
                                                        │   Rex Raymond │ Hazel Evine │
                                                        │  Hargadine   │  Erickson   │
                                                        │  1911–1995   │  1921–2015  │
                                                        └──────────┴──────────┘
                                                              │   483    │
┌─────────┬──────────────┐      ┌────────────┬──────────────┐
│ Roger   │ (unknown given│      │ David Paul │ Sharon Lee   │
│ Sharpe  │ name) Erica   │      │ Schmidt    │ Hargadine    │
└─────────┴──────────────┘      └────────────┴──────────────┘ 1948–
         │                                   │
    ┌─────────┐                        ┌──────────────┐
    │ Michael │                        │ 600          │
    │ Sharpe  │                        │Veronica Spring│
    └─────────┘                        │Ashley Dolan  │
              │         Married         │  1968–       │
                   ┌──────────────┐
                   │ Eric Michael │
                   │    Dolan     │
                   │    1989–     │
                   └──────────────┘
```

600.   Veronica Spring Ashley Dolan was born on Wednesday, August 21, 1968, in White Salmon, Klickitat County, Washington. She is the daughter of David Paul Schmidt and Sharon Lee Hargadine (483). David Paul Schmidt is her stepfather.

She married **Michael Sharpe**. They have one son. He is the son of Roger Sharpe and (unknown given name) Erica.

Son of Veronica Spring Ashley Dolan and Michael Sharpe:

m   I. **Eric Michael Dolan** was born in Tacoma, Pierce County, Washington, on March 04, 1989.

Family of Scott Boyens and Mary Cortez

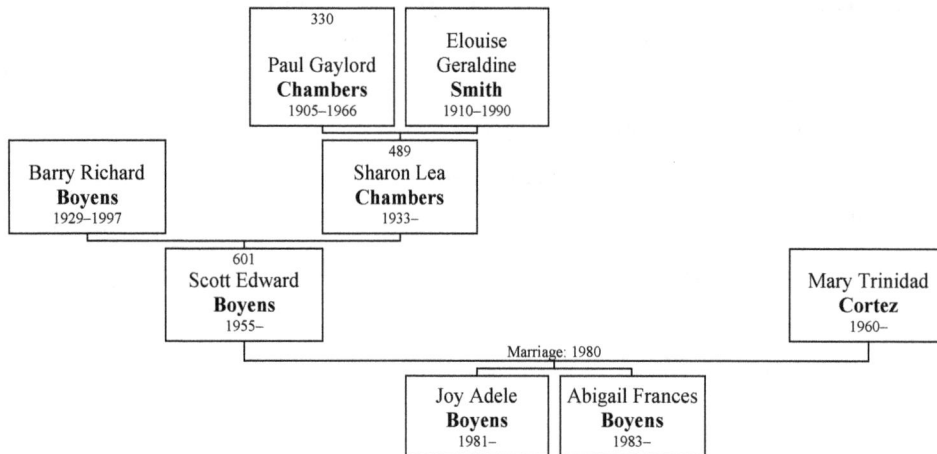

```
                     ┌──────────┬──────────┐
                     │   330    │ Elouise  │
                     │Paul Gaylord│Geraldine│
                     │ Chambers │  Smith   │
                     │1905–1966 │1910–1990 │
                     └──────────┴──────────┘
┌────────────┐            │  489  │
│Barry Richard│     ┌──────────────┐
│  Boyens    │     │ Sharon Lea   │
│ 1929–1997  │     │ Chambers 1933–│
└────────────┘     └──────────────┘
         │   601                         ┌──────────────┐
    ┌─────────────┐                      │Mary Trinidad │
    │Scott Edward │                      │   Cortez     │
    │  Boyens     │                      │   1960–      │
    │  1955–      │    Marriage: 1980    └──────────────┘
    └─────────────┘
         ┌──────────┬──────────┐
         │Joy Adele │Abigail Frances│
         │ Boyens   │  Boyens   │
         │ 1981–    │  1983–    │
         └──────────┴──────────┘
```

601.   Scott Edward Boyens was born on Thursday, November 03, 1955, in Harvey, Cook County, Illinois. He is the son of Barry Richard Boyens and Sharon Lea Chambers (489).

At the age of 24, Scott Edward married **Mary Trinidad Cortez** on Saturday, February 02, 1980, in Escondido, San Diego County, California, when she was 19 years old. They have two daughters.

Mary Trinidad was born in Escondido, San Diego County, California, on Friday, May 27, 1960.

Daughters of Scott Edward Boyens and Mary Trinidad Cortez:

> f   I. **Joy Adele Boyens** was born in Escondido, San Diego County, California, on February 25, 1981.

> f   II. **Abigail Frances Boyens** was born in Escondido, San Diego County, California, on June 08, 1983.

Valerie Boyens

602.   **Valerie Jean Boyens** was born on Tuesday, February 26, 1957, in Harvey, Cook County, Illinois. She is the daughter of Barry Richard Boyens and Sharon Lea Chambers (489).

Marriages with James Alan Smith and Gary Lee Helmts (Page 580) are known.

Family of Valerie Boyens and James Smith

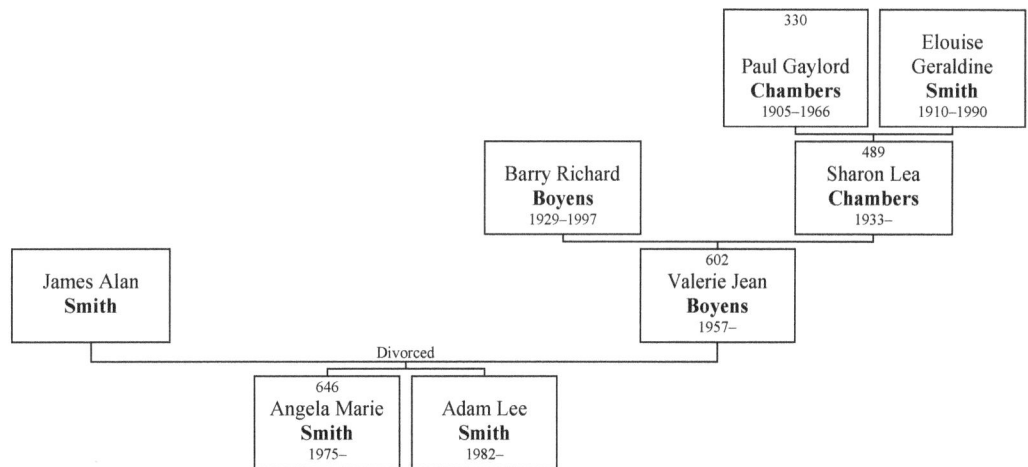

Here are the details about **Valerie Jean Boyens's** first marriage, with James Alan Smith. You can read more about Valerie Jean on page 579.

Valerie Jean Boyens married **James Alan Smith**. They are divorced. They have two children.

James Alan was born in California, USA.

Children of Valerie Jean Boyens and James Alan Smith:

> +   646   f   I. **Angela Marie Smith** was born in Escondido, San Diego County, California, on September 26, 1975. James Alan Smith is her stepfather. Her biological father is Gary Lee Helmts.

> m   II. **Adam Lee Smith** was born in Escondido, San Diego County, California, on January 20, 1982.

Family of Valerie Boyens and Gary Helmts

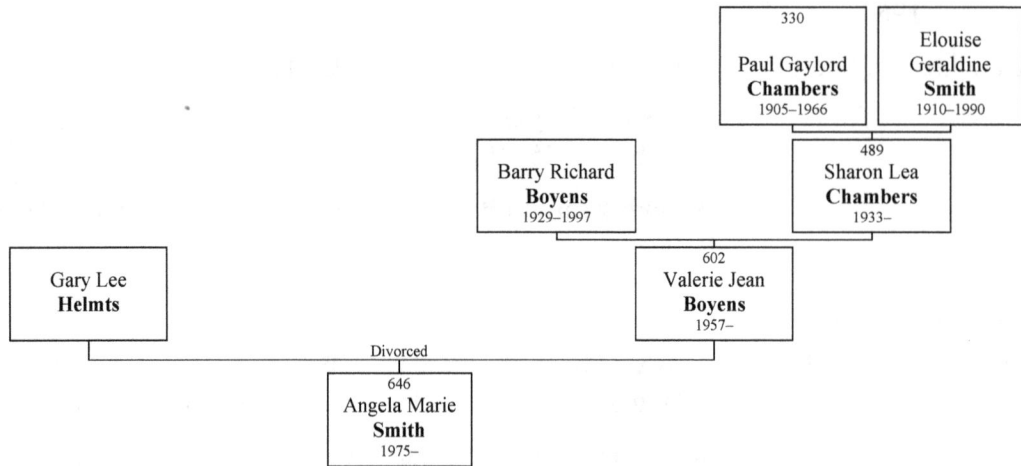

```
                                                    ┌──────────┬──────────┐
                                                    │   330    │ Elouise  │
                                                    │Paul Gaylord│Geraldine│
                                                    │ Chambers │  Smith   │
                                                    │1905–1966 │1910–1990 │
                                    ┌──────────┐    └──────────┴──────────┘
                                    │  Barry Richard │      489
                                    │   Boyens  │   Sharon Lea
                                    │ 1929–1997 │    Chambers
                                    └──────────┘      1933–
                    ┌──────────┐          602
                    │ Gary Lee │      Valerie Jean
                    │  Helmts  │        Boyens
                    │          │         1957–
                    └──────────┘
                              Divorced
                        ┌──────────┐
                        │   646    │
                        │Angela Marie│
                        │  Smith   │
                        │  1975–   │
                        └──────────┘
```

Here are the details about **Valerie Jean Boyens's** second marriage, with Gary Lee Helmts. You can read more about Valerie Jean on page 579.

Valerie Jean Boyens married **Gary Lee Helmts**. They later divorced. They had one daughter.

Gary Lee was born in Wisconsin, USA.

Daughter of Valerie Jean Boyens and Gary Lee Helmts:

+ 646   f   I. **Angela Marie Smith** was born in Escondido, San Diego County, California, on September 26, 1975.

Family of Andrea Boyens and Donald Milks

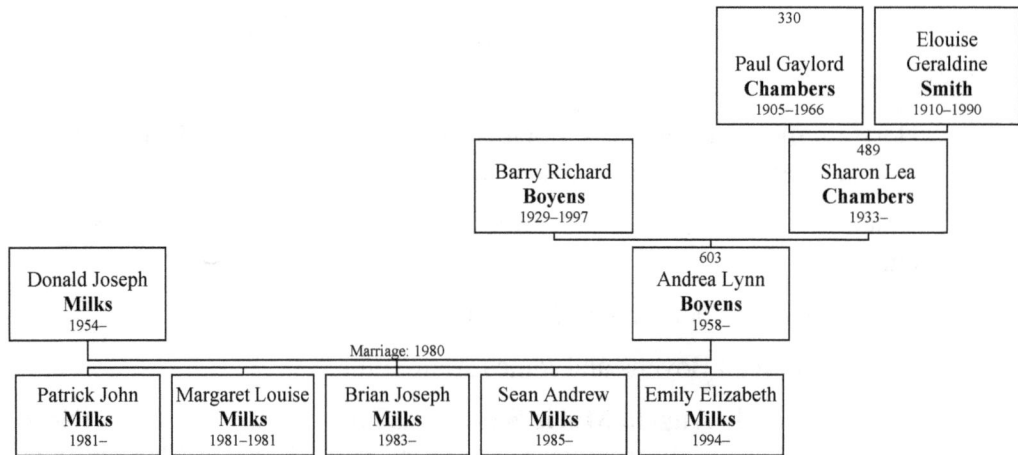

```
                                                    ┌──────────┬──────────┐
                                                    │   330    │ Elouise  │
                                                    │Paul Gaylord│Geraldine│
                                                    │ Chambers │  Smith   │
                                                    │1905–1966 │1910–1990 │
                                    ┌──────────┐    └──────────┴──────────┘
                                    │  Barry Richard │      489
                                    │   Boyens  │   Sharon Lea
                                    │ 1929–1997 │    Chambers
                                    └──────────┘      1933–
                    ┌──────────┐          603
                    │Donald Joseph│   Andrea Lynn
                    │  Milks   │        Boyens
                    │  1954–   │         1958–
                    └──────────┘
                              Marriage: 1980
  ┌──────────┬──────────┬──────────┬──────────┬──────────┐
  │Patrick John│Margaret Louise│Brian Joseph│Sean Andrew│Emily Elizabeth│
  │  Milks   │  Milks   │  Milks   │  Milks   │  Milks   │
  │  1981–   │1981–1981 │  1983–   │  1985–   │  1994–   │
  └──────────┴──────────┴──────────┴──────────┴──────────┘
```

603.   **Andrea Lynn Boyens** was born on Wednesday, February 05, 1958, in Harvey, Cook County, Illinois. She is the daughter of Barry Richard Boyens and Sharon Lea Chambers (489).

At the age of 22, Andrea Lynn married **Donald Joseph Milks** on Saturday, June 28, 1980, in Las Vegas, Clark County, Nevada, when he was 25 years old. They had five children.

Donald Joseph was born in Whittier, Los Angeles County, California, on Thursday, July 15, 1954.

Children of Andrea Lynn Boyens and Donald Joseph Milks:

m I. **Patrick John Milks** was born in Escondido, San Diego County, California, on January 06, 1981.

f II. **Margaret Louise Milks** was born in Escondido, San Diego County, California, on November 29, 1981. She died in Escondido, San Diego County, California, on November 29, 1981. Margaret Louise was buried in Oak Hill Cemetery, Escondido, San Diego County, California.

m III. **Brian Joseph Milks** was born in Escondido, San Diego County, California, on August 07, 1983.

m IV. **Sean Andrew Milks** was born in Escondido, San Diego County, California, on June 06, 1985.

f V. **Emily Elizabeth Milks** was born in Escondido, San Diego County, California, on May 07, 1994.

Family of Craig Boyens and Lisa Perez

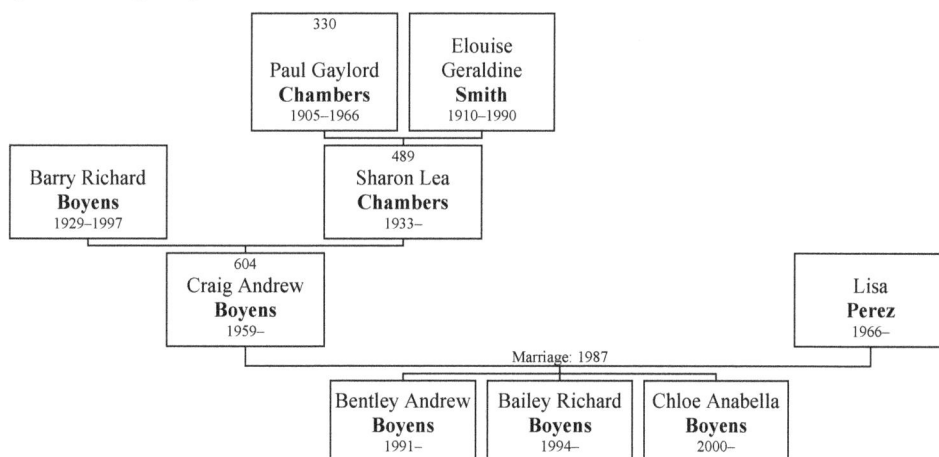

604. **Craig Andrew Boyens** was born on Tuesday, September 01, 1959, in Harvey, Cook County, Illinois. He is the son of Barry Richard Boyens and Sharon Lea Chambers (489).

At the age of 27, Craig Andrew married **Lisa Perez** on Saturday, January 03, 1987, in Las Vegas, Clark County, Nevada, when she was 20 years old. They have three children.

Lisa was born in San Pedro, Los Angeles County, California, on Monday, March 14, 1966.

Children of Craig Andrew Boyens and Lisa Perez:

m I. **Bentley Andrew Boyens** was born in Vista, San Diego County, California, on May 13, 1991.

m II. **Bailey Richard Boyens** was born in Victorville, San Bernardino County, California, on December 29, 1994.

f III. **Chloe Anabella Boyens** was born in Escondido, San Diego County, California, on July 16, 2000.

Jasen Boyens

605. **Jasen Charles Boyens** was born on Thursday, November 30, 1961, in Peoria, Peoria County, Illinois. He is the son of Barry Richard Boyens and Sharon Lea Chambers (489).

Relationships with Mindy Ann Crouch and Doreen Antoinette Alvarado (Page 583) are known.

Jasen Boyens and Mindy Crouch

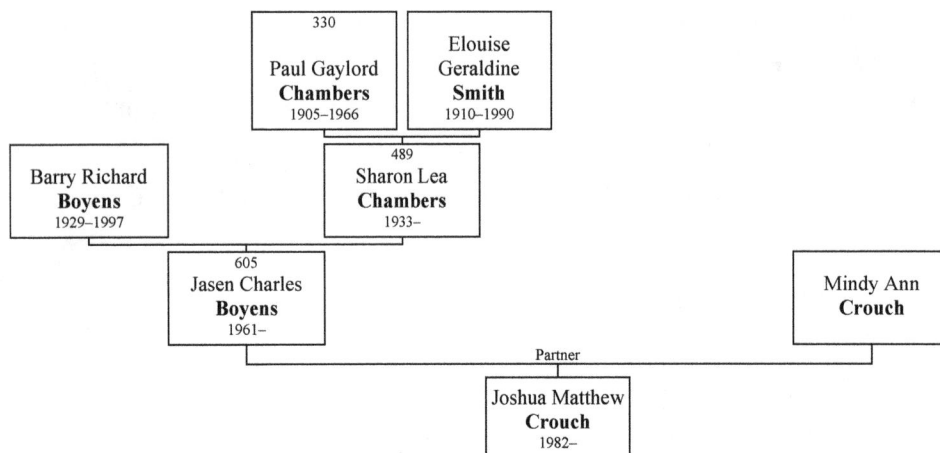

Here are the details about **Jasen Charles Boyens's** first relationship, with Mindy Ann Crouch. You can read more about Jasen Charles on page 582.

Jasen Charles Boyens is partnered with **Mindy Ann Crouch**. They have one son.

Son of Jasen Charles Boyens and Mindy Ann Crouch:

m I. **Joshua Matthew Crouch** was born in Escondido, San Diego County, California, on January 06, 1982.

Family of Jasen Boyens and Doreen Alvarado

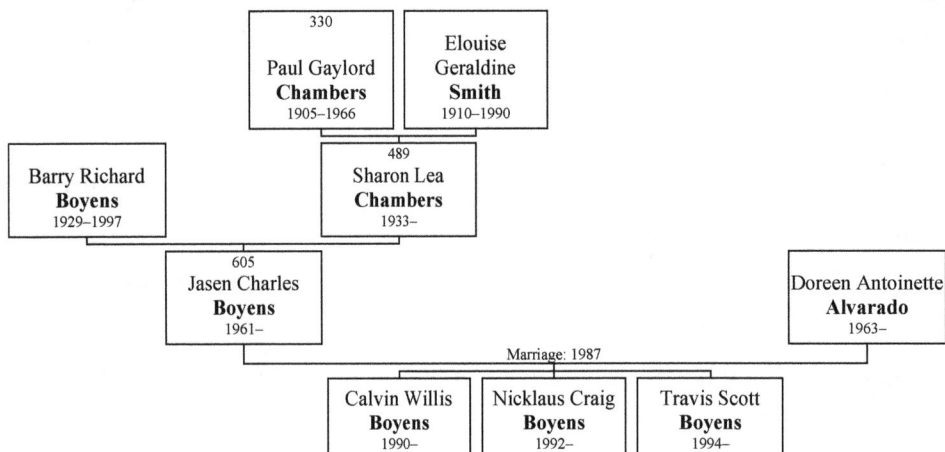

Here are the details about **Jasen Charles Boyens's** second relationship, with Doreen Antoinette Alvarado. You can read more about Jasen Charles on page 582.

At the age of 25, Jasen Charles Boyens married **Doreen Antoinette Alvarado** on Tuesday, February 03, 1987, in Vista, San Diego County, California, when she was 23 years old. They have three sons.

Doreen Antoinette was born in Escondido, San Diego County, California, on Thursday, December 26, 1963.

Sons of Jasen Charles Boyens and Doreen Antoinette Alvarado:

m   I. **Calvin Willis Boyens** was born in San Diego, San Diego County, California, on May 01, 1990. He is also known as **Calvin "Wil" Willis Boyens**.

m   II. **Nicklaus Craig Boyens** was born in San Diego, San Diego County, California, on September 15, 1992.

m   III. **Travis Scott Boyens** was born in San Diego, San Diego County, California, on December 28, 1994.

Family of Paula Boyens and Robert Gerchufsky

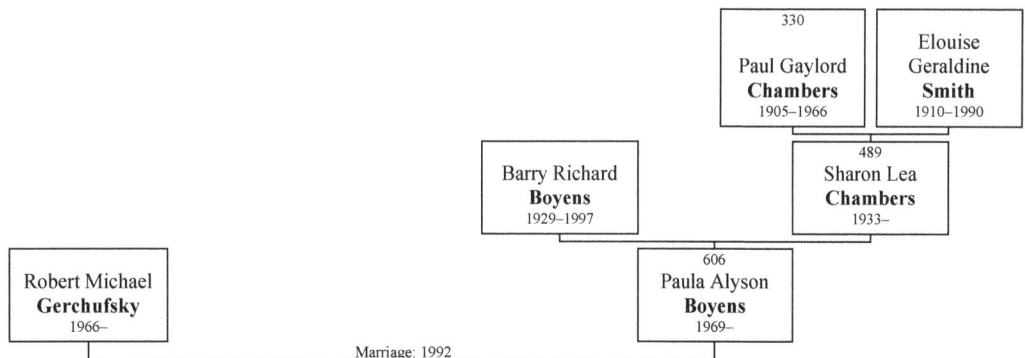

606.   **Paula Alyson Boyens** was born on Monday, September 22, 1969, in Harvey, Cook County, Illinois. She is the daughter of Barry Richard Boyens and Sharon Lea Chambers (489).

At the age of 22, Paula Alyson married **Robert Michael Gerchufsky** on Saturday, February 22, 1992, in Escondido, San Diego County, California, when he was 25 years old. Robert Michael was born in La Mesa, San Diego County, California, on Monday, August 22, 1966.

Family of Timothy Chambers and Dawn Ewing

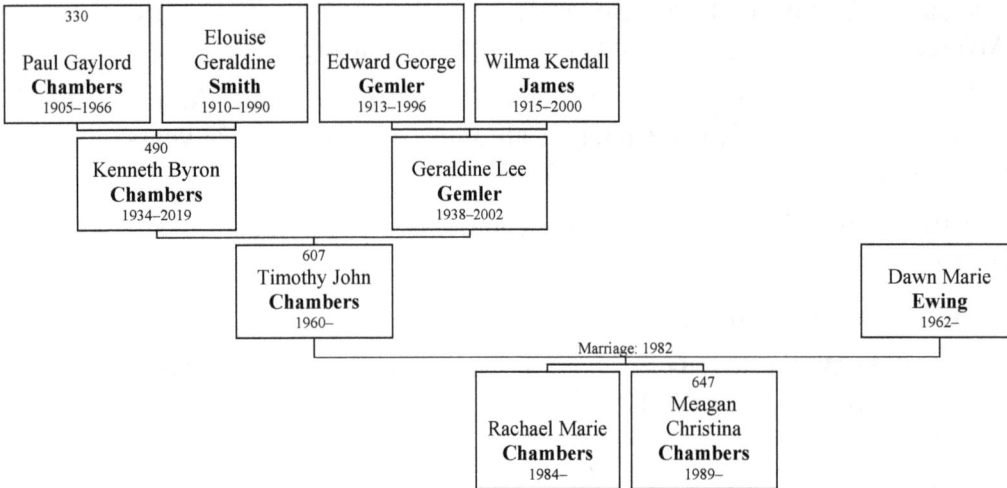

```
┌──────────┐ ┌──────────┐ ┌──────────┐ ┌──────────┐
│   330    │ │ Elouise  │ │  Edward  │ │  Wilma   │
│          │ │Geraldine │ │  George  │ │ Kendall  │
│Paul Gaylord│ │  Smith  │ │  Gemler  │ │  James   │
│ Chambers │ │1910–1990 │ │1913–1996 │ │1915–2000 │
│1905–1966 │ │          │ │          │ │          │
└──────────┘ └──────────┘ └──────────┘ └──────────┘
     ┌──────────┐         ┌──────────┐
     │   490    │         │Geraldine Lee│
     │Kenneth Byron│      │  Gemler  │
     │ Chambers │         │1938–2002 │
     │1934–2019 │         └──────────┘
     └──────────┘
          ┌──────────┐              ┌──────────┐
          │   607    │              │Dawn Marie│
          │Timothy John│            │  Ewing   │
          │ Chambers │              │  1962–   │
          │  1960–   │              └──────────┘
          └──────────┘
              Marriage: 1982
     ┌──────────┐ ┌──────────┐
     │Rachael Marie│ │   647   │
     │          │ │ Meagan   │
     │          │ │Christina │
     │ Chambers │ │ Chambers │
     │  1984–   │ │  1989–   │
     └──────────┘ └──────────┘
```

607.   **Timothy John Chambers** was born on Tuesday, March 01, 1960, in Harvey, Cook County, Illinois. He is the son of Kenneth Byron Chambers (490) and Geraldine Lee Gemler.

At the age of 22, Timothy John married **Dawn Marie Ewing** on Saturday, July 24, 1982, at St. Agnes Church in Chicago Heights, Cook County, Illinois, when she was 20 years old. They have two daughters.

Dawn Marie was born in Chicago, Cook County, Illinois, on Friday, June 29, 1962. [Chambers.GED]

Dawn and Tim were married at St. Agnes Church.. Chicago Heights, Illinois (Cook County) [Chambers.FTW]

Dawn and Tim were married at St. Agnes Church.. Chicago Heights, Illinois (Cook County)

Daughters of Timothy John Chambers and Dawn Marie Ewing:

      f   I. **Rachael Marie Chambers** was born in Hazel Crest, Cook County, Illinois, on March 25, 1984.

+ 647   f   II. **Meagan Christina Chambers** was born in Hazel Crest, Cook County, Illinois, on March 07, 1989.

Kevin Chambers

608.   **Kevin James Chambers** was born on Saturday, April 01, 1961, in Harvey, Cook County, Illinois. He is the son of Kenneth Byron Chambers (490) and Geraldine Lee Gemler.

Marriages with Lorraine Anne Grollemond and Sandra Lee Gawelczyk (Page 586) are known.

Family of Kevin Chambers and Lorraine Grollemond

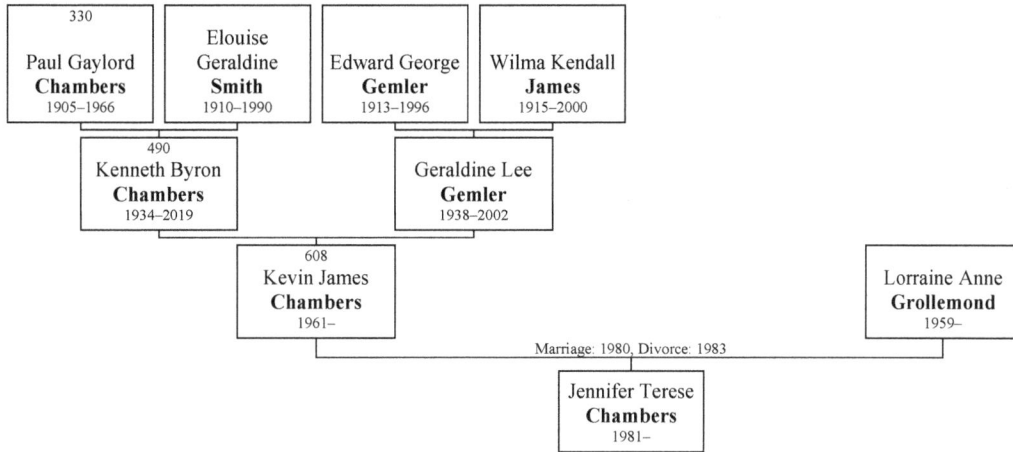

Here are the details about **Kevin James Chambers's** first marriage, with Lorraine Anne Grollemond. You can read more about Kevin James on page 584.

At the age of 19, Kevin James Chambers married **Lorraine Anne Grollemond** on Sunday, August 17, 1980, in Chicago Heights, Cook County, Illinois, when she was 20 years old. They were divorced in Steger, Cook County, Illinois, on September 11, 1983. They have one daughter.

Lorraine Anne was born on Tuesday, December 15, 1959.

Daughter of Kevin James Chambers and Lorraine Anne Grollemond:

  f   I. **Jennifer Terese Chambers** was born in Chicago Heights, Cook County, Illinois, on January 10, 1981.

Family of Kevin Chambers and Sandra Gawelczyk

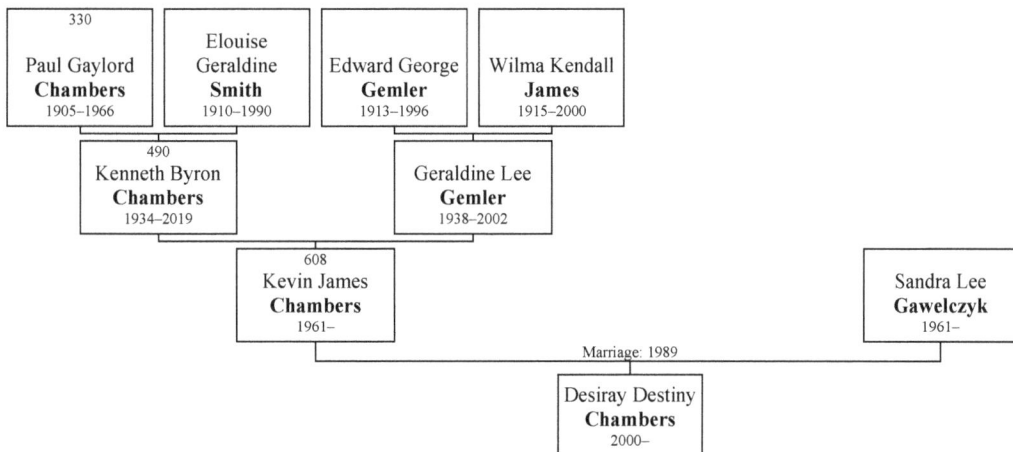

Here are the details about **Kevin James Chambers's** second marriage, with Sandra Lee Gawelczyk. You can read more about Kevin James on page 584.

At the age of 28, Kevin James Chambers married **Sandra Lee Gawelczyk** on Saturday, June 03, 1989, in Markham, Cook County, Illinois, when she was 28 years old. They have one daughter.

Sandra Lee was born in Chicago, Cook County, Illinois, on Monday, January 23, 1961.

Daughter of Kevin James Chambers and Sandra Lee Gawelczyk:

    f   I. **Desiray Destiny Chambers** was born in Hazel Crest, Cook County, Illinois, on January 17, 2000.

Family of Elizabeth Chambers and Anthony Mancuso

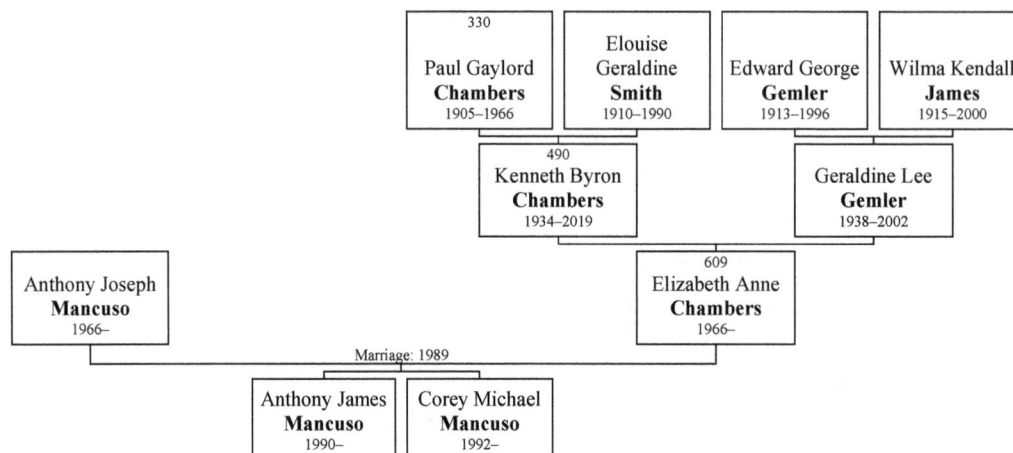

609. **Elizabeth Anne Chambers** was born on Thursday, January 06, 1966, in Harvey, Cook County, Illinois. She is the daughter of Kenneth Byron Chambers (490) and Geraldine Lee Gemler.

At the age of 23, Elizabeth Anne married **Anthony Joseph Mancuso** on Saturday, December 02, 1989, in Park Forest, Cook County, Illinois, when he was 23 years old. They have two sons.

Anthony Joseph was born in Blue Island, Cook County, Illinois, on Sunday, September 04, 1966.

Sons of Elizabeth Anne Chambers and Anthony Joseph Mancuso:

    m   I. **Anthony James Mancuso** was born in Hazel Crest, Cook County, Illinois, on November 11, 1990.

    m   II. **Corey Michael Mancuso** was born in Harvey, Cook County, Illinois, on March 23, 1992.

Family of Debra Chambers and Khori Dow

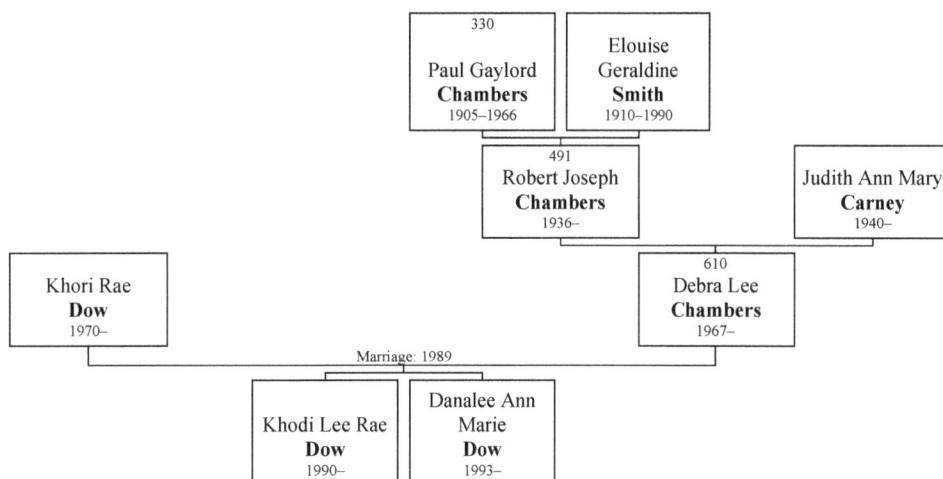

610. **Debra Lee Chambers** was born on Sunday, March 05, 1967, in Santa Monica, Los Angeles County, California. She is the daughter of Robert Joseph Chambers (491) and Judith Ann Mary Carney.

At the age of 22, Debra Lee married **Khori Rae Dow** on Sunday, October 15, 1989, in Elbe, Pierce County, Washington, when he was 19 years old. They have two children.

Khori Rae was born in Portland, Multnomah County, Oregon, on Tuesday, January 13, 1970.

Children of Debra Lee Chambers and Khori Rae Dow:

m   I.   **Khodi Lee Rae Dow** was born in Tacoma, Pierce County, Washington, on January 15, 1990.

f   II.   **Danalee Ann Marie Dow** was born in Centralia, Lewis County, Washington, on December 30, 1993.

Family of Jacquelyn Doyle and Steven Merlin

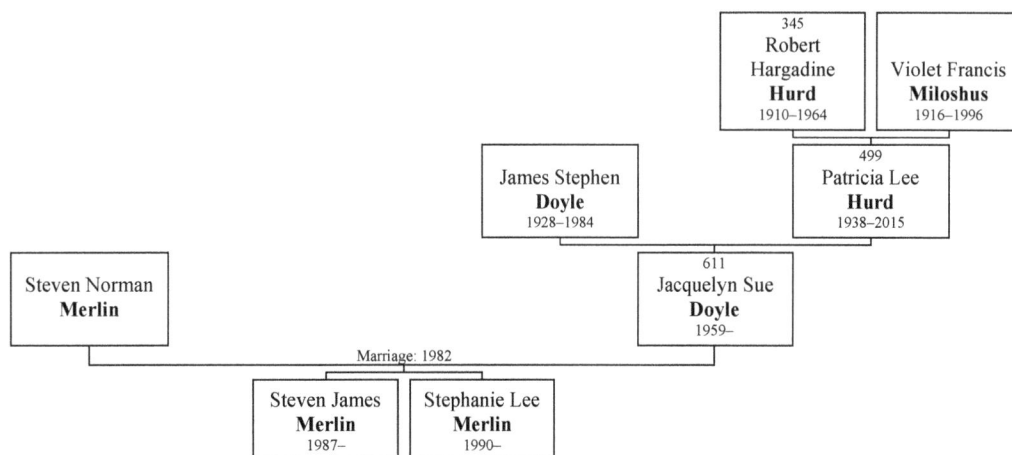

611. **Jacquelyn Sue Doyle** was born on Friday, July 31, 1959. She is the daughter of James Stephen Doyle and Patricia Lee Hurd (499). She is also known as **Jacki**.

Jacquelyn Sue married **Steven Norman Merlin** on Saturday, July 17, 1982. They have two children.

Children of Jacquelyn Sue Doyle and Steven Norman Merlin:

    m   I. **Steven James Merlin** was born on June 18, 1987.

    f   II. **Stephanie Lee Merlin** was born on February 04, 1990.

Therese Doyle

612. **Therese Lee Doyle** was born on Thursday, August 11, 1960. She is the daughter of James Stephen Doyle and Patricia Lee Hurd (499). She is also known as **Teri**.

Marriages with Steven John Macartney and Gregory Paul Duplessis (Page 589) are known.

Family of Therese Doyle and Steven Macartney

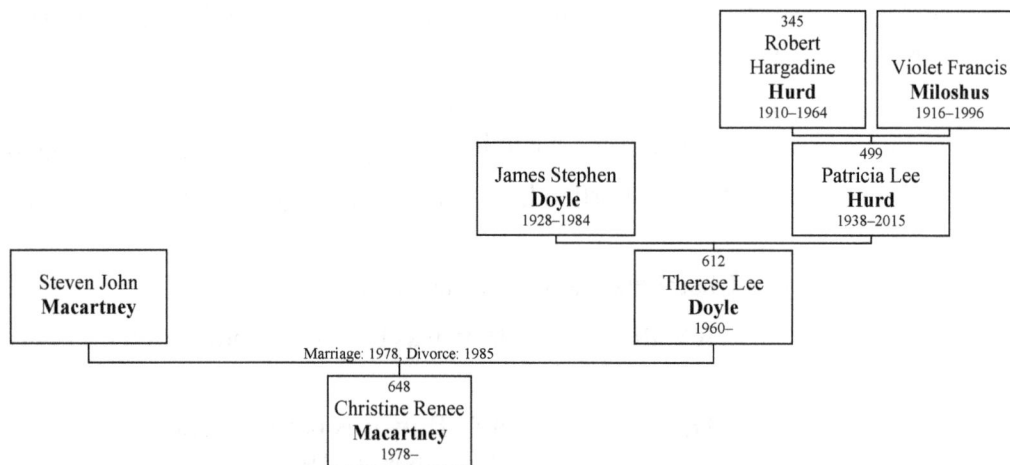

Here are the details about **Therese Lee Doyle's** first marriage, with Steven John Macartney. You can read more about Therese Lee on page 588.

Therese Lee Doyle married **Steven John Macartney** on Friday, May 26, 1978. They were divorced on September 19, 1985. They have one daughter.

Daughter of Therese Lee Doyle and Steven John Macartney:

+   648   f   I. **Christine Renee Macartney** was born on December 31, 1978.

Family of Therese Doyle and Gregory Duplessis

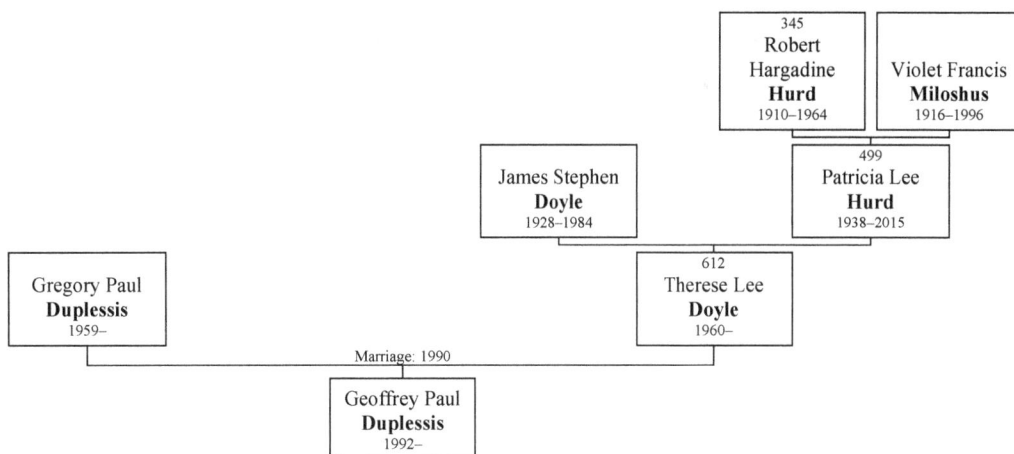

Here are the details about **Therese Lee Doyle's** second marriage, with Gregory Paul Duplessis. You can read more about Therese Lee on page 588.

Therese Lee Doyle married **Gregory Paul Duplessis** on Sunday, February 11, 1990, in Miami, Dade County, Florida. They have one son.

Gregory Paul was born in December 1959.

Son of Therese Lee Doyle and Gregory Paul Duplessis:

> m   I. **Geoffrey Paul Duplessis** was born on February 13, 1992.

Family of Nancy Doyle and Thomas Eden

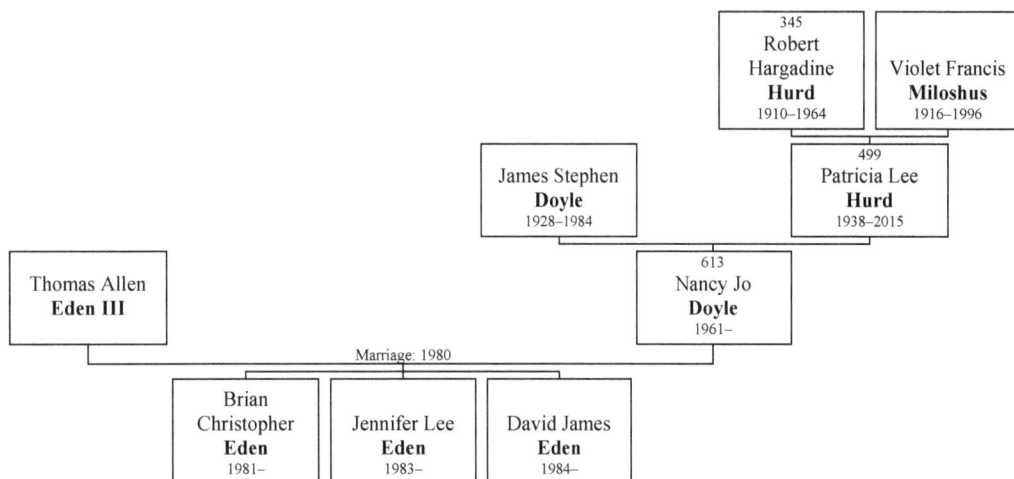

613.   **Nancy Jo Doyle** was born on Monday, October 09, 1961. She is the daughter of James Stephen Doyle and Patricia Lee Hurd (499).

Nancy Jo married **Thomas Allen Eden III** on Friday, May 30, 1980. They have three children.

Children of Nancy Jo Doyle and Thomas Allen Eden III:

> m   I. **Brian Christopher Eden** was born on October 08, 1981.

f   II. **Jennifer Lee Eden** was born on May 04, 1983.

f   III. **David James Eden** was born on November 01, 1984.

Family of Sharon Doyle and Edward Armesto

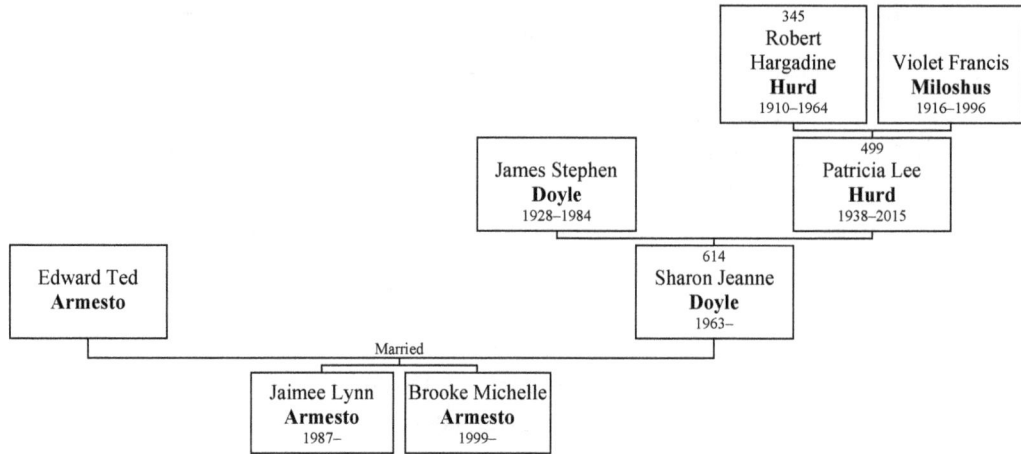

```
                                          ┌──────────┐
                                          │   345    │ ┌──────────┐
                                          │  Robert  │ │          │
                                          │ Hargadine│ │  Violet  │
                                          │   Hurd   │ │  Francis │
                                          │1910–1964 │ │ Miloshus │
                                          └──────────┘ │1916–1996 │
                           ┌──────────┐   ┌──────────┐ └──────────┘
                           │  James   │   │   499    │
                           │ Stephen  │   │ Patricia │
                           │  Doyle   │   │   Lee    │
                           │1928–1984 │   │   Hurd   │
                           └──────────┘   │1938–2015 │
                                          └──────────┘
                                    ┌──────────┐
              ┌──────────┐          │   614    │
              │ Edward   │          │  Sharon  │
              │   Ted    │          │  Jeanne  │
              │ Armesto  │          │  Doyle   │
              └──────────┘          │  1963–   │
                                    └──────────┘
                        Married
              ┌──────────┐┌──────────┐
              │ Jaimee   ││ Brooke   │
              │  Lynn    ││ Michelle │
              │ Armesto  ││ Armesto  │
              │  1987–   ││  1999–   │
              └──────────┘└──────────┘
```

614.   Sharon Jeanne Doyle was born on Thursday, August 01, 1963. She is the daughter of James Stephen Doyle and Patricia Lee Hurd (499).

She married **Edward Ted Armesto**. They have two daughters.

Daughters of Sharon Jeanne Doyle and Edward Ted Armesto:

f   I. **Jaimee Lynn Armesto** was born on May 03, 1987.

f   II. **Brooke Michelle Armesto** was born on October 10, 1999.

James Doyle

615.   James Francis Doyle was born on Friday, December 30, 1966. He is the son of James Stephen Doyle and Patricia Lee Hurd (499).

Marriages with Jody Annette McGee and Tracy Ann Prouty (Page 591) are known.

Family of James Doyle and Jody McGee

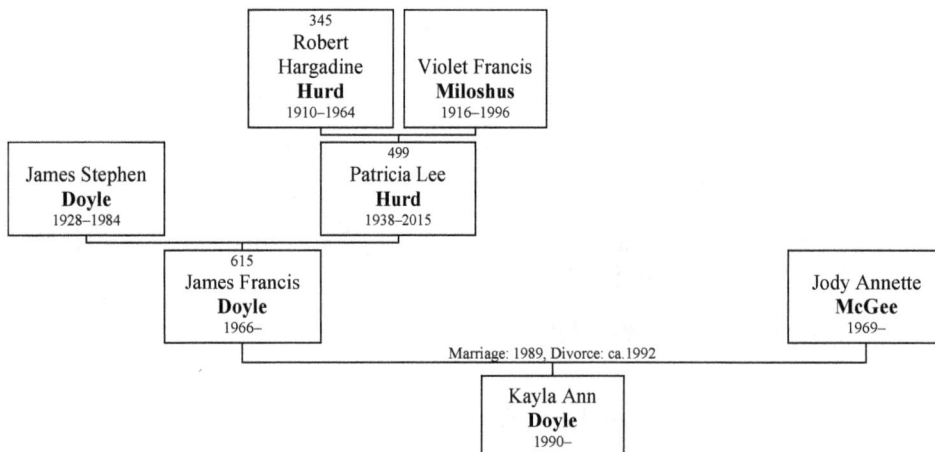

```
                        ┌──────────┐
                        │   345    │ ┌──────────┐
                        │  Robert  │ │  Violet  │
                        │ Hargadine│ │  Francis │
                        │   Hurd   │ │ Miloshus │
                        │1910–1964 │ │1916–1996 │
                        └──────────┘ └──────────┘
                        ┌──────────┐
        ┌──────────┐    │   499    │
        │  James   │    │ Patricia │
        │ Stephen  │    │   Lee    │
        │  Doyle   │    │   Hurd   │
        │1928–1984 │    │1938–2015 │
        └──────────┘    └──────────┘
              ┌──────────┐
              │   615    │              ┌──────────┐
              │  James   │              │   Jody   │
              │ Francis  │              │ Annette  │
              │  Doyle   │              │  McGee   │
              │  1966–   │              │  1969–   │
              └──────────┘              └──────────┘
               Marriage: 1989, Divorce: ca. 1992
                    ┌──────────┐
                    │  Kayla   │
                    │   Ann    │
                    │  Doyle   │
                    │  1990–   │
                    └──────────┘
```

Here are the details about **James Francis Doyle's** first marriage, with Jody Annette McGee. You can read more about James Francis on page 590.

At the age of 22, James Francis Doyle married **Jody Annette McGee** on Saturday, September 09, 1989, when she was 20 years old. They were divorced about 1992. They have one daughter.

Jody Annette was born on Monday, April 07, 1969.

Daughter of James Francis Doyle and Jody Annette McGee:

 f   I. **Kayla Ann Doyle** was born on June 25, 1990.

Family of James Doyle and Tracy Prouty

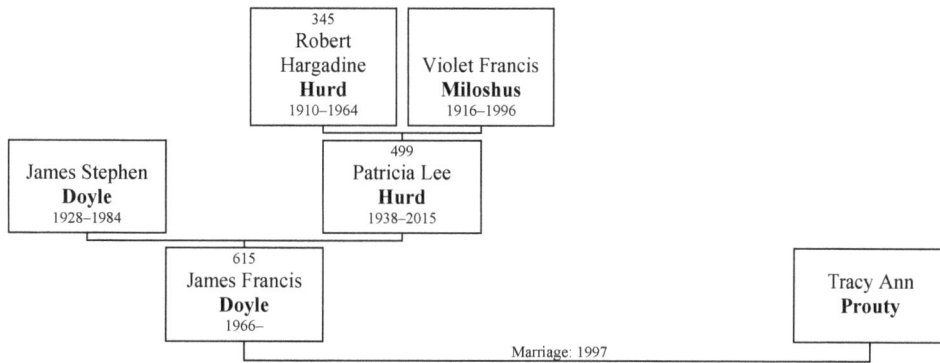

Here are the details about **James Francis Doyle's** second marriage, with Tracy Ann Prouty. You can read more about James Francis on page 590.

James Francis Doyle married **Tracy Ann Prouty** on Friday, December 26, 1997.

Family of Virginia Doyle and German Morales

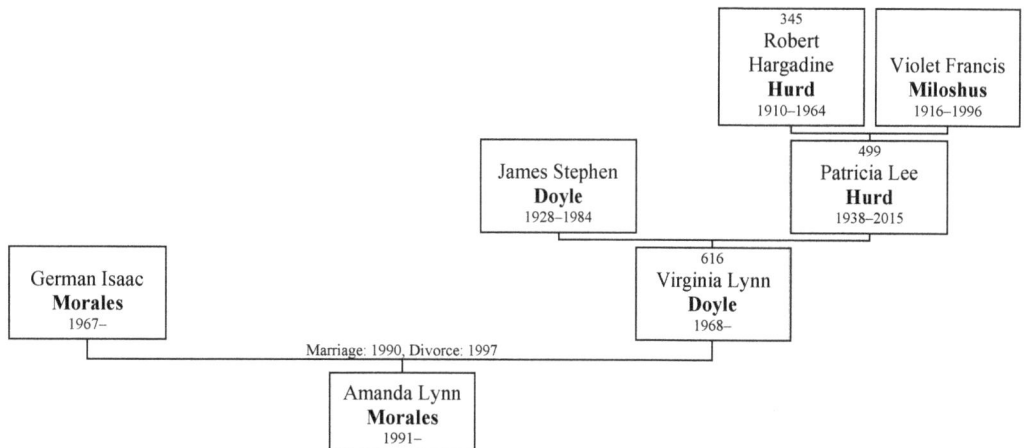

616. **Virginia Lynn Doyle** was born on Monday, June 03, 1968. She is the daughter of James Stephen Doyle and Patricia Lee Hurd (499).

At the age of 21, Virginia Lynn married **German Isaac Morales** on Saturday, May 19, 1990, when he was 22 years old. They were divorced on April 02, 1997. They have one daughter.

German Isaac was born on Sunday, December 31, 1967.

Daughter of Virginia Lynn Doyle and German Isaac Morales:

    f   I. **Amanda Lynn Morales** was born on September 29, 1991.

Donna Frederick

617.   **Donna Marie Frederick** was born on Monday, May 16, 1960. She was the daughter of Theodore A. Frederick and Patricia Millard Passwater (508).

Donna Marie died on January 29, 2005, at the age of 44. She was buried in Cathedral Cemetery, Wilmington, New Castle County, Delaware (Find a Grave ID 22909132).

Marriages with Bruce Shimp and John Edward Zielinski (Page 592) are known.

Family of Donna Frederick and Bruce Shimp

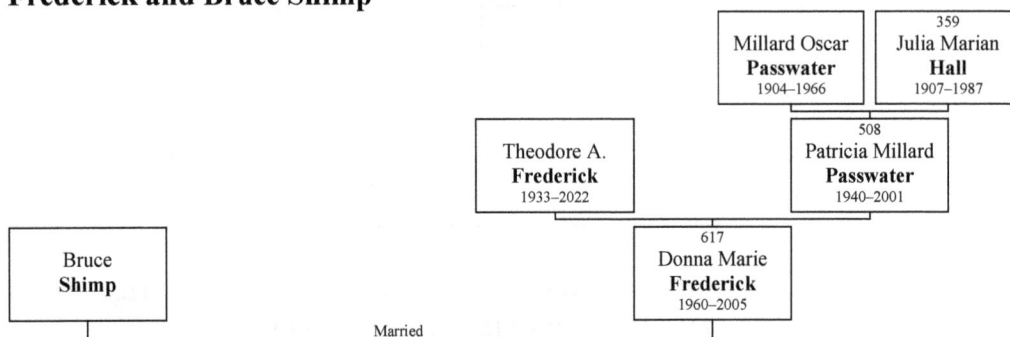

Here are the details about **Donna Marie Frederick's** first marriage, with Bruce Shimp. You can read more about Donna Marie on page 592.

Donna Marie Frederick married **Bruce Shimp**.

Family of Donna Frederick and John Zielinski

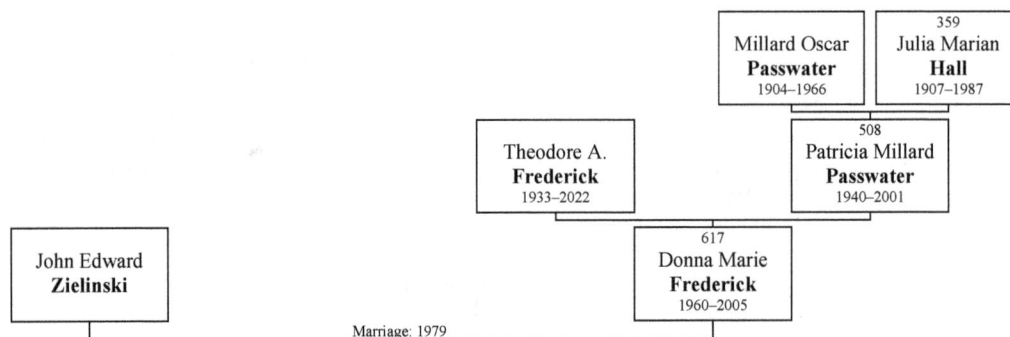

Here are the details about **Donna Marie Frederick's** second marriage, with John Edward Zielinski. You can read more about Donna Marie on page 592.

Donna Marie Frederick married **John Edward Zielinski** on Saturday, August 11, 1979.

Family of Kenneth Frederick and Niki Panos

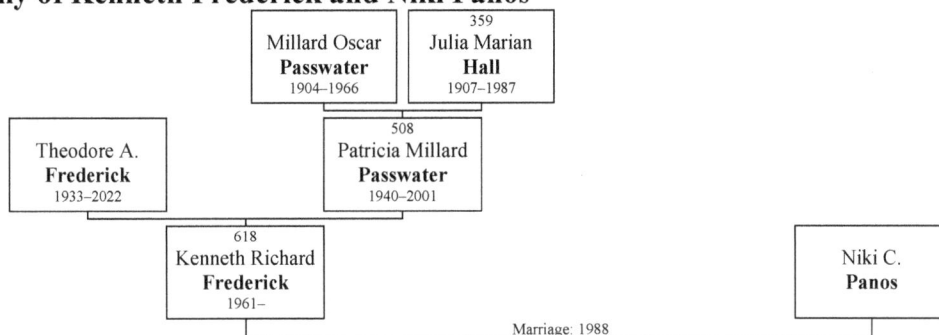

618. **Kenneth Richard Frederick** was born on Friday, June 09, 1961. He is the son of Theodore A. Frederick and Patricia Millard Passwater (508).

Kenneth Richard married **Niki C. Panos** on Saturday, May 14, 1988, at St. Hedwig's Catholic Church in Wilmington, New Castle County, Delaware.

Family of Daniel Frederick and Pauline Roberta

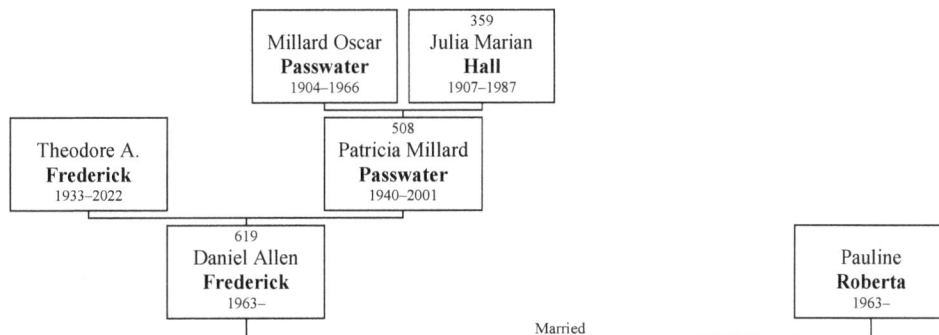

619. **Daniel Allen Frederick** was born on Friday, April 12, 1963. He is the son of Theodore A. Frederick and Patricia Millard Passwater (508).

He married **Pauline Roberta**. Pauline was born in September 1963.

Family of Roger Meekins and Ann McCurley

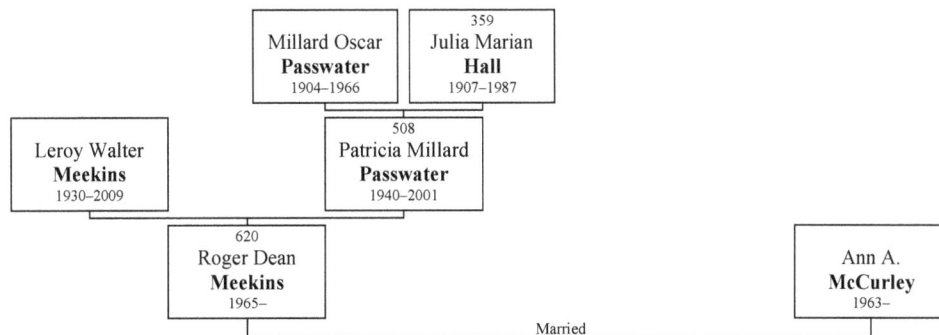

620. **Roger Dean Meekins** was born in December 1965. He is the son of Leroy Walter Meekins and Patricia Millard Passwater (508).

He married **Ann A. McCurley**. Ann A. was born on Thursday, March 07, 1963.

Family of Charles Meekins and Crystal Weddle

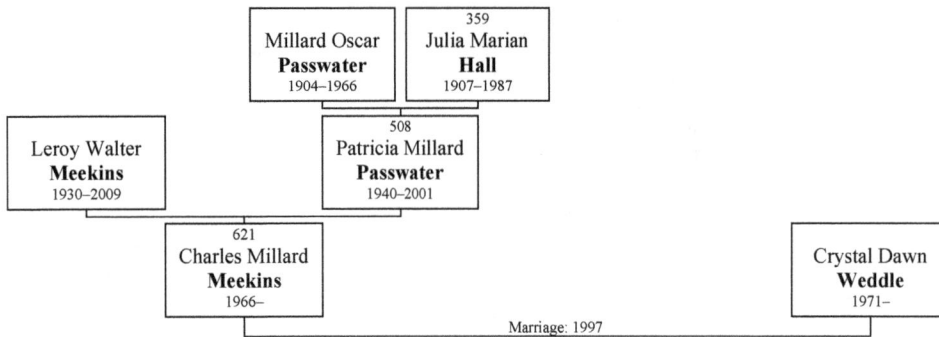

621. **Charles Millard Meekins** was born on Wednesday, November 30, 1966. He is the son of Leroy Walter Meekins and Patricia Millard Passwater (508).

Charles Millard married **Crystal Dawn Weddle** on Saturday, August 02, 1997, in Edinburgh, Johnson County, Indiana. Crystal Dawn was born in November 1971.

Family of Leigh Meekins and James Bodine

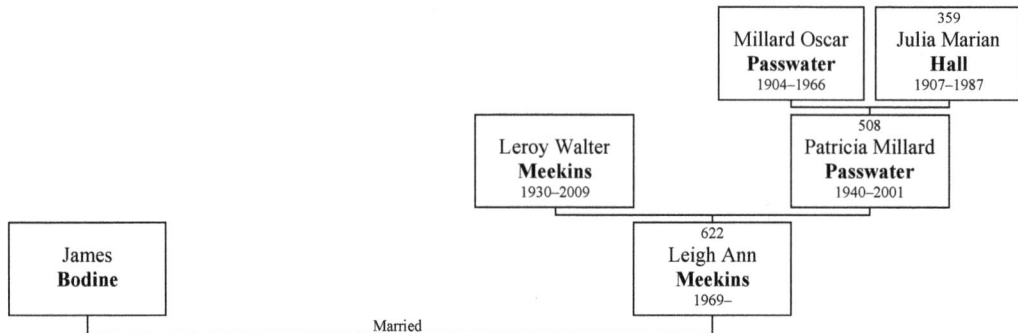

622. **Leigh Ann Meekins** was born on Thursday, July 10, 1969. She is the daughter of Leroy Walter Meekins and Patricia Millard Passwater (508).

She married **James Bodine**.

Michael Becker

623. **Michael Stephen Becker** was born on Saturday, May 08, 1965, in Independence, Jackson County, Missouri.[512] He is the son of Neil Stephen Becker (509) and Neta Rae Dull.

Marriages with Shelly A. Main and Denise Marie Sandoval (Page 596) are known.

---

512   Neil Becker.FTW, Date of Import: May 19, 2004.

Family of Michael Becker and Shelly Main

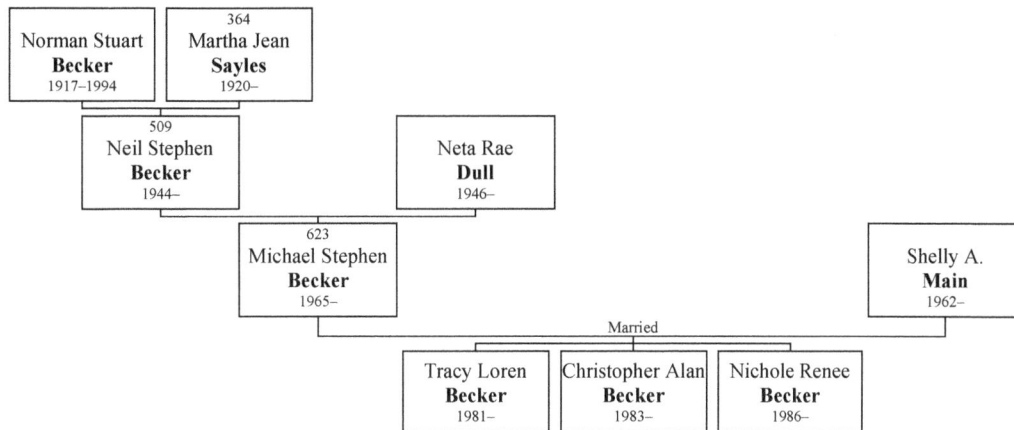

```
┌─────────────┐ ┌─────────────┐
│Norman Stuart│ │    364      │
│   Becker    │ │ Martha Jean │
│  1917–1994  │ │   Sayles    │
│             │ │   1920–     │
└─────────────┘ └─────────────┘
      ┌──────────────┐
      │     509      │      ┌─────────────┐
      │ Neil Stephen │      │  Neta Rae   │
      │   Becker     │      │    Dull     │
      │   1944–      │      │   1946–     │
      └──────────────┘      └─────────────┘
            ┌──────────────────┐
            │       623        │              ┌─────────────┐
            │ Michael Stephen  │              │  Shelly A.  │
            │     Becker       │              │    Main     │
            │     1965–        │              │   1962–     │
            └──────────────────┘              └─────────────┘
                        └─────── Married ──────┘
         ┌─────────────┐ ┌──────────────┐ ┌─────────────┐
         │Tracy Loren  │ │Christopher Alan│ │Nichole Renee│
         │   Becker    │ │    Becker    │ │   Becker    │
         │   1981–     │ │    1983–     │ │   1986–     │
         └─────────────┘ └──────────────┘ └─────────────┘
```

Here are the details about **Michael Stephen Becker's** first marriage, with Shelly A. Main. You can read more about Michael Stephen on page 594.

Michael Stephen Becker married **Shelly A. Main** in Reno, Washoe County, Nevada.[512] They have three children.

Shelly A. was born on Saturday, February 17, 1962.[512]

Children of Michael Stephen Becker and Shelly A. Main:

m   I. **Tracy Loren Becker** was born in Rifle, Garfield County, Colorado, on June 01, 1981.[512] Michael Stephen Becker is his adoptive father. He is also known as **Tracy Main**. Tracy Loren was adopted in Riley County, Kansas, on September 04, 1991.[512]

m   II. **Christopher Alan Becker** was born on January 30, 1983.[512] He is also known as **Speight**. Christopher Alan was adopted.[512] Unknown.

f   III. **Nichole Renee Becker** was born on July 17, 1986.[512]

Family of Michael Becker and Denise Sandoval

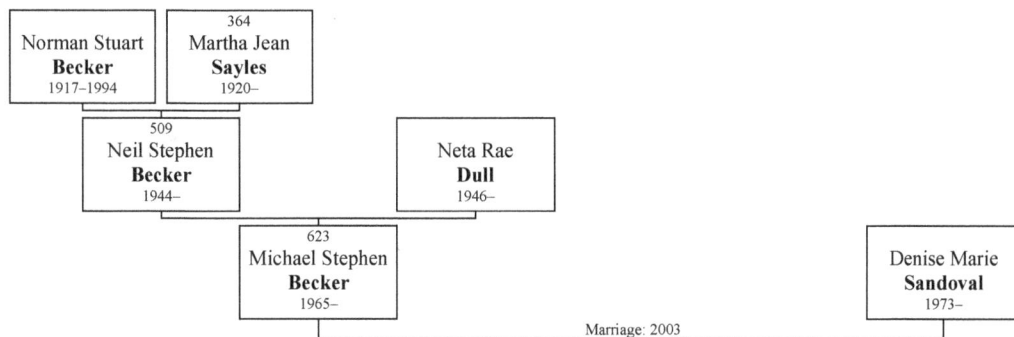

```
┌─────────────┐ ┌─────────────┐
│Norman Stuart│ │    364      │
│   Becker    │ │ Martha Jean │
│  1917–1994  │ │   Sayles    │
│             │ │   1920–     │
└─────────────┘ └─────────────┘
      ┌──────────────┐
      │     509      │      ┌─────────────┐
      │ Neil Stephen │      │  Neta Rae   │
      │   Becker     │      │    Dull     │
      │   1944–      │      │   1946–     │
      └──────────────┘      └─────────────┘
            ┌──────────────────┐
            │       623        │          ┌─────────────┐
            │ Michael Stephen  │          │Denise Marie │
            │     Becker       │          │  Sandoval   │
            │     1965–        │          │   1973–     │
            └──────────────────┘          └─────────────┘
                        └─── Marriage: 2003 ───┘
```

Here are the details about **Michael Stephen Becker's** second marriage, with Denise Marie Sandoval. You can read more about Michael Stephen on page 594.

At the age of 38, Michael Stephen Becker married **Denise Marie Sandoval** on Sunday, August 10, 2003, in Silver Spring, Lyon County, Nevada, when she was 30 years old.[512] Denise Marie was born on Thursday, April 05, 1973.[512]

Family of Christopher Becker and Amy Hoffman

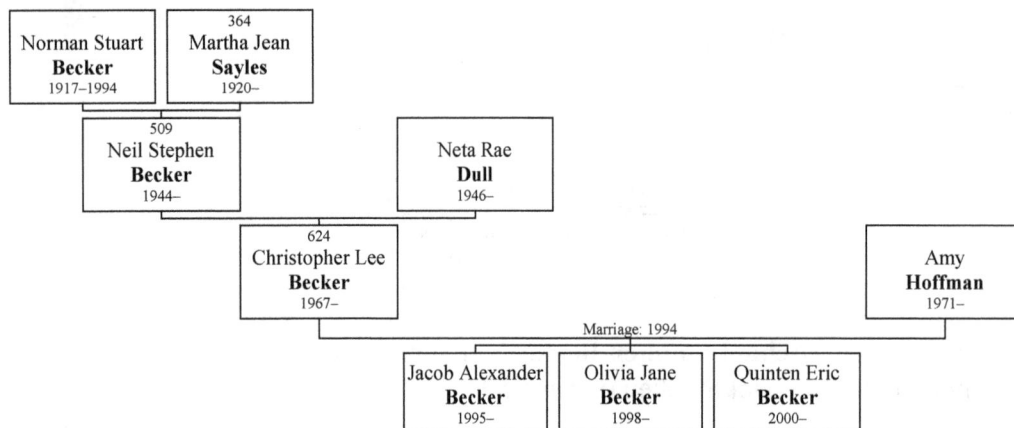

624. **Christopher Lee Becker** was born on Friday, October 13, 1967, in Independence, Jackson County, Missouri.[513] He is the son of Neil Stephen Becker (509) and Neta Rae Dull.

At the age of 26, Christopher Lee married **Amy Hoffman** on Saturday, September 24, 1994, in Kansas City, Missouri, when she was 23 years old.[513] They have three children.

Amy was born on Thursday, July 29, 1971.[513]

Children of Christopher Lee Becker and Amy Hoffman:

m   I. **Jacob Alexander Becker** was born on July 21, 1995.[513]

f   II. **Olivia Jane Becker** was born on May 18, 1998.[513]

m   III. **Quinten Eric Becker** was born on July 21, 2000.[513]

Family of Samuel Hargadine and Hillery Wheeler

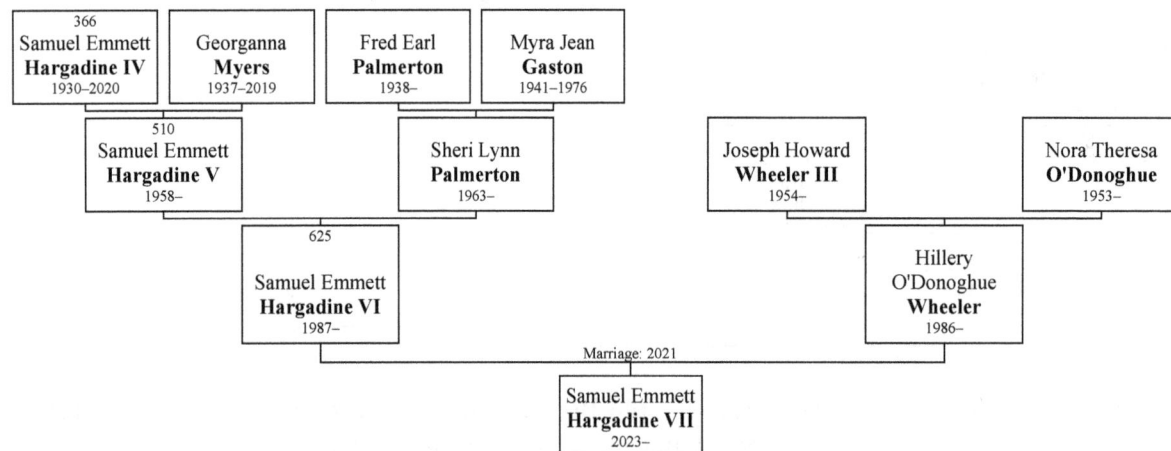

513   Neil Becker.FTW, Date of Import: May 19, 2004.

625. **Samuel Emmett Hargadine VI** was born on Thursday, July 23, 1987, at Boone Hospital Center in Columbia, Boone County, Missouri. He is the son of Samuel Emmett Hargadine V (510) and Sheri Lynn Palmerton. He is also known as **Sammy**.

At the age of 34, Samuel Emmett married **Hillery O'Donoghue Wheeler** on Saturday, July 31, 2021, at Civil Ceremony in Washington, District of Columbia, USA, when she was 35 years old. They have one son.

Hillery O'Donoghue was born in Hawaii, USA, on Saturday, June 28, 1986. She is the daughter of Joseph Howard Wheeler III and Nora Theresa O'Donoghue.

Son of Samuel Emmett Hargadine VI and Hillery O'Donoghue Wheeler:

m   I. **Samuel Emmett Hargadine VII** was born at George Washington University Hospital in Washington D.C. on December 16, 2023.

Family of Calvin Hargadine and Amber Beasley

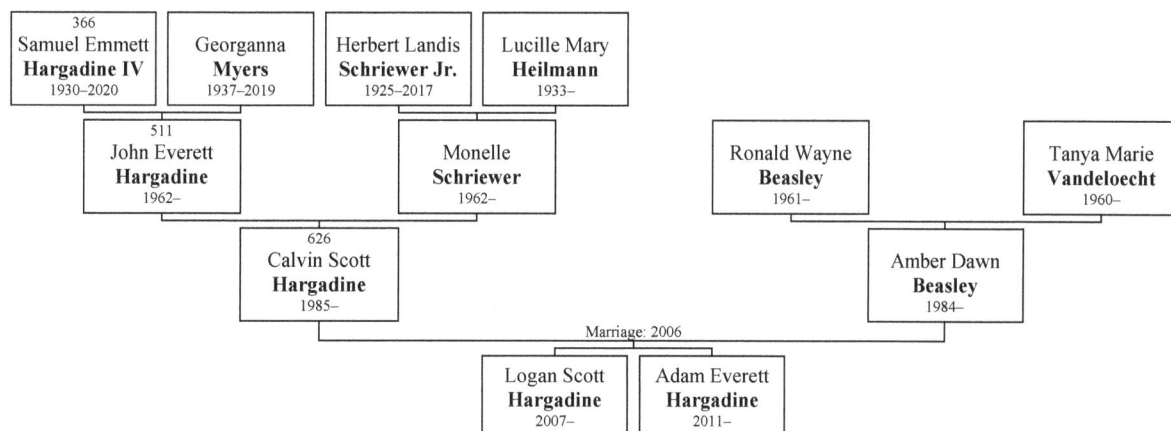

626. **Calvin Scott Hargadine** was born on Tuesday, October 22, 1985, in Sedalia, Pettis County, Missouri. He is the son of John Everett Hargadine (511) and Monelle Schriewer.

At the age of 20, Calvin Scott married **Amber Dawn Beasley** on Saturday, June 10, 2006, in Goose Creek, Berkeley County, South Carolina, when she was 21 years old. They have two sons.

Amber Dawn was born in Columbia, Boone County, Missouri, on Saturday, December 01, 1984.[514] She is the daughter of Ronald Wayne Beasley and Tanya Marie Vandeloecht.

Sons of Calvin Scott Hargadine and Amber Dawn Beasley:

m   I. **Logan Scott Hargadine** was born at Trident Hospital in North Charleston, Charleston County, South Carolina, on June 27, 2007.

m   II. **Adam Everett Hargadine** was born at Trident Hospital in North Charleston, Charleston County, South Carolina, on December 21, 2011.

---

514   Interview with Amber Hargadine.

Family of Mitchell Hargadine and Jenna McCracken

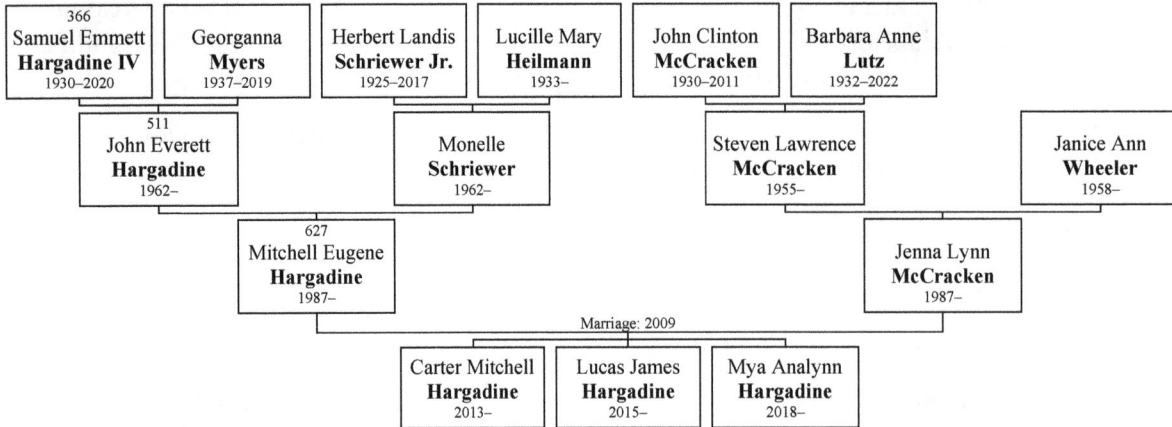

366 Samuel Emmett **Hargadine IV** 1930–2020	Georganna **Myers** 1937–2019	Herbert Landis **Schriewer Jr.** 1925–2017	Lucille Mary **Heilmann** 1933–	John Clinton **McCracken** 1930–2011	Barbara Anne **Lutz** 1932–2022

511 John Everett **Hargadine** 1962–	Monelle **Schriewer** 1962–	Steven Lawrence **McCracken** 1955–	Janice Ann **Wheeler** 1958–

627 Mitchell Eugene **Hargadine** 1987–

Jenna Lynn **McCracken** 1987–

Marriage: 2009

Carter Mitchell **Hargadine** 2013–	Lucas James **Hargadine** 2015–	Mya Analynn **Hargadine** 2018–

627. Mitchell Eugene Hargadine was born on Thursday, September 17, 1987, in Columbia, Boone County, Missouri. He is the son of John Everett Hargadine (511) and Monelle Schriewer.

At the age of 21, Mitchell Eugene married **Jenna Lynn McCracken** on Friday, May 22, 2009, in Saint Louis, Saint Louis County, Missouri, when she was 21 years old. They have three children.

Jenna Lynn was born in Fulton, Callaway County, Missouri, on Tuesday, September 01, 1987. She is the daughter of Steven Lawrence McCracken and Janice Ann Wheeler.

Children of Mitchell Eugene Hargadine and Jenna Lynn McCracken:

m   I. **Carter Mitchell Hargadine** was born in Concord, Cabarrus County, North Carolina, on April 24, 2013.

m   II. **Lucas James Hargadine** was born in Concord, Cabarrus County, North Carolina, on September 14, 2015.

f   III. **Mya Analynn Hargadine** was born in Concord, Cabarrus County, North Carolina, on September 12, 2018.

Family of Mary Hargadine and John Collins

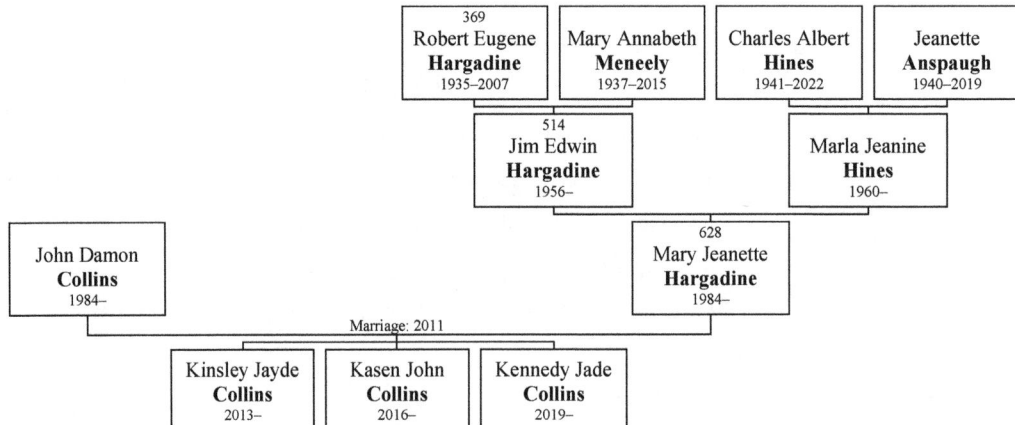

369 Robert Eugene **Hargadine** 1935–2007	Mary Annabeth **Meneely** 1937–2015	Charles Albert **Hines** 1941–2022	Jeanette **Anspaugh** 1940–2019

514 Jim Edwin **Hargadine** 1956–	Marla Jeanine **Hines** 1960–

628 Mary Jeanette **Hargadine** 1984–

John Damon **Collins** 1984–

Marriage: 2011

Kinsley Jayde **Collins** 2013–	Kasen John **Collins** 2016–	Kennedy Jade **Collins** 2019–

628. **Mary Jeanette Hargadine** was born on Wednesday, September 12, 1984, in Brookfield, Linn County, Missouri. She is the daughter of Jim Edwin Hargadine (514) and Marla Jeanine Hines.

More facts and events for Mary Jeanette Hargadine:

Individual Note: May 05, 2012   Central Methodist University
Masters in Education

At the age of 26, Mary Jeanette married **John Damon Collins** on Saturday, June 25, 2011, at Park Baptist Church in Brookfield, Linn County, Missouri, when he was 26 years old. They have three children.

John Damon was born in Brookfield, Linn County, Missouri, on Saturday, July 07, 1984.

Children of Mary Jeanette Hargadine and John Damon Collins:

    f   I. **Kinsley Jayde Collins** was born in Kirksville, Adair County, Missouri, on June 05, 2013.

    m   II. **Kasen John Collins** was born in Kirksville, Adair County, Missouri, on June 23, 2016.

    f   III. **Kennedy Jade Collins** was born in Kirksville, Adair County, Missouri, on August 06, 2019.

Family of Dustin Hargadine and Sara Comley

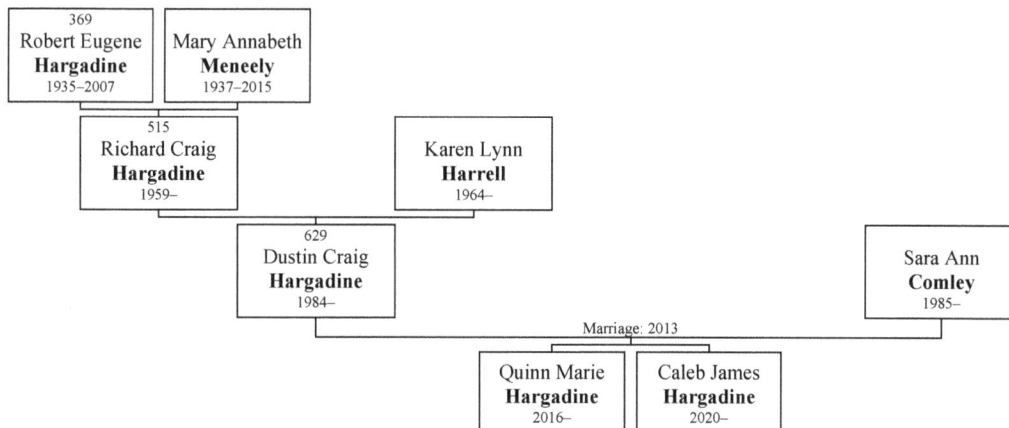

629. **Dustin Craig Hargadine** was born on Wednesday, October 10, 1984, in Chillicothe, Livingston County, Missouri. He is the son of Richard Craig Hargadine (515) and Karen Lynn Harrell.

At the age of 28, Dustin Craig married **Sara Ann Comley** on Saturday, April 13, 2013, when she was 27 years old. They have two children.

Sara Ann was born on Thursday, November 21, 1985.

Children of Dustin Craig Hargadine and Sara Ann Comley:

    f   I. **Quinn Marie Hargadine** was born at Missouri Baptist Medical Center in Saint Louis, Saint Louis County, Missouri, on April 12, 2016.

m   II. **Caleb James Hargadine** was born at Missouri Baptist Medical Center in Saint Louis, Saint Louis County, Missouri, on December 25, 2020.

Family of Heather Hargadine and Weston Lewis

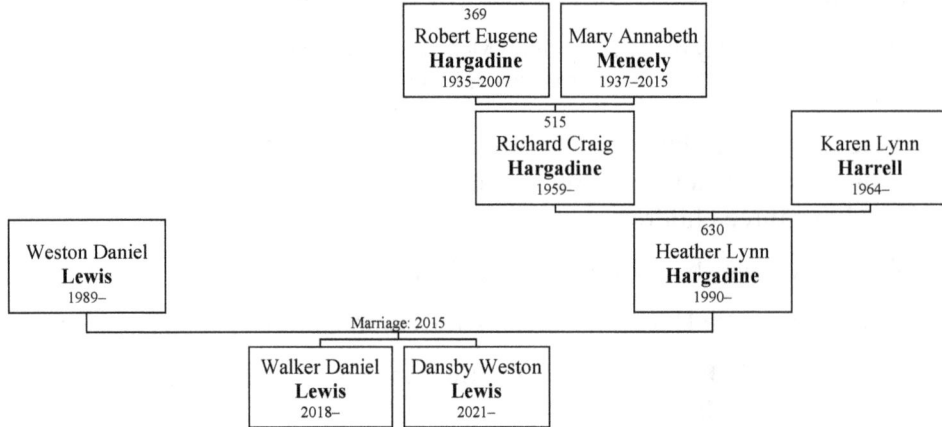

```
                                 ┌─────────────────┬─────────────────┐
                                 │      369        │                 │
                                 │ Robert Eugene   │ Mary Annabeth   │
                                 │   Hargadine     │    Meneely      │
                                 │   1935–2007     │   1937–2015     │
                                 └─────────────────┴─────────────────┘
                          ┌─────────────────┐          ┌─────────────────┐
                          │      515        │          │  Karen Lynn     │
                          │ Richard Craig   │          │   Harrell       │
                          │   Hargadine     │          │   1964–         │
                          │   1959–         │          └─────────────────┘
                          └─────────────────┘
                                              ┌─────────────────┐
  ┌─────────────────┐                         │      630        │
  │ Weston Daniel   │                         │ Heather Lynn    │
  │    Lewis        │                         │  Hargadine      │
  │   1989–         │                         │   1990–         │
  └─────────────────┘      Marriage: 2015     └─────────────────┘
              ┌─────────────────┬─────────────────┐
              │ Walker Daniel   │ Dansby Weston   │
              │    Lewis        │    Lewis        │
              │   2018–         │   2021–         │
              └─────────────────┴─────────────────┘
```

630.   **Heather Lynn Hargadine** was born on Tuesday, April 10, 1990, in Chillicothe, Livingston County, Missouri. She is the daughter of Richard Craig Hargadine (515) and Karen Lynn Harrell.

At the age of 25, Heather Lynn married **Weston Daniel Lewis** on Saturday, October 17, 2015, at United Methodist Church in Eureka, St. Louis County, Missouri, when he was 26 years old. They have two sons.

Weston Daniel was born on Thursday, July 27, 1989.

Sons of Heather Lynn Hargadine and Weston Daniel Lewis:

m   I. **Walker Daniel Lewis** was born in Saint Louis, Saint Louis County, Missouri, on July 06, 2018.

m   II. **Dansby Weston Lewis** was born in Saint Louis, Saint Louis County, Missouri, on March 26, 2021.

9th Generation

Family of Vickie Barker and Unknown Julien

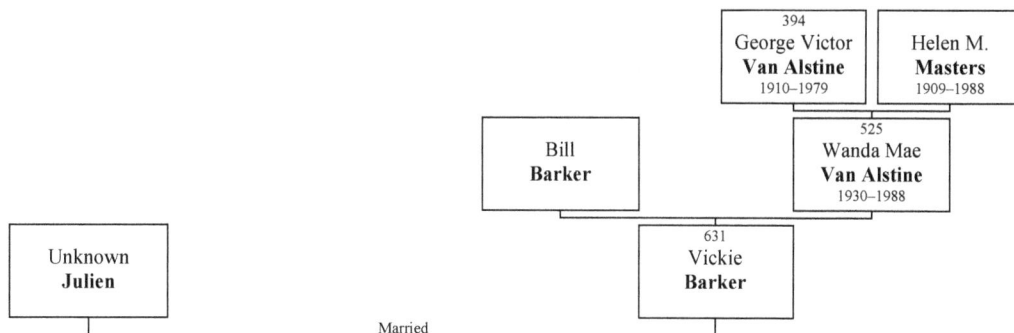

631.   **Vickie Barker.** She was the daughter of Bill Barker and Wanda Mae Van Alstine (525).

She married **Unknown Julien.**

Family of Lynn Hargadine and Jeremy Sims

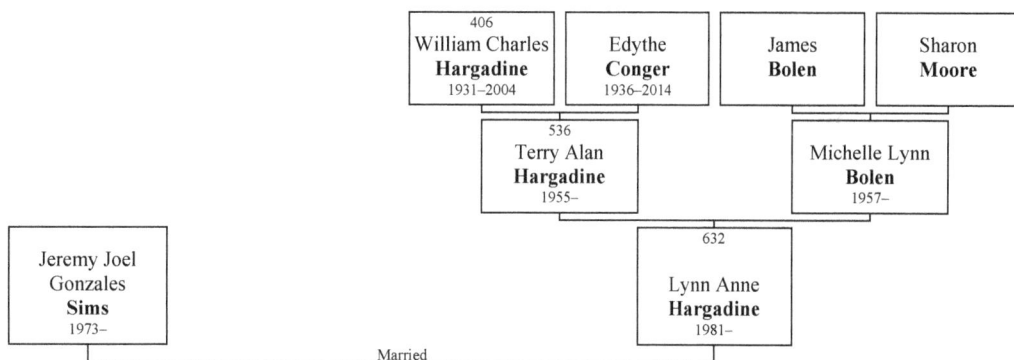

632.   **Lynn Anne Hargadine** was born on Tuesday, February 24, 1981. She is the daughter of Terry Alan Hargadine (536) and Michelle Lynn Bolen.

She married **Jeremy Joel Gonzales Sims.** Jeremy Joel Gonzales was born in June 1973.

Family of Sherry Hargadine and Chris Scaggiari

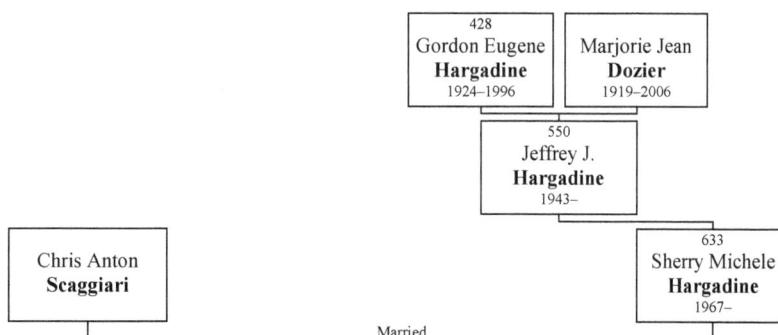

633. **Sherry Michele Hargadine** was born on Thursday, July 27, 1967. She is the daughter of Jeffrey J. Hargadine (550).

She married **Chris Anton Scaggiari**.

Family of Daron Hargadine and Rebecca Lamas

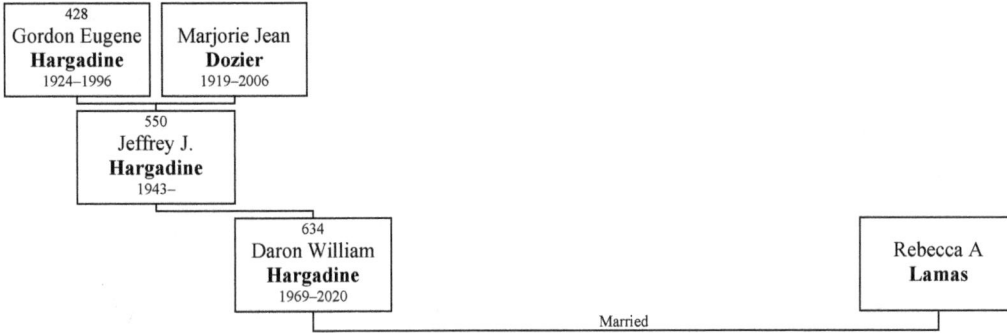

634. **Daron William Hargadine** was born on Tuesday, May 06, 1969, in Englewood, Arapahoe County, Colorado. He was the son of Jeffrey J. Hargadine (550).

Daron William died in Phoenix, Maricopa County, Arizona, on January 02, 2020, at the age of 50. He was cremated (Find a Grave ID 206084830).

He married **Rebecca A Lamas**.

Family of Thaddeus Hargadine and Kelsey Young

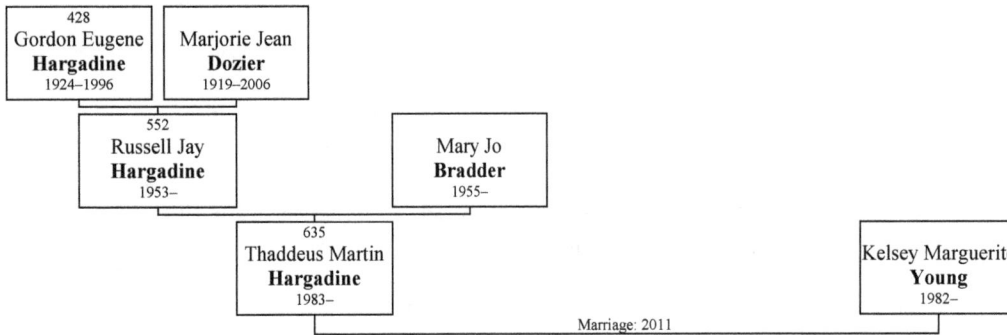

635. **Thaddeus Martin Hargadine** was born on Wednesday, December 07, 1983. He is the son of Russell Jay Hargadine (552) and Mary Jo Bradder.

Thaddeus Martin married **Kelsey Marguerite Young** on Tuesday, November 29, 2011. Kelsey Marguerite was born in July 1982.

Family of Peter Hargadine and Joelle Carlson

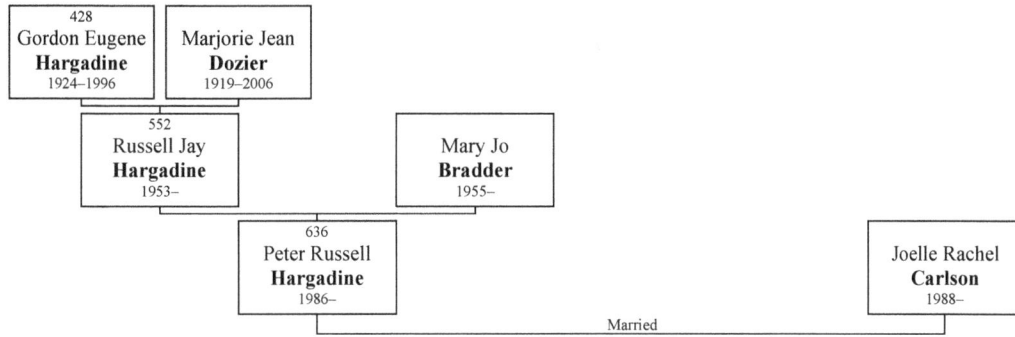

636. **Peter Russell Hargadine** was born in July 1986. He is the son of Russell Jay Hargadine (552) and Mary Jo Bradder.

He married **Joelle Rachel Carlson**. Joelle Rachel was born in 1988.

Family of Laura Hargadine and Peter Aukstolis

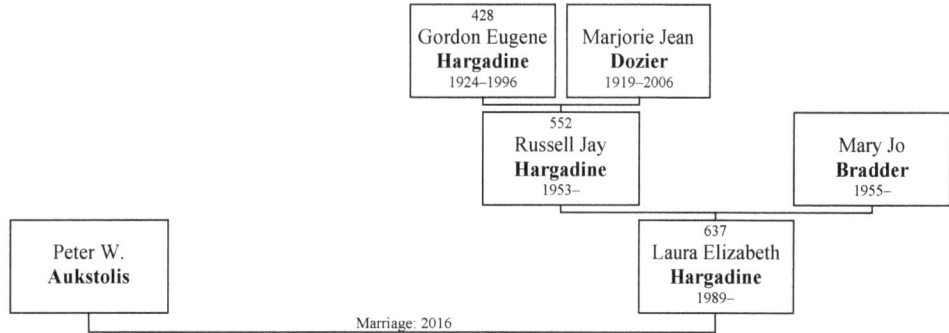

637. **Laura Elizabeth Hargadine** was born in 1989. She is the daughter of Russell Jay Hargadine (552) and Mary Jo Bradder.

Laura Elizabeth married **Peter W. Aukstolis** on Saturday, March 19, 2016, in Silverthorne, Summit County, Colorado.

Family of Sarah Grossarth and Christopher Stewart

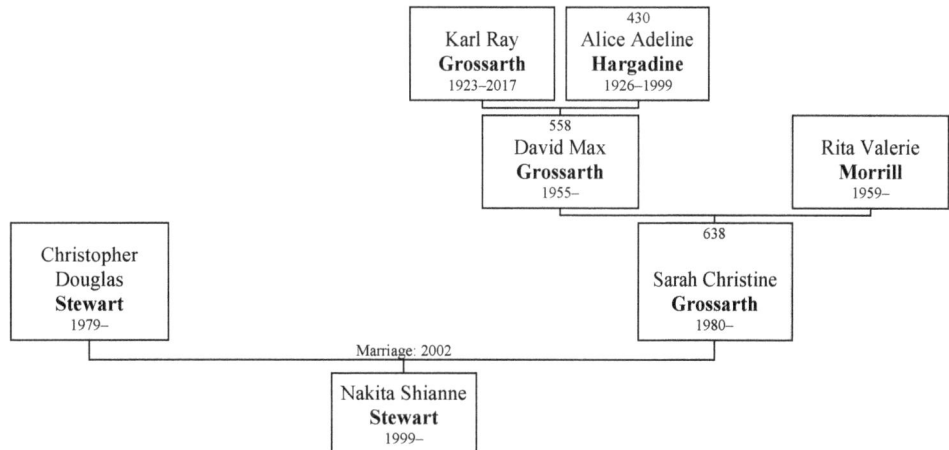

638. **Sarah Christine Grossarth** was born on Thursday, December 18, 1980. She is the daughter of David Max Grossarth (558) and Rita Valerie Morrill.

At the age of 21, Sarah Christine married **Christopher Douglas Stewart** on Friday, September 27, 2002, when he was 23 years old. They have one daughter.

Christopher Douglas was born on Thursday, August 16, 1979.

Daughter of Sarah Christine Grossarth and Christopher Douglas Stewart:

    f   I. **Nakita Shianne Stewart** was born on October 15, 1999.

Family of Brandon Hargadine and Katherine Baker

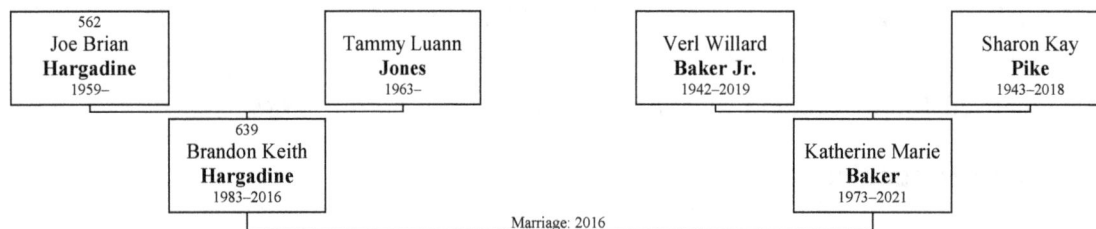

639. **Brandon Keith Hargadine** was born on Wednesday, November 09, 1983, in Paris, Lamar County, Texas. He was the son of Joe Brian Hargadine (562) and Tammy Luann Jones.

Brandon Keith died in Clarksville, Red River County, Texas, on December 31, 2016, at the age of 33. His cause of death was Spina Bifida. Brandon Keith was buried (Find a Grave ID 174800325).

At the age of 32, Brandon Keith married **Katherine Marie Baker** on Thursday, July 21, 2016, at Texas Marriage Index Record 114385 in Red River County, Texas, when she was 43 years old. Katherine Marie was born on Thursday, July 12, 1973. She was the daughter of Verl Willard Baker Jr. and Sharon Kay Pike.

Katherine Marie reached 48 years of age and died in Morgantown, Monongalia County, West Virginia, on November 16, 2021. She was cremated (Find a Grave ID 234113035).

Family of Bridgette Hargadine and Mohamed Belasli

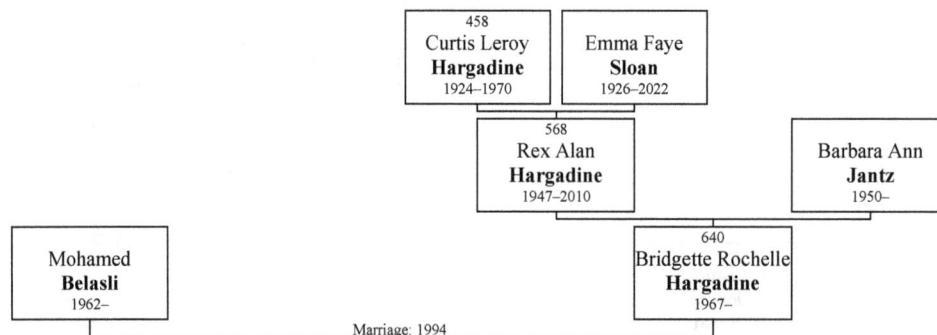

640. **Bridgette Rochelle Hargadine** was born on Saturday, January 07, 1967. She is the daughter of Rex Alan Hargadine (568) and Barbara Ann Jantz.

Bridgette Rochelle married **Mohamed Belasli** on Friday, January 07, 1994, in King County, Washington. Mohamed was born in March 1962.

Erika Hargadine

641.   **Erika Ann Hargadine** was born on Wednesday, July 28, 1971. She is the daughter of Rex Alan Hargadine (568) and Barbara Ann Jantz.

Marriages with Christos S. Christoforou and Keith Malcolm Bower (Page 605) are known.

Family of Erika Hargadine and Christos Christoforou

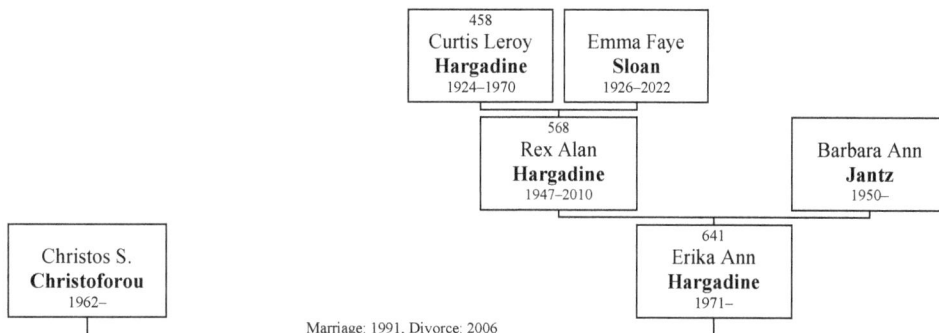

```
                              ┌─────────────────┬─────────────────┐
                              │      458        │   Emma Faye     │
                              │  Curtis Leroy   │                 │
                              │   Hargadine     │    Sloan        │
                              │   1924–1970     │   1926–2022     │
                              └─────────────────┴─────────────────┘
                                    ┌─────────────────┐             ┌─────────────────┐
                                    │      568        │             │   Barbara Ann   │
                                    │   Rex Alan      │             │                 │
                                    │   Hargadine     │             │    Jantz        │
                                    │   1947–2010     │             │    1950–        │
                                    └─────────────────┘             └─────────────────┘
    ┌─────────────────┐                          ┌─────────────────┐
    │  Christos S.    │                          │      641        │
    │                 │                          │   Erika Ann     │
    │  Christoforou   │                          │   Hargadine     │
    │    1962–        │                          │    1971–        │
    └─────────────────┘                          └─────────────────┘
              Marriage: 1991, Divorce: 2006
```

Here are the details about **Erika Ann Hargadine's** first marriage, with Christos S. Christoforou. You can read more about Erika Ann on page 605.

Erika Ann Hargadine married **Christos S. Christoforou** on Saturday, August 03, 1991, in King County, Washington. They were divorced in King County, Washington, on October 25, 2006.

Christos S. was born in March 1962.

Family of Erika Hargadine and Keith Bower

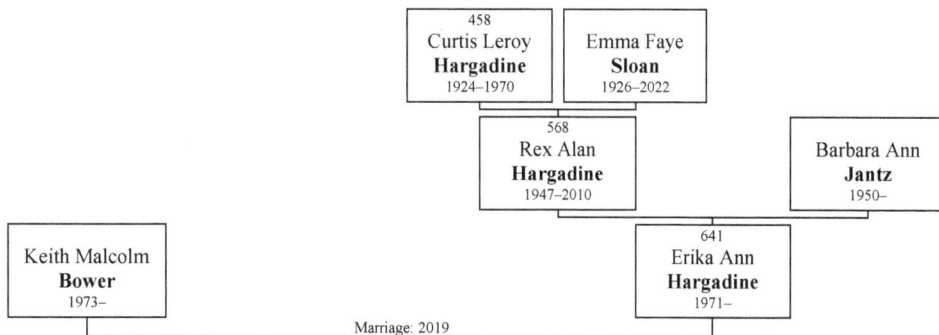

```
                              ┌─────────────────┬─────────────────┐
                              │      458        │   Emma Faye     │
                              │  Curtis Leroy   │                 │
                              │   Hargadine     │    Sloan        │
                              │   1924–1970     │   1926–2022     │
                              └─────────────────┴─────────────────┘
                                    ┌─────────────────┐             ┌─────────────────┐
                                    │      568        │             │   Barbara Ann   │
                                    │   Rex Alan      │             │                 │
                                    │   Hargadine     │             │    Jantz        │
                                    │   1947–2010     │             │    1950–        │
                                    └─────────────────┘             └─────────────────┘
    ┌─────────────────┐                          ┌─────────────────┐
    │ Keith Malcolm   │                          │      641        │
    │                 │                          │   Erika Ann     │
    │    Bower        │                          │   Hargadine     │
    │    1973–        │                          │    1971–        │
    └─────────────────┘                          └─────────────────┘
              Marriage: 2019
```

Here are the details about **Erika Ann Hargadine's** second marriage, with Keith Malcolm Bower. You can read more about Erika Ann on page 605.

Erika Ann Hargadine married **Keith Malcolm Bower** on Monday, January 14, 2019, in King County, Washington. Keith Malcolm was born in January 1973.

Family of Charles Elmore and Cynthia Reynolds

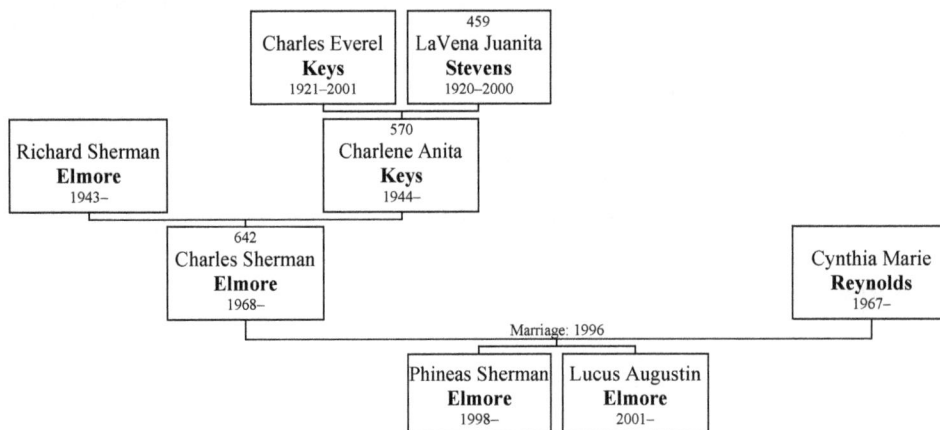

642. **Charles Sherman Elmore** was born on Thursday, September 12, 1968, in Greenville, Bond County, Illinois. He is the son of Richard Sherman Elmore and Charlene Anita Keys (570).

At the age of 27, Charles Sherman married **Cynthia Marie Reynolds** on Saturday, June 22, 1996, in Woodruff, Oneida County, Wisconsin, when she was 28 years old. They have two sons.

Cynthia Marie was born on Friday, August 04, 1967.

Sons of Charles Sherman Elmore and Cynthia Marie Reynolds:

    m   I. **Phineas Sherman Elmore** was born on December 13, 1998.

    m   II. **Lucus Augustin Elmore** was born on March 24, 2001.

Family of Melissa Keys and Nathan Zubal

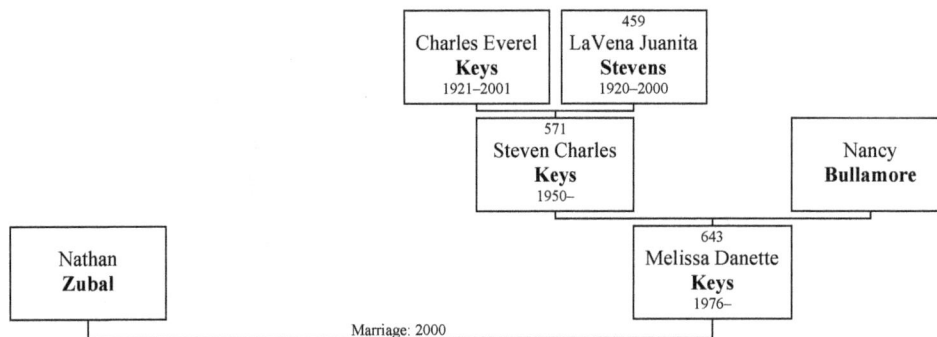

643. **Melissa Danette Keys** was born on Sunday, April 11, 1976. She is the daughter of Steven Charles Keys (571) and Nancy Bullamore.

Melissa Danette married **Nathan Zubal** on Saturday, March 11, 2000.

Family of Katrina Hargadine and Suraj Mahapatra

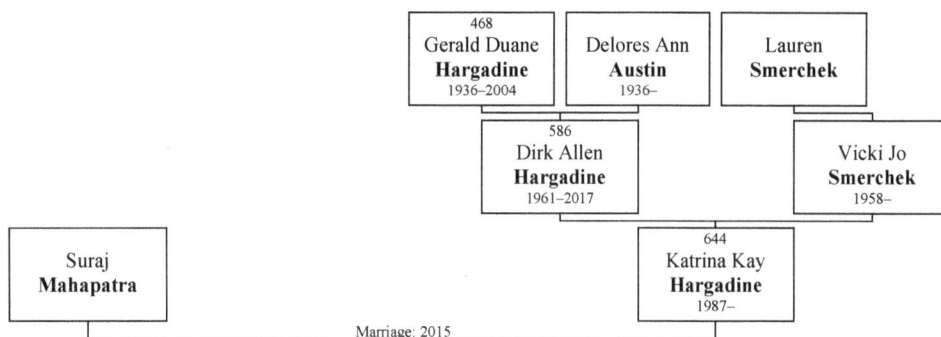

644. **Katrina Kay Hargadine** was born in August 1987. She is the daughter of Dirk Allen Hargadine (586) and Vicki Jo Smerchek.

Katrina Kay married **Suraj Mahapatra** on Saturday, September 12, 2015.

Family of David Archer and Amanda Roberts

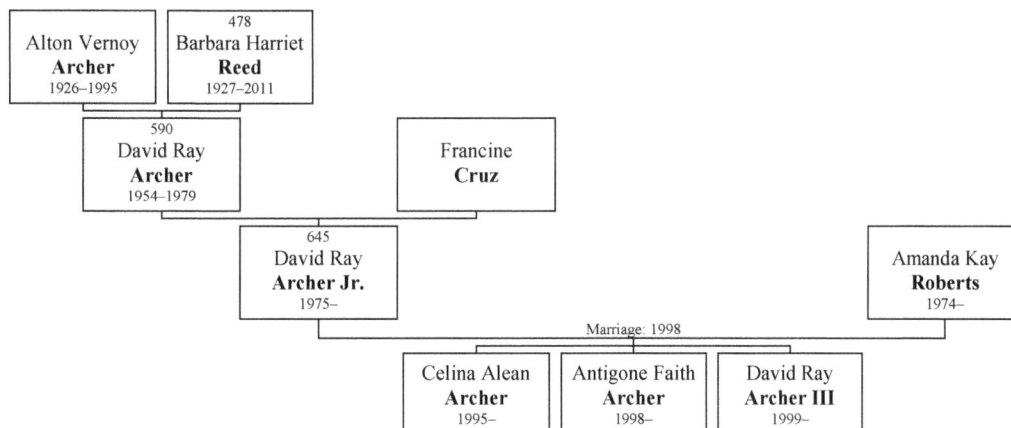

645. **David Ray Archer Jr.** was born on Thursday, December 04, 1975. He is the son of David Ray Archer (590) and Francine Cruz.

David Ray married **Amanda Kay Roberts** on Saturday, February 28, 1998. They have three children.

Amanda Kay was born in January 1974.

Children of David Ray Archer Jr. and Amanda Kay Roberts:

f	I.	**Celina Alean Archer** was born on August 03, 1995.
f	II.	**Antigone Faith Archer** was born on March 31, 1998.
m	III.	**David Ray Archer III** was born on February 28, 1999.

Angela Smith and Kevin Sullivan

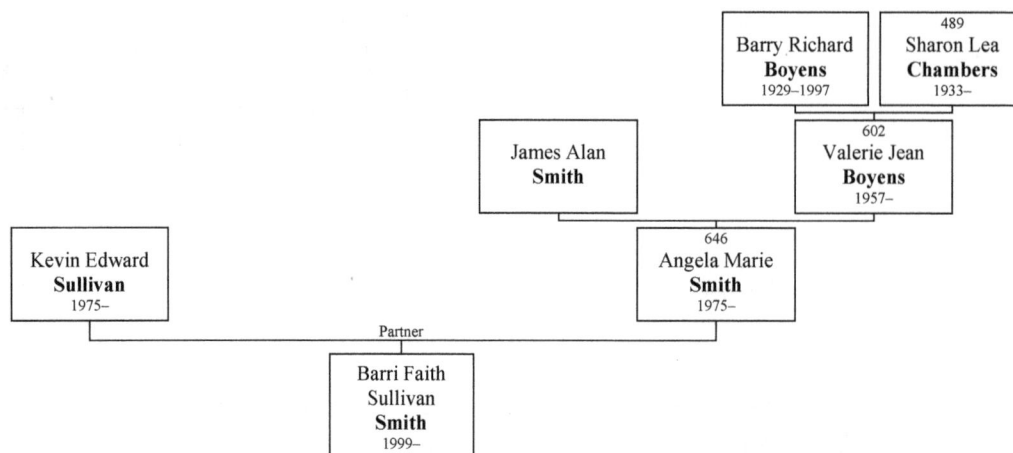

646. **Angela Marie Smith** was born on Friday, September 26, 1975, in Escondido, San Diego County, California. She is the daughter of James Alan Smith and Valerie Jean Boyens (602). James Alan Smith is her stepfather. Her biological father is Gary Lee Helmts.

She is partnered with **Kevin Edward Sullivan**. They have one daughter.

Kevin Edward was born on Friday, July 18, 1975.

Daughter of Angela Marie Smith and Kevin Edward Sullivan:

    f   I. **Barri Faith Sullivan Smith** was born on November 09, 1999.

Family of Meagan Chambers and Gilbert Savage

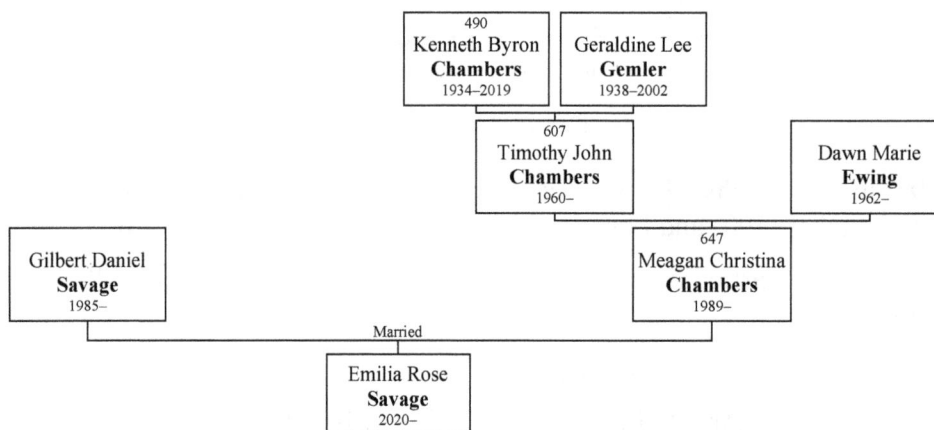

647. **Meagan Christina Chambers** was born on Tuesday, March 07, 1989, in Hazel Crest, Cook County, Illinois. She is the daughter of Timothy John Chambers (607) and Dawn Marie Ewing.

She married **Gilbert Daniel Savage**. They have one daughter.

Gilbert Daniel was born in Cook County, Illinois, on Wednesday, November 13, 1985.

Daughter of Meagan Christina Chambers and Gilbert Daniel Savage:

> f   I. **Emilia Rose Savage** was born in Hammond, Lake County, Indiana, on January 05, 2020.

Family of Christine Macartney and David Herr

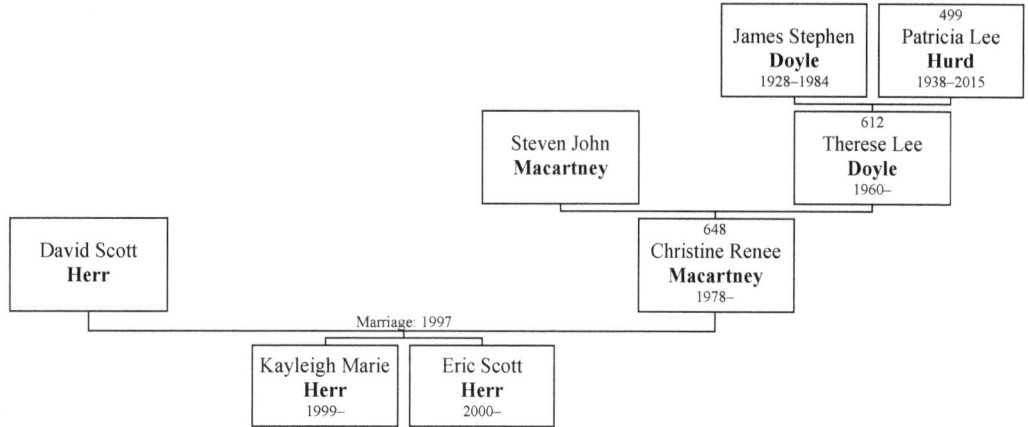

648.   **Christine Renee Macartney** was born on Sunday, December 31, 1978. She is the daughter of Steven John Macartney and Therese Lee Doyle (612).

Christine Renee married **David Scott Herr** on Wednesday, October 08, 1997. They have two children.

Children of Christine Renee Macartney and David Scott Herr:

> f   I. **Kayleigh Marie Herr** was born on August 18, 1999.
>
> m   II. **Eric Scott Herr** was born on October 06, 2000.

Index of Places

Bethel Methodist Episcopal Cemetery, Cheswold, Kent County, Delaware
(39.2323° N, 75.5838° W)

Bethesda Church Cemetery, Pearsons Corner, Kent County, Delaware
(39.1362° N, 75.6921° W)

Bingen, Klickitat County, Washington

Bingen, Skamania County, Washington

Bisbee, Cochise County, Arizona

Bismarck, Burleigh County, North Dakota

Bison, Garfield County, Oklahoma

Blackford, Jasper County, Indiana

Blackwell, Kay County, Oklahoma

Blair Cemetery, Blair, Washington County, Nebraska
(41.5508° N, 96.1186° W)

Blair, Washington County, Nebraska

Blanchard Cemetery, Blanchard, McClain County, Oklahoma
(35.1597° N, 97.6517° W)

Blanchard, Page County, Iowa

Bloom, Ford County, Kansas

Bloomington, McLean County, Illinois

Blue Island, Cook County, Illinois

Blue Rapids, Marshall County, Kansas

Blue Ridge Memorial Gardens, Roanoke, Roanoke County, Virginia
(37.3258° N, 79.9639° W)

Bluebonnet Hills Memorial Park, Colleyville, Tarrant County, Texas
(32.8942° N, 97.1419° W)

Boone County, Iowa

Boone County, Missouri

Bossier City, Louisiana

Boulder City, Clark County, Nevada

Bourbon County, Kentucky

Bowen, Hancock County, Illinos

Bowling Green City Cemetery, Pike County, Missouri
(39.3473° N, 91.1945° W)

Bowling Green, Pike County, Missouri

Breckenridge Cemetery, Harvey, Marion County, Iowa
(41.3024° N, 92.9944° W)

Clarinda, Page County, Iowa

Clark County, Nevada

Clark County, Ohio

Dellwood, Pinellas County, Florida

Deltona, Volusia County, Florida

Denton, Caroline County, Maryland

Denton, Denton County, Texas

Denver, Denver County, Colorado

Des Moines, Polk County, Iowa

Detroit, Jackson County, Michigan

Detroit, Wayne County, Michigan

Dunlap, Peoria County, Illinois

Dunlap, Radnor Twp., Peoria County, Illinois

Durham, Durham County, North Carolina

Durham, Marion County, Iowa

Earlham Cemetery, Earlham, Madison County, Iowa

(41.4906° N, 94.1119° W)

Earlham, Madison County, Iowa

East Grand Rapids, Michigan

East Haven, New Haven, Connecticut

East Lawn Cemetery, Urbana, Champaign County, Illinois

(40.1211° N, 88.2008° W)

East Lawn Palms Cemetery and Mortuary, Tucson, Pima County, Arizona

(32.2544° N, 110.8669° W)

East Peoria, Tazewell County, Illinois

Edelstein, Peoria County, Illinois

Edinburgh, Johnson County, Indiana

Edinburgh, Scotland

Edison, Furnas County, Nebraska

Edwards County, Kansas

Graceland Cemetery, Mitchell, Davison County, South Dakota
(43.7312° N, 98.0354° W)

Gracelawn Memorial Park, New Castle, New Castle County, Delaware
(39.6994° N, 75.5681° W)

Grand County, Colorado

Grand Island, Hall County, Nebraska

Grand Junction, Greene County, Iowa

Grand Junction, Mesa County, Colorado

Grandview Cemetery, Long Pine, Brown County, Nebraska
(42.5252° N, 99.702° W)

Grandview Cemetery, Wray, Yuma County, Colorado
(40.0672° N, 102.2131° W)

Highland Cemetery, Center Township, Clark County, Kansas
(37.1984° N, 99.7475° W)

Highland Cemetery, Glasgow, Valley County, Montana
(48.2011° N, 106.6206° W)

Highland Cemetery, Great Falls, Cascade County, Montana
(47.465° N, 111.2675° W)

Hillcrest Cemetery, Mountain Grove, Wright County, Missouri
(37.1497° N, 92.2653° W)

Hillcrest Cemetery, Mullinville, Kiowa County, Kansas
(37.5922° N, 99.4842° W)

Hillcrest Cemetery, Omaha, Douglas County, Nebraska
(41.2347° N, 95.9967° W)

Hillsboro, Caroline County, Maryland

Hillsboro, Montgomery County, Illinois

Hillsboro, Washington County, Oregon

Hillside Cemetery and Memorial Gardens, Roslyn, Montgomery County, Pennsylvania
(40.1242° N, 75.1431° W)

Hillside Cemetery, Fessenden, Wells County, North Dakota
(47.6595° N, 99.6501° W)

Hillside Cemetery, Kinsley, Edwards County, Kansas
(37.9375° N, 99.4486° W)

Hitchcock County, Nebraska

Hiteman, Iowa

Hobart, Meade County, Kansas

Hodges, Edwards County, Kansas

Holdrege, Phelps County, Nebraska

Hollywood, Broward, Florida

Hollywood, Dade County, Florida

Holt, Taylor County, Iowa

Holy Cross Catholic Cemetery, Dover, Kent County, Delaware

(39.1665° N, 75.5322° W)

Holy Cross Cemetery, Lincoln, Logan County, Illinois

(40.1347° N, 89.3886° W)

Holy Hope Cemetery and Mausoleum, Tucson, Pima County, Arizona

(32.2697° N, 110.9831° W)

Hutton Valley, Howell County, Missouri

Iberville Parish, Louisiana

Idaho Falls, Bannock County, Idaho

Illinois, USA

(39.7333° N, 88.5° W)

Imperial County, California

Imperial, Chase County, Nebraska

Independence, Jackson County, Missouri

Laclede County, Missouri

Laclede, Linn County, Missouri

Lacon, Marshall County, Illinois

Lafayette, Tippecanoe County, Indiana

LaGrange, Troup County, Georgia

Laguna Hills, Orange, California

Laird, Yuma County, Colorado

Lake Oswego, Oregon

Lake View Cemetery, Seattle, King County, Washington

(47.6342° N, 122.3144° W)

Lakeside Cemetery, Dover, Kent County, Delaware

(39.1708° N, 75.5286° W)

Medina, Peoria County, Illinois

Melcher, Marion County, Iowa

Memorial Gardens Cemetery and Mausoleum, Colorado Springs, El Paso County, Colorado

(38.8244° N, 104.7559° W)

Memorial Gardens Cemetery, Bowling Green, Pike County, Missouri

(39.3471° N, 91.1947° W)

Memorial Gardens, Grand Junction, Mesa County, Colorado

(39.079° N, 108.5022° W)

Memorial Park Cemetery, Dalhart, Dallam County, Texas

(36.0652° N, 102.5296° W)

Memorial Park Cemetery, Dalhart, Hartley County, Texas

(36.0652° N, 102.5296° W)

Memorial Park Cemetery, Hutchinson, Reno County, Kansas

(38.0536° N, 98.0217° W)

Memorial Park Cemetery, Saint Petersburg, Pinellas County, Florida

(27.8189° N, 82.7019° W)

Memory Cemetery, Page County, Iowa

(40.7221° N, 94.923° W)

Memory Gardens of the Valley, Santa Teresa, Doña Ana County, New Mexico

(31.8387° N, 106.6192° W)

Memphis, Shelby County, Tennessee

Merrionette Park, Cook County, Illinois

Mount Hawley Cemetery, Peoria, Peoria County, Illinois
(40.8161° N, 89.6122° W)

Mount Hope Cemetery, San Diego, San Diego County, California
(32.7112° N, 117.1122° W)

Mountain Grove, Wright County, Missouri

Mountain Home, Elmore County, Idaho

Mountain View Cemetery, Williams, Coconino County, Arizona
(35.2464° N, 112.2042° W)

Mullinville, Kiowa County, Kansas

Mullinville, Kiowa, Kansas, USA
(37.5861° N, 99.4757° W)

Multnomah County, Oregon

Multnomah, Oregon, USA
(45.5442° N, 122.414° W)

Munster Lake County, Indiana

Murray, Clarke County, Iowa

Myrtle Beach, Horry County, South Carolina

Oak Hill Cemetery, Washington, District of Columbia
(38.9128° N, 77.0567° W)

Oak View Memorial Park, Antioch, Contra Costa County, California
(38.0036° N, 121.7697° W)

Oakdale, Washington County, Minnesota

Oakland Cemetery, Iowa City, Johnson County, Iowa
(41.6702° N, 91.5201° W)

Oakland, Alameda County, California

Oakley, Logan, Kansas, USA
(39.1274° N, 100.8546° W)

Oakview Cemetery, Albia, Monroe County, Iowa
(41.0244° N, 92.8153° W)

Oakwood Cemetery, Corsicana, Navarro County, Texas
(32.0994° N, 96.4796° W)

Oakwood Cemetery, Macomb, McDonough County, Illinois
(40.4708° N, 90.6686° W)

Oakwood Cemetery, Syracuse, Onondaga County, New York
(43.0314° N, 76.1348° W)

Odd Fellows Cemetery

Odd Fellows Cemetery, Camden, Kent County, Delaware
(39.1128° N, 75.5337° W)

Odd Fellows Cemetery, Seaford, Sussex County, Delaware
(38.6468° N, 75.6121° W)

Ohio County, West Virginia

Ohio, USA
(40.2083° N, 81.325° W)

Oklahoma City, Oklahoma County, Oklahoma

Oklahoma, USA
(35.2917° N, 98.2583° W)

Okmulgee Cemetery, Okmulgee, Okmulgee County, Oklahoma
(35.5994° N, 95.9586° W)

Okmulgee County, Oklahoma

Okmulgee, Okmulgee County, Oklahoma

Olathe, Johnson County, Kansas

Old Carson Cemetery, Skamania County, Washington
(45.7376° N, 121.8155° W)

Old Highland Cemetery, Great Falls, Cascade County, Montana
(47.465° N, 111.2675° W)

Old Union Cemetery, Lincoln, Logan County, Illinois
(40.136° N, 89.3886° W)

Page County, Iowa

Page County, Virginia

Page, Coconino County, Arizona

Palisade Cemetery, Palisade, Hitchcock County, Nebraska
(40.3442° N, 101.0892° W)

Palisade, Mesa County, Colorado

Palmyra, Marion County, Missouri

Paris, Lamar County, Texas

Park Forest, Cook County, Illinois

Park Hill Cemetery and Mausoleum, Bloomington, McLean County, Illinois
(40.4678° N, 89.0066° W)

Parklawn Memory Gardens Cemetery, Brookfield, Linn County, Missouri
(39.7898° N, 93.0789° W)

Parksley Cemetery, Parksley, Accomack County, Virginia
(37.7858° N, 75.645° W)

Pekin, Tazewell County, Illinois

Ponca, Dixon County, Nebraska

Pontiac, Livingston County, Illinois

Pontotoc, Oklahoma, USA
(34.7236° N, 96.694° W)

Port Blakely Cemetery, Bainbridge Island, Kitsap County, Washington
(47.6011° N, 122.5199° W)

Port Charlotte, Charlotte County, Florida

Portage, Nebraska

Portland, Multnomah County, Oregon

Pottawattamie County, Iowa

Powell, Park County, Wyoming

Powhatan, Powhatan County, Virginia

Prairie Home Cemetery, Holdrege, Phelps County, Nebraska
(40.4547° N, 99.3492° W)

Prairie Lawn Cemetery, Wellington, Sumner County, Kansas
(37.2669° N, 97.3783° W)

Prairie Rose Cemetery, Corning, Adams County, Iowa
(40.9156° N, 94.7753° W)

Riverside Cemetery, Hastings, Barry County, Michigan
(42.6597° N, 85.3022° W)

Riverside Cemetery, Spencer, Clay County, Iowa
(43.1442° N, 95.1672° W)

Riverside County, California

Riverside, Riverside County, California

Roanoke County, Virginia

Roanoke, Roanoke County, Virginia

Rochester Cemetery, Topeka, Shawnee County, Kansas
(39.1044° N, 95.68° W)

Rochester, Monroe County, New York

Rochester, Thurston County, Washington

Rocky Ford, Otero County, Colorado, USA
(38.0525° N, 103.7202° W)

Rogers, Benton County, Arkansas

Rolla, Phelps County, Missouri

Rose Hill Cemetery, Brookfield, Linn County, Missouri
(39.7656° N, 93.065° W)

Rose Hill Memorial Gardens, Missouri Valley, Harrison County, Iowa
(41.5656° N, 95.8897° W)

Rose Hills Memorial Park, Whittier, Los Angeles County, California
(34.014° N, 118.0254° W)

Rosedale Cemetery, Ada, Pontotoc County, Oklahoma
(34.7953° N, 96.6867° W)

Rosefield Township, Peoria, Peoria County, Illinois

Rosehill Cemetery and Mausoleum, Chicago, Cook County, Illinois
(41.9861° N, 87.6819° W)

Rushville, Sheridan County, Nebraska

Russell, Russell County, Kansas

Sabetha, Nemaha County, Kansas

Sacramento County, California

Sacramento, Phelps County, Nebraska

Saint Elizabeth Ann Seton Catholic Cemetery, Hastings, Dakota County, Minnesota
(44.7169° N, 92.8505° W)

Saint Francis Catholic Cemetery, Phoenix, Maricopa County, Arizona
(33.4733° N, 111.9739° W)

Saint John's Parish, Hillsboro, Caroline County, Maryland

Saint Louis, Saint Louis County, Missouri

Saint Mary of the Woods Cemetery, Princeville, Peoria County, Illinois
(40.9481° N, 89.7545° W)

Saint Paul, Ramsey County, Minnesota

Taylor County, Florida

Taylor County, Iowa

Tekamah, Burt County, Nebraska

Templeville, Caroline County, Maryland

Templeville, Queen Annes County, Maryland

Tennessee

Tennessee, USA
(35.705° N, 84.9584° W)

Terre Haute, Vigo County, Indiana

Texarkana, Bowie County, Texas

Texas County, Missouri

Texas, USA
(31.1667° N, 98.925° W)

The Dalles, Wasco County, Oregon

Thibodaux, Lafourche Parish, Louisiana

Three Oaks, Berrien County, Michigan

Utah, USA
(39.5° N, 111.5° W)

Valley View Cemetery, Sutherlin, Douglas County, Oregon
(43.4° N, 123.2444° W)

Vancouver, Clark County, Washington

Vernon County, Missouri

Via Christi Regional Medical Center, Wichita, Sedgwick County, Kansas

Victorville, San Bernardino County, California

Villisca Cemetery, Villisca, Montgomery County, Iowa
(40.9389° N, 94.9747° W)

Villisca, Montgomery County, Iowa

Vinland Cemetery, Vinland, Douglas County, Kansas
(38.8486° N, 95.1764° W)

Viola, Kent County, Delaware

Virginia, USA
(38.0667° N, 78.5833° W)

Vista Memorial Gardens, Miami Lakes, Miami-Dade County, Florida
(25.9033° N, 80.2944° W)

Index of Individuals

Hargadine (Cont'd)

Hargadine (Cont'd)

Hargadine (Cont'd)

www.ingramcontent.com/pod-product-compliance
Lightning Source LLC
Chambersburg PA
CBHW061759260326
41914CB00006B/1166